THE DEVELOPMENT
OF CHILDREN

For our parents and our children, who have served as the medium of our development, and for Jonathan Cobb, loyal intellectual midwife whose experience of these birth pangs has brought a deeper understanding of development than he ever imagined.

The Development of Children

THIRD EDITION

MICHAEL COLE
University of California, San Diego

SHEILA R. COLE

W. H. Freeman and Company
New York

Acquisitions Editor:	Susan Finnemore Brennan
Development Editor:	Moira Lerner
Project Editor:	Christine Hastings
Text and Cover Designer:	Victoria Tomaselli
Illustration Coordinator:	Susan Wein
Production Coordinator:	Sheila E. Anderson
Illustration:	Academy Artworks, Inc.
	Rodd Ambroson
	Tomo Narashima
	Guy Porfirio
	Vantage Art, Inc.
Composition:	Progressive Information Technologies
Manufacturing:	R R Donnelley & Sons Company

Library of Congress Cataloging-in-Publication Data

Cole, Michael, 1938-
    The development of children / Michael Cole, Sheila Cole.
      p.   cm.
    Includes bibliographical references and index.
    ISBN 0-7167-2859-1
    1. Child development.   I. Cole, Sheila.   II. Title.
RJ131.C585 1996
305.23'1—dc20

96-32478
CIP

Printed in the United States of America

First printing, 1996

BRIEF CONTENTS

CONTENTS

CHAPTER 3

Prenatal Development and Birth   81

PART II
INFANCY   129

CHAPTER 4

Early Infancy: Initial Capacities and the Process of Change   133

CHAPTER 5

The Achievements of the First Year   185

PART III
EARLY CHILDHOOD 291

CHAPTER 8

Language Acquisition 295

CHAPTER 9

Early Childhood Thought: Islands of Competence   337

CHAPTER 10

Social Development in Early Childhood   381

CHAPTER 11

The Contexts of Early Childhood Development   427

PART IV
MIDDLE CHILDHOOD   471

CHAPTER 12

Cognitive and Biological Attainments of Middle Childhood   475

Coping with Increased Freedom and Responsibility   475

Biological Developments   480

**THE ROLES OF GENES AND ENVIRONMENT
IN GROWTH**   481
MOTOR DEVELOPMENT   481
BRAIN DEVELOPMENTS   483

A New Quality of Mind?   485

CHAPTER 13

Schooling and Development in Middle Childhood   513

The Contexts in Which Skills Are Taught   514

The Historical Development of Literacy and Schooling   516

Development and Academic Skills   519

CHAPTER 14

Social Development in Middle Childhood 563

PART V
ADOLESCENCE   617

CHAPTER 15

Biological and Social Foundations of Adolescence   621

CHAPTER 16

The Psychological Achievements of Adolescence   665

PREFACE

The task of writing a textbook to introduce students to the topic of human development poses a special challenge. In a sense, everyone who opens such a book is already an expert on the topic, for everyone has had firsthand experience with the process of growing up and vast opportunity to witness and to think about the development of other people as well. Our goal in writing this book, however, has been to show our readers how a broad scientific framework can enrich their understanding of development, add intellectual excitement to the learning process, and guide the practical applications of work in this dynamic field.

In our view, development is best understood as a fusion of biological, social, and psychological processes interacting in the unique medium of human culture. We have thus tried to show not only the role each of these factors plays but also how they interact in diverse cultural contexts to yield the striking similarities and important differences in individual children's development. Because development involves transformations that take place over time, we have adopted a chronological approach in our presentation. We begin with conception and trace the sequence of developmental changes from that instant into infancy, childhood, and adolescence.

Throughout, we have been guided by the belief that it is a mistake to make sharp distinctions between practical, theoretical, and research orientations to questions of development. Some textbooks focus on one orientation at the expense of others; we believe, however, that truly fundamental knowledge must draw on and illuminate all three orientations.

A Practical Orientation

The authors of *The Development of Children* have known each other since adolescence. We have shared an interest in children's development from the time we were teenagers working as camp counselors, and we have raised children of our own. We each have a professional interest in child development, as well. Sheila Cole is a journalist who has written articles about children and books for children. Michael Cole is a psychologist who has specialized in the study of children's learning and cognitive development.

Both personally and professionally, we are actively interested in discovering practical approaches for fostering the development of children. So it is natural that our book should focus continually on issues such as the benefits of special nutrition programs for children who have experienced malnutrition early in life; how to reduce aggression among children; controversies surrounding out-of-home care of young children; the importance of extended families in ameliorating the problems facing poor children; the special challenges of learning to read and to do arithmetic in school; and the special hazards of teenage pregnancy. We also include many examples drawn from the everyday lives of children to show how a society's beliefs influence its children's development by shaping both the laws and the social norms that govern child-rearing practices.

A Theoretical Orientation

There is much truth to the saying that nothing is so practical as a good theory. A deep understanding of how children develop requires familiarity not only with the observed phenomena but also with theories that provide coherent interpretations of the facts and suggest the consequences of various courses of action.

A major difficulty for students of child development is the number and diversity of theories that contribute significantly to our understanding of basic issues and phenomena. We have adopted two strategies to deal with this problem. First, we frame our presentation in terms of the enduring issues that all theories of development must resolve: how biological and environmental contributions (nature and nurture) are woven together; the extent to which the interaction of these factors results in continuities and discontinuities in the nature of the organism during the dynamic process of development; and the reasons for the individual differences among people. Second, we present competing theories in a constant dialogue with one another and with the practical issues they were designed to address. Rather than gloss over differences among theories, we have attempted to build an appreciation of the bases for their competing interpretations. Then we have tried to move beyond the differences to show how each theory contributes to an overall understanding of development.

A Research Orientation

The dialogue between theory and practice leads naturally to disputes about the facts of development and efforts to marshal facts in support of one perspective or another. Research is the process by which scholars gather evidence to settle such disputes and to challenge or support existing theories.

It is essential to understand research methods both as a means of judging the merits of the evidence that psychologists gather and as a means of thinking critically about the conclusions they draw. What is the evidence that sparing the rod spoils the child? How might we determine whether the differences between boys' and girls' games result from social pressures or from deep-seated biological predispositions? What links have been found between watching violent programs on television and subsequent aggressive behavior? And why is it so difficult for psychologists to answer enduring questions about development once and for all? Only through an awareness of the logic, methods, and indeed the shortcomings of psychological research can students come away from a course on development with the ability to evaluate for themselves the relative merits of different scientists' conclusions.

The kind of critical thinking needed to evaluate evidence and to appreciate the process of research does not develop spontaneously. It requires careful explanation and repeated exposure. Consequently, we have made the detailed discussion of relevant research a constant feature of the book.

A Focus on Culture

Our work has taken us to live in many parts of the world: West Africa, Mexico, Russia, Israel, Japan, and Great Britain. Within the United States, we have lived and worked in affluent suburbs and inner-city ghettos. Often our children have accompanied us, providing us with even richer opportunities for getting to know children in a wide variety of circumstances. Such experiences have led us to believe that culture must be a fundamental constituent of any comprehensive theory of development. To appreciate this truth fully, it is necessary to overcome as much as possible any ethnocentrism in one's view of children's development.

The task is by no means an easy one. For many Americans, the initial reaction to daily life in an African village, an Asian metropolis, or the slums of a large U.S. city is likely to be "culture shock," a sense of disorientation that stems from the difficulty of understanding why people in other cultures behave the way they do. Very often, culture shock is accompanied by a sense of cultural superiority; the way "we" do it (prepare our food, build our houses, care for our children) seems superior to the way "they" do it. With time and understanding, both the disorientation and the sense of superiority diminish.

An appreciation of culture's contribution to development requires more than attention to the ways people far away raise their children. Culture is fundamental to children's experience in *any* society—not something added on to the process of development, but an essential part of that process. Recognizing how difficult it is to think objectively about the nature of development in unfamiliar cultures, we have tried to keep our readers constantly aware of the diversity of human child-rearing practices. Only by considering our own culture as but one design for living among many can we arrive at a valid understanding of the principles that guide the development of all human beings.

A Focus on Biology

It may seem surprising that authors who profess a special interest in culture would simultaneously underscore, as we do, the importance of biology to human development; often the two sources of human variability are discussed as opposing each other, as if somehow, by virtue of living within a culture, human beings ceased to be biologically evolving creatures. In our opinion, this is a false opposition. Not only is the ability to create and use culture one of the most striking biological facts about our species, but there would be no development at all without biological maturation. Advances in the biological sciences have profoundly influenced human development through improved health care and advanced medical procedures. In addition, the biological sciences have increased our understanding of development by shedding light on critical issues such as the intimate links between biological changes in the brain and changes in children's cognitive capacities. The importance of such scientific contributions is made clear throughout this book.

A Focus on the Dynamic Interaction of Domains

The Development of Children combines traditional chronological and topical approaches to make as clear as possible the idea that development is a process involving the *whole child in a dynamically changing set of cultural contexts.* The book is chronological in its overall structure, describing development from conception to the threshold of adulthood, as befits our understanding of development as a process that unfolds over time. It also adopts traditional stage boundaries for each of its major sections.

The organization of the text is also topical in two respects. First, within broad, conventionally defined stages, it describes developments as occurring in the biological domain, the social domain, or the psychological domain (including affect and cognition), while at the same time tracing the ways in which these developments interweave with those in other domains. Second, it focuses on the way stagelike changes emerge from the convergence of events in the various developmental domains.

The chronological and topical perspectives correspond to the warp and the woof of development. The pattern that is woven from their combination is the story of development. It is that story we have attempted to tell in this book.

New to the Third Edition

Readers familiar with earlier editions will note several innovations introduced to make *The Development of Children* more effective than ever before. To make room for these changes we have reluctantly omitted the chapter on development during adulthood and old age. This was a difficult decision because the perspective we adopt assumes development to be a lifelong process. Many colleagues have told us, however, that their curricula simply do not permit them to address adult development in courses that, like this book, focus on childhood development. Sacrificing the treatment of adult development provided us with the opportunity to introduce a variety of changes that not only make the text more accessible to students and easier to teach from but amplify our treatment of key topics covered less fully in earlier editions.

- **An increased emphasis on issues of contemporary concern.** Throughout the text we have added to our already extensive discussions of practical issues by exploring genetic counseling, the consequences of maternal depression, childhood obesity and adolescent eating disorders, learning disabilities, the uses of computers in schools, adolescent risk taking, and more topics of current concern.

- **An increased emphasis on linking theory and practice.** A new epilogue specifically addresses the many ways in which knowledge of the principles of development can be used as a guide to everyday practice.

- **Increased attention to linkages between social, emotional, and cognitive development.** A major challenge facing developmentalists is to understand the interrelatedness of changes in different developmental domains. To this end we have devoted additional attention to examining how changes in social, biological, emotional, and cognitive domains occur as part of a single life process.

- **Innovative tables.** Tables are more readable and more numerous than ever. Special families of tables review Piagetian stages of cognitive development, summarize bio-social-behavioral shifts, and list important milestones of development. A new appendix, in table form, serves as a guide to discussions related to six key facets of development.

- **Integrative questions.** In place of suggestions for further reading (which can be found in the *Study Guide* and *Instructor's Manual*) we have introduced thought questions at the end of each chapter. These are intended to help students identify key issues in the chapter and integrate them with concepts presented earlier in the book.

- **Increased treatment of key traditional topics.** In response to suggestions from colleagues, we have increased our coverage of several traditional topics, including perceptual, socioemotional, and physical development, gender and ethnic identity formation, and information-processing approaches to cognitive development.

- **Valuing diversity.** With each new edition, we renew our commitment to communicating the significance of culture in human development. Like its predecessors, this edition of *The Development of Children* places special emphasis on the importance of understanding and appreciating the diversity of development as it occurs in many parts of the world. We are gratified that concern with cultural diversity has found a growing place in the study of child development, but we believe the urgency of understanding and appreciating the role of cultural diversity in human development is even greater today than ever before. Our third edition reflects this increased concern.

A Note to Instructors

The Development of Children has been designed to be taught within either a quarter or a semester system. For classes taught on the quarter system in which the curriculum is restricted to childhood, the final section of the book can be left to students to read or not, as they choose, and the remainder can be fitted comfortably into a 10-week course. For 10-week courses that include adolescence, sections rather than whole chapters in Part I can be read; Chapter 7 (on the way infant experience shapes later development) and Chapter 8 (on language) could also be skipped or assigned selectively without disrupting the general flow of the presentation.

Instructors who prefer to organize this course in a topical fashion may also wish to assign segments rather than entire chapters in Part I: these chapters present important foundational issues that can be explored to any depth that is deemed appropriate. Chapters 4 through 6 can be read in sequence, or topical issues from each can be abstracted for reading in connection with corresponding chapters in Parts III, IV, and V. The natural sequence of chapters for the remainder of the course then becomes 9, 12, 13, and 16, which emphasize cognitive development, and 10, 14, and 15, which emphasize social and personality development. Instructors planning to use this textbook in conjunction with a topical course will find it helpful to turn to the Appendix on page A-1, "Guide to Discussions of Specific Aspects of Development."

Supplements

An extensive package of supplements has been prepared, each corresponding to the third edition of *The Development of Children* in content, level, and organization.

- A *Study Guide*, by Stephanie Stolarz-Fantino of San Diego State University. In addition to reviewing the main points of each chapter, it provides a variety of practice questions and exercises to help integrate themes that reappear in various chapters. In our experience, this study guide helps students to read and retain the text material at a higher level than they are likely to achieve by reading the text alone.

- *Readings on the Development of Children*, Second Edition, by Mary Gauvain and Michael Cole, introduces students to a well-selected, representative survey of primary-source material.

- An *Instructor's Resource Manual* by Romy V. Spitz of University of Kansas, thoroughly revised for this edition. It contains teaching suggestions, ideas for student projects, a resource guide to films and books, and many transparency masters of key figures and tables from the text. It also contains a *Video Guide* prepared by Catherine King of Elon College.

- A *Test Bank* by Melvyn B. King of the State University of New York at Cortland and Debra E. Clark, containing hundreds of multiple-choice as well as numerous essay questions. The *Test Bank* is available in printed, Macintosh, and IBM versions.

- New to this edition, a full-color *Overhead Transparency Set* of the most important figures in the text.

- Also for the first time, a home page for this textbook on the W. H. Freeman Web site. The address for the home page is:
  www.whfreeman.com/thedevelopmentofchildren

Acknowledgments

A book of this scope and complexity could not be produced without the help of others. A great many people gave generously of their time and experience to deepen our treatment of various areas of development, particularly the many scholars who consented to review drafts of our manuscript and make suggestions for improvement. The remaining imperfections exist despite their best efforts.

For the foundations laid in earlier editions, we gratefully acknowledge the help of **Jeremy M. Anglin,** University of Waterloo; **Gay L. Bisanz,** University of Alberta, Edmonton; **Kathryn N. Black,** Purdue University; **Patricia C. Broderick,** Villanova

University; **Urie Bronfenbrenner,** Cornell University; **Ann L. Brown,** University of California, Berkeley; **Michaelanthony Brown-Cheatham,** San Diego State University; **Richard Canfield,** Cornell University; **Andrew C. Coyne,** Ohio State University; **William E. Cross, Jr.,** Cornell University; **Frank Curcio,** Boston University; **Judy S. Deloache,** University of Illinois at Urbana-Champaign; **Don Devers,** North Virginia Community College, Annandale; **Rosanne K. Dlugosz,** Scottsdale Community College; **Rebecca Eder,** University of California, Davis; **Jeffrey W. Elias,** Texas Tech University; **Shari Ellis,** Virginia Commonwealth University; **Beverly Fagot,** University of Oregon; **Sylvia Farnham-Diggory,** University of Delaware; **Jo Ann M. Farver,** University of Southern California; **Mark Feldmen,** Stanford University; **Brenda K. Fleming,** Family Service Agency, Phoenix; **Mary Gauvain,** University of California, Riverside; **Herbert P. Ginsburg,** Teachers College, Columbia University; **Sam Glucksberg,** Princeton University; **Artin Göncü,** University of Illinois at Chicago; **Alison Gopnik,** University of California, Berkeley; **Mark Grabe,** University of North Dakota; **Patricia M. Greenfield,** University of California, Los Angeles; **Harold D. Grotevant,** University of Minnesota; **William S. Hall,** University of Maryland, College Park; **Paul Harris,** University of Oxford; **Janis E. Jacobs,** University of Nebraska, Lincoln; **Jeannette L. Johnson,** University of Maryland, College Park; **Daniel P. Keating,** Ontario Institute for Studies in Education; **Claire Kopp,** University of California, Los Angeles; **Gisela Labouvie-Vief,** Wayne State University; **Alan W. Lanning,** College of DuPage; **Jacqueline Lerner,** Michigan State University; **Elizabeth Levin,** Laurentian University; **Zella Luria,** Tufts University; **Sandra Machida,** California State University, Chico; **Michael Maratsos,** University of Minnesota; **Patricia H. Miller,** University of Florida; **Shitala P. Mishra,** University of Arizona; **Joan Moyer,** Arizona State University; **Frank B. Murray,** University of Delaware; **Sharon Nelson-LeGall,** University of Pittsburgh; **Nora Newcombe,** Temple University; **Herbert L. Pick, Jr.,** University of Minnesota; **Ellen F. Potter,** University of South Carolina, Columbia; **Thomas M. Randall,** Rhode Island College; **Steven J. Reznick,** Yale University; **LeRoy P. Richardson,** Montgomery County Community College; **Christine M. Roberts,** University of Connecticut; **Barbara Rogoff,** University of California, Santa Cruz; **Marnie Roosevelt,** Santa Monica Community College; **Diane N. Ruble,** New York University; **Sylvia Scribner,** City University of New York; **Felicísima C. Seráfica,** Ohio State University; **Robert S. Siegler,** Carnegie Mellon University; **Jerome L. Singer,** Yale University; **Romy Spitz,** University of California, San Diego; **Doreen Steg,** Drexel University; **Stephanie Stolarz-Fantino,** San Diego State University; **Michael Tomasello,** Emory University; **Billy E. Vaughn,** California School of Professional Psychology, San Diego; **Lawrence J. Walker,** University of British Columbia; **Harriet S. Waters,** State University of New York at Stony Brook; **Thomas S. Weisner,** University of California, Los Angeles; **Patricia E. Worden,** California State University at San Marcos.

Paul Baltes (Max Planck Institute for Human Development, Berlin), **Joe Campos** (University of California, Berkeley), **Robbie Case** (Stanford University), **Carol Izard** (University of Delaware), and **Larry Nucci** (University of Illinois, Chicago) merit special thanks for providing us with valuable illustrative material and special advice for our various editions.

For the third edition we thank **Curt Acredolo,** University of California, Davis; **Karen Adolph,** Carnegie Mellon University; **Jeremy M. Anglin,** University of Waterloo; **Margarita Azmitia,** University of California, Santa Cruz; **MaryAnn Baenninger,** Trenton State College; **Ann E. Bigelow,** St. Francis Xavier University; **Jeffrey Bisanz,** University of Alberta; **Gordon Bronson,** University of California, Berkeley; **Angela Buchanan,** De Anza College; **Tara C. Callaghan,** St. Francis Xavier University; **William B. Carey,** Children's Hospital of Philadelphia; **David W. Carroll,** University of Wisconsin–Superior; **Robbie Case,** OISE; **David B. Conner,** Northeast Missouri State University; **David M. Day,** University of Toronto; **Anthony De Casper,** University of North Carolina, Greensboro; **Cathy Dent-Read,** University of California, Irvine; **Gregory T. Eells,** Oklahoma State University; **Peter**

Eimas, Brown University; **William Fabricius**, Arizona State University; **Jo Ann M. Farver**, University of Southern California; **David H. Feldman**, Tufts University; **Kurt Fischer**, Harvard University; **Constance Flanagan**, Pennsylvania State University; **Artin Göncü**, University of Illinois at Chicago; **Kathleen S. Gorman**, University of Vermont; **Steve Greene**, Princeton University; **Patricia Greenfield**, University of California, Los Angeles; **Kathleen L. Lemanek**, University of Kansas; **Jacqueline Lerner**, Michigan State University; **Lewis P. Lipsett**, Brown University; **Jean Mandler**, University of Calfornia, San Diego; **Sarah Mangelsdorf**, University of Illinois at Urbana-Champaign; **Shirley McGuire**, University of California, San Diego; **Andrew Meltzoff**, University of Washington; **Ageliki Nicolopoulou**, Smith College; **Willis Overton**, Temple University; **Elizabeth Pemberton**, University of Delaware; **David E. Powley**, University of Mobile; **Paul Quinn**, Washington and Jefferson College; **Jane L. Rankin**, Drake University; **Karl Rosengren**, University of Illinois at Urbana-Champaign; **Carolyn Saarni**, Sonoma State University; **Arnold Sameroff**, University of Michigan; **Robert Siegler**, Carnegie Mellon University; **Elizabeth Spelke**, Cornell University; **Romy Spitz**, Rutgers University; **Catherine Sophion**, University of Hawaii at Manoa; **Evelyn Thoman**, University of Connecticut; **Katherine Van Giffen**, California State University, Long Beach; **Terrie Varga**, Oklahoma State University; **Lawrence Walker**, University of British Columbia; **Nanci Weinberger**, Bryant College; **Phillip Sanford Zeskind**, Virginia Polytechnic University; **Patricia Zukow-Goldring**, University of California, Irvine.

We are also grateful to **Sheila Anderson, Travis Amos, Susan Brennan, Jonathan Cobb, Maria Epes, Christine Hastings, Moira Lerner, Larry Marcus, Mary Shuford, Vicki Tomaselli**, and **Susan Wein**, of W. H. Freeman and Company, who have shepherded us through the arduous process of production.

Solana Beach, California
July 1996

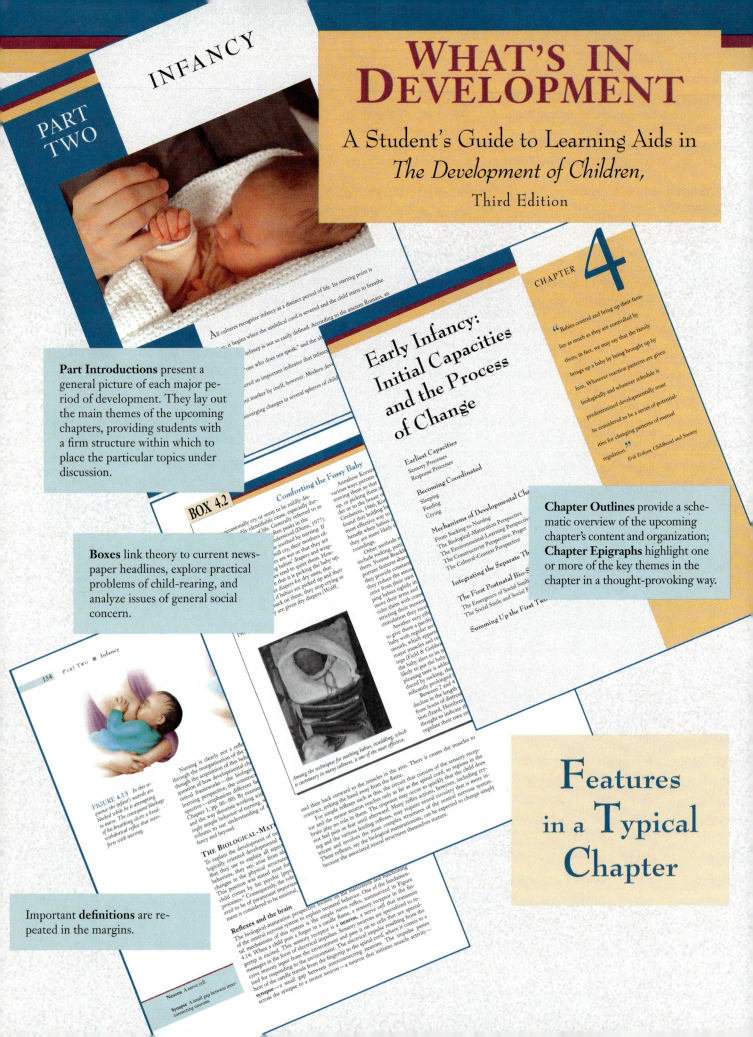

PART TWO

INFANCY

WHAT'S IN DEVELOPMENT

A Student's Guide to Learning Aids in
The Development of Children,
Third Edition

CHAPTER 4

Early Infancy:
Initial Capacities
and the Process
of Change

" Babies control and bring up their families as much as they are controlled by them; in fact, we may say that the family brings up a baby by being brought up by him. Whatever reaction patterns are given biologically and whatever schedule must be considered to be a series of potentialities for changing patterns of mutual regulation. "
Erik Erikson, Childhood and Society

Part Introductions present a general picture of each major period of development. They lay out the main themes of the upcoming chapters, providing students with a firm structure within which to place the particular topics under discussion.

Boxes link theory to current newspaper headlines, explore practical problems of child-rearing, and analyze issues of general social concern.

Chapter Outlines provide a schematic overview of the upcoming chapter's content and organization; **Chapter Epigraphs** highlight one or more of the key themes in the chapter in a thought-provoking way.

Important **definitions** are repeated in the margins.

Features in a Typical Chapter

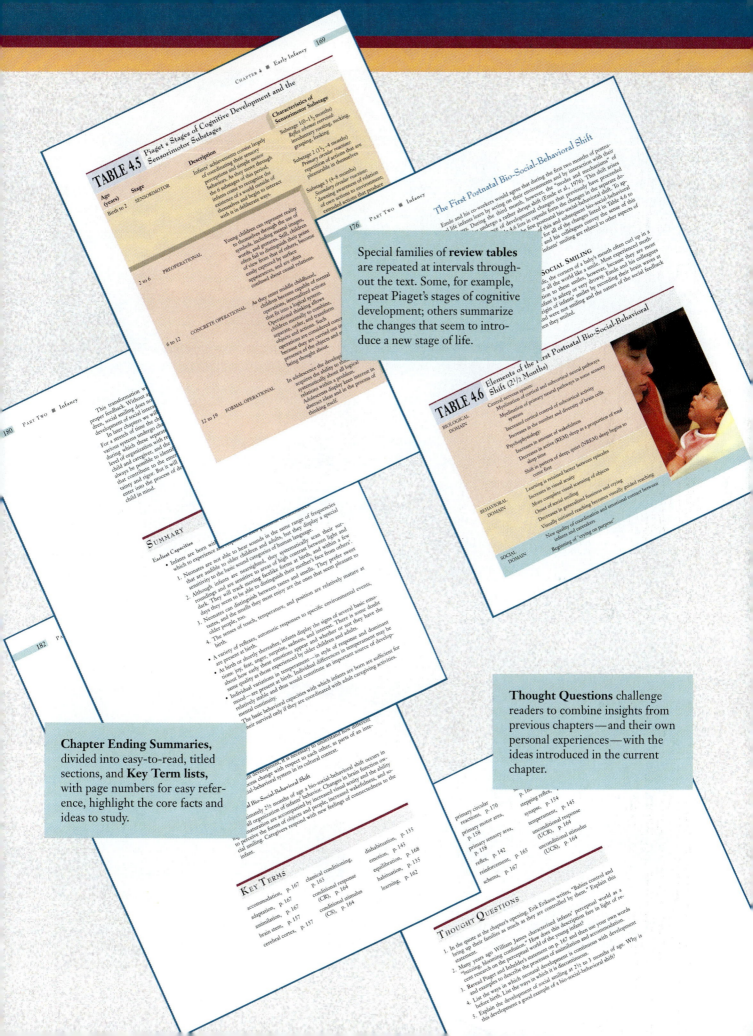

TABLE 4.5 Piaget's Stages of Cognitive Development and the Sensorimotor Substages

Age (years)	Stage	Description	Characteristics of Sensorimotor Substage
Birth to 2	SENSORIMOTOR	Infants' achievements consist largely of coordinating their sensory perceptions and simple motor behaviors. As they move through the 6 substages of this period, infants come to recognize the existence of a world outside of themselves and begin to interact with it in deliberate ways.	Substage 1(0–1½ months) *Reflex schemas exercised:* involuntary rooting, sucking, grasping, looking. Substage 2 (1½ –4 months) *Primary circular reactions:* repetition of actions that are pleasurable in themselves Substage 3 (4–8 months) *Secondary circular reactions:* dawning awareness of relation of own actions to environment; extended actions that produce
2 to 6	PREOPERATIONAL	Young children can represent reality to themselves through the use of symbols, including mental images, words, and gestures. Still, children often fail to distinguish their point of view from that of others, become easily captured by surface appearances, and are often confused about causal relations.	
6 to 12	CONCRETE OPERATIONAL	As they enter middle childhood, children become capable of mental operations, internalized actions that fit into a logical system. Operational thinking allows children mentally to combine, separate, order, and transform objects and actions. Such operations are considered concrete because they are carried out in the presence of the objects and events being thought about.	
12 to 19	FORMAL OPERATIONAL	In adolescence the developing person acquires the ability to think systematically about all logical relations within a problem. Adolescents display keen interest in abstract ideas and in the process of thinking itself.	

Special families of **review tables** are repeated at intervals throughout the text. Some, for example, repeat Piaget's stages of cognitive development; others summarize the changes that seem to introduce a new stage of life.

The First Postnatal Bio-Social-Behavioral Shift

Emde and his co-workers would agree that during the first two months of postnatal life infants learn by acting on their environments and by interaction with their caretakers. During the third month, however, the "modes and mechanisms" of this interaction undergo a rather abrupt shift (Emde et al., 1976). This shift arises as a consequence of a number of developmental changes that previously have proceeded separately. Table 4.6 lists in capsule form the changes in the separate domains that make up this first postnatal bio-social-behavioral shift. To appreciate the origin of this and subsequent bio-social-behavioral shift, we need to see how Emde and his colleagues believe that all of the changes listed in Table 4.6 are related to each other. The sense of this list may also be conveyed by the way in which the changes listed for all the separate domains are related to other aspects of infants' smiling are related to other aspects of

SOCIAL SMILING

During the first weeks of life, the corners of a baby's mouth often curl up in a pattern that looks for all the world like a smile. Most experienced mothers pay little attention to these smiles, however, because they are most likely to occur when the infant is asleep or very drowsy. Emde and his colleagues traced the developmental origin of infants' smiles by recording their brain waves at the same time that they noted when infants were and were not smiling and the nature of the social feedback that was provided to infants when they smiled.

TABLE 4.6 Elements of the First Postnatal Bio-Social-Behavioral Shift (2½ Months)

BIOLOGICAL DOMAIN	Central nervous system: Myelination of cortical and subcortical neural pathways Myelination of primary neural pathways in some sensory systems Increased cortical control of subcortical activity Increases in the number and diversity of brain cells Psychophysiology: Increases in amount of wakefulness Increases in active (REM) sleep as a proportion of total sleep time Decreases in amount of sleep; quiet (NREM) sleep begins to come first Shift in pattern of sleep; quiet (NREM) sleep begins to come first
BEHAVIORAL DOMAIN	Learning is retained better between episodes Increases in visual acuity More complete visual scanning of objects Onset of social smiling Decreases in generalized fussiness and crying Visually initiated reaching becomes visually guided reaching
SOCIAL DOMAIN	New quality of coordination and emotional contact between infants and caretakers Beginning of "crying on purpose"

Thought Questions challenge readers to combine insights from previous chapters—and their own personal experiences—with the ideas introduced in the current chapter.

SUMMARY

Earliest Capacities

• Infants are born with a host of sensory capacities, which to experience are... in the same range of frequencies which to experience allow... in the same range of frequencies that are audible to older children and adults, but they display a special sensitivity to the basic sound categories of human language.

1. Neonates are not able to hear sounds in the same range of frequencies that are audible to older children and adults, but they display a special sensitivity to the basic sound categories of human language.

2. Although infants are nearsighted, they systematically scan their surroundings. They will track moving facelike forms at birth, and within a few days they seem to be able to distinguish their mother's face from others' face. They prefer sweet tastes, and the smells they most enjoy are the ones that seem pleasant to older people, too.

3. Neonates can distinguish between tastes and smells. They prefer sweet tastes, and the smells they most enjoy are the ones that seem pleasant to older people, too.

4. The senses of touch, temperature, and position are relatively mature at birth.

• A variety of reflexes, automatic responses to specific environmental events, are present at birth.

• At birth or shortly thereafter, infants display the signs of several basic emotions: joy, fear, anger, surprise, sadness, and interest. There is some doubt about how early these emotions appear in older children and adults.

• Individual variations in temperament—in style of response and dominant mood—are present at birth. Individual differences in temperament may be relatively stable and thus would constitute an important source of developmental continuity.

The basic behavioral capacities with which infants are born are sufficient for their survival only if they are coordinated with adult caregiving activities.

Chapter Ending Summaries, divided into easy-to-read, titled sections, and **Key Term lists,** with page numbers for easy reference, highlight the core facts and ideas to study.

...velopment, it is necessary to understand how different...process change with respect to each other, as parts of an integrated system within its cultural context.

...social-Behavioral Shift

...imately 2½ months of age a bio-social-behavioral shift occurs in...all organization of infants' behavior. Changes in brain function overall maturation are accompanied by increased visual acuity and the ability to perceive the forms of objects and people, increased wakefulness, and social smiling. Caregivers respond with new feelings of connectedness to the infant.

KEY TERMS

accommodation, p. 167	classical conditioning, p. 163	dishabituation, p. 143
adaptation, p. 167	conditioned response (CR), p. 164	emotion, p. 143
assimilation, p. 157	conditioned stimulus (CS), p. 164	equilibration, p. 135
brain stem, p. 157		habituation, p. 135
cerebral cortex, p. 157		learning, p. 162
primary circular reactions, p. 170	stepping reflex, p. 165	
primary motor area, p. 158	synapse, p. 154	
primary sensory area, p. 158	temperament, p. 145	
reflex, p. 142	unconditioned response (UCR), p. 164	
reinforcement, p. 167	unconditioned stimulus (UCS), p. 164	
schema, p. 167		

THOUGHT QUESTIONS

1. In the quote at the chapter's opening, Erik Erikson writes, "Babies control and bring up their families as much as they are controlled by them." Explain this statement.

2. Many years ago William James characterized infants' perceptual world as a "buzzing, blooming confusion." How does this description fare in light of recent research on the perceptual world of the young infant?

3. Reread Piaget and Inhelder's statement on p. 167 and then use your own words and examples to describe the processes of assimilation and accommodation.

4. List the ways in which neonatal development is continuous with development before birth. List the ways in which it is discontinuous.

5. Explain the development of social smiling at 2½ to 3 months of age. Why is this development a good example of a bio-social-behavioral shift?

The Study of Human Development

> "The mature person is one of the most remarkable products that any society can bring forth. He or she is a living cathedral, the handiwork of many individuals over many years."
>
> *David W. Plath*, Long Engagements

Early one morning in the cold winter of 1800, a naked, dirty boy wandered into a hut at the edge of a French hamlet in the province of Aveyron to beg for food. Some of the people in the area had caught glimpses of the boy in the months before as he dug for roots, climbed trees, and ran at great speed on all fours. They said he was a wild beast. Word spread quickly when the boy appeared in the village, and everyone came to see him.

Among the curious was a government commissioner, who took the boy home and fed him. The child, who appeared to be about 12 years old, seemed ignorant of the civilized comforts that were offered to him. When clothes were put on him, he tore them off. He would not eat meat, preferring raw potatoes, roots, and nuts. He rarely made a sound and seemed indifferent to human voices. In his report, the commissioner concluded that the boy had lived alone since early childhood, "a stranger to social needs and practices. . . . [T]here is . . . something extraordinary in his behavior, which makes him seem close to the state of wild animals" (quoted in Lane, 1976, pp. 8–9).

When the commissioner's report reached Paris, it caused a sensation. Newspapers hailed the child as the "Wild Boy of Aveyron." People hoped that by studying the boy's traits and abilities they could resolve questions about the nature and development of human beings, a focus of philosophical and political disputes in Europe for many decades. Put in modern terms, these questions were

- How do we differ from other animals?
- What would we be like if we grew up totally isolated from human society?
- To what degree are we products of our upbringing and experience and to what degree is our character an expression of inborn traits?

A Child of Nature?

Many people hoped that the boy would have a noble character, which would support their claims that children are born good, only to be corrupted by society. But instead of a noble child of nature, examining physicians saw a disheveled creature who was unable to speak and who often moved about on all fours. The physicians diagnosed the boy as mentally deficient and suggested that he had been put out to die by his parents for that reason. They recommended that he be put in an asylum.

One person who disputed the diagnosis of retardation was a young physician, Jean-Marc Itard (1774–1838). Itard argued that the boy only appeared to be defective because he had been isolated from society and had not developed normal social skills. Perhaps as many as one in three normal children born in France in the late eighteenth century were abandoned by their parents, usually because the family was too poor to support another child (Kessen, 1965). Itard believed that what made the Wild Boy unusual was his remarkable ability to survive in the forests of Aveyron on his own.

Itard took personal charge of the boy. He thought that he could teach him to become a full-fledged Frenchman, master of the best of civilized knowledge. France had recently overthrown its monarchy and had embraced the political ideals of liberty, equality, and brotherhood. Itard and other supporters of the republic wanted to demonstrate that it is possible to change the course of peasant children's development by educating them and improving the conditions of their lives. To test his theory that it is the social environment that shapes human development, Itard devised an elaborate set of training procedures to teach the Wild Boy how to categorize objects, to reason, and to talk (Itard, 1801/1982).

(Top) *Victor, the Wild Boy of Aveyron.* (Bottom) *Jean-Marc Itard, who tried to transform the Wild Boy into a civilized Frenchman.*

Victor, as Itard named the Wild Boy, made rapid progress at first. He learned to communicate simple needs and to recognize and write several words. He also developed affection for the people who took care of him. But Victor never learned to speak and interact with other people normally.

After 5 years of intense work, Itard abandoned his experiment. Victor had not made enough progress to satisfy Itard's superiors, and Itard himself was unsure about how much more progress the boy could make. Victor was sent to live with a woman who was paid to care for him. He died in 1828, still referred to as the Wild Boy of Aveyron, leaving unsettled the large questions about human nature and the influence of civilized society that had aroused so many people's interest in him.

Most physicians and scholars of the time eventually concluded that Victor had indeed been mentally defective from birth. But doubts remain to this day. Victor spent many of his formative years alone. When found, he had already passed the age that appears to be the upper boundary for normal language acquisition. Some modern scholars believe that Itard may have been right in his belief that Victor was normal at birth but was stunted in his development as a result of his social isolation (Lane, 1976). Others believe that Victor suffered from autism, a pathological mental condition whose symptoms include a deficit in language and an inability to interact normally with others (Frith, 1989). It is also possible that Itard's teaching methods failed where different approaches might have succeeded. We can only guess.

The Legacy of Itard

In his pioneering work with Victor, Itard created methods for diagnosing mental and linguistic abilities. He combined these diagnostic procedures with a program of instruction that served simultaneously as a test of his scientific theories of human development as well as his social and political theories about how society should be organized and as a means to better the life of the individual child he was studying.

The modern science of developmental psychology did not arise until almost a century after Itard's attempts to promote Victor's development. But when the science of developmental psychology did come into being, its practitioners adopted many of Itard's specific techniques as well as his curiosity about the factors that shape development. Like Itard, they had faith that science would better the human condition.

Itard's carefully organized effort to improve Victor's behavior and language showed that systematic scientific research into the nature of human development can provide practical suggestions about raising children. It also demonstrated that broad philosophical and political debates shape both the questions that scientists ask and the conclusions they draw from their data.

Itard's fusion of science, philosophy, and public policy remains as relevant now as it was in his time. From one family and community to the next, decisions affecting children's development are influenced by people's assumptions about human nature, their opinions concerning the goals of development, and their beliefs about the factors that influence development. Whether handicapped children are enrolled in the same schools as their agemates or in separate facilities depends on opinions about the conditions under which healthy personality development and learning occur. The age at which children are taught to read will depend on the importance attached to reading as well as on assumptions about when children are mature enough to profit from reading instruction. Attitudes toward divorce are likely to influence beliefs about the effects of divorce on children's development at various ages. Decisions about whether to allow very young children to testify in court depend on beliefs about how accurately 4-year-olds can recall past events and about the possible harm of forcing them to relive painful experiences in public.

Modern developmental psychologists engage in research in an effort to provide objective evidence concerning these and many similar questions. The conclusions they reach affect not only the lives of individual children but also the policies of federal, state, and local governments, school boards, and the judicial system.

THE RISE OF A NEW DISCIPLINE

In Itard's day there was no scientific specialty called developmental psychology. But interest in children and their development was growing all during the nineteenth century. One stimulus to this trend was the Industrial Revolution, which brought broad social changes to Europe and North America. During the nineteenth century, the industrialization of these continents transformed the basic activities by which people earned their livings. Industrialization also transformed the role of children in society and the settings within which they developed. No longer did the vast majority of children grow up on farms, where they contributed their labor and were cared for by their mothers and fathers until they reached adulthood. Instead, many were employed in factories, alongside and sometimes in place of their parents (Hiner & Hawes, 1985).

Industrialization also fueled urbanization. Huge slums grew up in sprawling industrial cities. When urban children were not at work, they were a liability to their parents, who had little space to accommodate them and little money with which to feed them. They were also a liability to the community, which saw them as rowdy nuisances. As much for social control as for any academic reasons, public schools were established as places to supervise children's development when neither parents nor employers were supervising them.

Many young children worked long hours in factories and mines, under dangerous and unhealthy conditions. As these conditions became a matter of social concern, their effect on children became the focus of philanthropic, medical, and

Children doing piecework in their home near the turn of the century. The money they earned was usually a vital part of their family's income.

Children provided essential labor in many industries well into the twentieth century. These boys worked in the coal mines of Pennsylvania in 1911.

scientific activity. The close links among social problems, cultural values, and scientific research are evident in some of the earliest studies of children's growth. The Factories Inquiries Committee in England, for instance, conducted a study in 1833 to discover whether children could work 12 hours a day without suffering physical damage. The majority of the committee members decided that 12 hours was an acceptable workday for children. Those who thought a 10-hour workday would be preferable were concerned not about the effects of long work hours on small children's intellectual or emotional well-being but about their morals; these committee members recommended that 2 hours of religious and moral education a day replace 2 of the hours spent working in mine, factory, or shop (Lomax, Kagan, & Rosenkrantz, 1978).

The nineteenth-century pioneers of developmental psychology did more than address concerns arising from changes in society. They used the data they collected in their inquiries to clarify basic questions about human development and how to study it. The early studies of growth and work capacity, for example, showed how the environment affects development. Research found that children who worked in textile mills were shorter and weighed less than local nonworking children of corresponding ages, because of inadequate rest and nutrition and their long hours of work. Surveys of intellectual growth showed wide variations in children's achievements that seemed to depend on family background and individual experience. These findings fueled scientific and social debate about the factors that are primarily responsible for development. That debate continues to this day.

A crucial event that spurred interest in the scientific study of children was the publication of Charles Darwin's *Origin of Species*, in 1859. Scientists' acceptance of Darwin's thesis that human beings have evolved from species that developed earlier fundamentally changed the way people thought about children. Instead of imperfect adults to be seen and not heard, children came to be viewed as scientifically interesting because their behavior provided evidence that human beings are related to other species. It became fashionable, for example, to compare the be-

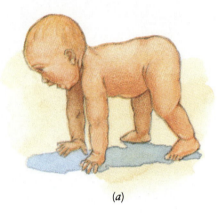

(a)

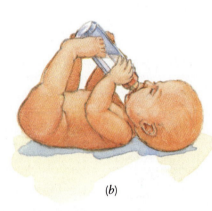

(b)

(c)

FIGURE 1.1 *Early evolutionists eagerly scrutinized the motor development of children for evidence that it recapitulated evolutionary stages. Here an infant (a) crawls about on all fours like many animals, (b) uses its feet for grasping as our primate ancestors did, and (c) sleeps in an animal-like crouch. (After Hrdlicka, 1931.)*

havior of children with the behavior of higher primates to see if individual children went through a "chimpanzee stage" similar to the one through which the human species was thought to have evolved (Gould, 1977b) (see Figure 1.1).

Late in the nineteenth century, developmental psychologists began to form organizations to promote their work. In the 1890s the Child-Study Association was founded by G. Stanley Hall, the first president of the American Psychological Association. The first journal devoted to child development, *Pedagogical Seminary*, appeared at this time. Near the turn of the century, various child welfare organizations were formed to raise money for hospitals and orphanages and to support social reform policies for the benefit of children. Believing that the knowledge gained from scientific research should reach as wide a public as possible, both government agencies and philanthropic foundations began to support specialized magazines such as *Infant Care* and *Parent's Magazine*. Today questions about child development are discussed in the popular media, an indication of broad acceptance of the idea that scientific research on children is a good way "to make this a better world through developing better people" (Young, 1990, p. 17).

A landmark in the institutionalization of concern about children was the creation in 1912 of the U.S. Children's Bureau to monitor the working conditions of children and to disseminate information about effective child-rearing practices. In addition, special institutes and departments devoted to the study of development began to spring up in major universities.

MODERN DEVELOPMENTAL PSYCHOLOGY

The core concern of developmental psychologists is to understand **development,** the sequence of physical and psychological changes that human beings undergo as they grow older. These changes begin with conception and continue throughout life. Interest in development rests on an ancient intuition about personal understanding and self-discovery: if we can discover our roots and the history of changes that brought us to the present moment, we can better understand ourselves. If we then combine insight into our past with information about our present characteristics and circumstances, we are in a better position to anticipate the future and to prepare to meet it on our own terms (see Table 1.1).

The discipline of developmental psychology translates these personal goals into systematic procedures for studying, predicting, and shaping the process of development. It also amasses knowledge that contributes to and profits from the insights of neighboring disciplines, such as biology, anthropology, linguistics, and sociology.

In the century since psychologists began to concern themselves with the systematic study of human development, they have accumulated a great deal of knowledge about the behavior of human beings at every age level, starting even before birth. They have devised a wide variety of research methods for learning about children, and they have made intensive efforts to explain the developmental processes responsible for the age-related changes that they study.

Developmental psychologists are also active in applying their knowledge to promote healthy development. They serve in hospitals, childcare centers, schools, recreational facilities, and clinics. They assess children's developmental status and prescribe measures for assisting children who are in difficulty. They design special environments, such as cribs for premature babies, therapeutic methods for children who find it difficult to control their tempers, and more effective techniques for teaching children to read. The many developmental psychologists who believe that development is a lifelong process also take an active interest in the well-being of people of middle age and the elderly (Fisher & Lerner, 1994).

The detailed knowledge that developmental psychologists have accumulated in the course of their research is important, as are the research methods them-

TABLE 1.1 — Recent Statistics Affecting the Lives of U.S. Children

- There are about 57 million children under 15 in the United States, roughly 22 percent of the population.
- The number of children per woman has decreased from 3.6 in 1960 to 2.0 in 1995.
- The United States has a higher percentage of low-birth-weight babies than Turkey, Iran, and Romania.
- Since 1950 the number of American children living in mother-only families has quadrupled, from about 5 million to 20 million.
- One of every six children is a stepchild.
- Average combined scores on the Scholastic Aptitude Test have dropped 78 points since 1963.
- In 1991, more teenagers and young adults died from suicide than from cancer, heart disease, AIDS, birth defects, pneumonia, influenza, stroke, and lung disease combined.
- Every day, 135,000 children take guns to school.
- In recent years, about 200,000 children under 14 immigrate to the United States each year.
- In 1992 there were more than 14 million U.S. children living in poverty, the worst percentage among 18 Western industrialized countries.
- Children spend an average of 3 hours a day with their parents, 40 percent less than in 1960. They spend 3 to 4 hours a day watching television and 26 minutes doing homework.
- An estimated one-third of children have a phone in their room.
- American kids ages 9 to 13 get a total of $1.3 billion a year in allowances.
- Eighty-three percent of 9- to 13-year-olds were able to identify Indiana Jones; 27 percent could identify the Holocaust.
- Seventy-one percent of 9- to 13-year-olds said they have close friends of a different ethnic origin.
- Ninety percent of 6- to 17-year-olds said they believe in God and Heaven.
- American girls between the ages of 2 and 10 own an average of eight Barbie dolls.

Source: Adapted from NY Times Sunday Magazine, October 8, 1995.

Development The sequence of physical, psychological, and social changes that human beings undergo as they grow older.

selves. As we investigate the facts generated by research and the skills required of developmental psychologists, it is just as important to keep firmly in mind the more general goal of the psychological sciences: to assemble the accumulating facts into larger patterns, called theories or frameworks, which increase our understanding of human nature and its development.

The Central Questions of Developmental Psychology

Despite great variety in the work they do and the theories that guide their research, developmental psychologists share an interest in three fundamental questions about the process of development:

1. *Continuity.* Is development a gradual process of change or is it punctuated by periods of rapid change and the sudden emergence of new forms of thought and action?
2. *Sources of development.* What are the contributions of the genes (nature) and the external environment (nurture) to the process of developmental change?
3. *Individual differences.* No two human beings are exactly alike. How do people come to have stable individual characteristics that make them different from all other people?

Psychologists are deeply divided on many aspects of these three fundamental issues. Their differing assumptions about continuity, sources of change, and individual differences give rise to competing theories.

QUESTIONS ABOUT CONTINUITY

Developmental psychologists ask three basic questions about continuity: How similar are human mental capacities and emotions to those of other species? Is individual development a process of the gradual accumulation of small quantitative changes, or do we undergo a series of qualitative transformations as we grow older? Last, are there periods in a person's life during which certain experiences are critical for continued normal development?

Are human beings distinctive?

For centuries people have debated the extent to which humans differ from other creatures and the closely related question of whether we are subject to the same natural laws as all other forms of life. This sort of question concerns **phylogeny,** the evolutionary history of a species.

Phylogeny The evolutionary history of a species.

The question of continuities and discontinuities between humans and other species is important because the way it is answered shapes our conclusions about the laws governing human development. Insofar as the relation of *Homo sapiens* to other species is continuous, the study of other animals can provide useful evidence about the processes of *human* development because the same principles of development are at work. To the extent that human beings are distinctive, research findings concerning the development of other species may be misleading when they are applied to humans.

When Charles Darwin (1809–1882) published *The Origin of Species,* the idea of evolution was already a subject of widespread speculation. Darwin's great achievement was to convince most of the Western scientific world, and eventually other people as well, that "the innumerable species, genera and families, with which this world is peopled, are all descended, each within its own class or group, from common parents, and all have been modified in the course of descent" (Darwin, 1859/1958, p. 425).

Darwin was a firm believer in continuity among species. He saw evolution as a slow, steady process of accumulating change. As he put it, the difference between *Homo sapiens* and our near neighbors is "one of degree, not of kind" (Darwin, 1859/1958, p. 107). Modern evolutionary theorists accept Darwin's claim that the origin of new species is a natural process, but many of them reject the idea that evolution is gradual and continuous (Eldredge & Gould, 1972). They claim that in relatively isolated environments new species have arisen quite rapidly and have been able to survive momentous environmental changes that have destroyed the species from which they evolved. Stephen Jay Gould (1980), a champion of the theory of *dis*continuous evolution, likens the process of evolutionary change to the boiling of water:

Although chimpanzees and human beings share more than 90 percent of their genetic material, the differences between the two species are enormous.

Change occurs in large leaps following a slow accumulation of stresses that a system resists until it reaches a breaking point. Heat water and it eventually boils. (pp. 184–185)

To test Darwin's claim that our species evolved gradually and continuously as a part of the natural order, scientists have searched for evidence of evolutionary links—intermediate forms that connect us with other forms of life—and have compared our genetic makeup and behavior with those of other organisms. On the side of continuity between ourselves and other animals, it has been established that we share as much as 99 percent of our genetic material with chimpanzees (Gribben & Cherfas, 1982). It is nevertheless clear that there is something distinctive about our species' characteristics. The difficult question is: What is that something?

One thing that distinguishes *Homo sapiens* is that we develop in an environment that has been shaped by countless earlier generations of people in their struggle for survival (Geertz, 1973; Donald, 1991). This special environment consists of artifacts (such as tools and clothing), knowledge about how to construct and use those artifacts, beliefs about the world, and values (ideas about what is worthwhile), all of which guide adults' interactions with the physical world and with each other and their children. Anthropologists call this accumulation of artifacts, knowledge, beliefs, and values **culture.** Culture is the "man-made" part of the environment that greets us at birth (Herskovitz, 1948) and the "design for living" that we acquire from our community (Kluckhohn & Kelly, 1945).

A key feature of culture is that it is made available to each succeeding generation through language. Thus it is not surprising that since antiquity, language has been proposed as a defining characteristic of our species. In the seventeenth century the philosopher René Descartes stated the traditional view eloquently:

Language is in effect the sole sure sign of latent thought in the body; all men use it, even those who are dull or deranged, who are missing a tongue, or who lack the voice organs, but no animal can use it, and this is why it is permissible

Culture The accumulated knowledge of a people as encoded in their language, physical artifacts, beliefs, values, customs, and activities that have been passed down for generations.

to take language as the true difference between man and beast. (Quoted in Lane, 1976, p. 23)

Even Darwin, who believed so strongly in the continuity of species, agreed that our distinctiveness, insofar as *Homo sapiens* is distinct, is the result of our capacity to communicate through language. In recent years scientists have demonstrated that chimpanzees and other primates have rudiments of culture and language (Savage-Rumbaugh et al., 1993; Wrangham et al., 1994). Still, as we will see in later chapters, the capacity for culture and for language use, considered as an ensemble, is far greater in humans than in other species.

Is individual development continuous?

The second major question about continuity concerns **ontogeny,** the development of the individual organism during its lifetime. As a rule, psychologists who believe ontogeny to be primarily a process of continuous, gradual accumulation of small changes emphasize *quantitative change*, such as growth in vocabulary or memory capacity. Those who view ontogeny as a process punctuated by abrupt, discontinuous changes emphasize the emergence of *qualitatively* new patterns at specific points in development, such as the change from babbling to talking. Qualitatively new patterns that emerge during development are referred to as developmental **stages.** The contrast between the continuity and discontinuity views is illustrated in Figure 1.2.

In everyday conversation, the concept of a developmental stage is sometimes misused to explain behavior. Susy, we may be told, "behaves wildly because she is

Ontogeny The course of development during an individual's lifetime.

Stage A distinctive period of development that is qualitatively different from the periods that come before and after.

FIGURE 1.2 (a) *The contrasting courses of development of sponges and flowers provide idealized examples of continuous and discontinuous development. According to the continuity view, development is a process of gradual growth (small sponge, bigger sponge, still bigger sponge), whereas according to the discontinuity view it is a series of stagelike transformations (seed, sprout, flowering plant).* (b) *Human beings appear to exhibit a mixture of the two types of development.*

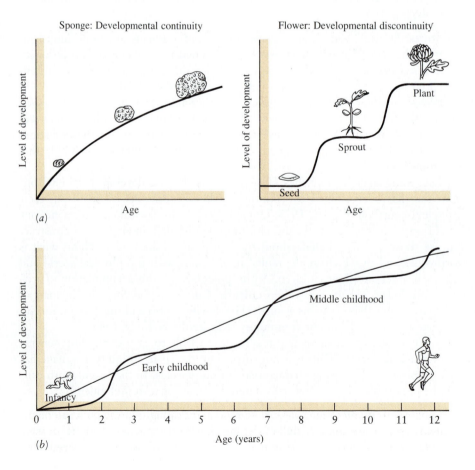

an adolescent." We would not be satisfied by the explanation that butterflies fly because they are in the butterfly, not the caterpillar, stage. We would want to know what it is about butterflies that enables them to fly and the mechanisms that brought about the transformation from caterpillar to butterfly.

The same rule applies to typical changes in humans. We seek to learn what it is about being an adolescent that makes Susy act "wild." Is it the freedom that comes with the right to drive a car? Is it the hormonal changes associated with puberty? Or perhaps Susy is responding to pressures from her peers. Without a careful specification of the processes that give rise to new patterns of behavior as children grow older, explanations of behavior that only name the stage the person is presumed to be in add nothing to our understanding.

Sensitive to this problem, psychologists who use the stage concept attempt to specify what they mean by a stage and how the psychological processes that they believe distinguish each stage are related to the behaviors that are characteristic of it (Brainerd, 1993; Flavell, 1971). The psychologist John Flavell suggests that four criteria are central to the concept of a developmental stage:

1. *Stages of development are distinguished by qualitative changes.* The change in motor activity associated with the transition from crawling to walking upright illustrates what is meant by a qualitative change to a new stage of development. Walking does not arise from the perfection of the movements used to crawl. Rather, the child undergoes a total reorganization of movement, using different muscles in different combinations.

2. *The transition from one stage to the next is marked by simultaneous changes in a great many, if not all, aspects of a child's behavior.* In the transition from infancy to early childhood, children begin to create grammatically complex utterances, talk about themselves as distinct individuals, and engage in pretend play.

3. *When the change from one stage to the next occurs, it is rapid.* Physical development in middle childhood (approximately ages 6 to 12), for example, is characterized by relatively slow growth followed by a dramatic spurt at the onset of puberty.

4. *The numerous behavioral and physical changes that mark the appearance of a stage form a coherent pattern.* The new forms of reasoning that arise during middle childhood, for example, are part of a pattern that includes new physical abilities, participation in peer groups, and new relationships with parents.

If development is characterized by discontinuous qualitative changes, then the way the child experiences the world and the way the world influences the child will differ from one stage to the next. In short, the process of change itself undergoes changes. Infants are especially sensitive to the sounds of language (Bornstein, 1992), for example, but they do not understand what is being said. Once they begin to understand and produce language themselves, the way they learn about the world appears to change fundamentally, and so does the way others interact with them. The discontinuity that accompanies the emergence of the child's active participation in conversation marks the boundary between infancy and early childhood in a great range of societies.

The psychologist Jerome Kagan (1984, p. 91) argues that "each life phase makes special demands, and so each phase is accompanied by a special set of qualities." Kagan believes that discontinuities between succeeding life phases are so marked that some of one's past history is actually "inhibited or discarded." This strong view of developmental discontinuities implies that early developmental problems do not inevitably lead to later developmental problems; in effect, each new stage presents its own opportunities.

Some psychologists deny that the stage concept is crucial for an understanding of development. Albert Bandura, for example, argues that the mechanisms by which people learn new behaviors are the same at all ages, so there is considerable continuity in the process of developmental change. According to this view, discontinuities in development are relatively rare occurrences that follow abrupt alterations in "social-training and other relevant biological or environmental variables" (Bandura & Walters, 1963, p. 25). Robert Siegler, a psychologist who specializes in studying the development of children's thinking, makes a similar argument: "Children's thinking," he writes, "is continually changing, and most of the changes seem to be gradual rather than sudden" (1991, p. 8).

During most of the twentieth century, stage theories of development have been more numerous and more influential than continuity theories. Yet stage theories are confronted with a variety of facts that appear to violate one or more of the criteria for developmental stages proposed by Flavell.

One acute problem for modern stage theories is that the stage a child appears to be in often varies from one situation to another. Four-year-olds often have difficulty taking another person's point of view, for example, but when they are speaking to a 2-year-old, they simplify their speech appropriately, apparently realizing that the 2-year-old may have difficulty understanding them. At 4 years of age children are also likely to overlook the needs of their siblings, yet they frequently become solicitous when the younger child appears to be upset (Eisenberg, 1992; Dunn, 1988). It is hard to reconcile the idea that a child can simultaneously exhibit behaviors associated with different stages with the idea that a given stage should define the child's general capabilities and psychological makeup.

Are there critical periods of development?

Another question about the continuity of individual development is whether there are **critical periods** of development—periods in the growth of an organism during which specific environmental or biological events *must* occur if development is to proceed normally. The existence of critical periods has been firmly established for some animals (see Figure 1.3) and for some aspects of human physical development as well. For example, if the newly formed gonads (sex glands) of a human embryo do not produce male hormones about 7 weeks after conception, the devel-

Critical periods Periods during which specific biological or environmental events must occur for normal development.

FIGURE 1.3 *The ethologist Konrad Lorenz proposed the existence of a critical period in the development of goslings. These baby geese would not have followed Lorenz had he not been the first moving thing they saw. Here they follow him in the water as he swims.*

opment of female genitalia is irreversibly set (Gilbert, 1991). The strongest evidence for critical periods in human psychological development comes from studies of the development of language (Emmorey, 1995; Morford, Singleton, & Goldin-Meadow, 1995). Children who for some reason have not had sufficient exposure to language to acquire one before the age of 6 or 7 years may never acquire a language. The Wild Boy of Aveyron's failure to acquire language might be explained by his isolation from other people during the critical period for learning language.

QUESTIONS ABOUT THE SOURCES OF DEVELOPMENT

The second major issue that preoccupies developmental psychologists is the way in which biological factors directed by the genes interact with environmental factors in human development. During much of the twentieth century, this issue has been posed in the form of a choice between "nature" and "nurture." **Nature** refers to the inborn biological capacities of the individual; **nurture** refers to the influences of the social environment on the individual, particularly those of the family and the community. Much of the argument about Victor, the Wild Boy of Aveyron, was about nature and nurture: Was Victor incapable of speech and other behaviors normal for a boy his age because of defective biological endowment (nature) or because of inadequate nurturing? (Early formulations of this issue are discussed in Box 1.1.)

Beliefs about the relative contributions of nature and nurture to development can have far-reaching effects on the way society treats children. If, for example, it is assumed that girls, by nature, lack interest and ability in mathematics and science, they are not likely to be encouraged to become mathematicians or scientists. If, on the other hand, it is assumed that mathematical and scientific talent is largely a result of nurture, a society may train girls and boys equally in these activities.

Modern psychologists emphasize that we cannot adequately describe development by considering either nature or nurture in isolation because the organism and its environment constitute a single life process (Gottlieb, 1992). Nonetheless, it is common practice to study living systems by separating definable influences and analyzing them independently. The problem, then, is twofold: (1) to determine the relative contributions of nature and nurture to various kinds of behavior and (2) to discover how the developing child emerges from the interaction of nature and nurture.

QUESTIONS ABOUT INDIVIDUAL DIFFERENCES

Every person is in some respects like all other people, like some other people, and like no other person (Kluckhohn, Murray, & Schneider, 1953). All humans are alike because we are all members of the same species; all humans are like some but not other people insofar as they share important biological characteristics (males are like each other and different from females) or cultural characteristics (Australian Aborigines are alike in comparison with the Inuit people of North America); and every person is psychologically and physically unique. Even identical twins, who have identical genetic constitutions, are not alike in every respect.

When we attempt to understand the nature of development, it is important to take into account two questions about individual differences: (1) What makes individuals different from one another? and (2) To what extent are individual characteristics stable over time?

The question of what makes individuals different from one another is really another form of the question about the sources of development: Are we different from one another because of our nature or because of our nurture? If baby Sam is fussy, is it because he inherited a tendency to be easily upset, or has he been af-

Nature The inborn, genetically coded biological capacities and limitations of individuals.

Nurture The influence of the environment exerted on the individual by the social group.

BOX 1.1

Philosophical Forefathers of Developmental Psychology

When Europeans first became conscious of the peoples of Africa and Asia, in the fifteenth and sixteenth centuries, they debated the source of the obvious physical and behavioral differences between those people and themselves. Were these creatures human? they wondered. Were they also God's children, and if so, why did they look and act so differently? In modern terms, were they different in their basic *nature*, or were they different because of the conditions of their *nurture?*

Europeans asked similar questions about one another. Were peasants and princes different because God willed them so? Or were they different because they had been exposed to different experiences after they entered the world? These were not abstract questions, of interest only to philosophers. They were questions of deep political significance. For centuries kings and nobles had claimed that they had a God-given right to rule over others because they were naturally superior by virtue of their birth.

At the beginning of the modern era, two philosophers whose writings were to have great influence on the history of child development, John Locke and Jean-Jacques Rousseau, challenged the view that human differences were determined primarily by birth. Their views of human differences and social inequality were directly connected to their beliefs about children's development.

John Locke

The English philosopher John Locke (1632–1704) proposed that the child's mind is a tabula rasa, a blank slate upon which experience writes its story. In *Some Thoughts Concerning Education* (1699/1938), Locke expressed the central intuition that guided his thinking:

The little, and almost insensible Impressions on our tender Infancies, have very important and lasting Consequences: And there 'tis, as in the Fountains of some Rivers, where a gentle Application of the Hand turns the flexible waters into Chanels, that make them take quite contrary Courses, and by this little Direction given them at first in the Source, they receive different Tendencies, and arrive at last, at very remote and distant Places. (pp. 1–2)

Locke did not deny that there are limits to what the "Application of the Hand" can achieve. One cannot make water run uphill. He believed that children are born with different "temperaments and propensities," and he advised that instruction be tailored to fit these differences, a view that remains central to modern theories of education. But Locke clearly asserted that nurture, in the form of adults who "channeled" children's initial impulses, was the key factor in the creation of the main differences between people.

Jean-Jacques Rousseau

The French philosopher Jean-Jacques Rousseau (1712–1778) also argued that differences among people were primarily the results of experience, but his view of children and the role of adults in their training differed from Locke's. Rousseau asserted that "natural man" was not born in sin but was corrupted by civilization. In the state of nature all people were equal; inequality appeared with the rise of agriculture, industry, and property. According to this view, the natives of the lands being explored by European seafarers were more

fected by his parents' anxiety or the fact that his mother was addicted to cocaine during her pregnancy? If baby Georgia has a large appetite, is it because she inherited a tendency to obesity, or is it because her food contains too much sugar? Powerful statistical techniques and ingenious methods of data collection have been used in an effort to tease apart the fundamental sources of individual variation, but disagreements of theory and fact remain (Jensen, 1980; Lewontin, 1994; Scarr, 1992).

Insofar as individual characteristics are stable, they provide a glimpse of what children will be like in the future. Determining the extent to which this is true is a major task facing developmentalists. If baby Sam is fussy, perhaps he will be an ir-

virtuous than their "discoverers," who took such pride in their own civilization.

Rousseau claimed for the child at birth what he had claimed for natural man—a nature unspoiled by civilization. In *Emile* (1762/1911), a book that was part novel and part treatise on education, he indicated his opinion of adults' attempts to bring the child "up" to virtue:

> God makes all things good. Man meddles with them and they become evil. He forces one soil to yield the products of another, one tree to bear another's fruit. He confuses and confounds time, place, and natural conditions. He mutilates his dog, his horse, and his slave. He destroys and defaces all things; . . . he will have nothing as nature made it, not even man himself, who must learn his paces like a saddlehorse, and be shaped to his master's taste like the trees in his garden. (p. 5)

In his tale of Emile's education, Rousseau provided a vision of childhood and education in which the role of the caretaker is to protect the child from the pressures of adult society. Emile, who stands for Everychild, is depicted not as an incomplete adult who must be perfected through instruction but as a whole human being whose capabilities are suited to his age. Emile passes through several natural stages of development. In each, his activities are appropriate to his needs at the time, and they are guided by an adult who uses suitably paced educational practices. As William Kessen (1965) points out, these ideas about stages of development were later taken up by developmental psychologists, and they remain influential to this day.

Locke, Rousseau, and the Modern World

Locke's notion of a tabula rasa and Rousseau's vision of natural man have been rightly criticized and sometimes ridiculed in the centuries that have passed since the two philosophers died. Modern research makes it clear that we are not blank slates when we are born; we enter the world with brains that are highly structured. Nor is it plausible that there ever existed a purely "natural" state of humankind, which the modern world corrupts. When Victor, the Wild Boy who really did grow up in a "state of nature," misbehaved outrageously during one of his outings with Itard, people joked, "If only Rousseau could see his noble savage now!"

The common wisdom underlying Locke's and Rousseau's views on the crucial role of experience in the shaping of human behavior remains valid, however. In 1776 the United States of America was founded as a republic based on a profound faith in the "self-evident" truth that "all men are created equal." In an earlier era, when kings and nobles ruled by "divine right," the open expression of such ideas would have been unthinkable. A clear indication of the political significance of the belief that human beings can shape the course of their development by arranging their environments is the fact that when the archbishop of Paris read *Emile*, he sought to have Rousseau arrested. Alerted by friends, Rousseau fled from France.

With the acceptance of the idea that children are born good, or at least not evil, came a deep obligation to confront obvious inequalities in the conditions of developing children's lives. Eventually, most people came to accept the idea that society must take some responsibility for children's welfare—and indeed, for the welfare of all people.

ritable child. If baby Georgia has a large appetite, maybe she will be a big eater as a teenager.

The idea that some of our psychological characteristics remain constant over extended periods of time is an appealing one. After all, we feel as if we are the same person we were when we were 10 years old, only we know more and are older. Demonstrating such stability scientifically, however, has proved difficult. The problem is that the indicators that seem appropriate for measuring memory or affability in an infant are not likely to be appropriate for measuring those traits in that same infant when he is an 8-year-old or a teenager. Perhaps for this reason, many studies have failed to support the idea of stable psychological traits (Eaton,

1994). The refinement of research techniques in recent years, however, has allowed some investigators to find moderately stable individual differences in psychological characteristics. There is evidence that children who are shy and uncertain at 21 months, for example, are likely to be timid and cautious at 5½ years (Kagan & Snidman, 1991 a,b), and that infants who rapidly process visual information at 7 months of age display rapid perceptual processing at the age of 11 years (Rose & Feldman, 1995).

The stability of children's psychological characteristics over time depends on stability in their environment in addition to any stable characteristics that might be attributed to their genetic makeup (Fischer, Kenny, & Pipp, 1990). Studies have found that children who remain in an orphanage that provides only minimal care from infancy through adolescence are lethargic and unintelligent. They are also at risk for intellectual and emotional difficulties as adults. But if the environment of these children is changed—that is, if they are given extra care and stimulating attention by the orphanage staff or if they are adopted into caring families—their condition improves markedly, and many of them become intellectually normal adults (Clarke & Clarke, 1986).

The Discipline of Developmental Psychology

Among the sciences that study development, psychology focuses on the individual human being, whereas sociology and anthropology focus on human groups, and the biological sciences encompass our species as a whole, viewing it in relation to other forms of life. This division of scientific labor creates a paradox. On the one hand, psychologists are supposed to seek to understand development in terms of the individual person; on the other hand, the natural sciences tradition, which has dominated psychology during this century, insists that humankind, not the individual human, is the relevant unit of scientific analysis (Danzinger, 1990). This paradox is eloquently described by the novelist-philosopher Walker Percy:

> There is a secret about the scientific method which every scientist knows and takes as a matter of course, but which the layman does not know. . . . The secret is this: Science cannot utter a single word about an individual molecule, thing, or creature insofar as it is an individual but only insofar as it is like other individuals. (1975, p. 22)

The difference between these two ways of knowing—one based on intimate knowledge of individual characteristics and biography, the other based on characteristics common to many people—is a source of constant tension in psychologists' attempts to understand development. The more psychologists want to know about individuals, the more they need to know about each person's life history and current circumstances. But the more they concentrate on unique histories and patterns of influence, the less they can generalize their findings to other individuals.

This trade-off requires psychologists to vary their research methods, choosing those that best suit their specific goal. If, for example, the goal is to create a beneficial environment for infants born prematurely or to understand the role of symbolic play in toddlers' intellectual development, the appropriate methods are those that treat all children as equivalent with respect to the issue in question. But if the goal is to help Johnny, who suddenly has started to fail in school and to misbehave in class, the psychologist may want to know about the circumstances of Johnny's birth, recent changes in his family life, and perhaps even the specific mix of children and activities Johnny is dealing with at school.

CRITERIA OF SCIENTIFIC DESCRIPTION

Every society has its own beliefs about the nature of children and the course of their development. Psychologists, however, are looking for scientific facts that can be universally applied. Like any other scientists, they may begin with common-sense observation and speculation. Then they attempt to test their ideas in ways that provide clear answers and that allow others to check their reasoning and procedures. Psychologists use four general criteria to judge the conclusions derived from investigations of children's behavior: *objectivity*, *reliability*, *validity*, and *replicability*.

To be useful in constructing a disciplined account of human development, data should be collected and analyzed with **objectivity;** that is, they should not be biased by the investigators' preconceptions. Total objectivity is impossible to achieve in practice because human beings come to the study of behavior with beliefs that influence their interpretations of what they see. But objectivity remains an important ideal toward which to work.

Data obtained in research should have **reliability** in two senses. First, the descriptions arrived at when the same behavior is observed on two or more occasions should be consistent. Second, independent observers should agree in their descriptions of the behavior. Suppose that one wants to know how upset infants become when a pacifier is taken from them while they are sucking on it (Goldsmith & Campos, 1982). Statements about the degree of an infant's distress are considered reliable in the first sense if the level of distress (manifested as crying or thrashing about) is found to be more or less the same on successive occasions when the baby's sucking is interrupted. The statements are considered reliable in the second sense if independent observers agree on how distressed the baby becomes each time the pacifier is taken away.

Validity means that the data being collected actually reflect the psychological process that the researcher claims they do. If this is so, one important test of validity is whether different ways of measuring the same characteristic yield the same outcome. Many psychologists believe, for example, that the distress infants display when their sucking is interrupted reflects an enduring predisposition to become irritable when frustrated (Kagan et al., 1994). Children who become upset when their pacifier is removed should also become irritable when a rattle is taken away or when they are not fed on time. If different measures do not converge on a single conclusion, doubt is cast on their validity.

Another important test of validity is whether the behavior exhibited at one time can be used to predict future behavior. If the same infants who appear greatly upset when their pacifier is removed also become upset when they are interrupted in future situations (when recess ends in the middle of a game, for example), that is evidence to support the validity of the claim about a predisposition to irritability when frustrated. If these same infants don't become upset easily in future situations in which they are frustrated, the original claim that the behavior is an indicator of an underlying temperamental predisposition to be irritable is suspect.

In scientific research, **replicability,** the fourth requirement, means that other researchers can use the same procedures as an initial investigator did and obtain the same results. In research on the ability to imitate, for example, some researchers report that newborns will imitate exaggerated facial expressions, whereas others have failed to elicit such imitation from newborns (see Chapter 4, pp. 162–163). Only if the same finding is obtained repeatedly by different investigators is it likely to be considered firmly established by the scientific community.

In addition to these four basic criteria, it is important that the group of people studied be a **representative sample** of the people about whom the psychologist wishes to answer questions. Conclusions drawn from data collected from one group of people may not be applicable to other people with different characteris-

Objectivity A requirement that scientific knowledge not be distorted by the investigator's preconceptions.

Reliability The scientific requirement that the phenomenon under study can be observed repeatedly and that different observers agree on what they observe.

Validity The scientific requirement that a description of behavior reflects the underlying psychological process that the investigator claims it does.

Replication A study is replicated when the same procedures are used on another occasion and the same results are obtained.

Representative sample A sample of individuals who are representative of the people about whom the psychologist wishes to answer questions.

tics. For example, a study of infants from middle-class families in Denver who manifest distress when they are separated from their mothers may yield different results than a study applying the same procedures to infants from working-class homes in Denver or middle-class homes in Tokyo.

TECHNIQUES OF DATA COLLECTION

Over the past hundred years, psychologists have refined a variety of techniques for gathering information about the development of children. Among the most widely used are self-reports, naturalistic observations, experiments, and clinical interviews. No one technique can answer all of our questions about human development. Each has a strategic role to play, its appropriateness depending on the topic. Often researchers use two or more methods in combination.

Self-reports

Self-report A method of gathering data in which people report on their own psychological states and behaviors.

Perhaps the most direct way to obtain information about psychological development is through **self-reports,** people's answers to questions about themselves. Psychologists usually conduct structured interviews to obtain self-reports, but written questionnaires are also common. Topics as diverse as adolescents' developing ideas about friendship and popularity (Savin-Williams & Berndt, 1990) and parents' ideas about child rearing (Sigel, McGillicuddy-DeLisi, & Goodnow, 1992) have been investigated in this manner. In one study (which we will describe further in Chapter 15), researchers went so far as to provide teenagers with beepers, which sounded at random intervals throughout the day to signal the teenagers to fill out a questionnaire about what they were doing and feeling at that moment (Csikszentmihalyi & Larson, 1984).

Self-reports obtained through interviews and questionnaires have the advantage of providing detailed accounts of the person's life experiences that might otherwise escape the investigator's notice. But they have a major limitation: there is good reason to expect self-reports to be inaccurate. This difficulty is obvious in the case of very young children, even after they have learned to talk. But it is a serious difficulty with adults, too (Brewin, Andrews, & Gotlib, 1993).

Evidence that parents are likely to be selective in what they remember (or at least in what they are willing to report) about themselves and their children comes from a study in which parents were asked to recall their child-rearing practices several years earlier, when their children were 3 years old (Robbins, 1963). The parents' reports could be checked against what they had actually done because they had participated in an earlier study in which their behavior had been observed. Parents' recall, Robbins found, was distorted to conform to their beliefs about optimum development. Some of the mothers, for example, claimed that their children had never sucked their thumbs, a practice disapproved of by experts at the time of the original observations, even though they were on record as having consulted with their physicians about their children's thumb-sucking.

To reduce such distortions in long-term retrospective reports, researchers now often ask parents to focus on specific ongoing behaviors, such as temper tantrums, disobedience, or the appearance of new words in a child's vocabulary, and ask for daily reports on these behaviors along with the parents' responses to them (Patterson, 1982; Zahn-Waxler & Radke-Yarrow, 1982). Even this precaution, however, does not solve the problem in all cases. There is good correspondence between observers and parents in some cases (the study of vocabulary development) (Fenson et al., 1994), but little agreement has been found in others (such as the study of temperament) (Seifer et al., 1994).

Naturalistic observations

The most natural way to gather objective information about children is to observe them in the course of their everyday lives and record what happens. Since the presence of a stranger is likely to be intrusive in many situations, however, the ideal strategy is to arrange to have the children observed by someone who ordinarily spends time with them—a parent or a teacher, for example.

In the nineteenth century, several scientists began to write **baby biographies,** diaries in which they recorded observations of their own children (Kessen, 1965). The most famous of these accounts is Darwin's (1877) daily record of the early development of his eldest son (Figure 1.4). By documenting characteristics shared by human beings and other species, Darwin hoped to support his thesis of human evolution. Darwin's baby biography and others such as W. F. Leopold's (1949) record of his daughter's language development and Jean Piaget's (1952b, 1954) descriptions of his children's mental development have proved to be of enduring scientific value.

At present baby biographies are rarely used outside the area of language development (where they are still a basic source of data) because even scientists usually cannot maintain objectivity when they describe their own children. As the psychologist William Kessen comments, "No one can distort as convincingly as a loving parent" (1965, p. 117).

Whether **naturalistic observations** are conducted by a nonprofessional parent or a trained observer who has no personal connection to the children being studied, their goal is detailed information about children's actual behavior in the real-world settings they inhabit, at home, in school, and elsewhere in the community.

Naturalistic observation is one of the major research tools used by developmental psychologists who consider themselves to be ethologists. **Ethology** is an interdisciplinary science that studies the biological, evolutionary foundations of behavior (Hinde, 1987). Ethologists place great emphasis on naturalistic observation because they believe that biologically important behaviors affecting human development are best studied in the settings that are significant to their daily lives (Savin-Williams, 1987).

F. Francis Strayer (1991) carried out naturalistic observations in this tradition when he studied the way children interact in preschool classrooms. By observing and recording who interacted with whom and the quality of the interactions, Strayer and his colleagues discovered that social hierarchies develop spontaneously in preschool classes much as they do in certain species of social animals. Once developed, these social hierarchies regulate the aggression that the children display toward one another. (We will return to this topic in Chapter 10).

Observation in Many Contexts Naturalistic observations can be confined to a single context or can be employed to gather data in many contexts. The latter type of observational strategy is often used to study a child's **ecology,** a term derived from the Greek word for "house." In the biological sciences, the "house" is the habitat of a population of plants or animals, and the ecology of that population is the pattern of its relationship with its environment. In psychology, "ecology" has come to refer to the range of situations in which people are actors, the roles they play, the predicaments they encounter, and the consequences of those encounters (see Figure 1.5) (Bronfenbrenner, 1979; Moen, Elder, & Lüsher, 1995).

Charles Super and Sarah Harkness (1986), who have studied children's development in Kenya as well as the United States, emphasize the links between children's development and the community within which they are born. They refer to the child's place within the community as a **developmental niche.** They suggest that every developmental niche be analyzed in terms of three components: (1) the physical and social context in which the child lives, (2) the culturally determined

FIGURE 1.4 *The naturalist Charles Darwin became famous for his theory of evolution. His observations of his son, which he recorded in a baby biography, provide one of the first systematic descriptions of infant development.*

Baby biography A parent's detailed record of an infant's behavior over a period of time.

Naturalistic observations Observations of the actual behavior of people in the real world settings they inhabit.

Ethology An interdisciplinary science that studies the biological bases of behavior and its evolutionary context.

Ecology The range of situations in which people are actors; the roles they play; and the predicaments they encounter.

Developmental niche The physical and social context in which the child lives, including child rearing and educational practices, as well as psychological characteristics of the child's parents.

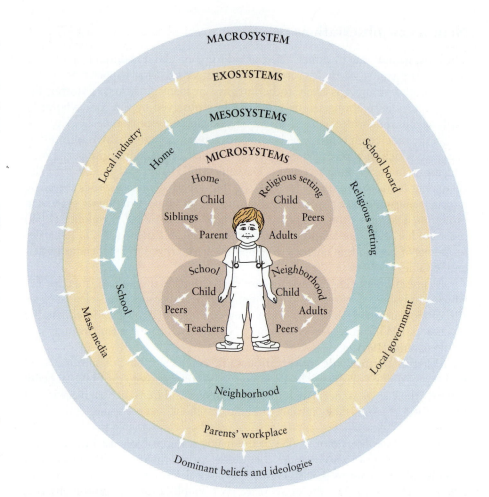

FIGURE 1.5 *The ecological approach sees children in the context of all the various settings they inhabit on a daily basis (microsystems). These settings are related to one another in a variety of ways (mesosystems), which are in turn linked to settings and social institutions where the children are not present but which have an important influence on their development (exosystems). All of these systems are organized in terms of the culture's dominant beliefs and ideologies (the macrosystem).*

child-rearing and educational practices of the child's society, and (3) the psychological characteristics of the child's parents. Thorough ecological descriptions of the variety of real-life experiences of children in their sociocultural contexts provide a sense of the whole child and the many influences that act on the child. They can tell us what difficulties loom largest in children's lives and how circumstances might be changed to foster their development.

The most ambitious project launched to study the ecology of human development was conducted by Roger Barker and Herbert Wright (1951, 1955). These researchers spent hundreds of hours observing and describing the natural ecology of schoolchildren in various communities in the United States and abroad. In one such study, they observed a single 7-year-old American boy from the time he awoke on April 26, 1949, until he went to sleep that night. They noted everything the boy did, everywhere he went, and everything that happened along the way. Barker and Wright found that this one child on just one day participated in approximately 1300 distinct activities in a wide variety of settings and involving hundreds of objects and dozens of people. These observations gave some idea of the wide range of skills children possess by the age of 7 and the many social demands made on them. (We will learn more about this study in Chapter 12.)

Barker and Wright made it a point to write down everything they could notice and get on paper about a child's daily behavior and the contexts in which it occurred. Other investigators who study children across a range of contexts are more selective. They usually decide in advance on a particular type of behavior to observe in different contexts, or they choose a few important contexts within which to make extensive observations of the various behaviors that children exhibit.

In a study of 160 Mayan children between 1 and 14 years of age in a village in Guatemala, for example, Barbara Rogoff (1981) sampled brief time periods to provide "snapshots" of children's activities. Rogoff drew up a list of the observations she planned to make and worked out a schedule that allowed her to observe each child for about 10 minutes several times a day on different days of the week. During these periods she noted whom a child was with and what the child was doing. Rogoff discovered that Mayan children, like U.S. children, spend much of their time apart from adults. When they do spend time with adults, however, their experiences are quite different from those of U.S. children. When Mayan children are with adults, they are expected to help with the grownups' usual jobs. In industrial societies such as our own, children cannot (or are not allowed to) help with many adult jobs. Instead, when U.S. children are with adults, they are likely to be instructed by them, even outside school (Schoggen, 1989).

Observations in a Single Context The very breadth of the ecological approach makes it time-consuming and expensive to apply. As a result, developmental psychologists often restrict their observations to a single social setting that is widely encountered and important in children's lives. They observe in minute detail the face-to-face interactions between children or between children and adults.

Lisa Serbin and her colleagues (1973), for instance, examined interactions between teachers and students in 15 preschool classrooms to see whether anything in the teacher's behavior might unwittingly be encouraging aggressiveness in boys and dependence in girls. They found that the teachers did not pay equal attention to the misbehavior of boys and girls. The teachers chastised the boys publicly for a greater proportion of their misdeeds than they did the girls for theirs. Often this selective treatment seemed to increase aggressiveness among the boys. In a parallel set of observations, the researchers discovered that the teachers rewarded dependent behavior in girls by paying more attention to those girls who were sitting closest to them; they paid equal amounts of attention to all the boys no matter where they were sitting in the classroom. Once such practices are discovered, new patterns of interaction can be suggested to the teachers that might foster more appropriate behavior in schoolchildren of both sexes. An important outgrowth of this line of research has been the introduction of all-girl classes in certain curriculum areas, such as mathematics, as a way of improving girls' educational performance.

Limitations of Naturalistic Observations Observational studies are a keystone of child development research and a crucial source of data about children's social development. What we can learn from them, however, is limited. Observers enter the scene with expectations about what they are going to see, and we all tend to observe selectively in accordance with our expectations. An observer cannot write down everything, so information is inevitably lost. In some studies, prearranged note-taking schemes specify what to look for and how to report it. The drawback of such schemes is that they are not flexible enough to take account of unexpected events, so details are often lost in this way, too. If time elapses between an event and note taking, observations may be further distorted because people's selective remembering accentuates the problem of selective observing (D'Andrade, 1974). Recordings of behavior on videotape or film are useful, but they are extremely time-consuming to analyze.

Cartoonist Gary Trudeau comments on the phenomenon, established in observational research, that teachers respond differently to boys and girls in their classrooms.

DOONESBURY By Garry Trudeau

BOX 1.2

Correlation and Causation

In their attempts to discover factors that influence development, psychologists often begin by determining if different factors are related. Two factors are said to be *correlated* with each other when changes in one are associated with changes in the other. In later chapters, we will see many examples of correlation: As children grow older, they display increased ability to remember lists of words; that is, age is correlated with memory. The higher the social class of the parents, the greater the achievement of their children in school; that is, school achievement is correlated with social class. These relationships are important hints about causal factors in development, but they fall short of specifying the actual mechanisms involved.

A coefficient of correlation (symbolized as *r*) provides a quantitative index of the *degree* of association between two factors; it enables psychologists to distinguish between relationships that occur by chance and those that occur with significant regularity. A coefficient of correlation that describes the relationship between factor *X* and factor *Y* can vary in both size and direction. When $r = 1.00$, there is a perfect positive correlation between the two factors: As factor *X* changes, factor *Y* changes in the same direction and at the same rate. When $r = -1.00$, there is a perfect negative correlation between factor *X* and factor *Y*. If every increase in age in a population were accompanied by an increase in weight, for example, the correlation between age and weight would be 1.00. If instead peo-

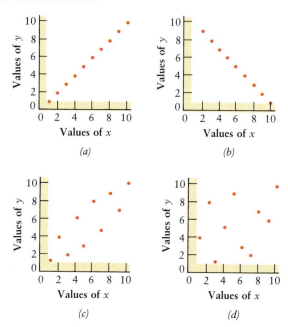

Four possible relationships between two variables: (a) *As values of* x *increase, values of* y *increase, producing a correlation of 1.00.* (b) *As values of* x *increase, values of* y *decrease, producing a correlation of* −1.00. (c) *As values of* x *increase, values of* y *often increase, but there are some exceptions, producing a correlation of .84.* (d) *As values of* x *increase, values of* y *show a weak but noticeable tendency to increase, producing a correlation of .33*

Another difficulty with observational research is that people's behavior changes when they know they are being watched, creating a false impression of their normal behavior (Zegiob, Arnold, & Forehand, 1975). A laboratory study of the interactions between mothers and their children confirmed this problem. Zoe Graves and Joseph Glick (1978) asked mothers to help their 18- to 25-month-old children put together a simple jigsaw puzzle. To determine the influence that being observed had on the mothers' behavior, Graves and Glick told half of them that the video equipment being used to record their interactions was not working. They found that the mothers who believed they were off camera were not so helpful to their children.

Perhaps the major problem with naturalistic observation is that it rarely allows researchers to establish the existence of causal relationships between phenomena, a basic aim of science. Collation and comparison of observations can establish whether a **correlation** exists between two factors; that is, whether changes in one factor vary with changes in another. But a correlation doesn't tell us whether one factor causes the other or whether both factors are caused by a third,

Correlation Two factors are said to be correlated with one another when changes in one factor are associated with changes in the other.

ple always got smaller as they aged, the correlation would be −1.00. If age and weight were not related at all, the correlation would be .00. Intermediate positive or negative values of a coefficient of correlation indicate intermediate levels of association. There is a correlation of approximately .50 between the heights of parents and their offspring, for example, indicating that tall parents tend to have tall offspring (Tanner, 1990).

A correlation may point to a causal relationship between two events, but correlation is not the same as causation; that is, a correlation does not establish that the occurrence of one event *depends* on the occurrence of the other. The difficulty of distinguishing correlation from causation is often a source of scientific controversy. In the case of the heights of parents and their children, the problem is not serious. We can be pretty certain that the height of a child does not cause the height of the parents. Nor is confusion likely to arise about the relationship between a child's age and weight, either. Age by itself cannot cause increases in weight because "age" is simply another term for the time that has elapsed since an agreed-upon starting point. Certainly, weight cannot cause an increase in age.

Other cases are less clear-cut. Among schoolchildren, for example, a correlation of about .30 has been found between height and scores on tests of mental ability; that is, taller children tend to score higher on intelligence tests than their shorter agemates (Tanner,

1990). Since nothing about children's height can plausibly be said to be a cause of their intelligence, or children's intelligence of their height, some other factor must be the cause of both.

The slipperiest cases to deal with are those in which a scientist has a strong theory about causal connections among the phenomena under study but only correlational data to work with. For example, there is a correlation of .50 between children's current grades in school and their scores on standard IQ tests (Minton & Schneider, 1980). It might be tempting to conclude that intelligence causes cognitive development. That conclusion does not follow from the correlational evidence, however, any more than the conclusion that age causes changes in weight, although it fits many people's notion that intelligence causes school achievement. It could just as plausibly be argued that students who work hard get their schoolwork done more often and learn more, thereby boosting their IQ scores.

The use of correlation coefficients to describe relationships among phenomena is important in the study of human development because so many of the factors of interest to psychologists (such as social class, ethnic origin, and genetic constitution) cannot be controlled experimentally. Because correlations often suggest causal relationships but do not provide crucial evidence of causation, controversies that have no clear resolution may arise, requiring developmental psychologists to exercise caution in the interpretation of their data.

undetermined factor (see Box 1.2). In their ecological study, for example, Barker and Wright revealed many relationships between the settings in which children find themselves and the characteristics of children's behavior in those settings; similarly, Serbin and her colleagues discovered interesting patterns in the ways teachers treat boys and girls in the classroom. Neither study, however, pinpoints the causes of the patterns it describes.

The difficulty in both these cases is that researchers have no means of telling from their observations alone which factors are causal. Did children in Barker and Wright's study act more grown up in church than in a drugstore because church attendance evokes religious feelings or because their parents were there to observe them? In the study by Serbin and her colleagues, did the teachers chastise the boys for their misbehavior more often than they chastised the girls because they had stereotyped the boys as troublemakers who needed discipline to be kept in line or because they simply noticed the boys' misbehavior more often than the girls'? Similar questions can be raised about almost any observational study of behavior. To attempt to resolve such questions, psychologists turn to experimental methods.

Experimental methods

An **experiment** in psychology usually consists of introducing some change in a person's or animal's experience and then measuring the effect of the change on the person's or animal's behavior. Ideally, all the other possible causal influences are held constant while the factor of interest is made to vary to determine if that factor makes a difference. If an experiment is well designed and executed, it should provide a means of confirming a scientific hypothesis about the causes of the behavior observed. A scientific **hypothesis** is an assumption that is precise enough to be tested and can be shown to be incorrect. If there is no way to disprove the hypothesis, it has little scientific value.

An investigation of the development of fear of high places by Joseph Campos and his colleagues (Bertenthal, Campos, & Barrett, 1984) demonstrates how the experimental method can help resolve uncertainties about causal factors in development. For many years it was believed that the fear of heights is innate in the human infant. According to this view, the fear of high places becomes apparent when infants begin to locomote, or move about under their own steam, not because either locomotion causes fear or fear causes locomotion, but because both result from general maturational factors and just happen to develop around the same time (Rader, Bausano, & Richards, 1980; Richards & Rader, 1981). Campos and his colleagues disagreed with this hypothesis. They believed that fear of heights is a result of experience, especially the experience that infants acquire when they start to crawl.

Initially Campos and his colleagues studied a group of infants who were between 6 and 8 months old, beginning a week or two after they began to crawl. They discovered that at the first few opportunities the infants were given, all would cross a visual cliff, a transparent platform that gives the illusion of a sharp drop in elevation (Figure 1.6). On subsequent trials, however, the infants became increasingly reluctant to cross over the visual cliff, even though nothing bad had happened when they crossed over it before. Something seemed to be building up in the infants' minds as they gained experience. But what was building up and what experience was causing it? To find answers to these questions, the investigators conducted an experiment.

Campos and his colleagues designed an experiment to test the hypothesis that the onset of the fear of heights results from the experience of moving about (Bertenthal et al., 1984). They located 92 infants who were near the age when they might be expected to start crawling and begin showing a fear of heights. The infants were randomly assigned to one of two groups. One group was designated as the **experimental group**—the group in an experiment whose environment is changed. Over several days the infants in this group were given more than 40 hours of experience moving about in special baby walkers before they learned to crawl (see Figure 1.7). The other children, called the **control group**—the group in an experiment that is treated as much as possible like the experimental group except that it does not participate in the experimental manipulation—were provided with no special experience in locomoting. If Campos and his colleagues were correct, the babies in the experimental group should respond differently to the visual cliff than the babies in the control group did because of their more extensive experience in moving about.

Forty hours of careening around a room in a walker may not seem like a lot of experience, but it apparently made a big

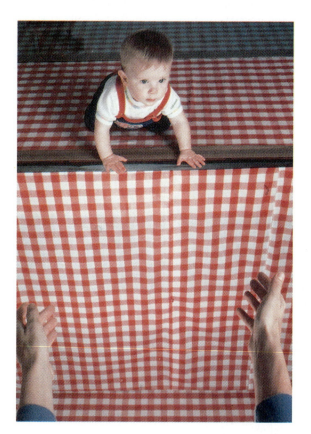

FIGURE 1.6 *A baby hesitates at the edge of a visual cliff, a transparent platform that makes it appear to the baby that there is a sharp drop just ahead.*

difference in the way the infants in the experimental group responded to the visual cliff. Although responses varied somewhat, in general the infants in the experimental group showed fear on their first exposure to the visual cliff, whereas the infants in the control group did not.

This experiment provided strong support for the hypothesis that the development of locomotion plays a large role in the development of the fear of heights. Additional research would be useful to rule out other possible factors that this research did not delve into. Suppose, for example, children were moved around in little vehicles that permitted them to explore the environment without locomotion; would they still become fearful when they were placed on the visual cliff? Such uncertainties about research results are almost inevitable. It is often necessary to carry out a series of experiments to isolate specific causes because the complexities of behavior exceed the researcher's ability to control all the relevant factors in a single experiment (Cole & Means, 1981).

In general, the clear strength of the experimental method is its ability to isolate causal factors in a way no other method of investigation can. Two main factors limit its usefulness as a source of information about development: for ethical reasons, many experiments should not be performed; and the very control of the environment that many experiments require may distort the validity of the results obtained.

Ethics and Experimentation   The central ethical tenet of all psychological research is: if a research procedure may harm anyone, it should not be carried out. Ethical issues in psychological research are not always so clear-cut as this tenet suggests, however. What is harmful, and how do we assess the risks? Practically any intervention in another person's life may involve some risk, so the judgment can be a difficult one. Furthermore, the factors taken into account often vary from one culture to the next and from one historical era to another. In 1920 John B. Watson, the behavior theorist, and Rosalie Rayner published the results of an experiment to demonstrate that children's fears of animals are not innate but are shaped by the environment. They showed a 9-month-old boy a series of animals (a rat, a white rabbit, a dog, etc.). According to these investigators, the baby showed no fear while he was playing with the animals. Then they hit a steel bar with a hammer behind the baby as he reached for the rabbit. The boy cried at the loud noise. After several such experiences, the baby cried whenever he saw the rabbit. Watson and Rayner reported that his fear of the white rabbit extended to many white, fuzzy objects, including a dog, a fur coat, and even a Santa Claus mask. Fear of white rabbits, fur coats, and Santa Claus masks is not inherited, they claimed, it is learned.

Watson and Rayner's research aroused little comment concerning its ethics at the time. In fact, it became a key piece of evidence in favor of environmental theories of development. Since then it has been severely criticized for its failure to conform to important scientific principles of experimentation. The investigators did not have an appropriate control group; they studied only one child, so they failed to replicate their results; and their reports of the procedures and results were inconsistent (Harris, 1979; Samelson, 1980). What is of interest here, however, is less Watson and Rayner's skill as experimenters than their apparent willingness to override ethical considerations in regard to the baby's welfare in the name of science. Watson's doctrine of learning led him to believe that if fear could be created by events in the environment, it also could be removed. But Watson and Rayner never proved this point in their experiment. They made no attempt to help the child overcome the fears they claimed to have induced in him.

Psychologists' judgments on the ethics of Watson and Rayner's experiment would almost certainly be different today than they were in the 1920s. Psycholo-

FIGURE 1.7 *Joseph Campos and his colleagues placed this infant in a walker to experience locomotion before having learned to crawl. Such experiences seemed to influence the onset of fear of the visual cliff.*

Experimental group The persons whose experience is changed as part of an experiment.

Control group The persons in an experiment who do not undergo the experimental manipulation.

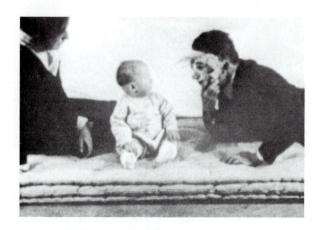

John B. Watson and Rosalie Rayner experimenting with infant fears. (Courtesy of Professor Benjamin Harris.)

gists now are less certain of their ability to turn psychological processes on and off, and they appreciate more fully that a scientifically proved hypothesis by no means equates with certain knowledge. To protect the rights of others, modern researchers are closely monitored by their own institutions and by government agencies. Before they can carry out their research, they must satisfy a committee of their peers that they will not harm the people who participate in their investigations and that the research promises some benefits to those people in the long run (see Box 1.3).

Experiments and Artificiality Sometimes people behave differently in an artificial, experimental situation than they would normally. This, of course, raises doubts about the worthiness of experimental results. Indeed, so pervasive is this problem that the psychologist Urie Bronfenbrenner (1979) has described many laboratory experiments involving children as studies of "the strange behavior of children in strange situations with strange adults for the briefest possible periods of time" (p. 19).

Often there is no simple way to eliminate artificiality from the experimental setting because the factors being studied in the experiment arise too seldom to be studied systematically in real life. In some cases, however, researchers have partially overcome the problem by introducing experimental variation in naturally occurring situations without significantly disrupting the usual course of events. To investigate how young children add new words to their vocabularies in ordinary circumstances, Elsa Bartlett (1977) and Susan Carey (1978) had a preschool teacher introduce an unusual color, olive, to her charges in the natural course of her classroom routine. To avoid the possibility that some children already knew the name of the color, the teacher referred to it as "chromium." The researchers found that when the new word was introduced casually—"Please pass the chromium crayon"—the children acquired it after very few exposures. Studies of word acquisition in the laboratory, in contrast, typically find that children require extensive instruction by an adult to learn a new word. Thus, by introducing new words to children in a natural way, Bartlett and Carey brought about a basic change in psychologists' understanding of a vitally important aspect of development. (We will return to their findings in Chapter 8.)

Clinical interview methods

Clinical method Research method in which questions are tailored to the individual.

All the research methods discussed thus far, with the exception of diary studies, are designed to apply uniform procedures of data collection to every individual observed. In this respect, clinical interview methods differ fundamentally from the others. The essence of the **clinical method** is to tailor questions to the individual subject. Each question depends on the answer to the one that precedes it.

As the term "clinical" implies, clinical interview methods are often used to investigate the problems of persons who are troubled or unwell. When developmental psychologists use clinical interview methods in this way, they, like medical clinicians, are seeking a set of appropriate remedies. The most famous application of clinical interview methods in developmental psychology comes from the work of Sigmund Freud, who considered the early family history of the child to be essential to later personality development. From a patient's account, he sought to identify crucial events that produced the difficulty from which that person was suffering. In Freud's use of the clinical method, this analysis was coupled with therapy;

Ethical Standards for Research with Children

The following guidelines are adapted and condensed from the Ethical Standards for Research with Children issued by the Society for Research in Child Development.

Children as research subjects present ethical problems for the investigator different from those presented by adult subjects. Not only are children often viewed as more vulnerable to stress, but, having less knowledge and experience, they are less able to evaluate what participation in research may mean. Consent of the parent for the study of the child, moreover, must be obtained in addition to the child's consent. These are some of the major differences between research with children and research with adults.

- No matter how young the children, their rights supersede the rights of the investigator.
- The final responsibility to establish and maintain ethical practices in research remains with the individual investigator.
- The investigator is responsible for the ethical practices of collaborators, assistants, students, and employees, all of whom, however, incur parallel obligations.
- The investigator should inform children of all features of the research that may affect their willingness to participate and should answer children's questions in terms appropriate to their comprehension.
- The investigator should respect children's freedom to choose to participate in research or not, as well as to discontinue participation at any time.
- Informed consent of parents or those who act in loco parentis (e.g., teachers, superintendents of institutions) similarly should be obtained, preferably in writing. Informed consent requires that parents or other responsible adults be told all features of the research that may affect their willingness to allow children to participate.
- The informed consent of any person whose interaction with the child is the subject of the study should also be obtained.
- The investigator may use no research operation that may harm children either physically or psychologically.

- Although we accept the ethical idea of full disclosure of information, a particular study may necessitate concealment or deception. Whenever concealment or deception is thought to be essential to the conduct of the study, investigators should satisfy a committee of their peers that their judgment is correct.
- The investigator should keep in confidence all information obtained about research participants.
- Immediately after the data are collected, the investigator should clarify for the research participant any misconceptions that may have arisen. The investigator also recognizes a duty to report general findings to participants in terms appropriate to their understanding. When scientific or humane values may justify withholding information, every effort should be made so that withholding the information has no damaging consequences for the participant.
- When, in the course of research, information comes to the investigator's attention that may seriously affect the child's well-being, the investigator has a responsibility to discuss the information with those expert in the field in order that the parents may arrange the necessary assistance for their child.
- When it is learned that research procedures may result in undesirable consequences for the participant, the investigator should employ appropriate measures to correct these consequences, and should consider redesigning the procedure.
- Investigators should be mindful of the social, political, and human implications of their research and should be especially careful in the presentation of their findings. This standard, however, in no way denies investigators the right to pursue any area of research or the right to observe proper standards of scientific reporting.
- When an experimental treatment under investigation is believed to be of benefit to children, control groups should be offered other beneficial alternative treatments, if available, instead of no treatment.

the analyst's theory was tested by the effectiveness of the treatment in resolving the person's difficulty.

Clinical methods are not restricted to pathology, however. The developmental psychologist Jean Piaget often used clinical interview techniques to explore children's developing understandings of the world. In the example to follow, note that it would have been impossible for Piaget to anticipate this 7½-year-old child's responses. Therefore, he adapted his questions to the flow of the conversation.

Piaget: . . . says that dreams come "from the night." Where do they go?
Child: Everywhere.
Piaget: What do you dream with?
Child: With the mouth.
Piaget: Where is the dream?
Child: In the night.
Piaget: Where does it happen?
Child: Everywhere. In rooms. In houses.
Piaget: Whereabouts?
Child: In the bed.
Piaget: Can you see it?
Child: No, because it is only at night.
Piaget: Would anyone know you are dreaming?
Child: No, because it's near us.
Piaget: Could you touch it?
Child: No, because you are asleep when you dream.

(Adapted from Piaget, 1929/1979, p. 93)

Piaget believed that by interviewing many children of different ages about such familiar phenomena, he could discover basic changes that knowledge undergoes over the course of development.

Alexander Luria (1902–1977), a Russian psychologist, showed that the clinical interview method could also be used to uncover qualitative differences in thinking in different cultural environments. In one study he presented people of varying ages who lived in a pastoral culture in Central Asia with drawings of four objects—a hammer, a saw, a log, and a hatchet—three of which could be grouped into the single category "tools." He then asked which of the objects did not fit with the others (1976, p. 58):

Subject: They all fit here! The saw has to saw the log, the hammer has to hammer it, and the hatchet has to chop it. And if you want to saw the log up really good, you need the hammer. You can't take any of these things away. There isn't any you don't need.

Luria: But one fellow told me that the log didn't belong here.

Subject: Why'd he say that? If we say the log isn't like the other things and put it off to one side, we'd be making a mistake. All these things are needed for the log.

Luria: But that other fellow said that the saw, hammer, and hatchet are all alike in some way, while the log isn't.

Subject: So what if they're not alike? They all work together and chop the log. Here everything works right, here everything's just fine.

Here we see a classic use of the clinical interview. The investigator probes the person's understanding by challenging various lines of reasoning and suggesting different (sometimes incorrect) alternatives depending on the person's prior responses. In this case, Luria has encountered someone for whom "similar" seems to mean "enters into the same activity." By contrasting this subject's answers with the answers given by people from other cultural backgrounds, Luria was able to formulate plausible conclusions about the ways in which culture influences the development of intellectual functions.

The strong point of clinical interview methods is that they provide insight into the dynamics of individual behavior. Each adult psychoanalyzed by Freud, each child interviewed by Piaget, and each Central Asian pastoralist interviewed by Luria provided a distinctive pattern of responses that corresponded to their individual experiences. To arrive at general conclusions, however, the clinician must ignore individual differences in order to distill the general pattern, and as the general pattern appears, the individual picture disappears. The heavy reliance on verbal expression of knowledge also runs the risk of underestimating what children can actually do.

RESEARCH DESIGNS

If psychological research is to illuminate the process of developmental change, it must be designed to reveal how the supposed factors work over time. There are two basic research designs that psychologists use for this purpose, longitudinal and cross-sectional. Each takes time into account in a distinctive way. The psychologist who uses the **longitudinal design** collects information about a group of children as they age over an extended span of time. The researcher who uses the **cross-sectional design** collects information about children of various ages at one time. These designs can be used in conjunction with each other and with any of the techniques of data collection just discussed. Each design has its own advantages and disadvantages.

Longitudinal designs

Researchers who choose a longitudinal design select a sample of the population they want to study and gather data from each person at two or more ages. The longitudinal design traces changes in persons over time and thus is consistent with the basic definition of development as the changes that occur in the physical structure and behavior of the organism during its lifetime. For example, a research team at the Fels Research Institute in Yellow Springs, Ohio, studied personality development in 71 children from their birth until they reached their middle teens (Kagan & Moss, 1962). Observations, tests of personality, and interviews repeated at various times allowed the Fels group to determine the stability of such characteristics as a tendency to become angry or upset when an ongoing activity is disturbed. Without longitudinal measurements, it would be impossible to discover if this particular behavior pattern remains constant or changes as a child grows older. Other influential longitudinal studies have focused on such varied topics as personality (Friedman et al., 1995), mental health (Werner & Smith, 1992), temperament and intelligence (DeFries, Plomin, & Fulker, 1994), language development (Fenson et al., 1994), and social adjustment (Cairns & Cairns, 1994).

Longitudinal designs would seem to be an ideal way to study development because they fit so closely the requirement that development be studied over time. Unfortunately, longitudinal research designs have some practical and methodological drawbacks that have restricted psychologists' reliance on them. They of-

Longitudinal design A research design in which data are gathered from the same group of people at several ages.

Cross-sectional design A research design in which children of different ages are studied at a single time.

Longitudinal designs follow the same persons through the years as they age.

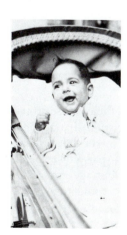

ten require a lengthy commitment on the part of the researcher, and they are expensive to carry out, particularly if they are to be conducted over several years. In addition, some parents may refuse to allow their children to participate in a lengthy study. If such refusals are more frequent in one social, economic, or ethnic group, they may make the sample unrepresentative of the population as a whole. Some of the children who do begin a study may drop out, further changing the sample in ways that weaken the conclusions that can be drawn from the study.

To circumvent these problems, some researchers use special procedures called **microgenetic methods.** These procedures attempt to provoke development in the course of a relatively brief time interval as a means of seeing basic mechanisms in action (Kuhn et al., 1995; Siegler & Crowley, 1991; Vygotsky, 1978). Annette Karmiloff-Smith (1992), for example, studied how children develop increasingly abstract methods of recording the correct pathways each time they go through a complex maze. The maze requires them to remember a complex sequence of left and right turns. To help them remember, they are given a pencil and paper to record the route. At first, children draw the entire maze. After they had traversed the maze several times, however, their recordings became more abstract and efficient until they arrived at a coded list of left and right turns.

Another difficulty with longitudinal designs is that the people in the sample may become used to the various testing and interviewing procedures; in other words, they may learn how they are expected to respond. As a consequence, it is difficult to know whether change in a person's responses over time represents normal development or simply the effect of practice in taking the tests.

Finally, longitudinal designs confound (mix together) the influence of age-related changes with other sources of change that relate specifically to the sample group's **cohort**—the population of persons born about the same time, who for that reason may share experiences that differ from those of people born earlier or later. For example, a longitudinal study of children's fears from birth onward that began in London in 1932 would coincide in its first years with the Great Depression. At the age of 9 or 10, many of these children would have been sent away from their parents (one or both of whom might later have been killed in World War II) to the countryside in an effort to keep them safe from Hitler's nightly bombings of the city. If the results of such a study indicated that the children's fears centered on hunger in their first years and that later, around the age of 9, they began to fear that they would lose their parents, it would not be possible to determine whether the observed age trends reflected general laws of development, true at any time and any place, or whether they were the result of growing up in a particular time and place, or both (Magnusson et al., 1991).

Because of these difficulties, some researchers have used a **cohort sequential design,** in which the longitudinal method is replicated with several cohorts, each of which is studied longitudinally. This modification of the longitudinal design allows age-related factors in developmental change to be separated from cohort-related factors.

Cross-sectional designs

The most widely used developmental research design is called the cross-sectional design because groups representing a cross section of ages are studied at a single time. To study the development of memory, for example, one might first test the way samples of 4-year-olds, 10-year-olds, 20-year-olds, and 60-year-olds remember a list of familiar words. By comparing how people in the four age groups go about the task and what the results of their efforts are, one could then form hypotheses about developmental changes in this basic cognitive process. (Figure 1.8 compares longitudinal and cross-sectional research designs.) In fact, a great

Microgenetic methods Experimental procedures that provoke change in the course of a relatively brief time interval.

Cohort A group of persons born about the same time who are therefore likely to share some common experiences.

Cohort sequential design An experimental design in which the longitudinal method is replicated with several cohorts.

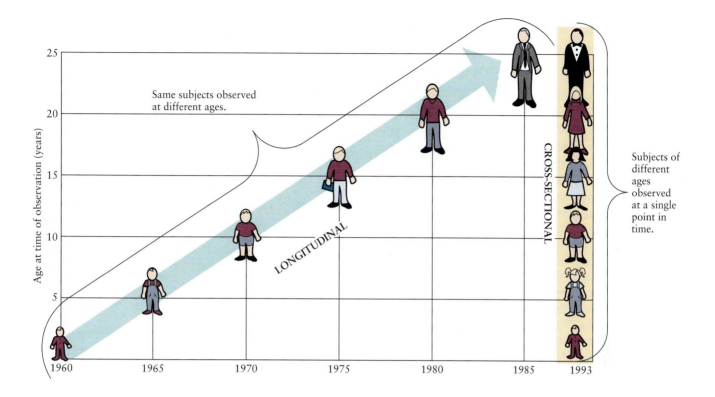

FIGURE 1.8 *A graphic representation of the difference between longitudinal and cross-sectional research designs.*

many cross-sectional studies of memory development have been carried out (Kail, 1990).

The advantages of the cross-sectional design are readily apparent. Because it samples several age levels at one time, this design takes less time and is less expensive than a longitudinal approach to the same question would be, but it can still yield important information. The limited time commitment required of the participants also makes it more likely that a representative sample will be recruited and that few participants will drop out of the study.

Despite these attractive features, cross-sectional designs also have drawbacks. Like longitudinal designs, cross-sectional designs can confound age-related changes and characteristics particular to a specific cohort. Only to the extent that people of different ages are equivalent in all relevant ways except for the factor of age will the study be likely to yield accurate information about development.

Consider the possibilities for the hypothetical study of memory development. Suppose that the study was conducted in 1985. Suppose further that the study showed that the 60-year-olds performed significantly more poorly than the 20-year-olds. These results might reflect a universal tendency for memory to decline with age. But the difference might also be caused by differences in childhood nutrition, which has been shown to affect intellectual development (Super, Herrera, & Mora, 1990); nutrition was generally not so good in 1925, when the 60-year-olds were babies, as it was in 1965, when the 20-year-olds were babies. The 60-year-olds are also likely to have received less education than the 20-year-olds. A college education was much more common in 1985 than it was in the 1930s, and education has been shown to increase performance on memory tests (Cole, 1990). In addition, because memory performance is maintained by the constant practice provided by schooling, it is possible that the 60-year-olds performed less well because they have been out of school a long time.

A second difficulty with cross-sectional designs is that, by sampling the behavior of different-aged people at one time, they inappropriately slice up development, an ongoing process, into a series of disconnected snapshots. While such a design may be used to contrast the general ways in which 4- and 10-year-olds remember a list of words, for example, it cannot take into account the developmental process by which one form of memory changes into another because it doesn't follow the same children over time. Thus when theorists formulate hypotheses about development on the basis of cross-sectional designs, they do a good deal of extrapolation and guesswork about processes of change.

RESEARCH DESIGNS AND DATA-COLLECTION TECHNIQUES IN PERSPECTIVE

Each design and each technique for data collection has its uses, but no single design or technique is likely to serve all purposes (Table 1.2). Longitudinal designs sample behavior of the same individuals over time, but unless they are supplemented by more complex procedures, there is a risk that they will confound age with cohort and that the samples will be biased. Cross-sectional designs are more efficient but may artificially break up the process of development. Self-reports provide unique insight into the process of development from the perspective of the individual, but they are sometimes of questionable validity. Systematically collected naturalistic observations yield essential information about the real-life activities of people, but they are weak when it comes to justifying causal statements about development. Experiments can isolate causal factors in specific settings, but the results obtained may not be generalizable beyond the artificial boundaries of the experimental situation. Clinical interview methods can reveal the dynamics of individual thought and feelings, but they are difficult to generalize beyond the individual case. In the chapters that follow, the advantages and problems of the various research methods will be discussed time and again as they apply to specific aspects of development.

TABLE 1.2 Research Techniques and Designs

	Advantages	Disadvantages
TECHNIQUE		
Self-report	Provides access to unique information	Unreliable and of uncertain validity
Naturalistic observation	Reveals full complexity of behavior and its ecology	Difficult to establish causal relations
Experiment	Best method of testing causal hypotheses	Sometimes impossible for ethical reasons Artificial procedures may distort validity of results
Clinical interview	Focuses on dynamics of individual development	Difficult to generalize beyond unique case or to establish causal relations
DESIGN		
Longitudinal	Traces development as a process occurring over time	Repeat testing may invalidate results Costly and difficult to use Results may be confounded with historical time
Cross-sectional	Takes relatively little time to administer Reveals age trends	Loses sense of continuity in development Findings are vulnerable to confounds with variables other than age

THE ROLE OF THEORY

Contrary to widely held belief, facts do not "speak for themselves." The facts that developmental psychologists collect help us to understand development only when they are brought together and interpreted in terms of a **theory,** a framework of ideas or body of principles that can be used to guide the collection and interpretation of facts. Like heredity and environment, facts and theories go together. Neither comes "first"; they arise and exist together.

When a newborn infant cries, the physical fact of crying is plain enough. But what does it mean? Is crying a reflex response to gastric pain or is it an expression of the newborn's distress at being wrenched from the mother's womb? Is the infant asking for help or just angry? We develop a theory to interpret crying; facts have no meaning outside the context of a theory. A theory provides a framework within which to investigate questions through research and reason.

Albert Einstein described the central role of theory in extending human knowledge of the physical world. Observation of the world may be useful, he said:

> But on principle, it is quite wrong to try founding a theory on observable magnitudes alone. In reality the very opposite occurs. It is the theory which decides what we can observe. (Quoted in Sameroff, 1983, p. 243)

Einstein's point applies to psychologists' attempts to understand the human world just as forcefully as it applies to investigations of the physical world. A deeper understanding of human development will not automatically come from the continuous accumulation of facts. Rather, it will come through new attempts to make sense of the accumulating evidence on development in the light of some theory.

At the present time, no broad theoretical perspective gives unity to the entire body of relevant scientific knowledge on human development. Instead, the field is approached from several theoretical perspectives. When these perspectives are characterized by the position taken on (1) the sources of development (nature and nurture), (2) the dynamics of developmental change (continuity versus discontinuity), and (3) the nature of individual differences, four broad theoretical frameworks emerge. Throughout this book we refer to these four broad frameworks as the biological-maturation, the environmental-learning, the constructivist, and the cultural-context frameworks (see Figure 1.9). In addition, a fifth framework, the **psychodynamic approach,** addresses these issues with clinical techniques designed to cure mental illness. Psychodynamic ideas have a continuing impact on the study of child development, but they have proved difficult to integrate with the discipline. As a matter of convenience, we will present psychodynamic ideas as appropriate within the four basic frameworks depicted in Figure 1.9.

Each of these broad frameworks encompasses many more specific theories that focus on particular aspects of human development, such as the growth of memory in the first months of life, the appearance of a distinctive sense of self at the end of infancy, or the emergence of new forms of play in middle childhood. What follows here is only a brief overview. Then in subsequent chapters we will return to the four broad frameworks and specific theoretical approaches within them to explore what they can tell us about particular aspects of development.

The biological-maturation framework

The crucial claim that unifies the theories of the biological-maturation framework is that the basic sequence of changes that characterize development is **endogenous**; that is, it comes from inside the organism as a consequence of the genes the organism inherits. The major cause of development from this viewpoint is **maturation,** genetically determined patterns of change that occur as individuals age

Modern-day psychologists use physiological measures in addition to measures of behavior in order to better understand the complex factors organizing development. Here a 4-month-old's brain waves are being measured as he watches tumbling balls.

Theory A broad framework or body of principles used to interpret a set of facts.

Endogenous causes Causes of development arising as a consequence of the organism's biological heritage.

Maturation The genetically determined patterns of change that occur as individuals age from conception through adulthood.

FIGURE 1.9 *Four frameworks for interpreting the influence of nature and nurture on individual development. In the first three frameworks, biological and environmental factors directly interact with each other to shape the individual. In the fourth, the cultural-context framework, biological inheritance and universal features of the environment act indirectly through the medium of culture.*

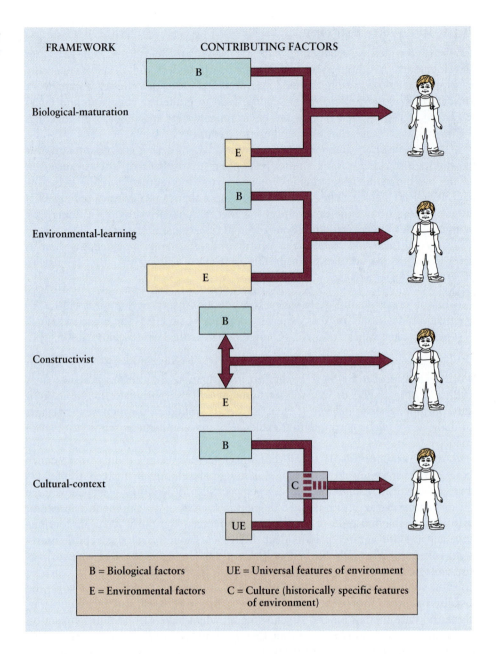

from their immature starting point at conception to full adulthood. Psychologists whose theories fall into the biological-maturation framework are likely to see psychological development as a progression of stagelike changes that accompany (and are caused by) stagelike changes in the biological structure of the organism.

That the environment has a secondary role in shaping the basic course of development according to the biological-maturation view is stated quite forcefully by Arnold Gesell (1880–1961), one of the most influential developmental psychologists of the early twentieth century:

> Environment . . . determines the occasion, the intensity, and the correlation of many aspects of behavior, but it does not engender the basic progressions of behavior development. These are determined by inherent, maturational mechanisms. (1940, p. 13)

As we noted earlier, the ideas of Sigmund Freud (1856–1939) have exerted a tremendous influence on modern ideas about human nature. Among theorists of

Arnold Gesell testing a child in the observation room at the Yale Child Study Center.

development, Freud was the first to emphasize the centrality of emotional life to the formation and function of human personality. Freud's well-known belief that sexual reproduction is the *primary* motive of human behavior places him among the biological-maturation theorists. When he considered the process of individual development, however, Freud, like Gesell, accorded some role to the environment. "The constitutional factor," he wrote, "must await experiences before it can make itself felt" (1905/1953a, p. 239). In other words, the basic human drives are biologically determined, but the social environment directs the way these drives will be satisfied, thereby fundamentally shaping individual personalities.

Biological-maturation theories of human development were out of favor at mid-century, but in recent decades they have enjoyed renewed attention. Again, modern studies of language acquisition are a prominent example, suggesting to some researchers that the environment plays only a triggering role in the realization of linguistic potential; the ability to use language appears to mature at a fixed pace and is inherited by all human beings (Pinker, 1994). In addition, researchers have shown that some aspects of personality and intelligence have a strong genetic basis (Plomin & McClearn, 1993). Several basic intellectual competencies appear to be present in embryonic form at or near birth, so it appears that their origin does not depend on interactions with the postnatal environment (Carey & Gelman, 1991).

The environmental-learning framework

Theories that fall into the environmental-learning perspective do not deny that biological factors provide a basic foundation for development, but they argue that the *major* causes of developmental change are **exogenous;** that is, they come from the environment, particularly from the adults who reward and punish the child's efforts. Thus **learning** is the major mechanism of development, according to the-

Exogenous causes Causes of development arising from the environment.

Learning The process by which an organism's behavior is modified by experience.

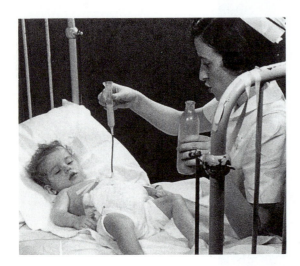

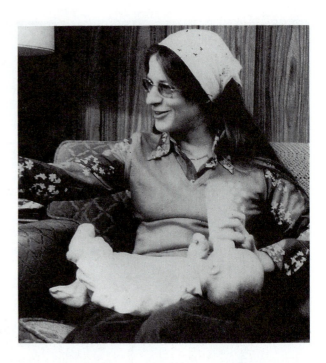

(Left) *Because of a birth defect requiring her to be fed through a tube directly into the stomach, Monica was never fed orally or held in arms while being fed during her first two years.* (Right) *When she was older, she fed her dolls and, later, bottlefed her infant daughters, who had no such defect, in the same position as she had been fed. For Monica, holding and feeding methods dominant in her culture never felt natural. The persistence of her unique behavior reflects the enduring importance of children's earliest learning experiences. (Courtesy G. L. Engel et al., 1985.)*

ories in this framework, where learning is defined as the process by which an organism's behavior is modified by experience. John B. Watson (1878–1958), an early behavior theorist, presented an extreme statement of this position:

> Give me a dozen healthy infants, well-formed, and my own specified world to bring them up in and I'll guarantee to take any one at random and train him to become any type of specialist I might select—doctor, lawyer, artist, merchant-chief, and, yes, even beggar-man and thief, regardless of his talents, penchants, tendencies, abilities, vocations, and race of his ancestors. (1930, p. 104)

Modern environmental-learning theories no longer ignore biological differences among children so completely. They are, however, characterized by the belief that the environment, acting through learning mechanisms, is overwhelmingly important in the shaping of development (Gewirtz & Pelaez-Nogueras, 1992). In support of such theories there is ample evidence that enriching the experience of children who have lived in isolation or who have been brought up in orphanages with little intellectual stimulation dramatically improves their later social and cognitive development (Clarke & Clarke, 1986); that certain styles of parenting appear to promote children's competence (Steinberg et al., 1994); and that television can influence aggressive behavior (Bandura, 1986).

Their focus on the environment as the primary influence on development leads many environmental-learning theorists to emphasize the gradual and continuous nature of developmental change. This intuition is captured nicely by B. F. Skinner's metaphorical description of how the environment gives rise to new forms:

> Operant conditioning [learning through rewards and punishments] shapes behavior as a sculptor shapes a lump of clay. Although at some point the sculptor seems to have produced an entirely novel object, we can always follow the process back to the original undifferentiated lump, and we can make the successive stages by which we return to this condition as small as we wish. At no point does anything emerge which is very different from what preceded it.

The final product seems to have a special unity or integrity of design, but we cannot find a point at which this suddenly appears. (Skinner, 1953, p. 91)

The constructivist framework

Psychologists whose theories fall into the constructivist view maintain that nature and nurture are equally necessary for development and find it inappropriate to attribute more importance to one factor or the other. A leading adherent of this view was the Swiss developmental psychologist Jean Piaget (1896–1980), who began his scientific career as a biologist. Piaget was very much concerned with biological development, much like a biological-maturation theorist. "Mental growth is inseparable from physical growth," he argued; "maturation of the nervous and endocrine systems, in particular, continues until the age of sixteen" (Piaget & Inhelder, 1969, p. vii). At the same time, Piaget, like supporters of the environmental-learning framework, believed that the environment's role in development goes well beyond triggering the child's innate potential:

> The human being is immersed right from birth in a social environment which affects him just as much as his physical environment. Society, even more, in a sense, than the physical environment, changes the very structure of the individual. . . . Every relation between individuals (from two onwards) literally modifies them. . . . (Piaget, 1973, p. 156)

Constructivist theories attribute to children a greater role in shaping their own development than do theories in either the environmental-learning or biological-maturation framework. "Knowledge is not a copy of reality," Piaget once wrote (1964, p. 8); the knowledge we acquire, in other words, results from the way we modify and transform the world. In the views of Piaget and other constructivists, by actively striving to master their environments, children *construct* higher levels of knowledge from elements contributed by *both* maturation and environmental circumstances.

Piaget and his followers also maintain that the environment does not influence children in the same way at all ages. Instead, the influences of the environment depend on the child's current stage of development. Development can be speeded up or slowed down by variations in the environment. However, all children go through the same basic sequence of changes. In this important sense, the processes of developmental change are the same in all human groups: they are universal in the species.

Contemporary psychologists who follow in the tradition established by Piaget have refined or amended a number of his ideas. Some have modified or elaborated on his explanations for why individual children at a given stage of development do not perform all intellectual tasks in a manner consistent with that level of development (contrary to the notion of stagelike change, according to which a child's level of competence is expected to remain consistent in all situations) (Fischer et al., 1993). Others have attempted to supplement his theory by including biological contributions to cognitive change (Case, 1991; Diamond, 1991). Still others have sought to specify the role of social interaction in the process of knowledge construction (Perret-Clermont, Perret, & Bell, 1991). All of the neo-Piagetians are, however, influenced by Piaget's idea that biology and the environment play reciprocal roles in developmental change.

Jean Piaget, whose work has had a profound influence on developmental psychology, observing children at play.

The cultural-context framework

Psychologists whose work falls within the three theoretical frameworks described thus far assume that development arises from the interaction of factors from two sources, biological heritage and the environment children experience. The frameworks diverge in the relative weight given to each of these two sources of influence on development and also in portraying how they interact to produce development.

Psychologists who work within the cultural-context framework also concur that biological and experiential factors influence each other in development. Like the constructivists, they believe that children construct their own development through their active engagement with the world. But they differ from the other theorists in insisting that the way biological or environmental factors influence children depends on the way they combine in a specific cultural-historical context. Pointing out that activities and patterns of living are shaped by the experiences of earlier generations passed down through culture, cultural-context theories include a third source of influences on development: the history of the child's social group, crystallized in the present in the form of its culture (Baltes, 1987; Bronfenbrenner, 1993; Bruner, 1990; Lerner, 1991; Rogoff, 1990; Valsiner, 1989; Vygotsky, 1978).

The term "culture" as it is used in discussions of development should not be confused with the "culture" popularly attributed to people who have acquired refined manners or an interest in the arts. As we suggested earlier, *culture* consists of

Cultural-context approaches pay special attention to variations in children's development arising from differences in the human-made parts of the environment.

human designs for living that are based on the accumulated knowledge of a people, encoded in their language, and embodied in the physical artifacts, beliefs, values, customs, and activities that have been passed down from one generation to the next.

The way culture influences development can be seen in children's development of mathematical understanding. The kinds of mathematical thinking children develop do not depend only on their ability to deal with abstractions and on adults' efforts to teach them mathematical concepts. They also depend on the adults' own knowledge of mathematics, which depends on their cultural heritage. A child growing up among the Oksapmin of New Guinea appears to have the same universal ability to grasp basic number concepts as a child growing up in Paris or Pittsburgh but learns a very different system of counting—counting by body parts. This system would be unwieldy for children who must solve arithmetic problems in school and later on in the money economy of Western culture; but it is no problem at all for a person dealing with the tasks of everyday life in traditional Oksapmin culture (Saxe, 1994). Culture also acts through the contexts within which mathematical knowledge is used. Brazilian market children, who do not attend school, develop remarkable mathematical skills in the course of everyday buying and selling. But these children have difficulties with the same problems when they are presented to them in a schoollike format (Nuñes, Schliemann,

Lev Vygotsky, a prominent theorist of the role of culture in development, and his daughter.

& Carraher, 1993). In each of these cases, culture has contributed to the course of development by arranging the conditions under which biological and environmental factors interact.

The cultural-context and constructivist points of view are similar in several respects. Both hold that the developing individual passes through distinctive stagelike changes in the course of development, and both emphasize that development is impossible without the individual's active striving. They differ, however, in three important respects. First, the cultural-context framework assumes that *both* children and their caretakers are active agents in the process of development. Development is, in this sense, "co-constructed." Second, this framework anticipates wide variability in a given individual's performance as the person moves from one kind of activity to another. Third, the cultural-context framework is more open to the idea that the sequence of developmental changes a child experiences and even the existence or nonexistence of a particular stage of development may depend on the child's cultural-historical circumstances.

Erik Erikson (1902–1994), a student of Freud, was a psychodynamic theorist who drew on evidence from many cultures. Erikson (1963) emphasized that the prior experiences of the society into which children are born, embodied in their current culture, play a major role in development. In these respects his point of view is similar to that of the cultural-context theorists.

Although adherents of competing approaches have been attempting to explain development all during the twentieth century, the central issues of developmental psychology remain unresolved. Nor is there agreement on a single "correct" framework or theory that should be used in efforts to resolve them. The modern discipline of developmental psychology can usefully be thought of as a social mechanism for organizing. It allows scholars with conflicting views to compare notes and learn from one another's work despite differing theories about specific phenomena. The resulting discussions about theories and methods encompass every aspect of the field—how observations are to be made, what methods best relate facts to theories, and how facts and theories translate into the ways we raise our children.

This Book and the Field of Developmental Psychology

The lack of a comprehensive and widely accepted developmental theory creates difficulties for anyone who seeks an integrated picture of the whole child in the dynamic processes of growth and change. Basic facts are interpreted differently within the various theoretical frameworks. In the face of these difficulties, this book adopts an integrative framework that provides a structured forum in which to evaluate different theorists' claims in a systematic way.

Our exploration of the field centers on the fundamental agreement that unites developmental psychologists: development is a process that emerges over time; it is *directional* in the sense that time is directional, moving irreversibly from past to future. To highlight the importance of this basic principle, we have organized this text chronologically, following development from conception onward.

In any chronological account of development, two major issues must be resolved. The first is how to segment the flow of time and how much significance to attribute to the various periods that are singled out. The second issue is the problem of keeping track of all the many aspects of development systematically, depicting how they combine and recombine to constitute a whole, living person.

The issue of how to divide the sequence of development into periods is easily settled because adherents of all major theoretical approaches refer to the same seven periods from conception to old age, although they may focus on only a few of them: the prenatal period (the months between conception and birth), infancy, early childhood, middle childhood, adolescence, adulthood, and old age.

Beyond this division of development into at least seven periods, consensus among psychologists breaks down. Some theorists believe that these divisions are little more than verbal conventions, whereas others (the so-called stage theorists) believe that they represent developmental stages that are both real and of essential importance for understanding the process of developmental change. Stage theorists themselves disagree as to whether significant subperiods should be distinguished. (Table 1.3 indicates how four well-known theorists treat the conventional periods of development.)

Anthropological and historical studies suggest that the seven developmental periods themselves may not be characteristic of children in all cultures and all historical eras. Many societies recognize no periods that correspond to early childhood and adolescence (Ariès, 1962; Whiting, Burbank, & Ratner, 1986). Modern industrial societies even provide evidence to support the subdivision of almost any of the seven conventional stages into smaller periods. Middle childhood, for example, might usefully be thought of as having early, middle, and late substages; adolescence could be divided into early and late substages; and youth could be seen as an early substage of adulthood.

In this book we follow psychological convention and divide the time between conception and the start of adulthood into five broad periods: the prenatal period, infancy, early childhood, middle childhood, and adolescence. Each is accorded a major section of the text. Within this chronological framework, our aim is to make clear how the fundamental biological, social, behavioral, and cultural aspects of development are woven together in the process of change from one period to the next. The text subdivides infancy, a period when change is particularly rapid, into three subperiods marked by important transition points where distinctively new and significant forms of behavior emerge. Robert Emde and his colleagues (Emde, Gaensbauer, & Harmon, 1976) refer to these transitions as bio-behavioral shifts because the resulting reorganization in the child's functioning emerges from the interaction of biological and behavioral factors. Modifying these researchers' ideas slightly, we refer to such transitions as **bio-social-behavioral shifts.** We add the social dimension because, as Emde and his colleagues themselves note, every bio-behavioral shift involves a change in the relationship between children and their social worlds. Not only do children experience the social environment in new ways as a result of the changes in their behavior and biological makeup; they also are treated differently by other people.

Bio-social-behavioral shift Transition points in development during which a convergence of biological, social, and behavioral changes gives rise to distinctively new forms of behavior.

TABLE 1.3 Stages of Development According to Four Theorists

Conventional	Piaget	Freud	Erikson	Vygotsky
Infancy (birth–2½ years)	Sensorimotor	Oral Anal	Trust vs. mistrust Autonomy vs. shame	Affiliation
Early childhood (2½–6 years)	Preoperations	Phallic	Initiative vs. guilt	Play
Middle childhood (6–12 years)	Concrete operations	Latency	Industry vs. inferiority	Learning
Adolescence (12–19 years)	Formal operations	Genital	Identity vs. role confusion Intimacy vs. isolation	Peer activity
Adulthood (19–65 years)			Generativity vs. stagnation	Work
Old age (65 years–death)			Ego integrity vs. despair	Theorizing

TABLE 1.4 Prominent Bio-Social-Behavioral Shifts in Development

Shift point	New developmental period
Conception: genetic material of parents combines to form unique individual	Prenatal period: formation of basic organs
Birth: transition to life outside the womb	Early infancy: becoming coordinated with the environment
2½ months: cortical-subcortical brain connections form; social smiling; new quality of maternal feeling	Middle infancy: increased memory and sensorimotor abilities
7–9 months: wariness of novelty; fear of strangers; attachment	Late infancy: symbolic thought; distinct sense of self
End of infancy (24–30 months): grammatical language	Early childhood (2½–6 years): strikingly uneven levels of performance; sex-role identity; sociodramatic play
5–7 years: assigned responsibility for tasks outside of adult supervision; deliberate instruction	Middle childhood: peer-group activity; rule-based games; systematic instruction
11–12 years: sexual maturation	Adolescence: sex-oriented social activity; identity integration; formal reasoning
19–21 years: shift toward primary responsibility for self and raising of next generation	Adulthood (19+)

In addition, we consider the cultural context of children's development to be an essential factor in the bio-social-behavioral shifts and the organization of human behavior as a whole at any age. From the earliest hours of life, cultural conceptions of what children are and what the future holds for them influence the way parents shape their children's experience. For example, parents who believe that girls are destined to be economically and socially dependent on their husbands are likely to treat their newborn daughters very differently from those whose fondest wish is for their daughter to become an airplane pilot or tennis champion. And as we mentioned earlier, in some cases the timing, the essential character, and even the existence of a developmental period may be strongly influenced by cultural factors (Berry et al., 1992; Whiting, Burbank, & Ratner, 1986).

Our adoption of a bio-social-behavioral framework for the study of development does not imply a commitment to a strict stage theory; rather, it provides a systematic way to keep in mind the intricate play of forces that combine to produce development. One must approach the notion of stages with caution because stagelike shifts in the functioning of the organism are rarely all-or-nothing phenomena. The state children are in at any given moment may determine whether they display the characteristics of a new stage or those of an earlier one (Fischer et al., 1993).

Table 1.4 outlines the bio-social-behavioral shifts that appear to be prominent in the development of the child from conception to adulthood. Not all of the shift points have been equally well established. Nevertheless, they provide a fruitful means of organizing discussions of development because they require us to consider both the sources of change and the evidence concerning developmental continuity and discontinuity in a systematic way.

Throughout the chapters that follow, the large questions of development that captivated Itard and his contemporaries are constantly recurring themes: What makes us human? Can our natures be remolded by experience, or must we be content with the characteristics inscribed in our genes at conception? Can we use our knowledge of development to help us plan our futures and guide the growth of our children? These questions are not likely to be satisfactorily answered until and unless a unified theory of development emerges. Because the issues are so complex and our knowledge is still so limited, we have tried to design each chapter to set forth basic facts, methods, and theories in a manner that will help the reader to think usefully about the fundamental questions of the field.

SUMMARY

A Child of Nature?

- The unusual case of the Wild Boy of Aveyron posed fundamental questions about human nature:
  1. What distinguishes humans from other animals?
  2. What would we be like if we grew up isolated from society?
  3. To what degree are we the product of our upbringing and experience and to what degree is our character the product of inborn traits?

The Legacy of Itard

- Both Itard's faith in the promise of scientific methods to resolve enduring questions about human nature and many of his specific techniques served as models for the scientific study of human development.
- The early history of developmental psychology is closely linked to social changes wrought by the Industrial Revolution, which fundamentally changed the nature of family life, education, and work.
- Darwin's thesis that human beings evolved from previously existing species inspired scientists to study children for evidence of evolution.
- Developmental psychology is a scientific discipline that studies the origins of human behavior and the laws of psychological change over the course of a lifetime.

The Central Questions of Developmental Psychology

- Many scientific and social questions about development revolve around three fundamental concerns:
  1. Is the process of development gradual and continuous, or is it marked by abrupt, stagelike discontinuities?
  2. How do nature and nurture interact to produce development?
  3. How do people come to have stable characteristics that differentiate them from one another?
- Questions about continuity branch into more specific questions:
  1. How alike and how different are we from our near neighbors in the animal kingdom?
  2. Are there qualitatively distinct stages of development?
  3. Are there critical periods in development?

- Questions about sources of development have given rise to competing views about the contributions of biology (nature) and the environment (nurture) to the process of development.
- The issue of individual differences focuses on two questions:
  1. What makes individuals different from one another?
  2. To what extent are individual characteristics stable over time?

The Discipline of Developmental Psychology

- Developmental psychologists use several data-collection techniques in their efforts to connect abstract theories to the concrete realities of people's everyday experience. These techniques are designed to ensure that the data used to explain development are objective, reliable, valid, and replicable.
- Prominent among the techniques of data collection used by developmental psychologists are a) self-reports, b) naturalistic observation, c) experimentation, and d) clinical interview methods.
- Research designs that include systematic comparisons among children of different ages enable researchers to establish relationships among developmental phenomena. Two basic research designs are:
  1. Longitudinal designs—the same children are studied repeatedly over a period of time.
  2. Cross-sectional designs—different children of different ages are studied at a single time.
- No one method or research design can supply the answers to all the questions that developmental psychologists seek to resolve. The choice of research design depends on the specific issue being addressed.
- Theory plays an important role in developmental psychology by providing a broad conceptual framework within which methods and research designs are organized and facts can be interpreted.
- Four major theoretical frameworks organize a large proportion of research in children's development.
  1. According to the biological-maturation framework, the sources of development are primarily endogenous, arising from the organism's biological heritage.
  2. According to the environmental-learning framework, developmental change is caused primarily by exogenous factors arising in the environment.
  3. According to the constructivist framework, development arises from the active adaptation of the organism to the environment. The roles of environmental and biological factors are of equal magnitude.
  4. The cultural-context framework accords importance to both biological and environmental factors in development. In addition, it emphasizes that the interactions out of which development emerges are crucially shaped by the history of the group as embodied in its culture.

This Book and the Field of Developmental Psychology

- The concept of the bio-social-behavioral shift highlights the ways in which biological, social, and behavioral factors interact in a cultural context to produce developmental change. Keeping these factors in mind helps us to maintain a picture of the whole developing child.

KEY TERMS

baby biography, p. 19

bio-social-behavioral shift, p. 41

clinical method, p. 26

cohort, p. 30

cohort sequential design, p. 30

control group, p. 24

correlation, p. 22

critical period, p. 12

cross-sectional design, p. 29

culture, p. 9

development, p. 7

developmental niche, p. 19

ecology, p. 19

endogenous, p. 33

ethology, p. 19

exogenous, p. 35

experiment, p. 24

experimental group, p. 24

hypothesis, p. 24

learning, p. 35

longitudinal design, p. 29

maturation, p. 33

microgenetic method, p. 30

naturalistic observation, p. 19

nature, p. 13

nurture, p. 13

objectivity, p. 17

ontogeny, p. 10

phylogeny, p. 8

reliability, p. 17

replicability, p. 17

representative sample, p. 17

self-report, p. 18

stage, p. 10

theory, p. 33

validity, p. 17

THOUGHT QUESTIONS

1. Using arguments from the four theoretical perspectives described in this chapter, give four possible explanations for the appearance and behavior of the Wild Boy of Aveyron.

2. On the basis of your own experience, give an example of how the scientific study of child development has affected the way the current generation of children in your neighborhood are being raised.

3. What is one question you have about the development of children? How do you think scientists might go about finding the answer?

4. List three ways in which the person you were at the age of 5 differed from the person you were at the age of 15. Label those differences as either qualitative or quantitative.

5. List two major ways in which you are like your best friend and two major ways in which the two of you are different. What causal factors do you think are primarily responsible for each of these similarities and differences?

PART ONE

IN THE BEGINNING

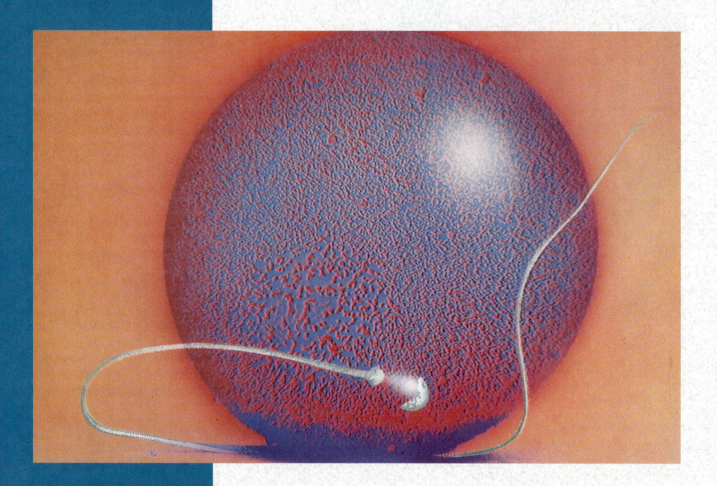

The development of every human being starts with the formation of a single cell at the time of conception. However, each individual human life is but a tiny drop in the vast stream of life that reaches back through thousands of generations and unimaginable millennia of evolutionary time. As such, it is a product of the evolutionary past of our species. Moreover, the environment each baby will experience is a product of the earth's history and the development of culture and society.

Science views the life process as a constant interplay of forces that create order and pattern, on the one hand, and forces that create variation and disorder, on the other. In the modern scientific view, the interaction of these competing forces is the engine of developmental change.

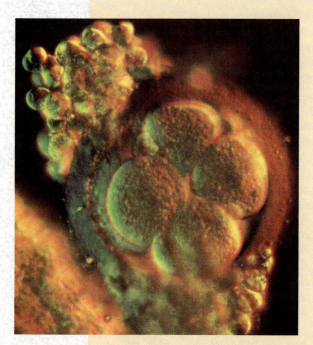

What are the forces that create order and diversity in human development? In Chapter 2 we will see that the beginning of an explanation can be found in our biological inheritance. Order, the ways in which all human beings are alike, initially arises from the finiteness of our species' pool of genetic possibilities. Variation initially arises through sexual reproduction, which in virtually every instance ensures that each individual will inherit a unique combination of genes from the common pool.

Chapter 2 describes the basic mechanisms of genetic transmission, the processes of gene–environment interaction, and some of the diseases that result from genetic abnormalities. It also discusses the contribution to our development of cultural evolution, a distinctly human mode of inheritance.

Chapter 3, which discusses prenatal development and birth, traces the changes that transform the single cell created at conception into a newborn infant with millions of cells of many kinds.

The process of prenatal development illustrates many principles that will recur in later chapters. For example, the changes in form and activity that distinguish the organism at 5 days from the organism at 5 weeks or 5 months after conception are excellent examples of *qualitative* changes, changes that distinguish one stage of development from another, as opposed to *quantitative* changes, which for the most part are merely increases in size. We will also see some important examples of *critical periods* of development, in particular the great sensitivity of the embryo at certain times to hormonal secretions, which trigger the development of new body organs, and to such external agents as drugs that act to disturb organ development.

After 9 months of growth and nurturing within the mother's body, chemical changes initiate the birth process. Birth constitutes the first major bio-social-behavioral shift in development. The baby is no longer able to obtain life-giving oxygen and nutrients automatically from the mother's body. Instead, biological capacities that developed during the prenatal period must now be used to breathe and eat. The behavioral changes that occur at birth are no less remarkable as babies begin to pay attention to the sights and sounds around them, and to provide some sights and sounds of their own! Without the support of parents who structure their baby's interactions with the environment according to culturally prescribed patterns, however, the baby would not survive. Parents must feed, clothe, and protect their offspring for many years before they are able to take care of themselves.

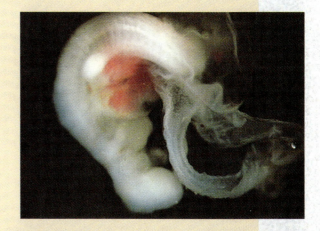

Thus begins the lifelong process in which the biological forces that created the new organism at conception interact with the forces of the culturally organized environment that greets the child at birth. Barring unforeseen calamities, in about 20 years the process will begin again with a new generation.

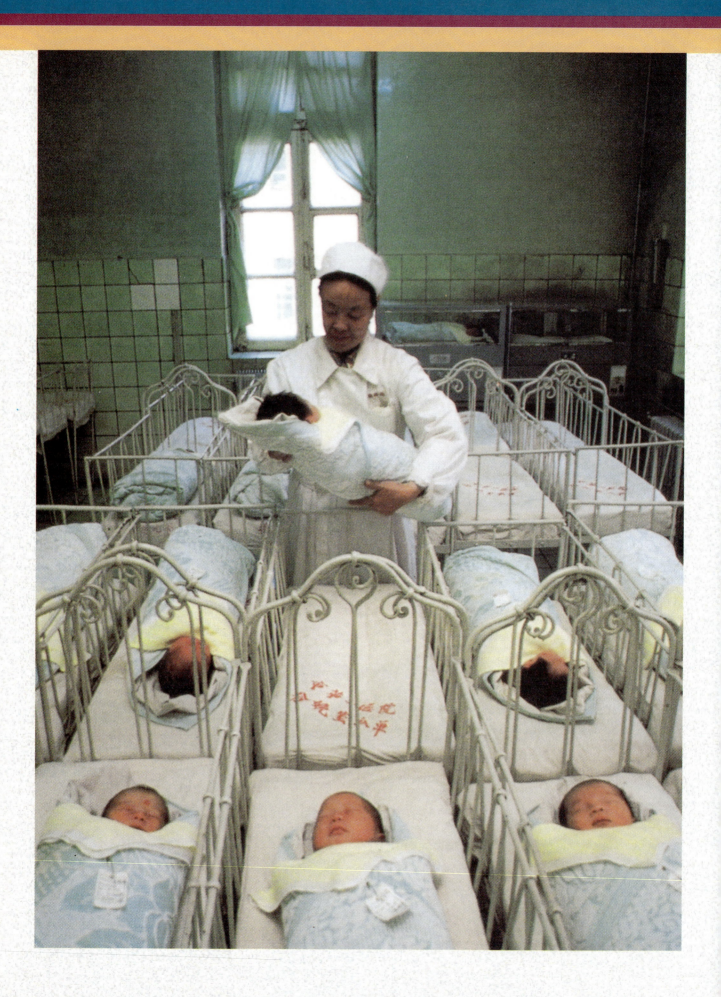

The Human Heritage: Genes and Environment

> **"** Every child conceived by a given couple is the result of a genetic lottery. He is merely one out of a large crowd of possible children, any one of whom might have been conceived on the same occasion if another of the millions of sperm cells emitted by the father had happened to fertilize the egg cell of the mother—an egg cell which is itself one among many. . . . If we go to all the trouble it takes to mix our genes with those of somebody else, it is in order to make sure that our child will be different from ourselves and from all our other children.**"**
>
> —*François Jacob*, The Possible and the Actual

A maternity-ward nursery provides an interesting setting for thinking about the origins and development of human beings. In some racially homogeneous communities, the babies may look so much alike that it is difficult for an observer to tell one from another. In other communities, some babies may be easily distinguished by their skin color. But beyond this, babies' features at birth give few clues about how each child will look later. Nevertheless, when these infants are mature adults, 30 years from now, the differences among them will have increased so much that it will be quite easy to tell them apart. Some will be men and some will be women; some will be tall, some short; some will have curly hair, some no hair at all. They may speak different languages, engage in different types of work, and enjoy different kinds of food. Some will be morose most of the time, whereas others will usually be cheerful; some will be impulsive, others reflective; some will be gifted at mathematics, others at growing rice or selling stocks. Despite this great variation, none will be mistaken for a member of any other species; all will clearly belong to *Homo sapiens*. Such observations raise a fundamental question about the sources of developmental change: What causes us to be so different from each other but at the same time more like each other than like members of any other species?

Both the similarities and the differences between people come ultimately from the interaction between environmental and genetic influences. The similarities that mark us as members of a single species arise, on the one hand, because we inherit from other human beings our **genes,** the molecular blueprints for our individual development. On the other hand, human beings are similar to one another because we have evolved in the common environment of the planet Earth. The differences among us come from the same two sources. The process of sexual reproduction ensures that the particular combination of genes each of us inherits is, with rare exceptions, unique. The environment further influences variations among people by determining which of their many characteristics will be called upon to deal with the specific conditions in which they live. For example, children born into families living deep in the forests of the Amazon basin, where people still live by hunting and gathering, must develop physical endurance and become close observers of nature. Conversely, children born into families living in a North American suburb must develop the ability to sit still for long hours in school and acquire the knowledge and skills they will need for economic success as adults. While historical and cultural circumstances promote general capacities in these ways, each individual also develops in a more immediate environment. Within a particular family, each child occupies a unique position; thus each child has a unique set of experiences that further shape the characteristics he or she develops (Dunn & McGuire, 1994).

We begin this chapter by discussing sexual reproduction, the mechanism for what François Jacob calls the "genetic lottery," and the basic laws of genetic inheritance to which that "lottery" is subject. Next we will discuss the lifelong process of interaction between genes and environment. The crucial importance of an individual's genetic constitution and the principles of gene–environment interaction will then be illustrated through a discussion of genetic abnormalities. Lastly, we will take a look at the way biology and culture interact in the process of human development.

Genes The segments on a DNA molecule that act as hereditary blueprints for the organism's development.

Chromosome A threadlike structure made up of genes; in humans there are 46 chromosomes in the nucleus of each cell.

Zygote The single cell formed at conception by the union of the 23 chromosomes of the sperm and the 23 chromosomes of the ovum.

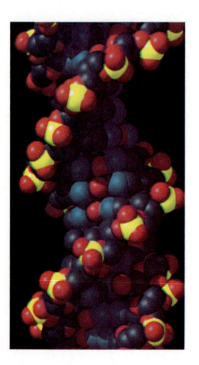

(Left) A computer rendering of deoxyribonucleic acid (DNA). Each chromosome is a single DNA molecule consisting of two strands twisted about each other and connected by cross steps to form a laddered spiral called a double helix. A gene is a segment on a strand of the DNA. When a parent DNA molecule replicates to form two identical daughter molecules, the two strands of the double helix separate. Each serves as a template for the synthesis of a complementary strand.

Sexual Reproduction and Genetic Transmission

At his climax during sexual intercourse, a man ejaculates about 350 million sperm into a woman's vagina. For the next several hours, the tiny tadpole-shaped sperm swim through the viscous fluid of the woman's uterus and fallopian tubes. The head of each sperm contains 23 **chromosomes**—threadlike structures consisting of approximately 20,000 genes each. These 23 chromosomes provide half of the genetic information necessary for the development of a new individual. The other half is provided by the woman's ovum (egg), which has developed from one of the 200,000 primary oocytes in her ovaries. If one of the man's sperm penetrates the woman's ovum, conception occurs, and the cell walls of the ovum and sperm fuse to form a **zygote,** a single cell containing 23 chromosomes from the father and 23 chromosomes from the mother. From this single cell with its 23 pairs of chromosomes will ultimately come all the cells that the child will have at birth.

MITOSIS: A PROCESS OF CELL REPLICATION

The zygote creates new cells through **mitosis,** the process of cell duplication and division that generates all the individual's cells except sperm and ova. Mitosis begins within a few hours of conception. The 46 chromosomes move to the middle of the zygote, where they produce exact copies of themselves—a process known as replication (see Figure 2.1). These chromosomes separate into two identical sets, which migrate to opposite sides of the cell. The cell then divides in the middle to form two daughter cells, each of which contains 23 pairs of chromosomes (46 chromosomes in all) identical to those inherited at conception. These two daughter cells go through the same process to create two new cells each, which themselves divide as the process repeats itself again and again. Mitosis is directed by the chromosomes themselves, complex molecules of deoxyribonucleic acid (DNA) on which the genes are located.

Mitosis continues throughout the life of an individual, creating new **somatic** (body) **cells** and replacing old ones. Each new somatic cell contains copies of the original 46 chromosomes inherited at conception. The genetic material carried by our chromosomes is not altered by the passage of time or by the experiences that shape our minds and bodies under the ordinary conditions of life, but is faithfully copied as mitosis takes place throughout the course of a lifetime. (There is increasing evidence, however, that direct exposure to radiation and to certain chemicals may alter genes. As we will see later in this chapter, the consequences of such changes can be disastrous.)

MEIOSIS: A SOURCE OF VARIABILITY

Recall that mitosis is responsible for the replication of somatic (body) cells, but not for **germ cells**—the sperm and ova. If mitosis governed the production of sperm and ova so that those cells each had 46 chromosomes, as the somatic cells do, at conception each zygote would receive a full set of 46 chromosomes from

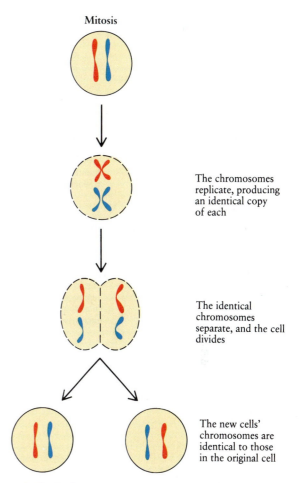

Mitosis

The chromosomes replicate, producing an identical copy of each

The identical chromosomes separate, and the cell divides

The new cells' chromosomes are identical to those in the original cell

FIGURE 2.1 *Mitosis is the process of cell division that generates all the cells of the body except the germ cells. During mitosis each chromosome replicates, producing another chromosome that is identical to the first. These chromosomes then separate in such a way that one is contributed to each new cell. Mitosis ensures that identical genetic information is maintained in the body cells over the life of the organism.*

Mitosis The process of cell duplication and division that generates all of an individual's cells except sperm and ova.

Somatic cells All the cells in the body except for the germ cells (ova and sperm).

Germ cells Sperm and ova; the cells specialized for sexual reproduction that have half the number of chromosomes normal for a species (23 in humans).

(a) Meiosis in the Male

(b) Meiosis in the Female

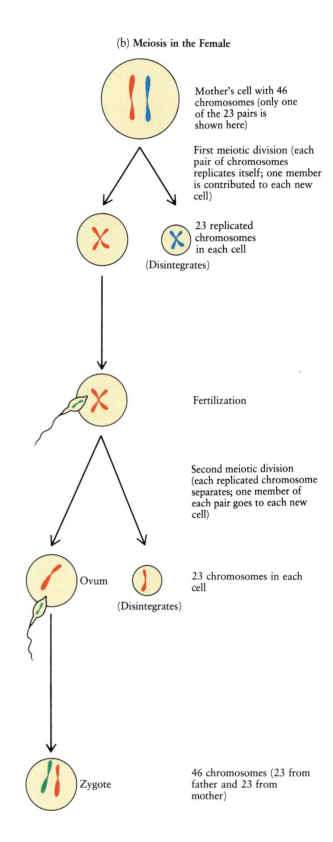

Father's cell with 46 chromosomes (only one of the 23 pairs is shown here)

First meiotic division (each pair of chromosomes replicates itself: one member is contributed to each new cell)

23 replicated chromosomes in each cell

Second meiotic division (each replicated chromosome separates; one member of each pair goes to each new cell)

23 chromosomes in each sperm

Mother's cell with 46 chromosomes (only one of the 23 pairs is shown here)

First meiotic division (each pair of chromosomes replicates itself; one member is contributed to each new cell)

23 replicated chromosomes in each cell

(Disintegrates)

Fertilization

Second meiotic division (each replicated chromosome separates; one member of each pair goes to each new cell)

Ovum

23 chromosomes in each cell

(Disintegrates)

Zygote

46 chromosomes (23 from father and 23 from mother)

FIGURE 2.2 (a) *Formation of sperm. As meiosis in the male begins, the chromosome pairs replicate, and one member of each pair is contributed to each new cell. Each new cell then divides and the replicated chromosomes separate. The result is four sperm cells, each of which contains one member (or a copy) of each of the original pairs of chromosomes.*
(b) *Formation of the ovum. Meiosis in the female differs slightly from meiosis in the male. When the first division occurs, the cytoplasm, the matter comprising most of the material of the cell, divides in such a way that the two resulting cells are unequal in size. The smaller of the two cells disintegrates. The large cell, the ovum, does not divide again unless it is fertilized. If fertilization occurs, the replicated chromosomes in the ovum separate into two new cells. Again the cytoplasm divides unequally, and the smaller of the resulting cells disintegrates. The 23 chromosomes of the larger cell fuse with the 23 chromosomes of the sperm to form the zygote with its 46 chromosomes.*

each parent for a total of 92, and in each succeeding generation the total number of chromosomes inherited by the offspring would double. Such doubling clearly does not occur. Except in abnormal cases, the number of chromosomes inherited by all members of the human species remains constant at 46.

The zygote contains only 46 chromosomes because the germ cells that are specialized for sexual reproduction contain only one set of 23 chromosomes, not two sets. Thus the zygote that is formed when sperm and ovum unite has just 46 chromosomes. Germ cells are formed not by mitosis but by a different cell-division process called **meiosis**. In the first phase of this process, the 23 pairs of chromosomes in the germproducing cells produce copies of themselves, just as in mitosis. But then the cell divides not once, as in mitosis, but twice, creating four daughter cells. Each of these daughter cells contains only 23 unpaired chromosomes—half of the parent cell's original set. Meiosis occurs somewhat differently in males and females, as Figure 2.2 explains.

Because the mother's ovum and the father's sperm contain only 23 chromosomes each, the zygote receives its full complement of 46 chromosomes (23 pairs) when the two germ cells unite at conception. Because half of the zygote's chromosomes come from each parent, each individual conceived is genetically different from both the father and the mother. This biological strategy creates genetic diversity across generations. Genetic diversity is further increased by **crossing over,** a process in which genetic material is exchanged between a pair of chromosomes during the first phase of meiosis. While the pair of chromosomes, each containing genes for the same characteristics, lie side by side, a section of one of the chromosomes may change places with the corresponding section of the other chromosome (see Figure 2.3). This exchange alters the genetic composition of each of the two chromosomes; genes originally carried on one chromosome are now carried on the other.

We can now better appreciate the extreme improbability that genes of any two children, even siblings, will be exactly alike, except in the special case of identical twins (see Box 2.1). Although we receive 23 chromosomes from each of our parents, it is a matter of chance which member of any pair of chromosomes ends up in a given germ cell during meiosis. According to the laws of probability, there are 2^{23}, or about 8 million, possible genetic combinations whenever a sperm and ovum unite. It is estimated that when the additional possibilities from crossing over are added, there is only 1 chance in 64 trillion that a particular genetic combination will be repeated (Scheinfeld, 1972).

Meiosis The reduction and division process that produces sperm and ova, each of which contains only half of the parent cell's original complement of 46 chromosomes.

Crossing over The process in which genetic material is exchanged between chromosomes containing genes for the same characteristic.

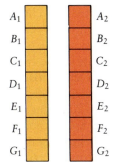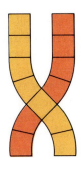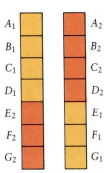

STEP 1
Each chromosome pair aligns before segregation into separate germ cells (letters designate different genes)

STEP 2
The chromosomes cross

STEP 3
Chromosomes break at the point of crossing, exchange genetic material, and segregate into separate germ cells

FIGURE 2.3 *The crossing-over process. (From Shaffer, 1985.)*

BOX 2.1

Twinning

During the first few mitotic divisions after the zygote is formed, the daughter cells occasionally separate completely and develop into separate individuals. When such a division results in two individuals, they are called **monozygotic twins,** because they are twins that have come from one zygote. Having come from the same fertilized egg, "identical twins" inherit identical genetic information. Thus they potentially have the same physical and psychological makeup, susceptibility to disease, and life expectancy. Monozygotic twins oc-

cur about once in every 250 conceptions. It is not understood what leads cells to separate after the first few mitotic divisions; neither the parents' race or heredity, the mother's age, nor the number of children she has had previously seems to be a factor.

Many twins originate not from a single fertilized ovum but rather from the fertilization by two sperm of two eggs that are released at the same time. The two fertilized eggs develop into **dizygotic** twins—twins that come from two zygotes. Though they shared the

Monozygotic twins not only look alike naturally, they are often dressed alike and treated similarly by others, so that their similarity is accentuated.

Monozygotic twins Twins that come from the same zygote and therefore have identical genotypes.

Dizygotic twins Twins that result from the fertilization by two sperm of two eggs that are released at the same time.

X and Y chromosomes The two chromosomes that determine the sex of the individual. Normal females have two X chromosomes, while normal males have one Y chromosome inherited from their fathers and one X inherited from their mothers.

SEXUAL DETERMINATION: A CASE OF VARIABILITY

In 22 of the 23 pairs of chromosomes found in a human cell, the two chromosomes are similar in type; chromosomes of the twenty-third pair, however, may differ. This pair of chromosomes determines a person's genetic sex, a crucial source of variety in our species. In normal females, both members of the twenty-third pair of chromosomes are of the *same type* and are called **X chromosomes.** The normal male, however, has just one X chromosome paired with a different, much smaller chromosome called a **Y chromosome** (see Figure 2.4). Since a female is always XX, each of her eggs contains an X chromosome. Sperm, however, may carry an X or a Y chromosome. If a sperm containing an X chromosome fertilizes the egg, the resulting child will be XX, a female. If the sperm contains a Y chromosome, the child will be XY, a male. The existence of both X and Y chromosomes in the male might suggest that each conception has a 50-50 chance of resulting in a boy or a girl. As Table 2.1 indicates, however, many more male than female zygotes are conceived, and slightly more boys than girls are actually born (Motulsky, 1986). In the end, though, as the table also indicates, fewer male babies

These dizygotic twins illustrate the great potential for variety of two individuals conceived by the same parents at the same time.

same uterus and were born at the same time, "fraternal twins" are no more alike at birth than are any other children of the same parents. The tendency to have

dizygotic twins is influenced by race, heredity, the mother's age, the number of prior pregnancies, and fertility drugs. African American women, mothers who are themselves fraternal twins, women between 35 and 40 years of age, women who have had four or more children, and those who have taken fertility drugs are all more likely to give birth to fraternal twins.

Twins are of special interest to psychologists because a knowledge of their characteristics can help answer questions about the influences of nature and nurture. By comparing resemblances between identical twins (who have the same genes) with resemblances between fraternal twins (whose genes are no more alike than those of any other siblings), researchers can estimate the influence of hereditary factors in the production of different characteristics. For example, Robert Plomin and his colleagues (Plomin & DeFries, 1985) compared identical and fraternal twins with respect to such temperamental characteristics as emotionality, level of activity, and sociability. They found that identical twins were somewhat similar in their expression of these characteristics: The correlation was .55. For fraternal twins, the correlation was zero; thus fraternal twins resembled each other in the expression of the characteristics no more than would any two children selected at random from the community. These findings indicate that inherited factors play a role in the development of temperament. Similar analyses by Thomas Bouchard, Jr. (1994) point to the same conclusion for a broad variety of personality characteristics.

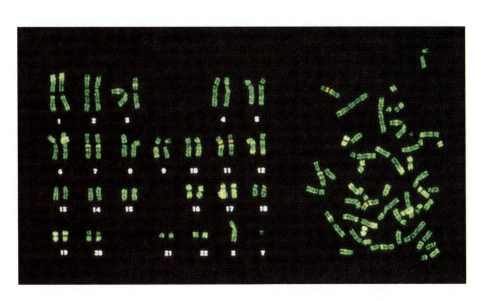

FIGURE 2.4 *Human chromosomes for a male arrayed in matched pairs, an arrangement called a karyotype. Note that the two members (X and Y) of the twenty-third pair for a male differ markedly in size, whereas they would be the same for a female (X and X).*

TABLE 2.1	Approximate Sex Ratios for the U.S. White Population

Age	Male : Female
Conception	120 : 100
Birth	106 : 100
18 Years	100 : 100
50 Years	95 : 100
67 Years	70 : 100
87 Years	50 : 100
100 Years	21 : 100

Source: Lerner & Libby, 1976.

Allele An alternate form of a gene coded for a particular trait.

Homozygous Having inherited two genes of the same allelic form for a single attribute.

Heterozygous Having inherited two genes of different allelic forms for the same attribute.

Dominant allele The allele that is expressed when an individual possesses two different alleles for the same trait.

Recessive allele The allele that is not expressed when an individual possesses two different alleles for the same trait.

Codominance A trait that is determined by two alleles but is qualitatively different from the trait produced by either of the contributing alleles alone.

are born than are conceived, and the ratio of males to females declines over the life span. This finding appears to reflect the greater vulnerability of males to genetic diseases and other problems that lead to death (McKusick, 1975).

A cultural factor that may influence the ratio of males to females at birth is the parents' preference for one sex or the other. With the recent development of methods for identifying the sex of the fetus, selective abortion has sometimes been used to prevent the birth of female babies. In South Korea, for example, the birth ratio in 1985 was 117 males to 100 females because, according to South Korean obstetricians, some mothers were aborting their female fetuses (Jameson, 1986).

The Laws of Genetic Inheritance

The mechanisms by which parents transmit their biological characteristics to the next generation were first studied scientifically by Gregor Mendel (1822–1884). From experiments in which he cross-bred varieties of garden peas, Mendel deduced that parents transmit certain traits unchanged to their offspring, and he proposed that they did so through discrete physical entities that he referred to as "characters." It was not until later that Mendel's hypothetical "characters" were shown to operate in humans as well and to correspond to actual physical structures—gene-carrying chromosomes in the nucleus of the cell.

In the simplest form of hereditary transmission, a single pair of genes, one from each parent, determines a particular inherited characteristic. Genes that control a particular trait (for example, the presence or absence of a cleft in the chin) can have alternative forms, called **alleles.** When the corresponding genes inherited from the two parents are of the same allelic form (both "cleft" or both "noncleft"), the person is said to be **homozygous** for the trait. When the alleles are different (one "cleft," one "noncleft"), the person is said to be **heterozygous** for the trait. The distinction between homozygous and heterozygous is essential for understanding how different combinations of genes produce different characteristics.

When a child is homozygous for a trait that is controlled by a single pair of alleles, only one outcome is possible: the child will display the characteristic specified by the allele. When a child is heterozygous for such a trait, one of three outcomes is possible:

1. The child will display the characteristic specified by only one of the two alleles. The allele whose characteristics are expressed is referred to as a **dominant allele,** and the allele whose characteristics are not expressed is called a **recessive allele.**

2. The child will show the effects of both alleles and will display a characteristic that is intermediate between the traits of children who are homozygous for one of the alleles and children who are homozygous for the other.

3. The child will display a characteristic that is contributed to by both alleles, but rather than being intermediate, the characteristic will be distinctively different from that specified by either contributing allele. This outcome is **codominance.**

The inheritance of blood type illustrates the homozygous outcome and two of the heterozygous outcomes. There are three alleles for blood type—A, B, and O—and four basic blood types—A, B, AB, and O. If children receive two type A, two type B, or two type O alleles, they are homozygous for the trait and will have

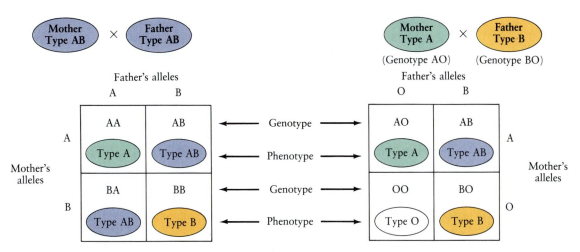

FIGURE 2.5 *The alternative forms of a gene for blood type, inherited in various combinations from parents, produce different blood phenotypes.*

type A, type B, or type O blood, respectively. But if they inherit either the type A or type B allele from one parent and the type O allele from the other, they will have type A or type B blood, even though their genetic code for blood type is AO or BO. The O allele is recessive, so it does not affect the exhibited blood type. Finally, if children inherit one type A allele and one type B allele, they will exhibit a codominant outcome—type AB blood, which is qualitatively different from either type A or type B blood. Figure 2.5 shows some of the outcomes of various combinations of the three alleles for blood type.

There is no intermediate outcome for blood type, but there is one for skin pigmentation and some other characteristics. The skin color of a child of a light-skinned mother and a dark-skinned father, say, may fall between those of the parents.

GENOTYPE AND PHENOTYPE

Because an individual's genetic code for blood type may be AO or BO but only the A or B allele is expressed in the blood type itself, knowledge of the person's actual blood type does not permit us to say what the individual's genetic code for blood type is. Such differences between the genetic code for a trait and the actual expression of that trait occur for a great many characteristics. As a consequence, geneticists must study organisms on two levels to discover the effects of genes. One level is the **genotype,** the individual's genetic endowment or, in other words, the particular alleles that the individual has inherited. The genotype is constant over the lifetime of the individual. The second level is that of the **phenotype,** the observable characteristics of the individual—his or her health, physical and personality traits, and behavior, which develop through interactions between the genotype and the environment.

Discussions about genetic influences on development rely heavily on inferences about genotypes based on observations of phenotypes. Making such inferences is a hazardous enterprise because it is usually impossible to isolate genetic from environmental variables. We will discuss some of these controversies, such as those about the degree to which temperament and intelligence are fixed by the genotype, in later chapters.

Determining genetic influences is further complicated by the fact that most human traits are **polygenic;** that is, they are caused not by a single gene but by the interaction of several genes. There is no specific gene for height, for instance;

Genotype The total set of genes that an individual inherits.

Phenotype The organism's observable characteristics that result from the interaction of the genotype with the environment.

Polygenic trait A genetic trait that is determined by the interaction of several genes.

height is believed to be controlled by many genes, each of which has a small effect (Tanner, 1990). What is more, most phenotypical characteristics that are determined by a number of genes are also subject to considerable influence by the environment (Futuyma, 1986).

Genes may interact in a variety of ways. Some genes modify the action of other genes. Many people mistakenly think that human eye color is controlled by a gene with two allelic forms, a dominant allele for brown eyes and a recessive allele for blue eyes. If this were actually the case, there would be no more than two eye colors: blue and brown. Many people, however, have eyes of other colors (gray, black, green, hazel), because **modifier genes**—genes that affect the action or expression of other genes—influence eye color. These modifier genes affect the amount of pigment in the iris, the tone of the pigment (which may be "light," "yellow," or "dark brown"), and the distribution of pigment (over the entire iris, in scattered spots, or in a ring around the outer edge) (Lerner & Libby, 1976).

In some cases, genes are **complementary** to one another—that is, more than one gene is necessary for the expression of a characteristic. Pea flowers are purple, for example, only when both the dominant allele for a gene, designated *C*, and the dominant allele for another gene, designated *P*, are present together. In the absence of either of these alleles, the flowers are always white.

In still other cases, one gene may mask the normal expression of another gene; appropriately, they are referred to as **masking genes.** The color of a guinea pig, for example, is affected by two genes. One determines whether melanin, the pigment that controls color, is produced; the other determines how much melanin is deposited. The latter gene has two alleles: one that causes a lot of melanin to be deposited, so that the animal has a black coat; and one that causes a moderate amount of melanin to be deposited, so that the guinea pig has a brown coat. If no melanin is produced, the guinea pig is an albino, and the gene that determines how much melanin is deposited cannot be expressed. In other words, the first gene can mask the second so that it has no effect on the phenotype.

Sex-Linked Genetic Effects

Some inherited human characteristics are determined by genes that are found only on the X or the Y chromosome and are thus called **sex-linked characteristics.** Most of these inherited sex-linked characteristics are carried on the X chromosome (we have seen that it is much larger than the Y chromosome). Because females receive two X chromosomes, they get two doses of X-chromosome sex-linked genes, one from each of their parents, as with the genes on any of the other chromosomes. Normal males receive only one X chromosome and therefore only one of each X-chromosome gene, which always comes from their mother. This asymmetry in genetic material leaves males susceptible to genetic defects that ordinarily do not affect females. If a daughter has a harmful recessive gene on one X chromosome, she will usually have a normal dominant gene on the other X chromosome to override it. Thus the recessive gene is not expressed. A son has no complementary allele to dominate the effects of a harmful recessive gene on his X chromosome, so the harmful gene is expressed.

Red-green color blindness is one sex-linked recessive trait. For a daughter to exhibit this trait, she must be homozygous for it; that is, she must have a father who is red-green color blind and a mother who is either color blind or heterozygous for the trait. By contrast, if a son receives the gene for red-green color blindness on the X chromosome he inherits from his mother, he will be unable to distinguish red from green because there is no corresponding gene on the Y chromosome to counteract the recessive gene.

Harmful sex-linked traits that primarily affect males include hemophilia (a defect that delays the clotting of the blood), certain types of night blindness, atrophy

Modifier gene A gene that influences the action or expression of other genes.

Complementary genes Genes that can only produce their phenotypical effect if they work in combination with other genes.

Masking gene A gene that masks the normal expression of another gene.

Sex-linked characteristic Attributes determined by genes that are found on the X or Y chromosome.

Gregor Mendel, discoverer of the basic principles of genetics.

of the optic nerve, hypogammaglobulin (the inability of the body to produce the antibodies necessary to fight bacterial infections), vitamin D resistance (which causes rickets), Duchenne's muscular dystrophy (a progressive wasting away of the muscles that leads to an early death), and some forms of diabetes, as well as color blindness (Motulsky, 1986).

The frequency of sex-linked abnormalities varies greatly depending on the particular trait and the population in which it occurs. For example, one form of genetically caused anemia, a condition in which the blood is deficient in red blood cells, occurs in 60 percent of male Kurdish Jews living in Israel, whereas only 0.5 percent of male European Jews have this condition (Lerner & Libby, 1976). The difference in the incidence of the disease reflects the different frequencies of the allele that causes it in the two gene pools. A **gene pool** is the total genetic information possessed by a sexually reproducing population.

Genes, the Organism, and the Environment

Knowledge about the laws of genetic inheritance is essential if we are to untangle the influences of nature and nurture on development. But this knowledge alone will not allow us to understand genetic influences on an individual's characteristics because it doesn't take into account the effects of the **environment:** the totality of things, conditions, and circumstances that surround the organism. Genes do not exist in isolation; they exist only within an environment. And only through the interactions of their genes with their environments do organisms develop.

STUDYING GENE–ENVIRONMENT INTERACTIONS

The relation of genes to their environment is complex and multileveled. Genes are merely chemical codes that specify the sequences of amino acids in the proteins produced by the cells. By doing so, they determine the form and functions of the cells. The cells, in turn, provide the immediate environment in which the genes exist. Thus the genes and the cell material are in constant interaction. The system of cells as a whole—the organism—is also in constant interaction with its environment. The interactions of the organism with its larger environment determine the conditions of the individual cells and hence the immediate environment of the genes (Futuyma, 1986).

Variations in the environment at any level can have profound effects on the development of the phenotype. Albert Winchester (1972) vividly demonstrated this phenomenon in a set of experiments with Himalayan rabbits. The Himalayan rabbit normally has a white body and black ears, nose, feet, and tail. If a patch of the white fur on a rabbit's back is removed and an ice pack is placed over the area, the new fur that grows there will be black (see Figure 2.6). This result shows that

Gene pool The total genetic information possessed by a sexually reproducing population.

Environment The totality of things, conditions, and circumstances that surround the organism.

FIGURE 2.6 *The effect of the environment on the expression of a gene for fur color in the Himalayan rabbit. Under normal conditions* (a) *only the rabbit's feet, tail, ears, and nose are black. If fur is removed from a patch on the rabbit's back and an ice pack is placed there* (b), *creating a cold local environment, the new fur that grows in is black* (c). *(Adapted from Winchester, 1972.)*

(a)   (b)   (c)

The kinds of gene–environment interaction that lead a child to perform well with a hoop depend greatly on the cultural context that specifies how it is to be used.

the fur-color phenotype depends on the temperature at the specific site where hair grows. The gene for black color is expressed only at low temperatures. But simply specifying the temperature of the rabbit's general environment is not sufficient to predict the color of its fur; the temperatures at *specific sites* on the rabbit are the relevant environments for predicting the expression of the gene for black fur. The rabbit's extremities are normally colder than the rest of its body, and this uneven distribution of temperatures causes the typical variations in its coat. This experiment makes it clear that when gene–environment interactions are investigated, the environment must be specified with as much care as the relevant genes.

In conducting research on gene–environment interactions in such organisms as plants, fruit flies, and mice, geneticists use two approaches. In one they attempt to *keep the environment constant* so that any variation in phenotype can be attributed to variations in the genes. In the other *they keep the genotype constant* while they vary the environment so that variations in the phenotype can be attributed to variations in the environment. The first procedure highlights genetic influences on development; the second highlights the influences of the environment. Either approach by itself would give us only a partial picture of gene–environment interaction.

By charting the changes that occur in the phenotype as the environment of a particular genotype is varied, researchers can discover the **range of reaction** for that genotype. Ideally, this range represents all the possible gene–environment relationships that are compatible with the continued life of the organism, so that it includes all the possible developmental outcomes. In the case of the Himalayan rabbit, the range of reaction for fur color would be bounded at one end by the temperature at which the rabbit would freeze to death and at the other end by the temperature that would be too high to permit it to live. As the temperature approaches the lower boundary, we would expect the rabbit's fur to be predominantly black. As the temperature approaches the higher boundary, even the extremities might remain white. The variations in the phenotypic expression of fur color as the temperature is varied from one extreme to the other is the range of reaction for the Himalayan rabbit's genotype for fur color.

CANALIZATION

The range of reaction focuses attention on the wide array of possible phenotypes that can result from the combination of a given genotype and the range of environments that can sustain the life of the organism. The developmental geneticist Conrad Waddington (1947) introduced the notion of **canalization** to highlight another aspect of gene–environment interactions—the fact that certain characteristics typical of a species may be restricted to a narrow range despite wide variations in environmental conditions. In other words, when development is "highly canalized," the genes may somehow be preventing the developmental process from varying more than a little in response to varying environmental events. Canalized processes also exhibit a strong tendency to *self-correction* after the organism is exposed to deviant experiences. When development is *not* highly canalized, variability in the environment produces more frequent and more marked differences between individuals, and self-correction is less likely to occur in the wake of any unusual experiences.

The capacity of developing children to acquire language is often cited as an example of a canalized developmental process. As we shall see in Chapter 8 (p. 327), children in all societies not only acquire language without needing deliberate instruction; they even acquire language when they suffer from mental retardation or when input from the environment is greatly reduced by loss of hearing. Only the most severe and prolonged deprivation of language input seems capable of deflecting language development from its species-typical developmental path.

Waddington thought that canalization was the product of genetic mechanisms, but Gilbert Gottlieb (1992) has argued that canalization can also result from early developmental experiences. He demonstrated that if mallard ducklings are not exposed early in life to the species-specific sounds of their mother's assembly call, they may instead respond to the call of a female of some other species and adhere to that species' call for the rest of their lives.

GENETIC INFLUENCES ON HUMAN BEHAVIOR

Geneticists believe that the principles of gene–environment interactions they have derived from their experiments with plants, insects, and animals also apply to human behavior. Researchers who seek to understand how genetic and environmental factors combine to produce individual differences in behavior are called **behavioral geneticists.**

When behavioral geneticists discuss individual differences, they commonly use the phrase "genetically influenced" to describe certain behavioral characteristics (mental retardation is an example). In some cases, this means that the geneticist has isolated a single gene that is crucial to expression of the actual behavior (the phenotype). In those instances, individual differences are an all-or-nothing affair: either one has the trait in question or one does not. Single-gene influences are rare, however; they usually involve a disease or disorder. PKU, discussed later in this chapter, is one form of mental retardation caused by a single gene. Another is galactosemia, a carbohydrate metabolic defect. Children who are homozygous for the recessive allele lack an enzyme to convert galactose to glucose. Usually such children die in infancy. Those who survive are severely mentally retarded unless they are fed a special diet. (Table 2.2, on p. 70, lists other examples.)

In contrast, any behavior that shows a large range of individual differences— shyness, say—has to be influenced by multiple genes in interaction with the environment. So to say that a characteristic such as shyness is genetically influenced does *not* mean that someone has discovered the genes that correspond to shyness. Nor does it mean that the environment plays no role in producing shyness. Rather, it means that there is a statistical correlation between individual differences on, say, a questionnaire measuring shyness and the range of genotypic differences in the population being studied. The extent to which a given behavior can be attributed to hereditary factors is referred to as the **heritability** of that behavioral characteristic.

An important restriction on the study of human behavioral genetics is the impossibility of carrying out the experimental manipulations needed to establish a range of reaction. To do so would require totalitarian control over people's lives and would expose children to dangerous environments purely for the purpose of scientific interest. Obviously, such experiments would be immoral and should not be carried out. (Other ethical implications of the study of behavioral genetics are discussed in Box 2.2.)

The ethical impossibility of measuring the ranges of reaction for human behavioral characteristics has led behavioral geneticists to rely on **family studies** for

Range of reaction All the possible phenotypes for a single genotype that are compatible with life.

Canalization The process that makes some characteristics relatively invulnerable to environmental influence during development.

Behavioral geneticist A researcher who seeks to understand how genetic and environmental factors combine to produce individual differences in behavior.

Heritability The extent to which a given behavior can be attributed to hereditary factors.

Family studies Studies that compare members of a family to see how similar they are in one or more traits.

BOX 2.2

Is a Gene Making You Read This?

Gina Kolata

Dr. Lee Silver, a biology professor at Princeton University, is among a growing number of scientists searching for genes that predispose people to complex behavioral traits, like aggression or a tendency toward alcoholism or drug abuse or even toward daydreaming or thrill seeking.

The work can lead to new treatments for alcohol and drug abuse or even for excessively aggressive behavior, but it also has implications that are profound, even troubling. And so it leads inevitably to the question: Is some research best not done at all?

Although the quest for genetic links to behavior is old, the difference now, scientists say, is that techniques are suddenly available to find such genes. Only last week, researchers announced they had found a gene that gives people an impulsive personality.

Researchers, however, say people are not slaves to their genes and that environment plays a role. "We are not talking about genes that determine behavior," said Dr. John Crabbe, a neuroscientist at Oregon Health Sciences University in Portland. "We are talking about genes that influence behavior." But as they get nearer to finding these genes, scientists are beginning to wonder what they have wrought. . . .

One fear is that society might abuse the results, stigmatizing people whose genes linked them with low intelligence or drug addiction. But an even deeper fear is that science will soon be able to intervene—soothe an impulsive personality, quell a rapist's tendencies

"The good news is that you will have a healthy baby girl.
The bad news is that she is a congenital liar."

Drawing by Handelsmann; © 1996.
The New Yorker Magazine, Inc.

or dull an alcoholic's craving. If every difficult behavior could be ameliorated, if every rough personality made smooth, "where is the core of the human soul?" Dr. Silver asked.

Several Princeton professors, including Dr. Silver, are passionately debating the issues partial answers to such questions. These studies compare members of a family to see how similar they are in one or more traits (Plomin, DeFries, & McClearn, 1990; Scarr, 1981). In the typical family study, people who live together in a household are compared with one another to determine how similar they are in a given attribute. If the attribute being studied (say shyness) is controlled largely by heredity, the similarity in shyness between any two people living in the same environment should increase as the degree to which they share the same genes increases. The ideal cases in family studies are those that compare identical (monozygotic) and fraternal (dizygotic) twins of the same sex. Identical twins have

surrounding genetically linked behavior, by E-mail and in discussion groups. . . .

Modern genetics has a tainted history in this country and Germany where early in this century scientists attempted to weed out the unfit and the feeble minded by sterilization. "When you find genetic bases for incurable conditions or behaviors that are socially not tolerated, you have to worry about what mechanisms are in place to help people," Dr. Adams said.

People with these genes might be rejected by insurance companies, Dr. Adams said, and be subjected to "restrictions on being able to reproduce."

Suggesting a different scenario, Dr. Silver said: "Let's say we could identify boys who have a tenfold higher potential to be rapists. What do you do with these children? On the one hand, you can restrict their freedom. You can imagine people saying they don't want that person in their neighborhood."

But, Dr. Silver said, "There's the alternative—there's what this research might lead to." If scientists find genes that increase the odds that a boy will grow up to be a rapist, they could probably find ways to block those genes, with drugs. Should the boys then be forced to take drugs although most would never rape?

Equally problematical are the implications of finding genes like the one for impulsiveness, Dr. Silver said. He said it is likely that scientists will find hundreds of such genes that together help determine personalities through subtle changes in brain chemistry. . . .

And so science will bring society face to face with an ancient question: What defines a human being? "If you are taking away all these things, if you are saying it is all just chemicals in the brain, then you keep chipping away at the soul," Dr. Silver said.

Despite these scenarios, scientists cannot bring themselves to say that they would voluntarily stop their work. The financial incentives—Federal grants and money pouring in from drug companies—are numerous. But scientists have to live with themselves, and they have a variety of reasons why they persevere.

Some point to the positive.

"Alcoholism kills and maims a lot of people every year," said Dr. Wade Berrettini, a researcher at Thomas Jefferson University in Philadelphia who is looking for genes linked to alcoholism. "We don't have good treatments now. In order to provide better treatments, we have to understand how it develops."

Others stress the metaphysical.

"Would I not do an experiment because I thought the information might be abused down the line?" Dr. Silver asked. "The cynical answer is, 'Well, if I don't do it, someone else will.' "

"I think that ultimately all knowledge is good for human beings. I don't think you can censor knowledge," he added. "I think scientists have an obligation to help society go in the right direction. But whether society listens to us is another story."

Adapted from The New York Times, *Sunday, January 7, 1996*

---

100 percent of their genes in common, whereas fraternal twins (and other siblings) share 50 percent of their genotypes. Insofar as genes control the trait being compared, identical twins raised together should show greater similarity to each other than do fraternal twins and siblings. By the same logic, fraternal twins and siblings who share, on the average, half their genetic material should differ less than half sisters and half brothers, who have only one parent in common and therefore share only about 25 percent of their genetic material. Many studies have shown that the patterns of similarity among kin decrease as the degree of genetic similarity decreases for such varied characteristics as personality (Bouchard, 1994), intel-

ligence test scores (Plomin & DeFries, 1983; Scarr & Weinberg, 1983), the perception of self-worth (McGuire et al., 1994), and susceptibility to schizophrenia (Gottesman, 1991).

Despite their usefulness, family studies, even those that permit comparison between identical and fraternal twins, are not without problems. It is possible, for example, that identical twins may be treated more similarly than fraternal twins or other siblings; to the extent that they are, identical twins may be more alike than fraternal twins for environmental rather than genetic reasons (Plomin, DeFries, & McClearn, 1990).

A family study that compares identical and fraternal twins seeks to assess the effects of variations in the genotype when the environment is held constant. A related research strategy, the **adoption study**, compares biologically identical or similar individuals who have been adopted into different families. The basic purpose of this strategy is to determine if adopted children are more similar to their *biological* parents and siblings, who share their genes, than to their *adoptive* parents and siblings, with whom they share a common environment. Data from adoption studies indicate that children are more like their biological parents than their adoptive parents with respect to such traits as intelligence and mental illness. Thus hereditary factors appear to figure significantly in the development of these traits. But adopted children also resemble the parents who adopted them to some degree, confirmation that the environment as well as heredity contributes significantly to human behavior.

From a rigorously scientific point of view, the biggest limitation of adoption studies is that children being studied do not inhabit the full range of environments available to our species, the condition necessary to establish a true range of reaction. Rather, adoption agencies are likely to make every attempt to place children in secure, loving homes, often with people whose social and cultural backgrounds match those of the biological parents (Scarr, 1981). Thus the extent to which adopted children are similar to their biological families cannot be attributed entirely to the similarity of their genes; it may also be due to the similarity of the environments in which the families live.

Behavioral geneticists have begun to focus attention on the fact that the environment, as well as the genes, works to create differences between members of a family. Judy Dunn and Robert Plomin describe the reasons for this shift in focus:

> From her research as well as observations of her own three children, who included a pair of twins, [Judy Dunn] believed that heredity could explain some of the differences between siblings growing up in the same family. But she was sure that sibling differences were not all to be explained by genetics—siblings are too different for that. They are first-degree relatives and thus share half their genes, which means that if a trait were entirely genetic, siblings should be 50 percent similar as well as 50 percent different. But siblings are much less than 50 percent similar. The difference between them must surely reflect differences in their experiences as well as differences in their heredity. But what were the key differences that led to brothers and sisters being so different? (Dunn & Plomin, 1990, p. xii)

Dunn and Plomin, as well as other researchers (Hetherington, Reiss, & Plomin, 1994), point to a variety of factors that account for the differences in the environments of siblings raised in the same family: not only do parents treat their children differently, but the siblings offer different environments for each other, and are likely to have different teachers at school and different friends (see Box 2.3).

Evidence that the distinctive environment of each individual has a profound effect on his or her development in no way minimizes the importance of genetic factors. Rather, it affirms the principle that genes and the environment are two as-

Adoption study Studies in which genetically related individuals who are raised in different family environments are compared to determine the extent to which heredity or environment controls a given trait.

pects of a single process of development. In later chapters, when we begin to examine the effects of the environment on development, it will be important to keep in mind the fact that each of us experiences the world in a distinctive way that depends not only on the unique combination of genes we inherited from our parents but on the unique environment each of us inhabits.

FEEDBACK IN GENE–ENVIRONMENT INTERACTIONS

Evidence gathered from family studies indicates that human genotypes interact with their environments in complex ways, leading psychologists to propose the existence of complex *feedback mechanisms* that mediate between children's genotypes, phenotypes, and environments. Sandra Scarr and Kathleen McCartney (1983) have proposed a model that encompasses a good deal of the current research on this topic.

The full Scarr-McCartney model is easiest to understand if we work up to it in steps. The simplest model, shown in Figure 2.7*a*, represents the common wisdom that the whole organism (the phenotype) is created through the interaction between its genes and its environment. For example, there is evidence that some people are genetically predisposed to irritability. Figure 2.7*a* represents the idea that the actual expression of irritability in a child will depend on the degree to which the environment interacts with the genetic predisposition for irritability to create irritable behavior.

Figure 2.7*b* reminds us that the picture is more complicated because the parents' genes not only contribute to their child's genotype but also, through their phenotypic expression in the parents, to their child's environment. If, for example, irritability is a highly expressed trait in a baby's mother and father, their presence in the baby's environment may well boost the expression of irritability in the baby. By contrast, if the parents maintain a calm environment in the home despite their own genetic predispositions to irritability, the expression of irritability in the baby may be reduced.

The model in Figure 2.7*c* comes still closer to real life. It shows that the child's expressed genetic characteristics feed back to influence the environment with which the child is interacting. Given enough provocation, even the most placid parents may become annoyed by an irritable baby and behave in a manner that will increase the baby's irritation. In that case, the infant's genotype is interacting with an environment that is shaped in part by her own phenotypic characteristics.

Finally, Scarr and McCartney add the possibility that the infant's genotype may influence the way the child experiences the environment. An irritable child, for example, may thrash and turn in a way that makes his environment more irritating, as he experiences the sight and feel of his own agitation and

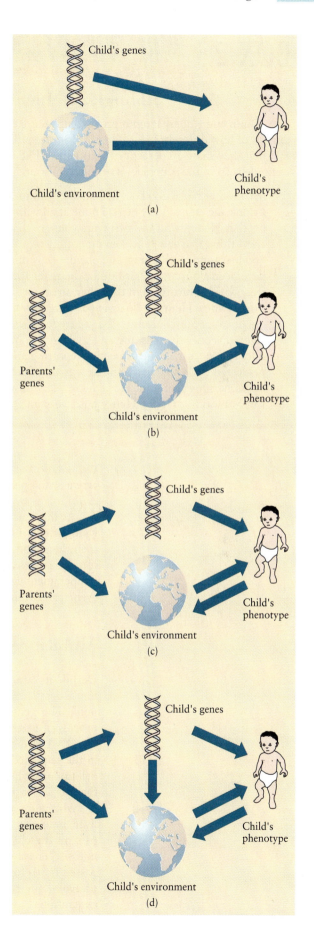

FIGURE 2.7 *The increasingly complex models of gene–environment interactions proposed by Scarr and McCartney.*

BOX 2.3

Siblings: So Much in Common, but So Diverse

Judy Dunn and Robert Plomin provide intriguing examples of how different two siblings can be, despite the fact that they share 50 percent of their genes. The first example is from the American writer Mark Twain.

> My mother had a good deal of trouble with me but I think she enjoyed it. She had none at all with my brother Henry, who was two years younger than I, and I think that the unbroken monotony of his goodness and truthfulness and obedience would have been a burden to her but for the relief and variety which I furnished in the other direction. . . . I never knew Henry to do a vicious thing toward me or toward anyone else—but he frequently did righteous ones that cost me as heavily. It was his duty to report me, when I needed reporting and neglected to do so myself, and he was very faithful in discharging that duty. He is Sid in *Tom Sawyer*. But Sid was not Henry. Henry was a very much finer and better boy than Sid ever was. (Quoted from Mark Twain, Dunn & Plomin, 1990, p. 1)

The second example is the poet Alfred (A. E.) Housman and his brother Laurence, who was a writer, described by the editor of Alfred's letters, Henry Maas.

> Alfred resembled Laurence only in the ability to write. Otherwise he was a complete contrast. Where Laurence was diffuse, impulsive, and warm-hearted, Alfred was precise, disciplined and reserved. Laurence lavished his gifts on too many books, Alfred constricted his poems within the bounds of a tiny *oeuvre* [body of work]. Laurence was always getting into trouble, Alfred carefully kept out of it. Laurence was a visionary and idealist, to whom his elder brother must at times have seemed a reactionary pedant. (Quoted in Dunn & Plomin, 1990, p. 3)

the agitation of the physical objects it causes. When this possibility is included, we arrive at the gene–environment interactions of the full model depicted in Figure 2.7d.

As the Scarr-McCartney model of gene–environment interactions suggests, a wide variety of factors lead each family member to react in specific ways to each of the others, and these different reactions contribute to the uniqueness of the environment that each child in the home inhabits. Gender, physical appearance, and temperamental variations, as well as illnesses, accidents, and other idiosyncratic events, all combine to make each person's environment unique.

Mutations and Genetic Abnormalities

Despite its fantastic power to produce diversity in human beings, sexual reproduction is restricted to recombining genes that are already present in the human gene pool. The gene pool can change, however, through **mutation,** an error in the process of gene replication that results in a change in the molecular structure of the DNA. A mutation can be a qualitative change in a particular gene or a change in the sequence of genes on a chromosome. It may also consist of an addition or deletion, as when part of a chromosome is duplicated or lost. Mutations change the overall set of genetic possibilities that sexual reproduction then rearranges.

Mutations sometimes occur in the somatic (body) cells—in cells of the skin, liver, brain, or bones, for example. The somatic cells that carry these mutations pass on the changed genetic instructions to the cells that descend from them by mitosis. These changes affect only the person in whom they occur; they are not passed on to following generations. When a mutation occurs in a parent's sperm or ovum, however, the changed genetic information may be passed on to the next generation.

Geneticists assume that spontaneous mutations have been occurring constantly and randomly since life on earth began, pouring new genes into the gene pool of every species. Indeed, mutation is the driving force behind the evolutionary processes by which new subspecies and species are formed. The fact that mutations are a natural and fundamental part of life does not, however, mean that they usually benefit the individual organisms in which they occur. Each living organism is an intricate whole in which the functionings of the separate parts are interdependent. It is little wonder, then, that the introduction of even a small change in the genes can have serious repercussions for the individual (Figure 2.8).

It is estimated that as many as half of all human conceptions have some sort of genetic or chromosomal abnormality. The majority of these mutations are lethal and result in early miscarriage (Connor & Ferguson-Smith, 1991). Still, about 3.5 percent of all babies born have some kind of genetic aberration (Ward, 1994). These genetic abnormalities tend to be recessive, so an individual who receives one from one parent usually receives a normal gene or chromosome from the other parent to counteract it. Some genetic abnormalities, though, do affect human beings. A few of the more significant conditions attributable to them are listed in Table 2.2.

Developmental psychologists are interested in studying mutations and genetic abnormalities for several reasons:

1. By disturbing the well-integrated mechanisms of development, mutations can help to reveal the intricate ways in which heredity and the environment interact.

2. If the existence of genetic abnormalities can be detected at a very early stage of development, ways may be found to prevent or ameliorate the birth defects that would normally result.

3. When children are born with genetic abnormalities, developmental psychologists are often responsible for finding ways to reduce the impact of the abnormalities on the children and their families.

These concerns are reflected in the current research being conducted on sickle-cell anemia, Down's syndrome, certain sex-linked chromosomal abnormalities, and phenylketonuria.

SICKLE-CELL ANEMIA: AN EXAMPLE OF GENE–ENVIRONMENT INTERACTION

In certain environments, some mutations are advantageous to people who are heterozygous for them. The recessive sickle-cell gene is a case in point.

People who inherit this gene from both of their parents, and thus are homozygous for it, suffer from *sickle-cell anemia*, a serious abnormality of the red blood cells. Normal red blood cells are round. In people with sickle-cell anemia, however, these cells take on a curved, sickle shape when the supply of oxygen to the blood is reduced, as it may be at high altitudes or during strenuous exercise (see Figure 2.9). These abnormal blood cells tend to clump together and clog the smaller blood vessels. Because sickle-cell anemia impairs circulation, people who suffer from the disease experience severe pains in the abdomen, back, head, and limbs. The disease causes the heart to enlarge and deprives the brain cells of blood. The deformed

> **Mutation** An error in the process by which a gene is replicated that results in a change in the molecular structure of the gene.

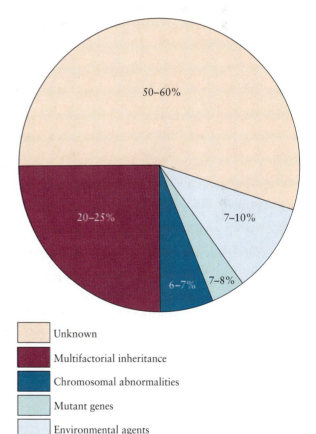

- Unknown
- Multifactorial inheritance
- Chromosomal abnormalities
- Mutant genes
- Environmental agents

FIGURE 2.8 *A graphic illustration of the leading causes of congenital anomalies. Note that the causes for most anomalies are unknown and that one quarter to one fifth are known to result from a combination of genetic and environmental factors. (Moore, Persaud, & Shiota, 1994.)*

TABLE 2.2   Common Genetic Diseases and Conditions

Disease or Condition	Description	Mode of Transmission	Incidence	Prognosis	Prenatal/Carrier Detections
Cystic fibrosis	Lack of an enzyme causes mucous obstruction, especially in lungs and digestive tract	Recessive gene	1 in 21,000 live births in U.S.; most common in people of Northern European descent	Few victims survive to adulthood	Yes/Yes
Diabetes mellitus (juvenile form)	Deficient metabolism of sugar because body does not produce adequate insulin	Thought to be polygenic	1 in 25 to 40 of all diabetics	Fatal if untreated; controllable by insulin and restricted diet	No/No
Down's syndrome	See text				
Hemophilia (bleeding disease)	Blood does not clot readily	X-linked gene; also occurs by spontaneous mutation	1 in 21,500 live births of males	Possible crippling and death from internal bleeding; transfusions ameliorate effects	No/Yes
Klinefelter's syndrome	See text (p. 72)				
Muscular dystrophy (Duchenne's type)	Weakening and wasting away of muscles	X-linked gene	1 in 200,000 males under age 20	Crippling; often fatal by age 20	Yes/Sometimes
Phenylketonuria (PKU)	See text (p. 72)				
Sickle-cell anemia	See text (p. 70)				
Tay-Sachs disease	Lack of an enzyme causes buildup of waste in brain	Recessive gene	1 in 3600 among Ashkenazi Jews in U.S.	Neurological degeneration leading to death before age 4	Yes/Yes
Thalassemia (Cooley's anemia)	Abnormal red blood cells	Recessive gene	1 in 100 births in populations from subtropical areas of Europe, Africa, Asia	Listlessness, enlarged liver and spleen, occasionally death; treatable by blood transfusions	Yes/Yes
Turner's syndrome	See text (p. 72)				

Sources: Bergsma, 1979; McKusick, 1986; Nightingale & Meister, 1987.

blood cells rupture easily, and the rupturing may lead to severe anemia and even to early death. As many as 80,000 African Americans are estimated to suffer from sickle-cell anemia (Connor & Ferguson-Smith, 1991).

People who are heterozygous for the sickle-cell gene have inherited the trait from only one parent and usually do not suffer the severe symptoms associated with sickle-cell anemia. Though they may encounter some circulatory problems (40 percent of their red blood cells may assume the sickle shape when the supply of oxygen to the blood is reduced), they are not at risk of death from the trait, as homozygous carriers are.

Because many people who suffer from sickle-cell anemia die before they have a chance to reproduce, one would expect that this mutation would eventually die out. This is exactly what is happening in the United States, where the incidence of the trait among African Americans is about 8 to 9 percent (Connor & Ferguson-Smith, 1991). But in West Africa, the area from which the ancestors of most African Americans were brought to this continent, the incidence of the sickle-cell trait is greater than 20 percent (Allison, 1954). For a long time these statistics puzzled scientists. Then investigators noticed that the areas in which the sickle-cell trait was most common also tend to have a high incidence of malaria, and they began to wonder whether this correspondence was more than a coincidence.

The link between the sickle-cell gene and malaria was established in 1954 by A. C. Allison of Oxford University, in England. Allison's studies showed that heterozygous carriers of the gene are highly resistant to the malaria parasite. Thus in malaria-infested areas such as the West African coast, people who do not carry the sickle-cell gene are at a disadvantage because they are more likely to suffer from malaria, which can be deadly. Because of the selective advantage the sickle-cell gene affords, its high frequency has been maintained in the population despite the losses caused by the early death of homozygous carriers.

Research by Dr. Samuel Charache and his colleagues (Leary, 1995) has provided the first treatment for sickle-cell anemia. They found that the drug hydroxyurea reduces the number of pain episodes and other symptoms by 50 percent. However, sufferers must take the drug every day, and the long-term effects of daily medication are not yet known, so much work remains to be done to improve the treatment of this genetically linked disease and perhaps someday to cure or eradicate it.

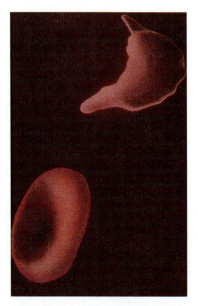

FIGURE 2.9 *A normal, round red blood cell (bottom) and a sickle-shaped red blood cell (top) from a person with sickle-cell anemia.*

DOWN'S SYNDROME: A CHROMOSOMAL ERROR

Down's syndrome was the first human disease to be linked with a specific chromosomal disorder. More than 95 percent of the children born with Down's syndrome have 47 chromosomes, one more than normal. Instead of two copies of chromosome 21, they have three. (For this reason, the disorder is sometimes called *trisomy 21*.) Children with Down's syndrome are mentally and physically retarded and have several distinctive physical characteristics: slanting eyes; a fold on the eyelids; a rather flat facial profile; ears lower than normal; a short neck; a protruding tongue; dental irregularities; short, broad hands; curved little fingers; a wider space between the toes than normal; and a crease running all the way across the palm (see Figure 2.10). On the average, children with this disorder are more likely than other children to suffer from heart, ear, and eye problems, and they are more susceptible to leukemia and to respiratory infections. As a result, they are more likely to die young (Bergsma, 1979).

Over 10 percent of the people in institutions for the retarded suffer from Down's syndrome (Plomin, DeFries, & McClearn, 1990); but how effectively Down's syndrome children function as they grow depends not only on the severity of their disorder but also on the environment in which they are raised. Intense intervention by concerned adults can markedly improve the intellectual function-

FIGURE 2.10 *A Down's syndrome child. (From Bob Daemmrich, The Image Works.)*

ing of some of these children. Thus this genotype apparently has a wide range of reaction.

Down's syndrome occurs in about 1 of every 1000 births in the United States (Pueschel, 1992). A strong relationship has been found between the incidence of Down's syndrome and the age of the parents, the mother in particular. Up to the age of 30 a woman's risk of giving birth to a live infant with Down's syndrome is less than 1 in 800. The risk increases to 1 in 100 by age 40, to 1 in 32 by age 45, and to 1 in 12 by age 49 (Hook, 1982). The risk is thought to increase because at birth the human female carries all the potential egg cells that she will ever produce. The ova are especially vulnerable to such environmental agents as viruses, radiation, and some chemicals, which can damage the chromosomes or interfere with the process of meiosis. The older a woman is, the more time she has had to be exposed to such harmful agents. This view is supported by the fact that the risk of other chromosomal anomalies, such as Klinefelter's syndrome, also increases with the mother's age.

SEX-LINKED CHROMOSOMAL ABNORMALITIES

Abnormalities of the chromosomes that determine sex are of special interest to developmental psychologists because they provide one means of obtaining information about the genetic basis of sex differences. The most common sex-linked chromosomal abnormality is *Klinefelter's syndrome*, a condition that affects only males. These babies are born with an extra X chromosome (XXY). It is estimated that this abnormality occurs in about 1 of every 1000 white males born in the United States (Connor & Ferguson-Smith, 1991). XXY males appear to develop normally until adolescence, but then, when they are expected to show signs of maturity, none appears: their sex organs do not mature, they do not acquire facial hair, their voices do not change, they have low levels of the male hormone testosterone, and they are sterile.

Another chromosomal anomaly, *fragile X syndrome*, has been found to account for 5 to 10 percent of the nation's cases of mental retardation. It is caused by a defect in the X chromosome that is estimated to occur in 1 of every 1250 men (Davies, 1989).

The most common sex-linked abnormality in females is *Turner's syndrome*. About 1 of every 5000 females is born with only one X chromosome (the genotype is designated as XO) (Connor & Ferguson-Smith, 1991). At puberty, girls with Turner's syndrome fail to produce the female hormone estrogen. As a result, they do not develop breasts or pubic hair, rarely menstruate, and are sterile. Such girls, as a group, have been found to be about average in verbal ability, although they frequently score below average on tests of spatial ability and have difficulty with such tasks as following a road map and copying a geometric design (Rovet & Netley, 1982).

PHENYLKETONURIA: A TREATABLE GENETIC DISEASE

The modern history of *phenylketonuria (PKU)*, an inherited metabolic disorder that often leads to severe mental retardation if it is not treated, shows dramatically how human beings can ameliorate the effects of a genetic defect by changing the environment in which a child develops. It is estimated that 1 in every 15,000 white infants born each year in the United States has PKU and that 1 in 100 people of European descent is a carrier of the recessive mutant gene (Hsia et al., 1956). The incidence of PKU is lower among blacks than among whites (Connor & Ferguson-Smith, 1991).

PKU was discovered in 1934 in Norway after Dr. Ashborn Følling found that two mentally retarded children who had been brought to him had abnormal amounts of phenylpyruvic acid in their urine. Spurred by this discovery, Dr. Følling tested other retarded children in institutions and found that some of them also had this symptom. We now know that PKU is caused by a defective recessive gene that leads to the absence of an enzyme necessary for the breakdown of certain proteins in the body. Because PKU children lack this enzyme, they accumulate phenylalanine and phenylpyruvic acid in the bloodstream, and these substances prevent their brain cells from developing normally.

Knowledge of the abnormal biochemistry of the condition led researchers to hypothesize that if the accumulation of phenylalanine and phenylpyruvic acid could be prevented, infants with PKU might develop normally. Physicians have tested this hypothesis by feeding PKU infants a diet low in phenylalanine. (Phenylalanine is highly concentrated in such basic foods as milk, eggs, bread, and fish.) In many cases the mental retardation that characterizes PKU can be significantly reduced through such intervention. The timing of the intervention is crucial. If phenylalanine intake is not restricted by the time a PKU infant is 1 to 3 months of age, the brain will already have suffered irreversible damage.

In 1961 Dr. Robert Guthrie devised a test to screen newborns for PKU so that preventive measures can be taken before phenylalanine and phenylpyruvic acid have a chance to accumulate. The test is now compulsory in most states. Hospital personnel draw blood from each baby's heel a few days after birth. The blood is then added to a bacterial culture that grows if the phenylalanine level in the baby's blood is high. The test is not infallible, however, so some PKU babies are not identified in time.

More recently a means has been developed to detect PKU prenatally (Nightingale & Meister, 1987). Researchers have also developed a test that can identify people who carry the recessive PKU gene. This test enables carriers of the gene to decide whether they want to risk having a child with the disease. (Box 2.4 discusses prenatal detection methods and genetic counseling.)

Biology and Culture

Today we know that mutations are the source of biological variation among species, but at the time Darwin wrote *The Origin of Species* (1859), the genetic basis of hereditary transmission was unknown. Ignorance of genetics and a limited knowledge of the fossil record helped to fuel a fundamental confusion about precisely how hereditary transmission works. In attempting to account for the differences observed among species and among peoples past and present (Figure 2.11), many scientists argued that the mechanisms that produced historical change and cultural differences were the same as those that produced biological change. Further examination of this confusion can give us a broader perspective on the relation between our genetic and environmental heritages and on why any attempts to separate the influences of nature and nurture are so problematic.

ACQUIRED CHARACTERISTICS

In the absence of knowledge about genetics, many prominent biologists in the nineteenth and early twentieth centuries hypothesized that characteristics acquired by individuals during

FIGURE 2.11 *The physical differences between people who live in different environments reflect evolutionary adaptations to those environments. The ratio of body surface area to body volume is very different for the Inuit, who live in the cold climate of northern North America and Greenland, than for the people of West Africa, who live in a warm climate. (From Howells, 1960.)*

BOX 2.4

Genetic Counseling

Thanks to recent advances in the field of genetics, many potential genetic problems can be avoided through genetic testing and counseling. The main responsibilities of genetic counselors are to test potential parents to learn whether they are carriers of a genetic disease and to determine the probability that a particular couple will bear a child with that disease.

Genetic counselors are often called on by couples who have had one child with a genetic defect and who want to know the likelihood that a second child will have the same abnormality. Genetic counselors also advise potential parents who have relatives with a genetic disease, who have physical anomalies they suspect are genetic, who have had several pregnancies that have ended in spontaneous abortion, or who are over the age of 35. Potential parents whose ancestors come from parts of the world where the incidence of a specific genetic disorder is high also use their services. Several inherited disorders are likely to be found in specific groups of people. For example, the recessive allele for *Tay-Sachs disease*, in which a missing enzyme inevitably leads to death before the age of 4, is carried by 1 in 30 Ashkenazi Jews in the United States. The recessive allele for thalassemia, a blood disease, is carried by 1 in 10 Americans of Greek or Italian descent (Omenn, 1978).

Detecting the carriers of the gene for some genetic disorders is relatively simple. The alleles for Tay-Sachs disease and *sickle-cell anemia*, an abnormality of the red blood cells that afflicts many people of African descent, can be detected through blood tests. Female carriers of *Lesch-Nyhan syndrome* (a metabolic disorder affecting male children that leads to the overproduction of uric acid) can be identified through an analysis of their hair follicles. Carriers of chromosomal abnormalities, such as the translocation of chromosome 21, which causes *Down's syndrome* (a condition that combines mental retardation with distinctive physical features) can be identified through the analysis of a cell from the body. The carriers of certain chromosomal disorders are sometimes signaled by specific patterns in the prints of their fingers and palms and the soles of their feet.

On the basis of test results and family histories, the genetic counselor tries to determine whether there is a potential problem and what the odds are that a child of the couple will be affected by it. Such predictions can now be made for diseases and traits that are caused by a single recessive or dominant gene or that are sex-linked, and in some cases for those caused by several genes acting together (polygenic defects). They cannot be made for defects caused by spontaneous mutations.

It must be kept in mind that genetic theory generates statistical probabilities that apply to whole populations. Thus a genetic counselor may not be able to say for certain in advance of conception that a particular couple will have a child who will suffer from a genetic abnormality. Once potential parents have been informed of the risks, they must make their own decision.

After conception, the principal techniques used to determine whether a given fetus suffers from a genetic defect are alpha-fetoprotein assay, sonograms, amniocentesis, sampling of the chorionic villi, and fetoscopy.

---

their lifetimes are transmitted biologically to the next generation. This belief raised concerns that parents who engaged in criminal activity, for example, would pass on a tendency to criminality to their children in the same way that they passed on the genes that determined the colors of their eyes and hair (Gould, 1977b).

The erroneous idea that acquired characteristics can be biologically inherited is referred to as *Lamarckism*, after a French biologist, Jean-Baptiste Lamarck (1744–1829), whose ideas were extremely influential among early evolutionary theorists. Although the inheritance of acquired characteristics has been discredited as a mechanism of biological evolution, the idea behind it is not irrelevant to the study of development: cultural evolution does operate in a Lamarckian way. Consider how the habit of making marks on objects has gradually evolved into symbol systems for writing and numerical calculation. Today the millions of children who are learning to read and do arithmetic in schools all over the world are mastering

The *alpha-fetoprotein assay* is a blood test that is used mainly to detect the presence of defects in the fetus's neural tube, which forms the spinal column and brain. Incomplete closure of the neural tube is the most common birth defect in the United States, occurring in 1 of every 1000 live births. When a fetus has a neural-tube defect, large amounts of alpha-fetoprotein pour out of the open spine or skull into the amniotic fluid. From there it enters the mother's bloodstream, where it can be detected. The results of this blood test are only suggestive, however. Women whose alpha-fetoprotein levels are abnormally high are usually offered sonograms and amniocentesis to verify or disconfirm the problem.

High-frequency sound waves are bounced off the fetus to provide a visible image in *sonograms*, or ultrasound. Sonograms are used to diagnose such malformations as an abnormally small head. They can also be used to diagnose multiple births, to estimate the fetus's age, to determine the rate of its growth, and to locate the placenta.

To perform an *amniocentesis*, the doctor first determines the position of the fetus by means of a sonogram. The doctor then inserts a long hollow needle into the mother's abdomen and extracts some of the amniotic fluid from the sac surrounding the fetus. The amniotic fluid contains cells and other substances from the fetus that can be analyzed for chemical abnormalities and for the presence of certain genetic disorders. Amniocentesis cannot be performed before the fourth month of pregnancy, and 2 weeks are needed to determine the results.

Another way to detect chromosomal disorders is to sample cells taken from the *villi* (hairlike projections) on the *chorion*, a tissue that forms the placenta. One advantage to such *chorionic villus sampling* is that it can be performed as early as the ninth week of pregnancy and its results are available within a few days; thus an abortion can be performed early, when it is safest, should the woman make that choice. Some controversy still surrounds the procedure with regard to both its safety and the accuracy of the findings (Kolata, 1987).

A physician performs a *fetoscopy* by piercing the uterus with a long, narrow tube through which a fetoscope is inserted. The physician then can observe the fetus and the placenta directly through the fetoscope. This procedure is most often used when a malformation is suspected. It can also be used to take blood or tissue samples from the fetus for diagnostic purposes.

When a genetic disorder is detected by any of these tests, parents usually have only two alternatives: the woman can carry the pregnancy to term and give birth to a child who is genetically defective in some way, or she can terminate the pregnancy. This is not an easy choice, especially since the diagnosis often fails to predict the degree of disability the affected child will suffer or the quality of life that can be expected. The severity of a neural-tube defect, for example, can vary greatly, and many people who suffer from such defects have lived productive lives. In some cases, fetal surgery and other kinds of prenatal and postnatal interventions, such as a special diet or blood transfusions, can ameliorate the effects of a defect.

symbol systems that are vastly more complex than those used by any humans as recently as 10,000 years ago. This increased sophistication is not a consequence of biological evolutionary change through the action of genes. Rather, it is the result of cultural evolution, in which the successful innovations of earlier generations—knowledge of when to hunt deer or to plant a field, of the alphabet, of the theorems of geometry—are passed on to succeeding generations through language and by example (Donald, 1991). Evidence of the transmission of innovative forms of behavior from one generation to the next is very meager in nonhuman species (Tomasello, 1990).

COEVOLUTION

For a great many years it was believed that the biological and cultural characteristics of *Homo sapiens* developed in a strict sequence: first the biological capacities we associate with humanity evolved to a critical point, and then an additional biologi-

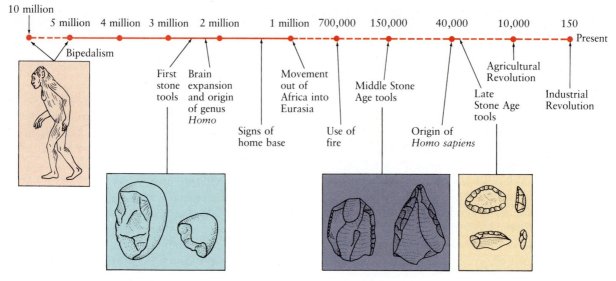

FIGURE 2.12   *The coevolution of toolmaking abilities and* Homo sapiens.

cal change occurred that allowed *Homo sapiens* to use language and generate culture. Now, however, the situation is believed to have been far more complicated. Contemporary studies of human origins have found evidence that rudimentary forms of culture were already present during early phases of human evolution (see Figure 2.12). *Australopithecus* (one of our primitive ancestors, who lived some 3 million years ago) domesticated fire, built shelters, engaged in organized hunting, and used tools—flint knives, cooking utensils, and notation systems (Tanner, 1981).

Such findings indicate that the biological evolution of our species did not end with the appearance of cultural objects. The brain of a modern person is about three times larger than the brain of *Australopithecus*. Most of this increase has occurred in the frontal lobes of the brain, those areas that govern complex, specifically human capacities (Donald, 1991). Insofar as the capacity to engage in cultural activities and to reason through the use of cultural tools—such as geometry, which permits navigation—confers a selective reproductive advantage, it is probable that the more effective users of culture have been more successful in passing on their genes to succeeding generations. In short, culture has influenced biology, and the two forms of evolution, biological and cultural, have interacted with each other in a process called **coevolution** (Futuyma, 1986).

As a consequence of the coevolution of human physical and cultural characteristics, attempts to separate the influences of nature and nurture in the development of contemporary children are even more problematic than our earlier discussion of the range of reaction suggests. The physical demands placed on people vary dramatically in different parts of the world. Furthermore, the cultural histories of people in different locales may have differed greatly for tens of thousands of years. These differences in environment and culture have clearly contributed to the physical differences among people, but whether they have also resulted in mental differences is by no means certain. When Japanese children excel at mathematics, for example, to what extent should their performance be attributed to their genetically transmitted characteristics and what part to the way they were raised in their culture (Gardner, 1983)? Are the extraordinary navigational abilities of Micronesian sailors, who can cross thousands of miles of ocean from one tiny island to another in small canoes without the aid of a compass, the result of ge-

Coevolution The combined process that emerges from the interaction of biological and cultural evolution.

netic heritage or cultural tradition (Gladwin, 1970)? There are no general formulas for determining the relative contributions of culture and genes in shaping such human abilities.

The complex interactions between genetic heritage and the environment begin when genes in the zygote start to express themselves and guide the creation of new cells. Each new human being is a variant within the overall range of possibilities that defines *Homo sapiens*. Chapter 3 follows the course of gene–environment interaction from the moment the genetic material of the mother and father come together. In later chapters, as we follow the general patterns of the development of children, we will repeatedly see instances of gene–environment interaction, with culture always playing a mediating role.

A cinder track with standardized obstacles provides an excellent standard running surface, but it is only one of the many possible environments within which running abilities may develop. That fact needs to be kept in mind when one investigates the genetic contribution to running speed.

Summary

Sexual Reproduction and Genetic Transmission

- The particular set of genes each human being inherits comes from his or her parents. Sexual reproduction rearranges the genetic combination in each new individual. With the exception of identical twins, every person inherits a unique combination of genes, so that great diversity among people is guaranteed.

- Throughout the life cycle new body cells are created by mitosis, a copying process that replicates the genetic material inherited at birth.

- The germ cells (sperm and ova) that unite at conception are formed by meiosis, a process of cell division that maintains a constant total of 46 chromosomes in each new individual.
- The sexes differ genetically in the composition of one pair of chromosomes. In females, the two chromosomes that make up the twenty-third pair are both X chromosomes. Males have one X and one Y chromosome.
- The genes carried by the twenty-third pair of chromosomes give rise to sex-linked characteristics. Because females receive two X chromosomes, they get two doses of X-linked genes, one from each parent. Normal males receive only one X chromosome, and therefore only one dose of genes on the X chromosome, which always comes from the mother. Thus men are susceptible to genetic defects that usually do not affect females.

The Laws of Genetic Inheritance

- It is not possible to determine individuals' genetic constitutions (genotypes) from their visible characteristics (phenotypes) because some genes are dominant and others are recessive and because a genotype can result in a wide variety of phenotypes, depending on the environment in which it develops.

Genes, the Organism, and the Environment

- The overall relationship between genotype and phenotype can be established only by exposure of the genotype to a variety of environments. By charting the changes that occur in the phenotype as the environment is varied, geneticists can establish a range of reaction. Ideally, such a range specifies all possible phenotypes that are compatible with life for a single genotype.
- Some characteristics, such as language development in human beings, appear to be canalized; that is, they are restricted to a narrow range of variation and show a strong tendency to self-correction after the organism is exposed to deviant experiences.
- The ranges of reaction of most human characteristics have not been established because few humans have identical genotypes and because moral precepts and ethical standards make it impossible to carry out investigations that would expose people to all of the environments that are compatible with human life.
- As a substitute for experimental studies to establish the ranges of reaction of human traits, behavioral geneticists rely on family studies and adoption studies, which allow them to estimate the relative influences of the genotype and experience on the phenotype.
- Family and adoption studies with human children indicate that there are complex feedback mechanisms among the genotype, phenotype, and environment in the process of development.

Mutations and Genetic Abnormalities

- Mutation is the ultimate source of variability in living organisms. Some mutations are compatible with normal life. Often, however, the changes brought about by mutation result in death or disorders.
- Studies of mutations and genetic abnormalities are of interest to developmentalists both for what they reveal about the process of development in general and because of the need to devise preventive techniques and methods of therapy.

Biology and Culture

- Culture provides human beings with a mode of adaptation that other species do not have. Cultural evolution occurs when adaptations that arise in one generation are learned and modified by the next.
- Cultural and biological evolution of human beings have interacted with each other in a process called coevolution, which greatly complicates attempts to separate the influences of nature and nurture in development.

KEY TERMS

adoption study, p. 66

allele, p. 58

behavioral geneticist, p. 63

canalization, p. 62

chromosome, p. 53

codominance, p. 58

coevolution, p. 76

complementary genes, p. 60

crossing over, p. 55

dizygotic twins, p. 56

dominant allele, p. 58

environment, p. 61

family studies, p. 63

gene pool, p. 61

genes, p. 52

genotype, p. 59

germ cells, p. 53

heritability, p. 63

heterozygous, p. 58

homozygous, p. 58

masking gene, p. 60

meiosis, p. 55

mitosis, p. 53

modifier gene, p. 60

monozygotic twins, p. 56

mutation, p. 68

phenotype, p. 59

polygenic traits, p. 59

range of reaction, p. 62

recessive allele, p. 58

sex-linked characteristics, p. 60

somatic cells, p. 53

X chromosome, p. 56

Y chromosome, p. 56

zygote, p. 53

THOUGHT QUESTIONS

1. Can you think of a way in which the cultural values and preferences of your own ancestors may have influenced your genetic makeup?
2. Name a behavioral tendency that you believe you have inherited. In what ways do you think this trait has been affected by your environment? Has it affected the way you have experienced your environment?
3. Reread the description of girls born with Turner's syndrome. Why might these symptoms be of interest to researchers studying child development?
4. Describe your family briefly three times, from the points of view of three of its members. What are some ways in which the three "environments" you have described differ from one another?

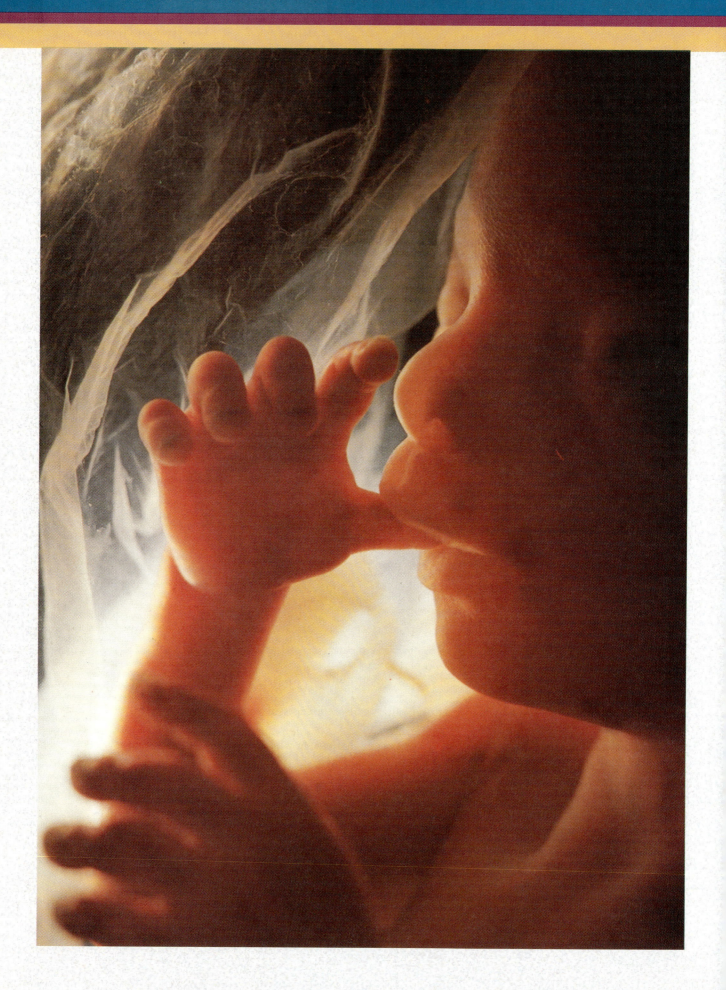

Prenatal Development and Birth

> "Every man is some months older than he bethinks him, for we live, move, have being, and are subject to the actions of the elements and the malice of disease, in that other world, the truest Microcosm, the womb of our mother."
>
> *Sir Thomas Browne,*
> Religio Medici *(1642)*

O f all our existence, the 9 months we live hidden from view inside our mother's womb are the most eventful for our growth and development. We begin as a zygote, a single cell 1/175 of an inch in diameter, about the size of a period on this page, weighing approximately fifteen-millionths of a gram. At birth we consist of some 2 billion cells and weigh, on the average, 3250 grams, or 7 pounds. The changes that occur in our form are no less remarkable than the increase in our size (see Figure 3.1). The first few cells to form from the zygote are all identical, but in a few weeks there will be many different kinds of cells arranged in intricately structured, interdependent organs. A basic task in the study of prenatal development is to explain how these changes in form and size take place.

Many developmental theorists look upon development during the prenatal period as a model for development during all subsequent periods, from birth to death. Indeed, many of the principles of developmental change are first seen in action during the prenatal period. For biological-maturational theorists such as Arnold Gesell (1945), all of development can be considered a process of *embryogenesis* (the technical name given to development that occurs before birth) in which the organism develops in a seemingly preordained manner, without significant shaping by its environment either in the womb or after birth.

Even psychologists who accord the environment a larger role in development may believe that the prenatal period provides a model for later development. Jean Piaget, who championed the view that development is a process of constructive interaction between the organism and the environment, claimed that understanding change in the prenatal period is a key to understanding development after birth. "Child psychology," he said, should be regarded as "the embryogenesis

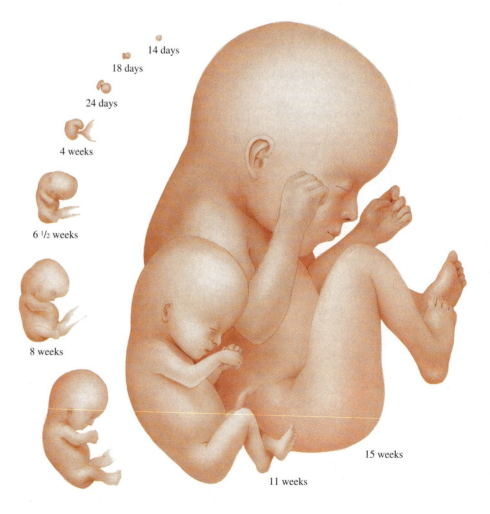

FIGURE 3.1 *Changes in the size and form of the human body from 14 days to 15 weeks after conception. (Adapted from Arey, 1974.)*

14 days

18 days

24 days

4 weeks

6 1/2 weeks

8 weeks

11 weeks

15 weeks

of organic as well as mental growth, up to the beginning of . . . the adult level" (Piaget & Inhelder, 1969, p. vii).

Understanding the prenatal period is important for practical as well as theoretical reasons. The developing organism can be adversely affected by the mother's nutritional status, health, drug and alcohol intake, emotions, and surrounding environment. Considerable research has been devoted to understanding how to prevent damage to the growing organism during this foundational period.

In order to understand the relation of prenatal development to later development, we first must look at the changes that take place as the organism progresses from zygote to newborn. Then we can look at how the developing organism can be adversely affected by the environment. Finally, we consider the circumstances surrounding the newborn's entrance into the world.

The Periods of Prenatal Development

Through a microscope, the fertilized ovum appears to be made up of small particles inside of larger ones. At the center of the cell, the chromosomes bearing the genes are contained within the nucleus. Surrounding the nucleus is the cell matter, which serves as the raw material for the first few cell divisions. The entire zygote is contained within the **zona pellucida,** a delicate envelope only a few molecules thick that forms its boundary.

No part of the zygote looks like a bone cell or a blood cell, let alone a newborn baby. Yet within the first few weeks after conception, this single cell will have subdivided many times to form many kinds of cells. In approximately 266 days it will have been transformed into a wriggling, crying infant. As a first step toward understanding this process, scientists often divide prenatal development into three broad periods, each characterized by distinctive patterns of growth and interaction between the organism and its environment.

1. The **germinal period** begins when the mother's and father's germ cells are joined at conception and lasts until the developing organism becomes attached to the wall of the uterus, about 8 to 10 days later.
2. The **period of the embryo** extends from the time the organism becomes attached to the uterus until the end of the eighth week, when all of the major organs have taken primitive shape.
3. The **period of the fetus** begins the ninth week after conception with the first signs of the hardening of the bones and continues until birth, an average of 30 weeks. During this period the primitive organ systems develop to the point where the baby can exist outside of the mother without medical support.

At any step in these prenatal periods, the process of development may stop. In an estimated 31 percent of cases, for example, the genetic material that comes together when a sperm and egg unite proves to be incompatible with life and the zygote fails to develop at all (Wilcox et al., 1988). If all goes well, however, the creation of a new human being is under way.

THE GERMINAL PERIOD

During the first 8 to 10 days after conception, the fertilized ovum moves slowly through the fallopian tube and into the uterus (see Figure 3.2). The timing of this journey is crucial. If the new organism enters the uterus too soon, the uterine environment will not be prepared and the organism will be destroyed. If it arrives too late, the proper conditions for attachment to the wall of the uterus will no longer be present, and the organism will pass out of the mother's body.

Zona pellucida The thin envelope that surrounds the zygote and later the morula.

Germinal period The period from conception to implantation.

Period of the embryo The period that begins when the organism becomes attached to the uterus and lasts until the end of the eighth week when the major organs have taken shape.

Period of the fetus The period from 9 weeks after conception until birth.

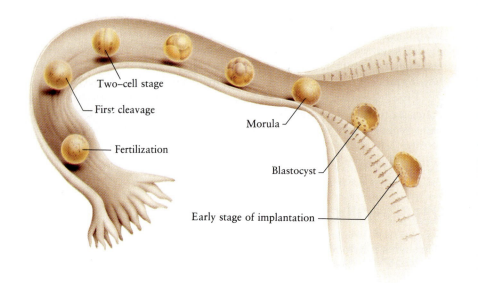

FIGURE 3.2 *Development of the human embryo in the mother's reproductive tract from fertilization to implantation. (Adapted from Tuchmann-Duplessis, David, & Haegel, 1971.)*

The first cells of life

Cleavage, the mitotic division of the zygote into several cells, begins about 24 hours after conception, as the fertilized ovum travels down the fallopian tube. (Mitosis is described in Chapter 2, p. 53.) The single-cell zygote divides to produce two daughter cells, each of which then divides to produce two more daughter cells, and so on (see Figure 3.3). Thanks to this periodic doubling, the developing organism will already consist of hundreds of cells by the time it reaches the uterus.

An important characteristic of cleavage is that the cells existing at any given moment do not divide simultaneously. Instead of proceeding in an orderly fashion from a two-cell stage to a four-cell stage and so on, the cells divide at different rates (Gilbert, 1991). This difference in the rates of change of different parts of the organism is called **heterochrony** (literally, "variability in time"). Because different parts of the organism change at different rates, the organism's behavior will be more or less mature depending on which of the organism's parts are most heavily involved. Thus the unevenness of development rates gives rise to another prominent feature of development, **heterogeneity,** or variability, in the *levels* of development of different parts of the organism. Both kinds of variability play an important role in the process of development throughout the life of the child.

FIGURE 3.3 *A zygote after two cleavages, resulting in four cells of equal size and appearance.*

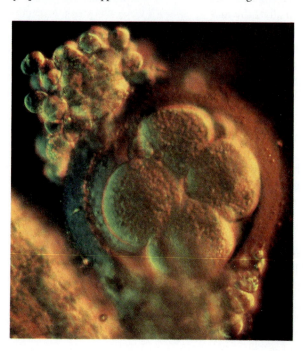

The emergence of new forms

As the first several cleavages occur, a cluster of cells called the **morula** takes shape inside the zona pellucida. For the first 4 or 5 days after conception, the cells in the morula become smaller and smaller with each cleavage until they are all approximately the size of the average body cell. Although the cells in each new "generation" have become smaller, they otherwise look identical to their parent cells and much like a large number of Ping-Pong balls crowded into a balloon.

At this point the cells begin to take in nutrients, their first interaction with the environment outside the zona pellucida.

If this interaction fails to occur, cleavage will cease and the organism will die. The first changes in the organism's internal form emerge simultaneously with these interactions between the organism (morula) and its environment (the fallopian tube).

The first noticeable change in form is the appearance of a fluid-filled cavity within the morula. Simultaneously two distinct kinds of cells can be distinguished for the first time (see Figure 3.4). This transformation of the morula into a **blastocyst** is the earliest instance of a repeating pattern in which development is manifested as a process of differentiation and reintegration. In this case, the identical cells of the morula are differentiated into two kinds of cells that are then reintegrated into the more mature form of the organism called the blastocyst.

The two kinds of cells in the blastocyst play different roles in development, corresponding to two kinds of interactions with the environment. Lumped along one side of the central cavity is a knot of small cells called the **inner cell mass.** This mass will give rise to the organism itself. Around the inner cell mass and the cavity, a double layer of large, flat cells called the **trophoblast** forms a protective barrier between the inner cell mass and the environment. Later the trophoblast will develop into the membranes that will protect the developing organism and transmit nutrients to it. (Appropriately, "trophoblast" is derived from the Greek *trophe*, "nourishment.") As the cells of the blastocyst differentiate, the zona pellucida surrounding it disintegrates. The trophoblast layer now serves as a kind of pump, filling the inner cavity with energy-giving fluid from the uterus, which enables the cells to continue to divide and the organism to grow.

Although it is easy enough to describe the transformation of the undifferentiated cells of the zygote, first into the two kinds of cells in the blastocyst and eventually into the multitudes of kinds of cells present at birth, the mechanisms by which it occurs remain the central puzzle of development. The explanation preferred by the leading scientists of the eighteenth century was that the very first cell created at conception contains minute organs—head, arms, legs, brain, liver, heart—already formed. According to this view, called **preformationism,** no new forms really develop; they are all there at the beginning.

Critics of the preformationists argued that a fertilized ovum does not look like a baby, so why claim that it "contains" the baby in a form that is simply too small to see? They preferred the idea that each new form emerges through the various kinds of interactions that take place between the preceding form and its environment, a process they called **epigenesis** (from a Greek expression meaning "at the time of generation"). This epigenetic explanation is now generally favored by embryologists, scientists whose specialty is early organic development (Gottlieb, 1992). The problem from the epigenetic view of development is to explain how various kinds of interactions account for, say, the emergence of the inner cell mass

Cleavage The initial mitotic divisions of the zygote into several cells.

Heterochrony The variability in the rates of change of different parts of the organism.

Heterogeneity The variability in the levels of development of different parts of the organism at a given time.

Morula The mass of cells that results from the cleavage of the zygote as it moves through the fallopian tube.

Blastocyst The hollow sphere of cells that results from the differentiation of the morula into the trophoblast and the inner cell mass.

Inner cell mass The knot of cells inside the blastocyst that becomes the embryo.

Trophoblast The outer cells of the blastocyst that develop into the membranes that support and protect the embryo.

Preformationism The hypothesis that the adult form is present in the cells out of which it develops.

Epigenesis The hypothesis that new forms emerge through the interactions between the preceding form and its environment.

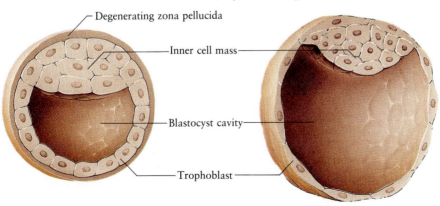

Degenerating zona pellucida

Inner cell mass

Blastocyst cavity

Trophoblast

Early blastocyst
(a)

Late blastocyst
(b)

FIGURE 3.4 *Two stages in the development of the blastocyst:* (a) *the formation of the inner cell mass in the early blastocyst stage, and* (b) *the differentiation of the trophoblast cells in the late blastocyst stage. By the late blastocyst stage, the zona pellucida has disappeared. (Adapted from Moore, 1982.)*

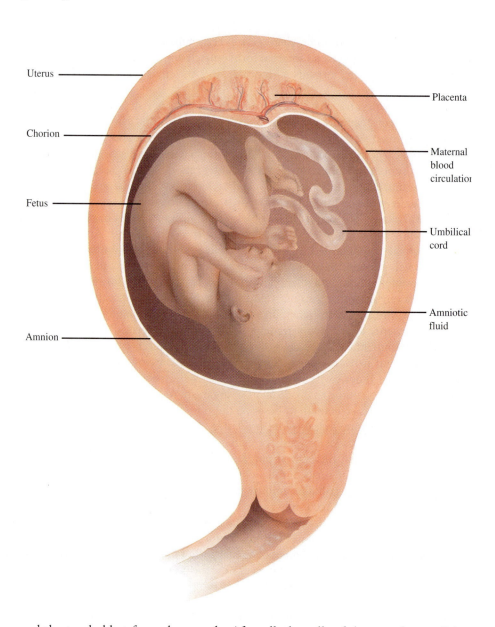

Uterus

Chorion

Fetus

Amnion

Placenta

Maternal blood circulation

Umbilical cord

Amniotic fluid

FIGURE 3.5 *The fetus in its protective environment. (Adapted from Curtis, 1979.)*

Implantation The process by which the blastocyst becomes attached to the uterus.

Amnion The membrane that holds the amniotic fluid surrounding the prenatal organism.

Chorion One of the membranes that develops out of the trophoblast. It forms the placenta.

and the trophoblast from the morula. After all, the cells of the morula are all inside the zona pellucida, which is inside the mother's reproductive tract. How can we say that one cell in the morula has a different kind of contact with the environment than any other cell does?

The answer is to think of "environment" as the immediate surroundings of each individual cell, rather than as the surroundings of the morula as a whole. The cells in the morula do not all have the same surroundings, just as children in the same family do not inhabit the same environment (see p. 67). The cells at the center of the morula are surrounded by other morula cells. Those on the outside have some contact with other morula cells, but on one side they are also in contact with the zona pellucida, which in turn is in contact with the mother's reproductive tract and its fluids.

These differences in location can have significant consequences. When the morula begins to take in nutrients, for example, those nutrients must pass through the cells on the outside to reach the cells on the inside. According to the epigenetic explanation, cell division under such different environmental conditions leads to the creation of different kinds of cells (Gilbert, 1991) and new forms of interaction between the organism and the environment. This pattern is repeated again and again in the course of an organism's development.

Scientists of the nineteenth and early twentieth centuries considered the old theory of preformation to have been little more than a mystical substitute for science. Currently, however, it is being remembered more favorably. As Stephen Jay Gould (1977a) points out, "the preformationists were . . . right in insisting that complexity cannot arise from formless raw material—that there must be something within the egg to regulate its development" (pp. 205–206). That something, however, is not a minuscule, preformed human being, as the early preformationists thought. Rather, what preexists in the zygote is now understood to be a set of coded instructions contained in the genes.

Implantation

As the blastocyst moves farther into the uterus, the trophoblast cells put out tiny branches that burrow into the spongy wall of the uterus until they come in contact with the mother's blood vessels. Thus begins **implantation,** the process by which the blastocyst becomes attached to the uterus. Implantation marks the transition between the germinal and embryonic periods. Like many of life's transitions (birth being an especially dramatic example), implantation is hazardous for the organism. The danger here arises because the blastocyst, being formed from the genes of *both* the father and the mother, differs genetically from the mother. If any other bit of alien tissue were introduced into a woman's uterus, it would be attacked by the mother's immune system. But for reasons not well understood, the blastocyst is usually not attacked, despite its genetic uniqueness (Scott & Branch, 1994).

THE EMBRYONIC PERIOD

If the blastocyst is successfully implanted, the developing organism enters the period of the embryo, which lasts for about 6 weeks. During this period, all of the basic organs of the body take shape, and the organism begins to respond to direct stimulation. Rapid growth is facilitated by the efficient way the mother now supplies nutrition.

Sources of nutrition and protection

The rapid growth of membranes from the trophoblast ensures that the requisites for the developing organism's survival—nutrients and protection from environmental trauma—are provided early in the embryonic period (see Figure 3.5). The **amnion,** a thin, tough, transparent membrane that holds the amniotic fluid ("bag of waters"), surrounds the embryo. The amniotic fluid protects the organism from hard surfaces and jolts as the mother moves about, provides liquid support for its weak muscles and soft bones, and gives it a medium in which it can move and change position.

Surrounding the amnion is another membrane, the **chorion,** which becomes the fetal component of the **placenta,** a complex organ made up of tissue from both the mother and the embryo. The placenta and the embryo are linked by the **umbilical cord.** Until birth, the placenta acts simultaneously as a barrier that prevents the bloodstreams of the mother and infant from coming into direct contact and as a filter that allows nutrients, oxygen, and waste products to be exchanged. It converts nutrients carried by the mother's blood into food for the embryo. It also enables the embryo's waste products to be absorbed by the mother's bloodstream, from which they are eventually extracted by her kidneys. Thus the mother literally eats, breathes, and urinates for two.

Placenta An organ made up of tissue from both the mother and the fetus that serves as a barrier and a filter between their bloodstreams.

Umbilical cord A soft tube containing blood vessels that connects the embryo to the placenta.

The human embryo at 3 weeks and 5 weeks after conception.

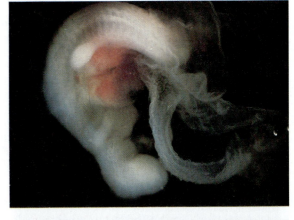

TABLE 3.1 Growth and Development of the Embryo

DAYS 10–13

Cells separate into ectoderm, endoderm, and mesoderm layers. The neural plate, which eventually will become the brain and the spinal cord, forms out of the ectoderm.

THIRD WEEK

The three major divisions of the brain—the hindbrain, the midbrain, and the forebrain—begin to differentiate by the end of the week. Primitive blood cells and blood vessels are present. The heart comes into being, and by the end of the week it is beating.

FOURTH WEEK

Limb buds are visible. Eyes, ears, and a digestive system begin to take form. The major veins and arteries are completed. Vertebrae are present, and nerves begin to take primitive form.

FIFTH WEEK

The umbilical cord takes shape. Bronchial buds, which eventually will become the lungs, take form. Premuscle masses are present in the head, trunk, and limbs. The hand plates are formed.

SIXTH WEEK

The head becomes dominant in size. The halves of the lower jawbone meet and fuse, and the components of the upper jaw are present. The external ear makes its appearance. The three main parts of the brain are distinct.

SEVENTH WEEK

The face and neck are beginning to take form. Eyelids take shape. The stomach is taking its final shape and position. Muscles are rapidly differentiating throughout the body and are assuming their final shapes and relationships. Neurons are developing at the rate of thousands per minute.

EIGHTH WEEK

The growth of the gut makes the body evenly round. The head is elevated and the neck is distinct. The external, middle, and inner ear assume their final forms. By the end of this week the fetus is capable of some movement and responds to stimulation around the mouth.

Ectoderm Cells of the inner cell mass that develop into the outer surface of the skin, the nails, part of the teeth, the lens of the eye, the inner ear, and the central nervous system.

Endoderm Cells of the inner cell mass that become the digestive system and the lungs.

Mesoderm Cells of the inner cell mass that become the muscles, the bones, the circulatory system, and the inner layers of the skin.

The growth of the embryo

While the trophoblast is forming the placenta and the other membranes that will supply and protect the embryo, the growing number of cells in the inner cell mass begin to differentiate into the various kinds of cells that eventually will become all the organs of the body. The first step in this process is the separation of the inner cell mass into two layers. The **ectoderm,** the outer layer, gives rise to the outer surface of the skin, the nails, part of the teeth, the lens of the eye, the inner ear, and the nervous system (the brain, the spinal cord, and the nerves). The **endoderm,** the inner layer, develops into the digestive system and the lungs. Shortly after these two layers form, a middle layer, the **mesoderm,** appears; eventually it becomes the muscles, the bones, the circulatory system, and the inner layers of the skin (Gilbert, 1991).

As Table 3.1 makes clear, the embryo develops at a breathtaking pace. The sequence in which the parts of the body form follows two patterns that are maintained until the organism reaches adolescence. In the first, the **cephalocaudal pattern,** development proceeds from the head down. The arm buds, for instance, appear before the leg buds. In the second, the **proximodistal pattern,** development proceeds from the middle of the organism out to the periphery. The spinal cord develops before the arm buds, the upper arm develops before the forearm, and so on. In general, the process of organ formation is the same for all human embryos, but in one major respect—sexual differentiation—it varies. This aspect of development is discussed in Box 3.1.

The emergence of embryonic movement

When the essential organ systems and the nerve cells of the spine have formed, the embryo becomes capable of its first organized responses to the environment. Studies of embryos as they were being removed from the womb during therapeutic abortions indicate that the 8-week-old embryo will turn its head and neck in response to a light touch to the area around the mouth. Its arms will quiver, the upper body will flex, and in many cases its mouth will open (de Vries, 1992). Within the womb, such movements are not detected by the mother because an 8-week-old embryo is still exceedingly small.

THE FETAL PERIOD

The fetal period begins once all the basic tissues and organs exist in rudimentary form and the tissue that will become the skeleton begins to harden, or ossify (Gilbert, 1991). During the fetal period, which lasts from the eighth or ninth week of pregnancy until birth, the fetus becomes 10 times larger and its proportions change dramatically (see Figure 3.6). Each of the organ systems increases in complexity, and the movements become more coordinated. The major events in fetal growth and development are detailed in Table 3.2.

Cephalocaudal pattern The sequence of body development from head to foot.

Proximodistal pattern The sequence of body development from the middle outward.

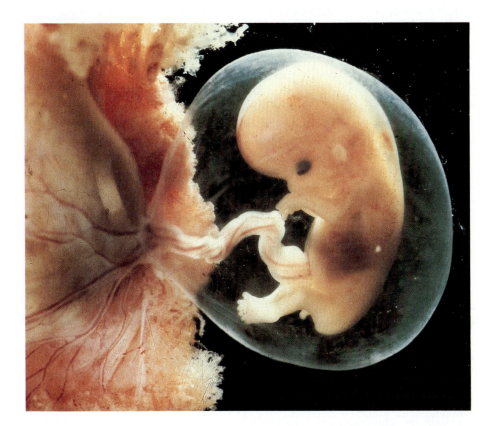

FIGURE 3.6 *The fetus at the beginning of the fetal period (approximately 9 weeks). The way the umbilical cord is attached to the placenta is clearly visible.*

BOX 3.1

The Development of Sexual Differentiation

Sexual differentiation provides a striking example of the ways in which nature and nurture interact over the course of an organism's development. At each stage of prenatal sexual development we find a new configuration of the parts that were present during the preceding stage and new mechanisms appear that will regulate sexual development in the next stage (Moore, 1982).

The genes that influence sexual determination are located on the X and Y chromosomes inherited at conception. Zygotes with one X and one Y chromosome are genetically male, whereas zygotes with two X chromosomes are genetically female. For the first 6 weeks after conception, however, there is no structural difference between genetically male and genetically female embryos. Both males and females have two ridges of tissue, called *gonadal ridges*, in the urogenital region. These give no clue to the sex of the embryo.

If the embryo is genetically male (XY), the process of sexual differentiation begins during the seventh week of life, when the gonadal ridges begin to form testes. If the embryo does not have a Y chromosome, no changes are apparent until several weeks later, when ovaries begin to form. Thus the genes inherited at the moment of conception determine whether the sex glands that develop from the gonadal ridges will be male testes or female ovaries. From this point on, though, it is not the presence of the Y chromosome itself but rather the presence or absence of male gonads that determines whether the embryo will develop male or female genital ducts. The male hormones produced by the male gonads, principally testosterone, determine maleness. Femaleness depends not on the secretion of hormones by the ovaries but on the absence of testosterone.

At the end of the seventh week after conception, genetically male and genetically female embryos have the same urogenital membrane and primitive phallus, the future penis or clitoris. If testosterone is present, the membranes are transformed into the male penis and scrotum. In its absence, the female external genitalia are formed. As many researchers have commented, it appears as though nature requires that something *be added* if the embryo is to become masculine (Halpern, 1986).

The influence of testosterone is not limited to the gonads and the genital tract. During the last 6 months of prenatal development, the presence of testosterone suppresses the natural rhythmic activity of the pituitary gland, located in the brain. If testosterone is absent, the pituitary gland establishes the cyclical pattern of hormone secretion that is characteristic of the female and eventually comes to control her menstrual cycle (Wilson, George, & Griffin, 1981).

Embryologists are still uncertain how the presence of testosterone creates differences in brain activity, but data from animal research suggest that it may shape the development of certain neural pathways in the brain (Toran-Allerand, 1984). These studies show that a dose of testosterone given to a rat at a critical period in the development of its brain will cause it to be responsive to male hormones and insensitive to female hormones from then on, no matter what its genetic sex. If the brain does not receive testosterone at this critical period, it will be responsive to female hormones.

Sensitivity to male rather than female hormones seems to have a striking effect on the organism's later behavior. After William Young and his colleagues (Young, Goy, & Phoenix, 1964) injected pregnant rhesus monkeys with testosterone, the female offspring they bore behaved more like young male monkeys: they threatened other monkeys, failed to withdraw when approached by other monkeys, and engaged in rough-and-tumble play. Their sexual behavior was also masculine in many respects.

During the prenatal period, the development of sexual differences is under strict biological control that is determined directly or indirectly by the genetic code. In later life, however, other factors come into play. Once the baby is born and the parents learn what kind of genitals it has, powerful social, cultural, and psychological factors begin to influence the child's sexual development through a long sequence of interactions between the child and the environments he or she encounters (MacLusky & Naftolin, 1981; Money & Ehrhardt, 1972).

Fetal activity

The increasing complexity of the organism during the fetal period is accompanied by changes in the level of its activity. The fetus begins to move its arms and head. At 10 weeks the fingers will close fleetingly when the palm is stimulated, and the toes will curl when the sole of the foot is touched. Over the next few weeks body

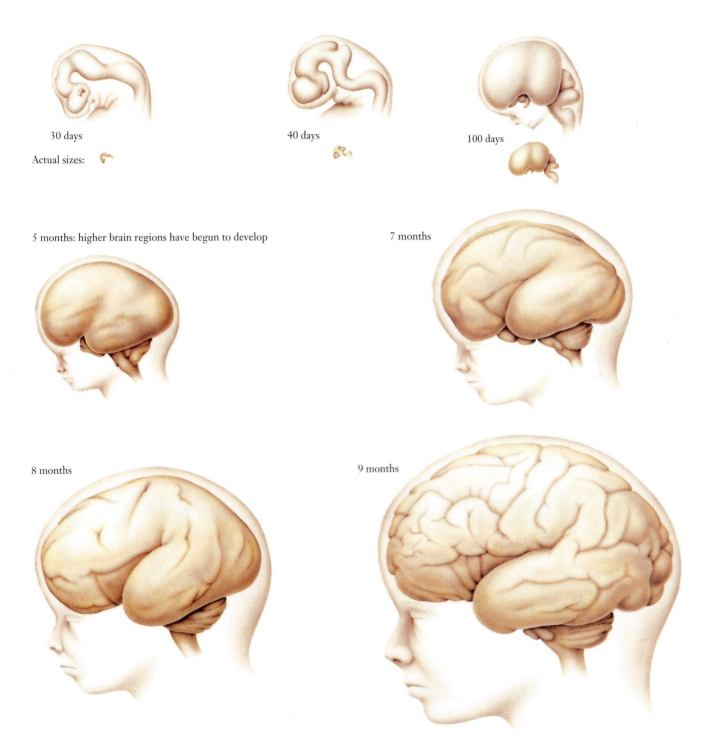

30 days

Actual sizes:

40 days

100 days

5 months: higher brain regions have begun to develop

7 months

8 months

9 months

movements become increasingly varied and smooth. Spontaneous jerks and thrusts of the limbs begin to be accompanied by slower squirming movements of the trunk. Toward the end of the fourth month the fetus is big enough so that the mother can feel its movements.

At 17 or 18 weeks after conception the fetus's activity declines markedly. This decline corresponds with the development of the higher regions of the brain (see Figure 3.7), which eventually makes more complex control of activity possible (Visser, 1992). As these brain regions mature, they begin to inhibit the primitive activity of the central nervous system characteristic of the less mature fetus. The thrusting and squirming movements of the fetus subside, and it becomes less

FIGURE 3.7 *The prenatal development of the brain. The primitive parts of the brain are present very early. The cerebral hemispheres, with their characteristic convolutions, do not make their appearance until the middle of pregnancy. (Adapted from Cowan, 1979.)*

TABLE 3.2 Growth and Development of the Fetus

TENTH WEEK

The head is erect. The intestines have assumed their characteristic position within the body. The spinal cord is a definite internal structure.

TWELFTH WEEK

Males and females are externally distinguishable. Blood begins to form in the bone marrow. The eyes take final form.

END OF MONTH 4

The fetus looks human. Hair begins to appear. The body has grown larger in relation to the head. The uterus and vagina are recognizable in females. In males, the testes are in position for later descent into the scrotum. Most of the bones are distinct, and the joints appear. The division between the two halves of the brain becomes visible. More reflexes become operational, including swallowing and sucking.

END OF MONTH 5

Brown fat, which will help the newborn stay warm, begins to form. New divisions differentiate within the brain. All of the nerve cells that the person will ever have are present. The sheathing of the nerve fibers begins, but it will not be completed until several years after birth.

END OF MONTH 6

The lungs begin to make surfactin, a chemical compound that prevents them from collapsing. The fissure between the two sides of the brain is very marked.

END OF MONTH 7

The lungs are capable of breathing air, and the central nervous system is sufficiently developed to direct rhythmic breathing movements. Considerable amounts of fat form, smoothing out the wrinkles in the skin. The eyes, which have been closed, open and can respond to light.

END OF MONTH 8

The fetus's skin is smooth, and the arms and legs have a chubby appearance. Many folds of the brain are present, although some will not form until after birth.

MONTH 9

The fetus becomes plumper, adding 50 percent of its weight in the last month. As birth approaches, growth slows. The brain becomes considerably more convoluted. Although the fetus has many reflexes and is active, there is no evidence that the cerebral cortex has any influence on behavior yet.

responsive to stimulation. This period of inhibited activity continues well into the sixth month, at which point the trend toward increasing fetal activity resumes.

As the time of birth draws near, the fetus becomes especially active, moving its limbs, changing its position, even sucking its finger (see the photograph on p. 80). In some cases, fetal activity appears to be *endogenous*; that is, it arises directly from the maturation of the organism's tissues. This is the case with the activity of the heart mentioned in Table 3.1. In other cases, it is clearly *exogenous*; that is, the activity arises in response to stimulation from the environment, as when the fetus makes a sudden movement in response to a loud sound.

Functions of fetal activity

Evidence discovered in recent decades indicates that fetal activity is important to development. Experiments with chick embryos, for example, suggest that their activity is crucial to normal limb development. Under normal circumstances, the spinal cord sends out many more neurons—nerve cells—to connect the limbs to the brain than the animal will need when it is fully coordinated. Many of these neurons die off, while the remainder are connected to muscles in an efficient way. If chick embryos are treated with drugs that prevent them from moving, however, the elimination of excess neurons that ordinarily accompanies neuromuscular development fails to occur. The results are disastrous. In as little as 1 or 2 days, the failure to prune away all but the neurons compatible with coordinated movement causes the joints of the chick embryos to become fixed into rigid structures, an indication that movement is necessary for proper articulation between the bones to develop (Provine, 1986).

Many uncertainties remain about the role of the organism's activity during the prenatal period. The data suggest fetal movement plays an important role in some species but not in all, and it has not been possible to gather direct evidence from species similar to *Homo sapiens* because such embryos are difficult or impossible to keep alive when their development is interfered with. It is clear, however, that the human fetus is both active and sensitive to its environment well before birth.

The Developing Organism in the Prenatal Environment

The marvelous ways in which the mother's body provides a protective and supportive environment for the growth of the human fetus can blind us to the realization that even in the womb the fetus is not independent of the larger world. Modern research makes it clear that the organism is affected not only by its immediate environment but by the world outside the womb as well.

The fetus can be influenced by its uterine environment in a variety of ways. The mother's digestive system and heart are sources of noise, and her movements provide motion stimuli. The fetus comes in contact with the world outside the mother through the wall of her abdomen and also, less directly, through the placenta and umbilical cord. Nutrients, oxygen, some viruses, and some potentially harmful chemicals all cross the placenta to the fetus. Through these biologically mediated routes a mother's experiences, emotions, illnesses, diet, and social circumstances can affect the child before it is born (Nijhuis, 1992).

Understanding the effect of the larger environment on the developing fetus is important for several reasons. First, substances and stimulation coming from the environment may have a significant impact on fetal development. Second, the fetus's responses to the environment provide clues about the behavioral capacities that the child will have at birth. Third, when the impact of the environment is detrimental to development, it is important for prospective parents to understand the dangers so that they can take preventive action.

THE FETUS'S SENSORY CAPACITIES

Using modern techniques of measurement and recording, researchers have begun to produce a detailed picture of the development of the human fetus's sensory capacities. This information is essential for determining how the fetus is influenced by its environment.

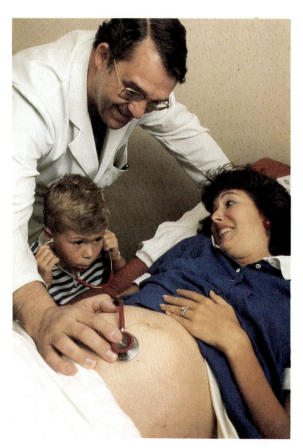

The idea that a baby is growing inside the mother becomes much less abstract when you listen to its heartbeat.

Motion

The vestibular system of the middle ear, which controls the sense of balance, begins to function in the human fetus about 5 months after conception and is fully mature at birth (Hepper, 1992). This early maturity means that the fetus is capable of sensing changes in the mother's posture as it floats inside the fluid-filled amniotic sac.

Vision

Little is known for certain about the extent of the fetus's visual experience. At 26 weeks of pregnancy, fetuses respond to light; it causes their heart rate to change and it causes them to move (Hepper, 1992). Aidan Macfarlane (1977) suggests that toward the end of pregnancy, the fetus may be able to see light that has penetrated the mother's stretched stomach wall. He likens the fetus's visual experience to the glow seen when the palm of the hand covers a flashlight.

Sound

Recent evidence indicates that at 4 months after conception the fetus is able to respond to sound (Hepper, 1992). Studies in which tiny microphones have been inserted into the uterus adjacent to the fetus's head reveal that the average sound level is approximately 75 decibels, about the level we experience when we ride in a car. This background noise is punctuated by the sound of air passing through the mother's stomach and, every second or so, by the more intense sound of the mother's heartbeat (Birnholz & Benacerraf, 1983). For many years it was believed that these sounds were so loud they would mask most noise coming from outside the mother's body. More recently, however, it has been found that fetuses do hear sounds coming from outside of the mother's body (Querleu et al., 1988).

Of all such sounds, the mother's voice is heard best because it is also transmitted as vibrations through her body. When the mother speaks brief sentences aloud, it is possible to detect changes in the fetus's heart rate (Lecanuet et al., 1992). Because external sounds must pass through the mother's abdomen and the amniotic fluid before the fetus can hear them, things sound different than they do outside the womb. At birth, babies prefer the sound of their mother's voice when it has been filtered to resemble how it sounded to them while they were in the womb (Fifer & Moon, 1995).

FETAL LEARNING

The folklore of many societies includes the belief that a pregnant woman's experiences have a significant effect on her child's postnatal development: whatever the mother desires, fears, or admires, the fetus and then the child will come to desire, fear, or admire (Verny & Kelly, 1981). Although such beliefs have met with considerable skepticism during the twentieth century (Carmichael, 1970), there is evidence that the fetus learns from at least some events both inside and outside the mother (Hepper, 1992).

One line of evidence for fetal learning comes from an unusual experiment by Lee Salk (1973). Working in a hospital where mothers and their newborn infants were customarily separated a good deal of the time, Salk arranged for three groups of infants to experience three different experimental conditions. One group was exposed to the sound of a normal heartbeat of 80 pulses per minute, the rate they would have heard while in the womb; another group heard a heart beating 120 times per minute; and a third group heard no special sounds at all. The infants who heard the accelerated heartbeat became so upset that Salk terminated their part in the experiment. The babies who heard the normal heartbeat, however, gained more weight and cried less over the 4 days that the experiment continued than did the group that heard no special sounds. The specific influence of the sound of the normal heartbeat suggests that the infants' experience in the womb had made this sound familiar and therefore reassuring. That newborns found the sound of the mother's heartbeat rewarding was later confirmed by Anthony De-Casper and A. D. Sigafoos (1983).

Salk's experiment suggests that fetuses learn from experiences that originate *inside* the mother. Evidence of similar learning from stimuli originating *outside* the mother comes from a study by Anthony DeCasper and Melanie Spence (1986). These researchers asked 16 pregnant women to read aloud a particular passage from *The Cat in the Hat*, a well-known rhyming children's story by Dr. Seuss, twice a day for the last month and a half before their babies were due. By the time the babies were born, the passage had been read to them for a total of about 3½ hours.

Two or three days after the babies were born, DeCasper and Spence tested them with a special pacifier that had been wired to record sucking rates (see Figure 3.8). First the baby was allowed to suck for 2 minutes to establish a baseline sucking rate. Afterward, changes in the rate of sucking turned a tape recording of their mothers reading a story on or off. For half of the babies, increased sucking rates turned on the passage from *The Cat in the Hat* that their mothers had previously read aloud, while decreasing their sucking rate turned on a story their mothers had not read. For the other half, increased sucking turned on the new story while decreased sucking produced *The Cat in the Hat*. The key finding was that the infants modified their rate of sucking in the direction that produced *The Cat in the Hat*. The investigators concluded that the babies had indeed heard the stories being read to them by their mothers and that their learning in the womb influenced the sounds they found rewarding after birth.

Recently DeCasper and his colleagues (1994) confirmed this conclusion by testing 17 pregnant women living in Paris. First they asked the women to read aloud a French children's rhyme called "La Poulette" ("The Chicken") three times a day for a month beginning 6 weeks before their babies were due. Four weeks later they brought the women to their laboratory and played tape recordings of "La Poulette" and an unfamiliar story over a speaker just above the women's stomachs. The researchers found that the fetuses' heart rates decreased when "La Poulette" was presented (a sign of attention in infants), but the new story produced no change in heartbeat. This evidence is not sufficient to support the claim that prenatal learning has a major impact on later development. Nevertheless, the evidence that some kinds of learning occur in the womb has led some psychologists to promote intensive programs for stimulating the fetus (Walmsley & Margolis, 1987).

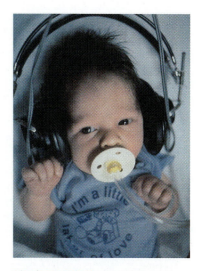

FIGURE 3.8 *This baby is listening to a recording of its mother reading a story. The apparatus permits recordings of changes in sucking to determine if newborns will react to stories read to them while they were in the womb.*

MATERNAL CONDITIONS AND PRENATAL DEVELOPMENT

In addition to stimuli that impinge directly on its senses, the fetus is affected by biochemical changes in the mother. Her body chemistry may be altered by factors as diverse as her attitude toward having the baby, her emotional state, the food she eats, and her general health. Many of these changes are transmitted to the fetus through the placenta.

BOX 3.2

Fathers and Pregnancy

"Pregnancy is a family affair," notes the psychologist Ross Parke (1981, p. 13). Although it is the mother who undergoes the most profound physical and mental changes as the new organism grows inside her body, fathers can play a significant role during pregnancy. In light of research indicating that maternal stress can have negative effects on prenatal development, special attention has been focused on ways the father can help create favorable conditions for the mother and the baby-to-be.

Several factors that commonly cause stress during pregnancy involve the father directly or indirectly. Among them are financial concerns, marital problems, and conception out of wedlock (Blomberg, 1980; Mowbray, Lanir, & Hulce, 1982). A father who denies paternity or refuses to support the mother greatly increases her burden; a father who is mature, flexible, supportive, and loving can greatly reduce her stress.

Harold Rausch and his colleagues (1974) report that many men try to react positively to their pregnant wives' need for emotional as well as financial support. The researchers observed how expectant couples settled minor disputes, such as deciding what television program to watch. They had seen some of these couples before the women became pregnant, so they were able to identify ways in which the pregnancy affected their interactions. In general, the expectant fathers were more conciliatory than before. Many men showed an increased interest in babies and parenting, taking childbirth and child-care classes with their wives and reading books about pregnancy and child rearing. Some took extra jobs to meet the increased financial obligations that come with having a child.

An important way in which the father can reduce both family tension and the mother's work load is to take a larger role in the care of the couple's other children. Many years ago, the psychologist Alfred Baldwin (1947) observed that when women who already have children become pregnant, they tend to spend less time with their children and behave less warmly toward them. The father's help with older children not only makes life more pleasant for the mother but also sets up a pattern of family interaction that improves the way the older children will react to their new sibling after it is born (Legg, Sherick, & Wadland, 1974).

In some preindustrial cultures, men mark the transition to fatherhood with special rituals called *couvade*, which are intended variously to deflect evil spirits that might harm the mother and baby and to establish paternity (Parke, 1981). As soon as a husband hears that his wife is in labor, he takes to his bed and simulates the pain of giving birth. During the last century it was reported that when a woman of the Erickala-Vandu, a tribe in southern India, went into labor,

The effects of maternal attitudes and psychological stress

Many physicians who care for pregnant women and newborn infants suspect that a woman's feelings of well-being and her attitude toward her pregnancy affect the well-being of the fetus she is carrying and the child after its birth. A sympathetic mate (see Box 3.2) and other supportive family members, adequate housing, and steady employment—factors that give a woman a basic sense of security—all appear to enhance the prospects for a healthy baby (Pritchard & MacDonald, 1980; Thompson, 1990).

An extensive investigation conducted in Czechoslovakia in the 1960s and 1970s provides the clearest evidence that negative attitudes can adversely affect prenatal development. Henry David (1981) followed up the lives of 220 children whose mothers indicated strong negative attitudes toward having them by twice asking for abortions to end the pregnancy. The refusal of the abortion was an indication that medical authorities believed these women to be capable of carrying through the pregnancy and raising the child.

The children were carefully matched with a control group of children whose mothers either planned for or accepted their pregnancies. The mothers in the two groups were matched for socioeconomic status and age; the children were

she informs her husband, who immediately takes some of her clothes, puts them on, places on his forehead the mark the women usually place on theirs, retires into a dark room where there is only a dim lamp, and lies down on the bed, covering himself with a long cloth. When the child is born, it is washed and placed on a cot beside the father. (Cain, 1874, quoted in Parke, 1992, p. 20)

Though expectant fathers in modern industrialized societies do not practice such formalized rituals as couvade, an estimated 15 to 20 percent experience what the British psychiatrist W. H. Trethowan and his colleague M. G. Conlon call the *couvade syndrome*: a set of physical symptoms that mimic some of the initial symptoms of pregnancy, including fatigue, backache, headache, loss of appetite, nausea, and vomiting (Trethowan & Conlon, 1965; Liebenberg, 1967). These physical symptoms are often accompanied by such psychological problems as depression, tension, insomnia, and irritability. All the symptoms disappear almost immediately after the mother gives birth.

Data collected by S. J. Bittman and S. R. Zalk (1978) show how difficult it can be for expectant couples to deal with pregnancy and the new responsibilities of parenthood. As a case in point, they describe Mr. A., a 28-year-old factory worker. Though Mr. A. described his wife's pregnancy of 7 months as "model," he admitted that he himself had been experiencing a great deal of physical discomfort from nausea, vomiting, alternating diarrhea and constipation, head and back pains, and leg cramps. In the course of the interview, he revealed that his wife felt that their apartment was too small for three people but was also concerned about the financial burden of a larger one. Worried about his ability to provide for the baby, Mr. A. was working overtime at a factory job he hated. Now he did not get home until after ten o'clock at night, and then his wife was usually exhausted and often asleep. Although his wife understood that the overtime would help pay for the baby furniture she wanted, she was unhappy about being left alone so long. She complained bitterly, accused Mr. A. of not loving her, and turned away from his embraces. According to Bittman and Zalk, Mr. A. may be an extreme case, especially with regard to the physical symptoms he suffered, but his worries about his ability to provide for his child and the conflicts and stresses he and his wife faced in adjusting to their impending parenthood are not at all unusual.

matched for sex, birth order, number of siblings, and date of birth. The unwanted children weighed less at birth and needed more medical help than the control group, even though their mothers had ready access to medical care and were judged to be in good health themselves. Fewer of the unwanted children were breast-fed, they had more difficulties in school, and they were referred for psychiatric help more often as teenagers.

More recently David and his colleagues (1988) compared wanted and unwanted children in several European countries. They found that children who had not been wanted are at increased risk for a variety of social and psychological dysfunctions into adulthood. They are more likely to be in jail, to abuse drugs or alcohol, and to find their own social relations unsatisfactory.

A moderate amount of stress can be expected to accompany any major life transition, even one that is welcomed (Holmes & Holmes, 1969). The expectant mother has to adjust her life to accommodate new responsibilities. One who decides to quit her job may have to cope with a reduced income. Another may be working so hard that she feels she does not have enough time to take care of herself, let alone her expected child. And if the pregnancy was unplanned, as many are, the stress that normally accompanies pregnancy may be magnified.

Studies have shown that a mother who is under stress or becomes emotionally upset secretes hormones, such as adrenaline and cortisone, that pass through the placenta and have a measurable effect on the fetus's motor activity (Van Den Bergh, 1992). When a woman is under extreme stress for a significant amount of time during her pregnancy, she is at increased risk for such complications as miscarriage, long and painful labor, and premature delivery (Blomberg, 1980; Sameroff & Chandler, 1975). She is also more likely to give birth to a child who is irritable and hyperactive and who has eating, sleeping, and digestive problems (Friedman & Sigman, 1980; Van Den Bergh, 1992).

In the relatively favored circumstances of middle-class life in industrialized countries, many women may experience little stress during pregnancy; but most of the world's women are poor, live in difficult circumstances, and must worry about how to provide for their child before and after its birth. Even with a sympathetic mate or relatives to ease the burden, stress seems unavoidable under such conditions and is indeed very much a part of a pattern of environmental circumstances that puts many women and their unborn children at risk.

Nutritional influences on prenatal development

Fetuses are totally dependent on their mothers for the nutrients that keep them alive and allow them to develop. Research indicates that a pregnant woman needs to consume between 2000 and 2800 calories daily in a well-balanced diet that includes all the essential vitamins and minerals (National Academy of Sciences, 1989). The importance of good maternal nutrition to normal prenatal development may seem obvious, but it is often difficult to demonstrate conclusively because maternal malnourishment is closely associated with a host of other factors that can also harm the fetus, such as poor maternal health (Worthington-Roberts & Klerman, 1990).

Extreme Malnutrition   The clearest evidence that insufficient maternal nutrition has a detrimental effect on fetal development comes from studies of sudden periods of famine. During the fall and winter of 1944–1945, for example, famine struck the large cities of western Holland when the Nazi occupation forces embargoed all food shipments because Dutch railway workers had gone on strike to aid the advancing Allied armies. During and after the famine, spontaneous abortions, stillbirths, malformations, and deaths at birth increased markedly. Those babies who were born alive weighed significantly less than normal, as Figure 3.9 indicates (Stein et al., 1975).

A more severe wartime famine occurred in the Soviet Union. In September 1941 Leningrad (now St. Petersburg) was encircled by the German army, and no supplies reached the city until February 1942. The standard daily food ration in late November 1941 was 250 grams (8.75 ounces) of bread for factory workers, 125 grams (two slices) for everybody else. The bread was 25 percent sawdust. The number of infants born in the first half of 1942 was much lower than normal, and stillbirths doubled. Very few infants were born in the second half of 1942, all of them to couples who had better access to food than the rest of the population did. These babies were, on the average, more than a pound lighter than babies born before the siege, and they were much more likely to be premature. They were also in very poor condition at birth; they had little vitality and were unable to maintain their body temperature adequately (Antonov, 1947).

The sudden famine in Leningrad produced nutritional variations so extreme that normal environmental influences on prenatal development were dwarfed by comparison. Con-

FIGURE 3.9 *Mean birth weights of children born and children conceived in Rotterdam, Holland, during a period of severe famine and in other parts of the country where conditions were less severe. (Adapted from Stein et al., 1975.)*

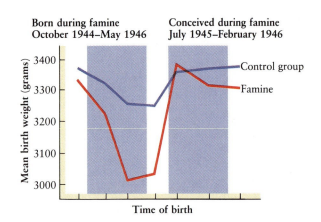

sequently, the specific effects of maternal malnutrition on the developing fetus during particular segments of the prenatal period could be isolated with a high degree of certainty. Severe nutritional deprivation during the first 3 months of pregnancy was most likely to result in abnormalities of the central nervous system, premature birth, and death. Deprivation during the last 3 months of pregnancy was more likely to retard fetal growth and result in low birth weight.

Undernourishment and Associated Factors   Studies of the relation between maternal nutrition, prenatal development, and neonatal health suggest that lesser degrees of malnourishment also increase risks to the fetus. It is difficult to single out the effects of poor nutrition, however, because malnourished mothers frequently live in impoverished environments where housing, sanitation, education, and medical care are also inadequate (Rosso, 1990; Worthington-Roberts & Klerman, 1990). (Table 3.3 shows just how important prenatal care can be for low-income mothers and their children.) Expectant mothers with low incomes are more likely to suffer from diseases or simply to be in a weakened state than women who live in more materially comfortable circumstances. Their babies are more likely to suffer from a wide variety of birth defects and illnesses and to be born prematurely (Luke, Johnson, & Petrie, 1993). Low-income mothers are also more likely to have babies who die at birth or soon after birth, according to a variety of studies conducted in many parts of the world, including the United States (Dott, Fort, & Arthur, 1975a, 1975b; Luke, Johnson, & Petrie, 1993).

Not all undernourishment can be attributed to the unavailability of food. Research in both industrial and nonindustrial societies demonstrates that cultural factors also play an important role in determining what foods expectant mothers eat. The Siriono of South America, for example, believe that the characteristics of any animal a woman eats while she is pregnant will be transferred to her unborn

TABLE 3.3	**Birth Complications for Low-Income Women in San Diego, California, Who Did and Did Not Receive Prenatal Medical Care (per 100 births)**	
Complication	**Women Who Received No Prenatal Care**	**Women Who Received Prenatal Care**
Premature rupture of membranes	13	2
Ominous fetal heart rate	10	5
Prematurity	13	2
Low birth weight (less than 2500 grams)	21	6
Low Apgar score (a measure of immediate risk)	8	2
Hospital stay of more than 3 days	24	12
Prenatal death	4	1

Source: Moore et al., 1986.

child. Pregnant women are therefore not allowed to eat the meat of the owl monkey because their children might develop a tendency to stay awake at night. Jaguar meat is also forbidden for fear that the child will be "quietly born" (stillborn).

In the United States, food choices vary even among people of the same social class. One study of the health of babies born to low-income rural women classified as having either "fair to good" or "poor to very poor" dietary habits found that expectant mothers who ate more nutritious food had markedly healthier babies (Jeans, Smith, & Stearns, 1955).

The possibility of preventing or at least reducing the damaging effects of malnutrition and an impoverished environment has been demonstrated by several studies. In the basic design of this type of research, expectant mothers and their offspring who receive supplemental food and medical attention are compared with those who do not. One of the largest intervention programs, designed to assess the effects of a massive supplemental food program for women, infants, and children—dubbed WIC—was initiated by the U.S. government in 1972 (Kotelchuck et al., 1984). Low-income women in the program were given vouchers for such staples as milk, eggs, fruit juices, and dried beans. The infants had significantly fewer health problems than infants born to a comparable group of women who were not in the program (Worthington-Roberts & Klerman, 1990).

A study that focused on 280 infants in Colombia supports the conclusion that food supplements started in mid-pregnancy and continued for 3½ years enhance the development of children in regions where malnourishment is prevalent (Super, Herrera, & Mora, 1990). When they were assessed at the age of 3, children who received food supplements were found to be somewhat taller and heavier than a group of children who had received no supplementary food. When food supplements were combined with a home-visiting program designed to help families stimulate their children's development, the gains were still evident 3 years after the program had ended.

Several studies indicate that maternal nutrition is important to the intellectual development as well as the physical health of the child (Kopp, 1983; Pollitt, 1994). Ernesto Pollitt and his colleagues (1993) have reported on a long-term study of the effects of nutritional supplements on the development of rural Guatemalan children. A nutritional supplement high in protein was given to mothers in one village beginning late in pregnancy and then to their infants for the first 2 years of life. When the intellectual performance of these children was compared with that of children in a nearby village who had received only a vitamin supplement, the children who received the protein supplement were found to perform at a higher level. These beneficial effects were still evident when the children became adolescents.

In a study of children whose mothers had participated in the WIC program in Louisiana, marked differences in the intellectual development of the children were found to depend on *when* their mothers began to receive food supplements (Hicks, Langham, & Takenaka, 1982). The children were evaluated on a variety of intellectual measures when they were 6 or 7 years old and were already enrolled in school. Those children whose mothers had received food supplements during the last 3 months of their pregnancies—the period when the fetal brain undergoes especially rapid development—outperformed the children of mothers who did not receive food supplements until after their children were born.

As important as adequate maternal nutrition is to the growth of the fetus, the long-term effects of prenatal malnutrition are also heavily influenced by the adequacy of the child's diet and environmental circumstances after birth. The most devastating consequences befall children who are both prenatally malnourished in the womb and inadequately nourished and cared for after they are born (Cravioto, De Licardie, & Birch, 1966). Such children are subject to continued health problems as well as deficits in intellectual functioning. However, when food supplements are combined with a program to teach parents how to interact effectively

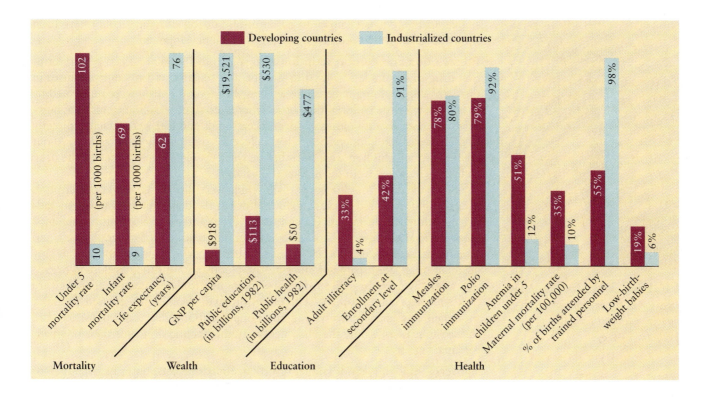

FIGURE 3.10 *In many countries of the world, poor economic conditions create a set of risk factors. For example, poor health conditions and lack of parents' education negatively influence child health and welfare. (Adapted from United Nations Children's Fund [UNICEF], 1995.)*

with their children, the negative effects of early malnutrition are significantly reduced (Grantham-McGregor et al., 1994).

Children who are born malnourished are typically apathetic, unresponsive, and irritable (Zeskind & Ramey, 1981). The negative consequences of this pattern of behavior are seen in a study that found that chronically undernourished toddlers in Santiago, Chile, were less likely to demonstrate a secure emotional attachment to their mothers than children whose weight was within the normal range for their age (Valenzuela, 1990). Apathy and irritability make babies difficult to interact with, a situation that can only intensify their problems.

These findings must be considered with some caution, because they are not always based on carefully controlled studies, but overall the evidence strongly suggests the damage that is done to millions of children throughout the world who are undernourished both before and after birth. Most of these children do not receive food supplements, and even fewer receive high-quality educational help. Quite the opposite. Instead, they experience a cascade of risk factors, of which malnutrition is only one (see Figure 3.10). Together such conditions lead to high rates of infant mortality and shorter life expectancies (Pollitt et al., 1993).

TERATOGENS: ENVIRONMENTAL SOURCES OF BIRTH DEFECTS

Other threats to the prenatal organism come from **teratogens**—environmental agents that can cause deviations in normal development and can lead to serious abnormalities or death (see Figure 3.11). (The term comes from the Greek *teras*, "monster.") Commonly encountered teratogens include certain drugs and infections, radiation, and pollution.

Teratogens Environmental agents that cause deviations in normal development and lead to serious abnormalities or death.

Drugs

As many as 60 percent of pregnant women in the United States take some medications during their pregnancy, primarily over-the-counter analgesics, antinauseants, and sleep medications (Schnoll, 1986). Some of the drugs they take are not generally thought of as drugs—caffeine, alcohol, the chemical substances in cigarette

FIGURE 3.11 *The devastating effects of agent orange, an environmental pollutant used during the Vietnam War.*

smoke. Caffeine is not known to be harmful, but tobacco and alcohol have been shown to have a variety of adverse effects on fetal development.

Prescription and Nonprescription Drugs   From 1956 until 1961, the prescription drug thalidomide was used in Europe as a sedative and to control nausea in the early stages of pregnancy. The women who took the drug were unharmed by it, and many of the children they bore suffered no ill effects. Some children, however, were born without arms and legs; their hands and feet were attached directly to their torsos like flippers. Some had defects of sight and hearing as well. About 8000 deformed children were born before their problems were traced to the drug and it was removed from the market (Persaud, 1977).

Since the disastrous effects of thalidomide were discovered, other prescription drugs have been found to cause abnormalities in the developing organism, including the antibiotics streptomycin and tetracycline, anticoagulants, anticonvulsants, most artificial hormones, Thorazine (used in the treatment of schizophrenia), and Valium (a tranquilizer). In large doses aspirin can also cause abnormalities. Indeed, all drugs are capable of entering the bloodstream of the developing organism, and only a few have been studied well enough to determine whether they are "safe" for expectant mothers. Therefore, pregnant women are advised to check with their physician before taking any nonprescription drug, and physicians are advised to prescribe only the most necessary therapeutic drugs for their pregnant patients.

Tobacco   Smoking is not known to produce birth defects, but a British study of 150,000 births found the rates of stillbirth and death at birth to be 28 percent higher among the children of mothers who smoked than among those of non-smokers (Bolton, 1983). Smoking is also associated with lower birth weight (see Table 3.4). This effect appears to be specific to smoking during pregnancy because the children of mothers who smoked during pregnancy were smaller than those born to the same women after they had abstained from smoking (Bolton, 1983). There is also a positive association between smoking and sudden infant death syndrome—a syndrome in which a seemingly healthy young infant stops breathing for no apparent reason. Both maternal smoking during pregnancy and smoking after pregnancy may play a role in increasing the risk of sudden infant death (Niebyl, 1994).

Alcohol   Alcohol is the most commonly abused drug. About 2 percent of all U.S. women of childbearing age suffer from alcoholism (Simpson & Golbus, 1992). In one study, 71 percent of the infants who were born to mothers who were heavy drinkers during pregnancy—that is, who ingested 3 ounces or more of 100-proof liquor a day—were abnormal in some way (Niebyl, 1994). Many suffered from **fetal alcohol syndrome,** a set of symptoms that includes an abnormally small head and underdeveloped brain, eye abnormalities, congenital heart disease, joint anomalies, and malformations of the face (see Figure 3.12). The physical growth and mental development of children with this syndrome are likely to be retarded throughout childhood (Jacobson et al., 1993; Niebyl, 1994). Women who drink heavily during the first trimester of pregnancy and then reduce their consumption of alcohol during the second and third trimesters do not reduce the risk of having children with this affliction (Vorhees & Mollnow, 1987).

The effects of lower levels of alcohol consumption on development are currently in dispute. Some research indicates that even moderate consumption affects prenatal development adversely. Other studies, however, have found no difference

TABLE 3.4	Mean Birth Weight (in grams) of Babies Born at Various Gestations to Smokers and Nonsmokers		
Maturity		**Cigarettes per Day**	
(weeks)	**Nonsmokers**	**1–20**	**Over 20**
31	2624	2415	1887
34	2798	2615	2488
37	3007	2848	2816
40	3341	3189	3188
43	3438	3274	3346

Source: Naeye, 1978.

between the babies of women who abstained from alcohol and those who had one or more drinks a day (Richardson, Day, & Taylor, 1989). Given the potential risks, health professionals advise women to stop drinking before they become pregnant.

Cocaine   Cocaine is an addictive stimulant that, in the concentrated form known as crack, became the drug of choice of many addicts in the late 1980s and is still in wide use today (Jones & Lopez, 1990). Cocaine rapidly produces addiction in the mother, and it is widely believed that when cocaine passes through the placenta it has a variety of destructive effects on the fetus, including spontaneous abortion, deficient growth, strokes, and birth defects (Niebyl, 1994). Babies born to cocaine-addicted mothers are described as being irritable, liable to react excessively to stimulation, uncoordinated, and slow learners (Alessandri et al., 1993).

Despite the justified concern about cocaine addiction, some researchers have been critical of claims that cocaine itself is the cause of these problems (Coles, 1993). These critics note that many studies fail to obtain evidence of long-term effects of maternal addiction. They point out that mothers who use cocaine also drink alcohol and use other drugs. Many are poor and live in stressful circumstances. All of these factors are known to contribute to symptoms such as those attributed to cocaine (Lester & Tronick, 1994; Richardson, Day, & McGauhey, 1993).

Methadone and Heroin   Babies of mothers who are addicted to either heroin or methadone are born addicted themselves and must be given heroin or methadone shortly after birth if they are not to undergo the often life-threatening ordeal of withdrawal. These babies are more likely to be premature, underweight, and vulnerable to respiratory illnesses. They are twice as likely to die soon after birth as are babies of nonaddicted mothers of the same socioeconomic class (Bolton, 1983).

While these babies are being weaned from the drugs to which they were born addicted, they are irritable and have tremors, their cries are abnormal, their sleep is disturbed, and their motor control is diminished. The effects of the addiction are still apparent in their motor control 4 months later. Even after a year their ability to pay attention is impaired (Jones & Lopez, 1990).

Infections and other conditions

A variety of infection-causing microorganisms can endanger the embryo, the fetus, and the newborn. Most infections spread from the mother to the unborn child across the placental barrier. In a few instances, however, the baby may become infected during the passage through the birth canal. Some of the more common infections and other maternal conditions that may affect the developing human organism are summarized below; Table 3.5 summarizes others.

Rubella   In 1941 Dr. N. M. Gregg, an Australian, noticed a sudden increase in the number of infants who were born blind. He interviewed their mothers and found that many of them recalled having had a mild rash, swollen lymph glands, and a low fever—all symptoms of rubella, or German measles—early in their pregnancies. Gregg wrote an article suggesting that there might be some connec-

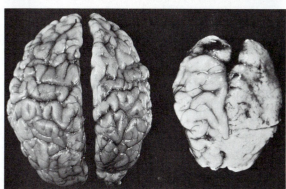

FIGURE 3.12   *Children who suffer from fetal alcohol syndrome do not merely look abnormal; their brains are underdeveloped and many are severely retarded. The brain of a child who suffered from fetal alcohol syndrome (lower right) lacks the convolutions characteristic of the brain of a normal child (lower left).*

Fetal alcohol syndrome   A syndrome found in babies whose mothers were heavy consumers of alcohol while pregnant.

TABLE 3.5 Some Maternal Diseases and Conditions That May Affect Prenatal Development

SEXUALLY TRANSMITTED DISEASES

Gonorrhea	The gonococcus organism may attack the eyes while the baby is passing through the infected birth canal. Silver nitrate eyedrops are administered immediately after birth to prevent blindness.
Herpes simplex (genital herpes)	Infection usually occurs at birth as the baby comes in contact with herpes lesions on the mother's genitals, although the virus may also cross the placental barrier to infect the fetus. Infection can lead to blindness and serious brain damage. There is no cure for the disease. Mothers with active genital herpes often have a cesarean delivery to avoid infecting their babies.
Syphilis	The effects of syphilis on the fetus can be devastating. An estimated 25 percent of infected fetuses are born dead. Those who survive may be deaf, mentally retarded, or deformed. Syphilis can be diagnosed by a blood test and can be cured before the fetus is affected, since the syphilis spirochete cannot penetrate the placental membrane before the 21st week of gestation.

OTHER DISEASES AND MATERNAL CONDITIONS

Chicken pox	Chicken pox may lead to spontaneous abortion or premature delivery, but it does not appear to cause malformations.
Cytomegalovirus	The most common source of prenatal infection, cytomegalovirus produces no symptoms in adults, but it may be fatal to the embryo. Infection later in intrauterine life has been related to brain damage, deafness, blindness, and cerebral palsy (a defect of motor coordination caused by brain damage).
Diabetes	Diabetic mothers face a greater risk of having a stillborn child or one who dies shortly after birth. Babies of diabetics are often very large because of the accumulation of fat during the third trimester. Diabetic mothers require special care to prevent these problems.
Hepatitis	Mothers who have hepatitis are likely to pass it on to their infants during birth.
Hypertension	Hypertension (chronic high blood pressure) increases the probability of miscarriage and infant death.
Influenza	The more virulent forms of influenza may lead to spontaneous abortion or may cause abnormalities during the early stages of pregnancy.
Mumps	Mumps is suspected of causing spontaneous abortion in the first trimester of pregnancy.
Toxemia	About 5 percent of pregnant women in the United States are affected during the third trimester by this disorder of unknown origin. Most common during first pregnancies, the condition mainly affects the mother. Symptoms are water retention, high blood pressure, rapid weight gain, and protein in the urine. If untreated, toxemia may cause convulsions, coma, and even death for the mother. Death of the fetus is not uncommon.
Toxoplasmosis	A mild disease in adults with symptoms similar to those of the common cold, toxoplasmosis is caused by a parasite that is present in raw meat and cat feces. It may cause spontaneous abortion or death. Babies who survive may have serious eye or brain damage.

Sources: Moore, 1982; Stevenson, 1977.

tion between the rubella epidemic of the summer of 1940 and the subsequent increase in the number of babies who were born blind, alerting the medical community to this danger for the first time (Gregg, 1941). Since then, researchers have found that rubella causes developmental defects in more than 50 percent of all babies born to mothers who suffer from the disease during the first months of pregnancy (Stevenson, 1977). Infection during the first 3 months of pregnancy often results in a syndrome of congenital heart disease, cataracts, deafness, and mental retardation. Infection during the second 3 months may lead to mental and motor retardation and to deafness. A rubella epidemic in the United States during the winter of 1964–1965 resulted in 30,000 stillbirths and 20,000 infants who suffered congenital defects (Lavigne, 1982).

The development of a vaccine for rubella in 1969 has greatly reduced the incidence of the disease, but it has not been eradicated. Women are advised to avoid becoming pregnant for at least 6 months after they receive the vaccine. A few states offer a test for immunity to rubella as part of the blood test given before a marriage license is issued.

Acquired Immunodeficiency Syndrome (AIDS)   The rapid spread of the AIDS virus in the 1980s has made this source of infection a major concern among physicians. Over 6000 pregnancies are complicated by AIDS annually in the United States (Wiesenfeld & Sweet, 1994). Approximately 50 percent of the babies born to mothers who test positive for the AIDS virus acquire this disease. The virus may be transmitted from the mother to her baby either by passing through the placental barrier or through exposure of the baby to the mother's infected blood during delivery (Whitely & Goldenberg, 1990; Wiesenfeld & Sweet, 1994). There is no known cure for AIDS, but recent research indicates that administering the drug AZT to pregnant women who test positive for the virus significantly reduces the chances that they will pass the disease to their unborn child (*San Francisco Chronicle*, 1995).

Rh Incompatibility   Rh is a complex substance on the surface of the red blood cells. One of its components is determined by a dominant gene, and people who have this component are said to be *Rh positive*. Fewer than one in six people inherit the two recessive genes that make them Rh negative (Connor & Ferguson-Smith, 1991).

When an Rh-negative woman conceives a child with an Rh-positive man, the child is likely to be Rh positive. During the birth of the baby, some of its blood cells usually pass into the mother's bloodstream while the placenta is separating from the uterine wall. The mother's immune system creates antibodies to fight this foreign substance, and the antibodies remain in her bloodstream after the birth. If the mother again becomes pregnant with an Rh-positive child, the antibodies produced during the birth of her first child will pass into the new baby's bloodstream, where they will attack and destroy its red blood cells. The resultant Rh disease can lead to serious birth defects and even death. Since it takes time for the mother's system to produce Rh antibodies, firstborn children are rarely affected, but the danger increases with each successive child. Fortunately, physicians can prevent Rh disease by giving the Rh-negative mother an injection of anti-Rh serum within 72 hours of the delivery of an Rh-positive child. The serum kills any Rh-positive blood cells in the mother's bloodstream so that she will not develop antibodies to attack them. Children who are born with Rh disease can be treated with periodic blood transfusions (Moore & Persaud, 1993).

Radiation   Massive doses of radiation often lead to serious malformations of the developing organism and in many cases cause prenatal death or spontaneous abortion (Moore & Persaud, 1993). Somewhat lesser doses may spare the life of the organism, but they may have a profound effect on its development. These dangers became tragically evident after the atomic blasts at Hiroshima and Nagasaki in 1945. Many of the pregnant women who were within 1500 meters of the blasts survived, but they later lost their babies. Of those babies who appeared to be normal at birth, 64 percent were later diagnosed as mentally retarded. The effects of radiation on the fetus's developing central nervous system were found to be greatest during the eighth through the fifteenth week of the prenatal period, a time of rapid proliferation of the cortical neurons (Vorhees & Mollnow, 1987). If the fetus's gonads receive doses of radiation, the germ cells may be affected, so that later generations may suffer genetic damage (Tuchmann-Duplessis, 1975).

The effects of low doses of radiation on human beings have not been firmly established. Because X rays may cause malformations in the embryo, physicians are likely to be cautious about X-raying pregnant women.

Industrial pollution is a growing health hazard for children. These children have been playing in an industrial dump site.

Pollution   Most of the thousands of chemicals that are used in industrial production and in the preparation of foods and cosmetics have never been tested to see if they are harmful to prenatal development, although some of these substances reach the embryo or fetus through the placenta (Ames, 1979). Some herbicides and pesticides have been shown to be harmful or even fatal to unborn rats, mice, rabbits, and chicks. Several pollutants in the atmosphere and in the water we drink also appear to be teratogenic. Moreover, some of the effects are cumulative, as concentrations of the chemicals build up in the body.

In 1953 it was discovered that the consumption of large quantities of fish from Minimata Bay in Japan was associated with a series of symptoms that have come to be known as *Minimata disease.* The symptoms include cerebral palsy (a disorder of the central nervous system), deformation of the skull, and sometimes an abnormally small head. The bay was polluted by mercury from waste discharged into the Minimata River from nearby industrial plants. The mercury passed in increasingly concentrated amounts through the food chain from the organisms eaten by fish to humans who ate the fish. Pregnant women who ate the contaminated fish then passed the mercury on to their unborn babies. "Minimata disease" has since become synonymous with mercury poisoning (Tuchmann-Duplessis, 1975).

The incidence of birth defects is also known to be abnormally high in areas of heavy atmospheric pollution. In the Brazilian industrial city of Cubatão, for instance, the air pollution from petrochemical and steel plants alone exceeds that generated by all the combined industries in the Los Angeles basin of California. During the 1970s, 65 of every 1000 babies born in Cubatão died shortly after birth because their brains had failed to develop, double the rate of this defect in neighboring communities that were not so heavily polluted (Freed, 1983). Fortunately, strong environmental safety efforts have greatly reduced the pollution in Cubatão, and the death rate of infants there has declined remarkably (Brooke, 1991).

Atmospheric pollution in such U.S. cities as Los Angeles, Elizabeth (New Jersey), Chicago, and Denver is not so high as it used to be in Cubatão, but it is still high enough to cause concern about its effects on prenatal development. And what are the risks to pregnant women and their unborn children who live near chemical dumps? What should a pregnant woman do to minimize these risks? More research is necessary before such questions can be answered.

Principles of teratogenic effects

Although the effects of teratogens on the developing organism vary with the teratogen, several general principles apply to all of them (Hogge, 1990; Moore & Persaud, 1993):

- *The susceptibility of a developing organism to a teratogenic agent varies with the developmental stage the organism is in at the time of exposure.* Overall, the gravest danger to life comes during the first 2 weeks, before the cells of the organism have undergone extensive differentiation and before most women are even aware that they are pregnant (see Figure 3.13). During this critical period, a teratogenic agent may completely destroy the organism. Once the various body systems have begun to form, each is most vulnerable at the time of its initial growth spurt. As Figure 3.13 indicates, the most vulnerable period for the central nervous system is from 15 to 36 days, whereas the upper and lower limbs are most vulnerable from 24 to 49 days after conception.

- *Each teratogenic agent acts in a specific way on specific developing tissue and therefore causes a particular pattern of abnormal development.* Thalidomide, for example, causes deformation of the legs and arms, and mercury compounds cause brain damage that is manifested as cerebral palsy.

- *Not all organisms are affected in the same way by exposure to a given amount of a particular teratogen.* The way a developing organism responds to teratogenic agents depends to some degree on its genotype and the genotype of its

FIGURE 3.13 *The critical periods in human prenatal development occur when the organs and other body parts are forming and therefore are most vulnerable to teratogens. Before implantation, teratogens either damage all or most of the cells of the organism, causing its death, or damage only a few cells, allowing the organism to recover without developing defects. The blue portions of the bars represent periods of highest risk of major structural abnormalities; the green portions of the bars represent periods of reduced sensitivity to teratogens. (Adapted from Moore, 1982.)*

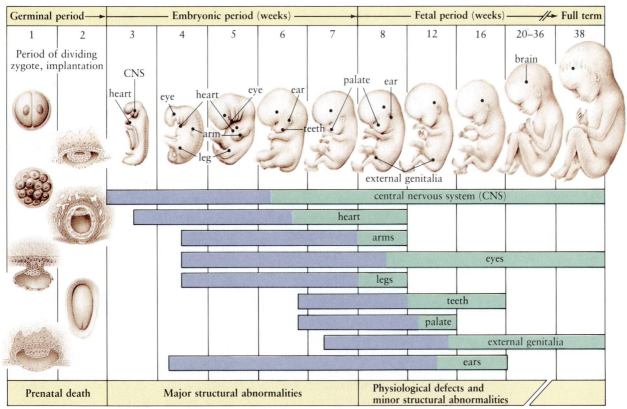

- Indicates common site of action of teratogen

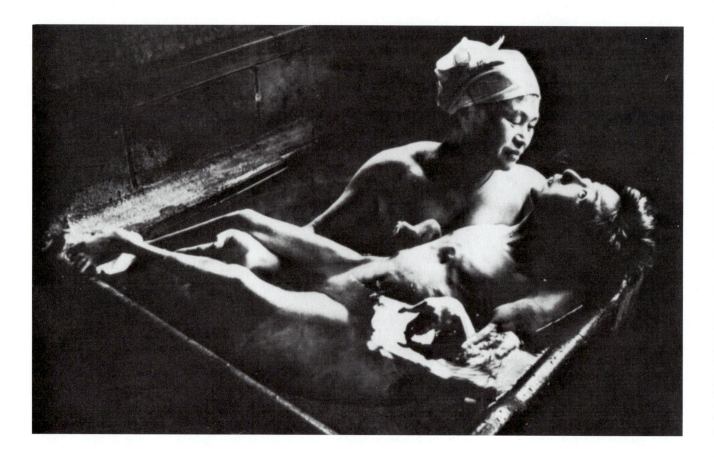

The tragic consequences of prenatal mercury poisoning, or Minimata disease. It first came to world attention because of the pollution in Minimata Bay, Japan.

mother. Fewer than one-quarter of the pregnant women who used thalidomide during the period when the embryo's limbs were forming gave birth to malformed babies.

- *Susceptibility to teratogenic agents depends on the physiological state of the mother.* The mother's age, nutrition, uterine condition, and hormonal balance all affect the action of teratogens on the developing organism. The risk of malformation is highest when the mother is younger than 20 or older than 40. The precise reason is not known. Nutritional deficiency in the mother intensifies the adverse effects of some teratogens. The impact of teratogens also appears to increase if the mother suffers from diabetes, toxemia, a metabolic imbalance, or liver dysfunction, among other disorders.

- *In general, the greater the concentration of teratogenic agents to which the organism has been exposed, the greater the risk of abnormal development.*

- *Levels of teratogens that can produce defects in the developing organism may affect the mother only mildly or not at all.* Some diseases and drugs that have little or only a temporary effect on the mother can lead to serious abnormalities in the developing organism.

Prenatal Development Reconsidered

As we noted earlier, many developmental psychologists view the prenatal period as a model for all subsequent development because many of the principles that explain prenatal development also explain development after birth. Before we move on to birth and life outside the uterus, it is worthwhile to review these explanatory principles as they apply to the prenatal period. They are ideas we will return to again and again throughout our study of child development.

- *Sequence is fundamental.* One cell must exist before there can be two. Muscles and bones must be present before nerves can coordinate movement. Gonads must secrete testosterone before further sexual differentiation can occur.

- *Timing is important.* If the ovum moves too rapidly or too slowly down the fallopian tube, pregnancy is terminated. If thalidomide is encountered after the first 3 months, the fetus is unlikely to be affected, but if it is encountered during the first 2 to 3 months of pregnancy, it may have a disastrous effect on the organism. The importance of timing implies the existence of critical periods for the formation of basic organ systems.

- *Development consists of differentiation and integration.* The single cell of the zygote becomes the many, apparently identical, cells of the morula. These cells then differentiate into two distinct kinds of cells, which later are integrated into a new configuration of cells called the blastocyst. Later arm buds will differentiate to form fingers, which will differ from each other in ways that make possible the finely articulate movements of the human hand.

- *Development is characterized by stagelike changes.* Changes in the form of the organism and in the ways it interacts with its environment suggest a series of stagelike transformations. The embryo not only looks altogether different from the blastocyst but also interacts with its environment in a different way.

- *Development proceeds unevenly.* From the earliest steps of cleavage, the various subsystems that make up the organism develop at their own rates. An important special case of such unevenness is physical development, which follows a cephalocaudal (from the head down) and proximodistal (from the center to the periphery) sequence.

- *The course of development seems to be punctuated by periods of regression.* Although development generally appears to progress through time, there are also periods of apparent regression. Regressions appear to reflect a process of reorganization, as when fetal activity decreases as higher regions of the brain are beginning to become active.

- *Development is still a mystery.* The process by which the human organism develops from a single cell into a squalling newborn baby continues to mystify investigators. In one sense, the results of development are present at the beginning, coded in the genetic materials of the zygote, which constrain the kinds of forms that can emerge out of the interactions between the organism and its environment. In this sense, the preformationist hypothesis is valid. But in another sense, new forms are constantly emerging out of the organism–environment interactions that sustain and propel development. In this sense, the epigenetic hypothesis is confirmed.

Birth: The First Bio-Social-Behavioral Shift

Among all of life's transitions, birth is the most radical. Before birth, the amniotic fluid provides a wet, warm environment, and the fetus receives continuous oxygen and nourishment through the umbilical cord. By contrast, the environment that greets the newborn as it emerges from the womb is dry and cold. When the umbilical cord is cut and tied, the automatic supply of oxygen and nourishment is

FIRST STAGE OF LABOR

Cervix   Birth canal

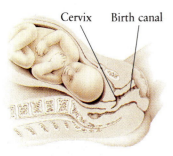

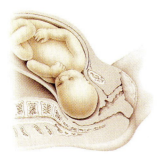

START OF SECOND STAGE

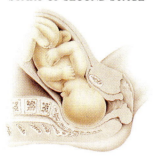

abruptly cut off. The lungs inflate to take in oxygen and exhale carbon dioxide for the first time, changing the pressure within the baby's circulatory system and causing the blood flow to reverse direction. Nourishment now comes only intermittently, and the baby must work for it by sucking. The baby no longer has the placenta to provide protection against disease-causing organisms.

The social and behavioral changes that occur at birth are no less pronounced than the biological ones, marking it as the first major bio-social-behavioral shift in human development. The newborn encounters other human beings directly for the first time, and the parents get their first glimpse of their child. From the moment of birth, neonates and parents begin to construct a social relationship.

THE STAGES OF LABOR

The biological process of birth begins with a series of changes in the mother's body that force the fetus through the birth canal. It ends when the mother expels the placenta after the baby has emerged. Labor normally begins approximately 280 days after the first day of a woman's last menstrual period, or 266 days after conception. It is customarily divided into three overlapping stages (see Figure 3.14).

The *first stage of labor* lasts from the first regular, intense contractions of the uterus until the *cervix*, the opening of the uterus into the vagina, is fully dilated and the connections between the bones of the mother's pelvis become more flexible. The length of this stage varies from woman to woman and from pregnancy to pregnancy: it may last anywhere from less than an hour to several days. The norm for first births is about 14 hours (Niswander & Evans, 1996). At the beginning, the muscle contractions come 15 to 20 minutes apart and last anywhere from 15 to 60 seconds. As labor proceeds, the contractions become more frequent and more intense and are longer in duration.

The baby's head is flexible because the bones of the skull have not yet fused. Once the cervix is fully dilated, the baby is pushed headfirst through the cervix into the vagina, beginning the *second stage of labor*. The contractions now usually come no more than a minute apart and last about a minute. The pressure of the baby and the powerful contractions of the uterus typically cause the mother to bear down and push the baby out. Usually the top of the baby's head and the brow are the first to emerge. Occasionally babies emerge in other positions, the most common being the *breech position*, with the feet or buttocks emerging first.

The final, *third stage of labor* occurs as the baby emerges from the vagina and the uterus contracts around its diminished contents. The placenta buckles and separates from the uterine wall, pulling the other fetal membranes with it. Contractions quickly expel them, and they are delivered as the *afterbirth*.

FIGURE 3.14 *During the first stage of labor, which usually lasts several hours, the cervix dilates. During the second stage, the birth canal widens, permitting the baby to emerge. The final stage (not shown) occurs when the placenta is delivered. (Adapted from Clarke-Stewart & Koch, 1983.)*

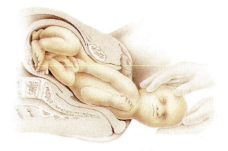

CULTURAL VARIATIONS IN CHILDBIRTH

As a biological process, labor occurs in roughly the same way everywhere. The *experience* of giving birth, however, varies with the traditions of the culture. These traditions provide the mother and the community with a prescribed set of procedures to follow during birthing and a set of expectations about how they are going to feel (Kaye, 1982).

In a few societies, giving birth is treated as an unremarkable process, a routine part of a woman's life. Consider the following description of birth among the !Kung, a hunting-and-gathering society in Africa's Kalahari Desert:

> Mother's stomach grew very large. The first labor pains
> came at night and stayed with her until dawn. That morning,
> everyone went gathering. Mother and I stayed behind. We
> sat together for a while, then I went and played with the other children. Later,
> I came back and ate the nuts she had cracked for me. She got up and started
> to get ready. I said, "Mommy, let's go to the water well, I'm thirsty." She said,
> "Uhn, uhn, I'm going to gather some mongongo nuts." I told the children
> that I was going and we left; there were no other adults around. We walked a
> short way, then she sat down by the base of a large nehn tree, leaned back
> against it, and little Kumsa was born. (Shostak, 1981, pp. 53–54).

These expectant parents are attending a class on how to deal with the process of birthing.

Such unassisted and unheralded birthing is relatively rare. It is far more common to find several people attending the mother during labor and delivery. Often a special house built outside the village is reserved for childbearing. Special practices, such as having the mother sit or lie in a particular posture as she gives birth or giving her herbal infusions to drink, are used to help her and her baby through the dangerous transition.

In many cultures, the specialists who assist the mother are called "doctors," although there is wide variation in what people believe "medicine" to be. The Onitsha Ibo of Nigeria regard childbirth as an illness. At the end of the third month, a woman places herself in the care of a traditional doctor and begins to take herbal medicines. Certain foods are prohibited and others (such as a soup made of leaves) are recommended (Henderson & Henderson, 1982).

The Ngoni women of East Africa consider themselves to be the childbirth experts, and men are totally excluded from the process. The women even conceal the fact that they are pregnant from their husbands as long as they can. "Men are little children. They are not able to hear those things which belong to pregnancy," the women claim (Read, 1960/1968, p. 20). When a woman learns that her daughter-in-law's labor has begun, she and other female kin move into the woman's hut, banish the husband, and take charge of the preparations. They remove everything that belongs to the husband—clothes, tools, and weapons—and all household articles except old mats and pots to be used during labor. Men are not allowed back into the hut until after the baby is born.

Fifty years ago the Navajo of the southwestern United States treated childbirth as a social event, opening their homes to the whole community when a child was being born. An anthropologist who worked among them at the time reported that "anyone who comes and lends moral support is invited to stay and partake of what food is available" (quoted in Mead & Newton, 1967, p. 171).

CHILDBIRTH IN THE UNITED STATES

Most babies in the United States today are born in a hospital. This emphasis on the medical aspects of childbirth represents a marked shift in cultural practices over the past century. In the nineteenth century, most births took place at home, attended only by a midwife, a woman recognized for her experience in assisting

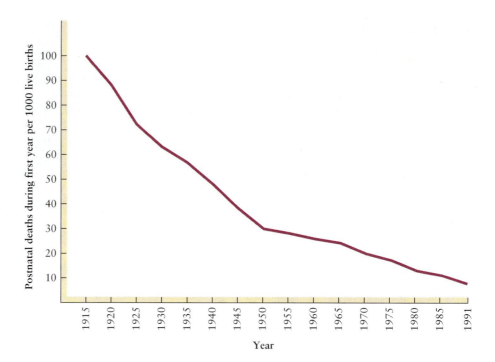

FIGURE 3.15 *During this century the death rate among children under 1 year of age has dropped dramatically in the United States.*

childbirth. By the middle of the twentieth century, 86 percent of all babies were born in hospitals and 95 percent were delivered by a physician (Gordon & Haire, 1981). Underlying this shift from home to hospital were two developments. First, many drugs were developed to relieve the pain of childbirth, and by law they could be administered only by physicians. Second, hospitals came to be better equipped to provide both antiseptic surroundings and specialized help to deal with any complications that might arise during labor and delivery (Cianfrani, 1960).

The lives of thousands of babies and mothers are saved each year by the intervention of doctors using modern drugs and special medical procedures (Figure 3.15). In 1915 approximately 100 of every 1000 babies died in their first year, and almost 7 of 1000 mothers died giving birth. By 1992, infant deaths had been reduced to fewer than 9 of every 1000 babies born (U.S. Bureau of the Census, 1995). In 1992, only 7.8 women of every 100,000 who gave birth in the United States died of causes related to pregnancy, childbirth, or complications after the birth (U.S. Bureau of the Census, 1995). Unfortunately, the reduction in death rates has not been evenly spread through all segments of the population. While the mortality rate has declined significantly for both African American and white infants, African American infants are still twice as likely to die during the first year of life as white infants. Moreover, African American mothers are more than twice as likely to die in childbirth as white mothers (U.S. Bureau of the Census, 1995).

Despite the reductions in maternal and infant mortality, health-care professionals and parents alike have pointed to problems arising from medical intervention during normal, uncomplicated births (U.S. Congress, Senate Committee on Human Resources, 1978). These concerns center on two questions: (1) What is the safest method for dealing with pain during childbirth? (2) What precautions are necessary to ensure the health of the mother and the baby?

Childbirth pain and its medication

Many drugs have been used to lessen the pain of labor and delivery. They include anesthetics (which dull feeling), analgesics (which reduce the perception of pain), and sedatives (which reduce anxiety). No national data are available on the current use of drugs during childbirth, but a 1974 poll of 18 large teaching hospitals in the

United States found that almost 95 percent of the births in those institutions took place under some form of medication (Brackbill, 1979).

Current evidence indicates that the drugs administered to the mother to control the pain of labor affect the baby when they pass through the placental barrier and enter the fetus's bloodstream (Troyer & Parisi, 1994). These drugs tend to reduce the mother's oxygen intake; the resultant drop in her blood pressure in turn reduces the supply of oxygen to the fetus and may cause the baby to have difficulty breathing after birth. The baby's immature liver and kidneys are unable to rid the body of these drugs efficiently, so that some of them remain to lodge in the neonate's brain (Wilson, 1977).

Obstetric medications seldom threaten the lives of healthy, full-term babies. But those drugs that have been tested have been found to affect neonatal behavior. The babies of mothers who receive one or another of a variety of drugs during labor and delivery are less attentive and more irritable, have poorer muscle tone, and are weaker than those whose mothers receive no medication (Aleksandrowicz, 1974; Brackbill, 1979; Sepkowski, 1985). The vigor of the newborn infant's sucking response has also been found to be reduced by some obstetric drugs (Brazelton, 1973). As one might imagine, the extent of these effects varies with the drug, the dosage, and the stage of labor at which it is administered (Brackbill, McManus, & Woodward, 1985; Lester, Als, & Brazelton, 1982).

The evidence that obstetric drugs affect the neonate has caused concern that they may have long-term effects on the child's development. Yvonne Brackbill and her colleagues claim, for example, that the heavy use of drugs during birth is implicated in a high incidence of learning disorders among U.S. schoolchildren (Brackbill, McManus, & Woodward, 1985). Most of the existing evidence indicates, however, that low levels of medication do not significantly affect healthy babies. It is only when substantial levels of medication are used in births of babies who are at risk for other reasons that medication may have longer-term effects (Brazelton, Nugent, & Lester, 1987). Because of their concern about the possible adverse effects of drugs on the neonate, many women in the United States and Western Europe are turning to alternative methods of controlling the pain of labor. All of these methods include educational classes that give the expectant mother an idea of what to expect during labor and delivery and teach her relaxation and breathing exercises to help counteract pain. They all recommend that the woman in labor not be left alone. Someone—her husband, a sympathetic friend, or a midwife—should be constantly at her side to provide comfort and emotional support.

Medical interventions during childbirth

In addition to administering drugs to ease the pain of labor, doctors may use medical procedures to safeguard the lives of mother and child. When the baby is significantly overdue or when the mother is confronted with some life-threatening situation, physicians commonly induce labor, either by rupturing the membranes of the amniotic sac or by giving the mother some form of the hormone oxytocin. Another commonly used procedure is the *cesarean section*, or surgical removal of the baby from the mother's uterus. This procedure is typically used in cases of difficult labor, when the baby is in distress during delivery, or when the baby is not in the headfirst position. The number of cesarean sections performed rose significantly during the 1970s. By 1993, 22 out of every 100 births in the United States were by cesarean section (U.S. Dept. of Health and Human Services, 1995).

Although modern medical techniques have made childbirth a great deal safer than it was in the past, some medical personnel claim that they are used more often than they should be (U.S. Congress, Senate Committee on Human Resources, 1978). These critics argue that many of the cesarean operations performed in the United States not only are unnecessary but raise the cost of childbirth, expose the

BOX 3.3

The Baby's Experience of Birth

What is birth like for the baby? For several hours the fetus is squeezed through the birth canal, where it is subjected to considerable pressure and occasionally is deprived of oxygen. Finally the newborn infant is delivered from the warm, dark shelter of the womb into a cold, bright hospital room. It is difficult to imagine this experience as anything but traumatic.

The psychiatrist Otto Rank (1929), one of Sigmund Freud's first and most valued students, believed that the birth trauma is the main source of neurotic anxiety in the adult, and that he could eliminate this problem by getting his patients to analyze and thereby overcome this "primal trauma." Freud (1937/1953) disagreed with Rank, and Freud's judgment has generally been sustained (Pratt, 1954). Nevertheless, concern continues over the possible long-term effects of the traumatic birth experience.

Modern research on the experience of birth has focused on the biological mechanisms that equip the baby to cope with the stress involved. Hugo Lagercrantz and Theodore Slotkin (1986) have suggested that as the birth process begins, a surge in the fetus's production of adrenaline and other "stress" hormones protects it from the adverse conditions—the pressure

on the head and the deprivation of oxygen—it experiences. They go on to suggest that the events that cause the production of stress hormones are of vital importance because these hormones prepare the infant to survive outside the womb.

In support of their hypothesis, Lagercrantz and Slotkin point out that infants delivered by cesarean section often have difficulty breathing. They believe that the procedure deprives babies of the experiences that produce high levels of adrenaline and other hormones in the hours before birth, hormones that facilitate the absorption of liquid from the lungs and the production of surfactin, which allow the lungs to function well. In addition, the hormones appear to produce an increase in the newborn's metabolic rate, which mobilizes readily usable fuel to nourish cells.

Lagercrantz and Slotkin also believe that the stress hormones are instrumental in increasing blood flow to such vital organs as the heart, lungs, and brain and thus increase the chances of survival of a baby who is experiencing breathing difficulties. Furthermore, these researchers speculate that the hormonal surge during the birth process puts the newborn in a state of alertness, which facilitates the attachment between mother and infant during its first hour of life.

mother to the risk of postoperative infection, and cause mothers to be separated from their infants while they heal from surgery. They may also be detrimental to the babies' well-being (see Box 3.3). Concerns about unnecessary medical intervention also extend to other procedures, such as induced labor and the electronic monitoring of the vital signs of the fetus during labor (Pernoll, Benda, & Babson, 1986).

In part because of such concerns, about 1 percent of U.S. women choose to have their babies at home. Although some of these home births are attended by physicians, most are overseen by certified nurse-midwives, who are specially trained to deal with childbirth. The mortality rate for such births is very low when the mothers have had good prenatal care and are healthy, the births are uncomplicated, and a well-trained medical professional is present (Schramm, Barnes, & Blakwell, 1987). But home births are not recommended for mothers who are at risk for complications of any kind.

The Newborn's Condition

To first-time parents, especially those who imagine that newborns look like the infants pictured on jars of baby food, the real neonate may cause alarm and disappointment. The baby's head is large in proportion to the rest of the body, and the limbs are relatively small and tightly flexed. Unless the baby has been delivered by cesarean section, the head may look misshapen after its tight squeeze through the birth canal. (The head usually regains its symmetry by the end of the first week after birth.) The baby's skin may be covered with *vernix caseosa*, a white, cheesy substance that protects it against bacterial infections, and it may be spotted with blood.

Medical personnel, accustomed to the way newborns look, are not distracted by the baby's temporarily unattractive appearance. They check the neonate for indications of danger so that immediate action can be taken if something is wrong. They take note of the size of the baby, check its vital signs, and look for evidence of normal capacities.

In the United States, neonates weigh an average of 3200 to 3400 grams (7 to 7½ pounds), although babies weighing anywhere from 5½ to 10 pounds are within the normal range. During their first days of life, most babies lose about 7 percent of their initial weight, primarily because of loss of fluid. They usually gain the weight back by the time they are 10 days old.

The average neonate is 20 inches long. To a large extent, the length of the newborn is determined by the size of the mother's uterus. It does not reflect the baby's genetic inheritance, because the genes that control height do not begin to express themselves until shortly after birth (Tanner, 1990).

ASSESSING THE BABY'S VIABILITY

A variety of scales and tests are used to assess the neonate's physical state and behavioral condition. The basic procedure in constructing such instruments is first to identify the characteristics that are essential to the newborn's immediate well-being and normal development. Ratings are then collected from a large number of infants to establish norms for comparison. These norms are then used to assess the relative condition of individual babies.

Physical state

In the 1950s Virginia Apgar (1953), an anesthesiologist who worked in the delivery room of a large metropolitan hospital, developed a quick and simple method of diagnosing the physical state of a newborn. The **Apgar Scale** is now widely used throughout the United States to determine if a baby requires emergency care.

The Apgar Scale is used to rate babies 1 minute after birth and again 5 minutes later on five vital signs: heart rate, respiratory effort, muscle tone, reflex responsivity, and color. Table 3.6 shows the criteria for scoring each of the signs.

Apgar Scale A quick, simple test used to diagnose the physical state of newborn infants.

TABLE 3.6   The Apgar Scoring System

	Rating		
Vital Sign	**0**	**1**	**2**
Heart rate	Absent	Slow (below 100)	Over 100
Respiratory effort	Absent	Slow, irregular	Good, crying
Muscle tone	Flaccid	Some flexion of extremities	Active motion
Reflex responsivity	No response	Grimace	Vigorous cry
Color	Blue, pale	Body pink, extremities blue	Completely pink

Source: Apgar, 1953.

The individual scores are totaled to give a measure of the baby's overall physical condition. A baby with a score of less than 4 is considered to be in poor condition and to require immediate medical attention.

Behavioral condition

During the past half century, many scales have been constructed to assess the more subtle behavioral aspects of the newborn's condition (Brazelton, 1973, 1978; Gesell & Amatruda, 1947; Graham, Matarazzo, & Caldwell, 1956). One of the most widely used is the **Brazelton Neonatal Assessment Scale,** developed by the pediatrician T. Berry Brazelton and his colleagues. A major purpose of this scale is to assess the newborn's neurological condition after the stress of labor and delivery. It is also used to assess the progress of premature infants, to compare the functioning of newborns of different cultures, and to evaluate the effectiveness of interventions designed to alleviate developmental difficulties (Brazelton, Nugent, & Lester, 1987).

Included in the Brazelton scale are tests of infants' reflexes, motor capacities, muscle tone, capacity for responding to objects and people, and capacity to control their own behavior and attention. The only equipment the tests require is a rattle, a bell, a flashlight, a pin, and a cloth. When scoring a newborn on such tests, the examiner must take note of the degree of the infant's alertness and, if necessary, repeat the tests when the baby is wide awake and calm. Here are some typical items on the Brazelton scale:

> *Orientation to animate objects—visual and auditory:* The examiner calls the baby's name repeatedly in a high-pitched voice while moving his head up and down and from side to side. Does the baby focus on the examiner? Does she follow the examiner with her eyes smoothly?
>
> *Pull-to-sit:* The examiner puts a forefinger in each of the infant's palms and pulls him to a sitting position. Does the baby try to right his head when he is in a seated position? How well is he able to do so?
>
> *Cuddliness:* The examiner holds the baby against her chest or up against her shoulder. How does the baby respond? Does she resist being held? Is she passive or does she cuddle up to the examiner?
>
> *Defensive movements:* The examiner places a cloth over the baby's face and holds it there. Does the baby try to remove the cloth from his face either by turning his head away or by swiping at it?
>
> *Self-quieting activity:* The examiner notes what the baby does to quiet herself when she is fussy. Does she suck her thumb, look around?

A lively controversy has developed about the usefulness of scales such as Brazelton's (Brazelton, Nugent, & Lester, 1987; Francis, Self, & Horowitz, 1987). Most of these scales are designed with two purposes in mind: (1) to screen for infants at risk and (2) to predict aspects of newborns' future development such as their temperaments or typical learning rates. Research over the past decade shows that they are satisfactory guides for determining when medical intervention is necessary (Francis, Self, & Horowitz, 1987). For predicting later development, however, they appear to be useful only when the newborn is tested repeatedly during the early days and weeks of life. Repeated testing makes it possible for the baby's early developmental progress to be estimated reliably (Brazelton, Nugent, & Lester, 1987). Even then, the predictions are not always accurate.

PROBLEMS AND COMPLICATIONS

Though most babies are born without any serious problems, some are in such poor physical condition that they soon die. Others are at risk for later developmental problems, sometimes fatal ones. Newborns are considered to be at risk if

Brazelton Neonatal Assessment Scale A scale used to assess the newborn's neurological condition.

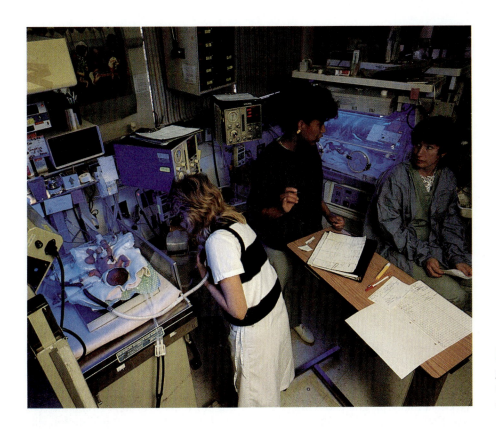

FIGURE 3.16 *Babies born prematurely may require intensive care in an incubator to sustain their early development.*

they suffer from any of a variety of problems, including asphyxiation or head injury during delivery (either of which may result in brain damage), acute difficulty breathing after birth, or difficulty digesting food owing to an immature digestive system (Korner, 1987). These are the kinds of problems that are likely to result in low scores on the Apgar Scale. Most of the newborns who are at risk are premature, abnormally underweight, or both (Witter & Keith, 1993).

Prematurity

The time that has passed between conception and birth is known as the baby's *gestational age*. The normal gestational age is 37 to 43 weeks. Babies born before the thirty-seventh week are considered to be **premature,** or preterm. In the United States, 10 percent of all births are premature (Witter, 1993). Disorders related to premature birth are the fourth leading cause of infant mortality. With the expert care now available in modern hospitals (see Figure 3.16), mortality rates for premature infants are declining. Eighty percent of those who weigh more than 1020 grams (2¼ pounds) now survive.

The leading cause of death among preterm infants is immature lungs (Witter & Keith, 1993). The other main obstacle to the survival of preterm infants is immaturity of their digestive and immune systems. Even babies of normal gestational age sometimes have difficulty coordinating sucking, swallowing, and breathing in the first few days after birth. These difficulties are likely to be more serious for preterm infants (see Figure 3.17). Their coordination may be so poor that they cannot be fed directly from breast or bottle, so that special equipment must be used to feed them. Moreover, their immature digestive systems often cannot handle normal baby formulas, so special formulas must be made.

A few of the factors that can lead to prematurity have been identified. Twins are likely to be born about 3 weeks early, triplets and quadruplets even earlier. Very young women whose reproductive systems are immature and women who

Premature Babies born before the thirty-seventh week of gestation are said to be premature.

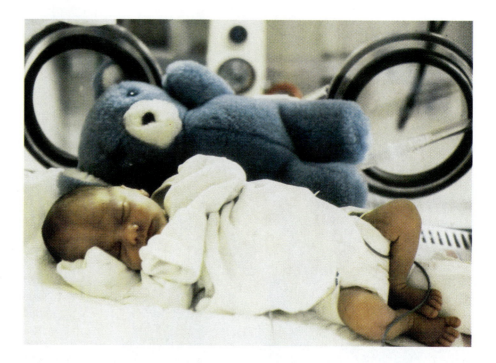

FIGURE 3.17 *Evidence that premature infants experience difficulty breathing led Evelyn Thoman and her colleagues to create a "breathing teddy bear" attached to an air pump outside the crib. The rhythmic stimulation provided by the bear not only improves the quality of infants' sleep but reduces crying and other expressions of negative emotions. (Ingersoll & Thoman, 1994.)*

have had many pregnancies close together are more likely to have premature babies. So are women who smoke, who are in poor health, or who have intrauterine infections. The chances of giving birth to a premature infant also vary with socioeconomic status (Witter & Keith, 1993). Poor women are twice as likely to give birth to small or preterm infants as are women who are more affluent. This disparity can be explained by the fact that poor women are more likely to be undernourished or chronically ill, to have inadequate health care before and during pregnancy, to suffer from infections, and to experience complications during pregnancy. (Figure 3.18 shows the increased risk of giving birth prematurely owing to fasts.)

Many of the causes of prematurity, however, are still not well understood. At least half of all premature births are not associated with any of the identified risk factors. These premature babies are born after otherwise normal pregnancies to healthy women who are in their prime childbearing years and have had good medical care.

Low birth weight

Low birth weight The term for babies whose weight is 2500 grams or less at birth.

Fetal growth retardation The term for babies who are especially small for their gestational age at birth.

Babies are considered to have a **low birth weight** if they weigh 2500 grams or less, whether or not they are premature. (Premature babies tend to be small, but not all small babies are premature.) Newborns whose birth weights are especially low for their gestational age are said to suffer from **fetal growth retardation;** in other words, they have not grown at the normal rate. Multiple births, intrauterine infections, chromosomal abnormalities, maternal smoking or use of narcotics, maternal malnutrition, and abnormalities of the placenta or umbilical cord have all been identified as probable causes of fetal growth retardation (Spellacy, 1994).

Developmental consequences

Intensive research has been conducted on the developmental consequences of prematurity and low birth weight (Liaw & Brooks-Gunn, 1993; Witter & Keith, 1993). Babies who fall into either category are at risk for later developmental problems, but they differ in the probable course of their development.

Low birth weight increases the risk of developmental difficulty whether the baby is premature or full-term. The smaller the baby, the more likely some sort of congenital abnormality, such as neurological impairment or a permanent impairment of growth potential (Pernoll, Benda, & Babson, 1986). Small babies are also more likely to die in the first year of life than are infants of the same gestational age who are of normal size (Congressional Research Service, 1983).

It is common for low-birth-weight babies to suffer some decrease in intellectual capacities. A comparison of 7-year-olds who were born prematurely at a weight of less than 3.3 pounds with full-term children born at a normal weight found that the premature children were three times more likely to need special education classes. They also performed more poorly on tests of intelligence, verbal ability, and memory (Ross, Lipper, & Auld, 1991).

Many premature babies catch up with full-term babies during infancy, but some do not (Brooks-Gunn et al., 1993). Two factors appear to be important in determining what happens to a premature baby in the long run: (1) whether the premature infant also suffers from some form of medical difficulty and (2) what the infant's environmental conditions are after birth. Premature babies who are of normal size for their gestational age are the ones most likely to catch up with full-term babies. It is those who also are low in birth weight and have medical complications who are most at risk for future developmental difficulties. Among premature babies who are particularly light for their gestational age, those who have very small heads at birth and whose heads grow slowly during the first 6 weeks of postnatal life are especially likely to suffer long-term developmental problems (Eckerman, Sturm, & Gross, 1985).

The importance of a supportive environment in overcoming the potential risks of prematurity is underscored by research on the social ecology of the families of premature and low-birth-weight infants. Babies who are raised in comfortable socioeconomic circumstances with an intact family and a mother who has had a good education are less likely to suffer negative effects from their condition at birth than are children who are raised without these benefits (Liaw & Brooks-Gunn, 1993). Social support programs can also have a beneficial effect (Brooks-Gunn et al., 1993).

The way parents react to their premature baby can profoundly affect its well-being. Premature babies look tiny and fragile, and they are less responsive and more irritable than full-term infants (Brazelton, Nugent, & Lester, 1987). These characteristics may make it more difficult for parents initially to become attached to them. Furthermore, many premature infants spend their first few weeks in the

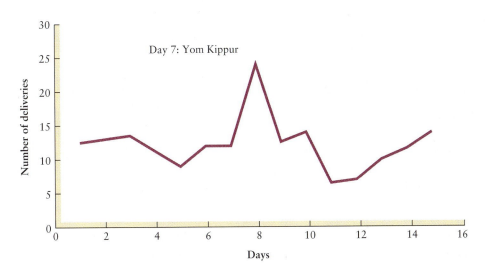

FIGURE 3.18 *A sudden drop in maternal food intake leads to hormonal changes that cause some woman to go into labor prematurely. The graph shows a doubling of the birthrate among Jewish women on the day following the 24-hour total food and water fast of Yom Kippur. (Adapted from Kaplan, Eidelman, & Aboulafia, 1983.)*

hospital in heated isolettes that maintain their body temperature and protect them from infection. Although the parents are encouraged to visit their babies often and to establish emotional ties with them, these visits are just that, visits, and then the parents go home and leave the babies alone. Once the mothers are able to take their premature infants home, however, they tend to spend more time with their babies than do mothers of full-term infants.

Although the evidence is somewhat contradictory, it currently appears that for the first year or so of life, premature babies develop more slowly than full-term babies. Keith Crnic and his colleagues (1983), for example, reported that low-birth-weight premature newborns lagged behind a comparison group of full-term babies with respect to motor, cognitive, and social-interactional indicators. In explaining this finding, they report that mothers and their premature babies had difficulty maintaining eye contact with each other. The mothers also seemed to have difficulty finding an appropriate level of stimulation for their premature infants, who were either overexcited or bored by their mothers' attempts to engage them. When Crnic and Mark Greenberg studied the same children a year later, however, they found that most of the differences between the two groups had disappeared (Greenberg & Crnic, 1988). Many of the mothers of the premature babies had developed especially positive attitudes toward their roles as parents and toward their babies. The researchers suggest that these positive attitudes helped the mothers to create more favorable environments for their babies, which in turn helped to compensate for the babies' vulnerability.

Beginning the Parent-Child Relationship

Once the crisis of birth is past, parents can turn their attention to the baby's future. Because human infants are helpless in many basic respects and their very survival depends on the active support and protection of their caretakers, the development of a close relationship between infants and their parents is crucial to infants' well-being. However, love between parent and child is neither inevitable nor automatic. The large numbers of infants who are neglected, abused, abandoned, even murdered the world over each year should convince even the most sentimental and optimistic observer of this harsh fact. In 1993, for example, nearly 3 million cases of child neglect and abuse were reported to local authorities in the United States (U.S. Bureau of the Census, 1995), and many knowledgeable people believe that the majority of cases are never reported.

Yet most parents love their babies. How is the bond between parent and child formed? And when no strong attachment develops, what has gone wrong? These are large questions that we will encounter again and again in subsequent chapters, because a close parent-child relationship is not formed in an instant; it develops over many years. Here we will examine the factors that come into play immediately after birth and that many people believe set the stage for the future: the initial reactions of the parents to their baby's appearance, the first hours of contact between parent and infant, and the expectations parents have for their babies.

THE BABY'S APPEARANCE

In their search for the sources of love between mother and infant, some psychologists have turned to ethology—the study of animal behavior and its evolutionary bases. These psychologists believe that examination of the factors that cause non-human mothers to protect or reject their young can shed light on the factors that influence human mothers. One important factor that seems to influence animals' responses to their young is their offspring's appearance. Konrad Lorenz (1943), a

German ethologist, noted that the newborns of many animal species have physical characteristics that distinguish them from the mature animal: a head that is large in relation to the body, a prominent forehead, large eyes that are positioned below the horizontal midline of the face, and round, full cheeks (see Figure 3.19). This combination of features, which Lorenz called *babyness*, seems to appeal to adults and, more significant, to evoke caregiving behaviors in them.

Evidence in support of Lorenz's hypothesis comes from a study by William Fullard and Ann Reiling (1976). These researchers asked people ranging in age from 7 years to young adulthood which of matched pairs of pictures, one depicting an adult and the other depicting an infant, they preferred. Some of the pictures were of human beings; others were of animals. They found that adults, especially women, were most likely to choose the pictures of infants. Children between the ages of 7 and 12 preferred the pictures of adults. Between the ages of 12 and 14, the preference of girls shifted quite markedly from adults to children. A similar shift was found among boys when they were between 14 and 16. These shifts in preference coincide with the average ages at which girls and boys undergo the physiological changes that make them capable of reproducing.

Patterned responses to the appearance of infants may explain why mothers find it difficult to care for malformed offspring. Mothers of dogs, cats, guinea pigs, and some other species will kill malformed offspring. Though human parents usually do not kill their malformed babies, they do interact more frequently and more lovingly with infants they consider attractive than with those they consider homely (Langlois, 1986). They also attribute greater competence to attractive babies (Stephan & Langlois, 1984). This pattern is particularly noticeable when the baby is a girl. While still in the hospital with their newborn girls, mothers of less attractive babies directed their attention to people other than their babies more often than those whose babies were attractive (Langlois et al., 1995).

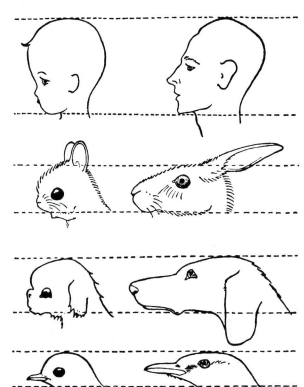

FIGURE 3.19 *Side-by-side sketches of the heads of infants and adults of four species make clear the distinguishing features of "babyness." (From Lorenz, 1943.)*

EARLY PARENT-INFANT CONTACT

It is popularly believed that the initial contacts between newborns and their parents, particularly their mothers, produce a special bond that has a profound effect on their future relationship. Recent research, however, has cast doubt on the importance of a special bonding process operating at birth for human babies and parents.

Evidence for the importance of initial contacts in animals is illustrated by the behavior of goats. If a baby goat is removed from its mother *immediately* after birth and returned, say, 2 hours later, the mother will attack it. But if the baby goat is allowed to stay with its mother for as little as 5 minutes after its birth before it is removed for a few hours, the mother will welcome its return (Klopfer, Adams, & Klopfer, 1964). Klopfer and his colleagues interpreted this phenomenon as evidence of a sensitive period during which the mother and baby became imprinted on each other.

Not long after Klopfer and his colleagues reported these results, Marshall Klaus, John Kennell, and their co-workers began research on mothers whose premature babies where being kept in incubators. Until the babies were mature enough to be held, the mothers had little contact with them. Some of these mothers lost interest in their babies, and the researchers thought that these infants might be especially at risk of being abused once they left the hospital. They speculated (1970) that the early sensitive period for mother-infant bonding among goats had its parallel in a similar sensitive period for the bonding of human mothers and their babies.

Next, in a widely publicized study, these same researchers divided 28 first-time mothers into an experimental and a control group. The mothers in the control group had the amount of contact with their newborn infants that was traditional in many hospitals in the late 1960s: a glimpse of the baby shortly after its birth, brief contact with it between 6 and 12 hours later, and then 20- to 30-minute visits for bottle feedings every 4 hours. In between these periods, the baby remained in the nursery. The mothers in the experimental group, however, were given their babies to hold for 1 hour within the first 3 hours after delivery. The babies were undressed so that their mothers could touch them. In addition, the mother and child spent 5 hours together each afternoon for the 3 days after delivery. Many of the mothers reported that, although they were already excited by being able to fondle their infants immediately after birth, their excitement rose higher when they succeeded in achieving eye contact with them.

When the mothers and babies in both groups returned to the hospital 1 month later, the mothers in the experimental group were more reluctant to leave their infants with other caretakers. They also seemed more interested in the examination of their infants, were better at soothing them, and seemed to gaze at and fondle their babies more than did the mothers in the control group. Eleven months later, the extended-contact mothers still seemed more attentive to their babies and more responsive to their cries than were the mothers in the control group (Kennell et al., 1974).

Drawing an analogy with animal behavior, Klaus and Kennell (1976) suggested that if a mother and child are allowed to be in close physical contact immediately after birth, "complex interactions between mother and infant help to lock them together" (p. 51). The researchers speculated that hormones generated by the mother's body during the birth process may make her more ready to form an emotional bond with her baby. If these hormones dissipate before the mother has any extended contact with her newborn, presumably she will be less responsive to it (Kennell, Voos, & Klaus, 1979).

These findings received a good deal of attention. Their publication coincided with a broad popular movement to reform hospital childbirth practices to allow mothers and fathers to have prolonged contact with their newborn babies. Pediatricians, nurses, and parents who supported these reforms found in Klaus and Kennell's work a strong rationale for the changes they wanted to make (Eyer, 1992). However, the research also provoked a lot of criticism. Klaus and Kennell were attacked on methodological grounds because their experimental and control groups were quite small (there were only 14 mothers in each) and composed entirely of unmarried African American women with low incomes, who could not, critics claimed, be considered representative of mothers in general. Furthermore, the mothers in the experimental group were probably aware of the special treatment they received, and some critics suggested that this awareness, rather than the extended contact with their babies, may have been the source of their behavior. In the years since the study was conducted, some follow-up studies have replicated Klaus and Kennell's findings, but others have failed to discover any long-lasting, significant differences between the mother-child relationships of experimental and control groups (Chess & Thomas, 1982; de Chateau, 1987; Lamb & Hwang, 1982).

Most researchers today agree that immediate contact is not crucial for the establishment of a long-term, positive emotional relationship between human mothers and normal infants. Parents who do not have immediate contact with their infants, for whatever reasons, almost always manage eventually to establish emotional ties to them. Most mothers who are anesthetized during delivery or suffer complications and who therefore do not see their babies for several hours or even days after their birth do not reject them; nor do mothers whose babies must be kept in incubators or fathers who are not present for their children's birth. In short, the great majority of mothers and fathers form attachments to their babies under all sorts of circumstances. (Eyer, 1992, reviews the evidence.)

SOCIAL EXPECTATIONS

When a baby is born among the Ngoni of East Africa, the mother-in-law announces its arrival by proclaiming, "A stranger has come!" In a sense, all newborn babies are strangers; they are newcomers no one has seen before. In important ways, however, babies are not total strangers.

While the mother is pregnant, most parents develop specific expectations about what their baby will be like. This is one reason a baby's death or deformity can be so devastating for the parents. But in normal circumstances, no sooner does a baby emerge from the womb than the parents begin to examine its looks and behaviors for hints of its future. Will she have Grandmother Cameron's high, round forehead? Does his lusty cry mean that he will have his father's quick temper?

Naturally, the baby will differ in some respects from the baby the parents have been imagining. Usually, though, the parents begin to accommodate themselves to the reality of their child at the moment of its birth. According to Aidan Macfarlane (1977), accommodation to the actual sex of the child when the other sex was wanted is one of the adjustments parents frequently have to make. The initial stages of such an adjustment can be seen in Box 3.4. Many people find the attitudes displayed in this dialogue offensive, but they are very common even today. When our own first child was born, the nurse expressed her regret, as if to console us for having a daughter.

Whether the baby is a boy or a girl, the parents' beliefs and expectations begin to shape their responses to the baby even before the child displays any truly distinctive features. One study found that parents who saw an ultrasound picture of their baby-to-be while it was still in the womb rated female fetuses as softer, littler, cuddlier, calmer, weaker, more delicate, and more beautiful than male fetuses (Sweeney & Bradbard, 1988). In another study, first-time mothers and fathers were asked to choose words that described their newborn babies within 24 hours after their birth (Rubin, Provenzano, & Luria, 1974). The male and female babies did not differ in length or weight or in their scores on the Apgar Scale. Nevertheless, the parents described their daughters as "little," "beautiful," "pretty," or "cute" and as resembling their mothers, whereas they described their sons as "big" and as resembling their fathers. Fathers, the researchers found, were more likely than mothers to sex-type their babies.

There is every reason for their baby's sex to be important to the parents. Children's sex determines what they are named, how they are dressed, how they are treated, and what will be expected of them in later life. There is a disconcerting side to this process, however. We like to think of ourselves as individuals, and we want to be treated with an awareness of who we are, not of what others expect us to be. It therefore comes as something of a shock to consider that so many important aspects of our future may be shaped so early by our parents' expectations.

Unless parental expectations are held so rigidly that they become destructive, they do not represent a failing on the parents' part. Rather, parents' responses to their newborns reflect the fact that human infants are not just biological organisms but cultural entities as well. For their parents and for other members of the community, infants have special meanings that are shaped by the culture's ideas about people and about the events that infants are likely to encounter as they grow

BOX 3.4

The Parents' Response to the Baby's Arrival

Aidan Macfarlane, an English pediatrician, recorded the following conversation in a delivery room as Mrs. B., age 27, gave birth to her first child. The concern it reveals about the baby's physical soundness is all but universal, and so is the power of the culture's belief system to shape the parents' initial responses to their newborn child.

Doctor: Come on, junior. Only a lady could cause so much trouble. Come on, little one.

[A baby is delivered]

Mother: A girl.

D: Well, it's got the right plumbing.

M: Oh, I'm sorry, darling.

Father: *[laughs]*

D: What are you sorry about?

M: He wanted a boy.

D: Well, you'll have to try again next week, won't you!

M: *[laughs]*

D: She looks great. Want to see her? Bloody and messy, but that's not from her.

M: Oh, she's gorgeous.

F: Looks like you.

[Mother kisses father]

M: Is she all right?

D: Why don't you ask her? She's quite capable of letting you know how she feels about the situation.

M: She's noisy, isn't she?

D: Yes, just like the modern generation.

F: Yes.

M: Well, Dr. Murphy, I was right. I had a sneaky feeling it was a girl, just because I wanted a boy.

F: Well, it will suit your mum, won't it?

M: *[laughs]*

D: Often tactically best to have a girl first—she can help with the washing up.

[Baby given to mother]

M: Hello, darling. Meet your dad. You're just like your dad. *[Baby yells.]*

F: I'm going home!

M: Oh you've gone quiet. *[laughs]* Oh darling, she's just like you—she's got your little tiny nose.

F: It'll grow like yours.

M: She's big, isn't she? What do you reckon?

D: She's quite good-looking, despite forceps marks on her head—but don't worry about that. She'll have little bruises around her ears—well, they usually have. I don't know if she does.

M: There's one—there. . . . Oh look, she's got hair. It's a girl—you're supposed to be all little.

D: What do you think she weighs, Richard? I think about seven and a half.

M: Oh, she's gorgeous, she's lovely. She's got blue eyes. You hold her. Come on.

F: No.

M: Why not? *[laughs]* You're all of a tremble, aren't you?

---

to adulthood. These meanings in turn shape the ways adults construct the environmental contexts within which children develop. When differences are found in the way boys and girls are treated, it is not just because parents think that infant boys and girls are different to begin with but, perhaps more significant, because they believe that men and women have different roles to play (Sigel et al., 1992).

This orientation to the future is expressed in clear symbolic form by the Zincantecos of south-central Mexico (Greenfield, Brazelton, & Childs, 1989). When a son is born he is given a digging stick, an ax, and a strip of palm used in weaving mats, in expectation of his adult role. Newborn girls are given a set of objects associated with the adult female role. Such future orientation is not only present in ritual; it is coded in a Zincantecan saying: "For in the newborn baby is the future of our world."

D: I dropped the first one I held.

F: Charming!

M: Oh look, oh mine. Hello, darling. Good lungs, hasn't she? She's got a dimple—where'd she get that from?

D: That's probably from the forceps. Actually, have you got dimples?

M: Oh no, neither of us have. Oh, you're lovely. Look . . . she's lovely.

M: I thought she'd be all mauve and crinkly.

D: Oh, she's in great nick.

M: Yes. I was expecting her to be all mauve and shriveled, but she's not, is she?

D: Not at all. In front of the cameras she's a real lady.

M: Oh dear. Having your photo taken, darling? Oh.

D: Ma'am, can I ask you to drop your ankles apart?

M: She doesn't go much on this.

[Nurse attaches name-tag to baby]

F: Like British Rail, labeling her like a parcel.

M: Oh look, darling, look at the size of her feet. She's got no toenails.

D: What do you mean, she hasn't got any toenails?

M: She hasn't got any toenails.

M: They're soft.

D: I don't think you'd like it scratching around inside you.

M: Look—fabulous. Aren't you pleased with her.

F: Yes, of course.

D: I'm not putting her back.

M: You said that if it was a girl it could go back.

D: Back to the manufacturers, yes.

M: Well, it came from him in the first place.

D: It's his spermatozoa that decides the sex.

M: Quite. *[kisses the baby and laughs]*

F: I shall be worried to death when she's eighteen.

M: You'll imagine her going out with all sorts of blokes like you were. *[laughs]* In a sort of odd way I was after his money really.

D: Yes?

M: All two quid. Go, go to dad.

(Macfarlane, 1977, pp. 61–67)

Mr. and Mrs. B. are not the only parents who find they must quickly change their plans and make a virtue out of having a daughter instead of a son. In the United States, it is a fairly common occurrence in spite of the changing attitudes about sex roles. Polls conducted in the United States indicate that most people want their first child to be a son, and if they were to have only one child, they preferred that child to be a boy (Frankiel, 1993). Despite their initial hopes and expectations, most parents eventually accept the sex of their newborns.

Organization of the present in terms of the future is a fundamental cultural source of developmental change and a powerful environmental source of developmental continuity. As the anthropologist Leslie White (1949) wrote, only among humans does the world of ideas come "to have a continuity and permanence that the external world of the senses can never have. It is not made up of the present only, but of a past and a future as well" (p. 372).

Just as infants arrive at childbirth with a set of genetically built-in capacities to learn about and to act upon the world, parents arrive at this moment with their own tendencies to respond in certain ways that have developed through their experience as members of their culture. The relationship between child and parents that begins at birth is an essential part of the foundation on which later development builds.

SUMMARY

The Periods of Prenatal Development

- Many developmental theorists look upon the prenatal period as a model for all periods of development from conception to death.
- Prenatal development is often divided into three broad periods:

  1. The germinal period, when the zygote moves into the uterus and becomes implanted there.
  2. The period of the embryo, which begins with implantation and ends with the first signs of ossification at the end of the eighth week. During this period the basic organs are formed.
  3. The period of the fetus, during which the brain grows extensively and the separate organ systems become integrated.

- As the organism grows from a single cell to a full-term newborn child, new forms constantly emerge. The preformationist hypothesis holds that all forms are already present in the organism's first cells. According to the epigenetic hypothesis, interactions between the cells and their environment generate the new forms.
- At implantation, the organism becomes directly dependent on the mother's body for sustenance.
- The embryo becomes active with the first pulses of a primitive heart, beginning about 1 month after conception.

The Developing Organism in the Prenatal Environment

- The fetus is subject to environmental influences originating from outside as well as inside the mother. The fetus sometimes experiences outside influences directly through its own sensory mechanisms, but often such influences work indirectly, through their effects on the mother.
- Babies' reactions to events they first experienced in the womb seem to indicate that fetuses are capable of learning.
- The mother's reactions to her environment—her feelings and attitudes—are associated with the fetus's well-being. Children born to mothers who do not want them or who are under stress are subject to developmental risk.
- The nutritional status of the mother is an important factor in fetal development. Extreme malnutrition in the mother has a devastating effect on her ability to produce a normal child. Lesser degrees of malnourishment associated with other forms of environmental deprivation also increase the risks to fetal and postnatal development.
- Teratogens (environmental agents that can cause deviations in fetal development) take many forms. Drugs, infections, radiation, and pollution all pose threats to the developing organism. Several basic principles apply to the effects of teratogens:

  1. The susceptibility of the organism depends on the stage of its development.
  2. A teratogen's effects are likely to be specific to a particular organ.
  3. Individual organisms vary in their susceptibility to teratogens.
  4. The physiological state of the mother influences the impact of a teratogen.

5. The greater the concentration of a teratogenic agent, the greater the risk.

6. Teratogens that adversely affect the developing organism may affect the mother little or not at all.

Prenatal Development Reconsidered

- Several basic principles of development are seen in the prenatal period:

  1. Sequence is fundamental.
  2. Timing is important.
  3. Development consists of differentiation and integration.
  4. Development is characterized by stagelike changes.
  5. Development proceeds unevenly.
  6. The course of development seems to be punctuated by periods of regression.

Birth: The First Bio-Social-Behavioral Shift

- Birth is the first bio-social-behavioral shift in human development.

- The process of birth begins approximately 266 days after conception, when changes in the mother's body force the fetus through the birth canal.

- Labor proceeds through three stages. It begins with the first regular, intense contractions of the uterus, and it ends when the baby is born, the umbilical cord is severed, and the afterbirth is delivered. Although the biological process of labor is roughly the same everywhere, there are marked cultural variations in the organization of childbearing.

- Drugs given to the mother to reduce pain may have negative effects on the neonate.

The Newborn's Condition

- The infant's physical state at birth is usually assessed by the Apgar Scale, which rates the infant's heart rate, respiratory effort, reflex responsivity, muscle tone, and color. Babies with low Apgar scores require immediate medical attention if they are to survive.

- Scales have been developed to assess the neonate's behavioral capacities. These scales are satisfactory for identifying neonates who require medical intervention; they appear to be modestly useful, at best, for predicting later patterns of development.

- Many premature babies who are of normal size for their gestational age can catch up with full-term infants if they are well cared for. Those who have low birth weights and small heads are especially at risk for long-term developmental problems.

Beginning the Parent-Child Relationship

- A newborn's appearance plays a significant role in the parents' responses to it.

- Some investigators believe that there is a critical period for emotional bonding between mothers and their infants shortly after birth. Attempts to replicate the study on which this claim is based have been only partially successful. Most researchers now believe that contact shortly after birth is not essential to long-term emotional attachment.

- The parents' expectations patterned by the culture's belief system influence the child's environment in ways that promote the continuation of cultural traits from one generation to another.

KEY TERMS

amnion,   p. 87

Apgar Scale,   p. 115

blastocyst,   p. 85

Brazelton Neonatal
 Assessment Scale,
 p. 116

cephalocaudal pattern,
 p. 88

chorion,   p. 87

cleavage,   p. 84

ectoderm,   p. 87

endoderm,   p. 87

epigenesis,   p. 85

fetal alcohol syndrome,
 p. 102

fetal growth retardation,
 p. 118

germinal period,   p. 83

heterochrony,   p. 84

heterogeneity,   p. 84

implantation,   p. 87

inner cell mass,   p. 85

low birth weight,   p. 118

mesoderm,   p. 88

morula,   p. 84

period of the embryo,
 p. 83

period of the fetus,
 p. 83

placenta,   p. 87

preformationism,   p. 85

premature,   p. 117

proximodistal pattern,
 p. 88

teratogens,   p. 101

trophoblast,   p. 85

umbilical cord,   p. 87

zona pellucida,   p. 83

THOUGHT QUESTIONS

1. Give examples of quantitative and qualitative changes that take place during prenatal development. What are the important differences between the two kinds of changes?

2. In what ways might your own physical, psychological, and social characteristics at the age of 10 illustrate the developmental principles of heterochrony and heterogeneity?

3. Propose an ethical, practicable research design to explore the effects of industrial pollutants on the health of newborn humans.

4. List six precautions that a woman and man might take to optimize the health of their future children.

5. Skim back through the chapter to list as many examples as you can in which the environment plays a significant role in prenatal development. Do you think that the role of the environment in development changes after birth? How?

PART TWO

INFANCY

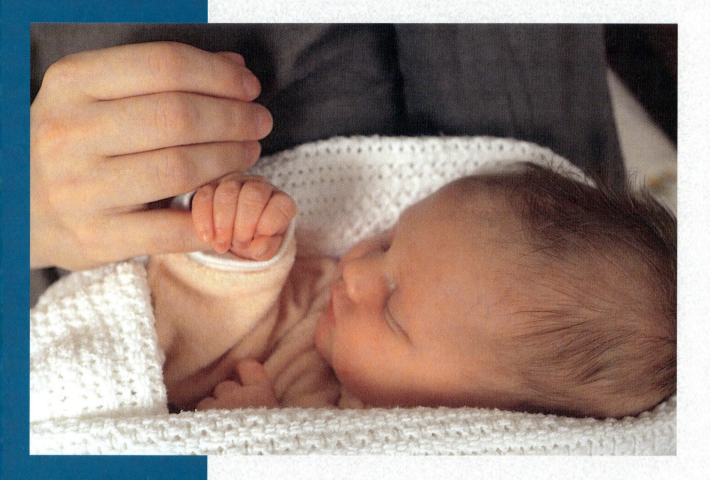

All cultures recognize infancy as a distinct period of life. Its starting point is clear; it begins when the umbilical cord is severed and the child starts to breathe. The end of infancy is not so easily defined. According to the ancient Romans, an infant is "one who does not speak," and the ability to speak a language is still considered an important indicator that infancy has come to an end. It is not a sufficient marker by itself, however. Modern developmental psychologists look for converging changes in several spheres of children's functioning to establish that one stage has ended and another begun. The acquisition of language is accompanied by changes in their physical capacities, modes of thought, and social relations. It is this ensemble of changes that transforms babies from helpless infants into children who, though still dependent upon adults, are on their way to independence.

The chapters in Part Two are organized to highlight the important sequences of changes in each sphere and the interactions among them. Chapter 4 begins with a description of infants' earliest capacities for perceiving and acting on the world. It then traces events in infant development from birth to the age of about 2½ months. An important requirement of this earliest postnatal period is that the behaviors of infants and their caretakers become sufficiently coordinated for adults to be able to provide infants with enough food and warmth to support their continued growth. This requirement is met through a wide variety of different cultural systems of infant care that call upon infants' basic capacities to learn from experience. If all goes well, the development of crucial brain structures by the end of this period enhances infants' abilities to experience the world and reorders the social and emotional interactions between infants and their caretakers. This ensemble of changes is the first bio-social-behavioral shift.

Between 2½ and 12 months of age, the period covered in Chapter 5, the infant's capacities in all spheres of development progress markedly. Increases in size and strength are accompanied by increases in coordination and mobility: the ability to sit independently appears at about 5 or 6 months, crawling at about 7 or 8 months, and walking at about 1 year. Both memory and problem-solving abilities improve, providing infants with a finer sense of their environment and how to act upon it. Sometime between 7 and 9 months, infants' increased physical ability and intellectual power bring about additional changes in their emotions and social relations. They are likely to become wary of strangers, they become upset when left alone, and they express strong emotional attachments to their caretakers. They also begin to make their first speechlike sounds. These changes mark what appears to be a second bio-social-behavioral shift during infancy.

Chapter 6 describes the changes that occur between 12 months and 2½ years, culminating in the bio-social-behavioral shift that signals the end of infancy. Rapid growth in the baby's ability to use language is accompanied by the emergence of pretend play and more sophisticated forms of problem solving. Toward the end of infancy, children begin to show a concern for adult standards and to attempt to meet those standards. Caretakers, for their part, view these changes as a sign that children are no longer "babies." They begin to reason with their children, to explain things to them, and to make demands upon them.

The coverage of infancy ends with Chapter 7, which takes up an enduring question concerning human development: Is the pattern of development that is established during infancy fixed and unchangeable, or can it be significantly altered by the maturational changes and experiences that will occur during later childhood and adolescence? This scientific question has a practical counterpart: Should society provide special supports for infants and their parents in order to reduce costly problems later on, or should infancy remain purely a family concern? As we shall see, opinions about these matters are sharply divided. Nevertheless, a look at the efforts of psychologists to study them underscores how important it is to consider the whole child in the context of both family and community if we are to gain a scientific understanding of development and make informed decisions about social policies that affect children.

CHAPTER 4

Early Infancy: Initial Capacities and the Process of Change

"Babies control and bring up their families as much as they are controlled by them; in fact, we may say that the family brings up a baby by being brought up by him. Whatever reaction patterns are given biologically and whatever schedule is predetermined developmentally must be considered to be a series of potentialities for changing patterns of mutual regulation."

Erik Erikson, Childhood and Society

In comparison with guinea pigs and other creatures that at birth are able to negotiate their environments almost as well as their parents, human beings are born in a state of marked immaturity. At birth, a baby's capacities are not adequate in themselves to ensure the baby's survival. The sucking reflex, for example, is of no help in obtaining food unless the infant's mouth is in touch with a source of milk, and newborns are incapable of arranging things so that the sucking reflex can come into play in an adaptive way. They must be physically aided to accomplish even such an elementary function as feeding. The relative helplessness of human babies at birth has two obvious consequences. First, human newborns must depend on their parents and other adults for many years for their survival. Second, in order to survive on their own and eventually reproduce, humans must acquire a vast repertoire of knowledge and skills they do not possess at birth.

This chapter describes the capacities of the child at birth and the processes of developmental change that occur in the initial period of infancy, a period beginning immediately after birth and ending some 2½ months later. During this time, significant changes take place in several important biological, behavioral, and social processes. These changes converge about 2½ months after birth to make new kinds of behavior possible, allowing a qualitatively different social and emotional relationship to develop between infants and their caregivers. This convergence of changes in different domains is the kind of *qualitative* reorganization in the child's functioning that we have designated a *bio-social-behavioral shift*.

Earliest Capacities

Nothing has fired the curiosity of developmental psychologists more strongly than the question of babies' psychological capacities when they emerge from the womb. How prepared are these newcomers to perceive the sights, smells, and sounds of the world around them? Is the newborn mind a tabula rasa (blank slate) on which the environment writes, as John Locke proposed? (See Box 1.1, pp. 14–15.) Or do infants come into the world already equipped with highly structured nervous systems, primed to experience and develop in an environment for which they have been shaped by their particular genetic endowment and cultural history?

At the beginning of this century, psychological opinion leaned in Locke's direction. The philosopher-psychologist William James (1890) summarized this view when he described the world the newborn child experiences as a "buzzing, blooming confusion." The new circumstances that greet the infant at birth may well be confusing, but as we will see, the research of recent decades has demonstrated that infants are by no means blank slates. They are born with remarkable capacities to engage the world and to behave in ways that promote their own survival.

SENSORY PROCESSES

The sensory systems of an organism are the primary means by which it receives information from the environment. Normal full-term newborns enter the world with all sensory systems functioning, but not all of these systems are at the same level of maturity. This unevenness illustrates the general rule of development that we remarked on with respect to the fetal period: the various organ systems develop at different rates (heterochrony) throughout the child's development.

The basic method used to evaluate an infant's sensory capacities is to introduce some change into the environment and observe how the child's physiological processes or behavior are affected by it (Bornstein, 1988). An investigator might sound a tone or flash a light, for example, and watch for an indication—a turn of the head, a variation in brain waves, a change in the rate at which the baby sucks on a nipple—that the newborn has sensed it. Sometimes the researcher presents two stimuli at once to determine if the baby will attend to one longer than to the other. If so, presumably the baby can tell the stimuli apart, and perhaps even prefers the one it attends to longer.

Another widely used technique is first to introduce and then repeat or continue a stimulus until the infant stops paying attention to it. This response pattern is called **habituation.** The next step is to make a change in some aspect of the stimulus: the frequency of the tone, the language being spoken, or the arrangement of elements within a visual array. If the infant's interest is renewed, the investigator can conclude that the infant sensed the change that was introduced. To begin paying attention again when some aspect of a stimulus has been changed is called **dishabituation.** If the infant continues to ignore the stimulus despite the change, the investigator cannot be certain whether the change in the stimulus was perceived or not.

Hearing

Make a loud noise and infants only minutes old will startle and may even cry. They will also turn their heads toward the source of the noise, an indication that they perceive sound as roughly localized in space (Weiss, Zelazo, & Swain, 1988). Yet newborns' hearing is not so acute for some parts of the sound spectrum as it will be when they are older (Werner & Vanden Boss, 1993). Sensitivity to sound improves dramatically in infancy and then more slowly until the age of 10, when it reaches adult levels.

Infants are able to distinguish the sound of the human voice from other kinds of sounds, and they seem to prefer it. They are especially interested in speech directed to them and spoken with the high pitch and slow, exaggerated pronunciation known as "baby talk" (Cooper & Aslin, 1990). There is even evidence that by the time they are 2 days old some babies would rather hear the language that has been spoken around them than a foreign language (Moon, Cooper, & Feiffer, 1993).

But consider the even more difficult problem newborn babies confront. Even if they have picked up a sense of the basic rhythms of their native language while in the womb, as studies discussed in Chapter 3 suggest (p. 94), infants are born into the world with very little experience of language. Yet within a year, and with no formal training, they will be making speechlike sounds, and by the end of the first year they will be able to produce three or four words (Fenson et al., 1994). What underlies human infants' prodigious ability to acquire language?

Part of the answer is that children have the ability to perceive basic language sounds at birth, or as early thereafter as the proper tests can be carried out (Marean, Werner, & Kuhl, 1992). One of the most striking discoveries about the hearing of very young infants is that they are particularly sensitive to the sound categories in human speech (Eimas, 1985), a capacity that appears to be essential for the acquisition of language. These basic language sounds are called **phonemes.** (Linguists denote phonemes and other language sounds by enclosing them in slashes, as we do.)

Phonemes vary from language to language. In Spanish, for example, /r/ and /rr/ are two phonemes; "pero" and "perro" sound different ("perro" has a "rolling" r) and have different meanings. In English, however, there is no such distinction. Similarly, /r/ and /l/ are different phonemes in English but not in Japanese. No wonder learning a new language often seems such a formidable undertaking! Peter Eimas and his colleagues arranged for 2-month-olds to suck on a nipple attached to a recording device in a special apparatus (see Figure 4.1). After establishing a baseline rate of sucking for each baby, they presented the speech sound /pa/ to the babies each time they sucked. At first the babies' rate of sucking increased as if they were excited by each presentation of the sound, but after a

Habituation The gradual decrease of attention paid to a repeated stimulus.

Dishabituation To begin paying attention again after habituation, as a result of a change in a repeating stimulus.

Phonemes The sound categories that signal differences between meaningful units in a language. Phonemes differ from language to language.

FIGURE 4.1 *Apparatus for presenting artificially manipulated speech sounds to young infants. The infant sucks on a pacifier connected to recording instruments as speech-like sounds are presented from a loudspeaker just above the Raggedy*

while they settled back to their baseline rate of sucking. When the infants had become thoroughly habituated to the sound of /pa/, some of them heard a new sound, /ba/, which differed from the original sound only in its initial phoneme—/b/ versus /p/. Others heard a sound that differed an equal amount from the original sound but remains within the /pa/ phoneme category (see Figure 4.2). The babies began sucking rapidly again only when they heard a phoneme of a different *category*, an indication that they were especially sensitive to the difference between the /b/ and /p/ sounds.

Other studies have shown that very young infants are able to perceive all the categorical sound distinctions used in all the world's various languages. Japanese babies, for example, can perceive the difference between /r/ and /l/, even though adult speakers of Japanese cannot. The ability to make phonemic distinctions apparently begins to narrow to just those distinctions that are present in one's native language at about 6 to 8 months of age (see Figure 4.3), the same age at which the baby's first halting articulations of language-like sounds are likely to begin (Eimas, 1985; Kuhl et al., 1992).

It is tempting to conclude that human infants are born with special perceptual skills that are pretuned to the properties of human speech, but studies indicate that other species can make similar distinctions (Kuhl & Miller, 1978). The difference is that humans use this ability as a stepping-stone to the mastery of language, an achievement that is beyond the capacities of other animals.

Vision

The basic anatomical elements of the visual system are present at birth, but they are not fully developed and they are not well coordinated (Aslin, 1987). The lens of the eye is still somewhat immature; it focuses images several millimeters behind the retina, so that the images on the retina are blurred. Also, the movements of the baby's eyes are not coordinated well enough to make the images on the two retinas sufficiently complementary to form a clear composite image. The immaturity of some of the neural pathways that relay information from the retina to the brain further limits the newborn's visual capacities (Atkinson & Braddick, 1982).

Color Perception Newborns seem to possess all, or nearly all, of the physiological prerequisites for seeing color, but psychologists disagree about precisely what colors newborns can perceive (Bornstein, 1976; Teller & Bornstein, 1987; Werner & Wooten, 1979). By 2 months of age, however, their color vision appears to be roughly equal to adults' (Bornstein, 1988).

Visual Acuity A basic question about infants' vision is how nearsighted they are. To determine newborns' visual acuity, Robert Fantz and his colleagues (Fantz, Ordy, & Udelf, 1962) developed a test based on the fact that when a striped visual field moves in front of the eyes, the eyes start to move in the same direction as the pattern. If the gaps between the stripes are so small that they cannot be perceived, the eyes do not move. By varying the width of the gaps and comparing the results obtained from newborns with those obtained from adults, these researchers were able to estimate that neonates have 20/300 vision—that is, they can see at 20 feet what an adult with normal vision can see at 300 feet. Other researchers estimate the visual acuity, or acuteness, of newborns to be closer to 20/800 (Cornell & McDonnell, 1986). Although these estimates are far apart, both suggest that the newborn is very nearsighted.

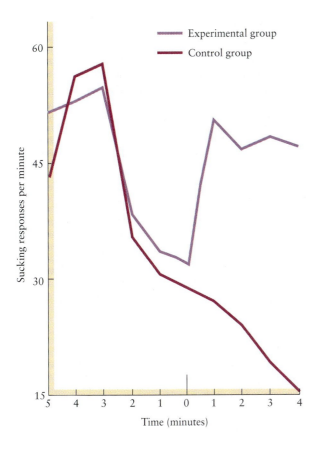

FIGURE 4.2 *When two groups of infants are repeatedly presented a single consonant over a 5-minute period, their rates of sucking decrease to just over 30 sucks per minute. For half of the infants (the experimental group) the consonant is changed at the time marked "0." Note that their rate of sucking increases sharply. For the remaining infants (the control group), who continued to hear the same consonant, the rate of sucking continues to decrease. (Adapted from Eimas, 1985.)*

Poor visual acuity is probably less troublesome to newborns than to older children and adults. After all, newborns are unable to move unless someone carries them, and they cannot hold their heads erect without support. Still, their visual system is tuned well enough to allow them to see objects a foot or so away—about the distance of their mother's face when they are nursing. This level of acuity allows them to make eye contact, which is important in establishing the social relationship between mother and child (Stern, 1977). By 7 or 8 months of age, when infants are able to crawl, their visual acuity is close to the adult level (Haith, 1990; Cornell & McDonnell, 1986).

Visual Scanning Despite their nearsightedness and their difficulty in focusing, newborns actively scan their surroundings from the earliest days of life (Bronson, 1991; Haith, 1980; Haith, Berman, & Moore, 1977). Marshall Haith and his colleagues developed recording techniques that allowed them to determine precisely where infants were looking and to monitor their eye movements in both light and dark rooms. They discovered that neonates scan with short eye movements even in a completely darkened room. Since no light is entering their eyes, this kind of

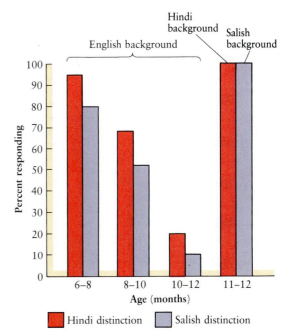

FIGURE 4.3 *Infants can distinguish among language sounds that do not occur in their native language. The proportion of infants from an English-speaking background who respond to consonants in Hindi and Salish (a North American Indian language) decreases markedly during the first year of life. In contrast, 1-year-old Hindi and Salish infants retain the capacity to perceive the linguistic contrasts native to their respective languages. (Adapted from Eimas, 1985.)*

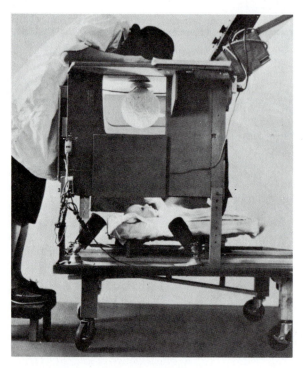

FIGURE 4.4 *The "looking chamber" that Robert Fantz used to test newborns' visual interests. The infant lies in a crib in the chamber, looking up at the stimuli attached to the ceiling. The observer, watching through a peephole, determines how long the infant looks at each stimulus.*

scanning cannot be caused by the visual environment. It must therefore be *endogenous*, originating in the neural activity of the central nervous system. Endogenous eye movements seem to be an initial, primitive basis for looking behavior.

Haith's studies also revealed that neonates exhibit an early form of *exogenous* looking; that is, looking that is stimulated by the external environment. When the lights are turned on after infants have been in the dark, they pause in their scanning when their gaze encounters an object or some change of brightness in the visual field. This very early sensitivity to changes in illumination, which is usually associated with the edges and angles of objects, appears to be an important component of the baby's developing ability to perceive visual forms (Haith, 1980).

Perception of Patterns   What do babies see when their eyes encounter an object? Are they able to see objects much as adults do?

Until the early 1960s it was widely believed that neonates perceived only a formless play of light. Robert Fantz (1961, 1963) dealt a severe blow to this assumption by demonstrating that babies less than 2 days old can distinguish among visual forms. The technique he used was very simple. Babies were placed on their backs in a specially designed "looking chamber" (see Figure 4.4) and shown various forms. An observer looked down through the top of the chamber and recorded how long the infants looked at each form. Because the infants spent more time looking at some forms than at others, presumably they could tell the forms apart and preferred the ones they looked at the longest. Fantz found that neonates would rather look at patterned figures, such as faces and concentric circles, than at plain ones (see Figure 4.5).

Fantz's findings set off a search to determine the extent of newborns' capacity to perceive form and the reasons they prefer some forms over others. That research has confirmed that infants visually perceive the world as more than random confusion, but it has also provided evidence that infants do not enter the world prepared to see it in the same way adults do. Gordon Bronson (1991), for example, studied the way 2-week-old and 12-week-old babies scan outline drawings of simple figures, such as a cross or a "v," on a lighted visual field. When adults are shown such figures, they scan the entire boundary, but Bronson found that babies 2 weeks of age appear to focus only on areas of high contrast, such as lines and angles (see Figure 4.6). This kind of looking behavior is clearly not random, but it does not constitute evidence that children are born with the ability to perceive basic patterns. At

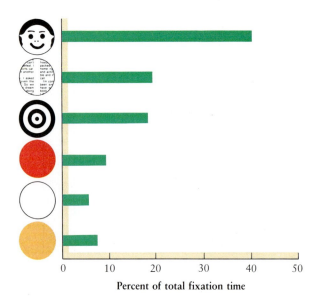

FIGURE 4.5   *Infants tested during the first weeks of life show a preference for patterned stimuli over plain stimuli. The length of each bar indicates the relative amount of time the babies spent looking at the corresponding stimulus. (Adapted from Fantz, 1961.)*

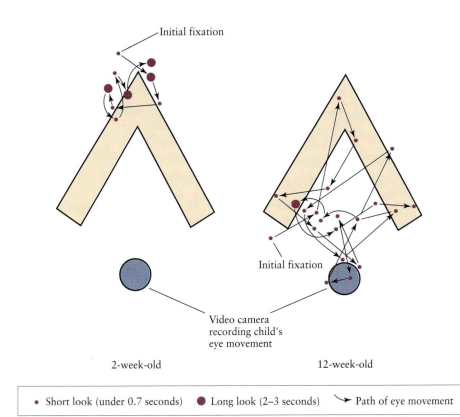

Initial fixation

Initial fixation

Video camera
recording child's
eye movement

2-week-old

12-week-old

• Short look (under 0.7 seconds)   ● Long look (2–3 seconds)   ↘ Path of eye movement

FIGURE 4.6 *Visual scanning of a triangle by young infants. The triangle was mounted on a wall. A video camera was mounted just beneath it, positioned to record the eye movements of an infant as it gazed at the triangle. Note that the 2-week-olds concentrated their gaze on only one part of the figure, whereas the 12-week-olds visually explored the figure more fully. Large dots indicate long fixation times. Small dots represent short fixation times. (Adapted from Bronson, 1991.)*

12 weeks of age, as Figure 4.6 indicates, infants scan more of the figure, although their scanning movements are sometimes off the mark and may still be arrested by areas of high contrast. In a follow-up study, Bronson (1994) found that 13-week-old infants scanned more rapidly and extensively than infants 10 weeks and under. The developmental change was so marked that "by 3 months of age [the] infants appear[ed] to be quite different organisms, at least with respect to their scanning characteristics" (p. 1260). Bronson suggests that as the nervous system matures, it becomes more sophisticated and can begin to control visual scanning.

Perception of Faces   In Fantz's early studies, one of the complex forms presented to the babies was a schematic human face. The fact that infants looked longer at this form than at any of the others suggested that newborn infants can perceive faces and like to look at them. When Fantz (1961, 1963) presented newborn infants with a schematic face and a form in which facial elements had been scrambled, he found that the infants apparently could distinguish the schematic face from the jumbled face (see Figure 4.7). This suggestion that newborns have an unlearned preference for a biologically significant form naturally attracted great interest. As Figure 4.7 shows, however, the preference for the schematic face over the scrambled face is small. Compare it with the difference in preference for a complex figure (line *a* or *b*) over a plain one (line *c*). In the years since Fantz conducted his studies, there has been much debate about whether newborns actually perceive faces or are simply visually attracted to complex figures.

The evidence from early follow-up studies ran against the idea that neonates are primed to respond to "faceness." Lonnie Sherrod (1979) replicated Fantz's research, controlling carefully for such factors as the degree of brightness, the contrast between the forms and their background, and the number of turns and angles

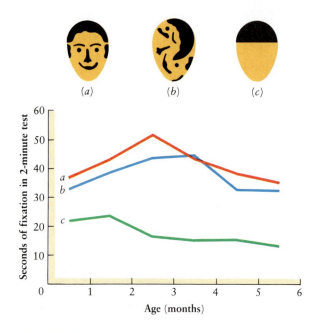

FIGURE 4.7 *Visual preferences of infants for* (a) *a schematic face,* (b) *a scrambled schematic face,* and (c) *a nonfacelike figure, all having equal amounts of light and dark areas. The infants preferred both facelike forms over the nonfacelike form, and they accorded the "real" face slightly more attention than the scrambled face. (Adapted from Fantz, 1961.)*

within the schematic and scrambled faces. His conclusion, supported by others (Haaf, Smith, & Smitely, 1983), was that the presence of highly contrasting elements or many turns and angles, not "faceness" itself, accounted for Fantz's findings. A follow-up of this line of research by James Dannemiller and Benjamin Stephens (1988) used a computer-generated display that allowed the researchers to equate their stimuli in all relevant factors except "faceness." They found that 6-week-olds did not show a preference for one figure over another, but 12-week-olds showed a preference for the face stimulus.

Subsequent studies have shown that motion has a critical influence on a newborn's preference for facelike stimuli. In Fantz's studies and the later replications we have described, researchers used only stationary schematic representations of faces. Several other studies indicate that babies as young as 9 minutes old will turn their heads to gaze at a schematic face if it *moves* in front of them, and will look at it longer than at a moving scrambled face (Goren, Sarty, & Wu, 1975; Morton & Johnson, 1991). John Morton and Mark Johnson suggest that the very early recognition of faces is a primitive reflex-like response controlled by lower levels of the brain, but that the preference for faces among infants older than 2 months arises because the visual cortex has matured and the infants have begun to learn about faces.

In real life, people move both their heads and the features of their faces. Under these naturalistic conditions, newborns only 2 days old demonstrate an ability to recognize the face they have seen most often, usually their mother's (Bushnell, Sai, & Mullin, 1989; Field et al., 1984). However, this recognition may amount to little more than their ability to detect differences in hairline contours (Pascalis et al., 1995).

Taste and smell

Neonates have a well-developed sense of smell (Engen, Lipsitt, & Kaye, 1963; Steiner, 1977, 1979). Trygg Engen and his colleagues demonstrated this sensory capacity in newborns by placing 2-day-old infants on a "stabilometer," an apparatus that measures physical activity. The experimenters held either an odorless cotton swab or a swab soaked in one of various aromatic solutions under the newborns' noses. Babies were judged to react to an odor if their activity increased over the level it had reached in response to the odorless cotton swab. The infants reacted strongly to some odors, such as garlic and vinegar, and less strongly to others, such as licorice and alcohol. Their responses indicated not only that they were sensitive to odors but also that they could tell one odor from another. This early sensitivity to odors has been confirmed in a more naturalistic way by Aidan Macfarlane (1975), who showed that by 5 days of age newborns will turn toward a pad soaked with breast milk, and by 8 to 10 days they will show a preference for the smell of their mother's milk over the milk of another woman.

Newborns' sense of taste, like their sense of smell, is acute. They prefer sweet to sour tastes (Lipsitt, 1977). They will also suck longer, and pause for shorter periods, on a bottle containing sweet substances than on one containing plain water. The characteristic facial expressions they make in response to various tastes look remarkably like those adults make when they encounter the same tastes, evidence that these expressions are innate (Rosenstein & Oster, 1988) (see Figure 4.8).

Touch, temperature, and position

The abilities to detect a touch to the skin, changes in temperature, and changes in physical position develop very early in the prenatal period. Although these sensory capacities have not received as much attention as vision and hearing, they are no less important to the baby's survival.

Newborns show that they sense they have been touched by making a distinctive movement, such as withdrawing the part touched or turning toward the touch. Some evidence suggests that sensitivity to touch increases in the days after birth (Lipsitt & Levy, 1959). Little is known, however, about whether neonates can distinguish between different tactile stimuli or tell what part of the body is being touched or about how such capacities might develop.

Neonates indicate that they are sensitive to changes in temperature by becoming more active if there is a sudden lowering of the temperature (Pratt, 1954). They respond to abrupt changes in their physical position, such as being suddenly dropped, with distinctive reflex-like movements. Such responses indicate that the mechanism for detecting changes in position, which is located in the middle ear, is operating.

Overall, there is extensive evidence that babies come into the world with sensory capacities in good working order and far more structured than they were once thought to be. (Infants' sensory capacities are summarized in Table 4.1.) The question then arises: What capacities do infants have for *acting* on the world? By studying the ability of infants to take in information from the environment and to act on it, researchers may be able to determine the starting point of postnatal psychological development.

RESPONSE PROCESSES

Infants are born with a variety of ways of acting on, and responding to, the world around them. Here we will examine infants' capacities as displayed in their reflexes, emotions, and temperament.

Reflexes

Newborn babies come equipped with a variety of **reflexes**—specific well-integrated, automatic (involuntary) responses to specific types of stimulation.

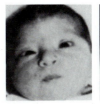

(a)

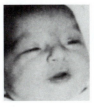

(b)

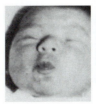

(c)

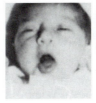

(d)

FIGURE 4.8 *Facial expressions evoked by various tastes are very similar in infants and adults: (a) a neutral expression follows the presentation of distilled water; (b) a hint of a smile follows the presentation of a sweet stimulus; (c) the pucker comes in response to a sour stimulus; (d) a bitter stimulus evokes a distinctive grimace.*

Reflexes Specific, well-integrated responses that are automatically elicited by specific aspects of the environment.

TABLE 4.1 Early Sensory Capacities

Sense	Capacity
Hearing	Ability to distinguish phonemes Preference for native language
Vision	Slightly blurred, slightly double vision at birth Color vision by 2 months of age Ability to distinguish patterned stimuli from plain Preference for moving, facelike stimuli
Smell	Ability to differentiate odors well at birth
Taste	Ability to differentiate tastes well at birth
Touch	Response to touch at birth
Temperature	Sensitivity to changes in temperature at birth
Position	Sensitivity to changes in position at birth

Some of the reflexes with which infants are born are described in Table 4.2. Virtually all psychologists agree that reflexes are important building blocks out of which various complex behavioral capacities of later life are constructed. They disagree, however, about the nature of reflexes and how they contribute to the development of more complex capacities.

Some reflexes are clearly part of the baby's elementary survival kit. The eyeblink reflex, for example, has a clear function: it protects the eye from overly bright lights and foreign objects that might damage it. The sucking and swallowing reflexes are essential to feeding. The purpose of some other reflexes, such as the grasping reflex (closing fingers around an object that is pressed against the palm) and the Moro reflex (grasping with the arms when suddenly dropped), is not as clear. Some biologically oriented developmental theorists believe that these reflexes serve no purpose now but were functional during early evolutionary stages, when infants needed to cling to their mothers in order to survive (Peiper, 1963). Others, such as John Bowlby (1973), believe that they may still be functional because they promote a close relationship between mother and infant.

TABLE 4.2 Reflexes Present at Birth

Reflex	Description	Developmental Course	Significance
Babinski	When the bottom of the baby's foot is stroked, the toes fan out and then curl	Disappears in 8 to 12 months	Presence at birth and normal course of decline are a basic index of normal neurological condition
Breathing	Repetitive, rhythmic inhalation and exhalation	Permanent	Provides oxygen and removes carbon dioxide
Crawling	When the baby is placed on his stomach and pressure is applied to the soles of his feet, his arms and legs move rhythmically	Disappears after 3 to 4 months; possible reappearance at 6 to 7 months as a component of voluntary crawling	Uncertain
Eyeblink	Rapid closing of eyes	Permanent	Protection against aversive stimuli such as bright lights and foreign objects
Grasping	When a finger or some other object is pressed against the baby's palm, her fingers close around it	Disappears in 3 to 4 months; replaced by voluntary grasping	Presence at birth and later disappearance is a basic sign of normal neurological development
Moro	If the baby is allowed to drop unexpectedly while being held, or if there is a loud noise, she will throw her arms outward while arching her back, and then bring her arms together as if grasping something	Disappears in 6 to 7 months (although startle to loud noises is permanent)	Disputed; its presence at birth and later disappearance are a basic sign of normal neurological development; possibly functions as facilitator of mother-infant bonding
Rooting	The baby turns his head and opens his mouth when he is touched on the cheek	Disappears between 3 and 6 months	Component of nursing
Stepping	When the baby is held upright over a flat surface, he makes rhythmic leg movements	Disappears in first 2 months but can be reinstated in special contexts	Disputed; it may be only a kicking motion, or it may be a component of later voluntary walking
Sucking	The baby sucks when something is put into her mouth	Disappears and is replaced by voluntary sucking	Fundamental component of nursing

Emotions

When we talk about emotions for purposes of everyday conversation, we are usually referring to the *feelings* aroused by an experience. If we unexpectedly win a prize, we feel happy and excited. When we say good-bye to a loved one whom we will not see for some time, we feel sadness and perhaps love. If someone prevents us from achieving a goal, we become angry.

Psychologists believe that the feelings aroused by an experience are only one aspect of emotion. In addition, emotions have a physiological aspect; they are accompanied by identifiable *physiological reactions* such as a change in heart rate or breathing. Emotions also communicate our internal feeling state to others through facial expressions and distinctive forms of behavior (Barrett & Campos, 1987). Lastly, emotions move us to action. They alert us and prepare us to respond. When something frightens us, for example, our senses become heightened and we become tense, ready to fight or flee. Technically speaking, then, **emotion** can be defined as a feeling state associated with distinctive physiological responses that motivates action, communicates, and regulates interaction with others.

Emotion The feeling tone, or affect, with which people respond to their circumstances.

Psychologists have long been divided on the question of which emotions are present at birth. Some favor the view that all people are born with a core set of *primary* emotions. To investigate this idea, these theorists have relied heavily on the assumption that the expression on one's face is a reliable indicator of one's emotional state. Specifically, they believe that certain facial expressions universally communicate a basic set of emotional states to others and that the facial expressions of very young infants signal the presence in them of the corresponding basic emotion. On the basis of their babies' facial expressions and vocalizations, for example, the mothers interviewed in one study reported that their infants were expressing several emotions by the age of 1 month, including joy, fear, anger, surprise, sadness, and interest (Johnson et al., 1982).

Mothers' reports about their babies are notorious for being biased, as we noted in Chapter 1 (p. 18). Recognizing this problem, Carroll Izard and his colleagues videotaped infants' responses to a variety of emotion-arousing events such as having an inoculation or the approach of a smiling mother (Izard, 1994; Izard et al., 1980). He showed the videotapes, or stills from them, to college students and nurses (see Figure 4.9), who agreed fairly consistently about which facial expressions communicated interest, joy, surprise, and sadness. To a somewhat lesser extent, they also agreed on which expressions showed anger, disgust, and contempt.

Additional support for the idea that there is a universal set of basic emotions and corresponding facial expressions comes from the cross-cultural research of Paul Ekman and his associates (Ekman, 1984, 1994). These researchers asked people in various literate and nonliterate cultures to pose expressions appropriate to such events as the death of a loved one and being reunited with a close friend. Both literate and nonliterate adults configured their faces in the same way to express each emotion. When shown photographs of actors posing the different expressions, the literate and nonliterate adults agreed on the photographs that represented happiness, sadness, anger, and disgust. The nonliterate adults did not distinguish fear from surprise, although they did distinguish them from the other expressions.

Yet facial expressions, no matter how universal their meanings among adults, may not be valid indicators of the same emotional states among newborns. Newborns may frown simply because they are hungry or cold. Their facial expressions and associated emotions are responses to immediate physical circumstances. An adult may frown, however, because she has just lost her job and is worried about how she will support herself. Her emotion involves the synthesis of information about her current circumstances and her anticipation of future events. This

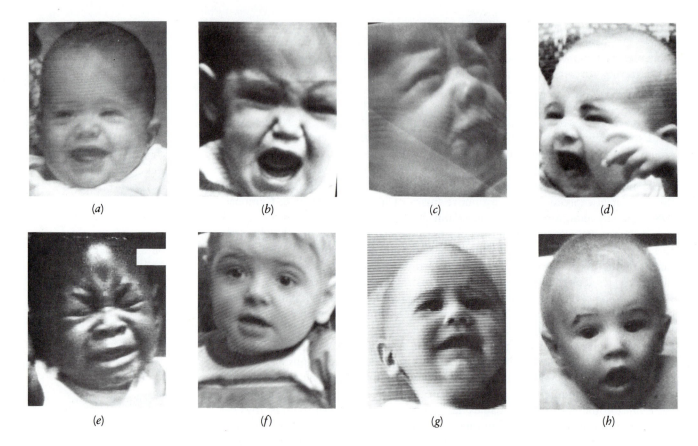

(a)   (b)   (c)   (d)

(e)   (f)   (g)   (h)

FIGURE 4.9 *Images from a videotaped recording of infants' facial expressions used by Carroll Izard and his colleagues to assess the possible universal relation between emotion and facial expression. What emotion do you think each facial expression represents? The responses most of Izard's adult subjects gave are printed upside down:*

əsıɹdɹns (ɥ) ʻɹɐəɟ (ƃ) ʻ1sə-ɹə1uı (ɟ) ʻuıɐd/ssəɹ1sıp (ə) ʻ1sn8sıp (p) ʻssəupɐs (ɔ) ʻɹə8uɐ (q) ʻʎoɾ (ɐ)

synthesis requires the accumulation of experience and interaction among the higher brain centers, which are immature at birth. Consequently, the processes that underlie the facial expressions of newborns may differ from those reflected by the same facial expressions in older infants, children, and adults.

It is this type of uncertainty that motivates the psychologists who question the claim that the primary emotions are there *at the beginning*. Adherents of this *differentiation approach to emotional development* assume that newborns experience only two general kinds of emotion, one positive (contentment), the other negative (distress). Additional emotions arise by splitting off, or differentiating themselves, from the original two states as the baby develops: joy becomes differentiated from contentment at about 3 months, anger and fear differentiate from discontent at about 4 months, and so on (Fischer et al., 1990; Lewis, 1993).

Whatever their views about the initial repertoire of emotions present at birth, psychologists agree that the feeling states associated with emotions and modes of emotional expression change and develop throughout the course of childhood. As infants grow older, their initial repertoire of emotions becomes entwined with their developing intellectual capacities and new kinds of social relations. Consequently, new emotions emerge to motivate the infants to act, communicate, and relate to others in new ways. Thus, in the chapters ahead, we will frequently find ourselves considering the development of emotions in connection with the development of the intellectual, social, and physical aspects of development.

Temperament

A commonly held intuition about human nature is that individual people differ from one another and are consistently like them*selves* in the ways they respond to the world around them and in their predispositions toward particular kinds of emotion. Our daughter, for example, has a tendency to approach life with boundless energy and an optimistic demeanor. Confronted with barriers, she rarely gives up, but finds some way to surmount them or to go around them. Her brother, by contrast, is a dreamier person. He is more likely to intellectualize a problem and more likely to vent his frustration. These stable individual styles of responding to the environment are encompassed by the word **temperament** (Allport, 1937; Bates, 1989; Goldsmith, 1987).

A wide variety of characteristics seen in babies have been interpreted as evidence of infants' temperamental qualities. They include the newborns' activity level, the ease with which they become upset, the intensity of their reactions, their characteristic reaction when something unusual happens, and their sociability (Bates, 1994). Such temperamental characteristics are believed to be core elements in the formation of a child's personality.

Pioneering studies of temperament and development were conducted by Alexander Thomas, Stella Chess, and their colleagues. Their work has had great influence over the years, both because the techniques they used to assess temperament have come to be widely used and because they followed the children's development into early adulthood. They began their research in the late 1950s with a group of 141 middle- and upper-class children in the United States. Later they broadened their longitudinal study to include 95 working-class Puerto Rican children and several groups of children suffering from diseases, neurological impairments, and mental retardation (Thomas et al., 1963; Thomas & Chess, 1977, 1984). The researchers asked the parents of the children to fill out questionnaires periodically, beginning shortly after the birth of their child. Included were questions about such matters as how the child reacted to the first bath, to wet diapers, and to the first taste of solid food. As the children grew older, the questionnaires were supplemented by interviews with teachers and by tests of the children.

When Chess and Thomas analyzed their data, they found they could identify nine behavioral traits that, taken together, provided an overall description of a child's temperament (see Table 4.3). After scoring the children on each of these nine traits, they found that most of the children could be classified in one of three broad temperament categories from the time they were infants:

- **Easy babies** are *playful, regular* in their biological functions, and *adapt readily* to new circumstances.
- **Difficult babies** are *irregular* in their biological functions, *irritable*, and often *respond intensely and negatively* to new situations or try to withdraw from them.
- **Slow-to-warm-up babies** are *low in activity* level and their responses are typically *mild*. They tend to *withdraw* from new situations, but in a mild way, and require more time than the easy babies to adapt to change.

There is widespread agreement that genetic factors contribute to the kinds of individual differences referred to as temperament (Bates, 1994; Buss & Plomin, 1984; Kagan et al., 1994). The strongest evidence for the heritability of temperamental traits comes from twin studies. For example, Arnold Buss and Robert Plomin (1984) found that ratings of emotionality, activity level, and sociability were strikingly similar in identical twins (who have identical genes) but not in fraternal twins (who inherit different mixes of genes from their parents). H. H. Goldsmith and Irving Gottesman (1981) obtained similar findings in respect to individual differences in activity level.

Daniel Freedman (1974) has documented ethnic differences in excitability among newborn infants, suggesting that excitability has a significant genetic component. He found that during the first days of life Chinese American babies tend to be more placid and more difficult to perturb than Anglo American or African American babies. In one set of observations, Freedman placed a cloth over the babies' noses and observed their reactions. Most African American and Anglo

Temperament The basic style with which an individual responds to the environment, as well as his or her dominant mood.

TABLE 4.3   Basic Indicators of Temperament According to Chess and Thomas

Trait	Definition	Example
Activity level	The level of movement typical of a given child's actions and the relative amount of time spent in action and inaction	Even in the uterus some babies kick and move around a lot while others are relatively still; similar differences are seen in the level and frequency of arm waving and kicking in early infancy and in the tendency of some young children to spend most of their waking hours in rapid motion
Rhythmicity	The degree of regularity and predictability of basic biological functions	Beginning shortly after birth, marked individual differences can be seen in the ease with which babies adapt to regular feeding and sleeping schedules and to bodily functions such as defecation
Approach–withdrawal	The nature of the baby's initial response to something new	Novel experiences such as the first substitution of a bottle for the breast, meeting a strange person, or the sudden appearance of a jack-in-the-box cause some children to be fearful and withdraw, while others actively explore and seek further stimulation
Adaptability	The ease with which a baby's initial responses to a situation are modified	Whether they initially withdraw from or take to a new experience, babies differ in how rapidly the novelty wears off and how easily they adjust to new circumstances, such as being given solid food in place of milk or being left with a baby-sitter
Threshold of responsiveness	The intensity level required in order for a stimulus to evoke a response	It takes very little noise to make some babies awaken from a nap or very little moisture in their diapers to make them cry, whereas others appear to react only when the stimulation becomes relatively intense
Intensity of reaction	The energy level of a response	It seems that whatever the circumstances, whether pleasant or unpleasant, some babies remain relatively placid in their responses, cooing when pleased and frowning when upset, whereas others laugh heartily and cry vigorously
Quality of mood	The amount of joyful, pleasant, and friendly behaviors in comparison to unpleasant and unfriendly behaviors	Some babies laugh frequently and tend to smile at the world, whereas others seem to be unhappy an unusual amount of the time
Distractibility	The extent to which novel stimuli disrupt or alter ongoing behaviors	Parents often seek to distract a crying baby by offering a pacifier or teddy bear, but such tactics work best with distractible babies
Attention span/persistence	The extent to which an activity, once undertaken, is maintained	Some babies will stare at a mobile or play happily with their favorite toy for a long time, whereas others quickly lose interest and move frequently from one activity to another

Source: Chess & Thomas, 1982.

American babies quickly turned their heads aside or swiped at the cloth with their hands. In contrast, the Chinese American babies usually lay quietly with the cloth covering their noses and breathed through their mouths. Two decades later, the substance of these results was supported in a comparison between Chinese, American, and Irish infants: the Chinese infants were significantly less active, less irritable, and less vocal than their Caucasian counterparts in a variety of situations (Kagan et al., 1994).

The possibility that temperamental traits are stable physiological "biases" in the way individuals respond to their environment implies that if the right measurements are taken in early infancy, it should be possible to predict the characteristic style with which individuals will behave at later stages of development (Kagan & Snidman, 1991a). Evidence for the stability of temperamental characteristics comes from a study by Cynthia Stifter and Nathan Fox (1990), who sampled ratings from physiological measures (such as heart rate), behavioral measures (such as the degree to which infants became upset when they were interrupted while sucking on a nipple), and parents' judgments about various traits (such as irritability, resistance to soothing, and cheerfulness). The researchers reported significant temperamental stability over the 5 months between the tests. Even longer periods of stability have been reported by Robert Plomin and his colleagues (Plomin, Emde, Braungart, & Campos, 1993).

Despite these interesting findings, a good deal of controversy still surrounds the study of temperament (Bates & Wachs, 1994). The first problem is how to describe the basic types of temperament. Though the three Chess and Thomas categories of temperament are widely used, there are other influential approaches that assume five or more basic temperament types (Rothbart et al., 1994).

A second problem concerns the stability of temperamental traits during the course of development. Even when statistical evidence supports the claim that temperamental traits remain somewhat the same from one time to the next, most studies find that the degree of stability is modest. Some researchers attribute the limited stability of temperamental traits over time to the uneven development of the biological systems that are responsible for temperament (Slabach, Morrow, & Wachs, 1991). Others suggest that the stability of children's temperamental traits is also influenced to some degree by the stability of their environment (Thomas & Chess, 1984).

Taken as a whole, newborns' initial resources for experiencing and acting on the world are quite impressive. Newborns are finely tuned to the sound categories and rhythms of human language, although their own ability to communicate is restricted largely to crying. Their taste, smell, and touch receptors all provide information about the immediate environment. They possess a limited but useful set of initial reflexes. They can learn new forms of behavior, and under some circumstances they can remember what they have learned between experiences. They have a small repertoire of basic emotions that motivate their actions, and they often display characteristic ways of responding that are precursors to temperamental characteristics.

Newborns are also, of course, nearsighted, uncoordinated, and extremely vulnerable. Without special care and the efforts of family members to make a place for them in the community, they cannot thrive and develop. In this respect, the initial resources of the infant, considered in isolation, are not a sufficient basis for development. Sources of development in the child's social world are also necessary.

Becoming Coordinated

Parents cannot always be hovering over their baby, anticipating every need before it is expressed. They must find a way to meet their infant's needs within the confines of their own rhythms of life and work. Whether parents work the land and must be up with the sun or work in an office where they are expected to appear at 9 A.M. sharp, they need to sleep at night. If it is the custom to eat a large meal at midday and take a nap before returning to work, that is the schedule they continue to follow. Such circumstances cause parents to attempt to modify their babies' patterns of eating and sleeping so they will fit into the life patterns of the household and the community.

In the United States such attempts to modify an infant's initial pattern of behavior are often referred to as "getting the baby on a schedule." Getting the baby on a schedule is more than a convenience. Through the coordination of activities that results, babies and parents create a system of mutual expectations that serves as the foundation for later developmental change.

Achieving a mutually satisfactory schedule is by no means easy or automatic. Babies come into the world with their own rhythms of activity, and those rhythms frequently do not coincide with their parents'. Every system of mutual accommodation causes some stress and strain. But when, eventually, families and newborns do achieve a common schedule and begin to coordinate their activities more smoothly, the general feeling of well-being that is produced helps to make the baby a welcome addition (Sprunger, Boyce, & Gaines, 1985).

Parents' efforts to achieve a common schedule with their baby focus on the infant's sleeping and eating. Crying is the baby's earliest means of signaling when these efforts fall short.

Sleeping

As with adults, the extent of newborns' arousal varies from complete rest to frantic activity. The patterns of their rest and activity are quite different from those of adults, however, particularly in the first weeks after birth. To find out about newborns' arousal patterns, Peter Wolff (1966) studied babies during their first weeks after birth. On the basis of such observable behaviors as muscle activity and eye movement, Wolff was able to distinguish seven states of arousal. (They are described in Table 4.4.) Additional research has shown that a distinctive pattern of brain activity is associated with each state of arousal (Berg & Berg, 1987; Emde, Gaensbauer, & Harmon, 1976). In this kind of research, a device called an electroencephalograph (EEG) is used to record the tiny electrical currents generated by the brain's cells, which are detected by electrodes placed on the scalp.

EEG recordings of infants' brain waves made shortly after birth distinguish two kinds of sleep that are the precursors of adult sleeping patterns: (1) an active pattern, called rapid-eye-movement (REM) sleep, which is characterized by uneven breathing; low-level, rapid brain-wave activity; and a good deal of eye and limb movement; and (2) a quiet pattern, called non-rapid-eye-movement (NREM) sleep, in which breathing is regular, brain waves are larger and slower, and the baby barely moves (see Figure 4.10). During the first 2 to 3 months of life, infants begin their sleep with active (REM) sleep and only gradually fall into quiet (NREM) sleep (Emde, Gaensbauer, & Harmon, 1976). After the first 2 or 3 months, the sequence reverses, and NREM sleep precedes REM sleep. Although this reversal is of little significance to parents, who are most concerned with their child's overall pattern of sleeping and waking, it is an important sign of developmental change because it shows a shift toward the adult pattern.

Neonates spend most of their time asleep, though the amount of sleep they need gradually decreases. This trend is clearly evident in a study in which mothers were asked to keep a record of their babies' sleep time for several weeks after birth (Emde, Gaensbauer, & Harmon, 1976; Thoman & Whitney, 1989). Babies sleep about 16½ hours a day during the first week of life. By the end of 4 weeks, they sleep a little more than 15 hours a day; and by the end of 4 months, they sleep a little less than 14 hours a day.

If babies sleep most of the time, why do parents lose so much sleep? The reason is that though newborns tend to sleep slightly more at night than during the day from the very beginning, they sleep in snatches that last anywhere from a few minutes to a few hours. Thus they may be awake at any time of the day or night.

TABLE 4.4 States of Arousal in Infants

State	Characteristics
Non-rapid-eye-movement (NREM) sleep	Full rest; low muscle tone and motor activity; eyelids closed and eyes still; regular breathing (about 36 times per minute)
Rapid-eye-movement (REM) sleep	Increased muscle tone and motor activity; facial grimaces and smiles; occasional eye movements; irregular breathing (about 48 times per minute)
Periodic sleep	Intermediate between REM and NREM sleep—bursts of deep, slow breathing alternating with bouts of rapid, shallow breathing
Drowsiness	More active than NREM sleep but less active than REM or periodic sleep; eyes open and close; eyes glazed when open; breathing variable but more rapid than in NREM sleep
Alert inactivity	Slight activity; face relaxed; eyes open and bright; breathing regular and more rapid than in NREM sleep
Active alert	Frequent diffuse motor activity; vocalizations; skin flushed; irregular breathing
Distress	Vigorous diffuse motor activity; facial grimaces; red skin; crying

Source: Wolff, 1966.

As babies grow older, their sleeping and waking periods lengthen and coincide more and more with the night/day schedule common among adults (see Figure 4.11).

A marked shift toward the night/day cycle occurs in the first weeks after birth among many babies born in the United States; by the end of the second week, their combined periods of sleep average 8½ hours between 7 P.M. and 7 A.M. (Kleitman, 1963). But their sleep pattern still results in some loss of sleep for their parents because the longest sleep period may be only 3 or 4 hours.

Although babies' adoption of the night/day sleep cycle seems natural to people who live in industrialized countries and urban settings, studies of infants raised

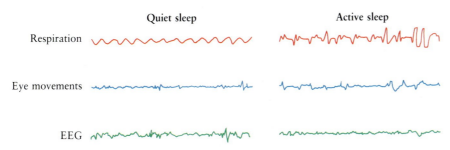

FIGURE 4.10 *The contrast between quiet and active sleep patterns in newborns is seen in the patterns of respiration, eye movements, and brain activity (EEG). Active sleep is characterized by irregular breathing, frequent eye movements, and continuous low-voltage brain activity. (Adapted from Parmelee et al., 1968.)*

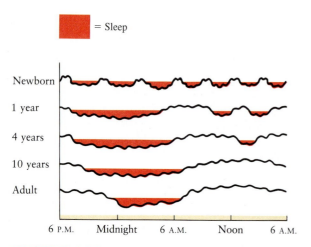

☐ = Sleep

Newborn

1 year

4 years

10 years

Adult

6 P.M.   Midnight   6 A.M.   Noon   6 A.M.

FIGURE 4.11   *The pattern of sleep/wake cycles among babies in the United States changes rapidly during infancy. A long period of sleep comes to replace many brief periods of alternating sleep and wakefulness. (From Kleitman, 1963.)*

in other cultures suggest that it is at least partly a function of culturally patterned social influence on the infant. We see the role of social pressure in rearranging the newborn's sleep (such as putting the baby to bed at certain hours and not picking it up when it wakes during the night) when we contrast U.S. patterns with the development of the sleep/wake behavior of Kipsigis babies in rural Kenya. These infants are almost always with their mothers. During the day they sleep when they can, often while being carried on their mothers' backs as the mothers go about their daily round of farming, household chores, and social activities. During the night they sleep with their mothers and are permitted to nurse whenever they wake up (see Box 4.1). Among Kipsigis infants, the longest period of sleep reported at 1 month is only about 3 hours; many shorter periods of sleep are sprinkled throughout the day and night. Eventually Kipsigis infants begin to sleep through the night, but not until many months after American infants have done so. Even as adults the Kipsigis are more flexible than Americans in their sleeping hours (Super & Harkness, 1972).

In the United States, the length of the longest sleep period is often used as an index of the infant's maturation. Charles Super and Sara Harkness (1972) suggest that parents' expectations that children will sleep for long periods of time during the early weeks of life may be pushing the limits of what young infants can adapt to. They suggest that the many changes that occur in a newborn's state of arousal in every 24-hour period reflect the immaturity of the infant's brain, which sets a limit on how quickly the child can conform to an adult routine. This may be the explanation for the failure of some infants in industrialized countries to adopt a night/day pattern of sleeping and waking as quickly and easily as their parents would like them to.

FEEDING

Besides attempting to regulate their babies' sleeping patterns, parents encourage their infants to adjust to a regular pattern of feeding. Pediatricians' recommendations as to when babies should be fed have changed significantly over the years. Today pediatricians often tell parents to feed their newborn babies as often as every 2 to 3 hours. But from the early 1920s through the 1940s, mothers were advised to feed their babies only every 4 hours, even if they showed signs of hunger long before the prescribed time had elapsed.

> Feed him at exactly the same hours every day.
> Do not feed him just because he cries.
> Let him wait until the right time.
> If you make him wait, his stomach will learn to wait.
> (Weill, 1930, p. 1)

For a very small infant, 4 hours can be a long time to go without food. Mothers in Cambridge, England, were asked to keep records of their babies' behaviors and their own caregiving activities. Included were the time their babies spent in their cradles, the hours at which they were fed, the time the mothers spent bathing their babies and changing their diapers, and the time their babies spent crying. All the mothers were advised to feed their babies on a strict 4-hour schedule, but not all followed the advice. The less experienced mothers tended to stick to the schedule, but the more experienced mothers sometimes fed their babies as soon as 1 hour after a scheduled feeding. Not surprisingly, the reports of the less experienced mothers showed that their babies cried the most (Bernal, 1972).

BOX 4.1

Sleeping Arrangements

One of the benefits of comparisons across cultures is that they make us aware of practices that are so common in our own culture that we assume they are the only way things can possibly be done. The ability of cross-cultural research to teach us about ourselves is nicely illustrated by studies to determine where and with whom young infants sleep.

Among middle-class, educated families in the United States it is common for babies to sleep alone, but this practice is quite unusual. The anthropologist John Whiting (1964) found that mothers sleep with their infants (a practice called *co-sleeping*) in two-thirds of the societies around the world that he surveyed. In the remainder, the babies usually slept in the same room as their parents. In an earlier survey of 100 societies, Michael Burton and Whiting (1961) had found that the United States was the only country where it was common to maintain separate quarters for young babies. Societies where co-sleeping is practiced include other highly technological countries, such as Japan and Italy, as well as rural communities in many countries.

Though the practice of co-sleeping is rare among college-educated, middle-class American families, it is widely practiced by other social groups in the United States and varies according to the region of the country. Among a group of newborns in eastern Kentucky, 36 percent shared their parents' bed and 48 percent shared their parents' room. Space did not seem to be the issue (Abbott, 1992). African American babies are more likely than Caucasian children to fall asleep with a caregiver present, to sleep in their parents' room, and to spend at least part of the night in their parents' bed (Lozoff et al., 1984).

Gilda Morelli and her colleagues (1992) interviewed rural Mayan peasants in Guatemala and middle-class American mothers about their infants' sleeping arrangements. None of the American parents in this study had the infant sleep with them. Many parents kept the sleeping child in a nearby crib for the first few months but soon moved the baby to a separate room. They gave various reasons for their arrangements:

- "We might roll over and hurt him . . . he might get smothered."
- "I think he would be more dependent . . . if he was constantly with us like that."
- "I think it would have made any separation harder if he wasn't even separated from us at night."

The Mayan mothers always had each new child sleep in the same bed with them until the next baby was born. They insisted that this was the only right thing to do. When they were told about the typical U.S. practice, they expressed shock and disapproval at the parents' behavior and pity for the children. They seemed to think the American mothers were neglecting their children. Similar sentiments have been voiced by Japanese mothers, who also sleep with their infants.

Sleeping practices are related to broader themes in the organization of interpersonal relations. Whereas American mothers talked about the need to train babies to be independent and self-reliant, mothers in societies where co-sleeping is the norm emphasize the need for babies to learn to be *inter*dependent, to be able to get along with and be sensitive to the needs of others (Caudill & Plath, 1966).

The object of such comparisons is not to show that one arrangement is better or worse for infants. Whether the infant sleeps in a bed alone or with its mother does not seem to make a great deal of difference *at the time*. All cultural systems are relatively successful in seeing that infants get enough sleep.

The point, rather, in describing the many differing cultural practices in regard to family sleeping arrangements is that they are all organized with a view to the ways in which children will be expected to act *at a later time*. This is another case, like parents' discussions about their baby's future as the child emerges from the womb (Chapter 3, p. 124), where cultural beliefs organize the current environment to accord with people's expectations for the future.

What happens if babies are fed "on demand"? In one study, the majority of newborn babies allowed to feed on demand preferred a 3-hour schedule (Aldrich & Hewitt, 1947). The interval gradually increased as the babies grew older. At 2½ months, most of the infants were feeding on a 4-hour schedule. By 7 or 8 months, the majority had come to approximate the normal adult schedule and were choosing to feed about four times a day. (Some parents reported the four feedings as "three meals and a snack.") It should be noted, however, that the figures given here are averages; at every age studied, about 40 percent of the babies did not fit the norm.

CRYING

One of the most difficult problems parents face in establishing a pattern of care for their babies is how to interpret their infants' needs. Parents can ask their newborn babies how they are feeling, but babies cannot answer. Infants do, however, have one important way of signaling that something is wrong—they can cry.

Crying is a complex behavior that involves the coordination of breathing and movements of the vocal tract that will later produce speech. Initially this coordination is provided by structures in the brain stem, but within a few months the cerebral cortex becomes involved and babies can cry voluntarily. This change in the neural organization of crying is accompanied by physical changes in the vocal tract that lower the pitch of infants' cries. At this point, parents begin to report that their infants are "crying on purpose," either to get attention or because they are bored (Lester, Boukydis, & Zachariah, 1992).

Babies' cries have a powerful effect on those who hear them. Experienced parents and childless adults alike respond to infants' cries with increases in heart rate and blood pressure, both of which are physiological signs of anxiety (Bleichfeld & Moely, 1984). New parents react even more strongly to infants' cries than childless adults or experienced parents do (Boukydis & Burgess, 1982). When nursing mothers hear babies' cries, even on recordings, their milk may start to flow (Newton & Newton, 1972).

When newborns cry, it is usually because something is causing them discomfort. The problem for the anxious parent is to figure out what that something is. The cries themselves can sometimes indicate possible causes of distress. At birth two kinds of cries can be distinguished by their distinctive sound patterns: (1) pain cries evoked by such stimuli as the prick of a pin or stomach cramps and (2) cries evoked by hunger (see Figure 4.12). Although there is disagreement about how they do it, adult listeners, even those who are not regularly in contact with newborn babies, can distinguish among these cries (Gustafson & Harris, 1990; Zeskind et al., 1985). Listeners in a variety of cultures can also distinguish the cries of normal infants from the cries of those at risk for a variety of developmental difficulties (Lester & Zeskind, 1982; Zeskind, 1983; Zeskind et al., 1985). These findings have led researchers to develop neonatal assessment techniques based on close analysis of cry patterns.

In spite of their ability to distinguish between types of crying, even experienced parents often cannot tell precisely why their baby is distressed. One reason is that prolonged crying of all kinds eventually slips into the rhythmic pattern of the hunger cry. In many instances, then, only the intensity of the distress is evident. Hunger is, of course, a common reason for a newborn baby to cry. Studies of crying before and after feedings confirm that babies cry less after they are fed (St. James-Roberts et al., 1993; Wolff, 1969). Circumstantial evidence suggests that some crying is the result of gastrointestinal pain. Babies will temporarily stop crying after they spit up, are burped, or pass gas, for example.

FIGURE 4.12 *Sound spectrograms graphically display the physical differences among the cries that provide adults with information about the causes of babies' distress. (From Wasz-Hokert et al., 1968.)*

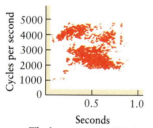
The best-recognized birth cry

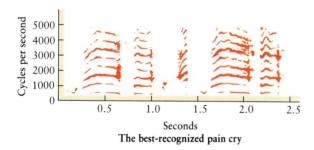
The best-recognized pain cry

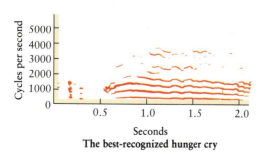
The best-recognized hunger cry

All these uncertainties make it difficult for parents to know what to do when their baby cries, especially when the cry does not signal acute pain. One natural response is to seek to comfort the infant (see Box 4.2). When parents are under stress or the crying is persistent, however, the uncertainty about how to comfort the child and the negative emotions that crying evokes in adults are sometimes too much to bear, and some parents respond by physically abusing their infants (Frodi, 1985).

Caregivers' efforts to get babies on a schedule and to comfort them when they are distressed continue as the months go by. These parenting activities are so commonplace that it is easy to overlook their significance; but they are crucially important for establishing the background for the more obviously dramatic changes of the first months of life.

Mechanisms of Developmental Change

Almost immediately after birth, the behavioral repertoire of neonates begins to expand, enabling them to interact ever more effectively with the world around them. The changes in behavior that occur during the first months of life are partly a matter of perfecting capacities that already exist. As infants become able to suck more effectively, for example, they obtain more food, so they can go longer between feedings without distress. The perfecting of existing behaviors does not, however, explain how new behaviors arise. By the age of 2½ months, infants raise their heads to look around, smile in response to the smiles of others, and shake rattles put into their hands. A major goal of developmental psychology is to explain how these new forms of behavior arise.

FROM SUCKING TO NURSING

One new behavior that appears in early infancy is nursing. When we compare the way newborn infants feed with the nursing behavior of 6-week-old infants, a striking contrast is evident. Newborns possess several reflexes that are relevant to feeding: rooting (turning the head in the direction of a touch on the cheek), sucking, swallowing, and breathing. These component behaviors are not well integrated, however, so babies' early feeding experiences are likely to be discoordinated affairs. When newborns are first held to the breast, a touch to the cheek will make them turn their heads and open their mouths, but they root around in a disorganized way. When they do find the nipple, they may lose it again almost immediately, or the act of sucking may cause their upper lip to fold back and block their nostrils, eliciting a sharp head-withdrawal reflex (see Figure 4.13). Furthermore, breathing and sucking are not well coordinated at first, so newborns are likely to have to stop sucking to come up for air.

By the time infants are 6 weeks old, a qualitative change is evident in their feeding behavior, a change that is more than just a perfection of the sucking reflex. For one thing, the infants anticipate being fed when they are picked up. More significant, they have worked out the coordination of all the component behaviors of feeding—sucking, swallowing, and breathing—so that they can perform them in a smooth, integrated sequence (Bruner, 1968). Feeding has become nursing. In fact, babies become so efficient at nursing that they can accomplish in less than 10 minutes what originally took them as long as an hour.

Nursing is clearly not a reflex. It is a new form of behavior that develops through the reorganization of the various reflexes with which infants are born. Although the acquisition of this behavior is commonplace, it raises in clear form the question of how developmental change comes about. Each of the four broad theoretical frameworks—the biological-maturation perspective, the environmental-

This infant's cries are likely to be taken as a peremptory command for someone to do something quickly.

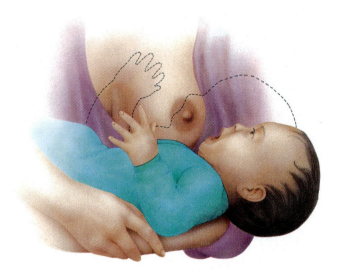

FIGURE 4.13 *In this sequence the infant's nostrils are blocked while he is attempting to nurse. The consequent blockage of his breathing elicits a head-withdrawal reflex that interferes with nursing.*

learning perspective, the constructivist perspective, and the cultural-context perspective—emphasizes different factors in its efforts to explain development (see Chapter 1, pp. 33–40). By examining phenomena spotlighted by each perspective and the way theorists working within them explain the development of the seemingly simple behavior of nursing, we can gain a sense of how each perspective contributes to our understanding of the development of other behaviors during infancy and beyond.

THE BIOLOGICAL-MATURATION PERSPECTIVE

To explain the development of nursing and other new behaviors after birth, biologically oriented developmental theorists invoke precisely the same mechanism that they use to explain all aspects of prenatal development—maturation. New behaviors, they say, arise from old behaviors as a result of distinct maturational changes in the physical structures and physiological processes of the organism. This position was stated most forcefully by Arnold Gesell (1945, p. 167). "The child comes by his psychic [psychological] constitution through embryological processes." Consequently, the role of the organism's genetic inheritance is considered to be of paramount importance, and the role of the environment in development is considered to be minimal, just as during the prenatal period.

Reflexes and the brain

The biological-maturation perspective focuses on the maturation and functioning of the central nervous system to explain neonatal behavior. One of the fundamental mechanisms of this system is the simple nerve reflex, summarized in Figure 4.14. When a child puts a finger in a candle flame, a sensory receptor in the fingertip is excited. This sensory receptor is a **neuron,** a nerve cell that transmits messages in the form of electrical impulses. Sensory neurons are specialized to receive sensory input from the environment and pass it on to cells that are specialized for responding to the environment. The electrical impulse resulting from the heat of the candle travels from the fingertip to the spinal cord, where it comes to a **synapse**—a small gap between interconnecting neurons. The impulse passes across the synapse to a motor neuron—a neuron that initiates muscle activity—and then back outward to the muscles in the arm. There it causes the muscles to contract, jerking the hand away from the flame.

For simple reflexes such as this, the circuit that consists of the sensory receptor and the motor neuron reaches only as far as the spinal cord, so regions in the brain play no role in them. The response may occur so quickly that the child does

Neuron A nerve cell.

Synapse A small gap between interconnecting neurons.

BOX 4.2

Comforting the Fussy Baby

All infants occasionally cry or seem to be mildly distressed for no readily identifiable cause, especially during the first 2½ months of life. Generally referred to as fussiness, or *colic*, this distress often peaks in the evenings for reasons not yet understood (Dunn, 1977). Sometimes fussy babies can be soothed by nursing. If they have just been fed and still cry, their mothers often assume that their diapers are wet or that they are cold. And indeed, changing babies' diapers and wrapping them up warmly does tend to quiet them. However, research has shown that it is picking the baby up, not the exchange of wet diapers for dry ones, that makes the difference; if babies are picked up and their wet diapers are put back on them, they stop crying as frequently as if they are given dry diapers (Wolff, 1969).

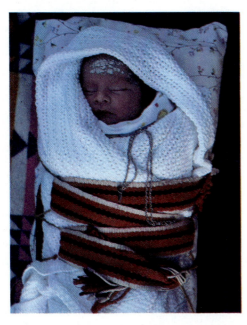

Among the techniques for soothing babies, swaddling, which is customary in many cultures, is one of the most effective.

Annaliese Korner and her associates compared the various ways parents move and hold crying babies—moving them so that they are lying prone, sitting them up, or picking them up and holding them to the shoulder or to the breast or in an embrace (Korner & Grobstein, 1966; Korner & Thoman, 1970). They found that holding babies to the shoulder is by far the most effective way to make them stop crying. An added benefit when babies are held to the shoulder is that they are more likely to become attentive to their surroundings.

Other methods mothers use to calm crying infants include rocking, patting, cuddling, and swaddling them. Yvonne Brackbill (1971) has found that the important features shared by these techniques are that they provide constant or rhythmic stimulation or that they reduce the amount of stimulation the babies receive from their own movements. *Swaddling*, or wrapping babies tightly in a blanket so that they cannot move their arms and legs, does both. The blanket provides them with constant touch stimulation and, by restricting their movements, reduces the amount of stimulation they receive from those movements.

Another very effective way to calm crying babies is to give them a pacifier to suck on. Sucking provides the baby with regular and rhythmic stimulation of the mouth, which apparently relaxes both the gut and the major muscles and reduces the baby's random thrashings (Field & Goldson, 1984). Whereas rocking makes the baby alert to its surroundings, sucking is more likely to put the baby to sleep (Campos, 1994). When a pleasing taste is added to the rhythmic stimulation produced by sucking, the calming effect appears to be significantly prolonged (Blass & Ciaramitaro, 1994).

Between 2 and 4 months of age, there is a sharp decline in the length of time it takes infants to recover from bouts of distress, such as that caused by an injection (Izard, Hembree, & Huebner, 1987). This shift is thought to indicate the beginning of infants' ability to regulate their own emotions.

not feel pain or fear until afterward. Many reflex actions, however, including crying and the various feeding reflexes, may require neural circuitry that is more intricate and involves the more complex structures of the central nervous system. These reflexes, say the biological maturationists, can be expected to change simply because the associated neural structures themselves mature.

In human beings and many other species, the upper end of the spinal cord thickens to form the **brain stem** (see Figure 4.15). Clusters of neurons within the brain stem begin to function during the fetal period. By birth the brain stem is one of the most highly developed areas of the brain. It controls such inborn reflexes as rooting and sucking, as well as such vital functions as breathing and sleeping. The

Brain stem The brain structure at the upper end of the spinal cord that controls vital functions and inborn reflexes.

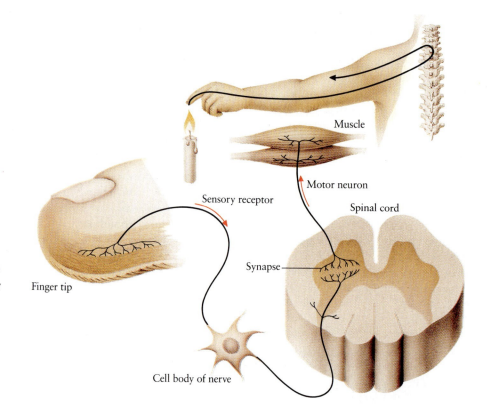

FIGURE 4.14   *How a simple reflex works. The heat of the candle flame sends a sensory message to the spinal cord. The spinal cord sends a message to the arm muscles to pull the hand from the heat. This happens before a person is consciously aware of being burned. (Adapted from Church, 1974.)*

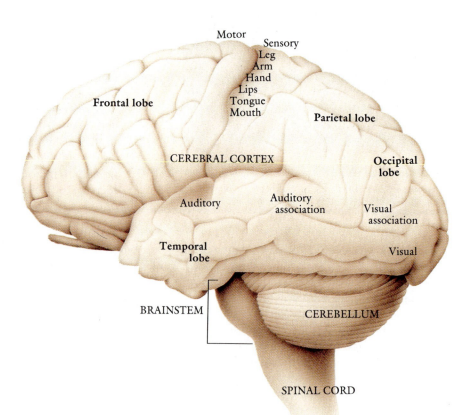

FIGURE 4.15   *A schematic view of the brain, showing the major lobes, or divisions, of the cerebral cortex (including the areas where some functions are localized), the brain stem, the cerebellum, and the spinal cord. (Adapted from Tanner, 1978.)*

brain stem also contains neural structures that are associated with the emotions.

The nerves of the brain stem do not respond to specific forms of sensory input in a precise, one-to-one manner such that different sensory inputs arrive at the brain as isolated signals. Instead, the brain stem contains neural pathways that *mix* various sources of sensory inputs with impulses from other regions of the brain and the body. Stimulation that reaches the brain stem from the environment is modulated and reorganized within these pathways. The fact that inputs from various stimuli follow different pathways allows for activities that are more complex and sustained than those characteristic of the simple reflexes that involve only the spinal cord.

In addition to the spinal cord and the brain stem, the activity of a third major area of the central nervous system is essential to early development—the **cerebral cortex** (Figure 4.15). In the cerebral cortex, stimulation from the environment travels through a network of interacting neurons so complex that scientists have thus far found it impossible to trace completely the fate of a single stimulus event, such as a touch on the cheek. This complex network of neurons integrates information from several sensory sources with memories of past experiences, processing old and new information and integrating them in a way that results in the development of new behaviors.

The cerebral cortex is the area of the brain that most clearly distinguishes human beings from other animals. Within the cortex are regions specialized for the analysis of time, space, and language as well as for motor functions and sensory discriminations. Large areas of the human cortical mass, however, are not prewired to respond directly to external stimulation in any discernible way (see Figure 4.16). These "uncommitted" areas provide humans with the capacity to synthesize sensory information in unique ways, making possible such higher psychological functions characteristic of the human adult as voluntary remembering, logical deduction, and written language (Luria, 1973).

Neonates' central nervous systems undergo many changes, in a continuing process that began during the fetal period. The number, size, complexity, and even the kinds of cells in the brain increase after birth (Diamond, 1990b; Dawson & Fischer, 1994) (see Figure 4.17). For example, the hippocampus, a brain structure that is located in the brain stem and plays an important role in memory, is estimated to be 40 percent mature at birth, 50 percent mature at 6 weeks, and fully mature at about 1½ years (Kretschmann et al., 1986).

A developmental change in the nervous system that has received much attention is **myelination,** the process by which the neurons become covered by **myelin,** a sheath of fatty cells that insulates the neurons and speeds transmission of nerve impulses along them. Cortical nerve cells, including those that connect the cerebral cortex with the brain stem, are not myelinated at birth. Consequently, the circuitry of the cortex is only tenuously connected to the lower-lying parts of the nervous system that receive stimulation from the environment. At birth these lower-lying areas, which are more mature, can mediate motor reflexes and visual responses without cortical involvement (Woodruf-Pak, Logan, & Thompson, 1990). As the nerve fibers connecting the cortex with regions below the cortex become myelinated, the infant's abilities expand. Myelinated axons transmit signals anywhere from 10 to 100 times faster than unmyelinated axons, making possible more effective interconnections between parts of the brain and more complicated forms of thought and action.

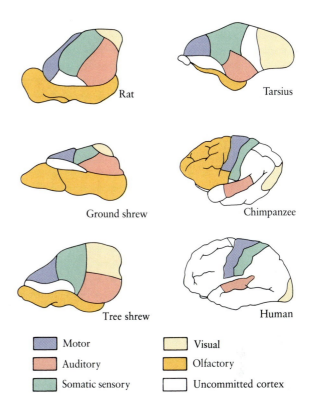

Rat

Tarsius

Ground shrew

Chimpanzee

Tree shrew

Human

■ Motor   ■ Visual
■ Auditory   ■ Olfactory
■ Somatic sensory   □ Uncommitted cortex

FIGURE 4.16 *In these six mammalian species the proportions of the brain mass that are devoted to different functions vary widely. The areas designated "uncommitted cortex" are not dedicated to any particular sensory or motor functions and are available for integrating information of many kinds. (Adapted from Fishbein, 1976.)*

Cerebral cortex The uppermost part of the central nervous system. Within it are specialized regions for the analysis of time, space, and language; as well as for motor functions and sensory discriminations.

Myelination The process by which myelin covers nerve cells.

Myelin The sheath of fatty cells that covers the neurons, stabilizing them and speeding the transmission of impulses.

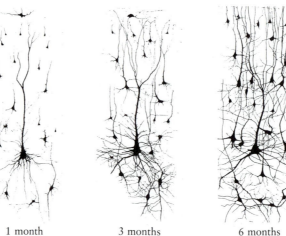
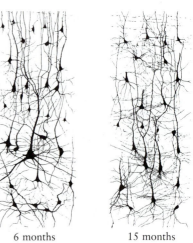

1 month   3 months   6 months   15 months

FIGURE 4.17 *These drawings from photomicrographs of infant brain tissue show the marked increases in the size and number of cerebral neurons during the first 15 months of postnatal life. (From Conel, 1939/1963.)*

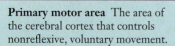

Primary motor area The area of the cerebral cortex that controls nonreflexive, voluntary movement.

Primary sensory area Those areas of the brain that are responsible for the initial analysis of sensory information.

Moro reflex In response to an abrupt noise or to the sensation of being dropped, infants fling their arms out with fingers spread and then bring them back toward their bodies with fingers bent as if to grab something.

FIGURE 4.18 *Even babies born with little or no cerebral cortex display basic reflexes such as sucking. (Courtesy of the New York Academy of Medicine Library.)*

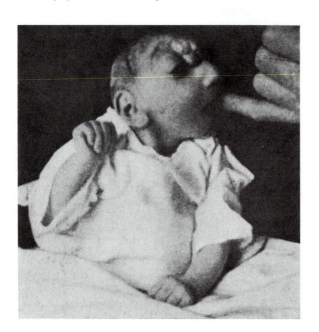

Different parts of the cerebral cortex continue to develop at different times throughout infancy and well into childhood and adolescence (Thatcher, 1994). Using criteria such as the number and size of neurons and the degree of myelination, scientists who study the anatomy of the nervous system estimate that the first area of the cerebral cortex to undergo important developmental change is the **primary motor area,** which is the area responsible for nonreflexive, or voluntary, movement (Kolb & Whishaw, 1990). Within the primary motor area, the first cells to become functional are those that control the arms and the trunk. By about 1 month, the neurons in this area are becoming myelinated, so they can now conduct neural impulses more efficiently. The region of the primary motor area that governs leg movements is the last to develop; it is not fully developed until sometime in the second year (Tanner, 1990).

The development of voluntary movement in the arms and legs thus follows the *cephalocaudal* (from the head down) pattern, introduced on page 88. At the end of the first month, many infants can raise their heads while lying on their stomachs. At 3 months they show more voluntary movements of the muscles that move the upper trunk, shoulders, arms, and forearms. Voluntary control of leg movements does not come until a few months later.

The **primary sensory areas** of the cortex—those areas that are responsible for the initial analysis of sensory information—also mature in the months after birth. The nerve fibers responsible for touch are the first to become active, followed by those in the primary visual area and then those in the primary auditory area (Huttenlocher, 1990). By 3 months, all of the primary sensory areas are relatively mature (Tanner, 1990).

The frontal cortex, which is essential in a wide variety of voluntary behaviors and behaviors that require planning, begins to function in infancy but continues to develop throughout childhood (Diamond, 1990a; Fischer & Rose, 1995).

According to the biological-maturation perspective, the baby becomes able to interact with the environment in more complicated and refined ways because the brain matures. In this view, the infant's increasing success at nursing, like the gradual lengthening of the intervals between feedings and between periods of sleep, appears to depend at least in part on the maturation of underlying brain structures. Two lines of evidence, one from studies of developmental abnormalities and the other from studies of the relation of reflexes to later behavior, support this view.

Evidence from studies of babies with abnormalities

In rare cases, infants are born without a cerebral cortex. Such babies may have normal reflexes at birth (see Figure 4.18). E. Gamper (1926/1959), for example, observed an infant who was born with an intact brain stem but little or no cerebral cortex. The baby could suck, yawn, stretch, cry, and follow a visual stimulus with his eyes. Robert Emde and Robert Harmon (1972) report REM smiles in such a baby.

Babies born without a cerebral cortex seldom live long. Those that do live more than a few days fail to develop the complex, well-coordinated behaviors seen in normal babies. This observation strongly suggests that the cerebral cortex plays an essential role in the development of such coordinated actions as nursing (Emde & Harmon, 1972; Kolb & Whishaw, 1990).

Evidence from studies of reflexes and later behavior

Within the first few months after birth, several of the reflexes infants are born with disappear, never to return (see Table 4.2, p. 142). Others disappear for awhile and then reappear as part of a more mature behavior. Still others are transformed into more complex behaviors without first disappearing for a time. Many researchers see these changes in the structure of early reflexes as important evidence about the way the maturation of higher brain centers changes behavior (Fox & Bell, 1990; Oppenheim, 1981).

The **Moro reflex** is a response to a sudden noise or to the sensation of being dropped: infants fling their arms out with their fingers spread and then bring their arms back in toward their bodies with their fingers bent as if to hug something. The Moro reflex usually disappears by the time babies are 4 or 5 months old. It is seen again only in the event of injury to the central nervous system. Some researchers conclude that its disappearance is the result of the maturation of higher brain centers (Prechtl, 1977).

When newborn babies are held in an upright position with their feet touching a flat surface, they make rhythmic leg movements as if they were walking (see Figure 4.19). For a long time this kind of movement was referred to as a **stepping reflex** (see Table 4.2, p. 142). This kind of behavior ordinarily disappears at around 2 months of age. At about 1 year of age, babies use similar motions as a component of walking, a voluntary activity that is acquired with practice.

A lively debate is in progress about these rhythmic leg movements. According to Philip Zelazo (1983), the new born's movements are a genuine reflex; he interprets their disappearance as an instance of the suppression of a lower reflex by the maturation of higher cortical functions. After a period of reorganization, he argues, the old reflex reappears in a new form as a component of voluntary walking.

Esther Thelen and her colleagues reject this explanation; they believe that the stepping reflex is really a form of kicking (Thelen, 1995; Thelen, Ulrich, & Jensen, 1989). According to these researchers, early kicking behavior disappears because of changes in the baby's muscle mass and weight, not because of changes in the cortex. They believe that the voluntary walking that appears a year or so after the stepping reflex disappears is not the same movement; it requires not only the maturation of the cortex but also a

FIGURE 4.19 *Babies held upright with their feet touching the ground move their legs in a fashion that looks like walking. Called the stepping reflex, this form of behavior is currently the subject of debate concerning its origins and subsequent developmental history.*

Stepping reflex The rhythmic leg movements newborn infants make when held upright with their feet touching a flat surface.

This neonate is exhibiting the grasping reflex present at birth.

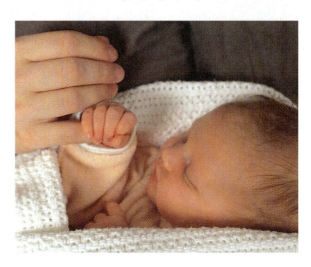

BOX 4.3

Experience and Development of the Brain

When we attempt to understand the relationship between the brain and psychological development, it seems no more than common sense to expect that increases in the complexity of the brain will precede, or at least accompany, increases in behavioral complexity. An example of such a relationship is the development of social smiling: the cells of the visual cortex and connections between the visual cortex and the brain stem must become functional before children can see others smiling and so be able to smile in return. What this simplified account leaves out, though, is that without visual input from the environment, the cells of the visual cortex will not continue to develop normally. In other words, the principle that development emerges from the *interaction* of the organism and the environment applies no less to the development of the brain than to the development of behavior (Gottlieb, 1992; Greenough, 1991).

Early demonstrations of how experience influences the brain were provided by studies that Austin Riesen (1950) carried out with normal chimpanzees raised for the first 16 months of their lives in total darkness. When the chimpanzees were then placed in a normally lighted environment, they were unable to learn simple pattern and color discriminations, and their visual acuity was severely impaired. Eye examinations revealed that their retinas had failed to develop normally. Subsequently, anatomical and biochemical analyses have shown that animals deprived of visual experience suffer disturbances of protein synthesis in the visual cortex; as a result, the neurons of the visual cortex have fewer and shorter branches and up to 70 percent fewer synapses than normal (Blakemore & Mitchell, 1973). Signifi-

cantly, the degree and duration of these effects depend on the age at which the animal is deprived of light. If the deprivation ends early enough, recovery is possible. This finding is consistent with the idea of critical periods.

Additional animal research has shown other ways in which visual experience shapes the neural connections between the eyes and the visual cortex. Certain cells in a cat's brain, for example, normally respond best to horizontal lines, whereas other cells respond best to vertical lines. Both kinds of cells are present in large numbers in kittens that have not yet opened their eyes (Hubel & Wiesel, 1979). When kittens are raised in an environment that allows them to see only horizontal lines for several months, they produce far fewer of the nerve cells that respond to vertical lines than do normal kittens, so their ability to detect vertical lines does not develop normally (Hirsch & Spinelli, 1971).

The visual cortex is not the only part of the brain to be affected by experience. In pioneering studies by Mark Rosenzweig and his colleagues (summarized in Rosenzweig, 1984), groups of young male laboratory rats from the same litter were raised in three different environments. The first group was housed individually in standard laboratory cages. Members of the second group were housed together in standard laboratory cages. The third group was provided with enriched conditions. Its members were housed in a large cage that was furnished with a variety of objects they could play with. A new set of playthings, drawn from a pool of 25 objects, was placed in the cage every day. Often the animals in this group were given formal training in a maze or were exposed to a toy-filled open field.

---

number of concurrent developments, including increased strength and the ability to balance upright.

Prereaching A reflexlike movement in which newborns reach toward an object and simultaneously make grasping movements.

A reflex that does not disappear but is instead transformed is **prereaching**, or *visually initiated reaching*: newborns reach toward an object that catches their attention and simultaneously make grasping movements (Bushnell, 1985; Von Hofsten, 1984). Reaching and grasping are uncoordinated just after birth and appear to be independently functioning reflexes. Infants often fail to grasp an object even after repeated attempts because their hands close too early or too late. Even at this very early age, however, movements of the two arms are surprisingly well coordinated (Von Hofsten & Siddiqui, 1993).

At about 3 months of age, and coincident with maturational changes in the visual and motor areas of the cerebral cortex, the visually *initiated* reaching reflex is transformed into a voluntary behavior; once infants locate an object by either seeing or hearing it, they can use feedback from their own movements to adjust the trajectory of their reach and get their hands close to the object (Clifton et

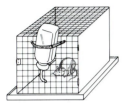

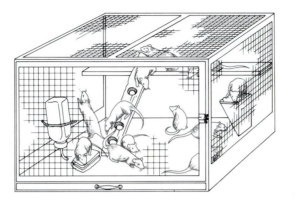

The standard laboratory cage in which laboratory rats are typically housed (left) provides little opportunity for complex interactions with the environment in comparison with a cage that provides for an enriched environment (right). (Adapted from Rosenzweig, Bennet, & Diamond, 1972.)

At the end of the experimental period, which lasted anywhere from a few weeks to several months, behavioral tests and examinations of the animals' brains revealed differences that favored the animals raised in enriched conditions. The rats of the third group demonstrated:

- Increased rates of learning in standard laboratory tasks, such as learning a maze.
- Increased overall weight of the cerebral cortex.
- Increased amounts of acetylcholinesterase, a brain enzyme that enhances learning.
- Larger neuronal cell bodies and glial (supportive) cells.
- More synaptic connections.

When rats were housed singly in small cages within an enriched environment so that they could do no more than observe what was going on around them, their learning capacity differed in no way from that of the animals that were housed in individual cages away from the enriched environment (Forgays & Forgays, 1952). These findings confirm an earlier study showing that *active interaction* with the environment is a crucial factor in the production of these changes.

Although these results were obtained with nonhuman animal species, they are consistent with what is known about human development and the importance of active involvement with the environment for human development. They show that behavioral changes should not be thought of as secondary consequences of changes that occur in the brain. Behavioral changes induced by environmental stimulation can themselves lead to changes in the brain that then support more complex forms of behavior.

al., 1993). A short time thereafter, infants begin to open their hands as soon as they begin to reach for an object and begin to close their hands a brief interval before they touch it, clear evidence that they have begun to coordinate reaching and grasping (Von Hofsten & Rönnqvist, 1988).

Although no one has yet identified the cortical areas responsible for such new behaviors as nursing and visually guided reaching, it seems safe to say that the maturation of the baby's cortical structures (along with development of the baby's muscles) must be an important factor in their development. At the same time, it is not clear that all of the brain connections associated with coordinated reaching and nursing develop before the baby begins to reach and nurse, or that they develop in complete independence of environmental influence, as some biological maturationists seem to imply. Rather, some of these brain developments appear to grow out of infants' interactions with their environment (see Box 4.3).

BOX 4.4

Imitation in the Newborn?

When we consider newborns' limited visual capacities and uncoordinated movements, the notion that neonates can imitate actions they see may seem far-fetched. Yet several studies appear to show that babies are capable of rudimentary forms of imitation from birth (Anisfeld, 1991; Meltzoff & Moore, 1977, 1989, 1994). These studies have generated intense interest among developmental psychologists because it had long been believed that imitation does not become possible until several months after birth (Abravanel, Levan-Goldschmidt, & Stevenson, 1976; Piaget, 1962).

If the capacity for true imitation does exist in newborns, it provides them with an important avenue for learning about the world that they were not previously known to possess.

All that seems necessary to determine whether newborns are capable of imitating is for the researcher to present some behavior to newborns and then observe whether or not they repeat it. Yet a good deal of research has failed to resolve the question of imitation in newborns definitively. Part of the problem is to find behaviors that are within newborns' capacities.

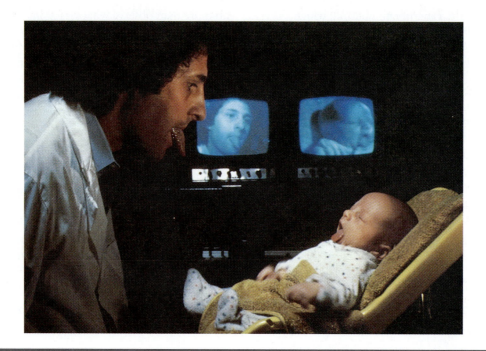

THE ENVIRONMENTAL-LEARNING PERSPECTIVE

Whatever biology may contribute to an infant's development of nursing behavior, some form of adaptation to the environment is also clearly necessary. Thus, a mother does not have to continue to ensure that her breast is always presented in precisely the position required to elicit the sucking reflex throughout her child's infancy. Babies quickly become accustomed to nursing in any number of situations, adjusting to each for maximum comfort and efficiency.

How do a baby's innate reflexes become coordinated with one another and with appropriate stimuli in the environment to transform reflex sucking into nursing? Environmental-learning theorists argue that such coordinations require **learning,** a relatively permanent change in behavior brought about by the experience of events in the environment. Several types of learning are believed to

Learning The process by which an organism's behavior is modified by experience.

In research conducted by Andrew Meltzoff and Keith Moore (1977, 1989, 1994), an adult would loom above alert newborn babies and make distinctive facial expressions, such as opening his mouth very wide and sticking out his tongue. Meltzoff and Moore reported that the infants often imitated the facial expression of the adult. Aware that their claims were going to be viewed skeptically, Meltzoff and Moore took special precautions to ensure that their results could not be attributed to procedural errors. As a check of their findings, they photographed the infants and the adult model independently. They then asked judges who had not been present during the experimental sessions to look at the photographs of the infants and guess what sort of face the adult had made. The judges guessed correctly more often than they could have done by chance. The implication is that the infants did indeed imitate the distinctive adult facial expressions they saw.

Yet the results were not so clear-cut as the report of the findings suggests. On the 97 trials when the researcher stuck out his tongue, for example, the babies "most often" stuck out their tongues in return. But the "most often" means that they stuck out their tongues 30 times; they opened their mouths 20 times, and they puckered their lips or moved their fingers on the remaining trials. The imitative response won out, but just barely.

Meltzoff and Moore's research has generated many follow-up studies. Tiffany Field and her colleagues (1982) found support for Meltzoff and Moore's conclusions when they used somewhat different procedures and responses (see the photos below). They arranged for an adult to model three facial expressions—happy, sad, and surprised—for babies who were an average of 36 hours old. The babies showed that they could distinguish among the model's facial expressions by the fact that they habituated to the repeated presentation of a single expression but then began to pay close attention again when the model presented them with a different facial expression. Most important, the babies appeared to imitate these new expressions. An observer who could not see the model and who did not know what expressions were being presented to the babies was able to determine the facial expression of the model from the facial movements of the babies on a statistically reliable basis. These results are difficult to explain without assuming that the infants somehow matched what they did with what they saw the model doing. Precisely how infants accomplished this matching remains uncertain.

Not everyone who has attempted to replicate Meltzoff and Moore's study has been successful (Anisfeld, 1991). Some researchers suggest that either there was some peculiarity in Meltzoff and Moore's procedures or the behavior they observed is a very special form of imitation (Abravanel & Sigafoos, 1984; Kaitz et al., 1988).

Meltzoff and Moore respond to this criticism by continued demonstrations that certain facial gestures can be evoked with reasonable regularity. They have suggested that faces are especially attractive and meaningful to infants because the infants recognize their own felt experiences in another person, and that recognition provides the foundations for the development of social identity (Meltzoff & Moore, 1994).

operate throughout development, including habituation (described on p. 135), classical conditioning, operant conditioning, and perhaps imitation (see Box 4.4).

Classical conditioning

Classical conditioning is the process by which an organism learns which events in its environment go with each other. Carolyn Rovee-Collier (1987), a researcher who has been influential in promoting the study of classical conditioning in infancy, points out, "Because many events in nature occur in an orderly fashion, classical conditioning permits organisms to exploit this orderliness and anticipate events instead of simply reacting to them" (p. 107).

The existence of this very basic learning mechanism was demonstrated at the turn of the century by the Russian physiologist Ivan Pavlov (1849–1936). Pavlov

Classical conditioning The process by which an organism learns which events in its environment go with others. It is the establishment of a connection between a response and a previously neutral stimulus, resulting from the neutral stimulus being paired with an unconditional stimulus.

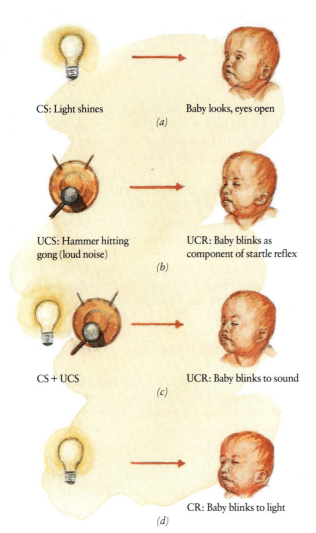

CS: Light shines   Baby looks, eyes open

(a)

UCS: Hammer hitting   UCR: Baby blinks as
gong (loud noise)   component of startle reflex

(b)

CS + UCS   UCR: Baby blinks to sound

(c)

                                    CR: Baby blinks to light

(d)

FIGURE 4.20 *Classical conditioning. In the top panel (a) the sight of a light (CS) elicits no particular response. In (b) the loud sound of a gong (UCS) causes the baby to blink his eyes (UCR). In (c) the sight of the light (CS) is paired with the loud sound of the gong (UCS), which evokes an eyeblink (UCR). Finally (d), the sight of the light (CS) is sufficient to cause the baby to blink (CR), demonstrating that learning has occurred.*

(1927) showed that after several experiences of hearing a tone just before food was placed in its mouth, a dog would begin to salivate in response to the tone, before it received any food. In everyday language, the dog began to expect food when it heard the tone, and its mouth watered at the thought.

In the terminology of environmental learning theories, Pavlov paired a **conditional stimulus (CS)**—a tone—with an **unconditional stimulus (UCS)**—food in the mouth. The food is called an unconditional stimulus because it "unconditionally" causes salivation, salivation being a reflex response to food in the mouth. Salivation, in turn, is called an **unconditional response (UCR)** because it is automatically and invariantly (that is, unconditionally) elicited by food in the mouth. The tone is called a conditional stimulus because the behavior it elicits depends on (is conditional on) the way it has been paired with the unconditional stimulus. When the unconditional response (salivation in response to food in the mouth) occurs in response to the CS (the tone), it is called a **conditional response (CR)** because it depends on the pairing of the CS (the tone) and the UCS (the food). The key indicator that learning has occurred is that the CS (tone) elicits the CR (salivation) before the presentation of the UCS (food) (see Figure 4.20).

A number of psychologists seized on Pavlov's demonstrations as a possible model for the way infants learn about their environments. One of Pavlov's co-workers demonstrated conditioned feeding responses in a 14-month-old infant (Krasnogorski, 1907/1967). The baby opened his mouth and made sucking motions (CRs) at the sight of a glass of milk (CS). When a bell (a new CS) was sounded on several occasions just before the glass of milk was presented, the baby began to open his mouth and suck at the sound of the bell, an indication that classical conditioning built expectations in the infant by a process of association. The crucial point to these observations is that there is no *biological* connection between the sight of a glass of milk or the sound of a bell and the mouth-opening and sucking responses they elicited. Rather, the fact that the new stimuli elicited these responses shows that learning has occurred.

Pavlov's ideas soon won a large following in the United States, and several studies were conducted with the intention of demonstrating the importance of classical conditioning as a mechanism of infant learning. In a study mentioned in Chapter 1 (pp. 25–26), John Watson and Rosalie Rayner purported to show that infants learn to fear through the process of classical conditioning. Dorothy Marquis (1931), in one of the early studies of classical conditioning in newborn infants, showed that sucking motions could be conditioned to the sound of a buzzer if the buzzer sounded just before the baby was given a bottle.

These early studies were criticized because they did not entirely rule out other possible causes for the babies' behavior. The babies in Marquis's study, for example, may have opened their mouths and made sucking motions simply because they were excited by the buzzer and not because they made a specific association between the buzzer and food. These criticisms took on additional force when several well-controlled experiments failed to show classical conditioning until infants were 2 or 3 months old. During the past 15 years, however, intensive research has demonstrated that classical conditioning can occur within hours of birth. These researchers used stimuli that are biologically significant to an infant, and they made certain that the infant subjects were alert at the time the experiments were performed.

Elliott Blass and his associates, for example, conditioned infants to suck whenever their foreheads were stroked (Blass, Ganchrow, & Steiner, 1984). These researchers assumed that such tactile stimulation occurs naturally during feeding but that it does not ordinarily produce sucking. The infants were only a few hours old when the experimenters began to stroke their foreheads and then feed them a small dose of sugar water (sucrose) through a pipette. Infants in a control group were also stroked and given sugar water, but the researchers performed the two acts independently and at variable intervals to preclude the possibility that the infants would form an association between them. The infants in the experimental group began to suck and pucker their faces—a response pattern the researchers dubbed a "pucker-suck"—when they were stroked on the forehead. The infants in the control group did not. One of the most convincing bits of evidence that classical conditioning had occurred was the way the infants reacted when the investigators later stroked their foreheads but did not give them sugar water. The first or second time this happened, the infants in the experimental group responded by frowning or making an angry face and then crying or whimpering. The researchers also stopped giving sugar water to the infants in the control group, but when their foreheads were stroked, they did not express anger or cry. Rovee-Collier (1987) comments that this finding "suggests that infants in the experimental group had learned the predictive relation between stroking and sucrose delivery and cried because their expectancy was violated" (p. 113).

Lewis Lipsitt (1990) and his colleagues have succeeded in showing that neonates will also form a conditioned reflex to a noxious stimulus—a puff of air to the eye. Infants 10, 20, and 30 days of age learned to shut their eyes in anticipation of an air puff that came $1\frac{1}{2}$ seconds after a tone sounded. The youngest infants did not seem to retain what they had learned, but those 20 and 30 days old showed indications of remembering the experience 10 days later.

Operant conditioning

Classical conditioning is a process by which previously existing behaviors come to be elicited by new stimuli. It explains how infants begin to build up expectations about the connections between events in their environment, but it does little to explain how even the simplest changes take place in infants' behavioral repertoires. The kind of conditioning that gives rise to new and more complex behaviors is called *operant*, or *instrumental*, conditioning because the learned response enables the organism to *operate* more effectively on its environment in order to bring about desired changes.

The basic idea of **operant conditioning** is that changes in behavior occur as a result of the positive or negative consequences the behavior produces; that is, organisms will tend to repeat behaviors that lead to rewards and will tend to give up behaviors that fail to produce rewards or that lead to punishment (Skinner, 1938; Thorndike, 1911). A consequence (such as receiving a reward) that increases the likelihood that a behavior will be repeated is called a **reinforcement.** According to an operant explanation of the development of nursing, such behaviors as turning the head away from the bottle or burying the nose in the mother's breast will become less probable because they do not lead to a result the infant would find satisfying: milk. At the same time, well-coordinated breathing, sucking, and swallowing will increase in strength and probability because they are likely to be rewarded with milk.

Until the 1960s, it was generally believed that newborns are capable of simple, reflexive behaviors only, so no one did research on operant conditioning in young infants. Since that time, it has been demonstrated that newborn infants are

Conditional stimulus (CS) In classical conditioning, a stimulus that evokes no particular response but which comes to elicit a response after training.

Unconditional stimulus (UCS) In classical conditioning, a stimulus that invariably elicits a particular response.

Unconditional response (UCR) In classical conditioning, a response that occurs whenever a particular stimulus is present. Salivation, for example, is the unconditional response to food in the mouth.

Conditional response (CR) In classical conditioning, a response that occurs following a previously neutral stimulus as a result of pairing the neutral stimulus with an unconditional stimulus.

Operant conditioning The modification of behavior as a result of the positive or negative consequences that the behavior produces.

Reinforcement In operant conditioning, reinforcement refers to the consequences of a behavior that increase the likelihood that the behavior will be repeated.

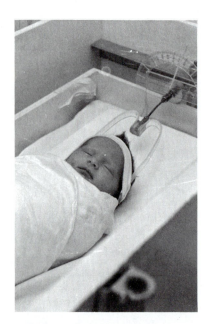

FIGURE 4.21 *A newborn with a specially designed headpiece that records head turning. Head turns of more than 10 degrees were reinforced by the opportunity to suck on a pacifier.*

indeed capable of operant learning, which can be reinforced in them by such varied stimuli as milk, sweet substances, an interesting visual display, a pacifier, and the sound of a heartbeat or the mother's voice (DeCasper & Fifer, 1980; DeCasper & Sigafoos, 1983; Rovee-Collier, 1987; Moon & Fifer, 1990).

An experiment by Einar Siqueland (1968), for example, demonstrated that neonates can learn to turn their heads in order to suck on a pacifier. The key requirement of operant learning is that a behavior has to occur before it can be reinforced. Head turning is ideal in this respect because it is something even the youngest neonates do. While the babies lay in laboratory cribs, Siqueland placed a band around their heads that was connected to a device for recording the degree their heads moved to either side (see Figure 4.21). Whenever the designated response occurred, the baby was given a pacifier to suck on.

In the first phase of his study, Siqueland recorded how often the babies naturally turned their heads. Once this baseline rate was established, he set his apparatus to signal when the babies had turned their heads at least 10 degrees to either side. As soon as they did, they were given the pacifier to suck on. After only 25 occasions on which the head turning was reinforced with the pacifier, most of the babies had tripled the rate at which they turned their heads.

To make certain that the increase in babies' head turning was not due to the excitement of being placed in the crib, Siqueland included another group of infants in his experiment who were rewarded with a pacifier for holding their heads still. These infants learned to move their heads less during the course of the experiment.

Sidney Bijou and Donald Baer (1966), two prominent environmental-learning theorists, summarize the developmental importance of operant conditioning this way:

> Operant conditioning is involved in a vast change in the form and complexity of the infant's responses which may be described as the stringing together of a collection of operants in a chain. An infant may be capable of a variety of arm motions. These may be linked in slightly different order to produce behavior described as a wave or a pat, making patti-cake, beating a drum, grabbing a cookie, fending off, sweeping away, etc. (p. 83)

Support for the argument that learning is an important contributor to behavioral development comes from studies that show that even very young infants are capable of remembering what they have learned from one testing session to the next (Rovee-Collier & Boller, 1995; Swain, Zelazo, & Clifton, 1993). These studies also suggest that memory for newly learned behaviors improves markedly during the first several months of life, a finding to which we will return at the end of this chapter and again in Chapter 5 (pp. 208–209).

The environmental-learning theorists' emphasis on the power of the environment to shape behavior provides an important counterweight to the biological-maturation theorists' emphasis on the primacy of genetic influences in determining the course of development. But the environmental-learning explanations of developmental change also have some significant shortcomings. In effect, this approach makes no distinction between learning and development; it views development as simply the accumulation of learned modifications in behavior. It acknowledges no qualitative differences that distinguish older and younger children, only quantitative differences in the number and complexity of the behaviors they have acquired. It also fails to deal adequately with individual differences in behavior, including differences associated with sex and temperament. According to this perspective, such differences can be accounted for only by differences in the experiences of individuals; the effects of genetic variation are discounted. Contemporary research on individual differences has made this extreme view difficult to justify.

THE CONSTRUCTIVIST PERSPECTIVE: PIAGET

Jean Piaget, the most prominent champion of a constructivist perspective, sought to understand how children come to know the world and to act effectively within it. He objected to both the biological-maturation and environmental-learning theories of his day. He criticized biological explanations for their failure to spell out how the environment of human infants interacts with their biological capacities to produce developmental change (Piaget & Inhelder, 1969). At the same time, he was critical of environmental-learning explanations because they assumed that the environment is the originator of developmental change, they gave too little emphasis to the role of children's actions in producing development, and they denied the existence of qualitative, stagelike changes during development.

Piaget's theory of developmental change

In Piaget's view, knowledge is acquired (in his words "constructed") through action. Consequently, to understand development one must begin at the beginning with the most elementary potentials for action present at birth.

Piaget chose early reflexes as the beginning point of his analysis. To Piaget, a reflex is a primitive schema, the basic unit of psychological functioning in his theory. The concept of a schema will appear frequently in later chapters because it figures prominently in many modern approaches to development, often with slightly different meanings attached to it. For the present, a **schema** can be thought of as a mental structure that provides an organism with a model for action in similar or analogous circumstances (Piaget & Inhelder, 1969).

During the first month of life, the "reflex schemas" babies are born with provide them with a kind of skeleton for action that is gradually fleshed out by experience. Eventually these initial schemas are strengthened and transformed into new schemas through **adaptation,** a twofold process involving what Piaget termed assimilation and accommodation.

During **assimilation,** various experiences are absorbed by the organism and are transformed to fit its existing schemas, strengthening those schemas and making them work more efficiently. Piaget used the process of digestion as an analogy to help clarify what he meant by assimilation. Reflex schemas, he explained, assimilate experience in much the same way the human body assimilates food. Various kinds of food taken in by the body are assimilated through the process of digestion into such existing physical structures as bone, blood, and brain tissue (Piaget, 1952b).

Sucking is one such primitive schema. It is initially closely tied to a small group of eliciting stimuli, such as a nipple placed in the mouth or a touch on the cheek, but it does not remain strictly bound to particular eliciting conditions for long. At some point babies are likely to find, say, a pacifier instead of a nipple touching their face and start sucking on it. Since a pacifier is similar to a nipple, the infants can adjust the way their mouths fit around the pacifier so that they can suck on it in pretty much the same way they suck on the nipple. In other words, they assimilate the pacifier, a new object, to their existing sucking schema.

Not every object babies encounter can be assimilated to an existing schema. When babies encounter a blanket, for instance, they may try to suck on it. However, because the qualities of the blanket—the satin binding, perhaps, or the cloth of the blanket itself—are so unlike the qualities of a nipple or a thumb, they are unable to assimilate the blanket as an object to suck on. They will therefore make some **accommodation;** that is, they will modify the way they suck, perhaps by choosing a corner of the blanket and sucking on that, using approximately but not exactly the same schema as they had used to suck on a nipple. In its modified form, the sucking schema can now be applied to old and new environmental experiences. If a baby encounters a toy truck and tries to suck on it, accommodation is

Schema A mental structure that provides an organism with a model for action in similar circumstances.

Adaptation In Piaget's theory, the twofold process consisting of assimilation and accommodation.

Assimilation In Piaget's theory, the process by which children incorporate new experiences into their existing schemas.

Accommodation In Piaget's theory, the process by which children modify their existing schemas in order to adapt to new experiences.

unlikely to occur because the toy is so difficult to suck on; in this case, the baby's sucking schema will be unmodified.

Piaget and Barbel Inhelder (1969) expressed the two-sided nature of the process that, in their view, leads to developmental change in the following way:

> [Our] view of assimilation presupposes a reciprocity between S–R [stimulus and response]; that is to say, the input, the stimulus, is filtered through a structure that consists of the action schemes, . . . which in turn are modified and enriched when the subject's behavioral repertoire is accommodated to the demands of reality. The filtering or modification of the input is called assimilation; the modification of the internal schemes is called accommodation. (p. 6)

One way to summarize Piaget's theory is to view development as a constant tug-of-war between assimilation and accommodation during action on the world. Piaget referred to this back-and-forth process of seeking a fit between the child's existing schemas and new environmental experiences as **equilibration,** which is basically the process of achieving a balance, or equilibrium, between the individual and the environment. At certain times a new balance between assimilation and accommodation creates a more inclusive, more complicated form of knowledge, bringing the child to a new level of development. But during childhood the balance does not last for long because the process of biological maturation and the accumulation of experience/knowledge leads to new imbalances, initiating a new tug-of-war between assimilation and accommodation in the search for a new equilibrium and a higher level of adaptation.

Piaget was a *stage theorist,* someone who maintains that development proceeds by a sequence of *qualitative transformations.* He saw the transformations as occurring in the overall knowledge structure of the child. He believed that there are four major developmental stages between birth and adulthood, corresponding to infancy, early childhood, middle childhood, and adolescence.

Table 4.5 provides a summary of the four stages of development described by Piaget. The sensorimotor stage, which occurs during infancy, is discussed below and in Chapters 5 and 6. We then examine the preoperational, concrete operational, and formal operational stages in Chapters 9, 12, and 16, respectively.

The sensorimotor period and its substages

Piaget (1952b) referred to infancy as the **sensorimotor stage** because during this period the process of adaptation consists largely of coordinating *sensory* perceptions and simple *motor* behaviors to acquire knowledge of the world: reaching for an object, for example, or starting to nurse at the mother's breast. This stage lasts from birth to about the age of 2 years. Within the *sensorimotor period* Piaget identified six substages, each of which builds on the accomplishments of the one before (see Table 4.5). We will discuss the first two substages of the sensorimotor period here because they correspond to the early months of postnatal life.

Substage 1 lasts from birth to approximately 1 to 1½ months. It is the stage during which infants *learn to control and coordinate their reflexes.* Piaget believed that the reflexes present at birth provide the initial connection between infants and their environments, but at that point the reflexes add nothing new to development because they have undergone very little accommodation and so still reflect the "preestablished boundaries of the hereditary apparatus" (Piaget & Inhelder, 1969, p. 7).

The initial reflexes provide the impetus for their own change, however, because they *produce* stimulation in addition to being responses to stimuli. When infants suck, for example, they experience tactile pressure on the roof of the mouth, which stimulates further sucking, which produces more tactile pressure, and so on. This stimulus-producing aspect of basic reflexes is the key to the development of

Equilibration The cognitive balance achieved through the back and forth process between assimilation of new experiences to prior schemas and the accommodation of schemas to new experiences.

Sensorimotor stage The first of Piaget's four developmental stages, characterized by the beginnings of coordination between the infant's sensory experiences and simple motor behaviors.

TABLE 4.5 Piaget's Stages of Cognitive Development and the Sensorimotor Substages

Age (years)	Stage	Description	Characteristics of Sensorimotor Substage
Birth to 2	SENSORIMOTOR	Infants' achievements consist largely of coordinating their sensory perceptions and simple motor behaviors. As they move through the 6 substages of this period, infants come to recognize the existence of a world outside of themselves and begin to interact with it in deliberate ways.	Substage 1 (0–1½ months) *Reflex schemas exercised*: involuntary rooting, sucking, grasping, looking Substage 2 (1½–4 months) *Primary circular reactions*: repetition of actions that are pleasurable in themselves
2 to 6	PREOPERATIONAL	Young children can represent reality to themselves through the use of symbols, including mental images, words, and gestures. Still, children often fail to distinguish their point of view from that of others, become easily captured by surface appearances, and are often confused about causal relations.	Substage 3 (4–8 months) *Secondary circular reactions*: dawning awareness of relation of own actions to environment; extended actions that produce interesting change in the environment Substage 4 (8–12 months) *Coordination of secondary circular reactions*: combining schemas to achieve a desired effect; earliest form of problem solving
6 to 12	CONCRETE OPERATIONAL	As they enter middle childhood, children become capable of mental operations, internalized actions that fit into a logical system. Operational thinking allows children mentally to combine, separate, order, and transform objects and actions. Such operations are considered concrete because they are carried out in the presence of the objects and events being thought about.	Substage 5 (12–18 months) *Tertiary circular reactions*: deliberate variation of problem-solving means; experimentation to see what the consequences will be
12 to 19	FORMAL OPERATIONAL	In adolescence the developing person acquires the ability to think systematically about all logical relations within a problem. Adolescents display keen interest in abstract ideas and in the process of thinking itself.	Substage 6 (18–24 months) *Beginnings of symbolic representation*: images and words come to stand for familiar objects; invention of new means of problem solving through symbolic combinations

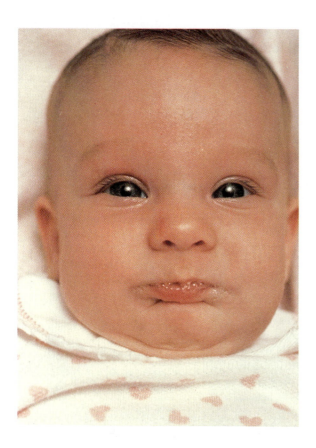

Blowing bubbles is an early instance of a primary circular reaction in which an accidental aspect of sucking is prolonged for the pleasure of continuing the sensation.

Primary circular reaction Behavior characteristic of the second substage of Piaget's sensorimotor period in which the baby repeats simple actions for their own sake.

the second sensorimotor substage because it results in the earliest extensions of the reflexes the baby is born with.

Substage 2 lasts from about 1 month to about 4 months. The first hints of new forms of behavior are found in the way *existing reflexes are extended in time* (as when infants suck between feedings) *or are applied to new objects.* Piaget and Inhelder (1969) offered thumb-sucking as an example of the extension of a reflex to accommodate a new object. They noted that babies may suck their thumbs accidentally as early as the first day of life. (We now know they may do so even before birth; see Chapter 3, p. 80.) They believed, however, that the thumb-sucking seen during substage 2 (from about 2 to 4 months of age) reflects a qualitatively new form of behavior.

Piaget used the term **primary circular reaction** to characterize the behavior characteristic of this second substage of sensorimotor development. In this substage infants repeat pleasurable actions for their own sake. In substage 1, infants suck their thumbs, but only when they accidentally touch their mouth with their hands. Now, if the thumb falls from the mouth, the infant takes the initiative to search out the hand, thereby producing for itself the stimulation needed for thumb-sucking. These actions are called *primary* because the objects at which they are directed are parts of the baby's own body; they are called *circular* because they lead only back to themselves. (Table 4.5 lists all of Piaget's sensorimotor substages and the behaviors characteristic of each.)

Piaget was a keen observer of his own infants, and evidence in support of many of his ideas about the earliest substages of the sensorimotor period can be seen in the notes he kept about their behavior. The following observations illustrate the kind of behaviors he referred to as primary circular reactions:

> After having learned to suck his thumb, Laurent continues to play with his tongue and to suck, but intermittently. On the other hand, his skill increases. Thus at 1 month, 20 days, I notice he grimaces while placing his tongue between gums and lips and in bulging his lips, as well as making a clapping sound when quickly closing his mouth after these exercises.
>
> From 2 months, 18 days Laurent plays with his saliva, letting it accumulate within his half-open lips and then abruptly swallowing it. About the same period he makes sucking-like movements, without putting out his tongue. (1952b, p. 65)

Piaget believed that such primary circular reactions are important because they offer the first evidence of cognitive development. "The basic law of dawning psychological activity," he wrote, "could be said to be the search for the maintenance or repetition of interesting states of consciousness" (1977, p. 202).

Over the first few months of life, these circular reactions undergo *differentiation*—infants learn to use different grasps for different objects and learn not to suck on toy trucks—and *integration*—infants can grasp their mother's arm with one hand while sucking on a bottle in a newly coordinated way. All the while, infants' experiences are providing more nourishment for their existing schemas and are forcing them to modify those schemas, permitting them to master more of the world.

In contrast to the infants portrayed by biological-maturation and environmental-learning approaches, Piagetian infants are active, problem-solving beings who from the beginning are busy acting on the environment in the process of adapting to it. All three perspectives discussed thus far designate inborn reflexes as the starting point for development, but they view the significance of these reflexes in different ways. Because Piaget saw reflexes as schemas for action, he downplayed the role of the environment in evoking or reinforcing particular behaviors and instead emphasized the infant's constructive activity in shaping the way the environment will exert its effects.

Piaget's theory and the social environment

Piaget acknowledged that the social environment is an important influence on early development, yet discussions of social context are virtually absent from his writing about the early development of reflexes. Nevertheless, a close look at the acquisition of new forms of behavior during the first 2½ months of life reveals that changes in a baby's behavior are accompanied by changes in the mother's behavior. These changes in maternal behaviors appear to be just as essential to the infant's development as are the changes that occur in the infant's relations to objects or in its brain functioning.

Nursing clearly demonstrates how the mother's behavior contributes to the infant's development. In the beginning, the mother's nursing behavior may not be much more coordinated than her baby's. She must learn how to hold the baby and adjust herself so that the nipple is placed at exactly the right spot against the baby's mouth to elicit the sucking reflex. She must also learn not to press the baby so tightly to her breast that its breathing is disrupted and the head-withdrawal reflex is brought into play.

When the mother breast-feeds, her reflexes in response to the baby's (reflex) sucking combine with her voluntary efforts to maximize the amount of milk the baby receives. This system of mutually facilitating reflexes in infant and mother, which changes the consequences of reflex sucking, is illustrated in Figure 4.22. The infant's sucking not only transports milk from nipple to mouth but also stimulates the production of more milk, thereby increasing the sucking reflex's adaptive value.

FIGURE 4.22 *The reflexes that establish a reciprocal relationship between the infant being fed and the mother. The infant's sucking stimulates the release of hormones that increase milk production and help to trigger the ejection of milk from the mammary glands. (From Cairns, 1979.)*

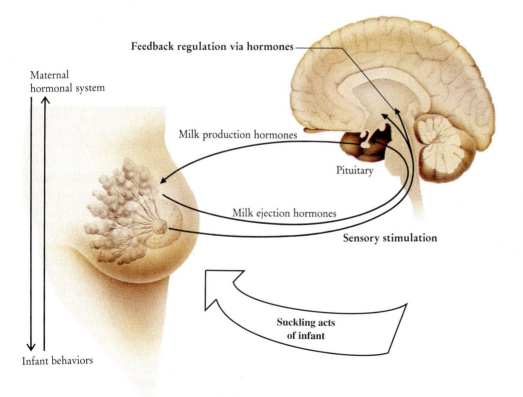

Feedback regulation via hormones

Maternal hormonal system

Milk production hormones

Pituitary

Milk ejection hormones

Sensory stimulation

Suckling acts of infant

Infant behaviors

A different type of mutual facilitation arises from the physical movements mothers make while they are feeding their infants by either breast or bottle. Kenneth Kaye (1982) and his colleagues found that even during the very first feeding, mothers occasionally jiggle their baby or the bottle. These jiggles come not at random intervals but during the pauses between the infant's bursts of sucking. The jiggles increase the probability of sucking and prolong the feeding session, thereby increasing the amount of milk the neonate receives.

Sucking in response to jiggling is not a reflex in the sense that rooting is a reflex. Rooting is an automatic, involuntary response to being touched on the side of the mouth. There are no known neural connections that make sucking an inevitable response to the mother's jiggle. Yet jiggling happens, it is to some extent automatic, and it has clear adaptive value. Scholars do not know for sure where such adaptive patterns come from. Kaye calls them "preadapted responses," implying that they may have arisen in the course of human evolution.

Kaye speculates that the mother's jiggle between her infant's bursts of sucking is her way of intuitively "conversing" with her baby by filling in her "turn" during the pauses in the baby's rhythmic sucking. Mothers' reports support Kaye's view. Although they are not aware that they are jiggling their babies in a systematic way, mothers report that they actively try to help their babies nurse. They notice and disapprove of the pauses between bursts of sucking. When mothers are asked about their jiggling behavior, a typical response is that the baby "gets lazy, or dozes off, so I jiggle her to get her going again."

This demonstration of one of the myriad ways mothers actively structure their children's experiences leads us to consider a point that Piaget does not raise: both the child *and* the child's environment actively participate in the process of interaction through which development occurs. But in one essential respect, the forms of interaction advanced by Kaye and Piaget are the same; both investigators assumed that the interaction processes they described are universal features of human behavior and thus apply to children everywhere. The cultural-context theorists challenge this assumption.

THE CULTURAL-CONTEXT PERSPECTIVE

As we indicated in Chapter 1 (p. 38), the cultural-context perspective shares Piaget's beliefs that (1) development occurs as individuals act on their environment and (2) biology and experience play equal and reciprocal roles in the creation of a human being. However, cultural-context theorists also consider two additional sources of developmental change: (1) the active contribution of other people in the child's community and (2) the cultural "designs for living" accumulated over the history of the social group. Such designs for living are present in all human societies, and in this sense they are universal. But their particular shape varies from one society to the next, giving rise to culturally specific modes of interaction. These culture-specific variations encourage development along certain lines while discouraging it along others, thereby producing distinctive patterns of behavior (Laboratory of Comparative Human Cognition, 1983). Let us look once again at the process through which sucking develops into organized feeding, this time to see how the universal facts of maturation, learning, and maternal support vary culturally in ways that shape infants' behavior in the present and give hints of further changes to come.

In their discussion of culture and development, Margaret Mead and Frances Macgregor (1951) noted that cultures "differ from each other in the way in which the growth process is interwoven with learning" (p. 26). This principle, they went on to explain, first operates in the various ways adults of different cultures respond to such basic neonatal capacities as the sucking reflex:

> The existence of the sucking reflex at birth . . . will be taken advantage of in some cultures by putting the baby at once to the mother's breast, so that the

infant's sucking is used to stimulate the flow of the mother's milk while the infant itself remains hungry, or the infant may be put at the breast of a wet nurse with a well-established flow of milk, in which case the infant's sucking behavior is reinforced but the mother is left without the stimulation that it would have provided. As another alternative, the infant may be starved until the mother has milk, and as still another, the infant may be given a bottle with a different kind of nipple. (p. 26)

These different feeding practices are equivalent in that they are all ways in which parents arrange for infants' innate sucking reflexes to become part of nursing. In this respect, nursing is universal—in every culture, some arrangement is made for the infant's sucking reflex to become a part of nursing (Figure 4.23).

Every culture works out its own best way to transport babies.

FIGURE 4.23 *Although babies are nursed in all cultures, there are wide variations in the way babies' nursing behavior is organized.*

According to the cultural-context perspective, however, cultural variations in the way nursing is handled may have a direct effect on the infant's early experience and an indirect effect on later experiences. To continue with the example provided by Mead and Macgregor, if a baby is bottle-fed until the mother's milk begins to flow, changes in the baby's sucking that are adaptive to bottle-feeding may interfere with subsequent breast-feeding. If the interference is great, breast-feeding may be given up altogether. This outcome will alter both the kind of milk that the infant receives and the forms of social interaction between infant and mother that are a part of feeding. When a specific cultural practice, such as bottle-feeding or the use of a wetnurse, is linked to a larger pattern of interaction that will shape the child's future experiences, the child's later development is likely to be affected. For example, if a mother who stays at home gives her baby a bottle because she believes that bottled milk is more nutritious than her own, the use of a bottle rather than breast-feeding may have no differential impact on the development of social relations between the mother and child. However, if the mother leaves her baby at a day-care center because she is working in an office or factory that makes no provision for on-site child care, the relationship between mother and baby is less than exclusive. For this baby, bottle-feeding is likely to become part of a pattern of social interactions with peers and a succession of caregivers. In either case, the immediate consequences of the specific feeding practice are less important than the larger patterns of life with which they are associated.

An important implication of the cultural-context perspective that is not captured by the example of nursing is that cultures provide people with a framework for interpreting their experiences that even influences their view of their own babies. The way newborn babies are treated depends very much on what a culture defines babies to be. In the United States today, for example, well-educated, middle-class adults tend to have a higher opinion of the psychological capacities of young infants than do adults of many other cultures and even of some subcultures within the United States (Siegel et al., 1992). When the behavioral consequences of this cultural belief are viewed in isolation from usual child-care contexts, they can be quite striking. The pediatrician T. Berry Brazelton and his colleagues placed 1-week-old infants in infant seats in the laboratory and asked their mothers to spend several minutes interacting with them. Here's how the scene unfolded:

> Our mothers were faced with the problem of communicating with infants who, if they were not crying or thrashing, were often hanging limply in the infant seat with closed or semiclosed eyes or, just as frequently, were "frozen" motionless in some strange and uninterpretable posture—staring at nothing. . . . Perhaps the most interesting response to the challenge of facing an unresponsive infant is this. The mother takes on facial expressions, motions, and postures indicative of emotion, as though the infant were behaving intentionally or as though she and he were communicating. Frequently, in response to a motionless infant, she suddenly acquires an expression of great admiration, moving back and forth in front of him with great enthusiasm; or again in response to an unmoving infant, she takes on an expression of great surprise, moving backward in mock astonishment; or in the most exaggerated manner, she greets the infant and, furthermore, carries on an animated extended greeting interchange, bobbing and nodding enthusiastically exactly as though her greeting were currently being reciprocated. (Brazelton, Koslowski, & Main, 1974, p. 67–68)

In sum, most mothers in the United States are unwilling or unable to deal with neonatal behaviors as though they were meaningless or unintentional. Instead, they endow the smallest movements with highly personal meaning and react to them affectively. They insist on joining in and enlarging on even the least possibly interactive behaviors, through imitation. And they perform as if highly significant interaction had taken place when there has been no interaction at all.

The Kaluli, who live in the rain forests of Papua New Guinea, have a far different set of beliefs about babies than middle-class Americans do, and they treat their babies quite differently as a result. As Eleanor Ochs and Bambi Schieffelin (1984) report, the Kaluli see their babies as helpless creatures who have "no understanding." Although they may greet their infants by name, they do not talk to them in the way middle-class American adults do. Nor do Kaluli mothers engage in extended eye contact with their babies, because the Kaluli believe that it is impolite to gaze at the person you are talking to. Kaluli mothers hold their infants facing outward so they can see, be seen by, and interact with other members of the social group. Instead of speaking to their infants, Kaluli mothers speak for them. As Ochs and Schieffelin point out, "in taking this role the mother does for the infant what the infant cannot do for itself, that is appear to act in a controlled and competent manner, using language" (p. 290).

Notice that the words Ochs and Schieffelin use to describe the intent of the Kaluli mothers could also be applied to the U.S. mothers, even though the specific actions involved are quite different. In both cultures, beliefs about what babies are, what they can do, and what they will need to do in the future affect the way babies are treated by those around them and thus the way they experience the environment. In short, different cultural patterns lead to different child-rearing practices, which have quite different effects on further development, as we will see in later chapters. For this reason it is important to keep cultural factors in mind when we consider the mechanisms of developmental change (Harkness & Super, 1996).

Integrating the Separate Threads of Development

The complexities of the various factors that account for the way nursing develops during the first months of life provide some idea of the enormous difficulties facing anyone who seeks to explain human development as a whole. Even for a behavior as seemingly simple as nursing, the contributions of biological and environmental factors, including cultural influences and the specific circumstances in which infants find themselves, must all be considered. And the difficulties do not end there. A child's various behaviors develop not in isolation but as parts of an integrated system. Thus psychologists must also study the parts of the system in relation to one another. Nursing, for instance, must be understood as but one element in a system of developing behaviors that includes increasingly longer sleeping and waking periods and the buildup of elementary expectations about the environment.

To meet this requirement that developing behaviors be considered both individually and as parts of a larger whole, the analytical strategy developed by Robert Emde and his associates is especially useful (Emde, Gaensbauer, & Harmon, 1976). As we mentioned in Chapter 1 (pp. 41–42), this strategy involves tracing developments in the biological, behavioral, and social domains *as they relate to one another*. It allows the identification of bio-social-behavioral shifts, those periods when changes in the separate domains converge to create the kind of qualitative reorganization in the overall pattern of behaviors that signals the onset of a new stage of development. We can see the usefulness of this approach by examining the first bio-social-behavioral shift after birth, which occurs when a full-term baby is about 2½ months old.

The First Postnatal Bio-Social-Behavioral Shift

Emde and his co-workers would agree that during the first two months of postnatal life infants learn by acting on their environments and by interaction with their caregivers. During the third month, however, the "modes and mechanisms" of their behavior undergo a rather abrupt shift (Emde et al., 1976). This shift arises from the convergence of developmental changes that previously have proceeded in relative isolation. Table 4.6 lists in capsule form the changes in the separate domains that converge to create the first postnatal bio-social-behavioral shift. To appreciate the far-reaching significance of this and subsequent bio-social-behavioral shifts, we must visualize what it means for all of the changes listed in Table 4.6 to occur at about the same time. Emde and his colleagues convey the sense of this meaning by tracing how changes in infants' smiling are related to other aspects of their development.

THE EMERGENCE OF SOCIAL SMILING

During the earliest weeks of life, the corners of a baby's mouth often curl up in a facial expression that looks for all the world like a smile. Most experienced mothers do not pay much attention to these smiles, however, because they are most likely to come when the infant is asleep or very drowsy. Emde and his colleagues studied the nature and origin of infants' smiles by recording their brain waves at times when they were and were not smiling and the nature of the social feedback the infants received when they smiled.

TABLE 4.6	Elements of the First Postnatal Bio-Social-Behavioral Shift (2½ Months)	

BIOLOGICAL DOMAIN	Central nervous system:
	    Myelination of cortical and subcortical neural pathways
	    Myelination of primary neural pathways in some sensory systems
	    Increased cortical control of subcortical activity
	    Increases in the number and diversity of brain cells
	Psychophysiology:
	    Increases in amount of wakefulness
	    Decreases in active (REM) sleep as a proportion of total sleep time
	    Shift in pattern of sleep; quiet (NREM) sleep begins to come first
		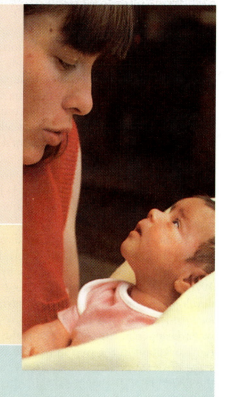

BEHAVIORAL DOMAIN	Learning is retained better between episodes Increases in visual acuity More complete visual scanning of objects Onset of social smiling Decreases in generalized fussiness and crying Visually initiated reaching becomes visually guided reaching	
SOCIAL DOMAIN	New quality of coordination and emotional contact between infants and caretakers Beginning of "crying on purpose"	

The researchers found that in the days after birth the babies' smiles came primarily during REM sleep and were accompanied by bursts of brain-wave activity originating in the brain stem. Emde and Jean Robinson (1979) call these endogenous smiles REM smiles. During the second week, smiles began to appear when the infants were awake, but they did not correlate with any particular events in the environment. Emde and his colleagues found that even when the infants were awake their smiles were accompanied by the pattern of brain waves characteristic of drowsiness and REM sleep.

Emde and his colleagues reported that the frequency of REM smiles decreased rapidly during the next several weeks. In their place there appeared an exogenous smile, one that responds to stimulation from the environment. Between the ages of 1 month and 2½ months, infants smile indiscriminately at things or people they see, touch, or hear. Thus this earliest form of exogenous smiling is not really social, even though it is stimulated from the outside.

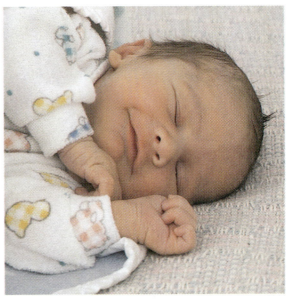

Smiling during REM sleep.

To become truly social, babies' smiles must be reciprocally related to the smiles of others; that is, the babies must both smile in response to the smiles of others and elicit others' smiles. This is precisely what begins to happen for the first time at the age of 2½ to 3 months as part of the first postnatal bio-social-behavioral shift. This new behavior depends in part on changes in the brain and the nervous system that result in marked increases in infants' visual acuity and in their ability to scan objects systematically. The improved visual capacity permits babies to focus their eyes, and thus their smiles, on people, so that early exogenous smiling can become truly social smiling.

The changes in infants' behavior that accompany the social smile are not lost on their parents. Quite the opposite; parents report a new emotional quality in their relationship with their child. The following remarks by two mothers concerning their feelings for their babies before and after the shift clearly illustrate the social and emotional implications of the new kind of smiling:

BEFORE THE SHIFT

I don't think there is interaction. . . . They are like in a little cage surrounded by glass and you are acting all around them but there is no real interaction. . . . I realized I was doing things for him he couldn't do for himself but I always felt that anyone else could do them and he wouldn't know the difference. (Robson & Moss, 1970, pp. 979–980)

AFTER THE SHIFT

His eyes locked on to hers, and together they held motionless. . . . This silent and almost motionless instant continued to hang until the mother suddenly shattered it by saying "Hey!" and simultaneously opening her eyes wider, raising her eyebrows further, and throwing her head up and toward the infant. Almost simultaneously the baby's eyes widened. His head tilted up . . . , his smile broadened. . . . Now she said, "Well hello! . . . heello, . . . heeelloooo!," so that her pitch rose and the "hellos" became longer and more stressed on each successive repetition. With each phrase the baby expressed more pleasure, and his body resonated almost like a balloon being pumped up. (Stern, 1977, p. 3)

When we contrast the "before" and "after" interactions, we see that the older child displays a new emotion, joy—expressed in his smile and his whole body—to help account for the mother's sense of a new and more connected relationship.

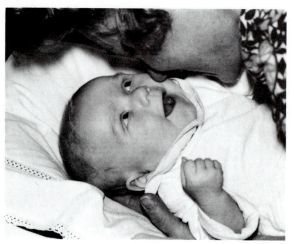

This 2½-month-old blind infant smiled and turned her face toward her mother upon hearing her mother's voice.

THE SOCIAL SMILE AND SOCIAL FEEDBACK

The importance of social feedback to the achievement of bio-social-behavioral shifts is dramatically demonstrated by research conducted by Selma Fraiberg (1974) on the development of congenitally blind infants. Like sighted infants, blind babies exhibit REM smiles. But unlike sighted infants, they may not exhibit the same shift to social smiling at 2½ months.

Under normal conditions of growth, the social smile is connected to visual exploration of the world. It depends on increased visual capacity and on visual feedback from people who smile back. Blind infants cannot explore the world visually and hence may not establish the feedback loop they need in order to develop social smiling.

The frequent failure of blind infants to make the expected shift toward social smiling also means that their sighted parents cannot use their baby's facial expressions as a gauge by which to evaluate their own efforts to help their infant. But it does not mean that blind infants receive no social feedback or that they *cannot* acquire social smiling. After all, their brains are maturing like those of sighted children. The problem is that they cannot express their increased capacities in visually related ways. In the absence of this major channel for social feedback, parents must find alternate ways to interact with their blind children.

The intuitive solution that some parents of blind children work out is to establish communication through touch. Fraiberg noticed that many of these parents bounce, nudge, and tickle their children far more than the parents of sighted children. At first all this manipulation struck Fraiberg as socially abnormal, but then she noticed that the touching made the children smile and realized that tactile stimulation was a good substitute for the smiling face that elicits the smiles of sighted babies. Through touch the parents had found a way to get the feedback that they needed from their infants—and to provide feedback that the infants needed from them. Fraiberg used this observation to design a training program to help blind infants and their parents (Fraiberg, 1974). Parents were taught to attend carefully to the way their children used their hands to signal their intentions and reactions and how to organize their baby's environment to encourage interaction. Once the children of these parents were provided with appropriate feedback, they began to develop social smiling.

The success of Fraiberg's training program indicates that social smiling does not arise simply from the fact that an infant's brain has matured to the point where social smiling is possible. For social smiling to emerge, appropriate interaction with others is necessary; when this new behavior does emerge, a new affective quality is able to develop between infants and their parents. As we will see in other periods of a child's life, development results from a complex interaction of biological, social, and behavioral changes. The notion of bio-social-behavioral shifts helps us to keep this important principle in mind.

Summing Up the First Two and a Half Months

Looking back over the first 2½ months or so of postnatal life, we can see a remarkable set of changes in infants' behaviors. Babies are born with a rudimentary ability to interact with their new environment. They have reflexes that enable them to take in oxygen and nutrients and expel waste products. They are able to perceive objects, including people, although they tend to focus on only a part of

The moment parents and their babies make eye contact is pleasurable for both parties.

the entire stimulus. They are sensitive to the sounds of human language, and they quickly develop a preference for the sound of their mother's voice. Although they sleep most of the time, they are occasionally quite alert.

From the moment of birth, infants interact with and are supported by their parents or other caregivers, who come equipped with the biological and cultural resources necessary to see that their babies receive food and protection. Despite these resources, the first interactions of babies and their caregivers are tentative and somewhat uncoordinated. Within a matter of days, however, a process of mutual adjustment has begun that will provide an essential framework for later development.

The developmental changes that characterize the first 10 to 12 weeks have clear origins in biology and in both the physical and social environments. In the domain of biology, there is rapid maturation of the central nervous system, particularly in the connections between the brain stem and the cerebral cortex. As a consequence of frequent feeding, the baby grows bigger and stronger. As a consequence of practice at feeding, the elementary reflex of sucking becomes efficient feeding, an accomplishment that owes a good deal to the complementary efforts of the baby's caregivers, primarily the mother.

Between the ages of 2½ and 3 months, several lines of development that have been proceeding more or less independently now converge. The consequences are qualitatively different forms of behavior and a new type of social relationship between babies and their caregivers. The story of the development of the seemingly simple behavior of social smiling illustrates the intricate way in which these different lines of development must relate to one another for a transition to a qualitatively new level of development to occur.

1. Maturation of the visual system enables a new level of visual acuity and a new ability to analyze the visual field.

2. As a consequence, smiling, a seemingly unrelated behavior, may be transformed.

3. With the advent of social smiling, parents report that they experience a new sense of connectedness with their babies and babies begin to express the emotion of joy.

This transformation will take place only if the infant's caregivers provide proper feedback. Without appropriate feedback, as in the case of some blind children, social smiling does not develop. And if social smiling does not develop, the development of social interactions may be disrupted.

In later chapters we will see versions of this pattern repeated again and again. For a stretch of time the child's overall level of development remains stable while various systems undergo changes in relative isolation. Then there is a brief period during which these separate lines of development converge, resulting in a new level of organization with regard to the child's behaviors, the interactions between child and caregiver, and the range of emotions that the child expresses. It will not always be possible to identify the specific biological, social, and behavioral factors that contribute to the emergence of new stages of development with equal certainty and rigor. But it will always be useful to consider the various domains that enter into the process of developmental change as a means of keeping the whole child in mind.

SUMMARY

Earliest Capacities

- Infants are born with remarkable sensory and behavioral capacities with which to experience and respond to their postnatal circumstances.

    1. Neonates are not able to hear sounds in the same range of frequencies that are audible to older children and adults, but they display a special sensitivity to the basic sound categories of human language.

    2. Although infants are nearsighted, they systematically scan their surroundings and are sensitive to areas of high contrast between light and dark. They will track moving facelike forms at birth, and within a few days they seem to be able to distinguish their mother's face from others'.

    3. Neonates can distinguish between tastes and smells. They prefer sweet tastes, and the smells they most enjoy are the ones that seem pleasant to older people, too.

    4. The senses of touch, temperature, and position are relatively mature at birth.

- A variety of reflexes, automatic responses to specific environmental events, are present at birth.

- At birth or shortly thereafter, infants display the signs of several basic emotions: joy, fear, anger, surprise, sadness, and interest. There is some doubt about how early these emotions appear and whether or not they have the same quality as those experienced by older children and adults.

- Individual variations in temperament—in style of response and dominant mood—are present at birth. Individual differences in temperament may be relatively stable and thus would constitute an important source of developmental continuity.

- The basic behavioral capacities with which infants are born are sufficient for their survival only if they are coordinated with adult caregiving activities.

Becoming Coordinated

- "Getting the baby on a schedule" is more than a convenience. By coordinating schedules, babies and their parents create a system of mutual expectations that supports further development.

- Newborn babies sleep approximately two-thirds of the time, but their periods of sleep are relatively brief and are distributed across all 24 hours of the day. All babies tend to sleep more at night than during the day from the outset, but the time that passes before they begin to sleep through the night depends on the sleep patterns of the adults who care for them, and those patterns vary from culture to culture.

- Newborn babies tend to eat about every 3 hours if they are given constant access to food. Babies fed only every 4 hours may have trouble adjusting to such a schedule, although most infants adopt a 4-hour schedule spontaneously by the time they reach 2½ months of age.

- Crying is a primitive means of communication that evokes a strong emotional response in adults and alerts them that something may be wrong. The distinctive sound patterns of early cries help cue caregivers as to possible sources of distress. In some cases they indicate serious illness.

Mechanisms of Developmental Change

- In the beginning, feeding is based on primitive reflex mechanisms that are not well coordinated. Within several weeks, this form of behavior is reorganized and becomes voluntary; the various constituent reflexes become integrated with one another and the baby becomes well coordinated with the mother.

- The four basic perspectives on development can all be applied to the earliest forms of infant development; each emphasizes a different way in which biological and environmental factors contribute to early developmental change.

- According to the biological-maturation perspective, postnatal development follows the same principles as prenatal development. New structures are said to arise from endogenous (inherited) capabilities that unfold as the baby matures. Changes in nursing as well as in other behaviors, according to this view, result from such factors as the increased myelination of the neurons and the growth of muscles.

- The maturation of brain structures contributes to the reorganization of early reflexes. Some of these early reflexes disappear completely within a few months of birth. Others may disappear and then reappear later as an element in a new form of activity. Still others remain and are transformed into voluntary behaviors under the control of the cerebral cortex.

- Environmental-learning theories assign the environment a leading role in the creation of new forms of behavior through the mechanism of learning.

- Infants' ability to learn from experience increases steadily during the first months of life. Classical conditioning permits infants to form expectations about the connections between events in their environment. Operant conditioning provides a mechanism for the emergence of new behaviors as a consequence of the positive or negative events they produce. Some studies appear to show that young infants can also learn through imitation, but this contention remains in dispute.

- Constructivist theories assign equal weight to biological and environmental factors in development. Reflexes, in this view, are coordinated patterns of action (schemas) that have differentiated from a more primitive state of global activity characteristic of the prenatal period.

- In the view of Jean Piaget, the leading constructivist of the twentieth century, developmental change is constructed through the interplay of assimilation (modification of the input to fit existing schemas) and accommodation (modification of existing schemas to fit the input). The interplay of accommodation and assimilation continues until a new form of equilibrium between the two processes is reached. New forms of equilibrium constitute qualitatively new forms of behavior; they are new stages of development.

- According to Piaget, infancy is characterized by sensorimotor ways of knowing. He divides the sensorimotor period into six substages, the first two of which occur during the first 10 to 12 weeks of postnatal life:

  1. Substage 1 is characterized by the exercise of basic reflexes.
  2. Substage 2 is characterized by the beginning of accommodation and the prolongation of pleasant sensations arising from reflex actions.

- Careful observations of interactions between mothers and infants reveal that some part of the work that Piaget attributed to infants is in fact contributed by the people with whom they interact.

- Cultural-context theories of development emphasize the active roles of the child and of the people around the child, and add historically accumulated "designs for living" as contributors to the process of developmental change.

- Significant and pervasive cultural variations in parents' everyday activities and their interactions with their newborn children influence both short-term and long-term development.

Integrating the Separate Threads of Development

- In order to explain development, it is necessary to understand how different parts of the process change with respect to each other, as parts of an integrated bio-social-behavioral system in its cultural context.

The First Postnatal Bio-Social-Behavioral Shift

- At approximately 2½ months of age a bio-social-behavioral shift occurs in the overall organization of infants' behavior. Changes in brain function owing to maturation are accompanied by increased visual acuity and the ability to perceive the forms of objects and people, increased wakefulness, and social smiling. Caregivers respond with new feelings of connectedness to the infant.

KEY TERMS

accommodation,   p. 167

adaptation,   p. 167

assimilation,   p. 167

brain stem,   p. 157

cerebral cortex,   p. 157

classical conditioning, p. 163

conditional response (CR),   p. 164

conditional stimulus (CS),   p. 164

dishabituation,   p. 135

emotion,   p. 143

equilibration,   p. 168

habituation,   p. 135

learning,   p. 162

THOUGHT QUESTIONS

1. In the quote at the chapter's opening, Erik Erikson writes, "Babies control and bring up their families as much as they are controlled by them." Explain this statement.

2. Many years ago William James characterized infants' perceptual world as a "buzzing, blooming confusion." How does this description fare in light of recent research on the perceptual world of the young infant?

3. Reread Piaget and Inhelder's statement on p. 168 and then use your own words and examples to describe the processes of assimilation and accommodation.

4. List the ways in which neonatal development is continuous with development before birth. List the ways in which it is discontinuous.

5. Explain the development of social smiling at 2½ to 3 months of age. Why is this development a good example of a bio-social-behavioral shift?

The Achievements of the First Year

"The question . . . is not where or when mind begins. Mind in some . . . form is there from the start, wherever 'there' may be."

Jerome Bruner, In Search of Mind

Two neighbors—Jake, who is about to celebrate his first birthday, and his mother, Barbara—have been out for a walk and have stopped by our house. Sheila is in the kitchen preparing dinner. Jake is sitting on his mother's lap at the kitchen table, drinking apple juice from a plastic cup while the two women chat.

Jake finishes his juice, some of which has dribbled onto his shirt, and puts the cup down on the table with a satisfied bang. He squirms around in his mother's lap so that he is facing her. He tries to get her attention by pulling at her face. When Barbara ignores him, Jake wriggles out of her lap to the floor, where he notices the dog.

"Wuff wuff," he says excitedly, pointing at the dog.

"Doggie," Barbara says. "What does the doggie say, Jake?"

"Wuff wuff," Jake repeats, still staring at the dog.

Following his pointing finger, Jake toddles toward the dog. His walk has a drunken, side-to-side quality, and he has a hard time bringing himself to a stop. Barbara grabs hold of Jake's extended hand, redirecting it from the dog's eyes.

"Pat the doggie, Jake."

Jake pats the dog's head.

The dog does not like the attention and escapes into the living room. Jake toddles after her like a pull toy on an invisible string. The dog leads him back into the kitchen, where Jake bumps into Sheila's legs and falls to a sitting position.

"Well, hello, Jake," Sheila says, as she bends over and picks him up. "Did you fall down? Go boom?"

Jake, who has not till then taken his eyes from the dog, turns, looks at Sheila with a smile, and points at the dog. "Wuff wuff," he repeats.

Suddenly Jake's body stiffens. He stares searchingly at Sheila's face for an instant, then turns his head away and holds his arms out to his mother.

Sheila hands Jake to Barbara, who says, "Did you get scared? It's only Sheila."

But Jake eyes Sheila warily and hides in his mother's arms for several minutes.

At almost 1 year of age, Jake behaves far differently than a baby of 2½ months. At that age, Jake's main activities were eating, sleeping, and gazing around the room. He could hold his head up and turn it from side to side, but he could not readily reach out and grasp objects or move around on his own. He took an interest in mobiles and other objects when they were immediately in front of him, but he quickly lost interest in them when they disappeared. Although he seemed most comfortable with his mother, he did not seem particularly unhappy when he was cared for by someone else. His communications were restricted to cries, frowns, and smiles. The contrast between Jake's behavior then and at 1 year gives us a picture of some of the amazing developmental changes that occur in the first year of infancy and present a challenge to the psychologists who seek to explain them.

This chapter explores the various kinds of changes that appear to be crucial to children's development between the ages of 2½ months and 1 year. Perhaps most obvious are the outwardly visible biological changes (see Figure 5.1). Jake is visibly larger and stronger at 12 months than he was at 2½ months. Invisible but essential maturation has also taken place in his nervous system, particularly the cerebral cortex and other parts of the brain.

Accompanying these changes are increases in mobility and coordination. At 3 months, infants are just beginning to be able to roll over. Their parents know that they will remain more or less wherever they are put down. At about 7 to 8 months they begin to crawl, and at about 1 year they begin to walk. All during this period, infants also become much more adept at reaching for objects and grasping them. They prod, bang, squeeze, push, and pull almost anything they can get their hands on, and they often put objects into their mouths to find out about them. Their parents, afraid that they will either harm themselves or destroy property, must be constantly on guard.

As infants near their first birthday, they also exhibit important new cognitive abilities. They learn and remember with markedly greater ease and effectiveness, for example, and they have come to recognize the existence of categories of objects. They can anticipate the course of simple, familiar events, and they act surprised when their expectations are not met. This new level of understanding makes it possible for them to play simple games such as peekaboo.

Finally, the social and emotional relationship between infants and their caregivers changes toward the end of the first year. Infants become upset when they are separated from their caregivers, and sometimes they are wary of strangers, as Jake was when he noticed Sheila. They begin to check their caregivers' faces for indications of how to behave in uncertain situations, and they also begin to comprehend a few words, extending the ways in which they can communicate and maintain contact with their caregivers.

As we shall see, these changes in biological makeup, motor behavior, cognitive capacities, range of emotions, and new forms of social relationship converge as babies approach their first birthdays to produce another bio-social-behavioral shift. The new qualities that emerge from this reorganization of developmental processes provide the context for a new stage of development that will bring children to the end of infancy.

FIGURE 5.1 *The differences in size, strength, shape and motor control between small infants and babies in their second year are evident in the contrast between the infant supported in this mother's arms and the older infant beginning to use a mortar and pestle.*

Biological Changes

The extensive changes in babies' motor behavior and cognitive abilities that occur between the ages of 2½ months and 1 year depend on changes in their body proportions, muscles, bones, and brain.

SIZE AND SHAPE

Most healthy babies triple in weight and grow approximately 10 inches during the first year. As Figure 5.2 shows, the rate of physical growth is greatest in the first months after birth; it then gradually tapers off through the rest of infancy and childhood.

Another brief growth spurt comes at the onset of adolescence. The rates at which individual children normally grow, however, vary as widely as the heights and weights they eventually attain (Tanner, 1990). Many factors contribute to these variations, including quantity and quality of food, family income level, exposure to sunlight (a source of vitamin D), and genetic constitution (Johnson, Borden, & MacVean, 1973).

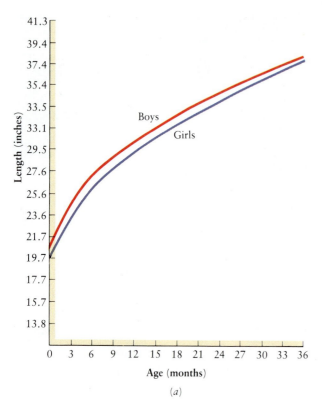

(a)

Increases in height and weight are accompanied by changes in body proportions (see Figure 5.3). At birth the head is 70 percent of its adult size and accounts for about 25 percent of the body's total length. At 1 year the head will account for 20 percent of the body's length, and in adulthood the proportion will be 12 percent. Infants' legs at birth are not much longer than their heads. By adulthood the legs account for about half of a person's total height. Changes in body proportions produce a lower center of gravity by about 12 months of age, making it easier for the child to balance on two legs and begin to walk (Thelen, 1995).

MUSCLE AND BONE

As babies grow, the bones and muscles needed to support their increasing bulk and mobility undergo corresponding growth. Most of a newborn's bones are relatively soft, and they harden only gradually as minerals are deposited in them in the months after birth. The bones in the hand and wrist are among the first to ossify (Tanner, 1989). They harden by the end of the first year, making it easier for a baby to grasp objects, pick them up, and play with them.

Although humans are born with all the muscle fibers they will ever have, their muscles change in length and thickness throughout childhood and into late adolescence. In infancy, increases in muscle mass are closely associated with the development of the baby's ability to stand alone and walk.

Sex differences in rate of growth

Research supports the common wisdom that girls mature faster than boys. The difference in the tempo of growth between the sexes starts even before birth. Halfway through the fetal period the skeleton of female children is some 3 weeks more advanced in development than that of male children. X rays of the growth centers (*epiphyses*) at the ends of bones show that at birth the female's skeleton is 4 to 6 weeks more mature than the male's and by puberty it is 2 years more advanced. Girls are more advanced in the development of other organ systems as well. Girls get their permanent teeth, go through puberty, and reach their full body size earlier than boys (Tanner, 1990). The earlier maturation of females is a characteristic human beings share with many other mammals.

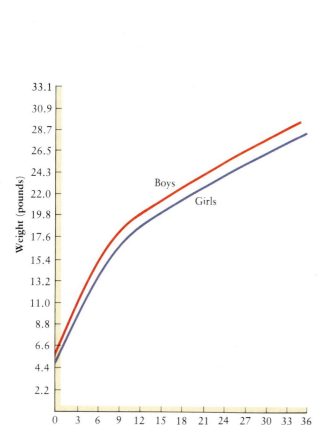

(b)

FIGURE 5.2 *Babies' length roughly doubles and their weight increases by 5 or 6 times during the first 3 years of life. (a) Average length by age. (b) Average weight by age. (From the U.S. Department of Health, Education, and Welfare, National Center for Health Statistics, 1976.)*

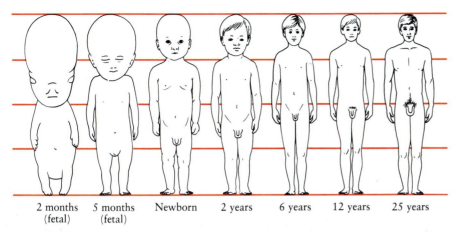

2 months   5 months   Newborn   2 years   6 years   12 years   25 years
(fetal)   (fetal)

FIGURE 5.3   *The proportions of body length accounted for by the head, trunk, and legs at different stages of development change remarkably. The disproportion is greatest during the fetal period, when the head accounts for as much as 50 percent of body length. The head decreases from 25 percent of body length at birth to 12 percent in adulthood. (From Robbins et al., 1929.)*

THE BRAIN

The entire nervous system continues to grow in size and complexity between the ages of 3 and 12 months (Bayer & Altman, 1991; Huttenlocher, 1990). Changes are especially notable in the frontal cortex, which plays a central role in bringing together information from the other parts of the brain and coordinating action (Luria, 1973).

A variety of evidence indicates that there is a spurt in frontal cortex development between roughly 7 and 9 months of age. During this brief period there are marked increases in various measures of electronic activity of the frontal cortex. The density of cell connections in that area increases rapidly as well. According to Kurt Fischer and Samuel Rose (1994), this developmental spurt in the frontal lobes gives the baby the ability to coordinate more complex forms of interaction.

The prefrontal area of the frontal cortex plays a particularly important role in the development of voluntary behavior. When this area begins to function in a new way sometime between 7 and 9 months, infants can inhibit their first impulses. They can stop themselves from grabbing the first attractive thing they see. With the ability to inhibit action, they become able to stop and think (Diamond, Cruttenden, & Neiderman, 1994).

Perceptual-Motor Development

One of the most dramatic developments of the first year of life is the enormous increase in infants' ability to explore their environment by looking at it, moving around in it, listening to it, and manipulating it. Perceiving and acting are intimately connected. It would be nearly impossible for babies to move from one place to another, for example, if their coordinated motor actions were not constantly modulated by perceptual information about the layout of the environment and their spatial orientation. Infants, no less than adults, perceive in order to obtain information about how to act and then act in order to get more information (Gibson, 1988).

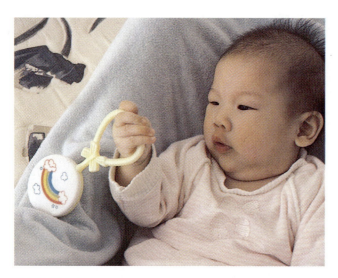

FIGURE 5.4 (Left) *In the first months after birth, eye-hand coordination takes effort.* (Right) *Only after a few months of attention and practice can infants perform such complex actions as eating with a spoon.*

REACHING AND GRASPING

In Chapter 4 (pp. 159–161) we saw evidence that shortly after birth perception and action are linked—when infants perceive an object moving in front of them, they reach for it. At first the perceptions and actions involved in reaching and grasping are not yet differentiated in a way that is functional. Infants may reach for an object but fail to close their hand around it. Then, as a part of the bio-social-behavioral shift at about 2½ months, babies begin to gain voluntary control over their movements when they reach for an object. At the same time, reaching and grasping begin to become coordinated in the proper sequence. At first, the coordination of reaching for and grasping that must be done to obtain the object requires concentration, and babies are likely to glance back and forth between the objects they wish to grasp and their hands. With practice, their perceptual-motor coordination gradually improves, although there are marked individual differences in the rapidity and vigor of their reaching movements (Thelen et al., 1993; Von Hofsten, 1992) (see Figure 5.4). At about 5 months they can gauge when an object is beyond their reach and they no longer attempt to reach for it (Yonas & Hartman, 1993). By the time they are 9 months old, most babies can guide their movements with a single glance, and the movements they use to reach for and grasp objects look as well integrated and automatic as a reflex (Mathew & Cook, 1990). About this same time caretakers need to "babyproof" their home by putting dangerous or fragile objects out of the infant's reach. They also have to watch out for the sudden appearance of unexpected items in the shopping cart if the baby is along for the ride.

In the period between 3 and 12 months of age, the hand and arm movements infants use to grasp and explore objects manually become more subtle and better coordinated. As Figure 5.5 indicates, 7-month-olds are still unable to use their thumbs in opposition to their fingers to pick up objects, but by 12 months they are able to move their thumbs and other fingers into positions appropriate to the size of the object they are trying to grasp. As their reaching and grasping become better coordinated and more precise, they can perform more complicated action sequences, such as drinking from a cup, eating with a spoon, and picking raisins out of a box (Connolly & Dalgleish, 1989).

Rachel Karniol (1989) found that there is an invariable sequence in the way babies manipulate objects as their fine motor skills increase during the first 9 months of life. They begin by simply rotating an object, then progress to moving it, shaking it, and holding it with one and then two hands, until they can use it as part of a sequence of actions to achieve a goal such as placing a block into a hole in a box.

Eleanor Gibson (1988) points out that as babies gain control over their hands, different objects invite them to explore in different ways: "Things can be displaced, banged, shaken, squeezed, and thrown—actions that have informative consequences about an object's properties" (p. 20). Babies appear to perceive that different objects invite different kinds of explorations and actions: they are more likely to imitate their mother when she shakes a rattle or rubs a cloth doll against her cheek than when she shakes the doll and rubs the rattle against her cheek (Von Hofsten & Siddiqui, 1993).

These studies of the development of reaching and grasping leave little doubt that the importance of babies' increasing skills goes beyond the capacity to grab hold of things. Perceptual-motor exploration is an all-important way to find out about the environment and to gain control over it.

LOCOMOTION

Progress in **locomotion**, the ability to move around on one's own, is central to the pattern of developmental changes that occur toward the end of the first year of postnatal life. As Selma Fraiberg (1959) puts it, "The first time the baby stands unsupported and the first wobbly, independent steps are milestones in personality development as well as in motor development" (p. 60). Babies' newfound motor abilities separate them from their mothers in a distinctive way that changes the basic conditions for further development.

Babies can reach out for and explore objects much earlier than they can move around on their own, however. Before any form of locomotion is achieved, they must be able to integrate the movements of many parts of their bodies.

Crawling, babies' first effective way of getting around, takes a few months to develop and progresses through several phases (see Figure 5.6). During the first month of life, when movements appear to be controlled primarily by subcortical reflexes, infants may inadvertently creep across a blanket, propelled by the rhythmic pushing movements of their toes or knees. At about 2 months of age this reflexive pushing disappears, but it will be another 5 or 6 months before babies can really crawl about on their own.

Although they can hold up their heads from about 2 months of age, young infants still have difficulty moving their arms in a coordinated way. Karniol (1989) places this milestone at about the end of the third month. Once they have managed to coordinate their arm movements, babies can pull themselves along, but their legs drag behind uselessly. Slightly later they can get on their hands and knees, but all they can do is rock back and forth because their arms and legs are not yet working together properly. Even as they enter the final phase of crawling at 8 to 9 months of age, their movements may lack precise coordination until, with practice, the various components are knitted into the well-coordinated action of the whole body.

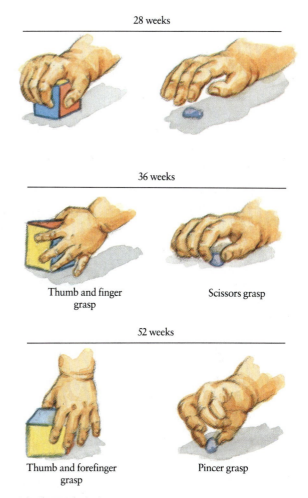

28 weeks

36 weeks

Thumb and finger grasp

Scissors grasp

52 weeks

Thumb and forefinger grasp

Pincer grasp

FIGURE 5.5 *Babies find ways to grasp objects from an early age, but good coordination of the thumb and forefinger requires at least a year to achieve. (Adapted from Halverson, 1931.)*

Locomotion The ability to move around on one's own.

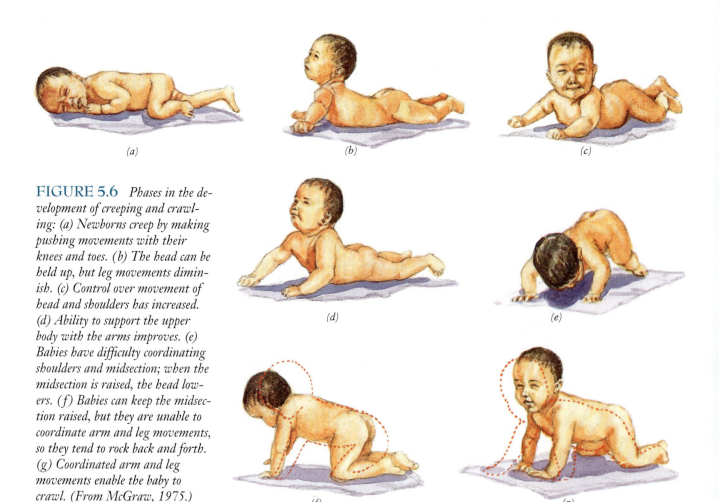

FIGURE 5.6 *Phases in the development of creeping and crawling: (a) Newborns creep by making pushing movements with their knees and toes. (b) The head can be held up, but leg movements diminish. (c) Control over movement of head and shoulders has increased. (d) Ability to support the upper body with the arms improves. (e) Babies have difficulty coordinating shoulders and midsection; when the midsection is raised, the head lowers. (f) Babies can keep the midsection raised, but they are unable to coordinate arm and leg movements, so they tend to rock back and forth. (g) Coordinated arm and leg movements enable the baby to crawl. (From McGraw, 1975.)*

Babies usually do not master walking until several months after they begin to crawl. The transition from crawling to walking requires a reorganization of component skills that is even more complex than the transformation from creeping to crawling (see Figure 5.7).

Table 5.1 shows some of the results of a large-scale study of the ages at which U.S. children achieve various milestones in motor development (Frankenburg & Dodds, 1967). Note the wide variations in the ages at which normal children are able to perform the various behaviors. Although 50 percent of the babies studied could walk by the time they were just over 1 year old, for example, some 10 percent were still not walking 2 months later.

THE ROLE OF PRACTICE IN MOTOR DEVELOPMENT

Studies of motor development were among psychologists' earliest strategies for discovering the relative roles of nature and nurture in development. During the 1930s and 1940s, when Arnold Gesell's infant scales were in wide use, it was commonly believed that learning and experience played little or no role in the development of such motor milestones as sitting and walking. One of the studies widely cited to bolster this view was conducted by Wayne and Margaret Dennis (1940) among Hopi families in the southwestern United States. In traditional Hopi families, babies were wrapped up tightly and strapped to a flat cradle board for the first several months of life. They were unwrapped only once or twice a day so that they could be washed and their clothes changed. The wrapping permitted very little movement of the arms and legs and no practice in such complex movements as rolling over. The Dennises compared the motor development of traditionally raised Hopi babies with that of the babies of less traditional parents who did not use cradle boards. The two groups of babies did not differ in the age at which they began to walk by themselves, which is consistent with the notion that this basic motor skill does not depend on practice for its development.

Observations of babies from other cultural settings, however, provide some evidence that practice can have an effect on the age at which babies reach universal motor milestones. Charles Super (1976) reports that among the Kipsigis people of rural Kenya, parents begin to teach their babies to sit up, stand, and walk shortly after birth. In teaching their children to sit up, for example, Kipsigis parents seat their babies in shallow holes in the ground that they have dug to support the infants' backs, or they nestle blankets around them to hold them upright. They repeat such procedures daily until the babies can sit up quite well by themselves. Training in walking begins in the eighth week. The babies are held under the arms with their feet touching the ground and are gradually propelled forward. Kipsigis babies reach the developmental milestones of sitting 5 weeks earlier and walking 3 weeks earlier, on the average, than babies in the United States. At the same time they are not advanced in skills they have not been taught or have not practiced. They learn to roll over or crawl no faster than American children, and they lag behind American children in their ability to negotiate stairs. Similar results have been reported among West Indian children, whose mothers put them through a culturally prescribed sequence of motor exercises during the early months of infancy (Hopkins & Westen, 1988).

The Ache, a nomadic people living in the rain forest of eastern Paraguay, discourage early motor achievement. Hilliard Kaplan and Heather Dove (1987) report that Ache children under 3 years of age spend 80 to 100 percent of their time in direct physical contact with their mothers and are almost never seen more than 3 feet away from them. A major reason is that Ache hunter-gatherer groups do not create clearings in the forest when they stop to make camp. Rather, they remove just enough ground cover to make room to sit down, leaving roots, trees, and bushes more or less where they found them. For safety's sake, mothers either carry their infants or keep them within arm's reach.

(a)

(b)

FIGURE 5.7 *(a) Babies who are just beginning to stand up find other people and furniture to be handy aids. Here a Balinese child is holding on to the anthropologist Margaret Mead. (b) The Filipino baby who lives in a house on stilts is being trained at an early age in the essential skill of climbing a ladder.*

TABLE 5.1
Ages at Which Infants Reach Selected Milestones in Motor Development

Motor milestone	Age (months)			
	25%	50%	75%	90%
Lifts head up	1.3	2.2	2.6	3.2
Rolls over	2.3	2.8	3.8	4.7
Sits without support	4.8	5.5	6.5	7.8
Pulls self to stand	6.0	7.6	9.5	10.0
Walks holding on to furniture	7.3	9.2	10.2	12.7
Walks well	11.3	12.1	13.3	14.3
Walks up steps	14.0	17.0	21.0	22.0
Kicks ball forward	15.0	20.0	22.3	24.0

Source: Frankenburg & Dodds, 1967.

FIGURE 5.8 *At the tender age of 7 months, 29 days, young Parks Bonifay is water-skiing. Waterskiing is a skill that requires practice to learn.*

Ache infants perform at North American norms on various tests of social ability, but they are markedly slower to acquire gross motor skills such as walking. They begin walking, on the average, at about 23 months of age, almost a full year later than children in the United States. At about the age of 5, however, when Ache children are deemed old enough to be allowed to move around on their own, they begin to spend many hours in complex play activities that serve to increase their motor skills. Within a few years they are skilled at scaling tall trees and at cutting vines and branches while they balance high above the ground in a manner that bespeaks normal, perhaps even exceptional, perceptual-motor skills.

Although special early practice does not appear to have any long-term advantages in the development of basic motor skills, there is some evidence that early practice in culture-specific skills, such as throwing a boomerang, playing tennis, roller-skating, and typing, does make a lasting difference. In one of the classic early studies of the role of experience in motor development, Myrtle McGraw (1935/1975) trained one of a pair of fraternal twins extensively in various activities that required specialized skills, such as riding a tricycle, swimming, and roller-skating. When he had attained proficiency, his twin brother was given training in the same activities. McGraw reported that the second twin caught up rather quickly with the first twin in general skill level. When the twins were adolescents and young adults, however, the first twin was more skilled in these activities and more enthusiastic about them.

As anyone knows who has tried some unfamiliar sport, specialized motor skills are not acquired without extensive practice and in some cases years of instruction as well. In recognition of this fact, specialized training in highly valued skills, such as playing a musical instrument or dancing, is begun quite early in many cultures, producing high levels of proficiency (see Figure 5.8).

Cognitive Changes

Just as most psychologists once believed that newborns experience the world as a confusing jumble of sensations, it was also believed that children slowly build an understanding of the basic properties of objects, people, and events over the course of infancy and early childhood. Certainly there is pervasive evidence that between 3 and 12 months of age infants are acquiring a greater ability to think systematically about their surroundings and to remember their experiences.

However, developmental psychologists are divided in their beliefs about the nature of infants' **cognitive processes**—the psychological processes through which they acquire, store, and use knowledge—during the first year of life. On the one hand, when infants are prompted to display their understanding by actually doing something such as searching for a missing object, they seem to be gradually constructing knowledge, much as Piaget claimed. On the other hand, when babies' psychological processes are assessed through techniques that require only minimal overt action on their part, such as a change in the interest they show (*habituation/dishabituation*), it appears that they have a rudimentary understanding of many basic properties of objects very early, possibly at birth. The importance of this difference in viewpoints goes well beyond a dispute about observable behavior; it speaks to the basic question of how babies' own actions relate to their development.

PIAGET'S CONSTRUCTIVIST EXPLANATION

As we saw in Chapter 4, Piaget held that new levels of cognition emerge from children's own efforts to master their environments; we come to know the world by acting on it. In his terms (p. 168), infants actively seek to *assimilate* their experiences to fit their existing action schemas (the forms in which their knowledge is structured). To the extent that their existing schemas are inadequate, they must *accommodate* those schemas or, in other words, modify them to suit the environmental realities they encounter. Development emerges from the interplay between assimilation and accommodation; sometimes we are able to deal with the world on our own terms—the world adjusts to us—and assimilation dominates. At other times, we must adjust to the world, and accommodation dominates. During those periods when accommodation and assimilation are in equilibrium, the nature of the cognitive process does not change. These periods of stability are what psychologists call "stages" or "substages."

Recall that within Piaget's constructivist framework, infancy is the stage when the child engages in *sensorimotor* actions, which combine perceiving and doing. During substages 1 and 2 (Chapter 4, pp. 168–170) of the *sensorimotor stage*, infants progress from simple reflex activity to the ability to prolong actions they find pleasurable *(primary circular reactions)*. Even at the end of the second substage, however, infants appear to have little or no understanding that their actions are separate from the environment. Piaget believed that it is between the ages of 4 or 5 months and 12 months that infants start to form an idea of an external reality. This occurs as they complete two more substages of sensorimotor development (see Table 5.2). This chapter describes these two substages in detail; the last two substages of the sensorimotor stage will be taken up in Chapter 6.

Substage 3: Secondary circular reactions (4 to 8 months)

In substage 3, infants are no longer restricted to the maintenance and modification of reflex or body-centered actions. Now they direct their attention to the *external* world—to objects and outcomes. Accordingly, the characteristic activity observed in infants during substage 3 is the repetition of actions that produce interesting changes in the *environment*. Piaget termed these new actions **secondary circular reactions** because their focus is on objects external to themselves. When babies kick a bar suspended above their crib and a bell rings, for instance, they will kick the bar repeatedly to make the bell ring again and again. Similarly, when babies make a noise and their mother answers, they will repeat the noise.

The change from primary circular reactions to secondary circular reactions indicated to Piaget that infants are beginning to realize that objects are more than extensions of their own actions. In this substage, however, babies still have only rudimentary notions of objects and space, and their discoveries about the world seem to have an accidental quality.

Substage 4: Coordination of secondary circular reactions (8 to 12 months)

The hallmark of the fourth sensorimotor substage is the emergence of goal-directed behaviors. In place of the accidental quality of object-oriented actions characteristic of earlier substages, infants begin to coordinate several secondary

Cognitive processes The psychological processes through which we acquire, store, and use knowledge.

Secondary circular reactions The behavior characteristic of the third substage of Piaget's sensorimotor stage in which babies repeat an action to produce an interesting change in their environment.

TABLE 5.2 Sensorimotor Substages and the Development of Object Permanence

Substage	Age Range (months)	Characteristics of Sensorimotor Substage	Developments in Object Permanence
1	0–1½	*Reflex schemas exercised:* involuntary rooting, sucking, grasping, looking.	Infant does not search for objects that have been removed from sight.
2	1½–4	*Primary circular reactions:* repetition of actions that are pleasurable in themselves.	Infant orients to place where objects have been removed from sight.
3	4–8	*Secondary circular reactions:* dawning awareness of relation of own actions to environment; extended actions that produce interesting changes in the environment.	Infant will reach for a partially hidden object but stops if it disappears.
4	8–12	*Coordination of secondary circular reactions:* combining schemas to achieve a desired effect; earliest form of problem solving.	Infant will search for a completely hidden object; keeps searching the original location of the object even if it is moved to another location in full view of the infant.
5	12–18	*Tertiary circular reactions:* deliberate variation of problem-solving means; experimentation to see what the consequences will be.	Infant will search for an object after seeing it moved but not if it is moved in secret.
6	18–24	*Beginnings of symbolic representation:* images and words come to stand for familiar objects; invention of new means of problem solving through symbolic combinations.	Infant will search for a hidden object, certain that it exists somewhere.

circular reactions in order to achieve a goal. Piaget believed that such coordination is the earliest form of true problem solving because it requires that two or more schemas be combined to achieve a desired effect.

When his son Laurent was 10 months old, Piaget gave him a small tin container, which Laurent dropped and picked up repeatedly (a secondary circular reaction characteristic of behavior in substage 3). Piaget then placed a washbasin a short distance from Laurent and struck it with the tin, producing an interesting sound. From earlier observations, Piaget knew that Laurent would repeatedly bang on the basin to make the interesting sound occur (another typical secondary circular reaction). This time Piaget wanted to see if Laurent would combine the newly acquired "dropping the tin box" schema with the previously acquired "make an interesting sound" schema. Here is his report of Laurent's behavior:

Now, at once, Laurent takes possession of the tin, holds out his arm and drops it over the basin. I moved the latter as a check. He nevertheless succeeded, several times in succession, in making the object fall on the basin. Hence this is a fine example of the coordination of two schemas of which the first serves as a "means" whereas the second assigns an end to the action. (Piaget, 1952b, p. 255)

According to Piaget, one of the clearest ways to show that children who enter substage 4 become capable of combining schemas to achieve a goal is to arrange for them to play with an attractive object and then hide the object behind a barrier. To achieve the goal of playing with the object again, the infant must combine the schemas of moving the barrier and grasping the object, an example of substage 4 behavior.

> **Object permanence** The understanding that objects have substance, are external to oneself, and continue to exist when out of sight.

PIAGET'S TEST FOR OBJECT PERMANENCE: OUT OF SIGHT, OUT OF MIND?

Piaget believed that when infants begin to combine elementary schemas into means-end sequences and to search for hidden objects, they are displaying an emerging understanding that objects have an existence independent of themselves. Psychologists usually test this idea by creating conditions in which the infant responds to objects that have been removed from their sight, touch, and hearing.

As adults, we believe that objects have substance, are external to ourselves, maintain their identity when they change location, and continue to exist when they are out of sight. Piaget called this understanding **object permanence,** and he found it lacking in infants until substage 4 of sensorimotor development, late in the first year of life. Young infants, he claimed, experience a world of discontinuous pictures that are constantly being "annihilated and resurrected." It is a world in which an object is "a mere image which reenters the void as soon as it vanishes, and emerges from it for no apparent reason" (1954, p. 11). That is, until babies understand that an object exists when they are not perceiving it, out of sight is literally out of mind, according to Piagetian theory.

Evidence consistent with Piaget's view that infants lack object permanence comes from observations of 5- and 6-month-old babies, such as the following:

OBSERVATION 1

A baby seated at a table is offered a soft toy. He grasps it. While he is still engrossed in the toy, the experimenter takes it from him and places it on the table behind a screen. The baby may begin to reach for the toy, but as soon as it disappears from sight he stops short, stares for a moment, and then looks away without attempting to move the screen (see Figure 5.9) (Piaget, 1954).

OBSERVATION 2

A baby is placed in an infant seat in a bare laboratory room. Her mother, who has been playing with her, disappears for a moment. When the mother reappears, the baby

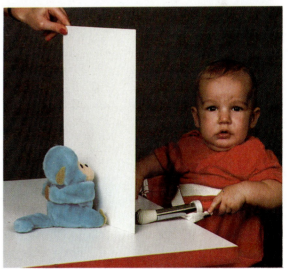

FIGURE 5.9 *Instead of searching behind the screen when his toy disappears, this infant looks dumbfounded. This kind of behavior led Piaget to conclude that objects no longer in view cease to exist for infants less than 8 months of age.*

Infant watches train approach tunnel.

Infant watches train enter tunnel.

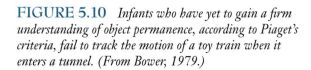

Infant's eyes remain fixed on tunnel's entrance.

FIGURE 5.10 *Infants who have yet to gain a firm understanding of object permanence, according to Piaget's criteria, fail to track the motion of a toy train when it enters a tunnel. (From Bower, 1979.)*

Infant notices train moving away from tunnel.

sees three of her, an illusion the experimenter has created through the use of carefully arranged mirrors. The baby displays no surprise as she babbles happily to her multiple mother (Bower, 1982).

OBSERVATION 3

From the comfort of his mother's lap, a baby follows a toy train with his eyes as it chugs along a track (see Figure 5.10). The baby watches as the train enters a tunnel. At that point, instead of continuing to follow the train's expected progress through the tunnel, his eyes remain fixed on the tunnel's entrance. When the train reappears at the other end of the tunnel, it takes him a few seconds to catch up with it. He shows no surprise when the train that comes out of the tunnel is a different color or shape (Bower, 1982).

Piaget maintained that infants respond in this manner because they cannot think of the object when it is absent. Only when they actively search for the absent object can we infer that babies understand that objects continue to exist when they are out of sight.

STAGES OF OBJECT PERMANENCE

Piaget proposed 6 stages in the development of object permanence, which correspond to the six substages of sensorimotor development (see Table 5.2). We will

No elaborate apparatus is necessary to discover babies' growing fascination with the appearance and disappearance of objects in the second half year of life. A simple game of peekaboo is enough to delight children at this age.

discuss the first four of these stages of object permanence in this chapter and the remaining two in Chapter 6.

Stages 1 and 2 (birth to 4 months)

Piaget observed that during the first 4 months of life babies begin to look toward the sources of sounds they hear. He also reported that during this period his own children continued to stare at the place where he was last visible to them (Piaget, 1952b). However, since they did not actively search for an object when it disappeared, but instead seemed quickly to turn their attention elsewhere, he denied that these behaviors were evidence that they had a conception of objects.

Stage 3 (4 to 8 months)

Babies 4 or 5 months of age can sit up with some support and can reach out to grasp objects with reasonable accuracy, but their ability to explore is still relatively restricted. Furthermore, their attention to events around them is often fleeting. This is the age of the children in our three observations. Objects that disappear completely seem quickly to be forgotten, and the appearance of the same object in several places causes no visible surprise. When objects are only partly hidden, however, the child will reach for them (Piaget, 1954).

Stage 4 (8 to 12 months)

At about 8 months of age, babies begin to show the first evidence, according to Piaget's criteria, that they know objects exist when they are out of sight: they begin to search for them. In searching for missing objects, however, babies in this stage tend to make a characteristic mistake that researchers have called the **A-not-B error**—babies reach for an object in the last place they found it even when they

A-not-B error A characteristic error 8- to 12-month-old babies make when searching for a hidden object. They look for the object in the last place they found it even if they have seen it moved to a new location.

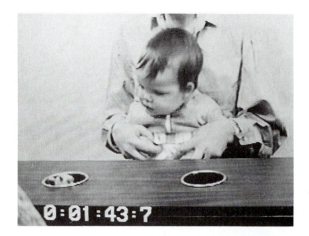

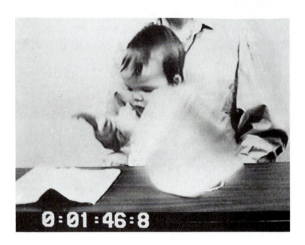
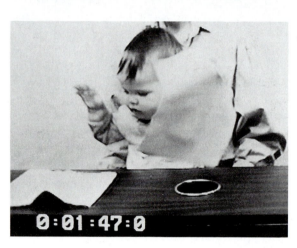

FIGURE 5.11 *In this movie sequence, an object is placed in the circle on the left (position B) and then both circles (positions A and B) are covered with a cloth while the baby watches. In a previous trial, the object had been placed in the right-hand circle (position A), and the baby had correctly retrieved it. This time, while remaining oriented toward the hidden object at position B, the baby nonetheless picks up the cloth at position A, where the object was hidden before. (Courtesy of A. Diamond.)*

have seen it moved to a new location. Suppose an object is hidden under cover A and the baby is allowed to retrieve it. Then, in full view of the baby, the object is placed under cover B. When allowed to retrieve the object this time, the baby will regularly look under cover A, where the object was found before, rather than under cover B, where the baby has seen it placed (Piaget, 1954) (see Figure 5.11). Infants tend to make this error until they are more than a year old.

EXPLAINING THE ACQUISITION OF OBJECT PERMANENCE

The sequence of changes in children's developing understanding of object permanence described by Piaget occurs so reliably that tests of object permanence have been standardized for use in assessing the development of children who are at risk because of disease, physical impairment, or extreme environmental deprivation (Decarie, 1969; Uzgiris & Hunt, 1975). Even so, more recent experiments indicate that babies appreciate the continued existence of objects that are out of sight much earlier than Piaget supposed. These controlled experiments have used techniques that require only minimal overt action on the babies' part, whereas Piaget depended on babies' active search behaviors to determine if babies appreciated object permanence.

Renée Baillargeon and her colleagues conducted several experiments that minimized the need for infants to engage in overt actions such as reaching and grasping to indicate their knowledge about an object's location. Their findings suggest that under some conditions 3½-month-old infants realize that objects continue to exist when they are hidden and can engage in elementary reasoning about them (Baillargeon, 1987, 1993; Baillargeon, Spelke, & Wasserman, 1985).

In one such study the researchers arranged for babies to watch a screen as it rotated slowly forward and backward through a 180-degree arc on a hinge attached to the floor of the viewing surface. In its upright position the screen was like a fence behind which an object might be hidden from view. The screen could rotate toward the babies until it was lying flat and away from them until it was again lying flat. (See Figure 5.12a.)

When the babies were first shown the rotating screen, they stared at it for almost a full minute, but after several trials they seemed to lose interest in it and looked at the display for only about 10 seconds. At this point, with the babies now *habituated* to the event, the experimenters placed a box behind the screen so that the screen obscured the box when it moved into its perpendicular position. Next, they did one of two things. For one group of babies, they rotated the screen until it reached the point where it should bump up against the box (see Figure 5.12b), then returned it to its flat starting position. For the second group, they secretly lowered the box through the floor of the apparatus as soon as the screen had hidden it from view. Then they rotated the screen through its full 180-degree arc as if it were moving right through the "hidden" box (see Figure 5.12c).

The researchers reasoned that if the babies thought the box still existed even when it was hidden by the screen, they would stare at the screen longer (*dishabituate*) when the screen moved through space where the box was supposed to be than they would when the screen seemed to bump into the box before returning to its starting point. The babies showed no special interest when the screen seemed to bump into the box (even if they had never observed this before), but they showed great interest when it appeared to pass right through the place where they thought the box was located. Their increased interest when the screen continued to rotate in its original manner is difficult to explain unless it is assumed that the babies continued to believe in the existence of the hidden object.

The babies' different responses to the rotating screen appear to indicate a realization that hidden objects do not cease to exist simply because they cannot be seen. But if babies know this, why do they behave as they do on tests of object permanence of the sort Piaget conducted? Psychologists' attempts to resolve this issue have focused on finding reasons for the A-not-B error.

Adele Diamond (1991) suggested that one reason they err is that they quickly forget. At 7½ to 8 months of age, the 2-second delay after moving the object from place A to place B is time enough to make the baby look in the wrong place. But by 9 months, they respond correctly after a 5-second delay, and by 12 months the delay must be 10 seconds or more before the baby will make the A-not-B error (Diamond, 1985). A second factor Diamond cites to explain the babies' errors is that they have trouble stopping themselves from reaching toward a place where they were just rewarded for reaching. Sometimes infants can be observed looking at position B (where they have just seen an object hidden) but reaching toward position A (where they successfully found the object before). If you refer to Figure 5.11, you will see that the baby displays the sort of behavior that Diamond describes. A third factor is that babies this age have difficulty executing deliberate goal-directed action sequences such as removing a barrier in order to get to the candy beneath it (Diamond, 1995).

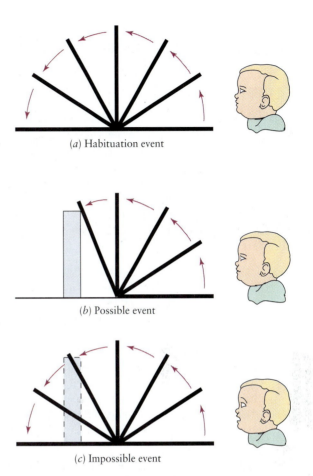

(a) Habituation event

(b) Possible event

(c) Impossible event

FIGURE 5.12 *The habituation and test events arranged for babies by Renée Baillargeon and her colleagues. In the habituation event (a), the screen is unimpeded and rotates 180 degrees. In the possible event (b), a box stands in the way of the screen and stops it from rotating the full distance. In the impossible event (c), a box stands in the way of the rotating screen but the screen appears to pass right through it. (From Baillargeon, 1987.)*

BOX 5.1

Action and Understanding

Piaget's hypothesis that children's own activities are the driving force of their development has led many psychologists to study the developmental consequences of restricted or enhanced movement early in life. A basic intuition guiding such research is the idea that locomotion not only allows babies to learn how to move their bodies in space but also provides them with a new understanding of the objects that fill space. Selma Fraiberg has written:

> Travel changes one's perspective. A chair, for example, is an object of one dimension when viewed by a six-month-old baby propped up on the sofa, or by an eight-month-old baby doing push-ups on a rug. It's even very likely that the child of this age confronted at various times with different perspectives of the same chair would see not one chair, but several chairs, corresponding to each perspective. It's when you start to get around under your own steam that you discover what a chair really is. (Fraiberg, 1959, p. 52)

A classic study demonstrating a close link between locomotor experience and the understanding of spatial relations was carried out by Richard Held and Alan Hein (1963) with kittens who were raised from birth in total darkness. When the kittens were old enough to walk, they were placed two at a time in an apparatus

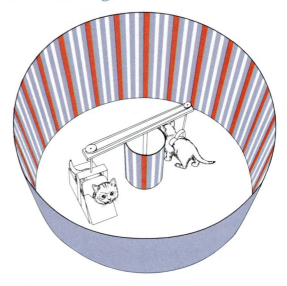

The kitten carousel used in Held and Hein's classic experiment demonstrating the importance of active experience to development. (From Held, 1965.)

called a "kitten carousel." One kitten, harnessed to pull the carousel, could use what it saw to control its movements, and its movements determined, to some extent, what it saw. The other kitten was carried in the gon-

However, none of these factors taken alone can account entirely for the babies' errors. When special procedures are adopted to simplify the task requirements, infants remember events over several minutes and sometimes many hours (Baillargeon & Graber, 1988; Meltzoff & Moore, 1994). Nor can the difficulty of inhibiting previous actions or of reaching around barriers alone explain errors, because 9-month-old infants have been observed to do both in some circumstances (Diamond, 1995; Wellman, Cross, & Bartsch, 1987).

Taken together, the data on the development of object permanence and motor skills between 3 and 12 months suggest the following general picture:

By 4 months of age, infants realize that objects do not cease to exist simply because they are out of sight, but they are unable to act on this realization except to register their surprise when their expectations are not met. At this stage, the act of reaching for and grasping an object takes considerable effort. Infants must concentrate on controlling their movements, and they are likely to encounter trouble when they try to reach around and under obstacles. Any such difficulty diverts the infants' attention from the object they are searching for and hastens their forgetting about it. By about 9 months, however, reaching and grasping have become well-integrated responses that no longer require special attention and therefore

dola of the carousel and had no active interactions with the world it saw. The experiences of the passive kitten were controlled largely by the actions of the kitten pulling the carousel. Each pair of kittens was given 3 hours of visual experience in the carousel every day for 42 days. Between these sessions, they were returned to the dark. Thus the only visual experience the kittens had, and hence the only opportunity they had to learn to coordinate vision and movement, was the time they spent in the carousel.

The influence of active versus passive movement on the kittens' responses to their environment became strikingly apparent when Held and Hein lowered them onto the surface of a visual cliff similar to the one shown in Figure 1.7 of Chapter 1 (p. 24). This apparatus had stripes painted on it like the stripes around the sides of the kitten carousel, except that they were painted to look as if one side of the apparatus were far below the other. The kittens that had been active in the carousel shied away from the deep side of the visual cliff and appropriately stretched out their legs to land on it. The passive kittens did not try to avoid the deep side of the cliff, nor did they make appropriate adjustments in the positions of their legs in anticipation of landing on it.

This finding fits well with the results of the experiment by Joseph Campos and his co-workers described in Chapter 1 (p. 25) that confirmed the importance of movement in human cognitive development (Bertenthal, Campos, & Barrett, 1984). In that study, 5-month-old babies who had not yet begun to crawl did not seem to be afraid of a visual cliff when they first saw it. They began to be afraid of heights only after they had begun to move around on their own or after they had gained experience in locomoting in baby walkers.

Campos and his co-workers have also shown that locomotion enhances the development of infants' memory for the locations of hidden objects. Babies who had extensive experience in moving around in baby walkers before they could move about on their own were more adept at locating hidden objects in standard object permanence tests than were children of the same age who had no such experience (Campos, Benson, & Rudy, 1986).

Finally, unusual support for the close connection between locomotion and development is provided by a study of the development of infants who suffered from a neural-tube defect that impeded locomotion (Telzrow et al., 1987). Such children were found to be delayed 5 to 6 months in their development of correct search behaviors. They began to search for hidden objects correctly only after they had begun to move voluntarily. The results of these experiments suggest that active engagement with the world does make a fundamental contribution to development.

no longer distract infants from their search. In addition, their memory has improved and they are better able to keep themselves from repeating actions that were successful the last time they did them. All these factors combine to help them keep the current location of a hidden object in mind long enough to act on it.

This overall picture of the development of object permanence contradicts Piaget's belief that infants under 8 months of age cannot keep in mind the continued existence of objects that they do not see. Instead it appears that infants have rudimentary but fleeting knowledge of objects' continued existence. That knowledge cannot yet serve to organize and sustain overt action, but it is detectable under specially simplified conditions. Still, Piaget's emphasis on action as essential to cognitive development has also received experimental support, as Box 5.1 reveals.

ADDITIONAL EVIDENCE FOR PERCEPTUAL ORIGINS OF EARLY KNOWLEDGE

Understanding that objects continue to exist even when they are out of sight is by no means all that babies know about them. A wide range of studies that focus on the ways infants perceive objects and events are pushing psychologists to consider the possibility that a baby comes into the world with considerably more initial knowledge than they previously believed. The same studies have also indicated that even newborns can acquire some kinds of knowledge of the world through observation in the absence of direct action.

Cross-modal perception

Developmental psychologists long assumed that newborn babies respond to the sight, sound, and other sense impressions of objects as if they were completely disconnected from one another. According to this view, infants must acquire a certain amount of experience with objects before they become able to associate the object's various sensory aspects. They would need to learn, for example, that the voice coming from the other room and the face they see a few moments later are two aspects of the same person, or that the gold color of the stuff on the spoon goes with its awful taste.

The understanding that certain features of an object perceived in one sensory mode go together with features perceived in a different sensory mode is known as **cross-modal perception.** Several ingenious studies have shown that cross-modal perception either does *not* have to be learned or is learned rapidly and quite early in infancy.

Elizabeth Spelke (1976, 1984) presented pairs of film strips to 4-month-old babies to see if they knew what sort of sound should accompany the event depicted in each film. To assess knowledge of sight-sound correspondences, she showed two films simultaneously, side by side. One depicted percussion instruments being played, and the other showed a game of peekaboo. A loudspeaker located between the two screens would sometimes play sounds appropriate to the percussion instruments, while at other times it played sounds appropriate to the game of peekaboo. The infants looked most often at whatever film corresponded to the loudspeaker's sounds, indicating they associated sounds with the appropriate sights.

In a later study, Arlette Streri and Elizabeth Spelke (1988) sought to determine if sight and touch are also closely linked in 4-month-old infants' perceptions of objects. In this case the researchers arranged for the infants to hold two rings, one in each hand, under a cloth that prevented them from seeing the rings or their own bodies (see Figure 5.13). In one case the rings were connected by a rigid bar and therefore moved together. In the other case the rings were connected by a flexible cord so that they moved independently. The infants were allowed to hold and *feel* one pair of connected rings, either rigidly or flexibly connected, until they had largely lost interest *(habituated)*; they were then *shown* both types of rings, one pair rigidly connected and the other with a flexible connection. The babies looked longer at the rings that were different from those they had been exploring with their hands. That is, babies who had been handling the independently moving rings looked longer at the rigid ones, while babies who had been holding the rigidly connected rings looked longer at the flexibly connected ones. These and other data (Meltzoff & Borton, 1979; Spelke, 1990; Spelke & Van de Walle, 1993) strongly suggest that infants perceive the sights, sounds, feel, and other basic properties of objects as being related aspects of the same object; they do not have to acquire this information through an extended process of associative learning.

Cross-modal perception The understanding that certain features of an object perceived in one sensory mode go together with features perceived in a different sensory mode.

FIGURE 5.13 *Objects (a) and apparatus (b) for experiments on the way infants use information gained in one sensory modality to recognize the same object in another. (a) Rings connected by rigid bar or flexible cord, one of which is presented until baby habituates. (b) This infant is feeling a rigid object that is hidden from sight and later will be able to recognize it by sight alone. (From Streri & Spelke, 1988.)*

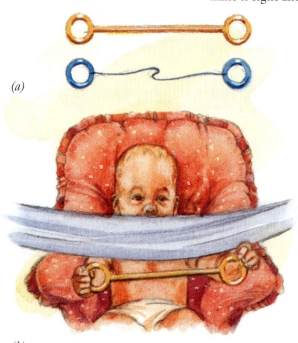

(a)

(b)

Perceiving number

Particularly striking evidence that even very young infants may directly perceive properties of objects and relations among them comes from studies showing that by the middle of the first year of life babies perceive the numerosity of a display and can, in some sense, even count small arrays of objects (Gallistel & Gelman, 1991; Simon et al., 1995; Wynn, 1992). Two examples illustrate the conditions under which this knowledge is tapped.

Infants 6 months old or younger have been habituated to visual displays containing two to six dots (the number differing for each group) and then shown a different dot pattern. The series of patterns was arranged to control for such potentially correlated cues as the length, density, and configuration of the array. The babies showed their sensitivity to number by staring longer in response when the number of dots changed so long as there were four dots or fewer (Antell & Keating, 1983).

Even more impressive sensitivity to number relations was found by Karen Wynn (1992), who showed 4-month-old babies the events depicted in Figure 5.14. First a mouse doll was placed on an empty stage while the baby watched. Then a screen was raised to hide the doll from the baby's view. Next, a hand holding an identical doll went behind the screen and then withdrew without the doll. The screen was then lowered. In half the cases there were two dolls behind the screen (the expected outcome). In the other half of the cases there was only one doll (the unexpected outcome). The babies looked longer at the unexpected outcome. Additional experiments showed that the babies expected 2 minus 1 to be 1 and 3 minus 2 to be 2.

There is still controversy about how preverbal infants process numbers. Some psychologists lean toward the explanation that a special primitive perceptual process allows direct perception of small quantities (Klein & Starkey, 1988). This

FIGURE 5.14 *After 4 month-olds observe the sequence of events at the top of the figure, they show surprise when the screen is removed and only one mouse remains. Apparently the babies not only remember the presence of the first mouse hidden behind the screen, but mentally add the second mouse and remember it.*

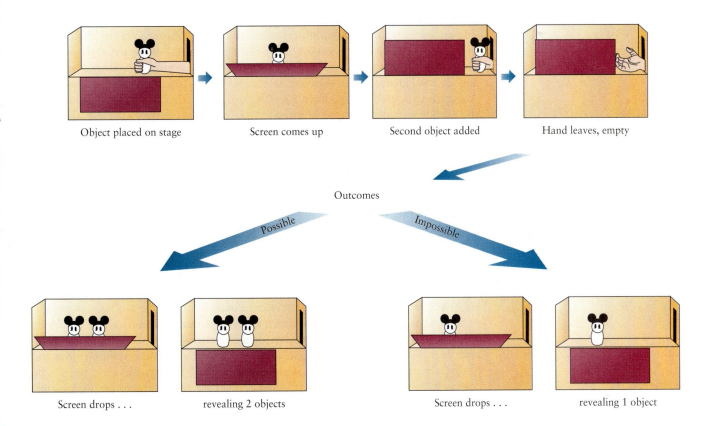

Object placed on stage   Screen comes up   Second object added   Hand leaves, empty

Outcomes

Possible   Impossible

Screen drops . . .   revealing 2 objects   Screen drops . . .   revealing 1 object

FIGURE 5.15 *A 3-month-old baby viewing a mobile whose A-shaped trinket moves when the baby kicks. After three 15-minute sessions, each with a different color A, the baby will kick a mobile with yet a fourth color. But if a new shape is used in the fourth session (for example, a B), the baby will not kick at first.*

Categorize To perceive objects or events that differ in various ways as equivalent.

Perceptual categories Categories that are based on perceptual similarities.

primitive process is then supplemented by a more elaborate counting procedure when children are older. Others believe that infants have what in fact amounts to a preverbal enumeration that serves as the foundation of a later arithmetic thinking system (Gallistel & Gelman, 1991). Whatever the ultimate explanation, some form of numerical knowledge appears to be present very early.

No techniques have been developed yet to determine if any of these perceptual abilities exist at birth, so the question of how early they develop is unresolved. Some investigators believe that infants are born with a great deal of innate knowledge about physical laws. Spelke (1994) argues that children are born knowing a number of physical principles—for example, that objects move as whole, bounded units; that they move on continuous paths; and that they can affect one another's motion only if they touch. Others have proposed that very young infants perceive causal relations between events and distinguish human motions from the motions of inanimate objects (Leslie, 1994; Premack, 1990). We will examine these and other claims when we discuss cognitive developments in later chapters. Insofar as they are correct, they cast doubt on Piaget's account of developmental change.

CATEGORIZING: KNOWLEDGE ABOUT KINDS OF THINGS

Categorizing is the process of responding to different objects in a similar way because of some perceived similarity between them. Categorization is fundamental to the acquisition of knowledge. It allows us to make inferences about novel objects in the absence of any direct experience. For example, if we classify a duck as a bird, we can infer that it will lay eggs, even if we have never seen it do so. We have already seen that newborn infants are able to perceive and respond to categories of speech sounds. What is more, they respond differently to sounds associated with human language than they do to other sounds. Over the course of the first year of life infants' ability to learn and use categories broadens enormously to encompass all of their developing knowledge.

Researchers have used a variety of techniques to study the development of categorizing abilities during early infancy. Carolyn Rovee-Collier and her colleagues used operant conditioning procedures to demonstrate that by the time infants are 3 months old they can readily form **perceptual categories;** that is, they categorize objects together on the basis of such perceptual similarities as shape and color (Hayne, Rovee-Collier, & Perris, 1987). Infants were initially shown A-shaped trinkets dangling from a mobile and taught that if they kicked their legs, the mobile would move (see Figure 5.15). In second and third sessions, the color of the A-shaped trinkets was changed (from blue to green to red, say). At the end of the three sessions, infants kicked at a consistently high rate to make the mobile with its A-shaped trinkets move. Lastly, the infants were shown test mobiles on which the trinkets either were of the same form but yet another color (a black A, say) or were different in both form and color (say, a black B). The infants responded at high rates to the test mobile with the same form and a novel color, but not to the mobile with the new form. Apparently they were categorizing the mobiles on the basis of the specific form of the trinkets, so when the form of the trinkets changed, they no longer responded to it.

Other studies of categorization make use of infants' proclivity to stare at the sights they find interesting for several seconds before turning away. This is the basis of the *habituation/dishabituation* method used in the studies of object permanence and other forms of object-related knowledge discussed earlier (p. 135). Peter Eimas and Paul Quinn (1994) used evidence of such differential looking to show that young infants rapidly form categories without any special training. Eimas and Quinn showed 3-month-olds a series of pictures of horses, two at a time. The horses in each pair were different, so the babies never saw the same horse twice. After the babies had seen pictures of six pairs of horses, the researchers showed them three new pictures of horses, but this time the horses were paired with cats,

Trial 1

Trial 2

Trial 3

Test trial

FIGURE 5.16 *Three-month-old babies shown a sequence of pictures of cats are surprised when they see a picture of a dog, indicating that they are sensitive to the category of cats.*

zebras, and giraffes. In all three cases, the infants looked longer at the pictures of the other animals than they did at the pictures of the horses. The same investigators found that when 3- and 4-month-olds were shown a series of pictures of cats (see Figure 5.16), they formed a category of cats that excluded lions and dogs (Quinn, Eimas, & Rosenkratz, 1993).

Given the limited ability of 3- and 4-month-old babies to grasp things with their hands and to move around, it is not surprising that the categories they form depend largely on the perceptual qualities of the things they are classifying—horses are classified together and separately from giraffes because of their appearance. When older children and adults use the category of horses, however, they

FIGURE 5.17 *Seven-month-old babies treat plastic toy birds or airplanes, which are perceptually similar, as if they are members of the same category. Babies 9 to 11 months old treat them as members of different categories, despite their perceptual similarity.*

Conceptual categories Categories that are based on conceptual similarities between different objects.

are not restricting the category to the animal's perceptual features. The category of horses becomes a **conceptual category** that includes the facts that horses are used for transportation, that they eat hay, and that they can be used to carry heavy loads. Consequently, when older children and adults treat horses and cats as members of different categories, they do so not only because horses and cats *look* different but because they have acquired a conceptual understanding of the many ways in which horses and cats *are* different.

Many psychologists believe that the beginning of conceptual categorizing begins in the period between 6 and 9 months of age (Bertenthal, Campos, & Barrett, 1984; Kagan & Hamburg, 1981; Mandler, 1995; Younger & Cohen, 1986). Jean Mandler and Laraine McDonough (1993), for example, showed that 9- and 11-month-olds treated toy birds and toy airplanes as members of different categories, even though the toy birds all had outstretched wings and looked like the airplanes (see Figure 5.17). Seven-month-old babies did not reliably make this category distinction, a finding consistent with the idea that visual similarity still ruled their construction of categories.

THE GROWTH OF MEMORY

Studies of the development of memory for past events have repeatedly found that young animals of many species, including human beings, forget rapidly (Spear, 1978). Using the same technique she used to study the formation of categories, Carolyn Rovee-Collier and her colleagues have demonstrated that increases in remembering are related to age during the first several months of life. These researchers trained infants to make a mobile move by kicking one of their legs, which was attached to the mobile by a ribbon (Greco et al., 1986; Hill, Borovsky, & Rovee-Collier, 1988). After the children had learned to kick vigorously as soon as their leg was attached to the mobile, they were removed from the crib and brought back at a later time. The researchers found that 2-month-olds remembered this experience for 1 day and started kicking immediately, but after 3 days the 2-month-olds seemed to have forgotten their training; they took just as long to start the mobile moving as they had taken when they were first trained to do so. Three-month-olds could remember for 8 days, but not for 13. Six-month-olds showed almost perfect recall for 14 days, but none at 21 days.

Later studies have shown that if infants are given a brief visual reminder, they can remember their earlier training much longer (Hayne & Rovee-Collier, 1995). In one such study, Rovee-Collier and her colleagues again trained a group of 3-month-old babies to activate a mobile by kicking. They then let a month elapse before putting the babies into the experimental situation again—more than enough time for the babies to forget their training. In this case, however, they showed them the mobile as a reminder (without allowing them to kick) 1 day before repeating the experience. When the babies were tested the next day, they started kicking as soon as they were placed in the crib and the ribbon was tied to their leg (Rovee-Collier et al., 1980). The mere sight of the mobile the day before seemed to remind the babies of what they had learned to do a month earlier.

RECALL AND WARINESS: EVIDENCE FOR A DEVELOPMENTAL DISCONTINUITY

The work of Rovee-Collier and her colleagues shows that babies begin to remember at a very early age and that their memory continues to improve steadily during the first year of life. On the basis of this evidence, these researchers have concluded that the improvement in memory over the course of the first year of life is a continuous process that does not involve any new principles of learning or remembering (Hayne & Rovee-Collier, 1995; Rovee-Collier, 1990).

Other investigators argue that sometime after 6 months of age babies begin to display a new form of remembering. Not only do they *recognize* what they have experienced before, they can call to mind *(recall)* absent objects and events even without any particular reminder (Kagan, Kearsley, & Zelazo, 1978; Mandler, 1990; Meltzoff, 1990). Recall memory is considered an especially important cognitive achievement because it seems to require the generation of a mental representation of something that is not present to the senses. According to Piaget's criteria, infants do not understand that objects continue to exist when they are out of sight before they are about a year old. Evidence of early recall memory would contradict his account of infant mental development.

The tendency of infants and young children to imitate the actions of others is the basis for one technique used to trace the early origin of recall memory. We discussed early forms of immediate imitation in Chapter 4 (pp. 162–163), and we will discuss the development of imitation more thoroughly in Chapter 6. For now it is sufficient to describe the procedures used to study memory through deferred, or delayed, imitation.

Andrew Meltzoff demonstrated three simple actions to 9-month-old infants seated on their parents' laps (Meltzoff, 1988b). First he took a small board attached in an upright position to a base by a hinge and pushed it until it lay flat on its base; then he pushed a black button that sounded a beeper; and then he rattled an orange plastic egg with nuts and bolts in it. After watching him do these things, the babies were taken home. The next day they were brought back to the laboratory and allowed to play with a few small toys. Then the board, the buzzer, and the plastic egg were brought out. Although the babies had never themselves done such things, most of them imitated one or more of the actions they had seen Meltzoff perform with these objects the day before (see Figure 5.18). They had recognized the items, and they had *recalled* Meltzoff's use of them. McDonough and Mandler (1989) obtained the same findings with 11-month-olds.

FIGURE 5.18 *Studies by Andrew Meltzoff have shown that young infants imitate live models and will also imitate actions they have seen on television (Meltzoff, 1988a). This child observes a televised adult model manipulate blocks and then immediately the child imitates the same actions. Meltzoff also demonstrated that infants who watch a televised model on one day will reproduce the model's behavior 24 hours later. (Courtesy of A. Meltzoff.)*

FIGURE 5.19 *The wide-eyed look this child is giving her disguised mother displays the wariness that infants develop sometime between the ages of 7 and 9 months.*

Sometime between the ages of 6 and 9 months, babies begin to be overtly wary and even afraid whenever something out of the ordinary happens (see Figure 5.19) (Rothbart, 1988). Some researchers believe that wariness would not be possible if infants had not first developed the ability to recall earlier events. To demonstrate this change in behavior, Rudolph Schaffer (1974) repeatedly presented babies between the ages of 4 and 9 months with a strange object until they became habituated to it. He then presented them with a new strange object, a plastic model of an ice cream sundae. Most 4-month-olds strained toward the sundae immediately, without any hesitation. Most 6-month-olds hesitated for a second or two, showing that they noticed the change, and then they reached for the sundae impulsively, often bringing it to their mouths. Nine-month-olds tended to hesitate longer, noting that it was unfamiliar. Some of them even turned away or started to cry.

Nathan Fox, Jerome Kagan, and Sally Weiskopf (1979) hypothesize that the 9-month-olds' wariness is caused by their newly acquired ability to compare current events with remembered past events in a systematic way that definitely fits the definition of recall. The babies not only note that the ice cream sundae is unfamiliar but search their memories to determine if it corresponds to any category of things they have seen before, and they become upset because it does not.

The issue of when recall memory first appears is by no means settled. Andrew Meltzoff and Keith Moore (1994) used their technique for eliciting imitation of facial expressions to argue that recall memory may appear as early as 6 weeks! They found that 6-week-old infants not only imitate a person who sticks out his tongue as soon as they see him do it, they repeat those movements when they see the same person 24 hours later, even though he does not make any funny faces this time. Meltzoff and Moore suggest that perhaps what is special about memory late in the first year of life is that it can operate on objects as well as people. Other investigators, such as Jean Mandler (1997), believe that early forms of imitation are largely reflexive and want to credit infants with recall only when they must deliberately bring prior information to mind. They believe that this achievement occurs late in the first year of life.

Considered as a whole, the data on object permanence, categorization, and the changing bases of remembering support the conclusion that the advances in cognitive development that occur in the latter part of the first year of life are closely interlinked, developing in tandem with the motor capacities and biological changes that we described earlier. The new cognitive capacities are also intimately linked with changes in the babies' social world, including their emotional relationships with their caregivers and their communicative abilities.

A New Relationship with the Social World

As infants acquire a better understanding of the properties of objects and their ability to remember improves, these changes are reflected in their relationships with other people. Jake's wariness of Sheila at 12 months, described at the start of this chapter, belongs to a new pattern of social behaviors that first appears around 7 months of age. When Jake was 2 months old, Sheila could care for him without Jake's showing any overt sign of distress. This does not mean, however, that he did not notice the difference. Keiko Mizukami and her colleagues (1990) have observed that the skin temperature of babies 2 to 4 months old drops—a physiological indicator that they are concerned—when their mother leaves and a stranger appears over their cribs. But at 1 year, Jake not only was surprised when he looked up and saw Sheila where he expected his mother to be; he was distressed, and he showed it by turning away and reaching for his mother.

Many developmental psychologists agree that in the second half of the first year babies' fear of an unfamiliar adult and their distress when their mothers disappear are closely connected to their increasing ability to move around, to categorize, and to remember (Bertenthal, Campos, & Barrett, 1984; Emde, Gaensbauer, & Harmon, 1976; Kagan, 1984).

THE ROLE OF UNCERTAINTY IN WARINESS

When we try to discover why the beginning of locomotion, an increased understanding of the nature of objects, and improved memory should be associated with overt wariness and fear, we have to remember the predicament babies are in. They are constantly encountering new situations and new objects, but they have little experience to guide their responses and little physical strength or coordination to respond with. They cannot eat, dress, or take off an uncomfortable diaper by themselves. What is more, since they have a vocabulary of only a few words at best, they have no reliable system of communication. Therefore, to get through each day reasonably well fed and comfortable, they must depend on adults and older siblings to know what needs to be done and how to do it, as the following case illustrates:

Amy, almost 4 months old, sat in her father's lap in a booth at the coffee shop. He was talking to a friend. Amy was teething on a hard rubber ring he had brought along for her. Her father supported Amy's back with his left arm, keeping his hand free. Twice he used that hand to catch the ring when it fell to her lap or his own lap. When Amy dropped the ring for the third time, he interrupted his conversation, said "Klutz," picked it up, and put it on the table. She leaned toward it, awkwardly reached out and touched it, but was not able to grasp it well enough to pick it up. Her father had returned to his conversation, and this time without interrupting it (though he was glancing back and forth between Amy's hand and his friend) he tilted the ring upward toward Amy so that she could get her thumb under it. She grasped the ring and pulled it away from him. Absorbed in chewing on the toy, Amy did not look at him. He went on talking and drinking his coffee, paying no further attention to her until he felt the toy drop into his lap once again. (Kaye, 1982 pp. 1–2)

Here we see a few of the ways in which adults who care for babies act for them and with them so that the babies can function effectively despite their relative ineptness. The adult's actions must be finely coordinated with the baby's abilities and needs or the baby will experience some form of difficulty.

The kind of finely tuned adult support that assists children in accomplishing actions that they will later come to accomplish independently creates what Lev Vygotsky (1978) called a **zone of proximal development**. Vygotsky attributed great significance to such child-adult interactions throughout development. The zone he referred to is the gap between what children can accomplish independently and what they can accomplish when they are interacting with others who are more competent. The term "proximal" (nearby) indicates that the assistance provided goes just slightly beyond the child's current competence, complementing and building on the child's existing abilities instead of directly teaching the child new behaviors. Notice, for example, that Amy's father did not put the teething

Zone of proximal development
The kind of support provided by adults that permits children to accomplish with assistance actions that they will later learn to accomplish independently.

ring in Amy's hand, nor did he hold it up to her mouth for her to teethe on. Instead, he tilted it upward so that she could grasp it herself, and he did so almost automatically while doing something else. To coordinate behaviors in this way, the adult must know what the child is trying to do and be sensitive to the child's abilities and signals.

By the time infants are 6 or 7 months old, they begin to play a more active role in getting adults to help them. Christine Mosier and Barbara Rogoff (1994) studied the development of help-seeking behavior in 6- to 13-month-old babies. They arranged for mothers to play out brief scripted events in which the infants would be likely to want their mothers' help. A toy was placed on a shelf, for example, or dropped on the floor out of the baby's reach. In about 40 percent of the trials with 6-month-olds, the infants glanced back and forth between the toy and their mothers and made sounds like "ugh" to get their mothers to give them the toy. The infants who were a year old sought their mothers' help in 75 percent of the episodes.

An important clue to the sources of infants' wariness of strangers was the finding that only a few 6-month-olds ever pointed or uttered a recognizable sound to communicate their goal, but that the older infants often did. As a consequence, the 6-month-olds had to depend almost exclusively on their mothers' understanding of what they wanted. One-year-olds also remained dependent on their mothers' special knowledge and goodwill to achieve their goals, but they were markedly more adept in signaling their needs through conventional sounds and words.

The adults they interact with every day provide a predictable and supportive environment for young infants whose communicative abilities are restricted. This helps explain the onset of wariness in their relations with strangers. There are only a few people 7-month-old babies can count on to arrange the environment appropriately and in accordance with their expectations. Before babies reach the age of 7 months, their capacity to classify people as "those who can be trusted to help" versus "unpredictable strangers" and to remember the likely implications for themselves is at best limited. Once infants can form such categories, however, and use them to compare a current situation with past ones, there is a qualitative change in the way they respond to strangers. Babies realize that strangers do not have routines for interacting with them and cannot be depended upon to notice and understand their signals or to do what they need them to do.

A NEW FORM OF EMOTIONAL RELATIONSHIP

All of the developments we have discussed in this chapter combine late in the first year of life to change the emotional relationship between parents and their infants. According to Joseph Campos and his colleagues, however, locomotion is the critical factor that organizes all the changes so as to produce a qualitative shift in developmental processes (Campos, Kermoian, & Zumbahlen, 1992). These researchers interviewed parents of 8-month-old infants, some of whom had begun to crawl and some of whom had not. Parents of children who had begun to crawl had more intense positive and negative feelings about their infants than did parents whose infants had not yet begun to crawl. The parents of children who were crawling said that they now gave their children tighter hugs, roughhoused with them more, and talked to them more affectionately. They also reported increased feelings of anger at their babies and increased attempts to control them with angry remarks.

Infants' expressions of emotion also seemed to change in conjunction with locomotion. The parents of babies who had begun to crawl reported that their babies now became more frequently and more intensely angry when their efforts to achieve a goal were frustrated. The babies who crawled also seemed to become more upset when their parents left their sides. One mother reported:

If I leave [the room] she gets upset unless she's busy and doesn't see it. But as soon as she notices, she starts hollering. I don't think it mattered the first four months. When she started doing more, sitting up, crawling, that's when she'd get upset when I would leave. (Campos et al., 1992, p. 33)

Many developmental psychologists believe that these new forms of emotional expression bespeak a new emotional bond, which they call **attachment.** Eleanor Maccoby (1980) lists four signs of attachment in babies and young children:

1. They seek to be near their primary caretaker. Before the age of 7 to 8 months few babies plan and make organized attempts to achieve contact with the other person; after this age, babies often follow their mothers closely, for example.
2. They show distress if separated from their caretaker. Before attachment begins, infants show little disturbance when their mothers walk out of the room.
3. They are happy when they are reunited with the person they are attached to.
4. They orient their actions to the other person, even when he or she is absent. Babies listen for their mother's voice and watch her while they play.

The special relationship with their mothers that babies begin to display between 7 and 9 months of age undergoes significant change during the remainder of infancy and beyond. We will take up these later events and describe some of the important research on attachment in Chapter 6.

THE CHANGING NATURE OF COMMUNICATION

As babies begin to be mobile and become wary of novel objects and strange people, the means by which they communicate with adults also undergo important changes.

By 3 months of age, as we saw in Chapter 4 (p. 177), infants and their caregivers are jointly experiencing pleasure in simple face-to-face interactions (recall Daniel Stern's description of the baby whose "body resonated [with pleasure] almost like a balloon being pumped up" during one such episode [1977, p. 3]). The advent of social smiling is accompanied by coordinated turn-taking. Colwyn Trevarthen (1980) refers to the emotional sharing that occurs between very young infants and their caregivers as **primary intersubjectivity.** This early form of communication is restricted to direct face-to-face interactions and still depends for most of its support on the efforts of the adult participant.

Around the age of 7 months babies begin to interact with others in a new and more complex way that Trevarthen calls **secondary intersubjectivity.** The hallmark of secondary intersubjectivity is the infant's and caregiver's sharing of understandings and emotions that refer beyond themselves to objects and other people. For example, if a mother and her 5-month-old baby are looking at each other and the mother suddenly looks to one side, the infant will not follow the mother's gaze; but at 7 or 8 months babies look in the direction their mothers are looking and engage in joint visual attention with her (Butterworth & Jarrett, 1991).

Social Referencing A phenomenon known as social referencing provides a striking example of secondary intersubjectivity, bespeaking the new emotional relationship between infants and their caregivers as well as the infants' increasingly complex communicative skills. **Social referencing** refers to babies' tendency to look at their caregiver for some indication of how they should feel and act when they come upon something unfamiliar. It becomes a common means of communication as soon as babies begin to move about on their own (Campos & Stenberg, 1981). When babies notice that their caregivers are looking at the same thing they

Attachment An enduring emotional bond between infants and specific people.

Primary intersubjectivity The coordinated turn king and emotional sharing between infants and their caregivers in face-to-face interactions.

Secondary intersubjectivity The sharing between infants and their caregivers of understandings and emotions that refer beyond themselves to objects and other people.

Social referencing The behavior in which babies keep a watchful eye on their caregivers to see how they should interpret unusual events.

This newcomer to the world of upright posture is looking back to see what his mother thinks of his exploits. His enquiring gaze is an example of social referencing.

Babbling A form of vocalizing by babies that includes consonant and vowel sounds like those used in speech.

Jargoning Vocalizations of strings of syllables that have the intonation and stress of actual utterances in the language that the baby will eventually speak.

are looking at and appear to be concerned, they hesitate and become wary. If their caregiver smiles and looks pleased about the new situation, the babies relax (Walden & Baxter, 1989). Babies will even check back to see how their mothers respond to an object after they have made their own appraisal of it (Rosen, Adamson, & Bakeman, 1992).

Researchers have found a difference in the ways baby boys and baby girls respond to their mother's worried looks. Baby girls are more likely than baby boys to move away from an object their mothers have looked at with fear. Perhaps as a result, mothers find it necessary to use more intensely fearful facial expressions when they communicate with their sons (Rosen, Adamson, & Bakeman, 1992).

Smiles and other facial expressions are only rudimentary means of communication. As babies become more mobile and more likely to wander out of their caregiver's sight and reach, facial expressions become less available as a source of information. A new means of interaction, one that will allow babies and caregivers to communicate at a distance, now becomes an urgent necessity. We refer, of course, to language.

The Beginnings of Speech At about 9 months of age, children begin to understand some words and expressions, such as "Do you want your bottle?" "Wave bye-bye," and "Cookie?" when they are used in highly specific, often ritualized situations. One little girl observed by Elizabeth Bates and her colleagues (1979) touched her head when asked, "Where are your little thoughts?" Another would bring her favorite doll when she was asked to "bring a dolly," but she did not understand the word "doll" to refer to any doll but her own.

The development of the ability to produce language can be traced back to the cooing and gurgling noises babies begin to make at 10 to 12 weeks of age. Soon thereafter, babies with normal hearing not only initiate cooing sounds but begin to respond with gurgles and coos to the voices of others. When they are imitated, they will answer with another coo, thereby engaging in a "conversation" in which turns are taken at vocalizing. They are most likely to vocalize with their mothers and other familiar people.

Babbling begins around 4 months of age in hearing children. It is a form of vocalizing that includes consonant and vowel sounds like those used in speech (Adamson, 1995). At first babbling amounts to no more than vocal play, as babies discover the wealth of sounds they can make with their tongue, teeth, palate, and vocal cords. They practice making these sound combinations endlessly, much as they practice grasping objects or rolling over. They even produce syllables they have never heard before and will not use when they learn to speak. Babbling during the first year of life is the same the world over, no matter what language the baby's family speaks (Blake & de Boysson-Bardies, 1992). At about 9 months of age, however, babies begin to narrow their babbling to the sounds produced in the language they will eventually speak. As babies often babble when they play alone, early babbling does not seem to be an attempt to communicate.

Toward the end of the first year, babies begin to vocalize strings of syllables that have the intonation and stress of actual utterances in the language they will eventually speak. Such vocalizations are called **jargoning.** John Dore (1978) found that before the end of the first year, babies start to repeat particular short utterances in particular situations, as if they had some meaning. When Jake was about 10 months old, for example, if he wanted the bottle of juice from the bag hanging on the back of his stroller, he would turn around in his seat, say, "Dah, dah," and reach toward the bag while looking up at his mother in appeal. She immediately knew what he wanted and gave it to him.

By about 12 months of age infants are able to comprehend about a dozen common phrases, such as "Give me a hug," "Stop it!" and "Let's go bye-bye." During the same period, the first distinguishable words make their appearance, although their use is restricted to only a few contexts or objects (Fenson et al., 1994).

The course of vocalizing by deaf children provides an instructive contrast to that of hearing children. It used to be thought that deaf children began to babble at the same age as hearing children (Lenneberg, Rebelsky, & Nichols, 1965). Work by D. Kimbrough Oller and Rebecca Eilers (1988), however, has shown that the vocalizations of deaf and hearing infants differ markedly in ways that indicate that only deaf children with residual hearing actually babble. By 1 year of age or so, deaf children rarely vocalize, but instead are seen to "babble" with their hands, making the movements that will become the elements of sign language (Pettito & Marentette, 1991).

These budding linguistic abilities, which we discuss in more detail in Chapters 6 and 8, are part and parcel of the reorganization of babies' perceptual-motor, cognitive, and social capacities that signals the advent of a new bio-social-behavioral shift in the latter half of the first year of life.

The pleasure this baby and mother take in their face-to-face interaction is an example of the kind of emotional sharing referred to as primary intersubjectivity.

A New Bio-Social-Behavioral Shift

Table 5.3 summarizes many of the changes that converge to create a bio-social-behavioral shift in infants' psychological processes between 7 and 9 months of age (Brazelton, 1990; Emde, Gaensbauer, & Harmon, 1976; Fischer & Rose, 1994). Whereas the crucial biological events at the 2½-month bio-social-behavioral shift centered on changes in the sensory pathways of the brain and the brain stem, the shift that occurs at 7 to 9 months involves changes in the frontal lobes of the cerebral cortex (which are essential for planning and executing deliberate action). Equally significant are increases in the strength of muscles and bones, which are necessary to support locomotion.

Locomotion appears to orchestrate the reorganization of many other functions that have been developing in parallel with it. For one thing, the acquisition of new motor skills leads infants to discover many properties and functions of objects in their immediate environment. They become capable of reaching for objects efficiently and picking them up, feeling them, tasting them, moving around them, and using them for various purposes of their own. As babies learn that some of the "objects" out there move and respond in coordination with them, their interactions with people take on a whole new dimension. Sympathetic adults buffer them against discomfort and danger. These adults can be counted on to understand their signals, to complete their actions for them, and to arrange things so that they can act more effectively for themselves.

These experiences would not amount to much, however, if memories of them did not accumulate adequately in infants' minds. Once babies are able to move away from the immediate presence of watchful adults, they can no longer rely on

TABLE 5.3   Elements of the Bio-Social-Behavioral Shift at 7 to 9 Months

BIOLOGICAL DOMAIN	Growth of muscles and hardening of bones Myelination of motor neurons to lower trunk, legs, and hands Myelination of cerebellum, hippocampus, and frontal lobes New forms of EEG activity in cortex
BEHAVIORAL DOMAIN	Onset of crawling Fear of heights Automated reaching and grasping Action sequences coordinated to achieve goals Object permanence displayed in actions Recall memory Wariness in response to novelty Babbling
SOCIAL DOMAIN	Wariness of strangers New emotional response to caregiver (attachment) Social referencing

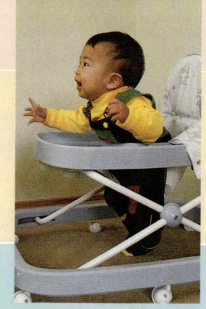

the adults' assistance and protection as they did before. It is not enough to recognize that one has seen an object before or to respond with curiosity if it is new. Babies must be able to recall ("bring to mind") their earlier experiences with objects, including people, in order to behave appropriately.

Both the baby and the caregiver must accommodate themselves to the uncertainties of their increasing separation as babies begin to move about on their own. Babies begin to exhibit emotions, such as anger when their efforts to reach a goal are frustrated, fear when confronted by strangers, and wariness when encountering unexpected, as well as strong feelings of attachment for their caregivers. Caregivers arrange the environment so that the baby is likely to come to no harm, and they keep a watchful eye (or ear) open for anything amiss. The babies, for their part, keep an eye on their caregiver's face and listen to the tone of the adult's voice, which communicates his or her evaluation of the situation.

As their first birthday approaches, many babies have progressed from crawling to walking upright. Walking increases both their independence and the importance of using all their accumulating cognitive and communicative abilities to coordinate their actions with those of their caregivers and other members of the community.

Sophisticated as 1-year-olds may be in comparison with babies of 2½ months, the pattern of adaptation that they have achieved is destined to change, and they will be meeting life's challenges in a fundamentally different way.

SUMMARY

Biological Changes

- Although there is great individual variation, most healthy babies triple in weight during the first year of life. Changes in size are accompanied by changes in overall body proportions that are important for the eventual achievement of balanced walking.

- Hardening of the bones and increases in muscle mass contribute to the development of crawling, walking, and coordinated movements of the arms and hands.

- Development in the prefrontal region of the frontal cortex of the brain makes possible the voluntary control and planning that make their appearance between 3 and 12 months of age.

Perceptual-Motor Development

- The initial stage of poorly coordinated reaching and grasping, controlled primarily by subcortical brain centers, is followed by a stage of visually guided reaching and grasping, which gives way to swift and accurate voluntary movements after several months of practice.

- Increasing skill in grasping objects with the hands makes possible the discovery of many new properties of objects.

- Locomotion, which begins during the second half of the first year of life, brings about a fundamental change in infants' relationships with their environments. Motor control of the body begins at the head and neck and proceeds gradually to the trunk and legs. At 7 to 8 months, infants begin to crawl or creep, using a combination of leg and arm movements. Walking is achieved a few months later, around the first birthday.

- Motor development can be speeded up by extensive practice, but practice has little influence on the eventual level of proficiency of basic motor skills.

Cognitive Changes

- According to Piaget, infants progress through two additional sensorimotor substages before the end of the first year. Between 4 and 8 months they pay increased attention to external objects and prolong actions that produce interesting changes in their environment (substage 3). Between 8 and 12 months of age, they acquire the ability to coordinate separate actions in order to achieve a goal (substage 4).

- Important changes occur in infants' ability to keep in mind and act upon objects that are out of sight:

  1. For the first 3 months of life, infants appear to forget objects not present to their senses.

  2. At 4 months, many infants behave as if objects exist even when they cannot see them, but they are incapable of acting on this knowledge. The object and its location are quickly forgotten.

  3. At about 8 months of age, infants begin to search for hidden objects but quickly become confused or forget their location, often remembering their own movements instead.

  4. Memory for the locations of objects continues to improve into the second year of life, as does the ability to search for hidden objects.

- By 3 to 4 months of age, infants are able to perceive the correspondence between such varied properties of objects as the way they look and how they feel. They also perceive the numerosity in small displays of objects. It is not known how early such understandings develop or what aspects of them are present at birth.

- The ability to perceive a variety of objects as members of a single category appears as early as 3 months of age. Early categories are based on similarity of perceptual features. Conceptual categories do not begin to appear until the end of the first year.

- Between the ages of 2½ and 12 months, memory increases steadily. When provided with a specific reminder of training received a month earlier, infants as young as 3 months of age remember how to make a mobile move.

- About the same time that babies begin to crawl, they show signs of being able to call to mind objects and people that are not present and activities they have not practiced.

A New Relationship with the Social World

- Changes in social and emotional behavior accompany changes in motor skills and cognition. Infants become wary of strangers and upset when they are separated from their primary caregivers, with whom they have formed an emotional bond called attachment.

- Locomotion is accompanied by a new form of communicative activity. Babies begin to monitor the expression on their caregiver's face to determine the caregiver's reaction to an object or event they are both attending to. Such social referencing helps babies to evaluate their environment.

A New Bio-Social-Behavioral Shift

- Events in the major developmental domains converge between the ages of 7 and 9 months in a bio-social-behavioral shift that ushers in a qualitatively new stage of development.

KEY TERMS

A-not-B error,   p. 199

attachment,   p. 213

babbling,   p. 214

categorizing,   p. 206

cognitive processes,   p. 194

conceptual category,   p. 208

cross-modal perception,   p. 204

jargoning,   p. 214

locomotion,   p. 191

object permanence,   p. 197

perceptual categories,   p. 206

primary intersubjectivity,   p. 213

secondary circular reactions,   p. 195

secondary intersubjectivity,   p. 213

social referencing,   p. 213

zone of proximal development,   p. 211

THOUGHT QUESTIONS

1. Give two examples illustrating close connections between perceiving and acting early in infancy.
2. List some of the physical and intellectual abilities a baby needs in order to eat a cookie without help from anyone else.
3. Selma Fraiberg (p. 202) writes that locomotion influences the development of the personality. Why might this be true?
4. What are some of the difficulties that researchers face in trying to assess the development of the concept of an object?
5. Why do psychologists believe that there is a link between wariness of strangers and the growth of cognitive abilities such as categorization and memory?

The End of Infancy

“The self and its boundaries are at the heart of philosophical speculation on human nature, and the sense of self and its counterpart, the sense of other, are universal phenomena that profoundly influence all our social experiences.”

—*Daniel Stern,*
The Interpersonal World of the Infant

J ust before Jake's second birthday, his mother, Barbara, and his father and sisters went to Switzerland for a few weeks. Barbara's sister, Retta, said it would be no trouble to look after Jake while they were gone. Before the trip, Barbara arranged to spend a week at her sister's with Jake so that he would have a chance to become familiar with the household.

At first Jake ignored everyone at his aunt's house except his mother and his 4-year-old cousin, Linda. The first afternoon in the sandbox with Linda, he sat and watched with fascination as she conducted a tea party for her teddy bear and bunny rabbit. After a while he placed several small containers in a row on the edge of the sandbox, filled a large container with sand, and then poured its contents into the smaller ones in perfect imitation of his cousin. Then Linda caught his eye. Calling, "Beep-beep! Get out of my way!" she took a toy truck and ran it along the edge of the sandbox, knocking over the teacups and stuffed animals. In an instant Jake was yelling, "Beep-beep!" and knocking over his containers with a toy car. Linda laughed wildly. Jake laughed too and chased her truck around the edge of the sandbox with his car.

From then on Jake followed Linda around the house. If she asked her mother for something to eat or drink, he was right behind her, waiting for his share. Jake did not talk to his aunt directly, and he would not permit her to change his diaper or help him. A lot of the time he refused help from anyone, but if he really couldn't manage, he said, "Mommy do it." Jake knew that Barbara was leaving. "You goin', Mommy?" he asked her several times during that week.

This child's first steps display the posture and uncertainty character-istic of toddlers.

At the airport Jake held Linda's hand and watched bravely as his mother disappeared into the plane. But that afternoon he cried. Linda tried to distract him, but he would not join her in play. Finally she brought him his favorite pillow, which he carried around for the next few days. Then he seemed to adjust to his mother's absence so well that he began to call his aunt "Mommy."

When Jake's family returned 20 days later, there was much excitement at the airport. No one paid any attention when Jake sat on his aunt's lap on the ride back to her house.

That afternoon Jake fell and scraped his knee while he was kicking a ball. He ran crying to his father. His father, who was busy at that moment, suggested that he ask his mother to put a Band-Aid on his scrape. Jake ran into the kitchen where his aunt and his mother were sitting. "Mommy fix it," he said, showing his injured knee to his aunt and ignoring his mother. When Barbara offered to help, Jake refused.

Later, in the swimming pool, Jake was showing his father all the new things he had learned to do. "Show Mommy," his father said, suspecting something. His suspicions were confirmed when Jake turned and tried to get his aunt's attention.

Jake had called his uncle "Daddy" throughout his stay, but as soon as his father was on the scene again, his uncle became "Uncle Len" and his father became "Daddy." No such switch occurred for "Mommy." For the 3 days that Jake's family remained at his aunt and uncle's house, Jake ignored his mother and refused to allow her to do anything for him. When they were preparing to

return to their own home, however, Jake looked up at his aunt and said, "Bye, Auntie Retta." Then, turning to his mother, he addressed her directly for the first time since she had returned. "Let's go, Mom," he said, raising his arms as a signal for her to pick him up.

The changes that have occurred in Jake's behavior since his first birthday reveal the new developments that mark the second year of life. At 12 months, Jake was just beginning to walk; at 24 months, he runs and climbs with ease. He is also far more skilled in manipulating small objects. His vocabulary at 12 months consisted primarily of single words and a few set phrases—"juice," "woof," "Mommy," "All gone"; now Jake's language skills enable him to communicate more effectively and to participate in imaginative play with another child. He is still wary of strange people and places, and he is still so strongly attached to his parents that it was difficult for him to adapt to being left at his aunt's home.

In this chapter we examine the events that complete the period of infancy and account for the increases in the complexity of children's behavior between the ages of 12 and 30 months. Changes occur in the brain and body; reasoning about the world of objects and people becomes increasingly sophisticated; the child acquires the ability to imitate sequences of actions, to engage in pretend play, to communicate using language; and social relationships between children and their caregivers take on a new form. Each of these facets of development is interesting in its own right. But more significant, each is a single thread in a tapestry; taken together they create a distinctive individual personality with its own distinctive sense of self. About the time infants celebrate their second birthday or soon thereafter, these biological, cognitive, and social changes converge to create a new bio-social-behavioral shift—the end of infancy—and a new stage of development emerges.

Biological Maturation

During the second and third years of life, children's bodies continue to grow rapidly, but the rate of their growth is considerably slower than it was in the first year (Eichorn, 1979; Tanner, 1990). During their second and third years, the average height of children raised in the United States in recent decades increases from 29 to 38 inches and their weight increases from 20 to 33 pounds, although there is considerable variation from one child to the next. These increases in overall size are accompanied by important changes in the structure of the brain and by increasing neuromuscular control.

Anatomical studies of the brains of children who have died at various ages during infancy show that several changes occur in the brain during the second year (Diamond, 1990a; Fuster, 1990). This evidence has encouraged developmental psychologists to seek links between changes in the brain and the emergence of new psychological capacities that characteristically appear during the same period.

For example, the second year brings accelerated myelination of brain cell connections both within the cerebral cortex and between the brain stem and the cerebral cortex (see Figure 4.15, p. 156). This development improves the functioning of the neurons that link the prefrontal cortex and frontal lobes to the centers in the brain stem where emotional responses are generated and to cortical centers where visual and auditory input is analyzed. These centers now begin to work in synchrony (Thatcher, 1994). Such changes are important for the development of the complex psychological functions that research has shown to be governed by the prefrontal portions of the cerebral cortex: the beginnings of self-awareness, more systematic problem solving, the voluntary control of behavior, and the acquisition of language, all widely held to define late infancy (Diamond, 1990a, 1990b; Fischer & Rose, 1994).

There is also evidence that toward the end of infancy the length and the degree of branching of the neurons in the cerebral cortex approach adult magnitudes: each neuron now has multiple connections with others. At this time, the various areas of the brain, which have been maturing at very different rates, reach similar levels of development. For the first time, the balance among the various brain systems begins to approximate that of adults (Lecours, 1975; Rabinowicz, 1979). The brain will undergo additional bursts of growth in later years, but after infancy the brain generally develops at a more modest pace. It appears that a great deal of the brain structure that eventually will support adult behavior is present by the end of the second year. This suggests that later developments are largely refinements of already existing structures.

Perceptual-Motor Coordination

Prominent consequences of the developments in the nervous system are the child's increased control of arm, hand, bladder, bowel, and leg muscles, and increased coordination of perceiving and acting.

FROM CRAWLING TO WALKING

In the transition from crawling to walking we see a new motor function developing in tandem with increased sensitivity to perceptual input from the environment. Karen Adolph and her colleagues (1993) demonstrated the confluence of these developments by arranging for 8½- and 14-month-old infants to move up and down ramps of varying steepness. The younger children were still crawling, while the older children had been walking for a few months. The researchers wanted to know if all the children would perceive the degree of slope and adjust their movements accordingly so as not to fall.

FIGURE 6.1 *Between the ages of 8 and 14 months, the transition from crawling to walking changes the way these two babies approach the task of going down a ramp. (a) The 8½-month-old sees that there is a slope but plunges down it all the same. (b) The toddler hesitates and feels the incline of the ramp with his foot before attempting to descend it.*

(a)

(b)

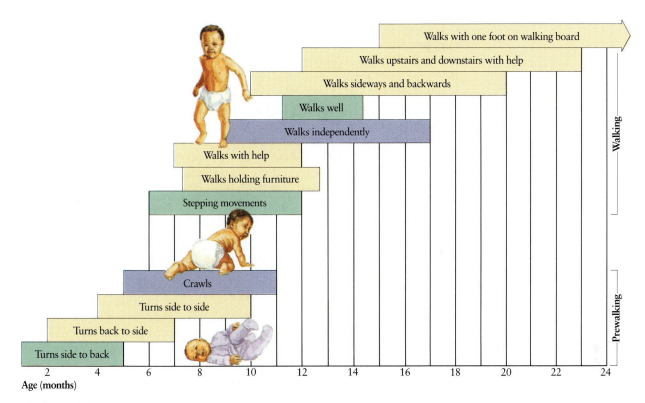

Age (months)

FIGURE 6.2 *The progression from creeping to crawling to walking follows a classic developmental sequence. Each new stage in locomotion allows children to move more rapidly and involves a qualitative change in the pattern of their behavior.*

When the 14-month-old toddlers encountered a gentle slope, they climbed it without hesitation. But when it was steeper, especially if it sloped downward, they hesitated and tried various alternative methods of getting down, finally either sitting and sliding down the slope or backing down slowly on their hands and knees (see Figure 6.1). The 8½-month-old babies, who did not yet walk, demonstrated that they perceived how steep the ramp was—they spent more time feeling the surface of the steeper ramps. But when they did try to crawl down the steep ramps, they seemed unable to adjust their movements accordingly. Many of them tumbled down the ramps into their mothers' waiting arms. They still did not adjust their movements even after they had fallen more than once.

Even in adulthood, walking safely means adjusting our movements in response to information we receive through our eyes. We have all had the experience of misjudging the depth of a step and turning an ankle as a consequence. Postural adjustment is only one of the many components of surefootedness, however.

In a series of studies, Esther Thelen and her colleagues (Thelen & Ulrich, 1991; Thelen, Ulrich, & Jensen, 1989) traced how a number of separately developing skills converge to enable the child to walk. One crucial element in this process is the ability to coordinate leg movements with shifts of body weight from one foot to the other as each foot steps forward in its turn. They found, for example, that if infants are stood on a treadmill and given the needed support, they can execute the pattern of leg movements needed for walking as early as 7 months of age. But babies this age cannot yet walk on a stationary surface, and without support they are unable to shift their weight and coordinate their arm and leg movements.

No one factor can be considered *the* cause of walking; rather, walking becomes possible only when all the component skills (upright posture, leg alternation, weight shifting, ability to evaluate the sensory information obtained while moving through space) have been developed and when the child has been able to practice them.

With their first steps babies become "toddlers"; the word describes the characteristic way they spread their legs and toddle from side to side. Most 1-year-olds are unbalanced and fall often, but falling does not stop them. The ground is not far away. Besides, walking is too exciting to give up on, so they simply get up and rush ahead to the next tumble. Once begun, relatively coordinated walking is achieved within a few months (Clark & Phillips, 1993).

Walking brings even more changes to babies' lives than crawling did. As Selma Fraiberg (1959) so eloquently puts it, walking represents

> a cutting of the moorings to the mother's body. . . . To the child who takes his first steps and finds himself walking alone, this moment must bring the first sharp sense of uniqueness and separateness of his body and his person, the discovery of the solitary self. (p. 61)

Many months must pass after babies have taken their first steps before they can go beyond walking to climb, kick, and jump in a coordinated fashion (see Figure 6.2). Most American children cannot walk up and down stairs until they are at least 17 months old, kick a ball forward until they are 20 months old, or jump until they are almost 24 months old (Frankenburg & Dodds, 1967; Gesell, 1929).

MANUAL DEXTERITY

One of the primary ways toddlers express independence is by taking their clothes off and, as their manual dexterity increases during the second year, by putting their clothes on by themselves.

Coordination of fine hand movements increases significantly between 12 and 30 months. Infants 1 year old can only roll a ball or fling it awkwardly; by the time they are 2½, they can throw it. They can also turn the pages of a book without tearing or creasing them, snip with scissors, string beads with a needle and thread, build a tower six blocks high with considerable ease, hold a cup of milk or a spoon of applesauce without spilling it, and dress themselves (as long as there are no buttons or shoelaces) (Gesell, 1929). Each of these accomplishments may seem minor in itself, but each skill requires a good deal of practice to master, and each increases infants' overall competence.

Even an act as elementary as using a spoon, which has been studied in detail by Kevin Connolly and Mary Dalgleish (1989), requires incredibly precise coordination. Figure 6.3 depicts the variety of ways in which infants between 10 and 23 months of age attempt to hold a spoon. After the spoon is dipped into the food, it must be held level so that nothing spills while it is raised to the lips. Then its contents must be emptied into the mouth. At 10 to 12 months babies can do only simple things with a spoon, such as banging it on the table or dipping it repeatedly into the bowl. Slightly older children can coordinate the actions of opening the mouth and bringing the spoon to it, but as often as not the spoon is empty when it arrives. This problem is the next to be solved, as infants learn to get food onto the spoon, carry it to the mouth without spilling it, and put the food in the mouth. Once this elementary sequence of actions is achieved, it is then adjusted until it is smooth and automatic. With all of these coordinated actions to be assembled, no wonder it takes two or more years before you can leave a child with a spoon and a bowl of cereal and expect much of the cereal to get into the child's mouth!

CONTROL OF ELIMINATION

Another important element in the growing ability of children to act on their own is the acquisition of voluntary control over the muscles that govern elimination. In the early months of life, elimination is involuntary. When the baby's bladder or

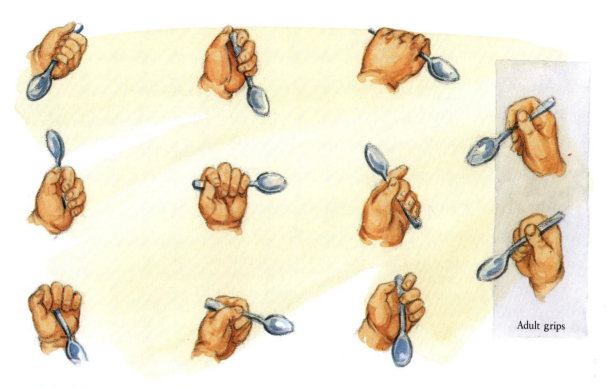

Adult grips

FIGURE 6.3 *Grip patterns. Babies initially grip a spoon in many different ways. As they accumulate experience and gain motor control, they eventually adopt an adult grip.*

bowels are full, the appropriate sphincter muscles open automatically and empty them. Before a baby can control these muscles voluntarily, the sensory pathways from the bladder and bowels must be mature enough to transmit signals to the cortex of the brain. Children must then learn to associate these signals with the need to eliminate. They must also learn to tighten their sphincters to prevent elimination and to loosen them to permit it. Children are usually not capable of voluntary postponement of elimination until they are at least 15 months of age, but they can be taught to eliminate when they are placed on a potty at 6 months of age by a caretaker who is sensitive to their bodily signals (De Vries & De Vries, 1977). As we will see shortly, several major developmental theorists attribute special importance to the events surrounding toilet training.

In the nineteenth and early twentieth centuries, toilet training was begun as early as possible, not only for convenience in an era before washing machines and disposable diapers but also because it was believed that early training would ensure bowel regularity, which was considered important for good health. The first edition of *Infant Care*, published by the U.S. Children's Bureau in 1914, advised mothers to begin bowel training by the third month or even earlier (Wolfenstein, 1953).

Because the neural basis for bladder and bowel control is still immature when children are very young, toilet training often takes a while to complete. One study found that toilet training begun before 5 months of age usually requires 10 months to complete; children learn in less than half that time when training is delayed until 20 months of age (Oppel, Harper, & Reder, 1968).

By the time they are 2 years old some children are able to remain dry during the day (Berk & Friman, 1990). Many children in the United States today, however, do not achieve this milestone until sometime later, and most do not manage to stay dry while they are asleep until they are 4 years old.

This little girl has brought along her teddy bear as she practices using a potty.

A New Mode of Thought

During the second year of life, as toddlers are perfecting their ability to get around on their own two legs, to eat with utensils, and to control their body functions, they also begin to display a qualitatively new mode of thinking. According to Piaget, this change signals the end of the sensorimotor period. Even psychologists who disagree with much of Piaget's theory agree that developments around the end of the second year enable children to think in a new way (Fischer & Knight, 1990; Kagan, 1982; Vygotsky, 1934/1987).

COMPLETING THE SENSORIMOTOR SUBSTAGES

As we saw in Chapter 4 (p. 170), babies are capable of repeating an action for its own sake during the first months of life, but they seem to be unaware of the relation of the action to the world beyond their own bodies (substages 1 and 2). And, as we saw in Chapter 5 (pp. 195–196), at about 4 months of age they begin to focus their actions on objects in the external world (substage 3). Then, between 8 and 12 months of age, they develop the ability to combine simple actions to achieve a simple goal (substage 4). Piaget believed that all of the actions of the first four substages are very much tied to the here and now, and that the ability of infants less than 1 year old to think about absent objects is limited.

Substage 5: Tertiary circular reactions (12–18 months)

The fifth substage of the sensorimotor period is characterized by an ability to vary systematically and flexibly the simple instrumental actions of substage 4. Piaget referred to this as the substage of **tertiary circular reactions.** Whereas primary circular reactions are centered on the child's body and secondary circular reactions are focused on objects, tertiary circular reactions are focused on the *relationship* between the two. Now, in addition to making interesting events last by using already established secondary circular reactions, infants become capable of deliberately varying their action sequences, thereby making their explorations of the world more complex. Piaget referred to tertiary circular reactions as "experiments in order to see" (1952b, p. 272) because children seem to be experimenting in order to find out about the nature of objects. Piaget observed this kind of behavior in his son Laurent, then aged 10 months and 11 days. Laurent is lying in his crib:

> He grasps in succession a celluloid swan, a box, etc., stretches out his arm and lets them fall. He distinctly varies the positions of the fall. . . . Sometimes he stretches out his arm vertically, sometimes he holds it obliquely, in front of or behind his eyes, etc. When the object falls in a new position (for example, on his pillow), he lets it fall two or three times more on the same place, as though to study the spatial relations; then he modifies the situation. (Piaget 1952b, p. 269)

This kind of trial-and-error exploration distinguishes tertiary circular reactions from secondary circular reactions, which involve only previously acquired schemas. But infants in substage 5 still do not seem able to *imagine* actions and their probable consequences; they are restricted to thinking about manipulating objects in their immediate physical environment.

Substage 6: Representation (18–24 months)

According to Piaget, the hallmark of substage 6, the final stage of the sensorimotor period, is that babies begin to base their actions on internal, mental symbols, or **representations,** of prior experiences. Before substage 6, children can act only on a "present" world. When they can re-present the world to themselves—that is,

Representation The capacity to go beyond actions in the immediate present world to "present" the world to oneself mentally.

TABLE 6.1 Sensorimotor Substages and Stages of Object Permanence

Substage	Age Range (months)	Characteristics of Sensorimotor Substage	Developments in Object Permanence
1	0–1½	*Reflex schemas exercised:* involuntary rooting, sucking, grasping, looking.	Infant does not search for objects that have been removed from sight.
2	1½–4	*Primary circular reactions:* repetition of actions that are pleasurable in themselves.	Infant orients to place where objects have been removed from sight.
3	4–8	*Secondary circular reactions:* dawning awareness of relation of own actions to environment; extension of actions that produce interesting changes in the environment.	Infant will reach for a partially hidden object but stops if it disappears.
4	8–12	*Coordination of secondary circular reactions:* combining schemas to achieve a desired effect; earliest form of problem solving.	Infant will search for a completely hidden object; keeps searching the original location of the object even if it is moved to another location in full view of the infant.
5	12–18	*Tertiary circular reactions:* deliberate variation of problem-solving means; experiments to see what the consequences will be.	Infant will search for an object after seeing it moved but not if it is moved in secret.
6	18–24	*Beginnings of symbolic representation:* images and words come to stand for familiar objects; invention of new means of problem solving through symbolic combinations.	Infant will search for a hidden object, certain that it exists somewhere.

when they can present it to themselves over again, mentally—they can be said to be engaging in true mental actions.

Piaget cited many new behaviors as evidence of the emergence of symbolic, representational thought. Chief among them are:

- the ability to imagine objects that are not present (shown by systematic search for hidden objects)
- the appearance of systematic problem solving
- the ability to imitate events well after they have occurred
- the use of language

The final substages of sensorimotor development, along with the earlier substages described in Chapters 4 and 5, are summarized in the third column of Table 6.1. The fourth column summarizes parallel developments in infants' search behavior in the object-permanence task.

(a) Infant sees apple

(b) Researcher hides apple as infant watches

(c) Researcher distracts infant and moves apple

(d) Infant is confused

(e) Infant searches for apple under wrong cloth

FIGURE 6.4 *Children in stage 5 of the development of object permanence cannot yet maintain a firm idea of the permanence of an object when its location is changed without their knowledge. (From Bower, 1982.)*

MASTERY OF OBJECT PERMANENCE

When they are about 1 year old, babies stop making the A-not-B error; that is, they no longer become confused when an object is first hidden in one location and is then hidden in a second location while they are watching. They now search for the object in its new location. This improved ability to keep track of an object's location marks stage 5 of the understanding of object permanence. However, a stage-5 baby still has trouble thinking about absent objects. If infants in substage 5 do not *see* the object moved, they continue to look where they last saw it, and when they do not find it, they are likely to become confused and stop searching. If you pretend to hide an object in your hand while you really hide it behind your back, for example, a stage-5 baby will continue to search for it in your hand, failing to reason that it must be somewhere else nearby. A version of this procedure used in many studies is shown in Figure 6.4.

Piaget (1952b) believed that infants enter stage 6, the final stage of object permanence, between the ages of 18 and 24 months. From that time on, they continue to search for a hidden object even if it has been moved without their knowledge. They appear to be able to reason, "Well, the toy wasn't where I expected, but it must be here somewhere," so they systematically check possible locations until they find it.

From then on infants are able to anticipate the trajectory of a moving object and the location of its reemergence if it goes behind a barrier. When a ball rolls under a couch, for example, a 2-year-old will go around to the other side of the couch to look for it instead of looking under the couch. Piaget argued that in order to perform successfully in a search for a hidden or moving object, babies must calculate its location mentally. They cannot rely solely on the immediate information given by their senses.

PROBLEM SOLVING

The ability to reason about the locations of unseen objects is accompanied by increased ability to solve a variety of other problems through systematic mental effort. Piaget's observations of his daughters nicely reveal how transformations in babies' understanding of objects and events permit them to solve problems systematically instead of by trial and error. Both girls confronted the same problem, Jacqueline when she was 15 months old and Lucienne when she was 13 months old. Both girls wanted to pull a stick through the bars of their playpen (see Figure 6.5), but they solved the problem in significantly different ways.

> Jacqueline is seated in her playpen. Outside is a stick 20 centimeters long, the distance of about three spaces between the bars. At first Jacqueline tries to pull the stick into her playpen horizontally, but it will not go through the bars. The second time, she accidentally tilts the stick a little in raising it. She perceives this and reaches through the bars and tilts the stick until it is sufficiently vertical to pass through the bars. But several subsequent attempts make it clear that this is an accidental success; she does not yet understand the principle involved. On the next several tries she grasps the stick by the middle and pulls it horizontally, against the bars. Unable to get it in that way, she then tilts it up. It is not until the seventeenth try that she tilts the stick up before it touches the bars, and not until the twentieth that she does so systematically. (Adapted from Piaget, 1952b, p. 305)

Jacqueline seemed to have a clear goal in mind because she was certainly persistent. She continued to work at the problem until it was solved. But her efforts were rather hit-or-miss. When she succeeded, she did not understand why. She grasped the solution only after many trials and many errors. This experience is typical of substage 5 of the sensorimotor period.

Although she was 2 months younger than Jacqueline was when she was presented with this problem, Lucienne's problem solving was more sophisticated, a reminder that age norms associated with Piagetian stages, like other developmental norms, are only approximate.

> Lucienne grasps the stick in the middle and pulls it horizontally. Noticing her failure, she withdraws the stick, tilts it up, and brings it through easily. When the stick is again placed on the floor, she grasps it by the middle and tilts it up before she pulls it through, or she grasps it by

FIGURE 6.5 *This child in substage 5 of the sensorimotor period carries out deliberate problem solving but still relies on trial and error.*

This child, who is "giving Godzilla a drink," is engaging in the kind of complicated symbolic play that appears to emerge between the ages of 18 and 24 months.

one end and brings it through easily. She does this with longer sticks and on successive days. Unlike her sister Jacqueline, who had to grope her way toward a solution, Lucienne profits from her failure at once. (Adapted from Piaget, 1952b, p. 336)

In Lucienne's actions we see the essence of substage 6 sensorimotor behavior; she seems to be using information that is not immediately available to her senses to solve the problem. Instead of going through the slow process of trial and error, as her sister did, Lucienne seems to have pictured a series of events in her mind before she acted. She imagined what would happen if she pulled the stick horizontally. She then inferred that if she turned the stick so that it was vertical and parallel to the bars, it would fit between them. Piaget singled out Lucienne's ability to solve the problem through inference alone as the key evidence for the existence of a new form of thought in substage 6.

PLAY

The early origins of play can be seen in the sensorimotor behavior of infants who kick their feet while being bathed for the sheer pleasure of the feel and sight of splashing water (a secondary circular reaction). Later play goes beyond the baby's own body to incorporate objects (tertiary circular reactions) and involve other people, as in peekaboo.

Peter Smith (1982, 1990) describes four major types of play that provide practice for later functions:

1. *Locomotor play*, which consists chiefly of strenuous use of the body's large muscles: running, jumping, leaping, and so on.
2. *Object play*, which focuses on exploration with the senses: pulling, tugging, shaking things, and so on.
3. *Social play*, in which the primary focus is interaction with another person. It can be divided into (a) play that involves physical contact, such as chasing and wrestling, and (b) play that does not, such as building with blocks.
4. *Fantasy play*, in which the meanings of objects and actions are transformed to fit an imaginary situation.

Smith points out that the first three kinds of play are very common among the young of many animal species but that clear instances of fantasy play are found exclusively among human beings. This species difference fits with the notion that the use of language and symbolic thought is the distinguishing characteristic of human beings, as well as with Piaget's belief that the advent of symbolic thought is the culminating achievement of cognitive development in the infant.

During the period from 12 to 30 months, behaviors that appear to reflect new mental abilities can be seen in new forms of play (Bretherton & Bates, 1985; Piaget, 1962; Zukow, 1986). At 12 to 13 months, babies use objects in play much as adults would use them in earnest; that is, they put spoons in their mouths and bang with hammers. Increasingly, however, babies begin to treat one thing as if it were another. They stir their "coffee" with a twig and comb the doll's hair with a toy rake or, as Jake and his cousin did, act as if the edge of a sandbox were a roadway. This kind of behavior is called **symbolic play** (also **pretend** or **fantasy play**): play in which one object stands for—that is, represents—another, as the rake stands for a comb.

Studies have shown that symbolic play becomes increasingly complex after it makes its appearance early in the second year (Howes et al., 1989; Hughes, 1995).

Symbolic play Play in which one object stands for another.

In the simplest case, children direct their play actions at themselves (for example, an infant pretends to feed *herself* with a spoon). In the most complicated cases, which are not usually seen until about 30 months of age, a toy (in developmental parlance, an "agent") is made to perform several actions fitting a social role (for example, the infant makes a mother doll feed her baby doll) (see Table 6.2).

Why all this scientific attention to something as seemingly frivolous as play? Many developmental psychologists believe that, though play may appear to be quite removed from the serious business of living, it actually serves important functions for the growing organism (Göncü, 1993; Nicolopoulou, 1993; Packer, 1994). They speculate that early forms of play provide opportunities to acquire abilities that will become important later, just as the seemingly aimless movements of the embryo are a vital part of the process of fetal development. Lev Vygotsky (1978) emphasized the importance of the social nature of fantasy play for development. He saw the imaginary situations created in play as zones of proximal development that operate as mental support systems. (We saw such a support system in Chapter 5, p. 211, where a father supports his infant daughter's attempts to grasp a teething ring before she is able to pick it up on her own.) According to this interpretation, the "as if" nature of social play and the active collusion of others allow children to perform actions that are developmentally more advanced than those they can perform on their own. Thus Jake can "pour tea" in a make-believe game with his cousin in which the demands for precision are far more lenient than they would be if he were to try to pour himself a glass of milk at the breakfast table.

As Vygotsky's approach would predict, the level of sophistication of infants' social play depends on the social context in which it occurs. Barbara Fiese (1990) found that children's play lasted longer and was more sophisticated when they played with their mothers than when they played by themselves. Other researchers found that mothers modeled possible pretend play topics—pretending, for example, to talk on a toy phone and then offering the toy phone to the child while encouraging the child to do the same thing. They also adjusted the level of their play to that of their children, maximizing its attractiveness (Tamis-LeMonda & Bornstein, 1994).

Toddlers' play is often more advanced with older siblings with whom they play frequently than it is when they play with their mothers, because the siblings are better able to enter into the fantasy than the adults (Farver & Wimbarti, 1995; Zukow-Goldring, 1995).

Despite the popularity of the belief that play facilitates general development, studies explicitly designed to demonstrate beneficial effects of play among infants are generally lacking. Peter Smith (1988), who has been active in this field of research, cautions that the belief that play is "good for babies" goes beyond the existing evidence. His doubts are supported by cross-cultural work indicating that Central American Mayan infants engage in less play in the first 2 years of life than North American infants but equal them in performance on standardized tests of development (Gaskins, 1990).

TABLE 6.2	Four Steps in the Development of Agent Use in Pretending
Type of Agent Use	**Example**
Self as agent	The infant puts his head on a pillow to pretend to go to sleep
Passive other agent	The infant puts a doll on a pillow to pretend that it goes to sleep
Passive substitute agent	The infant puts a block on a pillow to pretend that it goes to sleep
Active other agent	The infant has a doll lie down on the pillow and go to sleep, as if the doll were actually carrying out the action itself

Source: Watson & Fischer, 1980.

IMITATION

As we saw in Chapter 4 (Box 4.4, pp. 162–163), some psychologists claim that a rudimentary form of imitation is present at birth and that by 9 months of age infants are capable of **deferred imitation:** the ability to imitate something they saw

Deferred imitation In Piagetian terms, the imitation of actions that have occurred at an earlier time.

or heard many hours earlier. These claims are of special interest because for many years psychologists believed that (1) babies are incapable of deferred imitation until late in the second year of life and (2) when they do imitate something they saw or heard earlier, they are demonstrating the ability to represent events to themselves symbolically (Kaye, 1982; Maccoby & Martin, 1983; Piaget, 1962).

The following example, taken from Piaget's work (1962), illustrates both deferred imitation and the importance Piaget attributed to it as evidence that children are beginning to think in a new, more representational way. Jacqueline, now 16 months old, was astonished by the temper tantrum of an 18-month-old boy.

> He screamed as he tried to get out of his playpen and pushed it backwards, stamping his feet. J. stood watching him in amazement, never having witnessed such a scene before. The next day, she herself screamed in her playpen and tried to move it, stamping her foot lightly several times in succession. The imitation of the whole scene was most striking. Had it been immediate, [the imitation] would naturally not have involved representation, but coming as it did after an interval of more than twelve hours, it must have involved some representative or pre-representative element. (p. 63)

A key part of Piaget's argument for the significance of deferred imitation was that it seemed to him to appear during the same period when symbolic play begins. He believed that the two processes are related and that they signal the same underlying change in cognitive capacities, constituting, in effect, two sides of the same developmental coin.

Recall that in Piaget's framework, development results from the constant interplay between the assimilation of the environment into preexisting patterns of action (called schemas) and the accommodation of existing schemas to aspects of the environment. Piaget believed that imitation is closely linked to accommodation because it fits behavior to what is "out there" rather than molding the world to already existing, internal schemas, as play does.

Imitation may well represent a cognitive process in which accommodation plays the leading role, as Piaget believed. We have seen, however, that research by Jean Mandler (1990) and Andrew Meltzoff (1990) designed to demonstrate the origins of recall late in the first year of life (Chapter 5, p. 209) seems to contradict Piaget's claims that deferred imitation emerges only as infants approach their second birthday. Meltzoff's data indicate that deferred imitation of other people's actions on objects makes its first appearance late in the first year of life in conjunction with the ability to recall earlier experiences. While the capacity for deferred imitation may have existed before the second year, it now manifests itself in a far greater range of contexts.

THE GROWTH OF THE ABILITY TO CATEGORIZE

The abilities to engage in symbolic play and to imitate other people's actions provide circumstantial evidence that children in the middle of their second year are capable of the psychological process called mental representation. Little is known about the content or form of these mental representations, however, for they cannot be observed directly. The challenge for psychologists is to make good use of the clues provided by children's behavior to gain insight into the content and structure of these hidden processes.

As we saw in Chapter 5 (p. 207), when an experimenter presents babies with stimuli that are arranged according to adult categories, even very young babies can detect similarities between objects and categorize them on the basis of their *perceptual* features (Quinn, Eimas, & Rosenkratz, 1993). Using this same procedure, other investigators have found that around the time of their first birthdays, babies begin to categorize objects on the basis of their *conceptual* features as well (Mandler & McDonough, 1993). It is not until late in the second year of life, however, that children are able by themselves to *create* categories from a jumbled array of objects.

The growth of this capacity to generate categories was clearly demonstrated by Susan Sugarman (1983). She presented 12- to 30-month-old babies with a haphazard array of eight objects that could be classified and subclassified in various ways. (Figure 6.6 shows one such set of objects, composed of blue and red boats and blue and red dolls.) While sitting on their mother's lap, the toddlers were urged to "fix up" the random array of objects, to determine if they would create the same categories as adults. If this suggestion failed to produce results, Sugarman showed them ways to group the objects and then urged them to group the objects themselves. She noted four stages in the progression of categorizing behavior:

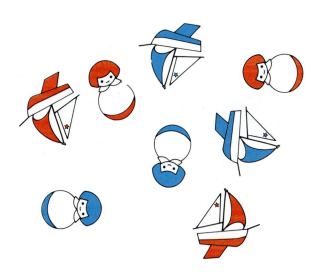

FIGURE 6.6 *The ability to categorize boats of one color and dolls of another and to subcategorize them according to color and form emerges slowly during late infancy. (From Sugarman, 1983.)*

1. One-year-olds would pick up one of the toys, look it over, and then touch it to the other toys one at a time. The only indication that they noticed the similarities between individual objects was that they were most likely to touch the toy they picked up to other toys that had the same shape.

2. The 18-month-olds would create a little work space in front of them and put two or three objects of the same kind in it.

3. The 24-month-old toddlers divided the objects into two distinct categories, working on one category at a time. For example, they would select all the boats first and then all the dolls. If Sugarman offered a boat to children of this age who were collecting dolls, they immediately set the boat aside and kept working on the dolls.

4. The 30-month-old children simultaneously coordinated their work on the two major categories and created subcategories in which the objects were grouped according to color as well. They began by making a work space in front of them and then created two categories within it. They filled the categories by picking up whatever toy was nearest at hand and adding it to the appropriate group. If these children were handed a doll right after they had placed a boat in its group, they put it with the other dolls.

It appears, then, that one of the key cognitive changes associated with the end of infancy is the ability to go beyond the mere *recognition* of conceptual relationships to make *active use* of these relationships. Children can now construct categories according to conceptual differences and correspondences in a flexible and systematic way.

THE APPEARANCE OF THE ABILITY TO USE MODELS

Another indication of a fundamental shift in children's thought processes at the end of infancy is highlighted in research by Judy De Loache (1987, 1995), who has made an extensive study of infants' ability to use models to guide their actions. De Loache asked 2½- and 3-year-olds to watch while she hid an attractive toy within a scale model of the room they were in. Then the children were asked to find an analogous toy that had been hidden in the corresponding place in the room itself. The 2½-year-olds could not use the model as a guide and were confused by the task; the 3-year-olds completed it rather easily (Figure 6.7).

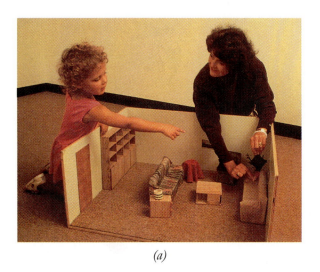

(a)

(b)

FIGURE 6.7 *The ability to guide one's behavior using a model emerges at the end of infancy. (a) The experimenter (Judy De Loache) hides a small toy troll in a scale model as a 3-year-old watches. (b) The child retrieves a larger toy troll that was hidden in the corresponding place in the room. (c) The child retrieves the small toy that she originally observed being hidden in the model.*

(c)

De Loache suspected that the younger children found this task difficult because they could not think of the scale model both as a symbol and as the thing itself. In a follow-up study, she and her colleagues arranged to convince half of a group of 2½-year-olds that it is possible (with a special machine) to shrink an actual tent into a small model replica or to expand the model into the real tent (De Loache, 1995). When the children believed that the model and tent were the same thing made large or small by the machine, they successfully used the model to find objects in the tent. But the children who were told that the model was a toy version of the tent could not use information about an object's location in one to help them locate a corresponding object in the other. De Loache believes that the key difficulty facing the 2½-year-olds is that they cannot keep in mind the dual nature of the model: it is both an interesting object in and of itself *and* it stands for the thing it models. When they interpret the model as a shrunken version of the original, it does not function for them psychologically as a symbol, so the complicating aspect of the task has been removed. Three-year-olds are able to see the model as both a symbol and an object, so they effectively use the model to find objects in the normal-size space and do not have to have the problem simplified for them.

THE CHANGING RELATIONS BETWEEN WORDS AND THOUGHTS

Longitudinal studies indicate a steady increase during the second year of life in the words and phrases that infants can understand and put to proper use (Fenson et al., 1994; McCall, Eichorn, & Hogarty, 1977). They can also label pictures of common animals and objects. By 21 months of age, toddlers are able to follow relatively complex verbal instructions. When told to "put the block under the doll's chair," for example, they can place the block in the correct location in relation to the chair. Their ability to create multiword sentences also increases, making possible the expression of more complex ideas.

The use of words that stand for people, objects, and events is sufficient by itself to show that children are beginning to engage in mental representation. But what especially intrigues developmental psychologists are the connections between children's use of representational words and the development of the other forms of mental representation discussed in this chapter—logical search for hidden objects, symbolic play, deferred imitation, and the ability to form categories (Bloom, Lifter, & Broughton, 1985; Bretherton & Bates, 1985; Gopnik & Meltzoff, 1987; McCall, Eichorn, & Hogarty, 1977; Piaget, 1962).

The link between deferred imitation and word acquisition is perhaps the most obvious; to a great extent, children's early use of words is closely tied to words they have heard adults speak. "More," for example, was one of the first words used by our daughter Jenny. Earlier, whenever she finished drinking a cup of milk or juice, Jenny would bang the empty cup on the tray of her highchair. We would then ask her, "Do you want some more?" Shortly before her first birthday, she began to hold up her cup and say "More" before anyone asked her if that was what she wanted.

Likewise, there is a clear association between language and symbolic play, both of which involve the representation of absent persons, objects, or actions. In symbolic play, arbitrary objects are used to stand for other objects—a banana is treated as a telephone, for example, or a sandbox railing becomes a highway; in language, arbitrary *sounds* are the substitutes. In the earliest stages, children's fantasy play is restricted to single actions and their utterances are restricted to single words. But at about 18 months of age they begin to combine two actions in play and to use two-word sentences (Bretherton & Bates, 1985; McCune-Nicolich & Bruskin, 1982). So, for example, about the same time that children begin to say "All-gone milk," they also begin to pretend that they are pouring water into a cup *and* helping a baby drink it.

Karen Lifter and Lois Bloom (1989) demonstrated close relationships between the early acquisition of vocabulary and the sophistication with which infants search for hidden objects and play with objects. They found that children's first words appeared at the same time that they first began to search for hidden objects, and that they underwent a spurt in the rate of acquiring new words at approximately the same time that they began to demonstrate logical search patterns. The same sort of linkages appeared when Lifter and Bloom looked at the sophistication of play; children who had not begun to talk moved toys around but did not combine them to construct new objects. Such combinatory play appeared with children's first words, and more complex constructions appeared in conjunction with a spurt in vocabulary.

Alison Gopnik and Andrew Meltzoff (1987) also found that the ability to classify objects into two groups, sophisticated behaviors in searching for objects, insightful problem solving, and a vocabulary spurt occur at approximately the same age. They report, however, that there is no precise ordering of achievements in the various cognitive tasks and vocabulary developments. Consequently, it is not possible to say that one of these achievements, or some other factor such as brain maturation, is the cause of this ensemble of changes; rather, they all make important contributions to the bio-social-behavioral shift that marks the end of infancy.

The Development of Child-Caregiver Relations

During the second year of life, children find novelty and excitement everywhere. A walk to the corner drugstore with a 1½-year-old can take forever. Each step presents new and interesting sights to explore: a bottle cap lying by the edge of the sidewalk requires close examination; a pigeon waddling across a neighbor's lawn invites a detour; even the cracks in the sidewalk may prompt sitting down to take a closer look.

As we saw in Chapter 5, however, things that attract babies may also cause them to be wary. To toddlers, whizzing cars, strange people, and novel objects are often frightening as well as fascinating. Both interest and fear must be kept in bounds as infants continue to explore and learn about the world. They cannot spend their entire lives in close proximity to their parents, but they cannot survive for long if they wander off on their own too soon. Research with both monkey and human mothers and babies is starting to show us how the balance between exploration and safety is created and maintained in ways that allow development to continue. A key element in this balance is the emotional bond that develops between children and their caregivers sometime between the ages of 7 and 9 months, which we briefly described at the end of Chapter 5 (p. 213). Explaining how this attachment comes about has proved to be a major challenge to developmental psychologists.

EXPLANATIONS OF ATTACHMENT

The fact that 7- to 9-month-old children everywhere begin to become upset when they are separated from their primary caregivers suggests that attachment is a universal feature of development (Grossmann & Grossmann, 1990). This possibility has led to a lively debate about the evolutionary reasons for attachment, the causes of changes in attachment as children grow older, and the influence of the quality of attachment on children's later development. Three major explanations of the basis of attachment have dominated this debate: Sigmund Freud's suggestion that infants become attached to the people who satisfy their need for food; Erik Erikson's idea that infants become attached to those they can trust to help them; and John Bowlby's somewhat similar hypothesis that infants become attached to those who provide them with a firm foundation for exploring the world.

Sigmund Freud's drive-reduction explanation

The process of attachment plays an important role in Sigmund Freud's theory of development. Freud held that the early interactions between children and their social environment, particularly the people who care for them, set the pattern for later personality and social development. He believed that human beings, like other organisms, are motivated in large part by **biological drives**—states of arousal, such as hunger or thirst, that urge the organism to obtain the basic prerequisites for its survival. When a drive is aroused, the organism seeks to satisfy the need that gives rise to it. Pleasure is felt as the drive is reduced, the need is satisfied, and the organism returns to a more comfortable biological equilibrium. In this sense, then, pleasure-seeking is a basic principle of existence.

Freud (1933/1964) identified the mouth as the primary locus of pleasure during the first year of life, which he dubbed the oral stage of development (Table 1.1 provides a complete list and timetable of Freud's and Erikson's stages). During this

Biological drives Aroused states, such as hunger and thirst, that urge the organism to obtain the basic requirements for survival.

stage, children become attached to the objects or persons that satisfy their hunger (Freud, 1940/1964). The first person infants become attached to is usually the mother, who is most likely to nourish them; "love has its origin in attachment to the satisfied need for nourishment" (p. 188). Freud believed that attachment to the mother is central to the formation of children's personalities as they progress through later stages of development. In adulthood, the relationship with the mother becomes "the prototype for all . . . love relations for both sexes" (p. 188).

According to Freud (1933/1964), the locus of children's pleasure-seeking shifts from the mouth to the anus during the second year after birth. In contrast to oral pleasures, which he characterized as receptive and dependent, Freud considered anal satisfaction to be basically expulsive and to reflect a drive for self-control and independence.

Freud's theory of early human attachment has not fared well. One major problem is that research has not substantiated his notion that attachment is caused by the reduction of the hunger drive, as we will soon see. Furthermore, his theory seems to imply that children should begin to act more independently once they enter the anal stage. Thus it fails to explain why children are increasingly likely to become distressed when they are separated from their mothers until well into the second year of life.

Erik Erikson's psychosocial explanation

A more promising explanation of attachment than Freud's, though still within the Freudian tradition, was proposed by Erik Erikson, one of Freud's most influential students. Erikson (1963), whose theory of development will figure in many discussions throughout the remainder of this book, believes that there are eight stages in the human life cycle, each characterized by a distinctive conflict that the individual must resolve. Through the resolution of the conflict at each stage of development, people acquire new skills, such as the ability to act independently of their parents and to do productive work, which open up new opportunities for them. These new opportunities, in turn, increase the demands made on them by society and create new conflicts. Individuals who do not resolve the conflict at each stage satisfactorily will continue to struggle with that conflict later in life.

The conflicts characteristic of the first two stages that Erikson proposes provide an explanation for the increase in children's anxiety when they are separated from their mothers late in the first year of life and its decline during the second year. According to Erikson's scheme, during the first stage of development, which lasts from birth to roughly 1 year of age, babies must develop a favorable balance between trust and mistrust: Will my mother come when I call? Can I trust her to take care of me? In Erikson's view, children become attached to the people who reliably minister to their needs and who foster a sense of trust. Once babies gain faith in their caregivers, usually during the second year, they enter the second stage and their need for autonomy increases; they cease to be distressed during brief separations because they understand that their caregiver will come back.

John Bowlby's ethological explanation

In the aftermath of the terrible destruction and loss of life of World War II, many public agencies became deeply concerned about the consequences of an early childhood deprived of normal maternal care. In 1950 the World Health Organization asked John Bowlby, a British psychiatrist, to undertake a

Many small children become strongly attached to a teddy bear, a blanket, or some other object. The British psychiatrist D. W. Winnicott (1971) has called such objects "transitional objects." They are the first objects that children perceive to be their very own. They support children in their attempts to understand and deal with the reality that exists beyond their own bodies. The strong attachment this little girl feels for her teddy bear is written all over the girl's smiling embrace.

study of the mental health problems of children who had been separated from their families and were cared for in institutions (Bowlby, 1969, 1973, 1980).

Bowlby reviewed observations of children in hospitals, nurseries, and orphanages who had either lost their parents or been separated from them for long periods of time. He also looked at reports of clinical interviews with psychologically troubled or delinquent adolescents and adults. He found a similar sequence of behaviors described in these various sources. When children are first separated from their mothers, they become frantic with fear. They cry, throw tantrums, and try to escape their surroundings. Then they go through a stage of despair and depression. If the separation continues and no new stable relationship is formed, these children seem to become indifferent to other people. Bowlby called this state of indifference *disattachment*.

In his attempt to explain the distress of young children when they are separated from their parents, Bowlby adopted a broad evolutionary perspective. His theory incorporated what was then known about mother-infant interactions among large, ground-living apes who defend themselves against predators by banding together with others of their species. Infancy among such primates lasts a long time. Because the growing infants are relatively helpless and vulnerable, they must remain close to their mothers if they are to survive. Counteracting this need for safety through proximity is the infants' urge to explore and play, activities that take them away from their mothers.

Bowlby hypothesized that some mechanism must exist to provide a balance between infants' need for safety and their need for varied learning experiences. He termed this mechanism *attachment* and hypothesized that once achieved, it works somewhat like a furnace's thermostat. In a thermostat, a switch is thrown to turn on the furnace whenever the temperature falls below a preset minimum. When the heat rises sufficiently, the switch is thrown again to turn the furnace off. As a result, temperature is maintained within comfortable limits.

Bowlby (1969) believed that attachment normally develops through four broad phases during the first two years of life, eventually producing a "dynamic equilibrium between the mother-child pair" (p. 236).

1. *The preattachment phase* (birth to 6 weeks). In the first few weeks of life, while infants and caregivers are working out the initial systems of coordination (see Chapter 4, pp. 148–153), infants remain in close contact with their caregivers, from whom they receive food and comfort. They do not seem to realize or to get upset when left alone with an unfamiliar caregiver.

2. *The "attachment-in-the-making" phase* (6 weeks to 6–8 months). Infants begin to respond differently to familiar and unfamiliar people, and start to show signs of wariness when confronted with unfamiliar objects and people (as discussed in Chapter 5, pp. 210–213).

3. *The "clear-cut attachment" phase* (6–8 months to 18–24 months) is the period during which children display full-blown **separation anxiety,** becoming visibly upset when their mother or other caregiver leaves the room. Once this phase of attachment is reached, it regulates the physical and emotional relationship between children and the objects of attachment. Whenever the distance between mother and child becomes too great, one or the other is likely to become upset and act to reduce that distance, for just as babies become upset if their mothers leave them, mothers become upset if their babies wander out of sight. Attachment provides the child with a feeling of security. The mother becomes a **secure base** from which babies can make exploratory excursions and to which they come back every so often to renew contact before returning to their explorations. During the early months of the attachment phase, the mother bears the greater responsibility for maintaining the equilibrium of the attachment system, because the infant's capacities to act and interact are quite restricted.

Separation anxiety The distress babies show when their mother leaves the room.

Secure base Bowlby's term for the security provided by the persons to whom a child is attached. A secure base helps to regulate the baby's explorations of the world.

4. *The phase of reciprocal relationships* (18–24 months and later). As the child becomes more mobile and spends increasing time away from the mother, the pair enter a reciprocal state in which they share responsibility for maintaining the equilibrium of the system. Among humans, this transitional phase lasts several years.

Once achieved, a firm, reciprocal emotional relationship between infants and caregivers helps children to retain feelings of security during the increasingly frequent periods of separation from their caregivers. It is interesting that this phase should coincide with the period in which mental representation becomes a dominant element in children's thought processes. According to Bowlby, the parent-child attachment relation now serves as an **internal working model** that children use as a standard to guide their interactions not only with caretakers but with other people as well.

> **Internal working model** A mental model that infants build as a result of their experience with their caregivers that they use to guide their behavior in other relationships.

Evidence from animal models

Ethical considerations make it difficult, if not impossible, to conduct experiments to determine the sources of human attachment. Therefore, scientists have taken to studying our near evolutionary kin, monkeys, whose behavior furnishes researchers with an animal model that appears to be somewhat analogous to our own.

Throughout the first half of the twentieth century, most American scholars who studied learning believed that animals learn in order to satisfy the needs basic to their and their species' survival—food, drink, freedom from pain, procreation. This drive-reduction theory is similar to Freud's explanation of why babies become attached to their mothers (Miller & Dollard, 1941).

To test the drive-reduction theory of attachment, Harry Harlow and his co-workers (Harlow & Harlow, 1969) carried out an extensive series of studies with rhesus monkeys. In one of these studies, the researchers separated eight baby monkeys from their mothers 12 hours or less after birth and placed them in individual cages with two inanimate surrogate mothers—one made of wire, the other of terry cloth (see Figure 6.8). Four of the infant monkeys received milk from the wire mothers, four from the terry-cloth mothers. The two types of surrogate mothers were equally effective as sources of nutrition, and all eight babies drank the same amount and gained weight at the same rate. Only the feel of the surrogate mothers differed.

Over the 165-day period when they lived with surrogate mothers, the baby monkeys showed a distinct preference for the cloth mothers. Even if they obtained all of their food from a wire mother, the babies would go to it only to feed and would then go back to cling to the terry-cloth mother. From the perspective of drive-reduction theory, it made no sense at all for the four infant monkeys who received their food from a wire mother to prefer to spend their time with a terry-cloth mother that might feel good but satisfied no apparent biological drive, such as hunger or thirst. Harlow concluded, "These results attest the importance—possibly the overwhelming importance—of bodily contact and the immediate comfort it supplies in forming the infant's attachment for its mother" (Harlow, 1959, p. 70).

In later investigations, Harlow and his colleagues (Harlow & Harlow, 1969) sought to determine whether attachment to their surrogate mothers had any effect on the infants' explorations, a crucial test of Bowlby's evolutionary theory. Knowing that normal human and monkey babies run to their mothers for comfort when faced with a strange situation, the researchers created such a situation for the monkeys who had received milk from the wire surrogate mothers. They placed in their cages a mechanical teddy bear that marched forward while beating a drum.

FIGURE 6.8 *This baby monkey spent most of its time clinging to the terry-cloth surrogate mother even when its nursing bottle was attached to a wire surrogate mother nearby. This preference indicates that bodily contact and the comfort it gives are important in the formation of the infant's attachment to its mother.*

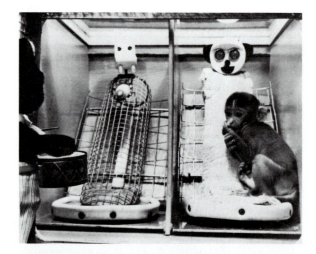

The terrified babies fled to the terry-cloth mothers, not to the wire ones (see Figure 6.9). Once the babies had overcome their fear by rubbing their bodies against the cloth mother, however, they turned to look at the bear with curiosity. Some even left the protection of the terry-cloth mother to approach the object that had so terrified them only moments before.

The infant monkeys demonstrated their attachment to the terry-cloth mothers after separations of up to a year. The researchers would place the monkeys in an apparatus in which pressure on a lever allowed them to look at the terry-cloth mother, the wire mother, or an empty box. The monkeys who had been raised with a wire mother that provided milk and a terry-cloth mother that did not spent more time pressing the lever to get a glimpse of the terry-cloth mother than the lever to see the wire mother. They were no more interested in the wire mother than in the empty box. Even monkeys who had been raised with only a wire mother showed no signs of attachment when they were given a chance to view it (Harlow & Zimmerman, 1959).

The studies of Harlow and his colleagues undermine the hypothesis that attachment is caused by drive reduction and that infants should become attached to the people who feed them. The idea that receives the most support is that soothing tactile sensations provide the baby with a sense of security that is more important than food to the formation of attachment.

Although soothing tactile sensations appear to be necessary for healthy development, they are not sufficient. As these monkeys grew older, the researchers found that they were either indifferent or abusive to other monkeys. None of them could copulate normally. The researchers concluded that

> the nourishment and contact comfort provided by the nursing cloth covered mother in infancy does not produce a normal adolescent or adult. The surrogate cannot cradle the baby or communicate monkey sounds and gestures. It cannot punish for misbehavior or attempt to break the infant's bodily attachment before it becomes a fixation. (Harlow & Harlow, 1962, p. 142)

The later social behavior of these monkeys supports Bowlby's belief that attachment is a highly evolved system of regulation between the mother and the infant. Such regulation is a two-sided process that requires social interaction for healthy emotional development. The infant monkeys clearly turned to the terry-cloth mothers for security, but in the absence of a live mother, all of the adjusting was left to the baby, and a proper regulatory system did not form.

FIGURE 6.9 Top: *This baby monkey clings to its terry-cloth surrogate mother and hides its eyes when it is frightened by the approach of a mechanical teddy bear.* Bottom: *After gaining reassurance, the baby monkey looks at the strange intruder. The fact that the terry-cloth mother, which does not provide nourishment, acts as a secure base rather than the wire mother, which does provide nourishment, contradicts drive-reduction theories of attachment.*

PATTERNS OF ATTACHMENT

The maladaptive social behavior of monkeys raised with inanimate surrogate mothers poses a pointed question: What kinds of interactions between mother and child provide the most effective basis for the development of healthy human social relations?

Because no two mother-infant pairs are alike and because the environmental conditions into which human babies are born vary enormously, we should not expect to find one "right" pattern of attachment that meets the basic requirements for social development in all cultures (Hinde, 1982). Many investigators believe, however, that it is possible to identify general patterns of mother-child interaction that are most conducive to development.

Research on the patterns of mother-child interaction has been greatly influenced by the work of Mary Ainsworth. On the basis of observations of mother-infant pairs in Africa and the United States, Ainsworth (1967, 1982) reports that there are consistent, qualitatively distinct patterns in the ways mothers and infants relate to each other during the second and third years of infancy. Most of the mother-infant pairs she observed seemed to have worked out a comfortable, secure relationship by the third year, but some of the relationships were characterized by persistent tension and difficulties in regulating joint activities.

Ainsworth designed a procedure called the **strange situation** as a means of testing the security of the mother-child relationship. The basic purpose of the procedure is to observe how babies respond to a stranger when they are with their mothers, when they are left alone, and when they are reunited with their mothers. Different patterns of reactions, she reasoned, would reflect different kinds of relationships. The following case study, summarized from research reported by Mary Ainsworth and Barbara Wittig (1969, p.116–118), illustrates the strange-situation procedure and how a typical 12-month-old middle-class North American child behaved in it.

Strange situation A procedure designed to assess children's attachment on the basis of their responses to a stranger when they are with their mother, when they are left alone, and when they are reunited with their mother.

An observer shows a mother and her baby into an experimental room that has toys scattered on the floor. "Brian had one arm hooked over his mother's shoulder as they came into the room. . . . He looked around soberly, but with interest, at the toys and at the observer."

The observer leaves the room. "After being put down, Brian immediately crept towards the toys and began to explore them [Figure 6.10*a*]. He was very active. . . . Although his attention was fixed on the playthings, he glanced up at his mother six times."

After three minutes the stranger enters, greets the mother, and sits down quietly in a chair. Brian "turned to look at the stranger . . . with a pleasant expression on his face. He played with the tube again, vocalized, smiled, and turned to glance at his mother. . . . When the stranger and his mother began to converse, he continued to explore actively. . . . When the stranger began her approach by leaning forward to offer him a toy, he smiled, crept towards her, and reached for it" [Figure 6.10*b*].

The mother leaves the room, leaving her purse on the chair, while the stranger distracts Brian's attention. "He did not notice his mother leave. He continued to watch the stranger and the toys. . . . Suddenly, he crept to his mother's chair, pulled himself up into a standing position, and looked at the stranger. She tried to distract him with a pull-toy . . . but he glanced again at his mother's empty chair. He was less active than he had been when alone with his mother, and after two minutes his activity ceased. He sat chewing the string of the pull-toy and glancing from the stranger to his mother's chair. He made an unhappy noise, then a cry-face, and then he cried. The stranger tried to distract him by offering him a block; he took it but then threw it away."

"When his mother opened the door . . . Brian looked at her immediately and vocalized loudly . . . then *he* crept to her quickly [italics added], and pulled himself up, with her help, to hold on to her knees. Then she picked him up, and he immediately put his arms around her neck, his face against her shoulder, and hugged her hard [Figure 6.10*c*]. . . . He resisted being

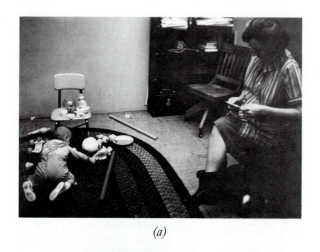

(a)

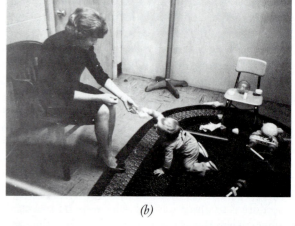

(b)

(c)

(d)

FIGURE 6.10 *Brian in the strange situation.*
(a) *Brian explores the toys.* (b) *Brian responds to the
stranger.* (c) *Brian hugs his mother when she returns to
the room after a brief absence.* (d) *Brian throws himself
on the floor when his mother puts him down.* (e) *Brian
cries and rocks back and forth when he is left alone again.*

(e)

put down; he tried to cling to her and protested loudly. Once on the floor,
he threw himself down, hid his face in the rug, and cried angrily [Figure
6.10*d*]. His mother knelt beside him and tried to interest him in the toys
again. He stopped crying and watched. After a moment she disengaged herself and got up to sit on her chair. He immediately threw himself down and
cried again."

Brian's mother gets up and leaves the room again. "As she said 'bye-bye'
and waved, Brian looked up with a little smile, but he shifted into a cry before she had quite closed the door. He sat crying, rocking himself back and
forth" [Figure 6.10*e*].

The stranger, who has earlier left the room, reenters. "Brian lulled slightly when he saw the stranger enter, but he continued to cry. She first tried to distract him, then offered her arms to him. Brian responded by raising his arms; she picked him up, and he stopped crying immediately. . . . Occasionally he gave a little sob, but for the most part he did not cry. But when she put him down, he screamed. She picked him up again, and he lulled.

"At the moment that his mother returned Brian was crying listlessly. He did not notice his mother. The stranger half-turned and pointed her out. Brian looked towards her, still crying, and then turned away. But he soon 'did a double take.' He looked back and vocalized a little protest. His mother offered her arms to him. He reached towards her, smiling, and leaned way out of the stranger's arms and his mother took him."

To permit systematic comparisons between children, Ainsworth and her colleagues worked out a method of categorizing infants' responses in the "strange situation" (Ainsworth, Bell, & Stayton, 1971; Ainsworth et al., 1978). The categories are based on the child's behaviors when the child and mother are alone in the playroom together, when the mother leaves the room, when a strange woman offers comfort, and when the mother returns. The researchers found that the way the child reacts to the return of the mother is the key element and that the responses fall into three categories:

Anxious/avoidant: During the time the mother and child are left alone together in the playroom, anxious/avoidant infants are more or less indifferent to where their mothers are sitting. They may or may not cry when their mothers leave the room. If they do become distressed, strangers are likely to be as effective at comforting them as their mothers. When the mother returns, these children may turn or look away from her instead of going to her to seek closeness and comfort. About 23 percent of U.S. middle-class children show this pattern of attachment.

Securely attached: As long as the mother is present, the securely attached child plays comfortably with the toys in the playroom and reacts positively to the stranger. These children become visibly and vocally upset when their mothers leave, and they are unlikely to be consoled by a stranger. When the mother reappears and they can climb into her arms, however, they quickly calm down and soon resume playing. This pattern of attachment is shown by about 65 percent of U.S. middle-class children.

Anxious/resistant: Anxious/resistant children have trouble from the start in the strange situation. They stay close to their mothers and appear anxious even when their mothers are near. They become very upset when the mother leaves, but they are not comforted by her return. Instead, they simultaneously seek renewed contact with their mother and resist her efforts to comfort them. They may cry angrily to be picked up with their arms outstretched, but they will struggle to climb down once they are in their mother's arms. These children do not readily resume playing after their mother returns. Instead, they keep a wary eye on her. About 12 percent of U.S. middle-class children show this pattern of attachment.

The joy of this mother and child at being reunited captures the special emotional feeling of attachment.

BOX 6.1

Attachment to Fathers and Others

Discussions of infant development tend to focus almost entirely on the role of mothers; other people with whom babies interact have been largely ignored. There are legitimate reasons for this one-sided treatment of babies' social environment.

Perhaps the most legitimate reason for focusing on the mother's role is that with few exceptions, the mother spends far more time with her infant than any other adult, not only in technologically advanced industrial societies but in most of the world's societies (Lamb, 1987). Michael Lamb and his colleagues (1987), working in the United States, reported that in two-parent families in which the mothers do not work outside the home, fathers spend only 25 to 30 percent as much time in one-to-one interaction with their infants as mothers do. Even when these fathers are with their children, they assume little or no responsibility for their day-to-day care or rearing.

This state of affairs results not from indifference or lack of ability but from the roles mothers and fathers assume in family life in the United States and in most other cultures. When fathers have been observed feeding their infants, for example, they respond as sensitively as do mothers to their babies' feeding rhythms and engage their babies in social episodes just as often (Parke & Tinsley, 1981). Moreover, the infants of fathers who are judged to be sensitive caretakers are likely to be as securely attached to them as to their mothers (Cox et al., 1992). But fathers are far more likely to play with their infants than to care for them. The vast majority of exchanges between fathers and their babies in the United States are brief play episodes that come at a specific period of the day (Lamb, 1987;

Children also form a strong attachment to their fathers, which provides them with an additional secure base for their continued development.

Roopnarine et al., 1990). Set aside as they are, these periods are likely to be memorable.

Given the differences between fathers and mothers in both the quantity and the quality of their interactions with their infants, psychologists have naturally been interested to learn if and how infants form attachments to their fathers. Although some early research indicated that attachment occurs earlier to mothers than to fathers (Kotelchuk, 1976), a large majority of the studies conducted in recent years find that children become attached to both parents at approximately the same time (Isabella, 1993; Pipp et al., 1993).

Anxious/avoidant and anxious/resistant children are sometimes labeled *insecurely attached* or simply *anxious.*

Accumulated experience has shown that the basic behaviors described by Ainsworth and her colleagues occur routinely in the strange situation and can be scored with reasonable reliability. Using this method of classifying modes of attachment, psychologists have spent more than two decades seeking to determine the causes of these patterns of behavior (Ainsworth, 1993; Bretherton, 1985; Isabella, 1993). Most of this research has focused on the mother-infant relationship, although other attachments that are important in children's lives have also been studied (see Box 6.1).

As often happens when a new scientific technique is introduced, research based on the strange situation has raised many new questions about social and emotional development. Two major questions have dominated the study of

Another question that has intrigued researchers is whether or not the attachments infants form to different caregivers are qualitatively the same. In a series of studies, Michael Lamb (1976, 1977a, 1979) observed infants in their homes to determine if they showed a preference for one or the other parent by staying near, approaching, touching, and asking to be held by one parent more than the other. Lamb found that infants displayed no general preference for either parent, but when they became distressed, they were more likely to turn to their mother for comfort.

Several studies have focused on how attachment to one parent affects attachment to the other. If attachment relations depend on infants' history of interactions with particular individuals, as some attachment theorists believe, attachment to one parent ought to be independent of attachment to the other. Yet in an analysis of 11 studies comparing attachment to mothers and fathers in the strange situation, Nathan Fox, Nancy Kimmerly, and William Schafer (1991) found that infants who were securely attached to one parent were also likely to be securely attached to the other.

Fox and his colleagues speculate that one reason for such a linkage is that infants form a **working model,** a mental schema for how to interact with familiar adults in general. Another explanation might be that children's temperaments lead them to interact similarly with their mothers and fathers, so that the emotional bonds are similar in quality.

A study by Frits Goossens and Marinus van IJzendoorn (1990) with a large group of 15-month-old Dutch infants indicates that if formation of a working model underpins attachment to parents, it is not as general as Fox and his colleagues believed. These investigators compared the behaviors displayed toward mothers, fathers, and day-care workers in the strange situation. Like Fox and his colleagues, Goossens and van IJzendoorn found that the attachment behaviors of infants toward mothers and fathers were linked. They found no such linkage, however, between babies' attachment behaviors directed toward their parents and those directed toward day-care workers with whom they spent many hours a day. This result contradicts the idea that the infants have formed a generalized working model of how to interact with familiar adults as well as the idea that their temperaments caused them to act similarly in all unusual circumstances.

Obviously many questions about the attachments that infants form to the significant adults in their lives remain to be answered. But the fact that such attachments exist and play an important role in children's social development is now well established.

Babies also form attachments with peers and siblings (Stewart & Marvin, 1984; Tronick, Winn, & Morelli, 1985). In some societies, such as that of the !Kung Bushmen of the Kalahari Desert, babies are cared for in groups of children of various ages beginning around the age of 1 year, so that their mothers can resume their work (Konner, 1977). Under such circumstances, babies form strong attachments to many older children in the group in addition to adults. In industrialized societies, babies are less upset and more sociable in strange surroundings when an older sibling is present (Dunn, 1984).

patterns of attachment. First, what are the causes of variations in the patterns of attachment? Second, do these variations have important consequences for later development? We will concentrate on the first question here. We address the consequences of different patterns of attachment for later development in Chapter 7.

The causes of variations in patterns of attachment

Research on what leads to variations in patterns of attachment has focused on several likely factors: the behavior of the mother toward the child, the capacities and temperamental disposition of the child, and the child-rearing patterns of the cultural group to which the mother and child belong.

Maternal Behaviors In an early study of the antecedents of attachment, Mary Ainsworth and Silvia Bell (1969) hypothesized that differences in the responsiveness of mothers to their infants' signals would result in different patterns of attachment. They found that the babies of mothers who responded quickly and appropriately to their cries when they were 3 months old and who were sensitive to their needs during feeding were likely to be evaluated as securely attached at 12 months.

Over the past three decades many studies have confirmed Ainsworth and Bell's basic findings. In comparison with mothers of insecurely attached infants, mothers of securely attached infants have been found to be more involved with their infants, more responsive to their signals, more appropriate in their responsiveness, and more positive in their emotional expression. (These findings are summarized in Isabella, 1993.) As might be expected, children raised by extremely insensitive mothers are especially likely to be rated as insecurely attached (Schneider-Rosen et al., 1985; van IJzendoorn et al., 1992).

Characteristics of the Child   Close observation of a mother and child's interactions reveals that interactional synchrony is a joint accomplishment: just as infants need a responsive mother to develop normally, mothers need responsive infants in order to achieve their full potential as caregivers (Campos et al., 1983). To test the idea that infant behaviors contribute to attachment relations, Michael Lewis and Candice Feiring (1989) observed 174 infant-mother pairs at home when the infants were 3 months old. They then evaluated the infants' reactions in a version of the strange situation 9 months later. They found that infants who had been observed to spend more time playing with objects than interacting sociably with their mothers were more likely later to display symptoms of insecure attachment.

Most of the research attempts to document the infant's role in the development of attachment have focused on the effects of the child's temperament. It seems intuitively reasonable, for example, that mothers would find it more difficult to establish interactional synchrony with fearful infants or ones who easily become upset. The data, however, are inconclusive. Some studies have found that newborns who become upset when their feeding is interrupted are likely to be evaluated as insecurely attached at 1 year (Miyake, Chen, & Campos, 1985). Others have found no relationship between temperament and attachment (Bates, Maslin, & Frankel, 1985; Bohlin et al., 1989; Vaughn et al., 1989). At present psychologists are seeking more adequate measures of both temperament and attachment in the hope of being able to clarify possible connections between them (Vaughn et al., 1992).

Cultural Influences   The pattern of attachment between children and their caregivers may also be influenced by the child-rearing practices of their culture. Children who grow up on Israeli kibbutzim (collective farms), for example, are raised communally from an early age. Although they see their parents daily, the adults who look after them are usually not family members. When, at the ages of 11 to 14 months, such communally raised children were placed in the strange situation with either a parent or a caregiver, many of them became very upset; half were classified as anxious/resistant, and only 37 percent appeared to be securely attached (Sagi et al., 1985). As we noted earlier, only about 12 percent of the middle-class U.S. children, most of whom were cared for by their parents, were judged to be anxious/resistant (Ainsworth et al., 1978).

A low percentage of securely attached babies has also been observed among German children. One study (Grossmann et al., 1985) found that 49 percent of the 1-year-olds tested were anxious/avoidant and only 33 percent were securely attached. Having made extensive observations of German home life, the researchers were able to reject the possibility that a large proportion of German parents are insensitive or indifferent to their children. Rather, German parents adhere to a cultural value that calls for the maintenance of a relatively large interpersonal distance and a cultural belief that babies should be weaned from bodily contact as soon as they become mobile. The researchers suggest that among German mothers, "the ideal is an independent, nonclinging infant who

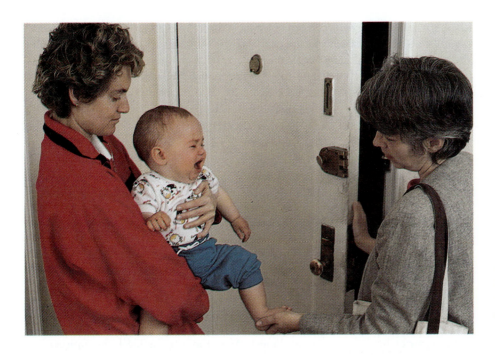

In resisting his mother's attempt to leave him in someone else's arms, this little boy is showing the distress that babies experience at being separated from their mothers.

does not make demands on the parents but rather unquestioningly obeys their commands" (p. 253).

A large proportion of anxious/resistant infants has been found among traditional Japanese families, but no anxious/avoidant infants at all (Miyake, Chen, & Campos, 1985). Kazuo Miyake and his colleagues explain this pattern by pointing out that traditional Japanese mothers rarely leave their children in the care of anyone else, and they behave toward them in ways that foster a strong sense of dependence. Consequently, the experience of being left alone with a stranger is unusual and upsetting to these children. This interpretation is supported by a study of nontraditional Japanese families in which the mothers were pursuing careers, which required them to leave their children in the care of others (Durrett, Otaki, & Richards, 1984). Among the children of these mothers, the distribution of the basic patterns of attachment was similar to that seen in the United States.

There is still no agreement about the significance of the different distributions of attachment patterns that have been found in different cultures. Some researchers believe that they indicate basic and important differences in psychological makeup (Grossmann & Grossmann, 1990). Others believe that cultural differences in the meaning attached to the strange situation make it difficult to infer the true nature of the emotional bonds between the mothers and their children, leading to false conclusions when patterns discovered in one culture are used to reason about another (Takahashi, 1990a, 1990b). Consequently, while current research clearly demonstrates major cultural differences in the ways infants and their caregivers interact in the strange situation, the psychological significance of these differences remains uncertain.

Stability of patterns of attachment

Studies of middle-class children in the United States and Germany have found that their pattern of attachment—whether anxious/avoidant, securely attached, or anxious/resistant—is likely to remain stable for at least several months (Grossmann et al., 1987; Lyons-Ruth et al., 1991; Main & Weston, 1981). Evidence is accumulating, however, that the stability of a pattern of attachment depends on the stability of the child's life circumstances. If the family is going through a difficult period because of unemployment, poverty, illness, or conflict between the adults, there is a good chance that the pattern of attachment displayed by children between the ages of 12 and 18 months will change. Researchers who studied families living below the poverty level found that the pattern of attachment changed for about one-third of the infants (Vaughn et al., 1979). When the level of family stress was high, securely attached infants became less so.

The developmental course of attachment

No single factor seems to account for the various patterns of attachment. The complicated interrelationships among the caregivers' behaviors, the innate characteristics of the children, the cultural context, and the children's life circumstances create many developmental paths. This point is made quite forcefully by Robert Hinde (1982), an eminent British ethologist, in his summary of research on human attachment.

> We must accept that individuals differ and society is complex, and that mothers and babies will be programmed not simply to form one sort of relationship but a range of possible relationships according to circumstances. So we must be concerned not with normal mothers and deviant mothers but with a range of styles and a capacity to select appropriately between them.
>
> At one level of approximation, there are general properties of mothering necessary whatever the circumstances. At a more precise level, the optimal mothering behavior will differ according to the sex of the infant, its ordinal position in the family, the mother's social status, caregiving contributions from other family members, the state of physical resources, and so on. *Natural selection must surely have operated to produce conditional maternal strategies, not stereotypy.* (p. 71; italics in original)

Much the same sort of complexity characterizes the long-term consequences of attachment. We will see when we discuss this hotly debated topic in Chapter 7 that there is conflicting evidence about the significance of the various patterns of attachment for later development.

As we noted, there are marked individual and cultural differences in the precise patterns of behavior that infants display in the various episodes *within* the strange situation. Interpretations of those differences are equally varied and a matter of debate among psychologists. The bottom line, however, is that infants all over the world, in every cultural setting, appear to show great consistency in the age at which they first express distress on being separated from their mothers. As Figure 6.11 indicates, 5-month-old babies do not appear to be distressed when

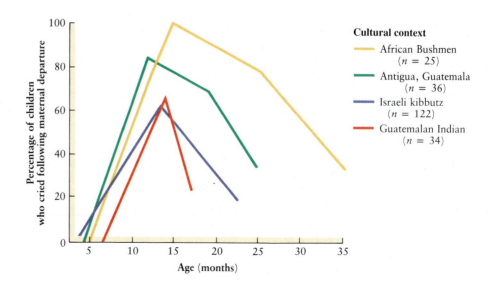

FIGURE 6.11　*The percentage of children of various ages from four cultures who cried after their mothers' departure from the room in the strange situation. (From Kagan, Kearsley, & Zelazo, 1978.)*

Cultural context
— African Bushmen (*n* = 25)
— Antigua, Guatemala (*n* = 36)
— Israeli kibbutz (*n* = 122)
— Guatemalan Indian (*n* = 34)

their mothers leave. It is not until they are about 7 months old that babies begin to show distress. After that age, the proportion of children who are upset when the mother leaves the room increases up to about 15 months and then begins to wane. This changing pattern of distress indicates that as time passes, the attachment relations established earlier in life become integrated in a new psychological system.

A New Sense of Self

By the time they are 6 months old, infants have acquired a great deal of experience interacting with objects and other people and have developed an intuitive sense of themselves as a result (Gibson, 1993). The ability to locomote provides them with still further experience of their separateness and promotes new forms of social relations. Infants at that age begin to learn that they can share experiences and compare reactions, especially through their emerging use of language (Trevarthen, 1993). As infancy comes to an end, around 24 months of age, the process of developing a distinctive sense of self undergoes yet another transformation, one that is recognized by parents the world over.

On the South Pacific island of Fiji, parents say that children gain *vakayalo*, sense, around their second birthday; they can be held responsible for their actions because they are supposed to be able to tell right from wrong. The Utku of the Hudson Bay area say that the 2-year-old has gained *ihuma*, reason. Parents in the United States focus instead on their infants' newly acquired independence and the dwindling of their own control over them, labeling the change as the onset of the "terrible twos."

However parents describe it, the distinctive pattern of behavior that tells people in many cultures that children have entered a new stage of development seems to comprise several interconnected elements: the ability to recognize physical features unique to oneself, a growing sensitivity to adults' standards of what is good and bad, a new awareness of their own ability to live up to those standards, an ability to create plans of their own that they then judge against adult standards, and a strong desire to see that their plans are not thwarted by adults (Kagan, 1981; Stern, 1985). As a result of all of these elements taken together, children begin to experience new emotions appropriate to their more active and complicated participation in the events of everyday life (Lewis, 1993). Their increasing competence provides the basis for the sense of autonomy that Erikson (1963) says characterizes this time of life.

SELF-RECOGNITION

Consciousness of self is among the major characteristics said to distinguish human beings from other species and 2-year-olds from younger children. This is an interesting idea, but finding a way to demonstrate it convincingly has been a problem.

In 1970 Gordon Gallup reported an ingenious series of mirror experiments with chimpanzees that has since been repeated with children. Gallup showed adolescent wild-born chimpanzees their images in a full-length mirror. At first the chimps acted as if another animal were in the room: they threatened, vocalized, and made conciliatory gestures to the "intruder." After a few days, however, they began to use the mirror to explore themselves; for example, they picked bits of food from their faces, which they could see only in the mirror.

To make certain of the meaning of these reactions, Gallup anesthetized several chimps and painted a bright, odorless dye above one eye and on the ear on the opposite side of the head. When they woke up and looked in the mirror, the chimps immediately began to explore the marked spots with their hands. Gallup concluded that they had learned to recognize themselves in the mirror.

Children's ability to recognize themselves in a mirror attests to the emergence of a new sense of self at the end of infancy.

This kind of self-recognition is by no means universal among monkey species. Gallup gave a wild-born macaque monkey over 2400 hours of exposure to a mirror over more than 5 months, but it never showed any sign of self-recognition. The problem was not simply dealing with the mirror image; the monkey quickly learned to use the mirror to find food that was out of sight. The monkey simply could not recognize itself.

Gallup's procedure has been used with human infants between the ages of 3 and 24 months. The results fit nicely with the evidence from other studies of the development of self-awareness (Bertenthal & Fischer, 1978; Lewis & Brooks-Gunn, 1979). This research reveals that there are several stages in learning to recognize oneself in a mirror. Before the age of 3 months, children held up to a mirror show little interest in their own images or in the image of anyone else. At about 4 months, if a toy or another person is reflected in the mirror, babies will reach out and touch the mirror image. At this stage, they clearly don't understand that they are seeing a reflection. Babies 10 months old will reach behind them if a toy is slowly lowered behind their back while they are looking in the mirror, but they will not try to rub off a red spot that has been surreptitiously applied to their nose. Not until children are 18 months old will they reach for their own nose when they see the red spot. Some try to rub the spot off; others ask, "What's that?" Within a few months, whenever someone points to the child's mirror image and asks, "Who's that?" the child will be able to answer unhesitatingly, "Me."

THE SELF AS ACTOR

When speech first emerges, most one-word utterances name objects in the visual field. Children point at or pick up an object and say its name. These first descriptions include no explicit reference to the self. Between the ages of 18 and 24 months, about the same time that children begin to use two-word utterances, they also begin to describe their own actions. A child completing a jigsaw puzzle exclaims, "Did it!" or "Becky finished." When blocks fall, a child exclaims, "Uh-oh. I fix." In these utterances we see not only children's ability to refer to themselves explicitly but also the ability to represent two aspects of an action in words—their recognition of adult standards of behavior and their desire to meet them.

A SENSE OF STANDARDS

As we have seen repeatedly, infants are sensitive to unusual changes in their environment. Even in the first days of life, babies become habituated to events that occur repeatedly and pay attention to unexpected changes in their surroundings. But around the age of 2 years, children also become emotionally sensitive to events that violate the way things are "supposed to be." Children at this age become upset if the plastic eye of their teddy bear is missing or if there is mud on the hem of a new dress. When 14-month-olds are brought to a playroom where some of the toys are damaged, they seem to be unaware of the flaws and play as if nothing were wrong. But 19-month-olds say disdainfully, "Yukky" or "Fix it" (Kagan, 1981, p. 47). Apparently their emerging ability to classify objects extends to an ability to classify events as proper and improper according to adult standards.

Children also express sensitivity to adult standards when they feel they are supposed to imitate an adult. In several studies, Jerome Kagan (1981) had an adult perform various activities in front of children in a play setting. The adult might make one toy monkey hug another monkey, or build a stack of blocks, or enact a small drama using toy blocks as animals. Many of the acts were too complex for 2-year-olds to imitate. Starting around 18 months of age, the children in Kagan's study seemed to feel that they were expected to do what the adult had done even when they couldn't. As a result, many of them started to fret, stopped playing, and clung to their mothers. Kagan concluded that their distress signaled a new ability to recognize adult standards and an associated sense of responsibility to live up to them.

Further evidence that toddlers develop a sense of standards comes from situations in which adults set goals for children or children set themselves a goal. It is not at all unusual to encounter 2½-year-olds struggling to use all the blocks in the room to build a tower or to fit every available doll into a single toy baby carriage so that all the babies can go on a trip. Merry Bullock and Paul Lütkenhaus (1989) traced the ability of infants to adhere to task standards set by adults. At 17 months the infants had difficulty even beginning to build a tower of blocks, dress a doll, or wash a blackboard. At 20 months, they started out to do the tasks according to adult standards, but got caught up by the materials and ended up playing according to their own whims. It was only at 26 months that they first showed that they could stick to the task until they met adult standards. But it was not until they approached their third birthday that this kind of self-control became the rule rather than the exception. This evidence suggested to the researchers that until children are able to represent themselves symbolically in relation to a future goal — "I dress the baby" — their problem solving is easily sidetracked.

Once children can set goals for themselves and realize that there are standards of performance that they must meet, they begin to interact with their parents in a new way: they actively seek their parents' help in reaching the goals and meeting the standards. When confronted with a task that appeared too difficult, one child is reported to have said, while clinging to his mother, "It's mommy's turn to play" (Kagan, 1981, p. 49). More routinely, children around 20 months of age begin to tell adults what they want them to do. Their success varies, of course, depending on the willingness of adults to let them have their way, which differs from family to family and from culture to culture.

THE EMERGENCE OF SECONDARY EMOTIONS

Whether they believe emotions to be present at birth or to develop in the months after birth, psychologists agree that babies experience and communicate six *primary emotions* — joy, fear, anger, surprise, sadness, and disgust — by the time they reach their first birthdays (see Chapter 4, p. 143). They also agree that sometime between the ages of 18 and 24 months, babies begin to experience the **secondary emotions** of embarrassment, pride, shame, guilt, and envy.

Secondary emotions The emotions of pride, embarrassment, shame, guilt, and envy that appear between 18 and 24 months. They are also referred to as self-conscious or social emotions.

Michael Lewis (1993) believes that the appearance of secondary emotions depends on babies' newly acquired abilities to recognize, talk about, and think about themselves in relation to other people. The primary emotions, Lewis argues, bear a simple and direct relation to the events that elicit them. Distress, for example, is a direct response to pain; we feel disgust when we taste or smell something terrible; fear is a response to a sudden loss of physical support. The secondary emotions, by contrast, are reflective and indirect. They do not appear until children are able to think about and to evaluate themselves in terms of some social standard, rule, or desired goal. In this sense, secondary emotions can be considered social emotions (Barrett, 1995). Because they involve either injury to or enhancement of the child's sense of self, Lewis refers to secondary emotions as *self-conscious emotions*.

Take pride. To feel pride, toddlers must be able to judge their own behavior as proper and admirable in the eyes of other people. Until they are about 18 months old, babies have no basis for feeling pride because they are incapable of thinking about other people's standards and their own behavior at the same time (Tomasello, 1993). But 2-year-olds can measure their behavior against the expectations of others. Pride can be observed in a toddler's self-satisfied smile as he places the topmost block on the stack or as she manages to slip into her shoes by herself. Shame or embarrassment can be seen when toddlers lower their eyes, hang their heads, and cover their faces with their hands or when they hide after doing something they know is "bad."

Adults and other members of the child's community play an important role in the development of secondary emotions. They provide the standards of behavior against which toddlers learn to measure themselves. By observing and learning from others, toddlers discover when it is appropriate to feel guilt, shame, pride, and other secondary emotions.

The secondary emotions play an important role in children's social development. Pride and shame, for example, enter into children's feelings about others as well as about themselves. Guilt functions to motivate children to make amends. Interpreted in this way, the development of secondary emotions can be seen as part of a larger ensemble of changes that mark the beginning of a new stage in the process of growing up.

The End of Infancy

The changes in children's autonomy and self-concept between the ages of 18 and 30 months—the decline in the level of distress they show when they are separated from their caregivers and the increase in their ability to engage in symbolic play, to adhere to adult standards, and to express themselves in elementary words and phrases—combine to produce a stagelike transition in overall behavior that we have identified as a bio-social-behavioral shift. Table 6.3 summarizes the changes that occur in the months surrounding a child's second birthday. It provides a timely reminder that the social and cognitive changes that have figured so prominently in this chapter are part and parcel of other, seemingly more mundane behavioral changes, such as coordinated walking and bladder control, that depend on the physical development of the body.

The new configuration of characteristics that emerges early in the third year does not, of course, permit children to survive on their own. Far from it. But it does set the stage for a new form of interdependence and a new system of interaction between children and their environments. If all goes well, the individual aspects of development will undergo further modification over time, and this new, distinctive stage of development will give way to the next.

TABLE 6.3 The Bio-Social-Behavioral Shift at the End of Infancy

BIOLOGICAL DOMAIN	Myelination of connections among brain areas
	Leveling off of brain growth
	Maturation of brain areas in roughly equal degrees
BEHAVIORAL DOMAIN	Walking becomes well coordinated
	Manual dexterity becomes adequate to pick up small objects
	Control over bladder and bowels
	Planful problem solving
	Symbolic play
	Conceptual representations
	Elementary vocabulary and beginning of word combinations
	Mastery smile
SOCIAL DOMAIN	Decline of distress at separation
	Distinctive sense of self
	Acceptance of adult standards

SUMMARY

- Sometime between their second and third birthdays, children complete the period of development called infancy. The end of infancy is marked by changes in biological processes, by expanding physical and mental abilities, and by the appearance of a new relationship with the social world.

Biological Maturation

- Important connections in the cerebral cortex and between the cortex and the brain stem become myelinated. Neurons in the brain begin to achieve adult length and density. The rate of overall brain growth slows.
- Children gain increasing control over several muscle systems, which makes it possible for them to walk upright, run, and jump.
- Increased manual dexterity makes it possible to execute such movements as eating with a spoon and picking up small objects.
- Voluntary control over elimination becomes possible, although total control is not achieved for some time.

A New Mode of Thought

- A new configuration of cognitive abilities is manifested in many domains: problem solving, play, categorization of objects, and communication.
- According to Piaget's theory, toddlers complete the sensorimotor stage of development:

  1. Systematic problem solving to achieve goals makes its appearance.
  2. Children engage in systematic search for hidden objects.

3. Solutions to problems are achieved without extensive overt trial and error.

- Play evolves from consisting primarily of variations in patterns of movements to the pretend use of objects in imaginary situations.

- Pretend play itself evolves. Children 1 to 1½ years old can use themselves as agents to carry out a single pretend act at a time. By the time they are 2 years old, children can carry out a sequence of pretend actions in which objects such as dolls are used as the agents.

- Piaget believed that infants become capable of deferred imitation toward the end of the second year of life as a result of the ability to represent absent objects. Current evidence indicates that deferred imitation can occur several months earlier.

- Coincident with the onset of pretend play is the appearance of a new form of categorizing. Presented with a collection of objects to group, toddlers create a separate work space and categorize objects in accordance with adult criteria.

- Toddlers' vocabularies grow rapidly at the same time that they begin to solve problems insightfully and to search logically for hidden objects.

- The ability to combine words to make elementary two-word sentences coincides with the ability to combine objects in pretend play.

The Development of Child-Caregiver Relations

- Developmental psychologists interpret infants' distress when they are separated from their mothers as an indicator of feelings of attachment. This distress increases steadily until sometime in the second year and then declines.

- A variety of theories offer competing explanations for the onset of attachment.

  1. Freud believed that attachment has its roots in the reduction of biological drives such as hunger.
  2. Erikson explains attachment as the establishment of a trusting relationship between parent and child.
  3. Bowlby hypothesizes that attachment serves to reduce fear by establishing a secure base of support from which children can explore their environments.

- Research with monkeys has disproved the drive-reduction theory by showing that infant monkeys can become attached to inanimate surrogate mothers that provide soothing tactile sensations but no food.

- The social incapacity of monkeys raised with inanimate surrogate mothers has focused research on the role of maternal responsiveness in the development of normal social interactions.

- The "strange situation" has been widely used to assess distinctive patterns of infants' attachment to their primary caregiver. Research has focused on the causes and consequences of three broad patterns of attachment: anxious/avoidant, securely attached, and anxious/resistant.

- The best predictor of secure attachment is attentive, sensitive caregiving. Abusive, neglectful, or inconsistent caregiving is likely to lead to insecure attachment.

- Children's own characteristics may contribute to the quality of their attachments. Children who are easily upset when their ongoing activity is interrupted or who display less interest in people than in objects may be more difficult for adults to coordinate with, so that secure attachments are not easily formed.

- There appear to be marked cultural variations in patterns of response in the strange situation. Traditions both of exclusive mothering and of communal upbringing can result in manifestations of anxiety in the strange situation. The psychological significance of these findings is uncertain.

A New Sense of Self

- A new sense of self appears around the time of a child's second birthday. It is manifested in:

  1. A growing sensitivity to adult standards.
  2. Concern about living up to those standards.
  3. A new ability to set one's own goals and standards.
  4. Self-reference in language.
  5. Immediate recognition of one's image in a mirror.
  6. The appearance of secondary emotions when the child assesses the self and others in relation to a set of social standards.

The End of Infancy

- The convergence of biological, perceptual-motor, cognitive, and social changes in the months surrounding a child's second birthday produces a new bio-social-behavioral shift and the beginning of a new stage of development.

KEY TERMS

biological drives, p. 238

deferred imitation, p. 233

internal working model, p. 241

representation, p. 228

secondary emotions, p. 253

secure base, p. 240

separation anxiety, p. 240

strange situation, p. 243

symbolic play (pretend, fantasy play), p. 232

tertiary circular reactions, p. 228

THOUGHT QUESTIONS

1. How do changes associated with the development of upright walking illustrate the close connection between changes in perceptual and motor abilities?
2. What common new ability appears to underlie the cognitive changes associated with the end of infancy?
3. How might each of Peter Smith's categories of play (p. 232) contribute to children's development?
4. What are some of the strengths and weaknesses of the "strange situation" as a way to investigate changing social and emotional relationships between infants and their caretakers in the second year of life?
5. What kinds of cognitive changes appear to be linked to the appearance of secondary emotions?

Early Experience and Later Life

> "Two roads diverged in a yellow wood,
>
> And sorry I could not travel both
>
> And be one traveler, long I stood
>
> And looked down one as far as I could
>
> To where it bent in the undergrowth;
>
> Then took the other, as just as fair,
>
> And having perhaps the better claim,
>
> Because it was grassy and wanted wear;
>
> Though as for that the passing there
>
> Had worn them really about the same,
>
> And both that morning equally lay
>
> In leaves no step had trodden black.
>
> Oh, I kept the first for another day!
>
> Yet knowing how way leads on to way,
>
> I doubted if I should ever come back.
>
> I shall be telling this with a sigh
>
> Somewhere ages and ages hence:
>
> Two roads diverged in a wood, and I—
>
> I took the one less traveled by,
>
> And that has made all the difference."
>
> —*Robert Frost*, "The Road Not Taken"

> "One of the most fundamental processes in development consists in the closing of doors . . . , in the progressive restriction of possible fates."
>
> —*Joseph Needham*, Order and Life

Primacy The idea that the earliest experiences of children determine their later development.

The poet and the scientist agree. Paths taken early in our lives launch us on a course that, once set, may be difficult to change. Insofar as children's fates are shaped by their experiences in the world, it seems reasonable to conclude that their earliest experiences, the paths they first travel down, will be the most significant for their later development. This idea is called **primacy.** We can find the concept in our proverbs—"As the twig is bent, so grows the tree"—and in our heritage from the Greeks. Plato (428–348 B.C.) expressed this view when he wrote:

> And the beginning, as you know, is always the most important part, especially in dealing with anything young and tender. That is the time when the character is being molded and easily takes any impress one may wish to stamp on it. (1945, p. 68)

During the twentieth century, primacy has come to be associated with the idea that children's experiences during infancy determine their future development. This line of thought was greatly influenced by Freud's claim that psychological illness in adulthood can be traced back to unresolved conflicts in the first years of life (Freud, 1940/1964). It is by no means restricted to Freudian theorists, however. In summarizing his research on intellectual development, the psychologist Burton White (1975) argues that *"to begin to look at a child's educational development when he is two years of age is already much too late,* particularly in the area of social skills and attitudes" (p. 4; italics added). Similarly, Alan Sroufe and June Fleeson (1986) maintain that the nature of children's first attachments greatly influences the way they form subsequent relationships.

In this chapter we focus on the questions whether and, if so, to what extent the experiences of infancy exert more influence than later experiences on the course of development. The answers to these questions have an important bearing on such issues as how society and parents can best provide for infants to ensure their optimal development and what can be done to improve the lives of children who have suffered deprivation early in life. As we will see, there is no doubt that infants' experiences have a significant effect on their later development. But in many cases there is good reason to doubt extreme claims that the trends begun during the first 2½ years of life are irreversible (Robbins & Rutter, 1990).

A few words of caution are in order about the nature of the research featured in this chapter. In many cases, the data come from studies of children who have suffered some kind of unusual deprivation that is not under the investigators' control: they have been raised in an orphanage, or in poverty, or by parents who are mentally unstable. In such studies, the basic principle of a true psychological experiment is violated: the subjects are not assigned at random to experimental and control conditions. As a consequence, it is not possible to conclude with certainty that any differences between these and other groups of children in later life are caused by the particular form of deprivation that the children experienced during infancy and early childhood: it is possible that some *covarying factor* (see Box 1.2, p. 22) is the real cause of the observed differences. For example, any differences found between children growing up in orphanages and in homes might actually reflect the fact that children in orphanages generally come from poorer families, where multiple physical and psychosocial risk factors are more frequently encountered; in this case, income and orphanage would be covarying.

Optimal Conditions for Infant Development

The widespread belief that the early experiences of infants have a major impact on the characteristics they will have as adults has led many researchers to attempt to identify the conditions that will best foster babies' initial growth and development. Such information could be very useful to parents who want to do all they can to ensure a happy and healthy life for their children, and to policy makers, who must sometimes pass laws concerning standards of care for children. Ideas about the nature of optimal development depend, of course, on cultural values, but in our society it is commonly held that the ideal conditions are those that will allow as many doors as possible to remain open for a child's future.

It is often suggested that development is best fostered when the mother, or whoever else cares for the baby, is sensitive and responsive to the baby's signals and states. We have encountered this idea in Chapter 6 (p. 248) in research on the conditions that promote secure attachment. A particularly powerful vision of the sensitive mother is provided by the nineteenth-century Danish philosopher Søren Kierkegaard:

> The loving mother teaches her child to walk alone. She is far enough from him so that she cannot actually support him, but she holds out her arms to him. She imitates his movements, and if he totters, she swiftly bends as if to seize him, so that the child might believe that he is not walking alone. . . . And yet, she does more. Her face beckons like a reward, an encouragement. Thus, the child walks alone with eyes fixed on his mother's face, not on the difficulties in his way. He supports himself by arms that do not hold him and constantly strives towards the refuge in his mother's embrace, little suspecting that in the very same moment he is emphasizing his need for her, he is proving that he can do without her, because he is walking alone. (Quoted in Sroufe, 1979, p. 462)

Kierkegaard's "loving mother" is so finely tuned to her child's needs that she creates the illusion of physical support where none exists. This illusion provides the child with a sense of capability and self-confidence that encourages maximum effort and courage. These character traits are widely admired in Western European and North American cultures. Consequently, the child-rearing behaviors that foster them are often considered the optimal conditions for development.

Kierkegaard's maternal ideal seems to be embodied in what Burton White and Jean Carew Watts (1973) call *A mothers*. The children of such mothers were judged to be more competent than their peers when they were in kindergarten, on the basis of their performance on a battery of tests and the researchers' observations. (Table 7.1 lists some of the characteristics the researchers evaluated.) The A mothers enjoyed being with their toddlers and talked to them in ways they could understand. They placed more importance on their children's happiness and learning than on the appearance of their homes, which were organized to be safe and interesting for toddlers. They allowed their children to take minor risks, but they set reasonable limits for them. They might allow their 1½-year-olds to negotiate stairs while holding on to the banister, for instance, but not to climb up on the edge of the bathtub. Their close attention to their children was complemented by their dominant mood: they were busy and happy rather than unoccupied and depressed.

The A mothers did not spend all day attending to their toddlers. In fact, they spent less than 10 percent of their time actually caring for them. Some had part-time jobs, and some had several other children. When they were at home, however, they were nearly always available to answer questions, set up a new activity, or give encouragement. The researchers concluded that neither a lot of money nor a lot of education

TABLE 7.1	Characteristics of Competent 3-Year-Olds

SOCIAL ABILITIES

Getting and holding an adult's attention in socially acceptable ways

Using adults as resources after concluding that they cannot handle the task themselves

Expressing affection and mild hostility

Engaging in role play

GENERAL INTELLECTUAL SKILLS

Understanding and communicating effectively

Engaging in complex problem solving, including finding materials and using them to make a product

Self-control in the absence of external constraints

Ability to plan for and prepare for an activity

Ability to explore novel objects and situations systematically

Source: White & Watts, 1973.

was necessary to be an A mother, although poverty did make a mother's work more difficult. Some of the A mothers were on welfare, and some of them had not graduated from high school.

White and Watts's description of "effective" maternal behaviors tells us something about the caretaking environments that foster successful early adaptation to a society in which behaving oneself and performing well in school are basic demands. But it does not help answer many important questions that parents and other caregivers must face: What is the "right" kind of responsiveness? How much support is too much, and how much is not enough? Will the same kind of responsiveness that prepares children to succeed in school also prepare them to cope with frustration, inadequate housing, discrimination, or extended periods of unemployment?

As we indicated earlier, answers to questions about what constitutes adequate preparation for later life depend on the historical and cultural circumstances into which a child is born. Japanese mothers, for example, like mothers in the United States, aspire for their children to develop into effective adults. But, by U.S. standards, Japanese mothers seem excessively responsive to their children; they seem, when viewed through an American cultural lens, to encourage considerable emotional dependence (Miyaki et al., 1986). Japanese mothers' high level of responsiveness, however, does not mean that they provide inappropriate environments for their children's development. Japanese society differs from American society. Japanese mothers are striving to foster a different overall pattern of adult characteristics in their children. It makes sense that their strategies for achieving their "optimal" pattern should differ as well.

A quite different set of circumstances prevails in the poverty-stricken areas of northeastern Brazil (Scheper-Hughes, 1992). The environment into which babies there are born is extremely hostile to survival: the drinking water is contaminated, there is little food to eat, there are no sanitary facilities, and there is little medical care. Almost 50 percent of the children born in these communities die before the age of 5 years. For those who survive, success in later life is rarely influenced by academic ability, since little schooling is available. Most of these children can look forward to labor as unskilled farmworkers, which affords no hope of economic advancement or even of a comfortable living.

In many parts of the world large numbers of children do not survive to celebrate their fifth birthday. Often they die of diseases that could be prevented with better sanitary conditions, nutrition, and health care.

These Rwandan children are searching in the dust for beans dropped when relief workers handed out food in their refugee camp in Tanzania.

In response to these conditions, according to Nancy Scheper-Hughes (1992), the mothers of this region have developed beliefs and behaviors about child rearing that seem harsh and uncaring by the standards of middle-class families in either the United States or Japan. They are fatalistic about their infants' well-being. Children who are developmentally delayed or who have a passive, quiet temperament may be neglected or simply left to die if they become sick, with no attempt to give them special care. The favored children are those who are precocious, active, and demanding. Children who have survived to the age of 5 or 6 years are expected to start contributing to the family's livelihood. The boys are allowed to roam the streets, searching for food and stealing if necessary. The girls are required to pick sugar cane or do housework. But as the report by Scheper-Hughes makes clear, these mothers are simply being practical; they are preparing their children to survive in an environment where weakness almost certainly leads to death.

SPOILING: RESPONDING TOO MUCH?

Even among middle-class families in the United States, beliefs about proper parental behaviors vary widely. One mother may ignore her toddler's requests for a treat at the store or cries in the middle of the night in the belief that too much responsiveness will foster an unhealthy attitude and spoil the child. Another mother may respond to her children's every whimper because she believes that she must buffer them against difficult circumstances until they are strong enough to cope on their own. Which mother is right? Is there a way of knowing how much parents should cater to the desires and distresses of their infants? Is it possible to spoil a child?

As we saw in Chapter 4 (p. 152), the meanings of newborns' cries are often ambiguous. Consequently, parents may worry that they will encourage fussiness if they pick up their babies every time they start to cry. Evidence on the short-term effects of being highly responsive to crying is mixed. Laboratory research shows that the duration of crying episodes decreases if the caregiver ignores the cries but responds quickly to other behaviors, such as smiling (Etzel & Gewirtz, 1967). Observations in home situations, however, suggest that crying may become more frequent if it is ignored. Silvia Bell and Mary Ainsworth (1972) studied the ways in

Berry's World

"Your honor, my client pleads not guilty, because, when he was a little boy, his parents allowed him to become a SPOILED BRAT."

Jim Berry, Newspaper Enterprise Association

Learned helplessness People's perception that their behavior does not matter because of their inability to affect events. As a consequence, they lose the desire to act.

which 26 mothers responded to their infants' cries. A member of the research team visited each home for 4 hours once every 3 weeks throughout the first year of each baby's life. During the visits the observer recorded how often the baby cried and how the mother responded. Contrary to the common wisdom, the mothers who responded quickly to their infants' cries had babies who cried relatively little. The mothers who ignored their babies' cries for long periods ended up with the babies who cried most often. Bell and Ainsworth suggest that the most important consequence of mothers' quick attention to their infants' cries is that it helps the babies to develop trust in the mother and in their own ability to control what happens to them.

There does not seem to be a serious risk of spoiling a child during infancy. Certainly there are some parents who cater to their children's every whim, thus giving them an exaggerated sense of their own power that will be maladaptive in the long run. In most cases, however, the everyday demands on parents to earn a living, to maintain a household, and to keep their children from doing things that are potentially dangerous make it almost inevitable that children eventually learn that they cannot always have their own way.

LEARNED HELPLESSNESS: RESPONDING TOO LITTLE

Parents' fear that they will create a baby tyrant if they respond to their infant's every demand is balanced by the competing concern that if they never respond on the baby's terms, but only on their own, they will create children who believe that they cannot influence the world around them. Support for the idea that a feeling of helplessness can be learned appeared first in studies of animals. In one such study Bruce Overmier and Martin Seligman (1967) administered a multitude of shocks to the forepaws of a group of dogs. These dogs received shocks no matter what they did. Then these dogs and a comparison group of dogs that had no experience with unavoidable shock were placed in a large box with a metal grid floor to which shocks could be delivered. If the animal crossed over to the other side of the box quickly enough, it could avoid being shocked altogether. Dogs who had no history of experiencing unavoidable shocks quickly learned to move back and forth across the box to avoid the shock. But the dogs that had previously been subject to an experience with inescapable shocks did not learn to avoid the shock; they lay down and whined. This is the effect known as **learned helplessness.**

Research on learned helplessness with human adults indicates that when people are put in situations in which they cannot control events, they too eventually become passive and lose even the desire to act (Fincham & Cain, 1986; Seligman, 1975).

Studies have shown that infants are capable of learning about their ability to control events, so it seems reasonable to assume that they might also be subject to learned helplessness, in the right circumstances. John S. Watson (not to be confused with John B. Watson, the founder of behaviorism mentioned in earlier chapters) set up an apparatus that allowed 8-week-old infants to move a mobile hanging above their cribs by pressing their heads against an air pillow. Because of the direct relationship between pressing down on the pillow and the movement of the mobile, the infants rapidly learned to make the mobile move (Watson, 1972).

Watson reported that once the infants learned to control the mobile, their daily activity levels increased in comparison with those of a control group whose actions had no effect on the mobile. The babies who were allowed to control the mobile also began to smile delightedly and coo at the sight of it. These observations led Watson to speculate that even very young infants find it pleasurable to control their environment because it gives them a feeling of personal effectiveness. On the basis of similar observations with infants and young children, the psychiatrist Robert White (1959) concluded that human beings have a basic drive to be in control of their environments. He called this drive the **competence motive.**

In another study, Watson (1971) contrasted the behavior of two groups of infants who were provided with mobiles for their cribs at home. One group could set the mobile in motion by pushing down on their pillows; the other group saw the mobile move equally often, but their own actions did not affect its movement. Later both groups were given an opportunity to make a similar mobile move in the laboratory. The infants who had learned to control the mobile at home soon learned to make the laboratory mobile move. The infants who could not control the mobile at home did not learn to control the laboratory mobile. In accord with the idea of learned helplessness, the experience of lack of control over an aspect of the environment in one situation seems to impair later learning in a similar situation.

Neal Finkelstein and Craig Ramey (1977) extended Watson's findings to show that babies who learn a particular behavior to control the environment in one situation may apply what they've learned to establish new behaviors. In the first stage of this study, the researchers placed 8-month-old babies in front of a panel that lit up and made interesting sounds. Half of the babies could produce the interesting outcome by pushing on the panel; the others could push the panel or not, as they pleased, and still see and hear the same things. As expected, the babies whose actions caused the change learned to press the panel, whereas the others did not.

In the second stage of the experiment, both groups could make the sights and sounds occur by engaging in an entirely different kind of behavior, vocalizing. The babies who had learned to push the panel to produce the lights and sounds also learned to activate the panel by vocalizing. But the babies who learned earlier that their behavior was irrelevant to the lights and sounds failed to learn this new way of producing them.

Findings such as Finkelstein and Ramey's suggest that even babies as young as 8 months of age learn more than the direct association between their own actions and specific outcomes, such as the connection between crying and being picked up or between sucking and obtaining nourishment. They also seem to learn something about their ability to control their environment. Although infants cannot tell us directly what they are feeling or thinking, their actions seem to indicate that such experiences shape their sense of personal effectiveness.

An important limitation of the research on spoiling and learned helplessness is that it does not indicate how to mix lessons in controlling the environment with lessons in accepting external control so as to provide infants with the optimum foundation for later development. There is no single recipe for the correct amount of responsiveness in every situation. That is why psychologists emphasize that parents' *sensitivity* to their individual children's needs is a key factor in promoting healthy development.

Competence motive A basic drive human beings have to control their environment.

Effects of Separation

A variety of circumstances can separate parents from their children for a time, and during those periods it is impossible for the parents to fine-tune their children's upbringing. The need to earn a living often separates parents from their young children for many hours several days a week. A family upheaval such as divorce,

Every day large numbers of children are orphaned as a result of war, famine, and disease. This child's father was killed during fighting between Croatians and Serbs after the breakup of Yugoslavia in 1992.

the death of a parent, or prolonged illness requiring hospitalization also separates children from their parents (Wolkind & Rutter, 1985). A major disaster—war, flood, famine—can dislocate a whole population.

Developmental psychologists have long been interested in the consequences of separating children from their parents (Rutter & Hersov, 1985, review the findings). They seek to understand how separation influences development at the time it occurs and how it may affect later development. This knowledge is essential both to help them understand the actual dynamics of development and to guide the search for effective therapies for children who have been adversely affected by such separations. In the following discussion, we will consider children who have experienced one or another of a wide range of separations, including enrollment in day care, hospitalization of themselves or their mothers, and residence in a foster home or orphanage.

TEMPORARY SEPARATION FROM PARENTS

Children who spend part of each weekday being cared for by a nonfamily member while their parents work are experiencing a relatively mild form of separation. Many researchers are convinced that high-quality day care has no lasting negative impact on infants' later development. Some, however, claim that no matter what its quality, extensive day care for babies under the age of 1 year does have lasting negative effects (Chase-Lansdale, 1994) (see Box 7.1). We will return to the subject of day care in Chapter 11, where we discuss its impact on slightly older children.

Another form of separation occurs when young children must spend time in a hospital. Several studies have evaluated the consequences of hospitalization on later emotional development. Michael Rutter (1976), for example, studied 400 10-year-olds to see if early hospitalization had influenced their later psychological adjustment. He found that a single hospital stay that lasted a week or less before the age of 5 produced no emotional or behavioral disturbances that could be detected at the age of 10. Repeated hospitalization, however, was found to be associated with behavior problems and delinquency in later childhood.

As we noted earlier, caution is in order when we interpret the results of studies in which differences in experience arise naturally rather than as a result of the experimenter's manipulation. Therefore, Rutter is careful to consider other possible explanations for his findings. For example, the later psychological problems may have resulted from the stress of continued ill health rather than from the children's separation from their parents. Another possibility suggested by subsequent research is that children who have been hospitalized repeatedly are more likely than children who have not been hospitalized to come from socially and economically disadvantaged families (Quinton & Rutter, 1976). The negative effect of repeated hospitalization may be less a reflection of disturbed social relations (owing to separation) than a reflection of chronically difficult home circumstances or ill health.

A more traumatic form of family separation often occurs in time of war. In the early 1940s, the German air force carried out an intensive bombing campaign against the civilian population of London and other English cities. Large numbers of English children were sent to live in the safer countryside with relatives, sponsoring families, or other children in special group living arrangements while their parents remained behind. Dorothy Burlingham and Anna Freud (1942) studied the reactions of a group of such children who ranged in age from a few months to 4 years. They found that many of the children were distressed at being separated from their parents. When these children were examined 20 years later, however, the researchers found no instances of severe mental illness among them; their behavior as young adults fell within normal limits (Maas, 1963).

EXTENDED SEPARATION FROM PARENTS

An extreme form of separation is experienced by children who spend their early lives in orphanages because their parents are dead or are unable to care for them. Because many orphanages keep good records of the children they care for, studies of orphanage-raised children provide some of the most systematic data on how separation from parents influences children's development. Among orphaned children, the risk is highest for those whose separation is coupled with residence in a facility with multiple caretakers and a suboptimal range of experiences.

Children of the crèche

A classic long-range study of orphanage-raised children was carried out by Wayne Dennis (1973) and his colleagues in a crèche (orphanage) in Lebanon. The children were brought to the crèche shortly after birth. Once there, they received little attention; there was only one caretaker for every ten children. These caretakers had themselves been brought up in the crèche until the age of 6, when they were transferred to another institution. According to Dennis, the caretakers showed little regard for the children's individual needs or temperaments. They rarely talked to the children, did not respond to their infrequent vocalizations, and seldom played with them while bathing, dressing, changing, or feeding them. Instead, they left the babies to lie on their backs in their cribs all day and the toddlers to sit in small playpens with only a ball to play with.

The harmful effects of this low level of stimulation and human contact were evident within a year. Although the children were normal at 2 months, as measured by an infant scale, Dennis found that they had developed intellectually at only half the normal rate when he tested them at the end of the first year.

The later developmental fates of these children depended on their subsequent care. Those who were adopted made a remarkable recovery. The children who were adopted before they were 2 years old were functioning normally when they were tested 2 to 3 years after their adoption, and those who were adopted between 2 and 6 years of age were only slightly retarded in their intellectual functioning.

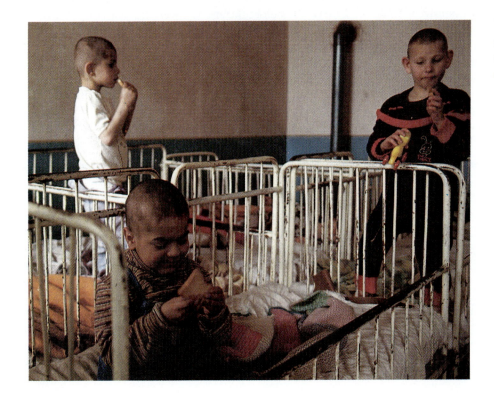

The conditions in orphanages such as this one provide insufficient stimulation for normal mental development.

BOX 7.1

Out-of-Home Care in the First Year of Life

Questions about the primacy of infancy reach beyond scientific research into the lives of individuals and the arena of public policy. The increasingly common practice in the United States of placing infants in the care of someone other than their parents during the first year of life has sparked a vigorous controversy with obvious political overtones. According to some experts, very early day-care experience puts children at risk for long-term social and emotional difficulties. According to others, little or no risk is associated with early high-quality child care (Belsky, 1990; Clarke-Stewart, 1989; Phillips et al., 1987).

The issue of out-of-home care for infants potentially affects the lives of many people because of two trends in American society: (1) the growing number of single-parent households and (2) the increasing economic need for both parents to work full-time. At the present time, women constitute the fastest-growing segment of the workforce, and a majority of mothers who work return to their jobs before their infants are 1 year old. If current trends continue, by the year 2000 the mothers of four out of every five infants under the age of 1 will be in the labor force.

Prominent among those who raise concerns about out-of-home care during the first year of life is Jay Belsky (1986, 1990). He bases his conclusions on evidence that children who have experienced extensive nonmaternal care (more than 20 hours a week) during the first year of life are more likely to exhibit insecure patterns of attachment in the "strange situation," are less compliant in meeting adults' demands, and are more aggressive in interactions with peers.

Belsky's concerns are supported by a study conducted by Peter Barglow, Brian Vaughn, and Nancy Molitor (1987). These researchers found that firstborn

children who had been placed in day-care arrangements before their first birthday were significantly more likely to display insecure forms of attachment when they were 12 to 13 months old than were children who stayed at home with their mothers.

Belsky's conclusions have also been criticized on several grounds. Alison Clarke-Stewart (1989) argues that the negative effects of early day care summarized by Belsky are very small in real-life terms. In support of day-care experience during the first year of life, she cites evidence that children enrolled in such care have higher scores on tests of intellectual development. In addition, she suggests that the behaviors labeled "non-compliant" might really reflect increased independence and self-confidence.

Deborah Phillips and her colleagues (1987) agree that Belsky's concerns are misplaced. They maintain that "early entry into day care may be less important than the kind and quality of care children receive while in day care" (p. 20).

A study by Carollee Howes (1990) supports this conclusion. Howes studied how the age at which children enter day care, the quality of the care they receive, and the characteristics of their families influence their social adjustment in preschool and kindergarten. She found that children who entered into low-quality day care before the age of 1 were the ones most likely to have difficulty with their peers in preschool; they were distractible, low in task orientation, and less considerate of others. However, children enrolled in high-quality day care, even during the first year of life, did not seem to be at any risk for such behavior problems. Howes also found that the families who enrolled their babies in low-quality day care early in infancy were under pressures that the other families she studied were

The children who remained institutionalized fared less well. At the age of 6, the girls were sent to one institution and the boys to another. The girls' institution, like the crèche, provided few stimulating experiences and virtually no personal attention. When these girls were tested at 12 to 16 years of age, they were found to be so retarded intellectually that they would be unable to function in modern society. They could barely read, they could not tell time, and they were not able to dial a seven-digit telephone number or to count out change in a store.

The outcome for the boys was quite different. The institution to which they were transferred provided far more intellectual stimulation and more varied experiences than did the crèche. What is more, they had frequent contact with the workers at the institution, who came from the surrounding communities. As a re-

With the majority of mothers returning to work within a year of the birth of their children, a growing number of babies are being cared for out of their homes before the age of 1. The effects of such care on their socioemotional development are the subject of intense debate among psychologists.

not. They were less likely to be connected with a supportive social network and they were more likely to be experiencing a variety of complex problems that had negative effects on their child-rearing efforts.

As Howes's study suggests, when a matter as complex as the effects of day care is at issue, the real-life circumstances of the people involved must be considered. If brief separations with high-quality care are the only disruptions in an otherwise secure family situation, the disruptions appear to have quite different consequences from those experienced by a child whose

family is under stress or who attends a poor-quality day-care facility. Unfortunately, recent studies indicate that a large percentage of day-care facilities are mediocre at best (Galinsky et al., 1994; Cost, Quality & Child Outcomes Study Team, 1995).

In accordance with mounting evidence on the cumulative impact of risk factors, Thomas Gamble and Edward Zigler (1986) conclude that when families are facing a variety of life stresses, substitute care during the first year of life increases the likelihood of insecure infant-parent attachment, which in turn makes the infants more vulnerable to stresses they encounter later in life.

The stakes in the debate are very high. On the one hand, everyone is aware that it is in the interests not only of the children in question but also of society as a whole to ensure that children grow up to be emotionally stable and socially competent people. If they do not, society will incur a huge toll in later social service costs and economic productivity. On the other hand, economic and social pressures are bringing many mothers into the workforce and keeping fathers there. The problem is how best to deal with these conflicting realities to maximize children's life chances. Belsky suggests that this goal could best be achieved if parents received support for staying home with their infants during their first year of life. Phillips and her colleagues argue that what is called for instead is better and more accessible day care.

Many millions of dollars will be spent to deal with the issue of infant and child care in the decades to come, and millions of parents and children will be affected by the policies that are eventually adopted. In fact, virtually everyone will be involved, if only in the role of taxpayer.

sult, when the boys were tested at 10 to 14 years of age they showed a substantial recovery from their initial intellectual lag. Although their performance on standardized tests was below the norm and below the performance of the children who had been adopted, it was within the range that would allow them to function in society.

Children reared in well-staffed orphanages

The grim picture painted by Dennis's research provoked further studies of orphanage-raised children in an effort to determine if the negative consequences he found were the result of particular forms of orphanage care. Barbara Tizard and her colleagues studied 65 English children of working-class backgrounds who were raised in residential nurseries from just after birth until at least the age of 2 years. (Tizard & Hodges, 1978; Tizard & Rees, 1975; Hodges & Tizard, 1989a, 1989b). The nurseries were considered to be of high quality. The children were fed well, the staff was trained, and toys and books were plentiful. The turnover and scheduling of staff members, however, discouraged the formation of close personal relationships between adults and children. Tizard and Hodges estimated that some 24 nurses had cared for each child by the time the children were 2 years old. By the age of 4½, each child had been cared for by as many as 50 nurses. This situation certainly appears to preclude the kind of intimate knowledge and caring that presumably underlie sensitive caregiving.

Tizard and her colleagues evaluated the developmental status of the children when they were 4½ years old and 8 years old, and again when they were 16 years old. They grouped the children into three categories:

1. Children who remained in the institutions.
2. Children who had returned to their families after the age of 2.
3. Children who were adopted between the ages of 2 and 8 years.

For comparison purposes, the researchers also evaluated a group of children with a similar working-class background who had always lived at home.

Leaving institutional care had a positive effect on the children, as Dennis's research might lead us to expect. But how much difference it made depended on what kind of environment they entered and what aspect of psychological functioning one looked at. One of the surprising findings was that the children who were restored to their biological families did not fare as well as the children who were adopted. The adopted children scored higher on standardized tests of intellectual achievement, and they were able to read at a more advanced level. The quality of the adopted children's relationships with their adoptive parents also appeared to be better. Almost all of the children who were adopted formed mutual attachments with their adoptive parents, no matter how old they were when they were adopted. This was not the case for the children who returned to their biological parents. The older they were when they left the nurseries, the less likely it was that mutual attachment developed.

One reason the adoptive homes may have been superior to the biological homes was that many of the families who took back their children were not alto-

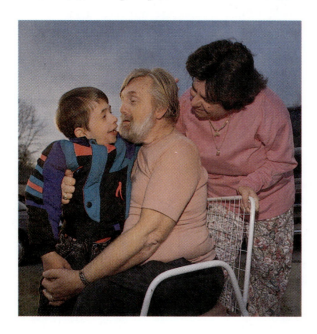

Evidence shows that children adopted by loving older parents are likely to fare better than those left in institutions. This child, who suffers from fetal alcohol syndrome, is shown with his adoptive parents.

gether happy to have them. Many of the mothers expressed misgivings, but they accepted the responsibility because the children were their own. Often the children returned to homes in which there were other children who required their mother's attention or a stepfather who was not interested in them. Most of the adoptive parents, by contrast, were older, childless couples who wanted the children and gave them a good deal of attention. Also, most of the adoptive families were financially better off than the children's biological families had been (Tizard & Hodges, 1978).

One area in which most of the institutionalized children were reported to suffer in comparison with the control group was their social relations at school. Here both groups of previously institutionalized children were seen to be "overly friendly." They had "an almost insatiable desire for adult attention, and a difficulty in forming good relationships with their peer group" (Tizard & Hodges, 1978, p. 114). Why these children experienced difficulties in social relations at school but not at home is not clear. Perhaps their early experiences in institutions gave them few clues about how to form peer relationships. Alternatively, they may have learned styles of interaction that were adaptive in the institutions but maladaptive outside them (Rutter & Garmezy, 1983).

When Hodges and Tizard (1989a, 1989b) contacted the children at the age of 16, they found a similar pattern. Children who had returned to their parents showed a high rate of antisocial behavior. Those adopted into new families did not, but even adopted children who developed normal attachment relations with their adoptive parents experienced difficulties dealing with their peers and society at large as teenagers.

The improvements seen in most children who leave institutional care speak against the theory that children can form emotional attachments only during a critical period in early infancy. Although the environment of the English nurseries prevented the children there from forming emotional attachments with their care-givers, most of the children who were adopted into new families formed attachments with their adoptive parents even though the children were well past their second birthday when they left the orphanage. At the same time, the research by Tizard and her colleagues confirms the idea that characteristics of children's environments during later periods of their life are influential in determining whether or not the lack of early attachments will prove to be an enduring problem, since the children who returned to indifferent biological parents were less likely to form attachments.

ISOLATED CHILDREN

The most extreme cases of neglect on record are those of children who have been separated not only from their parents but from other human beings as well. During the past 200 years several of these so-called feral children have been discovered, the most famous being the Wild Child, Victor, discussed in Chapter 1. Such children never fail to excite public interest because the idea of little children fending for themselves in nature is so dramatic. But the circumstances leading to such children's isolation and their condition before they became isolated are usually unknown. As a result, it is rarely possible to draw firm conclusions about the effects of their experiences during their isolation.

There are, however, a few well-documented modern cases of children who have been isolated early in life by sociopathic parents. Because public officials now keep good birth records and other health records, enough is known about the early lives of these children to permit more solidly based conclusions about the developmental impact of their bizarre circumstances (Skuse, 1984b).

Jarmila Koluchova (1972, 1976) studied one of these cases in Czechoslovakia. Identical twin boys were born in 1960 to a mother of normal intelligence who died shortly after their birth. When they were about 1½ years old their father remarried, and his new wife took an active dislike to them. The boys were forced to live in a small, bare closet without adequate food, exercise, or sunshine. They were not allowed to enter the parts of the house where other family members lived, and they were rarely visited.

The boys came to the attention of the authorities when they were 6 years old. They were abnormally small and suffered from rickets, a disease caused by a vitamin deficiency that leaves bones soft and bent. They could barely talk, they did not recognize common objects in photographs, and they were terrified of the new sights and sounds around them. The boys were taken to a children's home where they were housed with children younger than themselves in a nonthreatening environment and were well cared for. In these new circumstances, the twins soon began to gain weight, to take an active interest in their surroundings, and to learn to speak. When they were first tested at the age of 8 years, the boys' intelligence measured well below normal. But year by year their performance improved

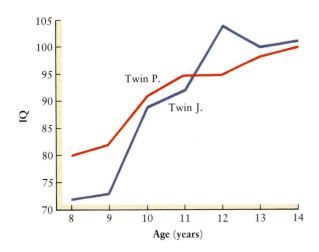

FIGURE 7.1 *After the twins studied by Koluchova were released from isolation, their intellectual abilities showed gradual recovery until they were normal. (Adapted from Koluchova, 1976.)*

until, at the age of 14, both of them manifested perfectly normal intelligence (see Figure 7.1).

An even more severely neglected child was Genie, who was locked in a room by herself sometime before her second birthday (Curtiss, 1977). For more than 11 years, Genie spent her days chained onto a potty and her nights tied up in a sleeping bag. No one spoke to her. When her father came to tie her in for the night or to bring her food, he growled at her like a beast and scratched her with his fingernails.

Genie was a pitiful creature when she was liberated from these horrible circumstances. Although she was 13 years old, she weighed only 59 pounds and was only 4 feet, 6 inches tall. She rarely made a sound and was not toilet trained. She could not walk normally; instead, she shuffled her feet and swayed from side to side. Remarkably, a battery of psychological tests revealed that Genie had an amazing ability to perceive and think about spatial relationships even though she could barely speak.

Genie learned to control her bowels and to walk normally, but she never developed normal language. She also learned a variety of appropriate social behaviors. When first found, she showed no emotion at all when people left her; eventually, though, she became attached to other people who lived in her hospital rehabilitation unit. She developed ways to make her visitors stay longer and became upset when they finally did leave. However, her social behavior never improved to the point where she could live outside of a special care facility.

Studies of isolated children leave little doubt that severe isolation can profoundly disrupt normal development, but they also show that early deprivation of caregiving and of normal interaction with the environment is not necessarily devastating to later development (Skuse, 1984a). Fortunately, such cases are so rare that we cannot know just how long and how severe a child's isolation has to be before the damage it causes is irreversible. The infrequency of such cases also makes it difficult to assess the impact of isolation on individual aspects of development. Emotional, intellectual, and physical development may all be affected by isolation, but probably not all are affected in the same way (Clarke & Clarke, 1986).

An important question raised, but not answered, by the studies of extreme isolation is: How do the conditions of the environment in which they were isolated interact with isolated children's predispositions to determine the extent of their later recovery? Is it important, for example, that the twins described by Koluchova had each other for company? Was Genie's aptitude for spatial thinking a special intellectual ability that would have shown up regardless of her isolation, or did it develop as a consequence of her immobility and her social isolation? The answers to such questions would help us understand the vulnerability to developmental disorders of children raised in less extreme but still adverse circumstances and the factors that enable them to recover despite these circumstances.

Vulnerability and Resilience

Even in times of relative peace and prosperity many adults find life a struggle. In trying to satisfy their own pressing needs, they create environments that are less than optimal for their children. Precisely because these situations are not extreme, they may persist for years and become permanent features of the family environment that shapes the development of the children. They may eventually contribute to delinquent behavior, failure in school, and mental health problems.

Michael Rutter and his colleagues (1975) conducted a large-scale study of the incidence of psychiatric disorders among 150 English families. They found four factors that, taken together, were strongly associated with childhood behavior problems and psychiatric disorders:

1. Family discord.
2. Parental social deviance of either a criminal or a psychiatric nature.
3. Social disadvantage, including low income, inadequate housing, and a large number of children close in age.
4. A poor school environment, including high rates of turnover and absence among staff and pupils and a large proportion of pupils from economically depressed homes.

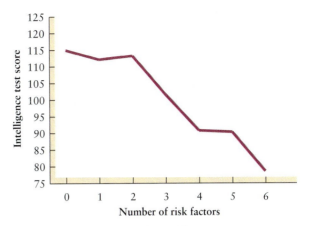

FIGURE 7.2 *The average IQ scores for 13-year-olds decrease markedly when their development is affected by more than two risk factors. (From Sameroff et al., 1993.)*

None of these factors by itself was strongly associated with psychiatric disorders in childhood. But if as few as two of them were present at the same time—for example, if one parent had a personality disorder and the family had a low income—the risk that the child would suffer from a psychiatric disorder increased 400 percent.

The emphasis Rutter and his colleagues placed on the cumulative nature of risk factors is substantiated by a growing body of research. Many studies have demonstrated that a combination of biological, social, and ecological factors, interacting over a considerable period of time, is required to cause serious developmental problems (Garmezy & Rutter, 1988; Kopp & Kaler, 1989; Sameroff et al., 1993; Shaw et al., 1994) (see Figure 7.2). At the same time, all of these researchers find marked individual differences among children who live in highly stressful circumstances. Some of these children seemed to have **resilience**—the ability to recover quickly from the adverse effects of early experience, or to persevere in the face of stress with no apparent special negative psychological consequences. Such observations led psychologists to search for the sources of children's resilience in the face of hardship (Cichetti & Garmezy, 1993).

CHARACTERISTICS OF THE FAMILY

The family is the main support system for the child. We would expect, then, that variations in the kinds of support that families provide for children should be associated with children's ability to withstand threats to their development. This idea is borne out by a variety of research (Fonagy et al., 1994, review the evidence). Many of the ways in which family characteristics influence risk factors and resilience can be seen in the results of an ambitious longitudinal study of a large, multiracial group of 689 children born on the Hawaiian island of Kauai in 1955 (Werner & Smith, 1982). Of these children, 201 were considered especially likely to suffer developmental problems because they experienced four or more risk factors by the time they were 2 years old. The risk factors included low-income families, higher than average rates of prematurity and stress during the birth process, low levels of maternal education, and parental psychopathology. The researchers found that the following circumstances reduced the risk of developmental difficulties:

- The family had no more than four children.
- More than 2 years separated the child studied and the next younger or older sibling.
- Alternate caregivers were available to the mother within the household (father, grandparents, or older siblings).

- The work load of the mother, even when she was employed outside the home, was not excessive.
- The child had a substantial amount of attention by caregivers during infancy.
- A sibling was available as a caregiver or confidant during childhood.
- The family provided structure and rules during the child's adolescence.
- The family was cohesive.
- The child had an informal, multigenerational network of kin and friends during adolescence.
- The cumulative number of chronic stressful life events experienced during childhood and adolescence was not great.

CHARACTERISTICS OF THE COMMUNITY

In general, children in poor communities are more likely to suffer from developmental difficulties than are children in affluent communities (Huston, McLoyd, & Coll, 1994; U.S. Department of Health and Human Services, 1991). Other characteristics of the communities in which children live also seem to affect the likelihood that they will develop problems. Those who live in poor inner-city neighborhoods, for example, have a significantly higher risk of developing a psychological disorder than do those who live in relatively poor small towns or rural areas (Richters & Martinez, 1993).

One factor found to reduce the impact of negative community characteristics is the strength of the social support networks provided by kin and social service agencies. Patricia Hashima and Paul Amato (1994) found that poor parents who had friends and neighbors they could call on in an emergency and turn to for advice engaged in significantly less punitive behavior aimed at their children. Similarly, Susan Crockenberg (1987) found that community-based social support services for parents provided by the National Health Service in England significantly increased the amount and quality of teenage mothers' interactions with their infants.

The fate of these children growing up in Bosnia is put in jeopardy by the horrendous conditions of war.

Another factor outside the home that helps to buffer children from stressful and depriving life circumstances is the school. Children in disadvantaged and discordant homes are less likely to develop psychological problems if they attend schools that have attentive personnel and good academic records (Rutter, 1987).

CHARACTERISTICS OF THE CHILD

Intelligence, an easy temperament, a capacity to plan, and a sense of humor are all associated with resilience in the face of poverty, family disruption, and other potentially damaging circumstances (Fonagy et al., 1994). Alexander Thomas and Stella Chess (1984) report that infants characterized as "difficult" because they displayed irregularity of biological functions, negative responses to new situations and people, and frequent negative moods are more likely to experience psychological problems as adults.

The temperamental characteristics most likely to put children at risk vary with age (Carey & McDevitt, 1995). In infancy and early childhood, the characteristics most likely to cause the child trouble are a difficult temperament and high activity level. As children enter middle childhood, lack of persistence, a short attention span, and lack of adaptability to new circumstances become more important. Box 7.2 discusses another factor that may put children at risk.

Whether a difficult temperament or lack of persistence are risk factors, however, also depends on cultural circumstances. A study by M. W. de Vries (1987) provides dramatic evidence that temperamental traits that would be considered "difficult" in one cultural setting can be crucial to development in another. De Vries administered a temperament questionnaire based on Chess and Thomas's ideas to the mothers of 48 4- to-5-month-old Masai children in East Africa. At the time this research was conducted, a severe drought was plaguing Masai country and many people left their villages in search of food. When de Vries returned several months later to conduct follow-up tests with the 10 most difficult and 10 least difficult infants identified by the earlier questionnaires, he could locate only 13 families, 7 from the "easy child" group and 6 from the "difficult child" group. To his distress, de Vries found that 5 of the 7 "easy" children had died. Five of the 6 "difficult" children remained alive. Coupled with the work of Scheper-Hughes (1992) in Brazil (p. 262), this study suggests that when young infants live in chronically deprived circumstances, the demandingness associated with a difficult temperament may actually aid survival.

Emmie Werner and Ruth Smith (1992) offer additional evidence that personal characteristics can help the child to survive difficult circumstances. On the basis of records provided by health, mental health, and social service agencies and educational institutions, as well as personal interviews and personality tests, they report that the children who were able to cope best with their life circumstances during their first two decades were those whom their mothers described as "very active" and "socially responsive" when they were infants. The mothers' reports were verified by independent observers, who noted that these children displayed "pronounced autonomy" and a "positive social orientation." When they were examined during their second year of life, these children scored especially well on a variety of tests, including measures of motor and language development.

TRANSACTIONAL MODELS OF DEVELOPMENT

We have seen that studies of developmental risk predict a greater likelihood of long-term developmental damage when several factors are present. These studies also point out the dangers of weighing the effect of any one factor in isolation. The various influences on development work in combination. Let us consider a study that found that infants characterized as "difficult" were more likely than those characterized as "easy" to suffer developmental problems, especially when

BOX 7.2

Maternal Depression as a Risk Factor

It is estimated that 10 to 15 percent of mothers experience a postpartum depression that is more prolonged than the "baby blues" and serious enough to interfere with daily functioning (O'Hara, Neunable, & Zekoski, 1984). Chronic maternal depression that lasts for 6 months or more is considered a risk factor in a child's development (Campbell, Cohn, & Meyers, 1995). Such prolonged depression is related to a variety of negative outcomes.

Depressed mothers spend less time talking to their babies and looking at them than mothers who are not depressed. They are also less responsive to their babies' cries, smiles, and fretting (Cohn et al., 1990). The babies of depressed mothers have lower activity levels, smile less, and frown more. They do not vocalize or play as much as other babies, and they tend to be more fussy and tense. They also are less likely to be securely attached to their mothers (Teti et al., 1995). The negative style of these babies' interactions with their mothers is carried over to their interactions with strangers who are not suffering from depression (Field, 1995).

Psychologists and psychiatrists who work with the children of depressed mothers are well aware of these facts but cannot be certain how to interpret them. The depressed behavior of these babies is enough like their mothers' behavior to suggest that they acquired it either through imitation of their mothers' treatment of them or in reaction to it. There is some evidence, however, that at least some babies who behave this way may have been depressive from birth. Tiffany Field and her colleagues studied a group of women who were diagnosed as suffering from depression while they were still pregnant (Field, 1994). When their babies were assessed by the Brazelton Neonatal Assessment Scale shortly after birth, they were found to have depressed activity levels and limited responses to social stimulation. The fact that some elements of depression are present at birth suggests that either prenatal influence or genetic heritage is involved (Cytryn et al., 1986).

Older children of depressed mothers are at risk not only for depression, but for a range of problems in situations that require emotional regulation (Hammen, 1991). They have difficulty with their peers and they get into trouble in school because their attention wanders, they fidget in class, and they fight with other children on the playground (Dodge, 1990).

Maternal depression, like all other risk factors, rarely occurs in isolation. It is most likely to occur in conjunction with marital strife, lack of social support, and such stresses as poverty and job loss (Fendrich, Warner, & Weissman, 1990).

The fact that not all children are affected by their mothers' depression has led researchers to look for the experiences and personal qualities that allow some children of depressed mothers to grow up relatively unscathed (Conrad & Hammen, 1993; Radke-Yarrow & Sherman, 1990). The most important protection factors include:

- Competence in school.
- A personality that is socially engaging.
- A close relationship with a parent or other adult who is not depressed.
- Close friendships with peers.

Some data show that if the mother recovers from her depression, it is possible for the child to begin to function more normally. If the mother's depression is persistent, however, or if it comes and goes in cycles, the children are especially at risk for long-term developmental problems. It is in these cases that the presence of supportive adults other than the depressed mother is so important (Carro et al., 1993).

To help prevent depression in infants, psychologists have been developing therapeutic techniques for modifying depressed mothers' behavior (Field, 1995). Some of the most effective interventions include teaching the depressed mother to imitate her baby's behaviors, to repeat words slowly when she talks to her baby, and to play games with her baby that are appropriate to the baby's developmental level. The babies whose mothers are given this kind of "interaction coaching" show increased eye contact and fewer expressions of distress (Field, 1995).

The boy in the picture is clearly upset by his parent's remarriage, but the eventual outcome of this change in his life will depend on the relationships that develop over the coming months and years.

they were subjected to parental conflict and other types of family stresses (Graham, Rutter, & George, 1973). The researchers suggest that temperamentally "difficult" children often become the targets of their family's distress and anger during periods of stress, which makes their already difficult situation worse, whereas "easy" children are able to stay out of the line of fire. An alternative explanation, however, may be that "easy" children simply fail to become upset by experiences, such as family disputes, that severely affect "difficult" children.

Several researchers have developed *transactional models* to describe the interplay among the various factors that influence development (Clarke & Clarke, 1986; Sameroff, 1995). These **transactional models** trace the ways in which the characteristics of the child and the characteristics of the child's environment interact across time ("transact") to determine developmental outcomes.

Thomas and Chess (1984) used a transactional model to explain the developmental implications of early temperamental patterns. To show how parents' interpretations can interact with a child's temperamental traits to influence the child's mental health, they describe a girl who

> had severe [neurotic] symptoms starting in her preschool years. She was temperamentally a difficult child, and her father responded with rigid demands for quick, positive adaptation and hostile criticisms and punishment when the girl could not meet his expectations. The mother was intimidated by both her husband and daughter and was vacillating and anxious in her handling of the child. With this extremely negative parent-child interaction, the girl's symptoms grew worse. Psychotherapy was instituted, with only modest improvement. But when she was 9–10 years of age, the girl blossomed forth with musical and dramatic talent, which brought her favorable attention and praise from teachers and other parents. This talent also ranked high in her parents' own hierarchy of desirable attributes. Her father now began to see his daughter's intense and explosive personality not as a sign of a "rotten kid," his previous label for her, but as evidence of a budding artist. He began to make allowances for her "artistic temperament," and with this the mother was able to relax and relate positively to her daughter. The girl was allowed to adapt at her own pace, and by adolescence all evidence of her neurotic symptoms and functioning had disappeared. (p. 7)

Transactional models Models of development that trace the ways in which the characteristics of the child and the characteristics of the child's environment interact across time to determine developmental outcomes.

Here, the initial negative child-parent interactions give rise to symptoms of mental illness in the girl that psychotherapy does little or nothing to overcome. When her drama and music talents are discovered, however, she acquires a new, positive social identity as a "talented kid." Her father now interprets her earlier behavior as a sign of talent (an "artistic temperament"), something in which he can take pride. This new interpretation brings about such changes in family interactions that the girl's negative symptoms disappear. Not all transactional histories have such happy outcomes, but all are characterized by complex interactions between a changing environmental context and the particular characteristics of the child that are highlighted in each new situation.

Transactional analysis is applied to groups of people as well as to individuals. Michael Rutter and his colleagues used a transactional model to explain the later life adjustments of young Londoners who had spent significant parts of their infancy and childhood in child-care facilities (Quinton & Rutter, 1985; Rutter, Quinton, & Hill, 1990). These children had been placed in institutions not because of any behavioral problems but because their parents could not cope with child rearing. Many of them remained in institutions throughout their infancy and early childhood. At 21 to 27 years old, they were compared with another group of the same age from the same part of London.

Focusing first on the "ex-care" (formerly institutionalized) women, Rutter and his colleagues found that these young adults had experienced difficulties that the women in the comparison group had not. To begin with, 42 percent had become pregnant before the age of 19, and 39 percent of them were no longer living with the fathers of their children. One-third had experienced a relatively serious breakdown in caring for their children. Only 5 percent of the women in the comparison group had become pregnant by the age of 19, all were living with the fathers of their children, and none had experienced a serious breakdown in the care of their children. When the women's current parenting practices were studied, the "ex-care" women were far more likely to receive poor ratings than were the women in the comparison group (see Table 7.2).

At first these findings may appear to be straightforward evidence of the long-term effects of early misfortune. But when they are viewed from the perspective of a transactional model, it becomes clear that the early misfortune set in motion a series of events that tended to perpetuate the difficulty. Institutional care led first to a lack of strong attachments during infancy and childhood and difficulties in

TABLE 7.2 Child-Care Behaviors of Mothers Raised in Institutions and of a Comparison Group of Mothers

Child-Care Difficulty	Ex-Care Group (n = 40)	Comparison Group (n = 43)
Lack of expression of warmth to children	45%	19%
Insensitivity	65%	28%
Lack of play with children	33%	16%
At least two of the above	59%	23%

Source: Quinton & Rutter, 1985.

forming good relationships with peers. These problems increased the likelihood of teenage pregnancy. The early pregnancy reduced the likelihood of further education or job training. The ensuing economic pressures created a disadvantaged environment, which in turn created the stresses that were the immediate cause of poor parenting.

Early institutionalization did not necessarily lead to continual misfortune, however. Those women raised in institutions who had supportive husbands were found to be just as effective at parenting as the women in the comparison group. These positive results led the researchers to conclude that institutionalization during infancy and childhood and the lack of strong personal attachments that goes with it do not necessarily doom women to become poor mothers. If the usual chain of consequences can be broken and favorable transactions established, normal behavior is likely to follow.

The profiles of the young men who had spent time in child-care institutions showed that positive later life experiences decreased their risk of long-term difficulties as well. One particularly interesting gender difference was that men were more likely than women to find a supportive spouse and to raise their children in an intact family, thus blocking the transmission of their own negative early experiences to the next generation (Rutter, Quinton, & Hill, 1990).

Recovery from Deprivation

The mounting evidence that the long-term consequences of misfortune depend to a significant degree on later circumstances has spurred a search for principles of successful intervention. A key element in any effort to repair developmental damage is removal from the damaging environment, but such a change alone is not sufficient for recovery. When the Lebanese children were moved from the crèche to other institutions, they did not reach normal levels of development, nor did Genie ever show sufficient recovery to become normal for her age. Could the Lebanese children or Genie have fared better? (See Box 7.3.) What conditions are necessary to foster more complete recovery from early deprivation? Is it possible that some as yet undiscovered environmental conditions might have allowed them to regain normal functioning? Or did their deprivation start too early and last too long to permit them ever to recover completely?

Such questions are impossible to answer in full because human babies cannot deliberately be assigned to live in potentially damaging circumstances to satisfy the quest for scientific knowledge. Research with monkeys, however, combined with scattered studies of human subjects, suggests what some of the aids to recovery might be.

HARLOW'S MONKEYS REVISITED

In Chapter 6 we examined Harry Harlow's studies of infant monkeys raised in isolation with inanimate surrogate mothers. One of Harlow's important findings was the difficulty the infant monkeys had developing normal social relations after they were introduced into cages with their peers. This was the case even with the monkeys who had become attached to surrogate terry-cloth mothers, although the severity of the behavioral disruption varied with the length of the isolation and the age of the monkey when the isolation began (Suomi & Harlow, 1972). Monkeys who were totally isolated for only the first 3 months of life, for example, did not seem to be permanently affected by the experience. When they were moved to a group cage, they were overwhelmed by the more complex environment at first, but within a month they had become accepted members of the social group.

BOX 7.3

Genie and the Wild Boy: Ethics Revisited

Genie, the girl who was locked away in a back room by her abusive father, strikingly demonstrates how scientific and ethical issues can conflict, even when no one involved in a research program seeks to hurt the subject of the research. The ethical controversy surrounding Genie focuses directly on this issue: Did the scientists who studied her development after she escaped from her confinement do all they could to ensure her recovery, or did their desire to solve a scientific puzzle lead them to subordinate Genie's well-being to the goal of scientific progress?

Russ Rymer (1993), who wrote a book about the case, argues that Genie's well-being was indeed sacrificed in the name of scientific inquiry. The scientists in charge of Genie's care deny any wrongdoing; they contend that Genie was treated as well as possible given the very unusual and difficult circumstances.

When Genie was first liberated, she was placed in Los Angeles Children's Hospital. It was quickly realized that she must have been isolated for many years; this was one of the most severe cases of child isolation on record. Her case quickly drew scientific interest. According to David Rigler, then chief psychiatrist at the hospital and the man who eventually became the principal investigator of Genie, human values and science alike called for a systematic study of Genie's development:

> Theories of child development hold that there are essential experiences for achievement of

normal psychological and physical growth. If this child can be assisted to develop in cognitive, linguistic and social, and other areas, this provides useful information regarding the critical role of early experience which is of potential benefit to other deprived children. The research interest inherently rests upon successful achievement of rehabilitative efforts. The research goals thus coincide with [Genie's] own welfare and happiness. (Rymer, 1993, p. 58)

Unfortunately for Genie, this is not how things worked out.

For the first several months after her liberation, Genie lived at Children's Hospital. David Rigler obtained a research grant to bring consultants together to decide what to do. The consultants disagreed. Some saw Genie as a scientific opportunity to answer questions about the development of language and thought. Inspired in part by the questions left unanswered by the case of Victor, the Wild Boy of Aveyron (a popular film based on Victor's story appeared just at that time), they wanted to use Genie to test the hypothesis that there is a critical period—up until puberty—after which language cannot be acquired.

Others argued that therapy for Genie should come first and everything else should be a secondary consideration. The psychologist David Elkind, one of the consultants, wrote, "Too much emphasis on language

Monkeys who were totally isolated for their first 6 months of life, in contrast, rocked, bit, or scratched themselves compulsively when they were placed in a cage with other monkeys. Monkeys who had been isolated during the second 6 months of life (but not the first) became aggressive and fearful when they were put back with other monkeys.

The long-term behavior of these groups of monkeys also differed. Those whose isolation began after 6 months of social interaction in the colony recovered quickly and were able to mate normally when they came of age. But those whose 6-month isolation started at birth recovered only partially. At 3 years of age, when they should have been able to mate, they proved to be incapable of normal sexual behavior.

Total isolation for the entire first year of life produced full-fledged social misfits who showed no propensities for social play or social interchange (Harlow & Novak, 1973). When they were placed in a group cage, these monkeys were often

could be detrimental if the child came to feel that love, attention, and acceptance were primarily dependent upon her speech" (Rymer, 1993, p. 59).

The decision was made to apply for a grant that focused on Genie's acquisition of language—not so much teaching Genie language as watching how she learned it. Shortly after this decision was made, Genie was exposed to rubella (German measles) while visiting the home of Jean Butler, her teacher at Children's Hospital. Rather than isolate Genie during her illness, the researchers decided that she should live with her teacher. In the next two months, Genie made enormous strides. But Jean Butler strongly objected to the intrusiveness of the scientists who were studying Genie. She said they were disrupting the girl's life and impeding her recovery. A battle for Genie's custody ensued. Butler applied to the Department of Public Social Services to become Genie's foster parent, but her request was denied in favor of David Rigler and his wife, Marilyn.

Genie lived in the Rigler household for four years. During that time she was treated as much as possible like a member of the family. She was taught how to chew solid food, to behave properly at the table, to express her emotions and indicate her desires appropriately, and to stop masturbating. But she was also being constantly observed and tested by linguists and psychologists.

Within a short time after her move to the Riglers' home, Genie's progress in language learning slowed to a standstill. Her speech resembled the language used in telegrams. She never learned to ask a real question or to form a proper negative sentence. Nor did she learn to behave normally in social situations. Scientists at the National Institutes of Mental Health, which sponsored the research on Genie, became dissatisfied with the project. Largely because it was a single case study based on anecdotal evidence and no controls were possible, they denied further funding for her study.

When the project ended, Genie was returned to her mother's custody. Her mother could not cope with Genie's disabilities and placed her in foster care. She is now residing in a home for mentally retarded adults in southern California. Overall, her behavior has significantly regressed. She is stooped and rarely makes eye contact. She cannot talk normally and continues to engage in inappropriate social behaviors.

Rigler and his colleagues chose to focus on Genie's language deprivation rather than on any of the other major domains of development. What if they had instead followed the lead of research on recovery from severe isolation? Would Genie have recovered more fully if they had provided her with social therapy emphasizing attachment and loving relations with others? There is no way to know. Russ Rymer titled his book *Genie: A Scientific Tragedy*. It tells the unfortunate sequel to the personal tragedy of a parent's inhuman treatment of a helpless child.

the targets of their peers' aggression. As time passed, they showed no signs of spontaneous recovery.

RECOVERY FROM THE EFFECTS OF ISOLATION

After their initial experiments, Harlow and his associates thought that the period from birth to 6 months of age might be critical for social development in these monkeys. If this were the case, recovery would be impossible for monkeys isolated throughout the 6-month period, regardless of any subsequent changes in their environment. The researchers tried various ways of aiding the adaptation of such monkeys to their new social world. One technique they used was to punish the monkeys for inappropriate behaviors by administering a mildly painful shock. Another approach was to introduce them to the new environment slowly, on the assumption that an abrupt change from total isolation to the busy activity of the

This mature female monkey, who was isolated for the first 6 months of life, finds it difficult to react to the baby monkey. But if the baby is sufficiently persistent in its attempts to interact with her, the older monkey may eventually learn to interact more or less normally with it.

group cage induced an "emergence trauma" that blocked recovery. The ineffectiveness of all these efforts seemed to support the idea that there was a critical period for social development. As it turned out, such was not the case at all.

The first hint that there might be an effective therapy for these monkeys came from observations of the maternal behaviors of the females, who had been artificially inseminated (Suomi, Harlow, & McKinney, 1972). Many of them beat their newborns and sat on them, and few of the babies survived. If a baby did live, however, the mother began to recover. As the researchers watched these babies with their mothers, they began to suspect how this change came about. If the baby monkeys could manage to cling to their mother's chest, as newborn infant monkeys normally do, they survived. While clinging, they not only had access to life-sustaining milk but also could usually escape their mothers' attempts to harm them. The longer they held on and the stronger they grew, the more time their mothers spent behaving in ways that were approximately normal, if not loving. By the end of the usual period of nursing, the mothers were no longer abusive and interacted more or less normally with their babies. Even more striking was the caregiving behavior of these mothers when they had a second baby. It was indistinguishable from that of their nondeprived peers. They had recovered normal social functioning.

The recovery of these mothers led Harlow and his colleagues to speculate that it might be possible to reverse the social pathologies of previously isolated monkeys by introducing them into a mother-infant type of relationship with a younger monkey (Harlow & Novak, 1973; Suomi & Harlow, 1972). The researchers introduced normal 2- to-3-month-old monkeys, who were strong enough to survive the abuse they were likely to receive, into a cage with monkeys who had been isolated for 12 months. The playful, love-seeking babies provided just what the older monkeys needed to learn appropriate social behaviors. Over a period of 18 weeks, the former isolates gradually stopped rocking and clasping themselves compulsively. They began to move around more, to explore their environments, and to engage in social play. In the end, all of the former isolates became so well adjusted that even experienced researchers could seldom tell them from monkeys who had been raised normally.

IMPLICATIONS FOR HUMAN RECOVERY

Harlow's research with monkeys suggests that placing previously isolated children in an environment in which they can interact with younger children may be therapeutic. This idea seems to be supported by the limited information available about the recovery of human children from extreme social deprivation. When the twins Koluchova (1972, 1976) studied were removed from their isolation, for example, they were at first placed in a special environment in which they lived with younger children. The twins recovered normal functioning despite their years of isolation.

Wyndol Furman, Donald Rahe, and Willard Hartup (1979) conducted a more formal test of the therapeutic potential of interactions with younger children. Through observations in day-care centers, the researchers identified 24 children between the ages of 2½ and 5 years who interacted so little with their peers that they were judged to be "socially isolated." These children were randomly assigned to three groups of eight children each. Each child in the first group participated in one-on-one play sessions with a child 1 to 1½ years old. The children in the second group participated in one-on-one play sessions with a child their own age.

The final group served as a control and received no special treatment. Each pair of children in the first two groups had 10 play sessions of 20 minutes each over a 6-week period. During each session, the two children were placed together in a room in which there were blocks, puppets, clothes to dress up in, and other toys that might promote positive social interaction. An observer sitting in the corner of the room took notes but otherwise tried not to interfere with the children.

After the last play session, the social interactions of all the children in the day-care classrooms were rated by observers who did not know which children had participated in the study. Their reports showed that the rate of peer interaction had almost doubled for the socially isolated children who had played with younger children. The children who had played with agemates showed some improvement, but they did not differ statistically from the control group. These results show that interactions with younger children, even for a relatively brief period, can reduce the effects of social isolation.

Such evidence of successful therapeutic intervention suggests the intriguing possibility that a given child's failure to recover may actually be due to adults' failure to arrange the proper therapeutic environment, not to some irreversible damage done to the child. The best environment for a formerly deprived or isolated child is not necessarily one that is common or easy to create. Adults ordinarily have limited time to spend with children, and they may not instinctively provide the special forms of attention and playfulness that will help deprived children to reorganize their patterns of social interaction.

This baby monkey is "comforting" an older monkey raised in isolation.

The Primacy of Infancy Reconsidered

Cases of significant recovery both in young animals and in children who have experienced extreme isolation or deprivation show that practitioners should not write such a child off; rather, a concerted effort should be made to give that child as therapeutic an environment as possible. When children are left to deal with undesirable life circumstances, however, especially circumstances that are abnormal for the society in which they live, it should be expected that negative experiences during infancy will have detectable effects on their later development. When children suffer severe and extended protein malnutrition during infancy, for example, studies have found disturbing evidence that effects remain at least into adolescence (Hoorweg & Stanfield, 1976; Galler, Ramsey, & Solimano, 1985).

Even the children described earlier as making remarkable recoveries showed some residual signs of their past deprivation. The children in Dennis's study who were adopted after infancy continued to exhibit somewhat depressed levels of intellectual ability, and Tizard and her colleagues found that the institutionalized children who were adopted continued to display problems in social adjustment.

In attempting to arrive at an overall conclusion about the primacy of infancy, it is helpful to return to the proverb "As the twig is bent, so grows the tree." If forces in the environment bend a sapling long enough, the tree may finally grow so low to the ground that its leaves cannot get the light they must have if the plant is to flower and hence to reproduce. But if the forces bending the tree are relieved in time, or if a gardener provides secure stakes to hold the tree upright, the only lasting effect may be a slight bend in the trunk. The tree will go on to flower and reproduce.

Three factors appear to be able to modify the impact of early experiences on the later development of human lives. The first is the one we have been focusing on: change in the environment. Whether these changes are positive (such as a supportive school environment or a community-based social support network) or negative (such as the outbreak of war or the death of a parent), they may create discontinuities in children's experiences that will set them on a new path into the future.

The second factor that may act to modify the long-term effects of experience in infancy is the bio-social-behavioral shift that reorganizes physical and psychological functions into qualitatively new patterns in human babies (but not twigs!) as infancy draws to a close. Such factors as the acquisition of language, new cognitive capacities, and a new relationship with the social world at the end of infancy result in a new way of experiencing and dealing with the world. A 12-month-old who is easily frustrated when she cannot get her own way may become a placid preschooler once she has learned to speak because she has acquired the ability to coordinate with her surroundings on her own terms. Alternatively, a placid baby who seems to take little interest in the world around him may suddenly display enormous curiosity and energy once he begins to walk.

The third factor is the change in the way children experience their environments as a result of their increased capacities. The separation anxiety shown by 1-year-olds when their caregivers are not present, for example, may be a realistic response for a helpless, relatively immobile infant because of the loss of crucial support that such separation entails. But 3-year-olds, who have a greater sense of autonomy because they can talk, walk, and run, are less dependent on their caregivers. Consequently, an experience that has a big effect on a 1-year-old may not affect a 3-year-old in the same way.

In recognition of the complicated interplay of the child's developing capacities, the changes these capacities bring about in the way the environment is experienced, and changes in the environment itself, psychologists who study the possible long-term effects of experience in infancy must also try to learn about:

1. The degree of discontinuity between infancy and later periods.
2. The significant threads of continuity between infancy and later life.
3. The mechanisms by which characteristics evident in early life are transformed or preserved in the transition from infancy to early childhood.

Two psychological domains that have been studied intensively with respect to these issues are attachment and cognition.

ATTACHMENT

In research on the long-term consequences of the various patterns of attachment, the basic strategy is to assess children's attachment just before their first birthday and then again several years later (Bretherton & Waters, 1985). The evidence concerning later developmental outcomes of particular attachment patterns is mixed (see Chapter 6, pp. 245–249).

Leah Matas, Richard Arend, and Alan Sroufe (1978) found that securely attached infants cooperate with their mothers in a difficult problem-solving task at the age of 2 years more effectively than children who manifest either anxious/avoidant or anxious/resistant attachment patterns. The securely attached babies also achieve higher scores on a scale of infant development (Main, 1973). Later, when they are 3½ years old, they are more curious, they play more effectively with their agemates, and they have better relationships with their teachers (Erikson, Sroufe, & Egeland, 1985; Frankel & Bates, 1990; Sroufe & Fleeson, 1986).

In follow-up observations over the next several years, Sroufe and his colleagues found that attachment classification during infancy predicted the quality of interactions into middle childhood and adolescence (Egeland, Carlson, &

The distress this French child exhibits as his mother drops him off at day care bespeaks the continued importance of attachment relations beyond infancy.

Sroufe, 1993; Sroufe, Carlson, & Shulman, 1993). When the children were 10, the researchers arranged for them to attend a summer camp where their interactions with peers and camp counselors could be observed. Children who were assessed as securely attached in infancy were more skillful socially, formed more friendships, displayed more self-confidence, and were less dependent than other campers, according to both their counselors' reports and the researchers' observations. Five years later the researchers arranged a camp reunion and found that the children initially assessed as securely attached were more open in expressing their feelings and in forming close relationships with other teenagers.

Despite reports such as these, many other investigators have not found that attachment status at 1 year of age predicts later behavior. John Bates, Christine Maslin, and Karen Frankel (1985) failed to find a relation between attachment behavior in the "strange situation" at 12 months and behavior problems at 3 years. Even studies that have found a general relationship between insecure attachment and later behavior problems sometimes report significant numbers of exceptions (Erikson, Sroufe, & Egeland, 1985).

Researchers who believe that patterns of attachment tend to remain consistent throughout development believe that children's attachment to their primary caregiver serves as the model for all later relationships. This view is similar to Freud's (see Chapter 6, p. 239). Inge Bretherton (1985) enlarges on this idea to explain how attachment patterns change. Drawing on a formulation by John Bowlby (1969), Bretherton proposed that infants build up an *internal working model* of the way to behave toward other people and then use it to figure out what to do each time they enter a new situation. As long as the people they interact with behave in ways that allow them to apply their internal working model effectively, children can be expected to continue to use it in all of their relationships (Sroufe & Fleeson, 1980). But if application of the internal working model leads to difficulties, it may change or be replaced. In short, continuity and discontinuity depend on the cumulative outcomes of everyday transactions between children and their environments.

To see how children's transactions influence developmental continuity, consider the finding that anxious/resistant children tend to cling to their mothers

(Chapter 6, p. 245). Suppose that we observe such a child in a preschool setting. If she is using her internal working model to guide her behavior, this little girl can be expected to try to stay close to the teacher. The consequences of her use of this internal working model at school will depend on how it is interpreted. If the teacher sees such behavior as politeness, cooperation, and eagerness to learn, the child will be likely to find this internal working model effective. Thus the same pattern of interaction will probably continue and may even be reinforced by the teacher. But suppose the teacher interprets the little girl's behavior as overly dependent. She may arrange for the girl to help younger, shyer children, thereby providing her with the experience of a new form of social interaction. As a result, the child's internal working model may change and her subsequent interactions with others may diverge from the earlier pattern.

Here we see, on the one hand, how internal working models of relationships can produce continuity in social interactions over time, and on the other hand, why it may be difficult to predict whether infants' patterns of interaction will be maintained in later life. The degree of continuity will depend on the nature of the initial internal working model and the extent to which it proves to be adaptive in children's transactions in the many contexts they encounter later in life.

COGNITIVE DEVELOPMENT

For many decades researchers believed that individual differences in infants' intellectual development did *not* predict later achievement, that there was little continuity in cognitive processes from infancy to later life. After reviewing many studies that attempted to correlate scores on infant developmental scales with later test scores, Claire Kopp and Robert McCall (1982) unequivocally concluded that "tests given during the first 18 months of life do not predict childhood IQ to any useful or interesting degree" (p. 35).

When young children were first given a standardized psychological test and years later a test of their cognitive abilities, the correlations between the test scores were better when the first test was administered after the children had reached the age of 24 months. Still, tests given at 3, 4, and 5 years of age were not sufficiently predictive of children's subsequent behavior to be useful unless the initial scores deviated a great deal from the norm (McCall, 1981; Sameroff, 1978).

In recent years psychologists have been somewhat more successful in demonstrating that individual cognitive characteristics measured in infancy do predict later intellectual abilities. The key difference between the earlier (generally unsuccessful) and more recent studies is that the earlier studies did not tap the same psychological processes both times the children were tested; standardized tests of infants' abilities focus heavily on the sensorimotor sphere, whereas tests of older children's intellectual ability focus on the conceptual sphere.

Several psychologists argue that it is possible to demonstrate a modest degree of continuity from infancy into childhood when appropriate behaviors are sampled and are measured sensitively (Laucht, Esser, & Schmidt, 1994; Rose et al., 1991; Sternberg, 1988). One line of support for claims of cognitive continuity between infancy and childhood comes from studies of the rate at which infants process visual information. It has been found, for example, that infants who habituate rapidly to repeated events are subsequently, in early childhood, more likely to display characteristics that psychologists associate with advanced intellectual development. These children are more likely to explore their environment rapidly, for instance, to play in relatively sophisticated ways, and to excel at various problem-solving and concept-formation tasks (Bornstein & Sigman, 1986).

Even in these cases, however, the degree of association between early and later cognitive performances, though statistically significant, is low enough to make it clear that such continuity is characteristic of only some children. Too little is known about the critical experiences that enhance, disrupt, or transform cognitive processes to enable us to specify the transactional mechanisms that work to sustain or disrupt those processes.

COMING TO TERMS WITH LIMITED PREDICTABILITY

Although recent research into continuity in various psychological spheres points to significant continuities between infancy and later developmental periods, it falls well short of implying that any trait is always continuous and predictable. The correlations between behaviors in infancy and later are generally very modest. Consequently, data showing marked recovery from early traumatic conditions (which suggest that psychological functioning can change markedly after infancy) and data showing a moderate correlation in individual behavioral traits over time (which imply continuity of functioning) should not be seen as contradictory. Together they provide evidence that a child's development is both continuous and discontinuous simultaneously.

Many years ago Sigmund Freud (1920/1924) pointed out that whether development seems continuous and predictable or discontinuous and uncertain depends to a certain extent on one's vantage point:

> So long as we trace the development [of a psychological process] from its final stage backwards, the connection appears continuous, and we feel we have gained an insight which is completely satisfactory or even exhaustive. But if we proceed the reverse way, if we start from the premises inferred from the analysis and try to follow these up to the final result, then we no longer get the impression of an inevitable sequence of events which could not be otherwise determined. We notice at once that there might have been another result. . . . (p. 226)

Figure 7.3 is a schematic representation of Freud's insight. If we start at some point in later life, E, and trace a person's history back to its beginnings, A, we can build a convincing case for why that precise life history proceeded as it did; the developmental state at time E resulted from events at time D, which resulted from events at time C, and so on. At each decision point, we can sort out the various contributing factors and discern which had the most influence. Only one route leads into the past at each point. But standing at the beginning, A, and looking ahead to the future, we cannot foresee the choices that will be made at points B, C, and D. To borrow Robert Frost's metaphor (p. 259), the bends in the diverging roads are hidden in the undergrowth.

For parents, the uncertainties about whether they are doing the right thing for their baby and whether their baby is developing normally are a natural source of anxiety. Research on primacy, however, shows us that this uncertainty has its good side. A perfectly predictable future holds no possibility of choice. Without the uncertainties that arise from changes in the environment and the changes in the child that accompany development, parents could not dream about influencing the course of their baby's future. It would be immutable. With these uncertainties come the possibility and the challenge of taking advantage of those changes to promote the child's welfare.

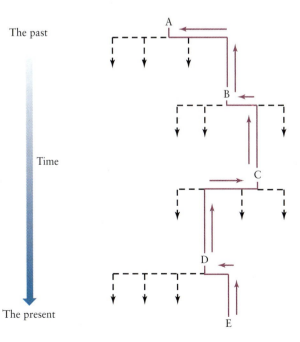

FIGURE 7.3   *It is relatively easy to trace development backward to its origins (red arrows). But the many decision points with uncertain outcomes that confront organisms during the life span defeat efforts to predict their futures. (Adapted from Emde, Gaensbauer, & Harmon, 1976.)*

The past

Time

The present

SUMMARY

- Many people believe that experiences in infancy are the most significant forces in the shaping of later behavior.

Optimal Conditions for Infant Development

- To foster optimal development, the caregiver must be sensitive and responsive to the infant's needs and signals. The kinds of sensitivity and responsiveness that are considered optimal in child rearing, and the way they are expressed, depend on the historical and cultural circumstances into which the child is born.

- Research does not support the belief that responsiveness to an infant's cries will spoil the child and cause unrealistic expectations that will result in antisocial behavior later.

- Paying too little attention to infants can result in learned helplessness, a state of mind that develops when children believe that nothing they do has any effect on what happens to them. Babies who develop learned helplessness fail to take initiative in their own behalf.

Effects of Separation

- Separation from parents is upsetting to babies. However, such separations have long-term negative consequences only when they are of long duration or are repeated.

- Experts dispute the consequences of short daily separations resulting from out-of-home care during the first year of life.

- Extended residence in a poorly staffed orphanage retards both mental and social development. Residence in a well-staffed orphanage produces less pronounced developmental difficulties. The degree to which children recover from such experiences depends on their subsequent environments and the age at which they leave the institution.

- Total isolation leads to severe mental and social retardation. If children are moved to a supportive environment before they are 6 or 7 years old, recovery is sometimes possible. If their circumstances are not changed until adolescence, full recovery appears to be impossible.

Vulnerability and Resilience

- Living in a home where a high level of discord is combined with social deviance or poverty and in a community where the school environment is poor puts a child at risk for later psychiatric disorders.

- Children's vulnerability to stressful circumstances depends to some extent on:

  1. Variations in temperament.
  2. Such family factors as the number of siblings, the mother's work load, and the presence of a network of kin and friends.
  3. Characteristics of the community, such as whether the neighborhood is in an urban slum or a rural area.
  4. The quality of the local school.

- The processes that lead to various developmental outcomes can be thought of as transactions between child and environment over an extended period of time.

Recovery from Deprivation

- Studies of monkeys suggest that recovery from early isolation can be achieved later than was once thought possible if an adequate therapeutic environment can be arranged. Research has shown that similar principles can be applied to socially isolated children.

The Primacy of Infancy Reconsidered

- Three factors limit the degree to which the psychological characteristics of older children and adults can be predicted from their characteristics as infants:
  1. Changes in the child's environment.
  2. The qualitative reorganization of the child's physical and psychological characteristics.
  3. An increase in the child's capacity to cope with the environment.

Key Terms

competence motive,
  p. 265

learned helplessness,
  p. 264

primacy,   p. 260

resilience,   p. 273

transactional models,
  p. 277

Thought Questions

1. Think of a time in your life when two pathways lay before you and consider what might have happened had you taken a different path. What makes it possible to imagine the alternative? What makes it hard to imagine?
2. Why might demonstrations of learned helplessness in dogs not apply to human development?
3. Imagine you are the director of an orphanage. In view of the information provided in Chapters 4 through 7, what are some of the practices you would promote to provide the best possible development for the children in your institution?
4. Imagine you are the director of a community program to improve the early experiences of children living in a poor community. What sorts of programs would you seek to promote? Give a research-based rationale for your suggestions.
5. How does a transactional approach to developmental change relate to the adage "As the twig is bent, so grows the tree"?

PART THREE

EARLY CHILDHOOD

By the age of 2½ or 3, children are clearly infants no longer. As they enter early childhood—the period between 2½ and 6—they lose their baby fat, their legs grow longer and thinner, and they move around the world with a great deal more confidence than they did only 6 months earlier. Within a short time they can usually ride a tricycle, control their bowels, and put on their own clothes. They can get out of bed quietly on Sunday morning and turn on the TV to amuse themselves while their parents still sleep. They can go over to a friend's house to play and take the role of flower girl or ring bearer at a wedding. Most 3-year-olds can talk an adult's ears off, even if their train of thought is difficult to follow, and they provide an avid audience for an interesting story. They can be bribed with promises of a later treat, but they won't necessarily accept the terms that are offered, and they may try to negotiate for a treat now as well as later. They develop theories about everything, which they constantly test against the realities around them.

Despite their developing independence, 3-year-olds need assistance from adults and older siblings in many areas. They cannot hold a pencil properly, string a loom, or tie their shoes. They do not yet have the ability to concentrate for long without a great deal of support. As a result, they often go off on tangents in their games, drawings, and conversations. One minute a 3-year-old may be mommy in a game of house, the next minute Cinderella, and the next a little girl in a hurry to go to the toilet. Children at this time still understand relatively little about the world in which they live and have little control over it. Thus they are prey to fears of monsters, the dark, dogs, and other apparent threats. They combat their awareness of being small and powerless by wishful, magical thinking that turns a little boy afraid of dogs into a big, brave, gun-toting cowboy who dominates the block.

Despite the long-term interest of developmental psychologists in early childhood, considerable uncertainty remains about how best to characterize this period of life. In some respects, it appears to be a distinctive stage with its own special modes of thinking, feeling, and acting. In other respects, it appears to be simply the beginning of a long period of gradual change that extends into adolescence and adulthood. In recent years early childhood has attracted special attention because 3- and 4-year-olds appear to be capable of doing some things that it was believed only children 7 or 8 could do, challenging long-held ideas about childhood development.

Our discussion of early childhood development covers four chapters. Chapter 8 examines the nature of language and its development. Once children begin to acquire language, they can experience the world in an entirely new way. Language is the medium through which they learn about their roles in the world, acceptable behavior, and their culture's assumptions about how the world works. Simultaneously, language enables children to ask questions, to explain their thoughts and desires, and to make more effective demands on the people around them.

Chapter 9 examines thinking during early childhood. Leading theories are compared for their ability to explain how young children can behave with logical self-possession at one moment only to become fanciful and dependent the next. The chapter considers whether their apparently illogical behavior is the result of their lack of experience or is governed by its own special logic.

Chapter 10 considers young children's social development and personality formation, their ideas about themselves, the way they think about rules of proper behavior, and their relations with the people around them. The chapter focuses on the acquisition of sex roles and on children's changing ability to get along with each other, particularly as they learn to balance their own desires with the demands of their social group.

With these general characteristics of early childhood as background, Chapter 11 addresses the influence of various contexts on preschoolers' development: first the family, where children come to learn about who they are and what adults expect of them, then day-care centers, preschools, and the media.

Language Acquisition

> **Girl:** *[on toy telephone]* David!
>
> **Boy:** *[not picking up second phone]* I'm not home.
>
> **Girl:** When you'll be back?
>
> **Boy:** I'm not here already.
>
> **Girl:** But *when will you be back?*
>
> **Boy:** Don't you know if I'm gone already, I went *before* so I can't talk to you!
>
> —*George Miller*, Language and Speech

> So here I am, in the middle way,
>
> having had twenty years—
>
> Twenty years largely wasted, the years of
>
> *l'entre deux guerres*—
>
> Trying to learn to use words, and every
>
> attempt
>
> Is a wholly new start, and a different kind
>
> of failure
>
> Because one has only learnt to get the
>
> better of words
>
> For the thing one no longer has to say, or
>
> the way in which
>
> One is no longer disposed to say it.
>
> —*T. S. Eliot*, "East Coker"

Both the real conversations of young children and the poet quoted in this chapter's epigraph testify that learning to "say it right" is a lifelong process. As we have seen, the first blossoming of language around the age of 2 years is a basic component of the bio-social-behavioral shift that separates infancy from early childhood. Language development is by no means complete by age 2½, however.

In the period between 2 and 6 years of age, children's mental and social lives are totally transformed by an explosive growth in the ability to comprehend and use language. They are estimated to be learning several words a day during this period, and by the time they are 6 years old their vocabularies have grown to anywhere between 8,000 and 14,000 words (Anglin, 1993; Templin, 1957). They can understand verbal instructions ("Go wash your face—and don't come back until it's clean"), chatter excitedly about the tiger they saw at the zoo, and insult their sisters and brothers. Although they will continue to acquire linguistic nuances and a more extensive vocabulary, 6-year-old children are competent language users. Without this achievement, they could not carry out the new cognitive tasks and social responsibilities that their society will now assign them.

We begin this chapter by reviewing and elaborating on the early foundations of linguistic communication that we discussed in earlier chapters. Next we trace the course of children's mastery of the four basic subsystems that constitute language: the sound system, the words, the grammar, and the uses to which language is put. With the facts of language development in hand, we turn to competing theories about the processes that underlie this unique and fundamental human capacity. Then we examine what is known about the necessary prerequisites for acquiring human language and how language affects thought.

Prelinguistic Communication

The evidence presented in Chapters 3 through 7 leaves little doubt that children are born into the world predisposed to attend to language and to communicate with the people around them. At birth they show a preference for language over other kinds of sounds and are capable of differentiating the basic sound categories or phonemes characteristic of the world's languages. Within a few days after birth they can distinguish the sounds of their native language from those of a foreign language. Well before they are able to speak intelligibly they have narrowed the range of sound distinctions they recognize to the sound categories of the languages they hear around them (p. 214).

The newborns' communicative abilities are initially limited to a small set of facial expressions and crying. Though variations in cry patterns are not particularly informative, they do provide caregivers with rudimentary information about the causes of distress. At about 2½ months, babies' communicative ability is enhanced by social smiles. Their sound repertoire expands to include cooing, which in turn is supplanted by *babbling* and then *jargoning*; each change brings the baby closer to producing recognizable words.

At the same time that babies' capacity to distinguish and produce linguistic signals increases, they are also becoming more adept at interacting with the people and objects around them. At birth their weak muscles and restricted vision make it difficult to carry out the most elementary functions, such as nursing and examining an object in a coordinated way. Within a few weeks, with a good deal of support from the parents, these functions become part of a daily routine that gives structure to babies' limited experiences. *Primary intersubjectivity*, the ability to match their behavior to that of another person and to share experiences in direct face-to-face interaction, emerges at about 3 months of age (Chapter 5, p. 213). It is evident in the rounds of helloing and smiling in which mothers and babies engage, to their mutual delight.

At around 9 months, babies acquire the ability to share mental states with another person when the joint focus of attention is a third person, an activity, or an object—an ability called *secondary intersubjectivity* (Chapter 5, p. 213). The close link between secondary intersubjectivity and communication is seen clearly in the form of behavior called *social referencing*, when babies check their mother's reactions to an uncertain event or an unfamiliar person and respond in accordance with her evaluation. *Secondary intersubjectivity* is a crucial precursor to language acquisition: when babies and their caregivers signal to one another, they are sharing knowledge about the objects and events that are the focus of their joint attention (Tomasello, 1992).

Between the ages of 9 and 12 months, babies begin to point at objects (Bruner, 1983a; Franco & Butterworth, 1991). Pointing is clearly a communicative act intended to create a joint focus of attention, but it is a primitive one. When 12-month-olds see a remote-controlled car roll past them, first they point at it and then they look to see how their mothers react to it (social referencing). At 18 months the function of pointing becomes communicative in a more complex way. Now the children are more likely first to look at their mothers to see if they are looking at the car and then to point to it. If babies this age are alone in the room when the electric car appears, they do not point until the adult walks back into the room, clearly demonstrating that their pointing has a purpose and is meant to communicate to another person.

During the second year of life children's repertoire of words accumulates, slowly to begin with and then at an increasing rate. As this is happening, they acquire greater ability to produce and understand more complex sentences.

In sum, when we look at development from birth to the start of the third year of life, we can see that the capacity for communication has already developed to a remarkable degree well before the child can actually hold a conversation.

The Puzzle of Language Development

A first step in any study of language is to recognize that although language is one of the most distinctive characteristics of our species, it is still very poorly understood. Linguists, specialists in the study of language, can tell us a great deal about the structure of adult language, the history and meanings of words, and the physical apparatus that transmits utterances from one person to another. But they have not been able to answer such basic questions as how children acquire language and how either children or adults compose and comprehend it. Developmental psychologists currently play a major part in the effort to understand both the nature of language and its role in the development of children. Two basic questions that have proved especially difficult to answer are: How do children discover what words mean? (the problem of reference) and How do they learn to arrange words and parts of words in a way that has meaning to others? (the problem of grammar).

THE PROBLEM OF REFERENCE

Perhaps the most basic intuition that we have about language is that each word refers to something; words name real or fancied objects and relationships in the world. This idea seems so commonsensical that it is difficult to grasp the mystery it conceals, a mystery that no philosopher, linguist, or psychologist has ever adequately explained: How, among all the many things or relations to which any word or phrase may refer, do we ever learn to pick out its intended referent—the object to which it refers?

FIGURE 8.1   *For children just learning to talk, the problem of knowing what words refer to is particularly acute.*

"Smotri, synochek, tam sidit ptitsa."

In Figure 8.1 we see the difficulty of determining what a word refers to. Imagine you are the child in the picture and try to decide what the Russian father is saying. It's a puzzle, isn't it?

Some people may argue that the example is unfair because the utterance is in a foreign language. A little more reflection reveals that the example may be fair after all; in the beginning, all languages are foreign to newborn children, who must somehow figure out that the sounds they hear are in fact meant to refer to something in the ongoing flow of experience—to indicate an actual object, event, or feeling.

To make the difficulty clearer, suppose you know all of the words that the father says except one: "Look, son, there sits a *ptitsa.*" Even this additional information does not tell us which of the objects in the scene is a *ptitsa.* The cat sitting on the wall? The helicopter sitting on the roof? Or the bird sitting in the tree? If you know Russian, you know that the father is pointing at the bird. But the language-learning child, even the Russian language-learning child, is not born knowing the meaning of the sound package *ptitsa.* Somehow the child must learn that when the father says *ptitsa* he is talking about the winged creature in the tree and not about any of the other objects.

The problem of how children come to know what words refer to is complicated by the fact that a single object or event has many parts and features, which can be referred to in a great many ways. George Miller (1991) illustrates this problem with the example in Figure 8.2. If an adult points to the object in Figure 8.2 and refers to it in the various ways indicated, how is the child to avoid the conclusion that "rabbit," "ear," "white," and "Harvey" are synonyms? Yet somehow, despite all the apparently confusing ways in which objects and actions are referred to, children learn the meanings associated with all of the different kinds of references.

"That's Harvey."

"That's an ear."

"That's a rabbit."

"That's a picture."

"That's the Easter Bunny."

"That's white."

"That's an animal."

FIGURE 8.2 *An adult can point to the animal in this picture or to many parts of the animal and apply the same kind of declaratory statement: "That's a _____." How do children know what is being referred to? (From Miller, 1991.)*

THE PROBLEM OF GRAMMAR

For words to be combined into a comprehensible sentence, they must be related not only to objects and events but to one another. The rules that govern both the sequence of words in a sentence and the ordering of parts of words (prefixes such as *pre-* begin words; suffixes such as *-ing* end words) are called the **grammar** of a language.

One clear indicator that even children as young as 2½ or 3 years old have some grasp of grammar comes from the errors they make when they string words together. When we hear a child make such statements as "My doggy runned away" or "Mommy, Johnny camed late," we know immediately that the child has confused one grammatical form with another. Such errors are so common that it is easy to overlook their significance. Children cannot have been taught to say such things, nor could they have learned them by simple imitation, because they virtually never hear such incorrect sentences uttered. Where could these sentences come from?

No less puzzling is the appearance in children's language of **recursion,** the embedding of sentences within each other. Recursion is one of the central properties of human language. It provides language with great economy and flexibility of expression. For example, the three sentences "The boy went to the beach," "He saw some fish," and "The boy got sunburned" can easily be combined to create "The boy who went to the beach saw some fish and got a sunburn": three sentences for the price of one. Only human communication exhibits this recursive capacity, and there is no evidence that it is ever consciously taught. How, then, do children develop it?

Here we see the central puzzle of language acquisition. On the one hand, almost all children, even many who are mentally retarded, acquire the ability to speak and communicate with words, so language appears to be a fundamental capacity that is easy for humans to acquire, like learning to walk. On the other hand, the complexities and subtleties of language are so great that it is difficult to understand how word meanings or grammatical rules could ever be acquired.

Somehow, in the space of a very few years, children accomplish something denied all other species. What is it they do, and how do they manage to do it?

With the early foundations of language and these puzzles in mind, it is now time to turn our attention to language itself, the system of communication fundamental to human life and human development.

Grammar The rules of a language that govern both the sequence of words in a sentence and the ordering of parts of words.

Recursion The embedding of sentences within each other.

Four Subsystems of Language

Language, according to *Webster's Ninth New Collegiate Dictionary*, is "the words, their pronunciation, and the methods of combining them used and understood by a considerable community." This definition identifies four central aspects of language: sounds, words, methods of combining words, and the communal uses that language serves. We will describe the development of each of these aspects separately, but it is important to keep in mind that language is a system: each of its aspects is connected to all of the others, and each aspect is itself a distinctive subsystem of elements. Unless some pathology interferes with normal development, these separate subsystems of language form a unified, organic whole.

SOUNDS

In the change from babbling to pronouncing words late in the first year, children give up their relative freedom to play with sounds and begin to vocalize the particular sounds and sound sequences that make up the words in their language community (Kuhl et al., 1992). Conformity to a restricted set of sounds brings with it both the ability to create meaningful distinctions between sounds and the freedom to speak rapidly. English-speaking adults talk at an average rate of about 150 words per minute. The words they use contain an average of 5 phones (speech sounds) each. This means that adults can easily produce about 12½ sounds per second, and with extra effort are capable of producing as many as 25 to 30 sounds per second. According to Philip Lieberman (1984), this feat would be impossible if the set of sounds and sound combinations were not organized, with permissible combinations drastically restricted. These same restrictions help children to discover the system of sounds in the language they hear.

It takes children several years to master the pronunciation of the separate words of their native language. Their first efforts may be no more than crude stabs at the right sound pattern, almost as if they were attempting to get the tune right at the same time that they are working on the meanings. One frequent simplification is to leave out parts of words (saying "ca" instead of "cat"). Multisyllable words are often turned into a repeating pattern. For example, a child may use the sound pattern "bubba" to say "button," "butter," "bubble," and "baby." A long word, such as "motorcycle," can come out sounding like almost anything: "momo," "motokaka," or even "lomacity" (Preisser, Hodson, & Paden, 1988).

Children's mastery of the sound system of their native language proceeds unevenly. Sometimes a particular sound will prove especially difficult, even after many words that employ that sound are well understood. At the age of 2½, for example, Alexander could not say /l/ sounds at the beginning of words, so he could not pronounce the name of his friend's dog, Lucky. Instead, he consistently pronounced the name "Yucky," much to the amusement of his family. This error didn't concern Alex at all; he knew what other people were talking about when they referred to Lucky, and Lucky didn't seem to notice. When Alex called him he came.

Neil Smith (1971) showed that such substitutions do not arise because children are incapable of pronouncing certain sounds. When he asked one young child to say the word "puddle" it came out as "puzzle," but when he asked for "puzzle" it became "puggle"! Another child would always say "fick" instead of "thick," but he had no difficulty in saying "thick" when he meant to say "sick." Both examples suggest that the basic sounds of a language are learned as parts of the larger system into which they fit, rather than as isolated instances of pronunciation.

Learning to make language sounds properly takes time and practice.

Evidently, newborn children can perceive the differences between the basic sounds of their language. This does not mean, however, that phonemes are "just there" at birth. When, for example, a child learns to employ the English phoneme /l/, more is involved than learning to reproduce a particular sound wave by creating a particular mouth shape. In reality, /l/ is a phoneme (sound category) of English because in our language it contrasts with other phonemes, such as /y/, as part of meaningful words. We hear /l/ and /y/ as different sounds only because they create different meanings: English speakers must learn that "lap" and "yap" or "lard" and "yard" are not simply variations in the pronunciation of a single word, as they could be in another language. Children's attention to the differences between sounds is not simply a mechanical skill, but develops along with their growing understanding of the meanings of words.

The close connection between phonemes and meanings becomes clear when one is attempting to learn a foreign language. Some native speakers of Spanish, for whom /b/ and /v/ sound much the same, find it difficult to produce or to hear any difference between them. To native English speakers "boat" and "vote" sound quite different; to Spanish speakers, these two words sound much the same and thus may be spoken interchangeably. Likewise, the English speaker frequently has difficulty hearing and producing the difference between the French *u* and *ou*, because that difference does not exist in English.

Although it is often convenient to think of words as the basic units of meaning in language, many words contain more than one meaning-bearing part, or *morpheme*. A morpheme may be a whole word or only a part of one. The word "transplanted," for example, is made up of three morphemes. The root of the word is "plant," which means "to fix in place." The morpheme "trans" means "across, over, beyond," and the morpheme "ed" is a marker of past tense. We do not stop to ponder all of these relations when we say a sentence with the word "transplanted" in it. In fact, until the rules are pointed out, we rarely stop to think about the parts of words or the way we compose them. Yet every child must acquire the ability to decipher and reproduce just such intricate interweavings of sound and meaning.

WORDS

It takes no effort at all to figure out when children make their first sounds; a shrill cry at birth settles that question. It is more difficult to decide when children first use actual words. Adults may be so eager to claim the power of speech for their children that they discover "words" in early cooing and babbling. Genuine words, however, appear only late in the first year, after children have been babbling for some time and after the contours of their sounds or of their hand movements, if they are learning American Sign Language, have gradually become more speech-like (as we saw in Chapter 5).

It is useful to think of the process of word formation as a peculiar sort of joint effort or collusion. Neither the adult nor the child really knows what the other is saying. Each tries to gather in a little meaning by supposing that the other's utterance fits a particular sound pattern that corresponds to a particular meaning. This joint effort, or collusion, may eventually result in something common, a word in a language that both can understand. This process may also fail. As the following examples make clear, the process can proceed in a variety of ways, depending on how the parent interprets the relation between the child's sounds and actions.

At 8 months Pablo began to say "dahdee." Although this "first" word sounds like "daddy," Pablo used "dahdee" for commands and requests when daddy was nowhere to be seen, so it must have had some other meaning for him. Adults interpreted "dahdee" to mean either "Take it from me" (when Pablo said it while he offered something to someone) or "Give it to me"; they ignored the fact that Pablo's first word sounded like "daddy." At about the age of 12 months, "dahdee" disappeared from Pablo's vocabulary (Shopen, 1980). A different fate befell Brenan's first word, "whey." Around 1 year of age, Brenan began to say "whey" after an adult had spoken. In this case, the adults' interpretation led them to incorporate the word when they spoke to Brenan. "Whey" not only sounded something like "why," it also came at a position in normal conversational turn-taking where "why" would be a possible (if not always appropriate) thing to say. Brenan's parents therefore responded to "whey" as if Brenan had asked a question and rephrased what they had said in order to "answer his question," expanding on their original utterance. Over time, Brenan pronounced and used "whey" more and more like a true "why" until it became a genuine "why" in the English language (Griffin, 1983).

Yet another route to the formation of the first word is taken by Samoans, who believe that once children begin to walk, they become cheeky and willful. In accordance with this belief, the only word that Samoan parents acknowledge as a child's first word is "tae," which is a Samoan curse word meaning "shit." They explain this remarkable agreement among their children as confirmation of Samoan common knowledge—that young children are defiant and angry. In fact, young Samoan children may make a number of sounds that might be interpreted as words, but Samoan adults choose to hear and acknowledge only "tae" (Ochs, 1982).

Each of these instances differs from the others in significant ways, but all are variations of a single process in which adults collude with each other and their children to create word meanings.

Words as mediators

From birth onward, infants' cries and coos express their emotional states. At some point, usually around 11 to 12 months of age, babies discover that the sound sequences they make can recruit adults' attention and help. What began as a process of making sounds that merely expressed emotion becomes a process of producing sounds that also anticipate, guide, and stimulate action and feeling. With the emergence of the capacity to use words, children acquire the ability to organize their activity in a new way.

This additional feature of language is illustrated in observations that Elizabeth Bates (1976) made of a 13-month-old girl:

> C. is seated in a corridor in front of the kitchen door. She looks toward her mother and calls with an acute sound *ha.* Mother comes over to her, and C. looks toward the kitchen, twisting her shoulders and upper body to do so. Mother carries her to the kitchen, and C. points toward the sink. Mother gives her a glass of water, and C. drinks it eagerly. (p. 55)

In this interaction we see several key features of the process of early word use. First, it is an excellent example of secondary intersubjectivity; initially the linguistic object, "ha," and then its referent, the glass of water, are jointly attended to by mother and child. Second, the episode illustrates clearly that it is the relation of the sound to action, and not just some property of the sound itself, that justifies the conclusion that a word has entered a person's vocabulary. Of course, in this case "ha," the "word" in question, functions in a very small community, the community of mother and child. Nonetheless, the child's use of "ha" displays an important new ability. Instead of seeking to operate directly on the object (by, for example, attempting to toddle over to the sink), the child operates indirectly through an idiosyncratic sound that evokes the desired behavior from the mother.

In this and the remaining chapters of this book, we will refer to the property of language illustrated in Bates's example as the *mediated,* or indirect, character of

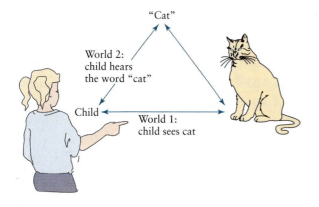

FIGURE 8.3 *Children experience the world in two distinctive ways once they acquire language: directly through their sensory contact with the physical environment (world 1) and indirectly (symbolically) through language (world 2).*

linguistic behavior. Until children acquire the ability to use and understand words, they are restricted to immediate, or direct, actions. But with the advent of language, they can also deliberately act indirectly, using words to mediate their actions. They can make something happen without doing the thing themselves. The same principle applies to the way children can be influenced by others; once they start to understand words, children can be influenced by others both directly, via nonverbal actions, and indirectly, through the mediating power of words and the culturally organized knowledge that words embody (see Figure 8.3).

Alexander Luria (1981) beautifully summarized the new intellectual power that human beings obtain when their behavior begins to be mediated by words:

> The enormous advantage is that their world doubles. In the absence of words, humans would have to deal only with those things which they could perceive and manipulate directly. With the help of language, they can deal with things which they have not perceived even indirectly and with things which were part of the experience of earlier generations. Thus, the word adds another dimension to the world of humans. . . . Animals have only one world, the world of objects and situations which can be perceived by the senses. Humans have a double world. (p. 35)

The earliest vocabulary

Evidence concerning children's earliest words comes from records kept by parents and tape recordings of children's speech in their homes or in organized play facilities (Bloom, 1993; Clark, 1995; Fenson et al., 1994).

One of the often-cited findings of this work is that words referring to objects occur frequently in the vocabularies of young children as they approach their second birthday (Bloom, Tinker, & Margoulis, 1993). For example, Katherine Nelson (1973) enlisted the aid of 18 families in keeping track of everything their children said during the months they were acquiring their first words. She found that most early words (65 percent) label things and classes of things at the same time, such as "doggie," "juice," and "ball," or particular things, such as "Mommy," "Daddy," and pet names.

Nelson (1976) points out that the first words acquired are often closely linked to actions that the child can accomplish with the things named. "Hat" and "sock" are common in the initial vocabularies of American children, but "sweater" and "diapers" are not, perhaps because little children can act more or less effectively on hats and socks, but sweaters and diapers are done to them. In addition, objects that can change and move (such as cars and animals) are likely to be named, whereas large, immobile objects such as trees and houses are "just there" and are not likely to be named. The fact that children tend to use words just at the moment when objects are changing and moving suggests a close link between words and actions in the young child's mind (Greenfield, 1991).

Though children use object labels fairly frequently, such words usually account for less than half of 2-year-olds' vocabularies (Bloom, 1993). What about the remaining words? Alison Gopnik and Andrew Meltzoff (1986) found that in addition to labeling things, young children use relational words to communicate about changes in the state or location of an object; "gone" may be said when an object disappears and "here" may announce its appearance. One of the most useful relational words in children's early vocabularies is "no," which can fulfill such important communicative functions as rejection, protest, and denial. "No" can also be used to comment on unfulfilled expectations and on an object's absence. Given these multiple functions, it is little wonder that "no" is among the earliest and most frequently used words in a child's initial vocabulary (Bloom, 1973).

Gopnik and Meltzoff (1986) identify an additional class of words that children use around the age of 2 to comment on their successes ("There!" "Hooray!") and failures ("Uh-oh"). This verbal evidence appears to fit well with the evidence that

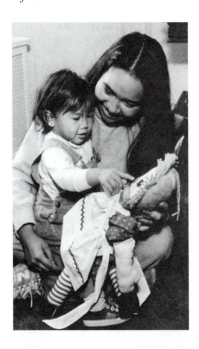

Many first words label familiar objects.

BOX 8.1

Gulliver among the Laputans

The common-sense idea that words can be identified only with things and have fixed, unique meanings is very difficult to overcome. In the following passage from *Gulliver's Travels*, Jonathan Swift highlights the absurdities to which such common sense leads. In the land of Laputa, the people have listened to their literal-minded philosophers too attentively. Swift's hero, Gulliver, tells us:

> Since Words are only names for Things, it would be more convenient for all Men to carry about them such Things as were necessary to express the particular Business they are to discourse on. . . . Many of the most Learned and Wise adhere to the new Scheme of expressing themselves by Things, which hath only this Inconvenience attending it; that if a Man's Business be very great, and of various Kinds, he must be obliged in Proportion to carry a greater Bundle of Things upon his Back, unless he can afford one or two strong Servants to attend him. I have often beheld two of these Sages almost sinking under the Weight of their Packs, like Peddlers among us, who when they meet in the Streets, would lay down their Loads, open their Sacks, and hold Conversation for an Hour together; then put up their Implements, help each other to resume their Burthens, and take their Leave. (Swift, 1726/1970, p. 158)

children this age become sensitive to social expectations and begin to set standards for themselves (see Chapter 6, p. 253).

Early word meanings

To understand how word meanings change during a child's development, it is useful to keep in mind that words do not have unique or fixed meanings. "Table," for example, can refer to an article of furniture or an arrangement of data in rows and columns, among other things. Nonetheless, the illusion that there is one word for each real-world referent remains strong. (See Jonathan Swift's satirical comment in Box 8.1.)

The ambiguity inherent in words can never be completely eradicated. But as children gain familiarity with the ways people around them use words, their own uses come to conform more and more closely to the general uses in their cultural group. They achieve this feat by narrowing the set of circumstances in which they use some words while at the same time broadening the applications of others (Anglin, 1986).

Overextensions   Adults are amused when a 2-year-old wanders into a room full of adults and proceeds to call each of the men there "daddy." This form of mislabeling is called an **overextension.** An overextension occurs whenever many members of a category are referred to by a single term that is conventionally used to label only one of them (Naigles & Gelman, 1995).

Children's early overextensions appear to be strongly influenced by perceptual features of the items named as well as by the way the things named function in children's actions (Naigles & Gelman, 1995). A word such as "kitty" may be extended to cover a wide variety of four-legged animals because of their common shape, or it may cover a variety of soft, furry objects because of their similar texture. (See Table 8.1.)

Underextensions   Children also commit the error of **underextension,** using words in a narrower way than adults do (Anglin, 1983). It is common, in fact, for early words to have a unique reference (Golinkoff, Mervis, & Hirsh-Pasek, 1994).

Overextension A term used for the error of applying verbal labels too broadly.

Underextension A term used for applying verbal labels too narrowly.

For example, 1½-year-old Emmy used "bottle" only for the plastic bottle she drank from, not other kinds of bottles. Young children may hotly deny that a lizard, a fish, or a mommy is an animal. They may also believe that "cat" applies only to their family's cat, not to cats in the neighborhood or on television.

Levels of Abstraction   In choosing how to refer to something, children must learn to deal with the fact that several words can be used to refer to the same object. In speaking of someone she sees at the supermarket, a child may point and say:

> "Mommy, look at Sally."
> "Mommy, look at that girl."
> "Mommy, look at her."
> "Mommy, look at that person."

All of these methods of referring are equally accurate, but not equally appropriate in all circumstances. If the girl being talked about is well known to the mother and daughter, it would be inappropriate to refer to her as "that person" or "that girl." It might be appropriate under some circumstances to refer to the girl as "her" instead of "Sally," but to do so would change the meaning of the utterance. Children rapidly learn to distinguish among such nuances if the appropriate words are in their vocabularies.

An interesting characteristic of the early words that children say is that they tend to refer to objects at an intermediate level of abstraction (*car*, for example, rather than *vehicle*, which has a more general meaning, or *Chevy*, which has a more specific meaning). Only later do children acquire words that are more general or more specific (Nelson, 1979). These early words seem to classify the world in categories that are neither too big nor too small.

Jeremy Anglin (1977) showed children posters that contained four pictures of objects that could be related at some level of abstraction and asked them for a label that applied to the whole set (see Figure 8.4). One poster might have four pictures of roses, which could be labeled by the relatively specific category "roses"; another might have a rose, a daisy, a carnation, and a pansy, which could

TABLE 8.1   Typical Overextensions in the Speech of Young Children

Child's Word	First Referent	Extensions	Possible Common Property
Bird	Sparrows	Cows, dogs, cats, any moving animal	Movement
Mooi	Moon	Cakes, round marks on window, round shapes in books, tooling on leather book covers, postmarks, letter O	Shape
Fly	Fly	Specks of dirt, dust, all small insects, his own toes, crumbs, small toad	Size
Koko	Cock crowing	Tunes played on a violin, piano, accordion, phonograph, all music, merry-go-round	Sound
Wau-wau	Dogs	All animals, toy dog, soft slippers, picture of old man in furs	Texture

Source: de Villiers & de Villiers, 1979.

Adult labels

Child labels

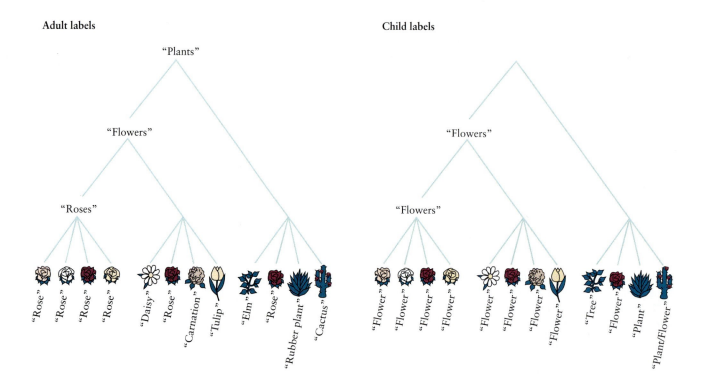

FIGURE 8.4 *Young children fail to differentiate levels of abstractness in the way they label sets of objects, using an intermediate level more frequently than adults do. (Adapted from Anglin, 1977.)*

be labeled at the intermediate category of abstraction as "flowers"; a third might have an elm, a rose, a rubber plant, and a cactus, which could be labeled at a higher level of abstraction as "plants." Anglin found that adults were able to vary the level of generality of their labels appropriately, whereas children between the ages of 2 and 5 tended to label all the sets at the same intermediate level of generality. They not only called the set containing the daisy, rose, carnation, and pansy "flowers," but also called all four roses "flowers," and were unable to provide a single label for the four plants. Most 4- and 5-year-olds were able both to name specific flowers and to use the general term "plants," but they too tended to use the intermediate term "flowers" far more than the adults did. These same results were obtained with many other category hierarchies, such as "animals, dogs, collies."

Children's limitations in labeling specific objects and general categories do not indicate that they fail to understand differences between objects. Even children who labeled all pictures of dogs and cats as "cat" could still pick out the picture of the proper animal when they were asked to do so (Fremgen & Fay, 1980). Moreover, Jean Mandler and Patricia Bauer (1988) have demonstrated that under some conditions, children less than 2 years of age will show knowledge of higher-level categories (vehicles) as well as basic-level categories (truck, train, airplane), even though they tend to stick to the basic level in the initial labels they use.

The changing structure of children's vocabularies

Clearly the growth of children's vocabularies involves more than a simple increase in the number of individual words they know and more than a simple improvement in the accuracy with which they apply labels to objects. Vocabulary growth is accompanied by fundamental changes in the ways children relate words to one another and in the contexts in which they use words, ultimately creating qualitatively new systems of meaning (Carey, 1985; Clark, 1995).

We can see the changing structure of word meanings by tracing the developmental course of a word such as "dog." The first words and phrases children use are likely to represent the specific circumstances of the first time they associate the sound and its referent, with their feelings playing as important a role as their thoughts. "Dog" may mean something terrible if the child has just been bitten; the same word may mean something wonderful if the dog lies on the rug and allows the child to burrow in its fur.

As children gain experience with dogs, the word "dog" begins to evoke a range of situations in which "dog" is only one element. The structure of the vocabulary at this stage is dominated by the pattern shown in Figure 8.5a. There "dog" is a unifying element in several situations: dog growls, dog barks, dog is petted, dog runs away, dog fights. Each situation is connected to "dog" in a specific way as part of a specific kind of action.

Further experience reveals that dogs are not the only creatures that bite. Cats bite too, and so do babies. At the same time, it becomes clear that cats do not bark (seals do) and they rarely take walks (but mommies do). Some of the things you can say about dogs you can just as easily say about cats (or seals or mommies), but some you cannot. When children are familiar with a large number of concrete situations in which the same word is used, words begin to acquire conceptual meanings that do not depend on any one context, or even on a real-world context. This aspect of language development is depicted in Figure 8.5b.

Once a word's meaning is influenced by the logical categories of the language, the word "dog" evokes more than the single emotion of fear or the single concrete image of Fido begging at the table. It has become part of an abstract system of word meanings independent of any particular situation. "Dog" becomes an instance of the category "domestic animal," or the more general category "animal," or the still more general category "living thing."

One of the simplest ways to assess the changing structure of children's vocabularies is to ask children of different ages to say the first word that comes to mind in response to a set of words. Early in development, children respond to "dog" with "bites" or "run," depending on the situation that the stimulus word evokes; later they respond to "dog" with "cat" or "animal" (Nelson, 1977). Very similar results are obtained when children are asked, "Tell me all you can about _____s" or "What kind of a thing is a _____?" (Anglin, 1985).

Although new forms of word meaning reshape the child's vocabulary, old forms do not disappear. Adults, no less than children, respond with fear, love, or some other emotion to "dog." And much of adults' use of language depends on a fine-tuned appreciation of the way words relate to each other in particular contexts. What distinguishes the adult's vocabulary from the child's, other than its greater size, is the presence of several alternative forms of meaning for each word, which provide a richer arsenal of linguistic tools for reasoning about dogs, cats, and everything else, and for talking about these things with other people (Anglin, 1985).

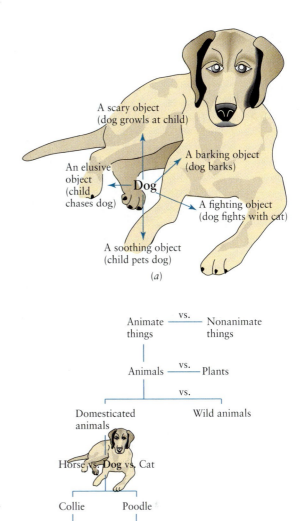

FIGURE 8.5 (a) *For the younger child, word meanings are dominated by the contexts of action in which the words have played a role.* (b) *As children acquire the formal conceptual categories of their language, the structure of word meanings changes accordingly. (Adapted from Luria, 1981.)*

Do early words stand for sentences?

The evidence presented so far indicates that children know something about the meanings of individual words very early. But this does not imply that they appreciate the new meanings that can arise from combinations of words or the possible changes of meaning that can be achieved by changes in word order ("John kissed Mary" versus "Mary kissed John").

This child is making clear the close connection between gestures and words.

Some investigators believe that even when children can utter only single words, these words stand for whole ideas and whole sentences. Such single-word sentences are called **holophrases.** By this account holophrases contain the germ of later, more differentiated language capacities (McNeill, 1970). As children's memory capacity develops and as they become more familiar with additional language forms, they begin to use increasing numbers of words to articulate the concepts they once packed into one-word utterances.

Patricia Greenfield and Joshua Smith (1976) offer a different interpretation of single-word utterances. They believe that a single-word utterance stands for one particular element of the situation the child wants to talk about, not the whole idea. Greenfield and Smith point out that children's single words are almost always accompanied by nonverbal elements, such as gestures and distinctive facial expressions. The single word *in conjunction with the gestures and facial expressions* is the equivalent of the whole sentence. By this account, the single word is not a holophrase, but one element in a complex of communication that includes nonverbal actions.

It is difficult to decide between competing theories of children's linguistic understanding at the stage of single-word utterances because too little information is available. Certainly, adults respond *as if* the child's single-word utterances are meaningful. A child says "Shoe," for example, and the father responds by saying, "Oh, you want Daddy to tie your shoelace." But how much of this meaning is the child's, and how much of it is the adult's interpretation of the utterance based on information gleaned from the context in which the child speaks? Until we have more to go on than a single word, it is especially difficult to determine where the child's word leaves off and the adult's interpretation begins. Although this problem of interpretation never completely disappears, it becomes less vexing when the child begins to string words together.

Holophrase A term for babies' single-word utterances that some believe stand for entire phrases or sentences.

SENTENCES

As we saw in Chapter 6, a watershed of language development is reached toward the end of infancy, when children begin to produce utterances consisting of two or more words. Although they seldom form grammatical sentences, even two-word utterances carry more than twice as much information about the child's meaning as a single word alone. Each of the two words provides hints about what the child is saying, just as the single word provided hints. But now, the relationship between the two words can also be used. With as few as two words children can indicate possession ("Daddy chair"), nonexistence ("All-gone cookie"), and a variety of other meanings. They can vary the order of the words to create different meanings ("Chase Daddy" and "Daddy chase"). This new potential for creating meaning by varying the arrangement of linguistic elements marks the birth of grammar. Grammatical expression develops over a long period of time.

TABLE 8.2	Sample Two-Word Utterances	
See boy	Mail come	
See sock	Mama come	
Night night office	Bunny do	
Night night boat	Want do	
More care	Boat off	
More sing	Water off	

Source: Braine, 1963.

Two-word utterances

Table 8.2 contains a sample of two-word utterances recorded in one of the first attempts to discover the earliest grammatical rules evident in children's speech (Braine, 1963). Several features of the English language stand out in these early "protosentences."

1. *Explicitness.* A child who can say "See boy" instead of being limited to the individual words "see" and "boy" has a better chance of communicating effectively to a listening adult, especially when the context does not make one specific interpretation obvious.

2. *Ordering.* Part of the gain in explicitness comes from the order in which the two words are used. "Boy see" or "Do bunny" does not convey the same meaning in English as "See boy" or "Bunny do." The gains in meaning that result from the order of elements in the utterance are the crucial evidence that something like grammar is beginning to organize the child's talk.

3. *Telegraphic quality.* In these two-word utterances children appear to be coding only the most obvious and essential parts of their ideas, in much the same way adults simplify their language when they send a telegram ("Mom. Cash low. All well. Send money. Love. Johnny"). Such utterances are more informative than single words, but they are often ambiguous.

The shortcomings of two-word utterances are illustrated in an amusing way by a series of incidents in *Higglety, Pigglety, Pop,* Maurice Sendak's tale of an adventurous dog who accepts a job as nanny for Baby, a child caught in the grip of the terrible twos. At first the dog attempts to get the baby to eat, and the baby says, "No eat!" When the dog decides to eat the food himself, the baby again says, "No eat!" Finally the baby and dog find themselves confronted by a lion, and the baby says for the third time, "No eat!"

As adults, we have ready interpretations of what the baby means in each instance. In the first case he appears to mean "I won't eat," in the second case he means "Don't eat my food," and in the third case he means "Don't eat me" (or, if he is feeling generous, "Don't eat us"). The difficulty with these two-word utterances is clear: the same sound pattern ("No eat") has at least three interpretations, and the utterance itself provides no clue to the meaning intended. The ambiguity of many two-word utterances is likely to restrict effective communication to occasions when listeners can reliably interpret the context in which the child is operating. Thus effective communication about absent or abstract subjects is not yet possible.

Increasing complexity

At the same time that children begin to string more and more words together to form complete sentences, they increase the complexity and the variety of words and grammatical devices they use. These changes are illustrated by the following prodigious sentence spoken by an excited 2-year-old: "You can't pick up a big kitty 'cos a big kitty might bite!" (de Villiers & de Villiers, 1978, p. 59).

This sentence is by no means typical of 2-year-olds, but it provides a good opportunity to assess how utterances that are more complex communicate more explicitly. The sentence communicates not only that the little girl doesn't want to pick up a big cat, but that no one should pick up a big cat; it also conveys her understanding that big cats sometimes bite but do not invariably do so. Such complex sentences communicate shades of meaning that help adults to respond sensitively to children's experiences.

As Figure 8.6 indicates, the length of 2-year-olds' utterances grows explosively, along with their vocabularies and grammatical abilities (Brown, 1973; Gopnik & Meltzoff, 1987). Note that the growth in the length of utterances is

FIGURE 8.6 *This graph shows the rapid increase in the mean length of utterances made by three children during the first four years of life. (From Brown, 1973.)*

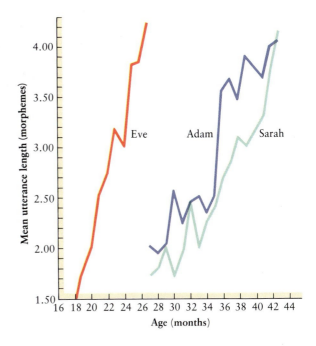

indicated by the average number of *morphemes* per utterance (or the "mean length of utterance" [MLU]), rather than by the average number of words. The phrase "That big bad boy plays ball," for example, contains six words and seven morphemes, whereas the phrase "Boys aren't playing" contains only three words but six morphemes *(boy, s, are, [not], play, ing)*. The procedure of counting morphemes rather than words provides an index of a child's total potential for making meaning in a particular utterance.

Grammatical Morphemes   The complexity of the little girl's long sentence quoted earlier is attributable in large measure to just those little words and word parts that are systematically absent in two-word utterances. The article "a" ("a big kitty") indicates that it is big cats in general, not just this particular big cat, that are worrisome. The word "'cos" connects two propositions and indicates the causal relationship between them. The contraction "can't" specifies a particular relationship of negation. These elements are called **grammatical morphemes** because they are units that create meaning by showing the relations between other elements within the sentence. Whether the rate of language acquisition is fast or slow, grammatical morphemes appear in roughly the same sequence in the speech of all children (at least those who acquire English as a first language).

As Table 8.3 indicates, the grammatical morpheme likely to appear first is *ing*, indicating the present progressive verb tense. This verb form allows children to describe their ongoing activity. Morphemes indicating location, possession, and number make their appearance next. Children have many opportunities to use these morphemes in the course of play with toys; blocks are stacked one on top of another, dolls go in their cribs, and a little girl's lunch belongs to her. Morphemes

> **Grammatical morphemes** Words and parts of words that create meaning by elaborating relations among elements in a sentence.

TABLE 8.3   Usual Order of Acquiring Grammatical Morphemes

Morpheme	Meaning	Example
Present progressive	Temporary duration	I walk*ing*
In	Containment	*In* basket
On	Support	*On* floor
Plural	Number	Two ball*s*
Past irregular	Prior occurrence	It *broke*
Possessive inflection	Possession	Adam*'s* ball
To be without contraction	Number; prior occurrence	There it *is*
Articles	Specific/nonspecific	That *a* book That *the* dog
Past regular	Prior occurrence	Adam walk*ed*
Third person regular	Number; prior occurrence	He walk*s*
Third person irregular	Number; prior occurrence	He *does* She *has*
Uncontractible progressive auxiliary	Temporary duration; number; prior occurrence	This *is going*
Contraction of *to be*	Number; prior occurrence	That*'s* book
Contractible progressive auxiliary	Temporary duration; prior occurrence	I*'m* walking

Source: Brown, 1973.

that mark complex relations, such as *am* in "I'm going" (which codes a relation between the subject of the action and the time of the action), are generally slower to emerge.

The appearance of grammatical morphemes is a strong indicator that children are implicitly beginning to distinguish nouns and verbs, because their speech conforms to adult rules that specify which morphemes should be attached to which words in a sentence. Children demonstrate their intuitive grasp of the rules for using grammatical morphemes by the fact that they do not apply a past-tense morpheme to a noun ("girled"); nor do they place articles before verbs ("a walked"). By the time they are 5 or 6 years old, most children will have implicit command of all of the standard parts of speech they will use as adults.

Complex Constructions   Between the ages of 2 and 6, children begin to use a great many grammatical devices, the "grammatical rules" that bedevil students in language classes throughout their schooldays. Some of these grammatical constructions obey rules of such subtlety that, although we follow them intuitively in our speech, we can't say why we use them as we do.

Small children's two- and three-word utterances may suggest that mastery of grammar requires no more than acquisition of a few ordering rules. But we need more than surface ordering principles to achieve competence in the use of language. Consider a common grammatical form known as the *tag question* (Dennis, Sugar, & Whitaker, 1982)—words added to the end of a declarative sentence to turn it into a question. "They won the prize, *didn't they?*" and "You will come, *won't you?*" are typical tag questions. It's no easy matter to provide a rule specifying how such questions are formed, is it?

A somewhat more complicated demonstration of the gap between our ability to use language and our ability to understand the principles that underlie our talk is provided by the following sentences:

1. John is easy to please.
2. John is willing to please.

Both sentences seem to follow a single ordering principle. But these sentences, despite their surface similarity, differ grammatically. We can clarify the difference by adding a single word to the end of each sentence while still preserving the order of elements. Compare the two new sentences:

3. John is willing to please Bill.
4. John is easy to please Bill.

Sentence 3 is just as acceptable in the English language as sentences 1 and 2, but sentence 4, despite the fact that the surface ordering principles are unchanged, is not grammatically acceptable, and we cannot interpret it.

Such examples suggest that acquiring the grammar of a language involves mastery of highly abstract rules that even adult speakers of a language cannot explain (unless they are linguists!). Yet such rules appear to be acquired by all normal children, regardless of the language they speak.

Children's difficulties in mastering the subtle grammatical constructions demanded by adult language have been studied by Carol Chomsky (1969). She tells of Lisa, 6½ years old, who was seated at a table on which there was a doll with a blindfold over its eyes.

Adult: Is this doll easy to see or hard to see?

Lisa: Hard to see.

Adult: Will you make her easy to see?

Lisa: If I can get this [blindfold] untied.

Adult: Will you explain why she was hard to see?

Lisa: *[to doll]* Because you had a blindfold over your eyes.

Adult: And what did you do?

Lisa: I took it off.

Before this interchange, Carol Chomsky had made certain that Lisa knew the meaning of "easy." Lisa knew that it is easy to sit in a chair but hard to climb a tree. What, then, was her difficulty in the case of the blindfolded doll? Chomsky argues that children still assume that the person mentioned at the beginning of a sentence is the one who carries out the action (in this case, that it is the doll who does the seeing). This assumption is often correct, but it is not correct in the case of "easy to see."

THE USES OF LANGUAGE

In order to communicate effectively, children must master more than the grammatical rules of their language and the meanings of its words. Such knowledge would be of little use if they did not simultaneously master the **pragmatic uses of language**—that is, the ability to select words and word orderings that are appropriate to their actions in particular contexts.

Conversational acts

One way of describing how language is used for pragmatic purposes is to think of utterances as **conversational acts,** actions that achieve goals through language. According to Elizabeth Bates and her colleagues (Bates, Camaioni, & Volterra, 1975), children's earliest conversational acts fall into two categories, proto-imperatives and proto-declaratives. *Proto-imperatives* are early ways of engaging another person to achieve a desired object. When our daughter, Jenny, first began holding up her cup and saying "More," she was using a proto-imperative.

Proto-declaratives are early ways of referring. Perhaps the earliest form of a proto-declarative is not verbal at all, but the act of pointing. Nonverbal pointing is soon accompanied by words, as when a baby points to a dog and says "Doggie." Another early form of proto-declarative conversation is giving. As babies master this form, they may be seen bringing all of their toys, one after another, to lay at a visitor's feet if each gift is acknowledged by a smile or a comment (Bates, O'Connell, & Shore, 1987).

Pragmatic uses of language The ability to select words and word orders that convey what the speaker intends to communicate.

Conversational acts The term used to describe how language is used for pragmatic purposes to achieve goals.

Young children take great delight in their ability to communicate by using their rapidly developing linguistic skills.

In the process of acquiring the pragmatic aspects of language, children also come to understand that a single sequence of words may accomplish several alternative goals. A sentence such as "Is the door shut?" has the grammatical form of a request for information (you want to know whether the door is open or shut). But "Is the door shut?" may also be a request for action or a criticism. In these cases, "Is the door shut?" is pragmatically equivalent to "Please shut the door" and "You have forgotten to shut the door again."

As children's vocabularies grow and their command of grammar improves, so does the range of actions they can be induced to perform and the actions they can carry out through language. Marilyn Shatz (1974, 1978) found that children as young as 2 years responded correctly to their mother's indirect commands, such as "Is the door shut?" Instead of responding to the surface grammatical form and answering "Yes" or "No," Shatz's toddlers went to shut the door. A 3-year-old observed by John Dore (1979) used three different ways to accomplish a single goal: "Get off the blocks!" "Why don't you stay away from my blocks?" and "You're standing on my blocks."

In the hope of getting a proper overall picture of language development, a number of scholars have attempted to catalog the full set of language functions that children have to master (Dore, Gearhart, & Newman, 1979). This task has proved to be formidable because there is so much variety in the uses of speech, even by 3-year-olds. The 3- and 4-year-olds these researchers studied have come a long way from mere pointing or the use of idiosyncratic "words" such as "ha." They can solicit information ("What happened?") or action ("Put the toy down!"). They can assert facts and rules ("We have a boat"), utter warnings ("Watch out!"), and clarify earlier statements.

Conversational conventions

As part of the task of learning how to achieve their goals through talking, children must come to appreciate basic rules that apply in any conversation. The master rule of ordinary conversation, according to the philosopher H. P. Grice (1975, p. 45), is the **cooperative principle:** make your contributions to conversation at the required time and for the accepted purpose of the talk exchange. Grice lists four maxims that must be honored if the cooperative principle is to operate effectively:

1. *The maxim of quantity:* Speak neither more nor less than is required.
2. *The maxim of quality:* Speak the truth and avoid falsehood.
3. *The maxim of relevance:* Speak in a relevant and informative way.
4. *The maxim of clarity:* Speak so as to avoid obscurity and ambiguity.

In conversation among adults everyone understands that these rules are often violated to make deliberately nonconventional statements. The act of encouraging a child, for example, may evoke an exaggerated statement such as "You can do it, Suzie. You're a big girl now, and you know that big girls try hard. They don't give up. I'm sure you can do it." This kind of talk might violate the maxim of quantity (the speaker is saying more than is required) except for the fact that it is acceptable for the special task of providing encouragement.

Some figurative uses of language (such as irony, in which someone says the obvious) depend on deliberate violation of a conversational maxim (see Box 8.2). Learning the circumstances in which the basic speech-act conventions do not apply requires years of additional experience (Winner, 1988).

Children must also acquire knowledge of the social conventions that regulate what is to be said and how to say it. These conventions may vary markedly from one culture to another. In the United States children are expected to say "please" when they request something and "thank you" when they are given something. But in a Colombian mestizo community such verbal formulas are frowned upon in

Cooperative principle The master rule of ordinary conversation: make your contributions to conversation at the required time and for the accepted purpose of the talk exchange.

BOX 8.2

Figurative Language

A 2½-year-old runs up to his parents, points at his yellow plastic baseball bat, and says with delight, "Corn, corn!" A 1½-year-old sends a toy car twisting along his mother's arm and exclaims, "Nake!" (snake). At first glance these children may appear to be overextending the meanings of their words. But a variety of evidence suggests that not long after children begin to name objects, they begin to use words figuratively as well as literally. They deliberately call objects by the name of something else to which it bears some striking resemblance. Such renamings are in fact deliberate metaphors (Winner et al., 1979). Significantly, the beginnings of metaphorical language coincide with the onset of symbolic play. In both forms of behavior, the 2-year-old child treats objects and events nonliterally.

Figurative use of words provides evidence that language production is a creative process, not a simple imitative one. As Ellen Winner and her colleagues point out, in order to generate a metaphor, children must recognize and express a similarity between two things in some novel way that they have never heard before.

Winner and her co-workers identify two distinct routes for the development of nonliteral, metaphoric speech. Some metaphors are closely tied to action: a 2-year-old rubs a fur teddy bear against a wooden armchair, then holds up the teddy bear and says, "Zucchini." Then he points to the arm of the chair and calls it "grater." A teddy bear does not look at all like a zucchini and most wooden chair arms do not look like vegetable graters; the resemblance that makes these words meaningful depends on the way the objects fit into a typical action sequence. Perceptual metaphors, by contrast, take on meaning from the physical similarities of the objects compared. When a little child exclaims, "Oh, mommy, how balloony your legs look!" or "Can't you see, I'm barefoot all over!" she is using perceptual metaphors (Chukovsky, 1968). Because adults base some of their metaphors on the same kinds of physical similarities that children use to form theirs, adults are often able to figure out what the child means.

Although children between the ages of 2 and 6 years use a good deal of figurative language, they often fail to understand the figurative meaning of adult speech that does not depend on simple actions or on an object's perceptual characteristics. Kornei Chukovsky, a Russian linguist, translator, and children's poet, was especially impressed by the special intelligence revealed by children's misunderstandings of adults' figurative speech. His examples are difficult to improve upon:

A woman . . . asked her 4-year-old, Natasha: "Tell me, what does it mean to say that a person is trying to drown another in a spoonful of water [a Russian expression]?"

"What did you say? In what kind of a spoon? Say that again."

The mother repeated the adage.

"That's impossible!" Natasha said categorically. "It can never happen!"

Right there and then she demonstrated the physical impossibility of such an act; she grabbed a spoon and quickly placed it on the floor.

"Look, here am I," and she stood on the spoon. "All right, drown me. There isn't enough room for a whole person—all of him will remain on top. . . . Let's not talk about it any more—it's such nonsense!"

Four-year-old Olia, who came with her mother to visit a Moscow aunt, looked closely at this aunt and her husband as they were all having tea, and soon remarked with obvious disappointment: "Mama! You said that uncle always sits on Aunt Aniuta's neck [a Russian expression for being bossy and controlling] but he has been sitting on a chair all the time that we've been here." (Chukovsky, 1968: pp. 12–13)

As children begin to master their native language and approach the age when they will be expected to acquire adult skills, their freewheeling use of figurative language declines. On the one hand, this narrowing of linguistic adventurism can be considered a good thing: children are learning what is conventional and acceptable in their community. On the other hand, a good deal of the creativity goes out of their speech. It may take some effort for them to regain their sense of delight in discovering new properties of the world through figurative language.

the belief that "please" and "thank you" signal the speaker's inferiority; obedience, not formulaic politeness, is what these adults expect of their children (Reichel-Dolmatoff & Reichel-Dolmatoff, 1961).

Taking account of the listener

The core meaning of the word *communicate* is "to place in common." Language is said to communicate when speakers and listeners come to share a common interpretation of what is said. Yet a major limitation of the language of young children, as we have seen, is that it leaves so much of the interpretive work to the listener. In this sense, children's language is not fully communicative. Children's increasing knowledge of word meanings and mastery of grammatical rules reduce this problem but by no means eliminate it.

One of the skills that children must master in order to make their language communicative is saying things in such a way that the meaning will be clear from the listener's point of view. An awareness of this necessity is evident at an early age in rudimentary form. The skills required develop slowly, however, in the years from 2½ to 8, and even adults sometimes fail to take their listener's knowledge and perspective into account.

Even 4-year-olds adapt their language when they speak to younger children.

Children as young as 2½ years of age show that they are able to take the listener into account by modifying what they say to include information important to the listener (Wellman & Lempers, 1977). By the time they are 3½ years old they are sufficiently mindful of what other people need to know that they provide extra information to someone who is blindfolded (Maratsos, 1973). They use simpler language when they talk to younger children than when they talk to adults, an indication that in some way they know the younger child's language ability is more primitive than their own (Tomasello & Mannle, 1985).

Marilyn Shatz and Rochel Gelman (1973) found that when 4-year-olds play with 2-year-olds, the older children shorten their sentences, speak more slowly, and simplify both their vocabulary and their grammar to make it easier for the younger children to understand. This ability to modify speech so that younger children can easily understand it does not depend on experience in talking to younger children. Only children are just as likely to simplify their speech as children with little brothers and sisters. Another study demonstrated that small children make the same kinds of simplifications in their speech when they play with a baby doll, but not when they play with a grown-up doll (Sachs & Devin, 1973).

Explanations of Language Acquisition

During much of the twentieth century, two widely divergent theories have organized a great deal of the research on language acquisition. These theories correspond roughly to the polar positions on the sources of human development—nature versus nurture—discussed in Chapter 1. The *learning-theory approach* attributes language to nurture; it accords the leading role in language acquisition to children's environments, especially to the language environment and teaching activities provided by adults. The *nativist approach* attributes language acquisition largely to nature; it assumes that children are born ready to learn language and that as they mature, their language-using capacity appears naturally, with only minimum input from the environment and without any need for special training.

TABLE 8.4   Major Approaches to Language Acquisition

Theory	Major Causal Factor	Mechanism	Major Phenomenon Explained
Learning	Environment	Imitation, conditioning	Word meaning
Nativist	Heredity	Triggering	Syntax
Interactionist (cognitive hypothesis)	Interaction of social and biological factors	Assimilation-accommodation	Correlation of cognitive and linguistic developments
Interactionist (cultural-context approach)	Cultural mediation of social-biological interaction	Coordination in cultural scripts	Language-thought relationships

In recent decades a variety of *interactionist approaches* to language acquisition have gained prominence. Interactionists hold that both nature and nurture play significant roles in the acquisition of language, as in other areas of human development. They also believe that the development of children's language is closely tied to their overall mental development. (Table 8.4 summarizes the basic concepts of the major competing approaches to the development of language.)

Two kinds of interactionist approach can be distinguished. The first, which is associated with Piaget's constructivism, emphasizes the way cognitive development sets the stage for language development. The second, which is associated with the cultural-context perspective, emphasizes the way the sociocultural environment enters into partnership with the child to change both language and cognition.

THE LEARNING-THEORY EXPLANATION

The basic assumption of the learning-theory view is that the development of language is just like the development of other behaviors and conforms to the same laws of learning. According to this point of view, language acquisition depends on imitation and on learning by association, through the mechanisms of classical and operant conditioning (Miller & Dollard, 1941; Skinner, 1957; Staats, 1968).

Perhaps the first statement of this view was provided by the early Christian philosopher St. Augustine (A.D. 354–430). Recalling his childhood, he wrote:

> When they named any thing, and as they spoke turned towards it, I saw and remembered that they called what one would point out by the name they uttered. . . . And thus by constantly hearing words, as they occurred in various sentences, I collected gradually for what they stood; and having broken in my mouth to these signs, I thereby gave utterance to my will. (Augustine, 1961, p. 4)

Classical conditioning

The process of associating objects and words described by St. Augustine is similar to the process that learning theorists refer to as *classical conditioning* (see Chapter 4, p. 164). Table 8.5 shows how the process operates in the acquisition of the word "candy."

A child who hears the word "candy" for the first time cannot know what it means. But if the sound "candy" is reliably paired with a sweet taste, the child begins to associate the sound and the object, thereby learning part of what the sound "candy" means. According to learning theorists, the child grasps the meaning of "candy" as the sum of all the associations that the word evokes after it has been paired with a wide variety of experiences (Mowrer, 1950).

Learning theorists use the classical conditioning model to account for the way children learn to *understand* language, but this mechanism does not account for a child's ability to *produce* language. To explain this aspect of language acquisition, learning theorists point to the mechanism of operant conditioning.

Operant conditioning

The operant explanation begins with the observation, described in Chapter 4 (p. 165), that children emit a rich repertoire of sounds more or less at random during the early phases of babbling. These sounds represent the initial elements of spoken language, which, according to the learning theorists, are gradually shaped through reinforcement and refined through the child's practice. The sound "da," for example, might be shaped into "dog" or "mo" into "more" by a parent's enthusiastic attention to the child's successively closer approximations to the sound of the word.

The process of language acquisition proposed by learning theorists applies to all societies at all times, but the particulars will vary from one language environment to another. An American child growing up in Boston will acquire a different way of pronouncing "Boston" ("Baaston") than a New Yorker ("Bawstin"). A Kpelle child growing up in West Africa will learn to be sensitive to the sound contours of words in order to pronounce the word "kali" with a rising tone on *a* to mean "hoe" and with a falling tone to mean "leopard"; an American child, whose history of reinforcement has rendered rising and falling tones insignificant as meaning-bearing features, may not even hear the difference.

TABLE 8.5	An Example of How Word Meaning Is Acquired through Classical Conditioning

Stimulus	Response
INITIAL STATE	
Sound of word "candy" ⟶	Orientation (look at candy)
Taste of candy in mouth ⟶	Salivation Sucking Pleasure
REPEATED PAIRING OF WORD AND OBJECT	
Sound of word "candy" and Taste of candy in mouth ⟶	Salivation Sucking Pleasure
AFTER REPEATED PAIRING	
Sound of word "candy" ⟶	Salivation Pleasure tastes good

Imitation

It seems obvious that imitation is involved in language acquisition if only because children acquire the languages they hear around them, rather than inventing totally new languages that adults cannot understand. Moreover, modern research has shown that young children often learn to name things by hearing someone else name them and then repeating what they hear (Leonard et al., 1983).

Simple imitation, however, does not appear to explain how children acquire the ability to compose complex grammatical patterns or the tendency to use grammatical forms they have never heard to express new ideas. Children often use a grammatical morpheme correctly the first several times they say it and then go through a period of incorrect usage before returning to the correct form. After months of using the correct plural form for "hand," for instance, children may go through a period in which they say "handses" before returning to "hands." They certainly never heard anyone say "handses," so while they may have learned to say "hands" by imitation, imitation cannot explain the development of their use of this grammatical form.

These and similar complexities have led researchers to a more complex description of how imitation participates in language learning. With respect to "handses," Gisela Speidel and Keith Nelson (1989) suggest that imitation has been selectively applied to different attributes of the referent. Initially the child may have attended to and imitated whole words. Then, as the child becomes sensitive to grammatical morphemes, the plural ending *es* becomes a target of imitation. Eventually the child learns to form some plurals with *s*, others with *es*, and still others in even more irregular ways (mouse/mice, goose/geese, and so on).

Pondering the mechanisms by which imitation is involved in language acquisition, Albert Bandura (1977, 1986), a leading learning theorist, described a kind of imitation called abstract modeling. Bandura called this kind of modeling *abstract* because, in his view, even when children imitate specific utterances, they abstract from them the general linguistic principles that underlie them. Thus a child repeating "Juana walked home" abstracts the grammatical principle of adding *ed* to show past tense and can then go on to say "Juana fixed the toy" without having to hear those exact words first.

THE NATIVIST EXPLANATION

The nativist view of language acquisition has been dominated by the work of the linguist Noam Chomsky (1975, 1986). According to Chomsky, because children produce a vast array of sentences that they have never before heard, it seems implausible that language could be acquired primarily through classical or operant conditioning. That children's early original utterances often violate grammatical rules in a systematic way also prompts Chomsky and other nativists to believe that imitation of the kind Bandura described cannot adequately explain language acquisition, although Chomsky does acknowledge that "children acquire a good deal of their verbal and non-verbal behavior by casual observation and imitation of adults and other children" (1959, p. 49).

Chomsky believes that the capacity to comprehend and generate language is innate, and that the principles by which it develops are not the same as those underlying other human behaviors. Instead, he argues, the capacity to comprehend and generate language is more like a special human organ with its own structure and function.

Chomsky's strategy for discovering the nature of language and the conditions for its acquisition is to determine the grammatical rules common to a variety of sentences despite variability from one utterance to the next. He refers to the actual sentences that people produce as the **surface structure** of the language. The restricted set of rules from which the surface structure can be derived is called the **deep structure** of the linguistic system.

Unlike researchers who collect their data by observing language in natural settings or in specially constructed experiments, Chomsky uses the intuitions of native speakers about whether a sample sentence is grammatical or not. Of course, native speakers cannot be familiar with an entire language, which by definition consists of an infinite set of utterances. But native speakers can judge whether any given utterance is a legitimate part of their language because this ability is a basic part of every language user's competence. For example, any adult English speaker of average intelligence is able to say that "Put the needles in the blue drawer" is grammatical, whereas "Put the needles in the drawer blue" is not.

Those who, like Chomsky, believe that language development is a maturational process argue that children get too little feedback on their early utterances to support a learning theory of language acquisition. Instead, they believe that there is some (inborn) linguistic structure that functions to guide children's language learning (Chomsky, 1980; Meisel, 1995; Pinker, 1994). Attempts to evaluate this argument have focused on documenting how much feedback about their use of language children actually receive. In an influential study of this kind, Roger Brown and Camille Hanlon (1970) sought to determine the degree to which parents show disapproval or correct their children when they say something like "Why the dog don't eat?" Brown and Hanlon found that most parents did not explicitly correct such errors.

Surface structure Chomsky's term for the actual sentences that people construct when using a language.

Deep structure The restricted set of rules of a language from which the actual sentences that people produce are derived.

Additional evidence that the development of language does not depend on direct feedback comes from reports that even when parents do attempt to correct erroneous grammar, the effort is likely to fail. The following exchange is reported by David McNeill (1966, pp. 106–107):

Child: Nobody don't like me.

Mother: No, say "nobody likes me."

Child: Nobody don't like me.

[This interchange is repeated several times. Then:]

Mother: No, now listen carefully; say "nobody likes me."

Child: Oh! Nobody don't like*s* me.

Extreme resistance to such corrections, even when the child is obviously trying to cooperate, combined with evidence that adults are unlikely to provide explicit feedback about correct and incorrect grammatical forms, undermines the idea that specific teaching is important to language acquisition and bolsters the nativist position that language acquisition depends only minimally on the environment.

In line with the analogy of language as an organ of the body, Chomsky proposes that every child is born with a **language acquisition device (LAD),** which is programmed to recognize the universal rules that underlie any particular language that a child might hear. The LAD is like a genetic code for the acquisition of language. At birth the child's language acquisition device is presumed to be still in an embryonic state. Chomsky theorizes that as the child matures and interacts with the environment, maturation of the LAD enables the child to fit increasingly complex language forms into the preexisting structure of the LAD. The eventual result of this process is the adult capacity to use language.

In summary, nativists contend that the essential structures that make language acquisition possible—the universals of grammar—are determined far more by the evolutionary history of our species than by the experiential history of particular children. Experience does of course determine which of the many possible human languages a child actually acquires. Children who never hear Chinese spoken will not grow up speaking Chinese, even though they are genetically capable of learning that language. The experience of hearing a particular language, however, does not modify the LAD; it only triggers the innate mechanisms designed for language acquisition.

Language acquisition device (LAD) The language acquisition device is Chomsky's term for an innate language-processing capacity that is programmed to recognize the universal grammar common to all languages.

INTERACTIONIST EXPLANATIONS

Surveying alternative explanations of language acquisition in the 1970s, George Miller, a leading researcher on the psychology of language, remarked wryly that psychologists were faced with two unsatisfactory explanations of language development. One of them, the idea that language is acquired from the environment through learning, was impossible. The other, nativism, was miraculous. Interactionist approaches to language acquisition may be viewed as attempts to create a bridge between the impossible and the miraculous explanations of language development (Bates, O'Connell, & Shore, 1987; Bloom, 1993; Bruner, 1982; Lock, 1980; Maratsos, 1983). Within this overall position, scholars differ significantly about exactly what the bridging mechanisms are and how they work.

Interactionists seek to explain children's language development by linking it, on the one hand, to the development of basic cognitive processes and, on the other hand, to support provided by the social environment (Bates, Bretherton, & Snyder, 1988; Meltzoff & Gopnik, 1989; Tomasello, 1992).

Meltzoff and Gopnik (1989), for example, suggest that the way children use words changes sometime around 18 months in conjunction with a change in the nature of their deferred imitations. Before 18 months, children use "social words" such as "Bye-bye" and "Hereyare" in connection with the events they are actually experiencing (a mother leaving for work, finding a searched-for toy); after 18 months they begin to acquire words for talking about the difference between actual experiences and possible experiences. As we noted earlier, they can now use such expressions as "Uh-oh" to mark the discrepancy between success and failure in the accomplishment of something they were trying to do.

Another interesting link between early cognitive development and language development is seen in the ability to categorize objects at different levels. As we saw in Chapter 6 (p. 235), at the age of about 30 months, children begin to place toy objects in categories and subcategories that relate them to one another in a systematic way. It is also at this age that children begin to identify a single object by two terms that differ in their generality. They may refer to a fir tree as both "tree" and "snow tree" and a dog as both "dog" and "Dalmatian dog" (Clark, 1995, p. 405).

Explaining the acquisition of grammar has proved particularly difficult for interactionists because grammatical structures appear to be well beyond the ability of young children (or many adults) to understand. The solution to this problem suggested by Elizabeth Bates and her colleagues is to treat the mastery of grammatical structures as a *by-product* of the ability to use language to get things done.

To illustrate how complex grammatical structures may arise from interactions that do not explicitly have the construction of those structures as their goal, Bates and Lynn Snyder (1987) point to the way a complex beehive is formed as a by-product of the process of collecting and storing honey. To make a structure to store the honey, bees deposit the wax that is carried in their heads. As they push their load up against the wax deposited by other bees, they create a honeycomb labyrinth made up of hexagonal cells. It may be tempting to assume that bees have a genetic predisposition to make hexagons to carry out their hive-building functions. But in fact, as Bates and Snyder point out, hexagons are inevitably created whenever circles or spheres are packed together under pressure from all sides. Applying this same logic to linguistic structures, Bates and Snyder propose that grammatical structures result from the packing together of people's various communicative intentions within the narrow confines of language in such a way as to communicate.

A great deal of language learning takes place in casual interactions between family members.

A cultural-context version of the interactionist approach to language acquisition is offered by scholars who emphasize that the social environment is organized to incorporate the child as a member of an already existing language-using group (Bruner, 1983a; Harkness, 1990; Nelson, 1988; Ochs & Schieffelin, 1995; Tomasello, 1992). Jerome Bruner (1982) refers to recurrent socially patterned activities in which adult and child do things together as **formats.** Simple formatted activities include such games as peekaboo and the routines surrounding bath, bedtime, and meals, which provide a structure for communicative interaction between babies and caretakers even before babies have learned any language and in this way serve as "crucial vehicles in the passage from communication to language" (p. 8).

Bruner (1982) nicely captured the cultural view of language development when he wrote that language acquisition cannot be reduced to

> either the virtuoso cracking of a linguistic code, or the spinoff of ordinary cognitive development, or the gradual takeover of adults' speech by the child through some impossible inductive *tour de force*. It is, rather, a subtle process by which adults artificially arrange the world so that the child can succeed culturally by doing what comes naturally, and with others similarly inclined. (p. 15)

He has suggested that as an ensemble, the formated events within which children acquire language constitute a **language acquisition support system (LASS),** which is the environmental complement to the innate, biologically constituted LAD emphasized by nativists.

Format The social patterning of activities in which the communicative interaction between children and adults takes place.

Language acquisition support system (LASS) Bruner's term for parental behaviors that structure children's language environment to support the development of language.

Essential Ingredients of Language Acquisition

None of the theories so far advanced provide an overarching explanation of all the processes at work in the development of language. Each approach, however, helps to explain one or more of the many elements of the overall phenomenon. To shed further light on the issues we have been considering thus far, three questions might be posed:

1. What biological properties must an organism have to be able to acquire human language?
2. What aspects of the environment are crucial to the development of language among human beings, and how do they operate?
3. How does the acquisition of language influence other aspects of development, particularly the development of thought?

THE BIOLOGICAL PREREQUISITES FOR LANGUAGE

The question of biological contributions to language acquisition has been addressed in two fundamentally different ways. The first is to inquire whether other species are capable of producing and comprehending language. If they are not, then membership in the human species is a biological prerequisite for language development. The second is to investigate children with marked biological deficits to see if and how those deficits affect their acquisition of language.

Is language uniquely human?

For most of human history it has seemed obvious that the basic requirement for acquiring language is that the learner be a human being. Many other species make a variety of communicative sounds and gestures, but none have evolved a system of communication as powerful and flexible as human language (Lieberman, 1991).

This chimp is using a specially designed keyboard composed of lexical symbols to communicate.

At this very basic level of analysis, virtually all developmental psychologists agree with Chomsky that the process of language development has a significant genetic basis. However, current research with chimpanzees is challenging the assumption that there is a sharp discontinuity between human and chimpanzee language abilities.

One strategy for testing the hypothesis that only human beings can acquire language is to raise a creature of another species in the home along with one's own children. Several researchers have done just that with chimpanzees, hoping that these near phylogenetic neighbors would acquire oral language if they were treated just like human beings. Early research with chimpanzees raised at home demonstrated that chimpanzees can learn to comprehend dozens of words and phrases (Kellogg & Kellogg, 1933; Hayes & Hayes, 1951). But the chimps never themselves produced language. Subsequent research that relied on manual signs instead of spoken words produced clear evidence that chimps can learn to use words to request and refer to things. However, the evidence that they have syntax (flexible, rule-bound variation in the ordering of their words to produce meaningful phrases) is still being disputed (Premack & Premack, 1983; Terrace, 1984).

Current optimism about the capacity of chimpanzees to understand and produce language has been inspired by the work of Sue Savage-Rumbaugh and Duane Rumbaugh (Savage-Rumbaugh & Rumbaugh, 1993; Rumbaugh, Savage-Rumbaugh, & Sevcik, 1994). The Rumbaughs combined several strategies that had been developed by others and added some of their own. Instead of insisting that the chimpanzees speak orally or sign, for example, they provided them with a "lexical keyboard" whose keys bore symbols that stood for words. They used standard operant learning reinforcement techniques to teach the chimpanzees the basic vocabulary symbols, but the people who worked with the chimpanzees also used natural language in everyday, routine activities such as feeding.

Their most successful student has been Kanzi, a pygmy chimpanzee. Kanzi initially learned to use the lexical keyboard by being present when his mother was being trained. He is able to use the keyboard to ask for things, to comment on activities he is engaged in, and to comprehend the meanings of lexigrams used by others. He has also learned to understand spoken English words and phrases (Savage-Rumbaugh & Rumbaugh, 1993).

Kanzi's comprehension of a wide variety of unusual sentences is roughly comparable to the performance of a 2-year-old child. For example, Kanzi correctly acted out the request to "feed your ball some tomato." He also responded correctly when asked to "give the shot [syringe] to Liz" and "give Liz a shot" by handing the syringe to the girl in the first case and by touching the syringe to the girl's arm in the second case.

Kanzi's ability to produce language is not so impressive as his comprehension, however. Most of his "utterances" on the lexical keyboard are single words that are closely linked to his ongoing actions. Most of them are requests. He also, however, uses two-word utterances in a wide variety of combinations and occasionally makes observations. For example, he produced the combination "car trailer" on one occasion when he was in the car and wanted (or so his caretakers believed) to be taken to the trailer rather than to walk there. He has created such phrases as "play yard Austin" when he wanted to visit a chimpanzee named Austin in the play yard and "potato oil" when a researcher put oil on him while he was eating a potato.

Despite these achievements, there remain important differences between the communicative behavior of chimpanzees and human language. After years of hard work, chimpanzees can learn several dozen signs; but children with no special training learn thousands of words. Chimpanzees also learn to construct sequences of signs analogous to babies' multiword utterances, but the internal complexity of these constructions remains rudimentary; as a consequence, even scholars who emphasize the language-learning abilities of primates are likely to refer to their accomplishments as "protolanguage," emphasizing its underdeveloped status (Greenfield & Savage-Rumbaugh, 1990).

Children with severe biological handicaps

In Chapter 2 (pp. 71–72) we briefly described Down's syndrome, a genetic disease that is associated with moderate to severe mental retardation. Although Down's children are able to hold a conversation, their vocabulary is relatively restricted and their talk is grammatically simple. When tested for the ability to produce and comprehend complex linguistic constructions, they fail. Such results suggest that normal language development requires normal cognitive functioning.

This conclusion is challenged, however, by research on children who suffer from a rare metabolic disorder called Williams syndrome. Children afflicted with Williams syndrome are also mentally retarded, yet many of them show nearly normal ability to produce sentences that are grammatical, clearly pronounced, and understandable, and are able to tell stories that are meaningful and display considerable subtlety in their portrayal of human feelings (Bellugi et al., 1990).

Data such as these strongly suggest that at least some aspects of language develop independently of general cognitive functioning. However, coordinated development of the phonetic, grammatical, semantic, and pragmatic aspects of language, all of which are essential to normal linguistic functioning, is clearly dependent on some minimum level of biological growth and inherited capacity.

THE ENVIRONMENT OF LANGUAGE DEVELOPMENT

Evidence from studies of nonhuman primates' abilities to communicate suggests one absolute biological precondition for full language acquisition: one must be a human being. Evidence from cases such as that of Genie, the girl who grew up in total isolation from normal human interaction and language (described in Chapter 7), suggests the corresponding precondition on the environmental side: one must grow up among humans who provide a LASS, a language acquisition support system. Beyond the specification of these two minimum requirements, however, important questions remain: Which aspects of the environment are necessary to trigger language? How are they arranged? What is the optimal support system for ensuring that the language capacity will be fully developed?

Partial deprivation

One way to answer such questions is to find children who are exposed to a great deal of language but are cut off from normal interaction with the speakers. There have been a few reports of children who are left alone for long periods of time with a television set broadcasting in a language other than the one spoken in the home. Scenes on television portray routine interactions involving normal language, so they might support the children's acquisition of the foreign language through imitation and the association of sound and action. While children raised in such homes can acquire vocabulary by watching television (Rice & Woodsmall, 1988), children for whom television provides the *only* exposure to language do not seem to acquire the crucial linguistic ability to create and comprehend an infinite number of sentences (Snow et al., 1976). The fact that language does not develop on the basis of television exposure alone contradicts the idea that mere exposure is all that is required to trigger language development. Children must also actively engage in speaking to others to see how their words affect others and themselves.

The crucial role of active participation in human activity is demonstrated by children who grow up in an environment without language but with normal human interaction. One such situation occurs in the case of deaf children whose hearing parents do not know sign language and discourage its use (Feldman, Goldin-Meadow, & Gleitman, 1978; Goldin-Meadow, 1985; Goldin-Meadow & Mylander, 1990). We know that the biological condition of deafness need not be

This little girl is signing the word "sleep." (Copyright Ursula Bellugi, The Salk Institute for Biological Studies; reprinted with permission.)

an impediment to normal language acquisition; deaf children born to deaf parents who communicate in sign language acquire language at least as rapidly and fully as hearing children born into hearing households (Padden & Humphries, 1989). So any delays and difficulties in deaf children's language development cannot be explained by their inability to hear; it must result from differences in the way the environment is organized to permit participation in language-mediated activity.

In the families studied by Susan Goldin-Meadow and her colleagues, the parents did not know sign language and refused to use it because they believed that their deaf children could and should learn to read lips and to vocalize sounds. As a consequence, at an age when other children are hearing (or seeing) language, these children received extremely restricted input in their home surroundings. However, they did participate in everyday, formated, routine activities coordinated through the language and cultural system of the adults.

Earlier studies had shown that deaf children raised under these circumstances will spontaneously begin to gesture in "home sign," a kind of communication through pantomime (Fant, 1972). Goldin-Meadow and her colleagues wanted to find out if the home-sign systems developed by the deaf children displayed the characteristic features of language acquisition. They discovered that, indeed, the gestures these children developed exhibited certain characteristics of language even though they had no one to show them the signs.

Home sign begins as pointing. The children gesture one sign at a time—at the same age when hearing children develop single-word utterances. Home-sign gestures seem to refer to the same kinds of objects and to fulfill the same functions as the early words of hearing children or of deaf children with signing parents. Remarkably, home-signing children go on to make patterns of two, three, and more signs around their second birthday, about the same time that hearing children utter multiword sentences.

Analysis of these multipart signs reveals ordering principles much like those seen at the two-word stage in hearing children. In addition, Goldin-Meadow reports that these deaf children were embedding sign sentences within each other ("You/Susan give me/Abe cookie that is round"). This is the property of recursion, which, as we pointed out at the beginning of this chapter, is characteristic of all human languages and absent from the communicative system of chimpanzees or other creatures even after long training.

Once these children are able to make two- to three-word "utterances" in their home sign and begin to embed sign sentences within each other, their language development appears to come to an end. They fail to acquire grammatical morphemes or to master complex grammatical distinctions. The mere fact of being raised in an environment where the actions of all the other participants are organized by human language and culture is sufficient to allow the child to acquire the basics of linguistic structure. But without access to the additional information provided by the sights (or sounds) of language in the environment, the child has no opportunity to discover its more subtle features (Goldin-Meadow, 1985). Confirmation of this conclusion comes from the case of a hearing child raised by deaf parents (Sachs, Bard, & Johnson, 1981). This child's parents exposed him to neither conventional oral nor conventional manual language input. He heard English only on TV and during a brief time spent in nursery school. The course of development for this child was precisely the same as for the deaf children of hearing parents: he developed the basic features of grammar, but not the more complex ones. Once he was introduced to normal American sign, at the age of 3 years and 9 months, he quickly acquired normal language ability.

Such research narrows the search for the critical environmental ingredients of language development. The beginnings of language may appear during the second year of life even in the absence of direct experience of language, as long as children are included in the everyday life of their family. The kind of language that appears under such linguistically impoverished conditions, however, resembles the language behavior of children at the two-word phase. Apparently participation in culturally organized activity, while necessary, is not always sufficient to enable the child to realize the full potential of language (Schaller, 1991).

How interaction contributes to language acquisition

The conclusion seems inescapable that if children are to acquire more than the rudiments of language, not only must they participate in family or community activity, they must also hear (or see) language as they mature. It is in everyday interactions that hearing children (or deaf children of signing parents) master language as a basic part of their activities, filling in the gaps between nonverbal actions. When researchers take account both of children's active efforts to make sense of language-mediated interactions and of adult communicative behaviors in the presence of children, the resulting analyses go a long way toward reducing the mystery of how children learn to understand and use words (see Figure 8.1, p. 298).

Fast Mapping Elsa Bartlett and Susan Carey's study of vocabulary development (mentioned in Chapter 1, p. 26) is one of many current attempts to understand how new words are acquired. These researchers made use of the normal routine of a preschool to find out what happens when a totally new word is introduced into conversation with children. They chose to study the acquisition of color terms. None of the 14 children in the classroom knew the name of the color that adults call olive; some children called it brown, others called it green, and some didn't refer to the color by name at all. Bartlett and Carey decided to give it an implausible name, chromium, just in case some children had partial knowledge of the real name that they had not revealed.

After the children had been tested to determine that they did not know the name of the color olive, one cup and one tray in the classroom were painted "chromium" (olive). While preparing for snacktime, the teacher found an opportunity to ask each child, "Please bring me the chromium cup; not the red one, the chromium one" or "Bring me the chromium tray; not the blue one, the chromium one."

This procedure worked. All of the children succeeded in picking the correct cup or tray, although they were likely to ask for confirmation ("You mean this one?"). Some of the children could be seen repeating the unfamiliar word to themselves.

One week after this single experience with the new word, the children were given a color-naming test with color chips. Two-thirds of the children showed that they had learned something about this odd term and its referents; when asked for chromium, they chose either the olive chip or a green one. Six weeks later many of the children still showed the influence of this single experience.

A variety of procedures have been used to confirm Bartlett and Carey's findings, including exposure of children to new words in a television program (Rice, 1990).

Bartlett and Carey's data on word learning do not support the idea that children acquire language because adults explicitly reward their efforts, nor do they support the idea that children learn by any simple process of imitation. Rather, when children hear an unfamiliar word in a familiar and structured and meaningful social interaction, they seem to form a quick idea of the word's meaning and the way it might fit into their existing repertoire. Psychologists refer to this form of rapid word acquisition as **fast mapping.** Fast mapping has been observed in

Fast mapping The way in which children quickly form an idea of the meaning of an unfamiliar word they hear in a familiar and highly structured situation.

children as young as 15 months of age in controlled experiments (Schafer & Plunkett, 1996). The challenge is to explain how participation in normal activities makes fast mapping possible.

The Child's Contribution   Psychologists have proposed several cognitive principles that young children could be following to make the fast mapping of word meanings possible (Clark, 1995; Golinkoff, Mervis, & Hirsch-Pasek, 1994). The whole object principle, for example, asserts that when a new word appears in connection with some object, the word applies to the whole object. Young children appear to assume, for example, that when a cup is used in conjunction with the word "cup," the new word applies to the entire cup, not just the handle.

A second principle might be termed the categorizing principle: except in the case of their very first words, children also appear to assume that object labels extend to classes of similar objects. For example, toddlers use the word "dog" not only when they are referring to the family dog, but for other dogs as well (Waxman & Hall, 1993).

A study by Sandra Waxman and Rochel Gelman (1986) clearly shows how very young children use the categorizing principle to help them figure out word meanings. Waxman and Gelman introduced children between the ages of 3 and 5 to three "very picky" hand puppets. Each hand puppet liked only one kind of thing—either animals, clothing, or food.

Waxman and Gelman found that if they simply told the children to give each puppet the things the puppet liked without using any labels, the children assigned items to the puppets at random, much as if they didn't realize that each puppet liked only one category of things. But if the researchers used a made-up word to label each category as part of the instructions, the children immediately gave each puppet only things of the kind "it would like to have." The totally unfamiliar label was just as effective in getting the children to recognize the categories as the words the children did know ("These are the animals, these are the clothes, these are foods"). In short, the children treated the adult's introduction of a label as an invitation to form a category.

From this "lexical principles" point of view, fast mapping is possible because children bring prior partial knowledge and cognitive strategies to the task of learning new words.

Contributions from the Social Context   When we begin to study the social context of early lexical development, we find another source of support for language acquisition. The situation created by Bartlett and Carey, in which children were asked to fetch a "chromium" tray, demonstrates how fast mapping occurs when new words are included in the interaction at precisely the right moment so that everything *but* the new word is treated routinely.

The crucial role of finely tuned and well-timed interaction in supporting word learning is seen in a series of studies by Michael Tomasello and his colleagues (Tomasello, 1988; Tomasello & Farrar, 1986). These researchers videotaped mothers interacting with their 1½- to 2-year-old children in order to identify the precise moment at which the mothers referred to objects in the immediate environment. They found that for the most part the mothers talked about objects that were already a part of the child's ongoing actions and the objects of joint attention, thus greatly reducing the child's problem in figuring out the referents of the mother's words. In a follow-up experimental study, these investigators deliberately taught new words to the children in one of two ways: for half the children, the adult labeled an object that was not the focus of the child's attention in an effort to direct the child's attention to it; for the other half, the adult labeled the object *after* the child had focused on it. The strategy of labeling an object after the child was already attending to it proved more effective than trying to get the child to attend to a new word and a new meaning at the same time. The social conditions that enable fast mapping clearly correspond well to the kinds of adult-guided constructive processes emphasized by cultural-context theorists (Bruner, 1983a; Ochs & Schieffelin, 1995). As cultural-context theorists see it, explicit rewards for learning language are unnecessary. The reinforcement comes from the children's increased success at communicating and the greater freedoms they experience once they can use new words.

Is there a role for deliberate instruction?

As we have described it thus far, language acquisition appears to require several elements, each of which is emphasized by one of the major theories:

1. A biologically programmed sensitivity to language present at birth, which develops as the child matures (the nativist view).
2. The ability to learn from and imitate the language behavior of others (the environmental-learning view).
3. Acquisition of basic cognitive capacities, including schemas for actions with objects, the ability to represent the world mentally, and the presence of lexical principles (the constructivist version of an interactionist view).
4. The inclusion of children in familiar routines in which language is one of many forms of interaction (the cultural-context version of an interactionist view).

Missing from this list is the role of deliberate instruction ("This is an apple," "This is a truck") or the use of explicit rewards for learning of the kind emphasized in some environmental-learning explanations of language acquisition. Are deliberate efforts to foster language development by teaching about language irrelevant?

Adults in many cultures certainly seem to think that it is important to teach their children how to talk (Ochs & Schieffelin, 1995). But the age at which they start such instruction varies widely among cultures. The Kaluli of New Guinea, for example, believe that children must be explicitly taught language just as they must be taught other culturally valued forms of behavior. The Kaluli make no effort to start teaching language until they believe the child is ready, a benchmark judged to be the time when the child has begun to use a few words. As soon as those first words are spoken, the parents begin to engage their babies in a form of speech activity called *elema*: the mother provides the utterance she wants the child to utter followed by the command "*Elema*" ("Say like this"). Eleanor Ochs (1982) described similar practices among Samoans, and Peggy Miller (1982) reported that working-class mothers in Baltimore, Maryland, follow a similar strategy with respect to teaching vocabulary.

Even in societies where adults do not engage in deliberate teaching strategies, many investigators have noted that adults sometimes use a special speech register when speaking to young children, dubbed **motherese**: they speak in a special high-pitched voice, emphasize boundaries between idea-bearing clauses, and use a simplified vocabulary when they talk to small children (Fernald, 1991; Snow, 1995).

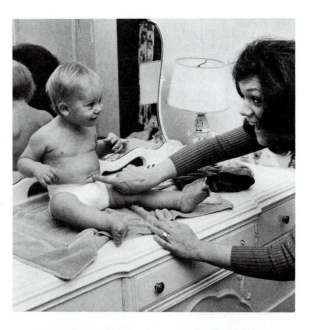
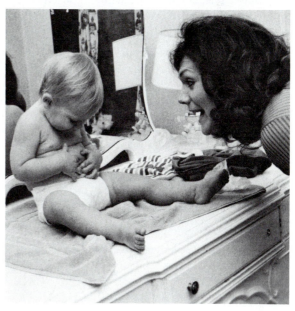

Language is acquired in the context of ongoing activity. This mother is talking and playing with her baby as a routine part of getting him dressed.

Motherese The special high-pitched voice, emphasis on the boundaries between idea-bearing clauses, and simplified vocabulary that adults use in speaking to small children.

TABLE 8.6 — Simplifications Used by Middle-Class U.S. Adults Speaking to Small Children

PHONOLOGICAL SIMPLIFICATIONS

Higher pitch and exaggerated intonation

Clear pronunciation

Slower speech

Distinct pauses between utterances

SYNTACTIC DIFFERENCES

Shorter and less varied utterance length

Almost all sentences well formed

Many partial or complete repetitions of child's utterances, sometimes with expansion

Fewer broken sentences

Less grammatical complexity

SEMANTIC DIFFERENCES

More limited vocabulary

Many special words and diminutives

Reference to concrete circumstances of here and now

Middle level of generality in naming objects

PRAGMATIC DIFFERENCES

More directives, imperatives, and questions

More utterances designed to draw attention to aspects of objects

Source: de Villiers & de Villiers, 1978.

As Table 8.6 indicates, middle-class parents in the United States simplify virtually every aspect of their language when they speak to their children. Several studies have shown that the complexity of adults' speech to children is graded to the level of complexity of the child's speech (Bohannon & Warren-Leubecker, 1988; Snow, 1995).

Catherine Snow (1972) shows how such tailoring processes can work. A child is putting away toys under the mother's direction. Note the sequence of the mother's directions: "Put the red truck in the box now. . . . The red truck. . . . No, the red truck. . . . In the box. . . . The red truck in the box." Snow argues that this kind of graded language environment, in which statements are gradually simplified and their meaning highlighted, isolates constituent phrases at the same time that it models the whole correct grammatical structure.

American adults not only simplify what they say as an aid to children's comprehension (and perhaps to aid them in the process of discovering how to use language); they also complicate what children say. This phenomenon was pointed out by Roger Brown and Ursula Bellugi (1964), who called this kind of adult speech *expansion* because it seemed to expand the child's utterance into a grammatically correct adult version. A child who says "Mommy wash," for example, might be responded to with "Yes, Mommy is washing her face"; the declaration "Daddy sleep" might evoke the caution "Yes, Daddy is sleeping. Don't wake him up."

Despite widespread belief that adult teaching, simplifying, and highlighting behaviors help children to master language, the necessity of such practices has been the subject of long-standing disagreement among scholars who study language acquisition.

As we noted earlier (p. 318), Brown and Hanlon (1970) found that adults rarely corrected their young children's grammatical errors in an explicit way. When Courtney Cazden (1965) attempted to "force-feed" children with a heavy diet of feedback by expanding and correcting their incorrect sentences, she found no special effect on language development. Subsequent studies have sometimes found effects of parental expansions or corrections (Farrar, 1992; Nelson, 1976; Hirsh-Pasek, Treiman, & Schneiderman, 1984), but failures to find such effects are at least as numerous (Gleitman, Newport, & Gleitman, 1984). Consequently, no firm conclusions about the influence of deliberate parental feedback are yet possible.

Perhaps the most important conclusion to come out of several decades of work on the relation between special adult behaviors and children's acquisition of language is that the differences in the everyday, intuitive practices of adults throughout the world make relatively little difference in the rate at which children acquire language: all normally developing children become competent language users. All cultural groups take into account the fact that small children do not understand language and make some provision for seeing that they have the opportunity to acquire it. However, it has not been possible to prove that a particular practice that might be called "teaching the child to speak" has an important impact on language acquisition or that one method of structuring children's language experience is universally essential.

Language and Thought

The research reviewed in this chapter makes it clear that language is complexly related to activity and the surrounding world. Children learn early to use this relationship to influence their interactions with the world. And all the time that their language capacities are growing, they are acquiring more knowledge. How are the development of language and the development of thought processes related?

THE ENVIRONMENTAL-LEARNING PERSPECTIVE

According to learning theorists such as Albert Bandura (1986) and B. F. Skinner (1957), children begin to grasp what different language forms signify by relating what they hear to what they understand to be going on. Eventually a great deal of their thought comes to be based on language. These theorists also believe that there are special advantages to such thinking.

> By manipulating symbols that convey relevant information, one can gain understanding of causal relationships, expand one's knowledge, solve problems, and deduce consequences of actions without actually performing them. The functional value of thought rests on the close correspondence between the symbolic system [in this case, language] and external events, so that the former can be substituted for the latter. (Bandura, 1986, p. 462)

Language, according to this view, is more than a means of communication with others. Words deepen a child's understanding of certain aspects of objects and of the subtle relations among various events. Associations among words provide a kind of mental map of the world, which shapes the way a child thinks. This view suggests that thinking should change markedly when children begin to acquire language.

THE PIAGETIAN INTERACTIONIST PERSPECTIVE

Piaget claimed that sensorimotor schemas accumulated by the end of infancy give rise to a new mode of representation, in which children begin to think in symbols (Chapter 6, p. 228). Language, he believed, is a verbal reflection of the individual's conceptual understanding (Piaget, 1926, 1983). The acquisition of language provides a means of thinking more rapidly, since a sequence of thoughts can often be carried out more quickly than a sequence of actions. But since language *reflects* thought, language developments cannot *cause* cognitive development. Rather, cognition determines language.

As we saw in Chapters 4 to 6, Piaget believed that cognitive development arises from the child's attempts to assimilate the environment, which are modified through subsequent accommodations. At the end of the sensorimotor period, children have developed a basic understanding that they are a part of a world that exists apart from them, but, as we will see in Chapter 9, they still have difficulty adopting other people's points of view. If language is determined by thought, it follows that early speech, like early thought, must be egocentric and fail to take into account others' points of view.

Early in his career, Piaget supported his hypothesis with data collected from preschool children's conversations. What struck him was that while preschoolers appear to be playing and conversing together, their remarks actually focus on what they are doing by themselves, with no real regard for their partner and with no apparent intention of actually communicating. Piaget (1926) called this type of language a **collective monologue.** He believed that collective monologues mirror a profoundly egocentric mode of thought. The following conversation between two American preschoolers illustrates his point:

Collective monologues The speech that occurs when children are playing near each other and each of them is talking with no real regard for their partner.

Jenny: They wiggle sideways when they kiss.

Chris: *(vaguely)* What?

Jenny: My bunny slippers. They are brown and red and sort of yellow and white. And they have eyes and ears and these noses that wiggle sideways when they kiss.

Chris: I have a piece of sugar in a red piece of paper. I'm gonna eat it but maybe it's for a horse.

Jenny: We bought them. My mommy did. We couldn't find the old ones. These are like the old ones. They were not in the trunk.

Chris: Can't eat the piece of sugar, not unless you take the paper off.

Jenny: And we found Mother Lamb. Oh, she was in Poughkeepsie in the trunk in the house in the woods where Mrs. Tiddywinkle lives.

Chris: Do I like sugar? I do, and so do horses.

Jenny: I play with my bunnies. They are real. We play in the woods. They have eyes. We all go in the woods. My teddy bear and the bunnies and the duck, to visit Mrs. Tiddywinkle. We play and play.

Chris: I guess I'll eat my sugar at lunch time. I can get more for the horses. Besides, I don't have no horses now. (Stone & Church, 1957, pp. 146–147)

Piaget believed that as children grow older, their ability to adopt others' points of view increases and collective monologues give way to genuine dialogues.

Piaget's idea that language depends on thought but thought is not influenced by language was tested by Hermione Sinclair de Zwart (1967), who taught French-speaking preschoolers the correct meanings of the terms for "more" and "less," then tested their ability to solve problems involving the relationships of more and less. She found that the children who had learned to use the words appropriately in the training situation showed no advantage over untrained children when these relationships were actually needed to solve a problem. This failure of language training to influence problem solving seems to confirm Piaget's theory that language does not affect thought.

THE NATIVIST PERSPECTIVE

Nativist theorists such as Noam Chomsky explicitly deny that it is possible for language to grow out of sensorimotor schemas, declaring that there are no known similarities between the principles of language and the principles of sensorimotor intelligence (Chomsky, 1980). Rather, as we explained earlier, Chomsky believes that language acquisition is made possible by a specifically human language acquisition device (LAD).

Chomsky (1980) has used the term **mental module** to indicate the self-contained nature of the capacity to use language. A mental module is a highly specific mental faculty that is tuned to particular kinds of environmental input. In claiming that language forms a distinctive mental module, Chomsky seems to be declaring that language and thought do not depend on each other. In support of this position, nativists note that some severely retarded children have relatively advanced linguistic abilities even though their other intellectual abilities are extremely limited (p. 323). However, Chomsky does not go so far as to say that there is no connection between these two domains of mind. When Piaget's colleague Barbel Inhelder challenged Chomsky on this issue, he replied:

> I take it for granted that thinking is a domain that is quite different from language, even though language is used for the expression of thought, and for a good deal of thinking we really need the mediation of language. (Chomsky, 1980, p. 174)

Mental modules Highly specific mental faculties tuned to particular kinds of environmental input.

A CULTURAL-CONTEXT PERSPECTIVE

The most prominent cultural theory of language and thought was developed by the Russian psychologist Lev Vygotsky (1934/1987, 1978). Pointing out that children's development always occurs in a context organized and watched over by adults, Vygotsky insisted that children's experience of language is social from the outset.

In accord with evidence we presented earlier, Vygotsky (1934/1987) argued that even children's initial words are communicative acts, mediating their interactions with the people around them. More generally, he believed that every new psychological function first appears during children's interactions with others who can support and nurture their efforts. These shared efforts are gradually taken over by the child and transformed into individual abilities. Applied to the area of language, this sequence suggests a progression from social and communicative speech to internal dialogue, or inner speech, in which thought and language are intimately interconnected. This is just the opposite of the way language, cognition, and the social world are related in Piaget's framework, and, as might be expected, Vygotsky's interpretation of collective monologues (or "egocentric speech") also differs from Piaget's.

Vygotsky and his colleagues conducted a series of studies to test Piaget's idea that egocentric speech serves no cognitive or communicative function (Vygotsky, 1934/1987). In one such study, they demonstrated that egocentric speech fulfills important cognitive functions: when children were faced with a difficulty in solving a problem, they raised the level of their overt self-regulatory speech. (This finding was replicated by Kohlberg, Yaeger, and Hjertholm [1968].) In a second study they demonstrated that egocentric speech serves a communicative function as well. In this case preschoolers were placed among deaf-mute children, with whom they had little chance of communicating. Vygotsky reasoned that if egocentric speech was really not intended to communicate, it would not be affected by potential listeners' inability to understand. Instead, the rate of egocentric speech decreased markedly from its level in the presence of hearing children (described in Wertsch, 1985).

Vygotsky saw the relationship between language and thought as changing over the course of development. Both language and thought develop, and so does the relationship between them. According to Vygotsky, during the first two years of life, language and thought develop along more or less parallel, relatively unrelated lines. Beginning around 2 years of age, however, thought and language begin to intermingle. This intermingling, wrote Vygotsky (1934/1987), fundamentally changes the nature of both thinking and language, providing the growing child with a uniquely human form of behavior in which language becomes intellectual and thinking becomes verbal (see Figure 8.7).

In Vygotsky's framework, language allows thought to be individual and social at the same time. It is the medium through which individual thought is communicated to others while at the same time it allows social reality to be converted into the idiosyncratic thought of the individual. This conversion of language from the social to the individual is never complete, even in the adult, whose individual thought processes continue to be shaped in part by the conventional meanings present in the lexicon and by the speech habits of the culture.

There appears to be reasonable agreement among developmental psychologists that language and thought are separable psychological functions; neither can be reduced to the other. There is also agreement that the two functions inter-

FIGURE 8.7 *A schematic representation of Vygotsky's idea that as children acquire language, both thinking and speech undergo transformations: language becomes an intellectual function while thinking becomes verbal.*

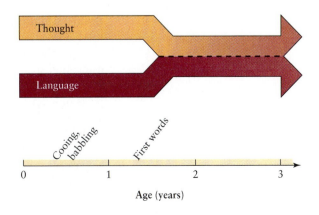

mingle in normal development. The field is still far from agreement, however, on the extent to which development in one domain influences development in the other and on their combined roles in the development of the child as a whole.

The Basic Puzzles of Language Acquisition Reconsidered

At the beginning of this chapter we introduced two basic questions about the way children acquire language: How do they come to understand what words mean and how do they acquire the ability to arrange words in acceptable sequences to express and understand the complex meanings needed to interact successfully with other people?

The information we have presented in this chapter does not definitively answer these questions because neither language nor the way children acquire it is fully understood. But research discussed in this chapter has at least narrowed the scope of the quest.

Consider the problem posed in Figure 8.1, in which the father and son are gazing out of a window and the father tells the boy to look at the *ptitsa* (bird). What this picture leaves out is a history of interaction between parent and child in the course of which they have developed many routines for understanding each other. It also leaves out any indication of what they were in the midst of doing when the father said, "Look, son, there sits a *ptitsa*." Perhaps they had been playing naming games, or perhaps they had been feeding their pet bird. A full account would also include the other words the child already knew, because, as we learned from the data on fast mapping (p. 325), children use the words they already know to help them figure out what new words mean.

Knowing these things would certainly reduce the mystery of how the child might come to understand the father but would not eliminate it entirely. No chimpanzee would be able to learn in such circumstances. It remains a uniquely human ability.

The puzzle of grammar remains even more mysterious. Perhaps, as nativist theorists claim, linguistic competence is achieved through an innate language acquisition device. But it is still unclear what minimal environmental conditions are needed to permit this device to function properly. Goldin-Meadow's work with deaf children in hearing households tells us that participation in normal cultural routines can be sufficient for the rudiments of language to appear. And evidence collected in both our own and other societies tells us that children acquire normal linguistic competence without special instruction if they can have access to language (either oral or sign) and if they are incorporated in routine, culturally organized activity, which serves as a language acquisition support system. As Jerome Bruner whimsically suggested, language is born from the union of the LAD and the LASS.

Although children 2½ to 3 years of age can properly be considered language-using human beings, we do not want to give the impression that their language development is complete (see Table 8.7). As we have indicated repeatedly, all aspects of language continue to develop all during childhood, and in some cases into adulthood. Moreover, we will see that as children begin to acquire the specialized skills they will need to cope with adult life in their culture, deliberate teaching may begin to play a conspicuous role in language development. Such specialized activities as reciting nursery rhymes, acting in a play, and writing an essay are all forms of language activity that require practice and instruction. We shall return to examine some of the more specialized language developments associated with middle childhood in Chapter 13.

TABLE 8.7 The Progress of Language Development

Approximate Age	Typical Behavior
Birth	Phoneme perception
	Discrimination of language from nonlanguage sounds
	Crying
3 months	Cooing
6 months	Babbling
	Loss of ability to discriminate between nonnative phonemes
9 months	First words
	Holophrases
12 months	Use of words to attract adults' attention
18 months	Vocabulary spurt
	First two-word sentences (telegraphic speech)
24 months	Correct responses to indirect requests ("Is the door shut?")
30 months	Creation of indirect requests (You're standing on my blocks!")
	Modification of speech to take listener into account
	Early awareness of grammatical categories
Early childhood	Rapid increase in grammatical complexity
	Overgeneralization of grammatical rules
Middle childhood	Understanding of passive forms ("The balls were taken by the boys")
	Acquisition of written language
Adolescence	Acquisition of specialized language functions

SUMMARY

Prelinguistic Communication

- Linguistic communication builds on an extensive foundation of prelinguistic communicative achievements, including babbling, turn-taking, and the ability to focus one's attention on objects and activities in concert with other people.

The Puzzle of Language Development

- Despite intensive investigation, scientists' understanding of language acquisition remains incomplete. No theory is able to explain satisfactorily how children come to understand either the meanings of words or the rules that govern their arrangement (grammar).

Four Subsystems of Language

- In the transition from babbling to talking, children begin to conform to the restricted set of sounds of the language their parents speak. The basic sounds of a language (phonemes) are those that distinguish one word from another.

- Early words for objects are associated with actions and with changes in an object's state or location.
- Early words indicate children's emerging ability to operate on the world indirectly (in a mediated way) as well as directly.
- Early word meanings often correspond to an intermediate level of abstraction. As a consequence, words may be used too broadly (overextension) or too narrowly (underextension) to conform to adult definitions.
- As children's vocabularies expand, their understanding of word meanings changes fundamentally; meanings embedded in particular contexts of action are supplemented by meanings dominated by logical categories.
- Children's first words are often nonconventional; interpretation depends to a great extent on the listener's knowledge of the context in which they are used.
- Two-word utterances allow children to take advantage of the relationships of words within utterances to convey meaning, marking the birth of grammar. As the length of utterances increases, so does the complexity of the grammatical rules governing the arrangement of words within sentences and of elements (morphemes) within words.
- The growth of children's vocabularies and their increased ability to use complex grammatical constructions are accompanied by a corresponding growth in their ability to engage in conversational acts that achieve a variety of goals.
- Central to the successful use of language is the ability to say things in a way that is understandable to one's partner in conversation. Children reveal at an early age their ability to tailor their language to their listeners' needs.

Explanations of Language Acquisition

- Three theories dominate late-twentieth-century explanations of language acquisition.

    1. Learning theories claim that words and patterns of words are learned through imitation and through classical and operant conditioning.
    2. Nativist theories claim that children are born with a language acquisition device (LAD), which is automatically activated by the environment when the child has matured sufficiently.
    3. Interactionist theories emphasize the cognitive preconditions for language acquisition and the role of the social environment in providing a language acquisition support system (LASS).

Essential Ingredients of Language Acquisition

- Language is a particularly human communicative ability, but aspects of language-like communication can be found among chimpanzees and other primates.
- Children acquire the basic elements of language with no special assistance from adults if they are raised in normal speaking or signing homes where communication is appropriate to the hearing ability of the child. Development of the full range of language abilities, however, requires both participation in human activity and exposure to language as part of that activity.

Language and Thought

- Each of the various theories of language acquisition has its own view of the relationship between language and thought.

1. According to environmental-learning theorists, language and thought are two aspects of a single process; hence the acquisition of language has a great impact on thinking and vice versa.

2. According to nativist theorists such as Chomsky, language and thought are independent of each other.

3. According to Piagetian interactionist theorists, developments in thought are the preconditions for language development.

4. According to cultural-context theorists such as Vygotsky, language and thought arise independently but fuse in early childhood to create specifically human modes of thinking and communication.

KEY TERMS

collective monologues, p. 329

conversational acts, p. 312

cooperative principle, p. 313

deep structure, p. 318

fast mapping, p. 325

format, p. 321

grammar, p. 299

grammatical morphemes, p. 310

holophrase, p. 308

language acquisition device (LAD), p. 319

language acquisition support system (LASS), p. 321

mental module, p. 330

motherese, p. 327

overextension, p. 304

pragmatic uses of language, p. 312

recursion, p. 299

surface structure, p. 318

underextension, p. 304

THOUGHT QUESTIONS

1. George Miller said that both the environmental-learning and nativist approaches to the acquisition of language were unsatisfactory, the first because it was impossible and the other because it was miraculous. What did he mean? Was this a fair statement of the problem?

2. Jerome Bruner characterized language acquisition as "a subtle process by which adults artificially arrange the world so that the child can succeed culturally by doing what comes naturally." What sorts of subtle arranging appear necessary for language acquisition to occur?

3. Once children move beyond the single-word stage of language development, how does their ability to combine two words to form a sentence affect their ability to create meaning?

4. Think about having dinner yesterday evening. What is the role of language in your thinking about the event? Are you able to think about this or any other event entirely without language?

5. Some developmental psycholinguists now claim that nonhuman primates can be trained to acquire a protolanguage that makes their communicative ability equivalent to that of a 2-to-2½-year-old child. How do the communicative capacities of such animals help us to gain a better understanding of the development of human language?

Early Childhood Thought: Islands of Competence

"In every sentence . . . , in every childish act [of the 2- to 5-year-old] is revealed complete ignorance of the simplest things. Of course, I cite these expressions not to scorn childish absurdities. On the contrary, they inspire me with respect because they are evidence of the gigantic work that goes on in the child's mind which, by the age of 7, results in the conquest of this mental chaos."

—Kornei Chukovsky, *From Two to Five*

A group of 5-year-old children have been listening to "Stone Soup," a folktale retold by Marcia Brown. "Stone Soup" is about three hungry soldiers who trick some selfish peasants into feeding them by pretending to make soup out of stones. "Do stones melt?" asks Rose, one of the children. Master Teacher Vivian Paley reports the conversation that followed this question:

"Do you think they melt, Rose?"

"Yes."

". . . Does anyone agree with Rose?"

"They will melt if you cook them," said Lisa.

"If you boil them," Eddie added.

No one doubted that the stones in the story had melted and that ours, too, would melt.

"We can cook them and find out," I said. "How will we be able to tell if they've melted?"

"They'll be smaller," said Deana.

The stones are placed in boiling water for an hour and then put on the table for inspection.

Ellen: They're much smaller.

Fred: Much, much. Almost melted.

Rose: I can't eat melted stones.

Teacher: Don't worry, Rose. You won't. But I'm not convinced they've melted. Can we prove it?

Ms. Paley suggests weighing the stones to see if they will lose weight as they boil. The children find that they weigh two pounds at the start. After they have been boiled again, the following conversation ensues:

Eddie: Still two [pounds]. But they are smaller.

Wally: Much smaller.

Teacher: They weigh the same. Two pounds before and two pounds now. That means they didn't lose weight.

Eddie: They only got a little bit smaller.

Wally: The scale can't see the stones. Hey, once in Michigan there were three stones in a fire and they melted away. They were gone. We saw it.

Deana: Maybe the stones in the story are magic.

Wally: But not these.

(Adapted from Paley, 1981, pp. 16–18)

We can see that when Ms. Paley entices the children into reconciling the world of the story and the world of their senses, their explanations are a mixture of sound physical theory and magical thinking. The children correctly believe that when things are "cooked down" they grow smaller and that small stones should be lighter than big ones. At the same time they are willing to believe that there really are such things as magical stones that melt, and so they miss the point of "Stone Soup." Their way of thinking appears to wobble back and forth between logic and magic, insight and ignorance, the reasoned and the unreasonable.

A similar patchwork of competence and incompetence can be found in preschoolers' ability to remember. It is quite common for young children to recall the names and descriptions of their favorite dinosaurs, details of trips to the

The experience of being read to during early childhood instills the idea that reading is a pleasurable activity. It also introduces the young child to a good deal of widely held cultural knowledge.

doctor's office, or the location of their favorite toy with an accuracy that can astound their parents (Baker-Ward et al., 1993; De Loache, Cassidy, & Brown, 1985). But they have difficulty recalling a set of toy objects immediately after they are asked to remember them (Rogoff & Mistry, 1990).

The patchwork-like quality of young children's intellectual performances raises in a new way the basic questions of development. Should early childhood be considered a distinct stage of development, and if so, how are we to account for the unevenness of young children's thinking? Are young children simply inconsistent? Or do their thought processes vary from one task to the next because they are more familiar with some tasks than with others? Or might it be that their abilities vary because some parts of their brain have matured more than others? In attempting to answer such questions psychologists must also be sensitive to the possibility that preschoolers only appear to be illogical or unable to remember things because their still-fragile language skills do not enable them to understand what is expected of them or to communicate their thoughts adequately.

We begin our discussion of these issues by describing Piaget's portrait of early childhood, which has dominated the study of mental development in the latter half of this century. In recent years Piaget's views on early childhood development have been increasingly questioned. Piaget's empirical observations continue to provoke extremely interesting questions, however, and his influence has been so great that even specialists who disagree with Piaget's theories use the phenomena he studied as the starting point for their own work.

Next we summarize research that calls into question Piaget's interpretations of the data he collected and points toward different interpretations of development during early childhood. At present it appears that young children are more competent than Piaget gave them credit for being, but sharp disagreements remain about both the nature of their abilities and the processes of cognitive change that are evident throughout the years of early childhood.

Piaget's Account of Mental Development in Early Childhood

In Piaget's theoretical framework, early childhood is a time of transition between infancy, when thinking is based on action (sensorimotor schemas), and middle childhood, when it is based on internalized (mental) actions (Piaget & Inhelder, 1969). When they complete the final sensorimotor substage (described in Chapter 6), children have acquired the rudiments of representational thought. Forever after, they are able to use one thing to stand for another, one of the fundamental capacities on which their newfound ability to use language is based. They no longer rely exclusively on overt trial and error to solve problems; they imitate actions that they have observed in quite diverse circumstances; they engage in pretend play.

A few years later, sometime around the age of 7 or 8, Piaget believed, children become capable of **mental operations,** mental "actions" such as combining, separating, and transforming information in a logical manner. Until they are able to engage in mental operations, their thinking is subject to limitations that lead to the "childish absurdities" to which Kornei Chukovsky refers in the epigraph of this chapter.

Piaget's belief that young children are led into error and confusion because they are still unable to engage in true mental operations is captured in the name that he gave to this period of development, the **preoperational stage.** The very name "preoperational" captures Piaget's basic idea. The thinking of 3-, 4-, and 5-year-old is not yet fully operational. Development during early childhood, then, can be seen as a process of overcoming cognitive limitations until mental operational thought is achieved.

The limitation that Piaget believed to be the key feature of thinking during early childhood is its "one-sidedness." Children of this age focus their attention (or "center," as he called it) on no more than one salient aspect of whatever they are trying to think about. Only after overcoming this limitation, he believed, do children make the transition to the stage of operational thinking, in which the ability to coordinate two perspectives emerges. Two classic examples from Piaget's work have greatly influenced all subsequent work on early childhood development; each is said to illustrate how centering on a single aspect of a problem to the exclusion of all others limits the young child's ability to reason.

The first example is perhaps Piaget's most famous demonstration of the difference between preoperational and concrete operational thinking (which appears in middle childhood). Children are presented with two identical beakers, each filled with exactly the same amount of water. While the child watches, the water in one of the beakers is poured into a third, narrower and taller beaker, so that the level of the water in the new beaker is higher. From this change in level, 3- and 4-year-olds conclude that the amount of water has somehow increased. Piaget maintained that young children err because they center on only a single dimension of the problem—in this case, the height of the water in the beaker. They are unable to consider the height and width of the beaker simultaneously. Once they are capable of mental operations, children firmly deny that the amount has changed, presumably because their thinking has become *de*centered and they can consider several aspects of the problem at once. Thus they are able to think through what would happen if the water were poured back into its original beaker at the same time that they keep track of the information about the new beaker. (We will return to research based on these examples in Chapter 12 because it also plays a central role in disputes about the nature of mental development in middle childhood.)

Mental operation In Piaget's terms the mental "actions" of combining, separating, and transforming information in a logical manner.

Preoperational stage In Piagetian theory, it is the stage following the sensorimotor stage. Children in the preoperational stage often fail to distinguish their point of view from that of others, become easily captured by surface appearances, and are easily confused about causal relations.

A different manifestation of the inability to coordinate two perspectives comes from a phenomenon mentioned in Chapter 1: young children appear to become confused about the relationship between a general class of objects and its subclasses. When shown a set of wooden beads, most of which are brown and the remainder white, young children fail to keep simultaneously in mind both the full set ("wooden beads") and the two subsets of differently colored members. When asked, "Which are there more of, brown beads or wooden beads?" they claim that there are more brown beads. According to Piaget, preschoolers make this mistake because they center on only one level of categorization at a time. They can think either about the beads as divided into two subclasses (brown versus white) or they can think about the united common class (wooden beads). When asked to think about both levels simultaneously, they become confused. In middle childhood, according to this line of thinking, children can keep the two levels of categorization in mind so they are not led into error.

Piaget considered this inability to keep two aspects of a problem in mind to be at the heart of what he saw as the three salient characteristics of a young child's way of thinking: (1) egocentrism, (2) the confusion of appearance and reality, and (3) nonlogical reasoning.

EGOCENTRISM

"Egocentrism" has a narrower meaning in Piaget's theory than in everyday speech. It does not mean selfish or arrogant. Rather, egocentrism means a tendency to consider the world entirely in terms of "ego's" point of view, to "center on one-self." In comparison with infants, who, according to Piaget, are totally centered on their own actions (and thus egocentric), preschoolers are far more anchored in external reality. Nevertheless, they are still trapped in their own point of view, so they tend to assume that everyone else sees things just as they do; they cannot "decenter."

The cognitive limitations that result from egocentrism were documented by Piaget and many later researchers who have been inspired by his work. Their particular manifestations depend on the specific task at hand.

Egocentrism The interpretation of the world from one's own (ego's) point of view without taking into consideration alternative perspectives.

Lack of spatial perspective taking

One way in which the egocentric nature of young children's thought shows itself is in the difficulty they have imagining what things look like from the perspective of another person's physical location. The classic example of this form of egocentrism is the three-mountain problem. Piaget and Inhelder (1956) confronted young children with a large diorama containing models of three distinctively marked mountains, each a different size and shape (see Figure 9.1). They first asked the children to walk around the diorama and become familiar with the landscape from all sides. Once the children were familiar with it, they were seated at one side and shown a doll. The doll was placed on the opposite side of the diorama, so that it had a "different view" of the landscape. The children were then shown pictures of the diorama from several perspectives and asked to identify the picture that corresponded to the doll's point of view. Despite the fact that they had traveled around the diorama, the children almost always chose the picture corresponding to their own point of view, not the doll's.

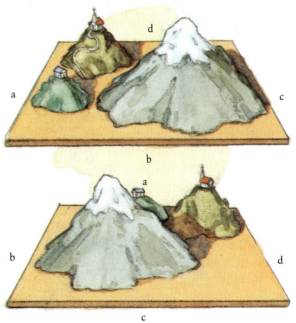

FIGURE 9.1 *Preschool children shown this diorama of three mountains with a distinctive landmark on each mountain were unable to say how the scene might look from perspectives other than the one they had adopted at the moment. (From Piaget & Inhelder, 1956.)*

FIGURE 9.2 *The task of keeping in mind what someone else needs to be told in order to communicate with that person effectively often defeats preschoolers. The girl on the left must describe the blocks on her side of the screen, being careful to mention their distinguishing features, so that the boy on the right will stack them in the same order she does. (From Krauss & Glucksberg, 1969.)*

example to parents
their voices of speaker listener
their questioning

Egocentric speech

The egocentric quality of children's thought also appears in their speech. Recall from Chapter 8, for example, the tendency of young children to engage in "collective monologues" rather than true dialogues when they play together. Piaget took such behavior to indicate that young children, owing to their entrapment in their own point of view, are not yet even trying to communicate. This same quality becomes evident when two youngsters are seated at a table and asked to communicate with each other about identical sets of objects arrayed before them. In experiments of this kind a small screen is placed between the children so that they cannot see each other. (Dickson, 1981, reviews the literature on this type of experiment.) One child is designated the speaker; the other is the listener. The speaker must describe the objects on her side of the screen one at a time, and the listener must choose the corresponding object from his own array. A typical experimental arrangement is shown in Figure 9.2.

Most 4- and 5-year-old children in the role of speaker provide too little information for the listener. If the objects are large and small toys in the shape of dogs, cats, and elephants, for example, the speaker might say only "This one is a dog," or even "Take this one," failing to realize that the listener doesn't have enough information to know exactly which object is being referred to. Young listeners also have difficulty with this task. Even when they are given the chance to ask for more information, 4- and 5-year-olds are unlikely to do so.

Failure to understand other minds

A different form of early childhood egocentrism involves difficulty reasoning about how other people think (Astington, 1993). According to Piaget's theory, until the age of 6 or 7, children have little appreciation of mental life. Psychologically speaking, the thoughts of other people do not exist. He found evidence for this conclusion in clinical interviews when he asked children such questions as

"Do you know what it means to think?" The following transcript is from an interview with a 7-year-old (Piaget, 1929/1979, p. 39).

Piaget: Do you know what it means to think?
Child: Yes.
Piaget: Then think of your house. What do you think with?
Child: The mouth.
Piaget: Can you think with your mouth shut?
Child: No.
Piaget: With the eyes shut?
Child: Yes.
Piaget: Now shut your mouth and think of your house. Are you thinking?
Child: Yes.
Piaget: What do you think with?
Child: The mouth.

One of the major methods currently being used to study the development of children's thinking about thought processes focuses on children's ability to understand that another person may hold a false belief. The false belief task is frequently presented as a story. At the end of the story, children are asked to make a judgment about how one of the characters will behave. The story and question are arranged so that the children's judgment will reflect their ability to engage in **mental perspective taking**—to think about what goes on in another person's mind. A typical story and subsequent question might be the following:

THE STORY:
Once there was a little boy who liked candy. One day he put a chocolate bar in a box on the table and went away for a while. While he was gone, his mother came. She took the candy out of the box and put it in the top drawer of the bureau where he kept his socks. The little boy came back. He was hungry and went to get his candy.

THE QUESTION:
Where do you think the little boy will look?

When 3-year-olds are asked the question, they respond as if the boy who left the room had the same information that they do; they say that the boy will look in the top drawer of the bureau. Five-year-olds are far more likely to say that the little boy will look in the box on the table; they understand that the child who left the room has a false belief about the location of the candy. A variety of evidence indicates that this ability to think about other people's mental states, often referred to as a **theory of mind,** comes into existence during the fourth year of life (Astington, 1993; Hirschfeld & Gelman, 1994).

The universality of the timing of this change in the ability to reason about other people's reasoning is suggested by the work of Jeremy Avis and Paul Harris (1991). They presented a version of the "hiding the candy bar" task to Baka children between the ages of 3 and 6. The Baka people are preliterate hunter-gatherers who live in southeast Cameroon, in West Africa. Avis and Harris found that the Baka children also make the transition to understanding that someone might have a false belief between the ages of 3 and 5.

Taken together, the evidence of young children's difficulty with spatial perspective taking (the three-mountain problem), their failure to provide adequate information to others in conversation, and their inability to appreciate that someone may have a false belief all provide support for Piaget's theory of the egocentric nature of young children's thinking.

Theory of mind The ability to think about other people's mental states is often referred to by psychologists as a theory of mind.

CONFUSING APPEARANCE AND REALITY

As we noted above, an important manifestation of the limitations of early childhood thought is children's tendency to focus exclusively on the most striking aspects of an object; that is, on its surface appearance (Figure 9.3). Piaget believed that this perceptual tendency makes it difficult for the young child to distinguish between the way things *seem* to be and the way they *are*. Because they have difficulty with the appearance-reality distinction, 2½-year-olds may become frightened when an older child puts on a mask at Halloween, as if the mask had actually changed the child into a witch or a dragon (Flavell, Miller, & Miller, 1993).

Rheta De Vries (1969) took advantage of small children's confusion about the reality behind masks to study the development of the appearance-reality distinction. In separate experimental sessions, each child was introduced to Maynard, an unusually well-behaved black cat. At the start of the experiment, each child was told, "I want to show you my pet. Do you know what it is?" All of the children were able to say that Maynard was a cat. They were encouraged to play with Maynard for a short while, and then De Vries hid Maynard's front half behind a screen while she strapped a realistic mask of a ferocious dog onto his head (see Figure 9.4a). The children were asked to keep their eyes on the cat's tail while the mask was put on so that they would be certain that she was not switching one animal for another. As she removed the screen, De Vries told each child, "Now this animal is going to look quite different. Look, it has a face like a dog."

De Vries went on to ask a set of questions designed to assess the children's ability to distinguish between the animal's real identity and its appearance: "What kind of animal is it now?" "Is it really a dog?" "Can it bark?" The strength of children's ability to distinguish appearance and reality was measured on an 11-point scale. Children who said that the cat had turned into a dog were given a score of 1, while children who said that the cat only appeared to turn into a dog but could never really become one were rated 11.

By and large, the 3-year-olds focused almost entirely on Maynard's appearance (see Figure 9.4b). They said he had actually become a ferocious dog, and some of them were afraid he would bite them. Most of the 6-year-olds scoffed at this idea, understanding that the cat only looked like a dog. The 4- and 5-year-olds showed considerable confusion. They didn't believe that a cat could become a dog, but they did not always answer De Vries's questions correctly.

Similar confusions between appearance and reality have been reported by John Flavell and his colleagues, who showed young children various objects that appeared to be one thing but were really another: a sponge that appeared to be a rock, a stone that appeared to be an egg, and a small piece of white paper placed behind a transparent piece of pink plastic so that the paper appeared to be pink. The children were shown the objects under a variety of conditions and asked to say what the object looked like and what it "really really" was (Flavell, Flavell, & Green, 1983; Flavell, Green, & Flavell, 1986).

Consistent with Piaget's claims about the difficulties that young children experience in distinguishing reality from appearance, these researchers found that American 3-year-olds are very likely to answer incorrectly. They say that the white paper under pink plastic really is pink or that the fake rock made from a sponge really really is a rock. Four-year-olds seem to be in a transition state; they sometimes answer correctly, sometimes incorrectly. Five-year-olds have a much firmer

FIGURE 9.3 *A phenomenon that requires the viewer to distinguish between appearance and reality is the bending of light that occurs when a straight stick is partially submerged in water: the stick looks broken, but we know that this appearance is not reality; it is an illusion. Young children, however, may believe the stick has actually changed.*

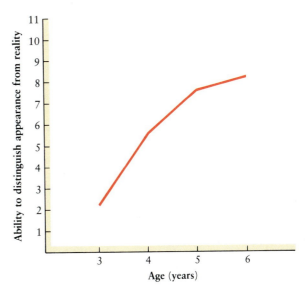

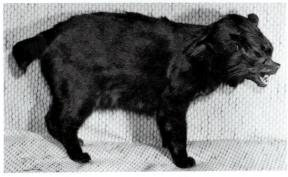

FIGURE 9.4 (a) *Maynard the cat, without and with a dog mask.* (b) *A chart plotting the growth of the ability to understand that Maynard remains a cat even when his appearance is changed so that he looks like a dog. (Adapted from De Vries, 1969.)*

grip on the appearance-reality distinction in these circumstances and usually answer the experimenters' questions correctly.

Flavell (1990, pp. 14–15) offers three lines of evidence to show that young children's difficulties with the appearance-reality distinction are "nontrivial, deep-seated, [and] genuinely intellectual ones."

1. Chinese, Japanese, and British 3-year-olds experience similar difficulties (Flavell et al., 1983; Harris & Gross, 1988).

2. Various attempts to simplify the task do not help young children over their difficulties (Flavell et al., 1987).

3. Attempts to train young children to make the appropriate distinctions have failed (Taylor & Hort, 1990).

PRECAUSAL REASONING

Nothing is more characteristic of preschoolers than their love for asking questions. "Why is the sky blue?" "What makes clouds?" "Where do babies come from?" Adults may not know the answers to such questions themselves or they may prefer not to answer them, but it seems self-evident that children are interested in the causes of things. Despite this interest, Piaget believed that young children are not yet capable of true mental operations, so they do not engage in cause-and-effect reasoning like older children and adults. Instead of reasoning from general premises to particular cases (deduction) or from specific cases to general ones (induction), he claimed, young children think *transductively*, from one particular to another, as his young daughter did when she missed her customary nap one afternoon and remarked, "I haven't had a nap, so it isn't afternoon." As a consequence of such reasoning, young children are likely to confuse cause and effect. Because transductive reasoning precedes true causal reasoning, he referred to this aspect of young children's thinking as **precausal thinking** (Piaget, 1930).

Precausal thinking According to Piaget, a form of thinking observed in young children in which they do not engage in cause-and-effect reasoning, but instead reason from one particular to another.

Our own daughter gave a splendid demonstration of the transductive reasoning that leads a young child to confuse cause and effect. At the age of 3½, Jenny happened to walk with us through an old graveyard. Listening to us read the inscriptions on the gravestones, she realized that somehow these old moss-covered stones represented people. "Where is she now?" she asked when we finished reading the inscription on one stone.

"She's dead," we told her.

"But where is she?" We tried to explain that after people die they are buried in the ground, in cemeteries. After that, Jenny steadfastly refused to go into cemeteries with us and would become upset when we were near one. At bedtime every evening, she repeatedly asked us about death, burial, and graveyards. We answered her questions as best we could, yet she kept asking the same questions and she was obviously upset by the topic. The reason for her fear became clear when we were moving to New York City. "Are there any graveyards in New York City?" she asked anxiously. We were exhausted by her insistent questions, and our belief that we should be candid and honest was crumbling.

"No," we lied. "There are no graveyards in New York City." At this response, Jenny visibly relaxed.

"Then people don't die in New York," she said a couple of minutes later. Jenny had reasoned that since graveyards are places where dead people are found, graveyards must be the cause of death. This reasoning led her to the comforting but incorrect conclusion that if you can stay away from graveyards, you are not in danger of dying.

The Study of Young Children's Thinking after Piaget

The examples we have provided thus far (summarized in Table 9.1) are only a sample of the phenomena supporting the idea that there is a distinctive mode of thought associated with early childhood. But the examples are sufficient to give the flavor of the sorts of evidence that influenced Piaget. There certainly appears to be something worthwhile in the idea that children's thinking is dominated by the inability to "decenter," to reason about two aspects of a thing simultaneously, or to see them as part of the same process. In recent years, however, a variety of other evidence has inspired a broad reexamination of Piaget's theory of early childhood thought processes (Case, 1992; Fischer et al., 1995; Wellman & Gelman, 1992).

THE PROBLEM OF UNEVEN LEVELS OF PERFORMANCE

Piaget was well aware that a child's performance could vary somewhat from one version of a problem to another, even though the problems seemed to require the same logical operations. He referred to such cases as instances of **horizontal décalage** (literally, horizontal misalignment). He found, for example, that children achieve conservation of number well before they achieve conservation of volume. He believed that subtle differences in the logical requirements of the different versions of a task accounted for these variations in children's performance in what appear to be logically identical cognitive tasks. He was also aware that the interview technique itself might produce an apparent unevenness in performance by obscuring the thought processes being studied, especially in young children who were still novices in the use of language (Piaget, 1929/1979). His own work convinced him, however, that he had overcome the problems of conversing with young children. Even when clinical interviewing is properly conducted, he believed, preoperational children fail to distinguish their point of view from that of someone else, become easily captured by surface appearances, and are often

Horizontal décalage Piaget's term for a child's uneven performance at a given stage of development when the same logical problem is presented in different forms.

TABLE 9.1 Piaget's Stages of Cognitive Development: Preoperational

Age (years)	Stage	Description	Characteristics and Examples
Birth to 2	SENSORIMOTOR	Infants' achievements consist largely of coordinating their sensory perceptions and simple motor behaviors. As they move through the 6 substages of this period, infants come to recognize the existence of a world outside of themselves and begin to interact with it in deliberate ways.	Centration, the tendency to focus (center) on the most salient aspect of whatever one is trying to think about. A major manifestation of this is egocentrism, or considering the world entirely in terms of one's own point of view. •Children engage in collective monologues, rather than dialogues, in each other's company. •Children have difficulty taking a listener's knowledge into account in order to communicate effectively. •Children fail to consider both the height and width of containers in order to compare their volumes. •Children confuse classes with subclasses. They cannot reliably say whether there are more wooden beads or more brown beads in a set of all wooden beads.
2 to 6	PREOPERATIONAL	Young children can represent reality to themselves through the use of symbols, including mental images, words, and gestures. Objects and events no longer have to be present to be thought about, but children often fail to distinguish their point of view from that of others, become easily captured by surface appearances, and are often confused about causal relations.	
6 to 12	CONCRETE OPERATIONAL	As they enter middle childhood, children become capable of mental operations, internalized actions that fit into a logical system. Operational thinking allows children mentally to combine, separate, order, and transform objects and actions. Such operations are considered concrete because they are carried out in the presence of the objects and events being thought about.	Confusion of appearance and reality. •Children act as if a Halloween mask actually changes the identity of the person wearing it. •Children may believe that a straight stick partially submerged in water actually does become bent. Precausal reasoning, characterized by illogical thinking and an indifference to cause-and-effect relations. •A child may think a graveyard is a cause of death because dead people are buried there.
12 to 19	FORMAL OPERATIONAL	In adolescence the developing person acquires the ability to think systematically about all logical relations within a problem. Adolescents display keen interest in abstract ideals and the process of thinking itself.	A form of moral reasoning that sees morality as being imposed from the outside and that does not take intentions into account.

FIGURE 9.5 *Borke's modification of Piaget's three-mountain perspective-taking task. When a diorama contains familiar objects, preschoolers are more likely to be able to say how it looks from a point of view other than their own.*

confused about causal relations. However, a variety of studies seem to show that young children are not so limited in their ability to decenter as Piaget thought. (Flavell, Miller, & Miller, 1993; and Gelman & Baillargeon, 1983, review the evidence.)

Nonegocentric reasoning about spatial perspectives

In one often-cited test of Piaget's ideas about spatial egocentrism, Helen Borke (1975) replicated Piaget and Inhelder's three-mountain experiment and then presented an alternative form of the problem. That is, one version of the task was precisely the same as Piaget and Inhelder's: children were shown a diorama of three mountains, one snowcapped, one with a church on it, and one with a house (Figure 9.1). In the other version, however, the landmarks were a small lake with a boat on it, a horse and cow, and a building, placed in approximately the same locations on the diorama as the three mountains (Figure 9.5).

In Borke's alternative version, Grover, a character from the television program "Sesame Street," drove around the landscape in a car. From time to time he would stop and take a look at the view. The child's task was to indicate what Grover's view of the scene looked like. Children as young as 3 years old performed well on Borke's farm-scene perspective-taking problem, but their performance on the three-mountain version of the problem was poor, as Piaget and Inhelder's work had suggested. These contrasting levels of performance led Borke to conclude that when easily differentiated objects are used and care is taken to make it easy for young children to express their understanding, they are able to imagine spatial perspectives other than their own. On the basis of similar results from similar experiments, Margaret Donaldson (1978) suggests that 3- to 5-year-old children can display nonegocentric spatial perspective taking, but the motives and intentions of the characters involved in the problem must be clear, so that the task makes what she calls "human sense."

Understanding other minds

We have seen that young children do not usually perform well when asked about story characters who hold false beliefs. Nevertheless, researchers have amassed ample evidence that children can appreciate the mental states of others well before Piaget thought they could.

Andrew Meltzoff (1995) locates the earliest evidence of a theory of mind in the ability of 18-month-old babies to understand other people's intentions. Meltzoff arranged for 18-month-old infants to observe an adult trying to pull the ends off a wooden dumbbell or trying to hang a bead necklace over a wooden cylinder. The adult succeeded in those tasks for half the children but did not complete the actions for the other half. The adult then gave the objects to the infants to see if they would imitate the actions they had just observed. The babies who had not seen the completed actions nevertheless "imitated" them just as frequently as those babies who had observed the completed actions. Since the first group never saw the complete action they produced, Meltzoff reasoned that they must have understood the adult's intentions.

To see if the attribution of intentions is domain specific, Meltzoff conducted a second study in which he substituted a mechanical device for the human model (see Figure 9.6). The infants showed no fear of the mechanical device as it either "tried and failed" or succeeded in removing the two end blocks from a wooden dumbbell; but only one in ten babies imitated the machine. Meltzoff argues that such behavior is evidence that babies attribute intentions only to other human beings, not to machines.

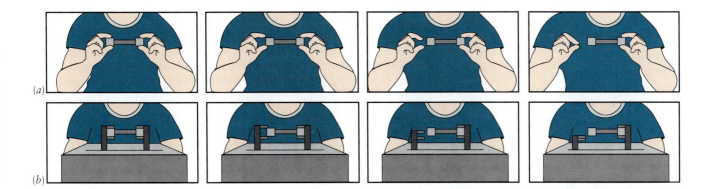

FIGURE 9.6 *Procedure used by Andrew Meltzoff to determine if infants imitate intended actions, even if they are not completed.* (a) *The two pictures to the left show an adult trying to pull the ends off the dumbbell; the two pictures to the right show the adult succeeding.* (b) *The analogous actions are being modelled by a mechanical device.*

Further evidence of an early appreciation of other people's mental states can be seen when young children try to deceive others. Michael Chandler and his colleagues (1989) created a game in which a treasure was hidden in a container by a doll who left a trail of inky footprints to the treasure. The child was asked to make it hard for someone who was out of the room while the treasure was being hidden to find it. A majority of the 2½- to 3-year-olds wiped up the ink to hide the telltale footprints leading to the treasure. Since deception is a process of instilling a false belief in someone else, Chandler and his colleagues argue that even children as young as 2½ must have some appreciation of other people's thought processes. Moreover, a variety of reports, such as the following, suggest that even young children can appreciate the difference between intentional and unintentional actions:

> A 3-year-old was helping to feed her baby brother. After spooning in a few mouthfuls of cereal, she took another spoonful and simply dumped it on the baby's head. Then she turned quickly to her very angry mother and claimed, "I didn't do it on purpose." (Shultz, 1990, p. 157)

When data from everyday life circumstances and experimental evidence are considered together, it appears that in some circumstances young children have a fine-tuned sense of the mental states of the people with whom they most often interact.

Distinguishing appearance from reality

In the studies by De Vries and Flavell described earlier (pp. 344–345), children began to make consistent distinctions between appearance and reality somewhere between the ages of 4 and 6. However, special features of the experimental procedures seem to be at least partly responsible for the difficulties experienced by the youngest children.

In a study designed to explore young children's ability to distinguish real and apparent emotions, 4-year-olds were presented with stories such as the following one:

> Diana wants to go outside, but she has a tummy ache. She knows that if she tells her mom that she has a tummy ache, her mom will say that she can't go out. She tries to hide the way she feels so that her mom will let her go outside.

When the researchers asked, "How did Diana really feel when she had a tummy ache?" and "How did she try to look on her face when she had a tummy ache?" they found that 4-year-olds were usually able to distinguish between real and displayed feelings. This ability was fragile, however, and the 4-year-olds were generally unable to provide reasonable justifications for their correct judgments (Harris et al., 1986).

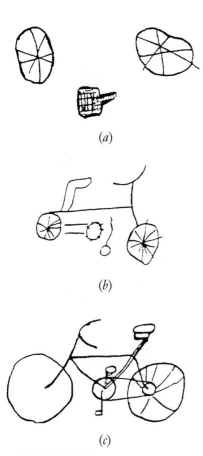

(a)

(b)

(c)

FIGURE 9.7 *These drawings show how children of different ages and mental abilities perceive the way a bicycle works. (a) The child who is 5 years and 3 months old has no clear idea how the different parts of the bicycle fit together. (b) A retarded 9-year-old has captured part of the mechanism in the illustration but fails to link the pedal to the cogwheel and chain. (c) An 8-year, 3-month-old child can represent all of the essential mechanisms. (After Piaget, 1930.)*

Perhaps the best evidence that under some circumstances children as young as 3 are able to distinguish between appearance and reality comes from experiments that are carefully designed to take children's inexperience with conversation into account. Recall from Chapter 8 (p. 313) that young children first acquire the basic conventions of conversation and only later learn to deal with violations of these conventions. In the experimental studies we have been reviewing in this chapter, the researchers characteristically presented the children with a large number of similar problems and questioned them repeatedly on each problem. Michael Siegal (1991) noted that this procedure violates the conventions of conversational norms that young children know. When a question is repeated, for example, the usual reason is either that the person didn't hear well or that the first answer was incorrect.

Siegal hypothesized that if the procedure were brought into line with familiar conversational conventions, younger children would not become confused. He reports that when he and his colleagues replicated the standard procedure, presenting a series of appearance-reality problems and asking the same kinds of questions over and over, 3-year-olds gave wrong answers. They seemed to confuse appearance and reality. If they were presented with only a single problem, however, and were not queried repeatedly about their responses, three out of four of the children answered correctly.

Children also distinguished appearance from reality correctly when asked to put themselves mentally in another child's place. Siegal presented the following story to a group of youngsters:

> A grown-up poured milk into a blue glass with a blue lid on top. She asked Sally, a girl your age, what color the milk was truly. Sally said the milk was truly blue. Did she say that because she really and truly thought the milk was blue or was she pretending? (Siegal, 1991, p. 75)

All of the 3-year-olds answered that Sally was only pretending, showing that they could make the appropriate distinction.

Two conclusions can be drawn from this research. First, many children are able to make the appearance-reality distinction well before the age of 6 or 7 years. Second, their ability to make such a distinction is fragile and may not appear unless special care is taken to avoid confusing them.

Effective causal reasoning

One of Piaget's best-known examples of precausal reasoning came from his interviews with children about how bicycles work. In the course of the interview, he also asked the children to draw a picture illustrating their explanations (see Figure 9.7). During the interview a bicycle was propped against a chair in front of the child. An interview with Grim, aged 5½, provides the kind of evidence that led Piaget to conclude that the reasoning of young children is precausal (Piaget, 1930, p. 206):

Piaget: How does the bicycle move along?
Grim: With the brakes on top of the bike.
Piaget: What is the brake for?
Grim: To make it go because you push.
Piaget: What do you push with?
Grim: With your feet.
Piaget: What does that do?
Grim: It makes it go.
Piaget: How?
Grim: With the brakes.

In the late 1920s Piaget visited the Malting House School in Cambridge, England, where Susan Isaacs was also conducting research on young children. Isaacs was skeptical about Piaget's ideas on preoperational thought. When she spotted one of her preschoolers riding by on a tricycle, she put her visitor's theory to an impromptu test:

> At that moment, Dan [aged 5 years, 9 months] happened to be sitting on a tricycle in the garden, back-pedaling. I went to him and said, "The tricycle is not moving forward, is it?" "Of course not, when I'm back-pedaling," he said. "Well," I asked, "how does it go forward when it does?" "Oh, well," he replied, "your feet press the pedals, that turns the crank round, and the cranks turn that round" (pointing to the cog-wheel), "and that makes the chain go round, and the chain turns the hub round, and then the wheels go round—and there you are!" (Isaacs, 1966, p. 44)

Isaacs offered this anecdote as evidence against Piaget's theory that young children are incapable of causal reasoning. Before accepting either conclusion, most developmental psychologists would require more information about both boys, their experience with tricycles and bicycles, and the way the interviews were conducted. Is Dan simply an especially advanced preschooler? Is the difference in their performances the result of differences in the way the problems were posed to them? Systematic answers to such questions require experiments that deliberately vary the way the problems are presented.

During the 1970s and 1980s, experiments by developmental psychologists provided ample evidence that when the task is sufficiently simplified, young children's understanding of causation far exceeds the level that Piaget thought typical (Bullock, 1984; Bullock & Gelman, 1979). Merry Bullock and Rochel Gelman, for example, tested the ability of 3- to 5-year-olds to understand the basic principle that causes come before effects, using the apparatus shown in Figure 9.8.

Children observed two sequences of events. In the first, a steel marble was dropped into one of two slots in a box, both of which were visible through the side of the box. Two seconds after the marble disappeared at the bottom of the slot, a Snoopy doll popped out of the hole in the apparatus's middle. At that moment, a second ball was dropped into the other slot. It too disappeared, with no further result. The children were then asked to say which of the balls had made Snoopy jump up and to provide an explanation.

Even the 3-year-olds were usually correct in selecting that the ball had caused Snoopy to jump up. The 5-year-olds had no difficulty with the task at all. However, there was a marked difference between the age groups in their ability to explain what had happened. Many of the 3-year-olds could give no explanation or said something completely irrelevant ("It's got big teeth"). Almost all of the 5-year-olds could provide at least a partial explanation of the principle that causes precede effects. This finding suggests one reason why Piaget may have underestimated the cognitive competence of young children: his research techniques relied heavily on verbally presented problems and verbal justifications of reasoning, both of which put young children at a disadvantage (see Box 9.1).

The evidence that young children's thinking is not so limited as Piaget thought has provided the starting point for several attempts to improve on both Piaget's theory and his methods of investigation. The different approaches draw on one or another of the four basic frameworks for understanding development summarized in Chapter 1 (pp. 33–40).

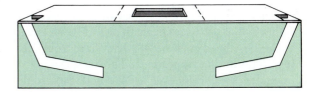

FIGURE 9.8 *The apparatus used by Bullock and Gelman to test preschoolers' understanding that cause precedes effect. A marble was dropped into one of the slots. Two seconds after the marble disappeared, a Snoopy doll popped out of the hole in the middle of the apparatus. At the same moment, a second marble was dropped into the other slot, where it disappeared, with no further result. Preschoolers are generally able to indicate which marble caused Snoopy to jump up. (From Bullock & Gelman, 1979.)*

BOX 9.1

Young Children as Witnesses

The nature of young children's thought processes becomes an important social issue when they are called upon to give testimony in a court of law. In some cases they may be witnesses to a crime; in others, suspected victims of a crime.

Adults have long been reluctant to believe the word of a young child. Psychologists have viewed children as suggestible (Stern, 1910); unable to distinguish fantasy from reality (Piaget, 1926, 1928; Werner, 1948); and prone to fantasize sexual events (Freud, 1905/1953a). Judges, lawyers, and prosecutors have also expressed reservations about children's reliability as witnesses (Goodman, 1984; Goodman et al., 1991). Legal rulings on the admissibility of children's testimony reflect these longstanding doubts. In many states, for example, the judge determines whether a child below a certain age (which varies from state to state) is competent to testify (King & Yuille, 1987).

Owing to growing concern about the prevalence of sexual and physical abuse of children in recent years, the legal community has reexamined the reliability of children's testimony. At the same time, psychologists are raising their own doubts about earlier conclusions that young children are unable to testify reliably about past events (Ceci, Toglia, & Ross, 1987).

At the heart of the current discussion of child testimony are two questions: How good are children's memories at various ages? How susceptible are young children to suggestions that change their memories? Reason for concern is provided by children's behavior both in actual trials and in experimental studies conducted by psychologists.

When young children are asked about events that have personal significance for them, such as whether or not they were given an injection when they went to the doctor's office, they are likely to provide correct answers (Goodman et al., 1990). They have trouble locating events in time, however, and giving specific examples of recurrent events (Nelson, 1986). Adults have a tendency to probe more deeply when a child appears not to remember, but such probes may lead to additional problems. When Katherine Nelson (1978) asked preschoolers about what happens when they eat lunch at school, she found that if she asked for information that children did not have ("Where did the lunch come from?"), they would provide responses that appeared to come from other scripted events, such as a visit to a restaurant or a market, rather than say that they did not know.

These difficulties are seen in a case in which the adults were eventually convicted of sexual abuse, but the child witnesses at first denied that anything unusual had happened. They later recalled events that led to the conviction of their baby-sitter and her husband. But in addition to their accurate testimony, they said outrageous, fanciful things—for example, that after assaulting the children, the baby-sitter and her husband ate them for dinner (Goodman, Aman, & Hirschman, 1987).

There are several ways in which the questioning procedures that are standard in criminal proceedings may lead the young child to make false statements. First, the questioning may affect the child's memory of what happened without the child's awareness. When an interviewer, probing a child's testimony, makes an erroneous suggestion about what happened, the suggestion may become blended with the child's original memory to produce a new, hybrid "memory." This hybrid memory can block the original memory so the child can no longer recall the actual events. It is also possible that the child remembers both what the adult suggested and what really happened but can no longer tell which memory is authentic (Ceci & Bruck, 1993).

Evidence of young children's vulnerability to suggestion is provided by an experiment in which 3- and 4-year-old children first witnessed a staged incident involving three men and a woman, and were then interviewed by an experienced police officer about the woman's appearance. One session went like this (Dent, 1982, pp. 290–291):

Q: Wearing a poncho and a cap?

A: I think it was a cap.

Q: What sort of a cap was it? Was it like a beret, or was it a peaked cap, or . . . ?

A: No, it had a sort of, it was flared with a little piece coming out. It was flared with a sort of button thing in the middle.

Q: What . . . Was it a peak like that, that sort of thing?

A: Ye—es.

Q: That's the sort of cap I'm thinking you're meaning, with a little peak out there.

A: Yes, that's the top view, yes.

Q: Smashing. Um—what colour?

A: Oh! Oh—I think it was black or brown.

Q: Think it was dark, shall we say?

A: Yes—it was dark colour I think, and I didn't see her hair.

In fact, the woman in the staged scene was wearing neither a poncho nor a hat. The child not only came to "remember" these items, but even added that the woman carried a dark purse to match her hat! As Elizabeth Loftus and Graham Davies (1984) point out, by persistent requests for details, the police officer led the child into error.

Besides pointing up the limitations on their ability to remember and recall information, such episodes may reflect the fact that young children are likely to believe that adults know more than they. When they are being questioned in a legal proceeding, they may incorporate the adult's suggestions in their answers because they want to please the adult, even when they know that the adult's suggestions are wrong. Asked the same questions more than once, they often change their answers because they assume that something was wrong with their first answer (Siegal, 1991).

Children are by no means the only ones whose memories are vulnerable to the suggestions of the people who question them. Adults, too, can be led astray in such situations (Loftus, 1979). Young children are considered to be especially susceptible, however, because of their limited ability to remember, their lack of experience with legal proceedings, and their tendency to try to please adults (Poole & White, 1993).

Three-year-old Amanda Conklin looks out at a crowded Van Nuys, California, courtroom as the judge questions her during the trial of her father for the murder of her mother.

NEO-PIAGETIAN THEORIES OF COGNITIVE DEVELOPMENT

There have been two major neo-Piagetian approaches to the problem of how best to use Piaget's ideas as the basis for a deeper understanding of cognitive development in early childhood. Adherents of the first approach retain Piaget's theory in more or less the original form. They believe that recent evidence appearing to contradict the theory has been misinterpreted; it can be incorporated into the theory with only minor modifications of Piaget's ideas.

John Flavell and his colleagues, for example, have modified Piaget's account of spatial perspective taking. Instead of seeing perspective taking as an all-or-nothing process, they distinguish two levels of difficulty in the process of adopting another's point of view (Flavell, 1986, 1990; Flavell, Green, & Flavell, 1990). The first level requires only that children realize that other people may be totally unable to see what they see. The second level requires children to realize that when they and another person both see an object, they see it differently, from a different point of view.

Flavell and his colleagues demonstrated the developmental significance of the two levels of perspective taking by showing children cards with pictures of different animals on the two sides (Figure 9.9). If a card with a cat on one side and a turtle on the other is shown to a 3-year-old child and then the card is held vertically between child and experimenter with the cat visible to the child, but not to the experimenter, the child will say that the experimenter cannot see the cat (this is level 1 perspective taking). However, if the picture is laid flat on the table so that both child and adult see the same picture from opposite positions, the same child is unlikely to say that it is upside down to the adult (which would require level 2 perspective taking). Such findings suggest that apparent variations in levels of children's performance occur because the experimenters have failed to analyze the cognitive demands of the tasks they use with sufficient precision. Flavell maintains that when very young children seem to succeed at such tasks, it is because the experimenter has distorted and simplified the tasks so drastically that they no longer tap the ability under investigation.

FIGURE 9.9 *The two conditions under which the child views the picture of an animal illustrate two levels in perspective-taking ability, according to John Flavell and his colleagues. In (a) the child knows that the adult does not see what she sees (a cat) and she does not see what the adult sees (a turtle is drawn on the other side of the card). This result shows that the child is capable of level 1 perspective taking. When a picture is presented as in (b), however, the child confuses the adult view of the picture with her own and assumes that they both see the turtle right side up. This more difficult (level 2) form of perspective taking does not develop until children are 4 to 5 years old.*

(a)   (b)

Adherents of the second branch of neo-Piagetian research retain Piaget's ideas that children construct knowledge through their active engagement with the world. They also agree that the growth of understanding goes through a series of distinctive changes. They argue, however, that Piaget's approach must be modified to take account of the new evidence on within-stage variability in young children's cognitive performance.

One such neo-Piagetian approach holds that stages in the acquisition of knowledge are confined to specific domains with their own logic and content, such as social reasoning, drawing, music, language, and mathematics (Demetriou, Shayer, & Efklides, 1992; Gardner, 1991). Thus a child may be an expert in the domain of chess or a whiz at arithmetic and yet solve typical Piagetian tasks such as class inclusion and conservation no better than her agemates (Feldman, 1994). The basic intuition of this approach is summarized by Jean Mandler (1983, p. 475): "It may well be that in many areas of thinking there is no generalized competence, only hard-won principles wrested anew from each domain as it is explored." According to this view, there may be little correspondence between the level of development children display in one situation and the developmental level they display in another because from the child's point of view, each domain has its own logic and content, both of which have to be mastered.

Kurt Fischer and his colleagues (Biddel & Fischer, 1995; Fischer et al., 1993) believe that within each domain the specific *level* of a child's achievement depends crucially on the support for performance offered by the child's local context. Fischer and his colleagues present various kinds of data to show that when *optimal* conditions for performance are provided, the process of change appears stagelike. When conditions for performance are suboptimal because, for example, the children lack relevant background knowledge or tasks are not explained clearly, their performance becomes uneven.

Robbie Case and his colleagues believe that in order to tease apart the specific and the general aspects of children's thinking it is necessary to gain a precise understanding of the knowledge required by each cognitive domain and to design diagnostic tasks specifically to tap into the child's knowledge in that domain (Case, 1992; Case & Okamoto, 1995). According to Case, when researchers make certain that tasks constructed from two domains present problems that are familiar, involve equally demanding content, and have the same logical structure, children will perform at the same level of ability in both domains, reflecting the level of their general cognitive development.

To demonstrate the possibility of such synchronous stage transitions in different domains, Case and his colleagues constructed two sets of problems with identical logical structures. The first required children to judge the "juiciness" of a drink made of different mixtures of orange juice and water. Would a mixture of five parts juice and three parts water, for example, taste as juicy as a mixture made of four parts juice and one part water?

The second, logically equivalent problem concerned two boys, each of whom was having a birthday party and each of whom wanted polished stones for his birthday (in the school where the investigators were conducting their research, polished stones were highly prized). The children were shown how many stones each boy wanted and how many he actually received. Then they were asked, "Which child would be happier?"

The researchers questioned children of different ages and found that their levels of performance go through a series of stagelike changes for each of the two kinds of problems. In addition, the estimated level of cognitive development of 89 percent of the children tested was either the same for both kinds of problems or only a single problem-solving stage off (Case et al., 1986). The fact that the children reached virtually the same levels of reasoning on two tasks that tapped different domains supports Piaget's hypothesis that the timing of changes in different domains is synchronous, bespeaking a general mechanism to complement domain-specific mechanisms of change.

INFORMATION-PROCESSING APPROACHES

The 1960s, when Piaget's ideas became popular among developmental psychologists, were also a time when many psychologists began to view thinking as a kind of information processing that can best be understood by analogy with the workings of a digital computer. Investigators who employ the metaphor of child-as-computer work in a tradition that has become known as an **information-processing approach.** They generally conceive of development as the result of changes both in children's "hardware," such as myelination of a new brain region, and in children's "software," such as the acquisition of a new strategy for remembering (Siegler, 1996).

David Klahr, a leading figure in this movement, expressed his dissatisfaction with Piagetian theorizing about development in colorful terms:

> For 40 years now we have had assimilation and accommodation, the mysterious and shadowy forces of equilibration, the "Batman and Robin" of the developmental processes. What are they? How do they operate? Why is it after all this time, we know no more about them than when they first sprang upon the scene? What we need is a way to get beyond vague verbal statements of the nature of the developmental process. (Klahr, 1982, p. 80)

Investigators who use the information-processing perspective and the child-as-computer metaphor are not necessarily committed to a particular point of view about the nature of development itself. Robbie Case (1992), for example, employs information-processing concepts to work out his neo-Piagetian view. Most psychologists who adopt the information-processing view, however, focus on the ways in which psychological processes are modified as the result of patterns of input from the environment. Following the environmental-learning path, many believe that development is a continuous process in which limitations on cognitive capacity are gradually overcome; long-term memory capacity gradually increases; behaviors are routinized; and strategies are developed to link input more effectively to output (Klahr & Wallace, 1976; Siegler, 1996).

Figure 9.10 is a simplified schematic diagram of a general information-processing approach to human thinking. At the left side is the presumed starting point of any problem-solving process. Some kind of stimulation ("input," in the language of computer programming) reaches the sensory organs that serve as the

Information-processing approach
A strategy of explaining cognitive development using the analogy of a modern computer.

FIGURE 9.10 *The major components of an information-processing model of mental actions. (Adapted from Atkinson & Shiffrin, 1980.)*

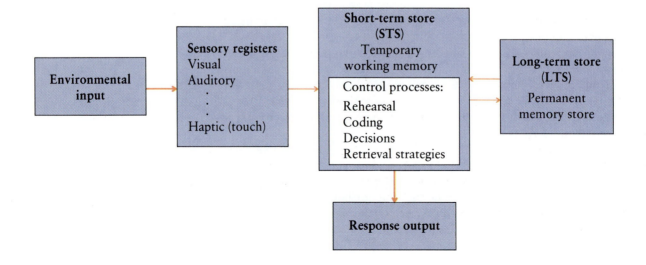

system's "sensory register." If the input is not attended to, it will disappear quickly, in a matter of seconds. If it *is* attended to and "read into" the system's sensory register, it will be stored temporarily in **short-term** (working) **memory,** where it can be retained for several seconds. The environmental information deposited in short-term memory can be combined there with memory of past experiences **(long-term memory)** or it can be forgotten. Short-term memory is continually monitored by control processes that determine how the information temporarily held there is to be applied to the problem at hand—for example, whether additional information must be gathered from the environment or whether long-term memory must be searched more thoroughly for a better response. Control processes also determine whether a piece of information in short-term memory needs to be retained or can be forgotten.

We can see the basic idea of this approach by considering what occurs when a mother asks her 4-year-old daughter to remember the family phone number, just in case she should get separated from the family during a visit to a shopping mall. The mother sits with the child at the phone and shows her the sequence of buttons to push, say, 543-1234. The child watches what the mother does and hears what her mother is saying.

At first the child registers the set of numbers as a sequence of sounds. Meanings corresponding to those sounds are retrieved from long-term memory and matched with the sounds in the short-term memory buffer; the child recognizes each number and "tries to remember." Remembering occurs when the information concerning the numerical sequence enters long-term memory, where forgetting is much slower than in short-term memory.

Despite differences among them, information-processing psychologists are united by the assumption that human beings, like computers, have limited information-processing capacities. The young child in our example may experience difficulty at any one of the phases of this process. She may pay insufficient attention to what her mother is saying. She may have a small (immature) short-term memory capacity. The speed with which she can transfer information from one memory store to another may be relatively slow. As a consequence, she may forget some of the numbers before they can get stored in long-term memory. Lastly, she may have had little experience with purposeful memorization and hence no repertoire of strategies for committing a series of numbers to memory.

Older children are likely not only to have larger memory stores and more rapid information-processing abilities, but also to have more effective strategies for overcoming their information-processing limitations. For example, older children are more likely to use their more powerful set of executive control processes to invent the strategy of rehearsing the number repeatedly or to analyze the number to find simplifying properties. In the case of 543-1234, recognition that the numbers go in descending and then ascending order makes the number easier to remember.

In sum, from this perspective, young children's cognitive difficulties are caused by limitations in knowledge, memory, and attentional control, as well as by limited strategies for acquiring and using information (Siegler, 1996). Performance improves in the course of development because these limitations are gradually reduced through maturation of the "hardware" and the development of more effective information-processing routines ("software").

The limitations of young children's information-processing abilities show up in many ways. First, their attention is easily captured by loud, flashy stimuli, so they are easy to distract. When they lose their train of thought in the middle of doing something, their performance naturally suffers.

Second, even when they are not distracted, young children are likely to explore an object in an incomplete and unsystematic way. This limitation was demonstrated some years ago by the Russian psychologist Vladimir Zinchenko

Short-term memory Working memory that retains new information for a period of several seconds; as opposed to long-term memory, in which information is held in storage.

Long-term memory Memory from past experience that is retained over long periods of time.

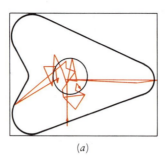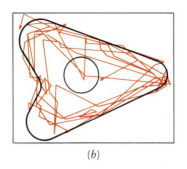

(a)   (b)

FIGURE 9.11 *Most 3-year-olds (a) asked to examine a novel figure for 20 seconds are less persistent and thorough than 6-year-olds (b) assigned the same task. (From Zinchenko, Chzhi-tsin, & Tarakanov, 1963.)*

and his colleagues (Zinchenko, Chzhi-tsin, & Tarakanov, 1963), who asked 3- and 6-year-olds to examine various objects and become familiar with them. As Figure 9.11 shows, the children's eye movements indicated that the 3-year-olds examined only a few points within the object, whereas the 6-year-olds gave it a thorough examination.

Third, children between the ages of 2½ and 6 have difficulty focusing on the most relevant features of a task if they receive no strong guiding hints from the environment. This limitation was demonstrated by Elaine Vurpillot (1968), who recorded the eye movements of children aged 3 to 10 while they examined pairs of line drawings of houses such as those shown in Figure 9.12. On some trials, children were shown identical houses; on others, the houses differed in one or more relatively subtle ways. The children were asked to say whether or not the houses were identical.

Vurpillot found that all of the children responded correctly when the houses were identical, but that the younger children were more likely to make mistakes when the houses differed, especially if they differed in only one particular. Her recordings of eye movements pinpointed the difficulty. The younger children scanned several windows in haphazard order, rather than making a systematic comparison. The older children scanned the windows row by row or column by column until they had checked almost all of them, sometimes scanning back again to check themselves. Younger children thus seem to have only limited ability to select and execute an effective scanning strategy.

The amount of information that young children take in and their ability to store and manipulate it is also limited, according to several studies. For example, Micheline Chi and David Klahr (1975) found that 5-year-olds could perceive no more than three objects flashed simultaneously on a screen, whereas adults could take in six or seven objects at a glance. Many studies have demonstrated age-related increases in the ability to hold several items of information in mind at one time. Thus older children and adults can work through various steps in complex problems without losing track of what they are doing, but young children cannot (Kail, 1990).

Finally, older children and adults have generally accumulated more knowledge than young children, process informa-

FIGURE 9.12 *Stimuli used by Vurpillot to assess visual search. Preschoolers' failure to scan systematically often leads them to claim that the top pair of houses are identical. (From Vurpillot, 1968.)*

tion more rapidly, and have more effective strategies for dealing with problems. As a consequence, they have more information available in long-term memory storage that can be speedily applied to new problems as they arise, so that they perform more competently (Chi & Koeske, 1983; Siegler, 1996).

This overview of the limitations on young children's ability to process information suggests that when they are interested in a task, when information is presented slowly, and when they have good background knowledge, their cognitive performance should be enhanced. These are precisely the characteristics of the experiments in which young children demonstrated unexpected competence on Piagetian tasks. Information-processing psychologists are thus encouraged to believe that their approach, by shifting the focus of study from a search for global stages of development to an assessment of a given task's information-processing demands, represents a genuine improvement on Piaget's.

BIOLOGICAL ACCOUNTS OF MENTAL DEVELOPMENT IN EARLY CHILDHOOD

So far in our discussion of the unevenness of young children's cognitive abilities, we have examined research focused on the content of tasks and the way they are presented: Do the tasks involve familiar content that is presented in a supportive and comfortable way, or are the tasks strange and is the way they are presented confusing? It is entirely possible, of course, that some, if not most, of the limitations on young children's mental abilities and the unevenness of their performance result primarily from variations in the rate of maturation of different parts of the central nervous system.

The growth of the brain

A promising line of evidence suggests that maturational changes in the brains of children between the ages of 2½ and 6 contribute to changes observed in their behavior (Case, 1992; Fischer & Rose, 1995). We have already reviewed evidence of similar correspondences in the bio-social-behavioral shifts that occur during infancy in Chapters 5, 6, and 7.

At the start of early childhood, the brain has attained about 50 percent of its adult weight. By the time the child is 6, it will have grown to 90 percent of its full weight (Huttenlocher, 1994; Lecours, 1982). Along with this overall enlargement, myelination occurs within and between several brain areas, and appears to play a particularly important role in the young child's cognitive development (Figure 4.15 provides an overview of major brain areas). The auditory area develops rapidly, for example, in accord with the speed with which language is acquired in early childhood. In addition, more effective connections are established between the temporal, occipital, and parietal lobes, areas that are crucially important for the processing of temporal, visual, and spatial information. The increased connections between these centers allows for more efficient synthesis of information about the various aspects of a problem. At the same time, all of these areas become more firmly linked with the speech areas of the brain, a development that fosters the growth of symbolizing and communication abilities. Other areas that undergo rapid myelination during early childhood include the hippocampus, which is important to short-term memory, and the fibers linking the cerebellum to the cerebral cortex, which allow for fine control of voluntary movements, such as those needed to tie a shoelace.

Mental modules

The widespread dissemination of Noam Chomsky's theory of language and its acquisition has brought the growth of the brain to the forefront of recent psychological theorizing about mental development. As we saw in Chapter 8, children acquire human language without any special tutoring by adults, an indication to Chomsky and his followers that the human brain contains an innate language acquisition device (LAD). Chomsky (1980, 1986) and others have proposed that the principles of language acquisition apply to many other cognitive phenomena as well. This line of thinking has become known as **modularity theory.**

Jerry Fodor (1983), for example, has suggested that the mind should be considered a vast collection of mental modules, highly specific mental faculties tuned to particular domains of environmental input. Recognition of faces, the concept of number, the perception of music, and the elementary perception of causality have all been offered as examples of mental modules (Carey & Gelman, 1991; Hirschfeld & Gelman, 1994). The concept of mental modules shares key assumptions with Chomsky's concept of the language faculty:

> **Modularity theory** A theory that emphasizes developmental changes within innately specified cognitive domains such as language, number, and space.

1. Psychological operations are presumed to be domain-specific. The mental operations required to perceive a tune are different from those required to recognize a face, and the principles of both are different from those that govern talking about perceiving a tune or a face.

2. The psychological principles that organize the operation of each module are assumed to be innately specified; that is, they are coded in the genes and need no special instruction to develop.

3. It is assumed that different modules do not interact directly; each represents a separate mental domain, only loosely connected to the rest.

According to modularity theorists, evidence for the modular origins of cognitive development is already observable in infancy. As we saw in Chapters 4 and 5, young infants display rudimentary knowledge of many physical principles and sensitivity to number operations within a few months of birth. These findings motivate a search for early origins of the various cognitive abilities that were long thought to emerge at the end of early childhood. Evidence concerning the development of causal reasoning and theory of mind illustrates the modularity approach.

Is causal reasoning modular?

Judging from evidence such as that offered by the preschoolers arguing over stone soup, Piaget seems justified in claiming that young children are subject to confusion about cause-effect relationships. However, the Scottish psychologist Alan Leslie and his colleagues have applied the concept of modularity to argue that while preschoolers may be confused about many causal relations, some aspects of a concept of causality are already present (Leslie, 1994; Leslie & Keeble, 1987). As we have seen, Piaget's belief that preschoolers are still precausal thinkers has been challenged by Rochel Gelman and her colleagues, who have shown that understanding of causal relations is present during early childhood. Leslie's goal was much more ambitious: he sought to show that a primitive sensitivity to physical causality is present as near to birth as could be tested for; that is, he wanted to show that the perception of causality is an innate mental module (point 2 above).

When we see a rolling billiard ball collide with a stationary billiard ball that then begins to roll, we perceive the movement of the second ball to have been caused by the collision with the first ball. This perception is so strong that when adults are shown a series of dots on a page arranged so that one dot draws closer to its neighbor and eventually "bumps into it," they experience the illusion that the first dot "causes" the second to move, even though they know that neither is really moving. Leslie and his colleagues studied the perception of such cause-effect relationships among infants.

The researchers presented 6-month-old children with a computer display in which one dot appeared to bump into a second and the second dot moved. In one case, the second dot moved immediately, suggesting causation. In the other case, there was a delay in the movement of the second dot, suggesting an absence of causation. The researchers showed the babies the causal event several times in a row and then showed them either a different causal event or the "noncausal" event. The babies stared longer at the *non*causal event than at the causal event, indicating that they were sensitive to causality in this restricted context.

Leslie and Stephanie Keeble (1987) suggest that this apparent capacity to perceive causality, even the illusory causality of the computer screen, serves as a template that guides children to develop genuine causal understanding even before they have much real-world knowledge. Although this primitive capacity is rigid and low-level, it points babies in the right direction when they attempt to interpret their experiences and thereby supports the later development of more complex causal knowledge.

A second line of evidence supporting the modularity position comes from prodigies, children whose overall level of development is normal but who demonstrate islands of brilliance. Wolfgang Mozart, for example, was an accomplished composer and musician while he was still a young child, but he was not markedly different from other children his age in other ways. The extraordinary accomplishments of Mozart and other prodigies appear to fit the idea of mental modules. Each of their accomplishments falls within a domain that has its own distinctive structure (music, language, arithmetic) (Feldman, 1994).

Autism and theory of mind

Another area in which the idea of modularity has proved helpful is the study of children who suffer from **autism,** a poorly understood condition that is defined primarily by an inability to relate normally to other people. Young autistic children rarely use language to communicate, do not engage in symbolic, pretend play, and do not respond appropriately to other human beings. They ordinarily score poorly on tests of intelligence (Baron-Cohen et al., 1993; Frith, 1989).

Autism A condition in which children are unable to interact with others normally, their language development is retarded, and their behavior is often ritualistic and compulsive.

For years autism was considered a form of childhood schizophrenia and many people believed that it was caused by cold, unemotional parenting practices. More recently, modularity theorists have argued that the fundamental deficit that accounts for the varied symptoms of autism is the failure of autistic children to develop the biological prerequisites for a theory of mind. Autistic children's inability to attribute mental states to others causes them to interact in asocial, inappropriate ways. Combining the evidence that autism arises from a specific cognitive defect with the neurological evidence of specific biological abnormalities associated with autism, Allen Leslie (1991) has proposed the existence of a "theory of mind module."

Several lines of evidence support this explanation (Astington, 1993). In an early study, Simon Baron-Cohen and his colleagues (1986) asked groups of children to arrange sequences of four picture cards into a story. There were three types of stories on the cards:

1. *Mechanical sequences* depicting physical interactions between people and objects: a man kicks a rock, which rolls down a hill, then splashes in the water (see Figure 9.13*a*).

2. *Behavioral sequences* depicting interactions among people: one child takes an ice cream cone from another and eats it (Figure 9.13*b*).

3. *Mentalistic sequences* depicting stories that involve mental events: a girl puts a toy down behind her while she picks a flower. Another person comes up behind her and takes the toy; the girl looks surprised when she turns around and finds the toy gone (Figure 9.13*c*).

Of the 4-years-olds studied, some were autistic, some were not autistic but were mentally retarded, and some were normal 4-year-old children. The autistic children outperformed the normal children when asked to create mechanical

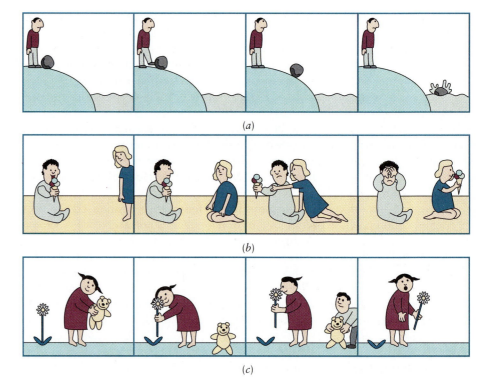

FIGURE 9.13 *Stimuli used to assess autistic children's ability to think about mental states. At the top of the figure is a* mechanical *sequence* (a) *showing a man kicking a rock, which rolls down a hill; the* middle behavioral *sequence* (b) *shows a girl taking an ice cream cone from a boy; the bottom* mentalistic *sequence* (c) *shows a boy taking a girl's teddy bear when her back is turned.*

sequences. But they were unable to create meaningful mentalistic sequences (see Figure 9.14). They did not attribute the mental state of surprise to the girl whose toy disappears while her back is turned (Figure 9.13c).

Additional evidence that autism involves the impairment of a specific "theory of mind" module comes from studies that make use of false-belief tasks, such as the one described earlier in this chapter. Children are told a story about a mother who moves a candy bar from one place to another while her child is absent (p. 343). They are then asked to say where the child will look for the candy when he returns and how he will feel when he looks there. Autistic children of various ages perform like typical 3-year-olds, failing to realize that the absent child has a false belief about the location of the candy and will be disappointed when he looks in the wrong location.

Assessing modularity explanations

The evidence that several mental capacities display the properties of modularity proposed by Fodor is too important to ignore. Variability in the rates at which different parts of the brain develop almost certainly contributes to the unevenness of behavior during early childhood.

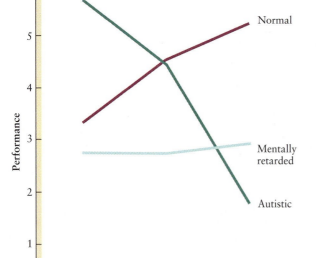

FIGURE 9.14 *The level of performance achieved by normal, mentally retarded, and autistic children when asked to create meaningful mechanical, behavioral, and mentalistic sequences. Note that the autistic children are especially good at creating mechanical sequences but have even greater difficulty than retarded children when asked to create mentalistic sequences.*

However, this approach too has its shortcomings. For example, Jerry Samet (1993) has argued that failure to develop a sense of self, not the absence of a "theory of mind module," explains the behavior of autistic children. Others argue that because we currently have no way of delineating either the full set of mental modules or the boundaries between modules, claims about modules and relations between them are unacceptably ambiguous (Fischer & Bidell, 1991; Karmiloff-Smith, 1992).

It is also difficult to imagine how the modularity approach would explain many of the uneven performances by young children that we have been describing. It seems implausible, for example, that there would be separate modules for taking another person's point of view, for deductive reasoning, for distinguishing between appearance and reality, and so on. But, given the present state of knowledge, modular brain processes appear to be an important source of development that a full theory of early childhood thought should take into account.

CULTURE AND MENTAL DEVELOPMENT IN EARLY CHILDHOOD

The cultural-context approach shares Piaget's insistence that children must be seen as active constructors of their own development. But in addition, cultural-context theory emphasizes that parents enter into the process of their children's development by selecting and shaping the environments in which their children grow up. The environments, in their turn, are structured by the parents' cultural beliefs, ways of earning a living, and social traditions. This two-sided process, in which both the environment and the child are seen as active agents, is referred to as **social co-construction** (Valsiner, 1988). Earlier we caught glimpses of the process of context-specific social co-construction in the mothers who jiggle their babies to encourage them to nurse (Chapter 4, p. 171), the father who supported his little daughter's attempts to play with a teething ring in a manner that allowed her to achieve a slightly more sophisticated level of play (Chapter 5, pp. 211), and the mother who encouraged her toddler son to walk (Chapter 7, p. 261).

The cultural-context view also focuses on specific domains of behavior, a trait it shares with the various neo-Piagetian and modularity theory approaches. Instead of emphasizing domains defined entirely by their logic or content, however, the cultural contextualists emphasize that contexts are organized in terms of cultural meaning systems that people use to interpret their experiences.

The intimate relationship among behavior, context, and cultural meaning systems can be seen in the simple act of waving a hand. This single motion can mean a wide variety of things, depending on its relation to the physical circumstances in which it occurs and the flow of events. A child who waves her hand may be waving good-bye to grandma, petting the cat, patting down Play-Doh to make a pancake, or swatting a fly. Which meaning the action has and its significance for later experience will depend on the relation of that act to what preceded it, what else is happening at the time, and what follows it. These relationships taken together create both the meaning and the context.

Cultural contexts vary not only from society to society but from one generation to the next. Even when particular activities occur in more than one culture (for example, eating), the ways in which the activity is carried out may create very different contexts and meanings. In one culture the men may eat by themselves while the women stay out of view in the kitchen, and the children must absent themselves until both the men and the women are through. In another culture children and parents may be expected to eat together, and conversation that includes the children may be considered very important (Ochs et al., 1991). Each of these patterns has consequences for the development of the child.

Social co-construction The two-sided process in which both the environment and the child are active in constructing the child's development.

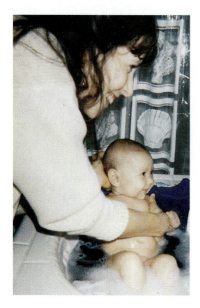

"Taking a bath" as done to an infant.

Scripts Generalized event representations developed by individuals as a result of their repeated participation in routine activities.

The mental representation of contexts

A major task of theories of development is to explain how structure in the environment is converted into mental structures during the course of a child's development. As we have seen, Piaget held that in the course of their activity, children construct *schemas*, organized patterns of individual knowledge that represent objects and their interrelationships. These schemas structure the way the child understands and acts; they develop in a logical progression.

Schemas are also important in cultural-context explanations of development, but they are conceived of somewhat differently. Katherine Nelson (1981, 1986) suggests that as a result of their participation in routine, culturally organized events, children acquire generalized event representations, or **scripts.** Scripts are schemas that specify the people who participate in an event, the social roles they play, the objects that are used during the event, and the sequence of actions that make up the event.

Participation in the activity we call "taking a bath" illustrates how script knowledge is acquired and how it functions. All during the process, the mother and child enact and elaborate the script in their joint activity. What changes is the respective contributions of the partners.

"Taking a bath" is done to a 2-month-old infant. An adult fills a sink or appropriate basin with warm water, lays out a towel, a clean diaper, and clothing, then slips the infant into the water, while holding tightly to keep the baby from drowning. The infant participates by wiggling and slipping in an effort to keep its head above water; the caretaker's role is to hold on to the baby for dear life. Gradually, however, as babies become familiar with the script of bath-taking (and their caretakers have perfected their role as bath-givers), they acquire more competence in parts of the activity and assume a greater role in the process.

By the age of 2 years, most children have "taken" many baths. Each time, roughly the same sequence is followed, the same kinds of objects are used, and the same cast of characters participates. Water is poured into a tub, clothes are taken off, the child gets into the water, soap is applied and rinsed off, the child gets out of the water, dries off, and dresses. There may be variations—a visiting friend may take a bath with the child, or the child may be allowed to play with her water toys after washing—but the basic sequence has a clear pattern to it.

During the preschool period, adults still play the important role of "bath-giver" in the scripted activity called "taking a bath." They initiate children's baths and come in to scrub their ears, to wash their hair, or to help them dry off. Not until adulthood will the child be responsible for the entire event, including scouring the tub and worrying about clean towels, hot water, and the money to pay for them.

Nelson points out that, as in the "taking a bath" script, children grow up inside of other people's scripts. As a consequence, human beings rarely, if ever, experience the natural environment "raw." Rather, they experience an environment that has been prepared (cooked up!) according to the recipes prescribed by their culture.

Nelson and her colleagues have studied the growth of scripted knowledge by interviewing children and by recording the conversations of children playing together. When she asked children to tell her about "going to a restaurant," for example, she obtained such reports as:

"Well, you eat and then go somewhere." (Boy aged 3 years, 1 month)

"Okay. Now, first we go to restaurants at nighttime and we, um, we, and we go and wait for a while, and then the waiter comes and gives us the little stuff with the dinners on it, and then we wait for a little bit, a half an hour or a few minutes or something, and, um, then our pizza comes or anything, and um, [interruption]. . . . [The adult says, "So then the food comes."] Then we eat

Participation in scripted activities, such as Catarina's birthday party in Tuscany, Italy, provides a context within which children can develop more complex understandings of their culture's basic concepts and ways of doing things.

it, and um, then when we're finished eating the salad that we order we get to eat our pizza when it's done, because we get the salad before the pizza's ready. So then when we're finished with all the pizza and all our salad, we just leave." (Girl aged 4 years, 10 months) (Nelson, 1981, p. 103)

Even these simple reports demonstrate that scripts represent generalized knowledge. For one thing, the children are describing *general content*: they are clearly referring to more than a single, unique meal. The 3-year-old uses the generalized form "You eat" rather than a specific reference to a particular time when he ate. The little girl's introduction ("First we go to restaurants at nighttime") indicates that she, too, is speaking of restaurant visits in general.

Besides containing general content, the scripts are organized into a *general structure*, similar to that of adult scripts. Even very young children know that the events involved in "eating at a restaurant" do not take place haphazardly. Instead they report, "First we do this, then we do that." Children evidently abstract the content of a script and its structure from many particular events and then use that knowledge to organize their behavior. But what really differentiates one script from another is the specifics of place, the particular contents, and the amount of detail that make the event a meaningful whole.

The functions of scripts

Scripts are guides to action. They are mental representations that children use to figure out what is likely to happen next in familiar circumstances. Until children have acquired a large repertoire of scripted knowledge, they must use a lot of mental effort to construct scripts as they participate in unfamiliar events. When they lack scripted knowledge, they must pay attention to the details of each new activity. As a consequence, they may be less likely to distinguish between the essential and the superficial features of a context. The little girl interviewed by Nelson, for example, seemed to think that eating pizza is a basic part of the "going to a restaurant" script, whereas paying for the meal was entirely absent. However, because the little girl has grasped a small part of the restaurant script, she will be free to attend to new aspects of the setting the next time she encounters it. Over time, she will gain a deeper understanding of the events she participates in and the contexts of which they are a part.

A second function of scripts is to allow people within a given social group to coordinate their actions more effectively. This function of scripts becomes possible because script knowledge is knowledge generally held in common. "Without shared scripts," Nelson says, "every social act would need to be negotiated afresh." In this sense, "the acquisition of scripts is central to the acquisition of culture" (Nelson, 1981, pp. 109, 110). When children go to the average restaurant in the United States, they learn that first you ask the host or hostess for a table and are assigned a seat. A somewhat different script applies to fast-food restaurants. Discoordination can result if the script is violated (for example, if the child were to enter a restaurant and to sit down at a table where an elderly stranger was midway through a meal).

A third function of scripts is to provide a means by which abstract concepts that apply to many kinds of events can be acquired and organized. When, for example, children acquire scripts for playing with blocks, playing in the sandbox, and playing house, they are accumulating specific examples of play that they can then subsume in a general category (Lucariello & Rifkin, 1986) (see Box 9.2).

Cultural context and the unevenness of development

Once children leave the confines of their caregivers' arms and their cribs, they begin all at once to experience a great variety of contexts that compel them to acquire a variety of new scripts, even as they refine their knowledge of the scripts with which they are already familiar. Thus it is natural, according to the cultural-context approach, that development during early childhood should appear to be so uneven. The content and structure of the new events in which young children participate will depend crucially on the contexts provided by their culture and on the roles they are expected to play within those contexts. In familiar contexts, where they know the expected sequence of actions and can properly interpret the requirements of the situation, young children are most likely to behave in a logical way and adhere to adult standards of thought. But when the contexts are unfamiliar, they may apply inappropriate scripts and resort to magical or illogical thinking.

Overall, cultures influence the unevenness of children's development in five basic ways (Feldman, 1994; Laboratory of Comparative Human Cognition, 1983):

1. By *arranging the occurrence and nonoccurrence of specific activities.* You cannot learn about something you do not observe and have not heard about. A 4-year-old growing up among the Bushmen of the Kalahari Desert is unlikely to learn about taking baths or pouring water from one glass to another; a child growing up in Seattle is unlikely to be skilled at tracking animals or finding water-bearing roots in a desert.

2. By *determining the frequency of basic activities.* Children growing up in Bali may be skilled dancers by the age of 4 (Mead & Macgregor, 1951), and Norwegian children are likely to become good skiers and skaters. In each case, adults arrange for children to practice these activities. Likewise, children growing up in a Mexican village famous for its pottery may work with clay day after day, whereas children living in a nearby town known for its weaving may encounter clay only rarely (Price-Williams, Gordon, & Ramirez, 1969). Insofar as practice makes perfect, the greater the frequency of practice, the higher the level of performance.

3. By *relating different activities.* If molding clay is associated with making pottery, it is experienced in the company of a whole host of related activities: digging from a quarry, firing clay, glazing clay, selling the products. Molding clay as part of a nursery school curriculum will be associated with an entirely different pattern of experience and knowledge.

The meaning of an activity such as weaving and the development of the skills needed to do it vary markedly from one culture to another.

4. *By regulating the difficulty of the child's role.* As in the script of taking a bath, adults decide how much responsibility the child will bear. Whatever the context, there are likely to be gradations in the contributions that a child must make, beginning with mere presence in the scene and proceeding, as the child grows and gains experience, to a central role with controlling responsibility.

5. *By emphasizing activities that promote widely held cultural values.* The activities that adults select for children to engage in most often and the ways of behaving they encourage in those contexts function to promote the values of the community. The study of these values reveals important information about the kinds of adult skills and knowledge that children will acquire.

Barbara Rogoff (1990), a prominent cultural-context theorist, calls the overall process by which adults select and shape young children's actions **guided participation.** The term is used to describe the ways adults and children collaborate in routine problem-solving activities and in the process develop a shared understanding of them. Through guided participation, children receive help in adapting their understanding to new situations, in structuring their problem-solving attempts, and eventually in achieving mastery.

Rogoff points out that the kind of guidance she is talking about is rarely explicit or designed specifically to instruct. Rather, it is a process deeply embedded in the casual interactions that are part of everyday activities. An interaction between Rogoff and her 3½-year-old daughter illustrates the implicit and two-sided nature of the process of guided participation.

> I was getting ready to leave the house, and I noticed that a run had started in the foot of my stocking. My daughter volunteered to help sew the run, but I was in a hurry and tried to avoid her involvement by explaining that I did not want the needle to jab my foot. I began to sew, but could hardly see where I was sewing because my daughter's head was in the way, peering at the sewing. Soon she suggested that *I* could put the needle into the stocking and *she* would pull it through, thus avoiding sticking my foot. I agreed, and we followed this division of labor for a number of stitches. (Rogoff, 1990, p. 109)

Guided participation The means by which adults shape young children's development through collaboration built upon shared understanding in routine problem-solving situations.

BOX 9.2

Sociodramatic Play

Play occupies a conspicuous role in young children's development, cognitive as well as physical and social. Dorothy and Jerome Singer (1990), researchers who have spent several decades studying the role of imagination in human behavior, refer to early childhood as the "high season of imaginative play."

By the end of infancy a child is able to pretend that a matchbox is a car that can zoom around the sandbox, or that a block is an iron. Such play, however, is largely solitary; even when several children are in a room together, their play is unlikely to be interconnected (Bretherton, 1984).

Pretend play is more social and more complex for preschool-aged children than for infants (Göncü & Kessel, 1988). Instead of solitary pretending, children begin to engage in *sociodramatic play*—make-believe games in which two or more children enact a variety of social roles. These games require shared understanding among the participants, which must be negotiated as part of the game.

Four girls in the doll corner have announced that they will play house and agree upon the roles: mother, sister, baby, and maid.

Karen: I'm hungry. Wa-a-ah!

Charlotte: Lie down, baby.

Karen: I'm a baby that sits up.

Charlotte: First you lie down and sister covers you and then I make your cereal and then you sit up.

Karen: Okay.

Karen: *(to Teddy, who has been observing)* You can be the father.

Charlotte: Are you the father?

Teddy: Yes.

Charlotte: Put on a red tie.

Janie: *(in the "maid's" falsetto voice)* I'll get it for you, honey. Now don't that baby look pretty? This is your daddy, baby. (Adapted from Paley, 1984, p. 1)

This transcript illustrates several features of young children's play. The children are enacting social roles and using scripts that they have encountered numerous times in their daily lives, on television, or in stories (Bretherton, 1989). Babies make stereotypic baby noises, maids get things for people, and fathers wear ties. At the same time that they are playing their roles

in the pretend world, the children are also outside it, giving stage directions to one another and commenting on the action. The "baby" who sits up has to be talked into lying down, and the boy is told what role he can play. Occasionally, however, the fantasy may become so real and threatening that children stop the game or refuse to join in (Garvey & Berndt, 1977).

Although children draw upon familiar scenes in their sociodramatic play, the scripts and social phenomena they act out are far from precise imitations. As Catherine Garvey (1977) notes, when a boy engaged in sociodramatic play walks into the house and announces, "Okay, I'm all through with work, honey. I brought home a thousand dollars," he has probably never heard that said before. Rather, he has abstracted certain behaviors characteristic of husbands and embellished them with fantasy.

In recent decades developmental psychologists have become intensely interested in sociodramatic play. Many are engaged in a lively controversy about its significance for cognitive and social development (Bretherton, 1989; Garvey, 1990; Nicolopoulou, 1993). The two main positions in this discussion are derived from the work of Piaget (1962) and Vygotsky (1978).

In Piaget's view, the special quality of play during the preoperational period derives directly from the characteristics of egocentrism. As he phrased it, "For egocentric thought, the supreme law is play" (Piaget, 1928, p. 401). Piaget minimized the significance of play for cognitive development because he assumed that in play, assimilation prevails over accommodation. He predicted that when egocentric thought gives way to logical thought in middle childhood, pretend play should give way to the kind of rule-bound play evident in board games and organized sports, reflecting changes in children's underlying level of cognitive competence.

Researchers have traced the rise and decline of pretend play during the years of early childhood by observing children and coding the kinds of play they engage in (Rubin, Fein, & Vandenberg, 1983). Though the results are not completely consistent, in general they have confirmed Piaget's belief that sociodramatic play should peak sometime in early childhood and then begin to decline. The disappearance of such play, however, does not mean that children stop pretending. Dorothy and Jerome Singer (1990) believe that once middle childhood is reached, pretend play "goes underground" because other forms of play are considered socially more acceptable. Douglas Hofstader (1979) believes that pretend play never disappears; throughout their lives people constantly create mental variants on the situations they face:

[The manufacture of "as-if" worlds] happens so casually, so naturally, that we hardly notice what we are doing. We select from our fantasy a world which is close, in some internal mental sense, to the real world. We compare what is real with what we perceive as almost real. In so doing what we gain is some intangible kind of perspective on reality. (p. 643)

Unlike Piaget, Lev Vygotsky (1978) believed that pretend play provides children with an important mental support system that allows them to think and act in more complex ways. In real life, children depend on adults to help them by providing the rules and by filling in for them in little ways, in what Vygotsky called the zone of proximal development. The freedom to negotiate reality—essential to games of "let's pretend"—provides children with analogous support. As a consequence, wrote Vygotsky, "In play a child is always above his average age, above his daily behavior; in play it is as though he were a head taller than himself" (p. 102).

M. G. Dias and Paul Harris (1988, 1990) provided interesting support for Vygotsky's idea that play creates a zone of proximal development in a study of the way pretending influences young children's ability to reason deductively. Dias and Harris presented 4- to 6-year-old children a series of logical problems in which they had to reason from two premises to reach a conclusion. Most children do not solve this kind of problem until they are considerably older. In fact, Piaget believed that such reasoning does not emerge until adolescence.

The problems presented by Dias and Harris were of the following kind:

All fishes live in trees.

Tot is a fish.

Does Tot live in the water?

These problems were presented to half of the children in a matter-of-fact tone of voice. With the other half of the children the experimenter started off by saying, "Let's pretend that I am from another planet," and went on to present the problem in the sort of dramatic voice that is ordinarily used in storytelling.

The children's ability to solve these reasoning problems varied greatly from one condition to the other. The children who were instructed in a matter-of-fact tone made many errors; they said that Tot the fish lives in the water. (While it is true that fish live in water, according to the logic of the problem, Tot lives in a tree.) These children justified their answers by going outside the boundaries of the problem to draw upon their knowledge of where fish live.

The children who participated in the "let's pretend" version of the problem were much more successful, and the way they justified their answers provided clear evidence that they entered into the hypothetical nature of the tasks. Typical justifications for their correct answers were such statements as "I said Tot lives in a tree because we're pretending that fishes live in trees."

Almost all of the research on pretend play has been carried out in industrially advanced countries where children are likely to attend a preschool (which serves as the setting for a great deal of the existing research). The few analogous studies of pretend play that have been carried out in nonindustrialized societies suggest that in these cultures sociodramatic play sticks much more closely to the models provided by actual adult practices and involves less imaginative transformation of reality (Gaskins & Göncü, 1992). Even in such cultures, however, when children are induced to adopt a "let's pretend" mode of behaving, their logical problem-solving capacities are enhanced (Dias, 1988).

Sociodramatic play is a leading activity for children from the age of 2½ to 6.

Assessing the cultural-context explanation

In the Piagetian view of development, cognitive structures undergo *generalized* transformations as children mature and gain experience. In the cultural-context view, by contrast, children are seen as developing *context-specific* abilities tied to the content and structure of the events in which they participate. The extent to which new and more sophisticated ways of thinking and acting become general depends crucially on the extent to which those psychological processes are useful in other settings as well (Laboratory of Comparative Human Cognition, 1983). According to cultural-context theorists, magical thinking, failure to take another's perspective, and confusion of appearance and reality are not unique to young children; they are also seen in older children and adults (Subbotski, 1991). If adults display these traits more rarely, they do so at least in part because they have much greater direct experience of the world. Adults also have more power than children to shape contexts to suit their own desires and a greater knowledge of the experiences and adaptive solutions of earlier generations.

Like the biological-modularity view, the cultural-context approach assumes that biological maturation is a basic prerequisite for development. The two approaches contrast markedly, however, in their conceptions of the mechanisms of change and the sources of variability in behavior. Modularity theorists assign a major role to biological maturation and a minimal role to the environment. The development of grammar provides the prototype: development of a rudimentary grammar "just happens" when the organism is ripe for it. Variations in the developmental level of children's behavior are assumed to depend on changes in the central nervous system that bring into being the specific biological prerequisites for the behavior in question.

Cultural-context theorists, on the other hand, believe that unless active sociocultural influences operate in tandem with biological ones, development will be stunted, much in the manner of the language of deaf children raised in households where the learning of sign is not permitted (see Chapter 8, p. 323).

Applying the Theoretical Perspectives

Each of the current theories of early childhood cognition provides a distinctive perspective from which to view development. When proponents of the various approaches attempt to explain the same phenomenon, we have an opportunity to compare the relative strengths and weaknesses of alternative views.

Drawing pictures—an activity with many cognitive components—is a case in point. Every theoretical viewpoint has something to say about it. In accord with Piaget's constructivist approach, children's drawing seems to go through a regular series of stages. In accord with an information-processing approach, changes in drawing can in some cases be tied closely to the ability to hold several aspects of an object in mind at one time. In accord with the modularity approach, children whose linguistic, mental, or social development is severely retarded may nonetheless draw at a high level of competence. And in accord with the cultural-context approach, the development of drawing ability depends on the opportunities the child is given to engage in that activity and the ways such opportunities are structured by adults.

CONSTRUCTING THE STAGES OF DRAWING

In every culture where children are given an opportunity to draw from an early age, their drawings appear to pass through the same sequence of stages (Gardner, 1980; Golomb, 1974; Kellogg, 1969). In the beginning they scribble. Children are

FIGURE 9.15 *Drawing of the human figure develops through a sequence of steps. At first a child draws a big circle that stands for a whole person. The child's global representation of a person soon evolves into a circle or an ellipse with the face in the upper part and two protruding lines underneath (a "tadpole figure"). Gradually the circle comes to represent only the head, and the body descends between the two vertical lines. Some months later, the child adds a second circle to represent the body, with another pair of lines extending from it as arms. (From Goodnow, 1977.)*

not "making pictures" when they scribble. What seems to matter to them is not the look of the product but the joy of moving their hands and the trail of their movements to which the scribbling bears witness.

Scribbling embodies both of the functions of art in a primitive form. It expresses a feeling—the exuberance of motion—and it leaves a trace of the movement, representing it for later examination. Scribbling is considered primitive because its expression is uncontrolled and unplanned and because it represents only itself.

Children take a giant step beyond scribbling around the age of 3, when they begin to recognize that their lines can represent things. At about this time children begin to draw circles and ellipses that are cleared of the whorls and lines that used to fill their scribble pictures. Most children interpret these circles as "things." The circular line encloses an inside area that seems more solid to them than the field it is on.

As children continue to gain experience with drawing, they are likely to adopt stereotyped ways of depicting objects: a house is a pentagon, a sun is a circle with lines extending from its surface, a flower is a circle surrounded by ellipses, humans and animals appear as tadpole figures (see Figure 9.15). Eventually children begin to combine representations of people and things to make scenes and stories or to depict a variety of experiences.

Between the ages of 7 and 11, children increasingly strive to be realistic in their drawings. At the same time they become more skilled at composition and the techniques of drawing (see Figure 9.16).

Many of these stages, observed in the drawings of North American and European children, can be found in all societies in which drawing is an expected activity. Such universals in the development of artistic representation are the kind of phenomena that are central to Piaget's theory of cognitive development.

AN INFORMATION-PROCESSING ACCOUNT OF DRAWING

People had been making drawings for thousands of years before techniques for representing objects in three dimensions became fully developed and exploited (Arnheim, 1954). Yet modern children who grow up with three-dimensional representations all around them acquire the ability to make such drawings at a very early age.

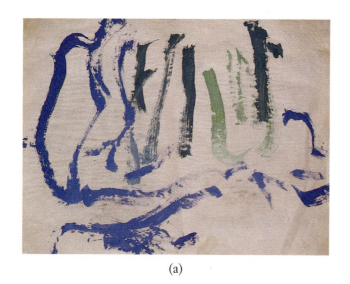

(a)

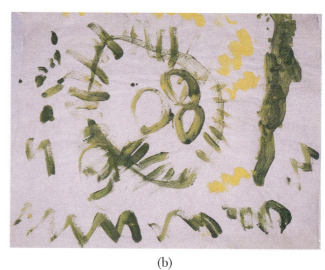

(b)

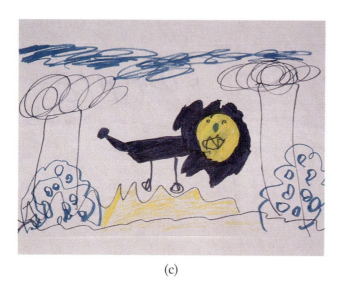

(c)

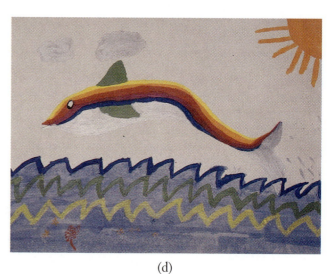

(d)

(e)

FIGURE 9.16 *A sequence of drawings by an American child: (a) at 2½ years, Carrie was drawing lines of different colors; (b) at 3½ years, she began to draw global representations of a person; (c) at 5 years, she added a body and legs to the creatures she drew, and she set her main figure in a scene; (d) motion, rhythm, and greater realism are evident in the drawings she produced at 7½ years; (e) at 12 years, she was able to draw a cartoon of a realistic scene. (Courtesy of Carrie Hogan.)*

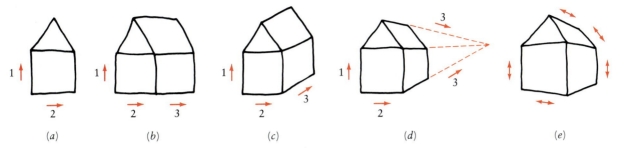

FIGURE 9.17 *The developmental sequence for drawing of an object in three dimensions. Drawing* (a) *leaves out the third dimension. Drawings* (b) *and* (c) *introduce the third dimension in partially correct ways. Drawings* (d) *and* (e) *represent the full three dimensions according to two conventions. (Adapted from Willats, 1987.)*

Figure 9.17 shows the developmental sequence that children go through in learning to draw a schematic house in three dimensions. The youngest children collapse three dimensions into two. Then the third dimension is partially added, but it is initially collapsed into one of the other two. Finally children acquire ways to represent the third dimension (Willats, 1987). From an information-processing perspective, this sequence follows directly from children's growing knowledge of drawing rules and their ability to remember the need to represent all three spatial coordinates in their drawings.

DRAWING AS A MENTAL MODULE

Although normally the development of children's ability to draw passes through the series of stages we have just described, some important exceptions suggest that drawing ability may be modular in some respects. A compelling example is provided by Nadia, an autistic child in Nottingham, England (Selfe, 1977). At first Nadia seemed to develop normally, but by the age of 3 she had forgotten the few words she had learned, her behavior was lethargic, and she did not engage in pretend play. At the age of 3½, Nadia began to display unusual artistic ability. Without any apparent practice, she began to incorporate the perspective and other artistic techniques when she copied pictures, an ability that usually is acquired only after years of experience in drawing (Figure 9.18). Nadia's dexterity when she was drawing was quite remarkable, yet her hand movements were otherwise uncoordinated. Extensive testing showed that Nadia had an extraordinary ability to form and remember visual images. She would often study a drawing for weeks before producing a version from memory herself. It seemed as if she were building up a mental image so that at some later time her "mind's eye" could guide her hand in re-creating the image on paper. Howard Gardner (1980), who has conducted research on the cognitive basis of art, uses terms reminiscent of Chomsky's and of Fodor's idea of mental modules in his discussion of Nadia's case:

> Nadia may have been operating with a high powered mental computational device—one seldom, if ever, exploited by others but perhaps available to at least a sample of the human species. (pp. 186–187)

Lorna Selfe (1983) reports that Nadia's unusual development is not unique. She has found a number of children whose language ability and general mental functioning were quite low but whose ability to create graphic images was exceptionally high. These cases fit nicely with the idea that mental modules, such as language and perception, can develop in relative isolation from one another.

FIGURE 9.18 *Nadia, an autistic preschooler with only minimal exposure to models, displayed an uncanny ability to capture form and movement in her drawings. This drawing is her copy of a picture of a horse.*

Evidence from less extreme cases also suggests that the ordinary sequence of stages is not necessary to mastery. Gardner (1980) reports that children deprived of the opportunity to draw during early childhood may skip the initial stages of drawing altogether when they finally do get an opportunity to draw. If true, this finding would run counter to the Piagetian position that stages follow each other in an invariant sequence.

A CULTURAL-CONTEXT ACCOUNT OF THE DEVELOPMENT OF DRAWING

A cultural-context view of the development of drawing takes for granted both that humans have an innate potential for drawing and that within any particular medium—drawing, writing, music—representations can be constructed at varying levels of complexity. To these axioms it adds its own idea of the processes that transform children's potential for drawing into the actual execution of specific kinds of meaningful representations.

An important indicator of the culturally organized nature of children's drawing is found in the ways adults talk to children about what they are doing. When American adults ask young children, "What are you drawing?" the very form of the question assumes that there is some thing to be drawn and that the child is attempting to represent it. When questions of this kind are posed, children often go along with the way the adult scripted the interaction by making up stories about what they have drawn *after the fact.* Initially, these stories are not tied to anything that an adult can perceive on the paper. After children have gained some experience, however, their explanations become connected to the discovery that the marks they have made resemble an actual object in the world—but this discovery is made only after the drawing is completed (Golomb, 1974).

The following dialogue between 3-year-olds Roslyn and Don, recorded in a U.S. preschool, illustrates the rudimentary nature of young children's understanding of drawing as well as some of the ways those understandings change (adapted from Gearhart & Newman, 1980, p. 172):

Roslyn: I got brown. *(Holds up her crayon)*

Don: I got another color. *(Draws short lines back and forth)*

Roslyn: I made a brown circle. *(Illustrates with counterclockwise gesture, holding crayon over the paper)*

Don: I got another color.

Roslyn: I, I, I made a big brown circ-er square. *(Repeats the illustrative gesture)*

Don: *(Makes a counterclockwise form on his paper)* Look what I'm making, Roslyn.

Roslyn: Huh! Ehh! *(Looks)*

Don: I, I went round like this. *(Illustrates with larger counterclockwise movements)*

Roslyn: Well. . . . Now watch what I am making, I'm making mountains. *(Immediately draws a series of short vertical lines)*

The development of drawing depends on the traditions of the culture into which the child is born. This drawing was done by a 7-year-old Chilean child.

Their words and actions clearly indicate that neither child has a fixed, individual drawing in mind. All of their talk refers either to something they have just done ("I made a brown circle") or something they are doing ("I'm making"). There is little talk about plans for their pictures. Each child imitates elements introduced by the other, with no overall plan of how that element might fit into the whole.

Even these children's drawings have progressed beyond scribbling, however. As they show each other crayons and figures, swapping comments and ideas, they are talking as if the drawings represented things (circles, squares, mountains) even if the correspondence is by no means clear to outsiders.

The way the teacher arranged for a picture to be called "finished" was also important in helping the children to discover what it means to draw a picture. Before writing the child's name on the picture and pinning it up on the board, she asked open-ended questions about what the child had been drawing, again behaving as if the child had been drawing a particular thing.

Teacher: Jeff? [Come] tell me about your picture. (*Jeffrey comes and looks at his drawing*)

Jeffrey: Uh, it has two mountains on orange, two orange circles.

Teacher: Two orange circles (*as she writes his name on the drawing*).

(Adapted from Gearhart & Newman, 1980, p. 182)

In this dialogue the teacher selectively accepts the part of the child's account (two orange circles) that accords with her notion of "thingness." The scribbled "mountains" are ignored. As a consequence, Jeffrey learns something about which sort of marks count as a drawing of a mountain or circles in the eyes of adults and which do not.

The existence of scripted activities for drawing does not contradict the possibility that there is a mental module for drawing or the idea that drawing goes through stages of increasing complexity. Rather, it suggests that the ways in which adults organize instruction provide essential opportunities for modular potential

How young children learn to represent reality in their drawings and paintings is of interest to psychologists.

to be triggered and stages constructed. Over the course of a year or two, the teacher's assumptions become second nature to the children. They learn not only the possibility of drawing pictures of "things" but a good many techniques for making those things take shape on the paper. Most important, they come to understand and share the teacher's concept of what "drawing a picture" means. This common understanding then becomes the basis for further instruction.

Reconciling Alternative Perspectives

Scholarly explanations of the phenomena of young children's thought are reminiscent of the parable of the blind men feeling an elephant: the man who feels the trunk believes that the creature is a snake; the man who feels the leg believes that the creature is a tree; and the man who feels the tail is certain that he has hold of a rope. Lacking a coordinated understanding, each man mistakes his part for the whole, which is distinctively different from the parts.

Piaget's young children are incomplete logicians. Having only recently learned to represent the world symbolically, they still have trouble constructing stable cause-effect schemas, and they are confused about what is real and what is not. They fail to distinguish their own point of view from the perspectives of others, so they are constantly led into error about what others think and say. It is several years before they can translate conflicting information into useful action- and language-based schemas.

Neo-Piagetian explanations of thinking during early childhood have sought to revise the negative description of young children as egocentric and prelogical. Neo-Piagetians show that young children can reason logically in familiar circumstances as long as their still-fragile verbal skills are not overstrained. Still very much at issue among these researchers, however, is whether Piaget's idea of global transformations of mind should be retained or replaced by a piecemeal, domain-specific picture of development.

The information-processing approach to young children's characteristic thought processes focuses on their limited knowledge, attention, and memory capacity and their lack of sophisticated problem-solving strategies. This theoretical framework may be viewed as either a rival to Piaget's theory or an alternative strategy for research. Some researchers (Case, 1992; Kitchener & Fischer, 1990) use information-processing ideas to support a neo-Piagetian theory. Others (Siegler, 1996) use similar ideas to arrive at a new theory in which cognitive development is seen as a nonstagelike, continuous process of change arising from the accumulation of specific knowledge and strategies.

One major alternative to the Piagetian and various neo-Piagetian approaches, modularity theory, denies that constructive interactions play a prominent role in cognitive development. Viewing the child's mental processes as a collection of separate computational modules, researchers in this tradition attribute the special characteristics of young children's thought primarily to the physical maturation of the brain. In some striking cases these researchers have shown that even infants display rudimentary forms of the cognitive abilities that Piaget denied to young children. From this perspective, the unevenness of behavior during early childhood mirrors unevenness in the rate of physical maturation. As basic brain structures approach maturity, extreme variations among modules decrease and behavior becomes more consistent and "adult."

Like those who work within a Piagetian or neo-Piagetian framework, cultural-context theorists believe that complex cognitive processes are constructed in social interaction. This approach, however, emphasizes that the process of construction, and hence the mechanism of cognitive development, is shared between children and older members of their communities in scripted activities organized, or at least supervised, by adults.

In our view these competing approaches are most usefully viewed as complementary. Certainly the various phenomena they focus on need to be accounted for in any comprehensive explanation of development during early childhood, even if no single theoretical framework has yet been able to encompass them all. At present a number of promising efforts to provide such a comprehensive explanatory framework are under way (Bidell & Fischer, 1995; Case & Okamoto, 1995; Siegler, 1996).

A child's total psychological development encompasses far more than the restricted abilities described here. Still to be explored are the ways young children think about themselves as members of their social worlds, their experiences in nursery school and day care (where they must learn to get along with children their own age under new circumstances), and their induction into the world of books and television.

SUMMARY

- Young children's thought processes are characterized by great unevenness; islands of competence exist in a sea of uncertainty and naiveté.

Piaget's Account of Mental Development in Early Childhood

- Piaget's explanation of thought during early childhood stresses how the inability to think about two aspects of a problem in relation to each other limits children's ability to engage in mental operations.
- Cognitive limitations resulting from the inability to decenter include the inability to take the perspective of another person, to reason about cause and effect, and to distinguish appearance from reality.

The Study of Young Children's Thinking after Piaget

- Piaget's theory fails to account satisfactorily for the unevenness of children's thought in what he called the preoperational stage. Some developmental psychologists want to refine his theory, while others have suggested alternatives.
- Neo-Piagetian explanations of young children's thought retain Piaget's theory of stages but account for uneven development by

   1. criticizing evidence concerning the extreme unevenness of development or
   2. proposing that stages occur within specific domains of knowledge.

- According to the information-processing view, cognitive development is a process of expanding the young child's limited attentional, memory, and problem-solving capacities. The unevenness of young children's thought is explained by differences in children's familiarity with specific task settings and in the demands made by the various settings.
- Biologically oriented theories hold that the brain is organized into mental modules that are domain-specific, innately structured, and relatively isolated from one another. They point to uneven rates of change in brain structures as the major cause of unevenness in young children's thought. The mental capacities of prodigies (children who excel in a single domain at an early age) and of some autistic children support this hypothesis.
- In the cultural-context view, contexts provide coherence to otherwise isolated actions. Children's interactions with the world are co-constructed within adult scripts and activities.
- Contexts are represented mentally in the form of scripts—conceptual structures that are guides to action, a means of coordination between people, and a framework in which abstract concepts applicable across contexts are formed.
- Culture mediates society's influence on mental development by:

   1. Arranging for the occurrence of specific contexts and associated scripts.
   2. Arranging which contexts a child will experience.
   3. Deciding which contexts are associated with particular activities.
   4. Regulating the level of the child's participation.
   5. Encouraging children to participate in activities that are widely valued.

Applying the Theoretical Perspectives

- Normally a child learning to draw passes through a series of stages. These stages are domain-specific in ways that fit with neo-Piagetian and modularity theories.
- As one stage follows another, the child's drawings represent more and more aspects of the objects drawn, in line with an information-processing approach.
- Learning to draw is culturally organized in ways that fit with cultural-context theories.

Reconciling Alternative Perspectives

- The various theories of early childhood development are best treated as complementary perspectives, rather than as competing explanations.

KEY TERMS

autism, p. 361

egocentrism, p. 341

guided participation, p. 367

horizontal décalage, p. 346

information-processing approach, p. 356

long-term memory, p. 357

mental operations, p. 340

mental perspective taking, p. 340

modularity theory, p. 360

precausal thinking, p. 345

preoperational stage, p. 340

scripts, p. 364

short-term memory, p. 357

social co-construction, p. 363

theory of mind, p. 343

THOUGHT QUESTIONS

1. Young children appear to become confused about the relationship between a general class of objects and its subclasses. How does this difficulty relate to features of linguistic development discussed in Chapter 8?

2. Suppose you were Piaget and you were confronted with evidence that even young infants appear to be surprised when the events they observe contradict laws of physical location. How might you interpret the data to fit your theory that young children are precausal thinkers?

3. In what ways is the biologically inspired concept of a mental module similar to the constructivist concept of a cognitive domain? In what ways do the two approaches differ?

4. How does the study of "theory of mind" among autistic children influence our understanding of normal children's cognitive development?

5. Write out your own going-to-a-restaurant script. In what ways does it differ from the scripts quoted on pages 364–365? What might be some of the reasons for those differences?

Social Development in Early Childhood

> "The incorporation of the individual as a member of a community, or his adaptation to it, seems like an almost unavoidable condition which has to be filled before he can attain the objective of happiness. . . . Individual development seems to us a product of the interplay of two trends, the striving for happiness, generally called 'egoistic,' and the impulse towards merging with others in the community, which we call 'altruistic.'"
>
> —*Sigmund Freud,*
> Civilization and Its Discontents

In the quote on the preceding page, Sigmund Freud is describing **social development,** a two-sided process in which children simultaneously become integrated into the larger social community and differentiated as distinctive individuals. One side of social development is **socialization,** the process by which children acquire the standards, values, and knowledge of their society. The other side of social development is *personality formation*, the process through which children come to have their own unique patterns of feeling, thinking, and behaving in a wide variety of circumstances.

The process of socialization begins as soon as a child is born and her mother says, for example, "She's never going to be a rugby player," or her father remarks, "I shall be worried to death when she's eighteen" (see Chapter 3, p. 125). Such predictions are not just idle talk. The beliefs that give rise to such statements lead parents to shape their child's experience in ways they deem appropriate. Socialization continues as an aspect of every encounter children have with other members of their society as they learn to eat and sleep on a schedule, to prefer clothes of pink or blue, to be polite to their elders, to take their vitamins, and to love their brother.

Both adults and children play active roles in social development. Adults communicate to children how they should behave, display pleasure or disapproval with the way they do behave, and reward, ignore, or punish them accordingly. Adults also select the contexts in which children learn about social categories and become conversant with their culture's funds of knowledge and rules of behavior. But children do not automatically or passively absorb the lessons adults intend. What children learn depends on how they interpret their experiences and what they select from the conflicting messages they receive. If 4-year-old Mark admires his older cousin Eric and wants to be like him, will he imitate Eric's socially appropriate style of dress, his socially inappropriate use of slang, or both?

In order to acquire an understanding of the social categories that apply to them, children must somehow figure out what people mean when they say such things as "You are my son" and "Act like a lady." These terms stand for **social roles** that reflect adult expectations about the child's rights, duties, and obligations, as well as appropriate forms of behavior. Consequently, it is not sufficient for children simply to learn what adults mean by words such as "son" and "lady"; it is also necessary for them to learn to fill these social roles in ways that correspond to adults' expectations. Although adults take such matters for granted, perhaps the most remarkable fact about the process of socialization is that most children come to accept the socially prescribed roles and rules as reasonable and even necessary.

The second side of social development, **personality,** is the unique pattern of temperament, emotions, and intellectual abilities that children develop in their social interactions with their kin and community. Since no two people have precisely the same experiences, no two people ever have precisely the same personality, not even identical twins. Even if two children are both nursery school students, friends, nieces, and Japanese Americans, each will have her own experiences, her own ways of interpreting how those experiences apply to her, and her own pattern of thinking, behaving, and feeling.

An important aspect of personality is the way children come to conceive of themselves in relation to other people—their **self-concept.** This intimate link between personality and social development was described at the turn of the century by one of the founders of developmental psychology, James Mark Baldwin:

The development of the child's personality could not go on at all without the constant modification of his sense of himself by suggestions from others. So

Social development A double-sided process in which children simultaneously become integrated into the larger social community and differentiated as distinctive individuals.

Socialization The process by which children acquire the standards, values, and knowledge of their society.

Social roles The social categories such as son, daughter, student that describe a person's relations to the social group and the person's rights, duties, and obligations in that role.

Personality The unique pattern of temperament, emotions, and intellectual abilities a child develops in his or her social interactions.

Self-concept The way individuals conceive of themselves in relation to other people.

he himself, at every stage, is really in part someone else, even in his own thought of himself. (1902, p. 23)

The early origins of personality are no less visible at birth than the presence of socializing influences. As we saw in Chapter 4 (p. 145), neonates display individual differences in characteristic levels of activity, responses to frustration, and readiness to engage in novel experiences. We referred to these patterns of responsivity and associated emotional states as *temperamental traits* and noted that temperament is moderately stable over time; children who draw back from novel experiences in infancy are likely to behave shyly when they first enter a nursery school.

Temperamental traits are the earliest visible manifestations of personality (Strelau, 1994; Thomas & Chess, 1989). But when children reach the age of 3 or 5 years, there is more to their personalities than temperament. We cannot say that a child is honest or compulsive at birth because there is no temperamental characteristic corresponding to honesty or compulsiveness, or to a host of other personality characteristics, such as stinginess, compliance, and a desire to please other people. Those characteristics are acquired over the course of a lifetime as children's initial styles of interacting with their environments (their temperaments) are integrated with their developing cognitive understanding, emotional responses, and habits.

These little flower girls are simultaneously fulfilling a traditional role in a wedding and learning about many important aspects of the social roles and behaviors expected of them when they grow up.

Personality formation and socialization are in constant tension as children discover the dilemma Freud wrote about—the fact that their individual desires and ideas often conflict with their culture's norms and the desires of others. A 5-year-old boy who sucks his thumb is likely to be discouraged from doing so by his parents and teased by his peers. A child who is jealous of the attention her baby brother receives must learn that she can't pinch him (or at least can't get caught pinching him!); she must find some socially acceptable way to gain her mother's attention and deal with her socially unacceptable feelings.

During early childhood, children learn a great deal about the roles they are expected to play and how to behave in accordance with them, how to control aggressive feelings, and how to respect the rights of others. At the same time, they develop a more explicit sense of themselves, their abilities, and the ways in which they are likely to react in a variety of circumstances. These changes in social development do not, of course, occur independently of the biological and cognitive changes discussed in Chapter 9. Socialization, personality formation, biological maturation, and cognitive development occur simultaneously. How does socialization emerge from their interactions?

Acquiring a Social and Personal Identity

Psychologists agree that **identification,** a psychological process in which children try to look, act, feel, and *be* like significant people in their social environment, is essential to the process of socialization. They disagree, however, about the mechanisms by which identification is achieved. Four proposed mechanisms have figured most prominently in discussions of this basic developmental process: differentiation, affiliation, imitation and social learning, and the formation of cognitive schemas.

> **Identification** A psychological process in which children try to look, act, feel, and be like significant people in their social environment. Identification is essential to the process of socialization.

These preschool girls are participating in a beauty contest. This kind of experience gives them an idea of what the adults in their community expect of girls.

The development of identification can be studied with respect to almost any social category—a family, a religious group, a neighborhood clique, or a nationality. The overwhelming majority of studies on identification in early childhood, however, focus on the acquisition of sex roles. Consequently, we will devote the lion's share of our attention to this social category before turning to ethnic identity, which is also an important social category in today's world.

SEX-ROLE IDENTITY

Because sexual identity is so central to adult experience, the question of how children acquire the understanding that they are a boy or a girl and how they interpret that sex role* is of great interest to developmental psychologists. The central issues in acquiring a sex-role identity are seen in the following conversations:

> "When I grow up," says [4-year-old] Jimmy at the dinner table, "I'm gonna marry Mama."
>
> "Jimmy's nuts," says the sensible voice of 8-year-old Jane. "You can't marry Mama and anyway, what would happen to Daddy?" Exasperating, logical female! Who cares about your good reasons and your dull good sense! There's an answer for that too. "He'll be old," says the dreamer, through a mouthful of string-beans. "And he'll be dead." Then, awed by the enormity of his words, the dreamer adds hastily, "But he might not be dead, and maybe I'll marry Marcia instead." (Fraiberg, 1959, pp. 202–203)

The next conversation took place when our daughter, Jenny, was 4 years old. She was lying on her mother's side of her parents' bed, watching her mother comb her hair.

---

* Some psychologists recommend the use of the word "gender" instead of "sex" when this topic is discussed because they believe that the term "sex" implies that all sex-typed behavior is ultimately determined by biology. Others argue against the term "gender," which they think implies that sex-linked behavior is ultimately determined by the environment (Gentile, 1993; Unger & Crawford, 1993). We will use both "sex" and "gender" in contexts where they appear most appropriate, without implying either that sex/gender roles are basically biological or that they are basically environmental.

Jenny: You know, Mommy, when you die I am going to marry Daddy.

Sheila: I don't think so.

Jenny: *(nodding her head gravely)* I am, too.

Sheila: You can't. It's against the laws of God and man.

Jenny: *(close to tears)* But I want to.

Sheila: *(going to comfort her)* You'll have your own husband when you grow up.

Jenny: No, I won't! I want Daddy. I don't like you, Mommy.

These stories are easy to understand. Both of these children have had several years to observe the family life around them. Jimmy knows that he is a boy and Jenny knows that she is a girl. Although neither has a deep understanding of what these labels imply, they know that they want the things that big boys and big girls have. The "big girl" in Jenny's household has a special relationship with Daddy. The "big boy" in Jimmy's household has a special relationship with Mommy. At this early stage of sex-role identification, the best way children can think of to get what they want is literally to take the place of the person they want to be like, to "stand in their shoes" (or sleep on their side of the bed).

Boys and girls in early childhood tend to choose same-sex parents as models to identify with. Yet the developmental paths that bring the two sexes to their respective identities differ in at least one respect. Although family configurations vary widely both within and among societies, the person who usually looms largest in the lives of both boys and girls during the first two years of life is their mother. She is likely to be the single greatest source of physical comfort, food, and attention for the very young child, whether a boy or a girl. She is, in Freud's terms, the "first love object," but while little girls soon begin to identify with their mothers, little boys do not.

As children enter their third year, their demonstrations of strong and obvious attachment to their mother diminish (see Chapter 6, p. 250). During this period of early childhood, the feeling of "wanting to be near" that dominates infancy is supplanted by "wanting to be like." (See Figure 10.1.)

For boys, becoming like their father requires that they become *different* from the person with whom they have had the closest relationship: their mother. Girls, on the other hand, seek to become *like* the person with whom they have had the closest relationship. Disagreements about the implications of this sex-linked difference in developmental tasks has sparked intense debate about the process by which children acquire the sex identification they will have as adults.

FIGURE 10.1 *In addition to wanting to be near their parents, young children want to be like them, especially the parent of the same sex.*

Identification through differentiation

By far the best-known account of identity formation is Sigmund Freud's (1921/1949, 1933/1964). Although many of Freud's specific hypotheses about development have not been substantiated, he remains an influential theorist because he was one of the few early psychologists to accord emotions a central role in development.

Freud believed that early in life, perhaps late in the first year, infants recognize that some objects in the external world are like themselves. He called this primitive recognition **primary identification.** The tendency of young infants to imitate other people, but not mechanical devices, is one example of primary identification (Meltzoff, 1995). During the third year of life comes **secondary identification,** which Freud defined as "the endeavor to mold a person's own ego after the fashion of one that has been taken as a model" (Freud, 1921/1949, p. 63). In other words, having noticed that a particular adult, or perhaps an older child, is somehow similar to themselves, children strive to take on his or her qualities. They "identify with" that person.

Primary identification In Freud's terms, the recognition by infants that some objects in the external world are like themselves.

Secondary identification In Freud's terms, the effort of a child to take on the qualities of a person with whom he or she identifies.

BOX 10.1

Sigmund Freud

Trained as a neurologist, Sigmund Freud (1856–1939) sought throughout his career to create a theory of human personality that would enable him to cure the patients who came to him with such symptoms as extreme fear, emotional trauma, and an inability to cope with everyday life. Although many of these symptoms appeared similar to neurological disorders, Freud found that he could best understand his patients' problems by tracing their symptoms back to traumatic, unresolved experiences in early childhood.

On the basis of his clinical data, Freud constructed a general theory of development that gave primacy to the manner in which children satisfy their basic drives—the drives that act to guarantee their survival. Survival of the individual child, however, is not sufficient for survival of the species. Influenced by Charles Darwin's theory of evolution, Freud reasoned that whatever their significance for individual adaptation, all biological drives have but a single goal: the survival and propagation of the species. Since reproduction, the necessary condition for the continuation of the species, is accomplished through sexual intercourse, it followed for Freud that, starting from the earliest days of life, all biological drives must ultimately serve the fundamental sex drive, on which the future of the species rests.

Although Freud believed the sexual nature of all gratification remains constant throughout life, the forms of that gratification change. Sexual gratification passes through an orderly series of stages defined in terms of the parts of the body that people use to satisfy their drives. Human beings strive to satisfy the drives that dominate the stage they are in at the moment. Freud held that the way children experience the conflicts they encounter in each of the early stages of development determines their later personality (1920/1955).

The first year of life is the *oral stage*, in which the

Sigmund Freud.

mouth is the primary source of pleasure. The mother's gratification of the baby's need to suck and gain nourishment is critically important.

In the second and third years of life, the *anal stage*, the child is preoccupied with gaining control of the smooth muscles involved in defecation.

Freud believed that during the fourth year children begin to focus their pleasure-seeking on the genital area. During this *phallic stage*, development for boys and girls diverges. Boys become aware that they have a penis. They develop sexual feelings toward their mothers and become jealous of their fathers. Girls become aware that they do not have a penis and begin to resent

---

Phallic stage In Freud's theory, the period around the fourth year when children begin to focus their pleasure seeking on the genital area.

By Freud's account, when Jimmy says that he wants to "marry Mama," he is playing out the universal male predicament of boys around the age of 3 or 4, the dilemma of the **phallic stage** of development (see Box 10.1). It is in this period, the time of secondary identification, that children begin to regard their own genitals as a major source of pleasure. Here's how Freud saw the conflict that these new pleasures and the new kind of identification evoke:

In a word, his early awakened masculinity seeks to take his father's place with [his mother]; his father has hitherto in any case been an envied model to the

their mothers for sending them out into the world "ill equipped." Freud believed that resolution of these conflicts produces the most basic form of sexual identification.

Between the ages of 6 and 7 years, the child enters the *latency stage*, which lasts until the beginning of puberty, 5 or 6 years later. During the latency stage sexual desires are suppressed and no new areas of bodily excitation emerge. Instead, sexual energy is channeled into the acquisition of technical skills that will be needed in adulthood for earning a living.

The physiological changes of puberty, the onset of sexual maturity, cause the repressed sexual urges to reappear in full force, marking the beginning of the *genital stage*. Now sexual urges are no longer directed toward the parents or repressed. This is the onset of adult sexuality, directed toward peers of the opposite sex for the ultimate purpose of reproduction.

Freud believed that from early childhood onward the personality is made up of three mental structures. The *id*, which is present at birth, is the main source of psychological energy. It is unconscious, energetic, and pleasure-seeking (1933/1964). The *ego* is the intermediary between the id and the social world. The ego emerges out of the id as the infant is forced by reality to cope with the fact that simply desiring something will not satisfy its drives. Action is necessary, but a form of action that accomplishes its purpose, that is productive rather than counterproductive. The work of the ego is seen clearly in the distinctive sense of self that children manifest around the age of 2, and it continues to develop throughout childhood and adolescence. The ego's primary task is self-preservation, which it accomplishes through voluntary movement, perception, logical thought, adaptation, and problem solving. It performs its tasks by bringing the instinctual demands of the id under control and deciding where, when, and how they are to be satisfied.

The *superego*, which begins to form during early childhood, becomes a major force in the personality during middle childhood. It represents the authority of the social group, embodied in the image of the father.

The three structures that make up human personality are rarely if ever in perfect equilibrium. Instead, dominance shifts as the superego and the id battle for control. The constant process of resolving these conflicts is the engine of developmental change, which Freud spoke of as *ego development*. The patterns of individual behavior that arise in this process constitute the personality.

Summarized in this brief fashion, Freud's theory may appear to be fanciful. His theory of infantile sexuality provoked outrage when he proposed it, and it remains controversial to this day. Freud's psychoanalytic method has been criticized as ineffective and unscientific. It must also be noted that all of Freud's claims about infancy and early childhood are based on his observations of disturbed adults. Freud is certainly vulnerable to criticism on both methodological and theoretical grounds, yet he remains one of the most influential forces in contemporary developmental theorizing.

Robert Emde (1992) points to several of Freud's enduring contributions to developmental psychology. First, Freud was among the most influential champions of the view that understanding of adult personality must rely on a developmental analysis. Thus he made a developmental approach the center of any theory of personality. Second, he emphasized the need to arrive at scientific generalization through intensive study of individual human beings. Third, he was among the first psychologists to point out and study the complex dynamics between unconscious motives and conscious understanding, between fantasy and reality. Finally, he insisted that a human being is a complex, dynamic creature who can be understood only by study of the person as a whole.

boy, owing to the physical strength he perceives in him and the authority with which he finds him clothed. His father now becomes a rival who stands in his way and whom he would like to get rid of. (1940/1964, p. 189)

These feelings cause Jimmy a lot of mental anguish. He is old enough to know that feelings like wanting your father to die are considered bad, and young enough to believe that his parents, who are powerful figures in his life, are always aware of what he is thinking. So he lives in fear of being punished and feels guilty about his bad thoughts.

Oedipus complex In Freudian terms, the fear, guilt, and conflict evoked by a little boy's desire to get rid of his father and take his place in his mother's affections.

Latency In Freudian theory, the stage that lasts from the age of 6 until puberty. During latency, sexual desires are suppressed and sexual energy is channeled into acquiring the technical skills that will be needed during adulthood.

Freud called this predicament the **Oedipus complex,** referring to the ancient Greek tragedy in which Oedipus, king of Thebes, unknowingly kills his father and marries his mother. Little boys do not, of course, literally repeat this tragedy. Rather, according to Freud, as they leave infancy and enter childhood, boys must mentally reorder their emotional attachments by distancing themselves from their mother and becoming closer to their father. In other words, they must differentiate themselves from their mother and affiliate with their father. This process is driven by complex social emotions such as guilt and envy.

According to Freud, male children achieve this differentiation in the transition between early childhood and middle childhood. He called the next stage of personality development the **latency stage** because it is a time when children's sexual desires are suppressed as a defense against the dangerous feelings they evoke and they display a great interest in learning the skills possessed by adults.

Identification through affiliation

Freud believed that female identification is also a defensive adaptation that propels girls into a latency stage, but the process takes place in a different way. According to Freud, the key event in the development of a girl's sexual identity is her discovery that she does not have a penis: the girl is "mortified by the comparison with boys' far superior equipment" (1933/1964, p. 126). She blames her mother for this "deficiency" and transfers her love to her father. Then she competes with her mother for her father's affection.

Now it's the girl's turn to feel guilty. She is afraid that her mother knows what she is thinking and that she will be punished by loss of her mother's love. She overcomes her fear and guilt by repressing her feelings for her father and identifying with her mother. As a result of this sequence, Freud said, a woman's psychological makeup never becomes as independent of its emotional wellsprings as does a man's because the object of her primary identification and the object of her secondary identification are the same person—her mother. He believed that this pattern of identity formation, in which women affiliate with their mothers, renders women "underdeveloped" versions of men because their attempts to differentiate themselves from their mothers were short-circuited. He concluded that women show less sense of justice than men, that they are less ready to submit to the great challenges of life, and that their judgments are more often colored by their emotions (1925/1961, pp. 257–258).

Not surprisingly, Freud's argument has been strongly attacked. Even people who support his general line of interpretation point out that his views depended heavily on the historical era in which he lived and were unduly influenced by its rigid sexual mores (Tyson & Tyson, 1990). In particular, Freud has been criticized for claiming that the lack of a penis makes girls feel inferior to boys, for assuming that a girl's sexual identification occurs only as a defense mechanism, and for concluding that women's path to identity renders them inferior to men.

Nancy Chodorow (1974), for example, acknowledges the difference in the two sexes' experience of early social interaction and their differing biological roles, but the conclusion she draws differs from Freud's. Chodorow considers identification a two-way process involving both the parent and the child. She argues that just as daughters identify with mothers, so mothers experience their daughters as like themselves. In contrast, "mothers experience their sons as a male opposite" (pp. 166–167). In defining themselves as masculine, boys reinforce their mothers' reactions to them and thereby facilitate the differentiation process. In defining themselves as feminine, daughters evoke further feelings of similarity in their mothers, fusing the process of attachment with the experience of sex-role identity. Because daughters do not have to go through the alienating experience of differentiating themselves from their mothers, they "emerge from this period with a basis for empathy built into their primary definition of self in a way that boys do not" (p. 167). Put differently, because girls' identity is based on affiliation with their mothers, girls have a built-in basis for understanding the needs of others.

In many respects Chodorow's formulation is similar to Freud's, but as Carol Gilligan (1982) points out, the difference in its emphasis is important. Freud assumed that because girls experience less differentiation from their mothers, they are less developed than boys the same age who have gone through the separation and reorientation to the father. Chodorow does not equate differentiation with development. By her account, the two paths to sexual identity result in two complementary developmental endpoints, each with its own strengths and weaknesses. Males achieve identity through separation; as a result, males see themselves as threatened by intimacy. Females, on the other hand, achieve identity through attachment. They see themselves as threatened by separation.

Whereas Chodorow reinterprets Freud's description of sex-role development, other developmental psychologists, even many who are generally supportive of Freud's ideas, believe that Freud's basic description of how sex roles are acquired is incorrect (Emde, 1992). First, they reject Freud's belief that female development is somehow secondary to male development. If any priority is to be given to one sex or the other, it is more likely to be the female. As we saw in Chapter 3 (p. 90), the sex organs and the brain of all human embryos initially follow a female path of development; these organs become male only if they are modified through the action of male hormones. Second, modern research indicates that children's sexual identities cannot be the *consequence* of resolving the Oedipus complex because aspects of identity formation can be discerned well before the age at which Freud assumed it to occur (Martin, 1993). Third, researchers now consider adults in the child's family, not the child, to be the primary carriers of sexual fantasies. Disturbances in identity formation currently are thought to result from psychological traumas caused by parents who are sexually abusive or seductive and not from children's inability to resolve infantile sexual desires (Cichetti & Carlson, 1989).

Freud's ideas, however, continue to influence popular thinking about the acquisition of sex roles. The challenge facing those who dispute his theories is to provide a better account of the processes at work.

Identification through observation and imitation

Freudian theories of identification assume that the process occurs indirectly and is driven by instinctual desires and strong emotions: children are caught in hidden conflicts between their fears and their desires. Identification is their way of resolving those conflicts.

Social-learning theorists have a very different perspective on how children adopt adult roles. They assume that the process of identification is not driven by inner conflict, but is simply a matter of observation and imitation. For example, as a 4-year-old, our son loved to run down the hallway and slide feet first into a pillow. He was not driven by desire for his mother, who disapproved strongly for fear that his sliding bothered the downstairs neighbors and out of certainty that he was wearing holes in his pants. Nor was his father's disapproval enough to stop him. Sasha was modeling his behavior on a baseball star who was being given prominence by the media at the time. He desired to be like that person, to be "in his shoes."

Social-learning theorists believe that behavior like Sasha's is acquired through *direct* observation and reinforcements (Bandura, 1969, 1986; Mischell, 1966). According to this view, children observe that male and female behavior differs. From this observation, children develop hypotheses about appropriate male and female behaviors. Further, children learn that adults reward boys and girls for different kinds of behavior, so they choose to engage in sex-appropriate behaviors that will lead to rewards (Perry & Bussey, 1984).

Bandura believed that the ability to learn from observation depends on several factors:

1. *Availability.* The behavior to be learned must be available in the child's environment, either directly or through a medium such as a book or television program.

2. *Attention.* Children cannot learn from observation unless they pay attention to the model (the mother, the father, or the fictional character) and perceive the significant features of the behavior in question. A child often needs to see a complex behavior more than once before determining its significant features. A boy who watches Daddy shave, for example, may at first see the application of shaving cream as the salient feature; he may have to watch his father shave several times before he realizes that using a razor is what signifies shaving.

3. *Memory.* Observation will have no lasting effect if children immediately forget what they observe. Bandura believes that when children have a name for modeled events, their observation becomes especially effective and memorable. Significantly, early childhood is the time when children are acquiring both language and knowledge of basic social categories—and their memory capacities are also increasing.

4. *Motor reproduction process.* Observation shows the child which behaviors to imitate. However, if a behavior is too complex (such as doing a backward flip off a diving board), the child will usually not try to perform it.

5. *Motivation.* For imitation and subsequent learning to occur, the observer must perceive some payoff. Children can become motivated to behave in certain ways by observing other people's experiences. When Ben, who wants to be thought well of by grownups, hears Daddy praise Lisa for taking her glass to the sink when she finishes her apple juice, he may be motivated to take his glass to the sink next time. If Daddy's good opinion means little to him, he probably will not be motivated to learn from this observation.

There is abundant evidence that parents not only provide models for children to imitate but also reward what they consider sex-appropriate behavior and punish cross-sex behavior. Beverly Fagot (1978a, 1978b), who observed children and their parents in their homes, found that many parents rewarded their daughters with smiles, attention, and praise for dressing up, dancing, playing with dolls, or simply following them around the house. By contrast, parents rewarded boys more than girls for playing with blocks. The same parents who criticized their girls for manipulating objects, running, jumping, and climbing criticized their boys for playing with dolls, asking for help, or volunteering to be helpful. Such findings support social-learning theorists' basic assumption that sex-appropriate behaviors are shaped by the distribution of rewards and punishments.

Despite many attractive features, social-learning theory has a serious problem in defining one of its central concepts: reward. To some degree, rewards, like beauty, are in the eye of the beholder. A 2-year-old boy and a 2-year-old girl may both be pleased when their grandparents give them a doll for good behavior. But 2 years later, while the girl may find another doll rewarding, the boy may turn away in disgust at "those girl things." Such incidents make it appear that children's conceptions about what is proper behavior for boys and girls shape their ideas of appropriate rewards for boys and girls. In short, the environment does not act directly on the child, it acts indirectly. Environmental effects are mediated through the child's prior understandings of the situation. Where do these prior conceptions come from?

Identification through cognition

The belief that a child's own conceptions are central to the formation of sexual identity is the cornerstone of the cognitive-developmental approach to sex-role acquisition proposed by Lawrence Kohlberg (1966). In contrast to the social-learning theorists, Kohlberg argues that "the child's sex-role concepts are the result of the child's active structuring of his own experience; they are not passive products of social training" (p. 85). In contrast to Freud, Kohlberg claimed that the "process of forming a constant sexual identity depends less on guilt and fear than on the general process of conceptual development."

Kohlberg believed that sex-role development goes through three stages:

1. *Basic sex-role identity.* By the time children are 3 years old, they are able to label themselves as boys or girls.
2. *Sex-role stability.* During early childhood, children begin to understand that sex roles are stable over time—boys grow up to be men and girls grow up to be women.
3. *Sex-role constancy.* Children's sex-role development is completed when they understand that their sex remains the same no matter what the situation. They know that even if they dress up as a member of the opposite sex for Halloween, they won't turn into a member of the opposite sex.

Whereas the social-learning theorists assume that the thought sequence of male children is "I want rewards, I am rewarded for doing boy things, therefore I want to be a boy," Kohlberg proposed the following sequence: "I am a boy; therefore I want to do boy things; therefore the opportunity to do boy things (and to gain approval for doing them) is rewarding" (1966, p. 89).

There is a good deal of evidence that the development of sex-role identity goes through the general sequence proposed by Kohlberg (Slaby & Frey, 1975; Frey & Ruble, 1992). Psychologists remain divided, however, about the processes that produce the sequence. Kohlberg himself believed that gender identity begins to guide thoughts and actions only after children attain sex-role constancy, because only then are they "categorically certain" that their gender identify is unchangeable (Kohlberg, 1966, p. 95).

Current data, however, do not support Kohlberg's strict adherence to gender constancy as the critical turning point in the development of sexual identity. For example, well before they attain gender constancy according to Kohlberg's criteria, children prefer the same toys as other members of their sex and imitate models of the same sex (Figure 10.2) (Bussey & Bandura, 1984, 1992; Carter & Levy, 1988).

A combined approach: Gender schema theory

To many psychologists it appears that an adequate explanation of how children's sexual identity develops must include features of both social learning and cognitive-developmental theories. One such approach is **gender schema theory.**

Gender schema theory is similar in some respects to Kohlberg's cognitive-developmental theory. Adherents of both approaches believe that the environment affects the child's understanding indirectly, through a schema, or cognitive structure. Once formed, this schema, or structure, guides the way information from the environment is selected and remembered. It also provides a model for action. A *gender* schema, then, can be considered a mental model containing information about males and females.

Gender schema theory A theory of how children's sexual identity develops that holds that the environment affects children indirectly through a schema which guides the way they select and remember information and provides a model for behavior.

July 12, 1995

Dear Santa Claus,

Here are the things that I forgot to put on the list last year, so here are the things I want most.

I want a vanity most and a pretend horse that is as big as grow-big Barbie, please. New ice skates with flowers on one side and hearts on the front and a basket for my tricycle and a new helmet so I'll like to ride my bike. I want a new heart key chain with a heart on it and a new jewelry box with diamonds and lace and any kind of sparkle stuff you can think of, with necklaces in it and rings and twist earrings. And also in the jewelry box, I want a ballerina that dances without turning a key and it comes alive like the Indian in the Cupboard. And I want a new Barbie wagon and a little coach for kids my size to go in and take rides and a coachman and two big pretend white stallions. And I want a plastic Prince Philip.

Santa Claus, I believe in you and I believe in magic too, even though some of the other kids don't. Please give me the courage to go downstairs by myself and be alone in the dark by myself, too.

Love,

Charlie

FIGURE 10.2 *This letter to Santa was dictated by a 5-year-old girl whose preferences seem to have been shaped by Barbie, the movies, and fairy-tale princesses.*

Gary Levy and Robin Fivush (1993) point out that children form gender schemas not only for objects and people but for familiar events as well. Accordingly, at the same time that they are discovering how to classify people and objects in terms of their gender, gender information is becoming a part of the scripts that boys and girls are expected to draw upon and apply in different circumstances (see Figure 10.3).

Gender schema theory departs from Kohlberg's cognitive-developmental theory in two ways:

1. Gender schema theorists believe that even in the earliest stages of gender development, children's developing schematic knowledge motivates and guides their gender-linked interests and behavior.
2. Gender schema theorists often use an information-processing approach to describe how the cognitive and learning elements of the system work together.

Carol Martin and Charles Halverson (1987) conceive gender schema theory in terms of the diagram in Figure 10.4. A little girl who can say that she is a girl and that her brother is a boy is presented with four objects to play with. Two of the objects are gender-neutral (an orange and an artichoke) and two are stereotypically male or female objects—a truck and a doll. When the girl is presented the doll, she must first decide if it is specifically relevant to her. She knows that "dolls are for girls" and that "I am a girl," so "dolls are relevant for me." As a result of this decision, write Martin and Halverson (1981, p. 1121), "she will approach the doll, explore it, ask questions about it, and play with it to obtain further information about it." This sequence is depicted by the thick blue line in the diagram.

When the little girl is presented with a truck, by contrast, she will think, "Trucks are for boys" and "I am a girl." This reasoning will lead her to decide that "trucks are not relevant for me." As a result, she will avoid the truck. She will not be interested in knowing anything else about the truck, except that it is for boys and not for her. Asked later about these toys, she will remember more about the doll than about the truck.

In their efforts to evaluate the merits of gender schema theory and its rivals, psychologists have tried to determine the precise relationships between children's increasingly complex understandings and their behaviors.

Sex-role behavior and sex-role knowledge

It is clear that long before boys and girls have any conceptual knowledge of sex roles, they behave differently. Male infants are more active than females (Eaton & Yu, 1989). This heightened activity level is believed to explain the fact that little boys engage in significantly more rough-and-tumble play than girls (Humphreys & Smith, 1987).

These gender differences are also visible when infants are placed together among toys and encouraged to interact. Carol Jacklin and Eleanor Maccoby (1978) found that when infant boys play together and get into a tug-of-war over a toy, for example, the tug-of-war is likely to become part of the game. But when a girl and boy get into the same kind of tug-of-war, the girl is likely to retreat and simply observe the boy playing. Maccoby is careful not to speculate on the source of these differences, restricting herself to the conclusion that even at 2 years of age, children "are already developing somewhat distinctive styles of play" (1980, p. 215). This basic result has been confirmed in several cultures (Leaper, 1994; Whiting & Edwards, 1988).

Not only do boys and girls play differently from an early age, they often prefer to play with different things. When children aged 1 to 3 years were observed in their own homes, researchers found that boys were more likely to play with trucks and cars while girls chose dolls and soft toys (Caldera, Huston, & O'Brien, 1989; O'Brien & Huston, 1985). The children spent more time playing with toys that fitted their sex-role stereotypes than with equally available toys that were not sex-typed. This finding suggests that the children had already developed sex-typed preferences.

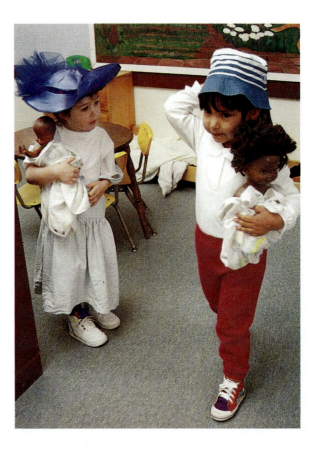

FIGURE 10.3 *Young children often adopt an extreme, stereotyped version of adult sex-role behavior in their dress-up play.*

FIGURE 10.4 *An example of an information-processing sequence associated with the process of gender schema formation. In this case, the child is a girl who has been offered a doll to play with. (Adapted from Martin & Halverson, 1981.)*

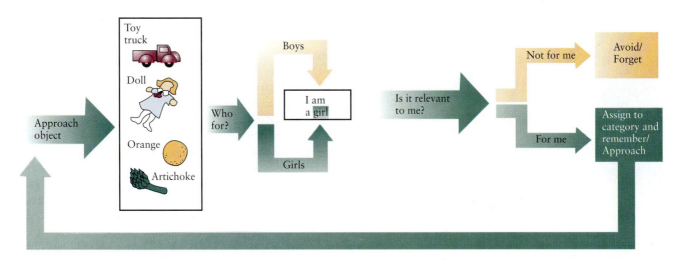

Between 2½ and 3 years, about the same time that children enter the earliest stage of gender schema formation, their talk shows the beginnings of a conceptual grasp of the more obvious attributes of sex roles in their culture. Judy Dunn, who observed young children in their homes, provided the following conversation between an older brother, a mother, and a 36-month-old girl. The children are arguing over who can play with a toy vacuum cleaner; it belongs to the girl, but the boy has just repaired it. As he plays with it, his sister tries to get it back:

Boy: *(to mother)* I wanted to do it because I fixed it up. And made it work.
Mother: *(to boy)* Well, you'll have to wait your turn.
Mother: *(to girl)* Are you going to let David have a turn?
Girl: I have to do it. Ladies do it. (Dunn, 1988, p. 57)

Even though they can say that ladies do certain things and men do others, young children's notions about sex roles are still fragmentary, as the following dialogue between two 3-year-olds in Vivian Paley's classroom reveals:

Mollie: Are you a sister, Margaret?
Margaret: I'm a brother's sister.
Mollie: They call a brother they sometimes call a boy.
Margaret: Brothers are boys, girls are girls.
Mollie: You're a girl, Margaret.
Margaret: So are you, Mollie. L-M-N-O. That spells "girl." (Paley, 1986, p. 35)

Beverly Fagot and her colleagues provided evidence that children's sex-role behaviors change after their gender identity schemas undergo changes (Fagot, Leinbach, & Hagen, 1986). These investigators asked children to identify the sex of boys, girls, men, and women in photographs. They found that children under 26 months of age were unlikely to label the pictures correctly, whereas those 36 months and older generally succeeded. Most important, once children of any age could correctly label the people in the photographs by sex, they were more likely to select children of their own sex to play with. This selectivity is evidence that their emerging gender schema is beginning to affect their behavior. Gender schema theory is also supported by the fact that girls who correctly labeled the photographs displayed less overt aggression than those who did not.

Such findings do not mean that the 3-year-olds had a deep understanding of the basis for the difference between boys and girls (see Box 10.2). Very few of the 2- and 3-year-old children who were able to label pictures of boys and girls could correctly identify which kinds of objects are usually associated with girls (such as flowers and butterflies) and which are usually associated with boys (such as fire engines and automobiles). Moreover, those children who *were* able to label pictures according to gender category did not always choose sex-stereotyped toys when they were allowed to play freely on their own (Fagot, Leinbach, & Hagen, 1986).

Once basic gender identity is achieved, however, both children's sex-role knowledge and their tendency to engage the world in sex-role-appropriate ways increase. One factor that promotes this development is children's increasing interest in the objects and activities that fit their gender identity schema. Mary Bradbard and her colleagues (1986) invited a group of children to explore several sets of objects, none clearly stereotyped according to gender: a burglar alarm, a shoe stretcher, and a number puzzle, for example. The children were given some information about each object and told to try to remember it, because they would be asked to come back

There is often very marked sex-role stereotyping in preschoolers' play.

BOX 10.2

How to Tell a Girl from a Boy

Sandra Bem (1989, p. 662) reports the kinds of difficulties that young children can encounter when their knowledge about the basis of sex-role categories is more (or less) sophisticated than that of their friends. Her young son, Jeremy, decided one day to wear barrettes to his nursery school. Another boy insisted repeatedly that he was a girl because "only girls wear barrettes." Although Jeremy argued that he was a boy because he had a penis and testicles, the other boy persisted in calling him a girl. Exasperated, Jeremy pulled down his pants to prove his sexual identity. The other boy was not impressed: "Everybody has a penis: only girls wear barrettes."

and try to recall it a week later. Although the objects were gender-neutral, the experimenters labeled one set of objects as "things for girls," another set as "things for boys and girls," and a third set as "things for boys." As gender schema theory would predict, the boys explored "boy things" more than "girl things" and the girls spent more time looking at "girl things." The results for the neutral "boy and girl" things fell between the two extremes. When the children were asked to remember all they could about each of the objects a week later, the same pattern held; their recall was better for the objects that fitted their own sexual identity.

The influence of children's developing sex-role identities on their behavior is confirmed by Vivian Paley's observations in her preschool classroom. She reports a marked increase in young children's sex-typed behavior and conceptions of sex roles in the years from 3 to 5.

> Domestic play looks remarkably alike for both sexes at age three. Costumes representing male and female roles are casually exchanged. Everyone cooks and eats pretend food together. Mother, father, and baby are the primary actors, but identities shift and participants seldom keep one another informed. . . . If asked, a boy will likely say he is father, but if he were to say mother, it would cause little concern. (Paley, 1984, p. x)

At the age of 4, boys become less comfortable playing in the doll corner, although they may sometimes do so, while girls, who sometimes adopt the role of Wonderwoman or Supergirl, prefer domestic play. In Paley's words, "the doll corner becomes the women's room" (p. xi). By the time the children are 5, the doll corner becomes a contested battleground, where girls struggle for domestic calm in the face of "boisterous" raids by boys in the guise of superheroes and bad guys. Now all the children seek to adhere to the cultural definition of what it means to be a boy or a girl, and the conflicts between bad guys and princesses are ever present in their play.

At this time there is no clear resolution of the theoretical disputes concerning children's acquisition of sex-role identity. No single theory appears to be able to encompass all of the data (see Table 10.1). The cognitive approaches that followed upon Kohlberg's work have established the importance of such signposts as the ability to label one's own sex and the realization that one's sex remains constant over time and while one is engaged in different kinds of activity. They do not, however, explain the fact that young children's toy preferences and behaviors become gender-appropriate even *before* they can label their own sex. It is difficult not to believe that, at least in part, the reason is that everyone around them is treating them either as little boys or little girls, and praising or criticizing them according to their adherence to the social expectations for their sex. That is, social learning

TABLE 10.1 Paths to Sex-Role Identity

Process	Influential Theorists	Hypotheses/Variations
Differentiation and integration	Freud	Boys differentiate from their mother and identify with their father through resolution of the Oedipus complex; girls identify with their mother after resolving their anger over the lack of a penis.
	Chodorow	A girl's path to identity formation is through affiliation providing a basis for development of intimacy. A boy's path is through differentiation; as a consequence boys tend to reject intimacy.
Observation and imitation	Bandura	Boys observe and imitate male behavior because they are rewarded for doing so, while girls are rewarded for female behavior. This ultimately produces observed gender differences.
Cognition	Kohlberg	Children first form a permanent schema of their gender and then define what is rewarding in terms of that schema.
Combined mechanisms	Gender schema theory (Martin & Halverson)	Sexual identity emerges from a combination of observation, imitation, and schema formation. The development of gender knowledge *both* depends on *and* is changed by the development of more sophisticated gender schemas.

is a part of the process from the very beginning. Nor can biological factors, such as sex differences in levels of activity, be ruled out. The challenge facing researchers who study gender and personality formation is to pinpoint the interplay between developing cognitive understandings and behavior in the overall process of social development (Bussey & Bandura, 1992; Martin, 1993).

A shortcoming shared by all of these approaches is the universally poor job they have done of accounting for the role of such emotions as guilt, fear, and envy in shaping sexual identity formation. As a consequence, many of the emotional phenomena that inspired the explanations of Freud and his followers remain to be incorporated into a comprehensive account of how sexual identities are formed.

How modifiable is the process of forming a sexual identity?

Uncertainties about the process of sexual identity make it difficult to know the extent to which adults can shape the final outcome of a child's sex-role development.

For somewhat different reasons, both Freudian and cognitive-developmental theorists believe that the child's sexual identification and subsequent sex-role behavior are unlikely to be affected by any but the most drastic changes in environmental circumstances. In Freud's famous phrase, "biology is destiny": males and females are biologically different forms of *Homo sapiens* that no cultural conditioning can change. In Kohlberg's version of the cognitive-developmental view, sexual identity grows out of universal forms of experience and laws of cognitive development; although cultural influence is not absent, it is not primary. Gender schema theorists accord more importance to environmental factors but still place great emphasis on universal mechanisms of information processing and schema formation. Finally, the social-learning view implies a greater role for culture in the shaping of sexual identification and behavior, thus suggesting that changes in the culture can produce significant changes in sex-role behavior. From this perspective, the essential requirement for changing behavior is a change in the models and rewards.

Just how flexible the definitions of "masculine" and "feminine" are remains a matter of dispute. A variety of studies show that individual adults may exert *some* influence on children's developing concepts of sex roles and associated behavior. Beverly Fagot and her colleagues (1986) reported that the mothers of children who learn early to label the people in pictures by sex were more likely to initiate play with their children by handing them a toy that fitted the stereotype for their sex. These mothers also expressed more traditional beliefs about sex roles. However, such influence often seems to be limited. Thomas Weisner and Jane Wilson-Mitchell (1990) studied families that sought to promote sex egalitarianism in their children to see how far they succeeded in modifying their children's sex-role stereotypes and behaviors. When they compared the sex-typed preferences for friends, toys, and modes of dress of children raised in such families with those of children whose families adhered to existing cultural norms, they found only scattered differences. A similar conclusion is suggested by Vivian Paley (1986), who devoted one school year to minimizing the development of sex-stereotyped play patterns among her preschoolers. Although she found that she could bring about changes so long as she remained directly in control of the children's actions, the children "reverted to type" as soon as she relaxed her controls.

This German 4-year-old is imitating his mother who is ironing, an activity that is stereotypically assigned to females. As he grows older, he will become increasingly less likely to imitate his mother.

Such results do not mean that sex-role acquisition is unaffected by social pressure. Comparisons of different cultural groups have shown that many attributes, including types of gestures, speech patterns, dress, activities, interests, and occupations, that are considered masculine in one society may be considered feminine in another (Rosaldo & Lamphere, 1974). Clearly such behaviors are learned from experience. In various countries and at various times in history, men have worn robes; in the United States, this form of dress is currently associated with femaleness. Such cases reveal that whatever the contribution of biology to the shaping of sex roles, at least part of our conception of sex roles and attitudes toward them depends on how sex is bound up with all of the customs and role categories present in our culture. In fact, the conclusion reached by Weisner and Wilson-Mitchell and by Paley is that the prevailing culture provides so many lessons in how to behave according to its sex-typed scripts that the family and preschool are not sufficiently powerful to make much of a difference.

ETHNIC AND RACIAL IDENTITY

In a world populated by many ethnic groups and races, children's developing sense of their own ethnic or racial identity is an important social issue. As a consequence, researchers have studied how children acquire the racial and ethnic categories prevalent in their community, identify their own race or ethnic group, and form stable attitudes toward their own and other groups (Cross, 1991; Harris, Blue, & Griffin, 1995; Spencer & Markstrom-Adams, 1990).

Several studies have demonstrated that by the time children are 4 years old, they can sort dolls and pictures into racial categories (Bigler & Liben, 1993; Hirschfeld, 1995). Controversy has centered on the way such categories influence the formation of ethnic stereotypes and the development of children's self-concepts.

Perhaps the most famous research on the development of ethnic and racial identity was carried out by Kenneth and Mamie Clark (1939, 1958), who asked American children of African and of European ancestry to choose between pairs of dolls. The children, who were 3 years old and older, were presented with pairs of dolls representing the two racial groups and asked to choose "which boy [doll] you would like to play with" or "which girl you don't like." The Clarks reported that most of the youngest children could distinguish between the categories of dolls. But more important, the African American children seemed to prefer the white dolls. These findings were used as evidence by the plaintiffs in the case of *Brown* v. *Board of Education of Topeka* (1954) in their argument that racial segregation in the schools leads to a negative sense of self among African American children. On the basis of this and other evidence, the U.S. Supreme Court ruled that racial segregation in the public schools is unconstitutional.

Since that time, the Clarks' empirical data about young children's conceptions of their racial and ethnic identity and their interpretation of the data have come under attack (Akbar, 1985; Spencer & Markstrom-Adams, 1990). One concern has been that the Clarks' original study did not produce statistically reliable results. Another concern is that too many psychologists jumped to the conclusion that African American children define themselves entirely in terms of the majority group, thereby denying the importance of their own families and communities in shaping their identities (Cross, 1991).

Studies conducted since the 1950s have confirmed the Clarks' findings (McAdoo, 1985; Spencer, 1988) and extended them to other groups, including Native Americans (Annis & Corenblum, 1987) and Bantu children in South Africa (Gregor & McPherson, 1966). Perhaps more important, however, these studies have also cast doubt on the notion that minority-group children acquire a generalized negative ethnic or racial self-concept. Ann Beuf (1977), for example, reports incident after incident in which Native American children who chose white dolls made evident their understanding of the economic and social circumstances that make their lives difficult in contrast to the lives of white people. In one study, 5-year-old Dom was given several dolls representing Caucasians and Native Americans (whose skins were represented as brown) to put into a toy classroom.

Dom: *(holding up a white doll)* The children's all here and now the teacher's coming in.

Interviewer: Is that the teacher?

Dom: Yeah.

Interviewer: *(holding up a brown doll)* Can she be the teacher?

Dom: No *way!* Her's just an *aide.* (Beuf, 1977, p. 80)

In Beuf's view, the children's choices were less a reflection of their self-concept than of their desire for the power and wealth of the white people with whom they had come in contact.

Other studies have shown that young children's expressed ethnic or racial preferences vary with the circumstances. Focusing on the interview situation itself, one study reports that Native American children show a greater preference for dolls representing their own group when they are tested in their native language (Annis & Corenblum, 1987). Harriette McAdoo (1985) reports that African American preschoolers' professed preference for white dolls has declined since the 1950s. She does not speculate on the reasons for this trend, but the end of racial segregation and several decades of political and cultural activism in the African American community are likely candidates. This conclusion is supported by Beuf's (1977) finding that young children of parents who were active in promoting Native American cultural awareness and social rights more often chose dolls representing Native Americans than children whose parents took little interest in Native American affairs.

Piaget: Why did he make a big blot?

Child: To be helpful.

Piaget: And why did the other make a little blot?

Child: Because he was always touching things. He made a little blot.

Piaget: Then which of them is the naughtiest?

Child: The one who made a big blot.

According to Piaget, as children enter middle childhood and begin increasingly to interact with their peers outside of situations directly controlled by adults, heteronomous morality gives way to a more **autonomous morality**. This new form of moral thinking is based on an understanding that rules are arbitrary agreements that can be challenged and even changed, if the people who are governed by them agree. (It will be discussed in Chapter 14, p. 574.)

INTERNALIZATION

Knowing the rules and knowing how to engage in proper behavior are both essential to the dual process of socialization and personality development. However, for socialization to be successful (that is, for the child to grow into an accepted member of the community) children must also *want* to be good; if they do not, they will be perceived as bad and treated accordingly.

Freud (1940/1964) describes the internalization of adult standards and its consequences for the development of self-control this way:

> [About the age of 5] a portion of the external world has, at least partially, been abandoned as an object and has instead, by identification, been taken into the ego and thus become an integral part of the internal world. This new psychical agency continues to carry on the functions which have hitherto been performed by the people [the abandoned objects] in the external world: it observes the ego, gives it orders, judges it and threatens it with punishments, exactly like the parents whose place it has taken. We call this agency the superego and are aware of it in its judicial functions as our conscience. (p. 205)

Internalization, then, is the process by which external culturally organized experience becomes transformed into interior psychological processes. **Conscience** is the new facet of the personality that emerges once children have internalized adult standards (Kochanska, Casey, & Fukumoto, 1995).

One sign that children are acquiring a conscience can be seen in such activities as toilet training, where young children know what they ought to do but are not always able to do it. When they put off going to the toilet because they are playing and then wet their pants, or when they climb up on the counter to help themselves to the cookies and knock over a dish, 3-year-olds know they have done something wrong and, as a consequence, feel guilty. In the view of Erik Erikson (see Box 10.3), early childhood is the time when children encounter, and must seek to resolve, the conflict between the need to take initiative and the negative feelings that arise when initiative leads to disapproval: "Conscience . . . forever divides the child within himself by establishing an inner voice of self-observation, self-guidance, and self-punishment" (1968b, p. 289).

Culture enters into the process of forming a conscience in two major ways. First, culture provides the specific roles, social rules, activities, and beliefs that are the *content* of conscience. Second, as Vygotsky (1978) has emphasized, culture sets the terms of the dialogue between the child and authority figures which becomes internalized as conscience.

Autonomous morality Morality based on the belief that rules are arbitrary agreements that can be changed if those governed by them agree.

Internalization The process by which children come to accept standards without being explicitly instructed or needing to wait for those in authority to respond.

Conscience The facet of the personality that emerges once children have internalized adult standards and know what is expected of them by those in authority.

BOX 10.3

Erik Erikson

Erik Erikson (1902–1994), a student of Freud's, combined a background in art, teaching, psychoanalysis, and anthropology in his approach to the process of development throughout the individual life span. Erikson is best known for adding an important social dimension to Freud's biological determinism.

Erikson's emphasis on the influence of society has expanded the scope of psychoanalysis, as has his addition of new methods for observing children, his cross-cultural comparisons, and his psychohistories. In his psychohistories he analyzed the psychological development of such well-known figures as Martin Luther and Mahatma Gandhi, basing his conclusions on their writings and on reports by people who knew them (Erikson, 1958, 1969).

Erikson built on many of Freud's basic ideas about development, including the importance of early childhood in the formation of personality, the existence of the three basic psychological structures (id, ego, and superego), and the existence of unconscious drives. He held that the main theme of life is the quest for identity, which he conceived of as the stable core of personality. *Identity* in Erikson's terms can be thought of as a relatively stable mental picture of the relation between the self and the social world in the various contexts of socialization. But unlike Freud, he saw identity formation as a lifelong process that goes through many stages. Each stage builds on, reconfigures, and elaborates on the stage from which it emerges. Throughout their lives people ask themselves "Who am I?" and at each stage of life they arrive at a different answer (Erikson, 1963, 1968b).

Whereas Freud's stages of development end in adolescence, Erikson proposed that human development passes through eight stages and continues throughout life. Freud's and Erikson's stages of development are outlined in the table on the facing page.

Each stage, Erikson believed, embodies a particular "main task" that the individual must accomplish in order to move on to the next stage of development. Erikson referred to these tasks as "crises" because they are the sources of conflict within the person experiencing them. Each person's sense of identity is formed in the resolution of these crises, which are periods of great vulnerability but also of heightened potential. Thus, whether a 2-year-old girl is successful in acquiring control over her desires and her body will determine whether she feels proud of herself and autonomous or ashamed and doubtful of her ability to

Erik Erikson.

control herself. At each stage, maturation opens up both new possibilities and increased social demands. A young girl's pleasure at being able to play the role of flower girl at an aunt's wedding, for example, is matched by the psychosocial demands from those around her that she stand still and follow directions without too much prompting.

Erikson believed that each crisis provides the individual with a "succession of potentialities," new ways of experiencing and interacting with the world. At the same time these potentialities are continuously being shaped by other individuals, who in turn are shaped by their culture and social institutions. The "widening circle" of significant individuals who interact with the developing person includes parents, siblings, peers, grandparents, aunts, uncles, teachers, teammates, mentors, colleagues, employers, employees, and grandchildren. The personality undergoes changes appropriate to the person's widening contacts with social institutions and cultural practices.

Each individual's life cycle unfolds in the context of a specific culture. While physical maturation writes the general timetable according to which a particular component of personality matures, culture provides the interpretive tools and the shape of social situations in which the crises and resolutions must be worked out.

Freud's Psychosexual Stages and Erikson's Psychosocial Stages Compared

Approximate Age	Freud (Psychosexual)	Erikson (Psychosocial)
First year	*Oral stage:* The mouth is the focus of pleasurable sensations as the baby sucks and bites.	*Trust vs. mistrust:* Infants learn to trust others to care for their basic needs or to mistrust them.
Second year	*Anal stage:* The anus is the focus of pleasurable sensations as the baby learns to control elimination.	*Autonomy vs. shame and doubt:* Children learn to exercise their will and to control themselves or they become uncertain and doubt that they can do things by themselves.
Third to sixth year	*Phallic stage:* Children develop sexual curiosity and obtain gratification when they masturbate. They have sexual fantasies about the parent of the opposite sex and feel guilt about their fantasies.	*Initiative vs. guilt:* Children learn to initiate their own activities, enjoy their accomplishments, and become purposeful. If they are not allowed to follow their own initiative, they feel guilty for their attempts to become independent.
Seventh year through puberty	*Latency:* Sexual urges are submerged. Children focus on mastery of skills valued by adults.	*Industry vs. inferiority:* Children learn to be competent and effective at activities valued by adults and peers or they feel inferior.
Adolescence	*Genital stage:* Adolescents have adult sexual desires, and they seek to satisfy them.	*Identity vs. role confusion:* Adolescents establish a sense of personal identity as part of their social group or they become confused about who they are and what they want to do in life.
Early adulthood		*Intimacy vs. isolation:* Young adults find an intimate life companion or they risk loneliness and isolation.
Middle age		*Generativity vs. stagnation:* Adults must be productive in their work and willing to raise a next generation or they risk stagnation.
Old age		*Integrity vs. despair:* People try to make sense of their prior experience and to assure themselves that their lives have been meaningful or they despair over their unachieved goals and ill-spent lives.

SELF-CONTROL

It is possible for children to know the kinds of behaviors that are expected of them and even to have internalized their society's standards, yet still fail to behave in a socially acceptable way. In addition to knowing what they should do, children must acquire the capacity to act in accordance with the expectations of their care-givers *even when they do not want to and are not being monitored*; this kind of compliance is called **self-control** (Kopp, 1987).

At the core of the development of all forms of self-control is the ability to inhibit one's initial impulses; in other words, to stop and think before acting. Eleanor Maccoby (1980) identifies four kinds of inhibition that children must eventually master:

1. *Inhibition of movement.* Studies have shown that it is easier for small children to start an action than to stop one already in progress (Luria, 1981). A child who does not know when or how to stop is likely to step on someone else's toes, both literally and figuratively. The same problem applies to verbal commands. In the follow-the-leader game "Simon says," for example, the leader's command is supposed to be obeyed only when it is preceded by the words "Simon says." Young children find it very difficult not to respond to the command whether they hear "Simon says" or not. Even first-graders continue to make errors in this game (Strommen, 1973).

2. *Inhibition of emotions.* During early childhood, children begin to gain control over the intensity of their emotions. Maccoby recounts an incident in which a mother found her 4-year-old with a cut on his hand that ordinarily would have led to tears. When she said to him, "Why, honey, you've hurt yourself! I didn't hear you crying," the youngster replied, "I didn't know you were home."

3. *Inhibition of conclusions.* Before the age of 6, children presented with a difficult problem tend to respond quickly, failing to recognize the difficulty of the task. A popular way to assess the ability to inhibit the impulse to jump to conclusions is to ask children to match a familiar figure with its mate in a set of confusing alternatives (Figure 10.5). Young children respond quickly to this task, and they perform poorly. As they grow older, children slow down to reflect on the problem and improve their performance (Figure 10.6) (Messer, 1976).

4. *Inhibition of choice.* An important element of adult self-control is the knowledge that it is often better to pass up short-term gratification for a larger long-term goal. Given a choice between eating a small candy bar immediately and a large candy bar the next day, kindergartners overwhelmingly take the small candy bar; not until they are about 12 years old do children choose to wait (Mischel, 1968).

An important consequence of the ability to inhibit immediate impulses is the ability to plan ahead. William Gardner and Barbara Rogoff (1990) asked young children to solve mazes such as the one shown in Figure 10.7. A glance at this maze will quickly reveal that a child who simply begins to trace a path from the nearest opening, without first scanning the maze to see what barriers lie ahead, is certain to fail. Instead of simply jumping in, successful problem-solvers first stop and look over the entire maze. Three-year-olds do not stop to consider what barriers lie ahead and do not solve such a maze. Although they are not always successful at solving the maze, 4- to 6-year-old children plan out their

Self-control The capacity to act in accordance with the expectations of those in authority even when one is not being monitored.

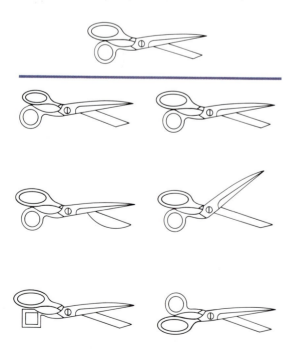

FIGURE 10.5 *An item from the Children's Matching Familiar Figures Test. Which of the six pairs of scissors at the bottom of the figure matches the model at the top? (Courtesy of Jerome Kagan.)*

routes in advance about half of the time, indicating the emergence of self-regulation.

Several researchers have studied the early development of children's compliance with adult norms (Kopp, 1987; Gralinski & Kopp, 1993; Kochanska & Aksan, 1995). Grazyna Kochanska and Nazan Aksan videotaped and analyzed the behavior of more than 100 children, 26 to 41 months old, interacting with their mothers in two situations. In the first, the mother and child were given a large number of attractive toys to play with in their own home. After the children played with the toys for a while, their mothers asked them to put them away.

Kochanska and Aksan noted three patterns in the children's responses to the request to put away the toys, from *committed compliance* (the children wholeheartedly embraced their mother's agenda) to outright defiance. Between these extremes was *situational compliance* (the children had to be prompted by their mothers to do as they were told). The children complied with their mothers' orders about 75 percent of the time and overtly disobeyed them only 10 percent of the time. Older children were generally more compliant than younger children, and girls were more compliant than boys. Committed compliance, however, was observed only half as frequently as situational compliance. The children clearly found it difficult to put away attractive toys with which they were still playing.

The second session took place in a laboratory arranged like a living room, where the children were also given toys to play with. The mothers were instructed to tell their children not to touch a set of especially attractive toys on a shelf. After the children had been playing for a while, the researchers asked each mother to come to an adjoining room to see if her child would continue to obey her even when she was not watching. At the end of the session, the mother returned and asked her child to put away the toys.

The injunction not to touch the forbidden toys turned out to be easier to obey than the command to put the toys away. At the end of the session, approximately 75 percent of the children complied with their mothers' request to put away the toys, just as they had done at home. And again as at home, most of their compliance was of the situational kind—the mothers had continually to remind the children to complete the cleanup. Not only did a somewhat larger proportion of the children continue to comply with their mothers' request not to touch the toys on the shelf, but most of them seemed to do so wholeheartedly. Some of the children were heard to talk to themselves, saying such things as "We don't touch these." Their use of the word "we" in such circumstances is a clear sign of identification with their mother and internalization of her request.

Another important finding was that the children who showed the highest level of compliance when asked to put the toys away were also the ones most likely to follow their mother's prohibitions even when she was absent. The self-control of these children in the absence of direct parental control suggests a direct link between compliance and internalization. Yet another important finding was that the quality of the children's compliance and level of internalization depended on the affective quality of the mother-child interactions during the observation sessions.

Studies such as Kochanska and Aksan's indicate a host of important changes between 2½ and 6 years of age. As children develop greater cognitive sophistication, including the ability to plan and to reason more systematically, they also develop a greater capacity for self-control. Thus they are increasingly able to comply with parental requests and cultural norms in the absence of overt control.

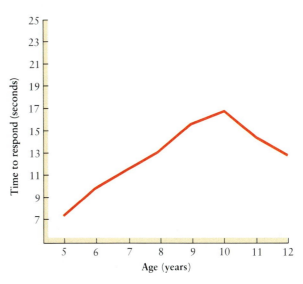

FIGURE 10.6 *Between the ages of 5 and 10, children become increasingly cautious in responding to the task of matching familiar figures. Children older than 10 respond more rapidly because the problems are relatively easy for them. (Adapted from Salkind & Nelson, 1980.)*

FIGURE 10.7 *A maze of the kind used by Gardner and Rogoff (1990) to assess children's ability to plan ahead. Trace the route from start to finish to get a feel for how planning is needed to avoid encountering a dead end.*

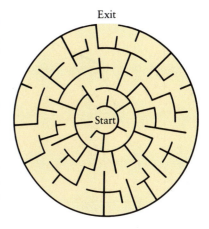

Aggression and Prosocial Behavior

Our discussion of internalization and compliance makes it clear that the development of conscience and self-control is more than an individual matter. These personal qualities take shape in social contexts. Thus far, however, the discussion has focused on situations in which toddlers are interacting with authority figures, usually their parents. An equally important aspect of social development in early childhood is the emerging ability of toddlers to behave themselves when they are interacting with other children their own age. In order to be accepted as members of their social group, children must learn to regulate their anger when their goals are thwarted and to subordinate their personal desires to the good of the group when the situation demands. Learning to control aggression and to help others are two of the most basic tasks of young children's social development.

As we saw in Chapter 4 (pp. 145–146), children begin to display the rudiments of both aggression and prosocial behavior shortly after birth. The earliest precursors of aggression are the angry cries and thrashing around of newborns whose rhythmic sucking has been interrupted. The first signs of prosocial behavior are manifested just as early, when newborns react to the cries of other babies by starting to cry themselves (Martin & Clark, 1987). It is widely believed that this "contagious crying" is the precursor of empathy, the sharing of another's feelings, which is the basis for helping and for a variety of other behaviors through which individual members contribute to the overall good of the group (Eisenberg, 1992; Radke-Yarrow, Zahn-Waxler, & Chapman, 1983).

THE DEVELOPMENT OF AGGRESSION

Aggression is difficult to define. At the core of its meaning is the idea of one person committing an action that hurts another—but not all of the ways a person can hurt another count as aggression. A teething baby who bites the mother's breast while nursing causes pain, as does a toddler who slips and falls on a friend, but these actions aren't usually considered aggressive. To be counted as aggressive, a behavior must be *intended* to harm someone (Parke & Slaby, 1983). Maccoby (1980) suggests that aggression begins only after children understand that they can be the cause of another person's distress and that they can get others to do what they want by causing them distress. This understanding seems to take shape very early, especially within the family.

As children mature, two forms of aggression enter their behavioral repertoire (Hartup, 1974). **Instrumental aggression** is directed at obtaining something desirable; for example, threatening or hitting another child to obtain a toy. **Hostile aggression,** sometimes called "person-oriented" aggression, is more specifically aimed at hurting another person, either for revenge or as a way of establishing dominance, which may gain the aggressor possessions in the long run.

Judy Dunn (1988), who observed young English children and their siblings in their homes, found that children between the ages of 1 and 2 showed a rapid increase in instrumental aggression toward their siblings (see Figure 10.8). Perhaps her most interesting finding is that until the age of about 18 months, teasing and physical aggression occur with equal frequency. But as children approach their second birthday, they are much more likely to tease their siblings than to hurt them physically. Teasing is a subtle form of aggression requiring the ability to understand the specific characteristics of another child. Dunn reports, for example, that 16- to 18-month-olds

Aggression An act in which someone intentionally hurts another.

Instrumental aggression Aggression committed in order to obtain a goal.

Hostile aggression An act aimed at hurting another, either for revenge or to establish dominance.

FIGURE 10.8 *Early in the second year of life, siblings are as likely to hurt each other physically as to tease each other; but as they approach their second birthday, teasing becomes much more frequent than physical aggression. (Adapted from Dunn, 1988.)*

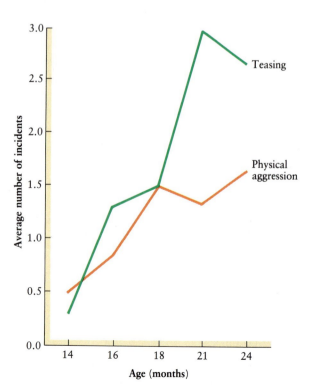

already know so well what will upset their siblings that they may leave a fight in order to go and destroy a sibling's cherished possessions.

One of the causes of the increased aggressiveness Dunn observed is that as children approach the age of 2 (just when a new and distinctive sense of self seems to emerge, as we saw in Chapter 6, p. 252), they begin to worry about "ownership rights." Taking toys then becomes a serious affair. To trace the early development of aggressive behavior, Wanda Bronson (1975) invited three or four 2-year-olds to a playroom as a group. She gave them toys to play with and she permitted their mothers to be present to give them a sense of security. As the children explored and played, Bronson watched for occasions when two children wanted the same toy.

She noted that often the 2-year-olds struggled over a toy that neither child had shown any interest in before and that neither cared about once the conflict ended. The fact of possession itself, as well as the possibility of "winning out," were new elements in their interactions. Reports from several cultures suggest that similar changes occur in all societies (Kagan, 1981; Ochs & Schieffelin, 1984; Raum, 1940/1967).

When Bronson observed older children, she identified changes between the ages of 3 and 6 that appeared to be interrelated. First, *physical* tussles over possessions decrease, while the amount of *verbal* aggression—threats, teasing, insults—continues to increase. Second, person-oriented or hostile aggression, makes its appearance—one child attempts to hurt another even though no possessions are at stake (Hartup, 1974).

Many studies of childhood aggression have reported that boys are more aggressive than girls in a wide variety of circumstances. They are more likely than girls to hit, push, hurl insults, and threaten to beat up other children (Crick & Grotpeter, 1995). This difference seems to emerge during the second and third years of life (Legault & Strayer, 1990; Fagot & Leinbach, 1989). As we see in Figure 10.9, which plots the frequency of overtly aggressive acts among young children, overt aggression by girls drops markedly as they approach their second birthday, while boys become slightly more likely to exhibit overt aggression at this time.

This does not mean that girls are not aggressive at all. Qualitative analysis of boys' and girls' social interactions has shown that both sexes engage in aggressive behavior, but the forms of their aggression differ (Crick & Grotpeter, 1995). Girls are more likely to harm another child's friendships or exclude that child from the group. This form of aggression, called **relational aggression,** can be heard in such statements as "We don't want to play with you," "I won't be your friend if you play with her," and "Emily says she doesn't like you anymore." As anyone who has been on the receiving end of such statements knows, they can hurt as much as a punch on the arm or a kick to the shin.

WHAT CAUSES AGGRESSION?

More people have died in wars during this century than in all earlier centuries combined. Every day our newspapers carry stories of people killing other people in search of money, to avenge a perceived wrong, or for no apparent reason at all. Among all the questions that can be asked about human social relations, none is more fraught with concern and uncertainty than the causes of aggression and the means of controlling it (see Box 10.4).

Explanations for the development of aggressive behavior focus on three contributing factors: the presence of aggression in the evolutionary precursors of our species, the ways societies reward aggressive behaviors, and the tendency of children to imitate the behavior of older role models.

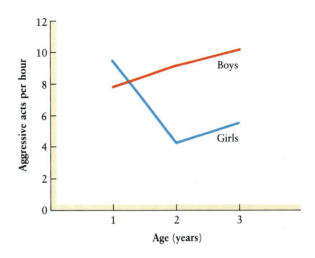

FIGURE 10.9 *As children in a nursery school approach their second birthday, acts of aggression decline significantly among girls but increase slightly among boys. (After Legault & Strayer, 1990.)*

Relational aggression Doing harm to another person's friendships or excluding them from a social group.

Teeth are a favorite weapon when preschoolers engage in person-oriented aggression.

The evolutionary argument

Noting that no group in the animal kingdom is free of aggression, many students of animal behavior have proposed that aggression is an important force in animal evolution (Lorenz, 1966). According to Darwin (1859/1958), a species gradually comes to assume the characteristics of its most successful individuals. Darwin defined as "successful" those individuals who manage to pass on their genetic characteristics to the next generation. Because each individual is, in some sense, competing with every other individual for the resources necessary for survival and reproduction, evolution would seem to favor competitive and selfish behaviors. Such animal behaviors as defense of a territory, which ensures that a mating pair will have access to food, have been interpreted as survival-oriented competition (Wilson, 1975). According to this interpretation of evolution, aggression is natural and necessary; its appearance automatically accompanies the biological maturation of the young.

Rewarding aggression

A second explanation, generally associated with the social-learning view, is that people learn to behave aggressively because they are often rewarded when they do so (Patterson, DeBaryshe, & Ramsey, 1989). G. R. Patterson and his colleagues (1967) spent many hours watching the aggressive behavior of nursery school children. Whenever they observed an incident of aggression, they noted who the aggressor was, who the victim was, and what the consequences were. They found that aggressive actions occurred several times an hour and that well over three-quarters of the aggressive acts they observed were followed by positive consequences for the aggressor: the victim either gave in or retreated. Each victory increased the probability that the aggressor would repeat the attack.

These researchers also found that parents of aggressive children often reinforce aggressive behaviors (Snyder & Patterson, 1986). In some cases, they provide positive reinforcement by paying more attention, laughing, or signaling approval when their children are aggressive. In other cases, children are successful at getting their parents to stop coercing them by becoming even more coercive themselves. Patterson and his colleagues (1989) remark that in coercive households aggressive behavior is functional because it makes it possible for the child to survive in punishing social circumstances.

Modeling

Social-learning theorists believe that in the act of punishing their children, parents may inadvertently teach them how to behave aggressively. One line of evidence for this mechanism comes from a famous series of experiments conducted by Albert Bandura and his co-workers (Bandura, Ross, & Ross, 1963; Bandura, 1965, 1973). They arranged for several groups of preschool children to watch as an adult yelled at a large, inflatable "Bobo" doll, hit it on the head with a mallet, threw it across the room, punched it, and otherwise abused it (see Figure 10.10). In some cases the children watched a normally dressed adult attacking the doll; in others, they saw a filmed version of the same events; in still another case, the model was costumed as a cartoon cat.

After the children watched the episodes of aggressive behavior, the experimenters arranged for them to engage in other activities for a while. Then they brought the children to a playroom containing a Bobo doll and invited them to play, in order to see if they would imitate the adult they had observed. As social-learning theory had led them to expect, the aggressive behavior of children who

BOX 10.4

Parental Beliefs about Causes of Aggression

The following anecdote comes from Ann McGillicuddy-DeLisi

My 4-year-old was practicing "pumping" himself on the swing and didn't want me distracting him, so I sat on a swing myself and watched the Frisbee game that two fathers were having around their 3-year-old sons. One of the little boys was getting all excited. He yelled "Hi-yahh!" and kicked karate-like at the other boy, who ran away laughing. One father threw the Frisbee to the karate kid, who spun around until he was dizzy and then released it. The fathers then went back to their Frisbee game and the two little boys ran around, making contact occasionally, falling and laughing, and then separating again.

The little kicker was getting more excited and more physical and aggressive with each interlude, however. I thought "That's the difference between mothers and fathers. A mother would see that this behavior is escalating and someone is bound to get hurt. She'd intervene now." I was wondering why mothers and fathers seem to react so differently to the same behavior from a child. The father called to the boy who had just connected a kick to his playmate's leg and threw the Frisbee again. The kid missed the Frisbee, ran to it and then ran off with it. The father caught him, wrestled playfully with him, took it away and resumed the steady back-and-forth toss with the other father.

Suddenly there were screams. The karate kid was sitting on his friend, swinging his little fists, pummeling his friend, and laughing while the other boy screamed. The father ran over, pulled the aggressor off the other child, and spanked him hard, three times. He shouted, "I told you never to hit! Now say you are sorry!" I was thinking, "Boy, this guy never heard of Bandura." I was about to go into a daydream concerning the beliefs parents hold about their children, and how this might affect their child-rearing strategies, when a neighbor on the swing next to me said, "It's really amazing, isn't it? I knew that kid was going to go wild." Aha . . . a kindred spirit who knew that this man behaved the way he did because he believed in negative feedback as a means of conveying messages regarding appropriate behavior, . . . giving little importance to the role of imitation, identification, and so forth in children's personal-social development. I said (in my best distancing voice), "Why do you think he did that?", looking for my neighbor's rationale for the father's behavior. My neighbor answered, "Boys are just so aggressive and physical. They can't help it."

She [the neighbor] watched exactly the same interactions as I did, and yet her construction of the event was different. I saw the child's activity level and physical aggressiveness as a learned behavior that continued to escalate as a result of the intermittent reinforcement of his father's attention following aggressive acts, as well as through imitation of the father's own physical aggressiveness with the boy. The neighbor saw the same behavior as an expression of an inborn trait that is characteristic of boys. She and I would have reacted to the child's behavior differently because we differed in our beliefs about the source to which the behavior was attributed. (1992, pp. 115–116)

---

had observed adult aggression was substantially higher than that of children in a control group who had watched nonaggressive interactions. Not only did the children who had been exposed to an aggressive model imitate specific forms of aggression, they also made up forms of their own, such as pretending to shoot the doll or spanking it. It made little difference whether the adult models were live or filmed, but the children were somewhat less likely to imitate the aggression of the cartoon character. The conclusion seems inescapable: once children are old enough to understand that they can get their way by harming others, they learn from adults both specific types of aggression and the general idea that acting aggressively may be acceptable (Figure 10.11).

A second line of evidence that children learn to behave aggressively by observing adults comes from cross-cultural research. Douglas Fry (1988) compared the levels of aggression of young children in two Zapotec Indian towns in central

FIGURE 10.10 *In the top row of photos, an adult behaves aggressively toward a Bobo doll. In the two lower rows, youngsters imitate her aggressive behavior.*

FIGURE 10.11 *Among the Dani of New Guinea, boys are socialized to be aggressive and warlike from an early age through organized practice sessions and many opportunities to observe admired older males in battle. These boys are watching men from their village fight against men from another village.*

Mexico. On the basis of anthropological reports, Fry chose one town that was notable for the degree to which violence was controlled and a second town that was notable for the fact that people often fought at public gatherings, husbands beat their wives, and adults punished children by beating them with sticks.

Fry and his wife established residences in both towns so that they could get to know the people and to establish enough rapport to be able to make their observations unobtrusively. They then collected several hours of observations of 12 children in each town as they played in their houses and around the neighborhood. When the researchers compared the aggressive acts of the children in the two towns, they found that those in the town with a reputation for violent behavior performed twice as many violent acts as the children in the other town.

Because these data were collected in naturally occurring interactions, it is not possible to assert that observational learning was the only factor in the levels of aggression displayed by the children. Fry reports, for example, that adults in the more violence-prone town sometimes directly encouraged their sons and daughters to be aggressive and did not always break up fights between their children. The differences he observed, however, could not plausibly be explained by reference to biological dispositions, so the results fit most comfortably within an environmental-learning or cultural-context approach. At the same time, it should not be overlooked that even in the town that discouraged aggression the children sometimes acted aggressively, a fact that is difficult to explain purely in terms of learning mechanisms.

Taken as a whole, the evidence concerning causes of aggression cautions us not to pit environmental and biological explanations of behavior against each other in a simplistic way. Such either/or thinking is not sufficient to explain a form of behavior as complex as aggression, which grows out of the interactions between deep-seated biological characteristics and culturally organized environmental influences. Nor can we understand aggression without looking at the various mechanisms that counteract it, since aggression is just one among several factors that regulate social behavior.

CONTROLLING HUMAN AGGRESSION

The same theories that attempt to explain aggression also point to mechanisms that are likely to be effective in controlling it. Three such mechanisms that have been extensively studied are the *evolution of hierarchical systems of control*, the use of *reward and punishment*, and *cognitive training*.

Evolutionary theories

While aggression is widespread among animal species, so are mechanisms that limit it. Changes in the aggressive behavior in litters of puppies, for example, follow a maturational timetable (James, 1951). At about 3 weeks, puppies begin to engage in rough-and-tumble play, mouthing and nipping one another. A week later the play has become rougher; the puppies growl and snarl when they bite, and the victims may yelp in pain. A few weeks later, if littermates are left together, their attacks become serious. Often the larger puppies concentrate their attacks on the runts of the litter, and among some breeds, the smallest animals will be killed if they are not removed. Once injurious attacks become really serious, however, a hierarchical social structure emerges, with some animals dominant and others subordinate. After such a **dominance hierarchy** is formed, the dominant puppy needs only to threaten in order to get its way; it has no need to attack. At this point, the frequency of fighting diminishes (Cairns, 1979). Throughout the animal kingdom one finds such hierarchies, which regulate interactions among members of the same species (see Figure 10.12).

Dominance hierarchy A hierarchical social structure in which some individuals are dominant and others subordinate to them; associated with the control of conflict.

The developmental history of aggression and its control among puppies is similar in some interesting ways to development in human children. F. F. Strayer and his colleagues (Strayer, 1980, 1991) observed a close connection between aggression and the formation of dominance hierarchies among 3- and 4-year-olds in a nursery school. They identified a specific pattern of hostile interactions among children: when one child would aggress, the other child would almost always submit by crying, running away, flinching, or seeking help from an adult. These dominance encounters led to an orderly pattern of social relationships within the group. One child who dominated another also dominated all children below that child in the dominance hierarchy of the group.

As dominance hierarchies in the nursery school take shape, they influence who fights with whom and under what circumstances. Once children know their position in such a hierarchy, they challenge only those whom it is safe for them to challenge. They leave others alone, thereby reducing the amount of aggression within the group.

The existence of similarities across species in these patterns of aggression and its control should not blind us to some important differences. The young of other species often must rely entirely on the dominance hierarchy, whereas human offspring are watched over by their parents and older siblings, who set limits to small children's initial expressions of aggression to keep them from harming others. These older members of the group also invoke rules about proper behavior which the children begin to internalize, thus helping to pave the way for self-control.

FIGURE 10.12 *Many species of animals have innate mechanisms for signaling defeat to allow the establishment of a social dominance hierarchy without bloodshed.*

Frustration and the catharsis myth

One of the most popular and persistent beliefs about aggression is that providing people with harmless ways to be aggressive will reduce their aggressive and hostile tendencies. This belief is based on the assumption that unless aggressive urges are "vented" in a safe way, they build up until they explode violently. Psychologists refer to this process of "blowing off steam" as **catharsis,** a general term for the release of fear, tension, or other intense negative emotions. According to this theory, the way to control aggression is to arrange for it to be vented before trouble erupts (Quanty, 1976).

Despite the popularity of this hypothesis in folk belief and clinical practice, there is little convincing evidence to support catharsis as a means of controlling aggression. In a rare experimental study of the efficacy of catharsis, Shahbaz Mallick and Boyd McCandless (1966) asked two groups of third-grade boys to build a house of blocks within a limited amount of time in order to win a cash prize. The activities of one group were interfered with by a boy who was a confederate of the experimenters. These children were angered because they lost the opportunity to win the prize. The other group was allowed to work uninterrupted. Some of the boys were then given the opportunity to shoot a play gun at animated targets of people and animals, or at a bull's-eye target. Others asked to solve arithmetic problems. Next, the boys were asked to administer uncomfortable shocks to the boy who had interrupted their building task (actually, no shocks were delivered to the boy). The number of "shocks" they gave was used as the measure of their aggression.

The experimenters found that frustration did appear to increase the children's aggression. The boys who had been interrupted administered more "shocks" than the other children. Contrary to the catharsis hypothesis, however, the opportunity to blow off steam did not reduce the boys' aggressive behavior; the boys who shot at targets delivered just as many "shocks" as the children who had solved arithmetic problems.

The ineffectiveness of catharsis contrasts sharply with a noncathartic treatment included as part of the experiment. Some of the boys were told that the child who had interrupted their building was "sleepy and upset." This sympathetic reinterpretation was sufficient to dissipate their anger. This finding underlines both the role of interpretation in human aggression and the specifically human possibilities for controlling aggression.

Punishment

Another common belief about aggressive behavior is that it can be eliminated if it is punished whenever it occurs. This tactic suppresses aggressive behavior under some circumstances, but often it does not. If punishment is used as a means of socialization, it is most likely to suppress aggressive behavior when the child identifies strongly with the person who does the punishing (Eron, Walder, & Lefkowitz, 1971) and when it is employed consistently. Used inconsistently, punishment is likely to provoke children to further aggression (Block, Block, & Morrison, 1981; Parke & Slaby, 1983).

Several studies have found that attempts to control children's behavior by means of physical punishment, or by threats to apply raw power, actually increase the children's aggressiveness (Dodge, 1994; Weiss et al., 1992). Gerald Patterson and his colleagues have observed how this effect is produced under natural conditions. They observed two groups of boys aged 3 to 13½ along with parents in their homes. The boys in the first group had been referred to the researchers by schools and clinics because of their excessively aggressive behavior. The second group of boys had not been referred for help. The investigators found that punitive child-rearing tactics were more frequent in the homes of the referred boys.

Catharsis The reduction of an urge, or an emotional release.

These tactics were often associated with a higher level of aggression in the family as a whole (Patterson, 1976, 1979, 1982). This approach depends on correlational data and does not isolate causal factors, but Patterson's findings indicate that such learning is likely to occur in the following way:

A younger brother hits his older sister in order to obtain a toy. His sister hits him back. He shouts at her and, while pulling on the toy, hits her again. She resists. Their mother comes running to see what is the matter. She shouts at them to stop, but they do not listen. Exasperated, she lashes out and slaps her son, and roughly shoves her daughter. The boy withdraws, breaking the cycle for the moment. If matters stopped here, this would be a simple case of punishment. But now the mother's behavior has been modified. Since the mother's slap successfully stopped the children's fighting, she is more likely to be aggressive at a later time. Since she models successful aggression, her children may also learn to interact in that way.

Patterson points out that in coercive interactions of this kind, children may inadvertently influence their parents to use physical punishment and make themselves still more aggressive as a result. He believes that coercive situations are counterproductive because they teach children both how to be aggressive and how to be the victim.

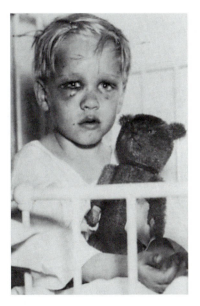

When a family adopts coercive child-rearing behaviors, the levels of violence may escalate to create patterns of serious abuse. Evidence suggests that such patterns may perpetuate themselves in the next generation when young parents who were abused as children abuse their own children. (Crowell, Evans, & O'Donnell, 1987).

Kenneth Dodge and his colleagues have conducted several studies on the mechanisms that link parental punishment to later aggression by their children (Dodge, 1994; Weiss et al., 1992; Strassberg et al., 1994). In one study they contacted 584 boys and girls at the time of their preregistration for kindergarten. In the spring before the children entered kindergarten a researcher went to the children's homes to interview their parents about the child's misbehavior. The researcher asked parents about their discipline practices—had they slapped, spanked, hit, or beaten their child? Had their child ever been physically harmed by an adult to the point of needing medical attention, or had the child ever been bruised? The researchers found that 12 percent of the children had been harmed.

In a separate interview, the children were shown short videos in which child actors carried out negative social actions, such as knocking over another child's building blocks or excluding another child from a group with which she wanted to play. In some cases, the video skits made it clear that these negative social acts were carried out on purpose. In other cases, the cause of the provocation was either clearly accidental or ambiguous. Immediately after seeing each video, the children were asked to recall what happened, how they might have behaved if they were in that situation, why they thought the children in the video behaved the way they did, and what they thought the probable outcome of the situation would be.

Six months later, after the children had entered kindergarten, each child was observed for twelve 5-minute periods on the playground and in the classroom by trained observers who did not know the child's punishment history. Within each time period, the observers recorded how many times the child engaged in one of three types of aggression:

1. *Instrumental aggression*, to obtain or retain a toy or another object.
2. *Reactive aggression*, in angry retaliation against another child for something done either by accident or on purpose.
3. *Bullying aggression*—an unprovoked attack on another child.

In addition, the child's teacher and peers were asked to rate the child's aggression.

In accord with the belief that physical punishment begets aggression, the data revealed that the children who had been physically harmed when they were disciplined were rated as more aggressive by both their peers and their teachers than the children who had not been harmed. These ratings were confirmed by the direct observations of the children in their classroom and on the playground.

Most often these children's aggression was *reactive*. Those who had been severely punished were three times more likely than other children to react to either real or imagined harm by lashing out against the other child with a shove, punch, or kick.

An interesting finding was that the children's aggression did not seem to be the *direct* result of learning to be aggressive, as learning theory suggests. Rather, the aggression seemed to be an *indirect* result of the way the children *interpreted* the events that provoked them. Children who had been severely punished appeared to misread the social events depicted in the videos. They were more likely than the other children to believe that accidental and ambiguous provocations were intentionally hostile, justifying an aggressive response.

Dodge and his colleagues believe that these results support the idea that children who are frequently and severely punished acquire chronic patterns of processing social information that incline them to interpret unpleasant interactions as hostile and directed at them. This pattern of interpretation tends to perpetuate itself, because when they respond in a hostile manner, they evoke hostility that falsely "confirms" their interpretation. The result is the development of chronic aggression.

Rewarding nonaggressive behaviors

Since young children sometimes become aggressive in order to gain attention, one strategy for reducing aggression has been to ignore it and to pay attention to children only when they are engaged in cooperative behavior.

One way for adults to employ this strategy is to step in between the children involved in an altercation and to pay attention only to the victim, ignoring the aggressor (Allen, Turner, & Everett, 1970). The adult may comfort the injured child, give the child something interesting to do, or suggest nonaggressive ways in which the victim might handle future attacks. Children are taught to say, for example, "No hitting" or "I'm playing with this now." When teachers are trained to use this selective-attention technique, aggression in their classroom declines significantly (Brown & Elliot, 1965).

In such selective-attention procedures the aggressor is not rewarded either by the adult's attention or by the victim's submission. The victim is taught how to deal with such attacks without becoming an aggressor, thus keeping the aggression from escalating. In addition, other children who may have observed the scene are shown that it is appropriate to be sympathetic to the victim of aggression and that nonviolent assertion in the face of aggression can be effective.

Cognitive training

Another way to control aggression is to use reason. Though it is sometimes difficult to hold a rational discussion with a 4-year-old who has just grabbed a toy away from a playmate, such discussions have been found to reduce aggression even at this early age.

Shoshana Zahavi and Steven Asher (1978) arranged for the teacher in a preschool program to take the most aggressive boys aside, one by one, and engage them in a 10-minute conversation aimed at teaching them that (1) aggression hurts another person and makes that person unhappy; (2) aggression does not solve problems, it only causes resentment in the other child; and (3) children can often resolve conflicts by sharing, taking turns, and playing together. The teacher taught each concept by asking the child leading questions and encouraging the desired response. After these conversations, the boys' aggressive behavior decreased dramatically and their positive behavior increased.

An important component of this technique was that the children were made aware of the feelings of those they aggressed against. All of the successful techniques for teaching children to control their aggression go beyond the mere suppression of aggressive impulses. Instead, children are encouraged to stop their direct attacks and to consider another way to behave.

THE DEVELOPMENT OF PROSOCIAL BEHAVIOR

When Charles Darwin published *The Origin of Species*, the public's understanding of evolution was dominated by such famous phrases as Herbert Spencer's "survival of the fittest" and Tennyson's "Nature, red in tooth and claw." Even Darwin said that Spencer's expression was "more accurate" than his own "natural selection" (1859/1958, chap. 3). Yet we recognize now that it presents an inaccurate, one-sided picture of evolution, for it takes no account of behaviors that offer no direct reward to the benefactor but do benefit the group. Such **prosocial behaviors**—altruism, cooperation, and helping—are common. When a preschooler offers her teddy bear to a friend who is crying because she scraped her knee or another brings candy to share with friends, they are engaging in prosocial behavior. Why do such behaviors occur and how do they develop?

> **Prosocial behaviors** Behaviors such as empathy, sharing, helping, and cooperation that benefit the group with no direct reward for the benefactor.

Evolutionary explanations

Prosocial behavior, like aggression, is not an exclusively human trait. Many animals, among them social insects, hunting dogs, and chimpanzees, exhibit behaviors that at least appear to reflect altruism. The challenge to theories of biological evolution is to show how these behaviors have evolved and how they apply to human beings.

Edward O. Wilson, a sociobiologist, has posed the problem and its solution as follows:

> . . . how can altruism, which by definition reduces personal fitness, possibly evolve by natural selection? The answer is kinship: if the genes causing the altruism are shared by two organisms because of common descent, and if the altruistic act by one organism increases the joint contribution of these genes to the next generation, the propensity to altruism will spread through the gene pool. This occurs even though the altruist makes less of a solitary contribution to the gene pool as the price of its altruistic act. (1975, pp. 3–4)

Wilson reasoned that if natural selection "looked for" altruism among lower animals, there must also be a direct genetic basis for altruism among human beings.

Wilson's argument set off a controversy that is still in progress. Among the animals Wilson studied, a biological explanation of altruism seems applicable because altruism is restricted to kin, individuals with genes very similar to one's own. But human beings extend altruism well beyond kin to total strangers. While it is possible to argue that altruism toward strangers may increase one's chance for survival because it may eventually be reciprocated (a modern version of the notion of casting one's bread upon the waters), to many investigators, the likelihood that such altruism will give one a selective advantage seems remote (Kitcher, 1985).

When we consider this aspect of social development, it is important to keep in mind that both antisocial and prosocial behaviors develop within a single integrated social system. Empathetic impulses develop in the context of social interactions, just as aggressive ones do; both are essential parts of a child's personality and both are subject to the process of socialization.

Empathy

The psychological state that corresponds to prosocial behavior in the way that anger corresponds to aggression is **empathy,** the sharing of another person's emotions and feelings. Empathy is widely believed to provide the essential foundations

> **Empathy** The sharing of another's emotional experience.

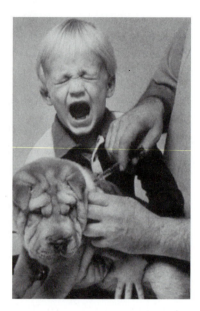

This child's empathy for his pet is so strong that one might think it was he, not the dog, that was being inoculated.

for prosocial behavior (Eisenberg, 1992; Hoffman, 1975, 1991). According to Martin Hoffman, a child can feel empathy for another person at any age. As children develop, however, their ability to empathize broadens and they become better able to interpret and respond appropriately to the distress of others.

Hoffman has proposed four stages in the development of empathy. The first stage occurs during the first year of life, even before a baby appears to be aware of the existence of others. As we noted earlier, babies as young as 2 days cry at the sound of another infant's cries (Martin & Clark, 1987). Nancy Eisenberg (1992) calls this phenomenon "emotional contagion." These early "sympathy cries" are akin to innate reflexes, since babies obviously can have no understanding of the feelings of others. Yet they respond as if they were having those feelings themselves.

As children gradually become aware of themselves as distinct individuals during the second year of life, their responses to others' distress change. Now when babies are confronted by someone who is distressed, they are capable of understanding that it is the other person who is upset, not they. This realization allows children to turn their attention from concern for their own comfort to comforting others. Since they have difficulty keeping other people's points of view in mind, however, some of their attempts to help may be inappropriate, such as giving a security blanket to a daddy who looks upset.

The third stage in the development of empathy, corresponding roughly to early childhood, is brought on by the child's increasing command of language and other symbols. Language allows children to empathize with people who are expressing their feelings more subtly, as well as with people who are not present. Information gained indirectly through stories, pictures, or television permits children to empathize with people whom they have never met.

The fourth stage in the development of empathy occurs sometime between the ages of 6 and 9. Children now appreciate not only that other people have feelings of their own but that these feelings occur within a larger set of experiences. Children at this stage begin to be concerned about the general conditions of others, their poverty, oppression, illness, or vulnerability, not just their momentary emotions. Since children in this age range are aware that there are classes of individuals, they are capable of empathizing with groups of people and thus can take a budding interest in political and social issues.

Note that Hoffman's theory of empathy is linked to Piaget's theory of cognitive development. Each new stage of empathy corresponds to a new stage of cognitive ability that allows children to understand themselves better in relation to others.

Perhaps because it is linked so closely to what children *understand*, Hoffman's explanation of the development of empathy tends to leave out how they *feel*. It is tacitly assumed that the more children understand, the more intensely they adopt the feelings of the person in distress. The catch, as Judy Dunn (1988) points out, is that children may understand perfectly well why another child is in distress and feel glad as a result.

Evidence on the development of prosocial behaviors

Several studies document the development of such prosocial behaviors as sharing, helping, caregiving, and showing compassion as early as the second year of life (see Figure 10.13). Carolyn Zahn-Waxler and Marion Radke-Yarrow (1982) studied the development of prosocial action over a 9-month period among three groups of children, who were 10, 15, and 20 months of age at the start of the observations. Their findings were based on mothers' reports of occasions when their children expressed sympathy for others.

In accord with Hoffman's theorizing, when confronted with someone else's distress, the youngest children responded by crying themselves. As the children grew older, crying decreased and was replaced by worried attention. In the period between 12 and 18 months of age, most children had progressed from diffuse emotional responses to active caregiving and comforting behavior in response to another's distress. The comforting behavior of 1½- and 2-year-olds was sometimes quite elaborate. Children this age did such things as try to put a Band-Aid on someone's cut or cover their resting mother with a blanket. They also began to express their concern verbally and to give suggestions about how to deal with the problem.

In another study, mothers report that their young children's helping, sharing, and comforting behaviors in response to another person's distress increase in frequency and variety during the second year of life (Zahn-Waxler et al., 1992). They express concern, attempt to comprehend the situation, and try to alleviate the other person's distress. These expressions of concern for others emerge about the same time children are able to recognize themselves in the mirror and begin to refer to themselves (see Chapter 6, p. 252). Zahn-Waxler and her colleagues speculate that these social cognitive capacities, as well as the emerging capacity to imagine and pretend, may help children to connect another's experience with their own and therefore understand it better.

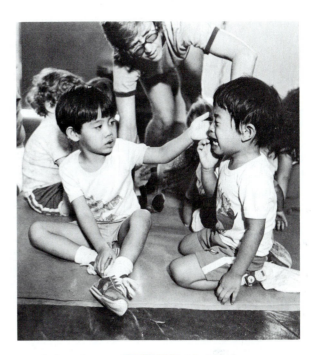

FIGURE 10.13 *One twin brother shows his sympathy for the other as he tries to comfort him.*

Dunn (1988) reports that the tendency of young children to comfort a sibling in distress increased between 15 and 36 months, as we would expect on the basis of the observations reported by Zahn-Waxler and her colleagues. But she found that such comforting occurred only when the child did not cause the sibling's distress in the first place. Moreover, children of all ages were sometimes observed to respond to a sibling's distress by laughing or seeking to make matters worse.

Such observations in the home make it clear that the way children respond to their siblings' distress depends to some degree on the nature of their prior relationship. Not surprisingly, the same can be said for their responses to their peers. In nursery school, 3- and 4-year-old children are more likely to respond prosocially to the distress of children with whom they have ongoing friendly relations than to others (Farver & Branstetter, 1994).

Other evidence about the development of prosocial behavior comes from observations of young children as they follow their parents through their daily rounds of activities, often trying or offering to help. Harriet Rheingold (1982) invited parents and their 18-, 24-, and 30-month-old children into a laboratory setting that simulated a home. The setting included several undone chores—a table to be set, scraps to be swept up, dusting to be done, a bed to be made, and laundry to be folded. The parents and other adults were instructed to do these chores without asking the children for help. Yet in a 25-minute session, all the 2-year-olds helped their mothers, and 18 of the 20 helped an unfamiliar woman. While they were helping, the children said things that indicated that they knew the goals of the tasks and were aware of themselves as working with others to achieve those goals. They worked spontaneously and eagerly, and went well beyond imitation in their helpfulness.

Promoting prosocial behavior

Adults are of course eager to encourage children's prosocial behavior. Research has identified many strategies that adults use in this endeavor. If we were to generalize from research on aggression, it would seem that one obvious tactic would be to reward children for prosocial behaviors. When Joan Grusec (1991) observed children in their homes, however, she found that rewards were not effective in increasing 4-year-olds' prosocial behavior. The 4-year-olds who were most inclined to act prosocially were those who received no recognition.

As a consequence of such findings, developmental psychologists suggest less direct means of promoting prosocial behavior. Two methods that recent research has shown to be effective are **explicit modeling,** in which adults behave in ways they desire the child to imitate, and **induction,** in which adults give explanations that appeal to children's pride, their desire to be grown up, and their concern for others (Eisenberg, 1992).

Most studies of explicit modeling contrast the behavior of two groups of children. In the "nonmodeling" group, no special arrangements are made for teachers to model prosocial behaviors such as helping and sharing. In the "modeling" group, teachers are told to stage periodic training sessions in which they demonstrate sharing and helping behaviors: they share candies among the children with explicit fairness, read stories about helping a child who is feeling sad or who is being teased, and so on. Such techniques have been found to increase prosocial behavior among children (Fukushima & Kato, 1976; Yarrow, Scott, & Waxler, 1973). Marion Yarrow and her colleagues also found that when the training was carried out in a nurturant, loving way, children showed the effects of the training as long as 2 weeks later—evidence that the effects of modeling can last for some time.

Studies of the efficacy of induction strategies, in which adults attempt to *reason* with children, have usually been carried out with older children. A study of early prosocial behaviors in the home found that younger children, too, performed more prosocial acts when their mothers attempted to induce prosocial behavior (Zahn-Waxler, Radke-Yarrow, & King, 1979). Reason by itself, however, was not the crucial factor; the most effective mothers combined reason with loving concern.

It is worth remembering that in real life, outside of research settings, the strategies to increase prosocial behavior do not occur in isolation from efforts to decrease aggressive behavior. Rather, a great variety of techniques are likely to be brought into play, interacting with and reinforcing one another to create overall patterns of socialization. (This patterning of socialization is discussed further in Chapter 11.)

Explicit modeling A method of increasing prosocial behavior in which adults behave in the ways they desire children to imitate.

Induction A method of increasing children's prosocial behavior through the use of explanations that appeal to their pride, concern for others, and their desire to be grown-up.

The Development and Regulation of Emotions

No discussion of personality and social development would be complete without a consideration of how children come to understand, regulate, and display the emotions that accompany and shape their relationships with others.

UNDERSTANDING THE EMOTIONS OF OTHERS

In order to behave properly in the many new social situations they encounter in early childhood, children must expand on their ability to understand the emotions of others. Recall that by the time they are 6 or 7 months old babies can read their mother's face as a guide to how they are expected to feel about a situation. By the time they are 2 years old, they know that other people feel bad when you hit them and that giving them something nice makes them feel good. At this early age, such statements as "Katie had tears. I pushed Katie out of the chair. I'm sorry" and "Daddy angry, I cry in crib" show that young children have some understanding of how others feel (Bretherton et al., 1986).

To track the development of children's ability to assess other people's emotions and the causes of those emotions, Richard Fabes and his colleagues (1991) observed a large number of 3- to 6-year-old children in a day-care center as they interacted over the course of the day. When the observers noted overt signs of emotion and its probable cause (Jennifer laughed because Suzy was tickling her), they approached one of the nearby children and asked, "How does Jennifer feel?" and "Why does Jennifer feel that way?" Even 3-year-olds could usually interpret other children's emotions correctly. By the time they were 5 or 6 years old, the children agreed with the adult's assessment of other children's emotional states and the events likely to have caused them more than 80 percent of the time.

Interview studies in which very young children are asked to interpret how other children would feel in hypothetical circumstances also indicate that they are able to assess other people's emotions remarkably well. Linda Michalson and Michael Lewis (1985) presented the pictures shown in Figure 10.14 to children between the ages of 2 and 5. Each picture was accompanied by a story about a little girl called Felicia. In Figure 10.14a, for example, Felicia is having a birthday party, and the children were asked to say how Felicia feels. At 2 years of age the children could say that Felicia was happy about the birthday party. But they could not say that Felicia was afraid when she was lost in the supermarket (Figure 10.14f) or sad when her dog ran away (Figure 10.14c). The older children were much better at assessing the emotions likely to be experienced in the more complicated situations.

FIGURE 10.14 *As children's understanding of social events increases, so does their ability to predict Felicia's feelings in these scenes.*

(a) Felicia has a birthday party

(b) Felicia's mother has pink hair

(c) Felicia's dog runs away

(d) Felicia's food tastes awful

(e) Her sister knocks over Felicia's tower of blocks

(f) Felicia gets lost in the supermarket

REGULATING ONE'S OWN EMOTIONS

Even very young babies are capable of modulating their emotions to some extent. They quiet themselves by sucking on their fingers, a pacifier, or the edge of a blanket, and by rocking themselves.

In the years from 2 to 6, children continue to use these strategies and develop others to help them keep their emotions under control (Bridges & Grolnik, 1995; Thompson, 1993). They avoid or reduce emotionally charged information by closing their eyes, turning away, and putting their hands over their ears. They use their budding language and cognitive skills to help them reinterpret events to create a more acceptable version of what is occurring ("I didn't want to play with her anyway; she's mean"), to reassure themselves ("Mommy said she'll be right back"), and to encourage themselves ("I'm a big girl; big girls can do it"). At the age of 3 our daughter Jenny displayed a useful strategy for regulating her emotions. Maurice Sendak's story *Where the Wild Things Are* frightened her, so she pushed the book out of reach behind the bookcase.

Situations in which young children are exposed to temptation provide another source of evidence about the development of the ability to regulate their emotions. Lisa Bridges and Wendey Grolnik (1995) arranged for 3½- to 4½-year-olds to visit a room in which they were shown an attractive toy but were told not to play with it. One of the strategies the children used to control themselves was to reorient their attention away from the tempting object to other toys and play with them in a focused way. This strategy, which the researchers called *active engagement*, was rarely used by children younger than 2 years. Between the ages of 2½ and 5, however, children become better able to distract themselves from temptation by playing on their own, and their use of active engagement increases accordingly.

LEARNING TO DISPLAY EMOTIONS APPROPRIATELY

The ability to display emotions in a socially appropriate way requires one to regulate the expression of whatever emotions one feels. Newborns display no such ability. They communicate their emotions directly, regardless of the circumstances. A 4-month-old who becomes upset during a wedding because he is hungry is not going to forgo crying until he is given a nipple to suck. From the earliest weeks of life, however, caretakers begin shaping babies' emotional expressions. A study of middle-class American mothers playing with their infants found that the mothers frequently reinforced their babies' positive emotional expressions by imitating them. The mothers rarely imitated expressions of negative emotion (Malatesta et al., 1986). Parents may also directly instruct their toddlers how to respond when they are attacked or feel angry at someone else (Miller & Sperry, 1987).

A young child who wants a puppy for Christmas and instead finds a videotape of the movie *101 Dalmatians* under the tree is unlikely to suppress her tears and pretend to be grateful; a somewhat older child will have the self-control to smile bravely and say thank you. Studies conducted in the United States indicate that American children cannot express an emotion that they do not feel until they are 3 years old, at least not when they are being interviewed rather formally by an adult (Lewis, Sullivan, & Vasen, 1987).

Even adults are not always able to control their displays of emotion. The expressions on the faces of the losers in a beauty pageant provide us with evidence that while the ability to control our displays of emotion increases with age, it is never perfectly achieved.

REGULATION OF EMOTIONS AND SOCIAL COMPETENCE

Two distinctive facts have emerged concerning the development and regulation of emotion in early childhood:

1. Each aspect of emotional development appears to go through a series of stages. In a variety of comparisons between 3-year-olds and 5-year-olds, the older children show a marked increase in the ability to read the emotional states of others, to control the emotions they feel, and to control the display of their own emotions.

2. Emotional development, social development, and cognitive development are intimately related. As we have seen, the emotions children experience always involve a cognitive assessment of ongoing goal-directed behavior. Cognition and emotion are closely intertwined psychological processes. Emotions shape the way we think and act, and our cognitive schemas shape the emotions we experience.

The term **socioemotional competence** denotes high levels of development in both the social and emotional spheres and the ability to deploy those resources effectively in real-life situations (Thompson, 1990). Carolyn Saarni (1990) proposed a set of 9 component skills that contribute to socioemotional competence, most of which are acquired in early childhood:

Socioemotional competence
High levels of development in the social and emotional spheres and the ability to deploy those resources in real circumstances.

1. Awareness of one's emotional state.
2. Ability to discern other people's emotions.
3. Ability to talk about emotion in the vocabulary typical for one's culture.
4. Capacity for empathetic involvement in others' emotions.
5. Realization that an inner emotional state may not correspond to outward expression.
6. Awareness of cultural display rules.
7. Ability to take account of unique personal information about others when one infers their emotional states.
8. Ability to understand that one's emotional-expressive behavior may affect another person and to take that fact into account in one's presentation of self.
9. Capacity to use self-regulation strategies to modify emotional states.

It should come as no surprise that preschool children who display the characteristics of socioemotional competence are better liked by both their peers and their teachers (Eisenberg et al., 1993). One reason may be that it is easier for other children to get along with them. During free play in a day-care center, socially competent 4½-year-olds were observed to respond to anger-inducing provocations by effectively regulating their emotions in order to minimize the damage to their social relationships (Fabes & Eisenberg, 1992).

In recent years psychologists have developed methods for categorizing and comparing children in terms of their level of socioemotional competence and for investigating the factors that promote it. These methods have led to the creation of experimental social programs for improving the competence of children who are having difficulty learning to behave in a socially acceptable manner.

Taking One's Place in the Social Group as a Distinct Individual

The kindergartners in Vivian Paley's classroom are discussing the fate of Tico, a wingless bird who is cared for by his black-winged friends. Their discussion reveals considerable sophistication about the dilemma described by Freud at the beginning of this chapter: How can a person achieve happiness as an individual and at the same time win acceptance as a member of the group?

In the story, the wishingbird visits Tico one night and grants him a wish. Tico wishes for golden wings. When his friends see his golden wings in the morning, they are angry. They abandon him because he wants to be better than they. Tico is upset by his rejection and wants to gain readmission to the group. He discovers that he can exchange his golden feathers for black ones by performing good deeds. When at last he has replaced all the golden feathers with black ones, he is granted readmission by the flock, who comment, "Now you are just like us" (Leoni, 1964).

Teacher: I don't think it's fair that Tico has to give up his golden wings.

Lisa: It is fair. See, he was nicer when he didn't have any wings. They didn't like him when he had gold.

Wally: He thinks he's better if he has golden wings.

Eddie: He is better.

Jill: But he's not supposed to be better. The wishingbird was wrong to give him those wings.

Deana: She has to give him his wish. He's the one who shouldn't have asked for golden wings.

Wally: He could put black wings on top of the golden wings and try to trick them.

Deana: They'd sneak up and see the gold. He should just give every bird one golden feather and keep one for himself.

Teacher: Why can't he decide for himself what kind of wings he wants?

Wally: He has to decide to have black wings. (Paley, 1981, pp. 25–26)

This conversation shows that the children understand that by wishing for golden wings, Tico has wished himself a vision of perfection. Each child has done the same thing countless times: "I'm the beautiful princess"; "I'm Superman; I'll save the world." For the blissful, magic moments when the world of play holds sway, perfection is attainable, even by a lowly bird or a preschool child. Wally and his friends also appreciate the dilemmas of perfection. In their eyes, Tico not only thinks he is better, he *is* better—but he is not supposed to be. Try as they may to conceive of a way for Tico to retain his prized possessions, the children realize that conformity is unavoidable. Wally's summary is difficult to improve upon: Tico has to choose to conform.

The children discussing the fate of Tico and his community of birds reveal more than an appreciation of the heavy hand of society as it is experienced by children everywhere. They are also able to see that individuals have a responsibility for regulating social relations. Since wishingbirds grant wishes, it is not the wishingbird's fault that Tico wished himself better than the others. Tico should have known better. He should have been able to control himself and make a reasonable wish.

This story returns us to the theme with which this chapter began—that social development and personality development are two aspects of a single process. When children engage in acts of sharing and comforting, they reveal their ability to know another person's mental state. At the same time, they are displaying their own ways of thinking and feeling—in other words, their personalities. As part of the process of personality formation within the social group, individual strengths and weaknesses, interests, and opportunities will lead to increasing differentiation between the self and others.

As they approach their sixth birthday, children have by no means completed the socialization process; but they have come a long way from infancy, when their sense of themselves and the social world was general and undifferentiated (Eder, 1989).

Before we turn in Part Four to the wide range of new roles and rules that children encounter in middle childhood and the corresponding changes that take place in their sense of themselves, we need to round out the discussion of early childhood by investigating the range of contexts and social influences that make up the world of the young child. As we shall see in Chapter 11, even young children are exposed to a great variety of social influences and cultural prescriptions. It is in the course of dealing with the variety of concrete circumstances that structure their everyday experiences that children create the synthesis of cognition and emotion called personality and acquire their social identities.

SUMMARY

Acquiring a Social and Personal Identity

- Social development is the two-sided process in which children become integrated into their community while differentiating themselves as distinct individuals.

- One side of social development is socialization, the process by which children acquire the standards, values, and knowledge of their society.

- The other side of social development is personality formation, the process by which children come to have distinctive and consistent ways of feeling and behaving in a wide variety of situations.

- Identification, the process of molding one's behavior to that of a person one admires, contributes to children's distinctive sense of themselves at the same time that it places each of them in a salient social category, such as male or female.

- Competing theories of identification emphasize four mechanisms:
  1. Identification as a process of differentiating oneself from others.
  2. Identification as a process of affiliation—empathy with and attachment to others.
  3. Identification resulting from observation and imitation of powerful others, and from the rewards gained by appropriate behavior.
  4. Identification resulting from the cognitive capacity to recognize oneself as a member of a social category and the desire to be like other members of that category.

- Sex-role identity goes through a sequence of cognitive milestones that begin with the early ability to identify oneself as a boy or girl, followed by understanding that one's identity does not change over time, and finally a full understanding that one's sex is a permanent characteristic.

- Current evidence indicates that both conceptual change and learning of appropriate behaviors contribute to the development of sex identity, but the precise relationship between these processes is not well understood.

- Children acquire a sense of ethnic identity around the age of 4. Their attitudes toward their race or ethnicity depend heavily on how their social group is perceived in the society as a whole.

Developing the Ability to Regulate Oneself

- Children's initial moral beliefs come from the social standards displayed by adult models with whom they identify.

- Internalization of social roles and standards of behavior provides children with a framework for controlling their own impulses.

- Self-control requires persistence and inhibition of action. Children develop four kinds of inhibition:
  1. Inhibition of motion.
  2. Inhibition of emotion.
  3. Inhibition of conclusions.
  4. Inhibition of choice.
- Early forms of self-control are situational. They require adult supervision. As children internalize adult standards, situational compliance is augmented by committed compliance.

Aggression and Prosocial Behavior

- Children display the rudiments of both aggression and altruism shortly after birth.
- Aggression in the sense of an act that is intended to hurt others does not appear until the second year of life.
- Aggression is observed among animals of many species. From an evolutionary perspective, aggression is seen as a natural consequence of competition for resources.
- Instrumental aggression is directed at obtaining desirable resources. Hostile aggression may also gain resources, but it is more directly aimed at causing pain to another person.
- Boys' and girls' aggressive behaviors often differ. Whereas boys tend to use instrumental aggression to cause physical pain, girls more often use relational aggression to create psychological pain.
- Aggressive behavior may increase among children either because they are directly rewarded for it or because children imitate the aggressive behavior of others.
- The development of aggression is accompanied by the development of social dominance hierarchies, which control aggression.
- Among humans, additional effective means for controlling aggression are rewards for nonaggressive behaviors and cognitive training that induces children to consider the negative consequences of aggressive behaviors.
- Physical punishment is generally an ineffective means of suppressing aggression because it often engenders more aggression.
- Our species is characterized as much by prosocial behavior as by aggression. Empathy—the ability to feel what another person is feeling—may be the basis for the development of prosocial behavior.
- The development of the ability to hurt other people is paralleled by and interacts with the ability to help others. Helping, sharing, and other prosocial behaviors can be observed as early as the first 3 years of life.

The Development and Regulation of Emotions

- Emotional development in early childhood requires children to understand their own and other people's emotions, to regulate their own emotions, and to control the way they display emotions.
- Children who quickly master these aspects of emotional regulation are more likely to get along well with others and to be considered socially competent.
- In acquiring a distinctive way of interacting with other people, both prosocially and antisocially, children acquire a sense of themselves and their own personalities.

KEY TERMS

aggression,   p. 406

autonomous morality,
   p. 401

catharsis,   p. 412

conscience,   p. 401

dominance hierarchy,
   p. 411

empathy,   p. 415

explicit modeling,
   p. 418

gender schema theory,
   p. 391

heteronomous morality,
   p. 400

hostile aggression,
   p. 406

identification,   p. 383

induction,   p. 418

instrumental aggression,
   p. 406

internalization,   p. 401

latency stage,   p. 388

Oedipus complex,
   p. 388

personality,   p. 382

phallic stage,   p. 386

primary identification,
   p. 385

prosocial behaviors,
   p. 415

relational aggression,
   p. 407

secondary identification,
   p. 385

self-concept,   p. 382

self-control,   p. 404

socialization,   p. 382

social development,
   p. 382

social role,   p. 382

socioemotional
   competence,   p. 421

THOUGHT QUESTIONS

1. James Mark Baldwin said that as children develop, they are "really in part someone else," even in their own thoughts of themselves. What does this characteristic of mental life imply for the development of personality?

2. In Kochanska and Aksan's study of compliance (p. 405), the children found it easier to adhere to the "don't touch" instructions than to the "clean up" instructions. Propose an explanation for this finding and design a study to test your ideas.

3. What basic cognitive abilities must children acquire before they will be able to tease a sibling deliberately?

4. Give examples of how 5-year-olds might demonstrate each of the components of socioemotional competence proposed by Saarni (p. 421).

5. Reread the children's discussion of Tico on page 422. How does it relate to Freud's statement about the process of individual development at the opening of the chapter?

The Contexts of Early Childhood Development

> "A new level of organization is in fact nothing more than a new relevant context."
>
> —*C. H. Waddington,*
> Organizers and Genes

Thus far we have treated the settings that children inhabit during early childhood primarily as background to our discussions of their cognitive, physical, and social development. In this chapter we alter our focus to highlight the ways in which the contexts of children's lives and the activities they engage in are part and parcel of their development.

As we shift our attention to the contexts of early childhood, it is helpful to refer once again to Figure 1.5 (p. 20), Urie Bronfenbrenner's scheme that represents the environments of development as a "nested arrangement of concentric structures, each contained within the next" (Bronfenbrenner, 1979, p. 22). The innermost circles in this diagram are the specific events and contexts of children's direct experience: eating dinner, playing on the jungle gym, having a drawing lesson, and so forth. These events take place in such community settings as the home, the church, the local park, and the preschool. On a somewhat more global level are settings and social institutions such as the parents' workplaces, government offices, and the mass media, which influence children either directly, as television does, or indirectly, through their impact on parents and other family members.

Each level of context in Bronfenbrenner's model is reciprocally related to its neighbors. Children are influenced by parents; they also influence their parents. The parents' behavior at home is influenced by the experiences they have at work and in their communities, while the society of which the community is a part both shapes and is shaped by its members.

The context that most directly influences young children's development is the family. Parents influence their children's development in two complementary ways. First, they shape their children's cognitive skills and personalities by the tasks they pose, the ways they respond to particular behaviors, the values they promote, and the patterns of behavior they model. But that is only part of the story. As the anthropologist Beatrice Whiting (1980) has observed, parents also influence their children's development by selecting many of the other contexts to which children are exposed, including the places they visit, the television programs they watch, and the other children they play with.

From the very beginning, of course, children are also shaping their parents' behavior: each child's distinctive emotional responsivity, appearance, verbal ability, and other characteristics all play their roles in the two-way process of social development (Goodnow, 1990; Wozniak, 1993).

We begin this discussion by summarizing some of the universal features of families as contexts for development. Then we compare family configurations and personality development in two markedly different societies. This cross-national comparison is followed by an examination of the major varieties of family configuration and child-rearing patterns in the United States. Next, we examine the influence of books and television—two communications media that link the family to the larger society. Finally, we discuss the socializing effects of two social institutions designed specifically to serve young children and their families in modern industrialized societies: day care, which substitutes for parental care at home; and preschools, which go beyond "minding" children to fostering their cognitive and social development.

The Family as a Context for Development

On the basis of his study of child-rearing practices in diverse cultures, the anthropologist Robert Le Vine (1988) has proposed that three major goals are shared by parents the world over:

1. *The survival goal:* to ensure that their children survive by providing for their health and safety.

Parents cannot directly control how successfully their children perform or the enthusiasm with which they enter new forms of activity.

2. *The economic goal:* to ensure that their children acquire the skills and other resources needed to be economically productive adults.

3. *The cultural goal:* to ensure that their children acquire the basic cultural values of the group.

These goals form a hierarchy. To begin with, parents' overriding concern is for their children's physical survival. It is not until the children's safety and health appear secure that they direct their child-rearing practices toward other goals. Although these basic goals are universal, the ways in which parents go about achieving them vary with the local circumstances.

It is important to remember that the social unit called a "family" varies considerably from one society to another around the world. During most of the twentieth century, the conventional image of a family in the United States has been a household with a husband, a wife, and two or three children (see Box 11.1). Anthropologists refer to this kind of family as the **nuclear family** (Murdock, 1949). Although such families can be found in most communities in the United States, they are by no means representative of the full range of family configurations that can be found here. In many households children are raised by a single parent (usually the mother) or by several adults in an extended family. When we consider variations in family configuration on a world scale, the nuclear family that is the American ideal is in a minority. *Polygyny*, in which one man is married simultaneously to more than one woman, is the dominant pattern (Stephens, 1963).

Nuclear family A family consisting of a husband and wife and their children.

A CROSS-CULTURAL STUDY OF FAMILY ORGANIZATION AND SOCIAL DEVELOPMENT

In a classic study, Beatrice and John Whiting (1975) organized teams of anthropologists to assess the role of culture in shaping children's personalities. The Whiting teams observed child rearing in six locales in the United States, India, Kenya, and Mexico. The families lived in societies that differed in social complexity, dominant economic activities, cultural belief systems, and domestic living arrangements.

A comparison of two of the groups studied by these teams, the Gusii of Nyansongo, Kenya, and Americans in a small New England town, shows how differences in life circumstances produce variations in basic economic activities and

BOX 11.1

Siblings and Socialization

Most theories of socialization concentrate on relations between one child and two parents when they address such questions as the development of sex-role identity, aggression, and prosocial behavior. But actual families and actual socialization are more complex. Single-child families are a distinct minority the world over. In North America, most families include at least two children.

Studies show that although parents are of primary importance in children's socialization, siblings also play significant roles in it (Dunn, 1988). The roles of siblings are most obvious in agricultural societies, where much of the child care is performed by older siblings or by the mother's younger sisters. It is through these child caretakers, who are sometimes no more than 4 years older than their charges, that many of the behaviors and beliefs of the social group are passed on (Zukow-Goldring, 1995). In industrialized societies, where families tend to have fewer children and those children attend school from the age of 5, boys and girls have less responsibility for their younger siblings. Nevertheless, siblings still influence one another's socialization in important ways.

Judy Dunn and Carol Kendrick (1979) studied the influence of siblings by observing 40 lower-middle-class English families in their homes from late in the mother's second pregnancy through the infancy of the second child. They visited the family again when the first child was 6 years old. Their observations, supplemented by reports from the mothers, reveal that siblings are prominent persons in one another's lives.

The birth of a second child is often upsetting for firstborns, especially if they are less than 4 years old. Since the firstborn had no competition until the second child arrived on the scene, this is understandable. In many families the added demands on the mother's attention reduce the amount of time she interacts with her firstborn child. The firstborn may respond to the mother's inattentiveness by being demanding and showing more negative behavior, by becoming more independent, by taking a larger role in initiating conversations and play, or by becoming more detached from the mother (Dunn, 1984). In Dunn's study, on fully 78 percent of the occasions when one of the parents interacted with the new baby, the older sibling joined in. Sometimes the older siblings were friendly and cooperative; at other times they were openly disruptive. Many instances were also observed in which the older sibling responded to signs that the baby was upset or was engaged in a forbidden act (Dunn, 1988).

There is ample evidence that younger children learn a lot from their older siblings. Margarita Azmitia and Joanne Hesser (1993) arranged for young children to play with building blocks while their older sibling and an older friend were block building too. The younger children spent more time imitating and consulting with their sibling than with the friend. Their older sibling, in turn, offered more spontaneous help than did the friend. When the two older children were asked to help the younger child to build a copy of a model out of blocks, the sibling again provided more explanations and encouragement. Additional observations showed that the younger children were to some extent responsible for the older sibling's helpfulness. They were more likely to pester the older sibling into helping than they were to impose on the friend.

Joseph Perner and his colleagues report that sibling relationships also appear to enhance children's social perspective-taking skills (Perner, Ruffman, & Leekham, 1994). They studied children with one or two siblings and only children. Each child was given the "false belief" task described in Chapter 9 (p. 343): a story in which someone returns to a room where an object last seen in one place has been moved to another place, and the child is asked to say where the person in the story will look for it. They found that the more siblings the children had, the more likely they were to understand that people may hold false beliefs. In the author's words, sibling relationships provide a "rich data base" for understanding the mental processes of other people.

Further evidence of links between cognitive development and the experience of sibling relationships comes from studies in which mothers and two siblings participated in a modified version of the "strange situation" described in Chapter 6 (p. 243) (Howe, 1991; Garner, Jones, & Palmer, 1994). The mother and two children spent some time in a room where the children could play. Then the mother left, asking the older child to look after the younger one for a few minutes. Children who scored higher on tests of the ability to take another person's perspective were also better able to comfort and distract their younger siblings during the mother's absence.

New babies are not only charges to be taken care of, they are people to play with. It is while they are playing together that siblings exert their greatest influence. A lot of the play is imitative. During the first year, it is the firstborn who imitates the new baby; then

the tables are turned and it is the little sibling who becomes the imitator (Abramovitch, Pepler, & Corter, 1982). Children take an increasingly active role in their relationships with their older siblings as they approach the age of 4, intervening more and more effectively in the interactions between their mothers and older siblings (Dunn & Shatz, 1989). They also become more interesting as conversation partners for their older siblings (Brown & Dunn, 1991). Even so, the older sibling continues to dominate the relationship and is the one who is most likely to initiate play, as well as altruistic and aggressive interactions (Abramovitch et al., 1986).

Sibling relationships are often ambivalent; it is not possible to characterize them as either consistently friendly or consistently hostile. The obvious explanation for the ambivalence is that brothers and sisters compete for their parents' love and attention. Beyond that, there is the issue of individual differences in personality and temperament (Stocker, Dunn, & Plomin, 1989). Children who have "difficult" temperaments, who are hostile, active, or intense, are more likely than children who have "easy" temperaments to have conflictual relationships with their siblings (Munn & Dunn, 1988). One might expect that the sexual composition of the sibling pair would affect the nature of the relationship, but the findings here are weak and inconsistent. Some studies show that same-sex sibling pairs get along better than mixed-sex pairs (Dunn & Kendrick, 1979) and some show the opposite (Abramovitch et al., 1986).

One factor that reliably affects the siblings' relationship is the emotional climate of their family (Brody & Stoneman, 1987). Siblings are more likely to fight when their parents are not getting along well together, when they divorce, and when a stepfather enters the family, especially if one or both of the siblings are boys (Hetherington, 1988).

Parents who favor one child over another contribute to their children's antagonism toward each other, according to the findings of several studies (Boer, 1990; Brody et al., 1992). One study of 200 pairs of siblings conducted in the Netherlands found that parental favoritism is related to increased hostility between the siblings, with both children acting negatively toward each other (Boer, 1990).

Faced with conflicts between their children, parents frequently intervene to try to settle their disputes. But several studies have found that the more often parents intervene in their children's disputes, the more disputes there are. What is not clear is what is cause and what is effect. Parental intervention may increase fighting between siblings because the children quarrel in order to get their parents' attention and because parental intervention deprives them of the opportunity to learn how to resolve their conflicts. But it may also be that parents intervene in their children's quarrels when they become intense; in this case, the proper conclusion would be that children who have intense quarrels also have frequent ones regardless of what their parents do (Dunn & McGuire, 1991).

family life that influence the way parents treat their children and affect the children's socialization and personality development.

At the time of the Whitings' work, the Gusii, who at one time were herders, were an agricultural people living in the fertile highlands of western Kenya. Women, who did most of the farmwork, usually lived in their own houses with their children, apart from their husbands. Men, no longer active as cattle herders, sometimes took wage-earning jobs but also spent a lot of time in local politics. Family groups were polygynous, with several wives living in separate houses within a single compound. The community had no specialized occupations, few specialized buildings, and almost no differences in social rank or wealth among its inhabitants.

Because of their farmwork, Gusii mothers were often separated from their infants, who were left in the care of older siblings and elderly family members. As is typical of agrarian societies, children's labor was valued for the production of food and the care of younger children. Beginning at the age of 3 or 4, Gusii children were expected to start helping their mothers with simple household tasks. By the age of 7, their economic contributions to the family were indispensable.

New England's "Orchard Town" of the 1950s represented the opposite extreme in family organization and social complexity. Most of the men of Orchard Town were jobholders who lived with their wives and children in single-family dwellings, each with its own yard. A few of the mothers had part-time jobs, but most of them spent their time caring for their children, their husbands, and their property. The town had many specialized buildings (see Figure 11.1) and a wide variety of specialized occupations—physician, firefighter, auto mechanic, teacher, librarian, merchant, and many more.

Children in Orchard Town were observed to spend more time in the company of adults than the children of Nyansongo did. At home, Orchard Town children played in the house or in the yard within earshot of their mother. At school they were constantly supervised by their teachers. In contrast to the Gusii children, Orchard Town children were rarely asked to do chores. Instead of contributing to their families economically, they were a drain on their families' income. (Raising children continues to be a costly affair in most technologically complex societies. It has been estimated that the cost of raising a child in the United States from birth to the age of 17 is approximately $133,000 [Lino, 1993].)

When the Whitings examined the children's behavior patterns, they found that most children in the two societies behaved in *both* prosocial *and* antisocial ways (see Table 11.1) but that the overall patterns of their behavior differed. The Gusii children were more likely to engage in what the Whitings called "nurturant-responsible" behaviors—offering help and support, and making responsible suggestions to others. Orchard Town children, on the other hand, were more often observed seeking help and attention or trying to dominate other children. The Whitings called this a "dependent–dominant" pattern of behavior. Though these two patterns are descriptive of some of the interactions the researchers observed, they fail to capture other prominent aspects of the children's behavior. Gusii children also reprimanded and assaulted others, behavior that the Whitings characterized as "authoritarian–aggressive." The Orchard Town children, by contrast, were more often observed engaging in sociable horseplay, touching others, and joining groups in an amiable way. This pattern was referred to as "sociable–intimate."

FIGURE 11.1 *The village of Orchard Town in New England in the 1950s. Each husband and wife lived with their children in their own house. (From Whiting & Whiting, 1975.)*

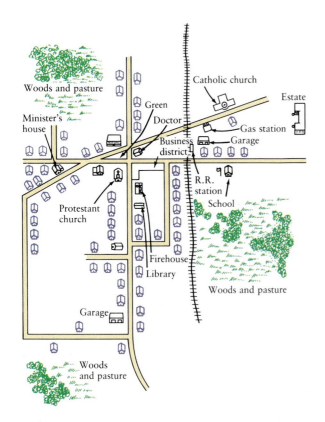

The important lesson to come from these comparisons is that it is inappropriate to conclude simply that Gusii children are prosocial while U.S. children are self-centered. To explain the social behavior of children in the two societies, both the nurturant–responsible versus dependent–dominant and the sociable–intimate versus authoritarian–aggressive dimensions of their behavior need to be related to conditions of family life in the two societies.

The Whitings believed that children of preindustrial societies, such as the Gusii, were more nurturant and responsible because the nature of their parents' work made it necessary for them to help at an early age. This conclusion has considerable support: many other researchers report that in societies where children are expected to contribute to the economic well-being of the community, adults encourage them to develop a sense of self based on social interdependence (Greenfield & Cocking, 1994; Le Vine, 1988).

The authoritarian–aggressive aspect of Gusii children's behavior was also shaped by their niche in Gusii family life. As sibling caregivers who are freeing their mothers to engage in essential economic activities, the older Gusii children have legitimate authority over their younger siblings. They exercise this authority to control their young charges and to teach them to adhere to cultural norms (including respect for one's elders). They may hit or tease in the exercise of these duties, but if they do so excessively, they will be punished by their elders (Zukow-Goldring, 1995).

According to the Whitings, children of industrialized societies, such as those in Orchard Town, were less nurturant and responsible because their chores were less clearly related to their families' economic welfare and may even have seemed arbitrary. Orchard Town children also spent most days in school, where, instead of helping other children, they competed with them for good grades and were encouraged to think of themselves as individuals rather than as members of a group. Like children in other urban technological societies, they were encouraged to develop a more autonomous and individualistic sense of self.

The same set of factors helps to explain why the Orchard Town children were more sociable-intimate than the children of Nyansongo. Orchard Town children lived in nuclear households. The father ate at the same table with his wife and children, slept with his wife, was likely to have been present when the children were born, and helped to care for them. These conditions, made possible and even necessary by the economic demands and cultural traditions of New England, helped create the intimacy within U.S. families. Gusii fathers, on the other hand, typically had more than one wife, and their marriages were exogenous (one could not marry a member of one's own clan). In addition, the Gusii lived in extended families headed by a grandfather. Property was owned by the family as a group. Children belonged to their father's clan, so that a man lived in the village where he grew up, surrounded by his parents, brothers, and other kin, whereas his wives left their home communities when they married. As Figure 11.2 indicates, each wife had her own house. Her husband may have slept in the same house with her periodically, but not in the same bed, and the preferred pattern was for him to sleep and eat in a separate house. By American

	Patterns of Social Behavior Distinguishing Gusii and U.S. Children
TABLE 11.1	

Specific Kinds of Behavior	Category of Behavior	Cultural Group
Offers help Offers support Makes responsible suggestions	Nurturant–responsible	Gusii
Seeks help Seeks dominance Seeks attention	Dependent–dominant	U.S.
Acts sociably Engages in horseplay Touches	Sociable–intimate	U.S.
Reprimands Assaults Insults	Authoritarian–aggressive	Gusii

Source: Whiting & Whiting, 1975.

FIGURE 11.2 *A plan of a typical residential compound in the village of Nyansongo, Kenya. Each wife lived in her own house. Older children also lived in separate houses. A husband might sleep in the house of one of his wives but did not share his bed with her. (From Whiting & Whiting, 1975.)*

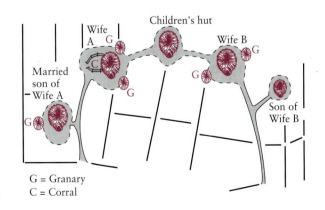

G = Granary
C = Corral

The responsible nurturing behavior demonstrated by this little girl can be expected to have a long-term impact on her personality development.

standards, there was little intimacy between husbands and wives or between fathers and children.

From a middle-class North American point of view, these arrangements may appear strange, even unpleasant. Most Americans believe it is immoral for a man to have more than one wife, and they are unlikely to approve when children behave in a way they consider authoritarian and aggressive. But the behavior and personality characteristics of Gusii children fit Gusii expectations and the Gusii way of life, so these arrangements seem both proper and desirable. In fact, when told about American child-rearing practices, Gusii parents are likely to express disapproval (Le Vine et al., 1994). In each case we encounter the power of culture to shape the socialization of its members.

FAMILY CONFIGURATIONS AND SOCIALIZATION PRACTICES IN NORTH AMERICA

Research in the United States has shown that while child-rearing practices vary widely, the dimensions along which they vary are fairly restricted. Precisely how many dimensions are identified and how they are best defined differ somewhat from one researcher to another. When Earl Schaefer (1959) carried out statistical analysis of his observations of parent-child interactions, he found that parental behavior varied along two dimensions. The first corresponds to the degree to which parents try to control the way their children behave—are they strictly controlling or do they allow a good deal of autonomy? The second dimension is the amount of affection that parents display toward their children—are they warm and loving or cool and indifferent? Eleanor Maccoby and John Martin (1983) have proposed a similar two-dimensional scheme that seeks to incorporate the basic properties of parental styles encountered in a variety of studies (see Table 11.2).

Recent studies of family socialization not only have sought to identify patterns, such as those seen in Table 11.2, but also have looked for answers to several related questions. How do parenting styles affect children's development? What mix of control, autonomy, and expression of affection is most supportive of healthy development? How are family socialization patterns influenced by social class and ethnicity? We begin our examination of these questions with research on the middle-class nuclear family. We then examine the socialization practices of other family types frequently encountered in North America at the end of the twentieth century.

Parenting styles in the middle-class North American nuclear family

In one of the best-known research programs on the developmental consequences of parenting styles, Diana Baumrind (1971, 1980) also found that families could be

TABLE 11.2	A Two-Dimensional Classification of Parenting Patterns	
	Accepting, Responsive, Child-Centered	**Rejecting, Unresponsive, Parent-Centered**
Demanding, Controlling	Authoritative–reciprocal High in bi-directional communication	Authoritarian Power assertive
Undemanding, Low in Control Attempts	Indulgent	Neglecting, ignoring, indifferent, uninvolved

Source: Maccoby & Martin, 1983.

TABLE 11.3	Sample Items from the Baumrind Rating Scale for Preschool Behavior Grouped into Statistically Related Clusters	
Hostile–friendly	Selfish	Understands other children's position in interaction
Resistive–cooperative	Impetuous and impulsive	Can be trusted
Domineering–tractable	Manipulates other children to enhance own position	Timid with other children
Dominant–submissive	Peer leader	Suggestible
Purposive–aimless	Confident	Spectator
Achievement-oriented– not achievement-oriented	Gives best to play and work	Does not persevere when encounters frustration
Independent–suggestive	Individualistic	Stereotyped in thinking

Source: Baumrind, 1971.

characterized by a small set of distinctive parenting styles such as those found in Table 11.2. Baumrind arranged for trained observers to record children's behavior during routine activities in a preschool. The observers rated the children's behavior on a 72-item scale and correlated these ratings to obtain seven clusters of scores, representing seven dimensions of preschool behavior (such as hostile vs. friendly, resistive vs. cooperative, domineering vs. tractable). The children's behavior could then be correlated with the teaching styles of their parents, as measured by observations and interviews (Table 11.3).

The researchers interviewed each child's parents, both separately and together, about their child-rearing beliefs and practices. Then they visited the children's homes twice to observe family interactions from just before dinner until after the child went to bed (Table 11.4).

When the interviews and observations were scored and analyzed, Baumrind and her colleagues found that parenting behaviors in 77 percent of their families fitted one of three patterns:

- Parents who follow an **authoritarian parenting pattern** try to shape, control, and evaluate the behavior and attitudes of their children according to a set traditional standard. They stress the importance of obedience to authority and discourage verbal give-and-take between themselves and their children. They favor punitive measures to curb their children's "willfulness" whenever their children's behavior conflicts with what they believe to be correct.

- Parents who demonstrate an **authoritative parenting pattern** take it for granted that although they have more knowledge and skill, control more resources, and have more physical power than their children, the children also have rights. Authoritative parents are less likely than authoritarian parents to use physical punishment and less likely to stress obedience to authority as a virtue in itself. Instead, these parents attempt to control their children by explaining their rules or decisions and by reasoning with them.

Authoritarian parenting pattern
Authoritarian parents try to shape and evaluate the behavior and attitudes of their children according to a set standard. They stress the importance of obedience to authority and favor punitive measures to bring about their children's compliance.

Authoritative parenting pattern
Authoritative parents try to control their children by explaining their rules or decisions, and by reasoning with them. They set high standards for their children's behavior.

They are willing to consider their child's point of view, even if they do not always accept it. Authoritative parents set high standards for their children's behavior and encourage them to be individualistic and independent.

- Parents who exhibit a **permissive parenting pattern** exercise less explicit control over their children's behavior than either authoritarian or authoritative parents, either because they believe children must learn how to behave through their own experience or because they do not take the trouble to provide discipline. They give their children a lot of leeway to determine their own schedules and activities, and often consult them about family policies. They do not demand the same levels of achievement and mature behavior that authoritative or authoritarian parents do.

Baumrind found that, on the average, each style of parenting was associated with a different pattern of children's behavior in the preschool:

- *Children of authoritarian parents* tended to lack social competence in dealing with other children. They frequently withdrew from social contact and rarely took initiative. In situations of moral conflict, they tended to look to outside authority to decide what was right. These children were often characterized as lacking spontaneity and intellectual curiosity.

- *Children of authoritative parents* appeared more self-reliant, self-controlled, and willing to explore, as well as more content than those raised by permissive or authoritarian parents. Baumrind believes that this difference is a result of the fact that, while authoritative parents set high standards for their children, they explain to them why they are being rewarded and punished. These explanations improve children's understanding and acceptance of the social rules.

- *Children of permissive parents* tended to be relatively immature; they had difficulty controlling their impulses, accepting responsibility for social actions, and acting independently.

Baumrind also reported differences in the way girls and boys responded to the major parenting patterns. The sons of authoritarian parents, for example, seemed to show more pronounced difficulties with social relations than the daughters did. They were also more likely than other boys to show anger and defiance toward people in authority. The daughters of authoritative parents were more likely to be independent than their brothers, while the boys were more likely to be socially responsible than the girls.

Research conducted in the years since Baumrind's initial publications has generally supported her observations and extended them to older children. Sanford Dornbusch and his colleagues found, for example, that authoritative parenting is associated with better school performance and better social adjustment than authoritarian parenting among high school students, just as it is among preschoolers (Dornbusch et al., 1987; Lamborn et al., 1991).

Despite the consistency of these findings, the conclusion that authoritative parenting is most conducive to intellectual and social competence must be qualified in two important ways. First, it is important to remember that the basic strategy for relating parental behaviors to child behaviors used in this

Permissive parenting pattern
Permissive parents exercise less control over their children's behavior and make relatively few demands on them. They give their children a lot of leeway to determine their own schedules and activities and often consult them about family policies.

TABLE 11.4
Sample Items in Baumrind's Scale of Parental Behaviors Observed in Home Interactions

Set regular tasks
Demand child put toys away
Provide intellectually stimulating environment
Set standards of excellence
Many restrictions on TV watching
Fixed bedtime hour
Mother has independent life
Encourage contact with other adults
Demand mature table behavior
Clear ideals for child
Stable, firm views
Cannot be coerced by child
Use negative sanctions when defied
Force confrontation when child disobeys
Parents' needs take precedence
Regard themselves as competent people
Encourage independent action
Solicit child's opinions
Give reasons with directives
Encourage verbal give and take
Inhibit annoyance or impatience when child dawdles or is annoying
Become inaccessible when displeased
Lack empathetic understanding

Source: Baumrind, 1971.

line of research relies on correlational data. Consequently, there can be no certainty that differences in parenting styles *caused* the differences in children's behavior (we discussed this problem in Chapter 1, pp. 22–23). Sandra Scarr (1993), among others, has pointed out that, in fact, preexisting differences among children may influence their parents' choice of child-rearing strategies. A particularly active and easily frustrated child, for example, may elicit authoritarian responses; the same parents might respond differently to an easygoing or timid child.

In support of this view, research on the personalities of biologically unrelated children in the same household has shown these children to be quite different from one another, even though they were being raised by the same parents (Plomin & Bergeman, 1991). Such findings imply one of two things: either patterns of caregiving do not have much effect on a child's behavior or parents' patterns of caregiving vary from one child to the next. Either conclusion undermines the idea that parental styles of socialization are the *causes* of variations in children's development.

Baumrind is well aware of these difficulties. She agrees that children's temperaments influence parenting styles, but she is convinced that her evidence shows clearly that parenting styles have a significant impact on children's personalities and later school achievement (Baumrind, 1980, 1991a). Researchers are currently using a variety of strategies to isolate the effects of parenting styles on patterns of child development (Crockenberg & Litman, 1991; Hoffman, 1991; Scarr, 1992; Sigel, 1993).

The use of verbal discipline coupled with explanation is characteristic of the authoritative pattern of parenting.

The second reason to qualify conclusions from Baumrind's research program is that her families were not representative of North American families as a whole: they were, in general, suburban, white, largely middle-class, two-parent families. If we are to get a broad understanding of the family as a context of development, we have to consider how various family configurations, in combination with educational experience, economic circumstances, ethnic heritage, and cultural context, influence socialization.

Baumrind herself was the first to raise this concern. She reported that the expected relationship between authoritarian parenting and personality development was not found among a group of 16 African American children and their families in her sample. She was particularly impressed that African American daughters of authoritarian parents took initiative and behaved assertively on the playground, yet could be self-controlled, polite, and quiet at a church meeting.

The replication of Baumrind's work by Sanford Dornbusch and his colleagues (1987) raised the same issue. Like Baumrind, Dornbusch found that authoritative parenting was associated with better school performance. However, Dornbusch and his colleagues also found that Asian American students, whose parents were reported to have the highest scores for authoritarian parenting practices, were the group that did best in school. The level of authoritarian parenting practices did not predict the school performance of these students as it did for white and Latino students.

In a follow-up study comparing Chinese American and European American families and their children, researchers encountered a major obstacle when they attempted to apply such categories as "authoritarian" and "authoritative" to two groups with different languages and cultural backgrounds: these words do not have the same meanings for both groups (Chao, 1994). In describing this study, Ruth Chao wrote that the English word "authoritarian" carries with it many negative connotations—such as hostility, aggressiveness, mistrust, dominance—that are not applicable to the core methods of socialization in the Chinese family. While it is true that Chinese place high value on obedience and parental control, the preferred Chinese process of socialization is a pattern closer to the American notion of "training." Chao also maintains that Chinese parents exercise control over their children and demand their obedience "in the context of a supportive, highly involved, and physically close mother-child relationship" (p. 112).

Chao tested her idea that Baumrind's parenting categories do not apply well to Chinese parenting patterns by administering a questionnaire to 50 Chinese American and 50 European American mothers. The questionnaire included standard questions such as those used by Baumrind plus a set of questions that related specifically to Chinese notions of training young children for life (the mothers were asked, for example, to indicate their level of agreement with the statement "Mothers must train their children to work very hard and to be disciplined"). As others had done before her, she found that the Chinese American mothers scored higher on the standard measures of control and authoritarianism. But the Chinese American and European American groups were best distinguished by the way their scores related to the Chinese concept of training.

If we think back to the cross-cultural comparison between the Gusii in Nyansongo and the Americans in Orchard Town, Chao's findings should come as no surprise. After all, the Whitings had demonstrated many years ago that the meanings of any terms used to describe parenting ("prosocial," "authoritarian") have to be interpreted in the light of local categories and cultural practices. What the more recent work on parenting styles and personality development in the United States has shown is that this lesson is equally applicable to the study of different ethnic groups in our heterogeneous society.

Patterns of socialization in single-parent families

In 1994, the last year for which statistics are available, approximately 28 percent of U.S. children were living in single-parent households, almost always with the mother (U.S. Bureau of the Census, 1995). Among African American families the percentage was 62 percent. What are the consequences of growing up with only one parent, especially when that parent is both young and unmarried?

Young Unmarried Mothers and Their Children   Many single women who are raising children are still teenagers. As Figure 11.3 indicates, the number of births among unmarried teenagers has grown rapidly over the past three decades. This situation is of great concern because research has shown that children of unmarried teenage mothers are at a developmental disadvantage. Preschool children of single teenage mothers have been found to be more aggressive, less self-controlled, and less cognitively advanced than the children of older, married mothers (Furstenberg, Brooks-Gunn, & Chase-Lansdale, 1989).

Frank Furstenberg and his colleagues (1992) believe that three factors contribute to the negative developmental effect of being raised by a young unmarried mother:

1. Young mothers tend to be less equipped emotionally to be competent parents.

2. Many young mothers are often less prepared to bring up children and have little interest in doing so. As a consequence, they tend to vocalize less with their babies than older mothers do. A lack of verbal communication seems to lead in turn to lowered cognitive ability in preschool and elementary school.

FIGURE 11.3 *The number of children born to unmarried teenage mothers in the United States, 1960–1992. (U. S. Bureau of the Census, 1995.)*

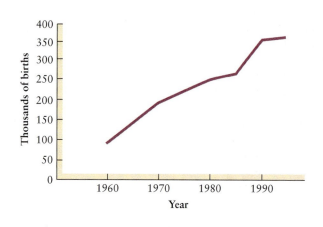

3. Young mothers, especially those without husbands, are likely to have very limited financial resources. As a consequence, they are likely to be poorly educated, to live in disadvantaged neighborhoods, to obtain poor health services for themselves and their children, and to be socially isolated.

It has proved difficult to specify how much each of these factors contributes to the developmental problems of children raised by young unmarried mothers because the factors are so closely intertwined.

We will return to the topic of young unmarried single mothers when we explore how poverty and racial prejudice shape family configurations and socialization practices (pp. 441–446).

The Consequences of Divorce More than half of all marriages in the United States end in divorce. It has been estimated that about 30 percent of the children born to married couples in the United States will see their parents divorce sometime before they are 18 years old (Furstenberg & Cherlin, 1991). While the divorce rate in the United States is by far the highest in the world, the rate of divorce in Canada and Europe is rising rapidly.

Many studies indicate that, at least in the short run, divorce has a negative effect on children's academic achievement and social development (Hetherington & Clingempeel, 1992; Hetherington, Stanley-Hagan, & Anderson, 1989). Some researchers have suggested that children in one-parent households do poorly in school because they tend to lack self-control and therefore become disruptive in the classroom (Guidubaldi et al., 1983). Mavis Hetherington (1989) agrees and attributes this lack of self-control to a breakdown in parenting after a divorce. Hetherington and her colleagues observed that immediately after a mother's marriage breaks up, she becomes both more coercive and more erratic in disciplining her children. She is less likely to explain her actions or to reason with her children, makes fewer demands on them, and does not communicate with them as often as she once did (Hetherington, Cox, & Cox, 1982).

Divorce leads to several other changes in children's life experiences that might be expected to harm their development. Many of the problems associated with divorce are of the same kind as those faced by unmarried single women. First, the average income of single-parent families created by divorce or separation falls by 37 percent within 4 months of the breakup, according to a study by the U.S. Bureau of the Census (1991). Only 44 percent of children living with their mothers receive child support from their absent fathers. As a consequence, many children whose parents' marriages have broken up find themselves living in poverty. (In 1995 the Census Bureau defined a family of four as poor if its annual income fell below $15,150.)

Second, a mother raising children alone is trying to accomplish by herself what is usually a demanding job for two adults. Divorce, separation, and widowhood force many mothers to enter the workforce at the same time that they and their children are adapting to a new family configuration. Seventy-eight percent of divorced mothers are in the labor force; most of them work full-time (U.S. Bureau of the Census, 1995). Because of the many demands on their mothers' time, children of divorce not only receive less guidance and assistance but tend to lose out on important kinds of social and intellectual stimulation (Medrich et al., 1982).

Third, the divorced mother is often socially isolated and lonely (Hetherington, Cox, & Cox, 1982). She has no one to support her when the children question her authority, nor does anyone act as a buffer between her and the children when she is not functioning well as a parent. Often fathers who see their children only occasionally are indulgent and permissive, making the mothers' task of parenting even more difficult.

Although it makes intuitive sense that the losses associated with the breakup of a family are the causes of these children's difficulties, a number of studies that collected data about children before their parents divorced have cast doubt on the belief that the divorce itself is the major cause of the problems that have been observed. Noting that divorce is a consequence of disharmony in the family, several researchers have suggested that it is conflict between the child's parents, and not divorce itself, that poses the greatest risk for children (Block, Block, & Gjerde, 1986).

This conclusion is confirmed by two longitudinal surveys of children conducted in Great Britain and the United States (Cherlin et al., 1991). The two studies began with a large sample of children living in intact families. All the parents were interviewed about their children's behavior when the children were 7 years old and again when they were 11 years old.

Children whose parents divorced or separated between the two interviews were compared with children whose families remained intact. Both studies found, in line with earlier research, that children whose parents had divorced between the two interviews had more behavior problems than children whose families had remained intact. However, when the researchers looked back at the reports on the same children when they were 7 years old and the family was still intact, they found that the children were already exhibiting many behavior problems, including tantrums, bad dreams, resistance to going to school, disobedience at home, and fighting with other children. These are the kinds of behaviors that tend to accompany parental conflict and may also contribute to it.

There is great diversity in the ways children respond to conflict between their parents and to their subsequent divorce, but some general patterns have emerged. The effects of marital disharmony and of divorce seem to be greater for boys than for girls (Hetherington et al., 1989). Boys who live with single mothers show a higher rate of behavior disorder and problems in their relations with others than girls who live with single mothers or children who live with both parents. Sometimes girls react to their parents' divorce with self-criticism, withdrawal, and crying, but it is more common for girls to become demanding and to seek attention. Boys, who tend to be more active, assertive, and less compliant than girls to begin with, react to the turmoil and stress of divorce by becoming unruly and angry.

In their attempts to regain control over their upset sons, mothers often respond to their unruly behavior with harsh and inconsistent discipline, which only makes the situation worse. The cycles of coercive interaction between divorced mothers and their sons often spread to sibling relations as well, so that quarreling, teasing, and hitting between siblings tend to increase (Baldwin & Skinner, 1989).

Temperamentally difficult children are also at special risk when their parents are in conflict or divorce (Hetherington, 1989). They are more likely to become targets of their parents' anger and criticism than are children who are more easygoing, and they have a harder time coping when that happens.

Children's age at the time of the marital conflict and divorce is another factor that plays a role in the way they adapt to their changing family situation. One study found that children who were young when their parents divorced initially blamed themselves for their parents' separation and were afraid of being abandoned. But when they were interviewed 10 years after the divorce, they could barely remember either the conflict between their parents or their own responses to it (Wallerstein, 1987). Adolescents are in a better position to assess the problems between parents at the time of a divorce and to cope with the attendant stresses. They are also better able than young children to take advantage of the support of friends and others outside their families. In fact, many adolescents do respond to their parents' marital problems by disengaging from their families (Hetherington, 1989). Whether the result is good or bad depends on the kind of people and activities the adolescent turns to. Unfortunately, it is not uncommon for adolescents to respond to intense family conflict by running away, playing truant, and breaking the law (Forehand et al., 1991).

By 2 or 3 years after the divorce, most children and parents have adapted to the new situation. The single most important factor in a child's adjustment after a divorce is how well the custodial parent deals with the stress of the divorce, shields the child from family conflicts, and provides the child with authoritative parenting. Children seem to do best when their parents put aside their disagreements and support each other in their parenting roles. Caring grandparents, aunts, uncles, and friends can ease the pain of the marital breakup and reduce children's stress.

In many families today, however, the equilibrium established after a divorce does not last long. Approximately two-thirds of divorced parents remarry within 5 years, requiring their children to cope with yet another major change in their family life, school, and peer group. Several studies have found that the early stages of remarriage are stressful for everyone, parents included, as the members of the blended family make the accommodations and adjustments necessary for them to live in the same house. Some members of the family, especially younger boys in households headed by mothers, seem to benefit from the presence of a stepfather in the home. Others, especially adolescent girls, are more likely to suffer in the new family configuration, seeing their stepfathers as interlopers who threaten their close relationship with their mother. They often react to their mother's remarriage by ignoring their stepfather and being sulky, resistant, and critical (Hetherington, 1989; Hetherington & Clingempeel, 1992).

Children's long-term adjustment to the new family configurations seems to be determined by several factors, including their sex, their age when the parent remarries, and the duration of the new marriage (Chase-Lansdale & Hetherington, 1990). Authoritative parenting that combines parental warmth, support, and involvement with the children and monitoring of their activities seems to be the key to their adjustment in the new families created by their parent's remarriage (Hetherington & Clingempeel, 1992).

The impact of poverty on child rearing

Poverty touches all aspects of family life: the quality of housing and health care, access to education and recreational facilities, and even one's safety as one walks along the street (Huston, McLoyd, & Coll, 1994). Studies in many parts of the

Chronic poverty such as that experienced by Irish tinkers creates multiple risk factors for children's development.

FIGURE 11.4 *An analytic model of how poverty and economic loss affect African American children. In this model, poverty increases psychological distress and weakens the marital bond. These factors also have an adverse effect on parents' social relations with their children, which may lead to socioemotional problems in the children. Special characteristics of the parents and the child and social support systems modify the way these effects play themselves out in individual cases. (After McLoyd, 1990.)*

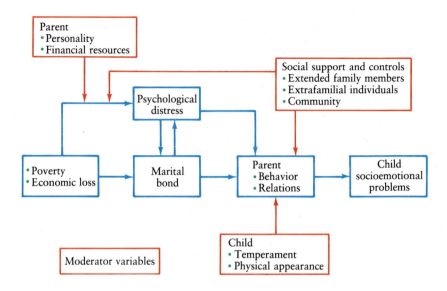

world have found that parents who live close to the subsistence level are likely to adopt controlling child-rearing practices akin to the authoritarian pattern described by Baumrind. According to the anthropologist Robert Le Vine (1974), parents who know what it means to eke out a living "see obedience as the means by which their children will be able to make their way in the world and establish themselves economically in young adulthood when the basis must be laid for the economic security of their nascent families" (p. 63).

An emphasis on obedience, among other features of authoritarian parenting, is also frequently encountered in poor families in the United States. Echoing Le Vine's conclusions concerning the child-rearing patterns of people living at a subsistence level in other countries, some researchers have suggested that poor minority mothers place a high value on unquestioning obedience and discourage their children's curiosity because the dangerous circumstances of daily life make mistaken judgment on the part of their children too risky (Silverstein & Krate, 1975).

One important way in which poverty influences adult socialization practices is by raising the level of stress. Adults who are under stress are less nurturant, more likely to resort to physical punishment, and less consistent when they interact with their children (see Figure 11.4 and the discussion of child abuse in Box 11.2). This relationship between stress and authoritarian parenting was observed by Forgatch and Wieder (summarized in Patterson, 1982), who studied interactions between mothers and children at home over the course of several days. The researchers obtained daily reports from the mothers about such stressful events in their lives as unexpectedly large bills, illness in the family, and quarrels with their husbands. A mother's irritability usually increased when things outside her relationship with her children were going badly, and at those times she was more likely to hit or scold her children and more likely to refuse their requests.

The kinds of stress documented by Forgatch and Wieder are by no means restricted to families living in poverty. But poverty makes these universal sources of stress more serious because it increases the likelihood that a variety of stresses are chronically present simultaneously (Duncan, Brooks-Gunn, & Klebanov, 1994). Poverty also decreases the likelihood that the family will have the resources to deal with multiple stresses.

Although multiple stresses and scant resources offer one explanation for obedience-oriented parenting styles, they are not the only factors. Several studies have shown that the kinds of work the parents engage in are directly related to the way they interact with their children at home (Crouter, 1994; Greenberger, O'Neil, & Nagel, 1994; Kohn, 1977). Middle-class occupations require the ability to work without close supervision. The content of such work is often complex and the flow of work is irregular; therefore workers must be self-directed. In the new forms of cooperative teamwork that are becoming widespread in American industry, work must be not only self-directed but also socially cooperative and democratic. Traditional working-class occupations, by contrast, demand obedience and punctuality. The flow of work is often so routinized that a robot can—and increasingly does—carry out the job just as efficiently as a human being (assembly-line jobs are a classic example). The high incidence of authoritarian parenting styles among the economically disadvantaged is perfectly understandable in light of the combined facts that working-class occupations require obedience in the face of routine work and that poverty creates stressful family circumstances. At the same time, the effects of traditional working-class occupations on family socialization create an additional obstacle—a lack of initiative and independence—which poor children have to overcome if they are to improve their socioeconomic situation. Robert Halpern pinpoints the problem when he remarks that "patterns of care and nurturance designed to prepare low-income children for the immediate contexts of their lives may not always be consonant with those that mainstream psychology offers as optimal" (1990, p. 7). In other words, the kind of care that middle-class psychologists recommend may not be appropriate to the real-life circumstances of poor people.

Coping with economic disadvantage: The extended family and social networks

Many scholars who study the socialization of poor minority children have found that the **extended family** acts as a problem-solving and stress-reducing social institution that can provide important resources to young children (Hashima & Amato, 1994; Wilson, 1995). An extended family is one in which not only parents and their children but other kin—grandparents, cousins, nephews, or more distant family relations—share a household. In some cases it includes children of other families who are sent for a time to trusted friends or business partners or godparents (Harrison et al., 1990).

> **Extended family** An extended family is one in which not only parents and their children but other kin—grandparents, cousins, nephews, or more distant relations—share a household.

It is uncertain just how widespread the phenomenon of extended families has become in recent decades. Melvin Wilson (1986) estimates that perhaps 10 percent of African American children live in extended families, and there are indications that the figure may be much higher when the mothers are young and single (Sandven & Resnick, 1990). Extended families are also common among Hispanic, Asian Pacific, and Native American households in the United States (Harrison et al., 1990).

Scholars identify two major sources for the formation of an extended family: cultural traditions and economic hardship. Extended family arrangements of various kinds were the norm among the African peoples brought to the Americas and sold into slavery. Strong family affiliations persisted during slavery, despite attempts to destroy them (Genovese, 1976). Richard Griswold del Castillo (1984) offers a similar explanation of the high incidence of extended families among Hispanic Americans. He traces the contemporary Hispanic American family back to the period before the Spanish conquest. Extended kin relations were a central feature of the cultures of these people's Amerindian ancestors.

Many scholars see the extended family as a natural strategy for dealing with the combined handicaps of low income and low social standing (Harrison et al., 1990; Huston et al., 1994). Extended families appear to play an especially important role in providing support for children born out of wedlock (Chase-Lansdale et al., 1994; Wilson, 1989). They provide income, child care, and help in

BOX 11.2

Child Maltreatment in the United States

Over the past three decades the public has become increasingly aware that many children in the United States are mistreated by their parents. Scarcely a day goes by without a story in the media about a child who has been neglected, maltreated, or even murdered by his or her parents. This concern is reflected in a report by a federal advisory panel to Congress and the Department of Health and Human Services which concludes that abuse and neglect of children by their parents constitute a national emergency in the United States (Cimons, 1990). According to the report, more than 2 million children "are starved and abandoned, burned and severely beaten, raped and sodomized, berated and belittled annually in the United States" (Advisory Board on Child Abuse and Neglect, 1990).

The mobilization of scientists, physicians, policy makers, and social workers to address the problem might lead one to believe that adult violence against children is a new problem. Yet infanticide was routinely practiced in ancient Greece, Rome, Arabia, and China. Earlier in this century, children were routinely beaten in schools and forced to work long hours at backbreaking tasks under the worst possible conditions (Zigler & Hall, 1989). It was not until the late 1960s that all 50 states had laws mandating the reporting of child maltreatment. Consequently, while it is possible that the maltreatment of children in the United States has skyrocketed in the past three decades, changing social attitudes toward parents' responsibilities and children's rights almost certainly play a role in the public's perception of the problem.

A major difficulty in all discussions of child maltreatment in our multicultural society is that different social groups have different conceptions of what constitutes child maltreatment. Nonetheless, faced with mounting public concern and the need to provide uniform standards for legal purposes, Congress passed the Child Abuse Prevention Act in 1974. The definition of child maltreatment provided in this bill remains the law of the land:

Child Abuse and Neglect means physical or mental injury, sexual abuse, negligent treatment, or maltreatment of any child under the age of eighteen by a person responsible for the child's welfare under circumstances which indicate the child's health or welfare is harmed or threatened thereby. (Public Law 93024, section 2)

The law lists five distinct kinds of maltreatment:

1. Physical abuse, such as beating or burning.
2. Physical neglect, such as failure to keep children warm and fed.
3. Mental abuse, such as constant teasing or hostility.
4. Mental neglect, or failure to attend to or talk to the child.
5. Sexual abuse, or subjecting children to sexual activity.

With the exception of sexual abuse, judgments about the applicability of these categories are likely to be difficult if the case is not severe. Take physical abuse. According to a variety of surveys, over 90 percent of all parents in the United States have spanked their children. The frequency and severity of physical punishment, however, varies dramatically from one parent to the next (Holden & Zambarano, 1992). The borders between "culturally acceptable" physical punishment and physical punishment that is defined as "maltreatment" depend very much on parents' beliefs about children and the modes of interaction sanctioned in the children's families and communities. Thus the judgment of a teacher, physician, or neighbor who suspects that a child is being maltreated is based on a definition that can fall anywhere on a continuum from the very narrow, which includes only intentional physical abuse so severe as to be life-threatening, to the very broad, which includes anything that interferes with a child's "optimal" development.

No matter how broadly or narrowly child maltreatment is defined, many cases of neglect, brutality, and sexual abuse go undetected by people outside the family and are not reported. Many experts consider the officially reported cases of abuse and neglect to be just the tip of the iceberg. The only certainty is that large numbers of children are harmed by their parents (Zuravin, 1991).

Who Is at Risk of Maltreatment?

Any child may be neglected or abused, but some children seem to be at greater risk than others. Age is one factor: children between 2 and 5 years old are slightly more likely to be abused than children who are older (U.S. Bureau of the Census, 1995). Poor health is a second factor. Premature and low-birth-weight infants are often irritable, unresponsive, and active, and thus difficult to care for. Premature infants make up nearly 25 percent of the population of battered infants, although they account for only 8 percent of all infants born (Parke & Collmer, 1975). Personality is a third factor: among babies and toddlers, it is the emotionally unresponsive, irritable, or hyperactive child who faces the greatest risks (Egeland & Sroufe, 1981; Sherrod et al., 1984). But passive, lethargic children are not immune; they are the ones who are most likely to be neglected (Belsky, 1980). Among older children, defiance in the face of discipline can lead some parents to escalate discipline until it becomes abusive. One study, in fact, found the incidence of physical abuse higher among adolescents then among younger children (National Center on Child Abuse and Neglect, 1988). Socioeconomic class is a fourth factor: children living in poverty are more likely than middle-class children to be abused (Barnett et al., 1993; Wilson & Saft, 1993). The sex of the child seems to be irrelevant to all forms of maltreatment but one: sexual abuse is committed four times more often against girls than against boys (U.S. Department of Health and Human Services, 1988).

It is important to remember, however, that most children who fall into these at-risk categories are not abused and that many healthy, even-tempered children are. Consequently, it is still necessary to determine why some adults are abusive and neglectful and others are not.

Who Does the Abusing?

A popular assumption is that people who abuse or neglect their children must be mentally ill. While a small percentage of those who abuse children are mentally ill (10 percent, according to one estimate), most are not (Kempe & Kempe, 1978).

Another widespread belief is that parents who physically abuse their children were abused as children themselves (Belsky, 1993; Kempe et al., 1962). Once again, the facts are not so simple. People who were physically abused as children are more likely to abuse their own children, but only about 30 percent of those who have a history of being abused as children mistreat their own children (Kaufman & Zigler, 1989). This history also fails to explain child abuse by parents who were not abused as children.

Sexual abuse is committed most often by men who know the children they are abusing. Often they are relatives (Finkelhor, 1994).

What Precipitates Child Maltreatment?

There is a good deal of evidence that children are much more likely to be maltreated when families are under stress. The stress factors can be of many kinds and compound one another: chronic poverty, recent job loss, marital discord, and social isolation have all been linked to increases in the incidence of child abuse (Pelton, 1994). The likelihood of abuse is also higher when the mother is very young, is poorly educated, abuses drugs or alcohol, or receives little financial support from the father (Pianta, Egeland, & Erickson, 1989; Sternberg, 1993).

Many scholars who have studied the physical abuse of children in the United States see it as a social disease that accompanies the acceptance of violence in families, local communities, and society at large (Belsky, 1993; Cicchetti & Toth, 1993). Two kinds of evidence support this position: (1) Most child abuse occurs when parents set out to discipline their children by punishing them physically and then end up hurting them (Zigler & Hall, 1989); (2) countries in which the physical punishment of children is frowned upon, such as Sweden and Japan, have very low rates of physical abuse of children (Belsky, 1993).

Sexual abuse of children is frequently seen in situations where the custodial parent divorces and remarries frequently or otherwise introduces multiple new partners into the home. But sexual abuse also occurs in relatively stable households (Gomes-Schwartz, Horowitz, & Cardarelli, 1990). Unlike neglect and physical abuse, sexual abuse is committed by parents of every income and educational level.

No single risk factor seems to be the overwhelming catalyst for child abuse and neglect, according to the National Research Council's Panel on Research on Child Abuse and Neglect (1993). Rather a complex interplay of multiple risk factors seems to set the stage.

Effects of Being Abused

Studies that compare the intellectual, social, and emotional consequences of child abuse attest to its negative effects (Belsky & Vondra, 1987, and Cicchetti & Carlson, 1989, review the research). In infancy, many maltreated infants are sad, fearful, and frequently angry. They rarely initiate social contact, and their attachment behavior in the strange situation is likely to be classified as insecure or avoidant (Toth & Cicchetti, 1993). In preschool, physically abused children find it

(Continued on following page)

BOX 11.2

Child Maltreatment in the United States *(Continued)*

difficult to get along with other children and are less well liked than their peers (Haskett & Kistner, 1991). Their popularity remains low in middle childhood, because their peers and teachers see them as more aggressive and less cooperative than other children (Salzinger et al., 1993). They are reported to be more afraid than other children of angry interactions between adults (Hennessy et al., 1994). A review of school and social service records found that maltreated children had poorer grades than their peers, performed poorly on standardized tests, and were more likely to have to repeat a grade (Eckenrode, Laird, & Doris, 1993). In short, there is little doubt that the effects of maltreatment extend well beyond any physical damage that the parents inflict.

Like children who have been abused in other ways, children who have been sexually abused tend to be anxious, depressed, withdrawn, and aggressive; these traits get them into trouble at school. They often show a precocious interest in sex and behave seductively (Haugaard & Reppucci, 1988; Kendall-Tackett, Willams, & Finkelhor, 1993). Some children, however, seem to emerge from the experience of sexual abuse without any symptoms (Kendall-Tackett et al., 1993). To a large degree, the psychological effects of sexual abuse depend on the age of the child, her relationship with the person who abused her, the severity and duration of the abuse, and the reactions of other people if the abuse becomes known (Kendall-Tackett et al., 1993).

What Can Be Done?

Intervention strategies have targeted virtually all known risk factors (Olds & Henderson, 1989; Skibinski, 1995). Some analysts have focused on changing the macrosystem, proposing a guaranteed minimum income as a way to reduce poverty or arguing for a reduction of violence in the media, but most programs intervene at a more local level. One strategy is to create social networks of support for hard-pressed parents: specially trained nurse–home visitors to provide emotional support as well as health and parenting education; hotlines for parents to call if they feel themselves getting too upset; and special organizations, such as Parents Anonymous. Another strategy is to use the medical establishment to provide special training programs before or soon after a child is born. A third strategy is to provide teenagers with extensive firsthand experience with children in a program of formal training for parenthood.

The long history of child abuse cautions us not to expect results from piecemeal efforts and expressions of community concern. A systematic campaign that attacks several risk factors simultaneously would appear to offer the best hope of eliminating the problem in the long run.

maintaining the household as well as less tangible assistance such as emotional support and counseling. In some circumstances, grandmothers provide care that is more responsive and less punitive than that of their teenaged daughters (Chase-Lansdale et al., 1994). Furthermore, the presence of other adults in the house makes it possible for the children's mothers to obtain additional education, which in turn improves the family's economic circumstances.

The evidence that extended family relations help to buffer children against the harmful effects of poverty has led psychologists to emphasize the importance of social networks in shaping parental behaviors toward their children (Cochran, 1990; Salzinger, 1990). When poor families are isolated from their communities, and especially when single young women attempt to raise their children without a social support system, the children are particularly at risk. By contrast, young mothers who belong to a social network that allows them to interact regularly with friends and neighbors, to attend church, and to participate in other community activities raise their children in a more nurturant and sensitive way (Hashima & Amato, 1994; McLoyd, 1990).

One of the most effective ways of giving children both a love of books and basic reading skills is to read with them, as this German family is doing.

Media Linking Community and Home

Parents are by no means the only ones in the home to shape children's behavior. Children are affected by their brothers and sisters, and sometimes by their grandparents, aunts, uncles, and cousins, as well as by people who come into the home as visitors, to perform services, or to bring news of the world outside. In modern societies like our own, the outside world also enters the home through letters, magazines, newspapers, television, radio, and books. The sheer magnitude of children's exposure to modern communications media makes it important to understand the impact of these media on child development.

Both the content of what children encounter through communications media (fairy tales, adventure stories, advertisements, news programs) and the form in which the information is presented (brief images flashed on a screen or stories read aloud) are widely claimed to have lasting effects on the development of children's interests, cognitive skills, and social behavior (Greenfield, 1993). Here we will discuss what is known about the developmental effects of watching television and of being read to.

TELEVISION: WHAT IS REAL? WHAT IS PRETEND?

It is estimated that a TV set is on for 6 or more hours each day in the average American home and that young children are to be found in front of it for 2 or more of those hours (Comstock & Paik, 1991). According to Dorothy and Jerome Singer (1990), "No other extraparental influence has penetrated the lives of children as television has."

The evidence that young children and even infants learn from watching TV is irrefutable. In Chapter 5 (p. 209) we saw how Andrew Meltzoff (1988a) demonstrated that infants only 14 months old will imitate actions they have seen on a TV screen. Meltzoff arranged for infants to watch an adult on television taking apart and reassembling an unfamiliar dumbbell-shaped object. When presented with this object the next day, many of the infants proceeded to take it apart and

The influence of media on children's play is evident here as this young Superman prepares to leap off his bed.

put it back together again. Infants also imitate the language they hear on TV. Dafna Lemish and Mabel Rice (1986) report that one 2-year-old they observed at home approached her father, pointed at the bottle of beer in his hand, and declared, "Diet Pepsi, one less calorie." Young children identify with superheroes and mythical creatures they see on television in their fantasy play, imitate their clothing, and eat the cereals they endorse—clear evidence that what children learn from television influences their everyday behavior.

A special concern about the influence of television viewing on young children arises from the fact that they easily confuse TV make-believe and reality. Research such as the cognitive studies summarized in Chapter 9 (pp. 344–345) has shown that young children have trouble distinguishing reality and appearance. Their confusion is compounded when they watch television entertainment because these programs are presented in a realistic format and show believable people engaging in behavior and events that could be happening. A fictitious story about a cowboy who goes to Dallas and rides in a rodeo may have real cowboys in the cast, and the filming may take place at a real rodeo in Dallas.

At the end of infancy, children show little understanding of the boundary between what they see on television and the rest of their perceptual environment. When an egg is broken on television, they are likely to try to clean it up (Jaglom & Gardner, 1981). Three-year-old children claimed that a bowl of popcorn shown on TV would spill if the TV set were turned upside down, but 4-year-olds seemed to understand that they were seeing pictures and not the people or objects themselves (Flavell et al., 1990). The investigators explain that the younger children's confusion results from their incomplete understanding that one thing can represent another.

By the time they are 5, children in the United States have a good feel for the various categories of programming they watch, such as news programs, dramas, educational programming, and cartoons. This information helps them decide when to take what they see on television as real and when to understand it as pretend. They are still susceptible to confusion, however. Aimee Dorr (1983) reports that children under the age of 7 often have difficulty understanding that when a bad guy is shot on television, the actor isn't really dead, or when a husband beats his wife, the actress isn't really hurt. Even 7- and 8-year-olds will claim that actors and actresses who play married couples must be friends, and they do not realize that fictional programs are rehearsed (Wright et al., 1994).

Confusion about the reality of television is not restricted to children. From time to time one reads of an irate adult assaulting an actor who portrays an evil character in a soap opera. But the problem is more acute for young children because they have little independent knowledge of the world with which to compare what they see on television. Some physical features of the medium and the way it is used may also confuse them.

The problem of television form

Television, like film, allows extraordinary flexibility in the way realistic visual images can be made and sequenced. Aware that the viewers' attention is attracted by movement and change, television directors use quick cuts from one scene or one camera angle to another, jolting expectations to keep us from turning away. The popular children's program "Sesame Street," for example, was deliberately designed to have a new cut on the average of every 30 seconds as a means of maintaining the attention of young children (Lesser, 1974).

Many techniques of television production help to focus adult viewers' attention and highlight the central message: close-up shots pick out essential details, camera placement gives hints about point of view, flashbacks fill in earlier parts of the story. These thought-shaping techniques are a great resource for conveying meaning, but they have their negative side as well, particularly for young children (Salomon, 1984).

Unless the subject matter is familiar, young children have difficulty interpreting sequences of quick scene changes without transitions. Juxtapositions of images intended to convey the relation of one action to another may also give them difficulty (see Figure 11.5). At the same time, some formal techniques, such as the use of lively music and sound effects, heighten young children's attention and interest in programming.

As a consequence of the limitations in their understanding, children often fail to comprehend a good deal of what they watch, although they do better when the program has been designed to take their special interpretive needs into account (Blosser & Roberts, 1985; Lorch, 1994). Comprehension improves markedly during middle childhood, but even 9- and 10-year-olds have difficulty understanding fast-paced programs that do not clearly show the continuity of action from one sequence to the next (Wright et al., 1984).

To the extent that television techniques communicate successfully and program content is remembered, a different concern arises. Television provides a prefabricated, alternative world that requires little mental effort on the part of viewers once they have sufficient background knowledge and mastery of its forms. Furthermore, its fast pace makes it impossible to stop and ponder what is being presented. Do these characteristics affect children's responses to the world beyond the television set? Evidence that they do has been reported by Gavriel Salomon (1984). He found that children socialized to learn from television had lower than normal expectations about the amount of mental work required to learn from written texts. As such a finding suggests, children who watch a great deal of television read less and fare relatively poorly when they get to school (Comstock & Paik, 1991).

The problem of television content

To the extent that children accept the ideas and behavior presented on television as appropriate models for their own behavior, there is good reason to be concerned about the content of what they view.

One major concern about television is the widespread presence of stereotyping: people who belong to an identifiable social category (Latinos, women, scientists) are portrayed as if they all had the same personality characteristics, lived in the same kinds of surroundings, and engaged in the same activities. In one of the earliest studies of ethnic stereotyping, Dallas Smythe (1954) found that African Americans (who made up only 2 percent of TV characters at the time) were portrayed only as servants, entertainers, or buffoons. By the 1980s, the proportion of African American characters appearing in television programming had increased markedly, but stereotyping had not disappeared, it had only changed. Although

FIGURE 11.5 *An item from a test that assesses children's ability to re-create an entire setting on the basis of partial glimpses. Each card corresponds to a camera angle used in films and television programs. Children are asked to put the four cards together to make a meaningful scene. (From Greenfield, 1984.)*

some African Americans appeared on television as positive characters, most appeared primarily as criminals or victims of crime (Barcus, 1983). The same was (and still is) true of portrayals of other minority groups in the United States, as well as characters depicted as foreigners; Italians are likely to be stereotyped as gangsters and Latin Americans as lazy or as drug-smuggling criminals (Berry & Asamen, 1993).

Television's stereotyping goes beyond ethnicity. Nancy Signorelli (1991, 1993) reports that men outnumber women about 4 to 1 in children's commercial programming. Men are portrayed as decisive and aggressive, while women are more likely to be victims. When women do appear as characters on television shows, they are mainly given supporting roles as wives, girlfriends, or other family members. If they are employed, they are more likely to be nurses or secretaries than doctors and CEOs. The elderly fare no better. They are seen relatively little on television, and when a comment is made about an elderly person on Saturday-morning programming for children, it is almost always negative (Kovaric, 1993).

Despite continuing pressure to make television for children more representative of everyday reality, the content of children's programming is remarkably stable. In a recent study of Saturday-morning commercial programs for children, Bradley Greenberg and Jeffrey Brand (1994) found only three that regularly featured African Americans, one that had a Latino character, and none representing other ethnic minorities. Greenberg and Brand comment wryly that "Saturday's commercial television programming schedule is fairly empty as a carrier of multicultural information" (p. 142).

The issue of stereotyping on television in general and in children's programming in particular is of concern because research indicates that the way various social groups are presented on TV influences young children's everyday behavior in the direction suggested by the TV portrayals. Greenberg and Brand (1994) report that when asked about their favorite programs and favorite characters, children identify with the protagonists who are members of their ethnic group. Given the generally negative depiction of women and minorities on children's television, the absence of positive role models is an obvious source of concern.

On the positive side, children who watch episodes of "Sesame Street," in which children of various ethnic groups are portrayed in positive ways, are increasingly willing to play with children of those groups (Gorn, Goldberg, & Kanango, 1976). Young children who watch televised episodes in which children play in non–sex-stereotyped ways are similarly affected. If the televised episodes

Parents often use television as a baby-sitter. Research shows, however, that children get more out of television viewing when their parents are there to discuss the programs with them, as is the case with this Swedish family.

portray children playing with dolls representing their own sex, sex-stereotyped toy selection increases; but if the televised children play with toys associated with the opposite sex, cross-sex toy selections increase (Comstock & Paik, 1991).

Special concerns about violence

The high level of violence on television has long been a social concern. Fully 80 percent of the television programs that young Americans watch include at least one violent event, and many contain more. To be sure, many of these images are in the form of cartoons, in which Roadrunner and the Coyote commit mayhem on each other. To the public at large, however, it seems obvious that a constant diet of violent behavior on television—even cartoon violence—fosters the attitude that violence is an acceptable way to settle disputes. Psychological research to assess the impact of television on aggressive behavior is not quite so conclusive.

Experimental studies show that after children watch a violent program, they act more aggressively in a laboratory playroom than children who have watched more benign programs. (Such work was described in the discussion of imitation in Chapter 10, p. 410). Critics have claimed, however, that the artificial circumstances of the experiment are so different from the way children view television at home that it is impossible to generalize the result to real-life circumstances.

Many studies also find a positive correlation between viewing television violence and acting aggressively. More aggressive children watch more violent programming. In this case critics remind us that correlation does not imply causation (Chapter 1, p. 22, discusses this principle) and that two very different conclusions are equally logical. The correlations alone give us no way of deciding whether children who already have a tendency to be aggressive enjoy watching violent action on television (and therefore seek it out) or whether television watching is the cause of their aggressiveness.

Some of the most convincing evidence that television watching increases aggressive behavior in children comes from "natural experiments" that reveal the impact of television on populations that have not been previously exposed to it. Tannis Williams (1986) conducted one such study in three small communities in Canada in the 1980s. One community had never had TV before, one had a single channel, and one had several available channels. He found that in the previously isolated community, elementary schoolchildren's behavior on the playground became more aggressive during the two years after the introduction of TV. The level of children's aggressiveness did *not* change in the two communities that already had television, an indication that the introduction of television was the causal factor.

Despite the technical difficulties of proving a causal link between viewing violence on television and engaging in violence, the current consensus is that watching violence on television does in fact increase violent behavior in many viewers, whether or not they were otherwise "predisposed" to it (Comstock & Paik, 1991; Gunter, 1994; Van Evra, 1990).

Family influences

The evidence that television affects children's behavior is complemented by equally strong evidence that the family can temper those influences. When Jerome and Dorothy Singer (1980) studied patterns of family viewing in a working-class community in the eastern United States, they found that the homes of highly aggressive preschoolers who watched a lot of television had relatively few books or records. These children were often permitted to stay up late to watch any program they wanted to. Their parents rarely took them out of the house, except to the market or to the movies. The families of less aggressive children, in contrast, tended to keep tighter control on the way their children spent their time. They restricted their children's television viewing to educational and children's

EDITING: THE BIONIC PUZZLE

Here are three pictures showing how a bionic jump is done. How does the bionic jump look on TV? You can find out by cutting out the three small pictures at the bottom of the page and pasting them onto the big TV screen.

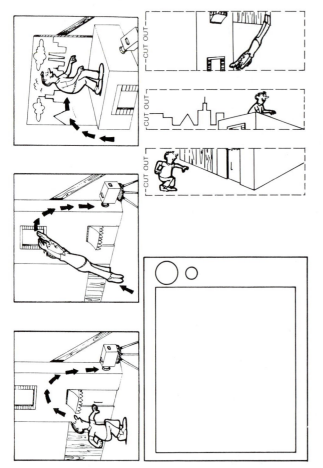

FIGURE 11.6 *Sample exercise to help people interpret the conventions of editing used in television production. (From Singer, Singer, & Zuckerman, 1981.)*

programs. Their children were more likely than those in the more aggressive group to go to bed early and to be taken to parks, museums, and cultural events.

When parents watch television with their children and talk about what they see, the children absorb more of the content (Signorelli, 1991). The parents can provide connections that the children miss and remind them of related events in their own lives, helping them to make sense of what is happening on the screen.

The message of these findings is that if parents are concerned about the negative effects of television on their children's behavior, they should restrict the amount of time the children spend watching television and increase the amount of time they join their children in front of the television set. Some informative guides have been written to help parents and children get the most out of watching television (see Figure 11.6) (Dorr, Graves, & Phelps, 1980; Singer & Kelley, 1984).

BOOKS

The belief that reading will enhance children's development is as pervasive as the worry that extensive television viewing may impede it. The positive opinion of reading comes in part from a belief that reading to children stimulates their mental development and in part from general approval of the content of the stories written for children.

In some ways being read to is much like watching television. In both cases, children must extract meaning from words and pictures that represent familiar elements of the everyday world. They encounter problems with both media when their limited experience of the world makes it difficult for them to arrive at a plausible interpretation of what they are seeing and hearing. The evidence on the effects of reading to children is not so extensive as that on television viewing, but the limited data available provide an instructive contrast between the two media.

The form of early literacy experiences

In the United States, young children of every social class are exposed to print in some form almost every day, even if only for a few minutes (Anderson & Stokes, 1984; McLane & McNamee, 1990). Sometimes the children are just "hanging around" while their parents read a letter or discuss their big sister's homework. But young children are also likely to be seen talking about the messages on cereal boxes, asking for help with a television schedule or instructions for a game, and carrying notes from preschool. These experiences teach them that the marks on paper somehow convey information, a form of knowledge about reading and writing that is currently referred to as "emergent literacy" (Teale & Sulzby, 1986) (see Figure 11.7).

Evidence indicates that young children who are often read to at home learn to read relatively easily once they start school (McLane & McNamee, 1990; Scarborough & Dobrich, 1994). Anat Ninio and Jerome Bruner's (1978) study of parents reading to their 1- to 2-year-old children suggests how such experiences might help children's later reading. For example, Richard, who is seated on his mother's lap, is engaged by his mother in a stylized, cyclical form of dialogue focused on the picture in a book. With few exceptions, each cycle in their conversation goes something like this:

Mother: *(pointing to a picture)* Look at this!
Richard: *(touches picture or gives some other indication of attention)*
Mother: What is it?
Richard: A doggy.
Mother: Right! *(turns pages and initiates a new round)*

Once children begin to attend school, the vast majority of their instructional experience will occur in a similar format:

Teacher: Who knows the capital city of France?
Student: Paris.
Teacher: That's right! *(then the teacher initiates a new round)*

When children are young, adults may fill in the labels for objects and accept any sort of contribution from the child as an adequate turn. As the child's knowledge increases, adults supply less help in keeping the game going. Instead they raise the stakes by choosing more complex texts and pictures, or by asking more complicated questions about old favorites (De Loache, 1984). This kind of tailored support that keeps changing to fit children's growing competence creates the "zone of proximal development" discussed in earlier chapters.

Parents who introduce their children to books in the way Ninio and Bruner described also talk to their children about the contents of books at odd times of the day when no books are present (Heath, 1982; Crago & Crago, 1983). These parents make it clear to their children that the pictures and texts in books are relevant to the world at large, thus helping them to acquire more powerful cognitive schemas.

Shirley Brice Heath (1982, 1984) has found that when parents seldom read picture and storybooks to their children, the whole structure and purpose of reading are likely to differ from the pattern described by Ninio and Bruner. In some families she observed, being read to was an occasion more for learning to sit still than for making sense of pictures and words. Children who learn that kind of lesson well may have trouble learning to read once they begin school, even if they sit very quietly and behave themselves in class.

This little boy who is pretending to read an upside-down newspaper has acquired part of the idea of what it means to read just by watching the people around him, but there are many crucial elements still to be learned.

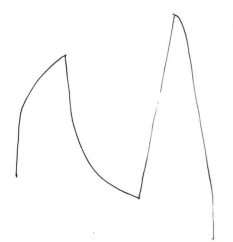

FIGURE 11.7 Left: *"An* M *. . . What does that spell? It spells* M *for Molly."* Right: *"And it could be a rabbit. See, it's got big ears."* Here 3½-year-old Molly uses the letter M *in two different ways as she begins to get the idea of writing. For Molly, the letter and the drawing are only fragilely differentiated (Gardner, Wolf, & Smith, 1982).*

Dialogic reading A form of reading in which the adults actively listen to the children read, asking questions, adding information of interest, and prompting the children to increase their contributions to the interaction until they are retelling the story in their own words.

Grover Whitehurst and his colleagues (1994) have developed a special form of joint reading they call **dialogic reading.** In dialogic reading the adult listens actively, asking questions, adding information of interest, and prompting the children to increase the complexity of their contributions until they are retelling the story in their own way. Whitehurst and his co-workers report that after 30 reading sessions spread over 6 weeks, young children speak more grammatically, express ideas better, and identify the component sounds of words more accurately. These achievements are known to be important to learning to read. Since the program has been effective across a wide range of family backgrounds, these researchers are urging that it be taught to parents as a means of promoting cognitive development.

Perhaps the most crucial difference between young children's viewing television and their being read to is seen in the degree to which adults control the content to which their children are exposed. Because few young children can read, most are exposed only to those books that adults deem appropriate and are willing to read to them. By contrast, once small children can toddle over to the television set and push the buttons, they are likely to hear and see programs that were not designed for them, including programs with relatively high levels of sex and violence.

From time to time books that have traditionally been read to children have come under fire for the harm they allegedly do to a child's view of the world. Most fairy tales and myths were created in the centuries before childhood was considered a special period of life and before any literature had been specifically devised for children (Sale, 1978). Adults have occasionally argued (echoing arguments about television) that fairy tales should not be read to children because they are brutal, cruel, and frightening, and are not realistic portrayals of the world. They condemn such stories as not sensible or "educational." Others, such as the psychoanalyst Bruno Bettelheim, have insisted that children need fairy tales. "Like all great art, fairy tales both delight and instruct; their special genius is that they do so in terms which speak directly to children" (Bettelheim, 1977, p. 56). Bettelheim believed that the very unreality of such stories allows children to use them to find solutions to their own inner conflicts; it is certainly less threatening to think about Cinderella's evil stepmother than to think consciously about real negative feelings toward one's own mother or father (see Box 11.3).

Another frequent complaint is that too many children's books ignore or misrepresent certain ethnic and racial groups, women, and working-class and poor people. As in the case of television, these concerns have frequently been supported by surveys of the contents of children's books (Weiss, 1983).

Whether in the form of a television situation comedy, an evening news bulletin, or a story about a beautiful princess, the larger world of adult pursuits enters the homes of children through a great variety of media. Evidence supports the conclusion that the influence of a particular form of mediated experience is neither good nor bad in any fixed, objective sense. How one assesses the value of, say, reading fairy tales or Bible stories or watching adult programming on television depends on the values one wishes to perpetuate in the home and the community and one's idea of the future life for which the child is being prepared.

The Young Child in the Community

As long as parents remain at home with their young children, they can retain relatively direct control over outside influences, even the influence of television. But when the parents leave their children in the care of other people for several hours a day, the nature of that control—not to mention the nature of their children's ex-

BOX 11.3

The Sense of Nonsense Verse

Kornei Chukovsky, a Russian author of poems for children, was sometimes accused of damaging children by his use of fantasy. The following letter is typical of the criticism he received during the Soviet years:

> Shame on you, Comrade Chukovsky, for filling the heads of our children with all kinds of nonsense, such as that trees grow shoes. I have read with indignation in one of your books such fantastic lines as:
>
> Frogs fly in the sky,
> Fish sit in fishermen's laps,
> Mice catch cats
> And lock them up in
> Mousetraps.
>
> Why do you distort realistic facts? Children need socially useful information and not fantastic stories about white bears who cry cock-a-doodle-doo.
>
> That is not what we expect from our children's authors. We want them to clarify for the

child the world that surrounds him, instead of confusing his brain with all kinds of nonsense.

In defense of his nonsense verse, Chukovsky had this to say of the man who sent the critical letter:

> Had he had other resources than "common sense," he would have realized that the nonsense that seemed to him so harmful not only does not interfere with the child's orientation to the world that surrounds him, but, on the contrary, strengthens in his mind a sense of the real; and that it is precisely in order to further the education of children in reality that such nonsense verse should be offered to them. For the child is so constituted that in the first years of his existence we can plant realism in his mind not only directly, by acquainting him with the realities in his surroundings, but also by means of fantasy. (1968, pp. 89–90)

periences—changes in a decisive way. In the United States and other industrialized countries, one of the most important tasks many parents face is to select the day care or preschool that will provide the upbringing of their children during those hours.

VARIETIES OF DAY CARE

At present more than 60 percent of U.S. mothers with children younger than 6 are working and have placed their children in some form of supervised care (U.S. Bureau of the Census, 1995). One of the most popular arrangements for children younger than 5 is **home care**—care provided in their own homes, primarily by their fathers or grandmothers—while their mothers are at work. **Day-care centers**—organized child-care facilities supervised by licensed professionals—have attracted the most public attention, yet they represent the arrangement least often used. The most commonly used is **family care**—child care provided in someone else's home, that of either a relative or a stranger (U.S. Bureau of the Census, 1994). The kind of care chosen depends in most cases on availability, cost, the parents' judgments about the quality of care offered, and the age and number of children in need of care (Belsky, Steinberg, & Walker, 1982) (see Figure 11.8).

Home care Child care provided in the child's own home either by a relative or by a paid babysitter.

Day-care centers Organized child-care facilities supervised by licensed professionals.

Family care Child care provided in the home of someone else who is either a relative or a stranger.

Home care

Because child care in the home is so private, relatively little is known about it. One study that compared various types of care confirmed what common sense might lead one to expect (Clarke-Stewart, 1993). Children cared for at home

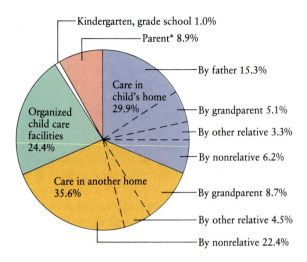

Kindergarten, grade school 1.0%
Parent* 8.9%
By father 15.3%
Care in child's home 29.9%
By grandparent 5.1%
Organized child care facilities 24.4%
By other relative 3.3%
By nonrelative 6.2%
Care in another home 35.6%
By grandparent 8.7%
By other relative 4.5%
By nonrelative 22.4%

*Includes mothers working at home or away from home.

FIGURE 11.8 *Primary child-care arrangements used by working mothers for children under 5 years of age in 1991. (From U.S. Bureau of the Census, Current Population Reports, Series P-70, 36 [1994].)*

experience the least change from normal routine: they eat food provided by their parents and take naps in their own beds. They also come in contact with relatively few children their own age.

Family day care

Family day care often exposes children not only to caretakers from outside the family circle but also to new settings and to children of other families. The children in a family day-care setting may range widely in age, forming a more diverse social group than is likely to exist at home. The routine of activities in family day care, however, is usually very similar to the routine at home (Clarke-Stewart, 1993).

State, county, or local government agencies grant licenses to family day-care homes that meet basic health and safety requirements and maintain acceptable adult-child ratios. A study that examined the quality of care in licensed family child-care homes with respect to the child's safety, the communication about the child between the parent of the child and the day-care provider, and the nature of the relationship between the day-care provider and the children found that licensing is no guarantee of high quality. Only 9 percent of the regulated child-care providers were found to offer good care, 56 percent were rated as providing minimal care, and 5 percent as providing inadequate care (Galinsky et al., 1994). Minority children and children whose family incomes are low are more likely to be in poor-quality family day-care homes than Anglo children and children whose parents have higher incomes (Galinsky et al., 1994).

The great majority of family day-care homes, however, are not licensed (Galinsky et al., 1994; Zigler & Finn-Stevenson, 1992). Observers have found that unlicensed providers are even less likely than licensed ones to give comfort, verbal stimulation, and guidance to the children in their care (Goelman, 1988).

Day-care centers

Licensed day-care centers generally offer a wider variety of formal learning experiences than family or home day care, and are likely to employ at least one trained caretaker. Waiting lists for places in day-care centers tend to be long, however, since the demand far exceeds the available openings.

Because licensed day-care centers often receive public financing, they have been more accessible to researchers, who have studied both their characteristics and the way these characteristics affect children's development. Here are some of the findings:

- Day-care centers with populations of more than 60 children place more emphasis on rules than smaller centers do, are relatively inflexible in their scheduling, and offer children fewer opportunities to initiate or control their own activities. Teachers in large centers tend to show less sensitivity to the needs of individual children, perhaps because there are so many children for them to supervise (Clarke-Stewart & Fein, 1983).

- The most important factor for 3- to 5-year-old children is the size of the day-care group and the ratio of adults to children (Howes et al., 1992). Groups of fewer than 15 to 18 children and ones in which there is at least one adult for every eight children allow for more individual contact and

These children at a day-care center are obtaining the kind of experience in getting along in groups that is one of the major features of the day-care experience.

more verbal interaction between children and adults, and for more active involvement in group activities (McCartney et al., 1985).

- A committed and stable staff that has been given some training and an administrator who is experienced increase the quality of a center's care (Cost, Quality, & Child Outcomes Study Team, 1995).

The programs offered by day-care centers vary in style and philosophy. Some offer an academic curriculum, emphasize discipline, and have a schoollike atmosphere. Others emphasize social development and allow children to exercise more initiative in their activities. In accord with the class differences in modes of parenting discussed earlier in this chapter, most lower-class parents have been found to prefer the more schoollike day-care centers, while middle-class parents are likely to choose the less structured centers (Joffe, 1977).

DEVELOPMENTAL EFFECTS OF DAY CARE

Psychologists disagree sharply about the developmental impact of day care on young children, just as they do about its impact on infants (see Box 7.1). Such notable figures in the field of child development as Selma Fraiberg (1977) and Burton L. White (1975) have claimed that prolonged daily separation of young children from their mothers is detrimental to their development. Others conclude that as long as day care is of high quality, it is not bad for young children and can even make positive contributions to their later intellectual and social development (Egeland & Heister, 1995; Kontos et al., 1994; Scarr, Phillips, & McCartney, 1990). Table 11.5 lists six features that are believed to contribute to high quality in day care.

Shortcomings of the evidence

These disagreements are difficult to resolve because intensive research on day care is still in its infancy, and many of the studies have been subject to some important limitations. First, a great deal of the early research on the effects of day care was

TABLE 11.5　Federal Interagency Day-Care Requirements

1. A planned daily program of activities that are developmentally appropriate and that are designed to promote children's intellectual, social, emotional, and physical development.
2. Caregivers with specialized training in child care who have also had an orientation to health and safety procedures for the particular setting.
3. Adequate and nutritious meals.
4. A health record for each child.
5. Opportunities for parents to observe the setting and to discuss the child's needs before enrollment and during the time the child attends the center.
6. Small group sizes and low child-to-staff ratios.

Source: Clarke-Stewart, 1992.

conducted in university-affiliated day-care centers of high quality. The experience of children in these centers is probably not representative. This problem is being redressed by comparative studies of children in high- and low-quality day care (McCartney, 1984; McCartney et al., 1985). But caution must be exercised when one attempts to generalize about the effects of programs that differ both in the backgrounds of the families involved *and* in the quality of care offered (Howes & Olenick, 1986).

Second, most research has looked only at the immediate effects of day care, leaving open the question of possible long-term effects. Finally, the families of children in day care are not a random sample of all families with young children. The lack of clear data comparing families that do and don't use day care raises the possibility that differences between children found at the end of the program were there at the beginning, and resulted not from day care but from other aspects of their family situation (Howes & Olenick, 1986). Despite these limitations, suggestive findings have emerged.

Intellectual effects

The intellectual development of middle-class children in adequately staffed and equipped day-care centers is at least as good as that of children raised at home by their parents (Clarke-Stewart, 1993; Clarke-Stewart & Fein, 1983) (see Figure 11.9).

Experience in high-quality day-care programs seems in some cases to lessen or prevent the decline in intellectual performance that sometimes occurs after the age of 2 when children of low-income families remain at home with poorly educated parents. Such programs may even lead to marked gains in language and cognitive development among these children (Burchinal, Lee, & Ramey, 1989; Caughy, DiPietro, & Strobino, 1994; McCartney et al., 1985; Wasik et al., 1990).

Impact on social development

Children who attend day-care centers in the United States tend to be more self-sufficient and more independent of parents and teachers, more helpful and cooperative with peers and mothers, more verbally expressive, more knowledgeable about the social world, and more comfortable in new situations. On the other hand, they tend to be less polite, less agreeable, less compliant with adults, and more aggressive than children who do not attend day-care centers (Haskins, 1985; Howes & Olenick, 1986). These effects seem to be related to the number of years a child spends in full-time nonparental care, with more extensive time being associated with more aggressive behavior (Honig & Park, 1993). This undesirable behavior seems to carry over to kindergarten. John Bates and his colleagues (1994) found that the more years children spent in day care, the more likely they were to have behavior problems in kindergarten.

The effects of day care may vary with the quality of care and the involvement of the child's parents. Many parents whose children are in low-quality day care have stressful lives and consequently are less involved in their children's activities than those whose children attend high-quality day-care centers (Howes & Olenick, 1986). By contrast, when there is strong government support for day care and financial support for parents, as there is in Sweden, day care may have a marked positive effect on social development, even day care that begins during the first year of life (Anderson, 1992).

It isn't necessary to look far for an explanation of day care's effects on a preschooler's social development. At home the wishes and needs of small children are often anticipated, their social incompetence is overlooked, and their failures at communication are filled in. Care supplied outside the home requires children to get along with adults who know less about their special likes and dislikes and who must fit several children into a common schedule. In addition, children who receive day care must learn to interact successfully with a variety of other children, often when few adults are present.

These children usually have more opportunities to turn to peers for companionship, affection, amusement, and a sense of identity and belonging. Experience with groups their own age helps children to learn about their strengths and weaknesses by comparing themselves with others. The flowering of language at the end of the second year and the beginning of the third adds an important dimension to children's social interactions that influences their experiences in day care. By the time children are 2½ they are able to manage interactions with one another that contain, in fledgling form, all the basic features of social interactions among older children and adults—sustained attention, turn-taking, and mutual responsiveness (Rubin, 1980).

Day-care arrangements of various kinds provide children with their first experiences at forming friendships with other children of the same age who are not kin. Carollee Howes (1987) found that friendship formation among preschoolers grows out of mutual social attraction in which the partners reciprocate and complement each other's behaviors, creating a "climate of agreement." Friendships provide children with experience at cooperating and communicating with others. According to Howes, preschoolers are able to carry out more complex actions with close friends of some duration than they can manage with other children, an indication that friendship has positive effects on children's cognitive abilities as well as on their social behavior.

Children's experiences with each other in day-care centers and preschools usually occur around a shared activity, such as playing fantasy games or building with blocks. Observations conducted by William Corsaro (1985) at a state university child-study center indicate that most voluntary interactions among groups of 3- and 4-year-olds are extremely fragile. Such group interactions usually last less than 10 minutes and often end abruptly when a playmate leaves the play area without warning. The fragility of such groups requires that children learn how to gain access to another group—or face the prospect of playing alone.

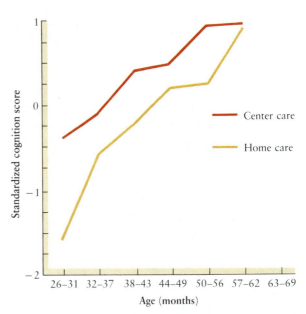

FIGURE 11.9 *Performance on tests of intellectual development by children cared for in day-care centers and by those cared for at home. The tests were specially constructed to assess children's ability to use language, form concepts, and remember information. (From Clarke-Stewart, 1984.)*

Learning to share toys with others is one of the difficult lessons young children have to confront.

An attempt to enter a preexisting group may be rebuffed, especially if the group is made up of good friends. Corsaro (1981) observed the outcome of 128 bids to gain access to a group's ongoing activities. More than 50 percent met with initial resistance. Typical of the reasons children gave for refusing admission to a newcomer are "We don't like you today" and "We only want boys here."

The key to success in entering a group seems to lie in understanding what is going on in the group, what its structure is, and who is doing what, and then using that knowledge to act as if one were already a member of the group. Good communication skills are also an asset (Hazen & Black, 1989). Children who ask socially inappropriate questions about what is going on, criticize what group members are doing, or tell the others how they feel are likely to be rejected when they try to join a group (Putallaz & Gottman, 1981).

Fearing rejection, most young children hover around the periphery of the group before making their first attempt to gain access to it (Corsaro, 1981). As their experience increases, they are more likely to become full participants in the group (Schindler, Moely, & Frank, 1987).

No matter how socially skilled a girl is, she can expect to have particular difficulty gaining entry to a group composed of boys. A little girl who asks to join two boys who are playing on the swings is likely to be told "No! We don't want girls here." At the start of early childhood, boys have a somewhat easier time joining a group of girls, but as they grow older they, too, encounter resistance.

Such exclusivity may be cruel, but according to Corsaro, it functions to preserve existing groups. By excluding others, the members of a group give themselves a special identity. They become "we," as opposed to outsiders, who are "they." Their rejections protect their ongoing interactions from the disruption of a newcomer, especially one who plays differently.

It is these kinds of experiences—gaining access to group activities, learning to become desirable companions, and dealing with rejection—that are the most likely social benefits of day care. On the negative side, some of the behavior children learn in day care may conflict with their parents' standards of appropriate behavior at home and elsewhere.

PRESCHOOL

Day care originated in response to the needs of adults who wanted their children supervised while they worked or went to school. By contrast, the purpose of preschool (which used to be called nursery school) is primarily educational. Preschools came into being early in the twentieth century out of educators' and physicians' concern that the complexities of urban life were overwhelming children and stunting their development. The preschool was conceived as "a protected environment scaled to [children's] developmental level and designed to promote experiences of mastery within a child-sized manageable world" (Prescott & Jones, 1971, p. 54). The basic intuition justifying preschools as environments for development is contained in the botanical metaphor of the child as a budding flower. At the age of 5 many children "graduate" from preschool to kindergarten, a "garden for children" (from the German *Kinder* [children] and *Garten* [garden]). To extend the metaphor, 3- and 4-year-old children are not ready for the rigors

of a garden where rain falls, wind blows, and birds forage for seeds. Like the seedlings at a local garden store (a nursery!), they are most likely to develop healthily if they are specially protected until they are ready for transplanting.

A typical preschool's layout and schedule reveal prevalent ideas of how best to foster development from the age of 2½ to 6 (see Box 11.4). There are likely to be several kinds of play areas: a sandbox, a water-play table, a doll corner, a block area, a large area with a rug where children can gather to listen to stories or sing songs, a cluster of low tables used for arts-and-crafts projects and for snacks, and an outdoor area with jungle gyms, slides, and swings. Each area provides an environment for developing a different aspect of children's overall potential: their ability to understand physical transformations in play materials; to control their own bodies; to create in language, song, clay, and paint; to adopt various social roles; and to get along with other children.

During the 2½ to 3 hours that children may spend in a preschool, they are guided from one activity area to another. The developmental spirit of preschools is reflected in their lack of pressure on children to perform correctly on preassigned tasks and in their emphasis on exploration.

Entering the play of children of the opposite sex presents special difficulties, but it is by no means impossible, especially if you have control of an attractive plaything.

Preschools and the "War on Poverty"

In the 1960s a variety of scientific and social factors combined to create great interest in preschools' potential to increase the educational chances of the poor. On the scientific side was a growing belief that environmental influence during the first few years of life is crucial to all later abilities, especially intellectual ones (see Chapter 7). This belief coincided with broader historical pressures to improve the status of ethnic and racial minorities and with widespread political concern that social barriers between the rich and the poor and between whites and blacks were

BOX 11.4

Cultural Variations in Preschool Education

When we compare the lives of young children in a traditional agricultural society and a modern industrialized society (as the Whitings did in their study of children in Kenya and New England), we are not surprised to discover that small children occupy vastly different developmental niches in the two societies. But when we look at two industrialized societies with apparently similar institutions for socializing children, we may not expect cultural variations to be so prominent. Yet when Joseph Tobin, David Wu, and Dana Davidson (1989) compared preschools in Japan and the United States, they found that even though the preschools were physically similar, the differences in the adults' socialization practices were very marked.

On the day Tobin and his colleagues were videotaping the 4-year-old group at Komatsudani Hoikuen, a Buddhist preschool in Kyoto, Hiroki was acting up. He greeted the visitors by exposing his penis and waving it at them. He initiated fights, disrupted other children's games, and made obscene comments.

American preschool teachers who observed the videotape disapproved of Hiroki's behavior, his teacher's handling of it, and many aspects of life in the Japanese classroom in general. They were shocked to see 30 preschoolers and only one teacher in the classroom. How could this be in a country as affluent as Japan? they asked. They could not understand why the teacher ignored Hiroki instead of isolating him or giving him "time out" as punishment.

The Japanese viewed the matter very differently. First, though Japanese teachers acknowledged that it would be very pleasant for them to have a smaller class, they believed it would be bad for the children. Children, they said, "need to have the experience of being in a large group in order to learn to relate to lots of children in lots of kinds of situations" (p. 37). When the Japanese teachers observed a tape of an American preschool with 18 children and two teachers, they worried for the children. "A class that size seems kind of sad and underpopulated," one remarked. Another added, "I wonder how you teach a child to become a member of a group in a class that small."

Members of the two cultures also had very different interpretations of the probable reasons for Hiroki's outrageous behavior. One American teacher speculated that perhaps Hiroki misbehaved because he was intellectually gifted and easily became bored. The Japanese educators rejected this notion out of hand. To them, "smart" and "intelligent" are almost synonymous with "well behaved" and "praiseworthy," neither of which applied to Hiroki. Hiroki, they believed, had a "dependency disorder." Because his mother was absent from the home, he had not learned how to be properly dependent, so he did not know how to be sensitive and obedient. Isolating Hiroki, they reasoned, would not help. Rather, he needed to learn to get along in his group. To this end his teacher encouraged the other children in the class to take responsibility for helping

creating a dangerous situation in the United States. In 1963, Michael Harrington warned that the United States was creating

> an enormous concentration of young people who, if they do not receive immediate help, may well be the source of a kind of hereditary poverty new to American society. If this analysis is correct, then the vicious circle of poverty is, if anything, becoming more intense, more crippling, and problematic. (1963, p. 188)

This combination of social, political, and scientific factors led the U.S. Congress to declare a "war on poverty" in 1964. One of the key programs in this "war" was Project Head Start. Its purpose was to intervene in the cycle of poverty at a crucial time in children's lives by providing them with important learning experiences that they might otherwise miss. Federal support enabled Head Start programs to offer these experiences at no charge to low-income families.

Hiroki to correct his behavior. Tobin and his colleagues point out that

> Japanese teachers and Japanese society place [great value] on equality and the notion that children's success and failure and their potential to become successful versus failed adults has more to do with effort and character and thus with what can be learned and taught in school than with raw inborn ability. (p. 24)

The Japanese preschool teachers who watched a videotape of an American preschool classroom disapproved of the individualism they observed, believing that "a child's humanity is realized most fully not so much in his ability to be independent from the group as his ability to cooperate and feel part of the group" (p. 39). But the very qualities the Japanese deplored in the Americans—independence, self-reliance—were the ones the Americans most wished to promote.

At the American preschool, disputes between children were negotiated daily, with the children "playing the roles of plaintiff, defendant, and attorney, and teachers playing the role of judge" (p. 166). This means of resolving classroom disputes struck some of the Japanese as cumbersome and heavy-handed. They believed that children should be left, as much as possible, to devise their own techniques for resolving conflicts. "I was surprised by the way the American teacher got right in the middle of the children's disputes," one Japanese teacher wrote after viewing a fight between two American boys. A Japanese school administrator added:

> For my taste there is something about the American approach [teachers take children who misbehave aside and talk to them] that is a bit too heavy, too adultlike, too severe and controlled for young children. (p. 53)

This comparison of American and Japanese preschools reveals a fundamental fact about the influence of culture on children's development. The difference in the sizes of the classes was not a result of necessity. The Japanese have the resources to limit their classes to 15 children if they chose to do so. The pattern of preschool education in each society is shaped by what the adults imagine the future will be for their charges, both in later grades and in later life. The American preschool educators imagine that it is desirable for the children in their classrooms to become self-sufficient and independent adults; the Japanese educators want their young charges to become sensitive adults who have a strong sense of interdependence with their group. Much as parents treat their newborn boys and girls differently, not because they are so very different but because they *will* be different as adults, the American and Japanese teachers are helping the children in their classrooms to develop the characteristics they imagine they will need as adults in their society.

This strategy of social reform through early childhood education rested on three crucial assumptions:

1. The environmental conditions of poverty-level homes are insufficient to prepare children to succeed in school.
2. Schooling is the social mechanism that permits children to succeed in our society.
3. Poor children could succeed in school, and thereby overcome their poverty, if they were given extra assistance in the preschool years.

When President Lyndon Johnson initiated Head Start, he declared that because of this project, "thirty million man-years—the combined life span of these youngsters—will be spent productively and rewardingly, rather than wasted in tax-supported institutions or welfare-supported lethargy."

Originally conceived as a summer program, Head Start soon began to operate year round, serving approximately 200,000 preschool children at a time

(Consortium for Longitudinal Studies, 1983). More than three decades later, Head Start programs continue to play an important role in the lives of many U.S. children (Kerr, 1995).

What difference does Head Start make?

Because preschools have gained considerable social acceptance since the 1960s, it might be assumed that the preschool experience proved to have positive benefits for children. The data are not so clear-cut.

Planners of Project Head Start and other preschool programs were sensitive to the need for scientific demonstrations of the usefulness of preschools (Zigler & Valentine, 1979). The logical requirements for providing such proof were simple enough: select a large sample of children; give half of them (the experimental group), chosen at random, the experimental preschool experience; and let the other half of the sample (the control group) stay home. But the demand for preschool was so great that every effort was made to provide a place for every child whose parent applied. No parents wanted their children to be part of a control group, so the logic of experimental design was bypassed. As a result, there has been a great deal of controversy over the developmental consequences of Head Start programs.

The first reports were promising. Children who attended a single summer program showed marked gains in standardized test scores. Hundreds of thousands of parents were involved in their children's school lives for the first time, whether as members of Head Start planning boards, as participants in special training programs for parents, or as classroom helpers. A great many children received better nutrition and health care through Head Start (Condry, 1983).

Doubts about the effectiveness of the program were soon heard, however. In 1969 it was reported that the effects of Head Start slowly disappeared during the first 3 years of elementary school (Grotberg, 1969). A widely publicized evaluation by the Westinghouse Learning Corporation (1969) concluded that although "full-year Head Start appears to be a more effective compensatory education program than summer Head Start, its benefits cannot be described as satisfactory" (p. 11).

These children attending a Head Start program are learning skills and acquiring attitudes that are intended to help them succeed in school in later years.

People who had never favored Head Start programs felt their doubts had been confirmed by the Westinghouse report. But supporters were by no means persuaded. They pointed out that the Westinghouse study lacked any proper control groups, substituting a variety of doubtful statistics instead.

In 1989 Ron Haskins, a psychologist and staff member of the Ways and Means Committee of the House of Representatives, reviewed all of the major studies of Head Start programs for which data concerning later developmental impact were available. The evidence included Head Start's model experimental preschool programs and the ordinary Head Start programs mounted without support from researchers. By 1989 it was possible to assess follow-up evaluations of children as they reached their early 20s and to include broader developmental indicators such as crime rates and earned income in the assessment.

This broad evaluation revealed a mixed picture. On the positive side, Haskins found that the children who had attended regular Head Start programs and special, model programs showed meaningful gains in intellectual performance and socioemotional development. Attendance at Head Start also reduced the likelihood that the children would be assigned to remedial special-education classes when they were in school. Only the model programs, however, yielded positive outcomes on such indicators as the rates of delinquency, teenage pregnancy, and employment. An important finding was that unless the preschool experience—whether in regular Head Start or a model program—is followed up by a special program later in the child's educational career, the impact of the "head start" grows smaller and smaller, and often fades out altogether.

Current evidence indicates that preschool experience for the children of low-income families can make a difference in their later school achievement, and perhaps in their later life success, but this positive outcome is by no means guaranteed. High-quality programs that are maintained longer than the initial "head start" are necessary to realize the hopes placed in preschool education by Head Start's founders (Bryant et al., 1994; Currie & Thomas, 1995).

The future of compensatory preschool programs

Head Start and other compensatory preschool programs face an uncertain future in the United States. In addition to uncertainty about the permanence of gains from programs that last only a year, two major philosophical objections have been raised to the propagation of compensatory preschool programs. First, there is the question of how public money should be spent. Congressional committees that oversee the uses of tax dollars have questioned whether even successful programs are successful enough to justify their costs. In his summary of the relationship between the costs and benefits of Head Start programs, Haskins (1989) concludes that the savings to taxpayers from Head Start programs (measured in the dollars that would otherwise have to be spent for special services and for law enforcement and the criminal justice system) are relatively small. This conclusion leads naturally to a search for more effective ways to use the funds. Second, some critics argue that educational programs cannot compensate for the damage caused by poor housing, inadequate nutrition, discrimination, and parental unemployment. They say that President Johnson and the planners and implementers of Project Head Start were misleading the public. Giving the children of the poor a "head start" would not reduce their poverty.

Despite uncertainty about the long-term effects and cost efficiency of the Head Start program, there are reasons to believe that the program may continue to play a role in the government's efforts in support of children. As Ron Haskins (1989) noted, the Head Start program has become a national symbol of the desire to help poor children advance through self-improvement. Head Start children receive much-needed food, health care, and dental care. They also obtain

An important aspect of the preschool experience is the opportunity to make friends with children one's own age.

intellectual stimulation that increases the chances that they will begin their formal schooling with a firmer foundation and greater hopes of long-term success.

On the Threshold

This chapter has by no means surveyed all of the contexts that significantly influence early childhood development: young children also learn from trips to the beach, attendance at houses of worship, and visits to the doctor's office. Each new context brings with it new social and intellectual challenges as the children gradually piece together a deeper understanding of their world and their place in it.

Recognizing the influence of context on early childhood development helps us make sense of the variable picture each young child presents to the world. In familiar contexts, where children know the appropriate scripts and their own roles in them, they may display mature reasoning and surprising competence. But often they find themselves novices in strange settings where they do not know the appropriate scripts, where they are expected to work out social relationships with strangers, and where they are set new tasks that require them to master new concepts. In these circumstances, their powers of self-expression and self-control are put under great strain, and their thought processes may be inadequate to the heavy demands placed on them.

The problem of being a novice is by no means unique to young children; people face it throughout their lives. But the difficulties are particularly acute at the beginning of early childhood because young children know so little about how their culture works. Consequently, children of this age need almost constant supervision. When they play together, they need some powerful organizing activity, such as pretend play, to support their fragile ability to coordinate with one another.

By the end of early childhood, children's vocabularies and command of grammatical forms have grown immensely. They have greater knowledge about a wide variety of contexts and a more sophisticated sense of themselves; and they are vastly more competent to think about the world, to control themselves, and to deal with other children. In these and many other ways they indicate a readiness to venture into new settings, to take on new social roles, and to accept the additional responsibilities that await them as they enter middle childhood.

SUMMARY

The Family as a Context for Development

- The factors that influence children's lives can be usefully thought of as a nested set of contexts that influence one another.

- The family influences children's development in two ways: by shaping their behavior within the family and by selecting other contexts for them to inhabit.

- Parenting everywhere has three goals: to ensure that the child
  1. Survives into adulthood.
  2. Acquires the skills and resources needed for economic self-sufficiency.
  3. Acquires the cultural values of the group.

- Cross-cultural comparisons of family life reveal that children's social behavior and personalities develop to fit the overall demands of economic activity and community life in their society.

- Family socialization patterns vary within societies, depending on such factors as the family configuration and the values, beliefs, education, income, and personalities of the family members.

- Patterns of socialization can be grouped for purposes of comparison. Child-rearing practices in the United States in most cases follow one of three patterns:
  1. Authoritarian families use set standards and emphasize conformity.
  2. Authoritative families emphasize control through reasoning and discussion.
  3. Permissive families avoid overt control and believe that children should make their own decisions.

- Among white middle-class two-parent families, authoritative child-rearing practices are associated with children who are more self-reliant, self-controlled, and willing to explore than those raised by permissive or authoritarian parents.

- Caution must be used in applying a single set of parenting categories to different cultural groups. Chinese American parenting, for example, is best characterized by an idea of "training" that is not found in European American families.

- A significant number of U.S. children grow up in single-parent families headed by a young unwed mother. These children tend to be more aggressive, less self-controlled, and less cognitively advanced than the children of older married couples.

- Children whose parents have divorced may display a variety of negative reactions, including sleep disturbances, irritability, and aggressiveness. The severity and duration of the dislocation resulting from divorce depend on a variety of factors, including the family income and the configuration of the new family that results if the custodial parent remarries.

- Poverty affects family life in many ways, increasing the stress on parents at the same time that it reduces their resources for dealing with it. Stress, in turn, is associated with authoritarian parenting styles.
- Extended family arrangements provide one means of coping with poverty. The presence of several adults reduces the stress on the parent or parents and provides resources for dealing with the causes of stress.

Media Linking Community and Home

- Influences from the community enter the family through such media as newspapers, television, radio, and books. Each medium of communication is assumed to influence children's development in specific ways.
- A major factor in television's influence on children is the great amount of time they spend watching it.
- Television's potential for realism makes it difficult for children to distinguish reality from fiction in television content, and their understanding of the content is confused by such cinematic techniques as rapid cuts and zoom shots.
- Television content influences people's basic beliefs about the world. Insofar as reality is distorted by television, children who watch television acquire false beliefs about the world.
- A variety of evidence suggests that violence depicted on television increases aggressiveness in children.
- Parents can influence television's impact on their children by controlling what their children watch and by watching with them and talking about what is happening on the screen.
- Reading to young children furnishes them with an early model of activities that will be important in school. Parents have far greater control over the pace and the content of the reading material that the child encounters than over what the child sees on television.

The Young Child in the Community

- Once children begin to spend time outside the home, their experience changes in fundamental ways.
- Day-care centers in the United States vary widely in social setting, philosophy, and physical facilities. The size of the group is of special importance to the quality in the United States of day care: the smaller the group, the higher the quality. Other factors that contribute to the quality of care are the stability, commitment, and training of the staff.
- Day care in the United States has more clear-cut effects on children's social behavior than on their cognitive behavior. The major effects are:
  1. Increased self-sufficiency and decreased compliance with adults' wishes.
  2. Increased ability to engage in peer-led group activity.
- Preschools evolved during the twentieth century as a means of promoting the development of children who had to cope with the complexities of urban life.
- Since the early 1960s, preschool education has been promoted as a means of combating school failure among people living in poverty.

On the Threshold

- The fact that children begin to spend extended time in unfamiliar contexts is a key feature of development in early childhood.

- Exposure to a variety of new contexts stimulates the social and intellectual development of young children.
- The fact that young children are novices in the new contexts they inhabit is one of the factors underpinning the unevenness that is characteristic of their thought and action.

KEY TERMS

authoritarian parenting pattern,   p. 435

authoritative parenting pattern,   p. 435

day-care centers,   p. 455

dialogic reading,   p. 454

extended family,   p. 443

family care,   p. 455

home care,   p. 455

nuclear family,   p. 429

permissive parenting pattern,   p. 436

THOUGHT QUESTIONS

1. A basic assumption of Bronfenbrenner's cultural-context approach is that contexts are reciprocally related. Give some examples from this chapter in which experiences in one context influence behavior in another.

2. Suggest a research design for isolating the causes and effects of different parenting styles (as a follow-up to Diana Baumrind's research program). What obstacles do you anticipate in carrying out your proposed study?

3. Drawing on the discussion in this chapter and in Chapter 10, how might you explain the psychological difficulties that young children experience when their mother or father remarries after a divorce?

4. Robert Halpern is quoted on p. 443 as saying that the child-rearing practices recommended by mainstream psychologists may not be appropriate for children of low-income families. Why might that be the case?

5. Why is there continuing controversy about the consequences of viewing violence on television?

PART FOUR

MIDDLE CHILDHOOD

Anthropologists' descriptions of a wide variety of cultures indicate that as children reach the age of 5 to 7 years they are no longer restricted to the home or to settings where they are carefully watched by adults. Instead, they become responsible for behaving themselves in a variety of new contexts. These can be divided into three principal types: *solitary contexts*, where children are expected to play or carry out chores on their own; *instructional contexts*, which are designed to impart culturally valued knowledge and are controlled by one or a few adults; and *peer contexts*, where children spend time together in the absence of adult supervision.

Alongside these cross-cultural regularities are important cultural differences in the particular activities that children engage in and in the age at which they are expected to begin accepting more grown-up responsibilities. Among some of the Mayan people in the highlands of Guatemala, boys go out to herd cattle, a solitary

activity that takes them well beyond the range of watchful adults, while girls spend more time at home helping their mothers and the older women of the village (Rogoff, 1978). In the United States, by contrast, boys and girls alike spend long hours in school, with their peers, receiving formal education. Barbara Rogoff (1995) describes a number of societies in which children as young as 3 or 4 are expected to help with child care and gardening, while in others such responsibilities are not assigned until children have reached the threshold of adolescence. In spite of such differences, however, the cross-cultural similarities are so impressive that the changes during the years from 5 to 7 seem to signal the emergence of a new developmental period (Sameroff & Haith, 1995).

At first glance, time spent in solitary activity or with peers when no adults are present may appear less important to development than time spent in educational settings. Solitary activities are often boring and undemanding (gathering wood, or chasing birds and small animals away from a growing rice crop, for example). A good deal of peer interaction is taken up with games, gossip, or simply "hanging out." But being left in charge of the family cornfield or engaging in informal interaction with peers provides children with important opportunities for learning what it means to take responsibility, for exploring social relationships, and for developing moral understanding and personal identity.

The changes in social context associated with the advent of middle childhood would be impossible for children to cope with if they did not also acquire the cognitive capacities needed to support their newly granted autonomy and responsibility. As we shall see, evidence from experiments, naturalistic observations, and clinical interviews makes it clear that the defining characteristics of middle childhood are a greatly increased ability to think more deeply and logically, to follow through on a problem once it is undertaken, and to keep track of more than one aspect of a situation at a time.

This section is divided into three chapters: Chapter 12 describes the nature of children's biological and cognitive capacities between the ages of 5 and 12. Chapter 13 examines the influence of schooling on development, with particular attention to the organization of school activities and to the intellectual capacities that schooling both demands and fosters. Chapter 14 focuses on the developmental significance of the new social relations that emerge during middle childhood, particularly among peers.

Cognitive and Biological Attainments of Middle Childhood

"Walking was my project before reading. The text I read was the town; the book I made up was a map. . . . I pushed at my map's edges. Alone at night I added newly memorized streets and blocks to old streets and blocks, and imagined connecting them on foot. . . . I felt that my life depended on keeping it all straight—remembering where on earth I lived, that is, in relation to where I walked. It was dead reckoning. On darkened evenings I came home exultant, secretive, often from some exotic leafy curb a mile beyond what I had known at lunch, where I had peered up at the street sign, hugging the cold pole, and fixed the intersection in my mind. What joy, what relief, eased me as I pushed open the heavy front door!—joy and relief because, from the very trackless waste, I had located home, family, and the dinner table once again.

An infant watches her hands and feels them move.

Gradually she fixes her own boundaries at the complex incurved rim of skin. Later she touches one palm to another and tries for a game to distinguish each hand's sensations of feeling and being felt. What is a house but a bigger skin, and a neighborhood map but the world's skin ever expanding?"

—*Annie Dillard,*
An American Childhood

I n societies around the world, adults begin to have new expectations when their children approach 6 years of age. Among the Ngoni of Malawi, in Central Africa, adults believe that the loss of milk teeth and the emergence of second teeth (which begins around the age of 6) signal that children are ready for a different kind of life. When this physical change occurs, adults expect children to begin to act more independently. Children of both sexes are held accountable for being discourteous. They are supposed to stop playing childish games and start learning skills that will be essential when they grow up. The boys leave the protection and control of women and move into dormitories, where they must adapt to a system of male dominance and male life. Margaret Read describes the associated stresses for Ngoni boys:

> There was no doubt that this abrupt transition, like the sudden weaning [several years earlier], was a shock for many boys between six-and-a-half and seven-and-a-half. From having been impudent, well fed, self-confident, and spoiled youngsters among the women many of them quickly became skinny, scruffy, subdued, and had a hunted expression. (1960/1968, p. 49)

Observations of life among the Ifaluk of Micronesia provide a similar picture. The Ifaluk believe that at the age of 6 years children acquire "social intelligence," which includes the acquisition of important cultural knowledge and skills, as well as the ability to work, to adhere to social norms, and to demonstrate compassion for others—all valued adult behaviors (Lutz, 1987).

Adults' increased expectations that 5- to 7-year-old children will begin to behave more maturely arise from a combination of ecological circumstances, cultural traditions, and adults' observations of how well their children now cope with new demands (see Figure 12.1) (Sameroff & Haith, 1996). The children are now strong and agile enough to catch a runaway goat or to carry their little sister on their hip. They know not to let the baby crawl into the fire. They can wait for the school bus without wandering off. They can, sometimes under duress, sit still for several hours at a time while adults attempt to instruct them, and they can carry out their chores in an acceptable manner. In short, they can perform tasks independently, formulate goals, and resist the temptation to abandon them.

Adults around the world assign children chores in middle childhood that call upon their increased physical strength as well as their ability to control themselves so that they can complete the assigned tasks.

Coping with Increased Freedom and Responsibility

One of the best ways to gain a sense of how children's lives change as they enter middle childhood is to observe how and where they spend their time. Roger Barker and Herbert Wright (1951) arranged for observers to follow one child living in "Midwest," a small community in the United States, through every minute of the waking day. The resulting portrait of 7-year-old Raymond Birch, titled *One Boy's Day*, is a classic in the literature of child development. The following account was adapted from it:

Raymond gets up, dresses himself (although his clothes have been laid out for him by his mother), and takes care of his own grooming. He eats breakfast with his mother and father. Then he helps his father to clear the dishes. He negotiates with his mother about the need to wear a jacket to school and grudgingly accepts her judgment that a jacket is in order. He decides on his own not to take his bike to school because it might rain.

After spending a few minutes casting a fishing rod with his father in the backyard (he is the only one who caught fish on their last outing), he accompanies his mother to the courthouse where she works. At the courthouse he greets adults politely, and holds the door open for a man who is going out at the same time he is. He plays by himself outside while his mother works. When it is time for him to go to school, he walks the few blocks by himself, crossing the street cautiously. On the playground, he and the other children are unsupervised. A few minutes before 9 A.M. he enters his classroom, which the second-graders share with the first grade. While waiting for school to begin, he draws on the board, looks at a book with a friend, and chats quietly with other children. When the teacher comes into

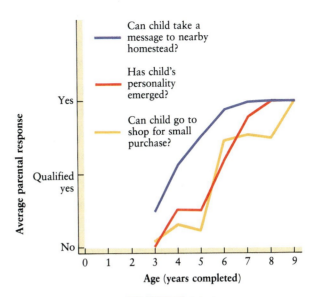

FIGURE 12.1 *The ages at which Kipsigis mothers in Kokwet, Kenya, believe their children undergo basic developmental changes. Note the sharp discontinuity in this culture's estimates of personality development and the ability to carry out an errand involving money. But according to this culture, there is continuity in the development of memory. (From Harkness & Super, 1983.)*

the room promptly at 9 A.M., he turns in his seat (all the seats are arranged in rows, facing front). While the teacher readies the first-graders to go to music, Raymond, who has become worried that he left his coat on the playground, asks permission to search for it. He has forgotten that he has hung it in the cloakroom. When he discovers this, he comes back and makes May baskets out of paper strips with the rest of the second-graders. He goes to music, listens to other children's stories, and goes outside for recess.

In the afternoon he does poorly on the spelling test. When another boy asks, "What did you get on your spelling?" he blushes and looks down at his desk. In a swift hoarse whisper he tells the boy that his grades are his own business. He seems embarrassed when he speaks. Close to dismissal time, the class searches for the money another boy has reported lost. When it turns out to have been in his desk all the time, Raymond smiles companionably at him and leans back to pat his hand. Then the boy pats Raymond's hand. They pat harder and harder, grinning broadly, until the teacher intervenes with a directive for the entire class.

While his mother is preparing dinner after work, Raymond pushes the lawn mower for a minute. He then joins his 11-year-old neighbor Stewart Evarts and Stewart's 3½-year-old nephew Clifford in the vacant lot across the street. Playing with their trucks in a pit that was once the basement of a house, Raymond discovers a dilapidated wooden crate about 5 feet long buried in the weeds. He drags the crate out, and the boys devise several ways to play with it, despite its unwieldy size. They lift it out of the pit and send it crashing back in, get in the crate and pretend it is a cage and that they are monkeys, and hang on with their hands and feet as it rocks and tumbles over and over. At the same time, the older boys are careful that Clifford is not harmed by their games.

FIGURE 12.2 *The average number of hours a day that people of various ages in "Midwest" spent in family and community settings. (From Wright, 1956.)*

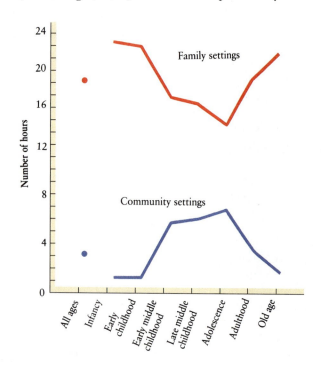

From such observations carried out with many children in the early 1950s, Barker and Wright (1955) concluded that the amount of time children spent unsupervised by adults increased markedly during the course of middle childhood (see Figure 12.2). In about one-third of the settings where children Raymond Birch's age spent their time—the streets between home and school and the empty lot across from Raymond's home, for example—they had no adult supervision (see Box 12.1). More recently, similar increases in unsupervised time have been reported in urban centers as well as the rural Midwest, among children born in different decades and in quite different societies in several parts of the world (Ellis, Rogoff, & Cromer, 1981; Whiting & Edwards, 1988). What distinguishes Raymond Birch's experiences from those of children in many parts of the world is that the major responsibility he was expected to take on as he entered middle childhood was the job of getting an education.

In the years since the observations of Raymond Birch were carried out, American society has undergone many changes that affect the way children spend their time, the amount of freedom they have to explore their communities, and the nature of their responsibilities. It is no longer considered safe, for example, to allow a school-aged child to roam the neighborhoods of a big city freely, as Annie Dillard roamed through Pittsburgh when she was a child (see the quote on p. 475)—although in small communities all over the

BOX 12.1

Way-Finding on the Home Range

Middle childhood is a time when children's activities take them farther and farther from home. It is the age at which children typically begin to walk by themselves to school, to their friends' houses, to the store, the library, the playground, and various other places in their neighborhoods. To find their way from place to place and return home safely requires several cognitive skills. They have to pay attention to where they are going and to such dangers as passing cars. They have to remember important landmarks, and they have to recognize these landmarks from a different perspective when they return.

The abilities of 6- and 12-year-old children to find their way back across a university campus were documented by Edward Cornell, C. Donald Heth, and Wanda L. Rowat (1992) and then compared with the performances of 22-year-old college students. First, the children were escorted across a corner of the campus of the University of Alberta. As they were walking, their escort instructed some of the children to stop at intervals and look back at where they had been. The idea was to show these children all the vistas that they would see when their direction of travel was reversed. The children were not yet told, however, that they would be asked to lead the way back, to prevent them from developing alternate strategies for remembering the route. (Anthropologists' observations of hunter-gatherer societies indicate that looking back is a common device used to remember routes. Novices are often instructed to glance back when they have reached an important sight or landmark [Gatty, 1958].) A second group of children were not told to look back, only that they were being led on a short tour of the university. After crossing the campus, both groups were asked to lead their escort all the way back to the place they began, along the same path they had just taken.

As might be expected, given their more limited cognitive abilities and way-finding experience, the 6-year-olds performed less well than either 12- or 22-year-olds. There were no significant differences between the performances of the two older groups. This result complements findings that the distance from home that a parent permits a child to venture independently (referred to as the *home range*) expands rapidly during the early elementary school years and remains stable after 10 or 12 years of age (Moore & Young, 1978).

The data that best explain the poor performance of the 6-year-olds are the results for those children who were instructed to stop and look back at crucial junctures. The 12- and 22-year-olds who were instructed to glance back at various landmarks performed significantly better than those who were given no special instructions. But the strategy of glancing back did not help the 6-year-olds; simple exposure to the memory strategy for that age group did not ensure an improvement in remembering.

Another experiment by Cornell and his colleagues further pinpointed the 6-year-olds' difficulty. If they were told to glance back at their path and were shown memorable landmarks as well, then the 6-year-olds' ability to remember the path they had followed increased significantly (Cornell, Heth, & Broda, 1989).

Finding your way across campus at the University of Alberta may be complicated, but there are no busy intersections and rapidly moving cars. When our own children began attending elementary school, we lived on the East Side of Manhattan. The question we faced at that time was "When are the kids old enough to cross 64th Street to go to the grocery or to cross Madison Avenue to catch the bus?" Our concern was not unreasonable. Thousands of children are killed crossing the street each year, four times the number reported for adults (O'Donoghue, 1988).

A study of children's ability to find safe ways to cross the road suggests strongly that it would be risky to send 5- to 7-year-olds on an errand if they would have to cross a busy road (Ampofo-Boateng et al., 1993). The researchers arranged to take children individually from their schools to sites close to a fairly busy two-lane road. One site was a crossroads where traffic converged from several directions; at three of the sites visibility was limited by an obstruction or a bend in the road. The children were told to imagine they wanted to cross to the other side of the road and had to select the safest way to get there. They were asked to point out the safest route and explain their choice.

Only 10 percent of the 5-year-olds and 21 percent of the 7-year-olds chose a safe route. Even 11-year-olds chose unsafe routes 25 percent of the time, with boys being more likely to make unsafe choices. The children's performance could be improved, however, by a special safety course that emphasized the importance of visibility and choosing the shortest possible route whenever possible. This research makes it clear that adults should take care to instruct children about environmental risks as the children's home range increases.

Children enjoy challenging games whether they are playing in an empty lot, a park, or a video arcade at the mall.

world it is still common to see children walking and riding their bikes to and from school without adult supervision. It is also likely that the 7-year-old Raymond Birches of today spend some time after school in front of a television or computer screen. These differences notwithstanding, middle childhood today, just as it was 50 years ago, is a time when the range of contexts children inhabit greatly expands, as does their responsibility to control their own behavior. Their varied activities and the contexts in which they occur provide a wealth of new challenges to children's developing cognitive abilities.

In this chapter we will investigate the changes in children's biological and cognitive functioning that justify adults' new demands and expectations. Are these changes the same all over the world, or do they vary from one society to the next? Are they signs of a distinctive new stage of cognitive and physical development, or are they better understood as the consequence of a continuous buildup of capacities already present in early childhood?

Biological Developments

Children's size and strength increase significantly during middle childhood, although more slowly than in earlier years. Average 6-year-olds in the United States are about 3½ feet tall and weigh about 50 pounds. At the start of adolescence, 6 or 7 years later, their average height will have increased to almost 5 feet and their weight to approximately 100 pounds.

These overall growth trends are based on group averages and give the impression that the course of growth between early childhood and adolescence is steady. Careful tracking of the height of individual children, however, tells another story. Instead of a steady course of growth, several periods of rapid growth are punctuated by lulls of much slower growth (Lampl, Veldhuis, & Johnson, 1992). A study of Scottish children whose heights were measured repeatedly between the ages of 3 and 11 found that girls tended to spurt ahead in their growth at ages 4½, 6½,

8½, and 10, whereas periods of rapid growth for boys occurred slightly later after the age of 4½, at ages 7, 9, and 10½ (Butler, McKie, & Ratcliffe, 1990).

THE ROLES OF GENES AND ENVIRONMENT IN GROWTH

Like all aspects of development, children's growth depends on the interaction of environmental and genetic factors. Tall parents tend to have tall children. Monozygotic twins reared together are very similar in their patterns of growth. Reared apart, they still tend to resemble each other more than dizygotic twins, who share only 50 percent of their genes. Cases have been reported, however, in which one monozygotic twin is significantly smaller than the other because of the effects of illness or a poor environment (Shields, 1962).

The genetic contribution to size can also be seen in the variations in the height and rate of growth typical of different populations. When Phyllis Eveleth and J. M. Tanner (1990) compared the heights of well-nourished European, Asian, and African American children from birth to age 18, they found that the Asian boys and girls were distinctively shorter than children of the other two groups. They also reported that African American and Asian children tend to reach their mature height earlier than North American Caucasian children, who in turn reach their full height sooner than European children.

Nutrition is one of the key environmental factors influencing a child's height and weight (see Box 12.2). Lower-class children, who have less access to food and good health care, are usually smaller than children of the same age in well-off families. One study found that during middle childhood the Nigerian sons of well-off parents were on average almost 4 inches taller than the boys in less advantaged families (Janes, 1975). In many industrialized countries where the population on the whole is better off, the gap in size between the children of the poor and those born into well-off families is much smaller. In some countries, such as Sweden and Norway, where the entire population has access to adequate food and medical care, the difference in height between children whose parents are wealthy and those born to less well-off parents has disappeared altogether (Eveleth & Tanner, 1990).

Illness also plays a role in a child's size. Growth slows during illnesses, even mild illnesses. When children are adequately nourished, this slowdown is usually followed by a period of rapid "catch-up growth," which quickly restores them to their genetically normative path of growth. When nutritional intake is inadequate, however, the children never do catch up, and their growth is stunted (Greene & Johnston, 1980). The fact that growth processes exhibit a strong tendency to correct themselves after short-term exposure to a deviant environment is an excellent illustration of the canalization process, discussed in Chapter 2 (p. 62).

MOTOR DEVELOPMENT

Walking along the beach one day, we saw a girl about 7 years old and her little brother following their father and 10-year-old brother. The father and older brother were tossing a ball back and forth as they walked. The girl was hopping along the sand on one foot, while her younger brother scrambled to keep up with her. Suddenly the little girl threw her arms up in the air, leaned over, threw her feet up, and did a cartwheel. She then did another cartwheel. Her younger brother stopped to watch her. Then he tried one. He fell over and rolled in the sand while she continued doing one perfect cartwheel after another. He picked himself up and ran ahead so that he was now between his father and his older brother. His father tossed the ball to him. He missed it. His older brother retrieved it and threw it back to the father, who caught it easily.

In such everyday scenes we can see the increase in motor skills, coordination, agility, and strength that occur over the course of middle childhood. Children

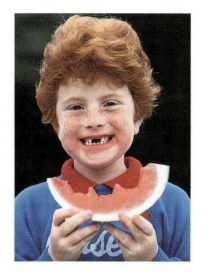

The loss of one's front teeth is a widely accepted sign that middle childhood is beginning.

BOX 12.2

Obesity in Middle Childhood

Despite the high value placed on thinness in our society, the number of obese children in the United States has increased markedly in recent decades. This increase has been greatest for African American children and for children whose family income is low (Wolfe et al., 1994).

Many obese children become obese adults. The older these children are and the more severe their weight problem, the greater their risk of being obese as an adult. Longitudinal studies of obese youngsters have found that approximately 27 percent of overweight 1- to 5-year-olds, 42 percent of overweight 3- to 9-year-olds, and 83 percent of overweight 10- to 13-year-olds remained overweight as adults (Kolata, 1986).

In addition to the psychological problems and damage to self-esteem that come from being fat in a society that frowns on obesity, obese children are more vulnerable to a variety of serious health problems. They have been shown to be at increased risk for asthma, heart disease, diabetes, respiratory disease, and orthopedic disorders (Unger et al., 1990).

The popular belief is that children are fat because they eat a lot. While there is some truth to this observation, not every child who eats large amounts of food is equally at risk for becoming obese. Body weight, like other physical attributes, is determined by an interaction of genetic and environmental factors. A study of 540 Danish adoptees found a strong correlation between the adoptees' weight as adults and the weight of their biological parents, especially their mothers (Stunkard et al., 1986). Twin studies and genetic mapping also point to a strong genetic contribution to obesity (Stunkard, Foch, & Hrubec, 1986).

Still, many people would argue that no one, not even children with a strong genetic propensity to becoming overweight, becomes obese without consuming more calories than the body needs. The difference between the caloric intake of a child whose weight is normal and that of a child who becomes obese need not be great. The consumption of as little as 50 extra calories a day can lead to an excess weight gain of 5 pounds over the course of a year (Kolata, 1986). This reasoning would lead one to assume that obese children eat more and are less active than other children. The data do not unequivocally support this assumption, however. Several studies report that children who are obese eat no more than their normal-weight peers (Klesges & Hanson, 1988; Shah & Jeffery, 1991).

What, then, is causing the increase in obesity among children? Dietary fat is one of the prime suspects. The diets of children who became obese have been found to have a higher percentage of calories from fats than those of other children. Another suspected culprit is a reduction in activity levels over time. Obese children tend to be less active. They also tend to watch more television than their normal-weight peers. Television watching has been found to dramatically lower the rate at which children burn calories (their metabolic rate) (Dietz & Gortmacher, 1985; Gortmaker, Dietz, & Cheung, 1990; Klesges et al., 1993). Decreases in fat intake and increases in physical activity were associated with decreases in children's weight gain (Klesges et al., 1995). Unfortunately, such changes are easier to prescribe than to put into action. Moreover, 80 percent of the obese children who do lose weight gain it back (Epstein et al., 1993).

The prevalence of obesity among children and the difficulty of designing therapeutic programs that enable them to attain and retain normal weight have inspired a good deal of research aimed at discovering the most effective forms of therapy. Leonard Epstein and his colleagues have found that successful programs target not only the obese children but also their parents (who are likely to be obese as well). The most effective programs also combine clear-cut procedures for identifying high-fat foods with carefully designed exercise programs that specify how many calories are burned up by each form of exercise. In a 5-year follow-up study of one such exemplary therapeutic effort, Epstein and his colleagues (1990) found that the children in the sample had sustained an average weight loss of 12 percent.

---

become stronger and more agile, and their balance improves. They run faster, throw balls farther, are more likely to catch them, and jump farther and higher than they did when they were younger. They also learn to skate, ride bikes, sail boats, dance, swim, and climb trees, and acquire a host of other physical skills during this period.

As a general rule, boys and girls differ in their physical skills. By the time they are 5 years old, boys can jump a little farther, run a bit faster, and throw a ball about 5 feet farther than girls. They are also better at batting, kicking, dribbling, and catching balls than girls. Girls, on the other hand, tend to be more agile than boys. Over the course of middle childhood these sex differences in motor skills

EEG coherence The synchronization of electrical activity in different areas of the brain.

become more pronounced (Cratty, 1970). Boys tend to be slightly advanced in motor abilities that require power and force, while girls often excel in fine motor skills such as drawing and writing, or in gross motor skills that combine balance and foot movement, such as skipping and hopping.

Boys have slightly greater muscle mass than girls and are slightly bigger—until about the age of 10½, when girls spurt ahead for a few years—but these sex-related physical differences are not large enough in themselves to account for the superiority of boys in many motor skills during middle childhood. It seems that cultural expectations also play a large role in shaping these differences in behavior. Being able to throw, catch, hit a ball, and run quickly are valued skills for boys in our culture. American parents encourage their sons to develop these skills by buying them balls, bats, and basketball hoops, taking them to ball games, talking about sports with them, playing with them, and encouraging them to practice these skills. Boys who are considered to be good athletes are more popular with their peers than those who show no athletic ability. While the participation of girls in such sports as baseball, soccer, and tennis has increased significantly in recent decades, girls are still not given the amount of encouragement and coaching that boys receive to develop skill in running, throwing, and catching, nor are they rewarded to the extent boys are for having those abilities.

BRAIN DEVELOPMENTS

The years between 6 and 8 witness the continued growth of the brain and the kinds of activity it manifests:

1. Myelination continues, particularly in the frontal cortex (Janowsky & Carper, 1996). (Recall from Chapter 4 that myelination provides each cortical neuron with an insulating sheath of tissue to speed transmission of nerve impulses along the neurons.)

2. The numbers of synapses at the ends of neurons increase, creating more connections between neurons, and the output of the chemical neurotransmitters that pass impulses from one neuron to the next also increases (Thatcher, 1991).

3. The dominant form of electrical activity measured by an EEG (electroencephalogram) undergoes a dramatic change (see Figure 12.3). Until the age of 5, EEGs recorded when children are awake display more theta activity (characteristic of adult sleep states) than alpha activity (characteristic of engaged attention). Between 5 and 7 years of age, the amounts of theta and alpha activity are about equal, but thereafter alpha activity (engaged attention) dominates (Corbin & Bickford, 1955).

4. The synchronization of electrical activity in different areas of the brain (called **EEG coherence**) increases significantly (see Figure 12.4). Particularly important, according to Robert Thatcher (1994), is evidence of increased coordination between the electrical activity of the frontal lobes and electrical activity in other parts of the brain.

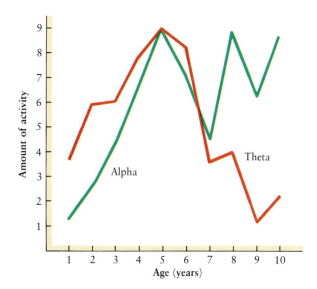

FIGURE 12.3 *Changes in the amount of theta (sleeplike) and alpha (alert) EEG activity during development. Note that alpha waves come to predominate over theta waves around the age of 7. (From Corbin & Bickford, 1955.)*

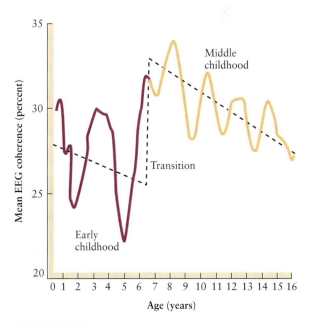

FIGURE 12.4 *Changes in EEG coherence in the transition from early to middle childhood. (From Thatcher, 1991.)*

FIGURE 12.5 *The rate of increase in the area of the frontal lobes and in the maturation of nerve cells during development. (From Luria, 1973.)*

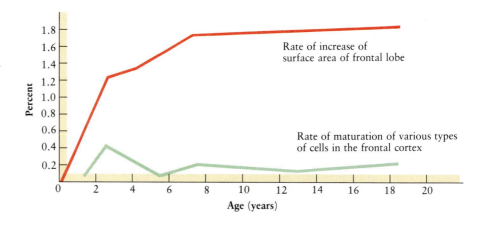

FIGURE 12.6 *A positron emission tomographic (PET) scan, used to assess the activity of different parts of the brain while a child is engaged in various forms of problem solving. This modern technique is based on the ability to detect the extent to which parts of the brain take up and use glucose. Orange and white on the scan indicate areas where more glucose is being taken up and used. By comparing the changing patterns of activity in different brain centers as children grow older, researchers can specify with greater precision the relation between brain changes and problem-solving activities.*

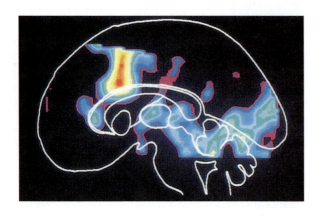

This pattern of changes in brain structure and function—particularly in the frontal lobes—suggests that maturation of the brain plays an important role in the development of thinking during this period. Robbie Case (1992) argues that the pattern of brain changes between the ages of 5 and 7 permits the frontal lobes to coordinate the activities of other brain centers in a qualitatively more complex way, enabling children to control their attention, to form explicit plans, and to engage in self-reflection, all behaviors that appear to undergo significant development in middle childhood (see Figure 12.5). This view is supported by the fact that when the frontal lobe is damaged in humans and in other animals, their behavior deteriorates in specific ways: they are unable to maintain goals; their actions become fragmentary and uncontrolled; and they respond to irrelevant stimuli and are easily thrown off track by interruptions and pauses. These deficits are similar to those attributed to young children (see Chapter 9), supporting the idea that the increasing role of the frontal lobes in overall brain organization accounts for the behavioral changes of middle childhood.

One of the most convincing demonstrations that changes in brain functioning lead to changes in problem-solving processes comes from a study in which 5- to 7-year-old children were asked to judge whether the amount of liquid in a glass increased, decreased, or remained the same when it was poured into a second glass (this experimental procedure was mentioned in Chapter 9 [p. 340] and will be discussed more fully on p. 487). The children wore caps that contained EEG recording electrodes, allowing the researchers to track the changes in brain activity that accompanied their problem-solving endeavors (see Figure 12.6). Some of the children at each age level solved the problems correctly; some did not. Those who solved the problems displayed a different pattern of brain activity, demonstrating that changes in the brain were associated with the differences in performance (Stauder, Molenaar, & Van der Molen, 1993).

Despite this evidence, we must be cautious about inferring direct causal links between particular changes in the brain and specific changes in behavior. The evidence we have cited is correlational: as children grow older, we observe changes in their brains *and* changes in their behavior, but the direction of causation remains uncertain. Do children perform in more sophisticated ways because of changes in their brains, or have their brains become larger and more complicated because they have experienced more challenging situations? (Evidence for the dependence of brain growth on experience is discussed in Box 5.1, pp. 202–203.)

A New Quality of Mind?

Whether we focus on ethnographic reports about adults' changing expectations of children's capabilities or on the data from electrophysiological measurements of changing brain activity, the evidence suggests that between the ages of 5 and 7 children develop more powerful cognitive abilities. Psychological research supports this conclusion, although disputes continue about the degree of discontinuity associated with the onset of middle childhood and the mechanisms of change.

CONCRETE OPERATIONS: NEW FORMS OF REASONING?

Piaget argued that the key to the increased cognitive capacities observed in middle childhood lies in the crystallization of a new form of thought, what he referred to as **concrete operations** (Piaget, 1983; Piaget & Inhelder, 1969; Piaget, 1952b). An *operation*, in Piaget's terminology, is an internalized (mental) action that is coordinated with other mental actions as part of a logical system (see Chapter 9, p. 340). These mental operations, summarized in Table 12.1, are termed "concrete" because they relate directly to tangible objects and thoughts about objects, not to abstract propositions or possible future states of affairs.

> **Concrete operations** In Piaget's theory, internalized mental actions that fit into a logical system. Such thinking allows the child to combine, separate, order, and transform objects in their minds.

R. Murray Thomas illustrates the difference between concrete operations and formal operations (which are said to appear in early adolescence) with the following two questions:

> *Concrete:* If Alice has two apples and Caroline gives her three more, how many will there be?
>
> *Formal:* Imagine that there are two quantities which together make up a whole. If we increase the first quantity but the whole remains the same, what has happened to the second quantity? (Thomas, 1992, p. 295)

In Piaget's account of cognitive development, concrete operations provide a transition between the preoperational thought of early childhood and the general logical structures of adult thought. Concrete operations are similar to action schemas in that they really are actions. But they are not external, physical actions such as pushing an object and observing its effect on another or grasping various objects. Rather, they are internalized actions, such as mentally comparing the sizes of several objects, coordinating two points of view, or assigning specific objects to more general categories of which they are members.

Piaget believed that while young children sometimes *appear* to be capable of concrete operations because they can physically carry out an action, this appearance does not correspond to psychological reality. As an example of the difference between physical and mental actions, he and his colleague Barbel Inhelder offer the following:

> Children of four and five often go by themselves from home to school and back every day even though the walk may be ten minutes or so in length. Yet if you ask them to represent their path by means of little three-dimensional cardboard objects (houses, church, streets, river, squares, etc.) or to indicate the plan of the school as it is seen facing the river, they are unable to reconstruct the topographical relationship, even though they constantly utilize them in action. (Piaget & Inhelder, 1969, p. 94)

In the transition from early to middle childhood, concrete operations transform all aspects of psychological functioning, according to Piaget. The physical world becomes more predictable because children come to understand that certain physical aspects of objects, such as size, density, length, and number, remain the same even when other aspects of their appearances have changed. Children's thinking also becomes more organized and flexible. They can think about

TABLE 12.1 Piaget's Stages of Cognitive Development: Concrete Operational

Age (years)	Stage	Description	Characteristics and Examples
Birth to 2	SENSORIMOTOR	Infants' achievements consist largely of coordinating their sensory perceptions and simple motor behaviors. As they move through the 6 substages of this period, infants come to recognize the existence of a world outside of themselves and begin to interact with it in deliberate ways.	New features of thinking • Decentration: Children can notice and consider more than one attribute of an object at a time and form categories according to multiple criteria. • Conservation: Children understand that certain properties of an object will remain the same even when other, superficial ones are altered. They know that when a tall, thin glass is emptied into a short, fat one, the amount of liquid remains the same. • Logical necessity: Children have acquired the conviction that it is logically necessary for certain qualities to be conserved despite changes in appearance. • Identity: Children realize that if nothing has been added or subtracted, the amount must remain the same.
2 to 6	PREOPERATIONAL	Young children can represent reality to themselves through the use of symbols, including mental images, words, and gestures. Objects and events no longer have to be present to be thought about, but children often fail to distinguish their point of view from that of others, become easily captured by surface appearances, and are often confused about causal relations.	
6 to 12	CONCRETE OPERATIONAL	As they enter middle childhood, children become capable of mental operations, internalized actions that fit into a logical system. Operational thinking allows children mentally to combine, separate, order, and transform objects and actions. Such operations are considered concrete because they are carried out in the presence of the objects and events being thought about.	• Compensation: Children can mentally compare changes in two aspects of a problem and see how one compensates for the other. • Reversibility: Children realize that certain operations can negate or reverse the effects of others. Declining egocentrism • Children can communicate more effectively about objects a listener cannot see. • Children can think about how others perceive them. • Children understand that a person can feel one way and act another.
12 to 19	FORMAL OPERATIONAL	In adolescence the developing person acquires the ability to think systematically about all logical relations within a problem. Adolescents display keen interest in abstract ideals and the process of thinking itself.	Changes in social relations • Children can regulate their interactions with each other through rules and begin to play rule-based games. • Children take intentions into account in judging behavior and believe the punishment must fit the crime.

alternatives when they try to solve problems, or mentally retrace their steps if they want to, as Raymond Birch did when he thought he had left his coat on the playground and asked permission to search for it.

Piaget believed that the advent of concrete operational thinking also changes children's social behavior: they gain an understanding of how to play games according to rules, and, as we shall see in Chapter 14, they have a better understanding of social and moral rules. In addition, children become less susceptible to being caught in their own point of view and more skilled at interpreting other people's intentions. With these new insights, the scope and complexity of their social relations increase.

Piaget invented a number of problem-solving tasks to enable him to diagnose the presence or absence of concrete operational thinking. Those involving *conservation of quantities* and *logical classification* demonstrate with special clarity his distinction between preoperational and concrete operational thinking (Inhelder & Piaget, 1964; Piaget & Inhelder, 1973).

Conservation

Conservation is Piaget's term for the understanding that some properties of an object or substance remain the same even when its appearance is altered in some superficial way. In the most famous version of his conservation task, touched on briefly in Chapter 9, children are presented with two identical glass beakers containing the same amounts of liquid (see Figure 12.7). The experimenter begins by asking, "Are the amounts of liquid in the two glasses the same?" If the child does not think so, the amounts are adjusted until the child agrees that the two glasses

> **Conservation** Piaget's term for the understanding that the properties of an object or a substance remain the same even though its appearance may have been altered in some superficial way.

Step 1: Present two beakers with equal amounts of liquid.

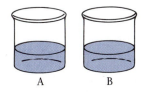

FIGURE 12.7 *The procedure Piaget used to test for the conservation of quantity.*

Step 2: Present taller, thinner beaker, and pour contents of B into it.

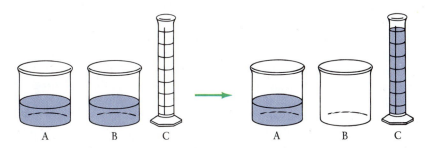

Step 3: Ask: "Which beaker has more liquid, A or C — or do they contain the same amount?"

contain exactly the same amounts. Then the experimenter pours the contents of one of the beakers into a third beaker that is taller and thinner. Naturally, the liquid rises higher in the new beaker. Now the experimenter asks the child, "Does the new beaker contain more liquid than the old beaker, does it contain the same amount, or does it contain less?"

In Piagetian interviews, 3- and 4-year-old children say that the amount of liquid has changed; the taller beaker has more. When asked why, they explain, "There's more because it's higher" or "There's more because it's bigger" or even "There's more because you poured it." They appear to focus their attention on a single aspect of the new beaker—its height. (Focusing on a single attribute of an object is the phenomenon of "centering," introduced in Chapter 9, p. 340). Even when the experimenter points out that no liquid was added or subtracted, and even after a demonstration that the amount has not changed when the liquid is poured back into the original beaker, 3- and 4-year-olds still claim that there is more liquid in the taller beaker. Piaget found that around the age of 5 or 6 years children's understanding of conservation goes through a transitional stage. At this point children seem to realize that it is necessary to consider both the height and the circumference of the beakers, but they have difficulty keeping both in mind simultaneously and coordinating the changes so that they can properly compare them.

According to Piaget, children begin to master the principle of conservation around the age of 8, when they understand not only that the new beaker is both taller and thinner but that a change in one dimension of the beaker is offset by a change in the other. Children who have acquired the concept of conservation of volume recognize that it is *logically necessary* for the amount of liquid to remain the same despite the change in appearance. When asked the reasons for their judgment, they make such statements as "The liquid *can't* change just because you poured it." When pressed further, they offer several arguments showing that they understand the logical relationships involved:

- "They were equal to start with and nothing was added, so they're the same." This mental operation is called **identity**; the child realizes that a change limited to outward appearance does not change the amounts involved.
- "The liquid is higher, but the glass is thinner." This mental operation is called **compensation;** changes in one aspect of a problem are mentally compared with and compensated for by changes in another.
- "If you pour it back, you'll see that it's the same." This mental operation is called negation or **reversibility;** the child realizes that one operation will negate, or reverse, the effects of another.

These ways of understanding all indicate that children have attained a new stage of cognitive development characterized by the appearance of logical thinking. As Piaget would say, they are now capable of concrete operations.

Children's developing understanding of number provides another example of the changes that occur when children acquire concrete operations. By "conservation of number" Piaget meant the ability to recognize one-to-one correspondence between two rows of objects, despite a difference in the sizes of the objects or in their spatial positions (Piaget, 1952a).

The basic procedure for testing children's ability to conserve number is to present them with two rows of objects such as those shown in Figure 12.8a. Both the numbers of objects and the lengths of the two lines are equal, and children are asked to affirm that they are. Then one of the rows is either spread out or compressed (see Figure 12.8b), and the children are asked if the numbers of objects in the two rows are still equal. Children below the age of 6 or 7 rarely display con-

Identity Used in Piagetian theory to mean a mental operation in which the child realizes that a change limited to outward appearance does not change the amounts involved.

Compensation A mental operation that allows the child to consider how changes in one aspect of a problem are related to changes in another.

Reversibility Piaget's term for mental operations in which children can think through an action and then reverse it.

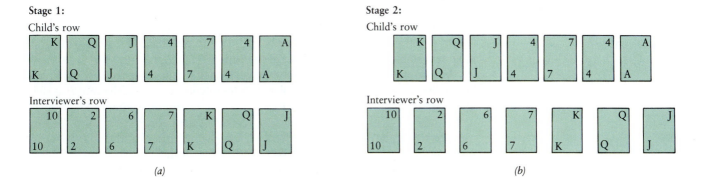

FIGURE 12.8 *The procedure used by Herbert Ginsburg to test for the conservation of number. (a) In stage 1, the child's and the interviewer's seven cards are arrayed at equal intervals. (b) In stage 2, the interviewer spreads out his cards and asks the child if she and the interviewer still have the same number of cards. (From Ginsburg, 1977.)*

servation of number, whereas older children realize that the number must remain the same.

The following interview with 6-year-old Deborah illustrates the typical pattern of confusion experienced by children who have not fully mastered concrete operations. In this case, one attribute that Deborah perceives—length—seems to overpower her ability to use logic.

The interviewer (I) placed seven playing cards in a line on the table in front of Deborah (D):

I: How many cards?

D: Seven.

I: Make another line of cards that's the same number.

Deborah counted out seven cards—"One, two, three, four, five, six, seven"—and placed them directly above the interviewer's cards. The interviewer pointed to the bottom row, saying it was his, and to the top row, identifying it as Deborah's.

I: Now does your line have just as many as my line? Is it just as many cards?

D: Yes.

I: All right, now watch what I do with my line.

The interviewer spread out his row of cards as Deborah watched. This is the "conservation" problem. The question is whether Deborah will conserve the initial equivalence despite the change in the appearance of the array.

I: See. Now do we both have as many cards? Does this line have as many cards as this line?

D: *(shakes her head no)*

I: Which line has more?

D: *(points to the interviewer's line)*

I: Why does this line have more?

D: Because it is out here. *(indicating that the interviewer's line is longer than hers)*

I: O.K. I see . . . but how many cards are in my line?

D: Seven.

I: How many cards are in your line?

D: Seven.

I: How come this one has more if they both have seven?

D: Because you spread them out. (Adapted from Ginsburg, 1977, pp. 26–27.)

In the first part of this interview, Deborah shows that she grasps the principle of one-to-one correspondence, which she uses to create a row of cards equal in number to the row created by the experimenter. When the lengths of the rows are made unequal because the experimenter spreads out his cards, however, Deborah fails to conserve the property of number of items in the row and instead makes her judgment on the basis of the length of the row.

In Piaget's view, once the child is capable of thinking operationally, individual bits of knowledge are no longer isolated or merely juxtaposed in the mind, as they were earlier. The capacity to perform concrete operations permits children to unify their experience into a coherent logical structure, which in turn enables them to think more systematically and effectively. In particular, the ability to perform the crucial operation of reversing something in their minds allows children to coordinate their representations of present and future states of objects and people. They can think ahead to see how actions may change the objects and then bring their thoughts back to the scene before them. If Deborah were able to apply concrete operations to the number conservation task, she would be able to say to herself, in effect, "There must be the same number of cards, because if the experimenter moved the cards in his row back to where they were at the beginning, nothing would have changed."

Alternative interpretations of conservation reasoning

It is difficult to overestimate the influence that Piaget's conservation experiments and his interpretations of the results have exerted on psychologists' interpretations of cognitive development. Dozens of books and hundreds of research papers have been written in attempts to extend, modify, or criticize Piaget's methods and conclusions about cognitive development in middle childhood.

By and large, when other investigators have replicated Piaget's methods, they have also replicated his results. But that has not prevented controversy over the conclusions he drew concerning young children's failure to reason about conservation.

We encountered one of the principal criticisms of Piaget's studies of children's thought in Chapter 9. There we saw that when problems are presented in simplified form with familiar materials and routines, 4- and 5-year-olds reason in ways previously thought possible only for 7- and 8-year-olds (see pp. 349–350). We titled that chapter "Early Childhood Thought: Islands of Competence" because children first begin to manifest new levels of cognitive ability in one or more restricted domains, only later coming to use them in a broader variety of contexts, so that psychologists conclude that a new level of cognitive development has been reached.

As we noted in Chapter 9 (p. 346), attempts to show that children acquire Piagetian stages earlier than he and his followers assumed have raised a difficult issue. Simplifications intended to make a task comprehensible to very young children may distort the task in such a way that the children can perform it well without having the kind of logical understanding that is the hallmark of Piaget's stage theory.

An early and influential study of this kind by Rochel Gelman (1972) directed at the issue of number conservation illustrates both the advantage of simplifying tasks and the shortcomings of this strategy as a means of explaining development.

Gelman's first method of simplification was to reduce greatly the number of objects in the two rows to be compared. Gelman presented a group of ten 3-year-old and ten 4-year-old children with two rows of three poker chips; this is the minimum number of objects needed to test for conservation. Each child was tested twice; in one case a row was lengthened, in the other case a row was shortened. The children were supposed to say that the number of chips remained the same in both cases.

The small numbers did not help the 3-year-olds. Almost all of them said that the number of poker chips changed when their row was made longer or shorter.

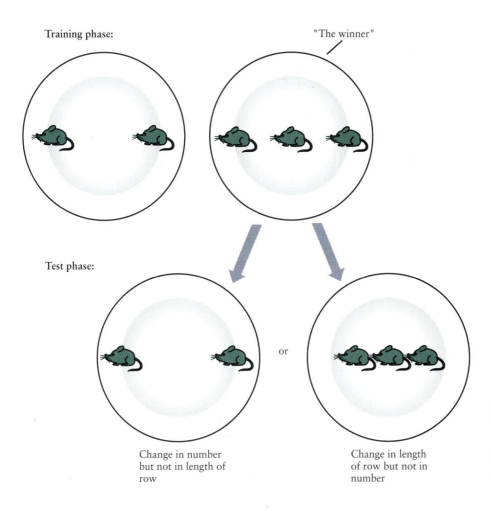

Training phase:

"The winner"

Test phase:

or

Change in number but not in length of row

Change in length of row but not in number

FIGURE 12.9 *The display used by Rochel Gelman to show that young children can conserve number under simplified conditions. (Gelman, 1972.)*

About half the 4-year-olds said the number of chips was the same, but they were unable to explain why; only two children justified their choices in terms of a logical operation such as reversibility. Reducing the number of objects to a bare minimum does not, by itself, solve the problem.

Gelman invented a different way to simplify the problem that seemed to make a difference. She created a kind of "magic show" in which the children were shown white plates to which two or three green plastic mice were attached (Figure 12.9). The mice could be placed close together or farther apart. Consequently, a row of three mice could be longer, the same length, or shorter than a row of two mice. At the start of the experiment, children were shown a plate with two mice and a plate with three mice and told that the plate with the three mice was "the winner." The plate with two mice was labeled "the loser." The children were then given several opportunities to identify the winners and losers to make sure that they knew the difference between the two displays. They all learned how to do this.

After several opportunities to show that they knew which display was the winner, the "magic trick" was implemented. Children were presented test trials on which the mice on the winner plate were either secretly displaced to make their row shorter or the number of mice was secretly reduced and again asked to identify "the winner." According to the logic of Piaget's conservation of number studies, these young children should be indifferent to a change in the *number* of mice, because they attend only to the length of the row of objects, not to their number.

Gelman found just the opposite: the children paid no attention to whether the mice were spread out or packed close together. What was critical to them now was that the number of mice remained the same—three in this case. This result

FIGURE 12.10 *A possible reason for wrong answers in conservation tasks. (From Siegal, 1991.)*

led Gelman to conclude that "the child clearly possesses a logical system for manipulating number before he reaches the stage of concrete operations" (1972, p. 89).

Other researchers have suggested that Gelman's simplifications distorted the problem and allowed the children to solve it without understanding conservation of number. For example, Gelman noted that some of the children counted the objects. By Piaget's criteria, children should not need to count in order to conserve number; they should know that *logically* nothing has changed. When follow-up studies have taken precautions to reduce the possibility that the children are counting, 6- and 7-year-olds continue to conserve number, indicating a logical understanding, but 3- and 4-year-olds do not, supporting Piaget's original proposition (Halford & Boyle, 1985). Despite these differences in interpretation, there seems little doubt that Gelman's study shows that 3- and 4-year-olds possess at least partial knowledge about number that Piagetian theory does not take into account.

A final line of evidence critical of Piaget's views comes from studies that hold the child's task constant but manipulate the social context. For example, it is common in conservation studies for children to be questioned about their judgments twice, once before the crucial transformation and once after. Michael Siegal (1991) suggested that some children believe that an adult who asks the same question a second time is implicitly suggesting that the first answer was wrong (see Figure 12.10 for a cartoon representation of how the child might reason).

Siegal assessed children's understanding indirectly, through their interpretations and explanations of other children's performance on the conservation task. After a child watched another child go through the conservation task with an adult, the child who was observing was asked, "Why do you think the child answered in that way? Did he say that because that is what he really believed, or did he say it to please the adult?" A significant proportion of the 3- and 4-year-olds who had failed conservation problems said that when the observed children gave a nonconservation response, they were doing it to please the adult. When the observed child gave a conservation response, the children said the child really believed it. Once again, it appears that children know more about the topic than Piagetian tests reveal.

Logical classification

As we have seen in earlier chapters, children arrive at middle childhood with a great deal of knowledge about the categories in their world. Much of this understanding is coded in their everyday language. By the end of infancy they can classify a collection of objects into two classes (such as blue objects and red objects), even when other attributes differ (some of the blue objects are toy boats, say, and others are wooden dolls) (Chapter 6, p. 235). During early childhood their vocabularies grow and differentiate to include a vast array of categorical distinctions organized around basic terms and hierarchies (see Figures 8.4 and 8.5, pp. 306 and 307). As a consequence, by the time they are 7 or 8 years old, they have a large fund of organized conceptual knowledge to draw upon in their thinking about the world.

Knowledge of the categories to which objects belong is crucial to the development of thought. It permits children to reason about individual category members, even ones they have never seen. Suppose, for example, that a child is invited over to her friend's house to see her new komondor. If the child has never encountered the word "komondor" before, she will have no idea what to expect. But if she asks, "What's a komondor?" and learns that it's a kind of dog, she will immediately know that the new object is likely to run around, wag its tail, bark, soil the rug until it is trained, and so on.

It was Piaget's belief that in the transition from early to middle childhood, there is a shift in the dominant mode that children use to categorize the elements of their experience. He believed that younger children cannot think of an object as belonging to two categories at the same time, the subordinate and the superordinate. Older children appreciate the fact that subclasses of superordinate categories can relate to one another and to the general class of which they are a part in multiple ways. The sort of classifying behavior that Piaget wrote about can be seen when children begin to collect stamps or baseball cards. Stamp collections can be organized according to multiple criteria. Stamps come from different countries. They are issued in different denominations and in different years. There are stamps depicting insects, animals, sports heroes, rock stars, and space exploration. Children who organize their stamps according to type of animal and country of origin (so that, for example, within "France," all the tigers are together, all the rabbits are together, and so on) are creating a multiple classification for their collections. Similarly, the child who groups baseball cards according to league, team, and position creates a multiple classification.

Piaget was particularly interested in children's ability to understand the hierarchical structure of classes and the logical relation of inclusion that holds between a superordinate class and its subclasses (for example, the subclass of cats is included in the superordinate class of mammals). As we saw in Chapter 9 (p. 341), when children 4 to 6 years old are shown a set of brown wooden beads and white wooden beads and asked, "Are there more brown beads, or more beads?" they are likely to say there are more brown beads than beads. According to Piaget, they answer this way because they cannot attend to the subclass (brown beads) and the superordinate class (beads) at the same time. Instead they compare one subclass (brown beads) with another subclass (white beads).

This result seems so counterintuitive (after all, the beads are right before the children's eyes!) that many investigators have tried to show that the children's errors are the result of a misunderstanding about what was being asked. For example, James McGarrigle and his colleagues (McGarrigle, Greaves, & Hughes, 1978) noted that the question about the subclass was linguistically marked by an adjective (*brown* beads) while the question about the superordinate class was not specially marked (beads). The researchers speculated that if the full set was also marked by an adjective, children might be clearer about what was being asked and would show that they understood class inclusion relations. The researchers repeated Piaget's experiment with black and white toy cows. The researchers asked half the children, "Are there more *black* cows or more cows?" just as Piaget would have done. The other half were shown all the cows lying down and asked, "Are there more *black* cows or more *sleeping* cows." Simply adding the adjective "sleeping" allowed more children to respond correctly, but 4- to 6-year-old children still answered incorrectly most of the time.

Systematic cataloguing of a rock collection requires the ability to classify according to multiple criteria.

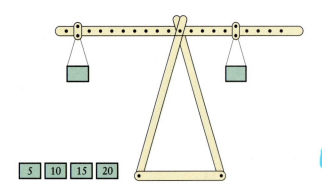

FIGURE 12.11 *A balance beam of the kind used to evaluate the development of logical reasoning.*

Other attempts to show that superficial communicative failures cause the young children's difficulties with class inclusion problems have obtained similar results. Under some circumstances even very young children correctly reason about class inclusion relationships. As a rule, though, they experience more difficulty than 7- to 8-year-olds (Winer, 1980). In line with expectations based on Piaget's approach, it is not until the age of 9 or 10 that children appear to be capable of thinking logically about the relationships of all the subcategories within a larger group in the standard tasks presented by psychologists (Chapman & McBride, 1992).

INFORMATION-PROCESSING APPROACHES TO PROBLEM SOLVING AND CLASSIFICATION

While Piagetian theorists consider the emergence of general problem-solving and classification abilities to be a key characteristic of cognitive development during middle childhood, psychologists who adopt an information-processing approach are more likely to view development as a piecemeal accumulation of knowledge, skills, and processing capacity.

Logical problem solving

One of the instruments that Piaget used to study the development of logical operations in problem solving was a balance beam (see Figure 12.11). Mature understanding of the balance beam problem requires understanding of the concept of *torque*, which is the product of weight times distance along the beam. Understanding of torque requires the ability to think simultaneously about two variables (weight and distance) and their interrelationship. It was Piaget's view that a child's developing grasp of this problem would mirror the logic of the problem: the child would attend first to one variable, then to two variables, and then would develop the ability to combine the two variables according to a single rule. He found that children younger than 7 or 8 failed to understand the problem because they focused only on weight. During middle childhood, he observed, they increasingly took into account both weight and distance. Only adolescents consistently took both weight and distance into account, and few of them achieved full understanding of torque.

Robert Siegler (1976) also used the balance beam to study cognitive development, but he analyzed the process in terms of changing strategies or rules. After analyzing the demands of the balance beam task in detail, he found it possible to formulate a set of rules, or cognitive strategies, that children might use for predicting the outcome of different arrangements of weights:

Rule 1: If the weight on one side is more, that side will go down. If the weights on the two sides are equal, they will balance.

Rule 2: If the weight on one side is more, that side will go down. If the weights are equal, the one farthest from the fulcrum goes down.

Rule 3: Always consider both weight and distance. If both weight and distance are equal, the beam will balance. If the dimensions are in conflict (for example, more weight on one side and distance on the other), muddle through. There is no rule for this case.

Rule 4: Proceed as in rule 3 but take both the distance and the weight into account by applying the torque concept: downward force equals the distance from the fulcrum times the weight on that side.

Siegler carried out a task analysis that identified six logical arrangements of weights and distances that yielded different specific patterns of errors and correct responses (see Table 12.2). As Table 12.2 indicates, when both weight and distance are equal, all rules provide correct answers. When weights are unequal but distances are equal, all rules are again correct.

The first problem that distinguishes between children of different ages comes when weights are equal and distances are not. Children who follow rule 1 should make wrong predictions, but those who follow rule 2 and consider distance will be correct. The remaining diagnostic problems are trickier to figure out. In the "conflict-weight" problem, the children who follow rules 1 and 2 get the right answer because neither of those rules is disconfirmed even though it is wrong. The children who follow rule 3 and try to take both weight and distance into account realize the problem is complicated, but they do not know the proper way to combine dimensions, so they must muddle through or guess. The "conflict-distance" and "conflict-balance" problems are set up so that if children are following rule 1 or 2 they will make the wrong response. Only rule 4 solves this problem reliably.

When Siegler tested children on the balance beam using the kinds of problems illustrated in Table 12.2, he found that he could assign almost all of the children's choice patterns to one of the rule categories. Most 5-year-olds used rule 1, most 9-year-olds used rule 2 or 3, and the 13- to 17-year-olds used predominantly rule 3. Very few of even the oldest participants used rule 4, an issue to which we will return in Chapter 16.

Siegler's analysis of how children at different ages cope with the problems in Table 12.2 demonstrates how the careful task analysis used by information-processing theorists can provide insights into the process of cognitive development. In a Piagetian analysis, all the problems are given equal weight in diagnosing children's underlying thought processes. Siegler's analysis, by contrast, leads to the unusual prediction that for some combinations of distance and weight, younger children, who follow rules 1 and 2 only, should actually outperform

TABLE 12.2 Correct Answers Predicted for Children Using Different Rules

	Rule			
Problem Type	**1**	**2**	**3**	**4**
Balance	100%	100%	100%	100%
Weight	100	100	100	100
Distance	0 (Will say "Sides balance")	100	100	100
Conflict-weight	100	100	33 (Lucky guess)	100
Conflict-distance	0 (Will say "Right side down")	0 (Will say "Right side down")	33 (Lucky guess)	100
Conflict-balance	0 (Will say "Right side down")	0 (Will say "Right side down")	33 (Lucky guess)	100

BOX 12.3

Perceiving Two Things at the Same Time

Clearly children cannot keep two things in mind or reason logically about relationships between two aspects of a problem if they do not *perceive* both of them in the first place. Research on perceptual development during childhood indicates that the ability to perceive two things at a time is one of the basic changes associated with the advent of concrete operational thinking.

A study by David Elkind (1978) demonstrates this change in perceptual ability. Elkind showed children the pictures depicted in the figure below, each of which is either ambiguous or made up of several elements. Children over 8 were generally able to see the alternative possibilities in the drawings right away. By contrast, 6-year-olds rarely gave more than one interpretation of each drawing unless the alternatives were pointed out to them. Among 4- and 5-year-olds, the tendency to latch on to a single interpretation was so strong that they did not perceive the alternative possibilities even when they were pointed out.

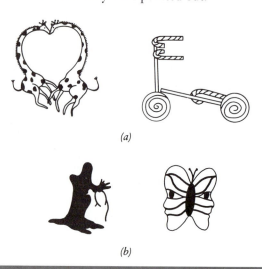

(a) *Parts and wholes: these figures depict objects constructed from other objects—a heart made of giraffes, a scooter made of candy canes and lollipops.* (b) *Ambiguous figures: a tree/swan and a butterfly/face. Until middle childhood, children are unlikely to perceive the double significance of these kinds of figures. (From Elkind, 1978.)*

children more than twice their age. When he examined the data for the relatively complicated "conflict-weight" problems, for example, he found that 5-year-olds, who are likely to follow rule 1, are correct 89 percent of the time, because rule 1 guides them to choose the side with the most weight. By contrast, 17-year-olds, most of whom were diagnosed as using rule 3, made the correct response only 51 percent of the time, an indication that they were doing a lot of guessing. This upside-down developmental pattern lends authority to Siegler's analysis. It is not predictable by Piaget's theory.

Siegler was not content to show only that the development of logical reasoning results from changes in the rules children use. He also investigated the factors that might explain the improved performance for the older children. He hypothesized that 5-year-olds have difficulty picking out the most important features of the task and forming a representation of them to use in reasoning, a process he called **encoding**. To test this hypothesis, he presented each child with a series of balance beam problems, but this time instead of asking the children to solve the problems, he covered the scale after a 10-second observation period and then gave them a new scale and asked them to reproduce the arrangement of weights and distances they had just seen. The 5-year-olds correctly remembered only the weights, not the distances, confirming his hypothesis that they had completely failed to encode distance (Box 12.3 discusses another aspect of this phenomenon). The 8-year-olds showed that they had encoded both weight and distance, even though they used only weight in their reasoning.

Encoding To pick the most important features of a task and to form a representation of them to use in reasoning about the task.

Siegler then trained each group of children on a series of problems that involved variations in both weight and distance. The 8-year-olds benefited from this training and began to use rules 2 and 3 to solve balance beam problems, while the 5-year-olds continued to use only rule 1—just the result to be expected if development of the ability to encode significant dimensions of the problem is essential to the development of reasoning. (Table 12.3 summarizes Siegler's ideas about the development of strategic thinking.)

Siegler's approach differs from Piaget's in three significant ways. First, it allows him to specify which of the many possible balance beam problems children will solve by using each rule. Second, unlike Piagetians, who expect patterns of performance to be consistent over a wide range of tasks, Siegler makes no assumption that children will solve every problem the same way; the rules are specific to the task. Third, while he does not downplay the role of logic in dealing with the problem, Siegler emphasizes the crucial importance of the way children encode the relevant features of the problem as they start to solve it, which influences the rule they will choose.

Siegler (1995, 1996) has extended his rule-based analysis to the development of conservation. He worked with 5-year-olds, who, according to Piaget, are too young to understand conservation but are in a transition phase where they are beginning to be able to consider two dimensions of a task at one time. Siegler reports that in the course of solving a long series of number conservation tasks, his 5-year-old subjects used a variety of strategies: sometimes they focused on the process of transforming a row of tokens by lengthening or shortening it; at other times they counted, or focused on the lengths of the rows, or said they didn't know. More than three-fourths of the children used at least three strategies, providing support for Siegler's view that in place of a single concept of number conservation, children have several concepts in their repertoires which compete with one another for use.

TABLE 12.3	**Six Types of Change That Contribute to the Development of Strategic Thinking**

1. The acquisition of new strategies.
2. Changes in the frequencies with which existing strategies are used.
3. Changes in the speed of executing strategies.
4. Changes in the accuracy with which strategies are carried out.
5. Changes in the degree to which strategies are used automatically.
6. Changes in the range of situations in which each strategy can be applied.

Source: From Lemaire & Siegler, 1995.

Logical classification

In place of the idea that a stagelike, global change at 5 to 7 years makes it possible for children to form complex categories, psychologists who use an information-processing approach contend that younger children can form complex categories and reason about them if the materials are presented in an appropriate manner.

Susan Carey (1985), for example, asked children to reason about the properties of various animals. She presented children between the ages of 4 and 10 and adults with pictures of such unfamiliar creatures as an aardvark, a dodo bird, and a stinkbug. As she showed each picture, she asked a series of questions about it (Does a dodo sleep? Does a stinkbug eat?). Carey found that up to the age of 7, the children judged an animal's behavior on the basis of its seeming similarity to human beings. By the age of 10, their judgments depended on the creature's biological category (bird, insect, and so on), an indication that significant cognitive change had occurred between the ages of 7 and 10 years.

Then, in a replication and extension of Carey's study, Frank Keil (1992) found that when he provided young children with a meaningful biological context for questions about biological properties, those children exhibited more advanced reasoning. For example, when he showed a picture of a person to a 4-year-old and said, "This person eats because he needs food to live and grow. If he doesn't eat, he will become thinner and thinner and will die," the child concluded that other

Middle childhood is a time when a combination of physical changes and extended practice enables children to acquire complex, culturally valued skills.

creatures must also eat food, regardless of their physical similarity to humans. The children were discriminating, too; they denied that plants have bones. These data fit well with the information-processing view that even young children can reason with biological concepts, but they apply them in a narrower range of contexts than do adults.

CHANGES IN REMEMBERING PROCESSES

Side by side with evidence that the transition from early to middle childhood is accompanied by increased ability to perceive and reason about two things at a time is evidence that children's overall memory capacities undergo significant changes. This increased ability to keep track of one's experiences offers another reason for adults' increased expectations of children at this age. The question is, what causes the changes in memory necessary to support the greater freedom of movement and responsibilities that are part of middle childhood?

Four factors, taken together, appear to bring about the memory changes characteristic of this period: (1) an increase in memory *capacity;* (2) an increase in *knowledge* about the things one is trying to remember; (3) the appearance of effective *strategies* for remembering; and (4) the appearance of the *ability to think about one's own memory processes* (Flavell, Miller, & Miller, 1993).

Memory capacity

In Chapter 9 (p. 357) we noted that as children mature, the number of randomly chosen numbers, words, or letters that they can keep in mind at one time increases steadily. This number, called a **memory span,** is used as a measure of children's short-term memory capacity. Memory span has been shown to grow continuously from early childhood into adolescence (Case, 1995). Most 4- and 5-year-olds can recall four digits presented one after another; most 9- and 10-year-olds can remember about six (Siegler, 1996).

While there is no doubt that children's memory span increases as time goes on, there is considerable uncertainty about how best to think of the underlying changes in psychological functioning (Halford et al., 1994). One possibility is that children's short-term memory storage capacity increases as the brain matures (Pascual-Leone, 1988). An alternative explanation offered by Robbie Case (1995) is that older children are able to recall more because their mental operations occur

Memory span The number of randomly chosen numbers, words, or letters that a child can keep in mind. A memory span test is used as a measure of short-term memory capacity.

more rapidly. As a consequence, they can encode, store, and retrieve information more rapidly and efficiently. In order to remember several numbers presented at random, for example, children must somehow represent each number to themselves, perhaps by silently repeating, "Ten, six, eight, two." Case and his colleagues have shown that young children take longer than older children simply to repeat a number such as 10 or 2. Because it takes them longer to say the second number, memory for the first number is more likely to decay and be lost. Older children name individual numbers quite quickly, reducing the time interval between numbers and increasing the likelihood of retaining the numbers in memory (Case, Kurland, & Goldberg, 1982) (see Figure 12.12).

Cross-cultural research enriches these conclusions. When Chuansheng Chen and Harold Stevenson (1988) compared the memory spans of U.S. and Chinese children aged 4 to 6 years, they found that the Chinese children were able to recall more digits at each of the ages tested. This finding might suggest that their working memory is larger. In line with the work of Case and his colleagues, however, Chen and Stevenson pointed to the fact that the Chinese words for the digits are shorter than the English words, so the task was easier for the Chinese children, just as it had been easier for the older American children. This hypothesis was supported by a study in which Stevenson and his colleagues (1985) used lists of objects whose names were equal in length in English and Chinese. When these words were presented for remembering, Chinese and American children were found to have equal memory capacities.

The ability of older children to repeat digits more quickly appears to be just one instance of a more general tendency for older children and adults to carry out cognitive operations of many kinds faster than younger children. In studies with both Americans and Koreans, Robert Kail and his colleagues have shown that the time it takes to retrieve information from memory decreases from early childhood well into adulthood. In comparison with young adults, 4- to 5-year olds generally respond 300 percent more slowly, 8-year-olds respond 200 percent more slowly, and 11-year-olds take 50 percent more time to respond (Kail, 1991; Kail & Park, 1994). As a consequence of this increase in mental processing speed, older children and adults can be expected to execute more cognitive operations in a given time span than younger children, and therefore to demonstrate increased intellectual effectiveness.

Knowledge base

A second factor that contributes to improved memory during childhood is the greater knowledge that older children are likely to have about any given topic simply because they have accumulated more experience in the world than younger children have. This experience provides older children with a richer **knowledge base,** or store of information, on which to draw in a new situation. As a consequence, when asked to remember new information, they have more prior information to relate it to.

The effect of prior knowledge on memory development is demonstrated by studies in which younger subjects who have a rich knowledge base are compared with older subjects who do not. In one such experiment, Michelene Chi (1978) compared memory for the arrangement of chess pieces among 10-year-old chess buffs with the memory abilities of college-age chess amateurs. The 10-year-olds recalled the chess arrangements that occurred in the course of a game better than the college students, though when the two groups were compared on their ability to recall a random series of numbers, the college students' performances were far

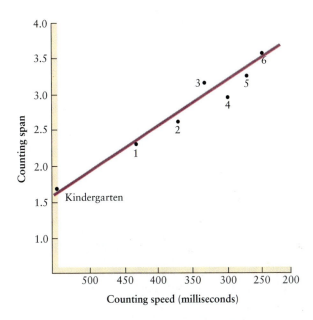

FIGURE 12.12 *Relationship between speed of naming and memory span. Note that as children grow older in grades kindergarten (K) through 6, their counting span increases accordingly. (From Case, Kurland, & Goldberg, 1982.)*

Knowledge base The store of information upon which the child can draw in a new situation in order to remember, reason, and solve problems.

Skill at cards requires the ability to remember the cards that have been previously dealt and the relative values of different hands, as well as the ability to use strategies to defeat your opponent.

Strategy A deliberate action performed for the purpose of attaining a particular goal.

Rehearsal A strategy for remembering that involves repetition of material.

superior. A replication of this study by German researchers confirmed the basic results and extended them by showing that when subjects were asked to remember *random* arrangements of chess pieces, rather than *meaningful* arrangements that might plausibly occur during a game (thereby removing the importance of knowledge of chess), the advantage of the chess experts was greatly reduced (Schneider et al., 1993).

A second study by Chi (Chi & Koeske, 1983) focused on a 4½-year-old boy's ability to recall the names of dinosaur species. Chi and Randi Koeske first elicited the names of all the dinosaurs the child knew (46 in all for this unusually well-versed child!) by questioning him on various occasions. They selected the 20 dinosaurs he mentioned most frequently and the 20 he mentioned least frequently in order to study how the child's comparative knowledge influenced his memory of each group.

The child's knowledge about these 40 dinosaurs was probed in a game in which the experimenter and the child took turns generating clues from which the other had to guess the dinosaur in question ("Lives in forest, eats plants, moves on four legs, is very big—what is it?"). The 20 dinosaurs the child mentioned most frequently were those he knew the most about.

Chi and Koeske then read the two lists of dinosaurs to the child three times each and at each reading asked him to memorize as many as he could. He recalled twice as many items from the list of dinosaurs he knew more about (an average of 9.7) as from the list with which he was less familiar (an average of 5.0). The researchers concluded that the more one knows about a topic, the easier it is to recall items that pertain to it. Consequently, the experiences children have accumulated by the time they reach middle childhood are likely to account for at least a part of the increase in their ability to remember.

Memory strategies

A **strategy** is a deliberately selected action performed for the purpose of attaining a particular goal (Paris, Newman, & Jacobs, 1985). When we say that children use memory strategies, we mean that they are able to engage in deliberate actions in order to remember something.

Even children younger than 2 years can be observed to use elementary memory strategies if just the right procedures are used. For example, Judy De Loache, Deborah Cassidy, and Ann Brown (1985) told 1½- to 2-year-old children to remember the location of an attractive stuffed animal that they hid while the children watched. The children were then induced to play with several attractive toys. After 4 minutes had elapsed, a bell rang and the children were urged to retrieve the stuffed animal. During the time they were playing with the toys, the children often interrupted themselves to look at, point at, peek at, or talk about the hidden stuffed animal. They did not engage in such behaviors when the stuffed animal was not hidden, indicating that their behaviors were specific to cases in which forgetting was a potential problem. De Loache and her colleagues point out that such behaviors are similar to well-known strategies observed in older children.

In many cases that appear to be relatively simple, however, such young children often fail to use special strategies to help them remember. A large number of studies have shown that children's spontaneous use of strategies for remembering undergoes a marked increase between the ages of 4 and 7 (Flavell, Miller, & Miller, 1993).

Two memory strategies whose development has been intensively studied are rehearsal and organization. **Rehearsal** is *repetition* of material that one is trying to memorize, such as a word list, a song, or a phone number. In order to study the development of rehearsal strategies in children, John Flavell and his colleagues (Keeney, Cannizzo, & Flavell, 1967) presented 5- and 10-year-olds with seven pictures of objects to be remembered. The children were asked to wear a "space helmet" with a visor that was pulled down over their eyes during the 15-second interval between the presentation of the pictures and the test for recall. The visor prevented the children from seeing the pictures and allowed the experimenter to watch their lips to see if they repeated to themselves what they had seen. Few of the 5-year-olds were observed to rehearse, but almost all of the 10-year-olds did. Within each age group, children who rehearsed the pictures recalled more than children who did not. When those who had not rehearsed were later taught to do so, they did as well on the memory task as those who had rehearsed on their own.

In a more recent study, children were videotaped as they were trying to remember, so the researchers could review the tapes and take note of more subtle indicators of rehearsal (McGilly & Siegler, 1989). They found that even kindergarten children are capable of rehearsing the things they want to remember. According to these investigators, widely observed increases in children's short-term memory in middle childhood result from increasingly effective use of strategies and not the sudden appearance of the ability to use a rehearsal strategy.

Marked changes are also found in a second memory strategy, **memory organization.** Children who use this strategy mentally *group* the materials to be remembered in meaningful clusters of closely associated items, so that they have only to remember one part of a cluster to gain access to the rest. Research has demonstrated that 7- and 8-year-olds are more likely than younger children to impose their own ordering principles on what they have to remember by grouping the items in easy-to-remember categories (Kail, 1990). The kinds of groupings that children impose on lists of things to be remembered also change. Younger children often use sound features, such as rhyme (cat, sat), or situational associations (cereal, bowl) to group words they are trying to remember. In middle childhood, children are more likely to link words according to the categories to which they belong, such as animals: cat, dog, horse; foods: cereal, milk, bananas; or geometric figures: triangle, square, circle (Super, 1991). The consequence of these changes is an enhanced ability to store and retrieve information deliberately and systematically.

Studies have demonstrated that children who do not spontaneously use rehearsal and organizing strategies to learn a given list of words can be taught to do so (Best, 1993; Lange & Pierce, 1992). The effectiveness of this training indicates that there is no unbridgeable gap between the memory performance of 4- to 5- and 7- to 8-year-olds or between children who use strategies spontaneously and those who do not.

Memory organization A strategy for remembering in which the materials to be remembered are grouped in meaningful clusters of closely associated items. This strategy does not come into use until middle childhood.

Metamemory Knowledge about one's own memory processes.

Metamemory

Most 7- and 8-year-olds not only know more about the world in general than preschoolers do but also are likely to know more about memory itself (knowledge referred to as **metamemory**). Even 5-year-olds, however, have some understanding of the process of remembering. In one study, the 5-year-olds said they knew that it was easier to remember a short list of words than a long one, to relearn something you once knew than to learn it from scratch, and to remember something that happened yesterday than something that happened last month (Kreutzer, Leonard, & Flavell, 1975).

Nevertheless, most 8-year-olds have a better understanding of the limitations of their own memories than most 5-year-olds. When shown a set of ten pictures and asked if they could remember them all (something most children at these ages generally cannot do), most of the 5-year-olds but only a few of the 8-year-olds claimed that they could. The 5-year-olds also failed to evaluate correctly how much progress they had made in remembering. Given unlimited time to master the set of pictures, the 5-year-olds announced that they were ready right away, even though they succeeded in remembering only a few of the items. The 8-year-olds, by contrast, knew enough to study the materials and to test themselves on their ability to remember (Flavell, Friedrichs, & Hoyt, 1970).

Even when children know that metacognitive knowledge can enhance remembering, they often do not use this knowledge, just as they don't always use rehearsal and organizational strategies when they know them (Bjorklund et al., 1994). William Fabricius and John Hagen (1984) created a situation in which all 6- and 7-year-olds used an organizational strategy on some trials and not on others. When the children used the strategy, they almost always remembered better. Did the children notice that the strategy was helpful? Fabricius and Hagen asked the children to tell them why they thought they were successful in remembering. Some of the children did not appear to understand that the organizing strategy was helpful, even though they had just used it successfully. They attributed their success to such strategies as slowing down and being more careful, or paying more attention to the stimuli. Other children did attribute their success to the deliberate use of an organizing strategy. When they were brought back for a second session of remembering in a slightly different situation, 99 percent of those children who displayed metacognitive understanding by attributing their success to the organizing strategy used the same strategy the second time around. Only 32 percent of the ones who attributed their success to some other factor used the organizing strategy. These and similar results indicate that familiarity with a good strategy does not automatically lead to its effective use. Some metamemory is also needed. Children need to notice and believe that the strategy has helped them remember better in the past.

The combined picture

These data on the development of memory capacity, knowledge, the use of remembering strategies, and metamemory all confirm that memory improves between early childhood and the age of 7 or 8. Considered one at a time, they also undermine the hypothesis that a *qualitatively* new form of remembering arises in middle childhood.

When familiar materials are presented to preschoolers in a simple format that they can understand easily, very young children are seen to use many of the strategies common in middle childhood, and their level of performance can be impressive. But such similarities between the memory abilities of young children and 7- or 8-year-olds should not be overstated. Memory experiments conducted for research purposes are designed to pare away all but one process. In a great many everyday circumstances the four aspects of remembering we have highlighted do not occur one at a time; two or more of them are likely to be relevant simultaneously. Children's ability to remember a list of words, for example, is affected by how rapidly they can store the words in short-term memory, how practiced they are at using such strategies as rehearsal and organization, and how well they can evaluate which parts of the list need the most attention. Because young children are less proficient at each of these processes, their performance outside of experiments is likely to suffer quite substantially.

When deliberate remembering is viewed as a kind of cognitive activity that recruits and deploys a variety of specific mental resources, older children's common propensity to remember well in a wide variety of circumstances contrasts sharply with a younger child's fleeting and fragile competence in highly restricted contexts. In the aggregate, several small, continuous changes can produce what appears to be a discontinuity; that is, a shift to a new stage and quality of remembering.

CULTURAL VARIATIONS IN COGNITIVE CHANGE

Cultural-context theorists warn repeatedly that an assessment of children's development cannot be considered valid unless it is carried out in the context of valued and customary activities that the children actually experience in their own culture. Yet the great majority of cross-cultural work on cognitive development uses standardized tasks to determine whether the patterns of change observed by the child psychologists of technologically sophisticated countries—Switzerland, Japan, the United States, and so on—also occur in the rest of the world's cultures.

When psychologists use their standard procedures to test the performances of children in nonindustrial societies, where literacy and schooling either are absent or have been introduced only in recent decades, they often find that children of different cultures perform at markedly different levels at the same age. Taken at face value, these data indicate that many children in some cultures do not display the cognitive changes characteristic of the transition to middle childhood in industrialized societies (Cole, 1996; Segall et al., 1990). But the data *cannot* be taken at face value. As we have seen repeatedly, variations in background knowledge about the domain being tested and the social arrangements of the testing itself make a difference in the way children perform. Consequently, cross-cultural data are often especially difficult to evaluate (Berry et al., 1992; Laboratory of Comparative Human Cognition, 1983).

Figure 12.13 summarizes the kinds of developmental growth curves that *might* distinguish development in one culture from development in another. The curve labeled *w* (for "Western, technologically sophisticated cultures") represents the performance typical of children such as those Piaget worked with in Geneva. As these children grow older, more and more of them show that they understand the concepts being tested, until the curve levels off at 100 percent.

Curves *a*, *b*, *c*, and *d* represent possible patterns that *might* be observed in comparison with the Western norm. Curves *a*, *b*, and *c* differ from curve *w* only in the rate of change: curve *a* represents earlier acquisition of the cognitive process; curve *b* represents development at essentially the same rate as the Western norm; curve *c* represents delayed development by Western standards. Curve *d* differs from the other curves not only in the rate of cognitive development but in the final level of performance, which remains significantly below 100 percent. Were researchers to discover a society in which the acquisition of a psychological function resembled curve *d*, it would indicate that people in that society never achieve the ability in question. Piaget (1966) assumed that the common phylogenetic heritage of our species ensures that children everywhere eventually attain the level of concrete operations. He expected culture to influence only the *rate* of development, the patterns represented by curves *a*, *b*, and *c*.

A great deal of research has been conducted in other cultures to test these speculations as they apply not only to concrete operations but to other cognitive

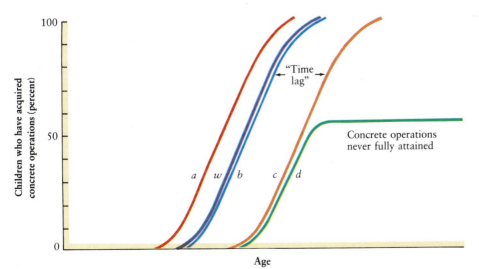

FIGURE 12.13 *Hypothetical curves representing the percentage of children who have acquired the concept of concrete operations at various ages. Curve* w *is assumed to be the developmental curve for a sample of children with a Western technological background. Curves* a, b, c, *and* d *are possible developmental curves derived from cross-cultural studies; their interpretation is discussed in the text. (From Dasen & Heron, 1981.)*

abilities as well (Berry et al., 1992). Two of the most frequently studied cognitive abilities are conservation (one of Piaget's concrete operations) and free-recall memory, each of which raises important questions about universal stagelike changes in children's development, the role of culture in development, and the ambiguities of using standard psychological methods to assess them.

Studies of concrete operations

Researchers who have used Piaget's conservation tasks to study cultural variations in cognitive development have often found that children in traditional, nonindustrial societies follow pattern *c*, lagging a year or more behind Western children in attaining the stage of concrete operations (Dasen & Heron, 1981). But in several cultures, investigators have encountered 12- and 13-year-old children and even adults who demonstrate no understanding of conservation in the Piagetian tasks (Dasen, 1982). Does this mean that they have failed to attain that level of development?

Patricia Greenfield (1966) conducted a series of conservation studies among Wolof children in the West African nation of Senegal that seemed to indicate a slower rate or lower level of development. Following the classical procedure, Greenfield first presented children ranging in age from 6 to 13 years with two beakers containing equal amounts of liquid, then poured the contents of one beaker into a taller, thinner beaker. Although the older children in the sample were more likely to display an understanding of conservation than the younger ones, only 50 percent of those 11 to 13 years old showed that they understood that the amount of liquid was not changed when it was poured from one beaker to another.

Similar results were obtained in studies of adults in settings as varied as central Australia, New Guinea, the Amazon jungle of Brazil, and rural Sardinia (Dasen, 1977a, 1977b). Reviewing the evidence available in the early 1970s, Pierre Dasen wrote, "It can no longer be assumed that adults of all societies reach the concrete operational stage" (1972, p. 31).

This conclusion was immediately challenged because of its wide-reaching implications. Adults who truly lacked concrete operations would be severely handicapped in everyday life. Like preschool-aged children, they would not be able to think through the implications of their actions and would believe that objects changed simply because of their spatial distribution. They would be unable to understand another person's social perspective or to engage in causal reasoning. If true, this conclusion would also justify the belief, popular in the nineteenth and early twentieth centuries, that "primitives think like children" (Hallpike, 1979).

Such implications led Gustav Jahoda (1980), a leading cross-cultural psychologist, to reject outright the possibility that in some cultures children do not eventually achieve the ability to think operationally. As Jahoda points out, it is difficult to see how a society could survive if its members were indifferent to causal relations, incapable of thinking through the implications of their actions, or unable to adopt other people's points of view. He concluded that "no society could function at the preoperational stage, and to suggest that a majority of any people are at that level is nonsense almost by definition" (1980, p. 116).

Words alone do not suffice to settle such questions, however. To resolve this issue, one would have to produce evidence that the findings produced by the research methods used in these studies, which seem straightforward enough, misrepresent their subjects' mental capacities.

One plausible explanation of the findings is that the people being tested failed to understand what was expected of them, either because they were unfamiliar with the test situation or because the experimenters did not make their intentions clear in an unfamiliar culture and language. This is the same line of reasoning

Although children from traditional agricultural societies sometimes perform poorly on psychological tests, their cognitive abilities are often manifested in other ways. This Ugandan boy has constructed his toy car out of bits of wire and some wooden wheels.

used to challenge Piaget's views on the thought processes of preschool-aged children (see Chapter 9). As might be expected, the same sorts of research methods are used to resolve the issue.

Dasen and his colleagues tackled the problem by training subjects to solve conservation tasks (Dasen, Ngini, & Lavallée, 1979). They reasoned that if subjects were truly able to engage in concrete operational thinking but did not display their ability because they were unfamiliar with the tests, training on similar tasks should be sufficient to change their performance.

In a series of studies, the researchers demonstrated that by the end of middle childhood, relatively brief training in procedures similar to the standard conservation task was sufficient to change the pattern of performance on the conservation task itself. One such result is shown in Figure 12.14, which compares rural Australian Aborigine children with children in the city of Canberra. Without training, half of the Aborigine children *appear* not to have acquired the concept of conservation of quantity at all (curve *d* in Figure 12.13). But when they are trained, their test results show that they do understand the basic concept of conservation of quantity. Even with training however, the Aborigine children exhibit curve *c* in Figure 12.13: in acquisition of the concept of conservation they lag behind the Canberra children by approximately 3 years, suggesting that their culture does not provide the kinds of experiences that accelerate the acquisition of this concept in other cultures.

This modified interpretation of cultural differences in the development of concrete operations is challenged by African psychologists who suggest that specialized training may be unnecessary and that no lags will appear if the researchers are of the same culture as the children they are testing and know the local language well. Psychologists native to the culture are able to follow the flexible questioning procedures that are the hallmark of Piaget's clinical interviews, procedures that seem to be even more effective than training in bringing out children's best performance.

Raphael Nyiti (1982), for example, compared the conservation performances of 10- and 11-year-old children of two cultural groups, both living on Cape Breton, Nova Scotia. Some of the children were of English-speaking European backgrounds and some were of the Micmac Indian tribe. The Micmac children all spoke Micmac at home, but they had spoken English in school since the first grade. The children of European backgrounds were all interviewed in English by

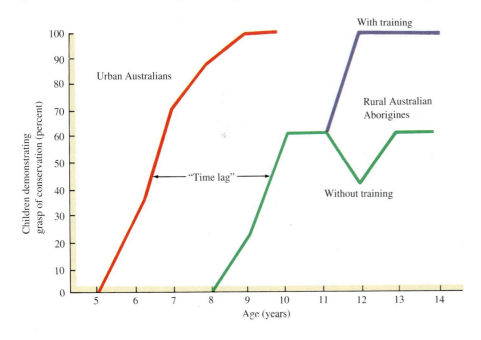

FIGURE 12.14 *Curves representing the actual percentages of Australian children who demonstrated a grasp of the concept of conservation. Australian Aborigines lagged behind urban Australian children with European backgrounds. Without training, 50 percent of the Aborigine children as old as 14 years failed to demonstrate an understanding of the concept of conservation. (From Dasen, Ngini, & Lavallée, 1979.)*

an English speaker of European background. The Micmac children were interviewed in English once and in Micmac once.

The results of Nyiti's experiment clearly suggest that inadequate communication between researchers and children can create the false impression that the children of some cultures lag in development. When all children were interviewed in their native languages, no difference at all was found in the performances of the two cultural groups. But when the Micmac children were interviewed in English, only half as many of them as of the other children seemed to understand the concept of conservation. Nyiti (1976) obtained similar results in a study of children in his native Tanzania, as did other researchers in the West African country of Sierra Leone (Kamara & Easley, 1977).

Other evidence has shown that when the content of the reasoning tasks is linked to domains in which children in a nonindustrial society have rich experience, they display more rapid cognitive development than the industrialized norm (curve *a* in Figure 12.13). For example, Gustav Jahoda (1983) studied the development of the concept of profit (which has been shown to develop through several Piagetian-like stages). Jahoda arranged for 107 fourth- to sixth-graders in the Central African country of Zimbabwe and 48 Scottish children of the same ages to act as shopkeepers in several mock business transactions. This task was assumed to be closer to the experience of the Zimbabwean children, all of whom had helped their parents with marketing and for whom trading was part of life.

Some of the hypothetical problems required the children to sell such goods as cloth and rice from a "store"; others required them to buy goods from a supplier. The main question was whether the children would know that they needed to sell the goods for more than they had paid for them, thereby demonstrating their understanding of the concept of profit. Jahoda hypothesized that the Scottish children would lag behind the children of Zimbabwe because they had less experience buying and selling at a profit. This was exactly what he found: fully 84 percent of the Zimbabwean children displayed full or partial understanding of the concept, compared to only 45 percent of the Scottish children.

Taken as a whole, recent evidence appears to demonstrate that when Piaget's clinical procedures are properly applied, concrete operations are a universal cognitive achievement of middle childhood, just as Piaget (1966/1974) assumed they were (Berry et al., 1992). However, there are quite dramatic cultural variations in

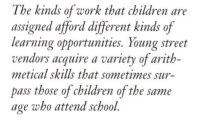

The kinds of work that children are assigned afford different kinds of learning opportunities. Young street vendors acquire a variety of arithmetical skills that sometimes surpass those of children of the same age who attend school.

children's familiarity with the contents of tests and with test procedures, and these variations clearly influence children's performances on the standard psychological tests.

Studies of memory development

Cross-cultural studies of memory call the universality of cognitive developments into question in a somewhat different way (Rogoff, 1982). Like the investigators of conservation, researchers who study memory in middle childhood also find that children's familiarity with test materials and procedures influences their performance. But unlike similar conservation research, memory tests that do make use of materials with which children are familiar still produce results that show cultural differences in the kind of remembering that takes place.

Michael Cole and his colleagues (1971; Cole & Scribner, 1974) studied the development of memory among tribal people in rural Liberia. To overcome the barriers of language and culture, these researchers observed everyday cognitive activities before conducting their experiments and worked closely with college-educated local people who acted as the experimenters. Even with these precautions, they found striking cultural differences in the way tribal people went about remembering and solving the problems presented by their experimental tasks.

The nature of these cultural differences can be seen in studies of the development of *free-recall memory*. In a free-recall task people are shown a large number of objects, one at a time, and then asked to remember them. This kind of memory is called "free" recall because people are free to recall the items in any order they wish.

Below is a list of objects used in several of these studies. The list shows that the objects appear to fall into four distinct categories. To make certain that American categories were not simply being imposed on Liberian reality, the researchers made preliminary investigations to ensure that Liberian subjects were familiar with the items used and that they readily separated these items into the four groups indicated in the list (Cole et al., 1971).

plate	potato	cutlass	trousers
calabash	onion	hoe	singlet
pot	banana	knife	headtie
pan	orange	file	shirt
cup	coconut	hammer	hat

The researchers found that tribal Liberian children, unlike children in industrial societies, showed no regular increase in memory performance during middle childhood—unless they had attended school for several years. The people who had never gone to school improved their performance on these tasks very little after the age of 9 or 10. These people remembered approximately ten items on the first trial, and managed to recall only two more items after 15 practice trials. The Liberian children who were attending school, by contrast, learned the materials rapidly, much the way schoolchildren of the same age did in the United States.

Important clues to the causes of these differences were revealed by detailed analyses of the order in which the items were recalled. Schoolchildren in Liberia and the United States not only learned the various items rapidly but used the categorical similarities between them to aid their recall. After the first trial they clustered their responses, recalling first, say, the items of clothing, then the items of food, and so on. The Liberians who had never attended school did very little such clustering, an indication that they were not using the categorical relationships of the items to help them remember.

To track down the source of this difference, the researchers varied aspects of the task. They found that if, instead of presenting a series of objects in random order, they presented the same objects in a meaningful way as part of a story, their nonschooled Liberian subjects recalled them easily, clustering the objects according to the roles they played in the story. When memory for traditional children's stories was tested, cultural differences were also absent (Mandler et al., 1980).

Similar results on tests of children's memorization skills have been obtained in research among Mayan people of rural Guatemala. When Mayan children were presented with a free-recall task, their performances lagged considerably behind those of agemates in the United States (Kagan et al., 1979). Their performances changed dramatically, however, when Barbara Rogoff and Kathryn Waddell (1982) gave them a memory task that was meaningful in local terms.

Rogoff and Waddell constructed a diorama of a Mayan village located near a mountain and a lake, similar to the locale in which the children lived. Each child watched as a local experimenter selected 20 miniature objects from a set of 80 and placed them in the diorama. The objects included cars, animals, people, and furniture—just the kinds of things that would be found in a real town. Then the 20 objects were returned to the group of 60 others remaining on the table. After a few minutes, the children were asked to reconstruct the full scene they had been shown. Under these conditions, the memory performance of the Mayan children was slightly superior to that of their U.S. counterparts.

The implication of these cross-cultural memory studies differs from that of the cross-cultural studies of concrete operational thinking. The latter studies probed basic mental operations presumed by Piaget and his followers to reflect the logic underlying everyday actions and reasoning in any culture. The ability to remember is also a universal intellectual requirement, but specific *forms* of remembering are not universal. The forms of memory most often studied by psychologists are usually associated with formal schooling.

Schooling presents children with specialized information-processing tasks—committing large amounts of information to memory in a short time, learning to manipulate abstract symbols in one's head and on paper, using logic to conduct experiments, and many more tasks that have few if any analogies in societies without formal schooling. The free-recall task that Cole and his colleagues initially used to assess memory among Liberian tribal people has no precise analogy in traditional Liberian cultures, so it is not surprising that the corresponding way of remembering would not be acquired.

The same conclusion applies to the vast majority of tasks psychologists use to assess other mental transformations that occur in middle childhood. Such tasks embody forms of activity that are specific to certain kinds of settings, especially schools and the modern technological workplace—settings that only some cultures provide. Performance on these tasks can be expected to be closely related to children's experience in school, but the relation of these tasks to other contexts of development is still poorly understood (Cole, 1996).

COGNITIVE DEVELOPMENT IN MIDDLE CHILDHOOD: COMPETING APPROACHES COMPARED

We opened this chapter by pointing out that, with the exception of increased size and strength and the loss of baby teeth, there is no visible physical evidence that 5- to 7-year-olds are capable of taking on greater responsibilities, yet adults in many parts of the world expect them to behave more responsibly and maturely. The adults do so because they notice a variety of changes in children's behavior that are related to their thought processes. Children become better able to keep track of where they are when they are sent on an errand to another neighborhood. They can keep in mind the fact that they are supposed to stop at the store on the way home from school to pick up milk for breakfast the next morning. They are more likely to think about the consequences of various actions and draw logical inferences from their growing knowledge of their culture's categories. In short, they are cognitively more competent.

Psychologists who study children's development see these same changes. The challenge they face is to provide a scientific explanation for the increases in children's competence and reliability.

One important *physical* change that cannot be seen without the help of sophisticated electrical recording equipment and detailed anatomical study is the greater maturity of the brain. Researchers have noted both quantitative differences, such as the greater speed with which information travels through the nervous system, and qualitative differences, such as the new patterns of electrical activity that arise because different parts of the brain begin to work in coordination with one another in new combinations.

There is as yet no consensus on how these changes in brain function relate to cognitive development. With respect to memory, there is now reasonable agreement that the greater maturity of the brain accounts for quantitative increases in such basic processes as memory span (Case, 1995; Siegler, 1996). It is not clear, however, how the changes that scientists have observed in the brain might account for such developments as the emergence of metacognitive understanding and the ability to use cognitive strategies such as rehearsing. One obstacle is that psychologists are still deeply divided about how best to conceive of these cognitive changes. Neo-Piagetians, in particular, have argued that there is a close link between the shift in patterns of cortical activity with age and the emergence of new skills and logical operations (Case, 1995; Fischer & Rose, 1995). Their argument rests on the assumption that cognitive development goes through a series of stagelike changes that correspond to parallel stagelike brain changes. Yet in both this chapter and in Chapter 9 (which discussed cognitive development in early childhood) we have encountered repeated demonstrations that for any claim that a new cognitive ability emerges around the age of 7 or 8, there is also evidence that the ability in question can be found at an earlier age—although it may appear only in simplified form and in highly restricted contexts. Such findings are incompatible with the idea of a one-to-one relationship between maturational changes and cognitive changes.

These complexities require us to withhold judgment on the competing views about the causes of the new behaviors seen in middle childhood. To address the question properly, we first need to reach beyond the relatively narrow range of tasks that have been featured in psychologists' studies of cognitive development and investigate the changes that children display in a variety of social contexts, especially in classrooms and peer groups, where children in middle childhood begin to spend so much of their time. Many psychologists believe that experiences in both of these contexts are crucial to the cognitive changes associated with middle childhood. What is the evidence to support such a claim? Once we have a more well-rounded picture of children's experiences, we can return to examine the central issue of the distinctiveness of middle childhood and the forms of thought that are said to characterize it.

SUMMARY

Coping with Increased Freedom and Responsibility

- The onset of middle childhood is recognized in cultures around the world. When children begin to lose their baby teeth, adults begin to assign them tasks that take them away from adult supervision and to hold them responsible for their own actions. This reorientation in adult behavior implies an increase in children's physical capacities, in their ability to follow instructions, and in their ability to keep track of what they are doing.

Biological Developments

- Size and strength increase significantly in the years from 6 to 12, but more slowly than during early childhood.
- There is a significant genetic contribution to growth; nutrition and general health factors are two important environmental contributors.
- Agility, balance, and coordination improve markedly during this period. Boys excel at motor abilities that emphasize power and force while girls excel in fine motor coordination and agility.
- Several significant developments in brain structure and function occur between the ages of 5 and 7:
    1. Myelination continues, particularly in the frontal cortex.
    2. The numbers of synapses and the output of neurotransmitters increase.
    3. Alpha activity comes to dominate theta activity.
    4. The synchronization of electrical activity in different parts of the brain increases significantly, producing marked coordination between the frontal lobes and other areas.

A New Quality of Mind?

- Piaget believed that around the age of 7 children become capable of concrete mental operations; they can now combine, separate, reorder, and transform objects mentally. One important manifestation of concrete operations is conservation, the understanding that the appearance of objects may change while their quantity or some other essential feature remains the same.
- Critics of Piaget have argued that when problems are sufficiently well explained and simplified, conservation appears far earlier than Piaget suspected.
- A second manifestation of concrete operations, the ability to classify objects according to multiple criteria, is another cognitive achievement characteristic of middle childhood. Logical classification permits children to think more systematically about the relation of one object to another.
- In place of a discontinuous, global change in cognition, information-processing theorists see the transition to middle childhood as a gradual accumulation of knowledge, skills, and information-processing capacity.
- Analyses of children's behavior in a variety of problem-solving tasks reveals the presence of more than one strategy at any given time. Development consists in the discovery of new strategies and changes in the frequency, spontaneity, and accuracy with which strategies are used.
- Information-processing analyses of the development of classification abilities indicate that children can reason effectively at an early age; what develops is the range of contexts in which they can do so.
- The ability to engage in deliberate remembering increases during middle childhood. Changes in memory ability are associated with
    1. The capacity to hold several items of information in mind at one time.
    2. Increased knowledge relevant to the information to be remembered.
    3. The use of memory strategies, such as organization and rehearsal.
    4. The ability to think about one's own memory processes.

- Cross-cultural research has identified cultures in which children in middle childhood fail to display the changes in mental abilities that are characteristic of children in industrialized societies.
- Cross-cultural differences on Piagetian conservation problems disappear when the subjects are provided special training or when the studies are conducted by experimenters who are fluent in the language of the people studied and familiar with their culture.
- Sizable variations in memory performance differentiate nonschooled people from those who attend school. These differences are most evident when the materials to be remembered are items selected at random or related to one another in ways that do not fit the patterns of the subjects' everyday activities. When the test materials are organized in ways meaningful to the subjects, however, no cross-cultural differences in performance can be detected.
- Cross-cultural evidence indicates that culture-specific contexts are important contributors to cognitive development. Consequently, study of schooling and peer groups is required to resolve questions about development in middle childhood.

KEY TERMS

compensation, p. 488

concrete operations,
  p. 485

conservation, p. 487

EEG coherence, p. 483

encoding, p. 496

identity, p. 488

knowledge base, p. 499

memory organization,
  p. 501

memory span, p. 498

metamemory, p. 501

rehearsal, p. 500

reversibility, p. 488

strategy, p. 500

THOUGHT QUESTIONS

1. In what significant ways have you observed middle childhood in your community to resemble and to differ from that of Raymond Birch?
2. What biological and cognitive features of middle childhood do you think are best described as discontinuous with the features of early childhood? Which do you consider to represent a chain of continuity?
3. Give specific examples of how various memory strategies might be used to learn the information presented in this chapter.
4. What are some of your everyday nonacademic tasks that require memorization? What memory strategies are you conscious of applying to them? Make a list of the ways in which these tasks differ from the remembering you do in school.

Schooling and Development in Middle Childhood

"I spent that first day picking holes in paper, then went home in a smoldering temper.

'What's the matter, Love? Didn't he like it at school, then?'

'They never gave me the present.'

'Present? What present?'

'They said they'd give me a present.'

'Well, now, I'm sure they didn't.'

'They did! They said: You're Laurie Lee, aren't you? Well you just sit there for the present. I sat there all day but I never got it. I ain't going back there again.'

—*Laurie Lee*,
Cider with Rosie

I
n many parts of the modern world, children are required by law to go to school from the ages of about 6 to 16. For nine or more months of the year, five or six days a week, children spend five to seven hours listening to teachers, answering questions, reading books, writing essays, solving arithmetic problems in workbooks, taking tests, and generally "being educated." Before they take their places as adult workers, most young Americans will have spent more than 15,000 hours in classrooms. In some countries the amount of time children spend in school is even greater (Stevenson & Stigler, 1992). It would be very surprising indeed if the activities that children engage in at school did not play a central role in defining the characteristics of their middle childhood and in shaping their later lives.

To determine the influence of schooling on children's development, we need to address a series of questions:

* What is the nature of school as a context for children's development, and under what historical conditions do schools arise?
* How does learning in school differ from learning in other contexts?
* How does schooling influence cognitive development?
* What special abilities does schooling require and what factors account for success in school?

Answers to these questions have far-reaching significance in modern societies. Children who fail to thrive in school or who drop out may be confined as adults to less interesting and less secure work as well as to substantially lower incomes than children who meet society's expectations by completing high school and higher levels of education (U.S. Bureau of the Census, 1995) (see Figure 13.1). Despite the emphasis society places on education, many millions of young people in the United States do not thrive in school. In the opinion of policy makers, resulting low levels of literacy and mathematical skills jeopardize the country's ability to compete effectively in the international arena (Educational Testing Service, 1988; U.S. Department of Education, 1983). These concerns have made the study of learning and development in the schools one of the most active areas of research in developmental psychology.

FIGURE 13.1   *The relationship between years of schooling and income in the United States. Note that at all levels of schooling, women were paid less than men in 1993. (From U.S. Bureau of the Census, 1995.)*

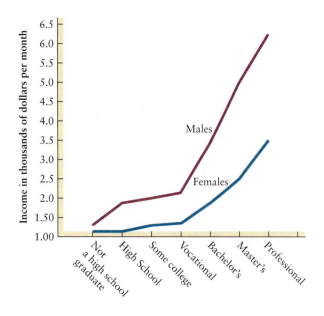

The Contexts in Which Skills Are Taught

In Chapter 10 we examined socialization in the family, concentrating on the ways in which young children are raised to acquire the basic knowledge, skills, and beliefs essential in their community. Socialization is a universal human process that has always been a part of human experience everywhere. In addition to the socialization that occurs within the family, as we discussed in Chapter 12, sometime around the sixth or seventh year of life, all societies begin to socialize children into new tasks that are designed to provide them with the skills necessary for adult life. What is not universal is the specific *content* of the preparation and the way it is socially organized. Although formal schooling is an enduring fact of life in industrialized countries, it is only one of several ways in which societies have arranged for children to acquire adult skills and knowledge.

Education is a form of socialization in which adults engage in *deliberate teaching* of the young to ensure the acquisition of specialized knowledge and skills. It is not known if education existed among the hunter-gatherer peoples who roamed the earth hundreds of thousands of years ago, but deliberate teaching is not a conspicuous part of socialization in contemporary hunter-gatherer cultures (Rogoff, 1990). Among the !Kung Bushmen of Africa's Kalahari Desert, for example, basic training in the skills expected of adults is embedded in everyday activity:

> There is . . . very little explicit teaching. . . . What the child knows, he learns from direct interaction with the adult community, whether it is learning to tell the age of the spoor left by a poisoned kudu buck, to straighten the shaft of an arrow, to build a fire, or to dig a spring hare out of its burrow. . . . It is all implicit. (Bruner, 1966, p. 59)

In cultures such as the !Kung, inclusion of children in grownups' activities is the basic means by which adults ensure that children acquire culturally valued skills and knowledge.

When societies achieve a certain degree of complexity and specialization in the roles people play, the tools they use, and the ways they secure food and housing, preparation for some occupations is likely to take the form of **apprenticeship,** a form of interaction intermediate between the implicit socialization of family life and formal education. A young apprentice spends an extended period of time working for an adult master while learning the trade on the job (Coy, 1989; Lave & Wenger, 1991). The settings in which apprentices learn are not organized primarily for the purpose of teaching. Rather, instruction and productive labor are combined; from the beginning, apprentices contribute to the work process.

Researchers have found that novice apprentices receive relatively little explicit instruction in their craft (Rogoff, 1990). Instead, they are given ample opportunity to observe skilled workers and to practice specific tasks. Manning Nash (1967) reported that in Guatemala novices learn to weave on a foot loom by sitting next to a skilled weaver for several weeks and observing him carefully. No explanations are offered.

In many societies the apprentice's relationship with the master is part of a larger web of family relationships. Sometimes the master is a relative who trains

Education A specialized form of socialization in which adults engage in deliberate teaching of the young to ensure the acquisition of knowledge and skills required in adult life.

Apprenticeship A special process of socialization in which a novice spends an extended period of time working for a master in a trade or craft while learning on the job.

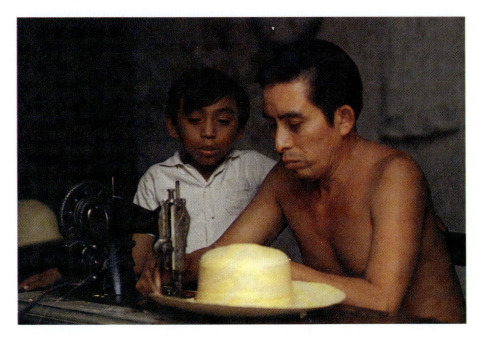

Apprenticeship arrangements in which children learn by observing adults and participating in their work are still an important form of education despite the spread of formal schooling.

the novice in exchange for training that the novice's parents give one of the master's children. Often the apprentice lives with the master and does farm or household chores to help pay for his upkeep. In this way the tasks of education and community building are woven together (Goody, 1989).

Although formal education has surpassed it as the primary form of acquiring proficiency in adult skills, apprenticeship is still important in the industrialized world. It is prevalent in such varied forms of adult work activity as the building trades, medicine, law, meat cutting, and navigating a ship, where it sometimes follows more formal instruction and sometimes accompanies it (Lave & Wenger, 1991; Hutchins, 1995).

Schooling differs from informal instruction in the family and from apprenticeship training in four main ways (Lave & Wenger, 1991; Scribner & Cole, 1973):

- *Motivation.* When students begin school, they must work for years to perfect their skills before they can put their knowledge to use in adult work.
- *Social relations.* Unlike masters of apprentices, schoolteachers are usually assigned a carefully restricted role in their pupils' upbringing that separates education from kinship obligations and economic contributions.
- *Social organization.* Apprentices are most likely to learn in a work setting among people of diverse ages and skill levels, so they have more than one person to turn to for assistance. At school, children have traditionally found themselves in a large room in the company of other children of about the same age and only one adult. As a rule they are expected to work individually rather than cooperatively.
- *Medium of instruction.* Apprenticeship instruction is usually conducted orally in the context of production. Speech is also important to formal schooling, but it is often speech of a special kind that requires children to acquire skills and knowledge through the manipulation of written symbols.

The Historical Development of Literacy and Schooling

To convey a deeper understanding of the distinctive nature of formal schooling as a context for development, we begin by examining the historical circumstances in which schooling came into being. This historical background makes it clear why literacy and numeracy are the foundations of the curriculum wherever formal education is encountered. Next we examine the process of acquiring three academic skills that are essential to successful mastery of the curriculum: reading, arithmetic, and the special forms of language that are commonly encountered in school. We also explore the consequences of acquiring these skills for cognitive development as a whole.

Wherever formal schooling has been introduced, large differences have been found in individual children's ability to master the curriculum, even the curriculum of the elementary grades, where basic skills are taught. It is this disparity that brought IQ tests into being. After summarizing the basic facts about IQ testing, we return to the broader context of the school in the community to examine how parents, peers, and school organization influence children's performance.

PRECURSORS OF LITERACY AND SCHOOLING

The earliest forms of writing have been traced back to around 4000 B.C., when changes in technology made it possible for one sector of a population to grow enough food to support a large number of others besides themselves. This fact made possible a substantial division of labor and the development of city-states.

In the ruins of such cities, archaeologists discovered symbols inscribed on clay tablets. This early writing system is referred to as *cuneiform writing* ("cuneiform" means "wedge-shaped," in reference to the shape of the symbols etched in clay) (Larsen, 1986; Schmandt-Besserat, 1978). The symbols inscribed on clay tablets included pictures representing objects supplemented by symbols representing the sounds of language (Olson, 1994).

Written symbols for words and numbers are direct extensions of the mediating capacity of spoken language. The essential advantage shared by all written notation systems is that they extend the power of language in time and space (Goody, 1977). Sounds disappear as soon as they are spoken, and even the loudest speakers can project their voices over only a short distance. Words that are written down, by contrast, can be carried great distances with no change in their physical characteristics. Writing freezes information in time; what is once written down can be referred to in its original form and thought about time and again. In this respect, written notations are a form of memory.

The new notation systems could be mastered only after long and systematic study. But so important were these new systems for keeping records that societies began to devote resources to support selected young men with the explicit purpose of making them scribes, people who could write. The places where young men were brought together for this purpose were the earliest schools. The social organization and content of the earliest schools were in some ways specific to the societies in which they arose and in other ways startlingly like our own. Two dozen or more students sat in rows facing a teacher, who lectured to them and drilled them in "the basics" while they scratched out their lessons on writing tablets. In addition to learning the rudiments of writing, reading, and arithmetic, these early students learned the record-keeping procedures they would use as civil servants after they graduated.

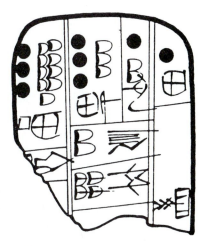

The earliest writings were symbols etched on clay tablets. This tablet records information about a herd of sheep. It is thought to be the annual account of a shepherd, who records that of the 33 sheep in the herd, 12 gave birth to lambs, 2 were taken away for some reason, and 4 died. (From Strauss, 1988.)

LITERACY AND SCHOOLING IN MODERN TIMES

For centuries the tradition of literacy and schooling in the Western world was confined largely to the children of the elite. Not until the nineteenth century, in response to the Industrial Revolution, did nations begin to institute mandatory schooling and strive for mass literacy.

Mastery of written symbol systems is the focus of most early education.

*"Now you're probably all asking yourselves,
'Why must I learn to read and write?'"*

Drawing by Bernard Schoenbaum; © 1994. The New Yorker Magazine, Inc.

The spread of schooling in the past two centuries has created a distinctive set of social problems with important implications for children's development. Two hundred years ago, when mass literacy programs were in their infancy, there were two kinds of education. "Higher education," intended for a small elite, included some mastery of classical literature and the rudiments of geometry and algebra. A tutor was hired to see that the children of the wealthy gained a degree of learning equal to their status in life. These children received individual attention and as much explanation as the tutor could provide.

The "mass education" provided to the great majority of children was quite different. It enabled them to recite from a religious text such as the Bible or the Koran, to write simple messages, and to calculate simple sums. The instruction provided the masses was not intended to give them a general education as we understand that term today. When teachers were confronted by 20, 40, or more students instead of one or two, instruction was based largely on drill and practice combined with oral imitation of the teacher (Resnick & Resnick, 1977). Today many societies expect all of their children to attain a level of education that was once reserved for small elites, but the children are still expected to do so in large classes in which they receive little or no individual instruction.

Even this brief historical background is sufficient to suggest two reasons why modern children confront a far more difficult task than that faced by their ancient predecessors in the Middle East or the children of the wealthy of more recent times. First, since the advent of literacy some 6000 years ago, scientific and technological knowledge has accelerated rapidly, adding significantly to the lessons that children have been asked to master as part of "the basics." Second, the social organization of instruction has failed to keep pace with the dramatic increases in the amount of knowledge children are expected to acquire. In an important sense, modern teachers and children are asked to accomplish more with fewer resources.

Development and Academic Skills

From the earliest schools of the ancient Middle East to neighborhood schools throughout the modern world, instruction has focused on the mastery of two basic symbol systems, written language and mathematics. Each challenges children in a special way.

LEARNING TO READ

The ability to read is the ability to interpret the world through print. There is broad agreement among psychologists that reading is not a unitary skill; it is a complex system of coordinated skills and knowledge (Adams, 1990; Crowder & Wagner, 1992). A good deal is known about how skilled readers translate marks on a page into meaningful messages. But despite intensive research efforts throughout this century, and especially over the past two decades, the process of *learning* to read is still not well understood. The problem is important because at present a great many children of normal intelligence fail to acquire reading skills deemed adequate for productive participation in a modern society (Miller, 1988).

The specific elements that must be coordinated in order to read depend on the way the orthography of the written language (its graphic symbols) is related to the spoken language. This relationship has developed in different ways in different parts of the world. The traditional Chinese writing system is *ideographic*—one written symbol *(grapheme)* corresponds to each distinct idea or meaning in the spoken language. The Japanese use two systems: the Chinese ideographic system, which represents meanings directly, and a *syllabic* system, in which each grapheme corresponds to a syllable in the spoken language. Most countries use an *alphabetic* system, in which each letter or grapheme corresponds to a significant sound variant *(phoneme)* in the spoken language. Here we will concentrate on the alphabet (named after the first two characters in the Greek system of writing, alpha and beta) (Olson, 1994).

An alphabetic writing system might seem very inefficient. For example, it takes three times as many symbols to represent "zygote" using the alphabet as it would using a syllabic system. But the alphabetic system is efficient in a different and powerful way. It can represent English, which has more than 8000 basic syllables, with only two dozen or so symbols and a few punctuation marks. A system that represented each syllable by its own symbol would make mastery of written English a formidable task indeed.

The economy of using phonemes, however, is offset by the fact that phonemes are abstractions; they cannot be pronounced in isolation, but only in combinations that we perceive as syllables. When we want to demonstrate the sound of the phoneme /t/, for example, we are likely to say something like "tuh," which is not the way the phoneme sounds in such words as "tomorrow" and "tattletale." As a consequence, it is difficult for teachers to give children a clear description of the basic correspondences they need to know in order to read.

Prereading

The first step that children must take in learning to read is to realize that there is some kind of correspondence between the marks on the printed page and the spoken language. Once they understand that each word is represented by a cluster of graphic signs, they still have to figure out what the actual rules of correspondence are. At first most children believe that there is one symbol for each word. Then they begin to focus on syllables. Eventually they realize that the letters are supposed to correspond to all of a word's phonemes.

Learning letter-sound correspondences so that written symbols can be decoded to find the corresponding sounds is one of the essential tasks confronting beginning readers.

Decoding In reading, the process by which letters of the alphabet are associated with corresponding phonemes of the spoken language.

Achieving the basic idea that letters of the alphabet correspond to the sounds that make up words is essential to learning to read. Now children are on the threshold of the really difficult task: to learn all of the specific sound-letter rules **(decoding)** and, while applying them, to use their knowledge of the spoken language to derive meaning from the text as a whole *(comprehension)*.

Decoding

In order to learn the letter-sound correspondences that are central to reading, children need to be skilled at analyzing sounds. That is, they must learn to "hear phonemes" ("*Balloon* begins with a *b*) just as they must come to "see letters" ("That letter is a *b*"). Mastery of the ability to hear phonemes does not appear to occur spontaneously without deliberate instruction; nonliterate adults in various parts of the world do not display an explicit awareness of them (Adams, 1990).

Peter Bryant (1993) summarizes a wealth of research demonstrating that children who find it difficult to break words into their constituent syllables and phonemes in a purely oral task have difficulty linking sounds and letters. This research has spawned special prereading educational programs that provide children with enriched experiences in oral language analysis before they are taught to read. The lessons include practice in rhyming, breaking words down into syllables, and special language games such as pig Latin, in which the first phoneme of each word is moved to the end of the word and then followed by an -ay (as in "igpay atinlay").

The results of such special instruction can be dramatic. Benita Blachman (1987) implemented a program that combined special language analysis exercises with lessons in linking sounds and letters. The program was administered in two inner-city schools during the first and second grades (and in the third grade for children who were still experiencing difficulty). Then the children were tested in the fourth grade. Before Blachman's program was introduced, the fourth-grade reading performance in the schools was seven months behind the national norm. The children in the experimental program, by contrast, scored seven months above the national norm, and the gains were even greater a year later. Such results not only support the theoretical link between language analysis and reading acquisition but show that the theory can be usefully applied in practice.

Even after they have acquired the ability to segment the spoken language into phonemes, children who are learning to read and write in English face an additional difficulty: there is no one-to-one relationship between letters of the alphabet and the phonemes that make up English words. Instead, the 26 letters of the English alphabet represent 52 basic phonemes (Henderson, 1982). So, for example, a child acquiring literacy in English must grasp the fact that while *t* remains *t*, it is not pronounced the same way in the words "tea" and "both," and such seemingly different letters as *g* and *f* can be used to produce a single sound, as in "muff" and "rough." Similar lessons must be mastered for the entire alphabet.*

A second difficulty is how to communicate about isolated phonemes. It is physically impossible to pronounce in isolation the sounds that correspond to the phonemes in a word, separating the *c* in cat from the *a*, for example, and the *a* from the *t*.

Faced with this problem, teachers may resort to a strategy called *blending.* They start out with a word such as "cat" and attempt to pronounce the phoneme that corresponds to each letter ("cuh," "ah," "tuh"). Note that even if children have learned the names of the three letters, "cee," "ay," and "tee," this demonstration may not help much because neither "cuh-ah-tuh" nor "cee-ay-tee" sounds much like "cat." Then the teacher pronounces the three letters faster and faster, gradually shifting from "cu-ah-tuh" to "cat." But this is only sleight-of-hand. No matter how quickly the children pronounce these names in sequence, the result will not blend the sounds to transform *c-a-t* into "cat." This circumstance makes it difficult to teach children who do not spontaneously "get the idea" (see Box 13.1).

Top-down vs. bottom-up processing

Thus far we have described the process of learning to read from the "bottom up." That is, we started by considering how children come to read words by first decoding the letters that compose the words. In this process, meaning comes when the child recognizes the oral word that corresponds to its full set of letters. Proceeding in this way, we could conceive of learning to read as a process in which the child decodes individual letters of a word to get access to its meaning, and then puts words together into phrases, then into sentences, then into paragraphs, and so on. While reading instruction may in fact be carried out in this way, a good deal of research in recent years has demonstrated that such bottom-up decoding processes are only half of the story (Adams, 1990; Crowder & Wagner, 1992). When adults read for meaning, the information supplied by words and phrases must simultaneously be integrated with the relevant knowledge they already have. Interpretation based on prior knowledge is often referred to as "top-down" processing because it begins with general knowledge that becomes increasingly focused as the reader combines it with the bottom-up information obtained from letters and words.

The kind of top-down information needed for meaningful reading can be seen in the following two passages. Although the words in each are of roughly equivalent difficulty (that is, the "bottom" components are similar), note how much more difficult it is to understand the second passage:

PASSAGE 1

When Mary arrived at the restaurant, the woman at the door greeted her and checked for her name. A few minutes later, Mary was escorted to her chair and was shown the day's menu. The attendant was helpful but brusque, almost

Once children catch on to reading, it can become a source of pleasure. This boy's comic book promises him not only the adventures of Tarzan but knowledge of the world of zoology as well.

---

* A famous example of the alphabet's complex relation to spoken English is attributed to the British writer George Bernard Shaw (1963). Shaw suggested that the word "fish" should be written "ghoti": *gh* as in "cough," *o* as in "women," *ti* as in "nation."

BOX 13.1

Learning Disabilities

Just as all children in the United States are legally required to attend school, the government is legally required to provide them with a free and appropriate education. To fulfill their part of the bargain, local and state governments provide specially designed educational programs for children who cannot cope with the demands of regular schooling. Children who are eligible for special assistance are those who are deaf, blind, motor-impaired, mentally retarded, emotionally disturbed (indicated by disruptive or withdrawn behavior), or learning disabled.

The children categorized as learning disabled offer special challenges to developmental psychologists and educators because, unlike children in other special-education categories, their difficulties are not readily apparent before they enter school. Even in school, children with learning disabilities are often difficult to spot, except when they are engaged in specific kinds of classroom work.

The federal government describes them this way:

> Children with special learning disabilities exhibit a disorder in one or more of the basic psychological processes involved in understanding or in using spoken or written language. These may be manifested in disorders of listening, thinking, talking, reading, writing, spelling, or arithmetic. They include conditions which have been referred to as perceptual handicaps, brain injury, minimal brain dysfunction, dyslexia, developmental aphasia, etc. (U.S. Office of Education, 1977)

Here we see the central problem that has dogged researchers seeking the causes and cures of learning disabilities—the list includes almost every facet of the learning required in schools! What, for example, distinguishes a child who has a disorder of "listening, thinking, talking, reading, writing, spelling, or arithmetic" from a retarded child? The key distinguishing characteristic is lurking in the word "or." To count as a learning disability and not mental retardation, the child

must be limited in only one or two of the academic areas in the list.

One method used to identify learning-disabled children is to analyze their performance on an intelligence test and on an academic achievement test that covers many parts of the curriculum. To qualify as learning disabled and not retarded, a child should have an overall IQ test score in the normal range but a large discrepancy between different parts of the test (for example, a high score on a subtest that taps verbal ability and low scores on subtests that tap quantitative ability and general knowledge). The child's academic performance should demonstrate the same discrepancies for a diagnosis of learning disabilities to be considered valid (Aram et al., 1992; Fletcher et al., 1992).

Sylvia Farnham-Diggory's (1992) description of "Kathy" illustrates this kind of diagnostic testing and the sort of special-education program that is recommended for a child with a specific pattern of difficulties. Kathy was administered the Wechsler Intelligence Scale for Children (WISC) and the Woodcock-Johnson test, which tests a broad range of academic skills. Kathy's overall IQ test score was 132, which places her in the top 98 percent of all children. Her score in a test that taps verbal ability was 111, which is somewhat above the average, but her performance on subtests that tap digit span, coding and arithmetic ability, and general knowledge produced a score of 147, which is very high indeed. With these kinds of abilities Kathy ought not to have had difficulty in school. In fact, she was performing significantly above her grade level in arithmetic and science. But she was having a very difficult time with reading, spelling, and writing. Her performance in these subjects was significantly below grade level.

Farnham-Diggory concluded that Kathy had *dyslexia*, a specific disorder of reading. (Some learning-disabled children have just the opposite pattern of difficulties: a normal level of reading and writing ability but extreme difficulty with simple calculations and word problems, a disorder called *dyscalcula*.) She recommended that Kathy be placed in a special educational program that explicitly taught letter-sound correspondences, which was believed to be her core difficulty. She emphasized that Kathy was a bright child, certainly capable of doing the work in such classes if she got special help with reading. It would be wrong to place Kathy in a class for slow learners or to take her out of content classes (such as social studies and science) for special reading instruction. Farnham-Diggory also recommended that Kathy's parents be sure to read to her, take her to museums, and enrich her knowledge in as many ways as possible. In time, with effort, Kathy would be able to read well enough to go to college and lead a normal working life.

The dominant theories about the causes of learning disabilities assume that the difficulties arise because of anomalies in brain development. Noting the tendency of dyslexic children to confuse one letter for another and to write letters backward, most reading researchers initially focused their attention on the visual cortex. Others believed that the difficulty involved short-term visual memory, which permitted information to drop out of short-term memory before it could be processed (Farnham-Diggory, 1992). Some kind of insult to the visual cortex is a possibility, but there are few direct data linking specific reading difficulties to specific brain lesions in this area. A new line of research suggests that the *auditory* cortex is involved in the problem as one instance of a more general information-processing deficit (Miller & Tallal, 1995; Tallal et al., 1993).

Paula Tallal and her colleagues discovered this possibility when they studied children who were experiencing difficulty in acquiring a first language. The children seemed to be unable to process very brief components of information when they entered the nervous system in rapid succession. Tallal and her colleagues began one experiment with a group of language-impaired children and a group of normal children by asking them to judge whether two tones, presented one right after the other, were the same or different. So long as the interval between the tones was half a second or more, there was little difference between the two groups; the children almost always judged correctly. But whenever the interval between the two tones was briefer than half a second, the performance of the language-impaired children plummeted and was little better than random guessing.

Next these researchers demonstrated that the language-impaired children had the same difficulty with the phonemes of spoken language and in fact with *any* rapid sequence of stimuli in any sensory modality. They also report research from magnetic resonance imaging (MRI) showing that language-impaired children have fewer cells in areas of the brain that support language.

When Tallal and her colleagues turned their attention to dyslexic children, they found they could be divided into two groups—those who showed general oral language impairment and those who did not. It appears very likely that the reason for the reading difficulties of the former children is a deficit in the ability to process critical information rapidly enough. The reasons for the difficulties of the dyslexic children who do not have an oral language impairment remain uncertain.

The work of this research group highlights a puzzling aspect of learning disabilities: the underlying deficit may be general but the problems it creates are quite specific. The disability of Tallal's language-impaired children appeared only when the children had to process small bits of information very rapidly, in small fractions of a second. In everyday interactions, a lot of information does not whizz by in this way, and when it does, there are likely to be enough redundancies in it and contextual clues supporting it for the language-impaired child to capture the gist. It is only in the specific case of learning to process written language that the children's general processing deficit presents a problem.

to the point of being rude. However, her meal was excellent, especially the main course. Later she paid the woman at the door and left.

PASSAGE 2

The procedure is really quite simple. First you arrange items into different groups. Of course, one pile may be sufficient depending on how much there is to do. If you have to go somewhere else due to lack of facilities that is the next step, otherwise you are pretty well set. It is important not to overdo things. That is, it is better to do too few things at once than too many. In the short run this may not seem important but complications can easily arise. A mistake can be expensive as well. . . . After the procedure is completed, one arranges the materials into different groups again. Then they can be put into their appropriate places. Eventually they will be used once more and the whole cycle will then have to be repeated. (Bransford, 1979, p. 135)

The first passage is easy to comprehend because we realize right away that it is about a restaurant. We have well-worked-out scripts for restaurants (see Chapter 9) that allow us to anticipate what will happen, thereby providing top-down constraints on our comprehension of the passage. The second passage is harder to read because it fails to provide a top-down indication of what it is about. You can verify this difference by trying to remember, without looking back, what the second passage says. As soon as you are told that the passage is about washing clothes, however, the separate sentences fall into place as you read, and the passage is easily interpreted. If readers cannot imagine what a passage is about, even if they can decode all of the words, the interpretation that is crucial to true reading does not occur.

Organizing instruction

When children are just learning to read, all three aspects of the process—low-level bottom-up information about letter-sound correspondences, high-level top-down general information, plus the act of combining the two to produce an

TABLE 13.1   Chall's Stages of Reading Development

Stage	Grade and Age Range	Major Qualitative Characteristics
Stage 0: Prereading or "pseudo reading"	Up to 6 years	Pretends to read, retells story while looking at familiar book, names letters of alphabet, recognizes signs and logos
Stage 1: Initial reading and decoding	Grade 1, ages 6–7	Learns relation between letters and sounds; can read simple text with familiar, high-frequency, phonetically regular words; can sound out one-syllable unfamiliar words
Stage 2: Confirmation of gains, increase in fluency	Grades 2 and 3, ages 7–8	Consolidation of decoding skills and sight vocabulary; reads simple, familiar stories with increasing fluency
Stage 3: Reading to learn	Grades 4–8, ages 9–14	Reads to gain new knowledge, experience new feelings, learn new attitudes, but generally from one point of view
Stage 4: Reading from multiple viewpoints	High school, ages 15–17	Reads widely from a broad range of complex materials representing a variety of viewpoints
Stage 5: Construction and reconstruction	College and beyond, age 18+	Reads to integrate and synthesize knowledge; reading is rapid and efficient

interpretation—can be sources of serious difficulty. If children are not skilled in assigning letters to sounds, they may struggle over the interpretation of specific words letter by letter ("c-c-che-check"). As the child struggles with the letter-sound correspondences, the knowledge that the passage is about a restaurant experience may be momentarily forgotten, and the child may substitute "cheek" for "check." After only a few such misreadings children can become confused and discouraged, and further reading becomes even more difficult. In order to avoid this problem, many psychologists argue, instruction should begin with a bottom-up approach: make sure that beginning readers have the ability to decode rapidly and automatically before they are asked to start comprehending.

Jean Chall, who wrote an influential summary of this debate, advocates the code-emphasis-first approach on the basis of her "developmental stage theory" of reading acquisition (Chall, 1983; Chall, Jacobs, & Baldwin, 1990). Chall describes reading not as a process that remains the same from the beginning to the mature stages, but as a process that changes as readers become more proficient (see Table 13.1).

The early stages in Chall's theory correspond to what we have already seen to be characteristic of the beginnings of reading. In the beginning children acquire the idea that there is a relation between the marks on paper and oral language, but they do not know what that relationship is. In stages 1 and 2 children learn to decode the arbitrary set of letters that make up the alphabet to discover their correspondence to the sounds of spoken language until they can read simple texts that contain familiar knowledge.

A major, qualitative change in the reading process is said to occur between stages 2 and 3. Once children no longer read letter by letter or word for word, they can begin to think about a topic while they are reading about it, a process that Chall refers to as "ungluing." When ungluing takes place, the process of reading is transformed from "learning to read" into "reading to learn." Chall summarizes this developmental change as follows:

> During Stages 1 and 2 what is learned concerns more the relating of print to speech while Stage 3 involves more the relating of print to ideas. Very little new information about the world is learned from reading before Stage 3; more is learned from listening and watching. It is with the beginning of Stage 3 that reading begins to compete with these other means of knowing. (1983, pp. 20–21)

The final two stages in Chall's theory are elaborations on the basic shift that occurred between stages 2 and 3. With extensive experience, readers are eventually able to juxtapose and compare different theories and facts and to reconcile different viewpoints in order to interpret a text's meaning. At the highest stage, readers are doing more than learning what the writer has to say. They are engaged in their own process of knowledge construction, in which written texts become aids in solving problems. At this stage readers know when to skim, when to reread, and when to take notes. As Chall phrases it, this highest level of reading entails "a struggle to balance one's comprehension of the ideas read, one's analysis of them, and one's own ideas about them" (1983, p. 24).

Many teachers adhere to some version of Chall's approach. In the early grades they emphasize "word-attack skills" and use a variety of workbook assignments to foster the ability to decode automatically (see Figure 13.2). The texts used in this approach are specially designed to give intensive practice in phonetic analysis and

Color the part brown if the word ends like ⬚. What is the surprise?

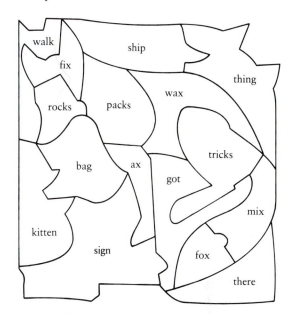

FIGURE 13.2 *A great deal of reading instruction in the elementary grades is carried out in workbook exercises, such as this one for building decoding skills.*

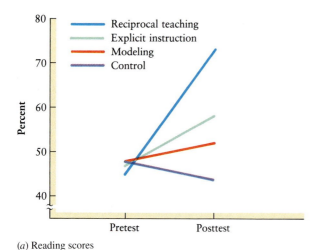

(a) Reading scores

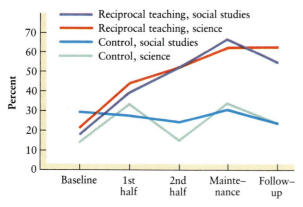

(b) Social studies and science scores

FIGURE 13.3 *Reciprocal teaching not only proved to be more effective than either explicit instruction or modeling (a) but also produced marked improvement in children's reading in social studies and science (b). All three forms of instruction led to improved reading, but reciprocal teaching was by far the most effective procedure. Students given practice in reciprocal reading showed large and sustained improvements in their social studies and science classes, whereas students who received no special reading instruction did quite poorly. (From Brown et al., 1992.)*

as a consequence do not make for very interesting reading. Aesop's tale of the tortoise and the hare, for example, has been presented like this:

Rabbit said, "I can run. I can run fast. You can't run fast."

Turtle said, "Look, Rabbit. See the park. You and I will run. We'll run to the park."

Rabbit said, "I want to stop. I'll stop here. I can run, but Turtle can't. I can get to the park fast."

Turtle said, "I can't run fast. But I will not stop. Rabbit can't see me. I'll get to the park." (Quoted in Green, 1984, p. 176)

Alternatives to the code-emphasis-first approach are based on the idea that reading is a special case of comprehending the world through symbols, an ability that children acquire when they learn language in the first place. Advocates of a comprehension-first approach argue that reading for comprehension should not be put off until the children are fluent decoders. Since children arrive at school already able to "read the world," the main requirement of a good reading curriculum is many rich opportunities to experience written language as a useful tool for exploring and problem solving. Emphasis on correct and automatic decoding is replaced by a belief that children should be allowed to invent their own spellings for words they do not know and to read any texts they perceive as instrumental to their goals. At first their spelling and text interpretation may not be strictly correct according to conventional standards, but that is not a matter for concern. What matters is that the children perceive reading and writing as good ways to achieve important goals; gradual mastery of conventional forms will follow.

Kenneth and Yetta Goodman refer to such a comprehension-based alternative as a *whole-language curriculum,* because reading is not taught in isolated lessons. Instead, literacy is made a part of the ongoing intellectual life of the classroom; when children begin to experience reading and writing as useful, these theorists argue, they will naturally incorporate it in their repertoire of cognitive skills (Goodman et al., 1987; Goodman & Goodman, 1990).

Evidence indicates that the most effective programs are those that provide a mixture of many different activities that, as an ensemble, engage and reinforce the separate components of the reading process in a coordinated way (Adams, 1990). The main task is to maintain children's interest in learning to read for the pleasure and power it can bring them while at the same time working on their skill at word recognition and decoding.

Reciprocal teaching

Reciprocal teaching, a method devised by Annemarie Palincsar and Ann Brown (1984), is one way instruction can be organized to integrate decoding skills and comprehension. In the **reciprocal teaching** procedure, a teacher and a small group of students read silently through a segment of text and then take turns leading a discussion of its meaning. The discussion leader (adult or child) begins by asking a question about the main idea and then summarizes the content in his or her own words. If members of the group disagree with the summary, the group rereads the passage and discusses its contents to clarify what it says. Finally, the leader asks for predictions about what will come next.

Note that each of the key elements in reciprocal teaching—asking questions about content, summarizing, clarifying, and predicting—presupposes that the purpose of the activity is to figure out what the text means. And because these strategies are talked about (and argued over), the children are able to see and hear the teacher and other children model the behaviors necessary for comprehension. As Brown and her colleagues (1992) point out, reciprocal teaching is an application of Vygotsky's notion of a "zone of proximal development" that allows children to participate in the act of reading for meaning even before they have acquired the full set of abilities that independent reading requires.

A number of studies (summarized in Rosenshine & Meister, 1994) have found reciprocal teaching to produce rapid and durable increases in children's reading skills. Figure 13.3 shows the findings of a study that successfully applied reciprocal teaching to help a group of junior high school students who had problems reading for meaning.

The work of Brown and her colleagues does not imply that decoding is irrelevant to mature reading; rather, it emphasizes the importance of integrating decoding with the process of comprehension. Most important, it provides relatively simple procedures that make a large difference in learning outcomes.

LEARNING ARITHMETIC

The teaching of mathematics, like the teaching of reading, has been the subject of intense investigation during most of this century. Rochel Gelman and her colleagues (Gelman, Meck, & Merkin, 1986) write that learning mathematics requires the acquisition and coordination of three kinds of knowledge:

1. **Conceptual knowledge,** or the ability to understand the principles that underpin the problem.
2. **Procedural knowledge,** or the ability to carry out a sequence of actions to solve a problem.
3. **Utilization knowledge,** or the ability to know when to apply particular procedures.

As we indicated in Chapter 12 (p. 490), most children arrive at school with some of each kind of knowledge, and cross-cultural research reveals that even societies with no tradition of schooling and literacy have their own characteristic methods of counting and solving arithmetic problems (see Figure 13.4). Young children know, for example, that numbers and objects can be put into one-to-one correspondence and that when they count the candies in a dish, the last number arrived at in the count stands for the total (conceptual knowledge). They have an intuitive grasp of how to add and subtract very small quantities (procedural knowledge). They also know that if Suzie has two candies and her mother gives her one more, they need to add, not subtract, to arrive at the total (utilization knowledge) (Klein & Starkey, 1987). These rudimentary kinds of knowledge provide an essential starting point for learning more advanced mathematics in school, but each must be constantly expanded to keep up with the increasingly complex forms of mathematics that schooling introduces.

Jeffrey Bisanz and Jo-Anne Lefevre (1990) provide a demonstration of the development of children's *conceptual knowledge* in their study of children's understanding of *inversion*. Inversion is the arithmetic principle that adding and subtracting the same number leaves the original quantity unchanged. They presented problems of the form "$a + b - b$" (for example, $10 + 8 - 8$) to subjects ranging in age from 6 years to adulthood. They found that between 6 and 9 years of age, calculating became progressively speedier, but some of the children did not seem to grasp inversion. Instead of creating a shortcut based on the inversion principle, they would dutifully add the second number to the first and then subtract the third number from the sum. The larger the second and third numbers, the longer

Reciprocal teaching A method of reading instruction in which a teacher and a small group of students read silently through a segment of text and then take turns leading a discussion of its meaning.

Conceptual knowledge The ability to understand the principles that underpin a problem.

Procedural knowledge The ability to carry out a sequence of actions to solve a problem.

Utilization knowledge The ability to know when to apply particular procedures in solving problems.

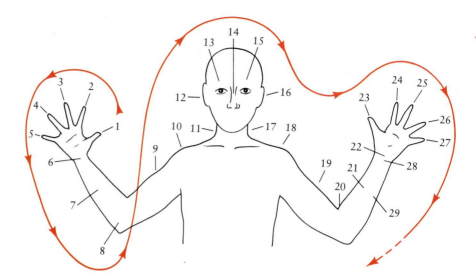

FIGURE 13.4 *The Oksapmin of New Guinea do their arithmetic by using a basic set of 29 numbers corresponding to a conventionalized sequence of body parts. (From Saxe, 1981.)*

it took them to get an answer (it required more time to figure out the answer to 4 + 9 − 9, for example, than to solve 4 + 5 − 5). Most 11-year-olds and virtually all adults ignored the particular value of the second and third numbers; they responded very rapidly, no matter how large the second and third numbers were, an indication that they had mastered the inversion principle.

Investigators have also documented the development of children's *procedural knowledge* in the course of mathematics instruction (Hughes, 1986; Siegler, 1991). Robert Siegler and his colleagues have studied the development of strategies that are essential to the mastery of addition, subtraction, and other mathematical operations (Siegler & Shrager, 1984; Siegler, 1996). To add two numbers, such as 4 and 3, first- and second-graders may count on their fingers starting with one (1-2-3-4 . . . 5-6-7). Eventually they may hit on the strategy of holding up fingers corresponding to the first of the pair and counting up (4 . . . 5-6-7). If asked to add 2 + 9, first-graders may start with 2 and then use their fingers to add 9 more; a year or so later children are more likely to convert 2 + 9 into 9 + 2, a strategy that both simplifies the task and shows their understanding of the principle that order is not important in addition. And, of course, if they think they know the sum "by heart," children will recall the answer (or what they believe to be the answer) directly. As children grow older and more knowledgeable, direct recall comes to dominate addition of small numbers, and a variety of paper-and-pencil procedures replace fingers as strategic tools under most circumstances.

Utilization knowledge (knowledge of which procedures to use to solve a given problem) increases as children grow older and receive more instruction, but it also depends a great deal on the particular way a problem is presented. This was made clear by Terezinha Nunes, Analucia Schliemann, and David Carraher (1993) when they studied mathematical problem solving among child street vendors in Recife, Brazil. Nunes and her colleagues first posed arithmetic problems to the children on street corners or at the market as part of the process of buying the goods the children were selling. A typical exchange with a 12-year-old child went like this:

Interviewer: How much is one coconut?

Child: 35.

Interviewer: I'd like ten. How much is that?

Child: *(Pause)* Three will be 105; with three more, that will be 210. *(Pause)* I need four more. That is . . . *(pause)* . . . I think it is 350. (Nunes et al., 1993, pp. 18–19)

After the interviewers posed a number of such questions, they gave the children a paper and pencil and asked them to solve identical problems. In the follow-up interview they presented two different kinds of problems. In some cases the problems were presented strictly as mathematical operations (How much is 10 times 35?) and in others the mathematical operations were presented as word problems. During the informal first interview, the children were correct 98 percent of the time. In the second interview they were correct on the word problems 74 percent of the time but could solve only 37 percent of those that required mathematical computation without any real-world connections.

Analysis revealed that in the formal interviews the children failed to use the successful computational strategies they had applied in their selling activity. One 9-year-old quickly responded to an offer to buy 12 lemons at 5 cruzeiros each by counting "10, 20, 30, 40, 50, 60" while separating out two lemons at a time. But when she was asked to solve the problem 12 × 5, she "brought down" first the 2, then the 5, and then the 1 and came up with an answer of 152. She failed to employ a strategy she knew to be effective and was unable to replace it with a correct, school-based form of computation. Such results indicate that the way problems are posed influences the extent to which children use their existing knowledge.

Counting on their fingers is a universal strategy for beginning arithmetic students.

Recommendations for effective teaching of mathematics cluster at two polar extremes, analogous to the dichotomy between code emphasis and meaning emphasis in reading instruction. At one end are psychologists who believe that instruction is best carried out through intensive drill and practice on small parts of the overall process; at the other end are psychologists who believe that learning should begin with understanding and then proceed to practice (Resnick & Ford, 1981).

The drill-and-practice approach is exemplified by the work of E. L. Thorndike (1922), a pioneer in educational research. Thorndike believed that learning arithmetic was a matter of building strength in a large number of specific habits. Once automated, the individual parts could fit into a total problem-solving organization. The alternative approach, learning with understanding, was championed by William Brownell (1928). Proper understanding, Brownell claimed, would enable students to go beyond the narrow confines of the practice problems and apply their knowledge in novel situations. Brownell's approach can be understood as advocating teaching methods that enable children to use their conceptual knowledge to support their procedural and utilization knowledge.

It is now agreed that both drill in computation and practice in generalizing computations to a variety of meaningful new problems are necessary. There is no single agreed-upon procedure for mixing these two aspects of instruction, but a variety of effective instructional procedures have been worked out for specific content domains (Dienes, 1966; Rasmussen, Hightower, & Rasmussen, 1964; Resnick & Ford, 1981). In recent years, computers have increasingly been used in attempts to create environments more conducive to instruction (see Box 13.2).

THE SPECIAL LANGUAGE OF SCHOOLING

As we noted in Chapter 8, by the time they are ready to enter school at the age of 6, children have acquired a vocabulary of perhaps 14,000 words, an intuitive grasp of their language's grammar, and many of the uses of language that are common in their communities. The forms of language used in school, however, are in some ways unlike those they have encountered in other contexts. Two such differences

BOX 13.2

Computers in Schools

Computers have become so pervasive in modern life that it comes as a surprise to learn that 50 years ago the word "computer" referred to a person who computed numbers. The present-day computer had its birth during World War II, when the rapidly developing technology of ballistics created an urgent need to calculate enormously complex equations. ENIAC, the first practical general-purpose electronic computer, began operation in 1946. It was still, in its essentials, "a calculator designed to work out ballistic firing tables" (Winston, 1986, p. 137).

For several decades, computers remained large, expensive high-speed calculators. They cost several million dollars and occupied the space of an average living room. But changes in technology eventually allowed the miniaturization of information storage on silicon chips, resulting in the first cheap, very powerful small computers. Subsequent advances in laser optical storage technologies and computer networking brought about the creation of multimedia programs and worldwide communication networks, leading to fundamental changes in the nature of manufacturing, sales, transportation, and finance, as well as a wide range of consumer products, from automobiles to children's toys.

When relatively inexpensive microcomputers first appeared, many education and development specialists recognized their potential for increasing the effectiveness of school-based instruction. And indeed, over the last two decades the growth of computer use in schools has been phenomenal. At present more than 95 percent of American schools have computers for instructional purposes, and in many schools computers play a large part in instruction (Baker & O'Neil, 1994).

Charles Crook (1994) identifies three approaches to the design of computer-based educational activities. Interestingly, they correspond to three of the theoretical approaches to development that we have discussed in this book. Each approach is based on a distinctive metaphor relating computers to the teaching process.

The Computer-as-Tutor: An Environmental-Learning and Information-Processing Approach

The earliest use of computers in education was based on the idea that the computer would do the work of a human teacher. The prototypic application of CAI—*computer-aided instruction*, as this approach is called—is to teach a series of foreign words, arithmetic problems, or geography facts. The items to be learned are presented one at a time. The child responds with a translation or a calculation or a place name. The computer records the response and gives feedback. This remains the commonest use of computers in education today (Scott, Cole, & Engel, 1992).

In its simplest forms, CAI is little different from the drill-and-practice workbooks used in schools for decades. The difference lies in the computer's ability to keep track of the individual child's exact performance and to respond accordingly. In a program designed by Patrick Suppes (1988), for example, the computer repeats items the child has forgotten more often than those the child remembers, and even presents "reminders" of previously learned materials on a special schedule to make sure that all of the information to be learned is firmly retained in the child's long-term memory. Such individualized instruction is impossible in a classroom with one teacher and 30 students sitting at their desks—a major argument for the application of computers to education.

The Computer-as-Pupil: A Constructionist Approach

While the computer-as-tutor fits well with environmental-learning and information-processing approaches to education, learners have little opportunity to act on their environment, except to answer each question it is given. Seymour Papert and his colleagues at MIT's Media Laboratory developed an approach based on Piaget's theory that children must construct their understandings through active exploration of their environments (Papert, 1980; Harel & Papert, 1991).

To make this idea practicable, Papert designed a special computer microworld in which it is possible to do interesting things such as drawing intricate patterns or designing an exercise to learn about fractions. Papert's microworld is called Turtle Logo. Logo is a simplified computer language that controls the actions of a symbol on the screen (the turtle). By learning to "teach the turtle" to carry out their instructions, children acquire several ideas that are fundamental not only to computer programming but to mathematics in general.

The Computer-as-Tool: A Cultural-Context Approach

A third group of psychologists emphasizes the fact that whatever its uniqueness, whatever may set it apart from other human technologies, the computer is, at bottom, simply a *tool*. It mediates the way people interact with the world and one another. Although it is often said that the computer is a *general-purpose* tool because it can be programmed to serve a wide variety of human goals, every use of a computer requires that it be tailored to the task at hand. Viewed in this way, computers have been used as tools to extend and enrich a variety of educational activities. The use of word processing programs, for example, can foster critical writing skills. The analysis of databases can teach science concepts and develop mathematical skills.

From a cultural-context perspective, the greatest potential of computers in the classroom is to reorganize children's interactions not only with the materials to be learned but with the teacher and one another, the school as an institution, and the world at large (Cognition and Technology Group, 1994; Newman, 1992). Two examples give the flavor of this approach.

Several research groups used computer networks to forge relationships between schools in different parts of the world, permitting children to engage in joint learning projects in which they measure and record levels of acid rain or compare the histories of their cultural groups in relation to each other (Levin et al., 1990; Scott, Cole, & Engel, 1992). These projects naturally promote work in small groups, mastery of many aspects of computer use, and the development of multiple academic skills. Teachers find that they do not need to urge children to attend to such studies; instead, it is common for children to ask permission to keep working on their projects during the lunch break and recess.

Another promising application of computers in classrooms takes advantage of the newly emerging combinations of interactive video disks and CD-ROM technology (Cognition and Technology Group, 1994). The curriculum is presented as a series of televised adventures and mysteries for the children to enter into. In one such program, called "The River Adventure," learners watch a video about a trip on a houseboat in which the protagonists must take into account such factors as the food and gas they will need, the docking facilities they will require, and so on. The video includes information about the boat (its size, cruising speed, fuel consumption), the route, the marinas along the way, and so on. Students are asked to determine when and why to use various kinds of data to help achieve such goals as docking at a particular marina and returning home quickly under various conditions.

Students who engage in this kind of multimedia problem solving acquire many kinds of expertise in using computers (file management, spreadsheets, databases, word processing skills) and a variety of academic skills as well. Just as important, their interest in school and their self-confidence as students have been shown to increase.

These and other studies have shown that computers *can* make a positive difference in the classroom. The challenge now is to *realize* this potential, making the new technology a routine part of every child's education.

are the way the act of speaking is structured in school and the way talk about numbers and operations on numbers is tied to the mathematical notation system.

Instructional discourse

Instructional discourse Language use in classrooms that gives students information about the content of the curriculum and feedback about their efforts, while providing teachers with information about student progress.

Initiation-reply-evaluation sequence A pattern of instructional discourse in which the teacher initiates an exchange, a student replies, and the teacher evaluates the student's reply.

Classroom conversation, or **instructional discourse,** differs in both structure and content from the ways adults and children speak in their everyday lives outside of school. The central goals of instructional discourse are to give children information stipulated by the curriculum and feedback about their efforts to learn it while providing teachers with information about their progress (Cazden, 1988; Wells, 1996).

One of the distinctive characteristics of instructional discourse is the **initiation-reply-evaluation sequence,** demonstrated in Table 13.2. In this pattern, the teacher initiates an exchange, usually by asking a question; a student replies; and then the teacher provides an evaluation.

The initiation-reply-evaluation sequence entails a form of question-asking that is rarely encountered in everyday conversation among adults, the "known-answer question." When the teacher asks Beth, "What does this word say?" that teacher already knows the answer; he or she is actually seeking information about Beth's ability to read, so the question is really a way to evaluate Beth's progress. Learning to respond easily to known-answer questions, in addition to learning the academic content of the curriculum, is an important early lesson of schooling (Mehan, 1979).

The initiation-reply-evaluation sequence can be quite flexible. When Ramona hesitates (Table 13.2), the teacher immediately calls on Kim, who provides the answer. This arrangement allows Ramona to learn from Kim's answer and the teacher's response to it at the same time that it allows the teacher to assess Ramona's need for more instruction.

Another special facet of school-based language is the emphasis placed on the linguistic form of students' replies, as we see in the lesson on the use of prepositions shown in Table 13.3. Note that the teacher gradually builds an understanding of the linguistic form that she considers appropriate by using the turn-taking rules of classroom discourse. Second, note that for the purposes of this lesson, the *truth* of what the children say is less important than the way they say it. Cindy gave her answer in the form the teacher was looking for, but, as Richard noticed, Cindy had named the wrong color! She was correct in school terms, although she clearly violated norms of everyday language use.

In everyday conversations one usually has ample opportunity to check one's expectations against reality. But in the closed world of the classroom, the real-world objects and events that are the content of the conversation are often

TABLE 13.2 Initiation-Reply-Evaluation Sequence

Initiation	Reply	Evaluation
T [Teacher]: . . . what does this word say? Beth.	**Beth:** One.	T: Very good.
T: What does this word say? Jenny.	**Jenny:** One.	T: Okay.
T: Now look up here. What does this word say? Ramona.	**Ramona:** Umm.	
T: Kim.	**Kim:** First.	T: Okay.

Source: Mehan, 1979.

TABLE 13.3 Lesson on Use of Prepositions

Initiation	Reply
T [Teacher]: Make a red flower under the tree. *(pause)* Okay, let's look at the red flower. Can you tell me where the red flower is?	**Children:** Right here, right here.
T: Dora?	**Dora:** Under the tree.
T: Tell me in a sentence.	**Dora:** It's under the tree.
T: What's under the tree, Dora?	**Children:** The flower.
T: Tell me, the flower . . .	**Dora:** The flower is under the tree.
T: Where is the red flower, Richard?	**Richard:** Under the tree.
T: Can you tell me in a sentence?	**Richard:** The flower is under the tree.
T: Cindy, where is the red flower?	**Cindy:** The red flower is under the tree.
Richard: *[noticing that Cindy actually drew the "red" flower with a yellow crayon]* Hey, that's not red.	

Source: Mehan, 1979.

unavailable to help children interpret what is being said. Consequently, in order to master the specialized knowledge taught in school, children must learn to focus on language itself as the vehicle of information. (Box 13.3 discusses the special problems that arise when children come to school speaking only a foreign language.)

Learning mathematical notation systems

The writing of numbers in mathematical notation systems is another distinctive feature of school language. One of the first tasks children face when they encounter mathematics at school is to learn to write the first ten digits. Since it is only a cultural convention that the symbol 9 should stand for the spoken word "nine," the first stage of this process requires memorization.

Once children learn the first ten digits, they must learn the conventions for writing larger quantities and the concept of place value that underpins our notation system. The required correspondences are not intuitively obvious. Some first-graders, for example, have written 23 as 203 (Ginsburg, 1977). This representation, although erroneous, follows the conventions of our way of speaking (20-3) and our system for representing spoken language in print ("twenty-three"). Unfortunately, from the child's point of view, conventions for representing place value in arithmetic do not follow the conventions of the writing system. While numbers such as 203 ("two hundred and three") are, so to speak, pronounced from left to right, they are actually constructed right to left from the decimal point, which is ordinarily written only when some fraction of a whole number is to be indicated. So, for example, "Two hundred and three and forty-five-hundredths" is written 203.45.

It takes most children several years to master these complexities, a fact that influences their ability to carry out such basic operations as addition and subtraction on paper. Common mistakes are to add numbers in the order in which they

BOX 13.3

Schooling in a Second Language

Over 2.5 million children in the United States begin school unable to understand or speak the English language. In a landmark decision in 1974, the U.S. Supreme Court declared that these children are denied equality of treatment even if they are given the same facilities, textbooks, and teachers as the native English-speaking students, because they are "effectively fore-closed from meaningful education" (*Lau v. Nichols*, p. 26). Since that time local school districts have spent well over $1 billion on programs intended to remedy this situation.

Although educators agree that the major goals of their programs are to increase these children's proficiency in the English language and promote their scholastic achievement, opinion continues to be sharply divided on *how* these goals should be achieved (McGroarty, 1992; Moll, 1992). On one side of the debate are those who believe that children should be immersed in the English language so that they can quickly achieve the competence necessary to participate in all aspects of the curriculum. Educators who favor this view believe that time spent communicating in the child's native language only postpones the day when the child will be fluent in English. On the other side are those who believe that a firm grounding in basic literacy and numeracy skills in the child's home language will serve as a foundation for later academic achievement in courses taught in English.

Research on this issue is clouded by the difficulty of conducting experiments in which ideal versions of the two strategies can be pitted against each other. It is simply not possible to set up a true experiment by controlling the school curricula and deciding what school each child attends (Hakuta & Garcia, 1989). Researchers have had to make do with the fact that some schools have adopted an "English-only" approach while others have provided instruction in children's native language for 2 or 3 years before moving them to English-based instruction. The difficulty with this kind of comparison is that it is impossible to ensure that the programs being compared differ only in the variable being studied—the use of English-only versus home-language-first instruction. Additional factors, such as the cultural and socioeconomic backgrounds of the children, the training and enthusiasm of the teachers, and the resources available for teaching, often vary in ways that undermine the logic of experimental comparisons.

Stephen Krashen and Douglas Biber (1988) summarize the evidence on the effectiveness of California's extensive bilingual education effort by declaring that "the fastest route to second language learning is through [use of] the first language" (p. 19). Acknowledging that bilingual education is not always successful, however, Krashen and Biber identify three characteristics of successful programs:

are said—from left to right—and to line up numbers from the left. Misunderstandings of this kind produce such errors as writing 123 + 1 as

$$\begin{array}{r} 123 \\ +\,1 \\ \hline 223 \end{array}$$

Children who produce such answers are behaving as they are expected to do in school in one important respect: they are applying previously acquired knowledge to solve new problems. As long as they don't become discouraged, they eventually catch on to the logic underlying the written number system their teachers present to them.

The Cognitive Consequences of Schooling

It seems reasonable to assume that many thousands of hours spent sitting in classrooms learning about the world through reading and writing should have considerable impact on cognitive development during middle childhood and beyond.

1. High-quality teaching of subject matter in the child's first language without translation.
2. A firm foundation of literacy in the first language.
3. After items 1 and 2 are accomplished, special teaching of English as a second language and supplementary subject-matter instruction in English.

Another important factor not mentioned by Krashen and Biber is the need to give the process of acquiring the second language enough time. This point is demonstrated in a study among Navajo children. Half the children were taught only in English (including special instruction in English as a second language). Their progress was compared with that of children in a bilingual program where they were first taught to read in Navajo and later transferred to English classes. Initially the children in the bilingual program fared poorly, but after three or four years the bilingual group was outperforming the children who had been instructed in English from the beginning (Rosier, 1977).

The need to allow time for children to learn enough English to take full advantage of school instruction is also highlighted in studies by Lily Wong-Fillmore (1985). She found that although minority-language children generally become reason-ably fluent in *spoken* English within two or three years of starting school in the United States, much more time is needed to become proficient in using the English vocabulary they encounter in school. Wong-Fillmore reported that as many as 4 to 5 years were required to master the language skills needed for academic success.

A major obstacle facing educators who seek to apply the lessons from this line of research is that there are far too few qualified bilingual teachers to teach the many languages represented by the school-aged population of the United States. In California, for example, nearly 1.5 million children for whom English was a second language were attending school in 1990. Almost 60 percent of them were judged to have limited proficiency in English, a situation that would seem to call for bilingual instruction if the current research is valid. But the schools have to contend with more than 50 languages! Except in districts that have a large concentration of children with the same linguistic background, the creation of high-quality bilingual programs is all but impossible. The great challenge facing these schools is to cope with the linguistic variety in their classrooms in a manner that works for children whose knowledge of English is limited.

After all, schooling expands children's knowledge base, gives them massive experience in deliberate remembering, and trains them in systematic problem solving, as we saw in Chapter 12.

When the cognitive performances of children who have attended school are compared with those who have not, it is possible to begin to identify the special contributions of schooling to cognitive development. One way to make such comparisons is to take advantage of bureaucratic rules concerning how old a child must be to attend school. Another is to conduct research in societies where schooling is not universal.

USING THE SCHOOL CUTOFF STRATEGY

In many countries school boards set a date by which the child must reach a certain age in order to begin attending school. To enter grade 1 in September of a given year, children in Edmonton, Alberta, Canada, must have passed their sixth birthday by March 1 of that year. Six-year-olds born after that date must attend kindergarten instead, and their formal education is delayed for a year. If researchers

compare the intellectual performances of children who turn 6 in January or February with those who turn 6 in March or April, first at the beginning and again at the end of the following school year, it is possible to assess the impact of schooling with age held virtually constant. This procedure is known as the **school cutoff strategy** (Morrison et al., 1995).

Researchers who have used this strategy find that schooling brings about a marked increase in the sophistication of some cognitive processes but not others. Frederick Morrison and his colleagues (1995), for example, compared the ability of first-graders and kindergartners to recall pictures of nine common objects. The first-graders were, on average, only a month older than the kindergartners, and at the start of the school year the performances of the two groups were virtually identical. At the end of the school year, however, the first-graders almost doubled the number of pictures they could remember, and they were seen to engage in active rehearsal strategies. The kindergartners did not improve at all, and for the most part did not engage in active rehearsal. Clearly, one year of schooling had brought about a marked change in performance. These researchers report similar results for such diverse skills as the ability to analyze the sound components of words, a cognitive skill that seems to be promoted by reading instruction, and to solve a variety of cognitive tasks that are often included in IQ tests.

There is an interesting exception to these findings. Jeffrey Bisanz and his colleagues (1995) tested children's responses to a standard Piagetian test of number conservation (see Chapter 12, p. 488) and also asked them to add small numbers. He found that performance in the conservation task improved largely as a consequence of age but that mental arithmetic improved almost exclusively as a consequence of schooling. These findings both confirm the importance of schooling in promoting a variety of relatively specific cognitive abilities and support Piaget's belief that the ability to conserve quantity develops without any special instruction at some time between the ages of 5 and 7.

CROSS-CULTURAL RESEARCH ON THE EFFECTS OF SCHOOLING

The school cutoff strategy provides an excellent way to assess the cognitive consequences of small amounts of schooling, but it is applicable for only one year. Societies where schooling is available to only a part of the population provide the other major route for assessing the contribution of formal education to cognitive development in middle childhood. Four cognitive domains have figured heavily in this research: concrete operations, lexical organization (the organization of word meanings), memory, and metacognitive skills (the ability to reflect upon one's own thought processes).

Despite wide variations among them, each of these settings is immediately recognizable as a school.

Concrete operations

As we saw in Chapter 12, studies of concrete operational thinking are more or less evenly split between those that find an advantage for children who have attended school and those that do not (Rogoff, 1981). When schoolchildren do well on the standard Piagetian tests, their success appears to have less to do with concrete operational thinking than with a greater familiarity with the circumstances of test taking. Such specialized knowledge includes familiarity with the forms in which questions are asked, a greater ease in speaking to unfamiliar adults, and an ability to speak the language when the testing is not conducted in the child's native language. Overall, this evidence, supplemented by Bisanz's findings, suggests that the development of concrete operational thinking increases with age and is relatively unaffected by schooling, in accord with Piaget's theory.

Lexical organization

We have seen that in contrast to children who are assigned to tend sheep, to care for younger siblings, or to weave rugs to be sold in the market, children who attend school spend vastly more time learning through talking and listening than through doing. Moreover, the talk encountered in school differs in content and form from the talk familiar to children who do not attend school. Not only does talk in school require the mastery of abstract concepts, it requires that mastery to be used away from the real-world contexts to which the concepts apply. A biology lesson about the way sunlight influences plant growth, for example, may be taught in a windowless room with no plants in it. As a consequence, children must learn to create meaning from subtle differences in the ways words are combined. This feature of schooling has led some psychologists to suggest that the underlying organization of children's lexicons—the total store of words in their vocabulary—is changed by schooling (Cole & D'Andrade, 1982).

The impact of schooling on lexical organization was demonstrated by Donald Sharp and his co-workers in a study of Mayan Indians on the Yucatan Peninsula of Mexico (Sharp, Cole, & Lave, 1979). When adolescents who had attended high school one or more years were asked which words they associated with the word "duck," they responded with other words in the same biological category, such as "fowl," "goose," "chicken," and "turkey." When adolescents in the same area who had not attended school were presented with the same word, their responses were dominated by words that describe what ducks do ("swim," "fly") or what people do with ducks ("eat").

The results of this study and findings from other parts of the world (such as Cole et al., 1971) suggest that schooling sensitizes children to the abstract, categorical meanings of words, in addition to building up their general knowledge. Not that word meaning fails to develop in children who have not attended school. The nonliterate Mayan farmers studied by Sharp and his colleagues knew perfectly well that ducks are a kind of fowl. Although they did not refer to this fact in the artificial circumstances of the free-association task, they readily displayed awareness of it when they talked about the kinds of animals their families kept.

Memory

In Chapter 12 we saw that during middle childhood children in some cultures do not show the same increase in memory skills that U.S. children do on the standard tests that psychologists generally use. Research comparing schooled and nonschooled children in other societies, like the comparative data on first-graders and kindergartners presented earlier in this chapter, has shown that schooling is the crucial experience underlying these cultural differences. When children in other cultures have had an opportunity to go to school, their memory performance on these standard tests is more similar to that of their American counterparts in the

School cutoff strategy A strategy for assessing the intellectual effects of schooling in which researchers compare the intellectual performance of first graders with that of children a few months younger who have not yet been admitted to school because of the school cutoff date.

Lexicon The total store of words in a person's vocabulary.

same grade than it is to that of their agemates in the same village (Cole et al., 1971).

A study by Daniel Wagner (1974) suggests the kind of memory-enhancing information-processing skills that children acquire as a consequence of schooling. Wagner conducted his study among educated and uneducated Mayans in Yucatan. He asked 248 people varying in age from 6 years to adulthood to recall the positions of picture cards laid out in a linear array (see Figure 13.5). The items pictured on the cards were taken from a local version of bingo called *lotería*, which uses pictures instead of numbers, so Wagner could be certain that all the pictures were familiar. On each trial, each of seven cards was displayed for two seconds and then turned face down. As soon as all seven cards had been presented, a duplicate of a picture on one of the cards was shown and people had to point to the position where they thought its twin was located. By selecting different duplicate pictures, Wagner in effect manipulated the length of time between the first presentation of a picture and the moment it was to be recalled.

Earlier research in the United States had demonstrated a marked increase in children's ability to remember the locations of cards after they reached middle childhood (Hagen, Meacham, & Mesibov, 1970). Wagner found that the performance of children who were attending school improved with age, just as in the earlier study by Hagen and his colleagues (see Figure 13.6). However, older children and adults who did not attend school remembered no better than young children, leading Wagner to conclude that it was schooling that made the difference. Additional analyses of the data revealed that the use of rehearsal by those who attended school was responsible for the improvement in their performance.

As with lexical organization, the evidence from studies of schooling's impact on memory should not be interpreted to mean that memory simply fails to develop among children who have not attended school. The difference between educated and uneducated children's performance in cross-cultural memory experiments is most noticeable after several years of schooling and when the materials to be learned are not related to one another according to any everyday script. When the materials to be remembered are part of a meaningful setting, as in Rogoff and Waddell's study of memory for objects placed in a diorama of the subjects' town (see Chapter 12, p. 508), the effects of schooling on memory performance disappear (see also Mandler et al., 1980). It appears that schooling helps children to develop specialized strategies for remembering and so enhances their ability to commit arbitrary material to memory for purposes of later testing. There is no evidence to support the conclusion that schooling increases an individual's memory capacity in general.

Metacognitive skills

Schooling appears to influence the ability to reflect on and talk about one's own thought processes (Luria, 1976; Rogoff, 1981; Tulviste, 1991). When children have been asked to explain how they arrived at the answer to a problem or what they did to make themselves remember something, those who have not attended school are likely to say something like "I did what my sense told me" or to offer no explanation at all. Schoolchildren seem better able to describe the mental activities and logic that underpin their cognitive activities. In other words, they display **metacognition.**

Schooling also seems to affect people's ability to think about their own language-using skills, their **metalinguistic awareness.** One line of evidence comes from the studies of phonemic recognition discussed earlier in connection with learning to read: people who have not been to school do not appear to acquire an explicit ability to separate their language into its basic sounds (Adams, 1990). A second line of evidence comes from the work of Sylvia Scribner and Michael Cole

Metacognition The ability to describe one's own mental activities and the logic underpinning one's attempts to solve problems.

Metalinguistic awareness The ability to think about your own language-using skills.

(a) Take a good look and turn the page

FIGURE 13.5 *Cards used to test short-term memory. Seven cards are selected and then turned face down. The person being tested is then shown a duplicate of one of the cards (see p. 540) and asked to select the card that corresponds to it from the seven that are face down. (From Wagner, 1978.)*

(1981), who asked educated and uneducated Vai people in Liberia to judge the grammatical correctness of several sentences spoken in Vai. Some of the sentences were grammatical, some not. Education had no effect on the ability to identify the ungrammatical sentences; but educated people could generally explain just what it was about a sentence that made it ungrammatical, whereas uneducated people could not.

The evidence in overview

Overall, the picture that emerges from extensive research on schooling provides only minimal support for the idea that schooling changes the cognitive processes associated with middle childhood in any deep and general way. In those cases in which schooling *has* been found to affect cognitive performance, the effect appears to be restricted to rather specific information-processing strategies or to a specific context that is relevant primarily, if not exclusively, to school itself (Cole, 1990).

This conclusion in no way detracts from the importance of schooling in modern life. Schooling need not produce a generalized increase in the level of cognitive ability to be of great significance for children's development. And indeed, the central goal of schooling is not to transform mental machinery but to make people more effective problem solvers and rememberers when they have pencils, books, and computer at hand. In many societies reading, writing, and calculating have real importance outside of school, and the impact of schooling may be more appropriately sought in people's everyday use of these skills than in any general mental transformations that schooling may produce. One particularly important consequence of schooling is its influence on child rearing (Le Vine et al., 1994); less-educated mothers raise their children to be obedient and respectful, while educated mothers emphasize cognitive and social engagement.

Perhaps the most important aspect of schooling for the majority of people is that it is a gateway to economic power and social status. Most work in modern industrial societies requires the level of literacy that a high school education usually provides, and most highly paid jobs require a college education and perhaps specialization beyond that. As we noted earlier in this chapter (Fig. 13.1, p. 514), the associations between years of schooling, income, and job status are strong (U.S. Census Bureau, 1995); on the average, the more years of

FIGURE 13.6 *Short-term memory performance as a function of age and number of years of education. In the absence of further education (as among the rural people tested in this study), performance does not improve with age. Thus schooling appears to be a key factor in one's ability to do well at this task. (Numbers in parentheses represent the average number of years of education for the designated group.) (From Wagner, 1974.)*

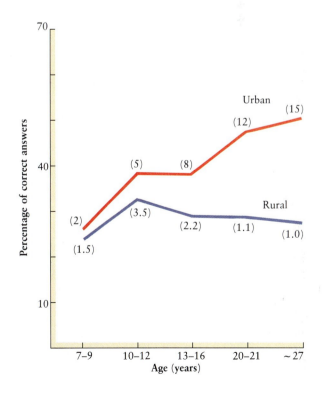

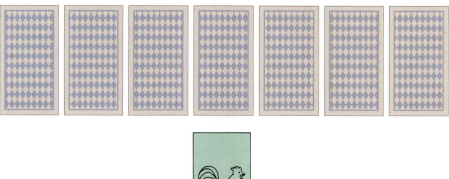

FIGURE 13.5   *(Continued)*

(*b*) Which card has a matching picture?

schooling people complete, the higher their incomes are and the more likely they are to obtain white-collar and professional jobs.

Success in school is such an important contributor to children's later economic well-being in literate societies that developmental psychologists and educators are greatly interested in understanding the factors that account for it. They have paid particular attention to the possibility that some children come equipped with a special "aptitude for schooling" that others lack. Considerable research has also been conducted on the ways the home, the community, and the school itself contribute to a child's performance in school.

Aptitude for Schooling

Although people need basic literacy and numeracy skills to function well in many modern societies, many youngsters leave school without having acquired them. It is estimated that as many as 22 percent of adults in the United States read so poorly that they cannot cope adequately with the demands of everyday life (National Center for Educational Statistics, 1993).

Why is it that some children experience exceptional difficulty in school while others do not? And what can be done to promote the kind of learning that takes place in school? All during this century, this inquiry has been influenced by the idea that people vary in an aptitude called "intelligence" and that these variations explain the differences in their school performance.

The concept of intelligence is very widely accepted. All languages have terms that describe individual differences in the way people solve problems and the kinds of problems they are good at solving (Serpell, 1993; Segall et al., 1990). But the precise meanings of these terms vary among cultures, and it has proved difficult—some people say impossible—to define intelligence so that it can be measured as precisely as weight or height. Nonetheless, almost all children growing up today in the United States can expect to take an intelligence test at some time before they complete their education. Such tests are used to decide the kind of education they will receive and the kind of work they will do, which in turn will influence the lives they will lead as adults. It is thus important to understand the nature of intelligence as a factor in children's development as well as the nature of intelligence testing.

THE ORIGINS OF INTELLIGENCE TESTING

Interest in measuring intelligence became widespread at the beginning of the twentieth century, when mass education was becoming the norm in industrialized countries. Though most children seemed to be able to profit from the instruction they were given, some seemed virtually unable to learn in school. Concerned educational officials sought to determine the causes and cures for these difficulties.

In 1904 the French minister of public instruction named a commission to ensure the benefits of instruction for what he termed "defective" children. The commission asked Alfred Binet, a professor of psychology at the Sorbonne, and Théophile Simon, a physician, to create a means of examining children to identify those who needed special instruction. Binet and Simon set out to construct a psychological examination to diagnose mental subnormality that would have all the precision and validity of a medical examination. They were especially concerned about children incorrectly diagnosed as subnormal, because, as they put it, "to be a member of a special class can never be a mark of distinction" (Binet & Simon, 1916, p. 10).

The diagnostic strategy adopted by Binet and Simon was to present children with a series of problems whose solution was considered indicative of intelligence in the culture of their time. The problems were tailored to differentiate between children at each age, so that children who were far behind could be identified and given special instruction. Binet and Simon surmised, for example, that one aspect of intelligence is the ability to follow directions while keeping several task components in mind at once. To test for this ability, they presented children aged 4 to 6 with tasks such as the following:

> Do you see this key? You are to put it on the chair over there (pointing to the chair); afterwards shut the door; afterwards you will see near the door a box which is on a chair. You will take that box and bring it to me. (1916, p. 206)

At 4 years of age, few children could carry out all parts of this task without help. At 5 years, about half of the children responded adequately, and at 6 years, almost all children passed. This age-linked pattern of achievement provided Binet and Simon with the test characteristics they needed. A 4-year-old who passed the test was considered precocious, while a 6-year-old who failed was considered retarded with respect to this ability.

Other tasks required children to identify the missing parts of a picture, to name colors, to copy geometric figures, to remember strings of random digits, to count backward from 20, to make change for 20 francs, and so on. After extensive pretesting, Binet and Simon tested slightly more than 200 children ranging in age from 3 to 12 years, giving a different set of questions to each age group. As they had hoped, almost precisely 50 percent of these children scored at the expected age level. Of the remainder, 43 percent were within 1 year of expectation and only 7 percent deviated above or below the norm by as much as 2 years.

Binet and Simon concluded that they had succeeded in constructing a scale of intelligence. They called the basic index of intelligence for this scale **mental age (MA).** A child who performed as well on the test as an average 7-year-old did was said to have an MA of 7, a child who did as well as an average 9-year-old was said to have an MA of 9, and so on. The MA provided Binet and Simon with a convenient way to characterize mental subnormality. A "dull" 7-year-old child was one who performed like a normal child one or more years younger.

To verify that their scale reflected more than a lucky selection of test items, Simon and Binet tested their conclusions against teachers' judgments. Their success in picking out the children judged most and least able by teachers confirmed their hopes.

Binet and Simon offered two explanations for school failure: a child might lack either the "natural intelligence" (the "nature") needed to succeed in school or the cultural background (the "nurture") presupposed by the school.

> A very intelligent child may be deprived of instruction by circumstances foreign to his intelligence. He may have lived far from school; he may have had a

Mental age A basic index of intelligence that indicates how children's performance relates to age-graded norms.

long illness . . . or maybe some parents have preferred to keep their children at home, to have them rinse bottles, serve the customers of a shop, care for a sick relative or herd the sheep. In such cases . . . it suffices to pass lightly the results of tests which are of a notably scholastic character, and to attach the greatest importance to those which express the natural intelligence. (1916, pp. 253–254)

This approach may appear intuitively plausible, but in fact it contains a crucial ambiguity: nowhere do Binet and Simon offer a definition of "natural intelligence" that would allow them to separate tests of natural intelligence from tests of a "scholastic character." Instead of defining natural intelligence in a way that distinguishes it from cultural experience (which they refer to as a problem of "fearful complexity"), they contented themselves with pointing out that whatever natural intelligence is, it is not equivalent to success in school. In their view, not only is there more to intelligence than schooling, there is also more to schooling—and to life—than intelligence:

Our examination of intelligence can not take account of all these qualities, attention, will, regularity, continuity, docility, and courage which play so important a part in school work, and also in after-life; for life is not so much a conflict of intelligences as a combat of characters. (1916, p. 256)

THE LEGACY OF BINET AND SIMON

Educators immediately adopted Binet and Simon's tests, and their use spread rapidly. By 1916 more than 20,000 test booklets translated into English had been distributed by a single American institution devoted to education of the retarded. This was only the beginning. The tests were later translated and used in such far-flung countries as Australia, China, the Soviet Union, and South Africa.

Many refinements of the original tests have been made in the years since then. In the United States, Lewis Terman at Stanford University modified the original scales to create the Stanford-Binet Intelligence Scale in an attempt to determine the origins of mental giftedness (Terman, 1925), and David Wechsler devised tests for use with both adults and children (Wechsler, 1939) (see Figure 13.7). Updated versions of these tests are still widely used today.

From mental age to IQ

William Stern (1912), a German developmental psychologist, introduced an important refinement in the way intelligence tests were thought about and applied. He suggested that intelligence be considered the ratio of children's mental age to their actual, or chronological, age (CA). Thus was born the unit of measurement that we use today, the "intelligence quotient" **(IQ):** IQ = (MA/CA)100. The stratagem of multiplying the relative magnitude of MA/CA by 100 is simply a convenience. Calculation of IQ in this fashion ensures that when children are performing precisely as expected for their age, the resulting score will be 100, so that 100 is an "average IQ" by definition (see Figure 13.8). A 9-year-old child with a mental age of 10, for example, is assigned an IQ of 111 (10/9 × 100 = 111), while a 10-year-old child with a mental age of 10 is assigned an IQ of 100 (10/10 × 100 = 100). Stern's IQ

FIGURE 13.7 *Simulated items from the Wechsler Intelligence Scale for Children. (Copyright © 1948, 1974, 1991 by the Psychological Corporation. Reproduced by permission. All rights reserved.)*

Information (30 items)

How many wings does a bird have?
What is steam made of?

Picture Completion (26 items)

What is the missing part of the picture?

Similarities (17 items)

In what way are a lion and a tiger alike?
In what way are an hour and a week alike?

Picture Arrangement (12 items made up of 3 to 5 picture cards each)

(The person is asked to arrange the cards so that the story of the woman weighing herself makes sense.)

Comprehension (17 items)

What should you do if you see someone forget his book when he leaves a restaurant?
What is the advantage of keeping money in a bank?

score was quickly adopted as the basic unit for comparison of mental performances because it provided psychologists and educators with a convenient index that could then be used to specify the correlation between intelligence test scores and grades in school. (Correlation is discussed in Chapter 1, pp. 22–23.)

In recent decades the method of calculating IQ has been refined to take into account the fact that mental development is more rapid early in life than later. Raw IQ scores do not take into account the fact that the difference in mental functioning between 4- and 5-year-olds, for example, is greater than the difference between 14- and 15-year-olds. To overcome this difficulty, psychologists now use a score referred to as a **deviation IQ** (Wechsler, 1974). Calculation of IQ scores as deviations takes advantage of the statistical fact, illustrated in Figure 13.9, that the raw IQ scores calculated for a large sample form an approximately normal distribution. When psychologists base the IQ scores assigned to children on the differences between their raw scores and the standardized mean of 100, they have a statistical standard that is the same for all children.

Despite various revisions, the logic of the procedures devised by Binet and Simon is still the basis of standardized intelligence tests. The key tasks in the creation of an IQ test are:

1. To select a set of items that produces a range of performances among children at the same age level.
2. To arrange the items in the order of difficulty, so that as children grow older, they are more likely to answer each successive item correctly.
3. To make certain that performance on the test corresponds to performance in school.

Only part of Binet and Simon's legacy is to be found in the adoption and refinement of their testing methods. Equally important have been the questions they left unresolved, three of which have dominated research on intelligence since the start of their pioneering efforts. The first question focuses on the nature of intelligence itself: How is intelligence to be defined? Is it a general characteristic of a person's entire mental life, or is it a bundle of relatively specific abilities? Second is the nature-nurture question: What causes variations in intelligence test scores? Third, why do variations in IQ scores predict variations in school performance?

The nature of intelligence: General or specific?

Although Binet and Simon were skeptical about the possibility of defining intelligence, the nature of their assignment forced them to attempt to specify the quality of mind they were trying to test for. They offered the following characterization:

> It seems to us that in intelligence there is a fundamental faculty, the alteration or lack of which is of the utmost importance for practical life. This faculty is judgment, otherwise called good sense, practical sense, initiative, the faculty of adapting oneself to circumstances. To judge well, to comprehend well, to reason well, these are the essential activities of intelligence. (1916, p. 43)

This definition served to guide Binet and Simon's choices of items for their test, but it did not by any means settle the question of the essential properties of intelligence.

In 1921, when educators were embracing intelligence tests with enthusiasm, the editors of the *Journal of Educational Psychology* asked a number of experts to give their views on the nature of intelligence. The contributors mentioned many different characteristics, but they agreed in one respect with Binet and Simon's early definition. In their view, intelligence, whatever it is, is a general

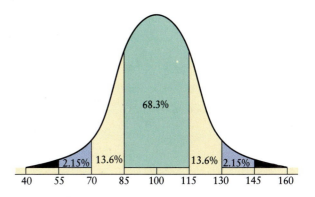

FIGURE 13.8 *An idealized bell-shaped curve of the distribution of IQ scores. A bell-shaped curve is a distribution of scores on a graph in which the most frequent value, the mode, is in the center and the less frequent values are distributed symmetrically on either side. By definition, the modal IQ score is 100.*

IQ A score on a test of intelligence; a child's mental age (as determined by the age at which average children pass the test items) divided by chronological age, multiplied by 100 (IQ = MA/CA × 100).

Deviation IQ A method of calculating IQ that recognizes that mental development is more rapid early in life than later. This method assigns IQ scores to children based on the difference between their raw scores and the standardized mean of 100.

characteristic. This view has been supported over the years by some statistical evidence that the separate tasks on the test are highly correlated with one another; people who score high on one task tend to score high on the others (Herrnstein & Murray, 1994; Spearman, 1927).

One participant in the 1921 symposium on intelligence, V. A. C. Henmon, disagreed with his colleagues. He believed that intelligence tests measure only "the special intelligence upon which the schools place a premium" (1921, p. 197). The idea that intelligence tests measure only school-specific aptitudes has been championed in recent years by a number of scholars (Ceci & Hembrooke, 1995).

Several characteristics seem to distinguish the intellectual tasks demanded by schools from tasks encountered in many other settings, as we have seen (see also Neisser, 1976; Scribner & Cole, 1973; Wagner & Sternberg, 1985):

- School tasks are formulated by other people.
- School tasks are generally of little or no intrinsic interest to the learner.
- As a rule, all the needed information is present at the start of a school task.
- School tasks are usually distinct from everyday experience elsewhere.
- School tasks are usually well defined, with a single correct answer.
- Often only one method for finding the solution to a school task is considered correct.
- School tasks are usually presented in written symbols (words, numbers).

These characteristics of school tasks have led several modern investigators to agree with Henmon that there is a special form of intelligence that is specific to such tasks. Ulric Neisser (1976) speaks of "academic" versus "everyday" intelligence. Robert Sternberg (1985) distinguishes academic and practical intelligence,

TABLE 13.4 The Multiple Intelligences Proposed by Howard Gardner

Kind of Intelligence	Characteristics
Linguistic	Special sensitivity to language, which allows one to choose precisely the right word or turn of phrase and to grasp new meanings easily
Musical	Sensitivity to pitch and tone, which allows one to detect and produce musical structure
Logical-mathematical	Ability to engage in abstract reasoning and manipulate symbols
Spatial	Ability to perceive relations among objects, to transform mentally what one sees, and to recreate visual images from memory
Bodily-kinesthetic	Ability to represent ideas in movement; characteristic of great dancers and mimes
Personal	Ability to gain access to one's own feelings and to understand the motivations of others
Social	Ability to understand the motives, feelings, and behaviors of other people

Source: Gardner, 1983.

both of which he considers to differ from a third kind of intelligence, which he calls wisdom.

More recently Howard Gardner (1983) has proposed a theory of multiple intelligences, each of which follows a separate developmental path (see Table 13.4). Musical intelligence often appears at an early age; logical mathematical intelligence seems to peak in late adolescence and early adulthood; the kind of spatial intelligence on which artists rely may reach its peak much later.

Population differences and the nature-nurture controversy

Along with their disagreements about whether intelligence is general or specific, theorists also disagree about *why* people's test performances vary. The current debate dates back to the beginning of World War I when Robert Yerkes proposed that all recruits be given an intelligence test to determine their fitness to serve in various military capacities as well as to generate data about the intelligence of the U.S. population as a whole. Approximately 1.75 million men were administered tests in groups—written tests for those who could read English,

FIGURE 13.9 *Items from the picture-completion test used by Robert Yerkes and his colleagues to test recruits during World War I. Each picture is incomplete in some way; the task is to identify what is missing. (From Yerkes, 1921.)*

a picture-completion test for those who could not (see Figure 13.9). Men who failed were given an individually administered version of the Binet and Simon scales (Yerkes, 1921). Never before had IQ tests been administered to such large groups of people at one time, or to people for whom the language of testing was not their native language.

Both because of the chaotic conditions of testing and because of the results, Yerkes's research began a controversy that has continued to the present time. Two results appeared to be particularly problematic. First, the average mental age of native-born white Americans was assessed at 13 years. Since, by the standards of the time, a mental age of 8 to 12 years was considered subnormal for an adult, it appeared that a substantial part of the white population consisted of "morons."

Second, there was a substantial difference between the scores obtained by European immigrants and African Americans. Overall, the average for recruits of European origin was a mental age of 13.7 years, although the recruits whose families came from southern and eastern Europe scored lower than northern Europeans, with an average mental age of about 11 years. African Americans scored lowest of all, with an average tested mental age of slightly more than 10 years.

Several of the pioneer mental testers interpreted such differences as the results of innate, immutable differences in natural intelligence ("nature"). According to this **innatist hypothesis of intelligence,** some people are born generally smarter than others and no amount of training or variation in the environment can alter this fact. The generally lower test scores of members of ethnic minority groups and the poor (who often, but not always, are the same people) were widely interpreted to mean that such groups were innately and irrevocably inferior (Hernnstein & Murray, 1994).

During the 1930s and 1940s scholarly opinion was seriously divided on this issue (Cronbach, 1975). The general-intelligence, innatist position was balanced by an **environmentalist hypothesis of intelligence** as both specific and heavily dependent on experience (Klineberg, 1980). It was demonstrated, for example, that after people had moved from rural areas to the city, their intelligence test scores rose (Klineberg, 1935), and that when orphans were removed from very restricted early environments, their intelligence test scores improved markedly (see Chapter 7).

The scientific and social debates about the differences in tested intelligence between ethnic groups and social classes erupted again when Arthur Jensen (1969) published an article with the title "How Much Can We Boost IQ and Scholastic Achievement?" Jensen was disenchanted with the federally sponsored Head Start program (see Chapter 11). He suggested that it was a mistake to expect scholastic improvements from Head Start because poor and minority children were genetically less capable of the mental processes demanded by school. His provocative thesis fueled a heated controversy. Jensen's critics charged that he used biased tests, misused statistical techniques, and misrepresented the data; Jensen disputed the charges (Block & Dworkin, 1976; Gould, 1981; Jensen, 1980).

IQ performance and the logic of testing

At the present time no responsible scholar believes that the variation in intelligence test scores from person to person can be attributed entirely to either environmental or genetic factors (Ceci & Hembrooke, 1995; Herrnstein & Murray, 1994; Plomin & McClearn, 1993). Even those who claim that genetic heritage makes a large contribution to academic success agree that all behavior, including performance on IQ tests and in school, is an aspect of a person's phenotype (that is, one's observable characteristics) and that the phenotype arises from the joint action of the genotype (the set of genes one inherits) and the environment.

As we pointed out in Chapter 2, the study of gene-environment interactions in human beings is especially difficult for several reasons. First, for ethical reasons,

Innatist hypothesis of IQ The belief that some people are born smarter than others and no amount of training or normal variation in the environment can alter this fact.

Environmentalist hypothesis of IQ The belief that intelligence is both specific and heavily dependent on experience.

it is impossible to study the full range of reaction. To do so would require us to expose some newborn children to hostile environments for the express purpose of satisfying our scientific curiosity. Second, almost all human characteristics are polygenic—that is, they are shaped by several genes acting in combination in a given set of environmental conditions. Thus, even when it has been possible to *estimate* the genetic contribution to a trait, little can be said about precisely which genes are interacting with the environment in what way. Third, the fact that parents contribute both to their children's genetic material *and* to the environment in which their children grow up complicates efforts to separate the various influences of nature and nurture on the phenotype. Finally, children actively shape their own environments, further complicating an already complicated situation (see Figure 2.7, p. 68, for a reminder of these complexities).

Attempts to understand how genetic and environmental factors combine to create the phenotypic behavior called "intelligence" face another, even greater difficulty. As we noted earlier, psychologists disagree profoundly about what, precisely, they are measuring when they administer an intelligence test. All they can say with any confidence is that these tests predict later school performance to a moderate degree. (The typical correlation between test performance and school performance is .50 [Neisser et al., 1996].) We can understand this problem better if we compare the gene-environment interactions that might determine intelligence with those that determine height.

To determine how environmental variation influences height, we might study sets of monozygotic (identical) and heterozygotic (fraternal) twins. Suppose that the twins to be studied were all born in Minnesota. Suppose further that some of the twins were separated, with the second member of each pair sent to live among the !Kung Bushmen of the Kalahari Desert. These environments do not represent the most extreme variations compatible with human life, but they are sufficiently different in climate, diet, daily activities, and other relevant factors to represent a plausible test of the relative importance of genetic and environmental contributions to height.

If, within this environmental range, genetic factors dominate the expression of the phenotype (measured height), then we would expect two facts to emerge:

- The heights of identical twins should be roughly as much alike when the twins are raised far apart as when they are raised in the same family.
- The similarity between the heights of identical twins should be greater than the similarity between the heights of fraternal twins. In fact, the similarity of the heights of identical twins raised in very different environments might be greater than that of fraternal twins raised in the same environment.

Note that whether the children are in Minnesota or in the Kalahari Desert, we can be pretty confident about our measure of height. Whether we use a yardstick or a metric scale, we have a valid standard for measuring the twins' heights, regardless of the context in which we use it. At first glance, IQ tests may appear to be standard measures logically similar to a yardstick. But this appearance is an illusion.

Precisely because intelligence tests take their meaning from their correlation with schoolwork, they are bound to the schooled society in which they are developed and to the graphic systems of representation that are central to all schooling. But these modes of representation are

"You can't build a hut, you don't know how to find edible roots and you know nothing about predicting the weather. In other words, you do *terribly* on our IQ test."

generally absent in nonliterate societies. To be administered to a !Kung child, every existing intelligence test would thus require some modification, if only translation from English to !Kung. If, for example, one of the test questions asks how many fingers are on two hands, the tester's first assumption might be that only minimal modification is necessary—but that assumption could be wrong. The number system used by the !Kung is not the same as that used by Minnesotans, and it plays a different role in their lives. What in !Kung society is the relative importance of knowing the number of fingers on a hand versus, say, knowing how to tie knots with those fingers?

When it comes to the tests that require interpretation of pictures or copying from written figures, even more serious difficulties arise. The !Kung have no tradition of either drawing or writing. Research with young children in the United States (Klapper & Birch, 1969) and with nonliterate peoples in several parts of the world (Berry et al., 1992) shows that people do not all automatically interpret two-dimensional pictures of objects as they would the objects themselves. So the tests that use pictures and require copying are inappropriate in many cultures, as are any tests that depend on the ability to read. We thus cannot assume that an IQ test is like a yardstick, yielding equivalent measures in all cultural environments.

Various attempts have been made to create "culture-free" tests (Cattell, 1949; Davis, 1948), but no generally satisfactory solution has yet been found: all tests of intelligence draw on a background of learning that is culture-specific (see Figure 13.10). (More recent attempts to deal with the difficulties of comparing intelligence across racial and cultural lines are described in Irvine & Berry, 1987, and Neisser et al., 1996.)

The fact that intelligence cannot be tested independently of the culture that gives rise to the test greatly limits the conclusions that can be drawn from IQ testing in different social and cultural groups. A number of studies have used compar-

FIGURE 13.10 *Items from a "culture-free" intelligence test. Note that though these test items do not require elaborate verbal formulation, they assume that the test taker is familiar with two-dimensional representations of figures, a convention that does not exist in many cultures. (From J. C. Raven,* Coloured Progressive Matrices *[London: H. K. Lewis & Co. Ltd., 1962]. Reprinted with permission of J. C. Raven Limited.)*

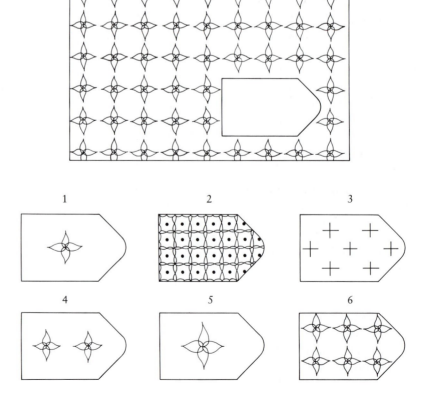

isons of identical and fraternal twins to distinguish genetic from environmental contributions to intelligence, but those studies suffer an important limitation. According to the logic of twin studies, the twins' environments must differ to such an extent that any consequences will be detected by the tests. But if the environmental variation is too great, as in the case of a child transported from Minnesota to the Kalahari Desert, both twins' intelligence cannot be validly measured by the same test.

Despite these difficulties, a large literature has grown up around studies of twins' IQ test performance, along with studies of children of interracial marriages and of children adopted across racial and ethnic lines (Mackenzie, 1984; Scarr, 1981). Controversy continues to attend this work, but the following conclusions appear to be the most defensible:

1. Some part of individual differences in performance on IQ tests is attributable to inheritance. The degree of heritability is in dispute: some investigators claim that it is very high (Herrnstein & Murray, 1994); some claim that it is very low or indeterminate (Bronfenbrenner & Ceci, 1994). One influential summary estimates that perhaps 50 percent of the variation in test performance within population groups is controlled by genetic factors (Plomin, 1990).

2. There are significant differences between the average IQ scores of African Americans and white Americans. Whites score approximately 15 points higher than African Americans; other ethnic groups in the United States, such as Native Americans and Hispanics, score at some intermediate level (Herrnstein & Murray, 1994).

3. There is no evidence that the average difference in scores between ethnic groups in the United States is the result of inherited differences in intelligence, however defined. Nonetheless, great uncertainty remains about precisely what environmental factors are involved in producing the group differences.

At first glance, the first two facts may appear to conflict with the third: if inheritance is responsible for a part of the differences between individuals in tested intelligence, and if there are differences between groups in tested intelligence, why wouldn't it be reasonable to conclude that the source of the differences between groups is the same as the source of the differences between individuals?

There are two answers to this question, one logical and the other empirical. The logical answer was provided by Richard Lewontin (1976). It can be illustrated by an example from plant genetics (see Figure 13.11). Suppose that a farmer has two fields, one fertile and the other depleted of nutrients. He randomly takes corn seed from a bag containing several genetic varieties and plants them in the two fields. He cares for them equally. When the plants have reached maturity he will discover that in each field some plants have grown taller than others. Since all the plants in a field experienced roughly the same environment, their variation can be attributed to genetic factors. But the farmer will also discover variation *between* the fields: the plants grown in the fertile field will be taller than the plants grown in the nutrient-poor field. The explanation for this average difference in the heights of the plants lies in their environments, even though the degrees of heritability in the two fields may be equal.

This same argument applies to variations in test performance between ethnic and racial groups. Even though the heritability of intelligence within ethnic or racial groups may be the

FIGURE 13.11 *The reason that differences within groups do not explain differences between groups. Here the difference in the heights of the plants in each box reflects genetic variations in the seeds planted in it. The difference between the average heights of the plants in the two boxes is best explained by the quality of the soil, an environmental factor. The same principle holds for IQ test scores of human groups. (Adapted from Gleitman, 1963.)*

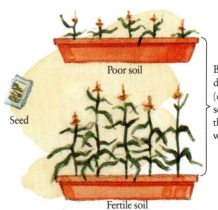

Poor soil

Seed

Between-group differences (cause: the soils in which the plants were grown)

Fertile soil

Within-group differences (cause: genetic variation in the seeds)

same, the average difference in performance between groups may still be caused not by their genetic endowment but by differences in the environments in which the children have been raised.

Lewontin's example illustrates another important point about heritability that applies equally to IQ. Heritability is a *population* statistic. It applies to groups, not to individuals. If the heritability statistic for a field of corn or a set of IQ scores is .50, it does not mean that 50 percent of the height of each corn plant or each IQ score is determined by genetic factors. It means rather that 50 percent of the *variation* in a field of corn or a group of IQ scores can be traced to genetic differences. The other 50 percent of the variation must be explained in some other way.

Research evidence also speaks strongly against the idea that ethnic, racial, and class differences in tested IQ can be explained by inheritance. In a particularly important study, Sandra Scarr and Richard Weinberg (1976, 1983) evaluated the impact on children of African American working-class parents of being adopted by white middle-class families. Had the African American children remained at home, they would be expected to achieve an average IQ score of 85. Raised in white middle-class families, these children had an average IQ score of 97, almost precisely the national average, despite the fact that they had been adopted more than a year after birth. Children adopted closer to birth had even higher scores. This kind of evidence points squarely to children's environment as a major factor in the development of the abilities tapped by standardized intelligence tests, abilities that are important to success in school.

A similar conclusion follows from a study of ethnicity and IQ among almost 500 5-year-old African American and white low-birth-weight premature children (Brooks-Gun, Klebanov, & Duncan, 1996). The families of these children were all relatively poor. The children were followed from birth. In addition to giving the children IQ tests when they were 5 years old, the researchers collected data on neighborhood and family poverty, the social structure of the family, maternal characteristics such as education and IQ, and the degree of stimulation in the home environment.

As many other studies have found, the African American children's IQ scores were significantly lower than the scores for the white children (85 vs. 103). When adjustments were made for ethnic-group differences in poverty, however, the difference was reduced by a little over half. When the differences in the stimulation provided in the home environment were also controlled for statistically, the ethnic differential was reduced by another 28 percent. As the authors note, these results do not imply that heredity has no role in IQ because they are not based on twin studies that allow estimates of heritability. They do show clearly, however, that when socioeconomic differences in the lives of African American and white children are taken into account, IQ differences between the groups are all but eliminated.

The School and the Community

In seeking to identify the environmental factors that contribute to IQ scores as well as school success, researchers have focused on factors operating in the family, in children's peer groups, and in the schools. (Box 13.4 takes an even broader cross-national look at factors that contribute to academic achievement.)

FAMILY INFLUENCES

Research described in Chapters 7 and 11 suggests some of the home characteristics that are likely to be influential in school achievement (Baumrind, 1989; White & Watts, 1973). Children whose parents encourage exploration, take care to explain what they are doing, listen to them, and tailor the difficulty of the environment to their abilities and interests tend to be more successful academically. Such results are not restricted to the United States; similar patterns of parental influence are found in Japan as well (Stevenson, Lee, & Stigler, 1986).

Another factor that has been found to influence children's success in school is the extent to which the patterns of language use in the home match those that teachers expect in the classroom. As we noted earlier in this chapter (p. 532), teachers ask a lot of questions to which they already know the answers.

Shirley Brice Heath, an anthropologist, spent several years comparing the language patterns characteristically employed in Anglo middle-class homes and working-class African American homes in a town in the southeastern United States (Brice Heath, 1982b, 1984). When she recorded the speech she heard in the Anglo homes, she found that there, as in the classroom, almost half of all the child-directed utterances she recorded were known-answer questions. When such children arrive at school, they are well versed in the special language of schooling. They understand what is expected of them and have developed skills in providing the proper kinds of answers.

The pattern of language use was quite different in the homes of the African American children. Questions made up only 10 percent of the talk directed at them. As Brice Heath put it, "children were more talked *at* than *with*". About the only times these children heard questions of the sort that make up so much of the repertoire of middle-class parents and teachers were the occasions when strangers such as social workers and bill collectors appeared; and the children were directly socialized *not* to answer those adults' questions.

The absence of known-answer questions in African Americans' speech to their children did not mean that the children were generally deprived of adult language input. Brice Heath documents many inventive uses of language in teasing and storytelling, for example. But the children never heard language used in the ways expected of them at school. Similar findings have been reported for Latino children (Vasquez et al., 1994).

Evidence that certain interaction patterns promote success in school does not mean that the socialization practices of home and school have to be closely matched before schools can teach children effectively. Studies carried out among Hawaiian children have shown that teachers can successfully build on some features of family socialization practices while ignoring or reversing others (Jordan, 1981; Weisner, Gallimore, & Jordan, 1988). These investigators found, for example, that they could build on the strong value Hawaiians place on cooperation and harmony by encouraging small groups of children to cooperate in carrying out school assignments. At the same time, they found that it was possible to ignore the fact that children speak a Creole dialect at home because this language variation did not interfere with their learning to read. By contrast, they advocated reversing the children's tendency to avoid looking directly at adults because eye contact is important in classroom discussion. This kind of culture-sensitive approach to the organization of classroom learning requires knowledgeable and flexible teaching, but when it is carried out by skilled teachers, it makes instruction more effective.

The family's role in academic achievement is strikingly evident in a different way among the refugees who fled to the United States from Vietnam, Cambodia, and Laos during the 1970s and 1980s. These people have been conspicuously successful in both economic and educational pursuits (Caplan, Whitmore, & Choy, 1989). Although they had lost from one to three years of formal education in refugee camps and most were unable to speak English when they entered school in the United States, eight out of ten students surveyed had a B average or better within three to six years. Almost half received A's in mathematics. These achievements are all the more noteworthy because they were attained in schools in low-income, inner-city areas traditionally associated with fewer resources and less motivated, more disruptive students.

BOX 13.4

Schooling in Three Cultures

Typical classrooms and curricula in schools appear very similar whether they are found in crowded cities such as New York and Tokyo or rural villages in West Africa and Australia. Yet many studies of classroom life and academic performance in different societies reveal that despite surface similarities, both the process and the products of schooling vary markedly from one culture to the next.

In the classrooms of rural Liberia, for example, children are taught basic reading, writing, and arithmetic through rote instruction (Cole et al., 1971). A favorite method used by Liberian teachers is to have the entire class recite lessons in unison, with little attention devoted to the meaning of the recitation. John Gay and Michael Cole (1967) report that when one of the children they studied was asked questions about arithmetic, he launched into a singsong patter ("La lala lala, la lala lala, la lala lala"). When asked what he was doing, he answered that he was adding numbers, but so far he had learned only the tune, not the words. Not surprisingly, the academic achievement of the typical Liberian child is low by U.S. standards.

But the achievement of American schoolchildren is itself low in comparison with that of children in other industrialized societies (McKnight et al., 1987). This finding has spurred attempts to identify the factors responsible for variations in children's achievement from one society to the next. A series of studies initiated by Harold Stevenson has provided a good deal of insight into the ways in which cultural differences in the conduct of elementary school education lead to variations in children's performance (Stevenson, Lee, & Stigler, 1986; Stevenson & Stigler, 1992; Stigler & Perry, 1990). These studies focused on classrooms in three countries: the United States, Japan, and Taiwan.

The accompanying diagrams provide a capsule look at schoolchildren's mathematical performance in the three societies on three tests of mathematical achievement: computational skill, word problems, and conceptual knowledge of mathematics. With the single exception of the test of conceptual understanding in the first grade, American children performed far below the level of both Asian groups. As might be expected, this evidence of marked national differences in the development of mathematical thinking has spurred a de-

bate about their causes. Richard Lynn (1982) argued, on the basis of comparative performance on IQ tests, that Japanese children enjoy a genetic superiority in intelligence. Careful evaluations of this hypothesis, however, have shown it to be false. Large comparative studies demonstrating differences in mathematics performance showed no corresponding differences in intelligence scores (Stevenson et al., 1985).

Acknowledging that other factors, such as encouragement of schoolwork at home and different forms of socialization, may contribute to the cultural differences observed, Stevenson and his colleagues have focused on the process of instruction in the classroom, arguing that a lot can be learned from study of these settings, whatever other factors may be at work. They found that the two factors in which American and Asian schooling differed the most were the amount of time spent in the teaching and learning of mathematics and the social organization of classroom interactions.

The Asian children in both the first and fifth grades attend school more days each year than the American children (240 days vs. 180). At the fifth-grade level, Japanese children go to school 44 hours a week, Chinese students 37 hours a week, and American children 30 hours a week. On each schoolday the two Asian groups spent as much time on mathematics as they did on reading and writing, but the American groups spent almost three times as much on language arts. As James Stigler and Michelle Perry (1990, p. 336) note, the disparity in the sheer number of hours spent on mathematics lessons is large enough to "go a long way toward explaining the differences in mathematics achievement."

But the differences are not restricted simply to gross amounts of time spent on mathematics; the Asian classrooms are organized quite differently from the American classrooms. By and large, classrooms in the two Asian countries are centrally organized and the teacher instructs the whole class at once. The American classrooms are generally more decentralized; often the teacher devotes attention to one group at a time while the other children work independently at their seats. Two important differences in the quality of teacher-student interactions are correlated with these differences in classroom organization. First, American

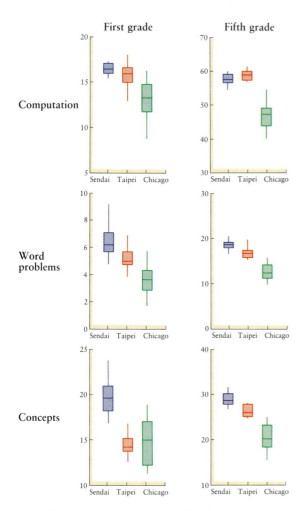

First grade   Fifth grade

Computation

Word problems

Concepts

Sendai   Taipei   Chicago

Distribution and mean number of correct answers on three mathematics-related tests in schools in Sendai (Japan), Taipei (Taiwan), and Chicago. (From Stigler & Perry, 1990.)

children spend a good deal of time being instructed by no one. This might not make much difference if the children were absorbed by their workbooks and truly working independently. But here another difference in students' behavior comes into play: to a significant de-gree American children do not use their independent study time well; they are out of their seats or engaged in inappropriate behavior such as gossiping with friends or causing mischief almost half of the time. Asian children spend far more time attending to schoolwork than their American counterparts do.

There are also differences in the content of the lessons. First, the Japanese teachers devote twice as much instruction time to helping children reflect on and analyze mathematics problems as the Chinese and American teachers do. Second, both the Chinese and Japanese teachers are more likely than their American counterparts to use concrete manipulable objects and to provide a meaningful context for the mathematics problems they teach. Third, the Asian teachers stress the connections between problems encountered at dif-ferent points in the lesson, or even between problems in one lesson and another, giving greater coherence to their teaching.

An attractive conclusion is that if American educa-tors want children to match the performance of their Asian counterparts, all they need to do is lengthen the school year and copy Japanese or Taiwanese classroom teaching methods. Proposals to extend the school year are on the agendas of many state legislatures and local school boards. It is not at all obvious, however, that a shift to teacher-led whole-group lessons will improve the quality of instruction or children's performance. In fact, a sizable body of evidence indicates that a curricu-lum organized around small-group activities can be es-pecially effective mode of instruction in American classrooms (Cole & Griffin, 1987).

Stigler and Perry (1990) sound a similar caution: their research suggests that instruction can be orga-nized so that children learn mathematics at a higher level than they are currently doing in American schools, but it does not indicate how to draw on Amer-ican cultural traditions to achieve this result. Quoting the sociologist Merry White (1987), they remind us that cross-cultural research does not provide a blue-print for improving the education of children. Rather, it provides a mirror that sharpens awareness of our own cultural practices and provides some hints about how they might be changed to make teaching and learning more effective.

In trying to account for the spectacular success of these immigrants, Nathan Caplan, John Whitmore, and Marcella Choy (1989) found the parents' involvement with their children to be crucial. Almost half of the parents surveyed said they read to their children, many in their native language. Apparently the parents' knowledge of English has less effect on the children's school performance than the emotional associations of being read to and the cultural wisdom they shared as they read the stories. The parents demonstrated their commitment to education not only by owning books and reading to their children but also by the number of hours of homework they required the children to do. Parents reported that their children spent an average of almost 3 hours of every weekday evening doing homework, twice the average for native-born American children.

Homework was also found to be a family affair. Caplan and his colleagues report that parents and older siblings took an active part in homework assignments. An interesting indicator of the effectiveness of this kind of involvement was the finding that the more children in the family, the higher their grade point averages. This result is just the opposite of the usual pattern in American households, where a large family is associated with poor school performance. Homework time was so much a family affair, in fact, that Caplan and his colleagues were unable to assess how much time each child spent on specific parts of the curriculum because they helped one another while they were doing their own work. The researchers comment that "a great amount of learning goes on in these homes in terms of course content and study habits, and it becomes understandable that children socialized in these settings would feel at home in school" (1989, p. 106).

PEER INFLUENCES

The possibility that peers will have a negative effect on a child's school performance is a common source of concern (Bishop, 1989). Evidence justifying this concern comes from a study by William Labov and Clarence Robbins (1969). Their research, carried out in central Harlem, focused on groups of boys in grades 4 to 10. Although these groups were not "gangs" in the sense that they did not fight other groups as a unit, fighting was common and conflict between groups was an important source of group cohesion.

The major values of group members were incompatible with those of the school, according to Labov and Robbins:

> Sources of prestige within the group are physical size, toughness, courage and skill in fighting; skill with language in ritual insults, verbal routines with girls, singing, jokes, and story-telling; knowledge of nationalist lore; skill and boldness in stealing. . . . Success in school is irrelevant to prestige within the group, and reading is rarely if ever used outside of school. (1969, p. 55)

By comparing the reading scores of group members and nonmembers at different grade levels, Labov and Robbins could assess the influence of participation in certain peer groups on academic achievement. They found that as boys who were not group members progressed through the grades, their reading scores rose steadily, whereas group members improved hardly at all.

On the other hand, Margarita Azmitia and Marion Perlmutter (1989) found that peers can also have positive effects on school performance. They reviewed a wide range of studies that assessed the effects of asking school-aged children to work collaboratively on academic tasks with their peers. Working with peers improved children's problem solving, they found, so long as the children got along well enough to collaborate in a mutually facilitating manner. It is particularly important that the children be able to reach agreement about the best way to tackle the problem and to agree when they have achieved a good result. But this outcome is by no means guaranteed. Consequently, current research is focusing on ways to make peer interactions more collaborative (Forman & McPhail, 1993).

SCHOOL ATMOSPHERE

Research demonstrates convincingly that the quality of children's experiences at school can make a decisive difference in their academic success. Michael Rutter and his colleagues (1979), for example, carried out a large-scale study of secondary schools in central London, where housing conditions are poor, unemployment and crime rates are high, levels of education among adults are low, and handicapping psychiatric disorders are common. These are just the conditions that one might expect would lead to poor educational achievement, and in many cases they do. Despite these unfavorable conditions, some schools were more successful than others in educating their students.

Rutter and his colleagues discovered that, contrary to expectations, the successful schools were not more modern, their teachers were not better trained or better paid, and their students did not have higher IQs or more favorable conditions at home. The differences were traced to educational conditions within the schools. Four conditions were found to be most important:

- *Academic emphasis.* Schools that clearly demonstrated an expectation that students were in school to master academic subjects produced higher levels of achievement. These expectations were communicated in a variety of ways, such as the assignment of homework and regular displays of excellent work on classroom bulletin boards. Figure 13.12 shows the relationship between the amount of homework assigned and the average examination score pupils achieved. (See also Box 13.5.)
- *Teachers' behaviors.* When teachers must stop to discipline individual children, everyone tends to lose the thread of the lesson. Successful classrooms were those where teachers could coordinate the entire class at one time; often these teachers expected their students to work silently, on their own.
- *Distribution of rewards and punishments.* The most successful classrooms were those where punishment was less frequent than praise.
- *Student conditions.* Schools in which students were free to use the buildings during breaks and at lunchtime, had access to a telephone, and were expected to keep the classrooms clean and pleasant produced better student achievement than schools that were run entirely by adults.

The most intriguing finding was that in the successful schools, each individual factor seemed to feed the others, creating an overall environment, or "school atmosphere," conducive to success. This positive school atmosphere cannot be legislated; it must be created by the staff and the students together. Each successful school arrived at its own conducive atmosphere in its own way, taking its own distinctive mix of approaches.

OUTSIDE OF SCHOOL

Literate societies have come to equate success with schooling, but we all know there is more to life than school. On weekday afternoons and evenings, on weekends and holidays, 6- to 12-year-old children are likely to be found among their friends, engaged in activities of their own choosing. Participation in these peer groups provides a kind of preparation for adult life that is quite different from that organized by adults in classrooms and at home. A full understanding of the nature of middle childhood requires investigation of this context as well,

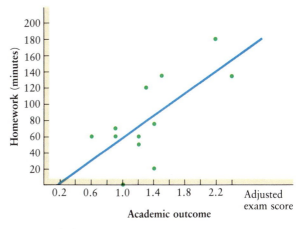

FIGURE 13.12 *As the amount of homework assigned each week increases (a measure of the academic emphasis of the school), students' grades improve. (From Rutter et al., 1979.)*

BOX 13.5

Teachers' Expectations and School Success

Most of us have spent more than a dozen years in classrooms and know from personal experience that teachers' attitudes toward students vary. Teachers expect some students to do better than others in mastering academic material. Modern research has shown that these attitudes and expectations influence students' performance in a variety of ways.

Perhaps the most famous, and certainly the most controversial, research on the effect of teachers' expectations was initiated in the 1960s by Robert Rosenthal and his colleagues (Rosenthal, 1987; Rosenthal & Rubin, 1978). These researchers found that a teacher's expectations about a child's academic ability may become a self-fulfilling prophecy, even when the expectations are groundless.

To demonstrate the power of teachers' expectations, Rosenthal and Lenore Jacobsen (1968) gave children in all six elementary grades a test that, they told the teachers, would identify children who were likely to "bloom" intellectually during the coming year. After the testing, teachers were given the names of those children who, the researchers said, would show a spurt in intellectual development during the school year. In fact, the names of the presumed "bloomers" were chosen at random (with a few exceptions, to be described in due course).

At the end of the school year the children were tested again. This time the researchers found that at the first- and second-grade levels there was in fact a difference between the "bloomers" and "nonbloomers": the children who had been randomly identified as likely candidates for rapid intellectual growth really did grow. They gained an average of 15 points on their IQ scores over their scores at the beginning of the school year, while their classmates' IQ scores remained unchanged. In this study, the IQs of children in grades 3 through 6 did not change, but in a follow-up study Rosenthal and his colleagues found that older schoolchildren's performance on IQ tests could also be influenced by the teachers' expectations (Rosenthal, Baratz, & Hall, 1974).

Since the children identified as those likely to bloom intellectually were chosen at random, Rosenthal and his colleagues concluded that teachers' expectations influence their own behavior and thus their students', so that their teaching is more effective with children they believe are academically able.

A particularly provocative finding in Rosenthal and Jacobsen's (1968) study concerned race, ethnic, and class differences in academic performance. Teachers often have lower expectations for the academic performance of minority-group and poor children than they do for their white, middle-class counterparts (Minuchin & Shapiro, 1983). To test the possibility that these lowered expectations actually lower minority and poor children's academic performance, Rosenthal and Jacobsen included a group of poor Mexican-American children among those they identified as likely to bloom during the coming year. These children made particularly large gains in IQ test performance. In fact, the children whom the teachers identified as most "Mexican-looking" made the largest gains, perhaps because they were the ones from whom the teachers would ordinarily have expected the least.

Such results immediately attracted the attention of researchers and the public at large. More than 500 studies have been conducted on the role of teachers' expectations in students' academic performance (Wineberg, 1987). Many school districts even have special training programs to ensure that their teachers are sensitive to the ways in which their expectations may negatively affect some children.

Despite general acceptance that teachers' expectations are a significant factor in children's academic performance, some psychologists and educators remain skeptical (Wineberg, 1987). One basis for doubt is that many studies fail to find any such effects. Why not? When researchers attempted to find out by observing teachers and children in interaction in classrooms, they found that teachers differ in their approach to the children of whom they expect little. Some teachers ignore those children and focus on the ones they consider more capable. But other teachers seem to compensate by giving extra help and encouragement to the children of whom they have low expectations, and still others are even-handed in apportioning attention (Good, Sikes, & Brophy, 1973). This research also makes it clear that children are not passive recipients of teachers' expectations. Children influence those expectations by their own classroom behavior (Brophy, 1983).

Research by Carol Dweck and her colleagues has shown one way in which the interplay between teachers' expectations and children's behavior may shape academic development. Dweck's research has focused on teachers' differing expectations for boys and girls. In general, girls are better behaved than boys during the elementary school years. Consequently, teachers expect boys to challenge classroom decorum and girls to support it. Dweck and her colleagues found that these differences in children's behavior and teachers' expectations led teachers to respond differently to boys

and girls (Dweck & Bush, 1976; Dweck et al., 1978; Dweck & Goetz, 1978). Overall, teachers criticize boys more than girls. Often this criticism focuses on boys' lack of decorum, their failure to do their work neatly, or their inattentiveness. Their criticism of girls, by contrast, is likely to focus on their ability and intellectual performance. At the same time, when teachers offer praise, its focus is likely to be girls' cooperative social behavior and boys' intellectual accomplishments.

These differences in teachers' expectations for boys and girls and in the kind of feedback they give them have been found to be related to the kinds of expectations that children form about their own behavior (Dweck & Elliott, 1983). When girls are told that they have failed, they usually believe that the teacher has correctly assessed their intellectual capacity, so they tend to stop trying. Boys interpret such criticism differently: they blame their poor performance on someone else or on their situation and retain faith in their own ability to do better next time.

Evidence that teachers may discourage children for whom expectations are low has prompted a variety of programs to encourage broad participation in academic work. This girl is participating in a program to encourage excellence in mathematics.

SUMMARY

- School is a specialized child-rearing environment that is specific to certain societies and historical eras.

The Contexts in Which Skills Are Taught

- Traditional hunter-gatherer and agricultural societies achieve the goals of education in the context of everyday activities. As societies become more complex, adults pay increasing attention to instructing children in the skills they will need as adults.

- Formal education in schools differs from traditional training, such as apprenticeship, in the motives for learning as well as in the social relations, the social organization, and the medium of instruction.

The Historical Development of Literacy and Schooling

- Schooling arose as a means of training large numbers of scribes to keep the records on which complex societies depend.

- The use of a written notation system is essential to formal education. The technology of writing has undergone a long evolution. The evolution of the written notation system called an alphabet decreased the number of symbols that people needed to learn but increased the abstractness of the resulting system for representing sounds.

Development and Academic Skills

- Mastery of two basic symbol systems, written language and mathematics, is essential to the process of schooling.

- Reading an alphabetic language is a complex cognitive skill in which information the reader obtains by learning the correspondences between letters and sounds must be coordinated with higher-order information about the content of the text.

- Researchers are divided in their ideas about how reading should be taught.
  1. Those who favor the code-emphasis-first approach believe that the ability to read is acquired in several stages. The transition around third or fourth grade from decoding individual words to reading for the purpose of learning something new is particularly difficult for many children.
  2. Those who favor the comprehension-first approach believe that from the outset decoding should be learned in the context of reading for meaning.

- Reading instruction has undergone changes in response to demands for higher levels of proficiency. Current curricula seek to balance an emphasis on decoding with an emphasis on reading for meaning. Special teaching methods, such as reciprocal teaching, have been devised to enable students to integrate their decoding skills with reading for meaning.

- Children arrive at school with rudimentary knowledge about practical arithmetic, including the idea of one-to-one correspondence between number words and objects and the ability to count.

- Learning mathematics in school requires students to acquire and coordinate three kinds of knowledge:
  1. Conceptual knowledge, or the understanding of mathematical principles.

2. Procedural knowledge, or the ability to carry out sequences of actions to solve a problem.

3. Utilization knowledge, or the knowledge of when to apply particular procedures.

- Theories of how best to teach mathematics vary between two extremes, one emphasizing the need for drill and practice, the other emphasizing the centrality of conceptual understanding. Most current teaching techniques attempt to balance drill with explanation.

- Classroom instruction is characterized by a special kind of talk.

1. With respect to spoken language, children must learn to acquire knowledge through verbal exchanges in which teachers ask questions, students reply, and teachers evaluate.

2. With respect to written language, children must learn to use notation systems that differ systematically from their spoken equivalents.

- The great emphasis placed on the use of correct linguistic forms in classroom discourse reinforces the hypothetical, "as if" nature of classroom problem solving.

The Cognitive Consequences of Schooling

- Research comparing the cognitive performances of schooled and unschooled children reveals that formal schooling in middle childhood enhances the development of certain cognitive skills, including lexical organization, memory, and metacognition.

- Positive cognitive consequences of schooling, however, turn out to be restricted to materials and procedures that closely match classroom practices.

- There is no evidence that schooling enhances cognitive development in general.

Aptitude for Schooling

- Tests of aptitude for schooling first appeared when education was extended to the population at large. The earliest tests were designed to identify children who needed special support to succeed in school.

- Binet and Simon's key innovation in constructing their test of school aptitude was to sort test items according to the age at which children could typically cope with them, thus producing a scale of "mental age."

- The aptitude measure called IQ represents a child's mental age (as determined by the age at which average children answer each test item correctly) divided by chronological age, with the result multiplied by 100 (a number arbitrarily chosen to represent the average IQ): $IQ = (MA/CA)100$.

- IQ test scores have been found to be correlated significantly with later school success.

- An important unresolved question about intelligence tests is the degree to which the aptitudes they tap are general across all domains of human activity or are closely related to specialized activities, such as those involved in schooling and music.

- Persistent class, racial, and ethnic differences in IQ test performance have inspired fierce debates about the possibility that some races, ethnic groups, and classes are genetically inferior.

- Modern research comparing the IQs of identical and fraternal twins indicates that IQ has a genetic component that accounts for perhaps 50 percent of the variation in test performance within groups.

- African American children adopted by white middle-class families develop normal IQs, an indication that average differences in IQ scores between groups are the result of environmental factors.

The School and the Community

- Children's school achievement is hindered when patterns of interaction and language use in the family do not match those of the school. When mismatches are recognized, school curricula can be modified to take advantage of family interaction patterns.
- Family support of children's schooling in the form of general encouragement and special arrangements for doing homework enhances children's achievement.
- Peer-group values antithetical to school values can exert a powerful negative effect on students' achievement. Peer groups can also be used to enhance classroom learning.
- Schools with a strong academic emphasis, teachers skilled in classroom management, an emphasis on praise over punishment, and a welcoming attitude toward students have positive effects on students' achievement in school.

KEY TERMS

apprenticeship,   p. 515

conceptual knowledge,
  p. 527

decoding,   p. 520

deviation IQ,   p. 543

education,   p. 515

environmentalist
  hypothesis of
  intelligence,   p. 546

initiation-reply-
  evaluation sequence,
  p. 532

innatist hypothesis of
  intelligence,   p. 546

instructional discourse,
  p. 532

IQ,   p. 542

lexicon,   p. 537

mental age (MA),
  p. 541

metacognition,   p. 538

metalinguistic awareness,
  p. 538

procedural knowledge,
  p. 527

reciprocal teaching,
  p. 526

school cutoff strategy,
  p. 536

utilization knowledge,
  p. 527

THOUGHT QUESTIONS

1. When you look back over your own work and school experiences so far, what personal examples can you recall of the differences between learning on the job and learning in school?

2. Suggest a research design for elucidating the process by which children acquire the ability to read. Include a comparison between two methods of teaching as a part of your design.

3. What factors might give rise to the special language of schooling? What might account for the fact that aspects of this way of using language are also found in some homes?

4. Paraphrase Binet and Simon's contention (quoted on p. 542) that "life is not so much a conflict of intelligences as a combat of characters." How does this idea bear on disputes about the significance of IQ testing as a means of assessing cognitive development?

5. Suppose you were assigned the task of creating a culture-free intelligence test. How would you go about it? What major obstacles would you expect to encounter?

Social Development in Middle Childhood

❝We went home and when somebody said, 'Where were you?' we said, 'Out,' and when somebody said, 'What were you doing until this hour of the night,' we said, as always, 'Nothing.'

But about this doing nothing: we swung on the swings. We went for walks. We lay on our backs in the backyards and chewed grass . . . and when we were done, he [my best friend] walked me home to my house, and when we got there I walked him back to his house, and then he—.

We watched things: we watched people build houses, we watched men fix cars, we watched each other patch bicycle tires with rubber bands . . . [we watched] our fathers playing cards, our mothers making jam, our sisters skipping rope, curling their hair. . . .

We sat in boxes; we sat under porches; we sat on roofs; we sat on limbs of trees.

We stood on boards over excavations; we stood on tops of piles of leaves; we stood under rain dripping from the eaves; we stood up to our ears in snow.

We looked at things like knives . . . and grasshoppers and clouds and dogs and people.

We skipped and hopped and jumped. Not going anywhere—just skipping and hopping and jumping and galloping.

We sang and whittled and hummed and screamed.

What I mean, Jack, we did a lot of nothing.❞

—*Robert Paul Smith*,
Where Did You Go? Out.
What Did You Do? Nothing.

etween the ages of 6 and 12, U.S. children typically spend more than 40 percent of their waking hours in the company of **peers,** children of their own age and status, often "doing nothing." This figure is more than double the amount of time they spent with peers when they were preschoolers. The increase in time spent among peers is accompanied by a complementary decrease in the time spent with parents (Hill & Stafford, 1980).

Comparisons of the same children's behavior in different settings suggest two obvious differences between contexts where adults supervise and contexts dominated by peers. First, *the content of the activity is different.* When adults preside over children's activities, some form of instruction or work is likely to take place; when several children get together with no adults present, they will probably play a game or "just hang out."

Second, *the forms of social control are different.* When children are under the watchful eyes of adults, either at home or in school, it is the adults who keep peace and maintain the social order. If Sarah takes more than her share of ice cream, or if Tom and Jimmy refuse to let Sam on the swings, the adult is there to invoke

Peers Individuals of comparable age and status.

Learning to get along without fighting is a difficult task, especially when a smaller child is threatened and one's honor is at stake.

These boys are playing in the ocean without any supervision by their parents, something that they would not have been allowed to do when they were younger.

society's rules ("Share and share alike"; "Everyone gets a turn") and to settle disputes. But when children are on their own in peer groups, they must establish the distribution of authority and responsibility themselves. Sometimes might makes right, and an especially strong child dominates the group. By and large, however, authority is established through negotiation, compromise, and discussion (Youniss, 1980). Power within the group may also shift with the children's activities. A leader in making mischief may not be the leader in organizing an afternoon trip to the movies (Sherif & Sherif, 1956).

Jeffrey Parker and his colleagues (1995) summarize current thinking among developmentalists about the significance of peer relations for development in the following straightforward terms:

> It is assumed that children who are successful with peers are on track for adaptive and psychologically healthy outcomes, whereas those who fail to adapt to the peer milieu are at risk for maladaptive outcomes. (p. 96)

The increased time that children spend among their peers is both a cause and an effect of their development during middle childhood. Adults begin to allow their children to spend extensive time with friends because they recognize the children's greater ability to think and act for themselves. At the same time, the new experiences with peers challenge children to master new cognitive and social skills (Hartup, 1992; Selman & Schultz, 1990).

Children's sense of themselves and their relations with others also change in middle childhood. So long as they spend their time primarily among family members, their place in the social world is determined for them. They are accepted as "Mrs. Smith's little girl, Suzie," or "Juan Lopez's brother Tony." When children spend more time among their peers, the sense of self they acquired in their families no longer suffices and they must learn to reconcile their old identities with the new ones they begin to form in the new contexts they inhabit (Damon & Hart, 1988). The responsible older sibling who watches the baby, the classroom comedian, the star volleyball player, and the kid who spends a lot of time reading adventure stories may well be one and the same person.

Middle childhood also brings changes in the quality of children's relations with their parents. Parents can no longer easily pick them up and physically remove them from danger or from sibling squabbles. Instead they must rely on their children's greater understanding of the consequences of their actions and on their desire to conform to adult standards. As a result, parents' socialization techniques become more indirect: they rely more on discussion and explanation than on physical force to influence their children's behavior.

Unfortunately, psychological research methods cannot always do justice to the greatly increased diversity of experience during middle childhood. In Chapter 9 we saw that scientists' study of preschoolers is impeded by the children's imprecise grasp of language; it is difficult to distinguish fact from fancy in what they say. At the same time, though, young children are almost always under adult supervision, and it is easy to observe them and record what they do. Moreover, the presence of an adult does not affect their spontaneity. Most 8- and 9-year-olds, in contrast, are perfectly capable conversationalists, but their behavior with their peers is likely to change radically when an adult observer appears on the scene.

Scientific knowledge about middle childhood is therefore fragmentary in several respects. We have extensive information about children's behavior in school, but systematic knowledge about their life in other contexts is often skimpy. A great many studies have been conducted on how children respond to questions about hypothetical moral dilemmas, their explicit conceptions of friendship, and the way they attempt to solve a variety of intellectual puzzles adults pose for them. But we have little systematic information about their actual moral behavior, their qualities as friends, or their ability to recognize and solve problems in everyday life. In this chapter we will discuss the evidence on the social aspects of middle childhood and then return at the end to the question of whether middle childhood represents a distinctive stage of development.

Games and Group Regulation

The appearance of peer groups among children 6 to 12 years old raises a central question about middle childhood: How do children learn to regulate their social relations when adults are not present? The precise psychological mechanisms are still uncertain, but it appears that one important arena for this development is *game playing* (Piaget, 1967; Hughes, 1995).

GAMES AND RULES

Like 4- and 5-year-olds, children who have entered middle childhood engage in fantasy role play, with each child taking a part in an imaginary situation: cops chase robbers, tree houses become havens for shipwrecked families, and forts hide runaway children (Singer & Singer, 1990). But now a new form of play comes into prominence as well—the playing of games based on rules.

The rules and the styles of interaction promoted by these games vary from culture to culture. In West Africa children divide into teams and challenge each other to remember the names of leaves gathered in the forest. Children in the United States are more likely to play Twenty Questions or Monopoly. In many cultures we find variations on games in which a ball is kicked, hit, or thrown as part of a team sport, or games that resemble tag or hopscotch (Roopnarine, Johnson, & Hooper, 1994). Even in societies in which children are more likely to begin to work than to attend school, middle childhood is the time when games with explicit rules make their appearance.

Although fantasy play is based on *roles* and games are based on *rules*, rules are not totally absent from fantasy play in early childhood, nor are roles totally absent from rule-based play. Rules are a part of young children's social pretend play in

Games with rules are prominent in the lives of children during middle childhood.

two ways. First, when young children perform their roles, they typically follow implicit social rules. The pretend teacher tells the pretend children to sit quietly; the children do not tell the teacher what to do.

Second, young children use rules to negotiate the roles they adopt and to maintain the make-believe context: "Only girls are allowed to be Superwoman"; "Go away, Darth Vader, we're having a birthday party and spacemen are not allowed at birthday parties" (Paley, 1984).

The balance between rules and roles is reversed in the games that become prominent during middle childhood. About the age of 7 or 8, rules become the essence of many games. In such games, the rules determine what roles are to be played and what one can and cannot do in playing those roles. Rules also enter differently into the content of the games of middle childhood. Preschool fantasy play can change from moment to moment on a whim. But in the games characteristic of older children, participants must agree ahead of time about the rules that will govern their activity. Anyone who changes the rules without common consent is "cheating."

Rule-based games seem to require the same kinds of mental abilities that form the basis for adults' assignment of new tasks and responsibilities to 6- and 7-year-olds (see Chapter 12). Children must be able to keep in mind the overall set of task conditions specified ahead of time as they pursue the goals of the moment. At the same time, they need to engage in social perspective-taking, understanding the relation between the thoughts of the other players and their own actions if they are going to be successful ("If I move my checker to this square, she'll double-jump me").

Rule-based games have a different purpose than fantasy play. In fantasy play, the play's the thing. Satisfaction comes from exercising the imagination in the company of others. In rule-based play, the object is to win through competition governed by rules (see Box 14.1). The following description of an attempt to involve a preschooler in a rule-based game captures beautifully this difference in orientation:

> The experimenter is playing hide-and-seek with a 3-year-old child. When the child has hidden, the experimenter does not "find" it immediately, but deliberately waits near the child for a minute or two pretending not to be able to find it. Then the tot cannot restrain itself from breaking the rule, and

BOX 14.1

Socialization for Adulthood: Little League Baseball

Little League Baseball is the best-known and most successful sports program for boys in the United States (although girls are now making inroads on this institution). Every spring and summer, well over half a million boys between the ages of 9 and 12 spend two or three afternoons a week learning "the American pastime." In addition to providing instruction in the skills of baseball, Little League coaches try to teach their players to work hard, to cooperate and compete with one another, to adhere to ideals of good sportsmanship, and to be good members of their communities.

For three seasons in the early 1980s the sociologist Gary Alan Fine (1987) was a frequent visitor to several Little League teams in various leagues. He not only attended practices and games but from time to time got together with the team members in other community settings. Although he rarely participated directly as a coach or an umpire, he won acceptance as a friendly outsider, "one of the boys," and his detailed field notes are a rich source of information about American boys growing up under the tutelage of older males in their community. Fine notes:

> If we hope to understand how adult sex roles are shaped, we must observe the blossoming of those roles in childhood peer groups. . . . Most nonfamilial guardians of boys are women; yet in sports, boys are taught to be men, and these men (at least in Little League) see themselves as having specific didactic roles. (1987, p. 1)

Fine discovered that participation in Little League provides many opportunities for socialization in basic community values.

- *Play and work* Playing baseball in Little League is a mixture of play and work. Once a boy becomes a member of a team, it is not enough for him simply to turn up at game time. He is expected to attend practices and to concentrate on building his skills even if he is bored or tired. During games he is expected to pay attention and provide encouragement to his teammates even if he is not in the game.

- *Effort* In an obvious sense, the object of playing baseball is to win. But Little League coaches make clear that it is at least as important to try hard as to win. Typical of coaches' comments is this one:

> Your goal for the year is to be a winner. That doesn't mean winning every game. Sometimes you will be up against teams that are better than you. It does mean to give everything you've got. If you give everything you've got, you're a winner in my book. (p. 62)

- *Sportsmanship* Although a coach may consider his players to be winners if they try hard, there is no avoiding the fact that losing is as much a part of the game as winning. When a boy strikes out or makes an error, he may feel a powerful urge to throw his bat or to cry. But the knowledge that he is performing in public provides an extra incentive at least to appear to take mistakes and losing gracefully.

When a player does lose his self-control—and it is not uncommon for a boy to become overtly upset or hostile—it is up to his coach and teammates to help him regain his equanimity. Of course, in the heat of the game, the coach himself may engage in unsportsmanlike conduct, yelling at the boys, suggesting underhanded ways for them to gain the advantage, or cursing other adults. Observation of several such scenes moved Fine to comment that "successful socialization is learning when to express the moral verities proclaimed by adults, discerning which ones they really mean, and knowing what moral rhetoric to adopt when caught red handed" (p. 60).

- *Teamwork* Perhaps no aspect of participation in Little League is so overtly linked to adult life as teamwork. One of the coaches whom Fine interviewed said that "teamwork is very important. That's one of the things that life is all about, is working with a team. Little League is that opportunity" (p. 71).

Supporters of Little League believe that this form of organized sports activity is good for the children who participate. The former major-league star Bob Feller sums up the view of many people when he says:

Little Leagues not only foster friendships, develop coordination and good health habits in boys, but they break down social barriers to make a more closely knit community. . . . No one pays attention to how much money a boy's father has, or his social standing. . . . Where else is there a more practical training for democracy? (p. 196)

Little League also has its critics. Noting that some coaches are so determined to win that they forget the lofty ideals of the organization, some observers argue that Little League is too competitive. Others suggest that the presence of umpires and fixed schedules robs children of the opportunity to engage in sports spontaneously and also exposes them to physical danger and to the tender mercies of untrained coaches.

Fine surveyed existing research on the impact of Little League on children's development and conducted an interview study of his own. By and large, the data he was able to gather appeared to be more supportive of Little League than critical of it. Parents generally think that Little League is beneficial for their

children, and fathers report that through Little League they spend more time with their sons engaged in mutually satisfying activity. Other research shows that participation in Little League is correlated with popularity, positive self-esteem, higher ratings of leadership ability by teachers, and reduced delinquency. In every case, however, the direction of causation is open to dispute, because Little League is a voluntary activity; boys don't have to play in Little League, they must want to. As a consequence, additional research will be needed to determine whether those desirable attributes (such as popularity and positive self-esteem) correlate with Little League because the more popular and self-confident children join Little League or whether they develop as a result of participation in Little League.

Surveying the results of his own and others' research on the merits and drawbacks of participation in Little League, Gary Alan Fine hands down a verdict of "not proven." On balance, his own personal opinion is positive: "Basically Little League is fun for those preadolescents who participate, and while we should never stop trying to curtail its flaws, we should be satisfied that it brings a little joy into the lives of our children" (p. 221).

almost immediately begins to shout: "Uncle, here I am!" A 6-year-old plays hide-and-seek quite differently. For it, the main thing is to stick to the rules. (Leontiev, 1981, p. 381)

The shift from fantasy play to rule-based games greatly expands both the number of children who can play together and the likely duration of their joint activity. In a typical preschool, only two or three children play together at a time, and their play episodes are likely to last less than 10 minutes (Corsaro, 1985). When larger groups gather, it is almost certainly because the teacher has taken the trouble to coordinate their activity. School-age children, by contrast, often play for hours in groups numbering up to 20 (Hartup, 1984). The increased duration and complexity of children's play provide evidence that at least under some conditions, children who have entered middle childhood are capable of regulating their own behavior according to agreed-upon social rules.

GAMES AND LIFE

The links between young children's pretend play and their social surroundings are fairly obvious because they use adult roles and familiar scripts as the basis of their fantasy. It is less obvious how a game of hopscotch or checkers relates to adult life. Nonetheless, the idea that rule-based games are preparation for life has widespread appeal, as Box 14.1 makes clear.

Piaget (1932/1965) believed that the appearance of rule-based games in middle childhood has a double significance for children's development. First, he saw the ability to engage in rule-based games as a *manifestation of concrete operations in the social sphere*, corresponding to decreasing egocentrism, the appearance of conservation, and other cognitive abilities discussed in Chapter 12. Second, he believed that such games create structured circumstances within which children obtain *practice in balancing their own desires against the rules of their society.*

Rule-based games are models of society for children in two closely related respects, Piaget argued. First, they are social institutions in that they remain the same as they are transmitted from one generation to the next. Like other social institutions—a school lesson, for example—rule-based games provide an already existing structure of rules about how to behave in specific social circumstances.

Second, like all social institutions, rule-based games can exist only if people agree to their existence. In order to play a game such as checkers or hide-and-seek, children must learn to subordinate their immediate desires and behavior to a socially agreed-upon system. Piaget linked this ability to work within a framework of rules to children's acquisition of respect for rules and a new level of moral understanding:

> All morality consists in a system of rules, and the essence of all morality is to be sought for in the respect which the individual acquires for these rules. . . . The rules of the game of marbles are handed down, just like so-called moral realities, from one generation to another, and are preserved solely by the respect that is felt for them by individuals. (1932/1965, pp. 13–14)

In Piaget's view, it is through the give-and-take of negotiating plans, settling disagreements, making and enforcing rules, and keeping and breaking promises that children come to develop an understanding that social rules provide a structure that makes cooperation with others possible (Piaget, 1932/1965).

On the basis of his observations of the way children play games, Piaget proposed a developmental progression in children's understanding of social rules. The game on which he based most of his discussion is marbles. He maintained that very young children play marbles with little regard for the rules and with no notion of competition. They pile marbles up or roll them around to suit their fancy. At this stage, marbles is not a true game at all.

In middle childhood they try to win according to preexisting rules. At first they tend to believe that the rules of the game have been handed down by such authority figures as older children, adults, or even God; therefore, the rules are sacred and cannot be changed. Piaget asked one 5½-year-old if it would be all right to allow little children to shoot their marbles from a position closer to the marbles they were trying to hit.

"No," answered Leh, "that wouldn't be fair." "Why not?"—"Because God would make the little boy's shot not reach the marbles and the big boy's shot would reach them." (1932/1965, p. 58)

Piaget suggested to Ben, aged 10, that he might invent a new version of marbles. Ben agreed reluctantly that it would be possible to think up new rules, and suggested one. Piaget asked if such a new rule would be acceptable:

Piaget: Then people could play that way?

Ben: Oh, no, because it would be cheating.

Piaget: But all your pals would like to, wouldn't they?

Ben: Yes, they all would.

Piaget: Then why would it be cheating?

Ben: Because I invented it: it isn't a rule! It's a wrong rule because it's outside of the rules. A fair rule is one that is in the game. (1932/1965, p. 63)

Most children begin to treat the rules of games with less awe sometime between the ages of 9 and 11, according to Piaget. They realize that game rules are social conventions resulting from mutual consent. The rules must be respected if you want to play together, "but it is permissible to alter the rules as long as general opinion is on your side" (1932/1965, p. 28).

In Geneva marbles was played almost exclusively by boys. Piaget wanted to show that the developmental progression he had encountered was universal, but he reported that he could not find any collective games played by girls that used as many rules and had as many fine-grained codifications as marbles. After observing many girls playing hopscotch, he remarked that girls seemed more interested in inventing new configurations of hopscotch squares than in elaborating the rules.

Piaget's observation that boys and girls not only play different games but play games differently has generated a good deal of subsequent research. When José Linaza (1984) observed English and Spanish boys and girls playing marbles, he found that though the boys might play marbles more often and more skillfully than girls, there were no marked sex differences in the children's understanding of the rules of the game. Janet Lever (1978), however, confirmed Piaget's finding that rules enter into the play of boys and girls differently (see Box 14.2). Overall, though, the research suggests that, despite some observed sex differences, middle childhood is a time when play based on explicit rules begins to assume prominence in the interactions of children of both sexes (Thorne, 1994).

Rules of Behavior

As the evidence concerning changes in children's games indicates, the transition to middle childhood is accompanied by an increased understanding of social rules and an increased ability to use such rules to guide behavior. Three major categories of social rules can be distinguished from one another in several ways. Particularly significant are the differences in the seriousness of the consequences if the rule is broken and the extent to which they apply to everyone alike, or only to members of specific social groups (Turiel, Killen, & Helwig, 1987) (see

BOX 14.2

Boys' Games, Girls' Games

Piaget's observation that during middle childhood boys are more likely than girls to engage in competitive games based on explicit rules was corroborated many years later by Janet Lever (1978). Lever observed children in the United States on playgrounds, interviewed them, and had them keep diaries of their after-school play. She then rated the children's play according to its complexity. She defined as complex those games that require each player to take a different role (such as baseball); that require a relatively large number of participants; that require players to compete for an explicit goal, such as scoring a goal in soccer or checkmating an opponent; that have a number of specified rules that are known by all the players before the game begins and whose violations are penalized; and that require teams.

According to Lever's data (see the accompanying table), both boys and girls engage in a wide variety of play activities, including complex games. But on the average, girls play less complex games with fewer participants than boys do. Boys are almost twice as likely as girls to engage in competitive games, even when they are not playing team sports. Girls tend to play cooperatively. When their games allow competition, as jump-rope and jacks do, it is indirect: each player acts independently, competing by turn against the others' scores, rather than in face-to-face confrontations, as boys do.

Not only are boys' games different from girls'; their play groups tend to be larger. Team sports, which they are more likely to engage in than girls, require from 10 to 25 participants to be played properly. Lever rarely observed girls playing in groups as large as 10; they favored such games as hopscotch and tag, which can be played with as few as two people and seldom include more than six. Some girls talked more than they played.

Lever conjectures that such differences provide girls and boys with markedly different sets of socialization experiences and social skills. Boys' games, she contends, provide them with the opportunity to deal with diversity, to coordinate with a large number of people, to cope with impersonal rule systems, and to work for

collective as well as personal goals. In particular, participation in team sports furnishes boys with the opportunity to be rewarded for improving their skills, to gain experience in leadership positions, and to deal with competition in a depersonalized fashion, as well as to maintain self-control.

Although systematic research is scanty, it is likely that girls gain the opportunity to learn these same skills through their participation in such activities as Girl Scouts, school governance, school plays, and informal clubs that they themselves create. In addition, there has been a marked increase in girls' participation in team sports.

Percent of Time Girls and Boys Were Observed Playing Games of Various Degrees of Complexity

	Girls	Boys
Complexity score 0 Roller skating, bike riding, listening to records	42%	27%
Complexity score 1 Singing, playing catch, bowling, racing electric cars	7	12
Complexity score 2 Indoor fantasy, jump-rope, tag, simple card games	31	15
Complexity score 3 Board games, checkers	8	15
Complexity score 4 Capture the flag	2	1
Complexity score 5 Team sports	10	30

Source: Lever, 1978.

TABLE 14.1 Sample Event Types and Infractions in the Domains of Moral Rules, Social Conventions, and Personal Rules

Sample Event Types	Sample Infractions
MORAL RULES	
Physical harm	Hitting, pushing, killing
Psychological harm	Hurting feelings, ridiculing
Fairness and rights	Stealing, breaking a promise
Prosocial behaviors	Never donating to charity, refusing help to someone in distress
SOCIAL CONVENTIONS	
School rules	Chewing gum in class, talking back to the teacher
Forms of address	Calling a physician "Mr." when he is working
Attire and appearance	Wearing pajamas to school
Sex roles	Boy wears barrette to keep hair out of eyes while playing football
Etiquette	Swearing, making loud noises while eating
PERSONAL RULES	
Hygiene	Not brushing teeth, forgetting to change sheets
Social	Neglecting to call parents, forgetting best friend's birthday
Financial	Overdrawing account at bank

Source: After Turiel, Killen, & Helwig, 1987.

Table 14.1). At the most general level are **moral rules,** social regulations based on principles of justice and the welfare of others. One important subset of moral rules applies to transgressions, such as the prohibition against killing another person. A second subset of moral rules applies to issues of fairness, such as the assumption that resources ought to be distributed equitably among people. Moral rules are often believed to derive from a divine source; they are obligations that cannot be transgressed. Such rules are found in some form in all societies (Kurtines & Gewirtz, 1991).

At the next level of generality are **social conventions**—rules that are particular to a given society, such as prescriptions about the kinds of behavior that are appropriate for males and females or the kind of clothes people should wear in public, as well as rules about who has authority over other people, how authority is exercised, and how it is acknowledged (Wainryb & Turiel, 1994). **Group norms,** a more restricted kind of social convention, apply to small groups such as peer groups. They include special modes of greeting (such as secret handshakes) and styles of dress. Social conventions coordinate the behavior of individuals within a social system, but vary from society to society and from group to group.

At the most specific level are **personal rules** governing particular events, such as "Do homework before watching TV" and "Brush teeth before going to bed every night." Personal rules are often created by individuals to regulate their own behavior.

North American children as young as 3 or 4 years can distinguish moral rules from social conventions. They respond quite differently to a rule violation such as

Moral rules Obligatory social regulations based on principles of justice and welfare.

Social conventions Rules that are specific to a given society.

Group norms Rules that apply to particular groups, such as peer groups or professional groups.

Personal rules Rules created by individuals to regulate their own behavior.

hitting another child or taking a favorite toy than to making noise during "quiet time" or standing up while eating (Nucci & Killen, 1991). By the time they reach middle childhood they can also make explicit judgments about the importance of different kinds of rules. To demonstrate this ability, Larry Nucci presented cartoon strips depicting violations of moral, conventional, and personal rules to children and adolescents (see Figure 14.1). Asked to judge the seriousness of each incident, subjects of all ages ranked moral violations the most serious; then came violations of social convention and finally violations of personal rules.

Understanding of social rules continues to develop throughout childhood. A major research goal is to determine the extent to which development within one rule domain is related to development within others, and to grasp how children's understanding of rules relates to their behavior in everyday life.

THOU SHALT NOT: REASONING ABOUT MORAL TRANSGRESSIONS

As we described briefly in Chapter 10 (p. 400), preschoolers believe that social rules are imposed by adults, so an act is bad in their view if it breaks the rules that adults formulate. Piaget referred to this kind of moral reasoning, in which morality is imposed from the outside, as the *morality of constraint*. According to his theory, when children later begin to understand that the rules of games can be changed if everyone agrees, children begin to base their judgments of good and bad behavior on *autonomous moral reasoning* instead. The key feature of autonomous moral reasoning is the belief that people have different points of view about social rules, so each person must arrive at his or her own conclusions concerning right and wrong and be prepared to test those views against the views of others (Piaget, 1932/1965). For Piaget, a core feature of autonomous moral reasoning is that it adopts a new standard of fairness, *reciprocity:* what applies to the others playing the game applies to oneself as well. One cannot double-jump in checkers if one's opponent cannot, for example. He believed that autonomous moral reasoning is achieved by approximately the age of 10.

Psychologists accept the general outline of Piaget's description of moral reasoning, along with his view that there is an intimate linkage between moral reasoning and other forms of cognitive action. However, as can be anticipated from our discussions of his ideas about cognitive development, it now appears that he underestimated young children's submission to adult authority as the sole source of morality (Asendorpf & Nunner-Winkler, 1992; Laupa, 1994). Moreover, a number of theorists have attempted to provide a more detailed analysis of how moral reasoning changes over the course of middle childhood (Hoffman, 1988).

The most influential attempt to build on Piaget's approach to moral development was carried out by Lawrence Kohlberg. In place of two stages during early and middle childhood, Kohlberg found evidence for three. He also extended his own stage theory of moral reasoning into adolescence and adulthood (Colby & Kohlberg, 1987; Kohlberg, 1969, 1976, 1984). We will focus here on the application of Kohlberg's ideas to middle childhood and postpone an overall evaluation of his approach until the discussion of adolescent development in Chapter 16. (Table 14.2 summarizes the first three stages according to Kohlberg's theory.)

Kohlberg's approach to moral reasoning was to create a series of story dilemmas, each of which embodies a traditional question of moral philosophy: the value of human life and property, people's obligations to each other, the meaning of laws and rules. The story dilemmas pose these abstract issues in a concrete, dramatic way to engage the subjects' interest.

In the manner of Piaget's clinical interview technique, Kohlberg would read the story, ask the child's opinion, and then probe the child's reasoning behind that opinion. Kohlberg's most famous story is the "Heinz dilemma":

(a) Kathy is playing with her doll.

Meg comes over and takes Kathy's doll away from her.

Kathy is upset. Meg is not supposed to take things away from other children.

(b) Karen is watching her very favorite TV program, "The Mickey Mouse Club."

Her big sister tells her, "Karen, you're not allowed to stay inside on sunny days. Mom says you have to go outside and play."

"Those are the rules."

(c) Larry is eating lunch in the school cafeteria. He is eating with his fingers.

Laura tells Larry, "You shouldn't eat meat with your fingers."

"You should use a knife and fork when you're eating in the cafeteria."

FIGURE 14.1 *Cartoon strips used to evaluate the relative importance that children attach to infractions of* (a) *moral rules,* (b) *personal rules, and* (c) *social conventions.* *(Courtesy of L. Nucci.)*

TABLE 14.2 Kohlberg's Six Moral Stages

Level and Stage	What Is Right	Reasons for Doing Right	Social Perspective
LEVEL I—PRECONVENTIONAL			
Stage 1—Heteronomous morality	• Adherence to rules backed by punishment. • Obedience for its own sake • Avoidance of physical damage to persons and property.	• Avoidance of punishment. • Superior power of authorities.	Egocentric point of view: Doesn't consider the interests of others or recognize that they differ from one's own; doesn't relate two points of view. Actions are considered in physical terms rather than in terms of psychological interests of others. Confusion of authority's perspective with one's own.
Stage 2— Instrumental morality	• Following rules only when it is to one's immediate interest. • Acting to meet one's own interests and needs and letting others do the same. • Seeing fairness as an equal exchange.	• To serve one's own needs or interests in a world where other people have their own interests.	Concrete individualistic perspective: Aware that all people have their own interests to pursue and these interests conflict, so that right is relative.
LEVEL II—CONVENTIONAL			
Stage 3— Good-child morality	• Living up to what is expected by people close to you. • Having good motives, and showing concern about others. • Keeping mutual relationships by such means as trust, loyalty, respect, and gratitude.	• The need to be a good person in one's own eyes and those of others. • Caring for others. • Belief in the Golden Rule. • Desire to maintain rules and authority that support stereotypical good behavior.	Perspective of an individual in relationships with other individuals: Aware of shared feelings, agreements, and expectations. Ability to relate points of view through the Golden Rule.
Stage 4—Law-and-order morality	• Upholding the law.	• To keep the institution going as a whole.	Perspective of an individual in relation to the social group.
LEVEL III—POSTCONVENTIONAL, OR PRINCIPLED			
Stage 5—Social-contract reasoning	• Being aware that people hold a variety of values and opinions.	• A sense of obligation to law because of one's social contract to act for the welfare of the group.	Prior-to-society perspective: Perspective of a rational individual aware of others' values and rights.
Stage 6—Universal ethical principles	• Following self-chosen ethical principles.	• A belief in the validity of universal moral principles.	Perspective of a moral point of view from which social arrangements derive.

Source: Adapted from Kohlberg, 1976.

In Europe, a woman was near death from cancer. One drug might save her, a form of radium that a druggist in the same town had recently discovered. The druggist was charging $2,000, ten times what the drug cost him to make. The sick woman's husband, Heinz, went to everyone he knew to borrow the money, but he could get together only about half of what it cost. He told the druggist that his wife was dying and asked him to sell it cheaper or let him pay later. But the druggist said no. The husband got desperate and broke into the man's store to steal the drug for his wife. Should the husband have done that? Why? (Kohlberg, 1969, p. 379)

Stage 1 in Kohlberg's theory coincides with the end of the preschool period and the beginning of middle childhood. Children at stage 1 adopt an *egocentric* point of view; they do not recognize the interests of others as distinct from their own. Moreover, their judgments about the rightness and wrongness of an action are based on its objective outcome, which in this case is how authorities would respond to it. Stage 1 children might assert that Heinz must not steal the medicine because he will be put in jail.

At stage 2, which ordinarily appears around 7 to 8 years, children continue to adopt a concrete, self-interested (egocentric) perspective but can recognize that other people have other perspectives. Justice is seen as an exchange system: you give as much as you receive. Kohlberg referred to the moral reasoning of children at this stage as **instrumental morality** because they believe it is perfectly acceptable to use others for their own interests. Children at this stage might respond to the Heinz dilemma by saying that Heinz should steal the drug because someday he might have cancer and would want someone to steal it for him.

At stage 3, which children begin to achieve around the age of 10 or 11, moral judgments are made on the basis of a **social-relational moral perspective.** At this stage, children see shared feelings and agreements, especially with people close to them, as more important than individual self-interest. One child quoted by Kohlberg said, "If I was Heinz, I would have stolen the drug for my wife. You can't put a price on love, no amount of gifts make love. You can't put a price on life either" (1984, p. 629).

Stage 3 is often equated with the kind of moral reasoning associated with the Golden Rule. In Jewish tradition, this precept is attributed to Rabbi Hillel, who lived in the decades just before the birth of Christ. Rabbi Hillel phrased this injunction as "Do not unto others what you would not have them do unto you." This same idea was expressed in positive form in the Sermon on the Mount, when Jesus exhorted his followers to "do unto others as you would have them do unto you" (Matt. 7:12).

Though stage 3 is undoubtedly a more humane way of thinking about morality than either stage 1 or 2, stage 2 is the key transition associated with the new ability to get along without adult supervision that appears during middle childhood. No longer do children depend on a strong external source to define right and wrong; instead, reciprocal relations between group members regulate behavior. Adults may not find the resulting behaviors desirable ("I won't tell your mom you went to see that R-rated movie if you won't tell mine"), but at least this form of thinking allows children to regulate their actions with each other.

THOU SHALT: REASONING ABOUT RULES OF FAIRNESS

Instead of examining situations that might lead to the breaking of rules, William Damon (1975, 1977, 1980) investigated children's conceptions of **positive justice:** how to divide resources or distribute rewards. In order to study age-related changes in forms of reasoning, Damon, too, adopted the popular technique of telling a story and then posing a series of questions. One of his stories went like this:

Instrumental morality Moral reasoning in which justice is seen as an exchange system; you give as much as you receive.

Social-relational moral perspective Moral judgments based on the belief that shared feelings and agreements, especially between people who are close, are more important than individual, self-interest.

Positive justice The process of reaching a decision about how to divide resources or distribute rewards fairly.

A classroom of children spent a day drawing pictures. Some children made a lot of drawings; some made fewer. Some children drew well; others did not draw as well. Some children were well-behaved and worked hard; others fooled around. Some children were poor, some were boys, some were girls, and so on. The class then sold the drawings at a school bazaar. How should the proceeds from the sale of the drawings be fairly distributed? (Adapted from Damon, 1975)

Damon probed the answers that children 4 to 12 years old gave to such questions, challenged them, and followed up with additional questions to determine the reasoning behind them. He found that children's conceptions of positive justice, like the moral judgments studied by Kohlberg, develop through a sequence of levels as children grow older (see Table 14.3). Although his initial studies were

TABLE 14.3   Levels of Reasoning about Positive Justice

LEVEL 0-A (AGE 4 AND UNDER)

Positive-justice choices derive from wish that an act occur. Reasons simply assert the wishes rather than attempting to justify them ("I should get it because I want to have it").

LEVEL 0-B (AGES 4 TO 5)

Choices still reflect desires but are now justified on the basis of external, observable realities such as size, sex, or other physical characteristics of persons (e.g., "We should get the most because we're girls"). Such justifications, however, are invoked in a fluctuating, after-the-fact manner and are self-serving in the end.

LEVEL 1-A (AGES 5 TO 7)

Positive-justice choices derive from notions of strict equality in actions (i.e., that everyone should get the same). Equality is seen as preventing complaining, fighting, "fussing," or other types of conflict.

LEVEL 1-B (AGES 6 TO 9)

Positive-justice choices derive from a notion of reciprocity in actions: that persons should be paid back in kind for doing good or bad things. Notions of merit and deserving emerge.

LEVEL 2-A (AGES 8 TO 10)

A moral relativity develops out of the understanding that different persons can have different yet equally valid justifications for their claims to justice. The claims of persons with special needs (e.g., the poor) are weighed heavily. Choices are attempts to reconcile competing claims.

LEVEL 2-B (AGES 10 AND UP)

Considerations of equality and reciprocity are coordinated so that choices take account of more than one person's claims and the demands of the specific situation. Choices are firm and clear-cut, yet justifications reflect the recognition that all persons should be given their due (though, in many situations, this does not mean equal treatment).

Source: Damon, 1980.

in the United States, Damon (1983) reported that this same sequence is found in Israel, Puerto Rico, and parts of Europe.

Before the age of 4, children do not give objective reasons for their choices; they simply state their wants. Most 4- and 5-year-olds still focus primarily on gratifying themselves, but now they begin to justify their decisions with appeals to such arbitrary characteristics as size and sex: "The biggest should get the most"; "We should all get some because we're girls."

Between the ages of 5 and 7, children begin to believe that all participants have a claim to the rewards. They usually assert that the way to resolve conflict is to give everyone an equal share. Their arguments recognize no mitigating circumstances; the only fair treatment is equal treatment.

From approximately the age of 8 onward, children begin to believe that some individuals within the group may have a legitimate claim to more than an equal share of the group's rewards if they contributed more to the group's work or if they are handicapped in some way, as by poverty or by a physical disability. However, it is still difficult for 8-year-olds to balance all of the competing considerations to produce a fair outcome. Changes after the age of 8 reflect children's increased sophistication at logically weighing all of the relevant factors (McGillicuddy-De Lisi, Watkins, & Vinchur, 1994).

The ability of children to take particular circumstances into consideration when they make decisions about fairness was tackled in a somewhat different way by Theresa Thorkildsen (1989). Instead of focusing on the distribution of rewards for contributions to an unusual group effort, she posed questions about the fairness involved in familiar events that the children encountered routinely in school.

Thorkildsen began from the observation that adults' judgments about fairness depend on the context of the actions being judged. She sought to determine if children's judgments of fairness depend on context in the same way. She told the children, who ranged in age from 6 to 11, about a classroom where everyone is trying hard to learn how to read, but some children finish the assignments more quickly than others. She then asked the children if it is fair for those who already read well to help those who are slower in each of three situations:

1. Is it fair for the teacher to ask the fast readers to help the slow readers during a reading lesson?
2. Is it fair for the good readers to help the slow readers by whispering answers during a spelling bee?
3. Is it fair for the good readers to help the slow readers during a test?

Children's judgments depended on the activity being described (see Figure 14.2). They thought it was fair to have a reading lesson in which children were told to work independently or to help each other, but it would be unfair to make the lesson competitive. If the activity was a spelling bee, they thought it was unfair to help. If the activity was a test, independent work was seen as the only fair alternative.

Thorkildsen found no substantial differences between the younger and older children. These results indicate that even 6-year-olds take the social context of an action into account when they judge fairness in circumstances with which they are very familiar.

FROM REASONING TO ACTING

Thus far the studies of moral reasoning we have discussed have been restricted to hypothetical situations. This restriction naturally raises the question of how children's abstract reasoning about moral issues is related to their actions in a

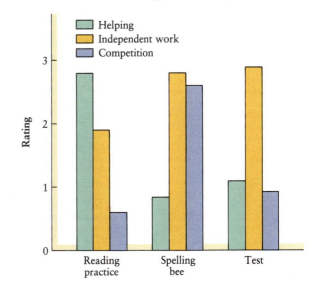

FIGURE 14.2 *Children 6 to 11 years old were asked to rate the fairness of helping, competition, and independent work in three different school activities: reading practice, a spelling bee, and a test. A rating of 0 indicates unfair; a rating of 3 indicates fair.*

TABLE 14.4 — Excerpts from Damon's Transcripts Comparing 6- and 10-Year-Olds' Reasoning about and Practice of Positive Justice

Three 6-Year-Olds: Jay, Juan, and Susan

Experimenter: So what Jay said is he put them out, three for him and three for Juan, two for Susan and two for Jennifer *[not present]*. And Susan said that's OK too. That's the way she did it.

Jay: *[to Juan]* You should think that's fair too. You have three, and I have three, and they have two.

Juan: I don't think that's fair.

Jay: Why?

Juan: We shouldn't give the boys more than the girls. We should break them in half and give the girls two, the boys two, and then . . .

Jay: No. No. No. I said ours were the prettiest, and that's why we get more.

Juan: Wait a second. Whose is this?

Jay: Yours.

Juan: No, it isn't.

Jay: See, we made the prettiest. I say we made the prettiest. Do you think that's a nice one? And you made the nice ones, and we made the prettiest. I think that's fair because we made the prettiest. . . .

E: What do you think, Susan? Didn't you at one point say you thought we should split them in half?

Susan: That's what I said. Now I say . . . *[Susan gives them out—three, three, two, two, as Jay wishes]*

E: What? This way?

Jay: Yeah. Because she thinks that we made the prettiest.

Juan: She got some in her lunch box. Do you have candy? . . .

E: Susan says it's OK. How about Jennifer?

Jay: I think she would say it's OK.

Juan: If she didn't leave, I think it wouldn't be OK. . . .

Jay: Think that would be fair! She would have three, and we would all have three.

E: We don't have eleven, we have ten.

Jay: But she only made one, and it's not pretty.

Juan: It's good. She's only in kindergarten. She would think it's fair, I think. Yeah, she would.

E: What are you guys going to do?

Jay: If you think it's fair, and Susan thinks it's fair, and I think it's fair, she *[Jennifer]* might think it's fair.

E: Well, let's see what Juan thinks. What do you suggest, Juan? What's the best way? What's the best thing to do with the candy bars?

Juan: I think that's *[three, three, two, two]* the best way, if she's only in kindergarten.

Jay: She had two, and we have three.

Juan: You made the most.

Jay: You see I had four bracelets.

Juan: I had the second most. Give these two candy bars to her.

Jay: You see, what I was thinking was, Juan and I get three 'cause we, ours are pretty and I made the most. Susan already has one in her lunch box.

Juan: And Jennifer's only in kindergarten.

Jay: She doesn't get more, 'cause she just made one and it's not pretty.

E: Do you agree, Susan?

Susan: OK.

real-life situation. How, for example, would children actually divide up the rewards if some had done more of the work than others? Would their actions fit their words?

To answer this question, Damon arranged for 144 children to be divided into groups of four. Each group was asked to make bracelets and at the end of the session he gave them ten candy bars to divide among themselves as payment for their work. Then he recorded what they did and said. As Table 14.4 indicates, the children's reasoning about fairness varied markedly depending on their age. In accord with other studies of reasoning about positive justice, the 6-year-olds insisted that fairness means equal outcomes, whereas the older children were better able to adjust the outcome to fit the profile of abilities and contributions in the group.

Damon compared the hypothetical reasoning of children with their actual behavior in this real situation. In half of the cases, the children's behavior matched their reasoning. About 10 percent of the children actually exhibited more advanced reasoning in the face of a real task, while almost 40 percent scored lower in reality than in their reasoning. It seems that when these children were faced with real candy bars, many of them gave in to temptation and claimed more than they would consider their due if they followed the reasoning they displayed in the hypothetical situation.

Three 10-Year-Olds: Craig, Norman, and Bonnie

E: . . . What do you think is the best way to give it out?

Craig: Would Dennis *[the younger child]* get some?

E: If you think so.

Norman: He has to be here too.

E: Well, you all decide among you.

Bonnie: I was thinking, we could give out one a bracelet, because Dennis did one and we all did three. Or give two and a half to everybody. That way everybody gets the same thing.

Craig: Maybe he *[Dennis]* should get one and we get three.

Norman: No. It ain't fair.

Bonnie: Also, Dennis is younger and he left earlier.

E: Well, what do you think? Is that the best way?

Norman: No.

E: Why not, Norman?

Norman: Because if he were here too, and he's a child too, so he should get even.

Bonnie: Yeah, well, lookit. His was bigger so it would have taken longer. And he used more black, but that made it shorter. But he left earlier, he's younger and, you know, didn't do it neat.

Norman: I know. That's beside the point. That means we don't expect much from him. . . .

Craig: Or give three to her *[Bonnie]*, three for Norman, and three for me, and one for Dennis.

E: And why do you think that is the best way, Craig?

Craig: *[No reply.]*

Norman: You're not putting his *[Dennis's]* mind into your little mind. . . .

Craig: Yes, I am.

Norman: Well, you're not reasoning about him. If we did that he would say *[mimics child's whining voice]* "Come, come, you guys got this and I only got this" and he'd start bawling his brains out.

Bonnie: Well, his isn't that neat or anything.

Norman: I know, but he is younger.

Bonnie: Well, wouldn't you say, supposing that you had a younger dog and an older dog, right? You could teach them both the same tricks. And if you had a box of dog bones, you'd give them a bone for every trick. Supposing the little one or even the big one just wanted the dog bones and he wouldn't do any tricks. You wouldn't give him one for that.

Norman: I know, but he did something. It's not like he didn't do anything. Least he did one. You're getting on the point like he didn't do anything.

Bonnie: No, I know he did something. He did the best he could.

Norman: Yeah, so he should get as much as we do.

Source: Damon, 1977.

Similar results have been obtained by other researchers who used similar tasks (Subbotsky, 1993). This slippage between moral reasoning and moral action is captured by the traditional parental advice to "do as I say, not as I do."

REASONING ABOUT SOCIAL CONVENTIONS

On the basis of evidence that by the time North American children are 4 or 5 years old they respond differently to moral rules and social conventions, Elliot Turiel and his colleagues concluded that moral reasoning and reasoning about social conventions are independent domains (Turiel, 1983; Turiel & Wainryb, 1994). In a series of studies, he and his colleagues provided evidence that social conventions are judged according to their own criteria and undergo their own sequence of developmental transformations (Tisak & Turiel, 1988; Turiel, 1983; Turiel, Killen, & Helwig, 1987).

Turiel's method, like that of other researchers who have probed children's reasoning about social rules, was to tell brief stories and then interview the children to investigate their reasoning about the stories. One story was about a young boy who wants to become a nurse and care for infants when he grows up, but his father doesn't want him to.

The following interview, based on the nurse story, illustrates the earliest stage of reasoning about social conventions. The child seems to believe that conventions reflect the natural order of things. To violate the convention would be to behave unnaturally.

> Joan (6 years, 5 months): (Should he become a nurse?) *Well, no, because he could easily be a doctor and he could take care of babies in the hospital.* (Why shouldn't he be a nurse?) *Well, because a nurse is a lady and the boys, the other men would just laugh at them.* (Why shouldn't a man be a nurse?) *Well, because it would sort of be silly because ladies wear those kind of dresses and those kind of shoes and hats. . . .* (Do you think his father was right?) *Yes, because, well, a nurse, she typewrites and stuff and all that.* (The man should not do that?) *No, because he would look silly in a dress.* (Turiel, 1978, pp. 62–63)

At the second level of reasoning about social conventions, evident around the age of 8 or 9, children realize that just because most doctors are men and most nurses are women, the empirical association of activities, roles, and modes of dress does not mean that other combinations are impossible. At this level, children reject the need for social conventions, believing that they play no useful role in society. They are even sophisticated enough to realize that traditional social conventions may mislead people:

> Emily (8 years, 11 months): (Why do you think his parents see that job as for women only?) *Being a nurse—because not many men are nurses so they get used to the routine. I know a lot of ladies who are doctors, but I don't know a man who is a nurse, but it is okay if they want to.* (Turiel, 1978, p. 64)

At level 3, children display a dawning awareness that social conventions, arbitrary though they are, have a legitimate role in the regulation of social life. Eventually, sometime in early adulthood, they come to view social conventions as a positive force because they facilitate the coordination of social interactions, which is essential to the functioning of any social group.

A current source of controversy among the developmental psychologists who study reasoning about social rules is whether children around the world think about moral rules and social conventions in the same way North American children do. Using culturally appropriate versions of Turiel's stories, some researchers have replicated his basic findings in a wide variety of societies (Nucci, Turiel, & Encarnacion-Gawrych, 1983; Song, Smetana, & Kim, 1987). Others, using somewhat different techniques to elicit judgments, have found that people in at least some cultures are more likely than North Americans to consider breaches of social convention to be moral issues (Shweder, Mahapatra, & Miller, 1987). The issue of cultural variations in the development of reasoning about noral rules and social conventions is discussed at some length in Chapter 16.

Relations with Other Children

Once children begin to spend significant amounts of time among their peers, they must learn to create a special place for themselves within the social group. Their greater appreciation of social rules and their increased ability to consider other people's points of view are essential resources for this new task. But no matter how sensitive or sophisticated they may be about social relations, there is no guarantee they will be accepted by their peers. In seeking friends, all children must come to terms with the possibility that they may not be liked, learn to compete for social status, and deal with the conflicts that inevitably arise.

FRIENDSHIP

Friendship is generally described as a relationship characterized by affection, reciprocity, and commitment between people who see themselves more or less as equals (Hartup, 1992). Willard Hartup identifies four developmental functions of friendships:

1. They are contexts in which children develop such basic social skills as communication, cooperation, and the ability to enter an already formed group.
2. They provide children with information about themselves, others, and the world.
3. They provide fun and help relieve the stress of everyday life.
4. They provide models of intimate relationships that will become important in later life.

Factors that influence the formation of friendships

Before you can become friends with someone, the two of you have to spend some time together, so it is no surprise that one of the major determinants of friendship between children is *proximity* (Epstein, 1989). But proximity cannot be the full story, because most children are in the company of other children several hours every day and become friends with only a few of them.

Children tend to pick friends who are *similar* to them in a variety of ways (Rubin et al., 1994). Friendships are most common among children who are of the same age, the same race, the same sex, and the same general skill level in various activities. Friends are also likely to feel the same way about school (a child who likes school and gets good grades is likely to have a friend who also likes school and gets good grades) and to like the same sports, music, movies, books, and so on.

Occasionally, though, children of different sexes, ages, and races become friends. Such cross-category friendships may arise when family friends get together, when there is a large project such as a school play to be put on, or when the children are simply "playing on the block"; that is, playing with the children who live closest to them (Ellis, Rogoff, & Cromer, 1981).

Being with friends is one of life's special pleasures.

John Gottman (1983) provides a detailed description of the process of becoming friends. Gottman arranged for pairs of children of the same age to meet and play together in one of the children's homes for three sessions within the space of a month. The children, who were strangers to each other at the start of the study, ranged from 3 to 9 years in age. In order to find out if the children became friends during the experiment, Gottman asked the mothers to fill out a questionnaire that probed the strength and quality of the children's relationship.

To determine how children make friends, Gottman tape-recorded each play session and analyzed the tapes, comparing children who became friends with those who did not. Five aspects of the children's social interaction appeared to distinguish pairs who became friendly from those who did not:

1. *Common-ground activity* The children who became friends were those who quickly found something they could do together. In addition, they explored their similarities and differences.

2. *Clear communication* Children who became friends were less likely to engage in what Piaget referred to as "collective monologues" (see Chapter 8, p. 329). They listened to each other, requested clarification when they did not understand, and spoke in ways that were relevant to the task at hand.

3. *Exchange of information* Children who became friends both asked for and provided information relevant to their partners.

4. *Resolution of conflicts* Children who became friends gave good reasons when they disagreed and were able to bring conflicts to a quick resolution.

5. *Reciprocity* Children who became friends were likely to respond to their partner's positive behaviors with an appropriate positive contribution of their own. A comparison of videotapes of pairs of sixth-grade friends and acquaintances found that during interactions friends were more attentive, emotionally positive, vocal, active, involved, relaxed, and playful with each other. They were also more likely to share the same mood than acquaintances (Field et al., 1992).

Children all over the world must learn how to sustain intimate and mutually supportive relationships with their peers. But in a great many societies, the children who become friends are not strangers who happen to have been placed in the same class at school or to be in the same car pool. Instead, friendships are formed between children who are part of the same family or kinship group. In these circumstances, children must understand where they and their friends belong in the network of kin, alliances, and feuds that make up their social world. They must also be able to incorporate their friends into their sibling group. In addition to playing with each other and gossiping together, the way friends in societies like our own do, children in less technological, village-based societies are likely to do their assigned tasks with their friends and to help one another with their work (Weisner, 1984).

Researchers have yet to collect detailed data about the psychological processes involved in friendships in such societies. Nevertheless, the general differences we have just described should be kept in mind as we explore friendships among children in industrially advanced countries.

What do friends do together?

In early childhood the focus of friendship is *pretend play*. Young children's descriptions of their actual friendships and of their beliefs about friendship in general reveal that they clearly place a premium on other children's potentials as playmates (Berndt, 1986). A good playmate is someone with whom the child can achieve a high level of coordination, leading to more fun, more solidarity, and more humor.

Belonging and social acceptance are the major themes of friendship in middle childhood. At this point in their lives children recognize that their agemates have different statuses and that play groups are hierarchically organized into leaders and followers. Children's awakened sensitivity to their relative status among their peers leads them to be particularly concerned about the possibility that they will be rejected or have their feelings hurt (Parker & Gottman, 1989).

As a result, according to Jeffrey Parker and John Gottman, gossip becomes "the mortar as well as much of the brick of friendship conversation during middle childhood" (1989, p. 114). It is through gossip that children now carry out the basic social reciprocities and information exchanges that are central to friendship. When a clear cultural norm is at issue (such as the norms that regulate sharing, aggression, and lying), gossip reaffirms the norm, as can be seen in a conversation between Erica and Mikaila as they gossip about Katie's bossiness:

M: She's mean. She beat me up once *[laughs]*. I could hardly breathe, she hit me in the stomach so hard.

E: She acts like . . .

M: She's the boss.

E: "Now do this." *[mimicking Katie]*

M: "And I'll . . . "

E: "And Erica, you do this. And you substitute for people who aren't here, Erica."

M: "And you do this, Mikaila. And you shouldn't do that, you shouldn't, you have to talk like this. You understand? Here. I'm the teacher here."

E: I know. She always acts like she's the boss. (Parker & Gottman, 1989, p. 114)

When a topic comes up that is not covered by a clear cultural norm, gossip allows children to find out what their friends think so that they can tailor their behavior accordingly.

Of course, childhood friends do more than just gossip. As they move toward adolescence, they increasingly exchange intimate personal knowledge. They are also more generous, cooperative, and helpful with each other. Perhaps because friends spend more time together, they also tend to quarrel more than children who are not friends. They are more likely than children who are not friends to negotiate their disagreements and to disengage, rather than to stand firm, however. They are also more likely to explain their positions; in addition, they criticize each other more (Rubin & Coplan, 1992).

Friends also compete with each other, go to school together, and hang out after school engaging in all those forms of "doing nothing" that Robert Paul Smith describes in the epigraph to this chapter.

Boys and girls as friends

During middle childhood, children of all cultures spend a great deal of time in sexually segregated groups. In nonindustrialized societies, sexual segregation may stem from the kinds of chores that children are assigned by adults. The girls help their mothers around the village by fetching water, doing the wash, sweeping, and helping to prepare food, while the boys watch the herds, hunt, and fish (Harkness & Super, 1985; Weisner, 1984; Whiting & Edwards, 1988). In industrialized societies, children's tendency to gather in same-sex groups appears to depend more on their preferences for different kinds of activities and styles of interaction. Studies that ask children to nominate a "best friend" have found that at 6 years of age roughly 68 percent choose a child of the same sex; and by the age of 12 this figure has grown to about 90 percent (Daniels-Beirness, 1989).

BOX 14.3

Border Work: Contact between the Sexes

When our son, Sasha, was 8 years old, we assigned him the task of looking after 6-year-old Tiana on the city bus that the two of them took to school. Tiana is the daughter of our closest friends and Sasha had known her from infancy. They shared a babysitter and over the years they spent countless hours playing together. They chatted, argued, and even played tag as they walked crosstown with Mike to catch the uptown bus. But once on the bus, they acted as if they didn't know each other. They never sat together or even spoke. When Mike found out about this, he asked them why. Tiana likes to sit up front and Sasha likes to sit way in the back: that was all the explanation he received.

Sasha and Tiana were displaying a kind of social behavior that is part of the code of behavior for school-aged children—they were maintaining the boundaries between the sexes (Thorne, 1993). They were by no means extreme in the way they did this. In fact, they were rather discrete in comparison with most of their peers.

When Courtney Cazden and Sarah Michaels (1985) introduced a computer mail system into a second-grade classroom in Boston as part of a study designed to promote children's writing, they found that throughout the 6-month study not one child wrote to a child of the opposite sex. Other researchers report that children become less willing to help children of the opposite sex in school during middle childhood (Nelson–Le Gall & De Cooke, 1987).

These strict gender boundaries are sometimes broken in interesting ways. Often contact between the two sexes occurs in the form of "raids" into enemy terri-

tory. From time to time, the boys will run through an area where the girls are playing and try to get the girls to chase them, or a couple of girls, shrieking with laughter, will threaten to kiss a boy. Calling a boy on the telephone and leaving a pseudo-romantic message on the family answering machine is another favorite border-crossing technique. These raids are accompanied by a lot of excitement.

When gender boundaries are crossed, children often behave as though they feel contaminated just by being near a member of the opposite sex and they engage in elaborate "cleansing rituals" to get rid of the "girl cooties" or the "boy germs."

Alan Sroufe and his colleagues (1993) report that a boy seen leaving the girls' tent at day camp (where he went to get his radio) was taunted, "Uuh, he's with the girls!"; "Did you kiss anyone, Charlie?" He had to chase and hit each boy in turn to reestablish his place in the group.

From their own and others' observations of children, Sroufe and his co-workers abstracted a number of rules under which school-aged children find it permissible to have contact with members of the opposite sex (see table). They then analyzed videotaped samples of the interactions between 47 9½- to 11½-year-old boys and girls at a day camp, looking for violations of those rules. The researchers noted who each child's friends were, had the children rated for social skill by their counselors, and interviewed each child about the popularity of others in the group.

The researchers found that most children maintained the boundaries between the sexes. The children who violated the gender boundaries were generally un-

Sex segregation is by no means total during middle childhood (Hartup, 1992; Whiting, 1986). Pamela Reynolds (1989), who observed children in a South African shantytown, estimated that boys and girls played together about 25 percent of the time. Sara Harkness and Charles Super (1985) report that in a Kipsigis village in Kenya, children's companions were often their kin from nearby homesteads and likely to vary in age and sex.

In many industrialized societies, boys and girls meet ritually in schoolyards and parks and on neighborhood streets. Some of these meetings have the qualities of a foray into enemy territory. Others, such as chase-and-kiss games and teasing, have sexual overtones. But there are also occasions when the two sexes naturally merge in joint activities (Adler et al., 1992; Thorne, 1994) (see Box 14.3).

Boys' and girls' experiences with peers often differ considerably, as we have already seen in the kinds of games they play. Observational studies of children on

popular with the other children. They were also judged by their counselors to be less socially competent than their peers.

According to Barrie Thorne and Zella Luria (1986), who refer to this kind of behavior as "border work," brief cross-gender encounters are a rehearsal for adult romantic relationships. Cross-cultural researchers seem to agree. When Brian Sutton-Smith and John Roberts (1973) examined ethnographic reports of border work in various societies to see who chased whom, they discovered that in societies where girls marry boys from their own communities, boys and girls chase each other. But in societies where girls marry outside their community, boys do the chasing, the pattern one would expect when the males must go outside their group in pursuit of a wife.

Knowing the Rules: Under What Circumstances Is It Permissible to Have Contact with the Other Gender in Middle Childhood?

Rule:	The contact is accidental.
Example:	You're not looking where you are going and you bump into someone.
Rule:	The contact is incidental.
Example:	You go to get some lemonade and wait while two children of the other gender get some. (There should be no conversation.)
Rule:	The contact is in the guise of some clear and necessary purpose.
Example:	You may say, "Pass the lemonade," to persons of the other gender at the next table. No interest in them is expressed.
Rule:	An adult compels you to have contact.
Example:	"Go get that map from X and Y and bring it to me."
Rule:	You are accompanied by someone of your own gender.
Example:	Two girls may talk to two boys, though physical closeness with your own partner must be maintained and intimacy with the others is disallowed.
Rule:	The interaction or contact is accompanied by disavowal.
Example:	You say someone is ugly or hurl some other insult or (more commonly for boys) push or throw something at them as you pass by.

Source: Sroufe et al., 1991.

playgrounds repeatedly find that girls congregate in groups of two or three, whereas boys move around in "swarms" (Daniels-Beirness, 1989). Girls tend to have fewer friends than boys and to make friends less rapidly (Eder & Hallinan, 1978). They seem to be more sensitive to the boundaries that differentiate close friends from acquaintances, and they are likely to be more reluctant to interact with children who are not their close friends. Girls' friendships are often more intimate than boys'; they are characterized by the sharing of feelings, exchanges of presents and compliments, and lengthy discussions of likes and dislikes, embarrassments and triumphs. Boys are more likely to have larger groups of friends and more friends of different ages. They are also more likely than girls to play physical, boisterous, competitive games with their friends (as we saw earlier) and to interact with one another in places where they are free from direct adult supervision (Beal, 1994).

These children playing during recess demonstrate the kind of sex segregation that appears during middle childhood.

A clear pattern of differences in sex-role socialization emerges from the existing data. Boys appear to be socialized to compete with one another in activities bound by rule systems, whereas girls are socialized for cooperation and interpersonal sensitivity in circumstances in which rules are only implicit. In the United States this pattern may be changing as it becomes more common for women to enter the workplace, where they compete with men. Girls may come to be socialized more for competition than they have been in the past, but if such a change is occurring, it is not yet visible in the social relations among peers during middle childhood.

Friendship and social competence

In Chapter 10 (p. 421) we introduced the concept of socioemotional competence, the ability to understand how others think and feel. The term itself expresses the close interconnection of social and emotional development. Psychologists who study the development of friendship use a similar term, **social competence,** to refer to the set of skills that collectively result in successful social functioning with peers (Howes, 1987). According to Jacqueline Goodnow and Ailsa Burns (1985, p. 134), the most important elements of social competence are these:

Social competence The set of skills that collectively result in successful social functioning.

1. Knowing how to make successful overtures.
2. Learning what is expected at various stages of friendship.
3. Working out which people are unlikely candidates for friendship.
4. Deepening one's relationships with people who are likely to be rewarding friends.
5. Keeping things going in a manner pleasing to both parties.
6. Making sure that each party puts a similar effort into the relationship, without keeping too close a tally.
7. Avoiding the risk of placing too much trust in someone likely to prove fickle.

8. Fighting off challenges from those who want to "steal" one's friends.
9. Avoiding getting stuck with friends one no longer finds appealing.
10. Avoiding a reputation for disloyalty and self-seeking.
11. Avoiding being stranded without friends.
12. Achieving resilience in the face of being dumped.

Becoming skilled at negotiating social interactions with one's peers depends on a child's growing ability to understand how others think (social perspective-taking) and feel (socioemotional competence). To assess developmental changes in the ability to understand others' thoughts and feelings, Robert Selman (1976, 1980) asked children to listen to a brief story and then to answer questions posed in a clinical interview format. Here is one of the stories Selman used:

> Holly is an 8-year-old girl who likes to climb trees. She is the best tree climber in the neighborhood. One day while climbing down from a tall tree she falls off the bottom branch but does not hurt herself. Her father sees her fall. He is upset and asks her to promise not to climb trees any more. Holly promises.
>
> Later that day, Holly and her friends meet Sean. Sean's kitten is caught up in a tree and cannot get down. Something has to be done right away or the kitten may fall. Holly is the only one who climbs trees well enough to reach the kitten and get it down, but she remembers her promise to her father. (1980, p. 36)

When the story was completed, children were asked to make judgments about the feelings and possible actions of the various characters. The comments of two children, one a preschooler, the other in middle childhood, indicate the differences in their understandings of other people's points of view.

A PRESCHOOLER'S UNDERSTANDING

Q: What do you think Holly will do, save the kitten or keep her promise?
A: She will save the kitten because she doesn't want the kitten to die.
Q: How will her father feel when he finds out?
A: Happy, he likes kittens.

A 9-YEAR-OLD'S UNDERSTANDING

Q: What punishment does Holly think is fair if she climbs the tree?
A: None.
Q: Why not?
A: She knows that her father will understand why she climbed the tree so she knows that he won't want to punish her at all. (Selman, 1976, pp. 303, 305)

The preschooler clearly fails to consider that Holly and her father may not have the same point of view. The 9-year-old is aware that each person in the story has a distinct point of view. Moreover, the 9-year-old's answer coordinates the points of view of Holly and her father in a plausible way. Note, however, that the older child still does not systematically take both persons' points of view into account. When children achieve the ability to be systematic about such questions, sometime in adolescence, they will find it difficult to say for certain how Holly's father will react. They will begin to realize that while the father may understand Holly's motive, he may not accept it.

In one set of studies designed to test his theory that the social skills needed for forming friendships depend on the ability to take other people's perspectives, Selman (1980) compared children's social perspective-taking skills (as revealed by their interpretations of stories) with their understanding of friendship (as revealed by structured clinical interviews). He found that children who responded at a high

TABLE 14.5   How Selman Relates Developmental Levels of Perspective-Taking to Developmental Levels of Friendship

Developmental Level in Coordination of Perspectives	Stage of Understanding Reflected in Close Friendships
LEVEL 0 (APPROXIMATELY AGES 3 TO 7)	STAGE 0
Egocentric or undifferentiated perspective. Children do not distinguish their own perspective from that of others. They do not yet recognize that others may interpret the same social experience or course of action differently from the way they do.	*Momentary playmates.* A close friend is someone who lives close by and with whom one is playing.
LEVEL 1 (APPROXIMATELY AGES 4 TO 9)	STAGE 1
Subjective or differentiated perspectives. The child understands that others' perspectives may differ from her own.	*One-way assistance.* A friend does what one wants. A close friend is someone who shares the same dislikes and likes.
LEVEL 2 (APPROXIMATELY AGES 6 TO 12)	STAGE 2
Self-reflective or reciprocal perspective. The child is now able to view his own thoughts and feelings from another's perspective.	*Fair-weather cooperation.* With their new awareness of the reciprocal nature of personal perspectives, children become concerned with coordinating their thoughts and actions, rather than adjusting them to a fixed standard, as they did before. Relationships depend on adjustment and cooperation and fall apart over arguments.
LEVEL 3 (APPROXIMATELY AGES 9 TO 15)	STAGE 3
Third-person or mutual perspective. The child at this level can step outside of an interaction and take the perspective of a third party.	*Intimate and mutually shared relationships.* Friendships are seen as the basic means of developing mutual intimacy and mutual support. At this stage friendship transcends momentary interactions, including conflicts. The primary limitation of this stage is possessiveness and jealousy.
LEVEL 4 (APPROXIMATELY AGES 12 TO ADULTHOOD)	STAGE 4
Societal or in-depth perspective. Children at this level are able to take the generalized perspective of society, the law, or morality.	*Autonomous, interdependent friendships.* This stage is characterized by an awareness of the interdependence of friends for support and a sense of identity and at the same time an acceptance of the other's need to establish relations with other people.

Source: Adapted from Selman, 1981.

level to perspective-taking problems were also likely to have more sophisticated ideas about friendship. Table 14.5, which summarizes Selman's findings, shows that children's reasoning in each domain develops from uncoordinated, individualistic understanding to understanding that coordinates two perspectives, and then to a stage in which individual perspectives are viewed in the context of a more complex system. This sequence fits closely with Piaget's theory that young children's egocentricity restricts them to their own point of view, whereas older children can keep two aspects of a problem in mind at the same time (see Chapter 9, p. 341, and Chapter 12, pp. 487–494).

To see if there was any connection between children's conceptions of friendship and their actual behavior as friends, Selman (1981) undertook research on interpersonal relations at a clinic for emotionally disturbed children. A notable characteristic of such children is that they have difficulty getting along with others and often behave immaturely. Not surprisingly, he found that the children who displayed lower levels of understanding in clinical interviews had difficulties forming and maintaining friendships because they failed to take the other's point of view or understand the reasons for the other's behavior. Some children reasoned at levels significantly higher than normal yet still ended up at the clinic because of interpersonal difficulties with their peers. Many of these children were disliked because they were bossy or hard to understand.

Overall it appears that higher levels of reasoning about interpersonal relationships, including friendships, provide children with **social repair mechanisms,** strategies that allow friends to remain friends even when serious differences temporarily drive them apart. Social repair mechanisms take on importance in middle childhood because of children's changed social circumstances. When no caretaker is present, children must settle conflicts on their own. Examples of social repair mechanisms include disengaging before a disagreement escalates into a fight, staying nearby after a fight, and minimizing the importance of a conflict once it is over. Each of these strategies increases the likelihood that when the conflict is over, the children will still be friends.

In this confluence of changed social circumstances and increased social competence we see that neither the social nor the cognitive characteristics of middle childhood could emerge without the other. They are two facets of a single developmental process.

PEER RELATIONS AND SOCIAL STATUS

Children, like adults, care deeply about how their peers feel about them, but not all members of a group are equally well liked. Whenever a group exists for a while, a social structure emerges in which it is possible to identify a few members whom almost all the others like, others who enjoy less popularity, and some who are actively disliked by most of the group. Developmental psychologists study children's social status with their peers as a means to understand the development of personality in relation to group processes. They are also interested in the influence of children's social status on later developmental outcomes (Dodge & Feldman, 1990; Crick & Dodge, 1994; Parker et al., 1995).

Researchers who study the relative social status of group members usually begin by asking children themselves about whom they like or dislike. Two techniques are widely used for this purpose. Sometimes both techniques are used in the same study as a means of evaluating the validity of the results.

When investigators use the **nomination procedure** they ask members of a group to name the children they would like to sit near, to play with, or to work with, or simply to name their friends in the group. They may also ask the children to name those whom they do not like. Alternatively, researchers may use a **rating scale** and ask children to rank one another according to a specific criterion, such as popularity or their desirability as a friend or teammate in sports.

When the nomination procedure is used, the resulting choices are compiled to create a **sociogram,** a graphic representation of how each child feels about every other child in the group (Asher & Dodge, 1986) (see Figure 14.3). The picture of social relations given by the sociogram and other *sociometric techniques* (measures of social relations) is then used to

Social repair mechanisms Strategies that allow friends to remain friends even when serious differences temporarily drive them apart.

Nomination procedure A method used to determine children's social status in which members of the group are asked who they would like to sit next to or play with, or who their friends are.

Rating scale A procedure in which children are asked to rank one another according to a specific criterion, such as popularity. It is used to determine children's relative social status in a group.

Sociogram The graphic representation of how each child relates to every other child in a group.

FIGURE 14.3 *A sociogram of the relationships among a group of fifth-grade boys and girls. Note that the one boy who has a friendship with a girl is only marginally related to the two groups of boys. The girl in this friendship, by contrast, is part of a group of girls. Two girls and one boy are social isolates, while a pair of boys have chosen each other in isolation from the group. (Adapted from Gronlund, 1959.)*

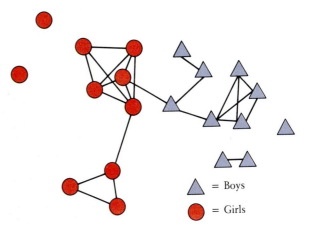

= Boys
= Girls

investigate the relation between children's individual characteristics and their group standing.

Using these techniques, psychologists have identified several categories of children defined by their position in their social group. One of the most influential category systems was constructed by Steven Asher and John Coie (1990):

- *Popular children* are those who receive the most positive nominations or highest ratings from their peers.
- *Rejected children* are those who receive few positive but many negative nominations from their peers. They are actively disliked.
- *Neglected children* are those who receive few nominations of any kind. These children seem to be ignored rather than disliked.
- *Controversial children*, as the label suggests, are those who receive both positive and negative nominations.

The causes and consequences of different social statuses

One of the most pervasive findings of sociometric research on children is that popularity is related to physical attractiveness (Langlois, 1986). In one study, boys were categorized in five subgroups on the basis of their popularity among their peers. Then adult raters who did not know the boys were asked to judge their attractiveness from photographs. In general, the lower the boys' ratings on attractiveness, the lower the popularity standing of their subgroup (Dodge, 1983). Brian Vaughn and Judith Langlois (1983) obtained similar results and found also that attractiveness and popularity are more highly correlated among girls than among

These French children of the 1950s are actively rejecting a peer because of the way he dresses and acts.

boys. Attractive children also appear to benefit from the stereotype that "beauty is good," which assumes that attractive individuals are generally superior even in the absence of any objective evidence (Ritts, Patterson, & Tubbs, 1992). There is more to popularity than good looks, however. Popular children perform better in school and score higher on intelligence tests (Green et al., 1980; Newcomb et al., 1993). They also display high levels of social competence (Sroufe et al., 1993).

The causes of rejection appear to be more complicated. Studies of children rejected by their peers reveal that the most conspicuous cause of rejection is aggression; children quite naturally do not like to be around others who bully them and behave unpleasantly. Rejection is especially likely to occur when aggressiveness is combined with lower levels of sociability and cognitive ability (Newcomb et al., 1993). But aggression is not the whole story; some extremely shy children are also rejected (Bierman et al., 1993).

Rejected children are aware of their social failure and value getting along with others as highly as other children do (Asher et al., 1990). Rejection makes them lonelier than other children, more dissatisfied with their social relations at school, and more distressed about them (Cassidy & Asher, 1992; Crick & Ladd, 1993).

Neglected children, like rejected children, are less sociable than their peers. But they are not as aggressive. A study conducted in Holland found that neglected children are more likely than rejected children to improve their social status among their classmates over the course of the school year (Cillessen et al., 1992). Neglected children also perform better academically than rejected children, are more compliant in school, and are better liked by their teachers (Wentzel & Asher, 1995). Rejected children, on the other hand, are more likely to be absent from school than other children, a circumstance that increases their difficulties (De Rosier, Kupersmidt, & Patterson, 1994).

Controversial children may behave even more aggressively than rejected children. But they compensate for their aggression by using greater social and cognitive skills to get along (Newcomb et al., 1993).

Unlike rejected children, controversial and neglected children tend not to be particularly distressed by their relative lack of social success (Coie & Dodge, 1983). Such children are usually liked by at least one other child. These friendships may be sufficient to prevent loneliness. Children without best friends, no matter how well they are accepted by their classmates, are lonelier than children with best friends (Parker & Asher, 1993).

How children achieve social status in interaction with each other

While the studies described above provide important information about the factors associated with different social statuses, they don't give a clear picture of how different social statuses arise and are maintained. To get a glimpse of the actual processes at work, researchers have brought children together in play groups to observe and videotape them for later analysis (Coie & Kupersmidt, 1983; Dodge, 1983).

Kenneth Dodge, for example, brought together unacquainted fourth-grade boys in play groups that met once a week for eight weeks. He videotaped the boys' interactions and at the end of the eight weeks asked them to name the two boys they liked most and the two they disliked most. To assess the role of attractiveness, ten college students rated photographs of the boys.

At first, of course, no one in these groups could be considered to be more popular than anyone else because the boys did not know one another. But by the end of the eight sessions it was possible to identify popular, neglected, and rejected boys on the basis of peer nominations. The videotapes enabled Dodge to observe the emergence of group structures and the behaviors that led to popularity, neglect, or rejection.

As expected, attractiveness played a role in the boys' preferences. Popular boys were judged to be more attractive than neglected boys, who in turn were judged to be more attractive than rejected boys. The children's behavior was also important. Boys who became popular were helpful, reminded others of the rules, provided suggestions in ambiguous and difficult situations, and were almost never aggressive. The rejected boys were more talkative, active, and aggressive than the other members of the group, and they often wandered off on their own. Boys who were neglected by the others interacted with their peers the least but rarely offended anyone.

Dodge and his colleagues (1986) found that rejected children did not seem to know how to enter the game. The kinds of difficulties the rejected children encountered are illustrated in the two following transcripts describing attempts to enter an existing group.

SUCCESSFUL ATTEMPT

Mark enters, pauses for a moment, and moves forward to the proximity of the two peer hosts (confederates), who are playing a board game.

Mark: Can I play?

Host 1: Okay.

Host 2: Okay.

Host 1: Get yourself a seat.

Mark seats himself.

Host 2: What grade you in?

Mark: Fourth. What grade are you in?

Host 2: Third.

Host 1: Third. I'm eight.

Mark: I'm nine.

Host 2: I'm eight.

Host 1: This—if I were—today was my birthday and if I was, if I was nine, I'd be as old as you.

UNSUCCESSFUL ATTEMPT

David enters, hovers, motionless, while looking down at the table. Hosts are seated. Host 1 motions to Host 2 to spin the dial for the game they are playing.

Host 2: Line.

Host 1: I get to go again.

Host 2: I know.

Host 2 looks at David, who is still standing. After a long pause, Host 2 speaks.

Host 2: What are you staring at?

David: Just watching . . . *[inaudible mumble].*

Host 2 giggles under his breath. The hosts continue playing the game. (Dodge et al., 1986, pp. 52–53)

Compared with the successful child, the unsuccessful child has difficulty making constructive contributions to the group conversation and taking advantage of the rules of social interaction. These children also had difficulty interpreting videotaped social scenes. These and other findings led Dodge and his colleagues to conclude that deficient social information processing contributes both to the children's disruptive and aggressive behavior and to their low social status (Crick & Dodge, 1994).

Observations of interactions of first-, third-, and fifth-graders on a school playground indicate that it takes more than social skill to gain entry to a group of children who are already playing, however. The researchers noted little difference in the skill with which low-status and high-status children (as determined by a sociometric questionnaire) sought entry to an ongoing game, yet the low-status children were more than twice as likely to be ignored as the high-status children. In the familiar setting of a school playground, apparently, children may be rejected because the group has already formed a negative opinion of them before they utter a word or make a move (Putallaz & Wasserman, 1990).

Evidence in favor of such a two-sided view of social rejection is reviewed by Shelley Hymel, Esther Wagner, and Lynda Butler (1990). They found that children's reputations ("He is always hitting"; "She never gives anyone else a turn") can become self-perpetuating. In a number of the cases they discuss, a peer group's expectations cause the members to interpret a child's behavior as aggressive or unfriendly even when, by objective standards, it is not. It is not difficult to imagine how such biased interpretations make the task of winning acceptance more difficult and how they might evoke the very behaviors that led the child to be rejected in the first place.

Emotional control and social status

Several studies have implicated emotional development as a factor that influences children's social status, as the discussion of socioemotional competence in Chapter 10 would lead one to expect (Hubbard & Coie, 1994). Rejected children appear to have difficulty both in reading the emotional states of others and in masking or controlling their own emotions (Dorsch & Keane, 1994; Underwood, Coie, & Herbsman, 1992). They are also more likely to see hostile intent in the behavior of others and to respond aggressively.

Overall, the evidence indicates that rejection by one's peers is the result of a bundle of characteristics, each of which influences a child to interact in socially inappropriate ways. The consequences are social isolation and loneliness, which only reinforce a difficult situation.

Concern for rejected children has evoked attempts to design programs to remedy their inappropriate social behavior (La Greca, 1993; Mize & Ladd, 1990). These programs include shaping desired behaviors through reinforcement, the teaching of social perspective-taking skills, and coaching in social situations. The results have been encouraging. Several such programs have produced improvements in social competence and acceptance by peers that have lasted up to a year.

Parental influences on children's status among peers

Peer-group interactions are never entirely free of adult influence. Teachers affect the peer preferences of children in their classrooms by their behavior. They also color the children's perceptions of one another. Parents influence their children's relations with peers intentionally by choosing where they go to school and by providing them with opportunities to interact with other children or by preventing them from doing so (Parke & Ladd, 1992). Parents also shape their children's peer experiences unintentionally through the settings they live in and their responses to their children's social behavior. Even when no adult is actually present, behavioral patterns that children have acquired at home and social norms accepted by the adult community are likely to influence children's behavior (Rubin & Sloman, 1984).

In Chapter 10 we reviewed evidence that parents may unwittingly encourage their children to behave aggressively when they themselves engage in coercive, power-assertive modes of socialization. Since aggressive behavior in children is associated with rejection by their peers, a number of researchers have investigated coercive family interaction patterns as a possible source of low social status in middle childhood (Dishion et al., 1994; Hart, Ladd, & Burleson, 1990; Putallaz & Heflin, 1990).

In one such study, Thomas Dishion (1990) collected information on social status by interviewing the teachers and classmates of over 200 boys between the ages of 9 and 10. He obtained evidence about family socialization patterns and the children's behavior from interviews with the parents and the boys themselves and through observations in the boys' homes.

Dishion found that the boys who seemed to be rejected by their peers at school were exposed to more coercive family experiences at home. These boys not only were more aggressive with their peers but also behaved badly in the classroom. Although boys from lower-income homes were more likely to fall within the rejected category, Dishion's data showed that socioeconomic class was not a *direct* cause of lower peer status or aggressive behavior. In accord with findings discussed in Chapter 11 (pp. 441–443), however, he found that poverty did affect social status and behavior *indirectly* by increasing the general level of stress within the family. When parents coped well enough with the pressures of poverty to treat their children in a noncoercive way, the children were less likely to have low social status among their peers.

The results of these studies linking children's social status to parenting styles appear to confirm the findings of research on the social behavior of younger children (Chapter 10, p. 409; MacDonald & Parke, 1984): the modes of interaction that children acquire at home tend to serve as models for their behavior with their peers, affecting their social status for better or for worse.

COMPETITION AND COOPERATION AMONG PEERS

Children's social behavior is influenced by the socialization patterns of a cultural group as well as by their parents. The particular aspect of social interaction that has been the focus of this research is the extent to which a culture values cooperation or competition among the members of a group.

Millard Madsen and his colleagues (Kagan & Madsen, 1971; Madsen & Shapira, 1970; Shapira & Madsen, 1969) studied the way members of small peer groups chose to cooperate or compete to solve a problem. The purpose of the studies was to contrast the problem-solving strategies of children whose cultures emphasize cooperation with the strategies of those whose cultures emphasize competition.

One of the early studies in this series contrasted two groups of Israeli children (Shapira & Madsen, 1969). One group was composed of children who lived in agricultural communes, or kibbutzim; the other group was made up of children from a middle-class urban neighborhood. Middle-class urban Israelis, like their U.S. counterparts, encourage their children to achieve as individuals. Kibbutzim, by contrast, prepare children from an early age to cooperate and work as a group. Kibbutz adults deliberately reward cooperation and punish failure to cooperate (Spiro, 1965). Competition is so discouraged that children may feel ashamed to be at the top of their class (Rabin, 1965).

Six- to 10-year-old children of both communities were brought together four at a time to play a game with the apparatus depicted in Figure 14.4. At the start of each round of the game, four children were seated at the corners of the board. In the center of the board was a pen connected to each corner by a string. Each child could pull the string to move the pen. The board itself was covered with a clean piece of paper, on which the pen left a mark as it moved.

The game called for the children to move the pen to specific places on the game board marked by four small circles. To bring the pen to one of these circles, the children had to

FIGURE 14.4 *Diagram of apparatus used to assess children's predispositions to compete or cooperate. The pen at the center of the board must be moved to the target circles, an act that requires changes in the lengths of the strings manipulated by all four players. (From Shapira & Madsen, 1969.)*

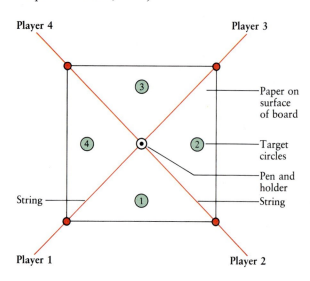

cooperate in pulling the strings; otherwise the pen would remain in the center or move erratically.

Each group of children was asked to play the game six times. For the first three trials Madsen and Ariella Shapira told them that the object of the game was to draw a line over the four circles in one minute. If they succeeded, each of them would get a prize. If they covered the four circles twice, they would get two prizes, and so on. But if they covered fewer than four circles, no one would receive a prize. Under these circumstances, children from both kinds of communities responded similarly, in a generally cooperative manner (see Figure 14.5).

After the first three trials, the experimenters changed the way rewards were given. Now, whenever the pen crossed the circle to the right of a child, that child received a reward. Under these new conditions, a cultural difference quickly became apparent. The urban children each started pulling the pen toward him- or herself. They persisted in competing even on the fifth trial, by which time they had ample opportunity to see that they were getting nowhere. In some cases the children would agree to cooperate, but the cooperation would break down as soon as one child pulled a little too hard on the string. As a result, their rate of success was greatly reduced.

The children from kibbutzim responded by quickly setting up cooperative rules, saying such things as "Okay, gang, let's go in turns." They also directed one another during the game with such suggestions as "We'll start here, then here. . . ." The kibbutz children were concerned that no one be rewarded more than the others, and they set up rules to see that they all shared equally in the prizes.

Madsen's studies, which have been repeated in other countries under varying conditions (Kagan & Madsen, 1971; Madsen & Shapira, 1970), show that the pattern of socialization that a culture fosters significantly influences the way peers work together. (Box 14.4 addresses a related issue: What factors make it possible for different peer groups to work together?)

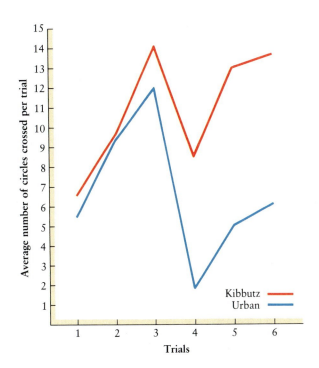

FIGURE 14.5 *The average number of successful attempts to cross a target circle by urban Israeli children and by Israeli children raised in a kibbutz. On the first three trials, children were rewarded for cooperating. On the second three trials, rewards were distributed for individual achievement. Children raised on a kibbutz continued to cooperate and succeed, but urban children began to compete, lowering their success rate. (From Shapira & Madsen, 1969.)*

Developmental consequences of peer interaction

Several lines of research suggest that children *need* peer interaction during middle childhood in order to develop adequate social cognitive skills and achieve social well-being (Perret-Clermont, 1980; Krappmann, 1989). Evidence that peer interaction promotes social competence is provided by Marida Hollos (Hollos, 1975; Hollos & Cowan, 1973), who studied children growing up in three distinctive social settings in Norway and Hungary: towns, villages, and isolated farms. Hollos sought to determine if differences in the children's experiences with peers led to distinctive patterns and rates of cognitive development.

Many Norwegian children live on isolated farms that are difficult to reach, especially during the winter, so they experience relatively little peer interaction. Except on holidays, young farm children rarely interact with children other than their brothers and sisters. At the age of 7, when they begin school, they are bused to a neighboring community three times a week and bused home again as soon as school is over, so they have no free time to play with the other children. At home they spend most of their time playing alone or watching their mothers work. Communication in their families is generally simple and direct, perhaps because the family members spend so much time in one another's company that they have little new to talk about.

BOX 14.4

Competition and Conflict between Groups

Except in small, widely separated communities, peer groups are unlikely to be isolated. In a single urban neighborhood there may be several groups, some based on common interests, others on membership in a church or athletic team, or simply residence on the same block. In some locales, children may become involved in street gangs in middle childhood, a social phenomenon that has aroused growing concern in recent decades.

When we turn from the study of interaction *within* a single peer group to interaction *between* two groups, many of the issues repeat themselves in a new form. Just as individual children must learn to get along with each other without strict adult control, so groups of children must find a way to regulate their interactions with other groups.

A classic series of studies by Muzafer and Carolyn Sherif (1953) provides the best evidence to date about the conditions that foster different kinds of interaction between peer groups. In the most famous of these studies, 11-year-old boys—all strangers to one another—were brought to one of two summer camps in Robbers Cave State Park in Oklahoma. The boys all came from stable middle-class homes. They were all in the upper half of their class in academic standing, and all were judged to be physically healthy and well adjusted.

The boys in the two encampments went canoeing, swam, played ball, and engaged in other typical camp activities. To ensure that the boys at each encampment formed a cohesive group, the adults arranged for them to encounter problems that the boys could solve only by cooperating. They provided ingredients for dinner, for example, but left it to the boys themselves to prepare and apportion the food. At the end of the week, friendships had formed and leaders had emerged within each group. Each had adopted a name: they were the Rattlers and the Eagles.

When it was clear that both the Rattlers and the Eagles had formed a stable pattern of group interactions, the adults let it be known that there was another group in the area. The boys expressed a keen desire to compete.

The adults arranged for a tournament, with prizes for the winners. At the end of the first day of competition, the Eagles lost a tug-of-war. Stung by their defeat, they burned a Rattlers flag that had been left behind. When the Rattlers returned the next morning and discovered the burned flag, they immediately seized the Eagles' flag. Scuffling and name-calling ensued. Over the next five days hostilities escalated. The Rattlers staged a raid on the Eagles' camp. The Eagles retaliated with a destructive raid of their own.

Once the intergroup hostility had reached a high level, the experimenters took steps to reverse it. First they tried bringing the boys together in a series of pleasant social gatherings—joint meals, attendance at a movie, setting off firecrackers—but these attempts all failed miserably. The boys used these occasions to escalate hostilities by throwing food and calling names.

Next the experimenters introduced a series of superordinate problems that affected the welfare of both groups equally, requiring them to combine efforts to reach a solution. The most successful application of this technique occurred during an overnight camping trip. The adults arranged for the truck that was to bring food to get stuck in a position where it could not be pushed. The boys came up with the idea of using their tug-of-war rope to pull the truck out of its predicament. The Sherifs describe the outcome:

> It took considerable effort to pull the truck. Several tries were necessary. During these efforts, a rhythmic chant of "Heave, heave" arose to accent the times of greatest effort. This rhythmic chant of "Heave, heave" had been used earlier by the Eagles during the tug-of-war contests in the period of intergroup competition and friction. Now it was being used in a cooperative activity involving both groups. When, after some strenuous efforts, the truck moved and started there was jubilation over the common success. (1956, pp. 322–323)

After this joint achievement, there seemed no point in preparing separate meals. The two groups cooperated without much discussion and with no outbreaks of name-calling or throwing of food. The experimenters arranged for the truck to get stuck again. This time the boys immediately knew what to do, and the two groups mixed freely as they organized the rope pull.

At the end of the series of joint-activity problems, the boys' opinions of each other had changed significantly. Mutual respect had largely replaced hostility, and several of the boys had formed friendships in the opposite group.

The Sherifs' experiment carries an important lesson. Cooperation and competition are not fixed biological characteristics of individuals or of groups. They are forms of interaction that can be found at some time in all social groups and in all individuals; they can be, and are, heavily influenced by social organization.

Young children living in villages and towns, by contrast, spend most of their free time playing with other children. They bicycle together all over, explore the waterfront, visit one another's homes, ski together in winter, and play out on the streets at all times of the year. They also interact with adults in shops, on the street, and in their friends' homes. Village children encounter fewer people than the town children do, but the peer interactions they experience are similar. Hollos found the same general patterns in Hungary.

To assess the impact of these different peer experiences on development, Hollos presented 7-, 8-, and 9-year-old children in these settings with a battery of tests drawn from two Piagetian categories. The first set consisted of classification and conservation tasks, designed to test the development of logical operations. The second set was designed to measure social perspective-taking and communication skills.

One perspective-taking task presented the child with a seven-picture cartoon sequence suggesting an obvious story that the child was asked to recount. Then three of the pictures were removed. The remaining four pictures suggested a different story. A second experimenter then entered the room and the child was asked to pretend to take the first experimenter's place and tell the story that the experimenter would tell. The key question was whether the child would simply repeat the first story or adjust to the new circumstances.

Hollos (1975) obtained similar results with both the Norwegian and the Hungarian children. As Figure 14.6 indicates, the scores of the three groups of Hungarian children were about equal on the test of logical operations. All groups improved with age. On the social perspective-taking tasks, however, the farm children, who spent little time interacting with others, did less well than the village and town children. In a study conducted in Iceland, other researchers also found that urban children's performance on social perspective-taking tests was superior to that of rural children (Edelstein, Keller, & Wahlen, 1984). Further evidence that peer interaction helps children develop the ability to take other people's perspectives comes from a study conducted in Canada, which found that elementary school children who played with their peers on the playground less often than their agemates also scored lower on social perspective-taking tests (Le Mare & Rubin, 1987).

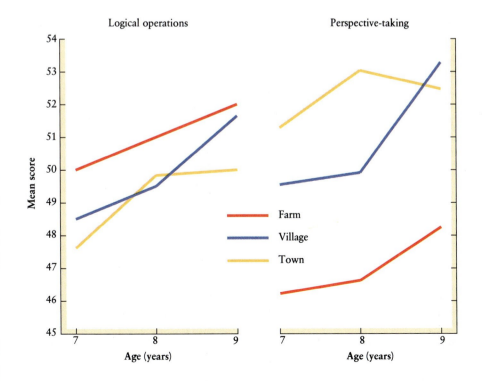

FIGURE 14.6 *The cognitive development of Hungarian children from isolated farms, villages, and towns. The graph on the left depicts their performance on tests of logical operations. The graph on the right depicts their performance on perspective-taking tasks. (From Hollos, 1975.)*

DEAR DR

I read the report in the Oct. 30 issue of _____ about your study of only children. I am an only child, now 57 years old and I want to tell you some things about my life. Not only was I an only child but I grew up in the country where there were no nearby children to play with. My mother did not want children around. She used to say 'I don't want my kid to bother anybody and I don't want nobody's kids bothering me.'

. . . From the first year of school I was teased and made fun of. For example, in about third or fourth grade I dreaded to get on the school bus to go to school because the other children on the bus called me 'Mommy's baby.' In about the second grade I heard the boys use a vulgar word. I asked what it meant and they made fun of me. So I learned a lesson—don't ask questions. This can lead to a lot of confusion to hear talk one doesn't understand and not be able to learn what it means . . .

I never went out with a girl while I was in school—in fact I hardly talked to them. In our school the boys and girls did not play together. Boys were sent to one part of the playground and girls to another. So, I didn't learn anything about girls. When we got into high school and the boys and girls started dating I could only listen to their stories about their experiences.

I could tell you a lot more but the important thing is I have never married or had any children. I have not been very successful in an occupation or vocation. I believe my troubles are not all due to being an only child, but I do believe you are right in recommending playmates for preschool children and I will add playmates for the school agers and not have them strictly supervised by adults. I believe I confirm the experiments with monkeys in being overly timid sometimes and overly aggressive sometimes. Parents of only children should make special efforts to provide playmates for [their children].

Sincerely yours,

FIGURE 14.7 *A letter from a friendless man giving his account of the importance of childhood friendships for development. (From Hartup, 1978.)*

A quite different kind of hypothesis about the consequences of peer relationships comes from the work of the psychiatrist Harry Stack Sullivan (1892–1949), who considered the experience of friendship during middle childhood to be an essential precursor to adult intimacy, with which it shares some important features:

> If you will look very closely at one of your children when he finally finds a chum . . . you will discover something very different in the relationship—namely, that your child begins to develop a new sensitivity to what matters to another person. And this is not in the sense of "what should I do to get what I want," but instead "what should I do to contribute to the happiness or to support the prestige and feeling of worth-whileness of my chum." So far as I have been ever able to discover, nothing remotely like this appears before the age of, say, 8½, and sometimes it appears decidedly later. (1953, pp. 245–246)

Sullivan believed that children's tendency to pick out one or a few other children with whom they feel this kind of special affinity is the childhood precursor of the need for interpersonal intimacy that will be called love when it is encountered again in adolescence. He further claimed that the failure to form such friendships in childhood creates a social deficit that is difficult to remedy later. As evidence, he cites several of his psychiatric patients who had failed to form friendships as children and who now were extremely uncomfortable in their business and social dealings with others. Figure 14.7 shows one person's interpretation of the consequences of failure to participate in a peer group.

Despite some weaknesses, the existing data support the belief that peer interactions and childhood friendships play an important part in development during middle childhood. It would be a mistake, however, to attribute all social development during this period to peer interactions. Children's relationships with their parents also continue to play an important role.

Changing Relations with Parents

When relationships between parents and 3-year-old children are compared with relationships between parents and their 9-year-olds, parents have been found to be less warm, more severe, and more critical of the 9-year-olds (Maccoby, 1984). Two related factors combine to account for this change in parental standards and behavior as children enter middle childhood. First, parents in every culture believe that the children should now be more capable and responsible (Goodnow et al., 1984; Warton & Goodnow, 1991). Second, the strategies parents adopt to correct their children's misbehavior change as their children's competence increases.

The precise ages at which parents expect children to be able to take on different tasks varies across cultures. Pamela Warton and Jacqueline Goodnow asked Japanese, American, Australian, and Australian Lebanese mothers the approximate age when they expected children to be capable of each of 38 kinds of behavior:

before the age of 4 years, between 4 and 6 years, or after 6 years of age. Table 14.6 shows the ages at which they expect their children to behave competently in various spheres. As the table indicates (note that low scores indicate late expectations of competence), Japanese mothers expected their children to display emotional maturity, compliance, and ritual forms of politeness at an earlier age than mothers in the other three groups. The American and Australian mothers expected their children to develop social skills and the ability to assert themselves verbally relatively early. The Australian Lebanese mothers were distinctive in their willingness to let the children attain the needed competencies in their own good time; their developmental timetables were usually later than those of the other groups. Despite cultural variations in the precise age at which the various competencies were expected to be achieved, all the parents expected their children to master these basic competencies sometime during middle childhood (Rogoff et al., 1980).

To learn how parental expectations concerning children's competencies affect the way parents react when their children misbehave, Theodore Dix and his colleagues (Dix, Ruble, & Zambarano, 1989) interviewed over 100 mothers of children ranging in age from 4 to 12 years. Each mother was read two descriptions of children the same age as her own who either stole quarters from a neighbor's house or ate the family's dessert at a picnic. Some of the descriptions were unclear

TABLE 14.6

Mean Ages at Which Mothers in Four Cultural Groups Expect Their Children to Attain Various Competencies
(1 = 6 years or older; 2 = 4–5 years; 3 = younger than 4 years)

Item	Japan	U.S.A.	Australia A*	Australia B†
EMOTIONAL MATURITY				
Does not cry easily	2.49	2.08	1.66	1.95
Can get over anger by self	2.67	1.69	1.93	1.38
Stands disappointment without crying	2.34	1.97	1.83	1.65
Does not use baby talk	2.07	1.91	2.66	2.76
COMPLIANCE				
Comes or answers when called	2.66	2.21	1.79	1.13
Stops misbehaving when told	2.57	2.33	2.28	1.57
Gives up reading/TV to help mother	1.33	1.54	1.59	1.51
POLITENESS				
Greets family courteously	2.90	2.22	2.69	2.38
Uses polite forms (please) to adults	2.08	2.37	2.76	2.73
INDEPENDENCE				
Stays home alone for an hour or so	1.78	1.04	1.10	1.05
Takes care of own clothes	2.17	1.87	1.55	1.35
Makes phone calls without help	1.41	1.21	1.14	1.21
Sits at table and eats without help	2.95	2.76	2.79	2.59
Does regular household tasks	2.03	1.97	2.07	1.32
Can entertain self alone	2.74	2.78	2.72	1.78
Plays outside without supervision	1.98	2.19	2.38	1.40
SOCIAL SKILLS				
Waits for turn in games	2.31	2.12	1.97	1.89
Shares toys with other children	2.62	2.72	2.72	1.73
Sympathetic to feelings of children	1.86	2.13	1.79	1.22
Resolves disagreement without fighting	1.41	1.70	1.45	1.11
Gets own way by persuading friends	1.40	1.94	1.97	1.30
Takes initiative in playing with others	1.59	2.48	2.24	1.73
VERBAL ASSERTIVENESS				
Answers a question clearly	2.10	1.98	2.14	1.46
States own preference when asked	1.72	2.25	2.00	1.30
Asks for explanation when in doubt	1.71	2.30	2.21	1.38
Can explain why s/he thinks so	1.48	2.09	1.76	1.32
Stands up for own rights with others	1.62	2.27	2.10	1.24
MISCELLANEOUS				
Uses scissors without supervision	2.00	1.54	1.52	1.11
Keeps feet off furniture	2.74	2.30	2.31	2.05
Disagrees without biting or throwing	2.43	2.34	2.38	1.92
Answers phone properly	1.52	1.49	2.10	1.98
Resolves quarrels without adult help	1.52	1.73	1.52	1.46

* Born in Australia.
† Born in Lebanon.
Source: Goodnow et al., 1984.

as to whether the child understood that the behavior was wrong; other descriptions made it obvious that the child understood. In the first case, mothers said that they would try to explain to the children how the behavior hurt other people, but that they were not likely to punish them. In the second case, mothers were more likely to say that the child should be punished, although they also thought that they should explain why the behavior was wrong. In accord with the findings on parental timetables described above, mothers believed that older children ought to be aware when they are misbehaving and consequently favored more severe responses to their transgressions.

Related to this change in parents' *expectations* is a change in the *issues* that arise between parents and children, according to Eleanor Maccoby (1980). Parents of young children are concerned with establishing daily routines and controlling temper tantrums and fights, as well as teaching children to care for, dress, feed, and groom themselves. Some of the issues of early childhood, such as fights among siblings, are still of concern during the years from 6 to 12. In addition, a whole new set of problems crop up when children start to take responsibility for chores at home, attend school, work, and spend increasing amounts of time away from adult supervision (see Box 14.5).

In economically developed countries, parents focus on their children's achievement during middle childhood, even though it may have no immediate economic consequences for the family. School is the arena in which children's achievement is most prominently judged. Parents worry about how involved they should become in their child's schoolwork, what they should do if a child has academic problems, and how to deal with behavior problems. Other concerns that emerge during middle childhood are whether to require children to do chores and what standards of performance should be expected of them, whether children should be paid for work they do around the house, and the extent to which parents should monitor their children's social life (Maccoby, 1984; Warton & Goodnow, 1991).

In less developed countries, where a family's survival often depends on putting children to work as early as possible, parents worry about their children's ability to take care of younger kin in the absence of adult supervision and to carry out important economic tasks such as the care of livestock or the hoeing of weeds (Weisner, 1984).

As children grow older and spend increasing amounts of time out of adults' sight, parents reason with their children more, appeal to their self-esteem ("You wouldn't do anything that stupid") or to their sense of humor, and seek to arouse their guilt. They remind children that they are responsible for themselves. In many societies, when school-aged children break rules and are punished, their parents are more likely to deprive them of privileges and confine them to the house or their room than to spank them (Newson & Newson, 1976).

As the parents' behavior changes, so does the children's (Collins, Harris, & Susman, 1995). Children openly express anger toward their parents less often than they did when they were younger. They are less likely to use such coercive behaviors as whining, yelling, hitting, and ignoring others' overtures. Now they argue with their parents, and point out their parents' inconsistencies. When conflict breaks out, however, or when they become angry, children do not recover so quickly as they did when they were younger. Parents report that children at this stage are often sulky, depressed, or passively noncooperative, and that they avoid them after an angry conflict.

In sum, parents increasingly share control with the children themselves. Maccoby (1984) terms this sharing of responsibility **coregulation.** Coregulation is built on parent-child cooperation. It requires parents to work out methods of monitoring, guiding, and supporting their children when adults are not present, using the time they are together to reinforce their children's understandings of

Coregulation The sharing of responsibility for the child's behavior between parent and child.

BOX 14.5

Maternal Employment and Child Welfare

All parents must rely on their children's good sense and self-control when they are not around to supervise, but such reliance becomes an urgent necessity when employed mothers are unavailable to their children during the greater part of each day. In the United States nearly 60 percent of all mothers of school-aged children are employed (see the accompanying table). The National Research Council formed a panel of scholars to review the research on how these children are affected by their mothers' employment.

Contrary to popular belief, this report concludes that available research "has not demonstrated that mothers' employment per se has consistent direct effects, either positive or negative, on children's development" (Hayes & Kamerman, 1983, p. 221). More recent research has confirmed this conclusion (Hoffman, 1989).

The effects of a mother's employment on her children depend on how her work interacts with other factors, including the family's income, race, family structure (are the parents married, divorced, single?), the parents' attitudes toward their roles as parents, their work and housework, as well as where the family lives (rural area, suburb, city, near relatives, etc.). It also depends on what happens to the children when their parents are at work. Although the data permit no sweeping generalizations, some specific findings are of interest.

As might be expected, school-aged children with employed mothers spend less time in their parents' company than children whose mothers are not employed. One survey found that mothers who were not employed outside the home spent roughly 13 hours each week in such primary child-care activities as feeding their children, taking them places, talking to them, and helping them with their homework, whereas mothers who worked 40 or more hours a week spent about 5 hours a week in such activities (Robinson, 1989). What might not be expected is that although children whose mothers are employed spend less time with their parents, the amount of time they spend actively doing things with them does not vary significantly from the average recorded for children whose mothers are not employed (Easterbrooks & Goldberg, 1985; Hoffman, 1984). One can only speculate about how children are affected by the amount of time they spend with their parents, and whether it matters if the time is spent actively doing something together or just being in each other's company.

Mothers who work outside the home are more likely to emphasize independence in training their children than mothers who are not employed. In line with this orientation, children of employed mothers have been found to spend somewhat more time on household chores than do their peers whose mothers do not work (Medrich et al., 1982). This emphasis on independence begins early. When both parents are wage earners, securely attached 18-month-olds show comparatively less dependency behavior than toddlers whose mothers are not employed (Weinraub, Jaeger, & Hoffman, 1988).

Socioeconomic status influences the way maternal employment affects children's development. Many children of single, impoverished, poorly educated mothers appear to benefit when their mothers hold a job. An increase in family income is one factor, but also important is the improvement in the mothers' social

right and wrong, what is safe and unsafe, and when they need to come to adults for help. For coregulation to succeed, children must be willing to inform their parents of their whereabouts, their activities, and their problems.

A New Sense of Self

The evidence reviewed thus far has documented the significant rearrangement of children's social lives that takes place in the transition from early to middle childhood. These changes in social relations are accompanied by equally striking developments in the children's sense of themselves.

circumstances, morale, and self-confidence (Bronfen-brenner, 1995). This finding is confirmed by a study that found that third- and fifth-grade children who were cared for after school by their single, nonemployed mothers had higher ratings for antisocial behaviors, anxiety, and peer conflicts and lower scores on a picture vocabulary test than their peers who were under other types of adult-supervised after-school care (Vandell & Ramanan, 1991).

Children are also affected by the number of hours their mothers work. Being employed more than 40 hours a week increases a mother's anxiety and affects the sensitivity of her mothering. It is also likely to have a negative effect on her child's achievement and adjustment (Gottfried, Gottfried, & Bathhurst, 1988; Owen & Cox, 1988).

Overall, it appears that maternal employment has a positive influence on girls. Daughters of employed mothers are reported to be more "independent, outgoing, higher achievers, to admire their mothers more, to have more respect for women's competence, and to show better social and personal adjustment" (Hoffman, 1984, p. 116).

Boys fare less well when their mothers hold jobs. The evidence suggests that in poor families these boys are less well adjusted than the sons of mothers who do not work outside the home, and in middle-class families they do not perform so well in school (Hoffman, 1989).

Since the general social trend in industrialized countries is toward full- and part-time maternal employment, considerable attention has been devoted to the evidence suggesting that in some conditions boys are at risk if the mother works outside the home (Hoffman, 1984); but precisely what those conditions are is not yet clear.

Percentage of Women in U.S. Labor Force with Children in Five Age Categories, 1990

| | | Children | | | |
	18 and Under	14–17	6–13	3–5	Under 3
All women	66.6%	76.4%	73.6%	64.4%	54.5%
White	66.9	77.2	73.9	64.4	54.8
Black	66.1	73.8	74.3	66.8	53.3
Hispanic	51.5	64.3	61.9	50.5	38.5

Source: U.S. Department of Labor, Bureau of Labor Statistics, Current Population Survey, March 1991.

Research on changes in children's sense of self in middle childhood has focused on how they define themselves, the emergence of a new level of sensitivity to their relative standing among peers, and their resulting efforts to maintain their self-esteem.

CONCEPTS OF THE SELF

Researchers have used a variety of methods, including interviews, story dilemmas, and questionnaires, to probe developmental changes in the way children think about themselves. Although results depend slightly on the procedure used, the evidence converges on the conclusion that the development of a sense of self undergoes a marked shift that parallels changes in cognition and social behavior during the period from 5 to 7 years of age (Harter, 1995).

Table 14.7 is based on an extensive study of changes in children's self-concept by William Damon and Daniel Hart (1988). It displays both the variety of children's answers when they are asked to describe themselves and the increasing complexity of their self-conception as they grow older. Damon and Hart report that children at all of the ages they studied refer to their appearance, their activities, their relations to others, and their psychological characteristics when they describe themselves; but both the importance they attach to the various characteristics and the complexity of their self-concept change with age. Children 6 to 7 years old sometimes describe themselves in terms of particular categories that apply to them ("I'm 6 years old") and sometimes in terms of others ("I'm older than she is"), but they do not combine the different descriptions.

Between 8 and 11 years of age, these two ways of thinking about themselves are expanded to include the interpersonal implications of whatever characteristics they have picked out. Instead of saying "I'm smarter than other kids," for example, children now begin to offer self-descriptions such as "I'm smarter than other kids, so they don't like to hang out with me."

Robert Selman (1980) probed children's reasoning about story dilemmas to determine how children's thinking about the self changes during middle childhood. One such story was the following:

Eight-year-old Tom is trying to decide what to buy his friend Mike for a birthday party. By chance, he meets Mike on the street and learns that Mike is

TABLE 14.7   A Developmental Model of Self-concept

Level of Self-concept	Area of Evaluation			
	Physical	Activity-Based	Social	Psychological
1. Categorical identification (4–7 years)	I have blue eyes. I'm 6 years old.	I play baseball. I play and read a lot.	I'm Catholic. I'm Sarah's friend.	I get funny ideas sometimes. I'm happy.
2. Comparative assessments (8–11 years)	I'm bigger than most kids. I have really light skin, because I'm Scandinavian.	I'm not very good at school. I'm good at math, but I'm not so good at art.	I like it when my mom and dad watch me play baseball. I do well in school because my parents respect me for it.	I'm not as smart as most kids. I get upset more easily than other kids.
3. Interpersonal implications (12–15 years)	I am a four-eyed person. Everyone makes fun of me. I have blonde hair, which is good because boys like blondes.	I play sports, which is important because all kids like athletes. I treat people well so I'll have friends when I need them.	I am an honest person, so people trust me. I'm very shy, so I don't have many friends.	I understand people, so they come to me with their problems. I'm the kind of person who loves being with my friends; they make me feel good about being me.

Source: After Damon & Hart, 1988.

The way one looks is often central to self-definition.

extremely upset because his dog, Pepper, has been lost for two weeks. In fact, Mike is so upset that he tells Tom, "I miss Pepper so much that I never want to look at another dog again." Tom goes off, only to pass a store with a sale on puppies: only two are left, and these will soon be gone. (1980, p. 94)

After telling this story, Selman asked children if Tom should buy a puppy for Mike and followed up the question with probes about each child's ideas concerning the self and others: "Is there an inside and an outside to a person?"; "Can you ever fool yourself into thinking that you feel one way when you really feel another?"

Before middle childhood, children take Mike's statement that he never wants to look at another dog at face value. They deny that what people say may not be what they think. Selman calls this conception of the self "physicalistic" because the self is equated with specific body parts. Children at this level, Selman reports, will say that their mouth tells their hand what to do or that their ideas come from their tongue (Selman, 1980).

About the age of 6, the children in Selman's study believed that inner experience and outward appearance are different but claimed that how a person feels and how they appear to feel must be consistent with each other. Then, at about the age of 8, they realized that the self can fool itself. Thus Mike may really want another puppy (the psychological experience), even though he says he doesn't (outer appearance). At this point children have developed the idea that each person has a private, subjective self that behavior does not always reveal.

The ability of 8- to 9-year-old children to think about their own unobservable, psychological characteristics, and those of others as well, is accompanied by an increased tendency to understand themselves and others in terms of psychological traits that remain the same from one setting to the next. In a study of Dutch children 5, 8, and 11 years of age, Tamara Ferguson and her colleagues (1986) presented brief stories in which characters behaved either helpfully (by carrying a heavy bag for another person) or aggressively (by kicking another child on the playground). The children were then told other stories with the same characters but this time asked to predict how the child would behave. The 8- and 11-year-olds based their predictions on the behavior of the characters in the first story, but the 5-year-olds did not, indicating that they did not interpret the characters' behavior to be a reflection of an underlying stable disposition.

SOCIAL COMPARISON

Social comparison A process in which children define themselves in comparison to their peers. Social comparison comes to prominence in middle childhood.

As Table 14.7 indicates, children entering middle childhood begin to define themselves by comparison with other children, a process referred to as **social comparison.** Of course, most preschoolers are not complete strangers to social comparison. When cookies are being distributed at snacktime in a day-care center, preschoolers make certain they get as many as their peers. Kindergartners are likely to know whether other children in their class can run faster than they can. And certainly jealousy among siblings reflects awareness of comparative levels of attention from parents. But around the age of 8 or 9 years, children's sensitivity to themselves in relation to others their own age increases significantly and they are able to formulate it in words (Ruble & Frey, 1991).

There is no mystery as to why social comparison begins to play a significant role in children's sense of themselves during middle childhood. The increased time they spend with their peers and their greater ability to understand others' points of view lead children to engage in a new kind of questioning about themselves. If the setting is the playground, they must decide "Am I good at sports?" "Am I a good friend?" "Do the other kids like me?" If the setting is the classroom, the comparison is likely to be along academic lines ("Am I good at math?"). Such questions have no absolute answer because there are no absolute criteria of success. Rather, success is defined by one's relation to the social group. From specific comparisons in a wide variety of settings, children begin to formulate a new overall sense of themselves.

To study the beginnings of one common form of social comparison, the extent of athletic ability, Diane Ruble and her colleagues (1980) arranged for 5-, 7-, and 9-year-old children to play a modified game of basketball, the objective of which was to throw the ball into a basketball hoop concealed behind a curtain. Because the children could not see for themselves if they were successful, they had to depend on what the experimenter told them. The unusual procedure was explained as a test of their ability to remember the location of the hoop when it was no longer visible. To make this story plausible, the children were given a brief practice session with the hoop visible.

Once the experimenters were satisfied that the children knew what was expected of them, each child was given four chances to throw the ball through the hoop. All the children were told that they were successful on the second and fourth throws. This part of the procedure set the stage for the social comparison manipulation to follow.

The children at each age level were divided into a "relative success group," a "relative failure group," and a control group. Each of these groups received different information about how they performed in relation to a hypothetical group of other children their own age. To make the comparison clear, the experimenter pasted paper symbols on a large scorecard to mark a child's performance. The child saw two balls and two X's pasted on the board to mark his or her two "hits" and two "misses." Children in the relative-success group also saw the hypothetical scores of eight other children, only one of whom scored even one hit. Children in the relative-failure group saw scores of eight children, all of whom scored three or more hits. Children in a control group saw only their own scores. The children were asked both how good they were at this game and how pleased they were with their performance.

If the children assessed their own performance by comparing their scores with others', one would expect that those who experienced relative failure would assess themselves as failures and those who experienced relative success would assess themselves highly. This is exactly what Ruble and her associates observed among the 9-year-olds. Nine-year-old children in the relative-success group had the highest self-assessment, followed by those in the control group; those in the relative-failure group gave themselves the lowest assessment. But these findings did not hold true for the 5- and 7-year-olds. These children did not seem to assess their own performances in relation to those of others. They were equally pleased with their performances whether they had experienced relative failure, relative success, or no social comparison at all.

In real life, children have a great deal of experience evaluating their relative abilities in all sorts of endeavors, from piano recitals to spelling bees and playground games, and the process of social comparison can be quite complex. The following example is taken from an interview with an aspiring ballet dancer. Gwen, who is 12½ years old, is in a special class from which members of a leading national ballet company are chosen. Gwen knows that she is constantly being graded, much as she might be in school.

> Partly because she is so much younger, Gwen is smaller and doesn't have as much strength and stamina as the other girls in her class. They also have more experience on toe than she does and she takes fewer classes than they do. "Mostly it doesn't really bother me that much," she says. "But sometimes I think I'm doing really badly and I start comparing myself to them. Then I say, Hey, look, I'm not as old. But I like having people a little bit older than me because that way I can look up to them and see what they're doing and then try to work up to that, instead of having kids my own age. Because when I was with the kids my own age I was always better than they were," she states matter-of-factly. Then, catching herself, she adds, "I feel badly saying that, but it's true." (Cole, 1980, p. 159)

When deliberate and pervasive social comparison becomes important around 8 years of age, children are initially inclined to make overt social comparisons in interaction with their peers, making such remarks as "My picture is the best." But they soon discover that this kind of comparison is perceived as bragging and is likely to evoke negative reactions. As a consequence, they begin to develop more subtle ways of making social comparisons, saving overt expressions for occasions when they are deliberately trying to make others feel bad (Pomerantz et al., 1995).

SELF-ESTEEM

As we mentioned in Chapter 10 (p. 403), Erik Erikson (1963) thought of middle childhood as the time when children have to resolve the crisis of industry versus inferiority. We discussed the "industry" side of this formulation at length in Chapters 12 and 13, which describe the new assignments adults give children who work or go to school. Here we focus on the "inferiority" side of the crisis by considering the challenges to self-esteem that arise from children's efforts to demonstrate that they are capable and worthy of love and admiration.

Self-esteem is considered to be an important index of mental health. High self-esteem during childhood has been linked to satisfaction and happiness in later life, while low self-esteem has been linked to depression, anxiety, and maladjustment both in school and in social relations (Harter, 1993).

To study self-evaluations, Susan Harter and Robin Pike (1984) presented 4-, 5-, 6-, and 7-year-old children with pairs of pictures like those in Figure 14.8 and asked them to say whether each picture was a lot or a little like them. Each picture was selected to tap the children's judgments in one of four domains thought to be important to self-esteem: cognitive competence, physical competence, peer acceptance, and maternal acceptance. All the children were presented comparable items, but the specific content was changed to be age-appropriate (for example, an

FIGURE 14.8 *A sample item to elicit information about children's self-esteem. Children were asked which picture corresponded most closely to themselves by marking the appropriate circle. The small circle means that the picture applies a little, the large circle that it applies a lot. (From Harter & Pike, 1984.)*

item such as "Knows the alphabet," used to assess cognitive competence in the 4- and 5-year-olds, corresponded to the item "Can read alone" for the 6- and 7-year-olds). Children's responses to these self-evaluation tasks revealed that they evaluated their own worth in terms of two broad categories—competence and acceptance. In effect, they lumped cognitive and physical competence together in a single category of competence and combined peer and maternal acceptance in the single category of acceptance. Nevertheless, the scale seemed to tap children's feelings of self-worth in a realistic way. Harter and Pike found, for example, that children who had been held back a grade rated themselves low in competence while newcomers to the school rated themselves low in acceptance.

In work with somewhat older children (8 to 12 years old), Harter (1982) presented the self-esteem questions in the written format shown in Figure 14.9. She found that these children were able to make more differentiated self-evaluations; for example, they distinguished between cognitive, social, and physical competence (Harter, 1987). Older children were also able to provide evaluations of their overall self-worth, whereas the younger children evaluated themselves only in specific domains. (Table 14.8 shows the content of sample items in each domain of self-esteem included in Harter's scale for 8- to 12-year-olds.)

Harter and others also report that there is an age-related change in the extent to which children's self-evaluations fit the views of others (Harter, 1983). Younger children are able to rate their peers' "smartness" at school in a way that agrees with teachers' evaluations. The way they rate themselves, however, does not correlate with either their teachers' or their peers' ratings. Around the age of 8, children's self-evaluations begin to fit with the judgments of both their peers and their teachers. This pattern of results fits nicely with the conclusion (discussed on p. 608) that an overall sense of oneself in relation to others arises around the age of 8.

A positive feature of young children's limited self-evaluations is that when they try hard at a task and fail, they may get discouraged, but they are likely to brush off the failure and be willing to try again the next time. By contrast, when children reach the age of 9 or 10 they increasingly tend to feel helpless and give up when they fail, because they attribute the failure to an enduring characteristic of the self, and not to situational factors. When this happens, they show reduced expectations for success, negative affect, and low persistence (Ruble & Dweck, 1995).

Self-esteem has also been linked to patterns of child rearing (Bishop & Ingersoll, 1989; Coopersmith, 1967). In an extensive study of 10- to 12-year-old boys, Stanley Coopersmith found that parents of boys with high self-esteem (as determined by their answers to a questionnaire and their teachers' ratings) employed a style of parenting strikingly similar to the "authoritative" pattern described by Diana Baumrind in her study of parenting (see Chapter 11). Recall that authoritative parents were distinguished by their mixture of firm control, promotion of high standards of behavior, encouragement of independence, and willingness to reason with their children. Coopersmith's data, taken from an older group of children, suggest that three parental characteristics combine to produce high self-esteem in late middle childhood:

Acceptance of their children The mothers of sons with high self-esteem had closer, more affectionate relationships with their children than mothers of children with low self-esteem. The children seemed to appreciate this

FIGURE 14.9 *A sample item from Harter's scale of self-esteem. Choices to the left of center indicate degrees of poor self-esteem; choices to the right indicate degrees of positive self-esteem. (From Harter, 1982.)*

Really true for me	Sort of true for me	Some kids often forget what they learn	but	Other kids can remember things easily	Sort of true for me	Really true for me
☐	☐				☐	☐

TABLE 14.8	Harter Self-esteem Scale for 8- to 12-Year-Olds	
Area of Self-Evaluation	**Content of Sample Items**	
Cognitive competence	Good at schoolwork, can figure out answers, remember easily, remember what is read	
Social competence	Have a lot of friends, popular, do things with kids, easy to like	
Physical competence	Do well at sports, good at games, chosen first for games	
General self-worth	Sure of myself, do things fine, I am a good person, I want to stay the same	

Source: Harter, 1982.

approval and to view their mother as favoring and supportive. They also tended to interpret their mother's interest as an indication of their personal importance, as a consequence of which they came to regard themselves favorably. "This is success in its most personal expression—the concern, attention, and time of significant others" (Coopersmith, 1967, p. 179).

Clearly defined limits When parents impose strict limits on their children's activities, they make it clear when deviations are likely to evoke action; enforcement of limits gives the child a sense that norms are real and significant, and contributes to the child's self-definition.

Respect for individuality Within the limits set by the parents' sense of standards and social norms, the children are allowed a good deal of individual self-expression. Parents show respect for their children by reasoning with them and taking their points of view into account.

Taken together, these data suggest that the key to high self-esteem is the feeling, transmitted in large part by the family, that one has some ability to control one's own future by controlling both oneself and one's environment (Harter, 1996). This feeling of control is not without bounds. Children who have a positive self-image know their boundaries, but this awareness does not detract from their feeling of effectiveness. Rather, it sets clear limits within which the person feels considerable assurance and freedom.

A strong and positive sense of who they are within the family context cannot completely shield children against buffeting by their peers, but it does provide a secure foundation for the trials they undergo when they are on their own.

Middle Childhood Reconsidered

With the evidence from this and the preceding two chapters before us, it is appropriate to return to the question of whether the transition from early to middle childhood constitutes a bio-social-behavioral shift. Is middle childhood a stage of development characterized by a common set of features in every culture?

TABLE 14.9	The Bio-Social-Behavioral Shift That Initiates Middle Childhood	
SOCIAL DOMAIN	Peer-group participation Rule-based games without direct adult supervision Deliberate instruction Golden Rule morality Coregulation of behavior between parent and child Social comparison	
BEHAVIORAL DOMAIN	Increased memory capacity; strategic remembering Concrete operations Logical classification Decreased egocentrism and improved perspective-taking	
BIOLOGICAL DOMAIN	Loss of baby teeth and gain of permanent teeth Growth spurt in frontal lobes and in overall brain size Sharp increase in EEG coherence	

Table 14.9 summarizes the changes that appear to distinguish middle childhood from early childhood. We have placed the social domain at the top because surveys of the world's cultures make it clear that adults everywhere assign 6- and 7-year-olds to a new social category and require them to behave themselves in new (and sometimes stressful) contexts. Whether individual children are fully prepared or not, they must adapt to their new duties and roles or face the displeasure of their parents and the scorn of their peers.

Another universal characteristic of middle childhood is the rise of the peer group as a major context for development. For the first time children must define their status within a group of relative equals without the intervention of adults. In many cultures, interactions with peers become coordinated, with games governed by rules serving as surrogates for adult control. The experience of negotiating these interactions and comparing themselves with peers contributes to children's mastery of the social conventions and moral rules that regulate their communities. Peer interactions also provide crucial contexts within which children arrive at a new, more complex and global sense of themselves.

The new cognitive capacities that develop at this time are less accessible to observation than changes in the social domain, but no less important in creating a qualitatively distinct stage of development. As we saw in Chapters 12 and 13, thought processes in middle childhood become more logical, deliberate, and consistent. Children become more capable of thinking through actions and their consequences; they are able to engage in concentrated acts of deliberate learning in the absence of tangible rewards; they keep in mind the points of view of other people in a wider variety of contexts; and they learn to inhibit actions and mask emotional reactions that would lead them into difficulty with their parents and their peers. As we have emphasized several times, these cognitive changes must be considered as both cause and effect of the social changes discussed in this chapter.

Least visible are the biological changes that underpin children's apparent new mental capacities and modes of social interaction. The fact that children are bigger, stronger, and better coordinated is obvious enough. But only recently has modern anatomical and neurophysiological research provided evidence of such subtle changes as the proliferation of brain circuitry, changing relations between different kinds of brain-wave activity, and the greatly expanded influence of the brain's frontal lobes. Without such biological changes, the cognitive and social changes we have reviewed would not be possible. By the same token, when children are deprived of experience, such biological changes do not occur normally.

If we were to consider each element in the transition to middle childhood separately, it would be difficult to sustain the argument that it is initiated by a bio-social-behavioral shift and represents a qualitatively stagelike change from earlier periods. After all, preschoolers are often found in neighborhood groups with older children when no adults are present. They have been shown to exhibit logical thinking and the use of memory strategies in some contexts, and their play contains elements of rules as well as social roles.

But the changes we have documented do *not* occur separately; they occur in the kind of loosely coordinated ensemble that we have come to expect of a bio-social-behavioral shift. Although the details vary from one culture and one child to the next, the overall pattern is consistent and thus suggests a distinctive stage of life.

The existence of a universal pattern of changes associated with middle childhood in no way contradicts the fact that there are significant variations among cultures in the particular ways they conceive of and organize 6- to 12-year-old children's lives. Societies in which formal schooling is a central arena for children's development are especially likely to encourage uniformity in the age at which children begin to enter into the mode of life typical of middle childhood. Rural agrarian societies in which the change in children's activities is less extreme are less precise in the specific age at which a child is accorded the responsibilities and rights of middle childhood. But a few months' variation in the occurrence of various elements in the bio-social-behavioral shift does not substantially change their significance in the overall process of development.

SUMMARY

Games and Group Regulation

- During the years from 6 to 12 children begin to spend significant amounts of time beyond direct adult control, in the company of children roughly their own age.

- During middle childhood the nature of children's play changes from role-based fantasy to games that require adherence to rules.

- Rule-based games serve as a model of society: they are transmitted from one generation to the next and they exist only through mutual agreement.

Rules of Behavior

- Social rules are of three types: moral rules, social conventions, and personal rules. Especially important for the functioning of peer groups are basic moral rules and social conventions.

- The distinction between moral rules and social conventions is understood during early childhood. Within each domain of rules, children's thinking goes through a sequence of developmental stages.

- Moral reasoning changes during middle childhood from a belief that right and wrong are based on a powerful outside authority (heteronomous morality) to an instrumental morality based on mutual support and, in some cases, to a belief in reciprocal responsibility (the Golden Rule).

- Ideas about the fair distribution of resources change from reliance on arbitrary criteria to a recognition of the rights of all to share in the group's resources. Further development consists of children's increasingly sophisticated ability to appreciate the legitimacy of distributing resources unequally under certain conditions.

- When children first reason about social conventions, they treat conventions as more or less equivalent to natural laws. With increased sophistication they begin to separate empirical associations ("Most nurses are women") from necessity ("A nurse has to be a woman"). Finally, children come to appreciate the usefulness of social conventions in the regulation of social interaction.

Relations with Other Children

- Children's conceptions of friendship develop from an emphasis on participating in joint activities to an emphasis on sharing interests, building mutual understanding, and creating trust.

- The development of conceptions of friendship is closely associated with an increased ability to adopt other people's points of view and to repair misunderstandings when they arise.

- Middle childhood is a period of relative segregation of the sexes. Boys tend to have more friends than girls, but girls' friendships tend to be more intimate than boys'.

- Social differentiation in peer groups creates preference patterns as to who likes to spend time with whom. Physical attractiveness is a major factor in popularity, but relevant social skills—such as making constructive contributions to group activity, adopting the group's frame of reference, and understanding social rules—also play important roles in it.

- Cultures vary in the value they place on cooperation versus competition in peer interactions.

- When conflicts arise between peer groups, the most likely way to reduce the tension is to involve both groups in solving a common problem.

- Participation in peer groups is important to later development because it fosters the ability to communicate, to understand others' points of view, and to get along with others.

Changing Relations with Parents

- As children begin to participate in peer groups, their relationship with their parents undergoes significant changes.
    1. Parents become more demanding of their children, with respect to both their domestic duties and their achievement in school.
    2. Parents shift from direct to indirect methods of control—to reasoning, humor, appeals to self-esteem, and the arousal of guilt.

A New Sense of Self

- Increased time spent among peers poses challenges to children's sense of themselves. Their basic conceptions of the self change from a fusion of the physical and the mental toward a recognition that people can feel one way and behave another.

- Special challenges to the sense of self arise from the process of social comparison, which occurs when children compete in games and in school.

- A strong sense of self-esteem is important to mental health. Family practices that emphasize acceptance of children, clearly defined limits, and respect for individuality are most likely to give rise to a firm sense of self-worth.

Middle Childhood Reconsidered

- Social development is an essential part of the bio-social-behavioral shift that occurs in the years between 5 and 7. Understood as a unique configuration of biological, social, and behavioral characteristics, middle childhood appears to be a universal stage of human development.

KEY TERMS

coregulation, p. 603

group norms, p. 573

instrumental morality, p. 577

moral rules, p. 573

nomination procedure p. 591

peers, p. 564

personal rules, p. 573

positive justice, p. 577

rating scale, p. 591

social comparison, p. 608

social competence, p. 588

social conventions, p. 573

social-relational moral perspective, p. 577

social repair mechanisms, p. 591

sociogram, p. 591

THOUGHT QUESTIONS

1. Developmentalists link the emergence of rule-based games in middle childhood to the willingness of adults to allow children to spend time without supervision. What is the psychological connection between these two aspects of development?

2. Piaget asserted that "all morality consists in a system of rules, and the essence of all morality is to be sought for in the respect which the individual acquires for these rules" (p. 570). What are the implications of this view for the relationship between moral and cognitive development?

3. Make up a moral dilemma based on your everyday experience that is logically equivalent to Kohlberg's "Heinz dilemma" (p. 577). Present yours and Kohlberg's version to a friend. How is the reasoning produced by the two versions of the dilemma the same and how does it differ? What gives rise to the differences?

4. Evidence shows that children tend to choose friends who are similar to themselves.

   (a) What might be the psychological basis for this convergence?

   (b) Think of two friends from your own childhood, one who is like you and one who is quite different. What qualities of the two friendships were different? Why?

PART FIVE

ADOLESCENCE

The cascade of biochemical events that begins around the end of the first decade of life alters the body's size, shape, and functioning. The most revolutionary of these alterations is the development of an entirely new potential, the ability to engage in biological reproduction. This biological fact has profound interpersonal implications for the simple reason that reproduction cannot be accomplished by one human being alone. As their reproductive organs reach maturity, boys and girls begin to engage in new forms of social behavior because they begin to find the opposite sex attractive.

There is more to human reproduction than sex, however. The process of biological reproduction, by itself, is not sufficient for the continuation of our species. Central to human reproduction is the fact that biological reproduction must be complemented by an extended period of cultural reproduction, in which the "designs for living" evolved by the group are handed down to the next generation. In addition to mastering the basic skills necessary for economic survival, young people must achieve new and more mature relations with agemates of both sexes, learn the appropriate masculine or feminine social roles associated with adult status, develop emotional independence from parents and other adults, acquire their culture's values and ethical system, and learn to behave in a socially responsible manner (Havighurst, 1967).

In the United States and other industrialized societies, a gap of 7 to 9 years typically separates the biological changes that mark the onset of sexual maturity from the social changes that confer adult status (such as the right to marry without parental consent and to run for elective office). This lengthy period is necessary because it takes young people many years to acquire the knowledge and skills that will ensure them economic independence and enable them to reproduce their culture. It is in developed societies that a well-formed concept of adolescence as an intermediate stage of development between middle childhood and adulthood is most likely to be found.

Some societies recognize little or no gap between the beginning of sexual maturity and the beginning of adulthood (Whiting, Burbank, & Ratner, 1986). These are usually societies in which biological maturity occurs late by our standards and in which the level of technology is relatively low. By the time biological reproduction becomes possible, about the age of 15 in many nonindustrial societies, young people already know how to farm, weave cloth, prepare food, and care for children. In such societies, there may be no commonly acknowledged stage of development equivalent to adolescence.

The wide variation from one society to another in the time that elapses between the achievement of sexual maturity and the attainment of adult status raises the possibility that adolescence is not a universal stage of development. Some historians of childhood argue that adolescence exists as a distinct stage of development only in societies where prolonged education is necessary for people to become fully competent members of the community (Ariès, 1962; Demos & Demos, 1969; Modell & Goodman, 1990). Other scholars argue that there is a period in every society during which children strive to attain adult status, and that this striving produces similar experiences wherever it occurs (Bloch & Niederhoffer, 1958; Schlegel & Barry, 1991). They believe, therefore, that adolescence should be considered a universal developmental stage.

We will return to the question of the universality of adolescence as a distinctive stage at the end of Chapter 16. First, however, in Chapter 15, we examine the advent of biological maturity and its intimate links with changes in social life, including changes in the nature of interactions with peers, of friendships, and of relationships with one's family, as well as with entry into the workforce. Chapter 16 concentrates on what have traditionally been thought of as the psychological characteristics of adolescence: the new modes of thought that are needed to perform the economic tasks and fulfill the social responsibilities of adulthood, the changed sense of personal identity that is occasioned by a transformed physique and altered social relationships, and the new beliefs about morality and the social order that accompany preparation for adulthood.

CHAPTER 15

Biological and Social Foundations of Adolescence

> "How is it that, in the human body, reproduction is the only function to be performed by an organ of which an individual carries only one half so that he has to spend an enormous amount of time and energy to find another half?"
> —*François Jacob*, The Possible and the Actual

One of the most poignant accounts of what it feels like to enter adolescence appears in the diary of Anne Frank, a Jewish girl who lived in Holland during the German occupation of World War II. Unable to leave her hiding place and go outside for fear of being captured, Anne turned her diary into the friend she longed for. The entries quoted here were written shortly before Anne and her family were discovered and sent to their deaths in a concentration camp.

WEDNESDAY, 5 JANUARY 1944

Yesterday I read an article about blushing by Sis Heyster. This article might have been addressed to me personally. Although I don't blush very easily, the other things in it certainly all fit me. She writes roughly something like this—that a girl in the years of puberty becomes quiet within and begins to think about the wonders that are happening to her body.

I experience that, too, and that is why I get the feeling lately of being embarrassed about Margot, Mummy, and Daddy. Funnily enough, Margot, who is much more shy than I am, isn't at all embarrassed.

I think what is happening to me is so wonderful, and not only what can be seen on my body, but all that is taking place inside. I never discuss myself or any of these things with anybody; that is why I have to talk to myself about them.

Each time I have a period—and that has only been three times—I have the feeling that in spite of all the pain, unpleasantness, and nastiness, I have a sweet secret, and that is why, although it is nothing but a nuisance to me in a way, I always long for the time that I shall feel that secret within me again. (1975, pp. 116–117)

THURSDAY, 6 JANUARY 1944

My longing to talk to someone became so intense that somehow or other I took it into my head to choose Peter.

Sometimes if I've been upstairs into Peter's room during the day, it always struck me as very snug, but because Peter is so retiring and would never turn anyone out who became a nuisance, I never dared stay long, because I was afraid he might think me a bore. I tried to think of an excuse to stay in his room and get him talking, without it being too noticeable, and my chance came yesterday. Peter has a mania for crossword puzzles at the moment and hardly does anything else. I helped him with them and we sat opposite each other at his little table, he on the chair and me on the divan.

It gave me a queer feeling each time I looked into his deep blue eyes, and he sat there with that mysterious laugh playing round his lips. I was able to read his inward thoughts. I could see on his face that look of helplessness and uncertainty as to how to behave, and at the same time, a trace of his sense of manhood. I noticed his shy manner and it made me feel very gentle; I couldn't refrain from meeting those dark eyes again and again, and with my whole heart I almost beseeched him: oh, tell me, what is going on inside you, oh can't you look beyond this ridiculous chatter?

But the evening passed and nothing happened, except that I told him about blushing—naturally not what I have written, but just that he would become more sure of himself as he grew older. (pp. 118–119)

These diary entries, written less than 24 hours apart when Anne was 14½ years old, vividly reveal the intimate connection between the physical changes of puberty and the social characteristics of adolescence. They touch on many aspects of the bio-social-behavioral shift that marks the end of middle childhood. First, the biological changes of puberty transform the size and shape of young people's bodies and evoke new, initially strange feelings. These changes are accompanied by changes in social life: after many years of relatively little interest in the opposite sex, boys and girls begin to find each other attractive, and their mutual attraction brings about changes in their interactions with peers and with close friends. Simultaneously, their relationships with their parents change, as if in recognition of the fact that independence, work, and the responsibility of caring for others must replace reliance on their parents' support. Lastly, the combination of biological and social developments is accompanied by changes in the way young people think about themselves and the world.

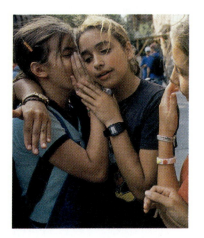

In attempting to gain a comprehensive picture of psychological development during adolescence, developmental psychologists face several difficulties. On the one hand, adolescents are able to talk more reflectively about their feelings and thought processes than are younger children. On the other hand, many of the topics that preoccupy them are socially awkward to talk about, and more of the things they do cannot be observed directly, so the actual facts of adolescents' behavior are difficult to document. Despite these difficulties, the nature of adolescence has long interested scholars, who have sought to understand its special characteristics both as a transition from middle childhood to adulthood and as a stage of development in its own right.

Societies' conceptions of adolescence are of vital importance to young people because they determine the demands made on them and the rights they are permitted to exercise. If they live in a society that considers puberty to be the onset of adulthood, they will be expected to maintain themselves economically, to care for others, and to be legally responsible for their actions. Conversely, if 15- and 16-year-olds are still considered children, they will be cared for by others and will remain free of many of the responsibilities adults must accept. But they will also be expected to acquiesce in adult demands as the price for their continued dependence.

Traditional Conceptions of Adolescence

Present-day conceptions of adolescence in Western cultures are still heavily influenced by the eighteenth- and nineteenth-century European scholars who wrote about adolescence as a distinct period of life. The first great theorist of adolescence was Jean-Jacques Rousseau (see Chapter 1, pp. 14–15). In *Emile* (1762/1911), his treatise on human nature and education, Rousseau suggested three characteristics of adolescence.

1. Adolescence is a period of heightened *instability* and emotional conflict that is brought on by biological maturation. As Rousseau phrased it:

As the roaring of the waves precedes the tempest so the murmur of rising passions announces this tumultuous change, a suppressed excitement warns us of the approaching danger. A change of temper, frequent outbreaks of anger, a perpetual stirring of the mind, make the child almost ungovernable. He becomes deaf to the voice he used to obey; he is a lion in a fever; he distrusts his keeper and refuses to be controlled. (p. 172)

2. The biological and social changes that figure prominently in adolescence are accompanied by a fundamental change in psychological processes. The transition to adolescence, Rousseau believed, brought with it *self-conscious thought* and the ability to reason logically.

3. In important respects, the changes that occur during adolescence are a re-birth. According to this view, adolescence *recapitulates*—repeats in concise form—the earlier stages of life through which the child has passed. Rousseau expressed this idea in this way: "We are born, so to speak, twice over; born into existence, and born into life; born a human being and born a man" (p. 172).

When developmental psychologists began to turn their attention to the phenomenon of adolescence at the end of the nineteenth century, Rousseau's ideas were picked up and modified by, among others, G. Stanley Hall, the first president of the American Psychological Association and a major figure in the shaping of developmental psychology (Cairns, 1983). Hall's goal was to construct a theory of individual development based on Darwin's ideas about the evolution of the species.

Hall, like Rousseau, described adolescence as a time of heightened emotionality and stress: stratospheric highs, deep depressions, and love of excitement. He too saw adolescence as a period of rebirth after childhood, although Hall, unlike Rousseau, believed that adolescence actually recapitulates earlier stages in the life of the *species*, not of the individual child. In the flush of late nineteenth-century enthusiasm for Darwinism, **recapitulationism**—the idea that each creature's individual development repeats the entire evolutionary history of the species—was so popular that it inspired a tongue-twisting aphorism: "Ontogeny recapitulates phylogeny."

According to Hall, middle childhood corresponds to an ancient period of historical development when human reason, morality, feelings of love toward others, and religion were presumably underdeveloped by modern standards. Adolescence seemed to him to repeat the evolutionary development of the highest human capacities and to be a period during which further human progress could be promoted.

Modern texts on adolescence tend to treat Hall as a figure of purely historical interest. His insistence that the young recapitulate the entire history of the human species has been discredited (Gould, 1977b; Medicus, 1992), and his portrait of adolescence as a period of emotional excess is considered to be exaggerated (Feldman & Elliott, 1990). But Hall's ideas, like Rousseau's, live on in our culture's stereotype of modern adolescence and appear in modified form in the ideas of several influential twentieth-century psychologists, including Freud, Gesell, Piaget, and Erikson.

> **Recapitulationism** The idea that human children repeat earlier stages of human evolution during their development. Freud and Erikson also maintained that older children recapitulate earlier stages of their own development.

Modern Theories of Adolescence

The challenge to modern theorists of adolescence is to understand the biological, social, behavioral, and cultural factors involved in the transition from childhood to adulthood and how they are woven together. Each of the four theoretical perspectives we have been examining offers insights into this question, but there is as yet no widely accepted, unified theory of adolescence, and a great many researchers do not identify themselves with any of the established theoretical perspectives (Brooks-Gunn, Lerner, & Petersen, 1991).

THE BIOLOGICAL-MATURATION PERSPECTIVE

Biological-maturation theories of adolescence, like similar theories of development during earlier periods, emphasize that development is primarily the unfolding of inherited biological potentials. Two early modern adherents of this view whose ideas we have been tracking are Arnold Gesell and Sigmund Freud.

Arnold Gesell

Gesell admitted that the environment may exert a more powerful influence during adolescence than it did during infancy, but he still maintained that environmental conditions do not alter the basic pattern of development during adolescence in any fundamental way:

> Neither he [the adolescent] nor his parents in their zeal can transcend the basic laws of development. He continues to grow essentially in the same manner in which he grew as he advanced from the toddling stage of two years through the paradoxical stage of two and a half, and the consolidating stage of three. (Gesell & Ilg, 1943, p. 256)

Gesell agreed with Hall that the child recapitulates the history of the species during the course of development. He asserted that the "higher human traits," such as abstract thinking, imagination, and self-control, make their appearance late in the development of the individual because they were acquired late in the history of the species. Although Gesell may be criticized for overemphasizing the effects of maturational changes on adolescents' behavior, his insistence that biological factors determine the basic pattern of psychological functioning in adolescence currently enjoys considerable support.

Sigmund Freud

As we saw in Chapter 1 (pp. 34–35), Freud's ideas are often best thought of as reflecting a maturational position with respect to the sources of development. In accord with the biological-maturational position, he viewed adolescence as a distinctive stage of development during which human beings can at last fulfill the biological imperative to reproduce themselves and hence the species. This evolutionary assumption underlay Freud's emphasis on sex as the master motive for all human behavior, even in the earliest stages of life. He called adolescence the **genital stage** because this is the period during which sexual intercourse becomes a major motive of behavior.

In Freud's theory, the emotional storminess widely believed to accompany the adolescent stage is the culmination of the psychological struggle between the three parts of the personality: the id, the ego, and the superego (see Chapter 10, pp. 386–387). As Freud saw it, the upsurge in sexual excitation that accompanies puberty reawakens primitive instincts, increases the power of the id, and upsets the psychological balance achieved during middle childhood. This imbalance produces psychological conflict and erratic behavior. The main developmental task of adolescence is therefore to reestablish the balance of psychological forces by reintegrating them in a new and more mature way that is compatible with the individual's new sexual capacities.

Freud, like Hall, was greatly influenced by the doctrine of recapitulationism (Gould, 1977b; Sulloway, 1979). He argued, for example, that when sexual maturation reawakens the oedipal urges that were repressed at the start of middle childhood, the young person must rework this old conflict under the new conditions.

Although Freud's theory of adolescence is rooted in biology, it does not ignore the social world. The superego is, after all, the internal representation of society, and the ego mediates between the social world embodied in the superego on the one hand and the demands of the id on the other. Consequently, personality development during adolescence, as in earlier periods, involves social as well as biological factors.

Genital stage In Freudian theory, the period of mature sexuality that begins with adolescence, in which sexual urges are directed to peers of the opposite sex.

Ethological approaches

A recent trend in the study of adolescence has been a growing interest in applying the theories and methods of *ethology;* that is, the study of animal behavior within an evolutionary framework (MacDonald, 1988). As we saw in our discussion of so-cial development in early childhood (Chapter 10, p. 411), there are striking simi-larities between the development of dominance relations in human children's so-cial interactions and in those of nonhuman species, and some psychologists hypothesize a common biological mechanism behind these similarities (Strayer, 1991). Research by Ritch Savin-Williams (1987) on the development of social hi-erarchies and aggressive behavior among teenagers suggests the continued impor-tance of such social control mechanisms during adolescence.

An interesting finding to emerge from studies of nonhuman primates is the presence of a transition period for males between the juvenile and adult stages of life. In some respects it resembles human adolescence (Montemayor, 1990). Non-human primate females enter adulthood as soon as they become sexually mature, but males go through a conflictual period in which they must aggressively fight for access to females. One investigator, impressed by the stress and danger of this transitional period, characterizes the adolescence of the nonhuman male primate as "the most dangerous and traumatic stage in his life" (Dolhinow, 1971, p. 383). In some human cultures, as we shall see, similar sex differences in the transition from childhood to adulthood can be observed.

THE ENVIRONMENTAL-LEARNING PERSPECTIVE

Beginning with the ascendance of behaviorist explanations of human behavior in the 1920s, biologically oriented accounts of development were criticized for un-derestimating the degree to which the social environment shapes children's behav-iors and for overestimating the degree of discontinuity that distinguishes adoles-cence from middle childhood. For example, Albert Bandura and Richard Walters (1959) argued that the aggressiveness that is often associated with adolescent boys is a product of societal reinforcement, not an innate predisposition. They found that aggressive boys were encouraged by their parents to be aggressive outside the home—to "stick up for their rights" and use their fists. The fathers of aggressive boys even seemed to get vicarious enjoyment from their sons' aggressive behavior. By being aggressive, then, the boys could have the satisfaction of pleasing their fa-thers. Similar findings have been reported by Gerald Patterson and his colleagues (1989).

Arguing that the same principles of learning that apply to human develop-ment at younger ages continue to apply during the teenage years, Bandura (1964) has been skeptical about claims that adolescence is a distinctive stage of develop-ment. He has been particularly critical of the idea that adolescence is inevitably a period of stress, tension, and rebellion, citing evidence that the rate of emotional difficulties is no higher among adolescents than among adults.

Investigators who give the most weight to environmental factors in develop-ment point to cultural variations in the behavior of teenagers as evidence that ado-lescent behaviors are shaped primarily by the social environment. One of the most famous studies in this tradition was undertaken by the anthropologist Margaret Mead (1901–1978), who went to the Pacific islands of Samoa in 1926. Mead as-sumed she would find young people going through adolescence but she ques-tioned whether the psychological characteristics associated with adolescence by Freud, Hall, and others would be universal. She posed the question to be an-swered by her research in a characteristically straightforward manner:

> Is adolescence a period of mental and emotional stress for the growing girl as
> inevitably as teething is a period of misery for the small baby? Can we think
> of adolescence as a time in the life history of every girl child which carries
> with it symptoms of conflict and stress as surely as it implies a change in the
> girl's body?

Her conclusion was equally straightforward:

> Following the Samoan girls through every aspect of their lives we have tried
> to answer this question and we found throughout that we had to answer it in
> the negative. The adolescent girl in Samoa differed from her sister who had
> not reached puberty in one chief respect, that in the older girl certain bodily
> changes were present which were absent in the younger girl. There were no
> other great differences to set off the group passing through adolescence from
> the group which would become adolescent in two years or the group which
> had become adolescent two years earlier. (1928/1973, p. 109)

Mead attributed the tranquility of Samoan adolescence to the general casual-
ness of Samoan society, particularly its relaxed attitude toward sexual relationships
among adolescents, in contrast to the wide variety of conflicting attitudes and
choices that confront young people in the United States and in Western European societies.

Although later investigators have claimed that there was a much higher level
of conflict and stress among Samoan girls than Mead recognized (Freeman, 1983;
Raum, 1940/1967), Mead's work has exerted enormous influence on modern ideas
about adolescence. She forced psychologists to pay serious attention to the cultural and social factors that contribute to the characteristics of adolescence proposed by Hall, Freud, and other biologically oriented psychologists.

A second environmental-learning approach to the study of adolescence is to
identify naturally occurring socio-environmental variations *within* cultural groups
or to create environmental variations experimentally and to look for ways in which
those variations might affect behavior. The first of these paths has been followed
by Diana Baumrind (1991), whose work on the influence of parenting behaviors
on young children's social, academic, and personality development was discussed
in Chapter 11 (pp. 434–436).

When Baumrind returned to her sample of families after the children entered
adolescence, she found that the children of "authoritative" parents (those who im-
parted clear standards, demanded high performance, and were responsive to their
children) were as "outstandingly competent" as adolescents as they had been earlier. The children of "directive," or "authoritarian," families achieved less in
school, engaged in more antisocial behavior, and precipitated more family conflict.
By this account, parenting styles are important environmental factors in the regulation of behavior during adolescence.

The second path to testing environmental-learning theories of adolescence is
seen in a persuasive experiment by Nancy Guerra and Ronald Slaby (1990). Following the lead of Kenneth Dodge (see Chapter 14, p. 594), Guerra and Slaby designed a 12-session program to teach inmates of a state juvenile correction facility
how to recognize important social cues, seek additional information when problems arose, generate alternative solutions to problems, and make good choices
among the alternatives they came up with. Even this relatively short training program produced marked reductions in aggression, impulsivity, and inflexibility in
the adolescents' everyday interactions outside the training environment, thus
demonstrating the power of the environment to shape development. A major
virtue of such approaches to the study of development is that they also provide
procedures for modifying behaviors that are unacceptable to society at large
(Eron, Gentry, & Schlegel, 1995).

PIAGET'S CONSTRUCTIVIST PERSPECTIVE

Piaget's approach to adolescence is a direct continuation of the line of theorizing
that we have traced in earlier chapters. He sought to reconcile the biological and
environmental-learning explanations of adolescence by showing how the distinc-

tive qualities of this period of development arise from the interaction of biological and social factors found in all societies, irrespective of their cultural organization.

At the core of Piaget's theory of adolescence is the idea that as young people begin to take on adult roles, they must begin to plan ahead and to think more systematically about the world. As we will see in Chapter 16, Barbel Inhelder and Piaget (1958) believed that the systematic nature of adolescent thinking indicates an advance from the concrete operational to the formal operational level. They argued that this new mode of thinking changes all aspects of psychological functioning, including adolescents' understanding of themselves, their relations with peers, their ability to work, and their attitudes toward social ideals.

ERIK ERIKSON'S APPROACH

As we mentioned in Chapter 1, Erik Erikson's theory of development is difficult to classify. Although he was a student of Freud, whose approach was more biologically oriented, Erikson was as concerned as Mead was to show that the development of human personality also depends heavily on the cultural organization of children's experience; in this respect he was similar to the environmental-learning and cultural-context theorists. Yet he accepted Freud's emphasis on the role of biological factors in shaping the characteristics of adolescence, and he too maintained that adolescence is a universal, qualitatively distinct period of development. His ideas about the cognitive characteristics of adolescence were also similar to Piaget's in some respects (Kegan, 1982; Kohlberg, 1984).

Erikson believed that the task for young people about to enter adulthood is to incorporate their new sexual drives and the social demands placed upon them into a fully integrated and healthy personality. The result of this integration is what Erikson called *identity*, which he defined as a "sense of personal sameness and historical continuity" (1968a, p. 17). Our identity tells us how we fit in with the people around us and with our selves of the past and future. Identity is not a single trait or belief. Rather, it is a *pattern* of beliefs about themselves that adolescents construct to reconcile the many ways in which they are like other people with the ways in which they differ from them.

The formation of identity becomes crucial during adolescence, in Erikson's view, because this is the time when the child's beliefs, abilities, and desires must be reconciled with adult norms; that is, individual identity and social identity must be made compatible so that the adolescent may eventually find a place in the adult world. For this reason, Erikson characterized the central crisis of adolescence as one of "identity versus identity confusion" (1968a, p. 94). Identity confusion leads to social deviance and conflict.

Erikson's approach to adolescence is also notable in that he did not view adolescence as the end point of development; like cultural-context theorists, he viewed development as a lifelong process. (It may be helpful to refer back to Table 1.1, p. 7, for a summary of the developmental stages posited by leading theorists, and Box 10.2, p. 403, for a summary of Erikson's stages.)

THE CULTURAL-CONTEXT PERSPECTIVE

The theories of adolescence discussed so far have differed from one another in several respects, including whether or not they consider development to end with adolescence, the emphasis they place on biological versus social factors as determinants of the psychological characteristics of the period, and the distinctiveness they attribute to the psychological characteristics of adolescence. The biological-maturation and Piagetian views are alike in their assumption that adolescence is a universal period of development that encompasses some part of the teenage years. Environmental-learning theorists also accept the universality of adolescence as a transition from childhood to adulthood but deny it has specific, universal, stagelike qualities. Developmentalists who take the cultural-context view contend that adolescence exists as a prominent stage of development only in societies where young people reach biological maturity before they have acquired the knowledge and skills needed to ensure cultural reproduction (Schlegel & Barry, 1991; Whiting, Burbank, & Ratner, 1986).

Among traditional !Kung San of the Kalahari Desert, for example, there is no delay between puberty and marriage. During middle childhood, !Kung San children become sufficiently competent at hunting animals and gathering wild plant products to sustain themselves. When they become ready for biological reproduction, they are also ready to engage in the tasks of cultural reproduction; they can sustain a family economically and can bring their children up to deal with the world as they know it (Shostak, 1981). When 13- and 14-year-olds in the United States have children, by contrast, both the parents and the children face great hardships because the parents cannot sustain either themselves or their children (McLoyd et al., 1994; Alan Guttmacher Institute, 1994).

According to the cultural-context view, the kinds of activities that must be mastered to carry out the full process of human reproduction in one's society shape the psychological characteristics that one develops at the end of childhood. The intellectual skills of a teenage girl in Detroit, say, who spends her days studying mathematics, the natural sciences, and literature, are likely to differ from those of a girl in a nonliterate society who spends her days helping her mother-in-law with farming, cooking, and child-rearing chores. She is also likely to have a distinctly different sense of herself and different relationships with her peers, parents, and other kin.

As we have found for each of the earlier periods of development, data that support one theoretical perspective do not require total rejection of rival perspectives. In some cases, when two different lines of research are asking similar questions and have gathered data in similar ways, theoretical disputes between researchers can be settled by further observation. But often the aspects of development addressed by rival theories differ too much to permit direct comparisons or choices among them.

With these words of caution, we will now turn to the major phenomena of the adolescent period that the alternative theories attempt to explain. We will start with a description of puberty, the biological changes that initiate the capacity for sexual reproduction. We will then turn to the reorganization of social life that the potential for biological reproduction requires as an essential part of the transition to adulthood. Other psychological changes, including cognitive and personality development, will be addressed in Chapter 16.

Puberty

During the second decade of life, the series of biological developments known as **puberty** transform individuals from a state of physical immaturity to one in which they are biologically mature and capable of sexual reproduction. Puberty begins with a signal from the hypothalamus, located at the base of the brain, that activates the pituitary gland, a pea-sized organ appended to the hypothalamus. The pituitary then increases its production of growth hormones, which in turn stimulate the growth of all body tissue. The pituitary gland also releases hormones that trigger a great increase in the manufacture of two gonadotrophic ("gonad-seeking") hormones. The **gonads,** or primary sex organs, are the ovaries in females and the testes in males. In females these hormones stimulate the ovaries to manufacture the hormones estrogen and progesterone, which trigger the numerous physical events, including the release of mature ova from the ovaries, that

Puberty Biological developments that transform individuals from a state of physical immaturity to one in which they are biologically mature and capable of reproduction.

Gonads The primary sex organs—the ovaries in females and the testes in males.

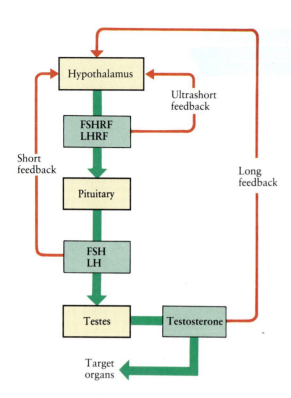

FIGURE 15.1 *Puberty in males is initiated by complex interactions among the hypothalamus, the pituitary gland, and the testes. When the hypothalamus releases gonadotropin-releasing factors (FSHRF, LHRF), it causes the pituitary to discharge the gonadotropins FSH and LH into the blood. These hormones stimulate the testes, promoting the production of testosterone, which in turn stimulates changes in other body organs and provides feedback to the hypothalamus. (From Katchadourian, 1977.)*

Primary sexual organs Those organs, like the ovaries in females and the testes in males, that are involved in reproduction.

Secondary sex characteristics The anatomical and physiological signs that outwardly distinguish males from females. They make their appearance as the primary sexual organs are maturing.

eventually allow for reproduction. In males, gonadotrophic hormones stimulate the testes and adrenal glands to manufacture the hormone testosterone, which brings about the manufacture of sperm (Katchadourian, 1977) (see Figure 15.1). While estrogen is usually considered to be the female hormone and testosterone the male hormone, both hormones are present in the two sexes. During puberty, both sexes experience an increase in these hormones, but the rate of increase is specific to each sex. Testosterone in boys increases to 18 times the level in middle childhood, while estrogen undergoes an eightfold increase in girls (Malina & Bouchard, 1991).

THE GROWTH SPURT

One of the first visible signs of puberty is a spurt in the rate of physical growth. Boys and girls grow more quickly now than at any other time since they were babies. A boy may grow as much as 9 inches taller and a girl as much as 6 to 7 inches taller during the 2 to 3 years of the growth spurt. Although adolescents continue to grow throughout puberty, they reach 98 percent of their ultimate adult height by the end of the growth spurt (Tanner, 1990).

Some parts of the body spurt ahead of others during adolescence. As a rule, leg length reaches its peak first, followed 6 to 9 months later by trunk length. Shoulder and chest breadths are the last to reach their peak. As J. M. Tanner has quipped, "A boy stops growing out of his trousers (at least in length) a year before he stops growing out of his jackets" (1978, p. 69).

Even the head, which has grown little since the age of 2, participates in the growth spurt. The skull bones thicken, lengthening and widening the head. The brain, which attains 90 percent of its adult weight by the age of 5, grows little during this period (Tanner, 1990).

Changes in physical size are accompanied by changes in overall shape. During puberty males and females acquire the distinctive physical features that characterize the two sexes. Girls develop breasts and their hips expand. Boys acquire wide shoulders and a muscular neck. Boys also lose fat during adolescence, and so appear more muscular and angular than girls. Girls continue to have a higher ratio of fat to muscle, so that they have a rounder, softer look.

Most boys not only appear to be stronger than girls after puberty, they *are* stronger. Before puberty, boys and girls of similar size differ little in strength. But by the end of this period, boys can exercise for longer periods and can exert more force per ounce of muscle than girls of the same size. Boys develop relatively larger hearts and lungs, which give them higher blood pressure when their heart muscles contract, a lower resting heart rate, and a greater capacity for carrying oxygen in the blood, which neutralizes the chemicals that lead to fatigue during physical exercise (Katchadourian, 1977).

The physiological differences between males and females may help to explain why males have traditionally been the warriors, hunters, and heavy laborers throughout human history. They also help to explain why most superior male athletes can outperform superior female athletes. In some important respects, however, females exhibit greater physical prowess than males: they are, on the average, healthier, longer lived, and better able to tolerate long-term stress (Hayflick, 1994).

SEXUAL DEVELOPMENT

During puberty all the **primary sex organs,** the organs involved in reproduction, enlarge and become functionally mature. In males the testes begin to produce sperm cells and the prostate begins to produce semen, the fluid that carries the sperm. They come together in the vas deferens. In females the ovaries begin to release mature ova into the fallopian tubes. When conception does not take place, menstruation occurs.

Secondary sex characteristics, the anatomical and physiological signs that outwardly distinguish males from females, appear at the same time that the primary sex organs are maturing (see Figure 15.2). The first signs that boys are entering puberty are an enlargement of the testes, a thickening and reddening of the skin of the scrotum, and the appearance of pubic hair. These changes usually occur about a year before boys begin their growth spurt. About the time the growth spurt begins, the penis begins to grow; it continues to do so for about 2 years. About a year after the penis begins to grow, boys become able to ejaculate semen. The first ejaculation often occurs spontaneously during sleep and is called a nocturnal emission. At first the sperm in the semen are less numerous and less fertile than in adult males (Katchadourian, 1977).

Underarm and facial hair usually appear about 2 years after a boy's pubic hair begins to grow, but in some individuals underarm and facial hair may appear first. Most men do not develop a hairy chest until late adolescence or early adulthood. A boy's voice usually does not deepen until late in puberty, and then does so gradually as the larynx expands and the vocal cords lengthen. During this process, cracks in a boy's voice announce to the world the changes that are taking place in his body.

The first visible sign that a girl is beginning to mature sexually is often the appearance of a small rise around the nipples called the breast bud. Pubic hair

FIGURE 15.2 *The hormonal changes that accompany puberty cause a wide variety of physical changes in both females and males. (Adapted from Netter, 1965.)*

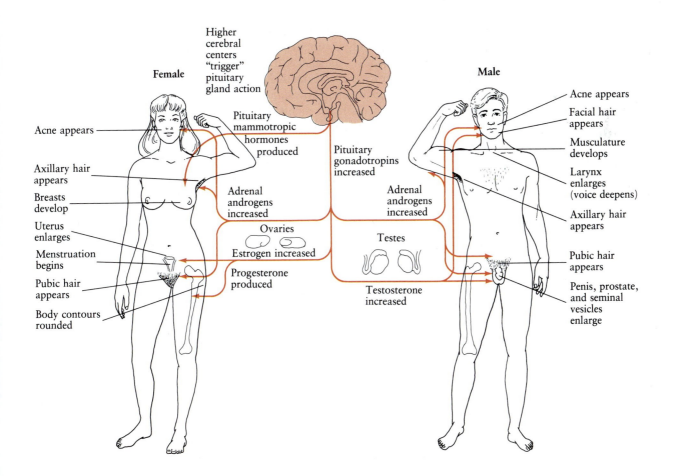

usually appears a little later, just before the growth spurt begins, but sometimes it appears first. About the same time that girls' outward appearance is beginning to change, their ovaries enlarge and the cells that eventually will evolve into ova begin to ripen. The uterus begins to grow and the vaginal lining thickens.

Girls' secondary sex characteristics develop throughout puberty. The breasts continue to grow with the development of the mammary glands, which allow for lactation, and the accumulation of adipose (fatty) tissue, which gives them their adult shape.

Menarche A girl's first menstrual period.

Usually **menarche**—the first menstrual period—occurs relatively late in puberty, about 18 months after the growth spurt has reached its peak velocity. Early menstrual periods tend to be irregular, and they often occur without ovulation—the release of a mature egg. Ovulation typically begins about 12 to 18 months after menarche (Boxer, Tobin-Richards, & Petersen, 1983).

THE TIMING OF PUBERTY

A glance around a seventh-grade classroom is sufficient to remind even the most casual observer of the wide variations in the age at which puberty begins. Some of the 12- and 13-year-old boys may look much as they did at the age of 9 or 10, whereas others may have the gangly look that often characterizes the growth spurt. Among the girls, who on the average begin to mature sexually somewhat earlier, some may look like mature women with fully developed breasts and rounded hips, some may still have the stature and shape of little girls, and some may be somewhere in between.

The timing of the changes of puberty depends, as do all events in development, on complex interactions between genetic and environmental factors. The importance of genetic factors is demonstrated by comparisons of identical and fraternal twins. The average difference in the age at which menarche occurs in identical twin sisters is only 2 months, whereas the average difference for fraternal twin sisters is 8 months (Marshall & Tanner, 1974).

Several studies have documented the importance of environmental factors in the timing of menarche. Michelle Warren and her colleagues (1991) report that adolescent dancers reach menarche later than other girls, and many studies show the same pattern in girls who participate in a high level of physical exercise (Calabrese et al., 1983).

A variety of other environmental factors, such as health, nutrition, stress, and psychological depression, also influence the age of menarche. One important stress factor is family conflict. Studies in the United States and New Zealand have found that adolescents who experience a high level of family conflict go through menarche earlier than those who live in more harmonious families (Graber et al., 1995; Moffit et al., 1992). At present researchers are uncertain about how these effects are produced. There is broad agreement that environmental stress affects children's developing hormonal systems. However, the exact mechanisms of these effects and the importance of the time at which they occur remain uncertain.

The age at which menarche is reached has also undergone striking historical changes. In industrialized countries and in some developing countries as well, the age when menstruation begins has been declining among all social groups (see Figure 15.3). In the 1840s the average age of menarche among European women was between 14 and 15 years, whereas today it is between 12 and 13 (Bullough, 1981). A similar trend is apparent in the United States, where menarche occurs more than 2 years earlier than it did in 1890.

Puberty also seems to be occurring earlier among males, but the evidence for this change is less direct. Fifty years ago the average American male gained his maximum height at the age of 26; now this marker of the end of puberty occurs, on average, at the age of 18 (Marshall & Tanner, 1974).

Studies of the physical changes associated with puberty indicate that it ordinarily lasts about 4 years (Tanner, 1990) (see Figure 15.4). The duration of puberty, however, is as variable as the age at which it begins. One boy may go through all the events of puberty in the time it takes another's genitals to develop.

THE DEVELOPMENTAL IMPACT OF PUBERTY

The biological changes associated with puberty are of special significance both to the young people themselves and to their community, but the way these changes are interpreted and portrayed varies with cultural circumstances and personal characteristics.

Rites of passage

In many societies the transition to adolescence is recognized by ritual. These ceremonies are often public events that herald the contributions to society the young person is expected to make in his or her adult life (Schlegel & Barry, 1991). When Margaret Mead visited the Arapesh of New Guinea several decades ago, a girl's first menstruation was accompanied by ceremonial rites that symbolized her emergence as a woman ready to become a productive member of the community. Here Mead describes the preparations for the ceremony, which takes place in the girl's husband's home:

> Her woven arm and leg bands, her earrings, her old lime gourd and lime spatula are taken from her. Her woven belt is taken off. If these are fairly new they are given away; if they are old they are cut off and destroyed. There

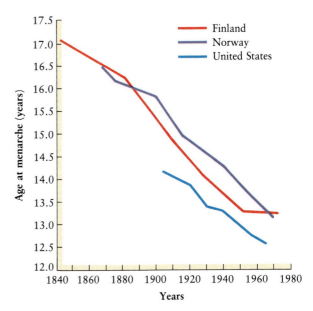

FIGURE 15.3   *The age of menarche has been declining in many countries during the past 150 years. (Adapted from Katchadourian, 1977.)*

FIGURE 15.4   *Diagram of the sequence of events at puberty in girls (left) and boys (right). (From Tanner, 1990.)*

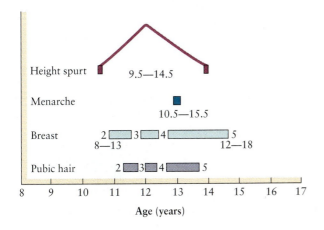

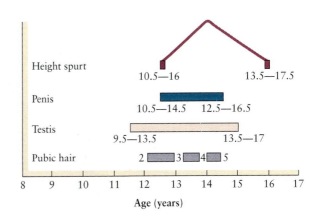

is no feeling that they themselves are contaminated, but only the desire to cut the girl's connection with her past.

The girl is attended by older women who are her own relatives or relatives of her husband. They rub her all over with stinging nettles. They tell her to roll one of the large nettle-leaves into a tube and thrust it into her vulva: this will ensure her breasts growing large and strong. The girl eats no food, nor does she drink water. On the third day, she comes out of the hut and stands against a tree while her mother's brother makes the decorative cuts on her shoulders and buttocks. . . . Each day the women rub the girl with nettles. It is well if she fasts for five or six days, but the women watch her anxiously, and if she becomes too weak they put an end to it. Fasting will make her strong, but too much of it might make her die, and the emergence ceremony is hastened. (1935, pp. 92–93)

Among the Mano in Liberia and in several other West African tribes, boys undergo a ceremonial "death" at puberty and are then spirited away by older men to an isolated grove deep in the forest. There they are taught the secret lore of the men, as well as farming and other skills they will need to earn a living. When they emerge from "behind the fence," in some cases several years later, they have a new name and a new identity (Harley, 1941).

Psychological responses to pubertal events

Modern societies have nothing that corresponds to a full initiation ceremony to mark the passage out of childhood. The events of puberty are rarely talked about publicly by the individuals who are experiencing them or by their community. Until fairly recently, when people recalled menarche or their first ejaculations it was often in negative or comic terms. By and large, the research done on adolescents' psychological responses to puberty has focused on the experiences of white middle-class adolescents.

When girls who had recently started to menstruate were asked how they felt about their first menstruation, about 20 percent reported feeling positive, about 20 percent said they felt negative, and another 20 percent were indefinite. The remaining 40 percent reported being both "excited and pleased" and "scared and

Every society has evolved customs that mark the end of childhood and the transition to adult status. Here Karla Chavez celebrates her quinceañera, her fifteenth birthday, in Houston with a mass followed by a dance.

upset," but for the most part their feelings were not very intense (Ruble & Brooks-Gunn, 1982).

In a series of studies (summarized in Brooks-Gunn & Reiter, 1990) Jeanne Brooks-Gunn and her colleagues have found that girls' attitudes and beliefs about menstruation are only in part a result of their direct experience. In fact, a girl's physical symptoms during menstruation are often correlated with the expectations she had *before* menarche (Brooks-Gunn, 1987). Girls who reported unpleasant symptoms were more likely to have been unprepared for menarche, to have matured early, and to have been told about menstruation by someone they perceived negatively.

Similarly, the responses of boys to their first ejaculations (**semenarche**) depend on the context in which it occurs. When semenarche occurs as a nocturnal emission (wet dream), boys report that their primary reactions are surprise and confusion. One boy recalled, "It reminded me of peeing in my pants—that was my first reaction even though I'd never done it" (Stein & Reisser, 1994, p. 377). If semenarche occurs during masturbation, the predominant reaction is more positive.

Both boys and girls are initially secretive about the onset of nocturnal emissions and menarche. Girls report telling far fewer friends that they have begun menstruating than they thought they would ahead of time. About one-fourth of all girls questioned report telling only their mothers. This reticence does not last, however. By the time they have been menstruating for 6 months, most have talked to their friends about it (Brooks-Gunn et al., 1986). Boys are far more likely to be reticent about the onset of puberty and thus receive far less social support from their parents and peers than girls do (Stein & Reisser, 1994).

Semenarche A boy's first ejaculation.

Consequences of early and late maturation

Several studies have sought to determine whether relatively early or late sexual maturation influences young people's peer relations, personality, and social adjustment (Figure 15.5). This research has produced a mixed picture (Richards, Abell, & Petersen, 1993).

One of the earliest of these studies, conducted by Mary Cover Jones and Nancy Bayley (1950), reported different consequences for early- and late-maturing boys in the United States. Using data from an ongoing longitudinal study of growth and development, these researchers identified 16 adolescent boys who

FIGURE 15.5 *Differences in the timing of puberty can result in startling differences in size between adolescents who are close in age.*

BOX 15.1

Eating Disorders

Gena was a chubby clarinet player who liked to read and play chess. She was more interested in computers than makeup and in stuffed animals than designer clothes. She walked to her first day of junior high with her pencils sharpened and her notebooks neatly labelled. She was ready to learn Spanish and algebra and to audition for the school orchestra. She came home sullen and shaken. The boy who had his locker next to hers had smashed into her with his locker door and sneered, "Move your fat ass."

That night she told her mother, "I hate my looks. I need to go on a diet."

Her mother thought, Is that what this boy saw? When he looked at my musical, idealistic Gena, did he see only her behind? (Pipher, 1994, p. 55)

The message to girls in our society comes across loud and clear: being beautiful means being thin. Images of tall, lithe models with boyish figures smile at us from the covers of fashion magazines. Thin young actresses are the objects of desire in popular movies. The media often represent heavy-set people as unhappy, unattractive people who lack self-control and deserve no respect or admiration. It is no wonder, then, that most adolescent girls in our society are afraid of being fat. They want to be beautiful; they want to look like models and actresses.

For better or for worse, the thin, prepubertal body shape idealized by the media is unattainable for most adolescents and women after puberty (Faust, 1983). One of the most dramatic physical changes associated with puberty for girls is the accumulation of fat in their subcutaneous tissues (Young, Sipin, & Rose, 1968). It has been estimated that during adolescence the average girl gains a little over 24 pounds in the form of body fat (Brooks-Gunn & Warren, 1985). This weight gain is perfectly normal.

As a result of the gap between the cultural ideal of thinness and the reality of normal development, many adolescent girls are dissatisfied with their new, more mature bodies; they see themselves as being "overweight" and "ugly" (Phelps et al., 1993). Many of them go to great lengths to lose weight. They go on fad diets, extreme regimens in which they may cut out entire classes of food, such as fats or carbohydrates; or take drugs to suppress their appetites; or induce vomiting and take laxatives to avoid gaining weight (Pipher, 1994). All of these practices endanger their health and in extreme forms can lead to psychiatric disorders known as eating disorders.

---

were maturing late and 16 who were maturing early, according to X-ray analyses of their bone growth. They then asked adults and peers who knew the boys to rate them on a variety of social and personality scales to see if the boys' state of physical maturation affected other people's perceptions of them.

Both adults and peers rated the early-maturing boys as more psychologically and socially mature. These boys did not appear to need to strive for status, and they were the group from which school leaders emerged. The boys who were slower to mature physically were rated as less mature both psychologically and socially. Both adults and peers thought that they often sought attention to compensate for their late development and that some of them tended to withdraw from social interaction. Other studies have confirmed some parts of this picture. In general, early-maturing boys seem to have a more favorable attitude toward their bodies, largely because their greater size and strength make them more capable athletes, and athletic prowess in turn brings them social recognition (Brooks-Gunn & Petersen, 1983; Simmons & Blyth, 1987).

Not all the effects of early maturation are positive for boys. On the basis of data from a longitudinal study that used a personality test to measure maturity instead of ratings by other people, Harvey Peskin (1967) found that early-maturing boys become significantly more somber, temporarily more anxious, less exploratory, less intellectually curious, and less active after the onset of puberty than do late-maturing boys. He argued that early-maturing boys are actually handicapped by the early end to childhood because they are less prepared for the hor-

One eating disorder that has received a great deal of attention from the psychiatric community is *anorexia nervosa*, a condition in which girls starve themselves until they lose 15 to 25 percent of their body weight. The malnutrition associated with anorexia produces such symptoms as cessation of menstruation, pale skin, the appearance of fine black hairs on the body, and extreme sensitivity to cold. Death due to kidney failure or heart damage occurs in about 3 percent of victims (Slaby & Dwenger, 1993). Anorexia is estimated to afflict only 4 out of a million adolescent girls, but it is more prevalent among the white middle and upper classes, where the incidence is as high as 1 in every 100 girls.

Bulimia nervosa is found in all classes and is more common than anorexia. Estimates are that 5 percent of all girls (and a smaller number of boys) are afflicted with this disorder (Graber et al., 1994). Girls suffering from bulimia are usually obsessed by their weight. They try to keep it at a suboptimal level by starving themselves, but the periods of starvation are broken by periods of "binge eating" during which they eat what they consider to be abnormal amounts. Typically these binges are followed by self-induced vomiting or the use of heavy doses of laxatives. Bulimia usually begins when a girl is in late adolescence, often when she leaves home for college, and continues into her 20s.

Jeanne Brooks-Gunn, Julia Graber, and their colleagues (1989, 1994) conducted a longitudinal study to determine the factors that lead to these and other eating problems. They followed 116 adolescent girls attending private schools in a major metropolitan area for 8 years, from the ages of 14 to 22. This age range spans the period when many girls of normal weight begin to diet. The girls filled out questionnaires about their attitudes toward food, their satisfaction with the way they looked, and their perception of social pressures to gain or lose weight. Their physical development and family relationships were also assessed.

The researchers found that several factors contribute to girls' obsession with weight and eating after the onset of puberty. First, as might be expected, those girls with the highest percentage of body fat were most likely to exhibit chronic eating disorders. But pubertal timing, body image, and family relationships also contributed to the onset of eating disorders. Among girls who entered puberty relatively early and who had poor body images, those who were in conflict with their families were at increased risk for chronic eating disorders. Personality factors also played a role: girls who tended toward high levels of psychological depression were more likely than their peers to develop an eating disorder.

monal and social changes taking place. Thus the experience of puberty is more intense and less manageable than it is for those who mature more slowly. In Peskin's view, the social advantages of maturing early also exact a price: later these boys tend to cling too rigidly to the patterns that brought them their early success.

Peskin's conclusions are supported by more recent research that associates early sexual maturation with lower self-control and less emotional stability, as measured by psychological tests (Sussman et al., 1985). Adolescent boys who reach puberty at a relatively early age are also more likely to smoke, drink, use drugs, and get in trouble with the law (Duncan et al., 1985).

The picture for girls is also mixed, but the overall effect of early maturation appears to be more negative (Brooks-Gunn & Petersen, 1983; Simmons & Blyth, 1987; Stattin & Magnusson, 1990). First of all, they are more likely to have negative feelings about their appearance (see Figure 15.6). They are larger than other children their age, especially boys, who generally enter puberty later, and this may be one reason why early-maturing girls are more likely than their peers to say that they are dissatisfied with their height and weight (see Box 15.1). In elementary school, girls who develop before their peers are often embarrassed about it. They wear big shirts to hide their breasts and assume a slouching posture.

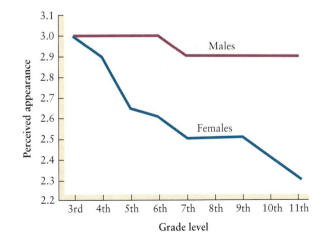

FIGURE 15.6 *The relationship of pubertal change to body image. While boys retain a basically positive image of their bodies as they go through puberty, girls' self-image declines precipitously.*

Second, studies in the United States have found that early-maturing girls tend to have somewhat lower emotional stability and self-control, perhaps as a consequence of the increased uncertainties and social pressures they experience (Richards, Abell, & Petersen, 1993). A longitudinal Swedish study of adolescent girls found that early-maturing girls are also more likely to get into trouble with adults because of a decline in their academic performance, truancy, drug and alcohol use, shoplifting, and running away (Stattin & Magnusson, 1990).

Such outcomes are not inevitable, however. They depend on the social context in which early maturation takes place. Avshalom Caspi and his colleagues (1993) compared the delinquent behavior of early- and late-maturing girls who attended either all-girls or mixed-sex secondary schools in New Zealand. They found attendance at an all-girls school reduced the incidence of delinquent behavior. They conclude that an all-girls school reduces girls' contact with boys, who are the major instigators of socially disapproved behavior.

Early maturation brings some girls greater social prestige based on sexual attractiveness. Girls who had reached puberty by the sixth or seventh grade considered themselves more popular with boys and more likely to be dating than girls who had not yet reached puberty (Simmons et al., 1987). In the Swedish study it was found that early-maturing girls were more likely to have a stable boyfriend and sexual experience by mid-adolescence and, perhaps as a consequence, were also more likely to have unwanted pregnancies than their later-maturing peers (Stattin & Magnusson, 1990).

Early-maturing children of both sexes tend to weigh more and to be slightly shorter than late-maturing children when they finish puberty, and this difference persists throughout life (Malina, 1975). This is an advantage for early-maturing boys, because robust males are considered attractive, but it is a disadvantage for early-maturing girls, who are less likely to fit Western industrialized society's current preference for a thin, long-legged, prepubertal body shape in women.

A relatively late passage through puberty may be a negative experience for girls at first, but the overall consequences are generally positive. Late-maturing sixth-grade girls in the United States report dissatisfaction with their appearance and their lack of popularity, but in a few years they may actually be more satisfied with their appearance and more popular than their early-maturing peers (Simmons & Blyth, 1987).

Unfortunately, evidence concerning the impact of the timing of puberty on later life is scant and inconclusive. On the basis of her study following early-maturing and late-maturing boys into their early 30s, Mary Cover Jones (1965) concluded that early maturation has positive psychological benefits that continue into manhood. She found the early-maturing boys to be poised, cooperative, and responsible; they held good positions at work and were leaders in their social organizations. The late developers were more likely to be impulsive, touchy, and nonconforming; they were not so successful, and some felt rejected and inferior. When John Clausen (1975) tested the same men at the age of 38, however, he could find only two differences between the groups: the early maturers took more pride in being objective and in being seen as conventional than did those who matured late. Hakan Stattin and David Magnusson (1990) found that the early-maturing Swedish girls they studied were likely to have children earlier and to complete fewer years of school than other girls their age.

The Reorganization of Social Life

The marked changes in young people's biological capacities are associated with equally marked changes in the way they interact with their families and their peers.

In the later stages of group development during adolescence, relationships become increasingly heterosexual.

A NEW RELATIONSHIP WITH PEERS

As children enter adolescence their social relationships with their peers undergo a marked reorganization. B. Bradford Brown (1990) identifies four major changes as a part of this reorganization in the lives of adolescents in technologically developed societies:

1. Peer interaction occupies an even larger proportion of time than it did during middle childhood. High school students spend twice as much time with their peers outside of school as they do with their parents or other adults.

2. Adolescent peer groups function with less guidance and control from adults. Instead of being confined to local neighborhoods, adolescent peer groups draw their members from many neighborhoods, and they are more likely to make sure that no parents or other adult authorities are observing their actions.

3. As adolescents increasingly distance themselves from adults, they seek out members of the opposite sex. This gender reorientation is generally believed to be a major reason for the reorganization of peer groups during adolescence.

4. Peer groups increase in size at the same time that friendships and other close relationships increase in intensity.

Friendship

Outside of school, teenagers in the United States spend an average of 22 hours a week with their peers. They report spending more time with their friends than they do with their families or by themselves, and the amount of time they spend this way increases over the course of adolescence (Csikszentmihalyi & Larson, 1984). It should come as no surprise, then, that teenagers typically say they enjoy the time they spend with their friends more than anything else they do (Youniss & Smollar, 1985). They feel their friends understand them and allow them to be themselves.

Because adolescents in the United States are more mobile than younger children and attend larger schools, they have more opportunities to meet peers of other social classes and ethnic backgrounds. Nevertheless, their close friends tend to be even more similar to them than they were in elementary school (Epstein, 1989), a trend that continues all during adolescence (Berndt & Keefe, 1995).

Several large-scale studies conducted in the United States document the changing basis of friendships as children enter adolescence (Berndt, 1988; Bigelow & La Gaipa, 1975; Youniss, 1980). Table 15.1 summarizes these changing expectations. Between the ages of 6 and 12 (grades 1 to 6), participation in common activities, including organized play, is a major reason given for considering a peer a friend. This criterion does not disappear in adolescence but is supplemented by other factors. In grade 7 (12 to 13 years of age), for example, common interests, similarity of attitudes and values, loyalty, and intimacy become important to friendship.

Teenagers choose friends who share their interests, values, beliefs, and attitudes because such friends are more likely to be supportive and understanding (Youniss & Smollar, 1985). High school friends tend to have similar feelings about drug use, drinking, and delinquency (McCord, 1990). They also tend to be similar in their views of school, their academic achievement, their dating, and other leisure-time activities (Berndt & Keefe, 1995; Berndt & Savin-Williams, 1993).

It is not difficult to understand why intimacy and loyalty become major criteria of friendships in adolescence, especially among girls. It is in the context of intimate, self-disclosing conversations with close friends that teenagers define themselves and explore their identities. According to Jeffrey Parker and John Gottman (1989), who observed and recorded teenage conversations, there is a difference between the self-disclosures of friends in middle childhood and those during

TABLE 15.1   Incidence of Various Types of Friendship, by Grade Level (Percent)

Type	Grade Level*							
	1	2	3	4	5	6	7	8
Help (friend as giver)	5	12†	14	7	14	25	33	35
Common activities	3	7	32	52	24	40	60	60
Propinquity	7	5	9	12	12	20	38	32
Stimulation value	2	3	12	23	30	51	52	61
Organized play	2	0	15	26	9	10	17	20
Demographic similarity	0	3	7	35	15	15	10	23
Evaluation	2	5	13	13	17	33	21	30
Acceptance	3	0	5	9	9	18	18	38
Admiration	0	0	5	23	17	24	32	41
Incremental prior interaction	2	7	4	10	10	17	32	34
Loyalty and commitment	0	0	2	5	10	20	40	34
Genuineness	0	3	0	2	5	12	10	32
Help (friend as receiver)	2	5	3	5	2	12	13	25
Intimacy potential	0	0	0	0	0	0	8	20
Common interests	0	0	5	7	0	5	30	18
Similarity of attitudes and values	0	0	0	0	2	3	10	8

* At each grade level, the number of subjects (*n*) = 60.
† An underlined score indicates the grade level at which the incidence of the type of friendship first becomes significant.
Source: Bigelow & La Gaipa, 1975.

adolescence. At younger ages, a self-disclosure prompts a statement of solidarity ("Oh, I know! Me too!"), but little else. In adolescence, self-disclosures occasion psychological attributions and lengthy discussions about the nature of the problem and possible avenues to its resolution. As evidence, Parker and Gottman offer the following excerpt from a conversation between two teenagers:

A: You missed two weeks of school.

B: I know. That's what Dad said. He said, "I guess London didn't help your grades," and I said . . .

A: No, and then you came back and were depressed and that didn't help school too much either. I mean, not wanting to be there doesn't help things at all.

B: I've got to get my grades up.

A: You're only allowed one B this quarter.

B: Yep.

A: You work your tail off in English.

B: Yeah, I'll get an A in English now.

A: OK. [That bad grade] was your fault.

B: *[giggle]*

A: Because you were a stubborn little twit. *[jokingly]* (Parker & Gottman, 1989, p. 121)

Because of the biological changes of puberty and growing involvement with the opposite sex, one of the most important aspects of the self that teenagers explore in their intimate conversations with their friends is their sexuality and how they feel about it:

A: *[joking]* I think you should take Randy to court for statutory rape.

B: I don't. I'm to the point of wondering what "that kind of girl" is. . . . I don't know about the whole scene.

A: The thing is . . .

B: It depends on the reasoning. And how long you've been going out with somebody.

A: Yeah. I'm satisfied with my morals. (Parker & Gottman, 1989, p. 119)

Obviously no one would want to have such a conversation with someone who was not loyal or who might gossip. Nor would one want to share such confidences with a person who was not understanding and supportive.

During the late teen years, girls' friendships seem to lose the feverish, jealous qualities that characterize them during the middle phase of adolescence. Elizabeth Douvan and Joseph Adelson suggest that "needing friendship less, they are less haunted by fears of being abandoned and betrayed" (1966, p. 192). By the time they are in their late teens, most girls show an increased capacity to tolerate friends who differ from them. This trend is consistent with the sequence of Selman's developmental stages of friendship (see Chapter 14, p. 590). According to Selman's (1981) evidence, there is a shift during adolescence from stage 3, in which friendships are seen as a means of developing mutual intimacy and support, to stage 4, which is characterized by a new acceptance of a friend's need to establish relations with other people.

The friendships of boys between the ages of 14 and 16 years are likely to be less close than those of girls, according to Douvan and Adelson (1966). They suggest that boys are more concerned with their relations to authority than girls are. To assert and maintain their independence of parents and other adults, boys need the alliance of a group of friends. Duane Buhrmester and Wyndol Furman

(1987) suggest that these sex differences in friendship are a matter more of style than of substance. They have found that boys form friendships "in which sensitivity to needs and validation of worth are achieved through actions and deeds, rather than through interpersonal disclosure of personal thoughts and feelings" (pp. 111–112). Their view is supported by findings that boys are generally less articulate than girls about the nature and meaning of friendship. Like girls of 11 to 13, the 14- to 16-year-old boys studied by Douvan and Adelson (1966) said that they wanted their friends to be amiable and cooperative, to be able to control their impulses, and to share their interests. Like girls in their late teens, they said they expected their friends to help them in times of trouble. What differed between the sexes was the kind of trouble they expected and therefore the kind of friendly support they sought. Girls wanted their friends to be people they could confide in about their relations with boys, whereas boys wanted their friends to support them when they got into trouble with authority.

Adolescent friendships for both boys and girls play a developmental role similar in certain respects to the role of attachment in infancy. During infancy babies engage in "social referencing"—continually looking to their mothers to see how they evaluate what is going on—and they use their mothers as a "secure base" to which they can retreat when they feel threatened as they explore their environment (see Chapters 5 and 6). During adolescence, friends help each other to confront and make sense of uncertain and often anxiety-provoking situations. The first time a boy calls up a girl for a date, his best friend may well be standing at his elbow. And no sooner has the girl hung up than she is likely to call her best friend. The two pairs of friends will decide together if the call was a success or a failure and lay plans for the next move. For both the infant and the adolescent, successful interaction with the world "out there" modifies the attachment bond; eventually the baby will leave the mother and the adolescent will begin to depend less on the best friend.

Evidence from a number of studies (summarized in Berndt & Savin-Williams, 1993) indicates that close friendships have a positive influence on adolescents' social and personality development. Adolescents who perceive their friends as supportive report fewer school-related and psychological problems, greater confidence in their social acceptance by peers, and less loneliness. Difficulty in making friends during adolescence is part of a broader syndrome of poor adjustment.

Cliques and crowds

Friendships are the smallest unit of peer interaction, a group of two. As children move into adolescence, two additional, more inclusive kinds of peer groups become prominent in some industrialized countries—cliques and crowds. A **clique** is a group with several members that remains small enough to enable the members to be in regular interaction with one another and to serve as the primary peer group (Brown, 1990). Cliques are made up of the people adolescents hang out with regularly. Dexter Dunphy (1963) noted that cliques are about the size of a two-child family with the grandparents present. "Their similarity in size to a family," Dunphy wrote, "facilitates the transference of the individual's allegiance to them and allows them to provide an alternative center of security" (p. 233).

Cliques differ from families in an important respect: they are voluntary groups that adolescents are free to leave, whereas membership in a family is not normally a matter of choice. The element of choice in clique membership reflects the increased control adolescents have in choosing the settings in which they find themselves, the people they associate with, and the things they do.

As children leave elementary school and middle childhood behind, cliques become part of a larger social unit, the crowd. **Crowds** are larger groupings of people who may or may not spend much time together. According to B. Bradford

Clique A group of about 5 or 6 that is small enough for its members to be in regular interaction with one another. It is the primary peer group during adolescence.

Crowd Reputation-based collectives of people who are similarly stereotyped by their peers because of their interests, activities, abilities, or attitudes.

Brown (1990), crowds are "reputation-based collectives" of people who are similarly stereotyped by their peers. Crowds are differentiated by, among other things, the interests, activities, abilities, and attitudes that their members have in common.

Although the labels differ from one locale to another, a relatively small set of stereotypic names are repeatedly encountered in the descriptions adolescents use to differentiate among crowds: jocks, brains, loners, druggies, nerds, and other not-so-flattering designations.

Being identified as a member of a particular crowd has a significant impact on adolescents' social status. James S. Coleman (1962) conducted a classic study of the factors that determine individual status and membership in high-prestige groups among U.S. high school students. He based his conclusions on an analysis of questionnaires distributed to thousands of students at ten high schools in small towns, small cities, large cities, and suburbs. In every school he studied, Coleman found that students could identify a "leading crowd" against which they evaluated themselves. The responses he obtained to the question "What does it take to get into the leading crowd in this school?" reveal some of the values of American adolescent society at the time and the characteristics that were considered important to be a success within it. Coleman found that both boys and girls said a "good personality" was the most important characteristic of people in the leading group. For boys, the next most important characteristics were having a good reputation, being a good athlete, being good-looking, wearing good clothes, and getting good grades. For girls, the most important characteristics after a good personality were good looks, good clothing, and a good reputation. Although Coleman's research was conducted many years ago, later research has confirmed Coleman's general point that there *is* a leading crowd in middle and high schools to which others are oriented (Brown, Mory, & Kinney, 1994).

The leading crowd seemed to have great influence in adolescents' lives. When Coleman asked for responses to the statement "If I could trade, I would be someone different from myself," he found that one out of five boys and girls expressed a desire to change themselves so that they would be accepted by the leading crowd. Being a member of the leading crowd was also associated with greater popularity (see Figure 15.7). Similar results have been reported in more recent research, although the ranking of characteristics that make someone popular has varied according to such factors as grade level, ethnicity, and socioeconomic status (Butcher, 1986; Sebald, 1981; Williams & White, 1983).

When data on the ethnic composition of crowds has been collected in schools with a diverse ethnic population, ethnicity has been found to be an important factor in crowd formation (Brown, 1990). In such cases, one-half to two-thirds of minority-group students were identified by their peers as members of ethnically defined crowds (African Americans, Latinos, Asians, etc.). The remaining students were identified as members of crowds based on reputation, such as jocks and nerds.

In some groups academic achievement leads to a decrease in popularity (Ishiyama & Chabassol, 1985). In some working-class African American communities, for example, academically able young people try to mask their abilities in order to avoid being labeled a "brain" and being ostracized (Fordham & Ogbu, 1986). As a rule, however, "brains" occupy a status somewhere between the elite groups and groups that are disparaged (Brown et al., 1994).

Calling a boy is likely to be a group project at first.

Peer pressure to conform

For many decades psychologists have worried that it may be unhealthy for adolescents to spend excessive time among their peers, beyond the observation and control of adults. The core of this concern was expressed by Urie Bronfenbrenner

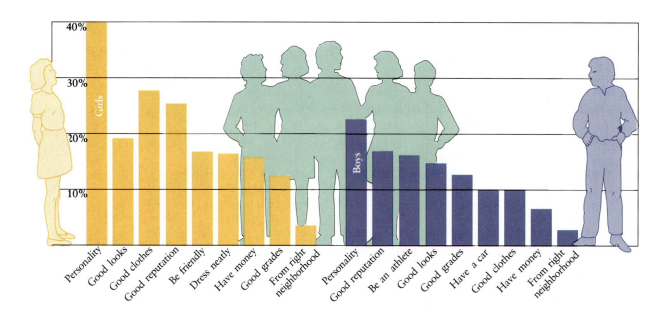

FIGURE 15.7 *The average ranks given by boys and girls to major criteria of popularity. (Adapted from Coleman, 1962.)*

(1970, p. 121): "If children have contact only with their own age-mates, there is no possibility for learning culturally-established patterns of cooperation and mutual concern." In short, left to themselves, adolescents are likely to engage in antisocial behavior.

There is a lot of evidence to support this belief. In a recent study Thomas Berndt and Keunho Keefe (1995) asked a large group of seventh- and eighth-graders to fill out a questionnaire about their involvement in school and any disruptive behaviors they engaged in both in the fall and in the spring of the school year. They were also asked to identify their friends. Their teachers were asked to fill out a questionnaire about each participant to check on the validity of the self-reports.

As one might expect, Berndt and Keefe found that students whose friends engaged in a high level of disruptive behavior in the fall reported an increase in the level of their own disruptive behavior in the spring. The girls were more susceptible to influence than the boys. Other studies show that if an adolescent's close friends use illegal drugs, are sexually active, or break the law, sooner or later the adolescent is likely to do these things, too (see Box 15.2) (Billy & Udry, 1985; Cairns & Cairns, 1994; Kandel & Andrews, 1987).

Such findings, however, are not sufficient to demonstrate that peer pressure *causes* friends to behave similarly. Social influence is a mutual process. Adolescents influence their friends at the same time that they are being influenced by them. They also choose friends who are like them (Cairns & Cairns, 1994). Moreover, adolescent friendships are not particularly stable. When adolescents behave in ways that their friends are uncomfortable with, the bonds of friendship loosen (Cairns & Cairns, 1994; Kandel, 1978). All this makes it hard to determine how much of an adolescent's behavior is influenced by peers.

An earlier study by Thomas Berndt (1979) found that teenagers may not be as susceptible to peer pressure as adults assume they are. In a study with third-through twelfth-graders, Berndt posed several hypothetical situations in which the adolescent could either choose or refuse to go along with the group. Some of the situations were neutral, while others involved more questionable behavior, such as the following:

You are with a couple of friends on Halloween. They're going to soap windows, but you're not sure whether you should or not. Your friends all say you should, because there is no way you could get caught. What would you really do? (p. 610)

As Figure 15.8 shows, Berndt found that the level of conformity to peer pressure to engage in antisocial acts increased between the third and ninth grades (roughly between the ages of 9 and 15) and then decreased. This pattern of increased susceptibility to peer pressure during adolescence followed by a decline has been found by other investigators (Brown, Clasen, & Eicher, 1986). Note three points, however. First, there is little increase in the conformity of adolescents *unless* the issue is whether to do something antisocial. Second, the level of conformity to peer pressure is *lower* for antisocial acts than for neutral ones. Third, overall the students were more likely to say they would *not* go along with their peers than to say they would.

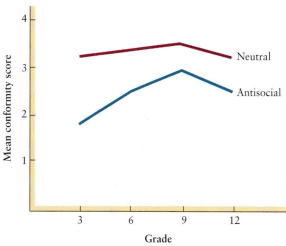

FIGURE 15.8 *Susceptibility to peer pressure increases during early adolescence and then begins to decline. A score of 3.5 indicates equal likelihood of succumbing to and rejecting peer pressure. (Adapted from Berndt, 1979.)*

Berndt also asked his subjects to evaluate the seriousness of various kinds of antisocial behaviors, such as stealing candy from a store. He found that the adolescents evaluated antisocial behaviors as being less bad than third-graders did. Third-graders were likely to say that stealing candy from a store is very bad, whereas ninth-graders did not seem to think it was particularly bad at all. Consequently, the increase in going along with peers displayed in Figure 15.8 may reflect not an increase in the influence of peer pressure but decreased concern that the action is wrong. As Berndt comments, the results "suggest that mid-adolescence is the period of least acceptance of conventional standards of behavior" (1979, p. 613).

As adolescents grow older, they are increasingly likely to drink alcoholic beverages, smoke cigarettes, and become sexually active. Adults disapprove of such activities for young people, though they think nothing of drinking or having sexual relations themselves. This situation has led Richard and Shirley Jessor (1977) to argue that age-related increases in drinking and other "grown-up" activities that some people might consider risk taking should be viewed not as social deviance but as an attempt to model accepted adult behavior.

Peer group organization and the transition to sexual relationships

Despite the fact that it was carried out many years ago, Dexter Dunphy's (1963) study of adolescent peer groups remains the field's most influential source of information about the transition to heterosexual social relationships during adolescence. Dunphy observed and interviewed 303 Australian young people between the ages of 13 and 21 over a 2-year period in largely middle-class areas of Sydney. He supplemented his notes and records with data from questionnaires and diaries kept by his subjects. He focused on the peer group's evolution from a same-sex clique at the start of adolescence to a heterosexual crowd later on. The crowds he studied ranged in size from 15 to 30 members, with an average of about 20.

As the adolescents Dunphy studied grew older, the dynamics within their cliques and crowds changed in a way that seemed to support their transition to heterosexual intimacy. Dunphy's diagram of the stages of this transition is shown in Figure 15.9. At stage 1 there are as yet no crowds, only isolated same-sex cliques. These cliques are, in effect, a continuation from the days of middle childhood.

Stage 2 represents the first movement toward heterosexual peer relations. At first the cliques come together to form crowds at such places as skating rinks, football games, swimming pools, and pizza parlors, where boys and girls get together under conditions in which anonymity precludes the likelihood of intimacy, which they fear.

BOX 15.2

Risk Taking and Social Deviance during Adolescence

While the extent of psychological storm and stress during adolescence continues to be debated, there is little debate that in modern industrial societies, adolescents engage in an exceptional level of socially disapproved behaviors that pose risks to their long-term well-being

(Arnett, 1992; Hechinger, 1992; U.S. Office of Technology Assessment, 1991).

- One in seven U.S. adolescents have contracted sexually transmitted diseases; this level is twice that of people in their 20s.
- Fifty-eight percent of all traffic accidents in Canada involve 16- to 21-year-olds, although this group accounts for just 21 percent of licensed drivers.
- Seventeen percent of high school students reported using alcohol or drugs while swimming or boating during the previous year.
- Adolescents are overrepresented in the commission of petty crimes.

These kinds of statistics, coupled with the fact that the levels of such behaviors seem to have risen sharply in recent years, have spurred efforts to understand and address what policy makers perceive as a crisis that may threaten the well-being of society as a whole (Carnegie Council on Adolescent Development, 1995).

In sharp contrast to these figures, cross-cultural evidence indicates that high levels of risk taking and antisocial behavior are not a universal feature of the transition to adulthood. In their survey of world cultures, Alice Schlegel and Herbert Barry (1991) report that such behaviors are typical of less than 50 percent of boys and less than 20 percent of girls. Two features distinguish societies where antisocial behavior is common from those where it is not. First, when adolescent boys spend most of their time with adult men at work and during leisure hours, antisocial behavior is absent. When boys spend most of their time in peer groups, the level of antisocial behavior is significantly elevated. Second, the nature of the interactions in a given peer group makes a difference. When peer groups are organized for competition and given special names, antisocial behavior is significantly higher than it is when peer relations are less formally organized and noncompetitive.

These results immediately indicate why high levels of antisocial behavior could be expected in the contemporary United States. Adolescents spend a great deal of time in peer groups that are often highly organized and competitive, gangs being an especially prominent example.

The cross-cultural data speak to the issue of antisocial behavior, but they do not shed light on the high level of risk-taking behavior that is so worrisome to contemporary policy makers in the United States. The leading hypotheses concerning that problem are being investigated in other ways.

One frequently offered explanation is that adolescents ignore or greatly underestimate the risks they are taking. In effect, according to this view, adolescents feel invulnerable and don't believe that anything bad can happen to them. To evaluate this possibility, Marilyn Quadrel and her colleagues (1993) conducted a study of adults, their adolescent children, and other adolescents living in treatment homes because they had gotten into trouble through their risky, antisocial behavior. Subjects were asked to estimate the risk they, their parents, and a friend would face with respect to such events as an automobile accident, an unplanned pregnancy, and alcohol dependency. Subjects in all three groups thought that they were at less risk than other people, but the adolescents were no more likely to make such judgments than the adults. These results speak against the idea that adolescents are especially prone to view themselves as invulnerable to risk.

Jeffrey Arnett (1992) argues that psychological characteristics common to adolescents in general combine with culturally specific forms of socialization (such as the promotion of competitiveness) to raise the levels of risk taking and antisocial behavior among teenagers in the United States. According to Arnett, an important psychological characteristic underpinning adolescent risk taking is *sensation seeking*, defined as "the need for varied, novel, and complex sensations and experiences and the willingness to take physical and social risks for the sake of such experiences" (Zuckerman, 1979, p. 10). He summarized a number of studies of adolescent brain function as well as enzyme and hormonal levels to argue that one important factor in the increase in sensation seeking is simply maturation. According to this view, the reason risk taking and antisocial behavior are less prevalent in societies where adolescents continue to spend their time with adults is that the adults act as a counterforce against the biological changes of adolescence.

Richard Jessor (1992) is critical of the sensation-seeking hypothesis. He argues:

Playing the game of "Chicken" on the highway, taking chances on avoiding detection during certain delinquent acts, or pursuing activities like rock climbing may be exemplars [of sensation-seeking behaviors]. *But the larger class of adolescent risk behavior does not lend itself to that kind of analysis.* Few adolescents continue cigarette smoking for the thrill of seeing whether or not they can avoid pulmonary disease; few engage in unprotected sexual intercourse for the thrill of beating the odds of contracting a sexually transmitted disease or becoming pregnant. Indeed a key concern of health educators is to make adolescents aware that there *are* risks associated with many of the behaviors they engage in. (p. 379)

The data Cynthia Lightfoot (1994) obtained when she interviewed 41 15- to 17-year-olds support Jessor's criticism of the sensation-seeking hypothesis. The adolescents she interviewed rejected the idea that they sought novelty for its own sake. They explained their risk taking as a way of testing the limits of what is possible in life and in themselves. One 17-year-old answered her question about the attractions of taking risks this way:

What's appealing? I think growth—inner growth. And a feeling of independence and maturity in trying something new. Even if I fail, I still kind of pat myself on the back and say, "hey, you tried it, and no one can blame you for sitting back and not participating." I want to be a participant. (p. 5)

At present psychologists have no satisfactory explanation or solution for adolescent risk taking. While it is clear that the social and cultural organization of modern life greatly increase adolescent risk taking and antisocial behavior, the complex ways in which these contextual factors contribute to the problem have eluded developmentalists and policy makers alike.

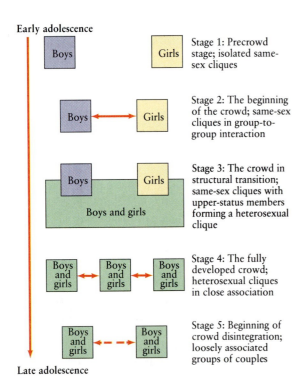

Early adolescence

Stage 1: Precrowd stage; isolated same-sex cliques

Stage 2: The beginning of the crowd; same-sex cliques in group-to-group interaction

Stage 3: The crowd in structural transition; same-sex cliques with upper-status members forming a heterosexual clique

Stage 4: The fully developed crowd; heterosexual cliques in close association

Stage 5: Beginning of crowd disintegration; loosely associated groups of couples

Late adolescence

FIGURE 15.9 *The stages of group development during adolescence. At the start of this period, peer-group interactions are largely segregated by sex; at the end, there is far more heterosexual peer-group interaction. (Adapted from Dunphy, 1963.)*

In stage 3 the members of the crowd with the highest status initiate heterosexual contacts across cliques while still maintaining membership in their same-sex cliques. At this stage boys and girls start going to parties and the movies together in groups, but they continue to spend a great deal of time with same-sex peers.

During stages 2 and 3, social events that require more intimate interaction, such as dances and parties, become prominent. Here again the size of the crowd is important. There is safety in numbers! The presence of others makes it less likely that anyone will overstep the bounds of propriety.

Eventually cross-clique pairing begins to transform the peer-group structures. In stage 4, same-sex cliques are transformed into heterosexual cliques, whose members are often paired. These arrangements allow a greater degree of intimacy, should the pair want it, but also provide a group of co-conspirators with whom each member can talk about what is going on.

Stage 5 sees the slow disintegration of the crowd.

A later study by B. Bradford Brown and his colleagues (1986), who interviewed 1300 adolescents in the United States, supports Dunphy's view that the importance of the crowd declines as teenagers grow older. However, cultural or historical variations in social relationships appear. On the basis of the data he collected in the late 1950s, Dunphy reported that the crowd disintegrated into groups of couples who were going steady or were engaged to get married. Forty years later this pattern may continue in some parts of the world, but it does not appear to be generally characteristic of contemporary industrialized societies. Instead, marriage is often postponed until several years after the initiation of sexual activity (see Figure 15.10) (Hofferth, 1990). Contemporary evidence also suggests that some crowds are made up entirely of males or females, contrary to Dunphy's emphasis on the crowd as an important social mechanism for structuring the transition to heterosexual relations (Urberg et al., 1995). Nonetheless, the general outline of the process he described continues to find considerable support (Berndt & Savin-Williams, 1993; Brown et al., 1994).

SEXUAL ACTIVITY

It should be clear by now that a great deal of the social behavior associated with sex roles must be learned from observation and practice. Less obvious, perhaps, is the fact that the physical act of uniting with another person sexually also requires a good deal of learning. Moreover, because boys and girls have different biological roles and social histories, the processes by which they learn to engage in sexual intercourse—often referred to as "coitus," from a Latin word meaning "to come together"—differ in important respects.

One line of evidence about the role of social experience in sexual intercourse comes from Harry Harlow's studies of monkeys raised in isolation. As we saw in Chapter 7 (p. 280), monkeys deprived of the opportunity to interact with their mothers and peers during the first 6 months of life were incapable of engaging in intercourse (Harlow & Novak, 1973).

A second line of evidence for the role of social learning in sexual activity comes from the wide range of behaviors that lead up to and accompany sexual intercourse. In the history of heterosexual activity, the changing incidence of petting—erotic caressing that does not include the union of male and female genitals—also reveals the role of social experience in sexual behavior. According to Dr. Alfred Kinsey and his associates, whose famous surveys of sexual behavior were published at mid-century (Kinsey, Pomeroy, & Martin, 1948; Kinsey et al.,

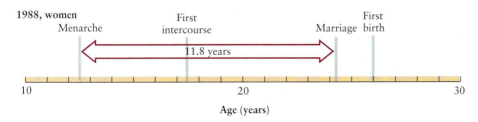

FIGURE 15.10 *The length of time between puberty, initiation of sexual activity, and marriage in the United States, 1890 and 1988. (Adapted from Alan Guttmacher Institute, 1994).*

1953), the practice of petting increased substantially among Americans born after 1900, and it has continued to increase in the decades since the Kinsey surveys (Scanzoni & Scanzoni, 1976).

Sex as a scripted activity

Petting is often viewed as part of a larger sequence of actions that make up sexual behavior in Western culture. John Gagnon and William Simon (1973) use the concept of scripts to describe this sequence, which in recent years proceeds from lip kissing to tongue kissing to caressing breasts through clothing to fondling breasts under the clothing to touching the genitals through clothing to touching genitals, and finally to genital contact. Oral sex, which has become fairly common, may or may not precede coitus (Katchadourian, 1990). This sequence is more common among white American adolescents than among African American teenagers, who are likely to move toward intercourse earlier and with fewer intervening steps (Smith & Udry, 1985).

In Chapter 9 we saw that the concept of scripts is important for understanding the mental development of preschool children. Scripts allow very small children, who clearly do not understand fully what is expected of them, to participate with adults in such activities as eating in a restaurant, attending a birthday party, and drawing a picture. A similar use of scripts is evident among adolescent boys and girls who are engaging in sexual activity for the first time. Their peer-group experiences, their observations of adults, and their general cultural knowledge provide them with a rough idea of the scripts they are supposed to follow and the roles they are supposed to play. In the United States, for example, the male is traditionally active and controls the interaction while the female responds. (Box 15.3 provides a glimpse of a very different way of organizing the transition to heterosexual behavior.)

A script also gives sexual meaning to individual acts that may have no such meaning in other contexts. Hand-holding, kissing, and unzipping one's pants are not inherently sexual acts; each occurs often in nonsexual contexts. It is only

BOX 15.3

The Traditional Kikuyu Script for Adolescent Sex

Among the Kikuyu people of central Kenya at the turn of the century, boys and girls underwent an initiation ceremony, or rite of passage, just before the start of puberty, after which the boys were considered to be junior warriors and the girls were considered to be maidens (Worthman & Whiting, 1987). For the next several years, approved sexual relations between the young men and women followed a script that differed in many ways from the scripts typically followed by teenagers in the United States.

In addition to helping their mothers with household chores and gardening, Kikuyu maidens were expected to strengthen the social cohesion of the group by entertaining the bachelor friends of their older brothers. The entertainment included not only dancing and feasting but a kind of lovemaking called *ngweko*. Jomo Kenyatta (1938), the first president of Kenya after it won its independence in 1962, described *ngweko*:

> The girls visit their boy-friends at a special hut, *thingira*, used as a rendezvous by the young men and women. . . .
>
> Girls may visit the *thingira* at any time, day or night. After eating, while engaged in conversation with the boys, one of the boys turns the talk dramatically to the subject of *ngweko*. If there are more boys than girls, the girls are asked to select whom they want as their companion. The selection is done in the most liberal way. . . . In such a case it is not necessary for girls to select their most intimate

friends, as this would be considered selfish and unsociable. . . .

> After the partners have been arranged, one of the boys gets up, saying *"ndathie kwenogora"* (I am going to stretch myself). His girl partner follows him to the bed. The boy removes all his clothing. The girl removes her upper garment . . . and retains her skirt, *motheru*, and her soft leather apron, *mwengo*, which she pulls back between her legs and tucks in together with her leather skirt, *motheru*. The two V-shaped tails of her *motheru* are pulled forward between her legs from behind and fastened to the waist, thus keeping the *mwengo* in position and forming an effective protection of her private parts. In this position, the lovers lie together facing each other, with their legs interwoven to prevent any movement of their hips. They begin to fondle each other, rubbing their breasts together, whilst at the same time engaged in love-making conversation until they gradually fall asleep. (pp. 157–158)

Sexual intercourse was explicitly not allowed as a part of this premarital sexual activity. In fact, both the boys and the girls were taught that if either of them directly touched the genitals of the other, they would become polluted and have to undergo a costly purification rite. Boys who did not adhere to this restriction were ostracized by their peers. Not until marriage was sexual intercourse sanctioned.

within the context of the larger script of dating or of coitus that these acts take on sexual meanings and give rise to sexual excitement.

Sexual expectations

Evidence from a wide variety of sources indicates that males and females come to sexual activity with different expectations as a result of their different histories (Beal, 1994). To begin with, biological differences between the two sexes set the stage for males and females to have divergent experiences with the erotic potential of their own bodies.

Sexual arousal is more obvious in males than in females because of its expression in clearly visible penile erection. Within 2 years after puberty, most males experience orgasm, usually through masturbation (Gagnon & Simon, 1973). Sexual arousal is more ambiguous in females. The clitoris, the center of female sexual pleasure, is small and hidden within the vulva, so girls are less likely to discover its erotic possibilities. In fact, Kinsey and his colleagues (1953) found that only

20 percent of the women they surveyed reported having masturbated to orgasm by the time they were 15 years old, as compared to 82 percent of the men.

According to Gagnon and Simon (1973), differences in the masturbatory behavior of boys and girls have consequences for later sexual behavior. First, masturbating to orgasm reinforces males' commitment to sexual behavior early in adolescence. Second, experience with masturbation tends to focus the male's feelings of sexual desire on the penis, whereas most females, lacking such experiences, do not localize their erotic responses in their genitals until much later, and then primarily as a result of sexual contacts with males.

These differences between male and female experience have led Gagnon and Simon to suggest that when males and females come together in later adolescence, the males are committed to sexuality but are relatively untrained in the rhetoric of romantic love, whereas the females are committed to romantic love but are relatively untrained in sexuality. As they put it, "Dating and courtship may well be considered processes in which persons train members of the opposite sex in the meaning and content of their respective commitments" (1973, p. 74).

Initial responses to sexual intercourse

Boys and girls differ in the ways they approach and respond to sexual intercourse, according to a survey of more than 1000 American adolescents conducted by Robert Coles and Geoffrey Stokes (1985). In all but a very few cases, girls and boys reported having their first intercourse with someone they knew, usually a boyfriend or girlfriend. However, the boys chose partners more casually than the girls. Thirty-two percent of the boys described their first partner as a friend, but for 75 percent of the girls the partner was definitely a boyfriend.

In general, boys responded more positively than girls to the first experience of intercourse. Very few said they were sorry, but the girls were more likely to say that they experienced pain and to express ambivalence (Table 15.2). Girls are less positive, and for a good reason: many young teenage girls are coerced into having sex. About 60 percent of the girls who have sex before they are 15 years old say that they did so involuntarily (Alan Guttmacher Institute, 1994).

Changing sexual habits

During the past quarter century there has been a clear trend toward increasing sexual activity among teenagers. Not only are more teenagers sexually active, they are becoming so at an earlier age (see Table 15.3). Although it has been suggested that the greater availability of contraceptive devices may play a role in this trend, contraception is unlikely to be the decisive factor.

Studies conducted in the 1970s and 1980s indicate that many teenagers made no attempt to prevent conception when they first had sexual intercourse (Sonenstein, Pleck, & Ku,

Even before they reach sexual maturity, children in many countries are the objects of sexual exploitation. These young Thai girls have been sold into prostitution.

TABLE 15.2 Feelings about First Intercourse (Percent)

	Sorry	Ambivalent	Glad	No Feelings
Boys	1%	34%	60%	5%
Girls	11	61	23	4

From Coles & Stokes, 1985.

TABLE 15.3 — Percentage of Never-Married Girls Who Are Sexually Active, United States, 1971–1990

Race and Age	1990	1982	1979	1976	1971	Percent Change, 1971–1990
All races	48.0%	42.2%	46.0%	39.2%	27.6%	+73.9%
15	31.9	17.8	22.5	18.6	14.4	+121.5
16	42.9	28.1	37.8	28.9	20.9	+105.2
17	52.7	41.0	48.5	42.9	26.1	+101.9
18	66.6	52.7	56.9	51.4	39.7	+67.8
19	n.a.	61.7	69.0	59.5	46.4	—
White	47.0	40.3	42.3	33.6	23.2	+102.6
Black	60.0	52.9	64.8	64.3	52.4	+14.5

Source: Zelnick & Kantner, 1980; U.S. Department of Health and Human Services, National Center for Health Statistics, 1992.

1991). The average delay between the initiation of sexual activity and the first use of prescription methods of birth control, which are the most effective, was reported to be about 1 year. More recently, surveys indicate that the use of condoms and other forms of birth control has increased among high school students, influenced at least in part by the increased awareness of the danger of AIDS and other sexually transmitted diseases. Still, more than half of those high school students who are sexually active do not protect themselves against these threats or the possibility of an unintended pregnancy (U.S. Dept. of Health and Human Services, 1992) (see Box 15.4).

CHANGING PARENT-CHILD RELATIONS

Family relations for both boys and girls change at the onset of puberty, according to a variety of studies conducted in the United States (Holmbeck et al., 1995). At the most general level, adolescents become more distant from their parents and more likely to turn to their peers than to their parents for advice on a variety of questions about how to conduct themselves (Paikoff & Brooks-Gunn, 1991; Steinberg & Silverberg, 1986).

For the first few months after a girl's menarche, both her parents are likely to increase their attempts to control her, and disagreements between the girl and her mother may increase (Hill, 1988). After a year or so has passed, the parents' attempts at control and the mother-daughter disagreements diminish markedly. The particular age when menarche begins does not seem to make a great deal of difference; it is pubertal status, not age, that seems to count. A similar pattern of mother-child dynamics is found among boys, but in the case of boys, age does make a difference. Early maturation is especially likely to increase a boy's conflict with his mother.

Adolescents' relations with their mothers change more noticeably than their relations with their fathers. Perhaps mothers have lower status than fathers in adolescents' eyes, so they assert their independence in their interactions with their mothers in the belief that their mothers will not challenge them. Or perhaps they have formed closer emotional relationships with the mother and so the process of achieving autonomy with respect to her is psychologically more difficult.

BOX 15.4

Teenage Pregnancy

According to a survey of 37 countries, the United States leads nearly all other developed nations in the incidence of pregnancy among girls between the ages of 15 and 19 (Alan Guttmacher Institute, 1994). Though the survey found that U.S. teenagers were no more sexually active than those in the other countries surveyed, they were far more likely to become pregnant. When asked why they delayed using contraception, the adolescents who came to a family planning clinic in Florida gave reasons that ranged from fear that their parents would discover their sexual activity to the wish to wait until their relationship with the boy in question was "closer" (Turner, 1991).

Government statisticians estimate that 10 percent of adolescent girls aged 15 to 19 become pregnant each year, but this trend may be slowing among older teenagers. Recently the birth rate among 18- and 19-year-olds has declined, while the rate for girls 15 through 17 has held steady at 37.8 per 1000 (U. S. Dept. of Health and Human Services, 1995).

Of the girls between the ages of 15 and 19 who become pregnant unintentionally, over a third choose to terminate their pregnancy by abortion; about 14 percent of these pregnancies end in miscarriages (Alan Guttmacher Institute, 1994). Of the girls who go on to give birth, an increasing number are unmarried. Unlike unwed mothers of earlier decades, these girls are more likely to keep and raise their babies than to give them up for adoption (National Research Council, 1987).

Race, social class, education, and the strength of religious beliefs all affect a teenager's decision about whether or not to have and keep her child. Black teenagers are more likely than white teenagers to become single mothers. White teenagers are more likely to choose to have an abortion or to get married before the baby is born. The more education a pregnant teenager's mother has (which is an indirect measure of her social class) and the better the teenager is doing in school, the more likely she is to decide to abort the pregnancy. Teenagers with strong religious convictions are likely to have and keep their babies, no matter what their race or social class (Eisen et al., 1983).

Several studies have found that teenage motherhood usually imposes lasting hardships on both the mother and the child (Ahn, 1994; Grogger & Bronars, 1993). Teenage mothers are, on the average, more likely to drop out of high school, to be poor, and to be dependent on welfare. Of the women under the age of 30 who receive benefits under Aid to Families with Dependent Children, 71 percent had their first child as teenagers (National Research Council, 1987). Rates of mortality, low birth weight, and illness are also higher among the babies of teenage mothers than among babies born to older women.

The high incidence of teenage pregnancy and childbearing has led to the organization of special programs to ensure that young mothers can complete their education.

Psychologists ask two broad questions about these changes in adolescents' relations with their parents:

1. What is the major source of these changes? Are they the result of factors operating primarily within the family or within the peer group? Or do the two spheres interact to produce changes in both spheres?
2. Are changes in parent-child relations best thought of as a process of breaking away from the family or as one of renegotiating an ongoing relationship?

The content and severity of adolescent-parent conflicts

A glance around any of the places where teenagers hang out might give the impression that, at least in today's technologically developed societies, there is a distinctive youth culture separate from the culture of the adult community. All the same, interviews with teenagers and data gathered from questionnaires reveal considerable continuity in the culture and values of adolescents and their parents.

When Denise Kandel and Gerald Lesser (1972) analyzed data from questionnaires filled out by more than a thousand teenagers and their mothers, they found that most teenagers report respect for their parents. Dialogue rather than outright conflict or rejection was the major method of resolving disagreements. When asked how they felt about their parents, approximately 60 percent of the adolescents said that they were "extremely" or "quite" close, and only 11 percent denied that they felt close at all. Almost 60 percent also said that they wanted to be like their parents in many or most ways.

Several years later, Kandel (1986) asserted that psychologists had been asking the wrong question about the influence of parents and peer groups during adolescence. Instead of pitting the general influence of peers against the general influence of parents, researchers should be asking: "What are the areas of influence for friends and what are the areas of influence for parents?" (p. 213).

Other researchers have reached the same conclusions. Ian Chand, Donald Crider, and Fern Willits (1975), for example, reported that adolescents and their parents tend to agree on issues related to religion and marriage, although they disagree about issues related to drugs and sex. Similarly, Robert Kelley (1972) found that parents and adolescents are in basic agreement about moral issues, but not about dress styles, hair length, and hours of sleep.

Additional questionnaire studies reveal that the topics adolescents discuss with their fathers are not those they discuss with their mothers (Gjerde, 1986; Kandel & Lesser, 1972; Smetana, 1989; Youniss & Smollar, 1985). James Youniss and Jacqueline Smollar describe a "family division of labor" in which fathers are authority figures who are responsible for providing their adolescent children with long-range goals. They are brought into personal matters only when special advice is needed. By contrast, adolescents talk to their mothers about personal topics both to obtain practical advice and to validate their feelings and impressions. These conversations may be argumentative. The adolescents studied by Kandel and Lesser reported that they disagreed with their mothers about the value of academic success, dating, involvement in athletics, financial independence, and popularity. On a great many issues, however, mothers and teenagers agreed: is important to plan for the future, to have a good reputation,

Adolescents are conspicuous for their unusual styles of dress and behavior, which change from one generation to the next. The only constant in these styles is their deviation from adult norms.

and to respect one's parents. Overall, the relationships of adolescents with their mothers were found to be considerably more intimate than those with their fathers.

Young people not only consult their parents frequently but also continue to spend time with them. From telephone interviews with 64 youngsters ranging in age from 12 to 15 Raymond Montemayor (1982) found that adolescents spend a good deal of time with their parents as well as their peers, but their activities in the two contexts are so different that Montemayor called them "contrasting social worlds." Time spent with parents is devoted largely to eating, shopping, and household chores, whereas relaxation and play are the leading activities with peers. That adolescents consider the time spent with parents to be important is shown by the fact that when they get into disagreements with one parent, they are not driven to spend more time with their peers. Instead, they spend more time with the other parent.

The findings from self-reports and questionnaire studies present a picture of relative adolescent-parent harmony. But as anyone who has gone through adolescence knows, the day-to-day interactions between adolescents and their parents tend not to be quite as smooth as these findings seem to indicate. Aware of this problem, Mihaly Csikszentmihalyi and Reed Larson (1984) asked adolescents to carry an electronic beeper with them for a week, from the time they got up in the morning until they went to sleep at night, as a means of gaining detailed information about the kinds of activities adolescents engage in at home as well as their moods and thoughts. At a randomly chosen moment every 2 hours or so the subjects were "beeped," at which point they filled out a standard report about what they were doing and experiencing (see Figure 15.11).

This technique provided detailed information about the kinds of activities adolescents engage in at home as well as their moods and their thoughts. The following sample of the responses to the question "As you were beeped, what were you thinking about?" gives some sense of the conflicts that occurred between the subjects and their parents:

- Why my mother manipulates the conversation to get me to hate her.
- How much of a bastard my father is to my sister.
- How ugly my mom's taste is.
- How incompetent my mom is.
- My bitchy mom.
- How pig-headed my mom and dad are.
- About my mom getting ice cream all over her.
- How f____ing stupid my mom is for making a big f____ing fuss.

Notice that these complaints are quite different from the issues highlighted in the questionnaire studies reviewed earlier. Instead of featuring grades and the undesirability of drinking, these questionnaires suggest that conflicts between adolescents and their parents often center on seemingly unimportant matters of taste. But the appearance of triviality is deceiving:

Asking a boy who has spent many days practicing a song on the guitar Why are you playing that trash? might not mean much to the father, but it can be a great blow to the son. The so-called "growth pains" of adolescence are no less real just because their causes appear to be without much substance to adults. In fact, this is exactly what the conflict is all about: What is to be taken seriously? (Csikszentmihalyi & Larson, 1984, p. 140)

Adults naturally try to structure adolescents' realities to correspond to their notions of how the world works. And adolescents, who are at the threshold of adulthood themselves, can see the shortcomings of their parents' realities. In large

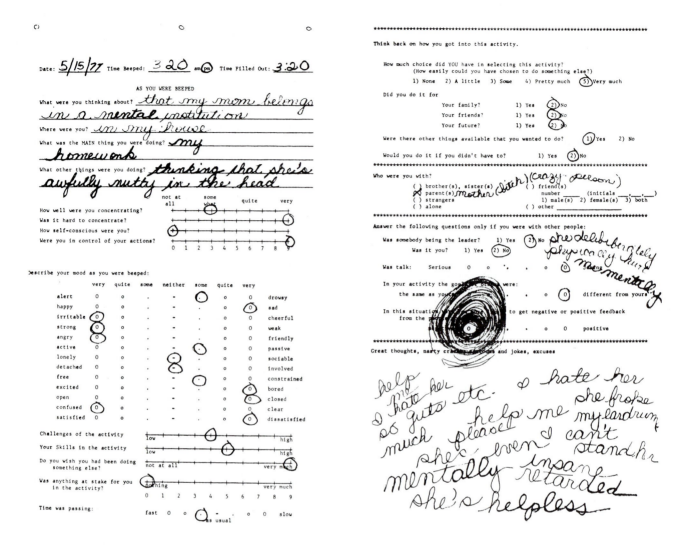

FIGURE 15.11 *A self-report filled out by a teenager at the time she was "beeped." (From Csikszentmihalyi & Larson, 1984.)*

and small ways, they resist having their realities defined for them on their parents' terms and seek to assert their own preferences. At the same time, adolescents realize they are dependent on their parents. When Robert Sorenson (1973) asked his national sample of adolescents between the ages of 13 and 19 to respond yes or no to the statement "I am not a child anymore, but I'm not an adult yet," 73 percent agreed with it. Approximately 50 percent agreed with the statement "If I had to go out into the world on my own right now, I think I would have a pretty hard time of it."

Here we see the real dilemma of adolescence and the major source of conflict between adolescents and their parents. Teenagers are caught between two worlds, one of dependence, the other of responsibility. Quite naturally, they would like to have the best of both worlds. But their parents, who pay the bills and pick up the clothing tossed on the floor, demand that independence be matched by responsibility. Once we realize that conflicts over "little things" are also disagreements about the major issues of growing up—the power to decide for oneself and to take responsibility for oneself—the issue of adolescent-parent conflict is brought into proper focus.

Parents versus peers

In the light of such contradictions—adolescents' tendency to adopt many of their parents' values and beliefs at the same time that they are arguing with their parents about their values and how they spend their time—some psychologists have suggested that adolescence is a time when the relationship between parent and child is renegotiated and transformed (Grotevant & Cooper, 1985).

A study of sixth- and seventh-graders by Andrew Fuligni and Jacquelynne Eccles (1993) gives us a picture of some of the factors that shape this transformation process. The young adolescents answered a questionnaire about their parents' strictness, their opportunities to make decisions on their own, and the extent to which their parents monitored their behavior (see Table 15.4). The questionnaire also included questions about their orientation to peers and their adjustment to junior high school.

Fuligni and Eccles found that the influences of peers and parents on adolescents' behavior are not separable. The extent to which adolescents report spending time with their peers and turning to them for advice depended on the way their parents' behavior changed in response to their growing up. When children perceived their parents as becoming stricter as they progressed into adolescence, they responded by turning to their peers. When they saw their parents as including them in family decisions and encouraging them to express their ideas, they did not orient themselves to their peers so much. At the same time, the children whose parents set a curfew for them and asked them to call if they were going to be late coming home were less peer-oriented than those whose parents did not monitor their behavior. In sum, adolescents retain a closer relationship with their parents when the parents behave in ways that are authoritative but not authoritarian.

As we saw from the follow-up study of Baumrind's work, discussed on page 436, the adolescent children of authoritative parents are also more competent in school than their peers and less likely to get into trouble. The positive effect of such parenting practices has even been found to extend beyond the family to the adolescent's friends, whose school performance and behavior are likely to improve as an indirect result (Fletcher et al., 1995; Steinberg & Darling, 1994).

TABLE 15.4 Sample Items Measuring Parent-Child Relationships

How does each of the following questions and statements apply to your situation?

PARENTAL STRICTNESS

My parents want me to follow their directions even if I disagree with them.
I have to ask my parents' permission to do most things.
My parents worry that I am up to something they won't like.

DECISION-MAKING OPPORTUNITIES

How often do you take part in family decisions concerning yourself?
My parents encourage me to give my ideas and opinions even if we might disagree.

PARENTAL MONITORING

When you go out at night, do you have a curfew?
When you are late getting home, do you have to call home?
Do your parents warn you it is dangerous to go out alone?

Source: From Fuligni & Eccles, 1993.

B. Bradford Brown and his colleagues (1993) argue that specific parenting practices not only have a direct influence on the adolescent's behavior but also have an indirect influence by determining what kind of crowd the adolescent is likely to join. In their observations of 695 young people from childhood through adolescence, Robert and Beverly Cairns (1994) found that again and again parents and teachers played a major role in realigning social groups so that they were consistent with family norms.

On the whole, current evidence indicates that the role of peer pressure in adolescents' social development is more limited and the family's role larger than they were once thought to be. Some adolescents really do break away and establish relationships outside the family that remove them from their parents physically and emotionally; but the more common pattern is for adolescents and their parents to negotiate a new form of interdependence that grants the adolescent a more equal role and more nearly equal responsibilities (Collins, 1990; Youniss, 1983). Neither the peer group nor the family can be assigned the primary role in this process. Instead, the two social contexts play complementary roles in reorganizing adolescents' social life.

WORK

The young person's gradual assumption of adult work responsibilities is another vital factor in the changing relations between parent and child. Until young people can participate in adult work—work that sustains them and their family—they will not gain adult status.

In many countries, including the United States, access to adult jobs and adult status comes only after a long period of preparation during which young people learn to work and acquire the skills that particular jobs require (Coy, 1989). American children's first work experience often consists of doing household chores, such as setting the table, washing dishes, and caring for pets, usually without pay. At about the age of 12 years, many children begin to work at odd jobs around the neighborhood—baby-sitting, delivering newspapers, mowing lawns. In most households, the money they earn from these jobs is theirs to spend with a minimum of adult supervision (Cole, 1980). By the age of 15, many adolescents have progressed from working in casual jobs to regular part-time employment (Mortimer, Shanahan, & Ryu, 1994).

Each successive job that an adolescent holds tends to be more substantial and more responsible. It also provides greater exposure to the options in the labor market. After high school, many adolescents gradually enter jobs in which they stay long enough to learn a skill, either formally or informally. Others seek career training in professional schools, colleges, public programs, or the military. By the time they are in their mid-20s, most young people have acquired vocational competence and are beginning to work in an adult career (Figure 15.12 shows the long transition from school to full-time work).

Some young people drop out of high school and plunge directly into the full-time labor market. According to the U.S. Bureau of the Census (1994), almost 10 percent of 16- and 17-year-olds dropped out of high school in 1992, but the figure was considerably higher in some inner-city neighborhoods.

No accurate count of student workers is possible because many teenagers work in jobs that the Labor Department does not monitor and because some are paid "off the books" by employers who want to avoid paying the minimum wage and

Part-time jobs do not usually provide young people with on-the-job training that will prove useful in adulthood, but they do provide young people with some practical knowledge about work in addition to giving them spending money and a sense of accomplishment.

social security taxes. Surveys indicate, however, that more than 75 percent of all high school seniors and juniors and as many as 60 percent of all tenth-graders are employed at some time during the school year (Bachman, Johnston, & O'Malley, 1987).

The employment rate is higher for white students than for minority groups. Among full-time students, 41.9 percent of the white 16- and 17-year-olds are employed but only 25 percent of African Americans the same ages (U.S. Bureau of Labor Statistics, 1993). White teenagers are more likely than minority teenagers to live near suburban shopping malls and other locations where part-time jobs can be found. They are also more likely to be successful in competing for the available jobs (Fine, Mortimer, & Roberts, 1990).

The number of hours that teenagers work each week varies with their social class and sex. When teenagers from minority and less advantaged homes find jobs, they tend to work longer hours than middle-class youths. Boys work at their jobs longer hours than girls. Among boys, sophomores typically work 15 hours a week, while seniors work 21 hours. By comparison, sophomore girls work 11 and senior girls 18 hours a week (Fine, Mortimer, & Roberts, 1990). Many teenagers work longer hours during school vacations.

It was once widely believed that extensive work experience during adolescence is all to the good. Government policy advisers contended that work is a good complement to school. Holding a job, so the argument went, teaches adolescents responsibility, develops positive attitudes toward work, provides on-the-job training, brings youngsters into contact with adults from whom they can learn, and keeps them out of trouble (Carnegie Commission on Policy Studies in Higher Education, 1980; National Commission on Youth, 1980; National Panel on High School and Adolescent Education, 1976).

This view is supported by high school students' responses to questionnaires. They report that they learn many practical skills at their part-time jobs. They say they have learned how to find and hold a job, how to manage money, and how the business world functions. They also report that their jobs teach them to be punctual and dependable, to budget their time, to take personal responsibility, and to assess their goals—Do they have the time to see their favorite television program and also get their homework done? Which is more important, working a few more hours a week or getting good grades? (Greenberger & Steinberg, 1986).

When they handle work situations well, young workers say, they feel proud and have a sense of accomplishment. Not surprisingly, even when they dislike their jobs, most adolescents enjoy the sense of power and independence they get from earning their own money. Dating and other social activities can be expensive. For most boys and for some girls, earning their own money is an essential prerequisite for participation in the social scene.

The picture is not all rosy, however. On the negative side, and contrary to the beliefs of many advocates of adolescent work experience, part-time jobs do not typically provide students with on-the-job training that will prove useful in adulthood, nor do they usually bring adolescents into contact with many adults. The vast majority of U.S. adolescents who are employed work in jobs that pay the minimum wage, offer no job protection, and provide few opportunities for advancement (Cole, 1980). Few adults can afford to work in jobs of this kind. As a result, adolescents frequently work with other adolescents in segregated sections of the labor market. They work primarily in food service, retail sales, clerical work, and

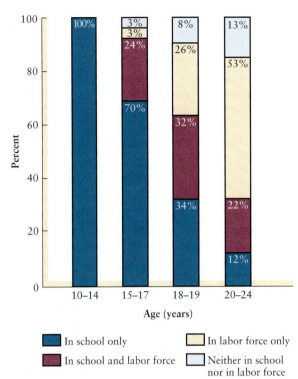

In school only

In school and labor force

In labor force only

Neither in school nor in labor force

FIGURE 15.12 *The slow transition to full-time work. (From Alan Guttmacher Institute, 1994).*

manual labor—all jobs that offer little formal instruction in work-related skills (Greenberger & Steinberg, 1986).

To complicate matters, part-time employment does not, as its advocates assume, keep teenagers out of trouble. A number of studies summarized by Laurence Steinberg and his colleagues (1993) have found that extensive part-time employment is associated with higher rates of alcohol and illegal drug use, psychological distress, and health problems, as well as more frequent delinquency.

Given the close correlation between years of schooling and the ability to find work as an adult, the data with perhaps the most serious negative implications for the future are those showing that adolescents who work are generally less involved in school than their classmates (D'Amico, 1984). It is not the mere fact of working that seems to cause the grades of teenagers to fall, however, but rather the number of hours they work. Five to ten hours of work may actually improve students' grades and behavior (Mortimer et al., 1994). This moderate level of work is also associated with an increase in the probability of completing high school.

Working long hours, however, often depresses high school students' grades (Bachman & Schulenberg, 1993; Steinberg, Fegley, & Dornbusch, 1993). Sophomores and juniors who work more than 20 hours a week during the school year are more likely to drop out of school than are their classmates who do not work so much (D'Amico, 1984). They also report being absent more and enjoying school less.

Longitudinal data indicate that work may not be the direct cause of these negative outcomes. Many adolescents who work long hours were less committed to school before they began working. Perhaps a better interpretation of the data is that working for more than 20 hours a week acts to further these students' disengagement from school (Bachman & Schulenberg, 1993; Steinberg et al., 1993).

Even as late as the high school years, many U.S. adolescents know little about the occupations available in their geographic region, the content of people's work, or their earnings (De Fleur & Menke, 1975). Adolescents' information about the labor force increases slowly as they begin to work themselves and as their network of working friends grows. Only gradually do they develop some sense of what work they want to do as adults.

The Biosocial Frame and Adolescent Development

The basic biosocial dilemma of adolescence is clear. Because biological maturity fundamentally changes the power relations between children and their parents, adolescence is a transition that one would expect to be difficult. It is especially difficult in societies where the assumption of adult rights and responsibilities is delayed well beyond puberty. Young people must then cope with bodies that allow mature sexual activity but social circumstances that keep them in a state of dependence and immaturity. Parents continue to exert considerable influence over their children, but this influence must be renegotiated—because, in a phrase, the children are "too big to be spanked."

In modern industrialized societies such as our own, the transition to adulthood is further complicated by two interrelated facts. First, the earlier onset of puberty and the increasingly longer years of education required for economic productivity have combined to lengthen adolescence even more. Second, the ways in which schooling and work are organized separate adolescents and adults, increasing the influence of peers and dividing generations.

Taken together, the biological and social reorganizations that define modern adolescence provide the essential conditions for the psychological changes that characterize this developmental period. In Chapter 16 we will first examine the special qualities of mind that develop as young people struggle to understand their new circumstances and to master the complex systems of technical knowledge that will structure their adult work lives. Then we will consider all three domains of developmental change—the biological, the social, and the psychological—simultaneously as an interacting system of influences in a cultural context.

SUMMARY

Traditional Conceptions of Adolescence

- Since the time of Rousseau, three key issues have preoccupied those who theorize about adolescence:

  1. The degree to which rapid biological changes increase psychological instability.
  2. The possibility that development in adolescence recapitulates earlier stages in achieving an integration appropriate to adulthood.
  3. The relation of biological and social changes to cognitive changes.

Modern Theories of Adolescence

- Common to all theories of adolescence is recognition of the child's need to integrate new biological capacities with new forms of social relations. Theories vary in this regard as they do in respect to earlier periods:

  1. Biological theories emphasize the universal physical changes in children's bodies as the central causes of adolescent behavior.
  2. Environmental-learning theories emphasize the continuity of adolescence with earlier periods and the power of society to shape its psychological characteristics.
  3. Constructivist theories emphasize the discontinuity of adolescence from earlier periods and the complementary roles of biological and social factors in provoking the emergence of a new level of psychological organization.
  4. Cultural-context theories do not assume that adolescence is a universal stage of development. Instead, they hold that it will appear only under conditions that create a delay between biological maturity and adulthood.

Puberty

- Puberty, the sum of the biological changes that lead to sexual maturity, is accompanied by a growth spurt during which boys and girls attain approximately 98 percent of their adult size. During puberty the bodies of males and females take on their distinctive shapes.
- Menarche, or the first menstrual period, usually occurs late in a girl's puberty, after her growth spurt has reached its peak. Among males, semenarche, the ability to ejaculate semen, signals the maturation of the primary sex organs.
- Both genetic and environmental factors affect the onset of puberty. For example, high levels of physical exercise delay the onset of menarche while family stress is associated with early menarche.
- The age at which biological maturation occurs influences a child's social standing with peers and adults.

- In general, the impact of early sexual maturation is negative for girls and positive for boys, although the impact varies with cultural circumstances.

The Reorganization of Social Life

- Four major changes occur as part of the reorganization of social life during adolescence:

  1. A great deal more time is spent with peers.
  2. Adult guidance is reduced and becomes more indirect.
  3. Cross-sex interactions increase markedly.
  4. Participation in large social groups becomes important.

- The dominant mode of peer relations at the start of adolescence is same-sex friendship focused on shared activities. As adolescence proceeds, same-sex friendship is increasingly characterized by an emphasis on trust, loyalty, and mutual understanding.
- Boys and girls have somewhat different expectations of friends. Girls seek confidantes with whom to share intimate knowledge and feelings while boys seek support when they come in conflict with authority.
- Social standing within one's peer group depends on social factors, such as membership in the leading crowd, and personal factors, such as girls' physical attractiveness and boys' athletic ability.
- Special susceptibility to peer pressure, especially antisocial peer pressure, is commonly believed to characterize adolescent behavior. Evidence for this concern is mixed.
- Sensitivity to peer pressure seems to peak around the age of 15.
- Most adolescents report that they are more likely to go along with peer pressure that is prosocial than with pressure to misbehave. The more pressure adolescents feel to engage in antisocial behavior, however, the more likely they are to do so.
- Two new forms of peer group come to prominence in adolescence, cliques and crowds. These new social forms are associated with the transition to sexual activity.
- The transition to two-person heterosexual relations goes through a number of stages. It begins with membership in small same-sex cliques and participation with the other members in social events that draw heterosexual crowds. Within these crowds, heterosexual cliques are formed, and couples begin the process of pairing off. As adult sexual relationships emerge, crowds become less prominent in adolescents' social lives.
- An intimate, mutually satisfactory heterosexual relationship requires the learning of culturally specified scripts and forms of behavior as well as biological maturation.
- The transition to heterosexual relations proceeds in opposite directions for males and females in our culture because of differences in their histories. Males begin with the highly developed goal of sexual satisfaction and only gradually learn to include a deeper social and emotional commitment in their heterosexual relations. Females begin with the highly developed goal of social and emotional affiliation and only gradually acquire the goal of sexual satisfaction.
- Biological maturation and the increasing time spent with peers alter parent-child relations. Parents' authority decreases in relation to the influence of peers, and they must now exercise their authority even more through persuasion than they did earlier.

- Contrary to the hypothesis of a separate youth culture, most adolescents share their parents' values. Dialogue, rather than outright conflict or rejection, is the major method of resolving disagreements between adolescents and their parents.
- Most U.S. adolescents have considerably more intimate relationships with their mothers than with their fathers. Typically, they turn to mothers for practical advice and validation of feelings while they turn to fathers for advice about long-range goals.
- Conflicts with parents during adolescence seem to center on matters of taste, though often they are actually about larger issues of control.
- Evidence concerning the developmental impact of work experience in the United States is mixed. Moderate amounts of work enhance feelings of independence and efficacy, but too much work reduces achievement in school.

The Biosocial Frame and Adolescent Development

- The biosocial shift to adulthood is complicated by the fact that sexual maturity does not necessarily coincide with adult status. The resulting conflict between biological and social forces gives this transition its unique psychological characteristics.

KEY TERMS

clique, p. 642

crowd, p. 642

genital stage,   p. 625

gonads, p. 629

menarche,   p. 631

primary sex organs,
  p. 630

puberty,   p. 629

recapitulationism,
  p. 624

secondary sex
  characteristics,   p. 631

semenarche,   p. 635

THOUGHT QUESTIONS

1. In the introduction to Part Five, "Adolescence," we commented, "there is more to human reproduction than sex" (p. 618). What more is there and what significance does your answer have for how you think about adolescence as a stage of development?

2. François Jacob calls reproduction the only bodily function for which the individual possesses only one-half of the necessary bodily organs. What might the consequences of this unique situation be?

3. According to the idea of a bio-social-behavioral shift, the biological changes associated with puberty, such as the growth spurt and the appearance of secondary sexual characteristics, are simultaneously relevant to social and behavioral change. Argue for or against this idea.

4. Provide several reasons to question the literature on peer influence during adolescence. What kind of research strategies might you propose to overcome these doubts?

5. Argue for or against the following proposition: for adolescents to complete childhood development effectively, conflict between them and their parents is essential.

CHAPTER 16

The Psychological Achievements of Adolescence

> "Now I look into myself and see the I of me, the weak and aimless thing which makes me. I is not strong and needs be, I needs to know direction, but has none. My I is not sure, there are too many wrongs and mixed truths within to know. I changes and does not know. I knows little reality and many dreams. What I am now is what will be used to build the later self. What I am is not what I want to be, although I am not sure what this is which I do not want.
>
> But then what is I? My I is an answer to every all of every people. It is this which I have to give to the waiting world and from here comes all that is different. I is to create."
>
> —*John D., Age 17,*
> *Quoted in Peter Blos*, On Adolescence

Theorists of adolescence have long agreed that the transition from middle childhood to adulthood is accompanied by the development of a new quality of mind. The basic logic behind this consensus is similar to the reasoning we used to explain earlier bio-social-behavioral shifts: changes in children's capacity for biological reproduction are necessarily accompanied by changes in social relations that propel them into a new social status, with new rights and responsibilities. These changes make it both possible and necessary for them to engage in the complex forms of economic activity on which the welfare of the community depends. Both the new forms of social relations and new economic responsibilities require more complex forms of thinking.

One manifestation of this new mode of thinking is adolescents' tendency to become critical of received wisdom and even more critical of the discrepancies between the ideals adults express and the way they actually behave. In response to this disillusionment with adult behavior, the adolescent may seek out adult

> models to imitate; heroes to worship. He also seeks out heroes of history and of biography. . . . Literature, art, religion take on new meanings and may create new confusions in his thinking. He has a strangely novel interest in abstract ideas. He pursues them in order to find himself. (Gesell & Ilg, 1943, p. 256)

In the end, neither slavish adherence to nor rejection of existing cultural expectations will suffice; rather, young people must reconcile their own desires and ways of doing things with their community's requirement that they become economically productive and law-abiding citizens. Viewed in this way, adolescents' thinking is, on the one hand, their most important psychological means of coming to grips with the tasks of adult life and, on the other hand, a result of their struggles to reconcile competing social demands. This process of reconciliation requires a level of systematic thought that strains or exceeds the capacity of younger children.

We begin this chapter by examining the experimental evidence for and against the idea that the thought processes of young people become more systematic and logical as they begin the transition to adulthood. This evidence raises a number of questions: Under what circumstances do adolescents engage in systematic, logical thinking? Is the quality of thinking exhibited in scientific experiments also revealed in the way young people think about such pressing issues as the laws that govern their society, their rights and obligations as citizens, and their own personal sense of identity? Is the new quality of mind that is observed among young people in modern industrialized societies universal or does it result from the extended schooling they receive? And finally, when the entire pattern of biological, social, and cognitive changes is examined in different cultural contexts, does it support the idea of adolescence as a universal stage of development?

Research on Adolescent Thought

Daniel Keating (1980) suggested five basic characteristics that distinguish adolescent thinking from thought during middle childhood:

1. *Thinking about possibilities* Unlike younger children, who are more at ease when reasoning about what they can directly observe, adolescents are likely to think about alternative possibilities that are not immediately present to their senses.

2. *Thinking ahead* Adolescence is a time when young people start thinking about what they will do when they grow up. Adolescents by no means

always plan ahead, but they do so more often and more systematically than younger children. Contemplating the upcoming summer holiday, an adolescent might think, "Well, I could go to Montana and work on a ranch. Or I could stay home and raise that D in algebra, which isn't going to look too good when I apply to college." A younger child would be more likely to focus only on having a good time and forget other responsibilities.

3. *Thinking through hypotheses* Adolescents are more likely than younger children to engage in thinking that requires them to generate and test hypotheses and to think about situations that are contrary to fact. In thinking about going to a beach party with a boy she does not know well, a teenage girl may reason, "What if they get drunk and rowdy? What will I do? I guess if things get out of hand, I can always ask someone to take me home. But then they'll think I'm a drag." A younger child would make a decision without contemplating the wide range of possible scenarios.

4. *Thinking about thought* During adolescence, thinking about one's own thought processes—the metacognitive thinking we described in Chapter 12—becomes increasingly complex. Adolescents also acquire the ability to engage in **second-order thinking,** the ability to think in terms of rules about rules and to hold two disparate rule systems in mind as they mull them over. At the same time, they can think more systematically and deeply than younger children about other people's points of view, a development seen in the changing nature of adolescent friendships (see Chapter 15, p. 639).

5. *Thinking beyond conventional limits* Adolescents use their newly sophisticated cognitive ability to rethink the fundamental issues of social relations, morality, politics, and religion—issues that are debated by the adults in their community and that have perplexed human beings since the dawn of history. Now acutely aware of the disparities between the ideals of their community and the behavior of individual adults around them, adolescents are highly motivated to figure out how to "do it right." Arnold Gesell and Frances Ilg, quoted on page 666, link this aspect of adolescent thought to youth's idealism and search for heroes.

Second-order thinking The ability to develop rules about rules and to hold competing thoughts in mind while mulling them over.

Formal operations The ability to think in a systematic manner about all the logical relations in a problem. It is the final stage in Piaget's theory of development.

One can certainly find adolescents in the United States displaying the characteristics that Keating describes. In addition, evidence from standardized tests shows that American adolescents can routinely solve problems that younger children cannot. Recent research, however, has raised basic questions about the distinctiveness and the universality of cognitive development during adolescence. When he reviewed the field again in 1990, Keating noted a change in experts' views: the idea that adolescents' thought processes could be characterized by a small set of general properties has given way to the belief that their thought processes depend heavily on the content of the problems they think about and the contexts in which they encounter those problems. This shift in opinion echoes many developmentalists' doubts about stagelike changes in cognition associated with the transition from early to middle childhood (Chapter 12).

The importance of content and context for understanding adolescent thought processes is nowhere more apparent than in current research on formal operational thinking.

FORMAL OPERATIONS

It was Piaget's contention that changes in the way adolescents think about themselves, their personal relationships, and the nature of their society have a common source: the development of a new logical structure that he called **formal operations** (see Table 16.1). As you will recall, an "operation" in Piaget's terminology is

TABLE 16.1   Piaget's Stages of Cognitive Development: Formal Operational

Age (years)	Stage	Description	Characteristics and Examples
Birth to 2	SENSORIMOTOR	Infants' achievements consist largely of coordinating their sensory perceptions and simple motor behaviors. As they move through the 6 substages of this period, infants come to recognize the existence of a world outside of themselves and begin to interact with it in deliberate ways.	Formal operational reasoning, in which each partial link in a chain of reasoning is related to the problem as a whole • Young people solve the combination-of-chemicals problem by systematically testing all possible combinations. • In forming a personal identity, young people take into account how they judge others, how others judge them, how they judge the judgment processes of others, and how all this corresponds to social categories available in the culture.
2 to 6	PREOPERATIONAL	Young children can represent reality to themselves through the use of symbols, including mental images, words, and gestures. Objects and events no longer have to be present to be thought about, but children often fail to distinguish their point of view from that of others, become easily captured by surface appearances, and are often confused about causal relations.	
6 to 12	CONCRETE OPERATIONAL	As they enter middle childhood, children become capable of mental operations, internalized actions that fit into a logical system. Operational thinking allows children mentally to combine, separate, order, and transform objects and actions. Such operations are considered concrete because they are carried out in the presence of the objects and events being thought about.	Application of the newly mastered logical and mathematical principles to a wide variety of life's problems • Young people think about politics and law in terms of abstract principles and are capable of seeing the beneficial, rather than just the punitive, side of laws. • Young people are interested in universal ethical principles and critical of adults' hypocrisies.
12 to 19	FORMAL OPERATIONAL	In adolescence the developing person acquires the ability to think systematically about all logical relations within a problem. Adolescents display keen interest in abstract ideals and in the process of thinking itself.	

a mental action that fits into a logical system. Inhelder and Piaget distinguished formal operations from the concrete operations characteristic of middle childhood in this way:

> Although concrete operations consist of organized systems (classifications, serial ordering, correspondences, etc.), [children in the concrete operational stage] proceed from one partial link to the next in step-by-step fashion, without relating each partial link to all the others. Formal operations differ in that all of the possible combinations are considered in each case. Consequently, each partial link is grouped in relation to the whole; in other words, reasoning moves continually as a function of a "structured whole." (Inhelder & Piaget, 1958, p. 16)

Formal operational thinking is the kind of thinking needed by anyone who has to solve problems systematically. This new ability is needed by the owner of a gasoline station who, in order to make a profit, has to take into account the price he pays for gasoline, the kinds of customers who pass by his station, the kinds of services he needs to offer, the hours he needs to stay open, and the cost of labor, supplies, rent, and utilities. A lawyer uses formal operations when she considers a wide variety of alternative developments and decides how best to present her client's case and counter the arguments of the attorney on the opposing side.

These young women are engaged in a task that requires them to combine variables in the manner Piaget associated with formal operations.

Reasoning by manipulating variables

Inhelder and Piaget's studies of formal operational thinking focused on the kinds of problems encountered in scientific laboratories. Typically these problems require subjects to hold one variable of a complex system constant while systematically searching mentally through all the other variables.

We introduced the "combination-of-variables" problems that Piaget and his colleagues used to study the development of formal operational thinking, the balance-beam problem, in Chapter 12 (p. 494). The solution to the balance-beam problem exemplifies the key properties of formal operational thinking because this problem requires the values of two key variables—weight and distance from the fulcrum—to be varied and combined systematically.

Perhaps the most widely cited example of a Piagetian problem designed to illustrate the nature of formal operations is the combination-of-chemicals problem, which requires the ability both to combine variables and to create in one's mind a "structured, psychological whole." According to Inhelder and Piaget, these are the key characteristics of formal operational thinking. At the start of the task, four large bottles, one indicator bottle, and two beakers are arrayed on a table in front of the child, as in Figure 16.1. Each bottle contains a clear liquid. The liquids are chosen so that when liquid from bottles 1 and 3 are combined in a beaker and then a drop of the chemical from the indicator bottle (g) is added, the mixture turns yellow. If the chemical in bottle 2 is added to a beaker containing liquid from both 1 and 3, the mixture remains yellow, but if 4 is then added, the liquid turns clear again.

The experimenter begins with two beakers already full of liquid. One contains liquid from bottles 1 and 3, the other liquid from bottle 2. He puts a drop from bottle g in each beaker, demonstrating that it produces a yellow color in one case but not in the other. Now the child is invited to try out various combinations in an attempt to determine which combination of chemicals will transform the color of the liquid.

Full set of chemicals to be combined

 1  2  3  4  g

Experimenter's demonstration

 g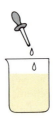

[Ren (7.1 years old) tries 4 × g, then 2 × g, and 3 × g.]

Ren: I think I did everything. I tried them all.

Exp [Experimenter]: What else could you have done?

Ren: I don't know. *[He is given the glasses again. He repeats 1 × g, etc.]*

Exp: You took each bottle separately. What else could you have done?

Ren: Take two bottles at a time? *[He tries 1 × 4 × g, then 2 × 3 × g, thus failing to cross over between the two sets of bottles. When we suggest that he add others, he puts 1 × g in the glass already containing 2 × 3, which results in the appearance of the color.]*

Exp: Try to make the color again.

Ren: Do I put in two or three? *[He tries 2 × 4 × g, then adds 3, then tries it with 1 × 4 × 2 × g.]*

Ren: No, I don't remember anymore.

[Eng (14.6 years old) begins with 2 × g, 1 × g, 3 × g, and 4 × g.]

Eng: No it doesn't turn yellow. So you have to mix them. *[He goes on to the six two–by–two combinations and at last hits 1 × 3 × g.]*

Eng: This time I think it works.

Exp: Why?

Eng: It's 1 and 3 and some water.

Exp: You think it's water?

Eng: Yes, no difference in odor. I think that it's water.

Exp: Can you show me? *[He replaces g with some water: 1 × 3 × water.]*

Eng: No, it's not water. It's a chemical product: it combines with 1 and 3 and then it turns into a yellow liquid. *[He goes on to three–by–three combinations beginning with the replacement of g by 2 and by 4—i.e., 1 × 3 × 2 and 1 × 3 × 4.]*

Eng: No, these two products aren't the same as the drops: they can't produce color with 1 and 3 *[Then he tries 1 × 3 × g × 4.]*

Eng: It turns white again: 4 is the opposite of g because 4 makes the color go away while g makes it appear.

FIGURE 16.1 *A 7-year-old and an adolescent tackle the combination-of-chemicals task. Note that the 7-year-old starts by testing only one chemical at a time. When it is suggested that he try working with two chemicals at a time, he becomes confused. The 14-year-old also starts with one chemical at a time but quickly realizes that he must create more complicated combinations, which he does in a systematic way until he arrives at the solution to the problem. (From Inhelder & Piaget, 1958.)*

Interviews with two of Inhelder and Piaget's subjects are shown at the bottom of Figure 16.1: one with a 7-year-old boy who does not have the kind of overall conceptual grasp of the problem that indicates the presence of a **structured whole** (a system of relationships that can be logically described and thought about) and one with a 14-year-old boy who does. The first child is unsystematic in his sampling of possible combinations, even with hints from the experimenter. The adolescent sets about his task systematically. He starts with the simplest possibility (that one of the chemicals, when combined with g, turns yellow), then proceeds to the next level of complexity—the possibility that two and later three chemicals must be combined. When he combines pairs, he discovers that when g is added to a mixture of 1 and 3, the yellow color appears, but because he is methodical in exploring all the logical possibilities, he also discovers that 4 counteracts g, thereby arriving at a systematic understanding of the miniature chemical system that Inhelder and Piaget have arranged for him. The adolescent is exhibiting formal operational thinking par excellence.

Reasoning by logical necessity

According to Piaget (1987), one of the consequences of acquiring second-order thinking is the ability to construct logical proofs in which conclusions follow from logical necessity. This ability underlies **deductive reasoning,** one of the central processes in scientific work. The simplest form of deductive reasoning begins with the statement of a general premise followed by the statement of a particular specific premise and then by a conclusion. If the premises are true, the conclusion must be true as well. Willis Overton (1990), who has studied the development of formal deductive reasoning, gives the following example of such a problem:

> *General premise:* All trains to Washington stop in Baltimore.
> *Specific premise:* The train on track 6 goes to Washington.
> *Conclusion:* Therefore, the train on track 6 stops in Baltimore.

To study developmental changes in formal logical reasoning, Overton and his colleagues have used a task in which children and adolescents must gauge whether an explicit rule is being followed or broken in a series of specific cases. The way children select the information with which to make a judgment provides the critical evidence about their use of deductive reasoning (Ward & Overton, 1990).

A sample problem is seen in Figure 16.2. The adolescent is given four cards that contain information relevant to a rule concerning the legal drinking age. A person is sitting at a table and drinking; is he doing so legally? Below the four pictured cards are instructions telling the subject to select the cards needed to determine if the rule regarding the legal drinking age is being broken or not. According to formal logic, it is necessary to turn over two of the cards in this problem, card 1 and card 3, to determine whether or not the rule is being broken. Information from the other cards is logically irrelevant to the conclusion. The crucial question is what cards the adolescent will choose to turn over to decide if the rule is being broken.

Several studies (summarized in Ward & Overton, 1990) find a steady increase in the percentage of subjects who display logical reasoning between the fourth and twelfth grades (roughly, 10 to 18 years of age) (see Figure 16.3). Note that formal

Structured whole A system of relationships that can be logically described and thought about.

Deductive reasoning A form of reasoning that moves from a general premise to a specific instance of that premise, followed by a conclusion. If the premises are true, then the conclusion must follow.

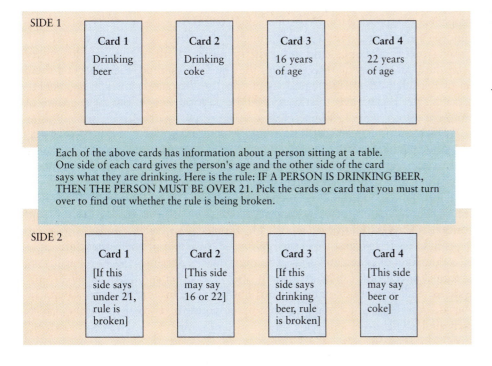

FIGURE 16.2 *One of the deductive reasoning problems used by Willis Overton and his colleagues to study the development of formal operational thinking.*

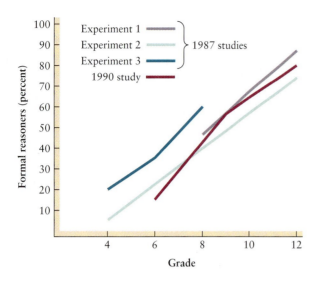

FIGURE 16.3 *The development of formal operational reasoning ability as indicated by responses to deductive reasoning problems in four experiments by Overton and his colleagues. Note how closely the different experiments replicate each other. (From Ward & Overton, 1990.)*

deductive reasoning is very rare before the sixth grade (11 to 12 years). On the basis of these results, Overton and his colleagues argue that "competence to reason deductively becomes available in adolescence" (Ward & Overton, 1990, p. 492).

Are formal operations universal?

Although Piaget and his colleagues selected the problems they used to study formal operational thinking from the domains of science and logic, their writings suggest both that formal operational thinking suffuses all domains of adolescent thought and that the social conditions that give rise to formal operational thinking—the demands of the adult roles and responsibilities the young person is preparing to shoulder—are just as universal a part of adolescence as puberty. One would thus expect to see formal operations characterizing adolescent and adult thought in all societies. The actual evidence tells a far more complicated story.

Studies among U.S. subjects

In studies of well-educated American teenagers, as few as 30 to 40 percent have solved such problems as the combination of chemicals and the balance beam, which, according to Piaget, exemplify universal characteristics of formal thinking (Keating, 1980; Linn, 1983). Such studies add to the controversy concerning Piaget's views of adolescents' abilities. A good deal of research has been carried out to determine whether formal operational thinking is or is not a universal achievement of adolescence, and what kinds of factors promote or block its development and expression. Robert Siegler and Robert Liebert (1975), for example, designed a combination-of-variables problem in which children ranging in age from 10 to 13 were asked to find the combination of open and closed positions on four switches needed to make a model train go along a track. This arrangement made the problem logically similar to Inhelder and Piaget's combination-of-chemicals problem.

Some children were introduced to the problem as Inhelder and Piaget would have presented it. The experimenters tutored other children, using one of two supplementary procedures. In the first supplementary procedure, they showed the children a systematic way to check through the various combinations of open and closed switches: all combinations of switch positions. In the second supplementary procedure, after showing the children the checking method, they coached them on two problems that were logically equivalent to the one they would be asked to solve. Siegler and Liebert then compared the performances of the three groups of children.

The tutoring helped. With no training or tutoring, none of the 10-year-olds and only 20 percent of the 13-year-olds searched systematically through all the alternatives, as formal operational thinkers are supposed to do. With training in checking but no tutoring in similar problems, the 13-year-olds showed only modest improvement and the 10-year-olds showed none at all. All the children who received both training and tutoring in analogous problems solved the problem correctly. (Similar findings are reported by Stone & Day, 1980.)

These results suggest that children on the threshold of adolescence are capable of the kind of systematic, logical manipulation of variables that is the hallmark of formal operations if they are given proper instruction and if the benefits of the systematic manipulation are made clear. But such coached performance cannot be considered evidence of the spontaneous development of a new mode of thought in early adolescence.

Difficulties with formal operational thinking do not disappear in later adolescence, nor do they show up only in laboratory problems. Noel Capon and Deanna Kuhn (1979) approached adult shoppers at a supermarket and asked them to judge which of two sizes of deodorant was a better buy: 8 ounces priced at $1.36 or 12 ounces priced at $2.11. The shoppers were provided with paper and pencil to help them reach a solution (see Figure 16.4).

Only 20 percent of the shoppers followed the formal operational procedure of determining the ratio of amount to price; most shoppers relied instead on the conventional belief that the bigger bottle must be a better buy. These results led Capon and Kuhn to conclude that "there does in fact exist significant variability in the level of logical reasoning among an adult population" (p. 451). Such widespread failure raises doubts as to whether this kind of thought process is universally acquired.

Sex differences in formal operations

A good deal of research in recent decades has sought to determine whether there are sex differences in the ability to engage in formal operational thought. The reasons for this interest are social as well as scientific. If formal operations are a universal capacity, both sexes can acquire this kind of reasoning. Yet the belief is pervasive that men have greater talent in such areas as mathematics, science, and engineering, fields that appear to require formal operational thinking. This stereotype is bolstered by (and bolsters) the fact that more men than women currently work in these fields.

Marcia Linn and Janet Hyde (1988) summarized the results of several meta-analyses of research on sex-related differences in spatial and mathematical thinking involving formal operational thought. A **meta-analysis** combines the results of many studies statistically in order to extract the overall trend they exhibit. Linn and Hyde looked at meta-analyses of studies that compared the performances of males and females during the 1970s and 1980s. They report that sex differences, which were generally small and confined to certain content areas in the 1970s, declined over the 20 years of research they surveyed. In many of the studies, no differences were found between the performances of males and females, but when sex differences were found, they generally favored males.

Several attempts have been made to discover why males sometimes perform better than females on experimental tasks that require formal operations. Joan Peskin (1980) investigated the possibility that the content of the usual Piagetian problem was boring for girls by creating "female-oriented" formal operational tasks. In place of the combination-of-chemicals task, for example, Peskin presented a logically identical problem in which it was necessary to figure out what combination of spices was responsible for creating an unusual-tasting stew. Another problem dealt with whether lipstick, eye shadow, or soap was causing an allergic skin reaction. Peskin found that high school girls in South Africa who reported little interest in science performed better on the female-oriented problems, whose content captured their interest. Female students interested in science, by contrast, performed no better on the special problems than on the standard Piagetian tasks. Since fewer girls than boys concentrate their studies in science, in contemporary American schools these findings suggest that documented sex differences may be caused by boys' greater interest in the content of the tasks used to assess formal operations, as well as by their greater familiarity with the procedures.

Current evidence favors the idea that the capacity to solve formal operational problems develops equally in males and females, but one's success in using this ability to solve particular problems depends on one's experience. This conclusion, as we will see, is supported by evidence from the other line of research on the

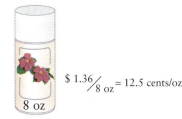

$\$1.36 / 8\ oz = 12.5\ cents/oz$

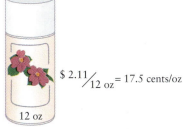

$\$2.11 / 12\ oz = 17.5\ cents/oz$

Caveat emptor! Buyer beware!

FIGURE 16.4 *One of the problems used by Capon and Kuhn to assess formal operational thinking. The subject's task is to determine the best buy among alternatives that differ in volume and price, requiring them to calculate the cost per unit.*

Meta-analysis An analysis that combines the results of several studies statistically in order to find an overall trend in the data.

universality of formal operations, which compares the performances of children from different cultures.

Cultural variations in formal operations

In Chapters 12 and 13 we reviewed research on cultural variability in the development of *concrete* operations in middle childhood. Some of the studies suggested that children who grow up without attending school are significantly delayed in the age at which they begin to use concrete operational reasoning to solve conservation problems. We also saw, however, that this variability seems to result from relatively superficial difficulties the children had in understanding the tasks because of their specific content or the ways they were presented. Concrete operational ability does appear to be universal and not dependent on schooling for its appearance.

Evidence concerning the development of *formal* operations in different cultures offers a more difficult challenge to the idea that the processes of cognitive development are universal. Unless they are among the relatively small part of the population that have attended high school or college, people in small, technologically unsophisticated societies rarely seem to use formal operations when they are tested with Piagetian methods (Hollos & Richards, 1993; Segall et al., 1990). But is it correct to conclude that they are incapable of this level of thinking?

In the course of his career Piaget shifted position on the universality of formal operational thinking. According to his general framework, the acquisition of formal operations should be universal, reflecting universal properties of biological growth and social interaction. Nonetheless, he did say that "in extremely disadvantageous conditions, [formal operational thought] will never really take shape" (Piaget, 1972, p. 7).

An alternative possibility, which Piaget also entertained, was that children progress through the invariant stages of intellectual development at different speeds, depending on the quality and frequency of intellectual stimulation available in their environment.

The conclusion that Piaget preferred toward the end of his life was that all normal people attain the level of formal operations. "However," he wrote,

> they reach this stage in different areas according to their aptitudes and their professional specializations (advanced studies or different types of apprenticeship for the various trades): the way in which these formal structures are used, however, is not necessarily the same in all cases. (1972, p. 10)

In other words, a lawyer might think in a formal manner about law cases but not when sorting the laundry, or a baseball manager might employ formal operational thinking to choose his batting lineup but fail to do so in the combination-of-chemicals task. Evidence in favor of this conclusion, which fits well with a cultural-context approach to cognitive development, comes from studies of a popular board game known as the "national game of Africa," in which opponents try to capture seeds from their opponents according to a complex set of rules (Cole et al., 1971; Retschitzki, 1989). The game is usually played by men and older boys. Analysis of the sequence of moves used by skilled players demonstrates that mastery is impossible by use of a good memory alone. Rather, it requires anticipation of the possible moves for several coming turns, balancing of defensive and offensive moves, and the calculations of complex trade-offs. On the basis of detailed clinical interviews with skilled players from Ivory Coast, Jean Retschitzki (1989) concluded that the strategies described by the players require the kind of logical thinking characteristic of formal operations.

ALTERNATIVE APPROACHES TO EXPLAINING ADOLESCENT THOUGHT

Investigators who question Piaget's account of adolescent cognition have sought alternative explanations for the kinds of results presented in the preceding sections. Those who work in the information-processing tradition have explained adolescents' improved performance on logical reasoning tasks in much the same way they attempt to explain advances in thought processes at earlier ages. Cumulative changes in memory capacity, relevant knowledge, effective strategies, and metacognitive understanding are the major mechanisms they invoke. Researchers from a variety of other traditions have suggested that adolescents discover a new relation between thought and language that is the key to their cognitive development during this period. Those who emphasize the importance of cultural context have pursued the path that Piaget himself suggested, concentrating on the way specialized practice in particular domains of experience gives rise to the kind of systematic thought that appears to underlie the new quality of adolescent cognition.

Information-processing theories

The explanations that information-processing theorists give of adolescent thinking are a direct extension of the explanations given of the development of thought during earlier periods of life. According to this view, in comparison with younger children, adolescents have developed more efficient strategies for solving problems and have become better able to retain information in their memory while they relate the components of a task to one another.

In Chapter 12 we discussed the application of Robert Siegler's (1996) information-processing approach to the balance-beam problem that Piaget and Inhelder offer as a model for the development of formal operational thinking. The impression one gets from Inhelder and Piaget's account is that this problem is a single logical puzzle that older children are able to master by applying more powerful logic. Siegler demonstrated, however, that what seems like a single logical problem can also be viewed as several tasks, each of which makes its own cognitive demands. Moreover, he found that only a quarter of the 17-year-olds he studied demonstrated the ability to solve the balance-beam problem in all its forms. Such evidence suggests that the increased problem-solving skills of adolescents, rather than demonstrating a global, qualitative change in modes of thinking, are better explained as the result of a gradual acquisition and implementation of more powerful rules and strategies. These rules can then be applied to particular problem-solving situations with increasing, but still incomplete, reliability.

Support for this view comes from a series of studies by Deanna Kuhn and her colleagues (1995) on the ability of 10-year-olds and adults to engage in logical inductive reasoning. The problems posed by these researchers required subjects to reason about the causes of events when several variables were potentially influential. One such problem was presented as a study by a board of education in a large city to determine the features of schools that do or do not make a difference in student achievement. Five features were presented as being potentially relevant:

- Teaching assistant (TA vs. no TA).
- Sex of principal (male or female).
- Noise in the classroom (noisy or quiet).
- Teacher's activity during recess (teacher on playground or in the lounge).
- Class size (small, medium, or large).

Subjects were presented with a large felt board and drawings with Velcro on the back that allowed them physically to represent and manipulate the features they thought important.

As each new problem was presented, subjects were asked to say what they thought the effect of each variable would be. Then they were given "data" to reason with. In the board-of-education problem, for example, they were given an extensive series of hypothetical profiles in which children were described as attending a school characterized by a particular combination of each of the five variables. Overall, each subject participated in 20 sessions over a 10-week period. Four problems were presented in each session.

The initial assessment of each subject's theories about the variables provided a baseline against which to assess cognitive change. Most children and adults responded to the board-of-education problem, for instance, by saying that having a TA present caused higher performance but that the sex of the principal was irrelevant. The problems were planned so that some of the variables would exert a simple, direct effect (for example, having a TA helped) but other effects occurred only in combinations (the effect of teacher activity during recess depended on whether there was a TA or not).

Some of the subjects' initial ideas about the causes of school achievement in the fictional school district turned out to be correct and some did not. Over time, as they gained information about how the variables affected performance, both the child and adult subjects refined their theories about which features were important. Moreover, subjects in both groups came to use more sophisticated strategies to pin down the causal relations as they acquired more practice with the problem. Neither the children nor the adults, however, were logically consistent in making inferences about either the same problem over time or different problems. In line with the results of Siegler's work with the balance beam described in Chapter 14, what differed among the two age groups and what changed as the subjects got more and more practice was the *mixture* of logical strategies they used. These results provide additional evidence in support of the information-processing view that the development of reasoning is a matter more of learning to select and implement logical strategies consistently than of acquiring a new quality of thought.

A changing relation of thought to language

Scholars who adhere to several theoretical traditions believe that an increased ability to use abstract verbal concepts is central to adolescents' increased ability to conceptualize alternative worlds and plan future ways of life (Vygotsky, 1934/1987; Werner & Kaplan, 1952). This new level of ability is evident both in the way adolescents make sense of unfamiliar words and in the way they make inferences from relations between familiar words.

Heinz Werner and Bernard Kaplan (1952) devised a clever way to show how children figure out the meanings of unfamiliar words. They made up a series of sentences, each of which contained a nonsense word whose meaning the child had to figure out from the context. The nonsense word has the same meaning in every sentence. For example:

1. You can't fill anything with a contavish.
2. The more you take out of a contavish, the larger it gets.
3. Before the house is finished, the walls must have contavishes.
4. You can't feel or touch a contavish.
5. A bottle has only one contavish.
6. John fell into a contavish in the road.

These sentences were presented one at a time. Each time a definition of "contavish" was decided on, and then the next sentence was presented, until the whole set was included. The children in the sample ranged from 9 to 12 years old. The 9- and 10-year-olds were more likely to try to figure out each sentence as a separate entity, ignoring the fact that the same word was present and must make sense in all the sentences. So, for example, a 9-year-old might respond to sentence 3 by saying that before the house is finished the walls must have paint and to sentence 4 by saying that you can't feel or touch air. Such children were unlikely to come up with a single definition of "contavish" that could be used in all of the sentences.

By contrast, while 11- and 12-year-old children often had difficulty coming up with a good definition of "contavish" in the first sentence or two (as did we when we first encountered this research), they were able to compare the possible meanings in the various sentences and eventually find a meaning that fitted all of the cases ("hole").

The complementary ability to build analogies such as "Day is to night as _____ is to dark" also seems to develop during adolescence (Levinson & Carpenter, 1974; Sternberg & Nigro, 1980). This kind of problem is encountered on many IQ tests and on the Miller Analogies Test, which is widely used in the United States as one of the criteria for evaluating candidates for admission to graduate school.

Philip Levinson and Robert Carpenter (1974) presented children 9 through 15 years old with two kinds of analogies in order to distinguish between abstract and concrete modes of thinking about words. The first kind of analogies, which they referred to as "real" or "true" analogies, were of the form "Bird is to air as fish is to _____ ." The concepts they embodied were expressed more concretely in the second kind of analogies, which the researchers referred to as quasi-analogies: "A bird uses air; a fish uses _____ ."

The 9-year-olds found the quasi-analogies significantly easier to grasp than the true analogies. The 15-year-olds found quasi-analogies and true analogies equally easy to solve. Since the true analogies require the coordination of isolated word meanings into a single logically consistent system, Levinson and Carpenter's results confirm this ability as a key achievement of adolescent thought.

The experiments on the development of verbal concepts suggest that new structures of word meaning begin to take shape during adolescence (Sternberg & Powell, 1983; Vygotsky, 1934/1987). These studies do not contradict Piaget's idea that a new form of logic contributes to adolescent thinking, but they demonstrate that changes in the ability to understand and use language, as well as the ability to use logic to solve problems, are important aspects of adolescent cognitive development.

The cultural-context perspective

The cultural-context approach to adolescent thought begins with an observation similar to Inhelder and Piaget's: new modes of thought become prominent as teenagers prepare to adopt adult roles. Both approaches start by analyzing the structure of adult activity. Whereas Piaget sought a single new logic underlying all adult thought, the cultural-context theorists emphasize variation in the contexts of adult activity and the consequent heterogeneity of adult thought processes. Thus these theorists believe that it is necessary to analyze the structure of activity and the scripts encountered in various kinds of settings that adults frequent (see Box 16.1).

To the extent that different contexts require different degrees of systematic thought, the cultural-context perspective leads one to expect variability in the kind of thinking exercised in different contexts; in particular, in the likelihood that someone would use formal operational thought. In this respect, the cultural-context position is similar to the approach Piaget (1972) adopted late in his life when he proposed that systematic, theoretically precise thinking is most likely to appear where it is most demanded. The cultural-context perspective differs from

BOX 16.1

Formal Operations in a Nonliterate Culture

In a great many of the situations that seem to call for the use of formal operations in our everyday lives, most of us use written notes as a means of keeping track of our thoughts. Even scientists, who are likely candidates for having achieved the stage of formal operations, routinely resort to paper and pencil or a computer when they have to sort through a large number of variables to solve a problem. Only rarely, as in a chess game or a psychological test, does the thinking have to go on entirely inside a person's head.

Attempts to determine the universality of a new mode of thinking associated with the transition to adulthood are undermined by the fact that many cultures do not have writing systems or the formal scientific procedures that tests of formal operations typically model. Consequently, the "standardized" test procedures are completely alien to many cultures. Fortunately, however, research by anthropologists familiar with psychological theories has begun to provide evidence on complex problem solving in a variety of settings (Hutchins, 1980; Rogoff & Lave, 1984).

An interesting instance of complex problem solving in a nonscientific culture is seen in the navigational practices of South Sea islanders (Goodenough, 1953; Gladwin, 1970). Until such devices as magnetic compasses became readily available after World War II, natives of Polynesia and Micronesia, groups of islands northeast of New Guinea, sailed their small outrigger canoes over hundreds of miles of ocean to get from one tiny island to another without the help of conventional instruments. Even very experienced sailors from other parts of the world would not presume to sail such distances without a compass for fear of sailing off into the vast Pacific and probable death.

The technique the islanders have developed for finding their way over the sea requires an external record-keeping system, a hypothetical reference point, and constant estimates of speed—all combined in a single problem-solving process that lasts as long as the voyage itself. It depends heavily on 14 distinctive "star paths"; that is, a set of stars that always rise from the same point on the eastern horizon and set at the same place in the west, appearing to move in an unvarying arc across the sky. Instruction in how to navigate with

this system begins in adolescence and continues for several years. A practiced navigator is able to construct the entire "star compass" mentally from a glimpse of two or three stars on the horizon (see diagram). As Edwin Hutchins phrases it, "The star compass is an abstraction which can be oriented as a whole by determining the orientation of any part" (1983, p. 195).

The star compass is only one part of the navigator's mental model of the voyage. An essential additional element is a "reference island" whose bearing on the star compass is known in relation to any island from which a boat might set out. The term "reference island" is placed in quotation marks because in many cases the island is purely hypothetical, a reference point needed only to make calculations of relative distance from the destination.

In the actual process of sailing, navigators mentally combine the information about the star paths, the loca-

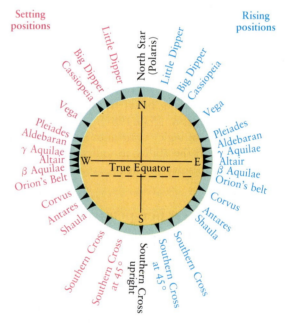

A schematic representation of the star compass used by navigators in the Caroline Islands to guide their outrigger canoes from one island to another. (From Goodenough, 1953.)

Navigators from one of the Caroline islands conduct a lesson in how to use the star compass.

tion of the reference island, and their rate of speed in order to discover their current position and distance from their destination. So skillful are they at making these calculations that they can tack away from their destination to catch the wind and still keep track of their location and find their way.

Some of the earlier researchers who investigated this kind of navigation believed that the navigators could not talk logically about the system they were using (Gladwin, 1970). Their explanations seemed to be inconsistent with the anthropologists' analysis of their navigational system. If they were indeed incapable of describing their own thought processes, the claim that their problem solving demonstrated formal operations would be considerably weakened.

Hutchins (1983) showed, however, that the navigators' explanations were perfectly logical for the system they were using. The apparent illogic arose from a basic cultural difference in the way people think about compasses and relative motion. It seemed obvious to Thomas Gladwin that the canoe moved across the water while the islands remained still. The navigators, however, had developed their system by imagining that the boat stood still while the reference island moved. When Hutchins took their accounts completely seri-

ously, he was able to show that the anthropologists had simply failed to work out the full system.

Although Micronesian navigators demonstrated that they can engage in formal operational thought at sea, they showed no such ability when they were presented with a standard Piagetian combination-of-variables task (Gladwin, 1970). Gladwin presented adolescents and adults with stacks of poker chips and asked them to find all the possible combinations of colors. Even expert navigators responded to this task at a very low level within Piaget's framework; most paired only a few colors, falling far short of the formal operational ideal. Only a few young men who had attended high school managed to display some aspects of systematic combinatorial activity. These young men, however, had not been trained in the sailors' system of navigation!

These results suggest that formal operational thinking may occur far more widely than the evidence from typical experiments suggests, and that this type of thinking may indeed be universal in human groups. At the same time, the data make it clear that formal operations do not uniformly replace earlier modes of thought. Their use remains highly restricted to contexts in which the individual has had considerable experience.

Piaget's, however, in its assumption that all cultures have contexts that require some formal operational thinking; thus adolescents in all cultures can be expected to use formal operational thought in some contexts. What is universal according to this perspective is the acquisition of the ability to think systematically about systems. What is variable are the contexts in which such ability will be used.

This approach emphasizes that Inhelder and Piaget's experiments are based on the kinds of activity that scientists are assumed to engage in and that school-children are exposed to when they are taught principles of science. According to the cultural-context perspective, it is inappropriate to use these specialized scientific procedures as the standard for assessing formal operations in general. Instead, formal operational thinking, like all other forms of thinking, should be regarded as dependent on the specific properties of an activity and the context in which it is occurring. Without denying that formal operational procedures can come to play a role in people's thinking in different cultures, psychologists who favor a cultural-context approach start by analyzing actual activities, finding occasions when formal operational thinking is required and therefore when it is likely to be manifested.

A common occasion in many cultures that requires formal operational thought is the event called "planning a holiday meal." The following example was provided by Peg Griffin (1983), a sociolinguist, who obtained it from a 40-year-old college-educated woman who believed, on the basis of reading Piaget, that she "did not have formal operations."

On the holiday in question it is customary to eat one of several main dishes: turkey, goose, or ham. The choice of the main course depends on several variables: What is available? How expensive is each of the alternatives? Is anyone coming who is on a low-cholesterol diet? Is anyone a vegetarian? Do the guests like to try new dishes, or are they meat-and-potatoes people? If turkey is on sale and a lot of people are expected, turkey can be very tempting. Goose, on the other hand, is more unusual, but the fattiness may bother guests who worry about cholesterol.

These calculations do not stop with the main course. If the hostess serves turkey, she has to serve cranberry sauce; with ham, Cumberland sauce is essential. What about starches? Stuffing? Rice? Potatoes? Sweet potatoes? What about the soup? Clam chowder goes with turkey, but will it go with goose, or would a clear broth be better?

Social factors also have to be taken into account. First, who is coming to dinner? Are all the guests old friends who expect a turkey, or are some "important personages" also invited? Social factors also include such elements as how to present and serve the food and how to keep everyone happy (who will sit next to chatty Aunt Betty or deaf Uncle Norm)?

The ability of this woman to engage in such thinking while she stands at the meat counter on the eve of a holiday illustrates several essential features of formal operational thinking. First, she is able to sort through several variables, holding one constant while she works on the others ("Hmmm, ham, candied sweet potatoes, cranberries . . . uh-oh, no cranberries, gotta start over again. . . . Besides, John keeps begging for goose, but will one goose be enough for 12 people? Two would make dinner too expensive. Well, let's see . . ."). Second, this kind of thinking clearly is a form of planning. Third, the plan results in a "structured whole" organized by concepts significant to the shopper; one of them is the concept "holiday meal." Finally, the shopper is able to reflect on and describe her thought processes.

This example differs from Inhelder and Piaget's characterization of formal operations in that the shopper fails to consider literally *all* of the possible combinations of relevant factors. Instead, she pursues each of the variables in her problem only long enough to come up with a usable solution. Nevertheless, the process by which she plans the meal clearly involves the kind of systematic variation of alternatives indicative of formal operations.

Several recent experimental studies suggest that it is quite common for people to reason differently in everyday situations than they do in formal experiments designed as logical puzzles (Lave, 1988; Linn, 1983; Tschirgi, 1980). Marcia Linn, Tina de Benedictus, and Kevin Delucchi (1982) tested a sample of adults on reasoning performance in Piagetian-style problems and on reasoning about the truthfulness of advertising. The researchers were questioning Piaget's hypothesis that once individuals can engage in formal reasoning, it becomes a general characteristic of their thinking. They found virtually no correlation between the quality of reasoning used in the Piagetian problems and that used in the advertising problems. Apparently, then, the participants did not use one single characteristic mode of thinking. In any case, their level of formal reasoning was so low for both kinds of problems that it cast doubt on the universality of this mode of thought among adults in the first place.

Judith Tschirgi (1980) found that even when two problems are analogous, the kind of reasoning used to solve each one depends on whether the outcome of the situation is one the subject views as positive (and hence wants to maintain) or negative (and hence wants to change). An example is seen in Figure 16.5. The boy has baked a cake with margarine, honey, and whole wheat flour, and the cake is a great success because it is so moist. The boy hypothesizes that the cause of the success is the honey. The question is: What should he change when he bakes another cake to check his hypothesis? In the negative case, the cake is too runny and the boy again hypothesizes that honey is the crucial factor. The question remains: What must be done to test this hypothesis?

The logic of these problems is the same. In each case, the best way to test the hypothesis is to hold the kind of shortening and flour constant while varying the

FIGURE 16.5 *A combination-of-variables task involving an everyday situation. Subjects were asked to choose one of the three problem-solving strategies. When the outcome of the original hypothetical event was positive, as in this case, neither children nor adults used rigorously logical testing procedures. (From Tschirgi, 1980.)*

Problem

John decided to bake a cake. But he ran out of some ingredients. So:
- He used margarine instead of butter for the shortening
- He used honey instead of sugar for the sweetening and
- He used brown whole wheat flour instead of regular white flour.

The cake turned out great because it was so moist.

John thought that the reason the cake was so great was the honey. He thought that the type of shortening (butter or margarine) or the type of flour really didn't matter.

 = Great cake

What should he do to prove this point?

Possible strategies

1. He can bake the cake again but use sugar instead of honey, and still use margarine and brown whole wheat flour.

2. He can bake the cake again but this time use sugar, butter, and regular white flour.

3. He can bake the cake again still using honey, but this time using butter and regular white flour.

kind of sweetener. But in this experiment, only when the cake was a failure did participants agree that the boy should substitute sugar for honey. When the cake was a success, they kept honey constant and changed other factors. College students were as likely to follow this pattern as second-graders, an indication that this illogical pattern may be a general characteristic of human reasoning. As Tschirgi comments, when people are confronted with an everyday problem, their expectations about the outcome, rather than their underlying cognitive competencies, control the way they reason (see also Linn, 1983).

The shortcuts taken by Griffin's shopper and the errors of the participants in Tschirgi's study do not conform to Piaget's idealized scientific solution. Even studies of the way experts solve problems suggest that such unscientific habits are typical (Chi, Glaser, & Rees, 1982). In fact, the systematic reasoning of the shopper displays more aspects of formal operations than skilled adults often display when they solve highly demanding intellectual problems. Expert chess players, for example, do not usually run through all possible combinations of moves, preferring instead to match the overall board pattern to a successful pattern they recall from past experience (Chase & Simon, 1973). Similarly, scientists follow their intuitions and take shortcuts that clearly violate the canons of scientific reasoning (Latour, 1987).

These data fit with Piaget's final speculation (1972) that the acquisition of formal operations is context-specific, casting doubt on his and Inhelder's earlier description of formal operational thinking as a totally systematic pattern that comes into routine use during adolescence.

The evidence from both the information-processing and cultural-context approaches has blurred the concept, central to traditional Piagetian theory, of a discontinuity between middle childhood and adolescence. According to these approaches, the improvements in cognitive ability during this transition may appear either continuous or discontinuous, depending on the depth of the young person's knowledge about a particular context or problem. Only if a qualitatively new mode of thinking appears across a broad range of contexts is it legitimate to conclude that a stagelike change has taken place. Consequently, to resolve the question whether thinking undergoes a stagelike change in adolescence, we turn now to assess the extent to which adolescent thinking is more systematic than younger children's thinking in a variety of social contexts and content areas.

Adolescent Thinking about the Social Order

The experimental tasks discussed thus far have been confined to the world of objects (chemicals, balance beams, groceries) and the logical relationships between events. In this section we examine the characteristics of adolescents' thought processes when they are asked to reason about issues of much greater personal concern: why their society is organized as it is; what might be done to improve it; how to be a moral person in a world where immoral behavior is so prevalent.

THINKING ABOUT POLITICS

Although children as young as 9 think seriously about the nature of society, they still have little understanding of political issues, according to Joseph Adelson (1991), who investigated how young people's reasoning about politics changes during the course of adolescence. To overcome national differences in knowledge about political figures and the fact that adolescents may have little specific knowledge about their political system, Adelson and his colleagues asked teenagers to imagine that a thousand people who have become disgusted with the way things

Their increased understanding makes teenagers critical of society and eager to suggest better ways of doing things.

are going in their country move to a Pacific island to set up a new society. The researchers then posed a series of questions about how the new society should be organized. Some questions required the young people to choose among different forms of government and to decide on the laws governing personal freedom and the rights of minorities. Others posed such hypothetical problems as whether a dissenting religious group should be allowed to refuse vaccinations.

These researchers found a major change in adolescents' reasoning about politics sometime around the age of 14 (Adelson & O'Neil, 1966; Adelson, Green, & O'Neil, 1969). This change, which occurred for members of both sexes and in all the countries where the study was conducted, was particularly evident in three areas: the way adolescents reason about laws, the level of social control they think appropriate, and the frequency with which they invoke overarching political ideals when they express their views.

Laws

Whereas 12- to 13-year-olds respond to questions about society in terms of concrete people and events, 15- to 16-year-olds respond in terms of abstract principles when asked, for example, "What is the purpose of laws?" (Adelson, 1972, p. 108):

A 12- TO 13-YEAR-OLD'S ANSWER

They do it, like in school, so that people don't get hurt. If we had no laws, people could go around killing people. So people don't steal or kill.

A 15- TO 16-YEAR-OLD'S ANSWER

To ensure safety and enforce the government. To limit what people can do. They are basically guidelines for people.

In their responses to questions about whether the law should allow the government to take private property for public use, the older adolescents demonstrated that they could reason hypothetically, taking many aspects of the problem into account. Adelson presented them with the case of a government that wanted to build a highway through land that an owner refused to sell. An older adolescent answers:

If it's a strategic point like the only way through a mountain maybe without tunneling, then I'm not too sure what I'd do. If it's a nice level stretch of plain that if you didn't have it you'd have to build a curve in the road, I think that the government might go ahead and put a curve in the road. (1972, p. 114)

Social control

The way 12- to 13-year-olds think about social control becomes evident when they are asked about crime, punishment, and retribution. In response after response, the youngest adolescents suggest that severe punishment is the best way to deal with lawbreakers, leading Adelson to conclude that "the young adolescent's authoritarianism is omnipresent" (1972, p. 119). One 13-year-old boy who was asked how to teach people not to commit crimes in the future answered:

Jail is usually the best thing, but there are others. . . . In the nineteenth century they used to torture people for doing things. Now I think the best place to teach people is in solitary confinement. (1972, p. 116)

As adolescents grow older, ideas of reform and rehabilitation begin to enter into their answers. Older adolescents also conceive of the beneficial side of laws, whereas younger ones think of laws only as a way of keeping people from behaving badly. When a law seems not to be working, older adolescents suggest that perhaps the law should be changed, while younger adolescents tend to say that the level of punishment should be increased.

The younger adolescents in Adelson's study seem to find it difficult to conceive of social and political regulation as a continually evolving process, assuming instead that "what is, has been; what is, will be." What "has been" for them is a world in which they were told what to do, so they project this regime into the future. The older adolescents, perhaps because they have experienced the need to be responsible for their own good behavior, seem capable of reasoning about a world in which they must formulate their own personal code of ethics.

Adelson points out that this mid-adolescent shift in reasoning about politics corresponds to changes that Inhelder and Piaget found in their studies of scientific problem solving. He suggests that the thinking of the younger adolescents, with its emphasis on finding one answer that is right in all cases, doesn't require formal operational thinking, whereas conceptions of modifiable, flexible, well-balanced political systems do.

Thinking about specific social problems

Developmental changes are also apparent when adolescents are asked to explain such widespread and troubling social phenomena as poverty, homelessness, and unemployment (Flanagan, 1995). Connie Flanagan asked adolescents ranging in age from 12 to 14 years and from 15 to 18 years such questions as "If you had to explain why some people are homeless, what would you say?" She found that the younger adolescents answered as if there were only one legitimate view, evaluating the issue in all-or-none terms without considering possible exceptions or qualifications. One young adolescent wrote, "I would tell them that it is many of their own faults and that they chose that lifestyle when they didn't take school work or whatever seriously."

In general, older adolescents offered explanations that included at least two distinct ways of interpreting the same question and treated several dimensions of the problem as legitimate explanations. This more complex thinking is reflected in answers such as "I would say that a lot of them got layed off and couldn't afford their homes anymore. Some of them were on welfare and got cut off, and the rest would be people who got into drugs and alcohol, and some who ran away from home."

Political idealism

In this century many adolescents have been attracted to visionary political and religious ideologies. Young people were prominent in the civil rights movement in the United States in the 1960s and in China in the late 1980s. According to many students of adolescence, young people are both pushed and pulled toward ideologies (Coles, 1967; Erikson, 1963; Inhelder & Piaget, 1958). They are pushed by their desire to become independent of their parents and to show that they can govern their own affairs; they are pulled by a seemingly coherent system that offers an alternative to the imperfections of the adult world.

Since no ideal political system has yet appeared on earth, adolescents' newly adopted ideologies are frequently utopian or religious. This proclivity was especially visible in the civil rights and commune movements of the 1960s, both of which drew heavily for support on adolescents who saw in them a consistent alternative to the imperfect society in which they lived (Berger, 1981; Coles, 1967).

Although adolescents have traditionally been viewed as idealistic and can think about ideal systems, most teenagers have not worked out any systematic alternatives to the existing political order for themselves. With rare exceptions, when asked directly to imagine an ideal society, teenage respondents came up with such platitudes as these:

> A society that everyone gets along and knows each other's problems and try to sit down and figure out each other's problem and get along like that.

> I think right now that the only society I would have would be the exact same one as we have now, although it does have its faults, I think we do have a good government now.

> Well, I would set up a society of helping out people like when there would be crime, . . . I would put these criminals in there for life because when they get out they would want to do it again and all that. (Adelson, 1975, pp. 74–75)

Many young people become cynical about political processes (Torney-Purta, 1990). They can see the problems and inconsistencies in political life but they are unable to work out practical solutions. Figure 16.6 shows adolescents' increasingly pessimistic responses to the question "Would it ever be possible to eliminate crime? poverty? racial prejudice?" In general, the older adolescents are pretty certain that political solutions to the world's ills are unlikely. At the same time, since they are in the process of defining themselves in contrast to their parents' generation, they are still attracted to the promises of someone who declares that, given the right beliefs and behavior, a more rational organization of life on earth is possible.

FIGURE 16.6 *Data indicating the increasing pessimism of young people about society's ability to eliminate crime, poverty, and racial prejudice. (From Torney-Purta, 1990.)*

THINKING ABOUT MORAL ISSUES

Regardless of their theoretical orientation, psychologists agree that adolescence is a time when young people become preoccupied by questions of moral behavior: What is right? What is wrong? What principles should I base my behavior on and use to judge the behavior of others? Evidence suggests that the processes used to think about such questions, like those used to think about science problems and politics, change during adolescence (Kurtines & Gewirtz, 1995).

For the last several decades, the study of moral reasoning during adolescence has been dominated by the work of Lawrence Kohlberg and his followers (Gibbs, Bassinger, & Fuller, 1992; Power, Higgins, & Kohlberg, 1989). Kohlberg,

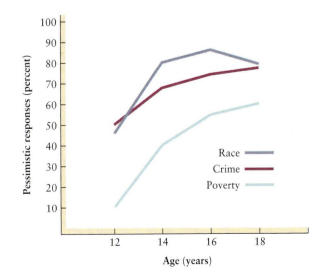

Both the experience of helping other people and formal instruction in issues of morality have been found to enhance moral development. The young people at top are volunteering at a food bank, while those at the bottom are listening to a lecture on intolerance.

it may be recalled (Chapter 14, p. 574), suggested that moral reasoning progresses through three broad levels during childhood and adolescence, each consisting of two stages (Table 16.2 summarizes these levels and stages). As they develop from one stage to the next, children make more adequate analyses of the moral obligations that prevail among individuals and between individuals and their social groups. Some aspects of Kohlberg's theory seem to have been borne out by research; others have not.

According to Kohlberg, moral reasoning at the start of middle childhood is at the *preconventional* level. In other words, children's reasoning in stages 1 and 2 is not based on social conventions or laws. They judge actions in the light of their own wants and fears and do not yet take into account the fact that social life requires shared standards of behavior. Toward the end of middle childhood, children attain the second level—the *conventional* level—in which they begin to take social conventions into account and recognize the existence of shared standards of right and wrong. Kohlberg called stage 3 reasoning (the first stage at this level) "good-child morality," because being moral now means living up to the expectations of one's family, teachers, and other significant people in one's life.

Moral reasoning at stage 4 is like that at stage 3 except its focus shifts from relations between individuals to relations between the individual and the group. People who reason at stage 4 believe that society has legitimate authority over individuals, and they feel an obligation to accept its laws, customs, and standards of decent behavior. Moral behavior from this point of view is behavior that maintains the social order. For this reason, stage 4 is sometimes referred to as the "law-and-order stage" (Brown & Herrnstein, 1975, p. 289). Stage 4 reasoning begins to appear during adolescence, but stage 3 is still the dominant mode of reasoning about moral questions until people reach their middle 20s (see Figure 16. 7) (Colby et al., 1983).

Kohlberg believed that moral thinking at stages 3 and 4 depends on partial ability to engage in formal operational reasoning, in particular the ability to consider simultaneously the various *existing* factors relevant to moral choices (Kohlberg, 1984). People who are reasoning at stages 3 and 4, however, are still reasoning concretely insofar as they do not yet consider all *possible* relations or form abstract hypotheses about what is moral.

With the transition from stage 4 to stage 5 in Kohlberg's scheme comes another basic shift in the level of moral judgment. Reasoning at stage 5 requires people to go beyond social conventions to more abstract principles of right and wrong. This perspective, which he called *postconventional*, involves a social-contract orientation to moral problems. People still accept and value the social system, but instead of insisting on maintaining it as it is, they are open to democratic processes of change and to continual exploration of possibilities for improving on the existing social contract. Recognizing that laws are sometimes in conflict with moral principles, they become creators as well as maintainers of laws. Kohlberg found that stage 5 moral reasoning does not appear until early adulthood, and then only rarely.

People reach stage 6 in Kohlberg's system when they make moral judgments in accordance with ethical principles that they believe transcend the rules of individual societies. Kohlberg and his colleagues failed to observe stage 6 reasoning in their research on moral dilemmas and he eventually concluded that it is more usefully thought of as a philosophical ideal than as a psychological reality. Nonetheless, under extraordinary circumstances, otherwise ordinary people have put their lives at risk because of moral beliefs guided by stage 6 reasoning. Such was the case during World War II, when many European gentiles rescued Jews destined for extermination. According to Samuel and Pearl Oliner (1988), most of them were motivated by ethical principles that they believed apply to all of humanity, the hallmark of stage 6 moral reasoning.

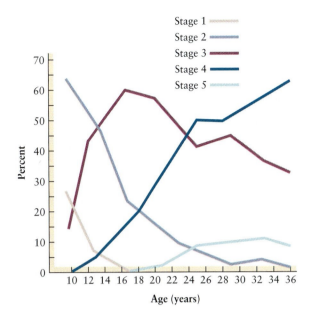

FIGURE 16.7 *Mean percentage of moral reasoning at each of Kohlberg's stages, by age group. (Adapted from Colby et al., 1983.)*

Evaluating Kohlberg's stage theory

By and large, researchers who have used Kohlberg's methods and criteria for assigning people to different stages have confirmed that children progress through Kohlberg's stages of moral reasoning in the predicted order (Kurtines & Gewirtz, 1991; Walker, 1986). However, success has not been uniform. Instead of steadily

TABLE 16.2   Kohlberg's Six Moral Stages

Level and Stage	What Is Right	Reasons for Doing Right	Social Perspective
LEVEL I—PRECONVENTIONAL			
Stage 1—Heteronomous morality	• Adherence to rules backed by punishment; obedience for its own sake.	• Avoidance of punishment.	Egocentric point of view.
Stage 2—Instrumental morality	• Acting to meet one's own interests and needs and letting others do the same.	• To serve one's own needs or interests.	Concrete individualistic perspective: Right is relative, an equal exchange, a deal, an agreement.
LEVEL II—CONVENTIONAL			
Stage 3— Good-child morality	• Living up to what others expect.	• The need to be a good person in one's own eyes and those of others.	Perspective of the individual sharing feelings, agreements, and expectations with others.
Stage 4—Law-and-order morality	• Fulfilling the actual duties to which one has agreed. • Upholding laws except in extreme cases when they conflict with other fixed social duties. • Contributing to society, group, or institution.	• To keep the institution going as a whole. • What would happen "if everyone did it"? • The imperative of conscience to meet one's defined obligations (easily confused with stage 3 belief in rules and authority).	Perspective of an individual in relation to the social group: takes the point of view of the system that defines roles and rules.
LEVEL III—POSTCONVENTIONAL, OR PRINCIPLED			
Stage 5—Social-contract reasoning	• Being aware that people hold a variety of values and opinions, most of which are relative to the group that holds them. • Upholding relative rules in the interest of impartiality and because they are the social contract. • Nonrelative values and rights such as *life*, and *liberty*, must be upheld in any society, regardless of majority opinion.	• A sense of obligation to law because of one's social contract to make and abide by laws for the welfare of all and for the protection of all people's rights. • A feeling of contractual commitment, freely entered upon, to family, friendship, trust, and work obligations. • Concern that laws and duties be based on rational calculation of overall utility, "the greatest good for the greatest number."	Prior-to-society perspective: Perspective of a rational individual aware of values and rights prior to social attachments and contracts. Integrates perspectives by formal mechanisms of agreement, contract, objective impartiality, and due process. Considers moral and legal points of view; recognizes that they sometimes conflict and finds it difficult to integrate them.

TABLE 16.2 (*Continued*)

Level and Stage	What Is Right	Reasons for Doing Right	Social Perspective
Stage 6—Universal ethical principles	• Following self-chosen ethical principles because they are universal principles of justice: the equality of human rights and respect for the dignity of human beings as individual persons. • Judging laws or social agreements by the extent to which they rest on such principles. • When laws violate principles, acting in accordance with the principle.	• A belief in the validity of universal moral principles. • A sense of personal commitment to those principles.	Perspective of a moral point of view from which social arrangements derive: Perspective is that of any rational individual recognizing the nature of morality or the fact that persons are ends in themselves and must be treated as such.

Source: Adapted from Kohlberg, 1976.

progressing from one stage to the next, subjects sometimes regress in their development or seem to skip a stage (Gilligan & Murphy, 1979; Kohlberg & Kramer, 1969; Kuhn, 1976; Kurtines & Grief, 1974).

One problem of evaluation arises from the procedures used to score the answers to Kohlberg's questions (Kurtines & Gewirtz, 1984). Recall from Chapter 14 that Kohlberg presented dilemmas in the form of stories and asked children to reason about them in a give-and-take interview session. Some investigators report having trouble sorting interview answers reliably into Kohlberg's six categories (Kurtines & Grief, 1974). Unreliable scoring makes it difficult to evaluate the accuracy with which the theory corresponds to reality. In response to this criticism, Ann Colby and Kohlberg (1984) created a standardized scoring scheme that they claim is both easy to use and reliable. Using the revised procedures, Lawrence Walker (1986) found improved correspondence between the theory and the data.

The difficulties in scoring the data from Kohlberg's moral dilemmas inspired other attempts to create more efficient ways to assess moral reasoning. John Gibbs and his colleagues (1992) created a paper-and-pencil testing procedure called the Sociomoral Reflection Measure (SRM), based on simple questions about moral issues instead of elaborate narrative descriptions of moral dilemmas (see Table 16.3). These researchers report that when they use this procedure to assign people to stages of moral development, the results correlate well with results obtained with Kohlberg's lengthy moral dilemmas.

In one respect, however, the data collected by Gibbs and his colleagues differ from Kohlberg's. They found too little evidence of moral reasoning higher than stage 4 to substantiate Kohlberg's idea of the existence of postconventional moral reasoning. This conclusion has drawn fire from researchers who believe that while stage 5 reasoning may appear in only 15 to 20 percent of the population, it is

TABLE 16.3   Socioemotional Reflection Questionnaire

INSTRUCTIONS

In this questionnaire, we want to find out about the things you think are important for people to do, and especially why you think these things (like keeping a promise) are important. Please try to explain your thinking by WRITING AS MUCH AS YOU CAN TO EXPLAIN—EVEN IF YOU HAVE TO WRITE YOUR EXPLANATIONS MORE THAN ONCE. Don't just write "same as before." If you use different words to show what you mean that will help us even more. Please answer all questions, especially the "why" questions . . .

(Every question is followed by the following requests for evaluation and explanation):

Circle one: very important   important   not important

WHY IS THAT VERY IMPORTANT/IMPORTANT/NOT IMPORTANT (WHICHEVER ONE YOU CIRCLED)

SAMPLE QUESTIONS

Think about when you've made a promise to a friend of yours. How important is it for people to keep promises, if they can, to friends?

Think about when you've helped your mother or your father. How important is it for children to help their parents?

In general, how important is it for people to tell the truth?

Let's say a friend of yours needs help and may even die, and you're the only person who can save him or her. How important is it for a person (without losing his or her own life) to save the life of a friend?

How important is it to live even if that person doesn't want to?

How important is it for people to obey the law?

Source: From Gibbs et al., Moral Maturity, Appendix 1.

---

nonetheless an important achievement that ought to be taken into account in theories of moral development (Snarey & Keljo, 1994).

Another point of contention is Kohlberg's belief that levels of moral reasoning correspond to the levels of cognitive development described by Piaget. The expected correspondences have been found by some researchers (Colby et al., 1983; Walker, 1986) but not others (Haan, Weiss, & Johnson, 1982). Some investigators (such as Hoffman, 1980) have taken the failures as evidence that Kohlberg's stage theory was incorrectly formulated, but others argue that the problem lies in the way the data have been interpreted (Walker, 1988).

An area of controversy that applies not only to Kohlberg's theory but to research on moral development as a whole is the question of how hypothetical reasoning about moral dilemmas is related to actual moral behavior (Saltzstein, 1994; Walker et al., 1995). It is commonly observed, for example, that perfectly respectable, law-abiding citizens who are likely to score at stage 3 or 4 on Kohlberg's scale sometimes fail to help strangers in need, or riot at football games, or commit terrible atrocities in times of war (Bandura, 1991; Kohlberg & Candee, 1984). Clearly the ability to reason about morality does not inevitably lead to moral behavior. A good many studies, however, do find a significant and some-

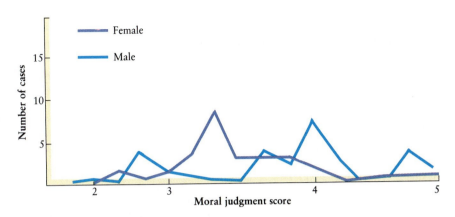

FIGURE 16.8 *The distribution of moral judgment scores for a sample of male and female 16-year-olds. Note that the most frequent score for girls is near level 3, whereas the most frequent score for boys is in the range of level 4. (From Holstein, 1976.)*

times strong relationship between the level of moral reasoning and observed behavior (Blasi, 1983; Turiel, 1990).

In a study of children making the transition from middle childhood to adolescence, Herbert Richards and his colleagues (1992) found that moral reasoning was related to the quality of their classroom behavior in a way that makes good sense in terms of Kohlberg's theory. They presented moral dilemmas to children in the fourth to eighth grades (roughly, 9 to 14 years of age). They found that children who responded at stage 1 (with reasoning based on obedience and punishment) or stage 3 (with reasoning based on acceptance of shared social norms) were the best-behaved children in the classroom. Those who used stage 2 reasoning (based on immediate interest) were the ones most likely to misbehave. This finding fits with those of earlier studies reporting that stage 2 reasoning is the most common form of moral reasoning encountered among juvenile delinquents (Trevethan & Walker, 1989).

Sex differences in moral reasoning

As much of the foregoing discussion suggests, Kohlberg's approach to moral development has been both influential and controversial. One additional area of controversy concerns questions of sex differences. Controversy over sex differences in moral reasoning was fueled by the fact that in some of the first tests of moral reasoning in adolescents, boys appeared to score higher than girls (Haan, Langer, & Kohlberg, 1976; Holstein, 1976). The data in Figure 16.8, taken from Constance Holstein's (1976) study of moral reasoning, show the pattern of results that sparked the controversy. Adolescent boys were most frequently found to be in stage 4, whereas adolescent girls most frequently scored at stage 3. In studies of adults, men's answers almost always displayed reasoning at a level higher than stage 3, whereas women's responses were hardly ever at the level of stage 5.

One response to these data was to suggest that Kohlberg's treatment of moral issues left out a dimension of morality of particular concern to women. Carol Gilligan (1977, 1982; Gilligan & Attanucci, 1988) argued that women's responses to moral dilemmas are lower on Kohlberg's scale than those of men because women's moral thinking is oriented toward interpersonal relationships and coupled with an ethic of caring and responsibility for other people. This difference in what she referred to as "moral orientation" would incline women to suggest altruism and self-sacrifice rather than to invoke rights and rules as the solutions to interpersonal problems and moral dilemmas. Because women are judged by criteria more appropriate to men, Gilligan argued, their orientation to care "creates a liability within Kohlberg's framework" (1986, p. 45).

Gilligan illustrated the difference between the two kinds of moral orientation by contrasting men's and women's responses to questions about the meaning of morality:

A 25-YEAR-OLD MAN'S RESPONSE TO THE QUESTION "WHAT DOES THE WORD MORALITY MEAN TO YOU?"

Nobody in the world knows the answer. I think it is recognizing the right of the individual, the rights of other individuals, not interfering with those rights. Act as fairly as you would have them treat you. I think it is basically to preserve the human being's right to existence. I think that is the most important. Secondly, the human being's right to do as he pleases, again without interfering with somebody else's rights.

A 25-YEAR-OLD WOMAN'S RESPONSE TO THE QUESTION "IS THERE REALLY SOME CORRECT SOLUTION TO MORAL PROBLEMS OR IS EVERYBODY'S OPINION EQUALLY CORRECT?"

No, I don't think that everyone's opinion is equally right. I think that in some situations there may be opinions that are equally valid, and one could conscientiously adopt one of several courses of action. But there are other situations in which I think there are right and wrong answers, that sort of inhere in the nature of existence, of all individuals here who need to live with each other to live. We need to depend upon each other, and hopefully it is not only a physical need but a need of fulfillment in ourselves, that a person's life is enriched by cooperating with other people and striving to live in harmony with everybody else, and to that end, there are right and wrong, there are things which promote that end and that move away from it. (1982, pp. 19–20)

In Gilligan's view, these answers capture the difference between male moral reasoning, which she sees as focused on individual rights, and female moral reasoning, which she believes is based on a sense of responsibility for other people.

Recent research has transformed this controversy and provided an enriched picture of the development of moral reasoning in both males and females. Contrary to expectations based on the earlier moral reasoning research or on Piaget's analysis of game playing, sex differences in moral reasoning have appeared rarely, and when they do appear, they are small (Nunner-Winkler, 1984; Snarey, 1985; Walker, 1986, 1988, 1995). In a review of 80 studies of moral reasoning involving 152 groups of subjects, Walker and de Vries (1985) found only 22 that showed significant sex differences, and in nine of them females scored higher on Kohlberg's scale than males.

Contrary to expectations based on Gilligan's ideas about two sex-linked moral orientations, additional research has shown that men as well as women are capable of displaying an orientation toward care and relationships. In order to test Gilligan's ideas that those who adopt a care orientation are likely to score poorly on Kohlberg's justice-oriented dilemmas, some studies have compared levels of performance on Kohlberg's moral dilemmas with reasoning about typical real-life moral conflicts. Contrary to the idea that the two orientations conflict, those who have a care-oriented approach to real-life dilemmas actually score as high or higher on Kohlberg's dilemmas as on real-life dilemmas (Walker, 1989). These results do not negate the possibility of gender-related differences in social relations and dominant moral concerns, but they do argue against the idea that one sex or the other is more capable of reasoning morally about issues of care or justice.

Cultural variations in moral reasoning

Standard studies of cross-cultural variability in moral reasoning, like those of formal operational reasoning, reveal far greater differences between cultural groups than between the two sexes (Kohlberg, 1969; Snarey, 1985). Although there are some exceptions (Shweder, Mahopatra, & Miller, 1987), most studies show that people who live in relatively small, face-to-face communities in technologically unsophisticated societies (and who have not received high levels of schooling that

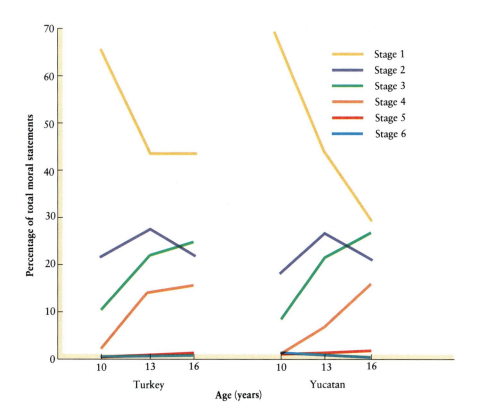

FIGURE 16.9 *Age trends in the moral judgments of boys in small isolated villages in two nations. Note the continuing high incidence of stage 1 responses even by 16-year-olds. (From Kohlberg, 1969.)*

take them outside of the traditional way of life) rarely reason beyond stage 3 on Kohlberg's scale. They most often justify their decisions at the level of stage 1 or 2 (Edwards, 1982; Tietjen & Walker, 1985; Walker & Moran, 1991). This difference can be seen by comparing the scores in Figure 16.9 with those in Figure 16.7).

Kohlberg explained cross-cultural data such as those in Figure 16.9 by suggesting that cultural differences in social stimulation produce differences in the ability to engage in formal operational reasoning, which in turn explain differences in moral reasoning:

> . . . an absence of cognitive stimulation necessary for developing formal logical reasoning may be important in explaining ceilings on moral level. In a Turkish village, for example, full formal operational reasoning appeared to be extremely rare (if the Piagetian technique for intellectual assessment can be considered usable in that setting). Accordingly, one would not expect that principled (Stage 5 or 6) moral reasoning, which requires formal thinking as a base, could develop in that cultural context. (1984, p. 198)

Critics have pointed out the unfortunate implications of Kohlberg's willingness to accept the validity of Piagetian techniques and to apply his own moral standards to different cultures. The anthropologist Richard Shweder (1982), for example, claims that culture-specific value judgments are built directly into Kohlberg's stage sequence, making it no more than a justification for the special cultural perspective of Anglo males, inheritors of the political ideology of liberal democracy. Are we to believe, such critics ask, that people who grow up in a traditional Third World village are less moral than the residents of a city in an industrially advanced country (Simpson, 1974)? Isn't it more reasonable to assume that because Turkish villagers live in face-to-face contact with the people who govern their fate, they are bound to give the greatest moral value to the Golden Rule, a morality of caring and responsibility?

The historian Howard Kaminsky (1984) expresses the same doubts:

> Is a Stage 6 refusal to support a friend who is wrong superior to a Stage 3 loyalty to that friend? A medieval nobleman would say no, and history suggests to us that if we repudiate the nobleman's sense of right, we are also repudiating the civilization created in resonance with his mentality, as well as those elements of the aristocratic ideal that have formed the modern sense of individuality. . . . [P]ersonal loyalty has obvious virtues that are lost when friendship or affection is made conditional on abstract rightness. (p. 410)

Kohlberg denied that bias in his scales fosters the conclusion that some societies, the United States among them, are more moral than others. He echoed the classical position of modern anthropology, that cultures should be thought of as unique configurations of beliefs and institutions that help the social group adapt to both local conditions and universal aspects of life on earth (Boas, 1911; Geertz, 1984). In accord with this relativist view, Kohlberg wrote that "we do not understand how a moral ranking of cultures could either be done or be scientifically useful" (1984, p. 311). In this view, a culture in which stage 3 was the height of moral reasoning would be considered "morally equivalent" to a culture dominated by stage 5 or 6 reasoning, even though the specific reasoning practices could be scored as less "developed" according to Kohlberg's universal criteria.

Kohlberg's position on cultural levels of moral development would be logically consistent, whatever else one thought of it, were it not for the nagging problem that he had already proposed that people of other cultures are at a lower level of cognitive development—not a relative matter. As a result of this crucial link between formal operational thinking and moral judgment, Kohlberg's view is vulnerable to his critics' claims that higher scores on his scale of moral development really do imply moral superiority at both individual and cultural levels (Liebert, 1984; Simpson, 1974).

Despite many uncertainties arising from disagreements about how data concerning "moral development" should be gathered and interpreted, evidence collected around the world indicates that by the time most people become adults, they are capable of reasoning at a level that corresponds at least to the Golden Rule.

Integration of the Self

One of the most widely held ideas about adolescence is that this is the period when the individual forges the basis for a stable adult personality. Teenagers' ability to take several factors into account when they think through a problem, their broader knowledge of society's norms and moral codes, and their increasing awareness that adulthood is approaching all contribute to the establishment of an integrated, adult sense of self.

CHANGING ATTRIBUTES OF THE SELF

In Chapter 14 we saw that at about the age of 6, when American children enter school, they begin to think of themselves in comparative terms: instead of saying (for example), "I am a girl who likes to skate," they begin to provide such self-descriptions as "I am a better skater than most of my class." A little later they begin explicitly to include the interpersonal consequences of their attributes: "I am a good skater so lots of kids like to skate with me" (see Table 14.7, p. 606).

During adolescence, a fourth kind of self-description makes its appearance, in which personal identity is expressed in terms of general beliefs, values, and life plans, as in the following dialogue:

Interviewer: What kind of person are you?

Adolescent: I am someone who believes that everybody is created equal.

Interviewer: Why is that important?

Adolescent: Because I want to work for equal rights for everybody.

Interviewer: What do you mean?

Adolescent: I am going to be a lawyer and take cases and see that everyone gets rights, even if he's very poor or the wrong color or something. (Damon & Hart, 1988, p. 69)

As children enter adolescence, their self-descriptions also shift from relatively concrete attributes (for instance, "I'm a good listener" or "I am easygoing") to more inclusive, higher-order concepts ("I am tolerant"). As Susan Harter (1990b, p. 355) points out, "To consider oneself sensitive, one must potentially combine such attributes as being understanding, friendly, and caring."

Another feature that distinguishes the self-concepts of adolescents from those of younger children is the greater variety of attributes they include. In middle childhood, children describe themselves in terms of either their cognitive, physical, and social competence or a global notion of self-worth (Harter, 1982). Adolescents describe themselves in terms of characteristics from many domains: scholastic competence, athletic competence, job competence, physical appearance, social acceptance, close friendship, romantic appeal, and conduct. These categories overlap but are not identical to those that are prominent in middle childhood (Harter, 1990a, 1990b).

Adolescents are also more likely to think of themselves with respect to the particular context they are being asked about. If they are asked what they are like when they are with their friends or in a class at school, their answers will differ from those they give when they are asked to describe what they are like when they are having dinner at home.

The appearance of "multiple selves" in adolescents' descriptions of themselves makes it necessary for them to deal with the fact that they are, in some sense, different people in different contexts. It is at this point that the question "Who is the real me?" comes to the fore.

On the basis of research among American adolescents, Susan Harter (1986) reports that the appearance of several selves, each depending on whom one is with and what role one is playing, is especially troublesome to 14- and 15-year-old Americans. When asked about the contradiction between being nice to some people but not to others, a 13-year-old responded, "I guess I just think about one thing about myself at a time and don't think about the other until the next day" (p. 45). By contrast, an older adolescent, when asked about problems in a romantic relationship, replied in a way that indicates her sensitivity to variations in herself as the situation changes: "I hate the fact that I get so nervous! I wish I wasn't so inhibited. The real me is talkative: I want to be natural, but I can't" (p. 45). Harter and her colleague Ann Monsour (1992) report that as young people move through adolescence, they become increasingly better at integrating the contradictory selves that they see themselves to be in different contexts.

ADOLESCENT SELF-ESTEEM

When adolescents begin routinely to notice the disparities between the way they behave and the way they ought to behave if they were being true to their "real selves," they begin to be preoccupied with what their "true" self is. Once they start dwelling on their own characteristics, they are confronted with the question "How much do I like myself?" To a considerable degree, attributes associated with high self-esteem in adolescents are the same ones they attribute to popular peers in earlier years. Attractiveness heads the list, especially for girls, followed by peer acceptance. All other characteristics trail behind.

This girl is displaying the increased concern with personal appearance that is a prominent feature of adolescence.

Identity formation According to Erikson, the developmental crisis faced by adolescents. To forge a secure identity, adolescents must bring about a resolution of the identity crisis in both the individual and the social spheres.

Developmental crisis In Erikson's theory, a set of choices and tests that individuals face as they become ready to confront a new life task.

This heavy emphasis on female attractiveness has an unfortunate impact on the self-esteem of girls, because many of them consider themselves to be unattractive. Studies in a wide range of countries have found that, on average, girls have a lower sense of self-esteem than boys (Baumeister, 1993).

Studies in the United States show a marked decline in overall self-esteem in early adolescence followed by a steady increase after the age of 14 or 15 (Harter, 1993). Researchers believe that this early decline in self-esteem is due in part to the transition from elementary school to junior high school, which confronts children with increased academic demands at the same time that it puts them at the bottom of the social ladder (Simmons & Blyth, 1987). The steady increase thereafter is less well understood; it may reflect the increasing freedom young people have to choose their friends, contexts, and activities, so that they can establish and live up to their own standards, or it may indicate that they are bringing their image of their ideal selves more into line with reality.

As adolescence comes to an end, young people face the task of reconciling the multiple, often conflicting self-images that have developed over the years. This so-called identity crisis, including the resolution of their sexual identity, is one of the most fundamental issues they must deal with during the transition from child to adult.

RESOLVING THE IDENTITY CRISIS

Recall from Chapter 15 that Erikson saw the fundamental task of adolescence to be **identity formation.** The adolescent must either achieve a secure sense of personal identity or confront a variety of psychological problems in later life (Erikson, 1968a; Kroger, 1989). Like Freud, Erikson believed that success in dealing with the developmental challenges of adolescence requires a reworking of previously resolved developmental crises. He explained the idea of a **developmental crisis** this way:

> At a given age, a human being, by dint of his physical, intellectual and emotional growth, becomes ready and eager to face a new life task, that is, a set of choices and tests which are in some traditional way prescribed and prepared for him by his society's structure. A new life task presents a *crisis* whose outcome can be a successful graduation, or alternatively, an impairment of the life cycle which will aggravate future crises. Each crisis prepares the next, as one step leads to another; and each crisis also lays one more cornerstone for the adult personality. (1958, p. 254; italics in original)

According to Erikson, adolescents must rework four earlier developmental crises:

1. *Establishing trust,* the problem that infants encounter as part of the attachment process, reappears in adolescence as the search for people to have faith in, people to whom one can prove one's own trustworthiness. This search goes on at several levels simultaneously, in both personal and social spheres. First, one seeks trustworthy and admirable friends. At the beginning of adolescence these are friends of the same sex who can be trusted to share your anxieties without making fun of you. Later, the focus shifts to partners of the opposite sex who will find you attractive and love you.

   In the larger social world, the need to establish trust takes the form of a search for political causes and leaders worth supporting. To succeed at this level, adolescents must think systematically about human nature and society in order to select an ideology in which to place their trust. The difficulties of this search are often expressed in mistrust of adult social institutions and cynical indifference to them.

Adolescents seek out heroes to worship and imitate. In the U.S. adolescents find many of the heroes they identify with among popular musicians.

2. *Establishing autonomy* was expressed at the end of infancy as the 2-year-old's demand to "do it myself!" Now autonomy means choosing one's own path in life instead of going along with decisions imposed by one's parents.

3. *Taking initiative*, which was expressed as pretend play during early childhood, now means setting goals for what one might become rather than settling for the limited reality that adults have arranged. The imaginary situations of preschool play find their counterparts in new dreams of greatness that the adolescent can seek to realize.

4. *Industry* takes on a new meaning toward the end of adolescence, quite different from its meaning during middle childhood. No longer will the tasks be set by the teacher; the relative independence of adulthood carries with it the duty to take responsibility for setting one's own goals and for the quality of one's work.

A special feature of the process of identity formation during adolescence is that for the first time physical maturation, cognitive skills, and social expectations come together in a way that makes it possible for young people to "sort through and synthesize their childhood identifications in order to construct a viable pathway toward adulthood" (Marcia, 1980, p. 160). In other words, trust, autonomy, initiative, and industry are blended to become the adult sense of self in relation to the social world.

As we noted earlier, Erikson saw this process of identity formation as involving the integration of more than the individual personality. In order to forge a secure sense of self, adolescents must resolve their identities in both the individual and the social spheres, or, as Erikson put it, establish "the identity of these two identities" (1968a, p. 22). Some idea of the intellectual complexity of this task can be gleaned from Erikson's attempt to specify the thought processes required to achieve identity formation:

In psychological terms, identity formation employs a process of simultaneous reflection and observation, a process taking place on all levels of mental functioning, by which the individual judges himself in the light of what he perceives to be the way in which others judge him in comparison to themselves

and to a typology significant to them; while he judges their way of judging him in the light of how he perceives himself in comparison to them and to types that have become relevant to him. (1968a, pp. 22–23)

Although Erikson's description of the kind of thinking required to achieve a sense of an integrated identity may seem unnecessarily convoluted, this passage is worth careful study. It corresponds closely to Piaget's descriptions of formal operational thinking, suggesting a link between Piaget's theory of cognitive development and Erikson's theory of personality development.

Erikson's core idea is that adolescents engage in an identity-forming process that depends on:

- How they judge others.
- How others judge them.
- How they judge the judgment processes of others.
- Their ability to keep in mind social categories ("typologies") available in the culture when they form judgments about other people.

Note that it is not enough to take only one or two of these elements into account—say, the fact that you base judgments of others on social categories of importance to you: "Sam is a jerk for allowing himself to be caught drinking beer behind the gym." If your judgment of Sam is to be complete with respect to your own identity, you must simultaneously consider both your own and other people's judgments, plus the perspective of society (embodied in the linguistic categories used to formulate the judgments). Sam may have been caught drinking behind the gym, but if you too drink beer, or if you also cut class, does that make you a jerk too? Or is getting caught the only way to be a jerk? And wouldn't Sam think you were a jerk for attending a dumb civics class just because you're the teacher's pet? And what would your teacher think if he knew whom you had been with at 11:30 last night and what you were doing?

Viewed in this way, Erikson's ideas about the mental processes involved in resolving the identity crisis of adolescence fit not only with Piaget's ideas of formal operational thinking but also with the findings of a variety of studies on the development of self-understanding during adolescence. As we noted earlier, adolescents begin to describe the self primarily in abstract, general terms, to be more self-reflective, and to show concern for integrating their past selves with an imagined future self (Damon & Hart, 1988; Selman, 1980).

Erikson's characterization of the developmental tasks of adolescence also makes it clear that the process of identity formation is likely to be difficult for families and friends as well as for adolescents themselves. (While this process is painful for many adolescents, it seems to be especially so for those who assume a homosexual identity. See Box 16.2.) Young people who are in the midst of working out a coherent notion of themselves sometimes take out their confusion on themselves and others, and the result can be antisocial, sometimes self-destructive, behavior (see Figure 16.10). As Erikson summarized it, a frequent result of identity confusion is that

youth after youth, bewildered by the incapacity to assume a role forced on him by the inexorable standardization of

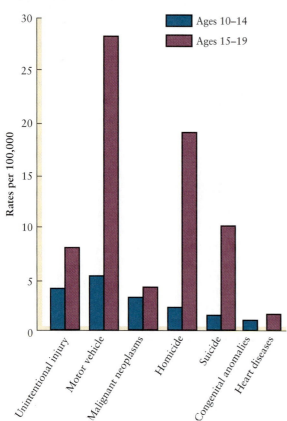

FIGURE 16.10 *Adolescence is a time when young people are at increasing risk of death by accident or suicide. Especially striking is the precipitous increase in male mortality. Experts believe that the increased availability of guns is a major factor in recent increases in the suicide rate. (Centers for Disease Control, 1995.)*

American adolescence, runs away in one form or another, dropping out of school, leaving jobs, staying out all night, or withdrawing into bizarre and inaccessible moods. (Erikson, 1968a, p. 132)

Here we have the Eriksonian version of Hall's and Freud's visions of an emotionally stormy adolescence (see Chapter 15, pp. 623, 625), clothed in more modern terminology.

It has proved difficult to create explicit, objective methods for testing Erikson's ideas about identity. Many threads enter into the process of establishing an identity, and each person must create a unique synthesis of all those disparate parts (Marcia, 1991; Waterman, 1985).

One of Erikson's favorite means of testing his ideas was the detailed biographical case study. His biographies of Martin Luther and Mahatma Gandhi (Erikson, 1958, 1969) produced fascinating interpretations of these historic men's psychological states. But to apply such a method to the everyday problems of contemporary teenagers who are experiencing identity confusion is time-consuming, expensive, and difficult.

The great popularity of Erikson's ideas has created a demand for simpler psychodiagnostic techniques that will achieve the same end, a portrait of an identity in the process of consolidation (Flum, 1994; Grotevant, 1986; Marcia, 1966; Waterman, 1985). James Marcia, for example, interviewed 86 male college students about their choice of occupation and their beliefs about religion and politics. Harold Grotevant, William Thorbecke, and Margaret Meyer (1982) extended Marcia's interview questions to include the interpersonal domains of friendship, dating, and sex roles. Their questions were designed to elicit information on the degree to which individuals have adopted and fully committed themselves to a point of view.

On the basis of the students' answers, Marcia (1966) identified four patterns of coping with the task of identity formation:

1. *Identity achievement* Adolescents who display this pattern have gone through a period of decision making about their choice of occupation, for example, or their political or religious commitment. They are now actively pursuing their own goals. When people in this group were asked about their political beliefs, they responded with such answers as "I've thought it over, and I've decided to be a _____ . Their program is the most sensible one for the country to be following."

2. *Foreclosure* Young people who display this pattern are also committed to occupational and ideological positions, but they show no signs of having gone through an identity crisis. In a sense they never really undergo a personality reorganization. Instead, they just take over patterns of identity from their parents. They respond to questions about their political beliefs with such answers as "I really never gave politics much thought. Our family always votes _____ , so that's how I vote."

3. *Moratorium* This pattern is displayed by adolescents who are currently experiencing an identity crisis. They are likely to answer a question about their political beliefs by saying, "I'm not sure. Both parties have their good points, but neither one seems to offer a better chance for my economic future."

4. *Identity diffusion* Adolescents who manifest this pattern have tried out several identities without being able to settle on one. They are likely to take a cynical attitude toward the issues confronting them, so they may answer questions about political commitment by declaring, "I stopped thinking about politics ages ago. There are no parties worth following."

When adolescents are struggling to achieve a stable identity, they often prefer to spend time by themselves.

BOX 16.2

Homosexuality

Although the dominant form of sexual behavior centers on the union of male and female, a sizable number of people exhibit a homosexual preference—that is, a preference for members of their own sex as sexual partners—at various times in their lives. Because of the social stigma attached to homosexuality in many societies and the resulting reticence about such matters, there is no way to know for sure how many people have engaged in homosexual practices. Still, that homosexual activity is common is borne out by survey data collected more than 40 years ago by Alfred Kinsey and his colleagues (1948, 1953). These researchers found that about a third of men and 13 percent of women reported having reached orgasm with a partner of the same sex at least once in their lives. Such behavior is by no means limited to our culture. It has been documented by anthropologists in most of the world's cultures (Ford & Beach, 1951).

While homosexual activity is widespread, only a small number of the people who engage in it consider themselves to be homosexuals. Both in the Kinsey surveys and in more recent investigations of adolescent sexual behavior, the young people who indicated that they had engaged in homosexual activity far outnumbered those who described themselves as homosexuals (Cole & Stokes, 1985).

In other cultures, adolescent homosexual behavior is only rarely viewed as an expression of a lifelong sexual identity (Gonsiorek & Weinrich, 1991; Herdt, 1989; Savin-Williams, 1990). Instead it is viewed as either necessary because of the separation between the sexes, as a way for young men to learn about sex, as part of the ritual of becoming a man, or as a playful acting out of the sex drive by young men who have excess energy.

Because of such disparities between sexual behavior and sexual identity, several contemporary researchers distinguish between homosexual orientation, homosexual behavior or practices, and homosexual identity. *Homosexual orientation* consists of a preponderance of sexual or erotic feelings, thoughts, fantasies, and behaviors involving members of the same sex. *Homosexual behavior* is sexual behavior between members of the same sex. *Homosexual identity* is an enduring integration of sexual orientation and sexual behavior into a homosexual sense of self (Savin-Williams, 1990). Some researchers maintain that a public declaration of one's homosexuality is a necessary part of assuming a homosexual identity; others disagree (Savin-Williams, 1990; Troiden, 1988).

In the United States, arrival at a heterosexual identity fits approved American social categories. Homosexuality is stigmatized in our society. How, then, do young men and women come to commit themselves to a homosexual identity?

Leading researchers seem to agree that for many people the development of a homosexual identity goes through several stages, such as those described by Richard Troiden (1988).

Stage 1: Sensitization; feeling different In retrospective reports one often encounters people who say that during middle childhood they had social experiences that made them feel different from other children and that served later to make homosexuality personally relevant to them, although they assumed at the time that they were heterosexual (Bell, Weinberg, & Hammersmith, 1981). Typical comments from girls: "I was very shy and unaggressive" (p. 148); "I felt different: unfeminine, ungraceful, not very pretty, kind of a mess" (p. 156). Typical comments from boys: "I couldn't stand sports, so naturally that made me different. A ball thrown at me was like a bomb" (p. 74); "I just didn't feel like I was like other boys. I was very fond of pretty things like ribbons and flowers and music" (p. 86).

Stage 2: Self-recognition; identity confusion When such children enter puberty, they realize that they are attracted to members of the same sex and begin to label such feelings as homosexual. This recognition is the source of considerable inner turmoil and identity confusion; they can no longer take their heterosexual identities as given, and they know that homosexuals are stigmatized.

"You are not sure who you are. You are confused about what sort of person you are and where your life is going. You ask yourself the questions 'Who am I,' 'Am I a homosexual,' 'Am I really a heterosexual?'" (Cass, 1984, p. 156)

By middle or late adolescence such young people begin to believe that they are probably homosexual because they are uninterested in the heterosexual activities of their peers. Many homosexual adults recall adolescence as a time when they were loners and social outcasts. This upsetting psychological and social situation provokes denial and attempts to rationalize their different sexual orientation in socially approved ways.

Stage 3: Identity assumption   Some young people who have had homosexual experiences and who recognize that they prefer sexual relations with members of their own sex do not act on their preference. Many others, however, move from private acknowledgment of their homosexual preference to admitting it openly, at least to other homosexuals. Although homosexual identity is assumed during the early stages of this process, it often is not fully accepted. Vivienne Cass (1984) describes people at this stage of identity formation:

"You feel sure you're a homosexual and you put up with, or tolerate this. You see yourself as homosexual for now, but you are not sure of how you will be in the future. You usually take care to put across a heterosexual image. You sometimes mix socially with homosexuals, or would like to do this. You feel a need to meet others like yourself." (p. 156)

People who have achieved this level of homosexual identity deal with it in a variety of ways. Some try to avoid homosexual contacts and attempt to pass as heterosexual because they are afraid of the stigma attached to homosexuality. Others adopt the broader society's stereotypes of homosexuals and behave in extreme ways that fit those stereotypes. Still others begin to align themselves with the homosexual community in an unobtrusive way.

Stage 4: Commitment; identity integration   This final level is reached by those who adopt homosexuality as a way of life. Identity integration is indicated by a fusion of one's sexuality and emotional commitments, by expressions of satisfaction with one's lifestyle, and by public disclosure of one's homosexual identity.

Troiden notes that commitment to a homosexual identity may vary from weak to strong, depending on such factors as the individual's success in forging satisfying personal relationships, being accepted by his or her family, and functioning well at work or in a career. By middle age, the inner and outer person may have become so well integrated that homosexuality ceases to be an important issue in the individual's life.

TABLE 16.4 — Percentage of Students Manifesting Four Identity Statuses in Domain of Vocational Choice, by Age Group

Age Group	Identity Achievement	Moratorium	Foreclosure	Identity Diffusion
Pre–high school years	5.2%	11.7%	36.6%	46.4%
High school underclass years	9.0	14.6	37.1	39.3
High school upperclass years	21.3	13.5	36.0	29.2
College underclass years	22.8	28.3	25.7	23.2
College upperclass years	39.7	15.5	31.3	13.5

Source: Waterman, 1985.

If Erikson's ideas about identity formation are successfully captured by Marcia's categories, and if both are accurate reflections of reality, research should show a consistent shift away from identity diffusion toward identity achievement as adolescents grow older. This expectation is confirmed by a large number of studies summarized by Jane Kroger (1989). The proportion of identity achievers increases steadily from the years before high school to the late college years, while the proportion manifesting identity diffusion decreases (Table 16.4 shows the relevant data in the realm of occupational choice). In agreement with Erikson's belief that identity formation is a process rather than a trait, researchers find a general shift toward identity achievement well into adulthood as individuals readjust their understandings of themselves to accord with their experiences (Waterman & Waterman, 1971).

A number of studies have explored the influence of family life on identity achievement. Harold Grotevant and Catherine Cooper (1985), for example, constructed a "family interaction task" to evaluate the way family interactions correlate with scores on identity achievement. In this task a mother, father, and their adolescent are asked to make plans for a 2-week vacation together. They have 20 minutes to arrive at a day-by-day plan that covers both the location and the activity for each day. The discussions are scored according to the way the family members express their individuality (for example, through stating their own point of view or through disagreeing with another family member) and their connectedness (as displayed by their responsiveness and sensitivity to others' points of view).

Grotevant and Cooper interviewed the adolescents in these families to find out how thoroughly they had explored a variety of options for their futures. They hypothesized that identity exploration would be related to individuality (the adolescent had to learn how to develop a distinctive point of view) and to connectedness (the family had to provide a secure base from which the adolescent could explore). In their study of white middle-class families, these researchers found that adolescents' interactions with their parents *were* associated with identity exploration as expected, but in different ways for sons and daughters. For sons, greater identity exploration was associated with their *father's openness*—his willingness to allow disagreement, to compromise, to modify his own suggestions in light of what the sons said—to engage in genuine give-and-take. For daughters, a higher degree of identity exploration was associated with *girls' assertiveness* as manifested in their expressions of disagreement with their parents and the assertiveness with which they made suggestions. Despite these different patterns for boys and girls, it appears safe to say that a family system that offers support and security while encouraging the adolescent to create a distinct identity appears to be most effective in promoting identity achievement.

The social support provided by friends also plays a role in identity formation. In fact, a study of 300 Dutch adolescents found that the support of friends was at least as influential as family factors in promoting identity achievement (Meuss, 1993).

SEXUAL IDENTITY

In the years of middle childhood, when most young people strongly prefer to spend time with members of their own sex, children's sense of self depends heavily on how other children of the same sex respond to them. Later, as a result of the changes brought on by puberty, the childhood sense of self is expected to change from one based on opposition to the opposite sex to one based on the interdependence of males and females. The work of Sigmund Freud and Erik Erikson has had an enduring influence on psychologists' thinking about this process.

As we noted in Chapter 15 (p. 625), Freudian psychologists view adolescence as a period when children reexperience the conflicts of earlier stages in new guises (Blos, 1962, 1972). In their view, unless these problems are worked through and resolved, the adult personality will be distorted. Erikson's theory is a good example of this view.

Central among the early developmental problems that must be reworked, according to Freud, is the child's primitive desire to possess the parent of the opposite sex. The way young children resolve this conflict, which Freud called the *Oedipus conflict*, is to repress illicit desire by identifying with the same-sex parent. Freud maintained that this infantile resolution is essential to proper sex-role identification (see Chapter 10, p. 388).

These early oedipal feelings are encountered again in adolescence, but repression and identification with members of the same sex are no longer the adaptive responses that they were at the end of infancy. Puberty, Freud argues, reawakens sexual desire at a time when adolescents are fully capable both of carrying out the forbidden acts and of understanding the incest taboo that denies them the parent as a sexual partner.

Freud held that the combination of awakened desire and social constraint leads the adolescent to search for people outside the family to love. The basis for this search was laid during the peer-group experience of middle childhood, but the adolescent's reorientation is nonetheless fraught with difficulties. To begin with, the young person has had little experience of friendship with opposite-sex peers and virtually no experience interacting with peers as sex partners; new modes of social behavior will have to be learned. Second, a shift in the object of affection from a parent to a peer requires emotional disengagement from the family, which has been the bedrock of emotional security since birth. Recognizing the difficulty of this task, Freud referred to the adolescent's reorientation of affection as "one of the most painful psychical achievements of the pubertal period" (Freud, 1905/1953a, p. 227).

Painful or not, the adolescent's reorientation from family to peers is viewed as essential by Freudian scholars. If, for example, a girl refuses to give up her dependence on her parents' love and authority, she may lack the capacity to love her husband. She may also, Freud claimed, become a sexually cold wife because she is fixated at a level of development where love is asexual. Similarly, a young man who fails to reorient his affections may find himself attracted only by older women and may later involve his mother too intimately in his marriage, angering and alienating his wife. Successful adjustment in adolescence, therefore, requires the reawakening of old conflicts and the subsequent attainment of a new equilibrium within socially acceptable constraints.

Freud believed that these demands and the stress they induce make the adolescent personality especially susceptible to disorders that may have lasting effects. Freud's daughter, Anna, an influential psychoanalyst herself, concentrated on the period of adolescence because of her concern about its special dangers. As she conceived it, to regain psychological balance the ego must avoid overassociation with either the superego or the id. If the ego "allies itself too closely with the superego" (to use her terminology), the adult will be inflexible in personal relations, a slave to social rules. Such a person will experience difficulty in forming attachments to the opposite sex. At the other extreme, if the ego sides too much with the id, "no trace will be left of the previous character of the individual and the entrance into adult life will be marked by a riot of uninhibited gratification of instinct" (A. Freud, 1946, p. 163).

SEXUAL VARIATIONS IN IDENTITY FORMATION

From a Freudian perspective, the psychosexual dynamics of development are different for the two sexes. In contrasting the adolescent resolution of males and females, the psychoanalyst Peter Blos has claimed that a boy's

> energies are directed outward toward control of and dominance over the physical world. The girl, in contrast, turns—either in fact or fantasy—with deep-felt emotionality, mixed of romantic tenderness, possessiveness, and envy, to the boy. While the boy sets out to master the physical world, the girl endeavors to deal with relationships. (1972, p. 61)

Erikson, too, claimed that there are significant sex differences in the process of forming an identity. He agreed with Freud that "anatomy is destiny." According to this view, a woman's biological makeup determines her social role as an adult, a role that assigns her the greater responsibility for child rearing and homemaking. At times Erikson softened his stance by noting that "nothing in our interpretation . . . is meant to claim that either sex is doomed to one . . . mode or another; rather . . . these modes come more naturally" (1968a, p. 273). In his view, adolescent girls, like adolescent boys, try out various roles and modes of life within the limits set by the norms of the social group.

War creates the conditions under which many adolescent males begin to assume an adult identity. These young adolescents are learning how to look and act like soldiers.

TABLE 16.5	Views of Adolescent Girls and Boys on Family and Career Priorities

Girls' Views

I might be a mother and not a wife. Having a husband is just like your father. You can't go out, can't do anything. You have to cook, clean, take care of the children and still work.

If I have a career and a husband who doesn't want me to work, I'll do what I want.

I intend to have a career. Being a wife is okay; it's not so much of a strain. Kids are a strain. Maybe I can talk him into adopting a 5-year-old; or stop my career. If I am into my career, especially at my peak, it would really hurt.

Boys' Views

If I was into sports, my wife and kids would have to travel and stay in a little room—but there's nothing that couldn't be worked out.

If I am a musician, on tour, my wife's going to get worried. I wouldn't try to bring it home. We'd talk and just give it some time. Sometimes it shouldn't interfere.

I would enjoy something like marriage and family. I'd love to have my own kid at the right time. I look forward to You have a wife to be with and share time with. Helping each other out. But you're tied down. Can't go out with the guys.

Source: Archer, 1985.

Recent research provides mixed evidence on Erikson's claims about sex differences in the process of identity formation. Waterman (1985) summarized several studies that used interviews of the kind designed by Marcia (1966). He found only "weak and inconsistent evidence" that boys and girls follow different paths to identity achievement in the domains of vocational choice, religious belief, political ideology, and sex roles. Several studies, however, have revealed sex differences in the particular domains in which boys or girls most quickly achieve identity status. Thorbecke and Grotevant (1982), for example, reported that adolescent girls score at higher levels of identity achievement than boys in the domain of friendship, and Sally Archer (1985) found that girls score higher in the domain of choices about combining career and family. Archer's interviews also reveal American girls' ambivalence and confusion as they confront the dilemmas that are inherent in the cultural expectations and standard social roles that await them (see Table 16.5). Jane Kroger (1993) found that restricted economic opportunities in New Zealand in the 1980s were reflected in a reduction of identity achievement for girls, who were particularly affected by it.

MINORITY-GROUP STATUS AND IDENTITY FORMATION

As Margaret Spencer and her colleagues note, the process of identity formation is particularly complicated among minority-group children in the United States owing to prejudice, discrimination, and accompanying barriers to economic opportunity (Spencer, Cunningham, & Swanson, 1995). The factors that influence this process for minority-group youngsters vary from one group to the next. Spencer and Markstrom-Adams (1990) note, for example, that skin color is more of an issue among African Americans and Native Americans than among Hispanics. Young people in all such groups, however, must contend with negative social

Graduation is an important event shaping one's sense of identity, regardless of one's ethnic background.

stereotypes and the generally low income and restricted life opportunities that accompany minority-group status.

As we saw in Chapter 10 (pp. 397–399), children entering middle childhood have acquired an awareness of their ethnic identity in the sense that they know the label and attributes that apply to their own ethnic group. During middle childhood and adolescence, children in ethnic minority groups undergo three additional stages of ethnic identity formation (Cross, 1996; Kim, 1981; Phinney, 1993). Although the specific labels they apply differ, researchers agree on the basic content of each stage and the general kinds of experiences associated with movement from one stage to the next (see Table 16.6). In this discussion we have adopted the labels suggested by Jean Phinney because she explicitly links the stages to those suggested by Marcia, whose methods (described on p. 699) have been widely generalized to the study of ethnic identity.

Stage 1: Unexamined Ethnic Identity   In this initial stage, children still accept and show a preference for the cultural values of the majority culture in which they find themselves. This acceptance may include a negative evaluation of their own group (see Chapter 10, p. 398). In some cases this initial stage appears to correspond to Marcia's category of foreclosure because the person refuses to consider the issues and adopts the views of others unquestioningly. One Mexican American male told Phinney, "I don't go looking for my culture. I just go by what my parents say and do, and what they tell me to do, the way they are" (p. 68). In other cases, the failure to examine questions of ethnic identity is more similar to identify diffusion. An example is provided by a young African American female, who responded "Why do I need to learn about who was the first black woman to do this or that? I'm just not too interested" (p. 68).

Stage 2: Ethnic Identity Search   Movement beyond Stage 1 is often initiated by an encounter in which the young person has a shocking experience in which she or he is rejected or humiliated because of ethnic background. The specifics of such encounters are quite varied (Cross, 1996; Fordham & Ogbu, 1986). A teacher may

TABLE 16.6 Labels for Stages of Ethnic Identity Formation According to Different Researchers

Researcher	Stage 1	Stage 2	Stage 3
Phinney (1989)	Unexamined ethnic identity	Ethnic identity search	Achieved ethnic identity
Cross (1978)	Preencounter	Encounter and immersion	Internalization
Kim (1981)	White-identified	Awakening to sociopolitical awareness and redirection to Asian consciousness	Incorporation

accuse a student of cheating when she does outstanding work, on the assumption that African Americans or Puerto Ricans or Samoans are incapable of such work; or a boy may be told he may no longer socialize with a girl he has been friends with for years because he has the wrong skin color, ethnic background, or religion. However, a shocking encounter is not necessary for young people to begin pondering their ethnic identity; it can also arise from a growing awareness that the values of the dominant group are not beneficial to ethnic minorities.

At this stage, young people show an intense concern for the personal implications of their ethnicity. They often engage in an active search for information about their own group. They are likely to become involved in social and political movements in which ethnicity is a core issue. They may also experience intense anger at the majority group and glorify their own heritage.

Signithia Fordham and John Ogbu (1986) describe several cases in which African American adolescents attempt to purge themselves of patterns of dress, speech, mannerisms, and attitudes associated with white American society and adopt an **oppositional identity.** These researchers believe that the process of oppositional identity formation provides one of the major explanations for the school failure of African American children. Evidence suggests that similar identity processes are at work in the development of adolescents of many minority groups (Phinney, 1995).

Stage 3: Ethnic Identity Achievement   Individuals who achieve a mature ethnic identity have resolved the conflicts characteristic of the prior stage and now accept their own ethnicity and have a positive self-concept. At this stage, which William Cross (1978) has termed "internalization," "tension, emotionality, and defensiveness are replaced by calm, secure demeanor. Ideological flexibility, psychological openness, and self-confidence about one's blackness are in evidence" (p. 18).

A word of caution is needed in regard to these findings. The economic inequalities that go with some minority-group statuses make it very difficult to isolate minority-group membership as the crucial variable in the development of members' personal and social identities, just as in the case of their IQs (Chapter 13, pp. 546–550). By and large, comparisons that are supposed to be about differences in ethnicity or race are also about socioeconomic class, because members of minority groups are disproportionately poor. As a consequence, we cannot be certain why foreclosure occurs more frequently among minority-group adolescents or why some of them appear to identify less with their own ethnic or racial group than with that of the dominant group in American society.

CROSS-CULTURAL VARIATIONS IN IDENTITY FORMATION

In contrast to investigations of identity formation within a single society, in which differences have been modest, many researchers have claimed that differences between cultures can be profound (Baumeister, 1987; Geertz, 1984; Markus & Kitayama, 1991; Rosaldo, 1984; Shweder & Bourne, 1984). In a review of cultural variations in concepts of the self, Hazel Markus and Shinobu Kitayama (1991) note that cultures can be ranked along a continuum. At one end they place cultures whose members see themselves primarily as individuals, as middle-class Americans do. At the other end they place cultures such as Japan's, whose members see themselves primarily in relation to the social group. Members of the first kind of culture are said to perceive themselves as independent, while those in the second see themselves as interdependent.

According to Markus and Kitayama, people whose cultures encourage an **independent sense of self** are oriented to being unique, to promoting their individual goals, and to expressing their own thoughts and opinions. People whose cultures emphasize an **interdependent sense of self,** by contrast, seek to fit into

Oppositional identity An identity forged by members of racial or ethnic minorities in which they reject patterns of dress, speech, mannerisms, and attitudes associated with the dominant group.

Interdependent sense of self A sense of self in which individuals try to fit into the group, to promote group goals, and to be sensitive to others.

Independent sense of self A sense of self that is described by such labels as "individualistic," "egocentric," "separate," "autonomous," "idiocentric," and "self contained."

TABLE 16.7 Key Differences between an Independent and an Interdependent Construal of Self

Feature Compared	Independent	Interdependent
Definition	Separate from social context	Connected with social context
Structure	Bounded, unitary, stable	Flexible, variable
Important features	Internal, private (abilities, thoughts, feelings)	External, public (statuses, roles, relationships)
Tasks	Be unique Express self Realize internal attributes Promote own goals Be direct; "say what's on your mind"	Belong, fit in Occupy one's proper place Engage in appropriate action Promote others' goals Be indirect; "read other's mind"
Role of others	Self-evaluation: others important for social comparison, reflected appraisal	Self-definition: relationships with others in specific contexts define the self
Basis of self-esteem[a]	Ability to express self, validate internal attributes	Ability to adjust, restrain self, maintain harmony with social context

[a] Esteeming the self may be primarily a Western phenomenon, and the concept of self-esteem should perhaps be replaced by self-satisfaction, or by a term that reflects the realization that one is fulfilling the culturally mandated task.
Source: Markus & Kitayama, 1991.

the group, to promote the goals of others (that is, of the group), and to develop the ability to "read" the minds of others (see Table 16.7).

A study by Steven Cousins (1989) among American and Japanese high school students reveals several contrasts between these two modes of self-perception. Students were asked to describe themselves in one of two circumstances. The first, context-free case presented them with the simple question "Who am I?" 20 times. The second, context-specific case asked the students to describe themselves in several specific situations (me at home, me at school, me with friends, etc.).

When asked to say 20 things about themselves in the context-free circumstance, the American students most often mentioned psychological traits or general attributes ("I am friendly," "I am a good athlete"). The Japanese students most often referred to kinds of behavior they engaged in ("I play tennis after school").

When the students were asked to answer the question "Who am I?" in particular contexts, the pattern of answers changed. This time it was the Japanese students who offered generalizations about themselves. Asked to say who they are in their families, for example, they might answer, "I am good-natured," whereas the American students qualified their answers. Cousins remarks that the American students' answers, such as "I am usually open with my brother," implied that just because they behave a certain way in one setting doesn't mean that they are always like that (see Figure 16.11).

As Markus and Kitayama point out, this difference in orientation to the self creates different sets of problems for the young person who is forging a unified sense of identity. For one thing, the American emphasis on the autonomous self presupposes that identity formation is an individual, personal process. In societies where the self is seen in relation to others, by contrast, others are included as an integral part of the self. Thus adolescents in collectivist societies do not have to make many of the decisions and choices that American adolescents must face in order to resolve their identity. It makes little sense to assert that healthy identity formation requires adolescents to make a "commitment to a sexual orientation, an ideological stance, and a vocational choice" (Marcia, 1980, p. 160) in societies in which marriages are arranged by the family, one's vocation is whatever one's father or mother does, and strict subordination to one's elders is a moral imperative.

Unfortunately, virtually no research has been done on the development of identity in nonindustrial societies that uses the methods that have been used to study it in technologically sophisticated societies. We have to turn to the reports of anthropologists who have concerned themselves with identity formation in small hunter-gatherer or agricultural societies, such as those found in parts of West Africa, the Arctic regions, and New Guinea (Condon, 1987; Harley, 1941; Raum, 1940/1967; Schlegel & Barry, 1991). The most distinctive fact about identity formation in such groups is that, as in the collectivist societies discussed by Markus and Kitayama, it involves little of the cognitive deliberation and personal choice that play such large roles in psychologists' accounts of identity formation in Western cultures. There are so few distinct adult roles in such societies that a young person has few decisions to make. The transition to adult identity in such societies, however, is often made in ritual initiation ceremonies that are obligatory and painful (see Chapter 15, p. 634). These circumstances must certainly influence identity formation, but existing psychological research does not permit us to draw conclusions about the processes involved.

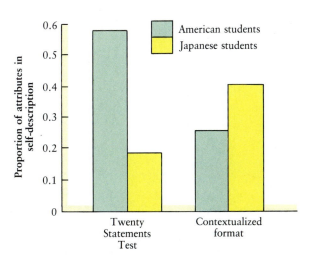

FIGURE 16.11 *Mean proportion of psychological attributes endorsed by American and Japanese students who were asked to give statements about themselves in two self-description tasks. One, the Twenty-Statements Test, was decontextualized; the other had a contextualized format that asked for self-descriptions in particular settings. (From Cousins, 1989.)*

The Transition to Adulthood

As we commented in the introduction to our discussion of adolescence, no developmental transition after birth is so well marked as the end of middle childhood. Profound changes in the size and shape of children's bodies are unmistakable signs that they are "ripening." Certainty about the end of middle childhood, however, is not the same as certainty that a distinctive stage intervenes between middle childhood and adulthood. Is adolescence really a stage in the same way that infancy or middle childhood is, or is it more like an uneven transition between stages, as Piaget sometimes conceived early childhood to be?

In examining the data concerning physical and social changes in Chapter 15 as well as cognitive and personality differences in this chapter, we saw evidence from other cultures suggesting that the transition to adult status universally involves conflict, anxiety, and uncertainty. At the same time, however, the data suggest equally strongly that adolescence is rarely as fraught with conflicts as the Western stereotype suggests. Moreover, the highly elaborated stage of adolescence encountered in modern industrial societies exists only under particular cultural circumstances (Whiting, Burbank, & Ratner, 1986). When researchers assume that adolescence exists in societies that have no concept of it and no set of social practices corresponding to it, they do violence to the facts.

The Inuit of the Canadian Arctic at the turn of the century, for example, used special terms to refer to boys and girls when they entered puberty, but these terms did not coincide with the usual notion of adolescence (Condon, 1987). Young women were considered adult at menarche, a change in status marked by the fact that they were likely to be married by this time and ready to start bearing children. Young men were considered fully grown as soon as they were able to build a snow house and kill large game unassisted. They might be able to do both shortly after the onset of puberty, but boys usually achieved adult status somewhat later because they had first to prove that they could support themselves and their families. In view of the life circumstances of these people, it is not surprising that they developed no special concept corresponding to adolescence that applied to boys and girls alike; such a concept did not correspond to their reality.

ADOLESCENCE IN MODERN SOCIETIES

Granted that a social category corresponding to adolescence may arise only in certain cultural circumstances, we are still left with the problem of understanding the developmental dynamics of young people who fit this category in modern industrialized societies. If we want to claim that adolescence is a stage of development in modern societies, does it adhere to the same rules of organization and transition as earlier stages, or is it unique in important respects?

When its roots in the United States and other modern industrialized societies are traced, adolescence appears to be closely associated with apprenticeship training or formal schooling; or with a period of waiting until the designated adult role becomes available, through either a marriage proposal or an inheritance (Ariès, 1962; Fox, 1977; Gillis, 1974; Kett, 1977). Although scattered instances of the concept of adolescence can be found in ancient civilizations, it was only during the nineteenth century, when formal schooling was introduced for the mass of boys and girls, that adolescence became a generally recognized and pervasive category defining children of a certain age regardless of sex and social class.

Two crucial factors are introduced by formal schooling. One is a long delay in achieving economic self-sufficiency. The other is prolongation of social experiences that take place in such contexts as a school or a community sports program, which are institutionally separated from the activities of adult life. In the United States, for example, young people are expected to attend school for 12 or more years and to abstain from starting a family until after they have graduated from high school. In these circumstances, there can be no doubt that adolescence as a stage of development is a social reality.

In fact, adolescence has been elaborated in such detail in the United States and other industrially advanced societies that psychologists who specialize in this developmental stage often distinguish three substages: early adolescence (11 to 14 years), middle adolescence (15 to 18 years), and late adolescence (18 to 21 years). As Larry Steinberg (1989) notes, these divisions correspond to the way modern societies group children in schools: early adolescence frequently corresponds roughly to middle or junior high school, middle adolescence to high school, and late adolescence to college.

This correspondence between age and the context of development presents analysts of adolescence with a problem: they can show that younger adolescents are more susceptible to peer pressure than older adolescents (Figure 15.9, p. 645) and reason differently about political processes (p. 682), but it is difficult to determine why. The differences may arise from some factor closely associated with age (such as density of brain cells or greater social experience) or perhaps from the differences in experience afforded by the various ways children's school life is organized.

A distinctive fact about adolescence in societies such as ours is that not all aspects of the bio-social-behavioral shift that initiates it coincide as they do in earlier stages. To be sure, biological maturation simultaneously gives rise to new desires and emotions and to new forms of social relationships. Intimate friendships with peers of the same sex are supplemented by, and in some cases supplanted by, intimate love relationships with members of the opposite sex. As these relationships develop, family ties loosen.

Yet an important element in the "social" part of the bio-social-behavioral shift that defines the transition to adulthood for Piaget and other stage theorists (see

TABLE 16.8 The Bio-Social-Behavioral Shift: Transition to Adulthood

BIOLOGICAL DOMAIN	Capacity for biological reproduction Development of secondary sex characteristics Attainment of adult size
BEHAVIORAL DOMAIN	Achievement of formal operations in some areas (systematic thinking) Formation of identity
SOCIAL DOMAIN	Sexual relations Shift toward primary responsibility for oneself Beginning of responsibility for next generation

Table 16.8) is the partial failure of part of the social system to change at the expected time. With some exceptions (such as peripheral participation in adult work), modern young people are offered carefully arranged substitutes for real adult roles. Instead of the responsibility for conducting real chemistry experiments, students are given exercises that model the ideal practice of chemists. Instead of responsibility for running their own school, students are given a student government with elected officers, laws, and legislatures but no power. Instead of responsibility for informing the community of important events, students are allowed to run student newspapers whose topics are carefully circumscribed by rule and custom. If modern adolescence is to be considered a separate stage of development, we must admit that it combines biological, social, and behavioral factors in a way we have not seen in any of the stages that precede it.

When adolescents throw themselves into an activity as if it were a lifetime commitment, or in those rare instances when they are allowed or required to take on an adult role (in a work situation, say, or when a mother falls ill), they may display the formal operational cognitive ability that is supposed to appear at this time. In many other situations, however, both their social roles and their thought processes can be expected to remain distinctly "adolescent."

LOOKING AHEAD

The modern trend toward extending and intensifying adolescence springs from the same forces that created the concept of adolescence in the first place. It is a virtual certainty that in the decades to come, young people will be expected to achieve higher levels of learning than ever before. This increased achievement will be sought in part through intensification of education in the lower grades, longer school hours, and more days of schooling per year. But to gain access to higher-paying and more secure jobs, young people will also be required to spend more years in school, which will further delay their independent working lives and prolong their economic dependence. These economic factors suggest that we will either see adolescence extended further or, as the psychologist Kenneth Keniston (1970) has suggested, invent a new stage of development between adolescence and adulthood, during which young people will achieve some forms of autonomy that adolescents are denied but will still stop short of taking on the full responsibilities of adults.

SUMMARY

Research on Adolescent Thought

- The thinking of adolescents often manifests five characteristics not usually observed in the thinking of younger children:
  1. Thinking about possibilities.
  2. Thinking through hypotheses.
  3. Thinking ahead.
  4. Thinking about thought.
  5. Thinking beyond conventional limits.
- Piagetian theory attributes these characteristics to the emergence of formal operations, in which all possible logical aspects of a problem are thought about as a structured whole. The core of Piaget's evidence comes from observations of adolescents working on problems modeled on scientific experiments and formal logical reasoning.
- Contrary to classical Piagetian theory, not everyone proves capable of solving Piagetian formal operational tasks consistently, even in adulthood.
- Studies of sex differences in formal operational thinking indicate that in some tasks males outperform females, but these differences have been decreasing in recent decades.
- Large cultural variations in formal operational thinking have been observed in traditional, nontechnological societies if children have not experienced relatively high levels of education. However, ability to reason in terms of formal operations appears in specific culturally valued domains.
- Difficulties with Piaget's explanations of adolescent thought processes have inspired attempts at alternative explanations.
  1. Theorists who take an information-processing approach hypothesize that increased memory capacity, increased efficiency in the use of strategies and rules, and the ability to form abstract verbal concepts, rather than changes in the logic of thought, account for adolescents' new thought processes.
  2. Theorists of several persuasions have suggested that developments in the domain of language are crucial to the emergence of new cognitive ability during adolescence.
  3. Cultural-context theorists propose that involvement in new activities creates the conditions for a new level of systematic thought. Systematic thought is assumed to occur in all societies but is always bound to the demands of particular contexts.

Adolescent Thinking about the Social Order

- Between the ages of 13 and 15 adolescents' thinking about the social order undergoes several changes.
  1. With respect to thinking about politics:
     a. Conceptions of the law become more abstract.
     b. An appreciation of the positive value of laws appears.
     c. There is increasing cynicism about the possibilities of solving social problems.
  2. With respect to thinking about moral issues:

a. The ability to reason about all *existing* factors relevant to moral choices is supplemented by the ability to think about all *possible* factors.

b. Reasoning about moral issues begins to go beyond social conventions to encompass more abstract principles of right and wrong.

- Though some psychologists assume that increased intellectual capacity results in a higher level of moral and political behavior, the evidence linking reasoning ability with actual behavior shows that many other factors are involved.

- Variability in the way males and females respond to moral reasoning problems has led some theorists to propose that there are sex differences in moral orientations rather than a single sequence of moral development.

- Members of small, face-to-face, traditional cultures generally do not engage in postconventional reasoning about moral issues but do attain the level associated with the Golden Rule.

Integration of the Self

- Personality development during adolescence requires that new sexual capacities and new social relations be integrated with the personality characteristics accumulated since birth.

- Adolescents describe themselves in more varied, generalized, and abstract ways than they did during middle childhood, an indication of the need to reconcile their "multiple selves."

- Self-esteem declines at the onset of adolescence, especially for girls in the United States, reflecting the difficulties of adjusting to social and biological changes. It then rises throughout the remainder of adolescence.

- According to Freud, the reintegration of personality begins when new sexual desires upset the balance of id, ego, and superego; the resolution of this imbalance requires the individual to find an appropriate person to love, bringing to a close the oedipal conflict of infancy.

- According to Erikson, adolescence is the time when the person recapitulates and resolves all earlier developmental crises in order to form an adult identity.

- According to both Freud and Erikson, failure to resolve past crises during adolescence leads to a neurotic adult personality.

- Both Freudian and Eriksonian theorists hypothesize sex differences in adolescent personality formation, but the evidence they offer about the course of female development is weak.

- The formation of ethnic identity in adolescence appears to go through three stages:

1. Unexamined ideas about ethnic identity.

2. Ethnic identity search.

3. Ethnic identity achievement.

- There is ample evidence that self-concepts vary with sociocultural circumstances, but evidence on cultural variations in the process of adolescent identity formation is generally lacking.

The Transition to Adulthood

- Historical variations in the cultural organization of young people's lives after middle childhood suggest that adolescence is not a universal stage of development. Rather, it arises as a social category when there is a gap between the ability to reproduce biologically and the ability to reproduce culturely.

- In modern industrial societies, where adolescence is an institutionalized stage of development, the discoordination of biological, social, and psychological changes creates a developmental configuration unlike those of earlier stages of development.

KEY TERMS

deductive reasoning, p. 671

developmental crisis, p. 696

formal operations, p. 667

identity formation, p. 696

independent sense of self, p. 707

interdependent sense of self,   p. 707

meta-analysis,   p. 673

oppositional identity, p. 707

second-order thinking, p. 667

structured whole, p. 670

THOUGHT QUESTIONS

1. What are the key features that distinguish formal operational thinking from concrete operational thinking?
2. Why is reasoning more likely to be logical in familiar situations than in contexts unrelated to one's everyday experience?
3. Monitor your activities for a day and make a list of all those in which you engaged in formal operational thinking to any extent. What characteristics seem to differentiate the contexts in which you use formal operational thinking from those in which you don't?
4. Draw comparisons between Troiden's stages of homosexual identity formation, Erikson's four preadolescent developmental crises, and Marcia's four patterns of identity development.
5. Increasing numbers of young adults in the United States are remaining in their parents' homes long after they have finished college and found employment. On the basis of material covered in Chapters 15 and 16, formulate three hypotheses about the psychological consequences of this trend.

Epilogue: Putting It Together

According to the framework presented here, development does not cease with the transition to adulthood. As the novelist Milan Kundera remarked, "We leave childhood without knowing what youth is, we marry without knowing what it is to be married, and even when we enter old age, we don't know what it is we are heading for" (1988:132–133). We are all, in short, developing.

Now that you have traced the process of development from conception to the threshold of adulthood, it is time to consider some of the general lessons you have learned. As we noted in our prefatory remarks, it is our conviction that knowledge about the process of development is not only of practical use to people who become responsible for children; it is useful in everyday life to anyone who comes in contact with children at all.

Relating Theory to Practice

The practice of developmental psychology cannot rely heavily on precise scientific formulas to explain and produce dependable solutions to problems the way the formulas of physics guide engineers. The application of principles of development to activity in the world is more comparable to the craft of the traditional family doctor as portrayed in old movies—the one who made house calls carrying a black bag, equipped with simple diagnostic tools, a small array of medications, and a vast store of understanding and experience. Developmental psychologists come to the practice of studying development and promoting the well-being of children with a tool kit of theoretical principles, diagnostic procedures, and remedial techniques. They then need to combine these principles and tools with their own practical experience to deal with the situation at hand.

A Preliminary Tool Kit

When one looks back over the contents of this book, it is possible to identify several principles that qualify for the "black bag" of the practicing developmental psychologist. The following list, by no means comprehensive, consists of six concepts that in our view are indispensable to an understanding of human development.

Sequence is fundamental At the core of the definition of development we offered in Chapter 1 (p. 61) is the idea that developmental changes follow one another in an orderly sequence: there must be one cell before there can be two; muscles and bones must be present before nerves can coordinate arm and leg movement; gonads must secrete testosterone before the sexual characteristics of genetically male infants can emerge. The same principle is equally apparent after birth. The primary emotions evident near or at birth must be present in order for the secondary emotions to arise with the acquisition of language. Children must be able to think operationally before they can develop the ability to think formally.

Owing to the sequential nature of development, the old proverb that "an ounce of prevention is worth a pound of cure" is especially relevant where children are concerned. When expectant mothers receive inadequate health care and give birth to premature and underweight babies, or when children begin their schooling without benefit of appropriate intellectual socialization at home, the long-term costs to society, as well as to the children, are vastly greater than the costs of preventing the problem in the first place.

Timing is important   Recall that if a fetus is exposed to thalidomide later than 3 months after conception, its development is unlikely to be affected by the drug. But if a fetus is exposed during the first 2 to 3 months of pregnancy, the thalidomide may have a disastrous effect. The timing of developmental change after birth is just as important. A child's ability to use language fails to develop fully if the child receives no linguistic input during the first few years of life. A girl's self-esteem is likely to suffer if she goes through the biological changes of puberty before her peers do.

However, children also show great resilience and ability to develop even when timing goes awry. A bad start does not necessarily foretell a bad end, so long as it falls within broad limits.

Development involves differentiation and integration   This principle is evident within hours of conception when the single cell of the zygote gives rise to the many apparently identical cells of the morula. These cells then differentiate into two distinct *kinds* of cells whose different shapes and functions become integrated into a new pattern in the blastocyst. Later cycles of differentiation and integration transform arm buds into the complex structure of the human hand.

After birth this double-sided process of differentiation and integration characterizes psychological development as well as physical development. Single-word utterances that stand for complete sentences are replaced by multiword sequences that are then integrated into the complex patterns of a language's grammar; the one-sided, egocentric thinking of preschoolers opens up to include the viewpoints of others and becomes reintegrated into a new way of thinking and solving problems.

Development is patterned   In Chapter 1 we noted that one of the fundamental issues debated by developmentalists is the relative importance of stagelike changes versus gradual cumulative change in the process of development (the continuity–discontinuity issue). Our review of the current evidence makes it clear that development is characterized by *both* qualitative, stagelike changes and quantitative, continuous change.

In part the argument between the two positions is a matter of scale. When you encounter your niece six years after last meeting her as a 2-year-old, it is crystal clear that the schoolgirl standing before you is a qualitatively different kind of person than she was as a toddler. But to someone who saw that child every day (such as her mother, father, live-in grandparent, or sibling) the process of change would have seemed almost seamlessly continuous and incremental.

The relative prominence of continuous and discontinuous change also depends on the phase of development that is the focus of interest. During prenatal development, major changes both in the appearance of the organism and in its interactions with the environment occur with stunning rapidity. The form of the embryo is altogether different from the form of the blastocyst. Implantation simultaneously reorders the fetus's interactions with its environment and gives rise to new, still more complicated physical forms. When such dramatic changes occur over a relatively short period of time, development indeed appears to be dominated by qualitative, stagelike episodes of change.

After birth the situation is more mixed; both qualitative and quantitative changes command our attention. The progression of changes that lead to walking, for example, has been described as a sequence of stagelike changes: from creeping to rocking on hands and knees to crawling, and finally to upright walking. Each of these forms of motion uses different combinations of muscles and skills and each results in qualitatively different interactions with the environment. Such stagelike changes appear in social behavior as well: the symbolic play of 4-year-olds requires a form of interaction with other persons that differs qualitatively both from the solitary motor play of infancy and the rule-bound games of school-age children.

Sequences of psychological changes, however, are not so clear-cut. It seems that for every claim of an abrupt stagelike change in the ability to remember, to think logically, or to classify, there is a counterclaim showing that the corresponding process of change is actually gradual and continuous. Moreover, for every claim that a child's psychological behavior in a given stage is uniform, someone can point to instances when the child remembered, reasoned, or classified according to one stage under some circumstances and according to another stage in other circumstances. This unevenness appears with particular clarity in early childhood, as we noted in Chapter 9, but it is evident in other periods as well.

Development emerges from multiple sources Just as the study of development pushes us to reject the view that development is either entirely continuous or entirely discontinuous, studies of the causes of development argue strongly for the view that *change emerges from the joint action of several sources acting more or less simultaneously and interactively.*

It is not helpful to claim that one source of development is generally more important than another—the traditional form of the nature-nurture debate. As data presented in Chapters 2 and 13 indicate, when statistical procedures are used to tease apart genetic and environmental contributions to an individual trait such as personality or intelligence, roughly half of the observed variations are attributed to genetic factors and half to the specific environments that individuals encounter after birth. Even these kinds of estimates are fraught with uncertainty, because they assume those two sources of variation to be independent contributors to development when in reality each contributes in subtle ways to the other.

Our use of the notion of a bio-social-behavioral shift to describe apparent turning points in development has been intended to emphasize the erroneousness of assigning causal priority to one or another source of development. It is tempting, for example, to envision the appearance of social smiling as the result of a sequence of factors: first biological changes in the infant's visual system reorder the potential for social interaction; then smiles become linked to social feedback; then changes occur in the affective tone of child-caretaker relations. However, when Robert Emde and his colleagues examined the relation between changes in brain waves and the advent of social smiling, they could find no strict sequence. Each kind of change—biological, cognitive, and social—is necessary for the others to occur.

Development is culturally mediated As we noted in Chapter 3, at the moment of birth everything changes—from the direction of the baby's blood flow to the way the baby is connected to the mother. Children are no longer bound to their environments through a *direct* biological connection. After birth, even essential biological processes are connected *indirectly*—they become mediated by culture. The baby's food no longer arrives predigested through the mother's bloodstream, but neither, generally speaking, is it "raw." Rather, it is transformed by some preparative process that is neither purely biological nor purely natural, a process that has been shaped as an integral part of the cultural history of the group.

In order to survive in an environment mediated by culture, the baby must act on its nurturing environment in a qualitatively different way than it did before birth. This is not to say that the baby is ever inactive. With the first heartbeat early in embryogenesis, the organism becomes and remains active until it dies.

Without such activity during the prenatal period, more complicated neural circuits needed for coordinated movement and thought could not develop adequately. However, the effects of the fetus's activity on the environment inside and outside its mother's womb are minimal.

After birth, the change in babies' impact on their environment is as marked as the change in the way the environment acts on them. They make urgent, vocal demands on their caretakers. They become social actors who reorder the social relations among the people around them. At birth, *development becomes a co-constructive process* in which both the social environment and the child are active agents.

Today one of the exciting things about the field of child development is the widespread desire to incorporate the cultural along with the biological, social, and psychological aspects of development in a single theoretical framework. For the present, however, there is no broad consensus about how to implement such an integration.

Using the Tool Kit in Everyday Life

The ways in which we put developmental theory into practice depend, of course, very much on each particular situation and our role in it. At the most general level, in our roles as citizens, the tool kit provided by developmental psychologists helps us to think critically about the constant stream of information concerning children that greets us daily when we open our newspaper or turn on the television set. When experts argue about the influence of television on children's behavior, we know that their failure to reach agreement is the result of their inability, for perfectly legitimate ethical reasons, to create the necessary conditions for a proper experimental study of the issue. When a politician advocates a simple plan for improving the reading scores of schoolchildren, we know that the children's performance is produced by a convergence of factors and is not likely to improve in response to any one-sided program. The tool kit of developmental psychology cannot solve every problem, but it can help prevent our wasting time and resources on policies that are poorly conceived.

The realization that children's lives are greatly affected by the developmental niches that they inhabit and the larger social contexts that shape those niches brings us to the arena of social policy from a different direction. As developmentalists we know that when adults are under stress, their ability to provide optimal conditions for their children's development suffers. The desire to promote children's development then forces us to be concerned about creating programs to provide parents with employment, safe housing, good health care, and supportive social networks so that they, in turn, can provide adequately for their children.

The people who assume professional responsibility for promoting children's development—those who work in schools, hospitals, clinics, youth clubs, family services, and the like—must use information from developmental studies in a different way. The comparison with the old-fashioned family doctor with the full satchel is most apt in the case of such child-development practitioners. A psychologist who works with visually impaired children, for example, has a variety of physical tools at his disposal: ways to test vision, intellectual development, language development, and so on. In this case, if he also knows that a child's development of social smiling depends on her getting the right kind of feedback regardless of the sensory medium, he then has a flexible tool for preventing a different kind of deficit: for a blind child, a well-timed tickling can be an adequate substitute for the sight of a smiling face. The same specialist can draw on other developmental research for guidance in organizing the child's social life, literacy instruction, and access to other valued cultural resources.

In the end, however, the effectiveness of the therapies prescribed by the specialist in the development of visually impaired children, like the effectiveness of the old-fashioned doctor's prescription for a cure, will depend on the specific case in question. Just how sick is the patient? Is the medicine known to work in such cases? Is the patient taking the medicine according to instructions? Are the surroundings otherwise healthful? Is the family doing all they can to help? In the face of such unique factors science is silenced because its methods depend on knowing how each individual is *like* all the rest. And inevitably every one of us is unique.

It is our hope that reading this book has helped readers to think more systematically about all of these issues. Beyond the potential practical utility of knowing more about the study of development, however, we also hope our readers will find our discussions useful in thinking about their own development, past, present, and future. Reading about adolescence may give them another perspective on the idealism, longing, self-consciousness, and conflicts that they themselves experienced during this period. Reading about sibling relationships may help them to understand the behaviors of their own brothers and sisters.

As parents we know from personal experience that the more one knows about processes of development, the more interesting interacting with children becomes. Raising children is often tiring and discouraging. When a 2-year-old screams in defiance, a 4-year-old refuses to go to bed without the lights on, a 9-year-old cannot seem to concentrate on her spelling lesson, it helps to understand the larger pattern of changes that the crisis of the moment fits into.

Finally, an appreciation of the process of development can be a direct source of pleasure. During a recent holiday visit, our granddaughter was just old enough to be entering the bio-social-behavioral shift at 10 weeks described in Chapter 4. She had not yet begun to exhibit social smiling, although her parents claimed that she sometimes smiled when they picked her up to feed her or to change her diaper. To see for ourselves if the baby was indeed at the threshold of social smiling, we repeatedly sought to amuse her. When she seemed alert and contented, one of us would bend over her crib or pick her up and start bobbing our heads in an eye-catching way, while at the same time smiling at her and talking to her in exaggerated, high-pitched "motherese." And sure enough, to everyone's delight, the baby reciprocated and a new level of social contact was reached; the parents were no less elated than the grandparents.

Appendix: Guide to Discussions of Specific Aspects of Development

GUIDE 1 Discussions of Physical Development

Period	Characteristic	Page Numbers
Early infancy	Hearing capacities at birth	pp. 135–136
	Early visual capacities	pp. 136–140
	Taste and smell	pp. 140–141
	Detection of touch, temperature, and position	p. 141
	Reflexes present at birth	pp. 142–143
	Maturation of sleeping patterns	pp. 148–150
	Maturation of the nervous system	pp. 154–161
	Growth and weight gain in first year	pp. 187–189
	Sex differences in rate of growth	p. 188
	Brain development in first year	p. 189
	Development of reaching and grasping	pp. 190–191
	Development of locomotion	pp. 191–192
	Effect of practice on early motor development	pp. 192–194
Later infancy	Height and weight during second year	p. 223
	Changes in brain during second year	p. 223
	Transition from crawling to walking	pp. 224–226
	Manual dexterity during second year	p. 226
	Control during elimination	pp. 226–227
	Biological prerequisites for language	pp. 321–323
Early childhood	Brain maturation	p. 359
Middle childhood	Physical growth	pp. 480–481
	Motor development	pp. 481–483
	Brain maturation	pp. 483–484
Adolescence	Puberty	pp. 629–633

GUIDE 3   Discussions of Language Development

Period	Characteristic	Page Numbers
General	Questions about language acquisition	pp. 297–299
	Language subsystems	pp. 300–315
	Theories of language acquisition	pp. 315–321
	Biological prerequisites	pp. 321–323
	Social prerequisites	pp. 323–329
	Relation between language and thought	pp. 329–330
	Cultural influences	pp. 331–332
Infancy	Language preferences at birth	pp. 135–136
	Distinguishing phonemic differences	pp. 300–301
	First words	pp. 301–303
Later infancy	Intersubjectivity and social referencing	pp. 213–214
	Beginnings of speech: cooing, babbling, jargoning	pp. 214–215
	Pointing	p. 312
Early childhood	Earliest vocabulary	pp. 303–304
	Early word meanings	pp. 304–308
	Constructing sentences	pp. 308–312
	Learning the uses of language	pp. 312–315
	Associations between early language development and early cognitive development	pp. 329–332
Middle childhood	Language of schooling	pp. 529–533
Adolescence	Relation between language and thought	pp. 676–677

GUIDE 4   Discussions of Emotional Development

Period	Characteristic	Page Numbers
General	Vulnerability and resilience	pp. 272–279
Early infancy	Evidence of emotions at birth	pp. 143–144
	Differentiation approach to emotional development	p. 144
	Evidence of temperament differences at birth	pp. 145–147
	Crying and parents' responses	pp. 152–153, 155
Later infancy	The onset of wariness	pp. 209–212
	Beginnings of attachment	pp. 212–213
	Explanations of attachment	pp. 238–242
	Patterns of attachment	pp. 243–251
	Emergence of secondary emotions	pp. 253–254
Early childhood	Regulation of emotions	pp. 404, 420
	Development of emotions	pp. 406, 418–419
	Beginnings of empathy	pp. 415–416
	Socio-emotional competence	pp. 420–421
Middle childhood	Emotional control and social status	p. 595
	Emotional maturity	p. 602
Adolescence	Traditional and modern conceptions of adolescents' emotions	pp. 623–625
	Psychological responses to puberty	pp. 634–635
	Emotional consequences of early and late maturation	pp. 635–638

GUIDE 5   Discussions of Cultural Influences on Development

Period	Characteristic	Page Numbers
General	Culture in language development	p. 331
	Family organization	pp. 429–434
	Socialization practices	pp. 434–438
	Social networks	p. 443
Early infancy	Coordination of feeding and sleep schedules	pp. 147–148, 150–152
	Nursing behaviors	pp. 172–175
	Adults' view and expectations of young infants	pp. 174–175
Later infancy	Maternal responsiveness	pp. 247–248
	Attachment patterns	pp. 248–249
	Effects of temperamental traits	pp. 262–263, 275
	Language instruction	pp. 327–328
Early childhood	Social co-construction	p. 363
	Scripts	p. 364
	Unevenness of development	pp. 366–370
	Guided participation	p. 367
	Sociodramatic play	pp. 368–369
	Acquiring a sex-role identity	pp. 396–397
	Acquiring ethnic and racial identity	pp. 397–399
	Internalization of adult standards	p. 401
	Causes of aggression	pp. 409–410
	Media	pp. 447–454
	Day care	pp. 454–459
	Variations in preschool environments	pp. 462–463
Middle childhood	Physical growth	p. 481
	Concrete operations	pp. 502–507
	Memory development	pp. 507–508
	Schooling	pp. 536–540, 552–553
	Intelligence testing	pp. 547–550
	Competition and cooperation among peers	pp. 596–597
Adolescence	Adolescence as a product of culture	pp. 628–629, 709–711
	Rites of passage	pp. 633–634
	Sex as scripted activity	pp. 649–650
	Formal operations	pp. 674, 677–682
	Moral reasoning	pp. 692–694
	Identity formation	pp. 707–709

GUIDE 6   Discussions of Cognitive Development

GLOSSARY

Accommodation In Piaget's theory, the process by which children modify their existing schemas in order to adapt to new experiences.

Adaptation In Piaget's theory, the twofold process consisting of assimilation and accommodation.

Adoption Study A study in which genetically related individuals who are raised in different family environments are compared to determine the extent to which heredity or environment controls a given trait.

Aggression Behavior that intentionally hurts another person.

Allele An alternate form of a gene coded for a particular trait.

Amnion The membrane that holds the amniotic fluid surrounding the prenatal organism.

A-Not-B Error A characteristic error made by 8- to 12-month-old babies when they search for a hidden object: they look for the object in the last place they found it even if they have seen it moved to a new location.

Apgar Scale A quick, simple scale used to rate the physical state of a newborn infant.

Apprenticeship A socialization process in which a novice learns a trade or craft by working for an extended period of time under a master.

Assimilation In Piaget's theory, the process by which children incorporate new experiences into their existing schemas.

Attachment An enduring emotional bond between an infant and another person.

Authoritarian Parenting Pattern A behavior pattern characterized by systematic attempts to shape and evaluate the behavior and attitudes of one's children according to a set standard; such parents stress the importance of obedience to authority and favor punitive measures to bring about their children's compliance.

Authoritative Parenting Pattern A behavior pattern characterized by systematic attempts to control one's children by explaining one's rules or decisions, and by reasoning with them; such parents set high standards for their children's behavior.

Autism A condition in which children are unable to interact with others normally, their language development is retarded, and their behavior is often ritualistic and compulsive.

Autonomous Morality Morality based on the belief that rules are arbitrary agreements that can be changed if the people governed by them agree.

Babbling A form of vocalizing by babies that includes the consonant and vowel sounds used in speech.

Baby Biography A parent's detailed record of an infant's behavior over a period of time.

Behavioral Geneticist A researcher who seeks to understand how genetic and environmental factors combine to produce individual behavior.

Bio-Social-Behavioral Shift A transition to distinctively new forms of behavior resulting in a convergence of biological, social, and behavioral changes.

Blastocyst The hollow sphere of cells that results from the differentiation of the morula into the trophoblast and the inner cell mass.

Brain Stem The brain structure at the upper end of the spinal cord that controls vital functions and inborn reflexes.

Brazelton Neonatal Assessment Scale A scale used to assess the newborn's neurological condition.

Canalization The process that makes some characteristics relatively invulnerable to environmental influence during development.

Categorize To perceive objects or events that differ in various ways as equivalent.

Catharsis The reduction of an urge; an emotional release.

Cephalocaudal Pattern The sequence of body development from head to foot.

Cerebral Cortex The uppermost part of the central nervous system, comprising specialized regions for the analysis of time, space, and language, as well as for motor functions and sensory discriminations.

Chorion A membrane that develops out of the trophoblast to form the placenta.

Chromosome A threadlike structure made up of genes; in humans there are 46 chromosomes in the nucleus of each cell.

Classical Conditioning The establishment of a connection between a response and a previously neutral stimulus, resulting from the pairing of the neutral stimulus with an unconditional stimulus; the process by which an organism learns which events in its environment go with others.

Cleavage The initial mitotic divisions of the zygote into several cells.

Clinical Method A research method in which questions are tailored to the individual, with each succeeding question depending on the answer to the previous one.

Clique A group of about 5 or 6 members, few enough so that they can be in regular interaction with one another. It is the primary peer group during adolescence.

Codominance A trait that is determined by two alleles but is qualitatively different from the trait produced by either contributing allele alone.

Coevolution The process that emerges from the interaction of biological and cultural evolution.

Cognitive Processes The psychological processes through which we acquire, store, and use knowledge.

Cohort A group of persons born about the same time who are therefore likely to share some common experiences.

Cohort Sequential Design An experimental design in which the longitudinal method is replicated with several cohorts.

Collective Monologue The speech of a child who is playing near another but is talking with no real regard for the other.

Compensation A mental operation that allows a child to consider how changes in one aspect of a problem are related to changes in another.

Competence Motive The basic human drive to control the immediate environment.

Complementary Genes Genes that can produce their phenotypical effect only in combination with each other.

Conceptual Category A category based on conceived similarities in different objects.

Conceptual Knowledge Understanding of the principles that can be used to solve a problem.

Concrete Operations In Piaget's theory, internalized mental actions that fit into a logical system. Such thinking allows children to combine, separate, order, and transform objects in their minds.

Conditional Response (CR) In classical conditioning, a response, such as an eyeblink, that follows a previously neutral stimulus, such as a tone, as a result of the pairing of the neutral stimulus with an unconditional stimulus.

Conditional Stimulus (CS) In classical conditioning, a stimulus that evokes no particular response but comes to elicit a response after training.

Conscience The facet of the personality that emerges when children have internalized adult standards and know what is expected of them by people in authority.

Conservation In Piaget's theory, the understanding that the properties of an object or a substance remain the same even though its appearance may have been altered in some superficial way.

Control Group The persons in an experiment who do not undergo the experimental manipulation.

Conversational Acts Utterances seen as actions that achieve goals through language.

Cooperative Principle The master rule of ordinary conversation: make your contributions to conversation at the required time and for the accepted purpose of the talk exchange.

Coregulation The sharing of responsibility for the child's behavior by parent and child.

Correlation A relation between two factors that vary with or are associated with each other in a way that is unlikely to occur by chance alone.

Critical Periods Periods during which specific biological or environmental events must occur if development is to proceed normally.

Crossing Over The process by which genetic material is exchanged between chromosomes containing genes for the same characteristic.

Cross-Modal Perception The understanding that certain features of an object perceived in one sensory mode go together with features perceived in another sensory mode.

Cross-Sectional Design A research design in which children of different ages are studied at a single time.

Crowd A reputation-based collective of people who are similarly stereotyped by their peers because of their interests, activities, abilities, or attitudes.

Culture The accumulated knowledge of a people as encoded in the language, physical artifacts, beliefs, values, customs, and activities that have been passed down through generations.

Day-Care Center An organized child-care facility supervised by a licensed professional.

Decoding In reading, the process by which letters of the alphabet are associated with corresponding phonemes of the spoken language.

Deductive Reasoning A form of reasoning that moves from a general premise to a specific instance of that premise and thence to a conclusion. If the premises are true, the conclusion must follow.

Deep Structure The restricted set of rules of a language from which the actual sentences that people produce are derived.

Development The sequence of physical, psychological, and social changes that human beings undergo as they grow older.

Developmental Crisis In Erikson's theory, a set of choices and tests that individuals face as they become ready to confront a new life task.

Developmental Niche The physical and social context in which a child lives, including child-rearing and educational practices and the psychological characteristics of the parents.

Deviation IQ An intelligence score based on the difference between the test taker's raw scores and the standardized mean of 100. This method recognizes that mental development is more rapid early in life than later.

Dialogic Reading A form of reading in which the adult actively listens to the child read, asks questions, adds information of interest, and encourages the child's contributions to the interaction until the child is retelling the story in his or her own words.

Dishabituation Renewal of attention after habituation, as a result of a change in a repeating stimulus.

Dizygotic Twins Twins that result from the fertilization by two sperm of two eggs that are released at the same time.

Dominance Hierarchy A hierarchical social structure in which some individuals are dominant and others subordinate to them; associated with the control of conflict.

Dominant Allele The allele that is expressed when an individual possesses two different alleles for the same trait.

Ecology The range of situations in which people are actors; the roles they play; and the predicaments they encounter.

Ectoderm Cells of the inner cell mass that develop into the outer surface of the skin, the nails, part of the teeth, the lens of the eye, the inner ear, and the central nervous system.

Education A specialized form of socialization in which adults engage in deliberate teaching of the young to ensure the acquisition of knowledge and skills required in adult life.

EEG Coherence The synchronization of electrical activity in different areas of the brain.

Egocentrism The interpretation of the world from one's own (ego's) point of view without consideration of alternative perspectives.

Emotion The feeling tone, or affect, with which people respond to their circumstances.

Empathy The sharing of another person's emotional experience.

Encode To pick the most important features of a task and form a representation of them to use in reasoning about the task.

Endoderm Cells of the embryo's inner cell mass that become the fetus's digestive system and the lungs.

Endogenous Causes Causes of development arising as a consequence of the organism's biological heritage.

Environment The totality of things, conditions, and circumstances that surround the organism.

Environmentalist Hypothesis of IQ The belief that intelligence is both specific and heavily dependent on experience.

Epigenesis The hypothesis that new forms of a developing organism emerge through its interactions with its environment.

Equilibration The cognitive balance achieved through the back-and-forth process between assimilation of new experiences to prior schemas and the accommodation of schemas to new experiences.

Ethology An interdisciplinary science that studies the biological bases of behavior and its evolutionary context.

Exogenous Causes Causes of development arising from the environment.

Experiment In psychology, research in which a change is introduced in a person's experience and the effect of that change is measured.

Experimental Group The persons whose experience is changed as part of an experiment.

Explicit Modeling A method of increasing prosocial behavior, in which adults behave in the ways they desire children to imitate.

Extended Family A family in which parents and their children share a household with grandparents, cousins, nephews, or more distant kin.

Family Care Child care provided in the home of a person who is not a member of the child's household.

Family Studies Studies that compare members of a family to see how similar they are in one or more traits.

Fast Mapping Rapid formation of an idea of the meaning of an unfamiliar word that a child hears in a familiar and highly structured situation.

Fetal Alcohol Syndrome A cluster of symptoms found in babies whose mothers were heavy consumers of alcohol during pregnancy.

Fetal Growth Retardation An instance of delayed or decreased development as evidenced by the unusually small size of a newborn baby for its gestational age.

Formal Operations Systematic mental processes that take into account all the logical relations in a problem; the final stage in Piaget's theory of development.

Format The social patterning of communicative interaction between children and their caretakers in activities such as bedtime or bathtime routines.

Gender Schema Theory The theory that children's sexual identity is a result of indirect effects of the environment on a schema that guides the way they select and remember information and provides a model for behavior.

Gene Pool The total genetic information possessed by a sexually reproducing population.

Genes The segments of DNA molecule that act as hereditary blueprints for the organism's development.

Genital Stage In Freud's theory, the period of mature sexuality that begins with adolescence, in which sexual urges are directed to peers of the opposite sex.

Genotype The total set of genes that an individual inherits.

Germ Cells Sperm and ova; the cells specialized for sexual reproduction, which have half the number of chromosomes normal for a species (23 in humans).

Germinal Period The period from fertilization of an ovum to its implantation in the wall of the uterus.

Gonads The primary sex organs—the ovaries in females and the testes in males.

Grammar The rules of a language that govern both the sequence of words in a sentence and the ordering of parts of words.

Grammatical Morphemes Words and parts of words that create meaning by elaborating relations among elements in a sentence.

Group Norms Rules that apply to a particular group, such as a peer group or a professional group.

Guided Participation Collaboration with a young child in routine activities to build shared understanding as a means to shape the child's development.

Habituation The gradual decrease of attention paid to a repeated stimulus.

Heritability The extent to which a given behavior can be attributed to hereditary factors.

Heterochrony The variability in the rates of change of different parts of the organism.

Heterogeneity The variability in the levels of development of different parts of the organism at a given time.

Heteronomous Morality In Piaget's theory, the morality of constraint characterized by unquestioning obedience to rules and to more powerful individuals; by attention to the letter of the law; and by a conception of responsibility in which outcomes are crucial and motives irrelevant.

Heterozygous Having inherited two genes of different allelic forms for a single attribute.

Holophrase A phrase or sentence believed to be encompassed by a baby's single-word utterance.

Home Care Child care provided in the child's own home either by a relative or by a paid baby-sitter.

Homozygous Having inherited two genes of the same allelic form for a particular attribute.

Horizontal Décalage In Piaget's theory, the unevenness of a child's performance at a given stage of development when a logical problem is presented in different forms.

Hostile Aggression Behavior aimed at hurting another person, either for revenge or to establish dominance.

Hypothesis An assumption that is precise enough to be tested to establish its validity or falsity.

Identification A psychological process, essential to socialization, in which children try to look, act, feel, and be like significant people in their social environment.

Identity In Piaget's theory, a mental operation in which the child realizes that a change limited to outward appearance does not change the amounts involved.

Identity Formation In Erikson's theory, the developmental crisis faced by adolescents, which they must resolve in both the individual and social spheres to forge a secure identity.

Implantation The process by which the blastocyst becomes attached to the uterus.

Independent Sense of Self A sense of self that is described by such labels as "individualistic," "egocentric," "separate," "autonomous," "idiosyncratic," and "self-contained."

Induction A method of increasing children's prosocial behavior through the use of explanations that appeal to their pride, concern for others, and desire to be grown up.

Information-Processing Approach A strategy for explaining cognitive development based on the analogy of a modern computer. Research in this tradition is aimed at providing a detailed analysis of a problem and the steps taken to solve it.

Initiation-Reply-Evaluation Sequence A pattern of instructional discourse in which the teacher initiates an exchange, a student replies, and the teacher evaluates the student's reply.

Innatist Hypothesis of IQ The assumption that intelligence is inborn, and that no amount of training or normal variation in the environment can alter the fact that some people are just born smarter than others.

Inner Cell Mass The knot of cells inside the blastocyst that becomes the embryo.

Instructional Discourse Language use in classrooms that gives students information about the content of the curriculum and feedback about their efforts, while providing teachers with information about the students' progress.

Instrumental Aggression Forceful behavior committed to attain a goal.

Instrumental Morality Morality based on the belief that justice is an exchange system: you give as much as you receive.

Interdependent Sense of Self A sense of self that impels the individual to try to fit into the group, to promote group goals, and to be sensitive to others.

Internalization The process by which a child comes to accept standards without being explicitly instructed or needing to wait for a person in authority to respond.

IQ A score on a test of intelligence; a child's mental age (as determined by the age at which average children answer the test items correctly) divided by chronological age, multiplied by 100 ($IQ = MA/CA \times 100$).

Jargoning Vocalizations of strings of syllables that have the intonation and stress of actual utterances in the language the baby will eventually speak.

Knowledge Base The store of information on which the child can draw in a new situation in order to remember, reason, and solve problems.

Language Acquisition Device (LAD) In Chomsky's theory, an innate language-processing capacity that is programmed to recognize the universal grammar common to all languages.

Language Acquisition Support System (LASS) In Bruner's theory, adult behaviors that structure children's language environment to support the development of language.

Latency In Freudian theory, the stage that lasts from the age of 6 until puberty, during which sexual desires are suppressed and sexual energy is channeled into acquiring the technical skills that will be needed during adulthood.

Learned Helplessness Passivity acquired as a result of repeated experiences that lead to the perception that one's behavior has no effect on events.

Learning The process by which an organism's behavior is modified by experience.

Lexicon The total store of words in a person's vocabulary.

Locomotion The ability to move about on one's own.

Longitudinal Design A research design in which data are gathered from one group of people at intervals over a span of years.

Long-Term Memory Memory that is retained over a long period of time.

Low Birth Weight A weight of 2500 grams or less at birth.

Masking Gene A gene that masks the normal expression of another gene.

Maturation The genetically determined patterns of change that occur as individuals age from conception through adulthood.

Meiosis The reduction and division process that produces sperm and ova, each of which contains only half of the parent cell's original complement of 46 chromosomes.

Memory Organization A strategy for remembering in which the materials to be remembered are grouped in meaningful clusters of closely associated items. This strategy does not come into use until middle childhood.

Memory Span The number of randomly chosen numbers, words, or letters that a child can keep in mind. A memory span test is used as a measure of short-term memory capacity.

Menarche A girl's first menstrual period.

Mental Age A basic index of intelligence that indicates how a child's performance relates to age-graded norms.

Mental Modules Highly specific, presumably innate mental faculties attuned to particular kinds of environmental input.

Mental Operation In Piaget's theory, mental process of combining, separating, or transforming information in a logical manner.

Mesoderm Cells of the inner cell mass that become the muscles, the bones, the circulatory system, and the inner layers of the skin.

Meta-Analysis An analysis in which the results of several studies are combined statistically in an effort to discern an overall trend in the data.

Metacognition Understanding of one's own mental activities and the logic underpinning one's attempts to solve problems.

Metalinguistic Awareness The ability to think about one's own language-using skills.

Metamemory Knowledge about one's own memory processes.

Microgenetic Method An experimental procedure that provokes change in a relatively brief time.

Mitosis The process of cell duplication and division that generates all of an individual's cells except sperm and ova.

Modifier Gene A gene that influences the action or expression of other genes.

Modularity Theory A theory that emphasizes developmental changes within innately specified cognitive domains such as language, number, and space.

Monozygotic Twins Siblings who developed from a single zygote and therefore have identical genotypes.

Moral Rules Obligatory social regulations based on principles of justice and welfare.

Moro Reflex An infant's instinctive response to an abrupt noise or to the sensation of being dropped: the arms are flung out with fingers spread and then brought back toward the body with fingers bent as if to clutch something.

Morula The mass of cells that results from the cleavage of the zygote as it moves through the fallopian tube.

Motherese The special high-pitched voice, emphasis on the boundaries between idea-bearing clauses, and simplified vocabulary that adults use in speaking to small children.

Mutation An error in the process by which a gene is replicated that results in a change in the molecular structure of the gene.

Myelin The sheath of fatty cells that covers the neurons, stabilizing them and speeding the transmission of impulses.

Myelination The process by which myelin covers nerve cells.

Naturalistic Observations Observations of the actual behavior of people in the real-world settings they inhabit.

Nature The inborn, genetically coded biological capacities and limitations of individuals.

Neuron A nerve cell.

Nomination Procedure A method used to determine children's social status, in which members of the group are asked who they would like to sit next to or play with, or who their friends are.

Nuclear Family A family consisting of a husband and wife and their children.

Nurture The environmental influence exerted on the individual by the social group.

Objectivity The extent to which an experimental procedure or measurement is free from distortion by prejudice, preconception, or interpretation, a requirement of scientific observations.

Object Permanence In Piaget's theory, the understanding that objects have substance, are external to oneself, and continue to exist when out of sight; an understanding that babies demonstrate when they begin to search actively for an object they no longer see.

Oedipus Complex In Freud's theory, the fear, guilt, and conflict evoked by a little boy's desire to eliminate his father and take his place in his mother's affections.

Ontogeny The course of development during an individual's lifetime.

Operant Conditioning Modification of behavior as a result of the positive or negative consequences that the behavior produces.

Oppositional Identity An identity forged by members of minority racial or ethnic groups characterized by rejection of patterns of dress, speech, mannerisms, and attitudes associated with the dominant group.

Overextension The application of a word denoting a member of a class of objects to all members of the class.

Peers Individuals of comparable age and status.

Perceptual Category A category based on perceived similarities.

Period of the Embryo The period that begins when the organism becomes attached to the uterus and lasts until the end of the eighth week, when the major organs have taken shape.

Period of the Fetus The period from 9 weeks after conception until birth.

Permissive Parenting Pattern The practice of exercising little control over children's behavior and making relatively few demands on them. Permissive parents give their children a lot of leeway to determine their own schedules and activities and often consult them about family policies.

Personality The unique pattern of temperament, emotions, and intellectual abilities that a child develops in his or her social interactions.

Personal Rules Rules created by individuals to regulate their own behavior.

Phallic Stage In Freud's theory, the period around the fourth year when children begin to focus their pleasure seeking on the genital area.

Phenotype The organism's observable characteristics that result from the interaction of the genotype with the environment.

Phonemes Units of the sound system of a language that are perceived as identical, and that function to indicate differences in meaning. Phonemes differ from language to language.

Phylogeny The evolutionary history of a species.

Placenta An organ made up of tissue from both the mother and the fetus that serves as a barrier and a filter between their bloodstreams.

Polygenic Trait A genetic trait that is determined by the interaction of several genes.

Positive Justice The process of reaching a decision about how to divide resources or distribute rewards fairly.

Pragmatic Uses of Language The ability to select words and word orders that convey what the speaker intends to communicate.

Precausal Thinking In Piaget's theory, a form of thinking observed in young children in which they reason not from cause to effect, but from one particular to another.

Preformationism The hypothesis that the adult form is present in the cells out of which it develops.

Premature Born before the thirty-seventh week of gestation.

Preoperational Stage In Piaget's theory, the stage that follows the sensorimotor stage, in which children often fail to distinguish their point of view from that of others, become easily captured by surface appearances, and are easily confused about causal relations.

Prereaching A reflexlike movement in which newborns reach toward an object and simultaneously make grasping movements.

Primacy The determinative influence of children's earliest experiences on their later development.

Primary Circular Reaction Behavior characteristic of the second substage of Piaget's sensorimotor period, in which the baby repeats simple actions for their own sake.

Primary Identification In Freud's theory, the recognition by infants that some objects in the external world are like themselves.

Primary Intersubjectivity The coordinated turn-taking and emotional sharing in face-to-face interactions between infants and their caregivers.

Primary Motor Area The area of the cerebral cortex that controls nonreflexive, voluntary movement.

Primary Sensory Area The area of the brain that is responsible for the initial analysis of sensory information.

Primary Sexual Organs The organs that are involved in reproduction—the ovaries in females and the testes in males.

Procedural Knowledge Understanding of the way to carry out a sequence of actions to solve a problem.

Prosocial Behaviors Behaviors such as empathy, sharing, helping, and cooperation, which benefit the group but bring no direct reward to the benefactor.

Proximodistal Pattern The sequence of body development from the middle outward.

Puberty The complex of biological developments that transform a child into a physically mature individual capable of reproduction.

Range of Reaction All the possible phenotypes for a single genotype that are compatible with life.

Rating Scale A scale on which children are asked to rank one another according to a specific criterion, such as popularity. It is used to determine the relative social status of members of a group.

Recapitulationism The idea that human children repeat earlier stages of human evolution during their development. Freud and Erikson also maintained that older children recapitulate earlier stages of their own development.

Recessive Allele The allele that is not expressed when an individual possesses two different alleles for the same trait.

Reciprocal Teaching A method of reading instruction in which a teacher and a small group of students read silently through a segment of text and then take turns leading a discussion of its meaning.

Recursion The embedding of sentences within each other.

Reflexes Specific, well-integrated responses that are automatically elicited by specific aspects of the environment.

Rehearsal The repetition of material that is being committed to memory; a strategy for remembering.

Reinforcement In operant conditioning, a consequence of a behavior that increases the likelihood that the behavior will be repeated.

Relational Aggression Behavior that interferes with another person's friendships or causes the person to be excluded from a social group.

Reliability The extent to which an experimental procedure or measurement produces the same result in repeated trials and when conducted by different observers; a requirement of scientific observations.

Replication Repetition of earlier results upon repetition of the procedures that yielded them.

Representative Sample A sample of people who are representative of a larger group that a researcher wishes to draw conclusions about.

Resilience The ability to recover quickly from the adverse effects of early experience or to persevere in the face of stress with no apparent negative psychological consequences.

Reversibility In Piaget's theory, mental operations by which children can think through an action and then its reverse.

Schema A mental structure that provides an organism with a model for action in similar circumstances.

School Cutoff Strategy A strategy for assessing the intellectual effects of schooling, in which researchers compare the intellectual performance of first-graders with that of children a few months younger who have not yet been admitted to school because of the school cutoff date.

Script A generalized representation of a routine activity developed by the people who engage in the activity, as a result of their repeated participation in it. A script specifies the people who appropriately participate in the activity, the social roles they play, the objects they use, and the sequence of their actions. It serves as a guide to behavior for the participants in the event and helps them to coordinate their actions.

Secondary Circular Reactions The behavior characteristic of the third substage of Piaget's sensorimotor stage, in which the baby repeats an action to produce an interesting change in its environment.

Secondary Identification In Freud's theory, a child's effort to take on the qualities of a person with whom he or she identifies.

Secondary Intersubjectivity The sharing between infants and their caregivers of understandings and emotions that refer beyond themselves to objects and other people.

Secondary Sex Characteristics The anatomical and physiological signs that outwardly distinguish males from females. They make their appearance as the primary sexual organs are maturing.

Second-Order Thinking The ability to develop rules about rules and to hold competing thoughts in mind while mulling them over.

Self-Concept The way individuals conceive of themselves in relation to other people.

Self-Control The capacity to act in accordance with the expectations of people in authority even when one is not being monitored.

Self-Report A method of gathering data in which people report on their own psychological states and behaviors.

Semenarche A boy's first ejaculation.

Sensorimotor Stage The first of Piaget's four developmental stages, characterized by the beginnings of coordination between the infant's sensory experiences and simple motor behaviors.

Sex-Linked Characteristics Attributes determined by genes that are found on the X or Y chromosome.

Short-Term Memory Working memory that retains new information for a period of several seconds; distinguished from long-term memory, which holds information in storage for later retrieval.

Social Co-construction The two-sided process in which both the environment and the child are active in constructing the child's development.

Social Comparison The process of defining oneself by comparison with one's peers. Social comparison comes to prominence in middle childhood.

Social Competence The set of skills that collectively results in successful social functioning.

Social Conventions Rules that are specific to a given society, such as prescriptions about the kinds of behavior that are appropriate to males and to females.

Social Development A two-sided process in which children simultaneously become integrated into the larger social community and differentiated as distinctive individuals.

Socialization The process by which children acquire the standards, values, and knowledge of their society.

Social Referencing Watchful attention to another person's expression as a cue to how one should react to an unusual event; a behavior characteristic of babies with their caregivers.

Social Relational Moral Perspective Moral judgment based on the belief that shared feelings and agreements, especially between people who are closely associated, are more important than individual self-interest.

Social Repair Mechanisms Strategies that allow friends to remain friends even when serious differences temporarily drive them apart.

Social Role A social category (such as son, daughter, student) that describes a person's relation to the social group, with accompanying rights, duties, and obligations.

Sociodramatic Play Make-believe games in which two or more children enact a variety of social roles.

Socioemotional Competence High levels of development in the social and emotional spheres and the ability to deploy those resources in real circumstances.

Sociogram A graphic representation that depicts how each child relates to every other child in a group.

Somatic Cells All the cells in the body except for the germ cells (ova and sperm).

Stage A distinctive period of development that differs qualitatively from the periods that come before and after it.

Stepping Reflex An automatic response of a newborn infant consisting of rhythmic leg movements when the child is held upright with the feet touching a flat surface.

Strategy A plan of action devised for the purpose of attaining a specific goal.

Structured Whole A system of relationships that can be logically described and thought about.

Surface Structure In Chomsky's theory, the actual sentences that people construct when they speak a language.

Synapse A small gap between interconnecting neurons.

Temperament The basic style with which an individual responds to the environment, as well as his or her dominant mood.

Teratogen An environmental agent that causes deviation in normal development and leads to serious abnormalities or death.

Theory A broad framework or body of principles used to interpret a set of facts.

Theory of Mind A framework for thinking about other people's mental states.

Transactional Models Models that trace the ways in which the characteristics of a child and the characteristics of the child's environment interact across time to determine developmental outcomes.

Trophoblast The outer cells of the blastocyst that develop into the membranes that support and protect the embryo.

Umbilical Cord A soft tube containing blood vessels that connects the embryo to the placenta.

Unconditional Response (UCR) In classical conditioning, a response that occurs whenever a particular stimulus is present. Salivation, for example, is the unconditional response to food in the mouth.

Unconditional Stimulus (UCS) In classical conditioning, a stimulus that invariably elicits a particular response. Food in the mouth is the unconditional stimulus for salivation.

Underextension A term used for applying verbal labels too narrowly.

Utilization Knowledge The understanding of when to apply particular procedures to solve problems.

Validity The extent to which measurements of a characteristic by a variety of means yield the same results and reliably predict future behavior; a requirement of scientific observations.

X and Y Chromosomes The two chromosomes that determine the sex of the individual. Normal females have two X chromosomes; normal males have one Y chromosome inherited from the father and one X inherited from the mother.

Zona Pellucida The thin envelope that surrounds the zygote and later the morula.

Zone of Proximal Development The gap between what a child can do independently and what a child can do with the support of someone more competent.

Zygote The single cell formed at conception by the union of the 23 chromosomes of the sperm and the 23 chromosomes of the ovum.

REFERENCES

Abbott, S. (1992). Holding on and pushing away: Comparative perspectives on an Eastern Kentucky child rearing practice. *Ethos, 20,* 33–65.

Abramovitch, R., Corter, C., Pepler, D., & Stanhope, L. (1986). Sibling and peer interaction: A final followup and comparison. *Child Development, 57,* 217–229.

Abramovitch, R., Pepler, D., & Corter, C. (1982). Patterns of sibling interaction among pre-school-aged children. In M. Lamb & B. Sutton-Smith (Eds.), *Sibling relationships: Their nature and significance across the lifespan.* Hillsdale, NJ: Erlbaum.

Abravanel, E., Levin-Goldschmidt, E., & Stevenson, M. B. (1976). Action imitation: The early phase of infancy. *Child Development, 47,* 1032–1044.

Abravanel, E., & Sigafoos, A. D. (1984). Exploring the presence of imitation during early infancy. *Child Development, 55,* 381–392.

Adams, M. J. (1990). *Learning to read: Thinking and learning about print.* Cambridge, MA: MIT Press.

Adamson, L.B. (1995). *Communication development during infancy.* Madison, WI.: Brown and Benchmark.

Adelson, J. (1972). The political imagination of the young adolescent. In J. Kagan & R. Coles (Eds.), *Twelve to sixteen: Early adolescence.* New York: W. W. Norton.

Adelson, J. (1991). Political development. In R. Lerner, A. C. Petersen, & J. Brooks-Gunn (Eds.), *Encyclopedia of adolescence.* New York: Garland Publishers.

Adelson, J., Green, B., & O'Neil, R. P. (1969). Growth of the idea of law in adolescence. *Developmental Psychology, 1,* 327–332.

Adelson, J., & O'Neil, R. P. (1966). Growth of political ideas in adolescence: The sense of community. *Journal of Personality and Social Psychology, 4,* 295–306.

Adler, P. A., Kless, S. J., & Adler, P. (1992). Socialization to gender roles: Popularity among elementary school boys and girls. *Sociology of Education, 65,* 169–187.

Adolph, K. E., Eppler, M. A., & Gibson, E. J. (1993). Crawling versus walking infants: Perceptions of affordances for locomotion over sloping surfaces. *Child Development, 64,* 1158–1174.

Advisory Board on Child Abuse and Neglect (1990). *Child abuse and neglect: Critical first steps in response to a national emergency.* Washington, DC: Department of Health and Human Services, Office of Human Development Services.

Ahn, N. (January–February, 1994). Teenage Childbearing and High school completion: Accounting for individual heterogeneity. *Family Planning Perspectives, 26,* 17–21.

Ainsworth, M. D. S. (1967). *Infancy in Uganda: Infant care and the growth of love.* Baltimore: Johns Hopkins Press.

Ainsworth, M. D. S. (1982). Attachment: Retrospect and prospect. In C. M. Parkes & J. Stevenson-Hinde (Eds.), *The place of attachment in human behavior.* New York: Basic Books.

Ainsworth, M. D. S. (1993). Attachment as related to the mother-infant interaction. In C. Rovee-Collier & L. P Lipsett (Eds.), *Advances in infancy research* (Vol. 8). Norwood, NJ: Ablex.

Ainsworth, M. D. S., & Bell, S. M. (1969). Some contemporary patterns of mother-infant interaction in the feeding situation. In A. Ambrose (Ed.), *Stimulation in Early Infancy.* New York: Academic Press.

Ainsworth, M. D. S., Bell, S. M., & Stayton, D. J. (1971). Individual differences in strange-situation behavior of one-year-olds. In H. R. Schaffer (Ed.), *The origins of human social relations.* New York: Academic Press.

Ainsworth, M. D. S., Blehar, M. C., Waters, E., & Wall, S. (1978). *Patterns of attachment: A psychological study of the strange situation.* Hillsdale, NJ: Erlbaum.

Ainsworth, M. D. S., & Wittig, B. A. (1969). Attachment and exploratory behavior of one-year-olds in a strange situation. In B. M. Foss (Ed.), *Determinants of infant behavior* (Vol. 4). London: Methuen.

Akbar, N. (1985). Our destiny: Authors of a scientific revolution. In H. P. McAdoo & J. L. McAdoo (Eds.), *Black children: Social, educational, and parental environments.* Beverly Hills, CA: Sage.

Alan Guttmacher Institute (1994). *Sex and America's teenagers.* New York.

Aldrich, C. A., & Hewitt, E. S. (1947). A self-regulating feeding program for infants. *Journal of the American Medical Association, 35,* 341.

Aleksandrowicz, M. K. (1974). The effect of pain-relieving drugs administered during labor and delivery on the behavior of the newborn: A review. *Merrill-Palmer Quarterly, 20,* 121–141.

Allen, K. E., Turner, K. D., & Everett, P. M. (1970). A behavior modification classroom for Head start children with problem behavior. *Exceptional Children, 37,* 119–127.

Allesandri, S. M., Sullivan, M. W., Imaizumi, S., & Lewis, M. (1993). Learning and emotional responsivity and cocaine-exposed infants. *Developmental Psychology, 29,* 989–997.

Allison, A. C. (1954). Protection afforded by sickle-cell trait against subtertian malarial infection. *British Medical Journal, 1,* 290–294.

Allport, G. (1937). *Personality: A psychological interpretation.* New York: Holt, Rinehart & Winston.

Ames, B. N. (1979). Identifying environmental chemicals causing mutations and cancer. *Science, 204,* 587–593.

Ampofo-Boateng, K., Thornson, J. A., Grieve, R., Pitcairn, T., Lee, D. N., & Demetre, J. D. (1993). A developmental training study of children's ability to find safe routes to cross the road. *British Journal of Developmental Psychology, 11,* 31–45.

Anderson, A., & Stokes, S. (1984). Social and institutional influences on the development and practice of literacy. In H. Goelman, A. Oberg, & F. Smith (Eds.), *Awakening to literacy.* Exeter, NH: Heinemann.

Anderson, B. E. (1992). Effect of day-care on cognitive and socioemotional competence of thirteen-year-old Swedish schoolchildren. *Child Development, 63,* 20–36.

Anglin, J. M. (1977). *Word, object, and conceptual development.* New York: W. W. Norton.

Anglin, J. M. (1983). Extensional aspects of the preschool child's word concepts. In T. Seiler & W. Wannenmacher (Eds.), *Concept development in the development of word meanings.* New York: Springer-Verlag.

Anglin, J. M. (1985). The child's expressible knowledge of word concepts: What preschoolers can say about the meanings of some nouns and verbs. In K. E. Nelson (Ed.), *Children's language* (Vol. 5). Hillsdale, NJ: Erlbaum.

Anglin, J. M. (1986). Semantic and conceptual knowledge underlying the child's words. In S. S. Kuczaj & M. D. Barrett (Eds.), *The development of word meaning.* New York: Springer-Verlag.

Anglin, J. (1993). Vocabulary development: A morphological analysis. *Monographs of the Society for Research in Child Development, 58,* (10, Serial No. 238).

Anisfeld, Moshe (1991). Neonatal imitation. *Developmental Review, 11,* 60–97.

Annis, R. C., & Corenblum, B. (1987). Effect of test language and experimenter race on Canadian Indian children's racial and self-identity. *Journal of Social Psychology, 126,* 761–773.

Antell, S. E., & Keating, D. P. (1983). Perception of numerical invariance in neonates. *Child Development, 54,* 695–701.

Antonov, A. N. (1947). Children born during the siege of Leningrad in 1942. *Journal of Pediatrics, 30,* 250.

Apgar, V. (1953). A proposal for a new method of evaluation of the newborn infant. *Current Researches in Anesthesia and Analgesics, 32,* 260–267.

Aram, D. M., Morris, R., & Hall, N. E. (1992). The validity of discrepancy criteria for identifying children with developmental language disorders. *Journal of Learning Disabilities, 25,* 549–554.

Archer, S. L. (1985). Identity and the choice of social roles. In A. S. Waterman (Ed.), *Identity in adolescence: Processes and contents (New directions for child development,* No. 30). San Francisco: Jossey-Bass.

Arey, L. B. (1974). *Developmental anatomy: A textbook and laboratory manual of embryology* (7th ed.). Philadelphia: Saunders.

Ariès, P. (1962). *Centuries of childhood: A social history of family life.* New York: Vintage Books.

Arnett, J. (1992). Reckless behavior in adolescence: A developmental perspective. *Developmental Review, 12,* 339–373.

Arnheim, R. (1954). *Art and visual perception.* Berkeley: University of California Press.

Ascher, M., & Ascher, S. R. (1981). *Code of the quipu.* Ann Arbor, MI: University of Michigan Press.

Asendorpf, J. B., & Nunner-Winkler, G. (1992). Children's moral motive strength and temperamental inhibition reduce their immoral behavior in real moral conflicts. *Child Development, 63,* 1223–1235.

Asher, S. R., & Coie, J. D., (Eds.). (1990). *Peer rejection in childhood.* New York: Cambridge University Press.

Asher, S. R., & Dodge, K. A. (1986). Identifying children who are rejected by their peers. *Developmental Psychology, 22,* 444–449.

Asher, S. R., Parkhurst, J. T., Hymel, S., & Williams, G. (1990). Peer rejection and loneliness in childhood. In S. R. Asher and J. D. Coie, *Peer rejection in childhood.* New York: Cambridge University Press.

Ashmead, D. H., & Perlmutter, M. (1979). *Infant memory in everyday life.* Paper presented at the meeting of the American Psychological Association, New York.

Aslin, R. N. (1987). Visual and auditory development in infancy. In J. D. Osofsky (Ed.), *Handbook of Infant Development* (2nd ed.). New York: Wiley.

Astington, J. W. (1993). *The child's discovery of the mind.* Cambridge, MA: Harvard University Press.

Atkinson, J., & Braddick, O. (1982). Sensory and perceptual capacities in the neonate. In P. Stratton (Ed.), *Psychology of the human newborn.* Chichester, England: Wiley.

Atkinson, R. C., & Shiffrin, R. M. (1980). The control of short-term memory. In R. L. Atkinson & R. C. Atkinson (Eds.), *Mind and behavior: Readings from Scientific American.* New York: W. H. Freeman.

Attie, I., & Brooks-Gunn, J. (1989). Development of eating problems in adolescent girls: A longitudinal study. *Developmental Psychology, 25,* 70–79.

Austin, C. R., & Short, R. V. (Eds.). (1972). *Reproduction in mammals: Embryonic and fetal development.* Cambridge: Cambridge University Press.

Avis, J., & Harris, P. L. (1991). Belief-desire reasoning among Baka children: Evidence for a universal conception of mind. *Child Development, 62,* 460–467.

Azmitia, M. & Hesser, J. (1993). Why siblings are important agents of cognitive development: A comparison of siblings and peers. *Child Development, 64,* 430–444.

Azmitia, M., & Perlmutter, M. (1989). Social influences on children's cognition: State of the art and future directions. *Advances in Child Development and Behavior, 22,* 89–144.

Bachman, J. G., Johnston, L. D., & O'Malley, P. M. (1987). *Monitoring the future: Questionnaire responses from the nation's high school seniors, 1986.* Ann Arbor, MI: Survey Research Center, Institute for Social Research.

Bachman, J. G., & Schulenberg, J. (1993). How part-time work intensity relates to drug use, problem behavior, time use, and satisfaction among high school seniors: Are there consequences or merely correlates? *Developmental Psychology, 29,* 220–235.

Baillargeon, R. (1987). Object permanence in 3½- and 4½-month-old infants. *Developmental Psychology, 23,* 655–664.

Baillargeon, R. (1993). The object concept revisited: New directions in the investigation of infants' physical knowledge. In C. Granrud (Ed.), *Visual perception and cognition in infancy. Carnegie Mellon symposia on cognition.* Hillsdale, NJ: Lawrence Erlbaum Associates.

Baillargeon, R., & Graber, M. (1988). Evidence of location memory in 8-month-old infants in a nonsearch AB task. *Developmental Psychology, 24,* 502–511.

Baillargeon, R., Spelke, E., & Wasserman, S. (1985). Object permanence in five-month-old infants. *Cognition, 20,* 191–208.

Baker, E. L., O'Neil, H. F. Jr. (Eds.), (1994). *Technology assessment in education and training.* Hillsdale, NJ: Lawrence Erlbaum Associates.

Baker-Ward, L., Gordon, B. N., Ornstein, P. A., Larus, D. M., & Clubb, P. A. (1993). Young children's long-term retention of a pediatric examination. *Child Development, 64,* 1519–1533.

Baldwin, A. L. (1946). Differences: Parent behavior toward three- and nine-year-old children. *Journal of Personality, 15,* 143–165.

Baldwin, A. L. (1947). Changes in parent behavior during pregnancy: An experiment in longitudinal analysis. *Child Development, 18,* 29–39.

Baldwin, A. L. (1955). *Behavior and development in childhood.* New York: Dryden Press.

Baldwin, D. V., & Skinner, M. L. (1989). Structural model for antisocial behavior: Generalization to single-mother families. *Developmental Psychology, 25,* 45–50.

Baldwin, J. M. (1902). *Social and ethical interpretations in mental development* (3rd ed.). New York: Macmillan.

Baltes, P. B. (1987). Theoretical propositions of life-span developmental psychology: On the dynamics between growth and decline. *Developmental Psychology, 23,* 611–626.

Bandura, A. (1964). The stormy decade: Fact or fiction. *Psychology in the School, 1,* 224–231.

Bandura, A. (1965). Influence of models' reinforcement contingencies on the acquisition of imitative responses. *Journal of Personality and Social Psychology, 1,* 587–595.

Bandura, A. (1969). Social-learning theory of identificatory processes. In D. A. Goslin (Ed.), *Handbook of socialization theory and research.* Chicago: Rand McNally.

Bandura, A. (1973). *Aggression: A social learning analysis.* Englewood Cliffs, NJ: Prentice-Hall.

Bandura, A. (1977). *Social learning theory*. Englewood Cliffs, NJ: Prentice-Hall.

Bandura, A. (1986). *Social foundations of thought and action: A social cognitive theory*. Englewood Cliffs, NJ: Prentice-Hall.

Bandura, A. (1991). Social cognitive theory of moral thought and action. In W. M. Kutines & J. L. Gewirtz, (Eds.), *Handbook of moral behavior and development: Volume I. Theory.* Hillsdale, N.J.: Lawrence Erlbaum.

Bandura, A., Ross, D., & Ross, S. A. (1963). Imitation of film-mediated aggressive models. *Journal of Abnormal and Social Psychology, 66,* 3–11.

Bandura, A., & Walters, R. H. (1959). *Adolescent aggression.* New York: Ronald Press.

Bandura, A., & Walters, R. H. (1963). *Social learning and personality development.* New York: Holt, Rinehart and Winston.

Banks, M. S., & Salapatek, P. (1983). Infant visual perception. In P. H. Mussen (Ed.), *Handbook of child psychology: Vol. 2. Infancy and developmental psychobiology.* New York: Wiley.

Barcus, F. E. (1983). *Images of life on children's television: Sex roles, minorities, and families.* New York: Praeger.

Barglow, P., Vaughn, B. E., & Molitor, N. (1987). Effects of maternal absence due to employment on the quality of infant-mother attachment in a low-risk sample. *Child Development, 58,* 945–953.

Barker, R. G., & Wright, H. F. (1951). *One boy's day: A specimen record of behavior.* New York: Harper Brothers.

Barker, R. G., & Wright, H. F. (1955). *Midwest and its children.* New York: Harper & Row.

Barnett, D., Manly, J. T., & Cicchetti, D. (1993). Defining child maltreatment. In D. Cicchetti & S. L. Toth (Eds.), *Child abuse, child development, and social policy: Advances in applied developmental psychology. 8.* Norwood, New Jersey: Ablex Publishing.

Baron-Cohen, S., Leslie, A. M., & Frith, U. (1986). Mechanical behavioral and intentional understanding of picture stories in autistic children. *British Journal of Developmental Psychology, 4,* 113–125.

Baron-Cohen, S., Tager-Flushing, H., & Cohen, D. J. (1993). *Understanding other minds: Perspectives from autism.* Oxford: Oxford University Press.

Barrett, K. C. (1995). A functionalist approach to shame and guilt. In J. P. Tangney & K. W. Fischer (Eds.), *Self-conscious emotions: The psychology of shame, guilt, embarrassment, and pride.* New York: Guilford Press.

Barrett, K. C., & Campos, J. J. (1987). Perspectives on emotional development: II. A functionalist approach to emotions. In J. D. Osofsky (Ed.), *Handbook of Infant Development* (2nd ed.). New York: Wiley.

Bartlett, E. (1977). The acquisition of the meaning of color terms. In P. T. Smith & R. N. Campbell (Eds.), *Proceedings of the Sterling Conference on the Psychology of Language.* New York: Plenum Press.

Bates, E. (1976). *Language and context: The acquisition of pragmatics.* New York: Academic Press.

Bates, E., Benigni, L., Bretherton, I., Camaioni, L., & Volterra, V. (1979). *The emergence of symbols: Cognition and communication in infancy.* New York: Academic Press.

Bates, E., Bretherton, I., & Snyder, L. (1988). *From first words to grammar.* Cambridge: Cambridge University Press.

Bates, E., Camaioni, L., & Volterra, V. (1975). The acquisition of performatives prior to speech. *Merrill Palmer Quarterly, 21,* 205–226.

Bates, E., & MacWhinney, B. (1982). A functionalist approach to grammatical development. In L. Gleitman & E. Wanner (Eds.), *Language acquisition: The state of the art.* Cambridge: Cambridge University Press.

Bates, E., O'Connell, B., & Shore, C. (1987). Language and communication. In J. D. Osofsky (Ed.), *Handbook of infant development* (2nd ed.). New York: Wiley.

Bates, E., & Snyder, L. (1987). The cognitive hypothesis in language development. In I. Uzgiris & J. McV. Hunt (Eds.), *Infant performance and experience: New findings with the ordinal scales.* Champaign, IL: University of Illinois Press.

Bates, J. E. (1989). Concepts and measures of temperament. In G. A. Kohnstamm, J. E. Bates, & M. K. Rothbart (Eds.), *Temperament In Childhood.* New York: Wiley.

Bates, J. (1994). Introduction. In J. E. Bates & T. D. Wachs (Eds.), *Individual differences at the interface of biology and behavior.* Washington, DC: American Psychological Association.

Bates, J. E., Maslin, C. A., & Frankel, K. A. (1985). Attachment, security, and temperament as predictors of behavior: Problem ratings at three years. *Monographs of the Society for Research in Child Development, 50* (Serial No. 209).

Bates, J. E., Marvinney, D., Kelly, T., Dodge, K. A., Ben-nett, D. S., & Pettit, G. S. (1994). Childcare history and kindergarten adjustment. *Developmental Psychology, 30,* 690–700.

Bates, J. E., & Wachs, T. D. (Eds.). (1994). *Individual differences at the interface of biology and behavior.* Washington, DC: American Psychological Association.

Baumeister, R. F. (1987). How the self became a problem: A psychological review of historical research. *Journal of Personality and Social Psychology, 52,* 163–176.

Baumeister, R. F. (Ed.), (1993). *Self-esteem: The puzzle of low self-regard.* New York: Plenum.

Baumrind, D. (1967). Child care practices anteceding three patterns of preschool behavior: *Genetic Psychology Monographs, 75,* 43–88.

Baumrind, D. (1971). Current patterns of parental authority. *Developmental Psychology Monographs, 4* (1, Pt. 2).

Baumrind, D. (1980). New directions in socialization research. *American Psychologist, 35,* 639–652.

Baumrind, D. (1989). Rearing competent children. In W. Damon (Ed.), *Child development today and tomorrow.* San Francisco: Jossey-Bass.

Baumrind, D. (1991a). To nurture nature. *Behavioral and Brain Sciences, 14,* 386.

Baumrind, D. (1991b). Parenting styles and adolescent development. In J. Brooks-Gunn, R. Lerner, & A. C. Peterson (Eds.), *The encyclopedia of adolescence.* New York: Garland.

Bayer, S. A., & Altman, J. (1991). *Neocortical development.* New York: Raven.

Beal, C. R. (1994). *Boys and girls: The development of gender roles.* New York: McGraw-Hill.

Bell, A. P., Weinberg, M. S., & Hammersmith, S. K. (1981). *Sexual preference: Its development in men and women.* Bloomington, IN: Indiana University Press.

Bell, S. M., & Ainsworth, M. (1972). Infant crying and maternal responsiveness. *Child Development, 43,* 1171–1190.

Bellugi, U., Bihrle, A., Jernigan, T., Trauner, D., & Doherty, S. (1990). Neuropsychological, neurological, and neuroanatomical profile of Williams Syndrome. *American Journal of Medical Genetics Supplement, 6,* 115–125.

Belsky, J. (1980). Child maltreatment: An ecological integration. *American Psychologist, 35,* 320–335.

Belsky, J. (1986). Infant day care: A cause for concern. *Zero to three, 6* (5), 1–9.

Belsky, J. (1990). Developmental risks associated with infant day care. In. S. Chehrazi (Ed.), *Psychosocial issues in day care*. Washington, DC: American Psychiatric Press.

Belsky, J. (1993). Etiology of child maltreatment: A developmental-ecological analysis. *Psychological Bulletin, 114*, 413–434.

Belsky, J., $ Steinberg, L. D. (1978). The effects of day care: A critical review. *Child Development 49*, 929–949.

Belsky, J., & Steinberg, L. D., & Walker, A. (1982). The ecology of day care. In M. E. Lamb (Ed.), *Nontraditional families: Parenting and child development*. Hillsdale, NJ: Erlbaum.

Belsky, J. & Vondra, J. (1987). Child maltreatment: Prevalence, consequences, causes, and interventions. In D. Crowell, I. Evans, & C. O'Donell (Eds.), *Childhood Aggression and Violence: Sources of Influence, Prevention and Control*. New York: Plenum Press.

Bem, S. L. (1989). Genital knowledge and gender constancy in preschool children. *Child Development, 60*, 649–662.

Berg, W. K., & Berg, K. M. (1987). Psychophysiological development in infancy: State, startle, and attention. In J. D. Osofsky (Ed.), *Handbook of infant development* (2nd ed.). New York: Wiley.

Berger, B. M. (1981). *The survival of a counterculture: Ideological work and everyday life among rural communards*. Berkeley: University of California Press.

Bergsma, D. (Ed.). (1979). *Birth defects compendium* (2nd ed.). New York: Alan R. Liss.

Berk, L. B., & Friman, P. C. (1990). Epidemiologic aspects of toilet training. *Clinical Pediatrics, 29*, 278–282.

Bernal, J. F. (1972). Crying during the first few days, and maternal responses. *Developmental Medicine and Child Neurology, 14*, 362–372.

Berndt, T. J. (1979). Developmental changes in conformity to peers and parents, *Developmental Psychology, 15*, 608–616.

Berndt, T. J. (1986). Children's comments about their friendships. In M. Perlmutter (Ed.), *Minnesota symposia on child psychology*. Vol. 18: Cognitive perspectives on children's social and behavioral development. Hillsdale, NJ: Erlbaum.

Berndt, T. J. (1988). The nature and significance of children's friendships. In R. Vasta (Ed.), *Annals of Child Development* (Vol. 5). Greenwich, CT: JAI Press.

Berndt, T. J., & Keefe, K. (1995). Friend's influence on adolescent's adjustment in school. *Child Development, 66*, 1312–1329.

Berndt, T. J., & Perry, T. B. (1990). Distinctive features and effects of early adolescent friendships. In R. Montemayor, G. R. Adams, & T. P. Gullotta (Eds.), *From childhood to adolescence: A transitional period? Advances in adolescent development: An annual book series, Vol. 2*. Newbury Park, CA: Sage Publications.

Berndt, T. J. & Savin-Williams, R. C. (1993). Peer relations and friendships. In P. H. Tolan, B. J. Cohler, (Eds.), *Handbook of clinical research and practice with adolescents*. New York: Wiley.

Berry, G. L., & Asamen, J. K. (1993). *Children and television*. Newbury Park: Sage.

Berry, J. W., Poortinga, Y. H., Segall, M. H., & Dasen, P. (1992). *Cross-cultural psychology: Research and application*. New York: Cambridge University Press.

Bertenthal, B. I., & Bai, D. L. (1989). Infants' sensitivity to optical flow for controlling posture. *Developmental Psychology, 25*, 936–945.

Bertenthal, B. I., Campos, J. J., & Barrett, K. C. (1984). Self-produced locomotions: An organizer of emotional, cognitive, and social development in infancy. In R. Emde & R. Harmon (Eds.), *Continuities and discontinuities in development*. New York: Plenum Press.

Bertenthal, B. I., & Fischer, K. W. (1978). Development of self-recognition in the infant. *Developmental Psychology, 14*, 44–50.

Best, D. (1993). Inducing children to generate mnemonic organizational strategies: An examination of long-term retention and materials. *Developmental Psychology, 29*, 324–336.

Bettelheim, B. (1977). *The uses of enchantment: The meaning and importance of fairytales*. New York: Vintage Books.

Beuf, A. H. (1977). *Red children in white America*. Philadelphia: University of Pennsylvania Press.

Bidell, T. R., & Fischer, K. W. (1995). Between nature and nurture. The role of agency in the epigenesis of intelligence. In R. Sternberg and E. Grigorenko (Eds.), *Intelligence: Heredity and environment*. New York: Cambridge University Press.

Bierman, K. L., Smoot, D. L., Aumiller, K. (1993). Characteristics of aggressive-rejected, aggressive (nonrejected), and rejected (nonaggressive) boys. *Child Development, 64*, 139–151.

Bigelow, B. J., & La Gaipa, J. J. (1975). Children's written descriptions of friendship: A multi-dimensional analysis. *Developmental Psychology, 41*, 857–858.

Bigler, R. S., & Liben, L. S. (1993). A cognitive-development approach to racial stereotyping and reconstructive memory in Euro-American children. *Child Development, 64*, 1507–1518.

Bijou, S. W., & Baer, D. M. (1966). *Child development: Vol. 2. The universal stage of infancy*. New York: Appleton-Century-Crofts.

Billy, J. O. G., & Udry, J. R. (1995). The influence of male and female best friends on adolescent sexual behavior. *Adolescence, 20*, 21–32.

Binet, A., & Simon, T. (1916). *The development of intelligence in children*. Vineland, NJ: Publications of the Training School at Vineland. (Reprinted by Williams Publishing Co., Nashville, TN, 1980.)

Birnholz, J. C., & Benacerraf, B. R. (1983). The development of human fetal hearing. *Science, 222*, 516–518.

Bisanz, J. (1989). *Development of arithmetic computation and number conservation skills*. Paper presented at the annual meeting of the American Educational Research Association, San Francisco.

Bisanz, J., & Lefevre, J. (1990). Mathematical cognition: Strategic processing as interactions among sources of knowledge. In D. P. Bjorkland (Ed.), *Children's strategies: Contemporary views of cognitive development*. Hillsdale, NJ: Erlbaum.

Bisanz, J., Morrison, F. J., & Dunn, M. (1995). Effects of age and schooling on the acquisition of elementary cognitive skills. *Developmental Psychology, 31*, 221–236.

Bishop, J. H. (1989). Why the apathy in American high schools? *Educational Researcher, 18*, 6–10.

Bishop, S. M., & Ingersoll, G. M. (1989). Effects of marital conflict and family structure on the self-concepts of pre- and early adolescents. *Journal of Youth and Adolescence, 18*, 25–38.

Bishop, J. M., & Krause, J. M. (1984). Depictions of aging and old age on Saturday morning television. *The Gerontologist, 24*, 91–94.

Bittman, S. J., & Zalk, S. R. (1978). *Expectant fathers*. New York: Hawthorn Books.

Bjorklund, D. F., Schneider, W., Cassel, W. S., & Ashley, E. (1994). Training and extension of a memory strategy: Evidence for utilization deficiences in the acquisition of an organizational strategy in high- and low-IQ children. *Child Development, 65*, 951–965.

Blackman, B. A. (1987). An alternative classroom reading program for learning disabled and other low-achieving children. In W. Ellis (Ed.), *Intimacy with language: A forgotten basic in teacher education*. Baltimore: Orton Dyslexia Society.

Blake, J., & De Boysson–Bardies, B. (1992). Patterns in babbling: A cross-linguistic study. *Journal of Child Language, 19*, 51–74.

Blakemore, C., & Mitchell, D. E. (1973). Environmental modification of the visual cortex and the neural basis of learning and memory. *Nature, 241*, 467–468.

Blasi, A. (1983). Moral cognition and moral action: A theoretical perspective. *Developmental Review, 3*, 178–210.

Blass, E. M., & Ciaramitaro, V. (1994). A new look at some old mechanisms in human newborns: Taste and tactile determinants of state, affect, and action. *Monographs of the Society for Research in Child Development, 59*, (No. 1, Serial No. 239).

Blass, E. M., Ganchrow, J. R, & Steiner, J. E. (1984). Classical conditioning in newborn humans 2–48 hours of age. *Infant Behavior and Development, 7*, 223–235.

Bleichfeld, B., & Moely, B. (1984). Psychophysiological response to an infant cry: Comparison of groups of women in different phases of the maternal cycle. *Developmental Psychology, 20*, 1082–1091.

Bloch, H. A., & Niederhoffer, A. (1958). *The gang: A study in adolescent behavior.* New York: Philosophical Library.

Block, J. H., Block, J., & Gjerde, P. (1986). The personality of children prior to divorce: A prospective study. *Child Development, 57*, 827–840.

Block, J. H., Block, J., & Morrison, A. (1981). Parental agreement–disagreement on child-rearing orientations and gender-related personality correlates in children. *Child Development, 52*, 965–974.

Blomberg, S. (1980). Influences of maternal distress during pregnancy on complications in labor and delivery. *Acta Psychiatria Scandinavia, 62*, 399–404.

Bloom, L. (1973). *One word at a time: The use of single-word utterances before syntax.* The Hague: Mouton.

Bloom, L. (1991). *Language development from two to three.* New York: Cambridge University Press.

Bloom, L. (1993). *The transition from infancy to language.* New York: Cambridge University Press.

Bloom, L., Lifter, K., & Broughten, J. (1985). The convergence of early cognition and language in the second year of life: Problems in conceptualization and measurement. In M. Barrett (Ed.), *Children's single-word speech.* New York: Wiley.

Bloom, L., Tinker, E., & Margulis, C. (1993). The words children learn: Evidence against a noun bias in early vocabularies. *Cognitive Development, 8*, 431–450.

Blos, P. (1962). *On adolescence.* New York: Free Press.

Blos, P. (1972). The child analyst looks at the young adolescent. In J. Kagan & R. Coles (Eds.), *Twelve to sixteen: Early adolescence.* New York: W. W. Norton.

Blosser, B. J., & Roberts, D. F. (1985). Age differences in children's perceptions of message intent: Responses to TV news, commercials, educational spots, and public service announcements. *Communication Research, 12*, 455–484.

Boas, F. (1911). *The mind of primitive man.* New York: Macmillan.

Boer, F. (1990). *Sibling relationships in middle childhood.* Leiden: DSWO University of Leiden Press.

Bohannon, J. N., III, & Warren-Leubecker, A. (1988). Recent developments in child-directed speech: We've come a long way baby-talk. *Language Sciences, 10*, 89–110.

Bohlin, G., Hagekull, B., Germer, M., Andersson, K., & Lindberg, L. (1989). Avoidant and resistant reunion behaviors as predicted by maternal interactive behavior and infant temperament. *Infant Behavior and Development, 12*, 105–118.

Bolton, P. J. (1983). Drugs of abuse. In D. F. Hawkins (Ed.), *Drugs and pregnancy: Human teratogenesis and related problems.* Edinburgh: Churchill Livingston.

Borke, H. (1975). Piaget's mountains revisited: Changes in the egocentric landscape. *Developmental Psychology, 11*, 240–443.

Bornstein, M. H. (1976). Infants are trichomats. *Journal of Experimental Child Psychology, 21*, 425–445.

Bornstein, M. H. (1988). Perceptual development across the life cycle. In M. H. Bornstein & M. E. Lamb (Eds.), *Developmental Psychology: An advanced textbook.* Hillsdale, NJ: Erlbaum.

Bornstein, M. H. (1989). Stability in early mental development: From attention and information processing in infancy to language and cognition in childhood. In M. H. Bornstein & N. A. Krasnegor (Eds.), *Stability and continuity in mental development: Behavioral and biological perspectives.* Hillsdale, NJ: Erlbaum.

Bornstein, M. H. (1992). Perceptions across the life span. In M. H. Bornstein & M. E. Lamb (Eds.), *Developmental psychology: An advanced textbook.* Hillsdale, NJ: Erlbaum.

Bornstein, M. H., & Sigman, M. D. (1986). Continuity in mental development from infancy. *Child Development, 57*, 251–274.

Bouchard T. J., Jr. (1994). Genes, environment, and personality. *Science, 264*, 1700–1701.

Boukydis, C. F. Z., & Burgess, R. L. (1982). Adult physiological response to infant cries: Effects of temperament of infant, parental status, and gender. *Child Development, 53*, 1291–1298.

Bower, T. G. R. (1979). *Human development.* San Francisco: W. H. Freeman.

Bower, T. G. R. (1982). *Development in human infancy.* New York: W. H. Freeman.

Bowlby, J. (1969). *Attachment and loss: Vol. 1. Attachment.* New York: Basic Books.

Bowlby, J. (1973). *Attachment and loss: Vol. 2. Separation.* New York: Basic Books.

Bowlby, J. (1980). *Attachment and loss: Vol 3. Loss, sadness, and depression.* New York: Basic Books.

Boxer, A. M., Tobin-Richards, M., & Petersen, A. C. (1983). Puberty: Physical change and its significance in early adolescence. *Theory into Practice, 22*, 85–90.

Brackbill, Y. (1971). Cumulative effects of continuous stimulation on arousal level in infants. *Child Development, 42*, 17–26.

Brackbill, Y. (1979). Obstetrical medication and infant behavior. In J. D. Osofsky (Ed.), *Handbook of infant development.* New York: Wiley.

Brackbill, Y., McManus, K., & Woodward, L. (1985). *Medication in maternity: Infant exposure and maternal information.* Ann Arbor, MI: University of Michigan Press.

Bradbard, M. R., Martin, C. L., Endsley, R. C., & Halverson, C. F. (1986). Influence of sex stereotypes on children's exploration and memory: A competence versus performance distinction. *Developmental Psychology, 22*, 481–486.

Braine, M. D. S. (1963). The ontogeny of English phrase structure: The first phase. *Language, 39*, 3–13.

Brainerd, C. J. (1993). Cognitive development is abrupt (but not stagelike). *Monographs of the Society for Child Development, 58(9)*, (Serial No. 237).

Bransford, J. D. (1979). *Human cognition: Learning, understanding, and remembering.* Belmont, CA: Wadsworth.

Brazelton, T. B. (1973). *Neonatal behavior assessment scale.* London: Spastics International Medical Publications.

Brazelton, T. B. (1978). Introduction. In A. Sameroff (Ed.), Organization and stability of newborn behavior: A commentary on the Brazelton neonatal behavior assessment scale. *Monographs of the Society for Research in Child Development, 43*, (5–6, Serial No. 177).

Brazelton, T. B. (1990). Saving the bathwater. *Child Development, 61*, 1661–1671.

Brazelton, T. B., Koslowski, B., & Main, M. (1974). The origin of reciprocity: The early mother-infant interaction. In M. Lewis &

L. Rosenblum (Eds.), *The effect of the infant on its caretaker.* New York: Wiley.

Brazelton, T. B., Nugent, K. J., & Lester, B. M. (1987). Neonatal behavioral assessment scale. In J. D. Osofsky (Ed.), *Handbook of Infant Development* (2nd ed.). New York: Wiley.

Bretherton, I. (1984). Representing the social world in symbolic play: Reality and fantasy. In I. Bretherton (Ed.), *Symbolic play: The development of social understanding.* New York: Academic Press.

Bretherton, I. (1985). Attachment theory: Retrospect and prospect. *Monographs of the Society for Research in Child Development, 50* (1–2, Serial No. 209).

Bretherton, I. (1989). Pretense: The form and function of make-believe play. *Developmental Review, 9*(4), 383–401.

Bretherton, I., & Bates, E. (1985). The development of representation from 10 to 28 months: Differential stability of language and symbolic play. In R. N. Emde & R. J. Harmon (Eds.), *Continuities and discontinuities in development.* New York: Plenum Press.

Bretherton, I., Fritz, J., Zahn-Waxler, C., & Ridgeway, D. (1986). Learning to talk about emotions. *Child Development, 57,* 529–548.

Bretherton, I., & Waters, E. (Eds.). (1985). Growing points in attachment theory. *Monographs of the Society for Research in Child Development, 50* (1–2, Serial No. 209).

Brewin, C. R., Andrews, B., & Gotlib, I. H. (1993). Psychopathology and early experience: A reappraisal of retrospective reports. *Psychological Bulletin, 113,* 82–98.

Bridges, L. J., & Grolnick, W. S. (1995). The development of emotional self-regulation in infancy and early childhood. In Nancy Eisenberg (Ed.), *Social development: Review of personality and social psychology.* Thousand Oaks, CA: Sage Publications.

Brody, G. H., Stoneman, Z., & Burke, M. (1987). Child temperaments, maternal differential behavior, and sibling relationships. *Developmental Psychology, 23,* 354–362.

Brody, G. H., Stoneman, Z., McCoy, J. K., & Forehand, R. (1992). Contemporaneous and longitudal associations of sibling conflict with family relationship assessments and family discussions about sibling problems. *Child Development, 63,* 391–400.

Bronfenbrenner, U. (1970). *Two worlds of childhood: U.S. and U.S.S.R.* (with the assistance of J. Condry). New York: Russell Sage Foundation.

Bronfenbrenner, U. (1979). *The ecology of human development.* Cambridge, MA: Harvard University Press.

Bronfenbrenner, U. (1986). Ecology of the family as a context for human development: Research perspectives. *Developmental Psychology, 22,* 723–742.

Bronfenbrenner, U. (1993). The ecology of cognitive development: Research models and figuritive findings. In R. H. Wozniak & K. W. Fischer (Eds.), *Development in context: Acting and thinking in specific environments.* Hillsdale, NJ: Erlbaum.

Bronfenbrenner, U., & Ceci, S. J. (1993). Heredity, environment, and the question, "How?": A first approximation. In R. Plomin & G. McClearn (Eds.), *Nature, nurture, and psychology.* Washington, DC: American Psychological Association.

Bronfenbrenner, U., & Crouter, A. C. (1983). The evolution of environmental models in developmental research. In P. H. Mussen (Ed.), *Handbook of child psychology: History, theory, and methods* (Vol. 1). New York: Wiley.

Bronson, G. (1991). Infant differences in rate of visual encoding. *Child Development, 62,* 44–54.

Bronson, G. W. (1994). Infants' transitions toward adult-like scanning. *Child Development, 65,* 1243–1261.

Bronson, W. C. (1975). Development of behavior with age-mates during the second year of life. In M. Lewis & L. A. Rosenblum (Eds.), *The origins of behavior: Friendship and peer relations.* New York: Wiley.

Brooke, J. (1991, June 15). Cubato journal: Signs of life in Brazil's industrial valley of death. *New York Times,* Pt. 1, p. 2.

Brooks-Gunn, J. (1987). Pubertal processes and girls' psychological adaptation. In R. Lerner & T. T. Foch (Eds.), *Biological-psychosocial interactions in early adolescence: A lifespan perspective.* Hillsdale, NJ: Erlbaum.

Brooks-Gunn, J., Attie, I, Burrow, C., & Rosso, J.T. (1989). The impact of puberty on body and eating concerns in athletic and nonathletic contexts. *Journal of Early Adolescence, 9,* 269–290.

Brooks-Gunn, J., Klebanov, P. K., & Duncan, G. J. (1996). Ethnic differences in children's test scores: Role of economic deprivation, home environment and maternal characteristics. *Child Development, 67,* 396–408.

Brooks-Gunn, J., Klebanov, P. K., Liaw, F. R., & Spiker, D. (1993). Enhancing the development of low-birthweight, premature infants: Changes in cognition and behavior over the first three years. *Child Development, 64,* 736–753.

Brooks-Gunn, J., Lerner, R., & Petersen, A. (Eds.). (1991). *The encyclopedia of adolescence.* New York: Garland.

Brooks-Gunn, J., & Petersen, A. (Eds.). (1983). *Girls at puberty: Biological and psychosocial perspectives.* New York: Plenum Press.

Brooks-Gunn, J., & Reiter, E. O. (1990). The role of pubertal processes in the early adolescent transition. In S. Feldman & G. Elliot (Eds.), *At the threshold: The developing adolescent.* Cambridge, MA: Harvard University Press.

Brooks-Gunn, J., & Warren, M. P. (1985). Measuring physical status and timing in early: A developmental perspective. *Journal of Youth and Adolescence, 14,* 163–184.

Brooks-Gunn, J., Warren, M. P., Samelson, M., & Fox, R. (1986). Physical similarity and the disclosure of menarcheal status to friends: Effects of grade and pubertal status. *Journal of Early Adolescence, 6,* 3–14.

Brophy, J. E. (1983). Research on the self-fulfilling prophecy and teacher expectations. *Journal of Educational Psychology, 75,* 631–661.

Brown, A. L., Campione, J. C., Reeve, R. A., Ferrara, R. A., & Palincsar, A. S. (1992). Interactive learning and individual understanding: The case of reading and mathematics. In L. T. Landsmann (Ed.), *Culture, schooling, and psychological development.* Hillsdale, NJ: Erlbaum.

Brown, B. B. (1990). Peer groups and peer cultures. In S. S. Feldman & G. R. Elliott (Eds.), *At the threshold: The developing adolescent.* Cambridge, MA: Harvard University Press.

Brown, B. B., Clasen, D. R., & Eicher, S. A. (1986). Perception of peer pressure, peer conformity dispositions, and self reported behavior among adolescents. *Developmental Psychology, 22,* 521–530.

Brown, B. B., Mory, M. S., & Kinney, D. (1994). Casting adolescent crowds in a relational perspective: Caricature, channel, and context. In R. Montemayor, G. Adams, & T. Gullotta (Eds.), *Personal relationships in adolescence: Advances in adolescent development* (Vol. 6). Thousand Oaks, CA: Sage.

Brown, B. B., Mounts, N., Lamborn, S. D., & Steinberg, L. (1993). Parenting practices and peer group affiliation in adolescence. *Child Development, 64,* 467–482.

Brown, J. R., & Dunn, J. (1991). 'You can cry, mum': The social and developmental implications of talk about internal states. *British Journal of Developmental Psychology, 9,* 237–256.

Brown, P., & Elliot, R. (1965). Control of aggression in a nursery school class. *Journal of Experimental Child Psychology, 2,* 103–107.

Brown, R. (1973). *A first language: The early stages.* Cambridge, MA: Harvard University Press.

Brown, R., & Bellugi, U. (1964). Three processes in the child's acquisition of syntax. *Harvard Educational Review, 34,* 133–151.

Brown, R., & Hanlon, C. (1970). Derivational complexity and the order of acquisition of child speech. In J. R. Hayes (Ed.), *Cognition and the development of language.* New York: Wiley.

Brown, R., & Herrnstein, R. J. (1975). *Psychology.* Boston: Little, Brown.

Brown v. Board of Education of Topeka, Kansas (1954). 347 U.S. 483; 7455 S.Ct. 686.

Browne, Sir Thomas (1642/1964). *Religio medici.* London: Oxford University Press.

Brownell, W. A. (1928). *The development of children's number ideas in the primary grades.* Chicago: University of Chicago Press.

Bruner, J. S. (1966). On cognitive growth. In J. S. Bruner, R. R. Olver, & P. M. Greenfield (Eds.), *Studies in cognitive growth.* New York: Wiley.

Bruner, J. S. (1968). *Process of cognitive growth: Infancy.* Worcester, MA: Clark University Press.

Bruner, J. S. (1982). Formats of language acquisition. *American Journal of Semiotics, 1,* 1–16.

Bruner, J. S. (1983). *Child's talk.* New York: W. W. Norton.

Bruner, J.S. (1990). *Acts of meaning.* Cambridge, MA: Harvard University Press.

Bryant, D. M. (1994). Family and classroom correlates of Head Start children's developmental outcomes. *Early Childhood Research Quarterly, 9,* 289–309.

Bryant, P. (1993). Reading in development. In C. Pratt & A. F. Garton (Eds.), *Systems of representation in children.* Chichester, England: Wiley.

Buhrmester, D., & Furman, W. (1987). The development of companionship and intimacy. *Child development, 58,* 1101–1113.

Bullock, M. (1984). Preschool children's understandings of causal connections. *British Journal of Developmental Psychology, 2,* 139–142.

Bullock, M., & Gelman, R. (1979). Preschool children's assumptions about cause and effect: Temporal ordering. *Child Development, 50,* 89–96.

Bullock, M., & Lütkenhaus, P. (1989). The development of volitional behavior in the toddler years. *Child Development, 59,* 664–674.

Bullough, V. (1981). Age of menarche: A misunderstanding. *Science, 213,* 365–366.

Burchinal, M., Lee, M., & Ramey, C. (1989). Type of day-care and preschool intellectual development in disadvantaged children. *Child Development, 60,* 128–138.

Burk, L., & Friman, P. (1990). Epidemiologic aspects of toilet training. *Clinical Pediatrics, 29*(5), 278–282.

Burlingham, D., & Freud, A. (1942). *Young children in wartime.* London: Allen and Unwin.

Burton, R., & Whiting, J. (1961). The absent father and cross-sex identity. *Merrill-Palmer Quarterly, 7,* 85–95.

Bushnell, I. W. R. (1985). The decline of visually guided reaching. *Infant Behavior and Development, 8,* 139–155.

Bushnell, I. W. R., Sai, F., & Mullin, J. T. (1989). Neonatal recognition of the mother's face. *British Journal of Developmental Psychology, 7,* 3–15.

Buss, A. H., & Plomin, R. (1975). *A temperament theory of personality development.* New York: Wiley.

Buss, A. H. & Plomin, R. (1984). *Temperament: Early developing personality traits.* Hillsdale, NJ: Erlbaum.

Bussey, K., & Bandura, A. (1984). Gender constancy, social power and sex linked modeling. *Journal of Personality and Social Psychology, 47,* 1242–1302.

Bussey, K., & Bandura, A. (1992). Self-regulatory mechanisms governing gender development. *Child Development, 63,* 1236–1250.

Butcher, J. (1986). Longitudinal analysis of adolescent girls' aspirations at school and perceptions of popularity. *Adolescence, 21,* 133–143.

Butler, G. E., McKie, M., & Ratcliffe, S. G. (1990). The cyclical nature of prepubertal growth. *Annals of Human Biology, 17,* 177–190.

Butterworth, G., & Jarret, N. (1991). What minds have in common in space: Spatial mechanisms serving joint visual attention in infancy. *British Journal of Developmental Psychology, 9,* 55–72.

Cahan, S., & Cohen, N. (1989). Age versus schooling effects on intelligence development. *Child Development, 60,* 1239–1249.

Cairns, R. B. (1979). *Social development: The origins of interchanges.* New York: W. H. Freeman.

Cairns, R. B. (1983). The emergence of developmental psychology. In P. H. Mussen (Ed.), *Handbook of child psychology: Vol. 1. History, theory and methods.* New York: Wiley.

Cairns, R. B., & Cairns, B. D. (1994). *Lifelines and risks: Pathways of youth in our times.* Cambridge: Cambridge University Press.

Cairns, R. B., Cairns, B. D., & Neckerman, H. J. (1989). Early school dropout: Configurations and determinants. *Child Development, 60,* 1437–1452.

Calabrese, L. H., Kirkendall, D. T., Floyd, M., Rapoport, S., Williams, G. W., Weiker, G. F., & Bergfeld, J. A. (1983). Menstrual abnormalities, nutritional patterns, and body composition in female classical ballet dancers. *Physician and Sports Medicine, 11,* 86–98.

Caldera, Y. M., Huston, A. C., & O'Brien, M. (1989). Social interactions and play patterns of parents and toddlers with feminine, masculine, and neutral toys. *Child Development, 60,* 70–76.

Campbell, S. B., Cohn, J. F., & Meyers, T. (1995). Depression in first-time mothers: Mother-infant interaction and depression chronicity. Special Section: Parental depression and distress: Implications for development in infancy, childhood, and adolescence. *Developmental Psychology, 31,* 349–357.

Campos, J. J., Barret, K. C., Lamb, M. E., Goldsmith, H. H., & Stenberg, C. (1983). Socioemotional development. In P. H. Mussen (Ed.), *Handbook of child psychology: Vol 2. Infancy and developmental psychobiology.* New York: Wiley.

Campos, J. J., Benson, J., & Rudy, L. (1986). *The role of self-produced locomotion in spatial behavior.* Poster paper presented at the meeting of the International Conference for Infant Studies, Beverly Hills, CA.

Campos, J. J., Kermoian, R., & Zumbahlen, M. R. (1992). Socioemotional transformations in the family system following infant crawling onset. In N. Eisenberg & R. A. Fabes (Eds.), *Emotion and its regulation in early development.* (*New directions for child development, 55*). San Francisco: Jossey-Bass.

Campos, J. J., & Stenberg, C. R. (1981). Perception, appraisal, and emotion: The onset of social referencing. In M. E. Lamb & L. R. Sherrod (Eds.), *Infants' social cognition: Empirical and social considerations.* Hillsdale, NJ: Erlbaum.

Campos, R. G. (1989). Soothing pain-elicited distress in infants with swaddling and pacifiers. *Child Development, 60,* 781–792.

Campos, R. G. (1994). Rocking and pacifiers: Two comforting interventions for heelstick pain. *Research in Nursing and Health, 17,* 321–331.

Caplan, N., Whitmore, J. K., & Choy, M. H. (1989). *The boat people and achievement in America: A study of family life, hard work, and cultural values.* Ann Arbor: University of Michigan Press.

Capon, N., & Kuhn, D. (1979). Logical reasoning in the supermarket: Adult females' use of proportional reasoning strategy in an everyday context. *Developmental Psychology, 15,* 450–452.

Carey, S. (1978). The child as word learner. In M. Halle, J. Bresnan, & G. A. Miller (Eds.), *Linguistic theory and psychological reality.* Cambridge, MA: MIT Press.

Carey, S. (1985). *Conceptual change in childhood.* Cambridge, MA: MIT Press.

Carey, S., & Gelman, R. (Eds.). (1991). *The epigenesis of mind: Essays on biology and cognition.* Hillsdale, NJ: Erlbaum.

Carey, W. B., & McDevitt, S. C. (1995). *Coping with children's temperament: A guide for professionals.* New York: Basic Books.

Carmichael, L. (1970). Onset and early development of behavior. In P. H. Mussen (Ed.), *Carmichael's manual of child psychology: Vol. I, Part I. Infancy and early experience.* New York: Wiley.

Carnegie Commission on Policy Studies in Higher Education. (1980). *Giving youth a better chance.* San Francisco: Jossey-Bass.

Carnegie Council on Adolescent Development (1995). *Great transitions: Preparing adolescents for a new century: Concluding report of the Carnegie Council on Adolescent Development.* New York: Carnegie Corporation.

Carro, M. G., Grant, K. E., Gotlib, I. H., & Compas, B. E. (1993). Postpartum depression and child development: An investigation of mothers and fathers as sources of risk and resilience. *Developmental Psychopathology, 5,* 567–579.

Carter, D. B., & Levy, G. D. (1988). Cognitive aspects of children's early sex-role development: The influence of gender schemes on preschoolers' memories and preferences for sex-typed toys and activities. *Child Development, 59,* 782–793.

Case, R. (1991). *The mind's staircase.* Hillsdale, NJ: Erlbaum.

Case, R. (1992). The role of the frontal lobes in the regulation of cognitive development. *Brain and Cognition, 20* (1), 51–73.

Case, R. (1995). Capacity based explanations of working memory growth: A brief history and reevaluation. In F. M. Weinert & W. Schneider (Eds.), *Memory performance and comeptencies: Issues in growth and development.* Mahwah, NJ: Lawrence Erlbaum.

Case, R., Kurland, D. M., & Goldberg, J. (1982). Operational efficiency and growth of short-term memory span. *Journal of Experimental Child Psychology, 33,* 386–404.

Case, R., Marini, Z., McKeough, A., Dennis, S., & Goldberg, J. (1986). Horizontal structure in middle childhood: Cross domain parallels in the course of cognitive growth. In I. Levin (Ed.), *Stage and structure: Reopening the debate.* Norwood, NJ: Ablex Publishing Corp.

Case, R., & Okamoto, Y. (1995). The role of central conceptual structures in the development of children's thought. *Monographs of the Society for Research in Child Development, 61,* (1–2, Serial No. 246).

Caspi, A., Lynam, D., Moffitt, T. E., & Silva, P. A. (1993). Unraveling girls' delinquency: Biological, dispositional, and contextual contributions to adolescent misbehavior. *Developmental Psychology, 29,* 19–30.

Cass, V. C. (1984). Homosexual identity formation: Testing a theoretical model. *Journal of Sex Research, 20,* 143–167.

Cassidy, J., & Asher, S. R. (1992). Loneliness and peer relations in young children. *Child Development, 63,* 350–365.

Cattell, R. B. (1949). *The culture-free intelligence test.* Champaign, IL: Institute for Personality and Ability Testing.

Caudill, W., & Plath, D. (1966). Who sleeps by whom?: Parent-child involvement in urban Japanese families. *Psychiatry, 29,* 344–366.

Caughy, M. O., Di Pietro, J. A., & Strobino, D. M. (1994). Daycare participation as a protective factor in the cognitive development of young children. *Child Development, 65,* 457–471.

Cazden, C. (1965). *Environmental assistance to the child's acquisition of grammar.* Unpublished doctoral dissertation, Harvard University.

Cazden, C. (1988). *Classroom discourse: The language of teaching and learning.* Portsmouth, NH: Heinemann.

Cazden, C. B., & Michaels, S. (1985). *Gender differences in sixth grade children's letters in an electronic mail system.* Paper presented at the Boston University Child Language Conference, Boston, MA.

Ceci, S. J., & Bruck, M. (1993). The suggestibility of the child witness: A historical review and synthesis. *Psychological Bulletin, 113,* 403–439.

Ceci, S. J., & Hembrooke, H. A. (1995). A bioecological model of intellectual development. In P. Moen, G. H. Elder, Jr. & K. Luscher (Eds.), *Examining lives in context: Perspectives on the ecology of human development.* Washington, DC: American Psychological Association.

Ceci, S. J., Toglia, M. P., & Ross, D. F. (Eds.). (1987). *Children's eyewitness memory.* New York: Springer-Verlag.

Chall, J. (1983). *Stages of reading development.* New York: McGraw-Hill.

Chall, J., Jacobs, V. A., & Baldwin, L. E. (1990). *The reading crisis: Why poor children fall behind.* Cambridge, MA: Harvard University Press.

Chand, I. P., Crider, D. M., & Willits, F. K. (1975). Parent-youth disagreement as perceived by youth: A longitudinal study. *Youth and Society, 6,* 365–375.

Chandler, M. J., Fritz, A. S., & Hala, S. M. (1989). Small-scale deceit: Deception as a marker of 2-, 3-, and 4-year-olds' early theories of mind. *Child Development, 60,* 1263–1277.

Chao, R. K. (1994). Beyond parental control and authoritarian parenting style: Understanding Chinese parenting through the cultural notion of training. *Child Development, 65,* 1111–1119.

Chapman, M., & McBride, M. L. (1992). Beyond competence and performance: Children's class inclusion strategies, superordinate class cues, and verbal justifications. *Developmental Psychology, 28,* 319–327.

Chase, W. G., & Simon, H. A. (1973). Perception in chess. *Cognitive Psychology, 4,* 55–81.

Chase-Lansdale, P. L. (1994). Families and maternal employment during infancy: New linkages. In R. D. Parke & S. G. Kellam (Eds.), *Exploring family relationships with other social contexts. Family research consortium: Advances in family research.* Hillsdale, NJ: Lawrence Erlbaum Associates.

Chase-Lansdale, P. L., Brooks-Gunn, J., & Zamsky, E. S. (1994). Young African-American multigenerational families in poverty: Qualities of mothering and grandmothering. *Child Development, 65,* 394–403.

Chase-Lansdale, P. L., & Hetherington, E. M. (1990). The impact of divorce on life-span development: Short-and long-term effects. In P. B. Baltes, D. L. Featherman, & R. M. Lerner (Eds.), *Life-span development and behavior,* (Vol. 10). Hillsdale, NJ: Erlbaum.

Chen, C., & Stevenson, H. W. (1988). Cross-linguistic differences in digit span of preschool children. *Journal of Experimental Child Psychology, 46,* 150–158.

Cherlin, A. J., Furstenberg, F. F., Jr., Chase-Lansdale, P. L.,

Kiernan, K. E., Robins, P. K., Morrison, D. R., & Teitler, J. O. (1991). Longitudinal studies of the effects of divorce on children in Great Britain and the United States. *Science, 252* (5011), 1386–1389.

Chess, S., & Thomas, A. (1982). Infant bonding: Mystique and reality. *American Journal of Orthopsychiatry, 52*, 213–221.

Chi, M. T. H. (1978). Knowledge structures and memory development. In R. S. Siegler (Ed.), *Children's thinking: What develops?* Hillsdale, NJ: Erlbaum.

Chi, M. T. H., Glaser, R., & Rees, E. (1982). Expertise in problem solving. In R. J. Sternberg (Ed.), *Advances in the psychology of human intelligence* (Vol. 1). Hillsdale, NJ: Erlbaum.

Chi, M. T. H., & Klahr, D. (1975). Span and rate of apprehension in children and adults. *Journal of Experimental Child Psychology, 19*, 434–439.

Chi, M. T. H., & Koeske, R. D. (1983). Network representation of a child's dinosaur knowledge. *Developmental Psychology, 19*, 29–39.

Chodorow, N. (1974). Family structure and feminine personality. In M. Z. Rosaldo & L. Lamphere (Eds.), *Women, culture and society.* Stanford, CA: Stanford University Press.

Chomsky, C. S. (1969). *Acquisition of syntax in children from 5 to 10.* Cambridge, MA: MIT Press.

Chomsky, N. (1959). Review of *Verbal Behavior* by B. F. Skinner. *Language, 35*, 26–58.

Chomsky, N. (1965). *Aspects of a theory of syntax.* Cambridge, MA: MIT Press.

Chomsky, N. (1975). *Reflections on language.* New York: Pantheon Books.

Chomsky, N. (1980). Initial states and steady states. In M. Piatelli-Palmerini (Ed.), *Language and learning: The debate between Jean Piaget and Noam Chomsky.* Cambridge, MA: Harvard University Press.

Chomsky, N. (1986). *Knowledge of language: Its nature, origins, and use.* New York: Praeger.

Chukovsky, K. (1968). *From two to five.* Berkeley: University of California Press.

Church, R. M. (1974). Reflex Action. *The World Book Encyclopedia* (Vol. 16). Chicago: Field Enterprises.

Cianfrani, T. (1960). *A short history of obstetrics and gynecology.* Springfield, IL: Charles Thomas.

Cicchetti, D., & Carlson, V. (Eds.). (1989). *Child maltreatment: Theory and research on the causes and consequences of child abuse and neglect.* Cambridge: Cambridge University Press.

Cicchetti, D., & Garmezy, N. (1993). Prospects and promises in the study of resilience. *Development & Psychopathology, 5*, 497–502.

Cicchetti, D., & Toth, S. L. (1993). Child maltreatment research and social policy: The neglected nexus. In D. Cicchetti & S. L. Toth (Eds.), Advances in applied developmental psychology series: Vol. 8. *Child abuse, child development, and social policy.* Norwood, NJ: Ablex.

Cillessen, A. H. N., Van Ijzendoorn, H. W., Van Lieshorst, C. F. M., & Hartup, W. W. (1992). Heterogenerty among peer-rejected boys: Subtypes and stabilities. *Child Development, 63*, 893–905.

Cimons, M. (1990, June 12). Panel Calls Child Abuse A National Emergency. *Los Angeles Times*, Section A, p. 12.

Clark, E. V. (1995). Later lexical development and word formation. In P. Fletcher & B. MacWhinney (Eds.), *The handbook of child language.* Cambridge, MA.: Basil Blackwell.

Clark, J. E., & Phillips, S. J. (1993). A longitudinal study of intralimb coordination in the first year of independent walking: A dynamical systems analysis. Special section: Developmental biodynamics: Brain, body, behavior connections. *Child Development, 64*, 1143–1157.

Clark, K., & Clark, M. (1939). The development of consciousness of self and the emergence of racial identity in Negro pre-school schoolchildren. *Journal of Social Psychology, 10*, 591–599.

Clarke, A. M., & Clarke, A. D. B. (1986). Thirty years of child psychology: A selective review. *Journal of Child Psychology and Psychiatry, 27*, 719–759.

Clarke-Stewart, A. (1984). Day-care: A new context for research and development. In M. Perlmutter (Ed.), *Parent-child interaction and parent-child relations in child development: The Minnesota Symposia on Child Psychology* (Vol. 17). Hillsdale, NJ: Erlbaum.

Clarke-Stewart, A. (1989). Infant day care: Maligned or malignant? *American Psychologist, 44*, 266–273.

Clarke-Stewart, A. (1993). *Daycare* (revised ed.). Cambridge, MA: Harvard University Press.

Clarke-Stewart, A., & Fein, G. G. (1983). Early childhood programs. In P. H. Mussen (Ed.), *Handbook of child psychology: Vol. 2. Infancy and developmental psychobiology.* New York: Wiley.

Clarke-Stewart, A., & Koch, J. B. (1983). *Children: Development through adolescence.* New York: Wiley.

Clausen, J. A. (1975). The social meaning of differential physical and sexual maturation. In S. E. Dragastin & G. E. Elder, Jr. (Eds.), *Adolescence in the life cycle.* Washington, DC: Hemisphere Press.

Clifton, R. K., Muir, D. W., Ashmead, D. H., & Clarkson, M. G. (1993). Is visually guided reading in early infancy a myth? *Child Development, 64*, 1099–1110.

Cochran, M. M. (1990). Personal social networks as a focus of support. *Prevention in Human Services, 9*, 45–67.

Cognition and Technology Group at Vanderbilt (1994). From visual word problems to learning communities: Changing conceptions of cognition research. In K. McGilly, (Ed.), *Classroom lessons: Integrating cognitive theory and classroom practice.* Cambridge, MA: MIT Press/Bradford Books.

Cohn, J. F., Campbell, S. B., Matias, R., & Hopkins, J. (1990). Face-to-face interactions of postpartum depressed and nondepressed mother-infant pairs at two months. *Developmental Psychology, 26*, 15–23.

Coie, J. D., & Dodge, K. A. (1983). Continuities and changes in children's social status: A five-year longitudinal study. *Merrill-Palmer Quarterly, 29*, 261–282.

Coie, J. D., & Kupersmidt, J. B. (1983). A behavioral analysis of emerging social status in boys' groups. *Child Development, 54*, 1400–1416.

Colby, A., & Kohlberg, L. (1984). Invariant sequence and internal consistency in moral judgement stages. In W. M. Kurtines & J. L. Gewirtz (Eds.), *Morality, moral behavior, and moral development.* New York: Wiley.

Colby, A., & Kohlberg, L., (1987). *The measurement of moral judgment.* New York: Cambridge University Press.

Colby, A., Kohlberg, L., Gibbs, J., & Lieberman, M. (1983). A longitudinal study of moral development. *Monographs of the Society for Research in Child Development, 48*, (1–2, Serial No. 200).

Cole, M. (1990). Cognitive development and formal schooling. In L. C. Moll (Ed.), *Vygotsky and education: Instructional implications and applications of sociohistorical psychology.* Cambridge: Cambridge University Press.

Cole, M. (1991). Culture in cognitive development. In M. Lamb and M. Bornstein (Eds.), *Developmental psychology: An advanced textbook.* Hillsdale, NJ: Erlbaum.

Cole, M. (1996). *Cultural psychology: A once and future discipline.* Cambridge, MA: Harvard University Press.

Cole, M., & D'Andrade, R. (1982). The influence of schooling on concept formation: Some preliminary conclusions. *Quarterly Newsletter of the Laboratory of Comparative Human Cognition, 4,* 14–26.

Cole, M., Gay, J., Glick, J. A., & Sharp, D. W. (1971). *The cultural context of learning and thinking.* New York: Basic Books.

Cole, M., & Griffin, P. (1987). *Contextual factors in education.* Madison: Wisconsin Center for Education Research.

Cole, M., & Means, B. (1981). *Comparative studies of how people think.* Cambridge, MA: Harvard University Press.

Cole, M., & Scribner, S. (1974). *Culture and thought.* New York: Wiley.

Cole, S. (1980). *Working kids on working.* New York: Lothrop, Lee & Shepard.

Coleman, J. C. (1980). *The nature of adolescence.* London: Methuen.

Coleman, J. S. (1962). *The adolescent society.* Glencoe, IL: Free Press.

Coles, C. D. (1993). Saying "goodbye" to the "crack baby." *Neurotoxicology and Teratology, 15,* 290–292.

Coles, R. (1967). *Children of crisis: A study of crisis and fear.* Boston: Atlantic–Little, Brown.

Coles, R., & Stokes, G. (1985). *Sex and the American teenager.* New York: Harper & Row.

Collins, W. A. (1990). Parent-child relationships in the transition to adolescence: Continuity and change in interaction, affects, and cognition. In R. Montemayor, G. Adams, & T. Gullota (Eds.), *Advances in adolescent development* (Vol. 2). Beverly Hills: Sage.

Collins, W. A., Harris, M. L., & Susman, A. (1995). Parenting during middle childhood. In M. H. Bornstein (Ed.), *Handbook of Parenting.* Hillsdale, NJ: Erlbaum.

Comstock, G., & Paik, H. (1991). *Television and the American child.* New York: Academic Press.

Condon, R. G. (1987). *Inuit youth.* New Brunswick, NJ: Rutgers University Press.

Condry, S. (1983). History and background of preschool intervention programs and the Consortium for Longitudinal Studies. In the Consortium for Longitudinal Studies (Ed.), *As the twig is bent . . .: Lasting effects of preschool programs.* Hillsdale, NJ: Erlbaum.

Conel, J. L. (1939/1967). *The postnatal development of the human cerebral cortex* (8 vols.). Cambridge, MA: Harvard University Press.

Congressional Research Service (1983, June). *Infant mortality.* Washington, DC: U.S. Government Printing Office.

Connolly, K., & Dalgleish, M. (1989). The emergence of a tool-using skill in infancy. *Developmental Psychology, 25,* 539–549.

Connor, J. M., & Ferguson-Smith, M. A. (1991). *Essential medical genetics* (3rd ed.). London: Blackwell Scientific Publications.

Conrad, M., & Hammen, C. (1993). Protective and resource factors in high- and low-risk children: A comparison of children with unipolar, bipolar, medically ill, and normal mothers. *Developmental Psychology, 5,* 593–607.

Consortium for Longitudinal Studies (1983). *As the twig is bent . . .: Lasting effects of preschool programs.* Hillsdale, NJ: Erlbaum.

Cooper, R. P., & Aslin, R. N. (1990). Preference for infant-directed speech in the first month after birth. *Child Development, 61,* 1584–1595.

Coopersmith, S. (1967). *The antecedents of self-esteem.* New York: W. H. Freeman.

Corbin, P. F., & Bickford, R. G. (1955). Studies of the electroencephalogram of normal children. *Electroencephalography and Clinical Neurology, 7,* 15–28.

Cornell, E. H., Heth, C. D., & Broda, L. S. (1989). Children's wayfinding: Response to instructions to use environmental landmarks. *Developmental Psychology, 25,* 755–764.

Cornell, E. H., Heth, C. D., & Rowat, W. L. (1992). Wayfinding by children and adults: Response to instructions to use look-back and retrace strategies. *Developmental Psychology, 28,* 328–336.

Cornell, E. H., & McDonnell, P. M. (1986). Infants' acuity at twenty feet. *Investigative Ophthalmology and Visual Science, 27,* 1417–1420.

Corsaro, W. A. (1981). Friendship in the nursery school: Social organization in a peer environment. In S. R. Asher & J. M. Gottman (Eds.), *The development of children's friendships.* Cambridge: Cambridge University Press.

Corsaro, W. A. (1985). *Friendship and peer culture in the early years.* Norwood, NJ: Ablex.

Cost, Quality, & Child Outcomes Study Team (1995). *Cost, quality, and child outcomes in child care centers, executive summary* (2nd ed.). Denver: Economics Department, University of Colorado at Denver.

Cousins, S. D. (1989). Culture and selfhood in Japan and the United States. *Journal of Personality and Social Research, 56,* 124–131.

Cowan, W. M. (1979). The development of the brain. *Scientific American, 241,* 112–133.

Cox, M. J., Owen, M. T., Henderson, V. K., & Margand, N. A. (1992). Prediction of infant-father and infant-mother attachment. *Developmental Psychology, 28,* 474–483.

Coy, M. (1989). *Apprenticeship: From theory to method and back again.* Albany, NY: SUNY Press.

Crago, M., & Crago, H. (1983). *Prelude to literacy.* Carbondale: Southern Illinois University Press.

Cratty, B. J. (1970). *Perceptual and motor development in infants and children.* New York: Macmillan.

Cravioto, J., De Licardie, E. R., & Birch, H. G. (1966). Nutrition, growth and neurointegrative development: An experimental and ecological study. *Pediatrics, 38,* 319–372.

Crick, N. R., & Dodge, K. A. (1994). A review and reformulation of social information-processing mechanisms in children's social adjustment. *Psychological Bulletin, 115,* 74–101.

Crick, N. R., & Grotpeter, N. (1995). Relational aggression, gender and social psychological adjustment. *Child Development, 66,* 710–722.

Crick, N. R., & Ladd, G. W. (1993). Children's perceptions of their peer experiences: Attributions, loneliness, social anxiety and social avoidance. *Developmental Psychology, 29,* 244–254.

Crnic, K. A., Ragozin, A. S., Greenberg, M. T., Robinson, N. M., & Basham, R. R. (1983). Social interaction and developmental compliance of preterm and full-term infants during first year of life. *Child Development, 54,* 1199–1210.

Crockenberg, S. (1987). Support for adolescent mothers during the postnatal period. In C. Boukydis (Ed.), *Research on support for parents and infants in the postnatal period.* Norwood, NJ: Ablex Publishing Corp.

Crockenberg, S., & Litman, C. (1991). Effects of maternal employment on maternal and two-year-old child behavior. *Child Development, 62,* 930–953.

Cronbach, L. J. (1975). Beyond the two disciplines of scientific psychology. *American Psychologist, 30,* 116–127.

Crook, C. (1994). *Computers and the collaborative experience of learning.* London: Routledge.

Cross, W. E., Jr. (1978). The Thomas and Cross models of psychological nigrescence: A review. *Journal of Black psychology, 5,* 13–31.

Cross, W. E., Jr. (1991). *Shades of black: Diversity in African-American identity.* Philadelphia: Temple University Press.

Cross, W. E., Jr. (1995). In search of Blackness and Afrocentricity: the psychology of Black identity change. In H. W. Harris, H. C. Blue, & E. H. Griffith (Eds.), *Racial and ethnic identity.* New York: Routledge.

Crouter, A. (1994). Processes linking families and work: Implications for behavior and development in both settings. In R. D. Parke & S. G. Killam (Eds.), *Exploring family relationships with other social contexts.* Hillsdale, NJ: Erlbaum.

Crowder, R. G., & Wagner, R. K. (1992). *The psychology of reading* (2nd ed.). New York: Oxford University Press.

Crowell, D. H., Evans, I. M., & O'Donnell, C. R. (Eds.). (1987). *Childhood aggression and violence: Sources of influence, prevention, and control.* New York, Plenum.

Csikszentmihalyi, M., & Larson, R. (1984). *Being adolescent: Conflict and growth in the teenage years.* New York: Basic Books.

Currie, J. & Thomas, D. (February, 1994). *Does Head Start make a difference? Labor and Population Program Working Paper Series 94-05.* Santa Monica, Ca.: Rand Corp.

Curtis, H. (1979). *Biology.* New York: Worth.

Curtiss, S. (1977). *Genie: A psychological study of a modern-day wild child.* New York: Academic Press.

Cytryn, L., McKnew, D. H., Zahn-Waxler, C., & Gershon, E. S. (1986). Developmental issues in risk research: The offspring of affectively ill parents. In Michael Rutter, Carroll E. Izard, & Peter B. Read (Eds.), *Depression in young people: Developmental and Clinical Perspectives.* New York: The Guilford Press.

D'Amico, R. (1984). Does employment during high school impair academic progress? *Sociology of Education, 57,* 152–164.

D'Andrade, R. G. (1974). Memory and assessment of behavior. In H. M. Blalock, Jr. (Ed.), *Measurement in the social sciences.* Chicago: Aldine.

Damon, W. (1975). Early conceptions of positive justice as related to the development of logical operations. *Child Development, 46,* 301–312.

Damon, W. (1977). *The social world of the child.* San Francisco: Jossey-Bass.

Damon, W. (1980). Patterns of change in children's social reasoning: A two-year longitudinal study. *Child Development, 51,* 1010–1017.

Damon, W. (1983). *Social and personality development: Infancy through adolescence.* New York: W. W. Norton.

Damon, W., & Hart, D. (1988). *Self-understanding in childhood and adolescence.* Cambridge: Cambridge University Press.

Daniels-Beirness, T. (1989). Measuring peer status in boys and girls: A problem of apples and oranges. In B. H. Schneider, G. Attili, J. Nadel, & R. P. Weissberg, (Eds.), (1989). *Social competence in developmental perspective.* Boston: Kluwer Academic Publishers.

Dannemiller, J. L., & Stephens, B. K. (1988). A critical test of infant pattern preference models. *Child Development, 59,* 210–216.

Danzinger, K. (1990). *Constructing the subject.* Cambridge: Cambridge University Press.

Darwin, C. (1859/1958). *The origin of species.* New York: Penguin.

Darwin, C. (1877). A biographical sketch of an infant. *Mind, 2,* 285–294.

Dasen, P. R. (1972). Cross-cultural Piagetian research: A summary. *Journal of Cross-Cultural Psychology, 3,* 29–39.

Dasen, P. R. (1977a). Are cognitive processes universal? A contribution to cross-cultural Piagetian psychology. In N. Warren (Ed.), *Studies in cross-cultural psychology* (Vol. 1). London: Academic Press.

Dasen, P. R. (1977b). *Piagetian psychology: Cross cultural contributions.* New York: Gardner.

Dasen, P. R. (1982). Cross-cultural data on operational development: Asymptotic development curves. In T. G. Bever (Ed.), *Regressions in Development.* Hillsdale, NJ: Erlbaum.

Dasen, P. R., & Heron, A. (1981). Cross-cultural tests of Piaget's theory. In H. Triandis & A. Heron (Eds.), *Handbook of cross-cultural psychology: Vol. 4. Developmental psychology.* Boston: Allyn and Bacon.

Dasen, P. R., Ngini, L., & Lavallée, M. (1979). Cross-cultural training studies of concrete operations. In L. H. Eckenberger, W. J. Lonner, & Y. H. Poortinga (Eds.), *Cross-cultural contributions to psychology.* Amsterdam: Swets & Zeilinger.

David, H. P. (1981). Unwantedness: Longitudinal studies of Prague children born to women twice denied abortions for the same pregnancy and matched controls. In P. Ahmed (Ed.), *Pregnancy, childbirth, and parenthood.* New York: Elsevier.

David, H. P., Dytrych, Z., Matejcek, Z., & Schuller, V. (1988). *Born unwanted: Developmental effects of denied abortion.* Prague: Avicenum, Czechoslovak Medical Press.

Davies, K. E. (1989). *The fragile X syndrome.* Oxford: Oxford University Press.

Davis, A. (1948). *Social class differences in learning.* Cambridge, MA: Harvard University Press.

Dawson, G., & Fischer, K. W. (1994). *Human behavior and the developing brain.* New York: Guilford Press.

Decarie, T. G. (1969). A study of the mental and emotional development of the thalidomide child. In B. M. Foss (Ed.), *Determinants of infant behavior* (Vol. 4). London: Methuen.

De Casper, A. J., & Fifer, W. P. (1980). Of human bonding: Newborns prefer their mother's voices. *Science, 208,* 1174–1176.

De Casper, A. J., Lecanuet, J. P., Busnel, M. C., Granier-Deferre, C., & Maugeais, R. (1994). Fetal reactions to recurrent maternal speech. *Infant Behavior and Development, 17,* 159–164.

De Casper, A. J., & Sigafoos, A. D. (1983). The intrauterine heartbeat: A potent reinforcer for newborns. *Infant Behavior and Development, 6,* 19–25.

De Casper, A. J., & Spence, M. J. (1986). Prenatal maternal speech influences newborn's perception of speech sounds. *Infant Behavior and Development, 9,* 133–150.

De Chateau, P. (1987). Parent-infant socialization in several Western European countries. In J. D. Osofsky (Ed.), *The handbook of infant development* (2nd ed.). New York: Wiley.

De Fleur, L., & Menke, B. (1975). Learning about the labor force: Occupational knowledge among high school males. *Sociology of Education, 48,* 324–345.

De Fries, J. C., Plomin, R., & Fulker, D. W. (Eds.). (1994). *Nature and nurture during middle childhood.* Cambridge, MA: Blackwell.

De Loache, J. S. (1984). What's this? Maternal questions in joint picture book reading with toddlers. *Quarterly Newsletter of the Laboratory of Comparative Human Cognition, 6,* 87–95.

De Loache, J. S. (1987). Rapid change in the symbolic functioning of very young children. *Science, 238,* 1556–1557.

De Loache, J. S. (1995). Early symbolic reasoning. In D. Medin (Ed.), *The Psychology Of Learning and Motivation.* (Vol. 32.) New York: Academic Press.

De Loache, J. S., Cassidy, D. J., & Brown, A. L. (1985). Precursors of mnemonic strategies in young children. *Child Development, 56*, 125–137.

Demetriou, A., Shayer, M., & Efklides, A. (1992). *Neo-Piagetian theories of cognitive development.* London: Routledge.

Demos, J., & Demos, V. (1969). Adolescence in historical perspective. *Journal of Marriage and the Family, 31*, 632–638.

Dennis, M., Sugar, J., & Whitaker, H. A. (1982). The acquisition of tag questions. *Child Development, 53*, 1254–1257.

Dennis, W. (1973). *Children of the creche.* New York: Appleton-Century-Crofts.

Dennis, W., & Dennis, M. (1940). The effect of cradling practices upon the onset of walking in Hopi children. *Journal of Genetic Psychology, 56*, 77–86.

Dent, H. R. (1982). The effects of interviewing strategies on the results of interviews with child witnesses. In A. Trankell (Ed.), *Reconstructing the past.* Deventer, the Netherlands: Kluwer.

De Rosier, M. E., Kupersmidt, J. B., & Patterson, C. J. (1994). Children's academic and behavioral adjustments as a function of the chronicity and proximity of peer rejections. *Child Development, 65*, 1799–1813.

De Villiers, J. G., & De Villiers, P. A. (1978). *Language acquisition.* Cambridge, MA: Harvard University Press.

De Villiers, J. G., & De Villiers, P. A. (1979). *Early language.* Cambridge, MA: Harvard University Press.

De Vries, J. I. P. (1992). The first Trimester. In J. G. Nijhuis (Ed.), *Fetal behavior: Developmental and perinatal aspects.* New York: Oxford University Press.

De Vries, M. W. (1987). Cry babies, culture, and catastrophe: Infant temperament among the Masai. In N. Scheper-Hughes (Ed.), *Child survival: Anthropological approaches to the treatment and maltreatment of children.* Boston: Reidel.

De Vries, M. W., & De Vries, M. R. (1977). The cultural relativity of toilet training readiness: A perspective from East Africa. *Pediatrics, 60* (2), 170–177.

De Vries, R. (1969). Constancy of genetic identity in the years three to six. *Monographs of the Society for Research in Child Development, 34*, (Serial No. 127).

Diamond, A. (1985). Development of the ability to use recall to guide action, as indicated by infants' performance on AB. *Child Development, 56*, 868–883.

Diamond, A. (1990a). Introduction. *Annals of the New York Academy of Sciences, 608*, xiiii–lvi.

Diamond, A. (Ed.). (1990b). The development and neural basis of higher cognitive functions. *Annals of the New York Academy of Sciences, 608*, 267–317.

Diamond, A. (1991). Frontal lobe involvement in cognitive changes during the first year of life. In K. Gibson, M. Konner, & A. Patterson (Eds.), *Brain and behavioral development.* Hillsdale, NJ: Erlbaum.

Diamond, A. (1995). Evidence of robust recognition memory early in life even when assessed by reaching behavior. Special issue: Early memory. *Journal of Experimental Child Psychology, 59*, 419–456.

Diamond, A., Cruttenden, L., & Neiderman, L. (1994). AB with multiple wells: 1. Why are multiple wells sometimes easier than two wells? 2. Memory or memory and inhibition. *Developmental Psychology, 30*, 195–205.

Dias, M. G. (1988). A comprensao de siligismos em criancas. (The understanding of syllogisms in children.) *Psicologia: Teoria e Pesquisa, 4*, 156–159.

Dias, M. G., & Harris, P. L. (1988). The effect of make-believe play on deductive reasoning. *British Journal of Developmental Psychology, 6* (3), 207–221.

Dias, M. G., & Harris, P. L. (1990). The influence of the imagination on reasoning by young children. *British Journal of Developmental Psychology, 8*, 305–318.

Dickson, P. (Ed.). (1981). *Children's oral communication skills.* New York: Academic Press.

Dienes, Z. P. (1966). *Mathematics in the primary school.* London: Macmillan.

Dietz, W. H., & Gortmacher, S. L. (1985). Do we fatten our children at the television set?: Obesity and television viewing in children and adolescents. *Pediatrics, 75*, 807–812.

Dillard, A. (1987). *An American childhood.* New York: Harper & Row.

Dishion, T. J. (1990). The family ecology of boys' peer relations in middle childhood. *Child Development, 61*, 874–892.

Dishion, T. J., Duncan, T. E., Eddy, M. J., Fagot, B. I., & Fetrow, R. (1994). The world of parents and peers: Coercive exchanges and children's social adaption. *Social Development, 3*, 255–268.

Dix, T., Ruble, D. N., & Zambarano, R. J. (1989). Mothers' implicit theories of discipline: Child effects, parent effects, and the attribution process. *Child Development, 60*, 1373–1391.

Dodge, K. A. (1983). Behavioral antecedents of peer social status. *Child Development, 54*, 1386–1399.

Dodge, K. A. (1990). Developmental psychopathology in children of depressed mothers. *Developmental Psychology, 26*, 3–6.

Dodge, K. A. (1994). Studying mechanisms in the cycle of violence. In C. Thompson & P. Cowas (Eds.), *Violence: Basic and clinical science.* Oxford: Butterworth-Hernemas.

Dodge, K. A., & Feldman, E. (1990). Issues in social cognition and sociometric status. In S. R. Asher & J. D. Coie (Eds.), *Peer rejection in childhood.* Cambridge: Cambridge University Press.

Dodge, K. A., Pettit, G. S., McClaskey, C. L., & Brown, M. M. (1986). Social competence in children. *Monographs of the Society for Research in Child Development, 51*, (2, Serial No. 213).

Dolhinow, P. (Ed.). (1972). *Primate patterns: Studies in Adaptation and Variability.* New York: Holt, Rinehart and Winston.

Donald, M. (1991). *Origins of the modern mind: Three stages in the evolution of culture and cognition.* Cambridge, MA: Harvard University Press.

Donaldson, M. (1978). *Children's minds.* New York: W. W. Norton.

Dore, J. (1978). Conditions for acquisition of speech acts. In I. Markova (Ed.), *The social concept of language.* New York: Wiley.

Dore, J. (1979). Conversational acts and the acquisition of language. In E. Ochs & B. B. Schieffelin (Eds.), *Developmental Pragmatics.* New York: Academic Press.

Dore, J., Gearhart, M., & Newman, D. (1979). The structure of nursery school conversation. In K. E. Nelson (Ed.), *Children's language* (Vol. 1). Hillsdale, NJ: Erlbaum.

Dornbusch, S. M., Ritter, P. L., Leiderman, P. H., Roberts, D. F., & Fraleigh, M. J. (1987). The relation of parenting style to adolescent school performance. *Child Development, 58*, 1244–1257.

Dorr, A. (1983). No shortcuts to judging reality. In P. E. Bryant & S. Anderson (Eds.), *Watching and understanding TV: Research on children's attention and comprehension.* New York: Academic Press.

Dorr, A., Graves, S. B., & Phelps, E. (1980). Television literacy for young children. *Journal of Communication, 30*, 71–83.

Dorsch, A., & Keane, S. P. (1994). Contextual factors in children's social information processing. *Developmental Psychology, 30*, 611–616.

Dott, A., Fort, B., & Arthur, T. (1975a). The effects of maternal demographic factors on infant mortality rates: Summary of the findings of the Louisiana Infant Mortality Study: Part 1. *American Journal of Obstetrics and Gynecology, 123,* 847–853.

Dott, A., Fort, B., & Arthur, T. (1975b). The effects of availability and utilization of prenatal care and hospital services on infant mortality rates: Summary of the findings of the Louisiana Infant Mortality Study: Part 2. *American Journal of Obstetrics and Gynecology, 123,* 854–860.

Douvan, E., & Adelson, J. (1966). *The adolescent experience.* New York: Wiley.

Duncan, G. J., Brooks-Gunn, J., & Klebanov, P. K. (1994). Economic deprivation and early childhood development. Special issue: Children and poverty. *Child Development, 65,* 296–318.

Duncan, P. D., Ritter, P. L., Dornbusch, S. M., Gross; R. T., & Carlsmith, J. M. (1985). The effects of pubertal timing on body image, school behavior, and deviance. *Journal of Youth and Adolescence, 14,* 227–235.

Dunn, J. (1977). *Distress and comfort.* Cambridge, MA: Harvard University Press.

Dunn, J. (1984). *Sisters and brothers.* Cambridge, MA: Harvard University Press.

Dunn, J. (1988). *The beginnings of social understanding.* Cambridge, MA: Harvard University Press.

Dunn, J., & Kendrick, C. (1979). Young siblings in the context of family relationships. In M. Lewis & L. A. Rosenblum (Eds.), *The child and its family.* New York: Plenum Press.

Dunn, J., & McGuire, S. (1992). Sibling and peer relationships in childhood. *Journal of Child Psychology and Psychiatry and Allied Disciplines, 33* (1), 67–105.

Dunn, J., & McGuire, S. (1994). Young children's nonshared experience: A summary of studies in Cambridge and Colorado. In E. Mavis Hethrington, David Reiss, & Robert Plomin (Eds.), *Separate social worlds of siblings: The impact of nonshared environment on development.* Hillsdale, NJ: Lawrence Erlbaum Associates.

Dunn, J., & Plomin, R. (1990). *Separate lives: Why siblings are so different.* New York: Basic Books.

Dunn, J., & Shatz, M. (1989). Becoming a conversationalist despite (or because of) having a sibling. *Child Development, 60,* 399–410.

Dunphy, D. C. (1963). The social structure of urban adolescent peer groups. *Sociometry, 26,* 230–246.

Durrett, M. E., Otaki, M., & Richards, P. (1984). Attachment and mothers' perception of support from the father. *Journal of the International Society for the Study of Behavioral Development, 7,* 167–176.

Dweck, C. S., & Bush, E. S. (1976). Sex differences in learned helplessness: I. Differential debilitation with peer and adult evaluators. *Developmental Psychology, 12,* 147–156.

Dweck, C. S., Davidson, W., Nelson, S., & Enna, B. (1978). Sex differences in learned helplessness: II. The contingencies of evaluative feedback in the classroom. III. An experimental analysis, *Developmental Psychology, 14,* 268–276.

Dweck, C. S., & Elliott, E. S. (1983). Achievement motivation. In P. H. Mussen (Ed.), *Handbook of child psychology: Vol. 4. Personality and social development.* New York: Wiley.

Dweck, C. S., & Goetz, T. E. (1978). Attributions and learned helplessness. In J. H. Harvey, W. Ickles, & R. F. Kidd (Eds.), *New directions in attribution research* (Vol. 2). Hillsdale, NJ: Erlbaum.

Easterbrooks, M. A., & Goldberg, W. A. (1985). Effects of early maternal employment on todders, mothers, and fathers. *Developmental Psychology, 21,* 774–783.

Eaton, W. O. (1994). Methodological implications of the impending engagement of temperament and biology. In J. E. Bates & T. D. Wachs (Eds.), Temperament: *Individual differences at the interface of biology and behavior.* Washington, DC: American Psychological Association.

Eaton, W. O., & Yu, A. P. (1989). Are sex differences in child motor activity level a function of sex differences in maturational status? *Child Development, 60,* 1005–1011.

Eckenrode, J., Laird, M., & Doris, J. (1993). School performance and disciplining problems among abused and neglected children. *Developmental Psychology, 29,* 53–62.

Eckerman, C. D., Sturm, L. A., & Gross, S. J. (1985). Different developmental courses for very-low-birth-weight infants differing in early head growth. *Developmental Psychology, 21,* 813–827.

Edelstein, W., Keller, M., & Wahlen, K. (1984). Structure and content in social cognition: Conceptual and empirical analysis. *Child Development, 55,* 1514–1526.

Eder, D., & Hallinan, M. T. (1978). Sex differences in children's friendships. *American Sociological Review, 43,* 237–250.

Eder, R. A. (1989). The emergent personologist: The structure and content of 3½-, 5½-, and 7½-year-olds' concepts of themselves and other persons. *Child Development, 60,* 1218–1228.

Educational Testing Service. National Assessment of Educational Progress (1988). *The mathematics report card: Are we measuring up?* Princeton, NJ: Educational Testing Service.

Edwards, C. P. (1982). Moral development in comparative cultural perspective. In D. Wagner & H. Stevenson (Eds.), *Cultural perspectives on child development.* New York: W. H. Freeman.

Egeland, B. R., Carlson, E., & Sroufe, L. A. (1993). Resilience as process. Special Issue: Milestones in the development of resilience. *Development & Psychopathology, 5,* 517–528.

Egeland, B. R., & Hiester, M. (1995). The long-term consequences of infant day-care and mother-infant attachment. *Child Development, 66,* 474–485.

Egeland, B. R., & Sroufe, L. A. (1981). Attachment and early maltreatment. *Child Development, 52,* 44–52.

Eibl-Eibesfeldt, I. (1970). *Ethology: The biology of behavior.* New York: Holt, Rinehart and Winston.

Eichorn, D. H. (1979). Physical development: Current foci of research. In J. Osofsky (Ed.), *The handbook of infant development.* New York: Wiley.

Eimas, P. D. (1985). The perception of speech in early infancy. *Scientific American, 204,* 66–72.

Eimas, P. D., & Quinn, P. C. (1994). Studies on the formation of perceptually base-level categories in young infants. *Child Development, 65,* 903–917.

Eisen, M., Zellman, G. I., Leibowitz, A., Chow, W. K., & Evans, J. R. (1983). Factors discriminating pregnancy resolution decisions of unmarried adolescents. *Genetic Psychology Monographs, 108,* 69–95.

Eisenberg, N. (1992). *The caring child.* Cambridge, MA: Harvard University Press.

Eisenberg, N., Fabes, R. A., Bernzweig, J., Karbon, M., Poulin, R., & Hanish, L. (1993). The relation of emotionality and regulation to preschoolers' social skills and sociometric status. *Child Development, 64,* 1418–1438.

Ekman, P. (1984). Expression and the nature of emotion. In P. Ekman & K. Scherer (Eds.), *Approaches to emotion.* Hillsdale, NJ: Erlbaum.

Ekman, P. (1994). Strong evidence for universal emotions in facial expressions: A reply to Russell's mistaken critique. *Psychological Bulletin, 115,* 268–287.

Eldredge, N., & Gould, S. J. (1972). Punctuated equilibria: An alternative to phyletic gradualism. In T. J. M. Schopf (Ed.), *Models in paleobiology.* New York: W. H. Freeman.

Eliot, T. S. (1971a). East Coker. In *The complete poems and plays: 1909 to 1950.* Orlando, FL: Harcourt Brace Jovanovich.

Eliot, T. S. (1971b). Little Gidding. In *The complete poems and plays: 1909 to 1950.* Orlando, FL: Harcourt Brace Jovanovich.

Elkind, D. (1978). *The child's reality: Three developmental themes.* Hillsdale, NJ: Erlbaum.

Ellis, S., Rogoff, B., & Cromer, C. (1981). Age segregation in children's interactions. *Developmental Psychology, 17,* 399–407.

Emde, R. N. (1992). Individual meaning and increasing complexity: Contributions of Sigmund Freud and René Spitz to developmental psychology. *Developmental Psychology, 28,* 347–359.

Emde, R. N., Gaensbauer, T. J., & Harmon, R. J. (1976). Emotional expression in infancy: *A behavioral study. Psychological Issues Monograph Series, 10,* (1, Serial No. 37).

Emde, R. N., & Harmon, R. J. (1972). Endogenous and exogenous smiling systems in early infancy. *Journal of the American Academy of Child Psychiatry, 11,* 77–100.

Emde, R. N., & Robinson, J. (1979). The first two months: Recent research in developmental psychobiology and the changing view of the newborn. In J. Noshpitz & J. Call (Eds.), *Basic handbook of child psychiatry.* New York: Basic Books.

Emmorey, K. (1995). Processing the dynamic visual-spatial morphology of signed languages. In L. B. Feldman (Ed.), *Morphological aspects of language processing.* Hillsdale, NJ: Lawrence Erlbaum Associates.

Engel, G. L., Reichsman, F., Harway, V. T., & Hess, D. W. (1985). Monica: Infant feeding behavior of a mother gastric fistula-fed as an infant. A 30-year longitudinal study of enduring effects. In E. J. Anthony & G. H. Pollock (Eds.), *Parental influences: In health and disease.* Boston: Little, Brown.

Engen, T., Lipsitt, L. P., & Kaye, H. (1963). Olfactory responses and adaptation in the human neonate. *Journal of Comparative and Physiological Psychology, 56,* 73–77.

Epstein, J. L. (1989). The selection of friends: Changes across the grades and in different school environments. In T. J. Berndt & G. W. Ladd (Eds.), *Peer relations in child development.* New York: Wiley.

Epstein, L. H., McCurley, J., Wing, R. R., & Valoski, A. (1990). A five-year follow-up of family-based behavioral treatments for childhood obesity. *Journal of Consulting and Clinical Psychology, 58,* 661–664.

Epstein, L. H., Valoski, A., & McCurley, J. (1993). Compliance and long-term follow-up for childhood obesity: Retrospective analysis. In N. A. Krasnegor, L. H. Epstein, S. B. Johnson, & S. J. Yaffe (Eds.), *Developmental aspects of health compliance behavior.* Hillsdale, NJ: Lawrence Erlbaum Associates.

Erikson, E. H. (1958). *Young man Luther.* New York: W. W. Norton.

Erikson, E. H. (1963). *Childhood and society* (2nd ed.). New York: W. W. Norton.

Erikson, E. H. (1968a). *Identity: Youth and crisis.* New York: W. W. Norton.

Erikson, E. H. (1968b). Life cycle. In D. L. Sills (Ed.), *International encyclopedia of the social sciences* (Vol. 9). New York: Crowell, Collier.

Erikson, E. H. (1969). *Gandhi's truth.* New York: W. W. Norton.

Erikson, M. F., Sroufe, L. A., & Egeland, B. (1985). The relationship between the quality of attachment and behavior problems in preschool in a high-risk sample. *Monographs of the Society for Research in Child Development, 50,* (1–2, Serial No. 209).

Eron, L. D., Gentry, J., & Schlegal, P. (Eds.), (1995). *Reason to hope: A psychological perspective on violence and youth.* Washington, DC: American Psychological Association.

Eron, L., Walder, L., & Lefkowitz, M. (1971). *Learning of aggression in children.* Boston: Little, Brown.

Etzel, B. C., & Gewirtz, J. L. (1967). Experimental modification of caregiver maintained high-rate operant crying in a 6-week- and a 20-week-old infant (Infant tyranno-tearus): Extinction of crying with reinforcement of eye contact and smiling. *Journal of Experimental Child Psychology, 5,* 303–317.

Eveleth, P. B., & Tanner, J. M. (1990). *Worldwide variation in human growth,* (2nd ed.). Cambridge: Cambridge University Press.

Eyer, D. E. (1992). *Mother-infant bonding: A scientific fiction.* New Haven, CT: Yale University Press.

Fabes, R. A., & Eisenberg, N. (1992). Young children's coping with interpersonal anger. *Child Development, 52,* 1119–1134.

Fabes, R. A., Eisenberg, N., Nyman, M., & Michaelieu, Q. (1991). Young children's approaches of other's spontaneous emotional reactions. *Developmental Psychology, 27,* 858–866.

Fabricus, W. V., & Hagen, J. W. (1984). Use of casual attributions about recall performance to assess metamemory and predict strategic memory behavior in young children. *Developmental Psychology, 20,* 975–987.

Fagot, B. I. (1978). Reinforcing contingencies for sex role behaviors: Effect of experience with children. *Child Development, 49,* 30–36.

Fagot, B. I., & Hagen, R. (1991). Observations of parent reactions to sex-stereotyped behaviors: Age and sex effects. *Child Development, 62,* 617–628.

Fagot, B. I., & Leinbach, M. D. (1993). Gender-role development in young children: From discrimination to labelling. *Developmental Review, 13,* 205–224.

Fagot, B. I., Leinbach, M. D., & Hagen, R. (1986). Gender labeling and adoption of sex-typed behaviors. *Developmental Psychology, 22,* 440–443.

Fagot, B. I., Leinbach, M. D., & O'Boyle C. (1992). Gender labelling, gender stereotyping, & parenting behaviors. *Developmental Psychology, 28,* 225–230.

Fant, L. (1972). *Ameslan.* Silver Springs, MD: National Association for the Deaf.

Fantz, R. L. (1961). The origins of form perception. *Scientific American, 204,* 66–72.

Fantz, R. L. (1963). Pattern vision in newborn infants. *Science, 140,* 296–297.

Fantz, R. L., Ordy, J. M., & Udelf, M. S. (1962). Maturation of pattern vision in infants during the first six months. *Journal of Comparative and Physiological Psychology, 55,* 907–917.

Farnham-Diggory, S. (1992). *The Learning Disabled Child.* Cambridge, MA: Harvard University Press.

Farrar, M. J. (1992). Negative evidence and grammatical morpheme acquisition. *Developmental Psychology, 28,* 90–98.

Farver, J. M., & Branstetter, W. H. (1994). Preschoolers' prosocial responses to their peers' distress. *Developmental Psychology, 30,* 334–341.

Farver, J. M., & Wimbarti, S. (1995). Indonesian children's play with their mothers and older siblings. *Child Development, 66,* 1493–1503.

Faust, M. S. (1983). Alternative constructions of adolescent growth. In J. Brooks-Gunn & A. C. Petersen (Eds.), *Girls at puberty: Biological and psychological perspectives.* New York: Plenum.

Feldman, D. H. (1994). *Beyond universal in cognitive development* (2nd ed.). Norwood, NJ: Ablex.

Feldman, H., Goldin-Meadow, S., & Gleitman, L. (1978). Beyond

Herodotus: The creation of language by linguistically deprived, deaf children. In A. Lock (Ed.), *Action, symbol, and gesture: The emergence of language.* New York: Academic Press.

Feldman, S. S., & Elliott, G. R. (Eds.). (1990). *At the threshold: The developing adolescent.* Cambridge, MA: Harvard University Press.

Fendrich, M., Warner, V., & Weissman, M. M. (1990). Family risk factors, parental depression, and psychopathology in offspring. *Developmental Psychology, 26,* 40–50.

Fenson, L., Dale, P. S., Reznick, J. S., Bates, E., Thal, O. J., & Pettnick, S. J. (1994). Variability in early communicative development. *Monographs of the Society for Research in Child Development, 59,* (5, Serial No. 242).

Ferguson, T. J., Van Roozendaal, J., & Rule, B. G. (1986). Information basis for children's impressions of others. *Developmental Psychology, 22,* 335–341.

Fernald, A. (1991). Prosody in speech to children: Prelinguistic and linguistic functions. In R. Vasta (Ed.), *Annals of child development* (Vol. 8). London: Jessica Kingsley Publishers.

Ferreiro, E., & Teberosky, A. (1982). *Literacy before schooling.* Portsmouth, NH: Heinemann Educational Books.

Field, T. (1990). *Infancy.* Cambridge, MA: Harvard University Press.

Field, T. (1995). Infants of depressed mothers. *Infant Behavior and Development, 18,* 1–13.

Field, T. M., Cohen, D., Garcia, R., & Greenberg, R. (1984). Infant response to facelike patterns under fixed trial and infant-control procedures. *Child Development, 54,* 172–177.

Field, T. M., & Goldson, E. (1984). Pacifying effects of nonnutritive sucking on term and preterm neonates during heelstick procedures. *Pediatrics, 74,* 1012–1015.

Field, T. M., Greenwald, P., Morrow, C., Healy, B., Foster, T., Guthertz, M., & Frost, P. (1992). Behavior state matching during interactions of preadolescent friends versus acquaintances. *Developmental Psychology, 28,* 242–250.

Field, T. M., Woodson, R., Greenberg, R., & Cohen, D. (1982). Discrimination and imitation of facial expressions by neonates. *Science, 218,* 179–182.

Fiese, B. H. (1990). Playful relationships: A contextual analysis of mother-toddler interaction and symbolic play. *Child Development, 61,* 1648–1656.

Fifer, W. P., & Moon, C. M. (1995). The effects of fetal experience with sound. In J. P. Lecanuet, W. P. Fifer, N. A. Krasnegor, & W. P. Smotherman (Eds.), *Fetal development: A psychobiological perspective.* Hillsdale, NJ: Lawrence Erlbaum Associates.

Fincham, F. D., & Cain, K. M. (1986). Learned helplessness in humans: A developmental analysis. *Developmental Review, 6,* 301–333.

Fine, G. A. (1987). *With the boys: Little League baseball and preadolescent culture.* Chicago: University of Chicago Press.

Fine, G. A., Mortimer, J. T., & Roberts, D. F. (1990). Leisure, work, and the mass media. In S. S. Feldman & G. R. Elliott (Eds.), At the threshold: *The developing adolescent.* Cambridge, MA: Harvard University Press.

Finkelhor, D. (1994). The international epidemiology of child sexual abuse. *Child Abuse and Neglect, 18,* 409–417.

Finkelstein, N. W., & Ramey, C. T. (1977). Learning to control the environment in infancy. *Child Development, 48,* 806–819.

Fischer, K. W. & Bidell, T. R. (1991). Constraining nativist inferences about cognitive capacities. In S. Carey & R. Gelman (Eds.), *The epigenesis of mind: Essays on biology and knowledge.* Hillsdale, NJ: Erlbaum.

Fischer, K. W., Bullock, D. H., Rotenberg, E. J., & Raya, P. (1993). The dynamics of competence: How context contributes directly to skill. In R. H. Wozniak & K. W. Fischer (Eds.), *Development in context: Acting and thinking in specific environments.* Hillsdale, NJ: Lawrence Erlbaum Associates.

Fischer, K. W., Kenny, S. L., & Pipp, S. L. (1990). How cognitive processes and environmental conditions organize discontinuities in the development of abstractions. In C. Alexander & E. Langer (Eds.), *Higher stages of human development: Perspectives on adult growth.* New York: Oxford University Press.

Fischer, K. W., & Knight, C. C. (1990). Cognitive development in real children: Levels and variations. In B. Presseisen (Ed.), *Styles of learning and thinking: Interactions in the classroom.* Washington, DC: National Education Association.

Fischer, K. W., & Rose, S. P. (1995). Dynamic growth cycles of brain and cognition development. In R. W. Thatcher, G. R. Lyon, J. Ramsey, & N. Krasnegor (Eds.), *Developmental neuroimaging: Mapping the development of brain and behavior.* New York: Academic Press.

Fishbein, H. D. (1976). *Evolution, development and children's learning.* Pacific Palisades, CA: Goodyear.

Fisher, C. B., & Lerner, R. M. (1994). *Applied Developmental Psychology.* New York: McGraw-Hill.

Flanagan, C. (1995, March). *Adolescents' explanations for poverty, unemployment, homelessness, and wealth.* Paper presented at the biennial meetings of the Society for Research on Child Development. Indianapolis, Indiana, March, 1995.

Flavell, J. H. (1971). Stage-related properties of cognitive development. *Cognitive Psychology, 2,* 421–453.

Flavell, J. H. (1985). *Cognitive development* (2nd ed.). Englewood Cliffs, NJ: Prentice-Hall.

Flavell, J. H. (1986). The development of children's knowledge about the appearance-reality distinction. *American Psychologist, 41,* 418–425.

Flavell, J. H. (1990, June 2). *Perspectives on perspective-taking.* Paper presented at the 20th Annual Symposium of the Jean Piaget Society, Philadelphia.

Flavell, J. H., Flavell, E. R., & Green, F. L. (1983). Development of the appearance-reality distinction. *Cognitive Psychology, 15,* 95–120.

Flavell, J. H., Flavell, E. R., & Green, F. L., & Korfmacher, J. E. (1990). Do young children think of television images as pictures or real objects? *Journal of Broadcasting & Electronic Media, 34,* 339–419.

Flavell, J. H., Friedrichs, A. G., & Hoyt, J. D. (1970). Developmental changes in memorization processes. *Cognitive Psychology, 1,* 324–340.

Flavell, J. H., Green, F. L., & Flavell, E. R. (1986). Development of knowledge about the appearance-reality distinction. *Monographs of the Society for Research in Child Development, 51,* (1, Serial No. 212).

Flavell, J. H., Green, F. L., & Flavell, E. R. (1990). Developmental changes in young children's knowledge about the mind. *Cognitive Development, 5,* 1–27.

Flavell, J. H., Green, F. L., Wahl, K. R., & Flavell, E. R. (1987). The effects of question clarification and memory aids on young children's performance on appearance-reality tasks. *Cognitive Development, 2,* 127–144.

Flavell, J. H., Miller, P. H., & Miller, S. A. (1993). *Cognitive development* (3rd ed.). Englewood Cliffs, NJ: Prentice Hall.

Fletcher, A. C., Darling, N.E., Steinberg, L., Dornbusch, S. (1995). The company they keep: Relation of adolescents' adjustment and behavior to their friends; perceptions of authoritative parenting in the social network. *Developmental Psychology, 31,* 300–310.

Fletcher, J. M., Francis, D. J., Rourke, B. P., & Shaywitz, S. E.

(1992). The validity of discrepancy-based definitions of reading disabilities. *Journal of Learning Disabilities, 25,* 551–561.

Flum, H. (1994). Styles of identity formation in early and middle adolescence. *Genetic, Social, and General Psychology Monographs, 120,* 435–467.

Fodor, J. (1983). *The modularity of mind.* Cambridge, MA: MIT Press.

Fonagy, P., Steele, M., Steele, H., Higgitt, A., & Target, M. (1994). The theory and practice of resilience. *Journal of Child Psychology and Psychiatry, 35,* 231–257.

Ford, C. S., & Beach, F. A. (1951). *Patterns of sexual behavior.* New York: Harper & Row.

Fordham, S., & Ogbu, J. U. (1986). Black students' school success: Coping with the "burden of 'acting white.'" *Urban Review, 18* (3), 176–206.

Forehand, R. L., Wierson, M., Frame, C., & Kempton, T. (1991). Juvenile delinquency entry and persistence: Do attention problems contribute to conduct problems? *Journal of Behavior Therapy and Experimental Psychiatry, 22,* 261–264.

Forgays, D. G., & Forgays, J. W. (1952). The nature of the effect of free-environmental experience in the rat. *Journal of Comparative and Physiological Psychology, 45,* 322–328.

Forman, E. A., & McPhail, J. (1993). Vygotskian perspective on children's collaborative problem-solving activities. In E. A. Forman, N. Minick, & C. A. Stone (Eds.), *Contexts for learning: Sociocultural dynamics in children's development.* New York: Oxford University Press.

Fox, N. (1977). Attachment of Kibbutz infants to mother and metapelet. *Child Development, 48,* 1228–1239.

Fox, N., & Bell, M. A. (1990). Electrophysiological indices of frontal lobe development. *Annals of the New York Academy of Sciences, 608,* 677–704.

Fox, N., Kagan, J., & Weiskopf, S. (1979). The growth of memory during infancy. *Genetic Psychology Monographs, 99,* 91–130.

Fox, N. A., Kimmerly, N. L., & Schafer, W. D. (1991). Attachment to mother/Attachment to father: A meta-analysis. *Child Development, 62,* 210–225.

Fox, V. C. (1977). Is adolescence a phenomenon of modern times? *Journal of Psychohistory, 5,* 271–295.

Fraiberg, S. H. (1959). *The magic years: Understanding and handling the problems of early childhood.* New York: Scribner.

Fraiberg, S. H. (1974). Blind infants and their mothers: An examination of the sign system. In M. Lewis & L. Rosenblum (Eds.), *The effect of the infant on its caregiver.* New York: Wiley.

Fraiberg, S. H. (1977). *Every child's birthright: In defense of mothering.* New York: Basic Books.

Francis, P. L., Self, P. A., & Horowitz, F. D. (1987). The behavioral assessment of the neonate: An overview. In J. D. Osofsky (Ed.), *Handbook of infant development* (2nd ed.). New York: Wiley.

Franco, F., & Butterworth, G. (1991, April). *Infant pointing: Prelinguistic reference and co-reference.* Paper presented at Society for Research in Child Development Biennial Meeting, Seattle, WA.

Frank, A. (1975). *The diary of a young girl.* New York: Pocket Books.

Frankel, K., & Bates, J. (1990). Mother-toddler problem solving: Antecedents in attachment, home behavior, and temperament. *Child Development, 61,* 810–819.

Frankenburg, W. K., & Dodds, J. B. (1967). The Denver developmental screening test. *The Journal of Pediatrics, 71,* 181–191.

Freed, K. (1983, March 14). Cubatao—a paradise lost to pollution. *Los Angeles Times,* pp. 1, 12, 13.

Freedman, D. (1974). *Human infancy: An evolutionary perspective.* Hillsdale, NJ: Erlbaum.

Freeman, D. (1983). *Margaret Mead and Samoa.* Cambridge, MA: Harvard University Press.

Fremgen, A., & Fay, D. (1980). Overextensions in production and comprehension: A methodological clarification. *Journal of Child Language, 7,* 201–211.

Frenkiel, N. (Nov. 11, 1993). Planning a family, down to a baby's sex. *New York Times,* B1, B4.

Freud, A. (1946). *Ego and the mechanisms of defense.* New York: International Universities Press.

Freud, S. (1905/1953a). Three essays on the theory of sexuality. In J. Strachey (Ed. and Trans.), *The standard edition of the complete psychological works of Sigmund Freud* (Vol. 7). London: Hogarth Press.

Freud, S. (1905/1953b). The transformation of puberty. In J. Strachey (Ed. & Trans.), *The standard edition of the complete psychological works of Sigmund Freud* (Vol. 7). London: Hogarth Press.

Freud, S. (1920/1924). The psychogenesis of a case of homosexuality in a woman. (B. Low & R. Gabler, Trans.). *Collected Papers* (Vol. 2). London: Hogarth Press.

Freud, S. (1920/1955). Beyond the pleasure principle. In J. Strachey (Ed. and Trans.), *The standard edition of the complete psychological works of Sigmund Freud* (Vol. 18). London: Hogarth Press.

Freud, S. (1921/1949). Group psychology and the analysis of the Ego. In J. Strachey (Ed. & Trans.), *The standard edition of the complete psychological works of Sigmund Freud* (Vol. 18). London: Hogarth Press.

Freud, S. (1925/1961). Some psychical consequences of the anatomical distinctions between the sexes. In J. Strachey (Ed. & Trans.), *The standard edition of the complete psychological works of Sigmund Freud* (Vol. 19). London: Hogarth Press.

Freud, S. (1930). Civilization and its discontents. In J. Strachey (Ed. & Trans.), *The standard edition of the complete psychological works of Sigmund Freud* (Vol. 21). London: Hogarth Press.

Freud, S. (1933/1964). New introductory lectures in psychoanalysis. (J. Strachey, Ed. & Trans.), *The standard edition of the complete psychological works of Sigmund Freud.* New York: W. W. Norton.

Freud, S. (1937/1953). Analysis terminable and interminable. In J. Strachey (Ed.), *The standard edition of the complete psychological works of Sigmund Freud.* (Vol. 5). London: Hogarth Press.

Freud, S. (1940/1964). An outline of psychoanalysis. In J. Strachey (Ed. and Trans.), *The standard edition of the complete psychological works of Sigmund Freud* (Vol. 23). London: Hogarth Press.

Frey, K. S., & Ruble, D. N. (1992). Gender constancy and the "cost" of sex-typed behavior: A test of the conflict hypothesis. *Development Psychology, 28,* 714–721.

Friedman, H. S., Tucker, J. S., Schwartz, J. E., Tomlinson-Keasey, C., Martin, L. R., Wingard, D. L., & Criqui, M. H. (1995). Psychosocial and behavioral predictors of longevity: The aging and death of the "Termites." *American Psychologist, 50,* 69–78.

Friedman, S. L., & Sigman, M. (Eds.). (1980). *Preterm birth and psychological development.* New York: Academic Press.

Frith, U. (1989). *Autism.* Oxford: Oxford University Press.

Frodi, A. (1985). When empathy fails: Aversive infant crying and children abuse. In B. M. Lester & C. F. Z. Boukydis (Eds.), *Infant crying: Theoretical and research prospectives.* New York: Plenum Press.

Frost, R. (1916/1969). The road not taken. In E. C. Lathem (Ed.), *The poetry of Robert Frost.* New York: Holt, Rinehart and Winston.

Fry, D. P. (1988). Intercommunity differences in aggression among Zapotec children. *Child Development, 59,* 1008–1018.

Fukushima, O., & Kato, M. (1976). The effects of vicarious experiences on children's altruistic behavior. *Bulletin of Tokyo Gakuge University*, 27 (Series 1), 90–94.

Fuligni, A. J., & Eccles, J. S. (1993). Perceived parent-child relationships and early adolescents' orientation toward peers. *Developmental Psychology*, 29, 622–632.

Fullard, W., & Reiling, A. M. (1976). An investigation of Lorenz's babyness. *Child Development*, 47, 1191–1193.

Furman, W., Rahe, D. F., & Hartup, W. W. (1979). Rehabilitation of socially withdrawn preschool children through mixed-age and same-age socialization. *Child Development*, 50, 915–922.

Furstenberg, F. F., Jr., Brooks-Gunn, J., & Chase-Lansdale, L. (1989). Teenage pregnancy and childbearing. *American Psychologist*, 44, 313–320.

Furstenberg, F. F., Jr., & Cherlin, A. J. (1991). *Divided families: What happens to children when parents part*. Cambridge, MA: Harvard University Press.

Furstenberg, F. F., Jr., Hughes, M. E., & Brooks-Gunn, J. (1992). The next generation: The children of teenage mothers grow up. In M. Rosenheim & M. F. Testa (Eds.), *Early parenthood and coming of age in the 1990's*. New Brunswick, NJ: Rutgers University Press.

Fuster, J. M. (1990). Prefrontal cortex and the bridging of temporal gaps in the perception-action cycle. *Annals of the New York Academy of Sciences*, 68, 318–336.

Futuyma, D. J. (1986). *Evolutionary biology* (2nd ed.). Sunderland, MA: Sinauer Associates.

Gagnon, J. H., & Simon, W. (1973). *Sexual conduct: The social sources of human sexuality*. Chicago: Aldine.

Galinsky, E., Howes, C., & Kontos, S. (1995). *The family child care training study: Highlights of the findings*. New York: Families and Work Institute.

Galinsky, E., Howes, C., Kontos, S., & Shinn, M. (1994). *The study of children in family child care and relative care: Highlights of the findings*. New York: Families and Work Institute.

Galler, J. R., Ramsey, F., & Solimano, G. (1985). A follow-up study of the effects of early malnutrition on subsequent development. II. Fine motor skills. *Pediatric Research*, 19, 524–527.

Gallistel, R., & Gelman, R. (1991). Preverbal and verbal counting and computation. *Cognition*, 44, 43–74.

Gallup, G. G., Jr. (1970). Chimpanzees: Self-recognition. *Science*, 167, 86–87.

Gamble, T., & Zigler, E. (1986). Effects of infant day care: Another look at the evidence. *American Journal of Orthopsychiatry*, 56, 26–42.

Gamper, E. (1926). Bau and Leistungen eines menschichen Mitteilhirnwesens (Arhinencephalie mit Encephalocele). Zugleich ein Beitrag zu Teratologie und Fasersystematik. *Zeitschr. f.d.ges. Neurol. u. Psychiat.*, vii, 154, civ. 149.

Gamper, E. (1926/1959). In J. Field, H. W. Magoun, & V. E. Hall (Eds.), *Handbook of Physiology* (Vol. 2). Washington, DC: American Physiology Society.

Gardner, H. (1980). *Artful scribbles: The significance of children's drawings*. New York: Basic Books.

Gardner, H. (1983). *Frames of mind: The theory of multiple intelligences*. New York: Basic Books.

Gardner, H. (1991). *The unschooled mind: How children think and how schools should teach*. New York: Basic Books.

Gardner, H., Wolf, D., & Smith, A. (1982). Max and Molly: Individual differences in early artistic symbolization. In H. Gardner (Ed.), *Art, mind and brain: A cognitive approach to creativity*. New York: Basic Books.

Gardner, W., & Rogoff, B. (1990). Children's deliberateness of planning according to task circumstances. *Developmental Psychology*, 26, 480–487.

Garmezy, N., & Rutter, M. (Eds.) (1988). *Stress, coping, and development in children*. Baltimore: Johns Hopkins Press.

Garner, P. W., Jones, D. C., & Palmer, D. J. (1994). Social cognitive correlates of preschool children's sibling caregiving behavior. *Developmental Psychology*, 30, 905–911.

Garvey, C. (1977). *Play*. Cambridge, MA: Harvard University Press.

Garvey, C. (1990). *Play* (enlarged ed.). Cambridge, MA: Harvard University Press.

Garvey, C., & Berndt, R. (1977). *Organization of pretend play*. Paper presented at the meetings of the American Psychological Association, Chicago, IL.

Gaskins, S. (1990). Exploratory play and development in Maya infants. *Unpublished doctoral dissertation*, University of Chicago.

Gaskins, S., & Göncü, A. (1992). Cultural variation in play: A challenge to Piaget and Vygotsky. *Quarterly Newsletter of the Laboratory of Comparative Human Cognition*, 14(3), 31–35.

Gatty, H. (1958). *Nature is your guide*. London: Collins.

Gay, J. & Cole, M. (1967). *The new mathematics and an old culture*. New York: Holt, Rinehart, & Winston.

Gearhart, M., & Newman, D. (1980). Learning to draw a picture: The social context of individual activity. *Discourse Processes*, 3, 169–184.

Geertz, C. (1973). *The interpretation of cultures*. New York: Basic Books.

Geertz, C. (1984). From the native's point of view: On the nature of anthropological understanding. In R. Shweder & R. Levine (Eds.), *Culture theory*. Cambridge: Cambridge University Press.

Gelman, R. (1972). Logical capacity of very young children: Number invariance rules. *Child Development*, 43, 75–90.

Gelman, R., & Baillargeon, R. (1983). A review of some Piagetian concepts. In P. Mussen (Ed.), *Handbook of child development: Vol. 3. Cognitive development*. New York: Wiley.

Gelman, R., Meck, E., & Merkin, S. (1986). Young children's mathematical competence. *Cognitive Development*, 1, 1–29.

Genovese, E. D. (1976). *Role, Jordan, Roll*. New York: Random House.

Gentile, D. A. (1993). Just what are sex and gender, anyway? A call for a new terminological standard. *Psychological Science*, 4, 120–122.

Gesell, A. (1929). *Infancy and human growth*. New York: Macmillan.

Gesell, A. (1940). *The first five years of life* (9th ed.). New York: Harper & Row.

Gesell, A. (1945). *The embryology of behavior*. New York: Harper & Row.

Gesell, A., & Amatruda, C. S. (1947). *Developmental diagnosis: Normal and abnormal child development* (3rd ed.). Hagerstown, MD: Hoeber.

Gesell, A., & Ilg, F. L. (1943). *Infant and child in the culture of today*. New York: Harper & Row.

Gewirtz, J. L., & Pelaez-Nogueros, M. (1992). B. F. Skinner's Legacy in human infant behavior and development. *American Psychologist*, 47, 1411–1422.

Gibbs, J. C., Basenger, K. S., & Fuller, R. L. (1992). *Moral maturity: Measuring the development of sociomoral reflection*. Hillsdale, NJ: Lawrence Erlbaum Associates.

Gibson, E. J. (1993). Ontogenesis of the perceived self. In U. Neisser (Ed.), *The perceived self: Ecological and interpersonal sources of self-knowledge*. Cambridge, MA: Cambridge University Press.

Gibson, K.R. (1991). Myelination and behavioral development: A comparative perspective on questions of neoteny, altriciality and intelligence. In K.R. Gibson & A.C. Petersen, (Eds.), *Brain maturation and cognitive development: Comparative and cross-cultural perspectives. Foundations of human behavior.* New York: Aldine de Gruyter. Gilbert, Scott F. (1991). Developmental biology (3rd ed.). Sunderland, MA: Sinaver.

Gilligan, C. (1977). In a different voice: Women's conceptions of the self and of morality. *Harvard Educational Review, 47,* 481–517.

Gilligan, C. (1982). *In a different voice: Psychological theory and women's development.* Cambridge, MA: Harvard University Press.

Gilligan, C. (1986). Remapping the moral domain: New images of the self in relationship. In J. C. Heller, M. Sosna, & D. E. Wellberg (Eds.), *Reconstructing individualism: Autonomy, individuality, and self in western thought.* Stanford, CA:Stanford University Press.

Gilligan, C., & Attanucci, J. (1988). Two moral orientations: Gender differences and similarities. *Merrill-Palmer Quarterly, 34,* 223–237.

Gilligan, C., & Murphy, J. M. (1979). Development from adolescence to adulthood: The philosopher and the "dilemma of the fact." In D. Kuhn (Ed.), *Intellectual development beyond childhood (New directions for child development,* No. 5). San Francisco: Jossey-Bass.

Gillis, J. R. (1974). *Youth and history: Tradition and change in European age relations 1770–present.* New York: Academic Press.

Ginsburg, H. (1977). *Children's arithmetic.* New York: Van Nostrand.

Gjerde, P. F. (1986). The interpersonal structure of family interaction settings: Parent-adolescent relations in dyads and triads. *Developmental Psychology, 22,* 297–304.

Gladwin, E. T. (1970). *East is a big bird.* Cambridge, MA: Harvard University Press.

Gleitman, H. (1963). *Psychology.* New York: W. W. Norton.

Gleitman, L., Newport, E., & Gleitman, H. (1984). The current status of the motherese hypothesis. *Journal of Child Language, 11,* 43–80.

Goelman, H. (1988). The relationship between structure and process variables in home and day care settings on children's language development. In A. R. Pence (Ed.), *Ecological research with children and families.* New York: Teachers College Press.

Goldin-Meadow, S. (1985). Language development under atypical learning conditions. In K. E. Nelson (Ed.), *Children's language* (Vol. 5). Hillsdale, NJ: Erlbaum.

Goldin-Meadow, S., & Mylander, C. (1990). The role of parental input in the development of a morphological system. *Journal of Child Language, 17,* 527–563.

Goldsmith, H. H. (1987). Roundtable: What is temperament? Four approaches. *Child Development, 58,* 505–529.

Goldsmith, H. H., & Campos, J. J. (1982). Toward a theory of infant temperament. In R. N. Emde & R. Harmon (Eds.), *The development of attachment and affiliative systems.* New York: Plenum Press.

Goldsmith, H. H., & Gottesman, I. I. (1981). Origins of variation in behavior style: A longitudinal study of young twins. *Child Development, 52,* 91–103.

Golinkoff, R. M., Mervis, C. B., & Hirsh-Pasek, K. (1994). Early object labels: The case for a developmental lexical principles framework. *Journal of Child Language, 21,* 125–155.

Golomb, C. (1974). *Young children's sculpture and drawing.* Cambridge, MA: Harvard University Press.

Gomes-Schwartz, B., Horowitz, J. M., & Cardarelli, A. P. (1990). *Child sexual abuse: Initial effects.* Newbury Park, CA: Sage Publications.

Göncü, A. (1993). Development of intersubjectivity in social pretend play. *Human Development, 36,* 185–198.

Göncü, A., & Kessel, F. S. (1988). Preschoolers' collaborative construction in planning and maintaining imaginative play. *International Journal of Behavioral Development, 11,* 327–344.

Gonsiorek, J. C., & Weinrich, J. D. (Eds.) (1991). *Homosexuality: Research implications for public policy.* Newbury Park, CA: Sage Publications.

Good, T. L., Sikes, J., & Brophy, J. (1973). Effects of teacher sex and student sex on classroom interaction. *Journal of Educational Psychology, 65,* 74–87.

Goodenough, W. H. (1953). *Native astronomy in the Central Carolines. Museum Monographs.* Philadelphia: University Museum, University of Pennsylvania.

Goodman, G. (1984). Children's testimony in historical perspective. *Journal of Social Issues, 40,* 9–31.

Goodman, G. S., Aman, C., & Hirschman, J. (1987). Child's sexual and physical abuse: Children's testimony. In S. J. Ceci, M. P. Toglia, & D. Ross (Eds.), *Children's eyewitness memory.* New York: Springer-Verlag.

Goodman, G. S., Levine, M., Melton, G. B., & Ogden, D. W. (1991). Child witnesses and the confrontation clause. *Law and Human Behavior, 15,* 13–29.

Goodman, G. S., Rudy, L., Bottoms, B. L., & Aman, C. (1990). Children's concerns and memory: Issues of ecological validity in the study of children's eyewitness testimony. In R. Fivush & J. A. Hudson (Eds.), *Knowing and remembering in young children.* New York: Cambridge University Press.

Goodman, K. S., Smith, E. B., Merideth, R., & Goodman, Y. E. (1987). *Language and thinking in school.* New York: Owen.

Goodman, Y. E., & Goodman, K. S. (1990). Vygotsky and the whole-language perspective. In L.C. Moll (Ed.), *Vygotsky and education: Instructional implications and applications of sociohistorical psychology.* New York: Cambridge University Press.

Goodnow, J. J. (1977). *Children drawing.* Cambridge, MA: Harvard University Press.

Goodnow, J. J. (1984). Parents' ideas about parenting and development. In A. L. Brown & B. Rogoff (Eds.), *Advances in developmental psychology* (Vol. 3). Hillsdale, NJ: Erlbaum.

Goodnow, J. J. (1990). The socialization of cognition: What's involved? In J. W. Stigler, R. A. Shweder, & G. Herdt (Eds.), *Cultural psychology: Essays on comparative human development.* New York: Cambridge University Press.

Goodnow, J. J., & Burns, A. (1985). *Home and school: A child's-eye view.* Sydney: Allen & Unwin.

Goodnow, J. J., Cashmore, J., Cotton, S., & Knight, R. (1984). Mothers' developmental timetables in two cultural groups. *International Journal of Psychology, 19,* 193–205.

Goody, E. N. (1989). Learning, apprenticeship, and the division of labor. In M. Coy (Ed.), *Apprenticeship: From theory to method and back again.* Albany, NY: SUNY Press.

Goody, J. (1977). *Domestication of the savage mind.* Cambridge: Cambridge University Press.

Goossens, F. A., & Van IJzendoorn, M. H. (1990). Quality of infants' attachments to professional caregivers: Relation to infant-parent attachment and day-care characteristics. *Child Development, 61,* 832–837.

Gopnik, A., & Meltzoff, A. N. (1986). Words, plans, things, and locations: Interactions between semantic and cognitive development at the one-word stage. In S. R. Kuczaj & M. D. Barrett

(Eds.), *The development of word meaning*. New York: Springer-Verlag.

Gopnik, A., & Meltzoff, A. N. (1987). Language and thought in the child: Early semantic developments and their relations to object permanence, means-ends understanding, and categorization. In K. Nelson & A. F. Van Kleeck (Eds.), *Children's language* (Vol. 6). Hillsdale, NJ: Erlbaum.

Gordon, J. S., & Haire, D. (1981). Alternatives in childbirth. In P. Ahmed (Ed.), *Pregnancy, childbirth, and parenthood*. New York: Elsevier.

Goren, C. C., Sarty, J., & Wu, P. Y. (1975). Visual following and pattern discrimination of face-like stimuli by newborn infants. *Pediatrics, 56*, 544–549.

Gorn, G. J., Goldberg, M. E., & Kanango, R. N. (1976). The role of educational television in changing intergroup attitudes of children. *Child Development, 47*, 277–280.

Gortmacher, S. L., Dietz, W. H., & Cheung, J. W. (1990). Inactivity, diet, and the fattening of America. *Journal of the American Dietetic Association, 90*, 1247–1252.

Gottesman, I. I. (1991). *Schizophrenia genesis: The origins of madness*. New York: W. H. Freeman.

Gottfried, A. E., Gottfried, A. W., & Bathhurst, K. (1988). Maternal employment, family environment and children's development: Infancy through the school years. In A. E. Gottfried & A. W. Gottfried (Eds.), *Maternal employment and children's development: Longitudinal research*. New York: Plenum Press.

Gottlieb, G. (1992). *Individual development and evolution: The genesis of novel behavior*. New York: Oxford University Press.

Gottman, J. M. (1983). How children become friends. *Monographs of the Society for Research in Child Development, 48* (3, Serial No. 201).

Gould, S. J. (1977a). *Ever since Darwin*. New York: W. W. Norton.

Gould, S. J. (1977b). *Ontogeny and phylogeny*. Cambridge, MA: Harvard University Press.

Gould, S. J. (1980). *The panda's thumb: More reflections in natural history*. New York, NY: Norton.

Gould, S. J. (1981). *The mismeasure of man*. New York: W. W. Norton.

Graber, J. A., Brooks-Gunn, J., Paikoff, R. L., & Warren, M. P. (1994). Prediction of eating problems: An 8-year study of adolescent girls. *Developmental Psychology, 30*, 823–834.

Graber, J. A., Brooks-Gunn, J., & Warren, M. (1995). The antecedants of menarcheal age: Heredity, family environment and stressful life events. *Child Development, 66*, 346–359.

Graham, F. K., Matarazzo, R. G., & Caldwell, B. M. (1956). Behavioral differences between normal and traumatized newborns: II. Standardization, reliability, and validity. *Psychological Monographs, 70* (21, Serial No. 428).

Graham, P., Rutter, M., & George, S. (1973). Temperamental characteristics as predictors of behavior disorders in children. *American Journal of Orthopsychiatry, 43*, 328–339.

Gralinski, H. J., & Kopp, C. B. (1993). Everyday rules for behavior: Mothers' requests to young children. *Developmental Psychology, 29*, 573–584.

Grantham-McGregor, S., Powell, C., Walker, S., Chang, S., & Fletcher, P. (1994). The long-term follow-up of severely malnourished children who participated in an intervention program. *Child Development, 65*, 428–439.

Graves, Z., & Glick, J. A. (1978). The effect of context on mother-child interaction: A progress report. *Quarterly Newsletter of the Laboratory of Comparative Human Cognition, 2*, 41–46.

Greco, C., Rovee-Collier, C., Hayne, H., & Griesler, P. (1986). Ontogeny of early event memory: I. Forgetting and retrieval by 2- and 3-month-olds. *Infant Behavior & Development, 9*, 441–460.

Green, G. (1984). On the appropriateness of adaptations in primary-level basal readers: Reactions to remarks by Bertran Bruce. In R. C. Anderson, J. Osborn & R. J. Tierney (Eds.), *Learning to read in American schools*. Hillsdale, NJ: Erlbaum.

Green, K. D., Forehand, R., Beck, P. J., & Vosk, B. (1980). An assessment of the relationship among measures of children's social competence and children's academic achievement. *Child Development, 51*, 1149–1156.

Greenberg, B. S., & Brand, J. E. (1994). Minorities and the mass media. In J. Bryant & D. Zillman (Eds.), *Media effects: Advances in theory and research*. Hillsdale, NJ: Erlbaum.

Greenberg, M. T., & Crnic, K. A. (1988). Longitudinal predictors of developmental status and social interaction in premature and full-term infants at age two. *Child Development, 59*, 554–570.

Greenberger, E., O'Neil, R., & Nagel, S.K. (1994). Linking workplace and homeplace: relations between nature of adults' work and their parenting behaviors. *Developmental Psychology, 30*, 990–1002.

Greenberger, E., & Steinberg, L. (1986). *When teenagers work: The psychological and social costs of adolescent employment*. New York: Basic Books.

Greene, L. S., & Johnston, F. E. (Eds.), (1980). *Social and biological predictors of nutritional status, physical growth and neurological development*. New York: Academic Press.

Greenfield, P. M. (1966). On culture and conservation. In J. S. Bruner, R. R. Olver, & P. M. Greenfield (Eds.), *Studies in cognitive growth*. New York: Wiley.

Greenfield, P. M. (1984). *Mind and media: The effects of television, video, games and computers*. Cambridge, MA: Harvard University Press.

Greenfield, P. M. (1991). Language, tools and brain: The ontogeny and phylogeny of hierarchically organized sequential behavior. *Behavioral and Brain Sciences, 14*, 531–594.

Greenfield, P. M. (1993). Representational competence in shared symbol systems: Electronic media from radio to video games. In R. R. Cocking & K. A. Renniger (Eds.), *The development and meaning of psychological distance*. Hillsdale, NJ: Erlbaum.

Greenfield, P. M., Brazelton, T. B., & Childs, C. P. (1989). From birth to maturity in Zinacantan: Ontogenesis in cultural context. In V. Bricker & G. Gossen (Eds.), *Ethnographic encounters in southern Mesoamerica: Celebratory essays in honor of Evon Z. Vogt*. Albany, NY: Institute of Mesoamerican Studies, State University of New York (1994).

Greenfield, P. M., & Cocking, R. R. (Eds.), *Cross-cultural roots of minority child development*. Hillsdale, NJ: Lawrence Erlbaum Associates.

Greenfield, P. M., & Savage-Rumbaugh, E. S. (1990). Grammatical combination in Pan paniscus: Processes of learning and invention in the evolution and development of language. In S. T. Parker & K. R. Gibson (Eds.), *Language and intelligence in monkeys and apes*. Cambridge: Cambridge University Press.

Greenfield, P. M., & Smith, J. H. (1976). *The structure of communication in early language development*. New York: Academic Press.

Greenough, W. T. (1991). Experience as a component of normal development: Evolutionary considerations. *Developmental Psychology, 27*, 14–17.

Gregg, N. M. (1941). Cogenital cataracts following German measles in mothers. *Transcripts of the Ophthalmological Society of Australia, 3*, 35.

Gregor, J. A., & McPherson, D. A. (1966). Racial preference and ego identity among White and Bantu children in the Republic of South Africa. *Genetic Psychology Monographs, 73,* 218–253.

Gribbin, J. R., & Cherfas, J. (1982). *The monkey puzzle: Reshaping the evolutionary tree.* New York: Pantheon Books.

Grice, H. P. (1975). Logic and conversation. In P. Cole & J. L. Morgan (Eds.), *Syntax and semantics: Vol. 3. Speech acts.* New York: Academic Press.

Griffin, P. (1983). Personal communication.

Grimwade, J. C., Walker, D. W., Bartlett, M., Gordon, S., & Wood, C. (1970). Human fetal heartrate change and move-ment-response to sound and vibration. *American Journal of Obstetrics and Gynecology, 109,* 86–90.

Griswold Del Castillo, R. (1984). *La familia: Chicano families in the urban southwest, 1848 to the present.* Notre Dame, IN: University of Notre Dame Press.

Grogger, J., & Bronars, S. (July–August, 1993). The socioeco-nomic consequences of teenage childbearing: Findings from a national experiment. *Family Planning Perspectives, 25,* 156–161.

Gronlund, N. E. (1959). *Sociometry in the classroom.* New York: Harper Brothers.

Grossmann, K. Fremmer-Bombik, E., Rudolph, J., & Grossmann, K. (1987, January). *Maternal attachment in relation to patterns of infant-mother attachment and maternal care during the first year.* Paper presented at Conference on Intrafamilial Relationships, Cambridge, England.

Grossmann, K., Grossmann, K. E., Spangler, S., Suess, G., & Unzner, L. (1985). Maternal sensitivity and newborn orienta-tion responses as related to quality of attachment in Northern Germany. *Monographs of the Society for Research in Child Development, 50* (1–2 Serial No. 209).

Grossman, K. E., & Grossman, K. (1990). The wider concept of attachment in cross-cultural research. *Human Development, 33,* 31–47.

Grotberg, E. (1969). *Review of Head Start research, 1965–1969.* Washington, DC: (OEO Pamphlet 1608:13 ED02308).

Grotevant, H. (1986). Assessment of identity development: Cur-rent issues and future directions. *Journal of Adolescent Research, 1,* 175–181.

Grotevant, H., & Cooper, C. (1985). Patterns of interaction in family relationships and the development of identity explo-ration in adolescence. *Developmental Psychology, 56,* 415–428.

Grotevant, H. D., Thorbecke, W., & Meyer, M. L. (1982). An ex-tension of Marcia's identity status interview in the interpersonal domain. *Journal of Youth and Adolescence, 11,* 33–47.

Grusec, J. E. (1991). Socializing concern for others in the home. *Developmental Psychology, 27,* 338–342.

Guerra, N. G., & Slaby, R. G. (1990). Cognitive mediators of ag-gression in adolescent offenders: 2. Intervention. *Developmental Psychology, 26,* 269–277.

Guidubaldi, J., Perry, J. D., Cleminshaw, H. K., & McLoughlin, C. S. (1983). The impact of parental divorce on children: Re-port of the nationwide NASP study. *School Psychology Review, 12*(3), 300–323.

Gunter, B. (1994). The question of media violence. In J. Bryant and D. Zillman (Eds.), *Media effects: Advances in theory and re-search.* Hillsdale, NJ: Lawrence Erlbaum Associates.

Gustafson, G. E., & Harris, K. L. (1990). Women's responses to young infants' cries. *Developmental Psychology, 26,* 144–152.

Haaf, R. A., Smith, P. H., & Smitely, S. (1983). Infant response to facelike patterns under fixed-trial and infant control procedures. *Child Development, 54,* 172–177.

Haan, N., Langer, J., & Kohlberg, L. (1976). Family patterns of moral reasoning. *Child Development, 47,* 1204–1206.

Haan, N., Weiss, R., & Johnson, V. (1982). The role of logic in moral reasoning and development. *Developmental Psychology, 18,* 245–256.

Hagen, J. W., Meacham, J. A., & Mesibov, G. (1970). Verbal label-ing, rehearsal, and short-term memory. *Cognitive Psychology, 1,* 47–58.

Haith, M. M. (1980). *Rules that babies look by: The organization of newborn visual activity.* Hillsdale, NJ: Erlbaum.

Haith, M. M. (1990). Progress in the understanding of sensory and perceptual processes in early infancy. *Merrill Palmer Quarterly, 36,* 1–26.

Haith, M. M., Berman, T., & Moore, M. J. (1977). Eye contact and face scanning in early infancy. *Science, 198,* 853–855.

Hakuta, K., & Garcia, E. E. Bilingualism and education. *American Psychologist, 44,* 374–379. (1989)

Halford, G. S., & Boyle, F. M. (1985). Do young children under-stand conservation of number? *Child Development, 56,* 165–176.

Halford, G. S., Mayberry, M. T., O'Hare, A. W., & Grant, P. (1994). The development of memory and processing capacity. *Child Development, 65,* 1338–1356.

Hallpike, C. R. (1979). *The foundations of primitive thought.* Oxford: Clarendon.

Halpern, D. F. (1986). *Sex differences in cognitive abilities.* Hillsdale, NJ: Erlbaum.

Halpern, R. (1990). Poverty and early childhood parenting: To-ward a framework for intervention. *American Journal of Or-thopsychiatry, 60*(1), 6–18.

Halverson, H. M. (1931). An experimental study of prehension in infants by means of cinema records. *Genetic Psychology Mono-graphs, 10,* (2–3, 107–286).

Hammen, C. (1991). *Depression runs in families: The social context of risk and resilience in children of depressed mothers.* New York: Springer-Verlag.

Harel, I., & Papert, S. (1991). *Constructionism.* Norwood, NJ: Ablex.

Harkness, S. (1990). A cultural model for the acquisition of lan-guage: Implications for the innateness debate. *Developmental Psychobiology, 23,* 727–740.

Harkness, S., & Super, C. M. (1983). The cultural construction of child development: A framework for the socialization of emo-tion. *Ethos, 11,* 221–231.

Harkness, S., & Super, C. M. (1985). The cultural context of gen-der segregation in children's peer groups. *Child Development, 56,* 219–224.

Harley, G. W. (1941). Notes on the Poro in Liberia. In B. B. Som-mer (Ed.), *Puberty and adolescence.* New York: Oxford University Press.

Harlow, H. (1959). Love in infant monkeys. *Scientific American, 200*(6), 68–74.

Harlow, H. F., & Harlow, M. K. (1962). Social deprivation in monkeys. *Scientific American, 207,* 136–146.

Harlow, H. F., & Harlow, M. K. (1969). Effects of various mother-infant relationships on rhesus monkey behaviors. In B. M. Foss (Ed.), *Determinants of infant behavior* (Vol. 4). London: Methuen.

Harlow, H. F., & Novak, M. A. (1973). Psychopathological per-spectives. *Perspectives in Biology and Medicine,* Spring, 461–478.

Harlow, H. F., & Zimmerman, R. (1959). Affectional responses in the infant monkey. *Science, 130,* 421–432.

Harrington, M. (1963). *The other America: Poverty in the United States.* New York: Macmillan.

Harris, B. (1979). Whatever happened to little Albert? *American Psychologist, 34,* 151–160.

Harris, H. W., Blue, H. C., & Griffith, E. H. (Eds.). (1995). *Racial and ethnic identity: Psychological development and creative expression*. New York: Routledge.

Harris, P. L., Donnelly, K., Guz, G. R., & Pitt-Watson, R. (1986). Children's understanding of the distinction between real and apparent emotion. *Child Development, 57*, 895–909.

Harris, P. L., & Gross, D. (1988). Children's understanding of real and apparent motion. In J. W. Astington, P. L. Harris, & D. R. Olson (Eds.), *Developing theories of mind*. New York: Cambridge University Press.

Harrison, A. O., Wilson, M. N., Pine, C. J., Chan, S. Q., & Buriel, R. (1990). Family ecologies of ethnic minority children. *Child Development, 61*, 347–362.

Hart, C. H., Ladd, G. W., & Burleson, B. R. (1990). Children's expectations of the outcomes of social strategies: Relations with sociometric status and maternal disciplinary styles. *Child Development, 61*, 127–137.

Harter, S. (1982). The perceived competence scale for children. *Child Development, 53*, 87–97.

Harter, S. (1983). Development perspectives on the self-system. In P. M. Mussen (Ed.), *Handbook of Child Psychology: Vol. 4. Socialization, personality, and social development*. New York: Wiley.

Harter, S. (1986). Cognitive-developmental processes in integration of concepts about emotion and the self. *Social Cognition, 4*, 119–151.

Harter, S. (1987). The determinants and mediational role of global self-worth in children. In N. Eisenberg (Ed.), *Contemporary topics in developmental psychology*. New York: Wiley.

Harter, S. (1990a). Issues in the development of the self-concept of children and adolescents. In A. LaGreca (Ed.), *Through the eyes of a child*. Boston: Allyn and Bacon.

Harter, S. (1990b). Self and identity development. In S. S. Feldman and G. R. Elliott (Eds.), *At the threshold: The developing adolescent*. Cambridge, MA: Harvard University Press.

Harter, S. (1993). Causes and consequences of low self-esteem in children and adolescents. In R.F. Baumeister (Ed.), *Self-esteem: The puzzle of low self-regard*. New York: Plenum.

Harter, S. (1996). The personal self in social context. In R. D. Ashmore & L. Jussim (Eds.), *Self and identity: Fundamental issues*. New York: Oxford University Press.

Harter, S., & Monsour, A. (1992). Developmental analysis of conflict caused by opposing attributes in the adolescent self-portrait. *Developmental Psychology, 28*, 251–260.

Harter, S., & Pike, R. (1984). The pictorial scale of perceived competence and social acceptance for young children. *Child Development, 55*, 1969–1982.

Hartup, W. W. (1974). Aggression in childhood. Developmental perspectives. *American Psychologist, 29*, 336–341.

Hartup, W. W. (1978). Children and their friends. In H. McGurk (Ed.), *Issues in childhood social development*. London: Methuen.

Hartup, W. W. (1984). The peer context in middle childhood. In A. Collins (Ed.), *Development during middle childhood: The years from six to twelve*. Washington, DC: National Academy Press.

Hartup, W. W. (1992). Friendships and their developmental significance. In H. McGurk, (Ed.), *Childhood social development: Contemporary perspectives*. London: Erlbaum.

Hashima, P. Y., & Amato, P. R. (1994). Poverty, social support, and parental behavior. Special issue: Children and poverty. *Child Development, 65*, 394–403.

Haskett, M. E., & Kistner, J. A. (1991). Social interactions and peer perception in young physically abused children. *Child Development, 62*, 979–990.

Haskins, R. (1985). Public school aggression among children with varying day-care experience. *Child Development, 56*, 687–703.

Haskins, R. (1989). Beyond metaphor: The efficacy of early childhood education. *American Psychologist, 44*, 274–282.

Haugaard, J. J., & Reppucci, N. D. (1988). *The sexual abuse of children*. San Francisco: Jossey-Bass.

Havighurst, R. J. (1967). *Developmental tasks and education*. New York: David McKay.

Hayes, C. D., & Kamerman, S. B. (Eds.). (1983). *Children of working parents: Experiences and outcomes*. Washington, DC: National Academy Press.

Hayes, K., & Hayes, C. (1951). The intellectual development of a home-raised chimpanzee. *Proceedings of the American Philosophical Society, 95*, 105–109.

Hayflick, L. (1994). *How and why we age*. New York: Ballantine Books.

Hayne, H., Greco-Vigorito, C., & Rovee-Collier, C. (1993). Forming contextual categories in infancy. *Cognitive Development, 8*, 63–82.

Hayne, H., & Rovee-Collier, C. (1995). The organization of reactivated memory in infancy. *Child Development, 66*, 893–906.

Hayne, H., Rovee-Collier, C., & Perris, E. E. (1987). Categorization and memory retrieval by three-month-olds. *Child Development, 58*, 750–767.

Hazen, N. L., & Black, B. (1989). Preschool peer communication skills: A longitudinal study. *Child Development, 60*, 867–876.

Heath, S. B. (1982). What no bedtime story means: Narrative skills at home and school. *Language in Society, 11*, 49–77.

Heath, S. B. (1984). *Ways with words: Language, life, and work in communities and classrooms*. Cambridge: Cambridge University Press.

Hechinger, F. M. (1992). *Fateful choices: Healthy youth for the 21st century*. Carnegie Council on Adolescent Development: Washington, D.C.

Held, R., & Hein, A. (1963). Movement-produced stimulation and the development of visually guided behaviors. *Journal of Comparative and Physiological Psychology, 56*, 872–876.

Henderson, H., & Henderson, R. (1982). Traditional Onitsha Ibo maternity beliefs and practices. In M. A. Kay (Ed.), *Anthropology of human birth*. Philadelphia: F. A. Davis.

Henderson, L. (1982). *Orthography and word recognition in reading*. New York: Academic Press.

Henmon, V. A. C. (1921). Intelligence and its measurement: A symposium. *Journal of Educational Psychology, 12*, 195–198.

Hennessy, K. D., Rabideau, G., Cicchetti, D., & Cummings, E. M. (1994). Responses of physically abused and nonabused children to different forms of interadult anger. *Child Development, 65*, 815–828.

Hepper, P. G. (1992). Fetal Psychology: An embryonic science. In J. G. Nijhuis (Ed.), *Fetal behavior: Development and perinatal aspects*. New York: Oxford University Press.

Herdt, G. (Ed.). (1989). *Gay and lesbian youth*. New York: Harrington Park Press.

Herrenkohl, L. R. (1988). The impact of prenatal stress on the developing fetus and child. In Richard N. Cohen, M. D. (Ed.), *Psychiatric consultation in childbirth settings: Parent and child oriented approaches*. New York: Plenum Medical Book Company.

Herrnstein, R. J., & Murray, C. (1994). *The bell curve: Intelligence and class structure in American life*. New York: Free Press.

Herskovitz, M. J. (1948). *Man and his works: The science of cultural anthropology*. New York: Knopf.

Hetherington, E. M. (1988). Parents, children, and siblings: Six years after divorce. In R. A. Hinde & J. Stevenson-Hinde (Eds.), *Relationships within families: Mutual influences.* Oxford: Oxford University Press.

Hetherington, E. M. (1989). Coping with family transitions: Winners, losers, and survivors. *Child Development, 60,* 1–14.

Hetherington, E. M., & Clingempeel, W. G. (1992). Coping with marital transitions. *Monographs of the Society for Research in Child Development, 57,* (2–3, Serial No. 227).

Hetherington, E. M., Cox, M., & Cox, R. (1982) Long-term effects of divorce and remarriage on the adjustment of children. *Journal of the American Academy of Child Psychiatry, 24,* 518–530.

Hetherington, E.M., Reiss, D., & Plomin, R. (Eds.), (1994). *Separate social worlds of siblings: The impact of nonshared environment on development.* Hillsdale, NJ: Lawrence Erlbaum.

Hetherington, E. M., Stanley-Hagen, M., & Anderson, E. R. (1989). Marital transitions. A child's perspective. *American Psychologist, 41,* 303–312.

Hicks, L. E., Langham, R. A., & Takenaka, J. (1982). Cognitive and health measures following early nutritional supplementation: A sibling study. *American Journal of Public Health, 72,* 1110–1118.

Hill, J. P. (1988). Adapting to menarche: Familial control and conflict. In M. R. Gunner, & W. A. Collins (Eds.), *Development during the transition to adolescence. Minnesota Symposia on Child Psychology* (Vol. 21). Hillsdale, NJ: Erlbaum.

Hill, R. C., & Stafford, F. P. (1980). Parental care of children: Time diary estimates of quantity, predictability, and variety. *Journal of Human Research, 15,* 219–239.

Hill, W. H., Borovsky, O. L., & Rovee-Collier, C. (1988). Continuities in infant memory development over the first half-year. *Developmental Psychologybiology, 21,* 43–62.

Hinde, R. A. (1982). Attachment: Some conceptual and biological issues. In C. Parkes & J. Stevenson-Hinde (Eds.), *The place of attachment in human behavior.* New York: Basic Books.

Hinde, R. A. (1987). *Relationships and culture: Links between ethology and the social sciences.* Cambridge: Cambridge University Press.

Hiner, N. R., & Hawes, J. M. (Eds.). (1985). *Growing up in America: Children in historical perspective.* Champaign, IL: University of Illinois Press.

Hirsch, H. V. B., & Spinelli, D. N. (1971). Modification of the distribution of receptive field orientation in cats by selective visual exposure during development. *Experimental Brain Research, 13,* 509–527.

Hirschfeld, L. A. (1995). Do children have a theory of race? *Cognition, 54,* 209–252.

Hirschfeld, L. A., & Gelman, S. (Eds.), (1994). *Mapping the mind: Domain specificity in cognition and culture.* New York: Cambridge University Press.

Hirsh-Pasek, K., Treiman, R., & Schneiderman, M. (1984). Brown and Hanlon revisited: Mothers' sensitivity to ungrammatical forms. *Journal of Child Language, 11,* 81–88.

Hodges, J., & Tizard, B. (1989a). IQ and behavioral adjustments of ex-institutional adolescents. *Journal of Child Psychology and Psychiatry, 30,* 53–75.

Hodges, J., & Tizard, B. (1989b). Social and family relationships of ex-institutional adolescents. *Journal of Child Psychology and Psychiatry, 30,* 77–97.

Hofferth, S. L. (1990). Trends in adolescent sexual activity, contraception and pregnancy in the United States. In J. Bancroft and J. M. Runesch (Eds.), *Adolescence and Puberty.* New York: Oxford University Press.

Hoffman, L. W. (1980). The effects of maternal employment on the academic attitudes and performance of school age children. *School Psychology Review, 9,* 319–335.

Hoffman, L. W. (1984). Maternal employment and the young child. In M. Perlmutter (Ed.), *Parent-child interactions and parent-child relations in child development. Minnesota Symposia on Child Psychology* (Vol. 17). Hillsdale, NJ: Erlbaum.

Hoffman, L. W. (1989). Effects of maternal employment in the two-parent family. *American Psychologist, 44,* 283–292.

Hoffman, L. W. (1991). The influence of the family environment on personality: Accounting for sibling differences. *Psychological Bulletin, 110,* 187–203.

Hoffman, M. L. (1970). Moral development. In P. H. Mussen (Ed.), *Carmichael's manual of child psychology: Vol. 2, Part 4.* Socialization (3rd ed.). New York: Wiley.

Hoffman, M. L. (1975). Altruistic behavior and the parent-child relationship. *Journal of Personality and Social Psychology, 31,* 937–943.

Hoffman, M. L. (1980). Moral development in adolescence. In J. Adelson (Ed.), *Handbook of adolescent psychology.* New York: Wiley.

Hoffman, M. L. (1988). Moral development. In M. H. Bornstein & M. E. Lamb (Eds.), *Developmental psychology: An advanced textbook 2nd ed.).* Hillsdale, NJ: Lawrence Erlbaum Associates.

Hofstader, D. (1979). *Godel, Escher, Bach: An eternal golden braid.* New York: Basic Books.

Hogge, A. W. (1990). Teratology. In I. R. Merkatz & J. E. Thompson (Eds.), *New perspectives on prenatal care.* New York: Elsevier.

Holden, G. W., & Zambarano, R. J. (1992). Passing the rod: Similarities between parents and their young children in orientations toward physical punishment. In I. E. Sigel, A. V. McGillicuddy, & J. J. Goodnow (Eds.) *Parental belief systems: The psychological consequences for children.* Hillsdale, NJ: Erlbaum.

Hollos, M. (1975). Logical operations and role-taking abilities in two cultures: Norway and Hungary. *Child Development, 46,* 638–649.

Hollos, M., & Cowan, P. A. (1973). Social isolation and cognitive development: Logical operations and role-taking abilities in three Norwegian social settings. *Child Development, 44,* 630–641.

Hollos, M., & Richards, F. A. (1993). Gender-associated development of formal operations in Nigerian adolescents. *Ethos, 21,* 24–52.

Holmbeck, G.N., Paikoff, R.L., & Brooks-Gunn, J. (1995). Parenting adolescents. In M. Bornstein (Ed.), *Handbook of parenting, Vol. I: Children and parenting.* Mahwah, NJ: Erlbaum.

Holmes, S. T., & Holmes, T. H. (1969). Short-term intrusions into the lifestyle routine. *Journal of Psychosomatic Research, 14,* 1–7.

Holstein, C. (1976). Development of moral judgment: A longitudinal study of males and females. *Child Development, 47,*51–61.

Honig, A. S., & Park, K. J. (1993). Effects of day care on preschool sex-rate development. *American Journal of Orthopsychiatry, 36,* 481–486.

Hook, E. B. (1982). Epidemiology of Down Syndrome. In S. M. Pueschel & J. E. Rynders (Eds.), *Down syndrome: Advances in biomedicine and behavioral sciences.* Cambridge, MA: Ware Press.

Hoorweg, J., & Stanfield, J. P. (1976). The effects of protein energy malnutrition in early childhood on intellectual and motor abilities in later childhood and adolescence. *Developmental Medicine and Child Neurology, 18,* 330–350.

Hopkins, B., & Westen, T. (1988). Maternal handling and motor development: *An intracultural study. Genetic Psychology Monographs, 14*, 377–420.

Howe, N. (1991). Sibling-directed internal state language, perspective taking, and affective behavior. *Child Development, 62*, 1503–1512.

Howells, W. H. (1960). The distribution of man. *Scientific American, 203*, 112–127.

Howes, C. (1987). Peer interaction of young children. *Monographs of the Society for Research in Child Development, 53*(1, Serial No. 217).

Howes, C. (1990). Can the age of entry into child care and the quality of child care predict adjustment in kindergarten? *Developmental Psychology, 26*, 292–303.

Howes, C., & Olenick, M. (1986). Family and childcare influences on toddlers' compliance. *Child Development, 57*, 202–216.

Howes, C., Phillips, D. A., & Whitebook, M. (1992). Thresholds of quality: Implications for the social development of children in center-based child care. *Child Development, 63*, 447–460.

Howes, C., Unger, O., & Seider, L. B. (1989). Social pretend play in toddlers: Parallels with social play and with solitary pretend. *Child Development, 60*, 77–84.

Hrdlicka, A. (1931). *Children who run on all fours, and other animal-like behaviors in the human child.* New York: Whittlesey House/McGraw Hill.

Hsia, D. Y., Driscoll, K. W., Troll, W., & Knox, W. E. (1956). Detection of phenylalanine tolerance tests heterozygous carriers of phenylketonuria. *Nature, 176*, 1239–1240.

Hubbard, J. A., & Cole, J. D. (1994). Emotional correlates of social competence in children's peer relationships. *Merrill-Palmer Quarterly, 40*, 1–20.

Hubel, D. H., & Wiesel, T. N. (1979). Brain mechanisms of vision. *Scientific American, 241*, 130–139.

Hughes, F. P. (1995). *Children, play, & development* (2nd ed.). Boston: Allyn and Bacon.

Hughes, M. (1986). *Children and number: Difficulties in learning mathematics.* New York: Blackwell.

Humphreys, A. P., & Smith, P. K. (1987). Rough and tumble, friendships, and dominance in school children: Evidence for continuity and change with age. *Child Development, 58*, 201–212.

Huston, A. C., McLoyd, V. C., & Coll, C. G. (1994). Children and poverty: Issues in contemporary research. *Child Development, 65*, 275–282.

Hutchins, E. (1980). *Culture and inference.* Cambridge, MA: Harvard University Press.

Hutchins, E. (1983). Understanding Micronesian navigation. In D. Gentner & A. Stevens (Eds.), *Mental models.* Hillsdale, NJ: Erlbaum.

Hutchins, E. (1995). *Cognition in the wild.* Cambridge, MA: MIT Press.

Huttenlocher, P. R. (1990). Morphometric study of human cerebral cortex development. *Neuropsychologia, 28*, 517–527.

Huttenlocher, P. R. (1994). Synaptogenesis in human cerebral cortex. In G. Dawson and K. W. Fischer (Eds.), *Human behavior and the developing brain.* New York: The Guilford Press.

Hyde, J. S., & Linn, M.C. (1988). Gender differentces in verbal ability: A meta-analysis. *Psychological Bulletin, 104*, 53–69.

Hymel, S., Wagner, E., & Butler, L. J. (1990). Reputational bias: View from the peer group. In S. R. Asher & J. D. Coie (Eds.), *Peer rejection in childhood.* Cambridge: Cambridge University Press.

Inhelder, B., & Piaget, J. (1958). *The growth of logical thinking from childhood to adolescence.* New York: Basic Books.

Inhelder, B., & Piaget, J. (1964). *The early growth of logic in the child.* New York: Harper & Row.

Irvine, S. H., & Berry, J. W. (1987). *Human abilities in cultural context.* New York: Cambridge University Press.

Isaacs, S. (1966). *Intellectual growth in young children.* New York: Schocken.

Isabella, R. A. (1993). Origins of attachment: Maternal interactive behavior across the first year. *Child Devlopment, 64*, 605–621.

Ishiyama, F. I., & Chabassol, D. J. (1985). Adolescents' fear of social consequences of academic success as a function of age and sex. *Adolescence, 14*, 37–46.

Itard, J. M. G. (1801/1982). *The wild boy of Aveyron* (G. Humphrey & M. Humphrey, Trans.). New York: Appleton-Century-Crofts.

Izard, C. (1994). Innate and universal facial expressions: Evidence from developmental and cross-cultural research. *Psychological Bulletin, 115*, 288–299.

Izard, C. E., Hembree, E. A., & Huebner, R. R. (1987). Infants' emotion expression to acute pain: Developmental change and stability of individual differences. *Developmental Psychology, 23*, 105–113.

Izard, C. E., Huebner, R. R., Risser, D., McGinnes, G. C., & Dougherty, L. M. (1980). The young infant's ability to produce discrete emotion expressions. *Developmental Psychology, 16*, 132–140.

Jacklin, C. N., & Maccoby, E. E. (1978). Social behavior at 33 months in same-sex and mixed-sex dyads. *Child Development, 49*, 557–569.

Jacob, F. (1982). *The possible and the actual.* New York: Pantheon Books.

Jacobson, S. W., Jacobson, J. L., Sokol, R. J., Martier, S. S., & Ager, J. W. (1993). Prenatal alcohol exposure and infant information processing ability. *Child Development, 64*, 1706–1721.

Jaglom, L. & Gardner, H. (1981). The preschool television viewer as anthropologist. In H. Kelly and H. Gardner (Eds.). *Viewing children through television. (New directions in child development. Vol. 13.).* San Francisco: Jossey-Bass.

Jahoda, G. (1980). Theoretical and systematic approaches in mass-cultural psychology. In H. C. Triandis & W. W. Lambert (Eds.), *Handbook of cross-cultural psychology* (Vol. 1). Boston: Allyn and Bacon.

Jahoda, G. (1983). European "lag" in the development of an economic concept: A study in Zimbabwe. *British Journal of Developmental Psychology, 1*, 113–120.

James, W. T. (1890). *The principles of psychology.* New York: Holt & Co.

James, W. T. (1951). Social organization among dogs of different temperaments: Terriers and beagles, reared together. *Journal of Comparative and Physiological Psychology, 44*, 71–77.

Jameson, S. (1986, July 11). South Korean parents tip birth ratio. *Los Angeles Times, p. 1*, 18.

Janes, M. D. (1975). Physical and psychological growth and development. *Environmental Child Health, 121*, 26–30.

Janowsky, J. S., & Carper, R. (1995). A neural basis for cognitive transitions in school-aged children. In M. Haith & A. Sameroff (Eds.), *Reason and responsibility: The passage through childhood.* Chicago: University of Chicago Press.

Jeans, P. C., Smith, M. B., & Stearns, G. (1955). Incidence of prematurity in relation to maternal nutrition. *Journal of the American Dietary Association, 31*, 576–581.

Jencks, C. (1972). Inequality: A reassessment of the effect of family and schooling in America. New York: Basic Books.

Jensen, A. R. (1969). How much can we boost I.Q. and scholastic achievement? *Harvard Educational Review, 29,* 1–123.

Jensen, A. R. (1980). *Bias in mental testing.* New York: Free Press.

Jessor, R. (1992). Risk behavior in adolescence: A psychosocial framework for understanding and action. *Developmental Review, 12,* 374–390.

Jessor, R., & Jessor, S. L. (1977). *Problem behavior and psychosocial development: A longitudinal study of youth.* New York: Academic Press.

Joffe, C. (1977). *Friendly intruders: Child care professionals and family life.* Berkeley: University of California Press.

Johnson, W., & Emde, R. N., Pannebecker, B., Stenberg, C., & Davis, M. (1982). Maternal perception of infant emotion from birth through 18 months. *Infant Behavior and Development, 5,* 313–322.

Johnston, F. E., Borden, M., & MacVean, R. B. (1973). Height, weight, and their growth velocities in Guatemalan private school children of high socioeconomic class. *Human Biology, 45,* 627–641.

Johnston, F. E., & Low, S. M. (1995). *Children of the urban poor.* Boulder: Westview.

Jones, C. L., & Lopez, R. E. (1990). Drug abuse and pregnancy. In I. R. Merkatz & J. E. Thompson (Eds.), *New perspectives on prenatal care.* New York: Elsevier.

Jones, M. C. (1965). Psychological correlates of somatic development. *Child Development, 36,* 899–911.

Jones, M. C., & Bayley, N. (1950). Physical maturing among boys as related to behavior. *Journal of Educational Psychology, 41,* 129–184.

Jordan, C. (1981). The selection of culturally compatible teaching practices. *Educational Perspectives, 20,* 16–19.

Kagan, J. (1981). *The second year.* Cambridge, MA: Harvard University Press.

Kagan, J. (1982). *Psychological research on the human infant: An evaluative summary.* New York: William T. Grant Foundation.

Kagan, J. (1984). *The nature of the child.* New York: Basic Books.

Kagan, J. (1994). *Galen's prophecy: Temperament in human nature.* New York: Basic Books.

Kagan, J., Arcus, D., Snidman, N., Feng, W. Y., Hendler, J., & Greene, S. (1994). Reactivity in infants: A cross-national comparison. *Developmental Psychology, 30,* 342–345.

Kagan, J., & Hamburg, M. (1981). The enhancement of memory in the first year. *Journal of Genetic Psychology, 138,* 3–14.

Kagan, J., Kearsley, R. B., & Zelazo, P. (1978). *Infancy: Its place in human development.* Cambridge, MA: Harvard University Press.

Kagan, J., Klein, R. E., Finley, G. E., Rogoff, B., & Nolan, E. (1979). A cross-cultural study of cognitive development. *Monographs of the Society for Research in Child Development, 44*(5, Serial No. 180).

Kagan, J., & Moss, H. A. (1962). *Birth to maturity.* New York: Wiley.

Kagan, J., & Snidman, N. (1991a). Infant predictors of inhibited and uninhibited profiles. *Psychological Science, 2,* 40–44.

Kagan, J., & Snidman, N. (1991b). Temperamental factors in human development. *American Psychologist, 46,* 856–862.

Kagan, J., Snidman, N., Arcus, D., & Reznick, J. S. (1994). *Galen's Prophecy: Temperament in human nature.* New York: Basic Books.

Kagan, S., & Madsen, M. C. (1971). Cooperation and competition of Mexican, Mexican-American, and Anglo-American children of two ages under four instructional sets. *Developmental Psychology, 5,* 32–39.

Kail, R. (1990). *The development of memory in children* (3rd. ed.). New York: W. H. Freeman.

Kail, R. (1991). Processing time declines exponentially during childhood and adolescence. *Developmental Psychology, 27,* 259–266.

Kail, R., & Park, Y. (1994). Processing time, articulation time, and memory span. *Journal of Experimental Child Psychology, 57,* 281–291.

Kaitz, M., Meschulach-Sarfaty, O., Auerbach, J., & Eidelman, A. (1988). A reexamination of newborns' ability to imitate facial expressions. *Developmental Psychology, 24,* 3–7.

Kamara, A. I., & Easley, J. A., Jr. (1977). Is the rate of cognitive development uniform across cultures? A methodological critique with new evidence from Themne children. In P. R. Dasen (Ed.), *Piagetian psychology: Cross-cultural contributions.* New York: Gardner.

Kaminsky, H. (1984). Moral development in historical perspective. In W. M. Kurtines & J. L. Gewirtz (Eds.), *Morality, moral behavior, and moral development.* New York: Wiley.

Kandel, D. B. (1978). Homophily, selection and socialization in adolescent friendships. *American Journal of Sociology, 84,* 427–436.

Kandel, D. B. (1986). Processes of peer influences in adolescence. In R. K. Silbereisen, K. Eyferth, & G. Rudinger (Eds.), *Development as action in context: Problem behavior and normal youth development.* Berlin: Springer-Verlag.

Kandel, D. B., & Andrews, K. (1987). Processes of adolescent socialization by parents and peers. *International Journal of the Addictions, 22,* 319–342.

Kandel, D. B., & Lesser, G. S. (1972). *Youth in two worlds: United States and Denmark.* San Francisco: Jossey-Bass.

Kaplan, H., & Dove, H. (1987) Infant development among the Ache of Eastern Paraguay. *Developmental Psychology, 23,* 190–198.

Kaplan, M., Eidelman, A. I., & Aboulafia, Y. (Sept. 9, 1983). Fasting and the precipitation of labor: The Yom Kippur effect. *Journal of the American Medical Association, 250* (10): 1317–1318.

Karmiloff-Smith, A. (1992). *Beyond modularity: A developmental approach to cognitive science.* Cambridge, MA: MIT Press.

Karniol, R. (1989). The role of manual manipulative stages in the infant's acquisition of perceived control over object. *Developmental Review, 9,* 205–233.

Katchadourian, H. A. (1977). *The biology of adolescence.* New York: W. H. Freeman.

Katchadourian, H. A. (1990). Sexuality. In S. S. Feldman & G. R. Elliott (Eds.), *At the threshold: The developing adolescent.* Cambridge, MA: Harvard University Press.

Kaufman, J., & Zigler, E. (1989). The intergenerational transmission of child abuse. In D. Cicchetti & V. Carlson (Eds.), *Child maltreatment: Theory and research on the causes and consequences of child abuse and neglect.* Cambridge: Cambridge University Press.

Kaye, K. (1982). *The mental and social life of babies.* Chicago: University of Chicago Press.

Keating, D. (1980). Thinking processes in adolescence. In J. Adelson (Ed.), *Handbook of adolescent psychology.* New York: Wiley.

Keating, D. (1990). Adolescent thinking. In S. S. Feldman & G. R. Elliott (Eds.), *At the threshold: The developing adolescent.* Cambridge, MA: Harvard University Press.

Keeney, T. J., Cannizzo, S. D., & Flavell, J. H. (1967). Spontaneous and induced verbal rehearsal in a recall task. *Child Development, 38,* 935–966.

Kegan, R. (1982). *The emerging self: Problem and process in human development.* Cambridge, MA: Harvard University Press.

Keil, F. C. (1992). The origins of an autonomous biology. M. R. Gunnar, M. Maratsos (Eds.), *Modularity and constraints in language and cognition. The Minnesota symposia on child psychiatry, Vol. 25.*

Kelley, R. K. (1972). The premarital sexual revolution: Comments on research. *Family Coordinator, 21,* 334–336.

Kellogg, R. (1969). *Analyzing children's art.* Palo Alto, CA: National Press Books.

Kellogg, W. N., & Kellogg, L. A. (1933). *The ape and the child: A study of environmental influences upon early behavior.* New York: Whittlesey House.

Kempe, R., & Kempe, C. H. (1978). *Child Abuse.* Cambridge, MA: Harvard University Press.

Kempe, C., Silverman, E., Steele, B., Droegemueller, W., & Silver, H. (1962). The battered child syndrome. *Journal of the American Medical Association, 181,* 17–24.

Kendall-Tackett, K. A., Williams, L. M., & Finkelhor, D. (1993). Impact of sexual abuse on children: A review and synthesis of recent empirical studies. *Psychological Bulletin, 113,* 164–180.

Keniston, K. (1970). Youth: As a stage of life. *American Scholar, 39,* 631–654.

Kennell, J. H., Jerauld, R., Wolfe, H., Chester, D., Kreger, N., McAlpine, W., Steffa, M., & Klaus, M. H. (1974). Maternal behavior one year after early and extended post-partum contact. *Developmental Medicine and Child Neurology, 16,* 172–179.

Kennell, J. H., Voos, D. K., & Klaus, M. H. (1979). Parent-infant bonding. In J. D. Osofsky (Ed.), *Handbook of infant development.* New York: Wiley.

Kenyatta, J. (1938). *Facing Mt. Kenya: The tribal life of the Kikuyu.* London: Secker & Warburg.

Kerr, T. (1995). Happy birthday Head Start. *Early Childhood News, VII,* 50–51.

Kessen, W. (1965). *The child.* New York: Wiley.

Kett, J. F. (1977). *Rites of passage: Adolescence in America, 1790 to the present.* New York: Basic Books.

Kim, J. (1981). *The process of Asian-American identity development: A study of Japanese American women's perceptions of their struggle to achieve positive identities.* Unpublished doctoral dissertation, University of Massachusetts.

King, M. A., & Yuille, J. C. (1987). Suggestibility and the child witness. In S. J. Ceci, M. P. Toglia, & D. F. Ross (Eds.), *Children's eyewitness memory.* New York: Springer-Verlag.

Kinsey, A. C., Pomeroy, W. B., & Martin, C. E. (1948). *Sexual behavior in the human male.* Philadelphia: Saunders.

Kinsey, A. C., Pomeroy, W. B., Martin, C. E., & Gebhard, P. H. (1953). *Sexual behavior in the human female.* Philadelphia: Saunders.

Kitchener, K. S., & Fischer, K. W. (1990). A skill approach to the development of reflective thinking. In D. Kuhn & S. Karger (eds.), Developmental perspectives on teaching and learning thinking skills. *Contributions to human development, v. 21.* Basel, Switzerland: Karger.

Kitcher, P. (1985). *Vaulting ambition: Sociobiology and the quest for human nature.* Cambridge, MA: MIT Press.

Klahr, D. (1982). Nonmonotone assessment of monotone development: An information processing analysis. In S. Strauss (Ed.), *U-shaped behavioral-growth.* New York: Academic Press.

Klahr, D., & Wallace, J. G. (1976). *Cognitive development: An information-processing view.* Hillsdale, NJ: Erlbaum.

Klapper, Z. S., & Birch, H. G. (1969). Perceptual and action equivalence of objects and photographs in children. *Perceptual and Motor Skills, 29,* 763–771.

Klaus, M. H., Kennell, J. H., Plumb, N., & Zuehlke, S. (1970). Human maternal behavior at the first contact with her young. *Pediatrics, 46,* 187.

Klaus, M. H., & Kennell, J. H. (1976). *Maternal-infant bonding: The impact of early separation or loss on family development.* St. Louis, MO: Mosby.

Klein, A., & Starkey, P. (1987). The origins and development of numerical cognition. In J. A. Sloboda & D. Rogers (Eds.), *Cognitive processes in mathematics.* Oxford: Clarendon Press.

Klein, A., & Starkey, P. (1988). Universals in the development of early arithmetic cognition. In G. B. Sax & M. Gearhart (Eds.), *Children's mathematics. New directions for child development,* Vol. 41. San Francisco, CA: Jossey Bass.

Kleitman, N. (1963). *Sleep and wakefulness.* Chicago: University of Chicago Press.

Klesges, R. C., & Hanson, C. L. (1988). Determining the environmental precursors and correlates of childhood obesity: Methodological issues and future research directions. In N. A. Krasnegor, G. D. Grav, & N. Kretchmer (Eds.), *Childhood obesity: A biobehavioral perspective.* New York: Telford Press.

Klesges, R. C., Klesges, L. M., Eck, L. H., & Shelton, M. L. (1995). A longitudinal analysis of accelerated weight gain in preschool children. *Pediatrics, 95 (1),* 126–130.

Klesges, R. C., Shelton, M. L., & Klesges, L. M. (1993). Effects of television on metabolic rate: Potential implications for childhood obesity. *Pediatrics, 91,* 281–286.

Klineberg, O. (1935). *Race differences.* New York: Harper.

Klineberg, O. (1980). Historical perspectives: Cross-cultural psychology before 1960. In H. Triandis & W. Lambert (Eds.), *Handbook of cross-cultural psychology* (Vol 1). Boston: Allyn and Bacon.

Klopfer, P. H., Adams, D. K., & Klopfer, M. S. (1964). Maternal imprinting in goats. *Proceedings of the National Academy of Sciences, 52,* 911–914.

Kluckhohn, C., & Kelly, W. H. (1945). The concept of culture. In R. Linton (Ed.), *The science of man in the world crisis.* New York: Columbia University Press.

Kluckhohn, C., Murray, H. A., & Schneider, D. M. (1953). *Personality in nature, society, and culture.* New York: Knopf.

Kochanska, G., & Askan, N. (1995). Mother-child mutually positive affect, the quality of child compliance to requests and prohibitions, and maternal control as correlates of early internalization. *Child Development, 66,* 236–254.

Kochanska, G., Casey, R. J., & Fukumoto, A. (1995). Toddler's sensitivity to standard violations. *Child Development, 66,* 643–656.

Kohlberg, L. (1966). A cognitive-developmental analysis of childrens' sex role concepts and attitudes. In E. E. Maccoby (Ed.), *The development of sex differences.* Stanford, CA: Stanford University Press.

Kohlberg, L. (1969). Stage and sequence: The cognitive-developmental approach to socialization. In D. A. Goslin (Ed.), *Handbook of socialization theory and research.* Chicago: Rand McNally.

Kohlberg, L. (1976). Moral stages and moralization: The cognitive-developmental approach. In J. Lickona (Ed.), *Moral development behavior: Theory, research and social issues.* New York: Holt, Rinehart and Winston.

Kohlberg, L. (1984). The psychology of moral development: *The nature and validity of moral stages* (Vol. 2). New York: Harper & Row.

Kohlberg, L. & Candee, D. (1984). The relationship of moral judgment to moral action. In W. M. Kurtines & J. L. Gewirtz (Eds.). *Morality, moral behavior, and moral development.* New York: Wiley.

Kohlberg, L., & Kramer, R. (1969). Continuities and discontinuities in childhood and adult moral development. *Human Development, 12*, 93–120.

Kohlberg, L., & Ryncarz, R. (1990). Beyond justice reasoning: Moral development and considerations of a seventh stage. In C. Alexander & E. Langer (Eds.), *Higher stages of human development: Perspectives on adult growth*. New York: Oxford University Press.

Kohlberg, L., Yaeger, J., & Hjertholm, E. (1968). Private speech: Four studies and a review of theories. *Child Development, 39*, 691–736.

Kohn, M. L. (1977). *Class and conformity* (2nd ed.). Chicago: University of Chicago Press.

Kolata, G. (1986). Obese children: A growing problem. *Science, 232*, 20–21.

Kolata, G. (1987, Sept. 22). Flaws reported in new prenatal test. *New York Times*, Section 1, p. 12.

Kolata, G. (1995, Jan. 7). Is a gene making you read this? *New York Times*, Section 4, p. 3.

Kolb, B., & Whishaw, I. Q. (1996). *Fundamentals of human neuropsychology* (4th ed.). New York: W. H. Freeman.

Koluchova, J. (1972). Severe deprivation in twins: A case study. *Journal of Child Psychology and Psychiatry, 13*, 107–114.

Koluchova, J. (1976). A report on the further development of twins after severe and prolonged deprivation. In A. M. Clarke & A. D. B. Clarke (Eds.), *Early experience: Myth and evidence*. London: Open Books.

Konner, M. (1977). Evolution in human behavior development. In P. H. Leiderman, S. Tulkin, & A. Rosenfeld (Eds.), *Culture and infancy: Variations in human experience*. New York: Academic Press.

Kontos, S., Hsu, H., & Dunn, L. (1994). Children's cognitive and social competence in child care centers and family day-care homes. Special Issue: Diversity and development of Asian Americans. *Journal of Applied Developmental Psychology, 15*, 387–411.

Kopp, C. B. (1983). Risk factors in development. In P. H. Mussen (Ed.), *Handbook of child development: Vol. 2. Infancy and developmental psychobiology*. New York: Wiley.

Kopp, C. B. (1987). The growth of self-regulation: Caregivers and children. In N. Eisenberg (Ed.), *Contemporary trends in developmental psychology*. New York: Wiley.

Kopp, C. B., & Kaler, S. R. (1989). Risk in infancy: Origins and implications. *American Psychologist, 44*, 224–230

Kopp, C. B., & McCall, R. B. (1982). Predicting later mental performance for normal, at-risk, and handicapped infants. In P. B. Baltes & O. G. Brim (Eds.), *Life span development and behavior* (Vol. 4). New York: Academic Press.

Korner, A. F. (1987). Preventive intervention with high-risk newborns: Theoretical conceptual and methodological perspectives. In J. D. Osofsky (Ed.), *Handbook of infant development* (2nd ed.). New York: Wiley.

Korner, A. F., & Grobstein, R. (1966). Visual alertness as related to soothing in neonates. *Child Development, 37*, 867–876.

Korner, A. F., & Thoman, E. (1970). Visual alertness in neonates as evoked by maternal care. *Journal of Experimental Child Psychology, 10*, 67–78.

Kotelchuck, M. (1976). The infant's relationship to the father: Experimental evidence. In M. E. Lamb (Ed.), *The role of the father in child development*. New York: Wiley.

Kotelchuck, M., Schwartz, J. B., Anderka, M. T., & Finison, K. S. (1984). WIC participation and pregnancy outcomes: Massachusetts statewide evaluation project. *American Journal of Public Health, 74*, 1086–1091.

Kovaric, P. M. (1993). Television, the portrayal of the elderly, and children's attitudes. In G. L. Barry & J. K. Asamen (Ed.), *Children and television*. Newbury Park: Sage.

Kozol, J. (1985). *Illiterate America*. Garden City, N. Y.: Double day.

Krappman, L. (1989). Family relationships and peer relationships in middle childhood: An exploratory study of the associations between children's integration into the social network of peers and family development. In K. Kreppner, R.M. Lerner (Eds.), *Family systems and life-span development*. Hillsdale, NJ: Lawrence Erlbaum.

Krashen, S., & Biber, D. (1988). *On course: Bilingual education's success in California*. Sacramento: California Association for Bilingual Education.

Krasnogorski, N. I. (1907/1967). The formation of artificial conditioned reflexes in young children. In Y. Brackbill & G. G. Thompson (Eds.), *Behavior in infancy and early childhood: A book of readings*. New York: Free Press.

Krauss, R. M., & Glucksberg, S. (1969). The development of communication: Competence as a function of age. *Child Development, 42*, 255–266.

Kretschmann, H. J., Kammradt, I., Krauthausen, I., Sauer, B., Wingert, F. (1986). Growth of the hippocampal formation in man. *Bibliotheca Anatomica, 28*, 27–52.

Kreutzer, M. A., Leonard, S. C., & Flavell, J. H. (1975). An interview study of children's knowledge about memory. *Monographs of the Society for Research in Child Development, 40*(1, Serial No. 159).

Kroger, J. (1989). *Identity in adolescence: The balance between self and other*. London: Routledge.

Kroger, J. (1993). Ego identity: An overview. In J. Kroger (Ed.). *Discussions on ego identity*. Hillsdale, N. J.: Erlbaum.

Kuhl, P. K., & Miller, J. D. (1978). Speech perception by the chinchilla: Identification functions for synthetic VOT stimuli. *Journal of the Acoustical Society of America, 63*, 905–917.

Kuhl, P. K., Williams, K. A., Lacerda, F., Stevens, K. N., & Lindblom, B. (1992). Linguistic experiences alters phonetic perception in infants by 6 months of age. *Science, 255*, 606–608.

Kuhn, D. (1976). Short-term longitudinal evidence for the sequentiality of Kohlberg's early stages of moral judgment. *Developmental Psychology, 12*, 162–166.

Kuhn, D., Garcia-Mila, M., Zohar, A., & Anderson, C. (1995). Strategies of knowledge acquisition. *Monographs of the Society for Research in Child Development, 60*, (Serial No. 245, 4).

Kundera, M. (1988). *The art of the novel*. New York: Grove Press.

Kupersmidt, J. B., Coie, J. D., & Dodge, K. A. (1990). The role of poor peer relationships in the development of disorder. In S. R. Asher & J. D. Coie (Eds.), *Peer rejection in childhood*. New York: Cambridge University Press.

Kurtines, W. M., & Gewirtz, J. L. (Eds.). (1984). *Morality, moral behavior, and moral development*. New York: Wiley.

Kurtines, W. M., & Gewirtz, J. L. (Eds.). (1991). *Handbook of moral behavior and development: Vol. 1. Theory*. Hillsdale, NJ: Erlbaum.

Kurtines, W. M., & Gewirtz, J. L. (Eds.). (1995). *Moral development: An introduction*. Boston: Allyn and Bacon.

Kurtines, W. M., & Grief, E. B. (1974). The development of moral thought: Review and evaluation of Kohlberg's approach. *Psychological Bulletin, 81*, 453–470.

La Greca, A. M., (1993). Social skills training with children: Where do we go from here? Presidential Address of the Annual Convention of the American Psychological Association (1992,

Washington, DC). *Journal of Clinical Child Psychology, 22,* 288–298.

Laboratory of Comparative Human Cognition. (1983). Culture and cognitive development. In P. Mussen (Ed.), *Handbook of child psychology: Vol. 1. History, theory, and methods.* New York: Wiley.

Labov, W., & Robbins, C. (1969). A note on the relation of reading failure to peer-group status in urban ghettos. *Florida Language Reporter, 167,* 54–57.

Ladygina-Kots, N. N. (1935). *Infant, ape, and human child.* Moscow: Darwin Museum.

Lagercrantz, H., & Slotkin, T. A. (1986). The "stress" of being born. *Scientific American, 254,* 100–107.

Lamb, M. E. (1976). Interactions between eight-month-old children and their fathers and mothers. In M. E. Lamb (Ed.), *The Role of the Father in Child Development.* New York: Wiley.

Lamb, M. E. (1977). The development of mother-infant and father-infant attachments in the second year of life. *Developmental Psychology, 13,* 637–648.

Lamb, M. E. (1979). Paternal influences and the father's role: A personal perspective. *American Psychologist, 34,* 938–943.

Lamb, M. E. (Ed.). (1987). *The Father's Role: Cross-Cultural Perspectives.* Hillsdale, NJ: Erlbaum.

Lamb, M. E., & Hwang, C. P. (1982). Maternal attachment and mother-neonate bonding: A critical review. In M. E. Lamb & A. L. Brown (Eds.), *Advances for developmental psychology* (Vol. 2). Hillsdale, NJ: Erlbaum.

Lamb, M. E., Pleck, J. H., Charnov, E. L., & Levine, J. A. (1987). A biosocial perspective on paternal behavior and involvement. In J. B. Lancaster, J. Altmann, A. Rossi, & L. R. Sherrod (Eds.), *Parenting across the lifespan: Biosocial perspectives.* Hawthorne, NY: Aldine de Gruyter.

Lamborn, S. D., Mounts, N. S., Steinberg, L., & Dornbusch, S. M. (1991). Patterns of competence and adjustment among adolescents from authoritarian, authoritative, indulgent, and neglectful families. *Child development, 62,* 1049–1065.

Lampl, M., Veldhuis, J. D., & Johnson, M. L. (1992). Saltation and stasis: A model of human growth. *Science, 258,* 801–803.

Landsbaum, J., & Willis, R. (1971). Conformity in early and late adolescence. *Developmental Psychology, 4,* 334–337.

Lane, H. (1976). *The wild boy of Aveyron.* Cambridge, MA: Harvard University Press.

Lange, G., & Pierce, S. H. (1992). Memory-strategy learning and maintainance in preschool children. *Development Psychology, 28,* 453–462.

Langlois, J. (1986). From the eye of the beholder to behavioral reality: Development of social behaviors and social relations as a function of physical attractiveness. In C. P. Herman, M. P. Zanna, & E. T. Higgins (Eds.), *Physical appearance, stigma, and social behavior: The Ontario Symposium* (Vol. 3). Hillsdale, NJ: Erlbaum.

Langlois, J. H., Ritter, J. M., Casey, R. J., & Sawin, D. B. (1995). Infant attractiveness predicts maternal behaviors and attitudes. *Developmental Psychology, 31,* 464–472.

Larsen, M. T. (1986). Writing on clay: From pictograph to alphabet. *Quarterly Newsletter of the Laboratory of Comparative Human Cognition, 8,* 3–9.

Latour, B. (1987). *Science in action.* Cambridge, MA: Harvard University Press.

Lau v. Nichols (1974). 414 U.S. 563.

Laucht, M., Esser, G., & Schmidt, M. H. (1994). Contrasting infant predictors of later cognitive functioning. *Journal of Child Psychology and Psychiatry, 35,* 649–662.

Laupa, M. (1994). "Who's in charge?" Preschool children's concepts of authority. *Early Childhood Research Quarterly, 9,* 1–17.

Lave, J. (1988). *Cognition in practice: Mind, mathematics, and culture in everyday life.* Cambridge: Cambridge University Press.

Lave, J., & Wenger, E. (1991). *Situated learning: Legitimate peripheral practice.* New York: Cambridge University Press.

Lavigne, M. (1982). Rubella's disabled children: Research and rehabilitation. *Columbia, 7,* 10–17.

Le Maire, P., & Siegler, R. S. (1995). Four aspects of strategic change: Contributions to children's learning of multipli-cation. *Journal of Experimental Psychology: General, 124,* 83–97.

Le Mare, L. J., & Rubin, K. H. (1987). Perspective taking and peer interaction: Structural and developmental analyses. *Child Development, 58,* 306–315.

Leaper, C. (Ed.), (1994). *Childhood gender segregation: Causes and consequences. New directions for child development, No. 65.* San Francisco: Jossey Bass.

Leary, W. E. (1995, Jan. 30). Sickle cell trail called success, halted early. *New York Times,* B5, B8.

Lecanuet, J. P., Granier-Deferre, C., Jacquet, A. Y., & Busnel, M. C. (1992). Decelerative cardiac responsiveness to acoustical stimulation in the near term foetus. *Quarterly Journal of Experimental Psychology, 44,* 279–303.

Lecours, A. R. (1975). Mylogenetic correlates of the development of speech and language. In E. H. Lenneberg & E. Lenneberg (Eds.), *Foundations of language development* (Vol. I). New York: Academic Press.

Lecours, A. R. (1982). Correlates of developmental behavior in brain maturation. In T. Bever (Ed.), *Regressions in mental development.* Hillsdale, NJ: Erlbaum.

Legault, F., & Strayer, F. F. (1990). The emergence of sex-segregation in preschool peer groups. In F. F. Strayer (Ed.), *Social interaction and behavioral development during early childhood.* Montreal: La Maison D'Ethologie de Montréal.

Legg, C., Sherick, I., & Wadland, W. (1974). Reaction of preschool children to the birth of a sibling. *Child Psychiatry and Human Development, 5,* 3–39.

Lemish, D., & Rice, M. L. (1986). Television as a talking picture book: A prop for language acquisition. *Journal of Child Language, 13,* 251–274.

Lenneberg, E. H., Rebelsky, F. G., & Nichols, I. A. (1965). The vocalizations of infants born to hearing and deaf parents. *Human Development, 8,* 23–27.

Leonard, L. B., Chapman, K., Rowan, L. E., & Weiss, A. L. (1983). Three hypotheses concerning young children's imitations of lexical items. *Developmental Psychology, 19,* 591–601.

Leoni, L. (1964). *Tico and the golden wings.* New York: Pantheon.

Leontiev, A. N. (1981). *Problems of the development of the mind.* Moscow: Progress Publishers.

Leopold, W. F. (1949). *Speech development of a bilingual child: A linguist's record. Vol. 2. Diary from age two.* Evanston, IL: Northwestern University Press.

Lerner, M. I., & Libby, W. J. (1976). *Heredity, evolution, and society.* New York: W. H. Freeman.

Lerner, R. M. (1991). Changing organism-context relations as the basic process of development: A development contextual perspective. *Developmental Psychology, 27,* 27–32.

Leslie, A. M. (1991). The theory of mind impairment in autism: Evidence for a modular mechanism of development? In A. Whiten, (ed.) *Natural theories of mind: Evolution, development, and simulation of everyday mindreading.* Oxford: Basil Blackwell.

Leslie, A. M. (1994). To MM, to BY, and agency: Core architecture and domain specificity. In L. A. Hirschfeld & S. Gelman (Eds.), *Mapping the mind: Domain specificity in cognition and culture.* New York: Cambridge University Press.

Leslie, A. M., & Keeble, S. (1987). Do six-month-old infants perceive causality? *Cognition, 25,* 265–288.

Lesser, G. S. (1974). *Children and television.* New York: Random House.

Lester, B. M., Als, H., & Brazelton, T. B. (1982). Regional obstetric anesthesia and newborn behavior: A reanalysis towards synergistic effects. *Child Development, 53,* 687–692.

Lester, B. M., & Boukydis, C. F., & Zachariah, C. (1992). No language but a cry. In H. Papousek, J. Jurgens, & M. Papousek (Eds.), *Nonverbal vocal communications: Comparative and developmental approaches.* New York: Cambridge University Press.

Lester, B. M., & Tronik, E. Z. (1994). The effect of prenatal cocaine exposure and child outcome. *Infant Mental Health Journal, 15,* 107–120.

Lester, B. M., & Zeskind, P. S. (1982). A biobehavioral perspective on crying in early infancy. In H. Fitzgerald, B. Lester, & M. Yogman (Eds.), *Theory and research in behavioral pediatrics* (Vol. 1). New York: Plenum Press.

Lever, J. (1978). Sex differences in the complexity of children's play and games. *American Sociological Review, 43,* 471–483.

Levin, J. A., Kim, H., & Riel, M. (1990). Analyzing instructional interactions on electronic message networks. In L. Harasim (Ed.), *On-line education: Perspectives on a new environment.* New York: Prager.

Le Vine, R. A. (1974). Parental goals: A cross cultural view. In H. J. Leichter (Ed.), *The family as educator.* New York: Teachers College Press.

Le Vine, R. A. (1988). Human parental care: Universal goals, cultural strategies, individual behavior. In R. A. Le Vine, P. M. Miller, & M. M. West (Eds.), *Parental behavior in diverse societies. New directions for child development, No. 40.* San Francisco, CA: Jossey-Bass, Inc.

Le Vine, R. A., Dixon, S., Le Vine, S., & Richman, A. (1994). *Child care and culture: Lessons from Africa.* New York: Cambridge University Press.

Levinson, P. J., & Carpenter, R. L. (1974). An analysis of analogical reasoning in children. *Child Development, 45,* 857–861.

Levy, G. D., & Fivush, R. (1993). Scripts and gender: A new approach for examining gender-role development. *Developmental Review, 13,* 126–146.

Lewis, M. (1993). Self-conscious emotions: Embarrassment, pride, shame and guilt. In M. Lewis and J. M. Haviland (Eds.), *Handbook of Emotions.* New York: The Guilford Press.

Lewis, M., & Brooks-Gunn, J. (1979). *Social cognition and the acquisition of self.* New York: Plenum Press.

Lewis, M., & Feiring, C. (1989). Infant, mother, and mother-infant interaction behavior and subsequent attachment. *Child Development, 60,* 831–837.

Lewis, M., Sullivan, M., & Vasen, M. (1987). Making faces: Age and emotional difference in the posing of emotional expressions. *Developmental Psychology, 23,* 690–697.

Lewontin, R. C. (1976). Race and intelligence. In N. J. Block & G. Dworkin (Eds.), *The IQ controversy.* New York: Pantheon.

Lewontin, R. C. (1994). *Inside and outside: Gene, environment and organisms.* Worcester, MA: Clark University Press.

Liaw, F. R., & Brooks-Gunn, J. (1993). Patterns of low-birthweight children's cognitive development. *Developmental Psychology, 29,* 1024–1035.

Liebenberg, B. (1967). Expectant fathers. *American Journal of Orthopsychiatry, 37,* 358–359.

Lieberman, P. (1984). *The biology and evolution of language.* Cambridge, MA: Harvard University Press.

Lieberman, P. (1991). *Uniquely human: The evolution of speech, thought, and selfless behavior.* Cambridge, MA: Harvard University Press.

Liebert, R. M. (1984). What develops in moral development? In W. K. Kurtines & J. L. Gewirtz (Eds.), *Morality, moral behavior, and moral development.* New York: Wiley.

Lifter, K., & Bloom, L. (1989). Object knowledge and the emergence of language. *Infant Behavior and Development, 12,* 395–424.

Lightfoot, C. C. (1994). *Playing with desire: An interpretive perspective on adolescent risk-taking.* Paper presented at the annual meeting of the American Educational Research Association. New Orleans, LA.

Linaza, J. (1984). Piaget's marbles: The study of children's games and their knowledge of rules. *Oxford Review of Education, 10,* 271–274.

Linn, M. C. (1983). Content, context, and process in reasoning. *Journal of Early Adolescence, 3,* 63–82.

Linn, M. C., De Benedictus, T., & Delucchi, K. (1982). Adolescent reasoning about advertisements: Preliminary investigations. *Child Development, 53,* 1599–1613.

Linn, M. C. & Hyde, J. S. (1989). Gender, mathematics, and science. *Educational Researcher, 18,* 17–27.

Linn, M. C., & Hyde, J. S. (1991). Cognitive and psychosocial gender differences trends. In R. Lerner, A. C. Petersen, & J. Brooks-Gunn (Eds.), *Encyclopedia of Adolescence.* New York: Garland Publishers.

Linn, M. C., & Sweeney, S. F., Jr. (1981). Individual differences in formal thought: Role of expectations and attitudes. *Journal of Educational Psychology, 73,* 274–286.

Lino, M. (1993). Expenditure on a child by families. *Family Economic Review, 7,* 2–19.

Lipsitt, L. P. (1977). Taste in human neonates: Its effects on sucking and heart rate. In J. M. Weiffenbach (Ed.), *Taste and development: The genesis of sweet preference.* Washington, DC: U.S. Government Printing Office.

Lipsitt, L. P. (1990). Learning and memory in infants. *Merrill Palmer Quarterly, 36,* 53–66.

Lipsitt, L. P., & Levy, N. (1959). Electrotactual threshold in the neonate. *Child Development, 30,* 547–554.

Lock, A. (1980). *The guided reinvention of language.* New York: Academic Press.

Locke, J. (1938). *Some thoughts concerning education.* London: Churchill. (Original work published 1699).

Loftus, E. F. (1979). *Eyewitness testimony.* Cambridge, MA: Harvard University Press.

Loftus, E. F., & Davies, G. M. (1984). Distortions in the memory of children. *Journal of Social Issues, 40,* 51–67.

Logan, R. K. (1986). *The alphabet effect.* New York: Morrow.

Lomax, E. M., Kagan, J., & Rosenkrantz, B. G. (1978). *Science and patterns of child care.* New York: W. H. Freeman.

Lorch, E. P. (1994). Measuring children's cognitive processing of television. In A. Lang (Ed.), *Measuring psychological responses to media.* Hillsdale, NJ: Erlbaum.

Lorenz, K. (1943). Die Angebornen Formen möglichen Erfahrung. *Zeitschrift für Tierpsychologie, 5,* 233–409.

Lorenz, K. (1966). *On aggression.* New York: Harcourt, Brace & World.

Lozoff, B., Wolf, A., & Davis, N. (1984). Cosleeping in urban families with young children in the United States. *Pediatrics, 74*(2), 171–182.

Lucariello, J., & Rifkin, A. (1986). Event representations as the basis of categorical knowledge. In K. Nelson (Ed.), *Event knowledge: Structure and function in development*. Hillsdale, NJ: Erlbaum.

Luke, B., Johnson, T. R. B., & Petrie, R. H. (1993). *Clinical maternal-fetal nutrition*. Boston: Little, Brown, & Company.

Luria, A. R. (1961). The role of speech in the regulation of normal and abnormal behavior. New York: Pergamon.

Luria, A. R. (1973). *The working brain*. New York: Basic Books.

Luria, A. R. (1976). *Cognitive development*. Cambridge, MA: Harvard University Press.

Luria, A. R. (1981). *Language and cognition*. New York: Wiley.

Lutz, C. (1987). Goals, events, and understanding Ifaluk emotion theory. In D. Holland & N. Quinn (Eds.), *Cultural models in language and thought*. Cambridge: Cambridge University Press.

Lynn, R. (1982). IQ in Japan and the United States shows a growing disparity. *Nature, 297*, 222–223.

Lyons-Ruth, K., Repacholi, B., McLeod, S., Silva, E. (1991). Disorganized attachment behavior in infancy: Short-term stability, maternal and infant correlates, and risk-related subtypes. *Development & Psychopathology, 3*, 377–396.

Maas, H. (1963). The young adult adjustment of twenty wartime residential nursery children. *Child Welfare, 42*, 57–72.

Maccoby, E. E. (1980). *Social development: Psychological growth and the parent-child relationship*. New York: Harcourt Brace Jovanovich.

Maccoby, E. E. (1984). Middle childhood in the context of the family. In W. A. Collins (Ed.), *Development during middle childhood: The years from six to twelve*. Washington, DC: National Academy Press.

Maccoby, E. E., & Martin, J. A. (1983). Socialization in the context of the family: Parent-child interaction. In P. H. Mussen (Ed.), *Handbook of child psychology: Vol. 4. Socialization, personality, and social behavior*. New York: Wiley.

MacDonald, K. (1988). *Social and personality development: An evolutionary synthesis*. New York: Plenum Press.

MacDonald, K., & Parke, R. (1984). Bridging the gap: Parent-child play interaction and peer interactive competence. *Child Development, 55*, 1265–1277.

MacFarlane, A. (1975). Olfaction in the development of social preferences in the human neonate. *Parent-infant interaction* (CIBA Foundation symposium 33). New York: Elsevier.

MacFarlane, A. (1977). *The psychology of childbirth*. Cambridge, MA: Harvard University Press.

MacKenzie, B. (1984). Explaining race differences in I.Q. *American Psychologist, 39*, 1214–1233.

Maclusky, N. J., & Naftolin, F. (1981). Sexual differentiation in the central nervous system. *Science, 211*, 1294–1303.

Madsen, M. C., & Shapira, A. (1970). Cooperative and competitive behavior of urban Afro-American, Anglo-American, Mexican-American, and Mexican village children. *Developmental Psychology, 3*, 16–20.

Magnusson, D., Bergman, L. R., Rudinger, G., & Törestad, B. (1991). *Problems and methods in longitudinal research: Stability and change*. New York: Cambridge University Press.

Main, M. (1973). *Play, exploration, and competence as related to child-adult attachment*. Unpublished doctoral dissertation, Johns Hopkins University.

Main, M., & Weston, D. (1981). The quality of the toddler's relationship to mother and father: Related to conflict behavior and the readiness to establish new relationships. *Child Development, 52*, 932–940.

Malatesta, C. Z., Grigoryev, P., Lamb, C., Albin, M., & Culver, C. (1986). Emotional socialization and expressive development in preterm and full term infants. *Child Development, 57*, 316–330.

Malina, R. M. (1975). *Growth and development: The first twenty years in man*. Minneapolis: Burgess.

Malina, R. M., & Bouchard, C. (1991). *Growth, maturation and physical activity*. Champaign, IL: Human Kinetics Books.

Mallick, S. K., & McCandless, B. R. (1966). A study of catharsis of aggression. *Journal of Personality and Social Psychology, 4*, 590–596.

Mandler, J. (1983). Representation. In P. H. Mussen (Ed.), *Handbook of child psychology: Vol 3. Cognitive development*. New York: Wiley.

Mandler, J. (1990). Recall of events by preverbal children. *Annals of the New York Academy of Sciences, 608*, 485–516.

Mandler, J. M. (1996). Development of categorization: Perceptual and conceptual categories. In G. Bremner, A. Slater, & G. Butterworth (Eds.), *Infant Development: Recent Advances*. Hove: Erlbaum.

Mandler, J. M., & Bauer., P. J. (1988). The cradle of categorization: Is the basic level basic? *Cognitive Development, 3*, 247–264.

Mandler, J. M., McDonough, L. (1993). Concept formation in infancy. *Cognitive Development, 8*, 291–318.

Mandler, J., Scribner, S., Cole, M., & De Forest, M. (1980). Cross-cultural invariance in story recall. *Child Development, 51*, 19–26.

Maratsos, M. (1973). Nonegocentric communication abilities in preschool children. *Child Development, 44*, 697–700.

Maratsos, M. (1983). Some issues in the study of the acquisition of grammar. In P. Mussen (Ed.), *Handbook of child psychology: Vol 3. Cognitive development*. New York: Wiley.

Marcia, J. E. (1966). Development and validation of ego identity status. *Journal of Personality and Social Psychology, 3*, 551–558.

Marcia, J. E. (1980). Identity in adolescence. In J. Adelson (Ed.), *Handbook of Adolescent Psychology*. New York: Wiley.

Marcia, J. E. (1991). Identity and self development. In R. Lerner, A. C. Petersen, & J. Brooks-Gunn (Eds.), *Encyclopedia of Adolescence*. New York: Garland Publishers.

Marean, G. C., Werner, L. A., & Kuhl, P. K. (1992). Vowel categorization by very young infants. *Developmental Psychology, 28*, 396–405.

Markus, H. R., & Kitayama, S. (1991). Culture and the self: Implications for cognition, emotion, and motivation. *Psychological Review, 98*, 224–253.

Marquis, D. (1931). Can conditioned reflexes be established in the newborn infant? *Journal of Genetic Psychology, 39*, 479–492.

Marshall, W. A., & Tanner, J. M. (1974). Puberty. In J. A. Davis & J. Dobbing (Eds.), *Scientific foundations of pediatrics*. Philadelphia: Saunders.

Martin, C.L. (1993). New directions for investigating children's gender knowledge. *Developmental Review, 13*, 184–204.

Martin, C. L., & Halverson, C. F. (1981). A schematic processing model of sextyping and stereotyping in children. *Child Development, 52*, 1119–1134.

Martin, C. L., & Halverson, C. F. (1987). The roles of cognition in sex role acquisition. In D. B. Carter, (ed.) *Current conceptions of sex roles and sex typing: Theory and research*. New York, NY: Praeger Publishers.

Martin, G. B., & Clark, R. D. (1987). Distress crying in neonates: Species and peer specificity. *Developmental Psychology, 18*, 3–9.

Matas, L., Arend, R., & Sroufe, L. A. (1978). Continuity of adaptation in the second year. The relationship between quality of attachment and later competence. *Child Development, 49*, 547–556.

Mathew, A., & Cook, M. (1990). The control of reaching movements by young infants. *Child Development, 61*, 1238–1257.

McAdoo, H. P. (1985). Racial attitude and self-concept of young black children over time. In H. P. McAdoo & J. L. McAdoo (Eds.), *Black children: Social, educational, and parental environments.* Beverly Hills: Sage.

McCall, R. B. (1981). Nature, nurture and the two realms of development: A proposed integration with respect to mental development. *Child Development, 52*, 1–12.

McCall, R. B., Eichorn, D. H., & Hogarty, P. S. (1977). Transitions in early mental development. *Monographs of Society for Research Child Development, 42*(3, Serial No. 171).

McCartney, K. (1984). The effect of quality of day care environment upon children's language development. *Developmental Psychology, 20*, 244–260.

McCartney, K., Scarr, S., Phillips, D., & Grajek, S. (1985). Day care as intervention: Comparisons of varying quality programs. *Journal of Applied Developmental Psychology, 6*, 247–260.

McCord, J. (1990). Problem Behaviors. In S. S. Feldman & G. R. Elliott (Eds.), *At the threshold: The developing adolescent.* Cambridge, MA: Harvard University Press.

McCune-Nicolich, L., & Bruskin, C. (1982). Combinatorial competency in symbolic play and language. In D. J. Pepler & K. H. Rubin (Eds.), *The play of children: Current theory and research.* Basil: S. Karger.

McDonough, L., & Mandler, J. M. (1989). *Immediate and deferred imitation with 11-month-olds: A comparison between novel and familiar actions.* Poster presented at the biennial meeting of the Society for Research in Child Development, Kansas City, MO.

McGarrigle, J., Greaves, R., & Hughes, M. (1978). Interpreting inclusion: A contribution to the study of the child's cognitive and linguistic development. *Journal of Experimental Child Psychology, 26*, 528–550.

McGillicuddy-De Lisi, A. V., Watkins, C., & Vinchur, A. J. (1994). The effect of relationship on children's distributive justice reasoning. *Child Development, 65*, 1694–1700.

McGilly, K., & Siegler, R. S. (1989). How children choose among serial recall strategies. *Child Development, 55*, 172–182.

McGraw, M. B. (1975). *Growth: A study of Johnny and Jimmy.* New York: Arno Press. (Original work published 1935).

McGroarty, M. (1992). The societal context of bilingual education. *Educational Researcher, 21*, 7–9.

McGuire, S., Neiderhiser, J. M., Reiss, D., & Hetherington, E. M. (1994). Genetics and environmental influences on perceptions of self-worth and competence in adolescence: A study of twins, full siblings, and step-siblings. *Child Development, 65*, 785–799.

McKnight, C. C., (Jan. 1987). *The underachieving curriculum: Assessing U. S. School mathematics from an international perspective.* A national report on the second international mathematics study. Illinois University, Urbana Dept. of Secondary Education. New York: International Association for the Evaluation of Educational Achievement.

McKusik, V. A. (1975). *Mendelian inheritance in man: Catalog of autosomal dominant, autosomal recession and x-linked phenotype* (4th ed.). Baltimore: Johns Hopkins University Press.

McKusick, V. A. (1986). *Mendelian inheritance in man: Catalog of autosomal dominant, autosomal recessive, and x-linked phenotypes* (8th ed.). Baltimore: Johns Hopkins University Press.

McLane, J. B., & McNamee, G. D. (1990). *Early literacy.* Cambridge, MA: Harvard University Press.

McLoyd, V. (1990). The impact of economic hardship on black families and children: Psychological distress, parenting, and socioemotional development. *Child Development, 61*, 311–346.

McLoyd, V., Jayaratne, T. E., Ceballo, R., & Borquez, J. (1994). Unemployment and work interruption among African American single mothers: Effects on parenting and adolescent socioemotional functioning. *Child Development, 65*, 562–589.

McMillen, M. M. (1979). Differential mortality by sex in fetal and neonatal deaths. *Science, 204*, 89–91.

McNeill, D. (1966). Developmental psycholinguistics. In S. Smith & G. A. Miller (Eds.), *The genesis of language: A psycholinguistic approach.* Cambridge, MA: MIT Press.

McNeill, D. (1970). *The acquisition of language: The study of developmental psycholinguistics.* New York: Harper & Row.

Mead, M. (1935). *Sex and temperament.* New York: William Morrow.

Mead, M. (1928/1973). *Coming of age in Samoa: A psychological study of primitive youth.* New York: American Museum of Natural History.

Mead, M., & MacGregor, F. C. (1951). *Growth and culture.* New York: Putnam.

Mead, M., & Newton, N. (1967). Cultural patterning of perinatal behavior. In S. Richardson & A. Guttmacher (Eds.), *Childbearing: Its social and psychological aspects.* Baltimore: Williams & Wilkins.

Medicus, G. (1992). The inapplicability of the biogenetic rule to behavioral development. *Human Development, 35*, 1–7.

Medrich, E. A., Roizen, J., Rubin, V., & Buckley, S. (1982). *The serious business of growing up.* Berkeley: University of California Press.

Meeus, W. (1993). Occupational identity development, school performance, and social support in adolescence: Findings of a Dutch study. *Adolescence, 28*, 809–818.

Mehan, H. (1979). What time is it, Denise? Asking known information questions in classroom discourse. *Theory into Practice, 18*, 285–294.

Meisel, J. M. (1995). Parameters in acquisition. In P. Fletcher & B. MacWhinney (Eds.), *The handbook of child language.* Oxford: Blackwell.

Meltzoff, A. N. (1988a). Imitation of televised models by infants. *Child Development, 59*, 1221–1229.

Meltzoff, A. N. (1988b). Infant imitation and memory: Nine-month-olds in immediate and deferred tests. *Child Development, 59*, 217–225.

Meltzoff, A. N. (1990). Towards a developmental cognitive science: The implications of cross-modal matching and imitation for the development of representation and memory in infancy. *Annals of the New York Academy of Sciences, 608*, 1–37.

Meltzoff, A. N. (1995). Understanding the intentions of others: Re-enactment of intended acts by 18-month-old children. *Developmental Psychology, 66*, 838–850.

Meltzoff, A. N., & Borton, R. W. (1979). Intermodal matching by human neonates. *Nature, 282*, 403–404.

Meltzoff, A. N., & Gopnik, A. (1989). On linking nonverbal imitation, representation, and language learning in the first two years of life. In G. E. Speidel & K. E. Nelson (Eds.), *The many faces of imitation in language learning.* New York: Springer-Verlag.

Meltzoff, A. N., & Moore, M. K. (1977). Imitation of facial and manual gestures by human neonates. *Science, 198*, 75–78.

Meltzoff, A. N., & Moore, M. K. (1989). Imitation in newborn infants: Exploring the range of gestures imitated and the underlying mechanisms. *Developmental Psychology, 25*, 954–962.

Meltzoff, A. N., & Moore, M. K. (1994). Imitation, memory, and the representation of persons. *Infant Behavior and Development, 17*, 83–99.

Merkatz, I. R., & Thompson, J. E. (Eds.). (1990). *New perspectives on prenatal care.* New York: Elsevier.

Messer, S. B. (1976). Reflection-impulsivity: A review. *Psychological Bulletin, 83*, 1026–1052.

Michalson, L., & Lewis, M. (1985). What do children know about emotions and when do they know it? In M. Lewis & C. Saarni (Eds.), *The socialization of emotions.* New York: Plenum Press.

Miller, G. A. (1981). *Language and speech.* New York: W. H. Freeman.

Miller, G. A. (1991). *The science of words.* New York: Scientific American Library.

Miller, N. E., & Dollard, J. (1941). *Social learning and imitation.* New Haven: Yale University Press.

Miller, P. (1982). *Amy, Wendy and Beth: Learning language in south Baltimore.* Austin: University of Texas Press.

Miller, P., & Sperry, L. J. (1987). The socialization of anger and aggression. *Merrill-Palmer Quarterly, 33*, 1–31.

Miller, S. L., & Tallal, P. (1995). A behavioral neuroscience approach to developmental language disorder: Evidence for a rapid temporal processing deficient. In C. D. Cicchetti & D. J. Cohen (Eds.), *Developmental Psychopathology, Vol. 2: Risk, disorder, and adaption.* New York: John Wiley & Sons.

Minton, H. L. & Schneider, F. W. (1980). *Differential psychiatry.* Monterey, CA: Brooks/Cole.

Minuchin, P. P., & Shapiro, E. K. (1983). The school as a context of social development. In P. H. Mussen (Ed.), *Handbook of child psychology: Vol. 4. Socialization, personality, and social development.* New York: Wiley.

Mischel, W. (1966). A social learning view of sex differences in behavior. In E. M. Maccoby (Ed.), *The development of sex differences.* Stanford: Stanford University Press.

Mischel, W. (1968). *Personality and assessment.* New York: Wiley.

Miyaki, K., Campos, J., Bradshaw, D. L., & Kagan, J. (1986). Issues in socioemotional development. In H. Stevenson, H. Azuma, & K. Hakuta (Eds.), *Child development and education in Japan.* New York: W. H. Freeman.

Miyake, K., Chen, S., & Campos, J. J. (1985). Infant temperament, mother's mode of interaction, and attachment in Japan. An interim report. *Monographs of the Society for Research in Child Development, 50*(1–2, Serial No. 209).

Mize, J., & Ladd, G. W. (1990). A cognitive-social learning approach to social skill training with low-status preschool children. *Developmental Psychology, 26*, 388–397.

Mizukami, K., Kobayashi, N., Ishii, T., & Iwata, H. (1990). First selective attachment begins in early infancy: A study using telethermography. *Infant Behavior and Development, 13*, 257–273.

Modell, J., & Goodman, M. (1990). Historical Perspectives. In S. S. Feldman & G. R. Elliott (Eds.), *At the threshold: The developing adolescent.* Cambridge, MA: Harvard University Press.

Moen, P., Elder, G. H., Jr., & Luscher, K. (Eds.), (1995). *Examining lives in context: Perspectives on the ecology of human development.* Washington, DC: American Psychological Association.

Moffit, T. E., Caspi, A., Belsky, J., & Silva, P. A. (1992). Childhood experience and the onset of menarche: A test of a sociobiological model. *Child Development, 63*, 47–58.

Moll, L. C. (1992). Bilingual classroom studies and community analysis. *Educational Researcher, 21*, 20–24.

Money, J., & Ehrhardt, A. A. (1972). *Man and woman, boy and girl.* Baltimore: Johns Hopkins University Press.

Montemayor, R. (1982). The relationship between parent-adolescent conflict and the amount of time adolescents spend alone and with their parents and peers. *Child Development, 53*, 1512–1519.

Montemayor, R. (1990). Continuity and change in the behavior of nonhuman primates during the transition to adolescence. In R.

Montemayor, G. Adams, & T. Gullota (Eds.), *From childhood to adolescence.* Newbury Park, CA: Sage.

Moon, C., Cooper, R. P., & Fifer, W. P. (1993). Two-day-olds prefer their native language. *Infant Behavior and Development, 16*, 495–500.

Moon, C., & Fifer, W. P. (1990). Syllables as signals for 2-day-old infants. *Infant Behavior and Development, 13*, 377–390.

Moore, K. L., & Persaud, T. V. N. (1993). *The developing human: Clinically oriented embryology* (5th ed.). Philadelphia: Saunders.

Moore, K. L., Persaud, T. V. N., & Shiota, K. (1994). *Color atlas of clinical embryology.* Philadelphia: W. B. Saunders.

Moore, R., & Young, D. (1978). Childhood outdoors: Toward a social ecology of the landscape. In I. Altman & J. Wahlwill (Eds.), *Human behavior and environment* (vol. 3). New York: Plenum Press.

Moore, T. R., Origel, W., Key, T. C., & Resnik, R. (1986). The perinatal and economic impact of prenatal care in a low socioeconomic population. *American Journal of Obstetrics and Gynecology, 154*, 29–33.

Morelli, G. A., Rogoff, B., Oppenheim, D., & Goldsmith, D. (1992). Cultural Variation in infants sleeping arrangements: Questions of independence. *Developmental Psychology, 28*, 604–613.

Morford, J. P., Singleton, J. L., & Goldin-Meadow, S. (1995). From homesign to ASL: Identifying the influences of self-generated childhood gesture system upon language proficiency in adulthood. In D. MacLaughlin & S. McEwen(Eds.), *Proceedings of the 19th Boston University conference on language development.* Somerville, MA: Cascadilla Press.

Morrison, F. J., Smith, L., & Dow-Ehrensberger, M. (1995). Education and cognitive development: A natural experiment. *Developmental Psychology, 31*, 789–799.

Mortimer, J. T., Shanahan, M., & Ryu, S. (1994). The effects of adolescent employment on school-related orientation and behavior. In R. K. Silbereisen & E. Todt (Eds.), *Adolescence in context: The interplay of family, school, peers and work in adjustment.* New York: Springer-Verlag.

Morton, J., & Johnson, M. H. (1991). CONSPEC and CONLEARN: A two-process theory of infant face recognition. *Psychological Review, 98*, 164–181.

Mosier, C. E., & Rogoff, B. (1994). Infant's instrumental use of their mother's to achieve their goals. *Child Development, 65*, 70–79.

Motulsky, V. (1986). *Human genetics: Problems and approaches.* (2nd ed.). New York: Springer-Verlag.

Mowbray, C. T., Lanir, S., & Hulce, M. (1982). Stress, mental health, and motherhood. *Birth Psychology Bulletin, 3*, 10–33.

Mowrer, O. H. (1950). *Learning theory and personality.* New York: Ronald Press.

Munn, P., & Dunn, J. (1988). Temperament and the developing relationship between siblings. *International Journal of Behavioral Development, 12*, 433–451.

Murdock, G. P. (1949). *Social structure.* New York: Macmillan.

Naigles L. G., & Gelman, S. A. (1995). Overextensions in comprehensions and production revisited: Preferential-looking in a study of dog, cat, and cow. *Journal of Child Language, 22*(1), 19–46.

Naeye, R. L. (1978). Effects of maternal cigarette smoking on the fetus and placenta. *Journal of Obstetrics and Gynecology of the British Commonwealth, 85*, 732–735.

Nash, M. (1967). *Machine age Maya.* Chicago: University of Chicago Press.

National Academy of Education, Commission on Reading (1985). *Becoming a nation of readers: The report of the Commission on reading.* Washington, DC: U.S. Department of Education.

National Academy of Sciences, Committee on Dietary Allowances, Food and Nutrition Board, National Research Council (1989). *Recommended dietary allowances.* Washington, DC: National Academy of Sciences.

National Center on Child Abuse and Neglect (1988). *Study findings: Study of national incidence and prevalence of child abuse and neglect.* Washington, DC:

National Center for Education Statistics. *Adult literacy in America.* Educational Testing Service. Princeton, NJ.

National Commission on Youth (1980). *The transition of youth to adulthood: A bridge too long.* Boulder, CO: Westview Press.

National Panel on High School and Adolescent Education. (1976). *The education of adolescents.* HEW Publication (OE) 76–00004. Washington, DC: U.S. Government Printing Office.

National Research Council (U.S.), Panel on Adolescent Pregnancy and Childbearing (1987). C. Hayes (Ed.), *Risking the future: Adolescent sexuality, pregnancy and childbearing.* Washington, DC: National Academy Press.

National Research Council, Panel on Research on Child Abuse and Neglect (1993). *Understanding Child Abuse and Neglect.* Washington, D,C: National Academy Press.

Needham, J. (1968). *Order and life.* Cambridge, MA: MIT Press.

Neimark, E. D. (1975). Longitudinal development of formal operational thought. *Genetic Psychology Monographs, 91,* 171–225.

Neisser, U. (1976). *General, academic, and artificial intelligence.* Hillsdale, NJ: Erlbaum.

Neisser, U., et al. (1996). Intelligence: Knowns and unknowns. *American Psychologist, 51,* 77–101.

Nelson, K. (1973). Structure and strategy in learning to talk. *Monographs of the Society for Research in Child Development, 38*(2, Serial No. 149).

Nelson, K. E. (1976). Facilitating syntax acquisition. *Developmental Psychology, 13,* 101–107.

Nelson, K. (1977). The syntagmatic-paradigmatic shift revisited: A review of research and theory. *Psychological Bulletin, 84,* 93–116.

Nelson, K. (1978). Semantic development and the development of semantic memory. In K. E. Nelson (Ed.), *Children's language* (Vol. 1). New York: Gardner Press.

Nelson, K. (1979). Exploration in the development of a functional system. In W. Collins (Ed.), *Children's language and communication. The Minnesota Symposia on Child Psychology, 12.* Hillsdale, NJ: Erlbaum.

Nelson, K. (1981). Social cognition in a script framework. In J. H. Flavell & L. Ross (Eds.), *Social cognitive development.* Cambridge: Cambridge University Press.

Nelson, K. (1986). *Event knowledge: Structure and function in development.* Hillsdale, NJ: Erlbaum.

Nelson, K. (1988). Constraints on word learning? *Cognitive Development, 3,* 221–246.

Nelson-Le Gault, S., & De Coake, P. A. (1987). Same-sex and cross-sex help exchanges in the classroom. *Journal of Educational Psychology, 79,* 67–71.

Nerlove, S. B., Roberts, J. M., Klein, R. E., Yarbrough, C. & Habicht, J. P. (1974). Natural indicators of cognitive ability. *Ethos, 2,* 265–295.

Netter, F. H. (1965). *The CIBA collection of medical illustrations.* Summit, NJ: Ciba Pharmaceutical Products.

Newcomb, A. F., Bukowski W. M., & Pattee, L. (1993). Children's peer relations: A meta-analytic review of popular, rejected, con-troversial, and average sociometric status. *Psychological Bulletin, 113,* 99–128.

Newman, D. (1992). Technology as support for school structure and school restructuring. *Phi Delta Kappan, 74,* 308–315.

Newson, J., & Newson, E. (1976). *Seven years old in the home environment.* New York: Wiley.

Newton, N., & Newton, M. (1972). Lactation: Its psychological component. In J. G. Howells (Ed.), *Modern perspectives in psycho-obstetrics.* New York: Brunner/Mazel.

Nicolopoulou, A. (1993). Play, cognitive development, and the social world: Piaget, Vygotsky, and beyond. *Human Development, 36,* 1–23.

Niebyl, J. R. (1994). Teratology and drug use during pregnancy-and lactation. In J. R. Scott, Philip J. DiSaia, Charles B. Hammond, & William N. Spellacy (Eds.), *Dansforth's obstetrics and gynecology* (7th ed.). Philadelphia: J. B. Lippincott.

Nightingale, E. O., & Meister, S. B. (1987). *Prenatal screening, policies and values: The example of neural tube defects.* Cambridge, MA: Harvard University Press.

Nijhuis, J. G. (Ed.) (1992). *Fetal behavior: Developmental and perinatal aspects.* New York: Oxford University Press.

Ninio, A., & Bruner, J. (1978). The achievement of antecedents of labelling. *Journal of Child Language, 5,* 1–5.

Niswander, K. R. & Evans, A. T. (Eds.), (1996). *Manual of obstetrics* (5th ed.). Boston: Little Brown.

Nucci, L. (1994). Conceptions of personal issues: A domain distinct from moral or societal concepts. In B. Puka (Ed.), Fundamental research in moral development. *Moral development: A compendium, Volume 2.* New York: Garland.

Nucci, L., & Killen, M. (1991). Social interactions in the preschool and the development of moral and social concepts. In B. Scales, M. Almy, A. Nicolopoulou, & S. Ervin-Tripp (Eds.), *Play and the social context of development in early care and education: Early childhood education series.* New York, NY: Teachers College Press.

Nucci, L., Turiel, E., & Encarnacion-Gawrych, G. E. (1983). Children's social interactions and social concepts: Analyses of morality and convention in the Virgin Islands. *Journal of Cross-cultural Psychology, 14,* 469–487.

Nunes, T., Schliemann, A. D., & Carraher, D. W. (1993). *Street mathematics and school mathematics.* Cambridge: Cambridge University Press.

Nunner-Winkler, G. (1984). Two moralities: A critical discussion of an ethic of care and responsibility versus an ethic of rights and justice. In W. M. Kurtines & J. L. Gewirtz (Eds.), *Morality, moral behavior, and moral development.* New York: Wiley.

Nyiti, R. M. (1976). The development of conservation in the Meru children of Tanzania. *Child Development, 47,* 1122–1129.

Nyiti, R. M. (1982). The validity of "cultural differences explanations" for cross-cultural variation in the rate of Piagetian cognitive development. In D. Wagner & H. Stevenson (Eds.), *Cultural perspectives on child development.* New York: W. H. Freeman.

O'Brien, M., & Huston, A. C. (1985). Development of sex-typed play behavior in toddlers. *Developmental Psychology, 21,* 866–871.

O'Connor, B. P. (1995). Identity development and perceived parental behavior as sources of adolescent egocentrism. *Journal of Youth & Adolscence, 24,* 205–227.

O'Donoghue, J. (1988). *Pedestrian casualties, road accidents, Great Britain 1987: The casualty report.* London: HMSO.

O'Hara, M. W., Neunaber, D. J., & Zekoski, E. M. (1984). Prospective study of postpartum depression: Prevalence, course, and predictive factors. *Journal of Abnormal Psychology, 93*, 158–171.

Ochs, E. (1982). Talking to children in Western Samoa. *Language in Society, 11*, 77–104.

Ochs, E., & Schieffelin, B. (1984). Language acquisition and socialization. Three developmental stories and their implications. In R. Shweder & R. LeVine (Eds.), *Culture theory*. Cambridge: Cambridge University Press.

Ochs, E., & Schieffelin (1995). The impact of language socialization or grammatical development. In P. Fletcher & B. MacWhinney (Eds.), *The handbook of child language*. Cambridge, MA: Basil Blackwell.

Ochs, E., Taylor, C., Rudolph, D., & Smith, R. (1991). Storytelling as a theory-building activity. *Discourse Processes, 15*(1), 37–72.

Olds, D. L., & Henderson, C. R., Jr. (1989). The prevention of maltreatment. In D. Cicchetti & V. Carlson (Eds.), *Child Maltreatment: Theory and research on the causes and consequences of child abuse and neglect*. New York: Cambridge University Press.

Oliner, S. B., & Oliner, P. (1988). *The altruistic personality: Rescuers of Jews in Nazi Germany*. New York: Macmillan.

Oller, D. K. (1978). The emergence of the sounds of speech in infancy. In G. H. Yenikomshian, J. F. Kavanaugh, & C. A. Ferguson (Eds.), *Child phonology: Perception and production*. New York: Academic Press.

Oller, D. K., & Eilers, R. E. (1988). The role of audition in infant babbling. *Child Development, 59*, 441–449.

Olson, D. R. (1978). The language of instruction. In S. Spiro (Ed.), *Schooling and the acquisition of knowledge*. Hillsdale, N. J.: Erlbaum.

Olson, D. R. (1994). *The world on paper*. New York: Cambridge University Press.

Omenn, G. S. (1978). Prenatal diagnosis of genetic disorders. *Science, 200*, 952–958.

Oppel, W. C., Harper, P. A., & Reder, R. V. (1968). The age of attaining bladder control. *Pediatrics, 42*(4), 614–626.

Oppenheim, R. W. (1981). Ontogenetic adaptation and retrogressive processes in the development of the nervous system and behavior: A neuroembryological perspective. In K. J. Connolly & H. F. R. Prechtl (Eds.), *Maturation and development: Biological and psychological perspectives*. Philadelphia: Lippincott.

Ostrea, E. M., & Chavez, C. J. (1979). Perinatal problems (excluding neonatal withdrawal) in maternal drug addiction: A study of 830 cases. *Journal of Pediatrics, 94*, 292–295.

Overmeir, J. B., & Seligman, M. E. P. (1967). Effects of inescapable shock upon subsequent escape and avoidance learning. *Journal of Comparative and Physiological Psychology, 63*, 23–33.

Overton, W. F. (1990). Competence and procedures: Constraints on the development of logical reasoning. In W. F. Overton (Ed.), *Reasoning, necessity, and logic: Developmental perspectives*. Hillsdale, NJ: Erlbaum.

Owen, M. T., & Cox, J. J. (1988). Maternal employment and the transition to parenthood. In A. E. Gottfried & A. W. Gottfried (Eds.), *Maternal employment and children's development*. New York: Plenum Press.

Packer, M. (1994). Cultural work on the kindergarten playground. *Human Development, 37*, 259–276.

Padden, C., & Humphries, T. (1989). *Deaf in America: Voices from a culture*. Cambridge, MA: Harvard University Press.

Paikoff, R. L., Brooks-Gunn, J. (1991). Do parent-child relationships change during puberty? *Psychological Bulletin, 110*, 47–66.

Paley, V. G. (1981). *Wally's stories*. Cambridge, MA: Harvard University Press.

Paley, V. G. (1984). *Boys and girls*. Chicago: University of Chicago Press.

Paley, V. G. (1986). *Mollie is three: Growing up in school*. Chicago: University of Chicago Press.

Palinscar, A. S., & Brown, A. L. (1984). Reciprocal teaching of comprehension fostering and monitoring activities. *Cognition and Instruction, 1*, 117–175.

Papert, S. (1980). *Mindstorms*. Brighton: Harvester Press.

Paris, S. G., Newman, R. S., & Jacobs, J. E. (1985). Social contexts and functions of children's remembering. In M. Pressley & C. Brainard (Eds.), *Cognitive learning and memory in children: Progress in cognitive development research*. Berlin: Springer-Verlag.

Parke, R. D. (1981). *Fathers*. Cambridge, MA: Harvard University Press.

Parke, R. D., & Collmer, C. (1975). Child abuse: An interdisciplinary review. In E. M. Hetherington (Ed.), *Review of child development research Vol 5*. Chicago: University of Chicago Press.

Parke, R. D., & Ladd, G. W. (Eds.). (1992). *Family-peer relationships*. Hillsdale, NJ: Erlbaum.

Parke, R. D. & Sawin D. B. (1975). Infant characteristics and behavior as initiators of maternal and paternal responsivity. Paper presented at the biennial meeting of the Society for Research in Child Development, Denver.

Parke, R. D., & Slaby, R. G. (1983). The development of aggression. In P. H. Mussen (Ed.), *Handbook of child psychology: Vol. 4. Socialization, personality, and social behavior*. New York: Wiley.

Parke, R. D., & Tinsley, B. R. (1981). The father's role in infancy: Determinants of involvement in caregiving and play. In M. E. Lamb (Ed.), *The role of the father in child development* (2nd ed.). New York: Wiley.

Parker, J. E. & Asher, S. R. (1987) Peer relations and later personal adjustment: Are low-accepted children "at risk"? *Psychological Bulletin, 102*, 357–389.

Parker, J. G., & Asher, S. R. (1993). Friendship and friendship quality in middle childhood: Links with peer acceptance and feelings of loneliness and social dissatisfaction. *Developmental Psychology, 29*, 611–621.

Parker, J. G., & Gottman, J. M. (1989). Social and emotional development in a relational context: friendship interactions from early childhood to adolescence. In T. J. Berndt & G. W. Ladd (Eds.), *Peer relationships in child development*. New York: Wiley.

Parker, J. G., Rubin, K. H., Price, J. M., & De Rosier, M. E. (1995). *Peer relationships, child development, and adjustment: A developmental psychopathology*. In D. Cicchetti & D. J. Cohen (Eds.), *Developmental psychopathology*. New York, NY: J. Wiley.

Parmalee, A. H., Jr., Akiyama, Y., Schultz, M. A., Wenner, W. H., Schulte, F. J., & Stern, E. (1968). The electroencephalogram in active and quiet sleep in infants. In P. Kellaway & I. Petersen (Eds.), *Clinical electroencephaly of children*. New York: Grune & Stratton.

Pascalis, O., DeSchonen, S., Morton, J., Deruelle, C. (1995). Mother's face recognition by neonates: A replication and an extension. *Infant Behavior and Development, 18*, 79–85.

Pascual-Leone, J. (1988). Organismic processes for neo-Piagetian theories: A dialetical causal account of cognitive development.

In A. Demetriou (Ed.), *The neo-Piagetian theories of cognitive development: Toward an integration*. Amsterdam: Elsevier.

Patten, B. M. (1968). *Human embryology* (3rd ed.). New York: McGraw-Hill.

Patterson, G. R. (1976). The aggressive child: Victim and architect of a coercive system. In E. J. Marsh, L. A. Hamerlynk, & L. C. Handy (Eds.), *Behavior modification and families: Vol. 1. Theory and research*. New York: Brunner/Mazel.

Patterson, G. R. (1979). A performance theory of coercive family interaction. In R. Cairns (Ed.), *Social Interaction: Methods*. Hillsdale, NJ: Erlbaum.

Patterson, G. R. (1982). *Coercive family processes*. Eugene, OR: Castalia Press.

Patterson, G. R., Debaryshe, B. D., & Ramsey, E. (1989). A developmental perspective on antisocial behavior. *American Psychologist, 44*, 329–348.

Patterson, G. R., Littman, R. A., & Bricker, W. (1967). Assertive behavior in young children: A step toward a theory of aggression. *Monographs of the Society for Research for Child Development, 32*(Serial No. 113).

Pavlov, I. P. (1927). *Conditioned reflexes*. Oxford: Oxford University Press.

Peiper, A. (1963). *Cerebral function in infancy and childhood*. New York: Consultants Bureau.

Pelton, L. H. (1994). The role of material factors in child abuse and neglect. In G.B. Melton & F. D. Barry (Eds.), *Protecting children from abuse: Foundations for a new strategy*. New York: Guilford Press.

Percy, W. (1975). *The message in the bottle*. New York: Farrar, Straus & Giroux.

Perner, J., Ruffman, T., & Leekam, S. R. (1994). Theory of mind is contagious: You catch it from your sibs. *Child Development, 65*, 1228–1238.

Pernoll, M. L., Benda, G. I., & Babson, S. G. (1986). *Diagnosis and management of the fetus and neonate at risk: A guide for team care*. (5th ed.). St. Louis: Mosby.

Perret-Clermont, A. N. (1980). *Social interaction and cognitive development in children*. New York: Academic Press.

Perret-Clermont, A. N., Perret, J. F., & Bell, N. (1991). The social construction of meaning and cognitive activity in elementary school children. In L. B. Resnick, J. M. Levine, & S. D. Teaseley (Eds.), *Perspectives on socially shared cognition*. Washington, DC: American Psychological Association.

Perry, D. G., & Bussey, K. (1984). *Social development*. Englewood Cliffs, NJ: Prentice-Hall.

Persaud, T. V. N. (1977). *Problems of birth defects: From Hippocrates to thalidomide and after*. Baltimore: University Park Press.

Peskin, H. (1967). Pubertal onset and ego functioning. *Journal of Abnormal Psychology, 72*, 1–15.

Peskin, J. (1980). Female performance and Inhelder's and Piaget's tests of formal operations. *Genetic Psychology Monographs, 101*, 245–256.

Pettito, L. A., & Marentette, P. F. (1991). Babbling in the manual mode: Evidence for the onotogeny of language. *Science, 251*, 1493–1496.

Phelps, L., Johnston, L. S., Jimenez, D. P., Wilczenski, F. L., Andrea, R. K., & Healy, R. W. (1993). Figure preference, body dissatisfaction and body distortion in adolescence. *Journal of Adolescent Research, 8*, 297–310.

Phillips, D., McCartney, K., Scarr, S., & Howes, C. (1987). Selective review of infant day care research: A cause for concern! *Zero to Three, 1*(3), 18–21.

Phinney, J. S. (1993). A three-stage model of ethnic identity development in adolescence. In M. E. Bernal & G. P. Knight (Eds.), *Ethnic identity: Formation and transmission among hispanics and other minorities*. Albany, NY: SUNY Press.

Phinney, J. (1995). Ethnic identity and self-esteem: A review and integration. In A. Padilla (Ed.). *Hispanic psychology: Critical issues in theory and research*. Thousand Oaks, CA: Sage.

Piaget, J. (1926). *The language and thought of the child*. New York: Meridian Books.

Piaget, J. (1928). *Judgment and reasoning in the child*. London: Routledge & Kegan Paul.

Piaget, J. (1930). *The child's conception of physical causality*. New York: Harcourt Brace.

Piaget, J. (1952a). *The child's conception of number*. New York: W. W. Norton.

Piaget, J. (1952b). *The origins of intelligence in children*. New York: International Universities Press.

Piaget, J. (1954). *The construction of reality in the child*. New York: Basic Books.

Piaget, J. (1962). *Play, dreams and imitation*. New York: W. W. Norton.

Piaget, J. (1932/1965). *The moral judgment of the child*. New York: Free Press.

Piaget, J. (1964). Development and learning. In R. E. Ripple & V. N. Rockcastle (Eds.), *Piaget rediscovered*. Conference on cognitive studies and curriculum development. Cornell University and University of California.

Piaget, J. (1967). *Six psychological studies*. New York: Random House.

Piaget, J. (1972). Intellectual evolution from adolescence to adulthood. *Human Development, 15*, 1–12.

Piaget, J. (1973). *The psychology of intelligence*. Totowa, NJ: Littlefield & Adams.

Piaget, J. (1966/1974). Necessite et signification des recherches comparatives en psychologie genetique. [Need and significance of cross-cultural studies in genetic psychology.] In. J. W. Berry & P. R. Dasen (Eds.), *Culture and Cognition*. London: Methuen.

Piaget, J. (1977). *The development of thought: Equilibration of cognitive structure*. New York: Viking.

Piaget, J. (1929/1979). *The child's conception of the world*. New York: Harcourt Brace.

Piaget, J. (1980). Schemes of action and language learning. In M. Piattelli-Palmarini (Ed.), *Language and Learning: The debate between Jean Piaget and Noam Chomsky*. Cambridge, MA: Harvard University Press.

Piaget, J. (1983). Piaget's theory. In P. H. Mussen (Ed.), *Handbook of child psychology: Vol 1. History, theory and methods*. New York: Wiley.

Piaget, J. (1987). *Possibility and necessity: Vol. 1, The role of possibility in cognitive development*. Minneapolis, MN: University of Minnesota Press.

Piaget, J., & Inhelder, B. (1956). *The child's conception of space*. London: Routledge & Kegan Paul.

Piaget, J., & Inhelder, B. (1969). *The psychology of the child*. New York: Basic Books.

Piaget, J., & Inhelder, B. (1973). *Memory and intelligence*. New York: Basic Books.

Pianta, R., Egeland, B., & Erickson, M. F. (1989). Results of the mother-child interaction research project. In D. Cicchetti & V. Carlson (Eds.), *Child Maltreatment: Theory and research on the causes and consequences of child abuse and neglect*. Cambridge: Cambridge University Press.

Piattelli-Palmarini, M. (1980). *Language and learning*. Cambridge, MA: Harvard University Press.

Pinker, S. (1989). *Learnability and cognition*. Cambridge, MA: MIT Press.

Pinker, S. (1994). *The language instinct.* New York, NY: W. Morrow and Company.

Pipher, M. (1994). *Reviving Ophelia: Saving the selves of adolescent girls.* New York: GP Putnam's Sons.

Pipp, S., Easterbrooks, M. A., & Brown, S. R. (1993). Attachment status and complexity of infants' self- and other-knowledge when tested with mother and father. *Social Development, 2,* 1–114.

Plath, D. W. (1980). *Long engagments: Maturity in modern Japan.* Stanford: Stanford University Press.

Plato (1945). *The republic.* (F. M. Cornford, Trans.). London: Oxford University Press.

Pleck, J. H., Sonenstein, F. L., & Ku, L. C. (1990). Contraceptive attitudes and intention to use condoms in sexually experienced and inexperienced adolescent males. *Journal of Family Issues, 11,* 294–312.

Plomin, R. (1990). *Nature and nurture: An introduction to human behavioral genetics.* Pacific Grove, CA: Brooks/Cole.

Plomin, R., & Bergeman, C. S. (1991). The nature of nuture: Genetic influence on "environmental" measures. *Behavioral and Brain Sciences, 14*(3), 373–427.

Plomin, R., & Daniels, D. (1987). Why are children in the same family so different from each other? *The Behavioral and Brain Sciences, 10,* 1–16.

Plomin, R., & Defries, J. C. (1983). The Colorado adoption project. *Child Development, 54,* 276–289.

Plomin, R., & De Fries, J. C. (1985). Origins of individual differences in infancy. New York: Academic Press.

Plomin, R., Defries, J. C., & Fulker, D. W. (1990). *Nature and nurture during infancy and early childhood.* Cambridge: Cambridge University Press.

Plomin, R., Defries, J. C., McClearn, G. E. & Rutter, M. (1997). *Behavioral genetics: A primer* (3d ed.). New York: W. H. Freeman.

Plomin, R., Emde, R. N., Braungart, J. M., & Campos, J. (1993). Genetic change and continuity from fourteen to twenty months: The MacArthur Longitudinal Twin Study. *Child Development, 64,* 1354–1376.

Plomin, R., & McClearn, G. E. (Eds.), (1993). *Nature, nurture, and psychology.* Washingtion, DC: American Psychological Association.

Pollitt, E. (1994). Poverty and child development: Relevance of research in developing countries to the United States. Special issue: Children and poverty. *Child Development, 65,* 283–295.

Pollitt, E., Gorman, K. S., Engle, P. L., Martorell, R., & Rivera, J. (1993). Early supplementary feeding and cognition. *Monographs of the Society for Research in Child Development, 58* (7, Serial No. 235).

Pomerantz, E. M., Ruble, D. N., Frey, K. S., & Greulich, F. (1995). Meeting goals and confrontinf conflict: Children's changing perceptions of social comparison. *Child Development, 66,* 723–738.

Poole, D. A., & White, L. T. (1993). Two years later: Effects of question repetition and retention interval on the eyewitness testimony of children and adults. *Developmental Psychology, 29,* 844–853.

Power, C., Higgins, A., & Kohlberg, L. (1989). *Lawrence Kohlberg's approach to moral education.* New York: Columbia University Press.

Pratt, H. (1954). The neonate. In L. Carmichael (Ed.), *Manual of child psychology* (2nd ed.). New York: Wiley.

Prechtl, H. (1977). *The neurological examination of the full-term newborn infant* (2nd ed.). Philadelphia: Lippincott.

Preisser, D. A., Hodson, B. W., & Paden, E. P. (1988). Developmental phonology: 18–29 months. *Journal of Speech and Hearing Disorders, 53,* 125–130.

Premack, D., & Premack, A. J. (1983). *The mind of an ape.* New York: W. W. Norton.

Premack, D. (1990). Words: What are they, and do animals have them? *Cognition, 37,* 197–212.

Prescott, E., & Jones, E. (1971). Day care of children—assets and liabilities. *Children, 18,* 54–58.

President's Science Advisory Committee (1974). Youth: *Transition to adulthood.* Chicago: University of Chicago Press.

Price-Williams, D., Gordon, W., & Ramirez, M. (1969). Skill and conservation: A study of pottery-making children. *Developmental Psychology, 1,* 769.

Pritchard, J. A., & MacDonald, P. C. (1980). *Williams' Obstetrics* (16th ed.). New York: Appleton-Century-Crofts.

Provine, R. R. (1986). Behavioral neuro-embryology: Motor perspectives. In W. J. Greenough & J. Juraska (Eds.), *Developmental neuropsychology.* New York: Academic Press.

Pueschel, S. M., & Hopmann, M. R. (1993). Speech and language abilities of children with Down Syndrome: A parent's perspective. In A. P. Kaiser & D. D. Gray (Eds.), *Enhancing children's communication: Vol 2.* Research Foundation for intervention. Baltimore: Paul H. Brookes.

Putallaz, M. & Heflin, A. H. (1990). Parent-child interaction. In S. R. Asher & J. D. Coie (Eds.), *Peer rejection in childhood.* New York: Cambridge University Press.

Putallaz, M., & Gottman, J. M. (1981). Social skills and group acceptance. In S. R. Asher & J. M. Gottman (Eds.), *The development of children's friendships.* Cambridge: Cambridge University Press.

Putallaz, M., & Wasserman, A. (1990). Children's entry behavior. In S. R. Asher & J. D. Coie (Eds.), *Peer rejection in childhood.* New York, NY: Cambridge University Press.

Quadrel, M. J., Fischoff, B., & Davis, W. (1993). Adolescent (in)vulnerability. *American Psychologist, 48,* 102–116.

Quanty, M. B. (1976). Aggression catharsis: Experimental investigations and implications. In R. G. Green & E. C. O'Neal (Eds.), *Perspectives on aggression.* New York: Academic Press.

Querleu, D., Renard, X., Versyp, F., Paris-Delrue, L., & Crepin, G. (1988). Fetal hearing. *European Journal of Obstetrics and Gynecology and Reproductive Biology, 29,* 191–212.

Quinn, P. C., Eimas, P. D., & Rosenkrantz, S. L. (1993). Evidence for representations of perceptually similar natural categories by 3-month-old and 4-month-old infants. *Perception, 22,* 463–475.

Quinton, D., & Rutter, M. (1976). Early hospital admissions and later disturbances of behavior: An attempted replication of Douglas' findings. *Developmental Medicine and Child Neurology, 18,* 447–459.

Quinton, D., & Rutter, M. (1985). Parenting behavior of mothers raised "in care." In A. R. Nicol (Ed.), *Longitudinal studies in child psychology and psychiatry: Practical lessons from research experience.* New York: Wiley.

Rabin, A. J. (1965). *Growing up in the kibbutz.* New York: Springer-Verlag.

Rabinowicz, T. (1979). The differentiate maturation of the human cerebral cortex. In F. Falkner & J. M. Tanner (Eds.), *Human growth: Vol. 3. Neurobiology and nutrition.* New York: Plenum Press.

Rader, N., Bausano, M., & Richards, J. (1980). On the nature of the visual-cliff avoidance response in human infants. *Child Development, 51*, 61–68.

Radke-Yarrow, M., & Sherman, T. (1990). Hard growing: Children who survive. In J. Rolf, A. S. Mastes, D. Cicchetti, K. H. Nuechterlein, & S. Weintraub (Eds.), *Risk and protective factors in the development of psychopathology*. New York: Cambridge University Press.

Radke-Yarrow, M., Zahn-Waxler, C., & Chapman, M. (1983). Children's prosocial dispositions and behavior. In P. H. Mussen (Ed.), *Handbook of child psychology: Vol. 4. Socialization, personality, and social behavior*. New York: Wiley.

Rank, O. (1929). *The trauma of birth*. New York: Harcourt Brace.

Rasmussen, L., Hightower, R., & Rassmussen, P. (1964). *Mathematics for the primary school teacher*. Chicago: Learning Materials.

Raum, O. F. (1940/1967). *Chaga childhood*. Oxford: Oxford University Press.

Rausch, W. A., Barry, R. K., Hertel, R. K., & Swain, M. A. (1974). *Communication, conflict, and marriage*. San Francisco: Jossey-Bass.

Raven, J. C. (1962). *Coloured progressive matrices*. London: H. K. Lewis & Co., Ltd.

Read, M. (1960/1968). *Children of their fathers: Growing up among the Ngoni of Malawi*. New York: Holt, Rinehart & Winston.

Reichel-Dolmatoff, G., & Reichel-Dolmatoff, A. (1961). *The people of Aritama*. London: Routledge & Kegan Paul.

Reiss, I. L. (1972). Premarital sexuality: Past, present and future. In I. L. Reiss (Ed.), *Readings on the family system*. New York: Holt, Rinehart & Winston.

Resnick, D. P., & Resnick, L. B. (1977). The nature of literacy: A historical exploration. *Harvard Educational Review, 47*, 370–385.

Resnick, L. B., & Ford, W. W. (1981). *The psychology of mathematics instruction*. Hillsdale, NJ: Erlbaum.

Retschitzki, J. (1989). Evidence of formal thinking in Baoule airele players. In D. M. Keats, D. Munro, & L. Mann (Eds.), *Heterogeneity in cross-cultural psychology*. Amsterdam: Swets & Zeitlinger.

Reynolds, P. (1989). *Childhood in crossroads: Cognition and society in South Africa*. Grand Rapids, MI: Eerdmans Publishing.

Rheingold, H. L. (1982). Little children's participation in the work of adults, a nascent prosocial behavior. *Child Development, 53*, 114–125.

Rice, M. L., & Woodsmall, L. (1988). Lessons from television: Children's word learning when viewing. *Child Development, 59*, 420–429.

Rice, M. L. (1990). Preschooler's QUIL: Quick incidental learning of words. In G. Conti Ramsden & C. E. Snow (Eds.), *Children's Language:* Vol. 7. Hillsdale, NJ: Erlbaum.

Richards, H. C., Bear, G. G., Stewart, A. L., & Norman, A. D. (1992). Moral reasoning and classroom conduct: Evidence of a curvilinear relationship. *Merrill-Palmer Quarterly, 38*, 176–190.

Richards, J., & Rader, N. (1981). Crawling-onset age predicts visual cliff avoidance in infants. *Journal of Experimental Psychology: Human Perception and Performance, 7*, 382–387.

Richards, M. H., Abell, S. N., & Petersen, A. C. (1993). Biological development. In P. H. Tolan & B. J. Cohler (Eds.), *Handbook of Clinical Research and Practice with adolescents*. New York: John Wiley & Sons.

Richardson, G. A., Day, N. L., & McGauhey, P. J. (1993). The impact of prenatal marijuana and cocaine use on the infant and child. *Clinical Obstetrics and Gynecology, 36*, 302–318.

Richardson, G. A., Day, N. L., & Taylor, P. M. (1989). The effects of prenatal alcohol, marijuana, and tobacco exposure. *Infant Behavior and Development, 12*, 199–210.

Richters, J. E., & Martinez, P. E. (1993). Violent communities, family choices, and children's chances: An algorithm for improving the odds. Special issue: Milestones in the development of resilience. *Development & Psychopathology, 5*, 609–627.

Riesen, A. H. (1950). Arrested vision. *Scientific American, 183*, 16–19.

Ritts, V., Patterson, M. L., & Tubbs, M. E. (1992). Expectations, impressions and judgements of physically attractive students: A review. *Review of Educational Research, 62*, 413–426.

Robbins, L. C. (1963). The accuracy of parental remembering of aspects of child development and of child rearing practices. *Journal of Abnormal and Social Psychology, 66*, 261–270.

Robbins, L. N., & Rutter, M. (1990). *Straight and devious paths from childhood to adulthood*. New York: Cambridge University Press.

Robbins, W. J., Brody, S., Hogan, A. G., Jackson, C. M., & Greene, C. W. (Eds.) (1929). *Growth*. New Haven, CT: Yale University Press.

Robinson, J. P. (1989). Caring for kids. *American Demographics, 11*, 52.

Robson, K. S., & Moss, H. A. (1970). Patterns and determinants of maternal attachment. *Journal of Pediatrics, 77*, 976–985.

Rochat, P. (1989). Object manipulation and exploration in 2- to 5-month-old infants. *Developmental Psychology, 25*, 871–886.

Rogoff, B. (1978). Spot observation: An introduction and examination. *Quarterly Newsletter of the Laboratory of Comparative Human Cognition, 2*, 21–26.

Rogoff, B. (1981). Schooling and the development of cognitive skills. In H. C. Triandis & A. Heron (Eds.), *Handbook of cross-cultural psychology* (Vol. 4). Boston: Allyn & Bacon.

Rogoff, B. (1982). Integrating context and cognitive development. In M. E. Lamb & A. L. Brown (Eds.), *Advances in developmental psychology* (Vol. 2). Hillsdale, NJ: Erlbaum.

Rogoff, B. (1990). *Apprenticeship in thinking: Cognitive development in social context*. Oxford: Oxford University Press.

Rogoff, B. (1995). Observing sociocultural activity on three planes: Participatory appropriation, guided participation, and apprenticeship. In J. V. Wertsch, P. Del Rio, & A. Alvarez. (Eds.), *Sociocultural studies of mind*. New York: Cambridge University Press.

Rogoff, B., & Lave, J. (1984). *Everyday cognition*. Cambridge, MA: Harvard University Press.

Rogoff, B., & Mistry, J. (1990). The social and functional context of children's remembering. In R. Fivush & J. A. Hudson (Eds.), *Knowing and remembering in young children*. New York: Cambridge University Press.

Rogoff, B., Newcombe, N., Fox, N., & Ellis, S. (1980). Transitions in children's roles and capabilities. *International Journal of Psychology, 15*, 181–200.

Rogoff, B., & Waddell, K. J. (1982). Memory for information organized in a scene by children from two cultures. *Child Development, 53*, 1224–1228.

Roopnarine, J. L., Johnson, J. E., & Hooper, F. H. (1994). *Children's play in diverse cultures*. Albany, NY: SUNY Press.

Roopnarine, J. L., Talukder, E., Jain, D., Joshi, P., & Srivastave, P. (1990). Characteristics of holding, patterns of play, and social behaviors between parents and infants in New Delhi, India. *Developmental Psychology, 26*, 667–673.

Rosaldo, M. Z., & Lamphere, L. (Eds.). (1974). *Women, culture, and society*. Stanford: Stanford University Press.

Rosaldo, M. Z. (1984). Toward an ethnography of self and feeling.

In R. Shweder & R. A. LeVine (Eds.), *Culture theory: Essays on mind, self, and emotion.* Cambridge: Cambridge University Press.

Rose, S. A., & Feldman, J. F. (1995). Prediction of IQ and specific cognitive abilities at 11 years from infancy measures. *Developmental Psychology, 31,* 531–539.

Rose, S. A., Feldman, J. F., Wallace, I. F., & McCarton, C. (1991). Information processing at 1 year: Relation to birth status and developmental outcome during the first 5 years. *Developmental Psychology, 27,* 723–737.

Rosen, W., Adamson, L., & Bakeman, R. (1992). An experimental investigation of infant social referencing: Mothers' messages and gender differences. *Developmental Psychology, 28,* 1172–1178.

Rosenshine, B., & Meister, C. (1994). Reciprocal Teaching: A review of the research. *Review of Educational Research, 64,* 479–530.

Rosenstein, D., & Oster, H. (1988). Differential facial responses to four basic tastes in newborns. *Child Development, 59,* 1555–1568.

Rosenthal, R. (1987). Pygmalian effects: Existence, magnitude, and social importance. *Educational Researcher, 16*(9), 37–41.

Rosenthal, R., Baratz, S. S., & Hall, C. M. (1974). Teacher behavior, teacher expectations, and gains in pupils' rated creativity. *Journal of Genetic Psychology, 124,* 115–121.

Rosenthal, R., & Jacobsen, L. (1968). *Pygmalion in the classroom: Teacher expectation and pupils' intellectual development.* New York: Holt, Rinehart & Winston.

Rosenthal, R., & Rubin, D. B. (1978). Interpersonal expectancy effects: The first 345 studies. *Behavioral and Brain Sciences, 3,* 377–415.

Rosenzweig, M. R. (1984). Experience, memory, and the brain. *American Psychologist, 39,* 365–376.

Rosenzweig, M. R., Bennett, E. L., & Diamond, M. C. (1972). Brain changes in response to experience. *The nature and nurture of behavior: Development psychobiology.* Readings from Scientific American. New York: W. H. Freeman.

Rosier, P. (1977). *A comparative study of two approaches of introducing initial reading to Navajo children: The direct method and the native language method.* Unpublished doctoral dissertation, Northern Arizona University.

Ross, G., Lipper, E. G., & Auld, P. A. M. (1991). Educational status and school-related abilities of very low-birthweight premature children. *Pediatrics, 88,* 1125–1134.

Rosso, P. (1990). *Nutrition and metabolism in pregnancy.* Oxford: Oxford University Press.

Rothbart, M. K. (1988). Temperament and the development of inhibited approach. *Child Development, 59,* 1241–1250.

Rothbart, M. K., Derryberry, D., & Posner, M. I. (1994). A psychobiological approach to the development of temperament. In J. E. Bates & T. D. Wachs (Eds.), *Individual differences at the interface of biology and behavior.* Washingtion, DC: American Psychological Association.

Rousseau, J. J. (1762/1911). *Emile; or On education.* London: Dent.

Rovee-Collier, C. K. (1987). Learning and memory. In J. D. Osofsky (Ed.), *Handbook of infant development* (2nd ed.). New York: Wiley.

Rovee-Collier, C. K. (1990). The "memory system" of prelinguistic infants. *Annals of the New York Academy of Sciences, 608,* 517–542.

Rovee-Collier, C. K., & Boller, K. (1995). Interference or facilitation in infant memory? In F. N. Dempster & C. J. Brainerd (Eds.), *Interference and inhibition in cognition.* San Diego, Ca.: Academic Press.

Rovee-Collier, C. K., Sullivan, M. W., Enright, M., Lucas, D., & Fagan, J. W. (1980). Reactivation of infant memory. *Science, 208,* 1159–1161.

Rovet, J., & Netley, C. (1982). Processing deficits in Turner's syndrome. *Developmental Psychology, 18,* 77–94.

Rubin, J. Z. (1980). *Children's friendships.* Cambridge, MA: Harvard University Press.

Rubin, J. Z., Provenzano, F. J., & Luria, Z. (1974). The eye of the beholder: Parents' view on sex of newborns. *American Journal of Orthopsychiatry, 44,* 512–519.

Rubin, K. H., & Coplan, R. J. (1992). Peer relations in childhood in M. H. Bornstein & M. E. Lamb (Eds.), *Developmental Psychology: An advanced textbook* (3rd edition). Hillsdale, NJ: Erlbaum.

Rubin, K. H., Fein, G. G., & Vandenberg, B. (1983). Play. In P. H. Mussen (Ed.), *Handbook of child psychology: Vol. 4. Socialization, personality, and social behavior.* New York: Wiley.

Rubin, K. H., Lynch, D., Coplan, R., Rose-Krasnor, L., & Booth, C. L. (1994). "Birds of a feather. . . ": Behavioral concordance and preferential personal attraction in children. *Child Development, 64,* 1778–1785.

Rubin, K. H., & Sloman, J. (1984). How parents influence their children's friendship. In M. Lewis (Ed.), *Beyond the dyad.* New York: Plenum Press.

Ruble, D. N., Boggiano, A. K., Feldman, N. S., & Loebl, J. H. (1980). Developmental analysis of the role of social comparison in self-evaluation. *Developmental Psychology, 16,* 105–115.

Ruble, D. N., & Brooks-Gunn, J. (1982). The experience of menarche. *Child Development, 53,* 1557–1666.

Ruble, D. N, & Dweck, C. S. (1995). Self-conceptions, person conceptions, and their development. In N. Eisenberg (Ed.), *Review of personality and social psychology,* Vol. 15. Thousand Oaks, CA: Sage.

Ruble, D. N., & Frey, K. S. (1991). Changing patterns of comparative behavior as skills are acquired: A functional model of self-evaluation. In J. Suls & T. H. Wells (Eds.), *Social comparison: Contemporary theory and research.* Hillsdale, NJ: Erlbaum.

Rumbaugh, D. M., Savage-Rumbaugh, E. S., & Sevcik, R. A. (1994). Biobehavioral roots of language: A comparative perspective on chimpanzee, child, and culture. In R. W. Wrangham, W. C. McGrew, F. B. M. de Waal, & P. G. Heltne (Eds.), *Chimpanzee cultures.* Cambridge, MA: Harvard University Press.

Ruopp, R., Travers, J., Glantz, F., & Coelen, C. (1979). *Children at the center: Final report of the national day care study.* Cambridge: Abt Books.

Rutter, M. (1976). Maternal deprivation, 1972–1978: New findings, new concepts, new approaches. *Child Development, 50,* 283–305.

Rutter, M. L. (1987). Continuities and discontinuities from infancy. In J. D. Osofsky (Ed.), *Handbook of infant development* (2nd ed.). New York: John Wiley & Sons.

Rutter, M. (1989). Pathways from childhood to adult life. *Journal of Child Psychology and Psychiatry, 30,* 23–51.

Rutter, M., & Garmezy, N. (1983). Developmental psychopathology. In P. H. Mussen (Ed.), *Handbook of child psychology: Vol. 4. Socialization, personality, and social development.* New York: Wiley.

Rutter, M., & Hersov, L. (1985). *Child and adolescent psychiatry: Modern approaches* (2nd. ed.). Oxford: Blackwell.

Rutter, M., Maughan, B., Mortimore, P., & Ouston, J. (1979). *Fifteen thousand hours: Secondary schools and their effects on children.* Cambridge, MA: Harvard University Press.

Rutter, M., Quinton, D., & Hill, J. (1990). Adult outcome of institution-reared children. In L. Robins & M. Rutter (Eds.), *Straight and devious pathways from childhood to adulthood.* Cambridge: Cambridge University Press.

Rutter, M., Yule, B., Quinton, D., Rowland, O., Yule, W., & Berger, M. (1975). Attainment and adjustment in two geographical areas: III. Some factors accounting for area differences. *British Journal of Psychiatry, 126,* 520–533.

Rymer, R. (1993). *Genie: A scientific tragedy.* New York: Harper-Collins.

Sachs, J., & Devin, J. (1973). *Young children's knowledge of age-appropriate speech styles.* Paper presented to Linguistic Society of America.

Sachs, J., Bard, B., & Johnson, M. (1981). Language learning with restricted input; Case studies of two hearing children of deaf parents. *Applied Psycholinguistics, 2,* 33–54.

Sagi, A., Lamb, M. E., Lewkowicz, K. S., Shoham, R., Dvir, R., & Estes, D. (1985). Security of infant-mother, -father, and metapelet attachments among kibbutz reared Israeli children. *Monographs of the Society for Research in Child Development, 50*(1–2, Serial No. 209).

Sale, R. (1978). *Fairy tales and after.* Cambridge, MA: Harvard University Press.

Salk, L. (1973). The role of the heartbeat in the relationship between mother and infant. *Scientific American, 228*(3), 24–29.

Salkind, N. J., & Nelson, C. F. (1980). A note on the developmental nature of reflection-impulsivity. *Developmental Psychology, 16,* 237–238.

Salomon, G. L. (1984). Television is "easy" and print is "tough": The differential investment of mental effort in learning as a function of perceptions and attributions. *Journal of Educational Psychology, 76,* 647–658.

Saltzstein, H. D. (1994). The relationship between judgement and behavior: A social-cognitive and decision-making analysis. *Human Development, 37,* 299–312.

Salzinger, S. (1990). Social networks in child rearing and child development. In S. M. Pfafflin, J. A. Sechzer, J. M. Fish, & R. L. Thompson (Eds.), *Psychology: Perspectives and practice.* New York: New York Academy of Science.

Salzinger, S., Feldman, R. S., Hammer, M., & Rosario, M. (1993). The effects of physical abuse on children's social relationships. *Child Development, 64,* 169–187.

Samelson, R. (1980). J. B. Watson's little Albert, Cyril Burt's twins, and the need for a critical science. *American Psychologist, 35,* 619–625.

Sameroff, A. (1978). Organization and stability of newborn behavior: A commentary on the Brazelton Neonatal Behavior Assessment Scale. *Monographs of Society for Research in Child Development, 43*(5–6, Serial No. 177).

Sameroff, A. J. (1983). Developmental systems: Contexts and evolutions. In P. H. Mussen (Ed.), *Handbook of child psychology: Vol. 1. History, theory and methods.* New York: Wiley.

Sameroff, A. J. (1989). Models of developmental regulation: The environtype. In D. Cicchetti (Ed.) The emergence of a disipline. (*Rochester Symposium on Developmental Psychopathology,* Vol. I.) Hillsdale, NJ: Erlbaum.

Sameroff, A. J. (1995). General systems theories and developmental psychopathology. In D. Cicchetti & D.J. Cohen, (Eds.), *Developmental psychopathology, Vol. 1: Theory and methods.* New York: Wiley.

Sameroff, A. J., & Chandler, M. J. (1975). Reproductive risk and the continuum of caretaking casualty. In F. D. Horowitz (Ed.), *Review of child development research,* Vol. 4. Chicago: University of Chicago Press.

Sameroff, A. J. & Haith, M. M. (Eds.) (1996). The age of reason and responsibility. The 5–7 year shift. Washington, DC: American Psychological Association.

Sameroff, A. J., Seifer, R., Baldwin A., & Baldwin, C. (1993). Stability of intelligence from preschool to adolescence: The influence of social and family risk factors. *Child Development, 64,* 80–97.

Samet, J. (1993). Autism and theory of mind: Some philosophical perspectives. In S. Baron-Cohen, H. Tager-Flusberg, & D. J. Cohen, (Eds.) *Understanding other minds: Perspectives from autism.* Oxford: Oxford University Press.

Sandven, K., & Resnick, M. (1990). Informal adoption among black adolescent mothers. *American Journal of Orthopsychiatry, 60,* 210–224.

Sarni, C. (1990). Emotional competence: How emotions and relationships become integrated. In R. A. Thompson (Ed.), Nebraska Symposium on Motivation: Vol. 36: *Socioemotional Development.* Lincoln: University Nebraska Press.

Savage-Rumbaugh, E. S., McDonald, K., Sevcik, R. A., Hopkins, W. D., & Rubert, E. (1986). Spontaneous symbol acquisition and communication use by pygmy chimpanzees. *Journal of Experimental Psychology, 115,* 211–235.

Savage-Rumbaugh, E. S., Murphy, J., Sevcik, R. A., Brakke, K. E., Williams, SL. L., & Rumbaugh, D. M. (1993). Language comprehension in ape and child. *Monographs of the society for research in child development, 58,* (Nos. 3–4, Serial No. 233).

Savage-Rumbaugh, E. S., & Rumbaugh, D. M. (1993). The emergence of language. In K. R. Gibson & T. Ingold (Eds.), *Tools, language and cognition in human evolution.* Cambridge, England: Cambridge University Press.

Savin-Williams, R. C. (1987). *Adolescence: An ethological perspective.* New York: Springer-Verlag.

Savin-Williams, R. C. (1990). *Gay and Lesbian Youth: Expressions of identity.* New York: Hemisphere Publishing Corporation.

Savin-Williams, R. C., & Berndt, T. J. (1990). Friendships and peer relations. In S. S. Feldman & G. R. Elliott (Eds.), *At the threshhold: The developing adolescent.* Cambridge, MA: Harvard University Press.

Saxe, G. B. (1981). Body parts as numerals: A developmental analysis of numeration among the Oksapmin in Papua, New Guinea. *Child Development, 52,* 306–316.

Saxe, G. (1994). Studying cognitive developments in sociocultural context: The development of a practice-based approach. Mind, *Culture, & Activity, 1,* 135–157.

Scanzoni, L., & Scanzoni, J. (1976). *Men, women and change: A sociology of marriage and family.* New York: McGraw-Hill.

Scarborough, H. S., & Dobrich, W. On the efficacy of reading to preschoolers. *Development Review, 14,* 245–302.

Scarr, S. (1981). *Race, social class and individual differences in I.Q.* Hillsdale, NJ: Erlbaum.

Scarr. S. (1992). Developmental theories for the 1990's: Development and individual differences. *Child Development, 63,* 1–19.

Scarr, S. (1993). Biological and cultural diversity: The legacy of Darwin for development. *Child Development, 64,* 1333–1353.

Scarr, S., & McCartney, K. (1983). How people make their own environments: A theory of genotype-environment effects. *Child Development, 54,* 424–435.

Scarr, S., Phillips, D., & McCartney, K. (1990). Facts, fantasies, and the future of child care in the United States. *Psychological Science, 1,* 26–35.

Scarr, S., & Weinberg, R. A. (1976). IQ performance of black children adopted by white families. *American Psychologist, 31,* 726–739.

Scarr, S., & Weinberg, R. A. (1977). Intellectual similarities within families of both adopted and biological children. *Intelligence, 2,* 170–191.

Scarr, S., & Weinberg, R. A. (1983). The Minnesota adoption studies: Genetic differences and malleability. *Child Development, 54,* 260–267.

Schaefer, E. S. (1959). A circumplex model for maternal behavior. *Journal of Abnormal and Social Psychology, 59,* 226–235.

Schaffer, H. R. (1974). Cognitive components of the infant's response to strangeness. In M. Lewis & L. Rosenblum (Eds.), The origins of fear. New York: Wiley.

Schaller, S. (1991). *A man without words.* New York: Summit.

Scheinfeld, A. (1972). *Heredity in humans.* Philadelphia: Lippincott.

Scheper-Hughes, N. (1992). *Death without weeping: The violence of everyday life in Brazil.* Berkeley: University of California Press.

Schindler, P. J., Moely, B., & Frank, A. L. (1987). Time in day care and social participation of young children. *Developmental Psychology, 23,* 255–261.

Schlegel, A., & Barry, H. (1991). *Adolescence: An anthropological inquiry.* New York: Free Press.

Schmandt-Besserat, D. (1978). The earliest precursor of writing. *Scientific American, 283,* 50–59.

Schneider, W., Gruber, H., Gold, A., & Opwis, K. (1993). Chess expertise and memory for chess positions in children and adults. *Journal of Experimental Child Psychology, 56,* 328–349.

Schneider-Rosen, K., Braunwald, K., Carlson, V., & Cicchetti, D. (1985). Current perspectives in attachment theory: Illustration from the study of maltreated infants. *Monographs of the Society for Research in Child Development, 50*(1–2, Serial No. 209).

Schnoll, S. H. (1986). Drug use in pregnancy: Mother and child. In I. J. Chasnoff (Ed.), *Pharmacologic basis of perinatal addiction.* Lancaster, England: MTP Press.

Schoggen, P. (1989). *Behavior settings: a revision and extension of Roger G. Barker's Ecological Psychology.* Stanford, CA: Stanford University Press.

Schramm, W., Barnes, D., & Blackwell, J. (1987). Neonatal mortality in Missouri home births. *American Journal of Public Health, 77,* 930–935.

Scott, J. R., & Branch, D. W. (1994). Immunologic disorders in pregnancy. In J. R. Scott, Philip J. DiSaia, Charles B. Hammond, & William N. Spellacy (Eds.), *Dansforth's obstetrics and gynecology* (7th ed.). Philadelphia: J. B. Lippincott.

Scott, T., Cole, M., & Engel, M. (1992). Computer and education: A cultural constructivist perspective. *Review of Research in Education, 18,* 191–251.

Scribner, S., & Cole, M. (1973). Cognitive consequences of formal and informal education. *Science, 182,* 553–559.

Scribner, S., & Cole, M., (1981). *The psychology of literacy.* Cambridge, MA.: Harvard University Press.

Sebald, H. (1981). Adolescent's concept of popularity and unpopularity: Comparing 1960 with 1976. *Adolescence, 16,* 187–193.

Segall, M. H., Dasen, P. R., Berry, J. W., & Poortinga, Y. H. (1990). *Human behavior in global perspective: An introduction to cross-cultural psychology.* New York: Pergamon Press.

Seifer, R., Sameroff, A. J., Barrett, L. C., & Krafchuk, E. (1994). Infant temperament measured by multiple observations and mother report. *Child Development, 65,* 1478–1490.

Selfe, L. (1977). *Nadia: A case of extraordinary drawing ability in an autistic child.* New York: Academic Press.

Selfe, L. (1983). *Normal and anomalous representational drawing ability in children.* New York: Academic Press.

Seligman, M. (1975). *Helplessness: On depression, development, and death.* New York: W. H. Freeman.

Selman, R. L. (1976). Social cognitive understanding. In T. Lickona (Ed.), *Moral development and behavior: Theory, research, and social issues.* New York: Holt, Rinehart & Winston.

Selman, R. L. (1980). *The growth of interpersonal understanding: Developmental and clinical analysis.* New York: Academic Press.

Selman, R. L. (1981). The child as a friendship philosopher. In S. R. Asher & J. M. Gottman (Eds.), *The development of children's friendships.* Cambridge: Cambridge University Press.

Selman, R. L., & Schultz, L. H. (1990). *Making a friend in youth: Developmental theory and pair therapy.* Chicago: University of Chicago Press.

Sepkowski. C. (1985). Maternal obstetric medication and newborn behavior. In J. W. Scanlon (Ed.), *Prenatal anesthesia.* London: Blackwell.

Serbin, L. A., O'Leary, K. D., Kent, R. N., & Tonick, I. J. (1973). A comparison of teacher response to the preacademic and problem behavior of boys and girls. *Child Development, 44,* 796–804.

Serpell, R. (1993). *The significance of schooling: Life journeys in an African Society.* Cambridge: Cambridge University Press.

Shaffer, D. R. (1985). *Developmental psychology: Theory, research, and application.* Monterey, CA: Brooks/Cole.

Shah, M., & Jeffrey, R. W. (1991). Is obesity due to overeating and inactivity, or to a defective metabolic rate? A Review. *Annals of Behavioral Medicine, 13,* 73–81.

Shapira, A., & Madsen, M. C. (1969). Cooperative and competitive behavior of kibbutz and urban children in Israel. *Child Development, 4,* 609–617.

Sharp, D. W., Cole, M., & Lave, C. (1979). Education and cognitive development: The evidence from experimental research. *Monographs of the Society for Research in Child Development, 4,* (1–2, Serial No. 178).

Shatz, M. (1974). *The comprehension of indirect directives: Can you shut the door?* Paper presented at Linguistics Society of America, Amherst, MA.

Shatz, M. (1978). Children's comprehension of question-directives. *Journal of Child Language, 5,* 39–46.

Shatz, M., & Gelman, R. (1973). The development of communication skills: Modification in the speech of young children as a function of listener. *Monographs of the Society for Research in Child Development, 38*(5, Serial No. 152).

Shaw, D. S., Vondra, J. I., Hommerding, K. D., Keenan, K., & Dunn (1994). Chronic family adversity and early child behavior problems: A longitudinal study of low income families. *Journal of Child Psychology and Psychiatry, 35,* 1109–1122.

Shaw, G. B. (1963). *George Bernard Shaw on language.* A. Tauben (Ed.). London: Peter Owen.

Sherif, M., & Sherif, C. W. (1953). *Groups in harmony and tension.* New York: Harper & Row.

Sherif, M., & Sherif, C. W. (1956). *An outline of social psychology.* New York: Harper & Row.

Sherrod, L. R. (1979). Social cognition in infants: Attention to the human face. *Infant Behavior and Development, 2,* 279–294.

Sherrod, K. B., O'Connor, S., Vietze, P. M., & Altemeier, W. A., III. (1984). Child health and maltreatment. *Child development, 55,* 1174–1183.

Shields, J. (1962). *Monozygotic twins brought up apart and brought up together.* New York: Oxford University Press.

Shopen, T. (1980). How Pablo says "love" and "store." In T.

Shopen & J. M. Williams (Eds.), *Standards and dialects in English*. Cambridge: Winthrop.

Shostak, M. (1981). *Nissa: The life and words of a !Kung woman*. Cambridge, MA: Harvard University Press.

Shultz, T. R. (1980). Development of the concept of intention. In N. A. Collins (Ed.), *Minnesota Symposium on child psychology, Vol. 13*. Hillsdale, NJ: Erlbaum.

Shweder, R. A. (1982). Liberalism as destiny. *Contemporary Psychology, 27*, 421–424.

Shweder, R. A., & Bourne, E. J. (1984). Does the concept of person vary cross-culturally? In R. A. Shweder & R. A. LeVine (Eds.) *Culture theory: Essays on mind, self, and emotion*. Cambridge: Cambridge University Press.

Shweder, R. A., Mahapatra, M., & Miller, J. G. (1987). Culture and moral development. In J. Kagan & S. Lamb (Eds.), *The emergence of morality in young children*. Chicago: University of Chicago Press.

Siegal, M. (1991). *Knowing children: Experiments in conversation and cognition*. Hillsdale, NJ: Erlbaum.

Siegler, R. S. (1976). Three aspects of cognitive development. *Cognitive Psychology, 8*, 481–520.

Siegler, R. S. (1983). Information processing approaches to development. In P. H. Mussen (Ed.), *Handbook of child psychology: Vol. I. History, theory, and methods*. New York: Wiley.

Siegler, R. S. (1991). *Children's thinking* (2nd ed.). Englewood Cliffs, NJ: Prentice-Hall.

Siegler, R. S. (1995). How does change occur? A microgenetic study of number conservation. *Cognitive Psychology, 28*, 225–273.

Siegler, R. S. (1996). *Emerging minds: The process of change in children's thinking*. New York, NY: Oxford University Press.

Siegler, R. S., & Crowley, K. (1991). The microgenetic method. *American Psychologist, 46*, 606–620.

Siegler, R. S., & Liebert, R. M. (1975). Acquisition of formal scientific reasoning by 10-and 13-year-olds: Designing a factorial experiment. *Developmental Psychology, 11*, 401–402.

Siegler, R. S., & Shrager, J. (1984). Strategy choices in addition and subtraction: How do children know what to do? In C. Sophian (Ed.), *Origins of cognitive skills*. Hillsdale, NJ: Erlbaum.

Sigel, I. E. (Ed.) (1985) *Parental belief systems* Hillsdale, NJ: Erlbaum.

Sigel, I. E. (1993). The centrality of a distancing model for *The development of representational competence*. In R. R. Cocking & K. A. Renninger (Eds.), *The development and meaning of psychological distance*. Hillsdale, NJ: Lawrence Erlbaum Associates.

Sigel, I. E., McGillicuddy-De Lisi, A. V., & Goodnow, J. J. (Eds.). (1992). *Parental belief systems: The psychological consequences for children*. Hillsdale, NJ: Erlbaum.

Signorelli, N. (1991). *A sourcebook on children and television*. Westport, CT: Greenwood.

Signorelli, N. (1993). Television, portrayals of women, and children's attitudes. In G. L. Barry & J. K. Asamen (Eds.), *Children and television*. Newbury Park: Sage.

Silverstein, B., & Krate, R. (1975). *Children of the dark ghetto: A developmental psychology*. New York: Praeger.

Simmons, R. G., & Blyth, D. A. (1987). *Moving into adolescence: The impact of pubertal change and school context*. Hawthorn, NY: Aldine.

Simmons, R. G., Burgeson, R., Carlton-Ford, S., & Blyth, D. (1987). The impact of cumulative change in early adolescence. *Child Development, 58*, 1220–1234.

Simon, T. J., Hespos, S. J., & Rochat, P. (1995). Do infants understand simple arithmatic? A replication of Wynn (1992). *Cognitive Development, 10*, 253–269.

Simpson, E. L. (1974). Moral development research: A case of scientific cultural bias. *Human Development, 17*, 81–106.

Simpson, J. L., & Golbus, M. S. (1992). *Genetics in obstetrics and gynecology* (2nd ed.). Philadelphia: W. B. Saunders and Company.

Sinclair, J., & Coulthard, R. M. (1975). *Towards an analysis of discourse: The English used by teachers and pupils*. Oxford: Oxford University Press.

Sinclair de Zwart, H. (1967). *Acquisition du langage et dévelopement de la pensée*. Paris: Dunod.

Singer, D., & Kelly, H. B. (1984). *Parents, children, and TV: A guide to using TV wisely*. Chicago, IL: National PTA.

Singer, D. G., & Singer, J. L. (1990). *The house of make-believe*. Cambridge, MA: Harvard University Press.

Singer, J. L., & Singer, D. G. (1980). Television viewing, family style and aggressive behavior in preschool children. In M. Green (Ed.), *Violence and the family: Psychiatric, sociological and historical implications*. Boulder, CO: Westview Press.

Singer, D. G., Singer, J. L., & Zuckerman, D. M. (1980). *Getting the most out of TV*. Santa Monica, CA: Goodyear.

Siqueland, E. R. (1968). Reinforcement patterns and extinction in human newborns. *Journal of Experimental Child Psychology, 6*, 431–432.

Skibinski, G. J. (1995). The influence of the family preservation model on child sexual abuse intervention strategies: Changes in child welfare worker tasks. *Child Welfare, 74*, 975–989.

Skinner, B. F. (1938). *The behavior of organisms*. New York: Appleton-Century-Crofts.

Skinner, B. F. (1953). *Science and human behavior*. New York: Appleton-Century-Crofts.

Skinner, B. F. (1957). *Verbal behavior*. New York: Appleton-Century-Crofts.

Skuse, D. (1984a). Extreme deprivation in early childhood-I. Diverse outcomes for three siblings from an extraordinary family. *Journal of Child Psychology and Psychiatry, 25*, 523–541.

Skuse, D. (1984b). Extreme deprivation in early childhood-II. Theoretical issues and a comparative review. *Journal of Child Psychology and Psychiatry, 25*, 543–572.

Slaby, E., Morrow, J., & Wachs, T. D. (1991). Questionnaire measurement of infant and child temperament. In J. Strelau & A. Angleitner (Eds.), *Explorations in temperament*. New York: Plenum.

Slaby, A. E., & Dwenger, R. (1993). History of anorexia nervosa. In A. J. Giannini and A. E. Slaby (Eds.), *The eating disorders*. New York: Springer-Verlag.

Slaby, R. G., & Frey, K. S. (1975). Development of gender constancy and selective attention to same-sex models. *Child Development, 46*, 849–856.

Smetana, J. G. (1989). Adolescents' and parents' reasoning about actual family conflict. *Child Development, 60*, 1052–1067.

Smith, E., & Udry, J. (1985). Coital and non-coital sexual behaviors of white and black adolescents. *American Journal of Public Health, 75*, 1200–1203.

Smith, L. K. (1989). The influence of education on memory development. Paper presented at the annual meeting of the American Educational Research Association, San Francisco.

Smith, M. E. (1926). An investigation of the development of the entence and the extent of vocabulary in young children. *University of Iowa Studies in Child Welfare, 3* (No. 5), 1–92

Smith, N. V. (1971, Oct. 2). How children learn to speak. *The Listener*.

Smith, P. K (1982). Does play matter? Functional and evolutionary aspects of animal and human play. *Behavioral and Brain Sciences, 5*, 139–184.

Smith, P. K. (1988). Children's play and its role in early development: A re-evaluation of the "play ethos." In A. D. Pellegrini (Ed.), *Psychological bases for early education*. New York: Wiley.

Smith, P. K. (1990). Rough-and-tumble play, aggression and dominance: Perception and behavior in children's encounters. *Human Development, 33*, 271–282.

Smith, R. P. (1958). *Where did you go? Out. What did you do? Nothing*. New York: W. W. Norton.

Smuts, H. B., & Hagen, J. W. (Eds.). (1985). History and research in child development. *Monographs of the Society for Research in Child Development, 50*(4–5, Serial No. 211).

Smythe, D. W. (1954). Reality as presented by television. *Public Opinion Quarterly, 18*, 143–156.

Snarey, J., & Keljo, K. (1994). Revitalizing the meaning and measurement of moral development. Essay review of Moral maturity: Measuring the development of sociomoral reflection by John C. Gibbs, Karen S. Basinger, & Dick Fuller. *Human Development, 37*, 181–186.

Snarey, J. R. (1985). Cross-cultural universality of social moral development: A critical review of Kohlbergian research. *Psychological Bulletin, 97*, 202–232.

Snow, C. (1995). Issues in the study of input: Finetuning, universality, individual and developmental differences, and necessary causes. In P. Fletcher and B. MacWhinney (Eds.), *The handbook of child language*. Oxford: Blackwell.

Snow, C. E. (1972). Mother's speech to children learning language. *Child Development, 43*, 549–565.

Snow, C. E., Arlman-Rupp, A., Massing, Y., Jobse, J., Joosken, J., & Vorster, J. (1976). Mother's speech in three social classes. *Journal of Psycholinguistic Research, 5*, 1–20.

Snyder, J. J., & Patterson, G. R. (1986). The effects of consequences on patterns of social interaction: A quasi-experimental approach to reinforcement in natural interaction. *Child Development, 57*, 1257–1268.

Song, M., Smetana, J. G., & Kim, S. Y. (1987). Korean children's conceptions of moral and conventional transgressions. *Developmental Psychology, 23*, 577–582.

Sonenstein, F. L., Pleck, J. H., & Ku, L. C. (July/August, 1990). Levels of sexual activity among adolescent males in the United States. *Family Planning Perspectives, 23*, 162–167.

Sorenson, R. C. (1973). *Adolescent sexuality in contemporary America*. New York: World.

Spear, N. (1978). *The processing of memories: Forgetting and retention*. New York: Wiley.

Spearman, C. (1927). *The abilities of man*. New York: Macmillan.

Speidel, G. E., & Nelson, K. E. (1989). A fresh look at imitation in language learning. In G. E. Speidel & K. E. Nelson (Eds.), *The many faces of imitation in language learning*. New York: Springer-Verlag.

Spelke, E. S. (1976). Infants' intermodal perception of events. *Cognitive Psychology, 8*, 553–560.

Spelke, E. S. (1984). The development of intermodal perception. In L. B. Cohen & P. Salapatek (Eds.), *Handbook of infant perception*. New York: Academic Press.

Spelke, E. S. (1990). Principles of object perception. *Cognitive Science, 14*, 29–56.

Spelke, E. (1994). Initial knowledge: Six suggestions. *Cognition, 50*, 431–445.

Spelke, E. S., & Van de Walle, G. A. (1993). Perceiving and reasoning about objects: Insights from infants. In N. Eilan, R. A. McCarthy, & B. Brewer (Eds.), *Spatial representation: Problems in philosophy and psychology*. Oxford: Blackwell Publishers.

Spellacy, W. N. (1994). Fetal growth retardation. In J. R. Scott, P. J. DiSaia, C. B. Hammond, & W. N. Spellacy (Eds.), *Dansforth's obstetrics and gynecology* (7th ed.). Philadelphia: J. B. Lippincott.

Spencer, M. B., Cunningham, M., & Swanson, D. P. (1995). Identity as coping: Adolescent African males' adaptive responses to high-risk environments. In H. W. Harris, H. C. Blue, & E. H. Griffin (Eds.), *Racial and ethnic identity*. New York: Routledge.

Spencer, M. B., & Horowitz, F. D. (1973). Effects of systematic social and token reinforcement on the modification of racial and color concept attitudes in black and white preschool children. *Developmental Psychology, 9*, 246–254.

Spencer, M. B., & Markstrom-Adams, C. (1990). Identity processes among racial and ethnic minority children in America. *Child Development, 61*, 290–310.

Spiro, M. E. (1965). *Children of the kibbutz*. New York: Schocken.

Sprunger, L., Boyce, W. T., & Gains, J. A. (1985). Family-infant congruence: Routines and rhythmicity in family adaptations to a young infant. *Child Development, 56*, 564–572.

Sroufe, L. A. (1979). Socioemotional development. In J. Osofsky (Ed.), *Handbook of infant development*. New York: Wiley.

Sroufe, L. A., Bennett, C., Englund, M., Urban, J., & Shulman, S. (1993). The significance of gender boundaries in preadolescence: Contemporary correlates and antecedants of boundary violations and maintenance. *Child Development, 64*, 455–466.

Sroufe, L. A., Carlson, E., & Shulman, S. (1993). Individuals in relationships: Development from infancy through adolescence. In D. C. Funder, R. D. Parke, C. Tomlinson-Keasey, & K. Widaman (Eds.), *Studying life through time: Personality and development*. Washington: American Psychological Association.

Sroufe, L. A., & Fleeson, J. (1986). Attachment and the construction of relationships. In W. W. Hartup & Z. Rubin (Eds.), *Relationships and development*. Hillsdale, NJ: Erlbaum.

St. Augustine (1961). *Confessions*. Baltimore: Penguin Books.

St. James-Roberts, I., Harris, G., Messer, D. (Eds.), (1993). *Infant crying, feeding and sleeping: Development, problems and treatments*. London: Wheatsheaf.

Staats, A. W. (1968). *Learning, language, and cognition*. New York: Holt, Rinehart & Winston.

Stattin, H., & Magnusson, D. (1990). *Pubertal maturation in female development*. Hillsdale, NJ: Erlbaum

Stauder, J. E., Molenaar, P. C., & Van der Molen, M. W. (1993). Scalp topography of event-related brain potentials and cognitive transition during childhood. *Child Development, 64*, 769–788.

Stein, J. H., & Reiser, L. W. (1994). A study of white middle-class adolescent boy's responses to "semenarche" (the first ejaculation). *Journal of Youth and Adolescence, 23*, 373–384.

Stein, Z., Susser, M., Saenger, G., & Marolla, F. (1975). *Famine and development: The Dutch hunger winter of 1944–1945*. Oxford: Oxford University Press.

Steinberg, L. (1989). Pubertal maturation and parent-adolescent distance: An evolutionary perspective. In G. Adams, R. Montemayor, & T. Gullota (Eds.), *Advances in adolescent development* (Vol. 1). Beverly Hills, CA: Sage Publications.

Steinberg, L., & Darling, N. E. (1994). The broader context of social influence in adolescence. In R. K. Silbereisen & E. Todt (Eds.), *Adolescence in Context*. New York: Springer-Verlag.

Steinberg, L., Fegley, S., & Dornbusch, S. M. (1993). Negative impact of part-time work on adolescent adjustment: Evidence from a longitudinal study. *Development Psychology, 29*, 171–180.

Steinberg, L., Lamborn, S. D., Darling, N., Mounts, N. S., & Dornbusch, S. M. (1994). Over-time changes in adjustment and competence among adolescents from authoritative, authoritarian, indulgent, and neglectful families. *Child Development, 65,* 754–770.

Steinberg, L., & Silverberg, S. B. (1986). The vicissitudes of autonomy in early adolescence. *Child Development, 57,* 841–851.

Steiner, J. E. (1977). Facial expressions of the neonate infant indicating the hedonics of food related chemical stimuli. In J. N. Weiffenbach (Ed.), *Taste and development: The genesis of sweet preference.* Washington, DC: U.S. Government Printing Office.

Steiner, J. E. (1979). Human facial expressions in response to taste and smell stimulation. In H. W. Reese & L. P. Lipsitt (Eds.), *Advances in child development and behavior* (Vol. 13). New York: Academic Press.

Stephan, C. W., & Langlois, J. H. (1984). Baby beautiful: Adult attributions of infant competence as a function of infant attractiveness. *Child Development, 55,* 576–585.

Stephens, W. N. (1963). *The family in cross-cultural perspective.* New York: Holt, Rinehart & Winston.

Stern, D. (1977). *The first relationship.* Cambridge, MA: Harvard University Press.

Stern, D. (1985). *The interpersonal world of the infant: A view from psychoanalysis and developmental psychology.* New York: Basic Books.

Stern, W. (1910). Abstracts of lectures on the psychology of testimony and on the study of individuality. *American Journal of Psychology, 21,* 273–282.

Stern, W. (1912). *Psychologische methoden der intelligenz-prüfung.* Leipzig: Barth.

Sternberg, K. J. (1993). Child maltreatment: Implications for policy from cross-cultural research. In D. Cicchetti & S. L. Toth (Eds.), *Child abuse, child development, and social policy: Advances in applied developmental psychology, 8.* Norwood, NJ: Ablex Publishing.

Sternberg, R. J. (1985). *Beyond IQ: A triarchic theory of human intelligence.* New York: Cambridge University Press.

Sternberg, R. J. (1988). What theorists of intellectual development among children can learn from their counterparts studying adults. In E. M. Hetherington, R. Lerner, & M. Perlmutter (Eds.), *Child development in life-span perspective.* Hillsdale, NJ: Erlbaum.

Sternberg, R. J., & Nigro, G. (1980). Developmental patterns in the solution of verbal analogies. *Child Development, 51,* 27–38.

Sternberg, R. J., & Powell, J. S. (1983). The development of intelligence. In P. H. Mussen (Ed.), *Handbook of child psychology: Vol. 3. Cognitive development.* New York: Wiley.

Stevens, J. (1984). Black grandmothers' and black adolescent mothers' knowledge and parenting. *Developmental Psychology, 20,* 1017–1025.

Stevenson, H. W., Lee, S., & Stigler, J. W. (1986). Mathematics achievement of Chinese, Japanese, and American children. *Science, 231,* 693–699.

Stevenson, H. W., & Stigler, J. W. (1992). *The learning gap: Why our schools are failing and what we can learn from Japanese and Chinese education.* New York: Summit Books.

Stevenson, H. W., Stigler, J. W., Lee, S., Lucker, G. W., Kitamura, S., & Hsu, C. (1985). Cognitive performance and academic achievement of Japanese, Chinese, and American children. *Child Development, 56,* 718–734.

Stevenson, R. (1977). *The fetus and newly born infant: Influences of prenatal environment* (2nd ed.). St. Louis: Mosby.

Stewart, R. B., & Marvin, R. S. (1984). Sibling relations: The role of conceptual perspective taking in the ontogeny of sibling caregiving. *Child Development, 55,* 1322–1332.

Stifter, C. A., & Fox, N. A. (1990). Infant reactivity: Physiological correlates of newborn and 5-month temperament. *Developmental Psychology, 26,* 582–588.

Stigler, J. W., & Perry, M. (1990). Mathematics learning in Japanese, Chinese, and American classrooms. In J. W. Stigler, R. A. Shweder & G. Herdt (Eds.), *Cultural psychology: Essays on comparative human development.* New York: Cambridge University Press.

Stocker, C., Dunn, J., & Plomin, R. (1989). Sibling relationships: Links with child temperament, maternal behavior, and family structure. *Child Development, 60,* 715–727.

Stone, C. A., & Day, M. C. (1980). Competence and performance models and the characterization of formal operational skills. *Human Development, 23,* 323–353.

Stone, J. L., & Church, J. (1957). *Childhood and adolescence: A psychology of the growing person.* New York: Random House.

Strassberg, G, Z., Dodge, K. A., Pettit, G. S., & Bates, J. E. (1994). Spanking in the home and children's subsequent aggression toward kindergarten peers. *Developmental Psychopathology, 6,* 445–461.

Strayer, F. F. (1980). Social ecology of the preschool peer group. In W. A. Collins (Ed.), *Development of cognition, affect, and social relations: Minnesota Symposia in Child Development* (Vol. 13). Hillsdale, NJ: Erlbaum.

Strayer, F. F. (1991). The development of agonistic and affiliative structures in preschool play groups. In J. Silverberg & P. Gray (Eds.), *To fight or not to fight: Violence and peacefulness in humans and other primates.* Oxford: Oxford University Press.

Strelau, J. (1994). The concepts of arousal and arousability as used in temperament studies. In J. E. Bates and T. D. Wachs (Eds.), *Temperament: Individual differences at the interface of biology and behavior.* Washington: American Psychological Association.

Streri, A., & Spelke, E. S. (1988). Haptic perception of objects in infancy. *Cognitive Psychology, 20,* 1–23.

Strommen, E. A. (1973). Verbal self-regulation in a children's game: Impulsive errors on "Simon Says." *Child Development, 44,* 849–853.

Stunkard, A. J., Foch, T. T., & Hrubec, Z. (1986). A twin study of human obesity. *Journal of the American Medical Association, 256,* (1), 51–53.

Stunkard, A. J., Sorenson, T. I., Hanis, C., Teasdale, T. W., Chakraborty, R., Schull, W. J., & Schulsinger, F. (1986). An adoption study of human obesity. *New England Journal of Medicine, 314,* 193–198.

Subbotskii, E. V. (1991). A life span approach to object permanence. *Human Development, 34,* 125–137.

Subbotsky, E. V. (1993). *The birth of personality: the development of independent and moral behavior in preschool children.* New York, NY: Harvester Wheatsheaf.

Sugarman, S. (1983). *Children's early thought.* Cambridge: Cambridge University Press.

Sullivan, H. S. (1953). *The interpersonal theory of psychiatry.* New York: W. W. Norton.

Sulloway, F. J. (1979). *Freud, biologist of the mind: Beyond the psychoanalytic legend.* New York: Basic Books.

Suomi, S. J., & Harlow, H. F. (1972). Social rehabilitation of isolate-reared monkeys. *Developmental Psychology, 6,* 487–496.

Suomi, S. J., Harlow, H. F., & McKinny, W. T., Jr. (1972). Monkey psychiatrists. *American Journal of Psychiatry, 128,* 927–932.

Super, C. M. (1976). Environmental effects on motor development: A case of African infant precocity. *Developmental Medicine and Child Neurology, 18,* 561–567.

Super, C. M. (1991). Developmental transitions in cognitive functioning in rural Kenya and metropolitan America. In K. Gibson, A. Petersen, & J. Lancester (Eds.), *Brain and development: Biosocial perspectives.* Hawthorne, NY: Aldine de Gruyter.

Super, C. M., & Harkness, S. (1972). The infant's niche in rural Kenya and metropolitan America. In L. Adler (Ed.), *Issues in cross-cultural research.* New York: Academic Press.

Super, C., & Harkness, S. (1986). The developmental niche: A conceptualization at the interface of society and the individual. International *Journal of Behavioral Development, 9,* 545–570.

Super, C. M., Herrera, M. G., & Mora, J. O. (1990). Long-term effects of food supplementation and psychosocial intervention on the physical growth of Colombian infants at risk of malnutrition. *Child Development, 61,* 29–49.

Suppes, P. (1988). Computer-assisted instructions. In D. Unwin & R. McAllese (Eds.), *The encyclopedia of educational media, communication and technology* (2nd edition). New York: Greenwood.

Sussman, E. J., Nottlemann, E. D., Inhoff-Germain, G. E., Dorn, L. D., Cutler, G. B., Jr., Loriaux, D. L., & Chrousos, G. P. (1985). The relation of development and social-emotional behavior in young adolescents. *Journal of Youth and Adolescence, 14,* 245–264.

Sutton-Smith, B., & Roberts, J. M. (1973). The cross-cultural and psychological study of games. In B. Sutton-Smith (Ed.), *The folkgames of children.* Austin, TX: University of Texas Press.

Swain, I. V., Zelazo, P. R., & Clifton, R. K. (1993). Newborn infants' memory for speech sounds retained over 24 hours. *Developmental Psychology, 29,* 312–323.

Sweeney, J., & Bradbard, M. R. (1988). Mothers' and fathers' changing perceptions of their male and female infants over the course of pregnancy. *Journal of Genetic Psychology, 149,* 393–404.

Swift, J. (1726/1970). *Gulliver's travels.* New York: W. W. Norton.

Takahashi, K. (1990). Are the key assumptions of the "strange situation" procedure universal? *Human Development, 33,* 23–30.

Tallal, P., Miller, S. L., & Fitch, R. H. (1993). The neurobiological basis of speech: A case for the preeminence of temporal processing. In P. Tallal, A. M. Galaburdn, R. R. Llinás, C. von Euler (Eds.), Temporal information processing in the nervous system: Special reference to Dyslexia and Dysphasia. *Annals of the New York Academy of Sciences, 682,* 27–47.

Tamis-Le Monda, C. S., & Bornstein, M. H. (1994). Specificity in mother-toddler language-play relations across the second year. *Developmental Psychology, 30,* 283–292.

Tanner, J. M. (1978). *Fetus into man: Physical growth from conception to maturity.* Cambridge, MA: Harvard University Press.

Tanner, J. M. (1990). *Fetus into Man: Physical growth from conception to maturity.* (revised edition). Cambridge, MA: Harvard University Press.

Tanner, N. M. (1981). *On becoming human.* Cambridge: Cambridge University Press.

Taylor, M., & Hort, B. C. (1990). Can children be trained to make the appearance reality distinction? *Cognitive Development, 5,* 89–99.

Teale, W. H., & Sulzby, E. (Eds.) (1986). *Emergent literacy: Writing and reading.* Norwood, NJ: Ablex.

Teller, D. Y., & Bornstein, M. H. (1987). Infant color vision and color perception. In P. Salapatek & L. B. Cohen (Eds), *Handbook of infant perception.* New York: Academic Press.

Telzrow, R. W., Campos, J. J., Shepherd, A., Bertenthal, B. I., & Atwater, S. (1987). Spatial understanding in infants with motor handicaps. In K. Jaffe (Ed.), *Childhood powered mobility: Developmental, technical and clinical perspectives.*

Templin, M. C. (1957). *Certain language skills in children.* Minneapolis: University of Minnesota Press.

Terman, L. M. (1925). *Genetic studies of genius.* Stanford: Stanford University Press.

Terrace, H. (1984). Apes who "talk": Language or projection of language by their teachers? In J. De Luce & H. T. Wilder (Eds.), *Language in primates.* New York: Springer-Verlag.

Teti, D. M., Gelfand, D. M., Messinger, D. S., & Isabella, R. (1995). Maternal depression and the quality of early attachment: An examination of infants, preschoolers, and their mothers. Special Section: Parental depression and distress: Implications for development. *Developmental Psychology, 31,* 364–376.

Thatcher, R. W. (1991) Maturation of the human frontal lobes: Physiological evidence for staging. *Developmental Neuropsychology, 7(3),* 397–419.

Thatcher, R. W. (1994). Cyclic cortical reorganization. In G. Dawson & K. W. Fischer (Eds.), *Human behavior and the developing brain.* New York: Guilford.

Thelen, E. (1995). Motor development: A new synthesis. *American Psychologist, 50,* 79–95.

Thelen, E., Corbetta, D., Kamm, K., Spencer, J. P., Schneider, K., & Zernicke, R. F. (1993). The transition to reaching: Mapping intention and intrinsic dynamics. *Child Development, 64,* 1099–1110.

Thelen, E, & Ulrich, B. D. (1991). Hidden skills. *Monographs of the Society for Research in Child Development, 56(1, Serial No. 223).*

Thelen, E., Ulrich, B. D., & Jensen, J. L. (1989). *The developmental origins of locomotion.* In M. Woollacott & A. Shumway-Cook (Eds.), *The development of posture and gait across the lifespan.* Columbia, SC: University of South Carolina Press.

Thoman, E. B., Hammond, K., Affleck, G., & De Silva, H. N. (1995). The breathing bear with preterm infants: Effects on sleep, respiration, and affect. *Infant Mental Health Journal, 16, 3,* 160–168.

Thoman, E. B., & Whitney, M. P. (1989). Sleep states of infants monitored in the home: Individual differences, develpmental trends, and origins of cyclicity. *Infant Behavior and Development, 12,* 59–75.

Thomas, A. & Chess, S. (1977). *Temperament and development.* New York: Brunner/Mazel.

Thomas, A., & Chess, S. (1984). Genesis and evaluation of behavioral disorders: From infancy to early adult life. *American Journal of Psychiatry, 141,* 1–9.

Thomas, A., & Chess, S. (1989). Temperament and personality. In G. A. Kohnstamm, J. E. Bates, & M. K. Rothbart (Eds.), *Temperament in childhood.* New York: Wiley.

Thomas, A., Chess, S., Birch, H. G., Hertzig, M. E., & Korn, S. (1963). *Behavioral individuality in early childhood.* New York: New York University Press.

Thomas, R. M. (1996). *Comparing theories of development* (4th ed.). Pacific Grove, CA: Brooks/Cole Publishing.

Thompson, J. E. (1990). Maternal stress, anxiety, and social support during pregnancy: Possible directions for prenatal intervention. In I. R. Merkatz & J. E. Thompson (Eds.), *New perspectives on prenatal care.* New York: Elsevier.

Thompson, R. A. (1990). Emotion and self-regulation. In R. A. Thompson (Ed.), *Nebraska Symposium on Motivation: Vol. 36: Socioemotional Development.* Lincoln: University of Nebraska Press.

Thompson, R. A. (1993). Socioemotional development: Enduring issues and new challenges. *Developmental Review, 13*, 372–402.

Thorbecke, W., & Grotevant, H. D. (1982). Gender differences in adolescent interpersonal identity formation. *Journal of Youth and Adolescence, 11*, 479–492.

Thorkildsen, T. A. (1989). Pluralism in children's moral reasoning about social justice. *Child Development, 60*, 965–972.

Thorndike, E. L. (1911). *Animal intelligence: Experimental studies.* New York: Macmillan.

Thorndike, E. L. (1922). *The psychology of arithmetic.* New York: Macmillan.

Thorne, B. (1993). *Gender play: Girls and boys in school.* New Brunswick, NJ: Rutgers University Press.

Thorne, B., & Luria, Z. (1986). Sexuality and gender in children's daily worlds. *Social Problems, 33*, 176–190.

Tietjen, A. M., & Walker, L. J. (1985). Moral reasoning and leadership among men in a Papua New Guinea society. *Child Development, 21*, 982–992.

Tisak, M. S., & Turiel, E. (1988). Variation in seriousness of transgression and children's moral and conventional concepts. *Developmental Psychology, 24*, 352–357.

Tizard, B., & Hodges, J. (1978). The effect of early institutional rearing on the development of eight-year-old children. *Journal of Child Psychology and Psychiatry, 19*, 99–118.

Tizard, B., & Rees, J. (1975). The effect of early institutional rearing on the behavioral problems and affectional relationship of four-year-old children. *Journal of Child Psychology and Psychiatry, 16*, 61–73.

Tobin, J. J., Wu, D. Y. H., & Davison, D. H. (1989). *Preschool in three cultures: Japan, China, and the United States.* New Haven: Yale University Press.

Tomasello, M., (1988). The role of joint attention in early language development. *Language Sciences, 11*, 69–88.

Tomasello, M. (1990). Cultural transmission in the tool use and communicatory signalling of chimpanzees? In S. Parker & E. Gibson (Eds.), *"Language" and intelligence in animals: Developmental perspectives.* Cambridge: Cambridge University Press.

Tomasello, M. (1992). The social bases of language acquisition. *Social Development, 1*, 67–87.

Tomasello, M. (1993). Infants' knowledge of self, other, and relationship. In U. Nusser (Ed.), *The perceived self: Ecological and interpersonal sources of self-knowledge.* Cambridge, MA: Cambridge University Press.

Tomasello, M., & Farrar, J. (1986). Joint attention and early language. *Child Development, 57*, 1454–1463.

Tomasello, M., & Manle, S. (1985). Pragmatics of sibling speech to one-year-olds. *Child Development, 56*, 911–917.

Toran-Allerand, C. D. (1984). Gonadal hormones and brain development: Implications for the genesis of sexual differentiation. *Annals of the New York Academy of Science, 435*, 101–110.

Torney-Purta, J. (1990). Youth in relation to social institutions. In S. S. Feldman & G. R. Elliott (Eds.), *At the threshold: The developing adolescent.* Cambridge, MA: Harvard University Press.

Toth, S. L., & Cicchetti, D. (1993). Where do we go from here in our treatment of victims? In D. Cicchetti & S. L. Toth (Eds.), *Advances in applied developmental psychology series:* Vol. 8, *Child abuse, child development, and social policy.* Norwood, NJ: Ablex.

Trethowan, W. H., & Conlon, M. F. (1965). The couvade syndrome. *British Journal of Psychiatry, 111*, 57–66.

Trevarthen, C. (1980). The foundations of intersubjectivity: Development of interpersonal and cooperative understanding in infants. In D. Olson (Ed.), *The social foundations of language and thought.* New York: W. W. Norton.

Trevarthan, C. (1993). On the interpersonal origins of self-concept. In U. Neisser (Ed.), *The perceived self: Ecological and interpersonal sources of self-knowledge.* Cambridge, MA: Cambridge University Press.

Trevethan, S. D., & Walker, L. J. (1989). Hypothetical versus real-life moral reasoning among psychopathic and delinquent youth. *Development & Psychopathology, 1*, 91–103.

Troiden, R. R. (1988). *Gay and lesbian identity: A sociological analysis.* Dix Hills, NY: General Hall, Inc.

Tronick, E. Z., Winn, S., & Morelli, G. A. (1985). Multiple care-taking in the context of human evolution: Why don't the Efe know the western prescription for child care? In M. Reite & T. Field (Eds.), *The Psychobiology of attachment and separation.* Orlando, FL: Academic Press.

Troyer, L. R., & Parisi, V. M. (1994). Managment of labor. In J. R. Scott, P. J. DiSaia, C. B. Hammond, & W. N. Spellacy (Eds.), *Dansforth's obstetrics and gynecology* (7th ed.). Philadelphia: J. B. Lippincott.

Tschirgi, J. E. (1980). Sensible reasoning: A hypothesis about hypotheses. *Child Development, 51*, 1–10.

Tuchmann-Duplessis, H., David, G., & Haegel, P. (1971). *Illustrated human embryology* (Vol. 1). New York: Springer-Verlag.

Tuchmann-Duplessis, H. (1975). *Drug effects on the fetus.* Acton, MA: Publishing Science Group Inc.

Tulviste, P. (1991). *The cultural-historical development of verbal thinking.* Commack, NY: Nova.

Turiel, E. (1978). Social regulation and domains of social concepts. In W. Damon (Ed.), *Social cognition: New directions for child development, 1.* San Francisco: Jossey-Bass.

Turiel, E. (1983). *The development of social knowledge: Morality and convention.* Cambridge: Cambridge University Press.

Turiel, E. (1990). Moral judgement, moral action, and development. In D. Schrader (Ed.), *The legacy of Lawrence Kohlberg: New Directions for Child Development, 47,* San Francisco: Jossey-Bass.

Turiel, E., Killen, M., & Helwig, C. C. (1987). Morality: Its structure, functions, and vagaries. In J. Kagan & S. Lamb (Eds.), *The emergence of morality.* Chicago: Chicago University Press.

Turner, R. (Nov/Dec, 1991). Fear of contraceptives, wish for closer relationship are major reasons teenagers delay clinic. *Family Planning Perspectives, 23*, 287–288.

Tyson, P., & Tyson, R. L. (1990). *Psychoanalytic theories of development: An integration.* New Haven: Yale University Press.

United Nations Childrens Fund (UNICEF) (1995). *The state of the world's children.* Oxford: Oxford University Press.

U.S. Bureau of the Census (1991). *Statistical Abstract of the United States: 1991* (111th ed.). Washington, DC: U.S. Government Printing Office.

U.S. Bureau of the Census (1991). Daily disruption and economic hardship; the shortrun picture for children. *Current Population Reports*, Series P-70, No. 3.

U.S. Bureau of the Census (1994). *More education higher career earnings.* (Statistical Brief). Washington, DC: US Department of Commerce.

U.S. Bureau of the Census (1994). Primary child care arrangements used by working mothers for children under five years of age in 1991, *Current Population Reports*, Series P. 70, 36.

U.S. Bureau of the Census (1994). *Statistical abstract of the United States: 1994* (114th ed.). Washington, DC: US Government Printing Office.

U.S. Bureau of the Census (1995). *Statistical abstract of the United States: 1995* (115th ed.). Washington, DC: US Government Printing Office.

U.S. Congress, Senate Committee on Human Resources (1978). Obstetrical practices in *U.S. Hearings before the subcommittee on Health and scientific research of the Committee on Human Resources.* Washington, DC: U.S. Government Printing Office.

U.S. Department of Education, National Commission on Excellence in Education (1983). *A nation at risk: The imperative for educational reform.* Washington, DC: U.S. Government Printing Office.

U.S. Department of Education, Office of Educational Research and Improvement (1991). *Youth indicators 1991: Trends in the well-being of American youth.* Washington, DC: U.S. Government Printing Office.

U.S. Department of Health and Human Services (1988). *Study of national incidence and prevalence of child abuse and neglect.* Washington, DC: U.S. Government Printing Office.

U. S. Department of Health and Human Services (1991). *Healthy people 2000.* Washington, DC: Government Printing Office (DHHS Publication No. PH591-50212).

U.S. Department of Health and Human Services , National Center for Health Statistics (1992, Jan. 13, 1992). *Monthly Vital Statistics Report, 40*(9), 1.

U.S. Department of Health and Human Services, National Centers for Disease Control (January, 1992). Sexual Behavior Among High School Students—United States, 1990. *Morbidity and Mortality Weekly Report, 40*, Nos. 51–52, 885–887.

U.S. Department of Health and Human Services. (February 9, 1995). 1995 Poverty Guidlines for all states except Alaska, Hawaii, and the District of Columbia. *Federal Register, 60, 27,* 7772.

U.S. Department of Health and Human Services, National Centers for Disease Control (April 21, 1995). Cesarean delivery in the United States in 1993. *Mortality and Morbidity Weekly Report, 44,* No.15, 303–304.

U.S. Department of Health and Human Services, National Centers for Disease Control (Sept. 22, 1995). State-specific pregnancy and birth rates among teenagers in the U.S. 1991–1992. *Morbidity and Mortality Weekly Report, 44,* No. 37, 677–685.

U.S. Department of Health and Human Services, National Centers for Health Statistics (annual). *Vital Statistics of the U.S.* Washington, DC: U.S. Government Printing Office.

U. S. Office of Education, (1977). "Procedures for evaluating specific learning disabilities." *Federal Register 42:65082–65085.*

U. S. Office of Technology Assessment (1991). *Adolescent health: Vol. 3 Cross-cutting issues in delivery of health and related services.* (Publication No. OTA-H-467). Washington, DC: U.S. Government Printing Office.

Underwood, M. K., Coie, J. D., & Herbsman, C. R. (1992). Display rules for anger and aggression in school-age children. *Child Development, 63,* 366–380.

Unger, R., Kreeger, L., & Christoffel, K. K. (1990). Childhood obesity: Medical and familial correlates and age of onset. *Clinical Pediatrics, 29,* 368–372.

Unger, R., Crawford, M. (1993). Commentary: Sex and gender: The troubled relationship between terms and concepts. *Psychological Science, 4,* 122–124.

Urberg, K., Degirmencioglu, S. M., Tolson, J. M., & Halliday-Scher, K. (1995). The structure of adolescent peer networks. *Developmental Psychology, 31,* 540–547.

Uzgiris, I. C., & Hunt, J. (1975). *Assessment in infancy: Ordinal scales of psychological development.* Champaign: University of Illinois Press.

Valenzuela, M. (1990). Attachment in chronically underweight young children. *Child Development, 61,* 1984–1996.

Valsiner, J. (1988). *Child development within culturally structured environments, Vol. 2: Social co-construction and environmental guidance in development.* Norwood, NJ: Ablex.

Valsiner, J. (1989). *Constructing the subject.* Lexington, MA: Lexington Books.

Vandell, D. L., & Ramanan, J. (1991). Children of the National Longitudinal Survey of Youth: Choices in after-school care and child development. *Developmental Psychology, 27,* 636–643.

Van Den Bergh, B. R. H. (1992). Maternal emotions during pregnancy and fetal and neonatal behavior. In J. G. Nijhuis (Ed.), *Fetal behavior: Development and perinatal aspects.* New York: Oxford University Press.

Van Evra, J. (1990). *Television and child development.* Hillsdale, NJ: Erlbaum.

Van IJzendoorn, M. H., Goldberg, S., Kroonenberg, P. M., & Frenkel, O. J. (1992). The relative effects of maternal and child problems on the quality of attachment: A meta-analysis of attachment in clinical samples. *Child Development, 63,* 840–858.

Vaughn, B., Egeland, B., Sroufe, L. A., & Waters, E. (1979). Individual differences in infant-mother attachment at twelve and eighteen months: Stability and change in families under stress. *Child Development, 50,* 971–975.

Vaughn, B. E., & Langlois, J. H. (1983). Physical attractiveness as a correlate of peer status and social competence in preschool children. *Developmental Psychology, 19,* 550–560.

Vaughn, B. E., Lefever, G. B., Seifer, R., & Barglow, P. (1989). Attachment behavior, attachment security, and temperament during infancy. *Child Development, 60,* 728–737.

Vaughn, B. E., Stevenson-Hinde, J., Waters, E., Kotsaftis, A., Lefeore, G. B., Shouldice, A., Trudel, M., & Belsky, J. (1992). Attachment security in infancy and early childhood: Some conceptual clarifications. *Developmental Psychology, 28,* 463–473.

Verny, T., & Kelly, J. (1981). *The secret life of the unborn child.* New York: Summit Books.

Visser, G. H. A. (1992). The second trimester. In J. G. Nijhuis (Ed.), *Fetal behavior: Development and perinatal aspects.* New York: Oxford University Press.

Von Hofsten, C. (1984). Developmental changes in the organization of prereaching movements. *Developmental Psychology, 20,* 369–382.

Von Hofsten, C. (1992). The gearing of early reaching to the environment. In G. E. Stelmach and J. Requin (Eds.), *Tutorials in motor behavior* II. Amsterdam: North Holland.

Von Hofsten, C., & Rönnqvist, L. (1988). Preparations for grasping an object: A developmental study. *Journal of Experimental Psychology, 14,* 610–621.

Von Hofsten, C., & Rönnqvist, L. (1993). The structuring of neonatal arm movements. Special Section: Develpomental biodynamics: Brain, body, behavior connections. *Child Development, 64,* 1046–1057.

Von Hofsten, C., & Siddiqui, A. (1993). Using the mother's actions as a reference for object exploration in 6- and 12-month-old infants. *British Journal of Developmental Psychology, 11,* 61–74.

Vorhees, C. V., & Mollnow, E. (1987). Behavior teratogenesis: Long-term influences on behavior. In J. D. Osofsky (Ed.), *Handbook of infant development* (2nd ed.). New York: Wiley.

Vurpillot, E. (1968). The development of scanning strategies and their relation to visual differentiation. *Journal of Experimental Child Psychology, 6,* 632–650.

Vygotsky, L. S. (1934/1987). Thinking and speech. In *The collected works of L. S. Vygotsky. Vol 1. Problems of general psychology.* (N. Minick, Trans.). New York: Plenum Press.

Vygotsky, L. S. (1978). *Mind in society.* Cambridge, MA: Harvard University Press.

Waddington, C. H. (1947). *Organizers and genes.* Cambridge: Cambridge University Press.

Wagner, D. A. (1974). The development of short-term and incidental memory: A cross cultural study. *Child Development, 48,* 389–396.

Wagner, D. A. (1978). Memories of Morocco: The influence of age, schooling, and environment on memory. *Cognitive Psychology, 10,* 1–28.

Wagner, R. K., & Sternberg, R. J. (1985). Practical intelligence in real-world pursuits: The role of tacit knowledge. *Journal of Personality and Social Psychology, 49,* 436–458.

Wainryb, C., & Turiel, E. (1994). Dominance, subordination, and concepts of personal entitlements in cultural contexts. *Child Development, 65,* 1701–1722.

Walden, T. A., & Baxter, A. (1989). The effect of context and age on social referencing. *Child Development, 60,* 1511–1518.

Waldman, I. D., Weinberg, R. A., & Scarr, S. (1994). Racial-group differences in IQ in the Minnesota Transracial Adoption Study: A reply to Levin and Lynn. *Intelligence, 19,* 29–44.

Walker, L. J. (1980). Sex differences in moral reasoning. In W. M. Kurtines & J. L. Gerwirtz (Eds.), *Handbook of moral behavior and development,* Vol. 2. Hillsdale, NJ: Erlbaum.

Walker, L. J. (1986). Sex differences in the development of moral reasoning: A rejoinder to Baumrind. *Child Development, 57,* 522–526.

Walker, L. J. (1988). The development of moral reasoning. *Annals of Child Development, 5,* 33–78.

Walker, L. J. (1989). A longitudinal study of moral reasoning. *Child Development, 60,* 157–166.

Walker, L. J. (1995). Sexism in Kohlberg's moral psychology. In W. M. Kurtines & J. L. Gewirtz (Eds.), *Moral development: An introduction.* Boston: Allyn & Bacon.

Walker, L. J., & De Vries, B. (1985). Moral stages/moral orientations: Do the sexes really differ? In C. Black (Ed.), *Gender differences in research in moral development.* Symposium conducted at the meetings of the American Psychological Association, Los Angeles.

Walker, L. J., & Moran, T. J. (1991). Moral reasoning in a communist Chinese society. *Journal of Moral Education, 20,* 139–155.

Walker, L. J., Pitts, R. C., Henning, K. H., & Matsuba, M. K. (1995). Reasoning about morality and real-life moral problems. In M. Keller & D. Hart (Eds.), *Morality in everyday life. Developmental perspectives.* Cambridge: Cambridge University Press.

Wallerstein, J. S. (1987). Children of divorce: Report of a ten-year follow-up of early latency-age children. *American Journal of Orthopsychiatry, 57*(2), 199–211.

Walmsley, J., & Margolis, J. (1987). *Hothouse people: Can we create super human beings?* London: Pan. A Channel Four Book.

Ward, K. (1994). Genetics and prenatal diagnosis. In James R. Scott, Philip J. DiSaia, Charles B. Hammond, & William N. Spellacy (Eds.), *Dansforth's obstetrics and gynecology* (7th ed.). Philadelphia: J. B. Lippincott.

Ward, S. L., & Overton, W. F. (1990). Semantic familiarity, relevance, and the development of deductive reasoning. *Developmental Psychology, 26,* 488–493.

Warren, M. P., Brooks-Gunn, J., Fox, R., Lancelot, C., Newman,

D., & Hamilton, W. G. (1991). Lack of bone accretion and amenarchea in young dancers: Evidence for a relative osteopenia in weight-bearing bones. *Journal of Clinical Endocrinology and Metabolism, 72,* 847–853.

Warton, P. M., & Goodnow, J. J. (1991). The nature of responsibility: Children's understanding of "Your Job." *Child Development, 62,* 156–165.

Wasik, B. H., Ramey, C. T., Bryant, D. M., & Sparling, J. J. (1990). A longitudinal study of two early intervention strategies: Project CARE. *Child Development, 61,* 1682–1696.

Wasz-Hockert, O., Lind, J., Vuorenkoski, V., Partanen, T., & Valanne, E. (1968). *The infant cry: A spectographic and auditory analysis. Clinics in developmental medicine,* No. 29. Lavenham, Suffolk: Spastics International Medical Publications and William Heinemann Medical Books, Ltd.

Waterman, A. S. (1985). Identity in the context of adolescent psychology. In A. S. Waterman (Ed.), *Identity in adolescence: Progress and contents: New directions for child development,* No. 30. San Francisco: Jossey-Bass.

Waterman, A. S., & Waterman, C. K. (1971). A longitudinal study of changes in ego identity status during the freshman year at college. *Developmental Psychology, 5,* 167–173.

Waters, E. (1978). The reliability and stability of individual differences in infant-mother attachment. *Child Development, 49,* 483–494.

Watson, J. B. (1930). *Behaviorism.* Chicago: Chicago University Press.

Watson, J. B., & Rayner, R. (1920). Conditioned emotional reactions. *Journal of Experimental Psychology, 3,* 1–14.

Watson, J. S. (1971). Cognitive-perceptual development in infancy: Setting for the seventies. *Merrill-Palmer Quarterly, 17,* 139–152.

Watson, J. S. (1972). Smiling, cooing and "the game." *Merrill-Palmer Quarterly, 18,* 323–340.

Watson, M. W., & Fischer, K. W. (1980). Development of social roles in elicited spontaneous behavior during the preschool years. *Developmental Psychology, 16,* 483–494.

Waxman, S. R., & Gelman, R. (1986). Preschoolers use of superordinate relations in classification. *Cognitive Development, 1,* 139–156.

Waxman, S. R., & Hall, G. D. (1993). The development of a linkage between count nouns and object categories: Evidence from fifteen-to twenty-one-month-old infants. *Child Development, 69,* 1242–1257.

Wechsler, D. (1939). *The measurement of adult intelligence.* Baltimore: Williams & Wilkins.

Wechsler, D. (1974). *Manual for the Wechsler intelligence scale for children.* New York: Psychology Corporation.

Weill, B. C. (1930). *Are you training your child to be happy? Lesson material in child management.* Washington, DC: U.S. Government Printing Office.

Weinbraub, M., Jaeger, E., & Hoffman, L. W. (1988). Predicting infant outcomes in families of employed and non-employed mothers. *Early Childhood Research Quarterly, 3,* 361–378.

Weisenfeld, H. C., & Sweet, R. L. (1994). Perinatal infections. In J. R. Scott, P. J. DiSaia, C. B. Hammond, & W. N. Spellacy (Eds.), *Dansforth's obstetrics and gynecology* (7th ed.). Philadelphia: J. B. Lippincott.

Weisner, T. S. (1984). Ecocultural niches of middle childhood. In W. A. Collins (Ed.), *Development during middle childhood: The years from six to twelve.* Washington, DC: National Academy Press.

Weisner, T. S., Gallimore, R., & Jordan, C. (1988). Unpackaging cultural effects on classroom learning: Hawaiian peer assistance and child-generated activity. *Anthropology and Education Quarterly, 19,* 327–353.

Weisner, T. S., & Wilson-Mitchell, J. (1990). Nonconventional family lifestyles and sex typing in six-year-olds. *Child Development, 62,* 1915–1933.

Weiss, B., Dodge, K., Bates, J., & Pettit, G. (1992). Some consequences of early harsh discipline: Child aggression and a maladaptive social information processing style. *Child Development, 63,* 1236–1250.

Weiss, J. S. (1983). *Prize-winning books for children: Themes and stereotypes in U. S. prizewinning prose fiction for children.* Lexington, MA: Lexington Books.

Weiss, M. J., Zelazo, P. R., & Swain, I. U. (1988). Newborn response to auditory stimulus discrepancy. *Child Development, 59,* 1530–1541.

Wellman, H. M., Cross, D., & Bartsch, K. (1987). Infant search and object permanence: A meta-analysis of the A-not-B error. *Monographs of the Society for Research in Child Development, 51* (Serial No. 214).

Wellman, H. M., & Gelman, S. A. (1992). Cognitive development: Foundational theories and core domains. *Annual Review of Psychology, 43,* 337–376.

Wellman, H., & Lempers, J. D. (1977). The naturalistic communication abilities of two-year-olds. *Child Development, 48,* 1052–1057.

Wells, G. (1994). Text, talk and inquiry: Schooling as semiotic apprenticeship. In N. Bird et al. (Eds.), *Language and learning.* Hong Kong: Institute of Language in Education.

Wentzel, K. R., & Asher, S. R. (1995). The academic level of neglected, rejected, popular and controversial children. *Child Development, 66,* 754–763.

Werner, E., & Smith, R. S. (1982). *Vulnerable but invincible: A longitudinal study of resilient children and youth.* New York: McGraw-Hill.

Werner, E. E., & Smith, R. S. (1992). *Overcoming the odds: High risk children from birth to adulthood.* Ithaca, NY: Cornell University Press.

Werner, H. (1948). *Comparative psychology of mental development.* New York: International Universities Press.

Werner, H., & Kaplan, B. (1952). The acquisition of word meanings: A developmental study. *Monographs of the Society for Research in Child Development, 15* (1, Serial No. 51).

Werner, J. S., & Wooten, B. R. (1979). Human infant color vision and color perception. *Infant Behavior and Development, 2,* 241–273.

Werner, L. A., & Vanden Boss, G. R. (1993). Developmental psychoacoustics: What infants and children hear. *Hospital and Community Psychiatry, 44*(7), 624–626.

Wertsch, J. (1985). *Vygotsky and the social formation of mind.* Cambridge, MA: Harvard University Press.

Westinghouse Learning Corporation. (1969). *The impact of Head Start: An evaluation of the effects of Head Start on children's cognitive and affectional development. Executive summary, Ohio University report to the Office of Economic Opportunity.* Washington, DC: Learning House for Federal Scientific and Technical Informations.

White, B. L. (1975). *The first three years of life.* Englewood Cliffs, NJ: Prentice-Hall.

White, B. L., & Watts, J. C. (1973). *Experience and environment: Major influences on the development of the young child.* Englewood Cliffs, NJ: Prentice-Hall.

White, L. A. (1949). *The science of culture.* New York: Grove Press.

White, M. (1987). *The Japanese education challenge: A commitment to children.* New York: Free Press.

White, M. L. (1976). *Children's literature: Criticism and response.* Columbus, OH: Charles E. Merrill.

White, R. W. (1959). Motivation re-considered: The concept of competence. *Psychological Review, 66,* 279–333.

Whitehurst, G. J., Arnold, D. S., Epstein, J. N., Angell, A. L., Smith, M., & Fischel, J. E. (1994). A picture book reading intervention in day-care and home for children from low-income families. *Developmental Psychology, 30,* 679–689.

Whitely, R. J., & Goldenberg, R. L. (1990). Infectious disease in the prenatal period and recommendations for screening. In I. R. Merkatz & J. E. Thompson (Eds.), *New perspectives on prenatal care.* New York: Elsevier.

Whiting, B. (1980). Culture and social behavior: A model for the development of social behavior. *Ethos, 8,* 95–116.

Whiting, B. B. (1986). The effect of experience on peer relationships. In E. C. Mueller, & C. R. Cooper (Eds.), *Process and outcome in peer relationships.* Orlando, FL: Academic Press.

Whiting, B. B., & Edwards, C. P. (1988). *Children of different worlds: The formation of social behavior.* Cambridge, MA: Harvard University Press.

Whiting, B. B., & Whiting, J. W. M. (1975). *Children of six cultures: A psycho-cultural analysis.* Cambridge, MA: Harvard University Press.

Whiting, J. W. M. (1964). The effects of climate in certaincultural practices. In W. H. Goodenough (Ed.), *Explorations in cultural anthropology: Essays in honor of George Peter Murdock.* New York: McGraw-Hill.

Whiting, J. W. M., Burbank, V. K., & Ratner, M. S. (1986). The duration of maidenhood. In J. B. Lancaster & B. A. Hamburg, (Eds.), *School age pregnancy and parenthood.* Hawthorne, NY: Aldine de Gruyter.

Wilcox, A. J., Weinberg, C. R., O'Conner, J. F., Baird, D. D., Schlatterer, J. P., Canfield, R. E., Armstrong, E. G., & Nisula, B. C. (1988). Incidence of early loss in pregnancy. *New England Journal of Medicine, 319*(4), 189–194.

Willats, J. (1987). Marr and pictures: An information processing account of children's drawings. *Archives de Psychologie, 55,* 105–125.

Williams, J. M., & White, K. A. (1983). Adolescent status system for males and females at three age levels. *Adolescence, 18,* 381–390.

Williams, T. M. (1986). *The impact of television: A natural experiment in three communities.* Orlando, FL: Academic Press.

Williams, T. M. (1985). Implications of a natural experiment inthe developed world for research on television in thedeveloping world. Special issue: Television in the developing world. *Journal of Cross-Cultural Psychology, 16,* 263–287.

Wilson, E. O. (1975). *Sociobiology: The new synthesis.* Cambridge, MA: Harvard University Press.

Wilson, J. D., George, F. W., & Griffin, J. E. (1981). The hormonal control of sexual development. *Science, 211,* 1278–1284.

Wilson, J. G. (1977). Current status of teratology. In J. G. Wilson & F. C. Fraser (Eds.), *Handbook of teratology* (Vol. 1). New York: Plenum Press.

Wilson, M. N. (1986). The black extended family: An analytical consideration. *Developmental Psychology, 22,* 246–258.

Wilson, M. N. (1989). Child development in the context of the black extended family. *American Psychologist, 44,* 380–383.

Wilson, M. N. (Ed). (1995). *African American family life: Its structural and ecological aspects. New directions for child development,* No. 68. San Francisco, CA: Jossey-Bass.

Wilson, M. N., & Saft, E. W. (1993). Child maltreatment in the African-American community. In D. Cicchetti & S. L. Toth (Eds.), *Child abuse, child development, and social policy: Advances in applied developmental psychology*, Vol. 8. Norwood, NJ: Ablex Publishing.

Winchester, A. M. (1972). *Genetics.* Boston: Houghton Mifflin.

Wineberg, S. S. (1987). The self-fulfillment of the self-fulfilling prophecy. *Educational Researcher, 16,* 28–36.

Winer, G. A. (1980). Class inclusion reasoning in children: A review of the empirical literature. *Child Development, 51,* 309–328.

Winner, E., McCarthy, M., Kleinman, S., & Gardner, H. (1979). First metaphors. In D. Wolfe (Ed.), *Early symbolization. New directions for child development,* No. 3. San Francisco: Jossey-Bass.

Winner, E. (1988). *The point of words.* Cambridge, MA: Harvard University Press.

Winston, B. (1986). *Misunderstanding media.* Cambridge, MA: Harvard University Press.

Witter, F. R. (1993). Epidemiology of prematurity. In F. R. Witter & L. G. Keith (Eds.), *Textbook of prematurity: Antecedents, treatment, & outcome.* Boston: Little, Brown, & Company.

Wolfe, W. S., Campbell, C. C., Frongillo, E. A., Haas, J. D., & Melnik, T. A. (1994). Overweight schoolchildren in New York state: Prevalence and characteristics. *American Journal of Public Health, 84,* (5), 807–813.

Wolfenstein, M. (1953). Trends in infant care. *American Journal of Orthopsychiatry, 33,* 120–130.

Wolff, P. H. (1966). The causes, controls, and organization of behavior in the neonate. *Psychological Issues, 5,* 1–105.

Wolff, P. H. (1969). The natural history of crying and other vocalizations in infancy. In B. M. Foss (Ed.), *Determinants of infant behavior* (Vol. 4). London: Methuen.

Wolkind, S., & Rutter, M. (1985). Separation, loss and family relationships. In M. Rutter & L. Hersov (Eds.), *Child and adolescent psychiatry.* Oxford: Blackwell.

Wong-Fillmore, L. (1985). Second language learning in children: A proposed model. In R. Eshch, & J. Provenzano (Eds.), *Issues in English language development.* Rosslyn, VA.: National Clearing House for Bilingual Education.

Woodruff-Pak, D. S., Logan, C. G., & Thompson, R. F. (1990). Neurobiological substrates of classical conditioning across the life-span. *Annals of the New York Academy of Sciences, 608,* 150–178.

Worthington-Roberts, B. S., & Klerman, L. V. (1990). Maternal nutrition. In I. R. Merkatz & J. E. Thompson (Eds.), *New perspectives on prenatal care.* New York: Elsevier.

Worthman, C. M., & Whiting, J. W. M. (1987). Social change in adolescent sexual behavior, mate selection, and premarital pregnancy rates in a Kikuyu community. *Ethos, 15, 145–165.*

Wozniak, R. H. (1993). Co-constructive metatheory for psychology: Implications for an analysis of families as specific social contexts for development. In R. H. Wozniak & K. W. Fischer (Eds.), *Development in context: Acting and thinking in specific environments.* Hillsdale, NJ: Erlbaum.

Wrangham, R. W., McGrew, W. C., DeWaal, F. B., & Heltne, P. G. (Eds.). (1994). *Chimpanzee cultures.* Cambridge, MA: Harvard University Press.

Wright, H. F. (1956). Psychological development in Midwest. *Child Development, 27,* 265–286.

Wright, J. C., & Huston, A. C. (1995). *Effects of educational TV viewing of lower income preschoolers on academic skills, school readiness, and school adjustment one to three years later.* Research Report. Center for Research on the influences of television on children. Lawrence, Kansas.

Wright, J. C., Huston, A. C., Reitz, A. L., & Pienyat, S. (1994). Young children's perceptions of television reality: Determinants and developmental differences. *Developmental Psychology, 30,* 229–239.

Wright, J. C., Huston, A. C., Ross, R. P., Clavert, S. L., Rolandelli, D., Weeks, L. A., Raeissi, P., & Potts, R. (1984). Pace and continuity of television programs: Effects on children's attention and comprehension. *Developmental Psychology, 20,* 653–666.

Wynn, K. (1992). Addition and subtraction by human infants. *Nature, 358,* 749–750.

Yakovlev, P. I., & Lecours, A. P. (1967). The myelogenetic cycles of regional maturation of the brain. In A. Menkowski (Ed.), *Regional development of the brain in early life.* Oxford: Blackwell.

Yarrow, M. R., Scott, P. M., & Waxler, C. Z. (1973). Learning concern for others. *Developmental Psychology, 8,* 240–260.

Yerkes, R. M. (Ed.). (1921). Psychological examining in the United States Army. *Memoirs of the National Academy of Sciences, 15.*

Yonas, A., & Hartman, B. (1993). Perceiving the affordance ofcontact in four-and five-month-old infants. *Child Development, 64,* 298–308.

Young, C. M., Sipin, S. S., & Rose, O. A. (1968). Density and skinfold measurements: Body composition of pre-adolescent girls. *Journal of the American Dietetic Association, 53,* 25–31.

Young, K. T. (1990). American conceptions of infant development from 1955 to 1984: What the experts are telling parents. *Child Development, 61,* 17–28.

Young, W. W., Goy, R., & Phoenix, C. (1964). Hormones and sexual behavior. *Science, 143,* 212–218.

Younger, B., & Cohen, L. B. (1986). Developmental change in infants' perception of correlation among attributes. *Child Development, 57,* 803–813.

Youniss, J. (1980). *Parents and peers in social development.* Chicago: University of Chicago Press.

Youniss, J. (1983). Social construction of adolescence by adolescents and their parents. In H. D. Grotevant & C. R. Cooper (Eds.), *Adolescent development in the family. New directions for child development,* No. 22. San Francisco: Jossey-Bass.

Youniss, J., & Smollar, J. (1985). *Adolescent relations with mothers, fathers, and friends.* Chicago: University of Chicago Press.

Zahavi, S., & Asher, S. R. (1978). The effects of verbal instruction on preschool children's aggressive behavior. *Journal of School Psychology, 16,* 146–153.

Zahn-Waxler, C., & Radke-Yarrow, M. (1982). The development of altruism: Alternative research strategies. In N. Eisenberg (Ed.), *The development of prosocial behavior.* New York: Academic Press.

Zahn-Waxler, C., Radke-Yarrow, M., & King, R. (1979). Child rearing and children's prosocial initiations toward victims of distress. *Child Development, 50,* 319–330.

Zahn-Waxler, C., Radke-Yarrow, M., Wagner, E., & Chapman, M. (1992). Development of concern for others. *Developmental Psychology, 28,* 126–136.

Zegiob, L. E., Arnold, S., & Forehand, R. (1975). An examination of observer effects in parent child interaction. *Child Development, 46,* 509–512.

Zelazo, P. R. (1983). The development of walking: New findings and old assumptions. *Journal of Motor Behavior, 15,* 99–137.

Zeskind, P. S. (1983). Cross-cultural differences in maternal perceptions of cries of low- and high-risk infants. *Child Development, 54,* 1119–1128.

Zeskind, P. S., & Ramey, C. T. (1981). Preventing intellectual and interactional sequelae of fetal malnutrition: A longitudinal, transactional and synergistic approach to development. *Child Development, 52,* 213–218.

Zeskind, P. S., Sale, J., Maio, M. C., Huntington, L., & Weiseman, J. R. (1985). Adult perceptions of pain and hunger cries: A synchrony of arousal. *Child Development, 56,* 549–554.

Zigler, E., & Hall, N. W. (1989). Physical child abuse in America: Past, present, and future. In D. Cicchetti & V. Carlson (Eds.), *Child maltreatment: Theory and research on the causes and consequences of child abuse and neglect.* New York: Cambridge University Press.

Zigler, E., & Finn-Stevenson, M. (1992). Applied Developmental Psychology. In M. H. Bornstein & M. E. Lamb (Eds.), *Developmental psychology: An advanced textbook,* (3rd ed.). Hillsdale, NJ: Lawrence Erlbaum & Associates.

Zigler, E., & Valentine, J. (Eds.). (1979). *Project Head Start: A legacy of the war on poverty.* New York: Free Press.

Zinchenko, V. P., Chzhi-Tsin, V., & Tarakanov, V. V. (1963). The formation and development of perceptual activity. *Soviet Psychology, 2,* 3–12.

Zuckerman, M. (1979). *Sensation seeking: Beyond the optimal level of arousal.* Hillsdale, NJ: Erlbaum.

Zukow, P. G. (1986). The relationship between interaction with the caregiver and the emergence of play activities during the one-word period. *British Journal of Developmental Psychology, 4,* 223–234.

Zukow, P. G. (1989). *Sibling interaction across cultures.* New York: Springer-Verlag.

Zukow-Goldring, P. (1995). Sibling caregiving. In M. Bornstein (Ed.), *Handbook of Parenting, Vol. III, Status and social conditions of parenting.* Hillsdale, NJ: Erlbaum.

Zuravin, S. J. (1991). Research definitions of child physical abuse and neglect, current problems. In R. H. Starr, Jr. & D. A. Wolfe (Eds.), *The effects of child abuse and neglect: Issues and research.* London: Guilford Press.

SOURCES OF PHOTOGRAPHS

CHAPTER 1

Opener: Lennart Nilsson, *A Child is Born,* 1990 ed., Dell Publishing Company; p. 2: Jean-Loup Charmet, Paris; p. 4: Library of Congress; p. 5: Lewis W. Hine Collection, NYPL; p. 9: Kari Rene Hall, Los Angeles Times; p. 12: Nina Leen, *Life* magazine © Time Inc.; p. 19: Down House and the Royal College of Surgeons of England; p. 21: Doonesbury copyright 1992 G. B. Trudeau. Reprinted with permission of UNIVERSAL PRESS SYNDICATE. All rights reserved; p. 24: Enrico Ferorelli; 25: Joseph Campos, University of Illinois; p. 26: Benjamin Harris; p. 33: Joe McNally/Sygma; p. 35: Herb Gehr, *Life* magazine © Time Inc.; p. 36: G. L. Engel, F. Reichman, V. T. Harway, D. W. Hess. Monica: Infant-feeding behavior of a mother gastric fistula-fed as an infant: A 30-year longitudinal study of enduring effects, pp. 29–90, in E. J. Anthony and G. H. Pollock (Eds.). *Parental Influences in Health and Disease.* Boston: Little, Brown & Co., 1985; p. 37: © 1979, Yves De Braine/Black Star; p. 38: *(top)* Shawn G. Henry/Material World; *(bottom)* Hiroyuki Matsumoto/Black Star; p. 39: *(top)* Macduff Everton; *(bottom)* V. Chiasson/Gamma Liaison; p. 40: Courtesy Gita Vgotskaya

PART I

Opener: David M. Phillips/Photo Researchers Inc.; p. 48: Copyright Lennart Nilsson, *A Child Is Born,* 1990 ed., Dell Publishing Company; p. 49: Copyright Lennart Nilsson, *Behold Man,* Little Brown and Co.

CHAPTER 2

Opener: Jim Brandenberg/Minden Pictures; p. 52: Julie Newdol, Computer Graphics Laboratory, UCSF Copyright © Regents University of California; p. 56: Kathryn Abbe and Frances McLaughlin-Gill; p. 57: *(top)* Barbara Rogoff; *(bottom)* David Ward, Yale School of Medicine; p. 60: Moravian Musem, Brno; p. 62: *(top)* Frank Siteman/Stock Boston, (middle) Joan Lifton, UNICEF, *(bottom)* Eastphoto; p. 71: Custom Medical Stock Photo; p. 77: Gary Mortimore/Tony Stone Worldwide

CHAPTER 3

Opener: Copyright Lennart Nilsson, *A Child Is Born,* 1990 ed., Dell Publishing Company; p. 84: Copyright Lennart Nilsson, *A Child Is Born,* 1990 ed., Dell Publishing Company; p. 87: Copyright Lennart Nilsson, *Behold Man,* Little, Brown & Co.; p. 89: Copyright Lennart Nilsson, *A Child Is Born,* 1976 ed., Dell Publishing Company; p. 94: Copyright Lennart Nilsson, *A Child Is Born,* 1990 ed., Dell Publishing Company; p. 95: Melanie Spence, University of Texas; p. 102: Marie Dorigny/REA; p. 103: *(top)* George Steinmetz; *(bottom)* from Ann Pytkowicz Streissguth et al. (18 July 1980). Teratogenic effects of alcohol in humans and laboratory animals, *Science* 209, 353–361, figs, 2,3,4. Copyright 1980 by the American Association for the Advancement of Science. Photographs courtesy University of Washington, School of Medicine; p. 106: Vincent Leloup/Gamma Liaison; p. 108: Aileen & W. Eugene Smith/Black Star; p. 111: Lawrence Migdale; p. 117: John Ficara/Woodfin Camp & Associates; p. 118: Evelyn Thoman, Infant Studies Laboratory

PART II

Opener: © Allen McInnis/Liaison International; p. 130: © 1995 Laura Dwight; p. 131: Elizabeth Crews

CHAPTER 4

Opener: Penny Genteieu/Tony Stone Images; p. 136: James Killkelly, *Scientific American,* 252, 46–52; p. 138: David Linton, *Scientific American,* 204, 66–72; p. 141: Courtesy Jacob E. Steiner, The Hebrew University–Hadassah School of Dental Medicine, Jerusalem; p. 144: Carroll Izard; p. 153: Elizabeth Crews; p. 155: Stephen Trimble; p. 158: E. Gamper

(1926), *Zeitschrift fur der gesamte Neurologie und Psychiatrie,* 104, 65, fig. 14; p. 159: *(top)* Elizabeth Crews; *(bottom)* © 1993, Allen McInnis/Liaison International; p. 162: Enrico Ferorelli; p. 166: Courtesy: Einar R. Siqueland, Brown University; p. 170: Laura Dwight; p. 173: *(top left)* Frans Lanting/Minden Pictures; *(middle)* David Turnley/Black Star; *(top right)* Comstock; *(bottom)* Bernard Wolff, UNICEF; p. 176: Elizabeth Crews; p. 177: ©1995 Laura Dwight; p. 178: D. G. Freedman, *Human Infancy: An Evolutionary Perspective,* Erlbaum, 1974; p. 179: © William Hubbell/Woodfin Camp & Associates

CHAPTER 5

Opener: Michael Newman/Photo Edit; p. 187: Penny Tweedie/Tony Stone Worldwide; p. 190: *(left)* © 1995 Laura Dwight; *(right)* © Laura Dwight; p. 193: *(top)* Library of Congress; *(bottom)* Martha Cooper; p. 194: Randy Taylor/Sygma; p. 197: D. Goodman/Monkmeyer; p. 199: Elizabeth Crews; p. 200: Adele Diamond; p. 206: Prof. Carolyn Rovee-Collier, Rutgers University; p. 207: *(top left, second from bottom left, second from top right)* Creszentia and Ted Allen; *(second from top left)* Hervé Chanmeton Chamaliers; *(bottom left)* Marc Henrie A.S.C.—London; *(top right)* Jal Duncan; *(bottom right)* Karl Wolffram; 208: Jean Mandler and Laraine McDonough; p. 209: A. N. Meltzoff (1988), *Child Development,* 59, 1221–1229. Photo A. N. Meltzoff; p. 210: Charles Gatewood/The Image Works; p. 214: Laura Dwight; p. 215: © Ursula Markus/Photo Researchers; p. 216: Elizabeth Crews

CHAPTER 6

Opener: Tony Freeman/Photo Edit; p. 222: Laura Dwight; p. 224: Photos courtesy of Karen Adolph, Carnegie Mellon; p. 226: © 1996 Laura Dwight; 227: Laura Dwight; p. 231: George S. Zimbel/Monkmeyer; p. 232: © 1995 Laura Dwight; p. 236: Courtesy Judy De Loache; p. 239 Sheila Cole; p. 241: Martin Rogers/Tony Stone Images; p. 242: Harlow Primate Laboratory, University of Wisconsin; p. 244 Mary D. Ainsworth; p. 245: Elizabeth Crews; p. 246: Catherine Karnow/Woodfin Camp & Associates; p. 249: © 1995 Laura Dwight; p. 252: © 1995 Laura Dwight

CHAPTER 7

Opener: Jon Jones/Sygma; p. 262: © 1983 Abbas/Magnum Photos, Inc.; p. 263: Witold Krassowski/© 1994 Network Matrix; p. 266: Christopher Morris/Black Star; p. 267: Anthony Suau/Black Star; p. 269: Gerd Ludwig/Woodfin Camp & Associates; p. 270: David Wells/JB Pictures; p. 274: © 1994 A. Boulat/Material World; p. 277: April Saul/*The Philadelphia Inquirer;* pp. 282–283: Harlow Primate Laboratory, University of Wisconsin; p. 285: © Stephanie Maze/Woodfin Camp & Associates

PART III

Opener: Elizabeth Crews; p. 292: Elizabeth Crews; p. 293: J. Guichard/Sygma

CHAPTER 8

Opener: Paul Damien/Tony Stone Worldwide; p. 300: Phiz Mezey/Taurus; p. 303: Beryl Goldberg; p. 308: Erika Stone; p. 312: Myrleen Ferguson/Photo Edit; p. 315: Novosti from Sovfoto; p. 320: © 1994D Peter Ginter/Material World; p. 322: Enrico Ferorelli; p. 324: © Ursula Bellugi, The Salk Institute for Biological Studies; p. 327: Erika Stone

CHAPTER 9

Opener: Laura Dwight; p. 339: Bonnie Kamin; p. 344: The Exploratorium, San Francisco; p. 353: Al Seib, *Los Angeles Times;* p. 364: Sheila Cole; p. 365: © 1994 Guglielmo De'Micheli/Material World; p. 367:

© 1994 Miguel Luis Fairbanks/Material World; p. 369: © 1995 Laura Dwight; p. 376: Lawrence Migdale

CHAPTER 10

Opener: Cotton Coulson/Woodfin Camp & Associates; p. 383: Sheila Cole; p. 384: 1993 © Karen Kasmauski/Matrix; p. 385: Lynn Johnson/ Black Star; p. 386: Austrian Press and Information Service; p. 389: Andy Sacks/Tony Stone Images; p. 393: Elizabeth Crews; p. 394: Marlene Wallace/Photo Edit; p. 397: Peter Ginter/Material World; p. 402: UPI/ Bettmann; p. 406: Herlinde Koelbl/Betty Dornheim Picture Service; p. 410: *(top)* Albert Bandura, Stanford University; *(bottom)*: Film Study Center, Harvard; p. 411: © 1996 Michael H. Francis; p. 413: UPI/ Bettmann Newsphotos; p. 416: *(top)* Janet Kelly/*Eagle-Times*, Reading, Pennsylvania; *(bottom)* David M. Grossman

CHAPTER 11

Opener: © 1993 Laura Dwight; p. 429: Arthur Pollack, *Boston Herald*; p. 431: © 1994D David Reed/Material World; p. 434: Eastcott/ Momatiuk/Woodfin Camp & Associates; p. 437: Tony Freeman/Photo Edit; p. 441: Peter Turnley/Black Star; p. 447: © 1994 Peter Ginter/Material World; p. 448: © Nan Goldin; p. 450: Joseph Rodriquez/Black Star; p. 453: Barbara Rios/Photo Researchers; p. 457: © Stephanie Maze, All rights reserved/Woodfin Camp & Associates; p. 460: J. Guichard/ Sygma; p. 461: *(top)* Elizabeth Crews; *(bottom)* Erika Stone; p. 465: Paul Conklin/Photo Edit

PART IV

Opener: Macduff Everton; p. 472: Elizabeth Crews; p. 473: Andy Sacks/ Tony Stone Images

CHAPTER 12

Opener: Franz Lanting/Minden Pictures; p. 476: Joe Traver/Gamma Liaison; p. 477: © 1994 Shawn G. Henry/Material World; p. 480: © 1994 Lynn Johnson/Material World; p. 481: Roger Werth/Woodfin Camp & Associates; p. 484: Adapted from: J. V. Pardo, P. J. Pardo, K. W. Janer, M. E. Raichle (1990). The anterior cingulate cortex medicates processing selection in the Stroop attentional conflict paradigm. *Proceedings of the National Academy of Sciences USA)* 87:256–259; p. 493: © 1994 Laura Dwight; p. 498: Lawrence Migdale; p. 500: Martha Cooper; p. 504: © 1994 Kirk McRoy/Material World; p. 506: Macduff Everton

CHAPTER 13

Opener: Tony Freeman/Photo Edit; p. 515: Macduff Everton; p. 517: Bonnie Kamin; p. 520: Lawrence Migdale; p. 526: Ulrike Welsch/Photo Researchers; p. 528: Elizabeth Crews; p. 536: *(top)* © 1994 Peter Ginter/Material World; *(2nd from top)* © Betty Press/Woodfin Camp & Associates; *(3rd from top)* Sygma; *(bottom)* © 1993D Peter Menzel/ Material World; p. 547: Sidney Harris; p. 557: Lawrence Migdale

CHAPTER 14

Opener: Andy Sacks/Tony Stone Images; p. 564: Shirley Zeiberg/Taurus; p. 565: Frans Lanting/Minden Pictures; p. 567: Lauren Greenfield/Sygma p. 569: Don Spiro/Tony Stone Worldwide; p. 583: Joseph Rodriquez/ Black Star; p. 588: Lawrence Migdale; p. 592: Robert Doisneau/Rapho; p. 601: E.A. Kennedy III; p. 607: Jean Marc Charles/Sygma

PART V

Opener: © 1987 Peter Menzel/Material World; p. 618: Alon Reininger/ Woodfin Camp & Associates; p. 619: Kaluzny/Thatcher/Tony Stone Images

CHAPTER 15

Opener: © 1994 Alexandra and Pierre Boulat/Material World; p. 632: Joseph Rodriquez/Black Star; p. 634: F. Carter Smith/*New York Times*; p. 639: Karen Kasmauski/Matrix; p 642: *(top)* Jon Riley/Tony Stone Images; *(bottom)* © Mark Peterson/SABA; p. 643: © 1994 Laura Dwight; p. 646: David Stewart/Tony Stone Images; p. 649: Nicholas Kristof/NYT Pictures; p. 653: Alon Reininger/Woodfin Camp & Associates; p. 654: Phil McCarten/Photo Edit; p. 658: Ron Levine/Black Star

CHAPTER 16

Opener: Arthur Tilley/Tony Stone Worldwide; p. 669: Air Products and Chemicals; p. 679: Stephen D. Thomas, *The Last Navigator*, Henry Holt & Co., 1987; p. 683: Alexis Duclos/Gamma Liaison; p. 686: *(top)* Momatiuk/Eastcott/Woodfin Camp & Associates; p. 696: © 1987 Peter Menzel; p. 697: Grant Haller/Seattle Post Intelligencer/Sygma; p. 698: Hays/Monkemeyer Press; p. 699: Terry Vine/Tony Stone WorldWide; p. 701: Jan Sonnenmair/NYT Pictures; p. 704: © Liliana Nieto Delrio/ JB Pictures; p. 706: Kaluzny/Thatcher/Tony Stone Images

NAME INDEX

Subject Index